W9-DAL-383

the food encyclopedia

the food encyclopedia

Over **8,000** ingredients, tools, techniques and people

Jacques L. Rolland
and Carol Sherman
with other contributors

For complete cataloguing information, see page 694.

Editor: Carol Sherman
Contributors: Christina Anson Mine, Jo Calvert, Judith Finlayson, Stephanie Ortenzi, Erik Tanner
Copy Editor: Linda Stulberg

Design & Production: PageWave Graphics Inc.
Illustrations: Alana Machnicki
Cover Photography: Colin Erricson
Food Stylist: Kathryn Robertson
Prop Stylist: Charlene Erricson
Photo Researchers: Linda Tanaka and Karen Becker

We acknowledge the financial support of the Government of Canada through the Book Publishing Industry Development Program (BPIDP) for our publishing activities.

Published by Robert Rose Inc.
120 Eglinton Avenue East, Suite 800, Toronto, Ontario, Canada M4P 1E2
Tel: (416) 322-6552 Fax: (416) 322-6936

Printed in Canada

1 2 3 4 5 6 7 8 9 TCP 12 11 10 09 08 07 06 05 04

Acknowledgments

Creating an encyclopedia that does justice to the ever-expanding world of food is both an exciting challenge and a gargantuan task involving a team of people. The contributors who helped compile and write this book are its lifeblood. Tina Anson Mine and Jo Calvert were on the front lines finding and defining important food terms including the latest culinary trends and techniques. Thanks to both for getting to the bottom of such complicated terms as manna and méthode champenoise, and such seemingly uncomplicated ones as B vitamins and salad bar, which were anything but. Thanks to Judith Finlayson and Stephanie Ortenzi for researching and writing the biographies and including not just contemporary chefs and cookbook authors but such important pioneers as Adelaide Hunter Hoodless and Ferdinand Carré. To Jacques L. Rolland who started the whole thing and quotes Pliny and Apicius with such aplomb. Linda Stulberg for her copy editing expertise and asking the right questions, and Erik Tanner for his writing and researching skills and making the best spaghetti sauce. Thanks to the team at PageWave Graphics — Andrew Smith and Joseph Gisini for designing such lovely colorful pages, and Kevin Cockburn and Daniella Zanchetta for all their care and attention to the book. Alana Machnicki for the charming illustrations, and Linda Tanaka and Karen Becker for photo research for the biographies. Thanks to Arden Boehm, Marian Jarkovich and Lisa Ekus, who all work so tirelessly to see that the book gets into the right hands. And, finally, thanks to publisher Bob Dees, who believed in the project and its long list of ingredients from the beginning.

— Carol Sherman

Introduction

"Tell me what you eat and I will tell you what you are."

– Jean Anthelme Brillat-Savarin, *The Physiology of Taste (La Physiologie du goût),* 1825

Although all animals eat, only humans discuss and write about this most basic need. Our survival and ability to thrive depend upon the nutrients food provides, and what we eat, not to mention how it is prepared, appreciated and remembered, is as deep and complex as any work of art. To learn about ourselves as consumers of food is to be in touch with the deepest aspects of our humanity.

Ever since Eve ate the apple in the Garden of Eden, our taste buds have influenced the course of world events. "The fate of nations depends upon the way they eat," concluded the French gourmand and epicurean Brillat-Savarin. Thoughts about the way we eat permeate culture, from literature, religion, philosophy and anthropology to science and medicine. In fact, food is such a fundamental part of our lives, we're likely to take it for granted, which would be a terrible mistake. The journey from our ancestors' discovery of fire to the fine art of gastronomy is the story of the human race, an eventful romp, loaded with lively anecdotes and startling information. Often it makes great bedtime reading.

Whether you're looking for an entertaining read or the answer to a specific culinary question, *The Food Encyclopedia* offers a unique vantage point from which to expand your knowledge of food and your appreciation of cooking. Food words, such as the names of fruits and vegetables, recipe titles and cooking techniques or terminology, rarely come about by chance. Insight into their historical origins is not only interesting — it makes the adventure of cooking all the more enjoyable. You likely recognize restaurant as a place to eat. But do you know its fascinating history? For the answer, turn to page 544.

Based on many years of research from a wide range of sources and containing more than 8,000 definitions of key food and beverage terms, techniques and biographies of prominent food people, including famous chefs, authors and inventors, as well as a wealth of historical background, this treasury of food lore is much more than an excellent resource. It's a book to browse through, one that will take both the interested amateur and the professional cook on a delightful journey through the world of food. We welcome your comments or suggestions so please contact us at foodencyclopedia@robertrose.ca.

How To Use This Book

This book has been organized with two main objectives in mind. Firstly, we encourage browsing. Culinary literature can be very entertaining, and we hope we've opened the door to an enjoyable journey through the world of food. The book should be a good read and fun to browse through. Secondly, we've worked hard to make this an excellent reference work, the first you'll turn to when you have a question about food. The answers to specific questions are easy to find and wherever possible will open the door to further exploration.

Here's some handy information to help you look up your favorite words.

ALPHABETICAL ORDER. All entries are in alphabetical order. When entries contain more than one word — for example, **à la carte** — they are treated as a single word **(àlacarte).** Thus, **akala** comes before **à la carte.**

CROSS-REFERENCING is indicated in **bold** when the word is unusual and the reader wants to learn more about it, such as **génoise,** which is mentioned under **cake.** It also has its own listing. For more information about **génoise,** go to G.

BOLD is also used for easy access to words within an entry when the reader has been referred to it.

ITALICS are used to indicate foreign phrases, genus names, and book and magazine titles.

MORE INFORMATION. Many entries end with a list of other entries to see for additional information about similar foods. For instance, under **cheese,** you'll find a comprehensive list of all the different cheeses listed throughout the book from ADMIRALS to YARG.

MULTIPLE MEANINGS. When a word has multiple meanings, the first entry is the most common usage followed by the other meaning(s).

MULTIPLE NAMES AND SPELLINGS (for example, **ajowan** - also **ajwain**) are in **bold.** Because many food terms have multiple names, they are listed under the most common usage and cross-referenced. For instance, **Queensland nut** will refer you to the more common usage **macadamia nut.**

SUBTOPICS are cross-referenced with listings of a larger scope — for example, **brown rice** will send you over to **rice** for a comprehensive look at this ancient grain.

VARIETIES. When a main entry such as **apples** has many different varieties, they are grouped together in a breakout box for easy reference.

Contributors

Jacques L. Rolland has a degree in culinary art and hotel management and is a certified sommelier. His appreciation and knowledge of food has been honed from the many cultures he has experienced. He is the author of *The Cook's Essential Kitchen Dictionary*.

Carol Sherman is an author and award-winning editor with a special interest in food and health. She has edited many bestselling cookbooks and food-reference books including *The Food Substitutions Bible*, winner of a 2006 International Association of Culinary Professionals (IACP) cookbook award. She was the managing editor of the travel magazine *Destinations* and founding editor of Thomson newspaper's *Healthfile*. She is the co-author of *Highlights: An Illustrated History of Cannabis* and *Yoga in a Muskoka Chair.*

Christina Anson Mine is the managing editor of *Canadian Living* and *Homemakers* magazines. She received a degree in Spanish from Washington's Georgetown University and spent her third year studying in Spain. After graduation, she lived for a year in Kyoto, Japan. Much of her professional life has been spent as a magazine editor, focused on food, nutrition, health and fitness as well as copy editing a variety of cookbooks and reference works for Robert Rose Inc. Her love of food was born during her childhood in Massachusetts and developed into a passion once she began to travel internationally.

Jo Calvert is a writer and senior editor at *Canadian Living* magazine specializing in gardening and crafts. One of her great pleasures is baking apple pies with fruit picked from the trees she planted herself. Jo dedicates her work in this book to Moira Gillette, who loved to cook unusual dishes for the usual crowd.

Judith Finlayson is a journalist and author who began her career writing feature food articles, reviewing restaurants and developing recipes for magazines. Her work has been published widely in Canadian newspapers and magazines and she is the author of ten books, six of which are bestselling cookbooks.

Stephanie Ortenzi is a Toronto writer who took a 15-year hiatus from editorial work to become a professional chef. She has cooked at a number of Distinguished Restaurants of North America (DIRONA) and returned to writing full-time in 2004. Her work has been published in business, news and lifestyle magazines.

a
artichoke

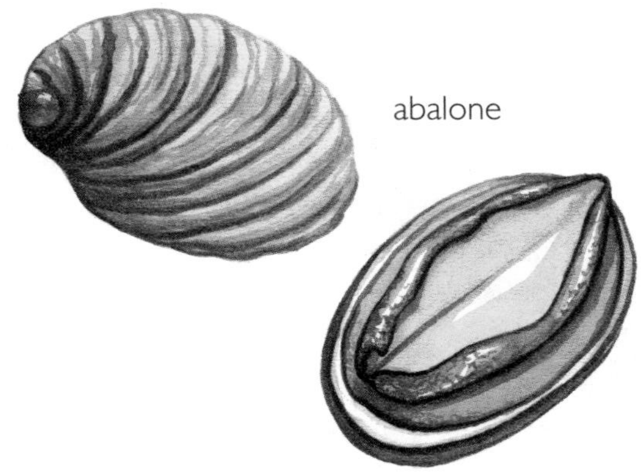
abalone

abalone - a large gastropod mollusk of the genus *Haliotis*, found in a variety of genera in the Atlantic, Mediterranean and Pacific. The edible part is the foot, or adductor muscle, with which the abalone clings to rocks. The muscle meat is tough so must be pounded before cooking. Known during the Roman Empire, abalone was a favorite dish of Aristotle, who mentioned it many times. This mollusk is also highly prized throughout Asia, especially in China and Japan. The Chinese suggest that its name, *bau yue*, sounds like the words for "guaranteed wealth," and abalone is eaten symbolically at the Lunar New Year and other celebrations. In New Zealand, it's known by the Maori name **paua.** In the English Channel, it's known as **ormer,** and in Australia as **muttonfish. Awabi** is the Japanese name for abalone, commonly seen on sushi menus in North America.

abbacchio - an Italian name for a milk-fed baby lamb.

Abernethy biscuit - a mildly flavored Scottish biscuit that purportedly takes its name from Dr. John Abernethy (1764–1831), who was accustomed to taking his lunch in a barbershop, where the barber would serve ordinary sea or ship biscuits that he baked. Growing tired of such a plain repast, Abernethy suggested that the barber add sugar and caraway seeds. About 1850, the barber became a baker, closing his barbershop and opening a biscuit factory, bestowing his customer's name on the (slightly) improved biscuit.

à blanc - a French term, literally "in white," denoting foods cooked without browning.

abruzzese - the Italian name for dishes cooked in the style of the Abruzzo region of Italy. Abruzzese cuisine centers around peasant dishes, such as *maccheroni alla chitarra* ("guitar pasta," roughly cut using a wooden box fitted with wires that looks like a guitar). Many of these dishes contain locally grown hot chiles.

absinthe - a bitter green high-**proof** liquor made from wormwood, anise and a variety of other herbs, called *La Fée Verte* in France, meaning The Green Fairy. This potent drink is traditionally served drizzled over a sugar cube, held in a special perforated spoon, over a glass of water, turning the liquid milky white. Absinthe was first bottled and promoted as a medicinal cure-all by the French physician **Pierre Ordinaire,** who fled the French Revolution in the 1790s and settled in Couvet, Switzerland, where wormwood grew wild. Ordinaire learned of absinthe from two sisters in Couvet, who were already making it before he arrived.

Popular in Europe in the 19th and early 20th century but banned in Switzerland (the ban was repealed in 2005), the aromatic liqueur was blamed for everything from gastrointestinal irritation to hallucinations to even death among habitual users. Many countries banned its sale including the U.S. in 1912 and France in 1915. It was no doubt a powerful liquor but many of the claims against absinthe were most likely a result of yellow journalism and the temper of the times. The active ingredient was said to be **thujone,** a neurotoxin, but modern studies of vintage absinthe show just trace amounts of it.

Absinthe enjoyed its greatest popularity in France in the late 1800s, with Vincent van Gogh, Paul Verlaine and Oscar Wilde among its most ardent imbibers. It also achieved great popularity in New Orleans, where it was widely consumed by artists, musicians and Storyville madams.

absolute alcohol - **1.** a pure, water-free alcohol, with specific gravity of 0.79359; boiling point 173°F (78°C). The North American standard is 200 proof, while the British standard is 175.1 proof. **2.** the total amount of alcohol contained in a beverage.

aca - a type of corn (maize) beverage brewed in Peru since at least 200 BC. It was both consumed by the common people and offered to the gods.

acacia - a small, often thorny shrub of the genus *Acacia*, which grows in deserts. It's used to make a gum that relieves coughs. In France, its fragrant yellow flowers (commonly known as mimosa and wattle) are made into fritters and a homemade liqueur. Honey is also made from acacia flowers. In Italy, a honey called *miele d'Abruzzo* is made by bees that feed primarily on acacia flowers.

acacia honey - see HONEY.

accidental food additive - see INCIDENTAL FOOD ADDITIVE.

accoub - a thistle, *Gundelia tournefortii*, native to Syria but found throughout the Mediterranean. The shoots, when mature, can be cooked like asparagus, while the buds are cooked in the same manner as new potatoes.

acephala - a name used for mollusks, such as the oyster, mussel and scallop, which do not have a distinct head.

acerola - also **Barbados cherry, Puerto Rican cherry, West Indian cherry.** The cherrylike, semisweet fruit of the shrubby *Malpighia punicifolia*. Indigenous to the Lesser Antilles and tropical South America, it naturalized throughout the American tropics and Caribbean after its introduction in the early 1900s. The fruit is so rich in vitamin C, that acerola seedlings were distributed for Victory Gardens during the Second World War.

acerola

acesulfame potassium - also **acesulfame-K.** A calorie-free artificial sweetener, about 200 times sweeter than sugar, approved for use in everything from beverages to baked goods. It doesn't break down when exposed to heat, as **aspartame** does, so it can be used in baking, similar to **sucralose.** It also has a long shelf life, so it is used widely in packaged foods and drinks. See also ARTIFICIAL SWEETENERS, SACCHARIN.

acetic acid - a clear acid that gives vinegar its distinctive taste, formed by bacteria's effect on the alcohol in wine, beer or cider.

achar - also **achaar.** A word used in India to refer to various types of salted or pickled relishes, which can be either sweet or hot.

achee - see ACKEE.

achilée - a wild herb, *Achillea ptarmica*, sometimes called either **milfoil** or **goose tongue,** a little of which (chopped like chervil) can be used in salads.

achiote seed - the seed of the annatto tree, *Bixa orellana*, which is bright or rusty red in color. Slightly bitter in taste, it is widely used in Latin American cooking. It provides a virtually tasteless dye, which has been used for centuries to color butter, margarine, Cheshire cheese, many types of Cheddar cheese and smoked fish. A red oil from these seeds was used by some Native Americans to protect their skins from the sun.

acid - any of a large group of substances that are essential to the working of the body and are found in many foods. All acids are sour to a greater or lesser degree. Foods containing acids include vinegar (acetic acid), lemon juice (citric acid), soured milk products (lactic acid) and wine (tartaric acid). Acids are also found in the human digestive tract, where they help break down foods. In cooking, acids are used in marinades as a tenderizer and as a preservative in pickling. The action of "cooking" food in an acidic preparation, such as for raw fish (**seviche**), is well known in some Mediterranean and South American countries.

acid curd cheese - also **lactic curd cheese.** A cheese, such as cottage cheese, made using only the lactic acid in sour milk or a lactic acid culture to initiate the curdling process. Acid curd cheeses do not use **rennet** to curdle them, so they are acceptable for strict vegetarians.

acid drops - an English acidic hard candy or boiled sweet.

acidity - the relative sourness of a wine due to its natural acid content. Acid is an important component in the taste of a wine: too much makes it sharp and harsh, too little makes it flat and uninteresting. A balanced wine contains just the right amount of acidity to complement its sweetness and alcohol content. Wines are made up of a variety of acids, some that form as a result of the fermentation process, and some, such as tartaric, malic and citric acids, that come from the grapes themselves. These acids are also crucial in preserving a fine wine and allowing it to age properly if it is cellared for an extended period of time.

acidophilus milk - milk that has been soured slightly by the *Lactobacillus acidophilus* bacteria, making the lactose in the milk easier to digest.

acidulated water - also **acid rinse.** This is water to which a small amount of some acid, such as vinegar or lemon juice, has been added to prevent discoloration in fruits and vegetables, such as apples and artichokes.

acine di pepe - see PASTA.

acitrón - the candied flesh or stem of the *biznaga* cactus, *Echinocactus grandis*, used in Mexican cooking. It's often shaped into bars and used for desserts and in some meat dishes. It does not have a distinct flavor of its own but does add texture. Candied citron may be substituted for acitrón in cooking.

ackee - also **achee, akee.** A bland, red or yellow fruit of a tropical evergreen tree, *Blighia sapida*, originally native to West Africa but now associated especially with Jamaica. It was introduced to the West Indies by Capt. William Bligh (of *Mutiny on the Bounty* fame), and its Latin name bears tribute to him. The peculiarity of the fruit is that, unless it has fully ripened, it's deadly poisonous, and all seeds need to be removed before consumption. After these precautions, it's edible either raw or cooked. It's traditionally cooked and eaten with saltfish as one of Jamaica's national dishes.

ackee

açorda - a Portuguese garlic bread porridge.

acorn - a nut borne by the oak tree of the genus *Quercus*. In North America, several species of oak are edible especially the California Black Oak, which gets high marks for taste. The sweetest varieties come from areas around the Mediterranean and W. Asia, called the *Quercus ilex* var. *rotundifolia*. In Greek legend, the acorn was a staple food during the Golden Age. Its high carbohydrate content led to its use as a pseudo-cereal by some Native Americans and by Europeans during times of famine. Acorns can also be ground and roasted to make a type of coffee.

acorn barnacle - a small shellfish, *Balanus balanoides*, which lives on rocks in temperate and cold salt water. The flesh is usually prepared like crabmeat.

acorn squash - see SQUASH.

acqua cotta - an Italian vegetable soup that originated in Tuscany, made of a variety of different vegetables, usually tomatoes, mushrooms, zucchini, carrots and/or onions, or anything else that is available or in season. The finished soup is poured over a slice or two of rustic **artisanal** bread and topped with a layer of grated Romano cheese, sometimes with egg beaten into the cheese for extra flavor and texture. The name means "cooked water" in Italian; it was a common dish of shepherds and the poor, for whom the soup might have been very thin at times.

acrid - a negative wine-tasting term used to describe a wine that contains excessive sulfur compounds, sometimes making it smell and taste like a rotten egg. An acrid wine is bitter, harsh-smelling and -tasting.

active dry yeast - a widely available form of dehydrated yeast sold as dry granules. See also DRIED BAKER'S YEAST, YEAST.

Acton, Eliza - see profile right.

adafina - see DAFINA.

additives - see FOOD ADDITIVES.

ade - a drink, such as lemonade, made by mixing citrus juice with water and sugar.

adjust - to modify the seasoning in a dish, especially just before serving and to the cook's individual taste. This is the final step in preparing food.

Acton, Eliza (1799–1859) - English poet and author of *Modern Cookery for Private Families* (1845), which introduced numerous innovations in style and method to recipe writing and was the most successful cookbook of its era. Acton was born in Sussex, England, and her story is far from typical for a woman of her time. It hints of an unconventional past and the possibility of a child born out of wedlock. She lived for a time in France, dabbled in social reform and tried her hand at journalism, eventually becoming a poet with a modest reputation. The daughter of a brewer, Acton never married and spent much of her life cooking and keeping house for her mother and herself. A poetry submission to her publishers evoked the suggestion that she write a cookbook, instead. Turning her poet's eye for detail and facility with language to the practicalities of cooking, she produced a classic, which **Elizabeth David** deemed "the greatest cookery book in our language."

Expansive in scope, her recipes, which include dishes of French and Jewish origin, as well as a section on "foreign cookery," were written for an audience of inexperienced housewives with few servants, the product of pre-industrial England's emerging middle class. Acton introduced a level of precision previously lacking in cookery books by listing ingredients with quantities, cooking times, and specific methodology in a consistent style. Summations of the recipe and particular observations (today these would likely be called "tips") enhanced the likelihood of a successful result. Although her book was a hit and remained in print for more than 50 years, it did not achieve the lasting recognition of some imitators, notably the *Book of Household Management* by **Isabella Beeton.** Much copied, if not plagiarized, Acton was well aware of "the unscrupulous manner in which large portions of my volume have been appropriated by contemporary authors." Fortunately, her achievement has once again been recognized and since the late 1960s, new editions of her book have been published in a scholarly context that has established her significance.

Admirals - a beautiful-looking English layered cheese, with pink port wine Cheddar surrounding layers of bluish-green Stilton. Admirals is considered an excellent after-dinner cheese, best eaten with a glass of port, red wine or dessert wine.

adobo - a national dish of the Philippines, consisting of pork and/or chicken marinated in vinegar, bay leaf, garlic and soy sauce. It's served with rice and can be eaten hot or cold. Adobos can also be made with other meats, as well as squid, catfish or shellfish.

adobo sauce - **1.** a Spanish marinade of vinegar and spices, most commonly oregano and paprika, used to flavor meat and fish before cooking. **2.** a dark red piquant Mexican sauce made from ground chiles, herbs and vinegar, used both as a marinade and a condiment.

Adrià, Ferrán - see profile on page 14.

adulteration - the addition of inferior or unnecessary substances to food. Once widespread, this practice has been eliminated or brought under control in many countries, especially in those that require ingredients to be listed on packaging.

advieh - the Persian name for a spice mixture made from a wide variety of spices and customized by individuals to suit the dishes they are preparing, from delicate to hearty. In one region of Persia, it is sprinkled over steamed rice and is likely to contain dried rose petals.

advocaat - a Dutch liqueur based on brandy and egg yolks.

adzuki bean - see AZUKI BEAN.

aebleflaesk - a Danish dish of fried salt pork or bacon with fried apple.

aeblepidsvin - a Danish dessert of apples, lemon juice and toasted almonds.

aebleskive - pl. **aebleskiver.** A small, round, puffy pancake flavored with apple, traditionally eaten in Denmark for holiday breakfasts or in the winter with spiced red wine. The pancakes can be plain, served with applesauce on top, or made with grated apple in the dough. The cakes are made in a special pan called an aebleskive pan, or sometimes ebelskiver iron, a modified cast-iron skillet with seven half-sphere depressions in it for cooking the puffy round pancakes.

Adrià, Ferrán (1962–) - Catalán chef whose culinary innovations have put him in a category all his own. French chef **Paul Bocuse** has said, "Adrià is doing the most exciting things in our profession today." Basque chef Juan Mari Arzak, considered the father of modern Spanish cuisine, says that Adrià "is the most innovative man in the history of cooking." In 1983, Adrià became an apprentice at El Bulli, the restaurant he eventually made famous and now owns, situated near the coastal town of Rosas, a short distance from the French border. Because the restaurant is open April to September, Adrià spends six months off-season experimenting in his "laboratory workshop," an über-modern facility in Barcelona, 92 miles (148 km) to the south. There, he teams up with a chemist, an industrial designer and a crew of chefs that includes his brother, Albert, experimenting and developing new dishes and techniques. Dining at El Bulli entails eating as many as 25 to 30 courses, most of them bite-size, presented on a spoon or in a miniature vessel, often manipulated into foams, sprays, gels and mists, produced by unique gadgets invented in the lab. Some recent experimentation involves atomizers for sweetening or salting at the table and spray-on sauces of wine or chocolate.

Aegle marmelos - see BAEL.

aemono - a Japanese word meaning "dressed foods," used to refer to salads or salad-like dishes served with a dressing, often used as appetizers or between meals. (The dressing, which is often made with a base of puréed tofu, may also be referred to as aemono.)

aerate - see SIFT.

aettekees - also **ettekees.** A Belgian cheese whose name is a dialectal corruption of *hardkees*, meaning "hard cheese." It's a strong-smelling fermented type of cream cheese, hardened and slightly salted. In Brussels, it goes by the nickname *stirkees*, meaning "stinking."

affinage - a French word that means both the art of ripening and curing a cheese.

affineur - the French term for an expert in *affinage*.

affogato - a dessert consisting of a shot of hot **espresso** poured over a scoop of vanilla **gelato** or ice cream. The name means "drowned" in Italian.

Afghan biscuit - made from a base of cream, cornflakes and cocoa, this biscuit is a reminder that everywhere the British went, they carried with them some form of this erstwhile biscuit, particularly in former British colonies, such as Afghanistan and New Zealand, where the biscuit is still made today.

African basil - see BASIL.

African horned cucumber - also **African horned melon.** See KIWANO.

afternoon tea - also **cream tea.** A quintessentially British, comparatively light afternoon meal, consisting of tea, sandwiches (especially cucumber sandwiches), scones and cakes with cream fillings. See also HIGH TEA.

aftersmell - an odor sensation that lingers after swallowing any alcoholic beverage.

aftertaste - the taste, odor and sensation that linger after swallowing a food or beverage, particularly alcoholic beverages.

agape - a French term from the Greek *agape*, meaning "love," originally used to describe a communal meal that the early Christians shared together. In modern France, the word *agape* denotes a meal among family or friends characterized by abundant food and conviviality. Every Masonic Lodge meeting finishes with a convivial agape.

agar-agar - also **agar, Bengal isinglass, Ceylon moss, Japanese moss, vegetable gelatin.** A gum obtained from an edible red seaweed of the genera *Eucheuma* or *Gelidium*. It's used as a gelling and thickening agent for certain food preparations, marked by its ability to set at room temperature (unlike gelatin) and to stay set at very high temperatures. The name is from Malay, meaning "jelly" or "gelatin." Salanganes, swallow-like Asian swiftlets, use agar-agar in the construction of their nests, which are used to make **bird's nest soup.** Agar-agar is also used as a medium for the experimental cultivation of bacteria.

agaric - the scientific classification Agaricales covers all the fungi that have a characteristic "mushroom" shape. In non-scientific usage, the term agaric is most correctly used in reference to cultivated mushrooms only. Because of these two sometimes conflicting meanings, the term can cause confusion. The name comes from the Latin *agaricum* and the Greek name for mushrooms, *Agarikon*, an allusion to the town of Agara, once famous for its mushrooms.

agar wood - a very fragrant wood, *Aquillaria agallocha*, which was mainly used as incense by Orthodox churches in the Orient. Modern Moroccan cuisine uses the wood as an ingredient in a spice mixture called *ras-el-hanout* or *oud kameira*.

agave - a plant of the genus *Agave*, of which there are several species, including the American aloe. **Tequila** is made from the blue agave in Mexico. It's also commonly known as the century plant because the plant lives for many years before flowering. Four major parts of the agave are edible: the flowers, leaves, stalks or basal rosettes and sap. Each plant can produce several pounds (1 kg) of sweet, edible flowers during the summer months. The leaves are eaten during the winter and spring, when they are full of sap. The plant is often infested with the larvae of *Megathymus stephousi*, the agave skipper butterfly, which were roasted with the leaves and then picked off and eaten as a delicacy by the Aztecs and Mayans (and still are today in South and Central America, especially Mexico). The stalks, which are picked in summer before the plants blossom, are also roasted and taste like molasses. After full maturation, the sap (*aguamiel*, or "honey water") drains down the stalk and is harvested, fermented and sometimes distilled. There are more than 400 varieties of the plant, including mescalines, and only six can produce a fairly decent wine. The Aztecs were making wine from this plant before the conquistadors showed them the process of distillation. The name comes from the Greek word *agunos*, meaning "noble." The Spaniards called the plant *maguey*.

agave

age - to store food or spirits under controlled conditions as a means of improving the flavor, etc. **1.** Many spirits and wines are aged in wooden barrels before bottling. In most cases, once a spirit is bottled, the aging process stops. This is why, for example, a Scotch that was aged for 12 years and sits on a shelf for 10 years unopened is still a 12-year-old Scotch. Some wines, such as **Bordeaux,** continue to age in the bottle.
2. Meat is aged by hanging in cold storage. The changes that occur are due to enzyme action that improves both the flavor and the tenderness of meat. Aged meats (both lean and fat) also brown better during cooking and are juicier than unripened cuts. However, aged meats may develop a grayer interior color than unripened meats, and too long an aging process may result in a strong, gamy or "off" flavor and odor.
3. Aging cheese affects both its flavor and its texture. Some cheeses are aged for many years.

agedashi - a Japanese dish of deep-fried tofu served with Asian radishes (**daikon**), dried **bonito** flakes, ginger and a soy-based dipping sauce.

agemono - a Japanese cooking term referring to deep-frying and the foods produced by this method, such as **tempura.**

aggregate fruit - see DRUPE FRUIT.

aggressive - a negative wine-tasting term used to describe a wine that has excessive **tannins** or **acidity,** making it harsh.

aglio e olio - the most basic Italian pasta sauce, meaning simply "garlic and oil." This simple combination is almost invariably served on long pasta, such as spaghetti or linguine. A small serving of the dish is believed by some to be a digestive aid after a large meal.

agliota - an Italian sauce made of garlic slices, bread crumbs and vinegar.

Aitken, Kate (1891–1971) - Canadian broadcaster, journalist and cookbook author. Born in a small town in Ontario, Kate Scott learned the domestic arts from her mother, an excellent cook and homemaker, before marrying her childhood sweetheart, Henry Aitken, in 1914. The young couple purchased land, and Kate soon established herself as a poultry farmer. She also launched a canning operation to process their produce, which developed into a business making 12,000 jars of preserves a year.

Personable and energetic, Aitken soon attracted government attention and became a spokesperson for the agricultural sector in Canada and abroad. During this period she developed her career as a journalist, fostering her domestic credentials by teaching cooking and running women's activities at the Canadian National Exhibition. In 1934, she launched her radio career with a show that was carried across Canada, first in syndication, then by the Canadian Broadcasting Corporation. She traveled the world interviewing such leaders as Benito Mussolini, Josef Stalin and Franklin Delano Roosevelt, while remaining in touch with her audience by assigning equal value to homemaking topics. When she published *Kate Aitken's Canadian Cook Book* in 1945, its comforting combination of traditional recipes and helpful hints, such as tips on canning, was an instant success. A marvel on many fronts, at the height of her career she employed 21 secretaries to deal with her mail. In 1958, she retired from broadcasting, although she continued her involvement as a board member of the CBC. She passed away on the family farm in 1971.

agnolotti - see PASTA.

agraz - a sour **sorbet**-like dessert of southern Spain and North Africa, similar in texture to a **granita,** made from ground almonds, sugar and **verjuice.** The name comes from the Spanish *agraz*, meaning "verjuice," and derived from the Latin *acrus*, meaning "sour."

agresto - the Italian version of **verjuice.** It's the juice of unripe grapes, used occasionally in some sauces instead of vinegar.

agrodolce - the favorite "sour-sweet" sauce of Italy, made with a few lumps of sugar steeped in vinegar and cooked until caramelized. Shallots, seedless raisins, capers and white wine are added, and the sauce is finally reduced with **demi-glace.** See also AIGRE-DOUX.

agua de jamaica - see JAMAICA.

aguardente - a Portuguese term for brandy.

aguardiente - a Spanish term for strong, but low-quality spirits made from sugarcane. In South America, it's also known as *aguardiente de caña*.

aguaxima - a variety of Brazilian black pepper.

ahi - a Hawaiian name for both the **bigeye tuna** and **yellowfin tuna.**

ahuatle - an aquatic insect that is toasted and eaten in Mexico. Its white eggs are called *ahuautli*. They are gathered in bunches, dried and then toasted, and eaten with chili and tortillas.

aigre-doux - a French word for a sauce containing both sour (aigre) and sweet (doux) ingredients, such as sugar and vinegar. See also AGRODOLCE.

aigrette - a French word used to describe savory deep-fried morsels, usually served as appetizers.

aïgroissade - in Provence, cooked vegetables mixed with a garlicky mayonnaise.

aiguillette - a French term, originally meaning "small needle," for a long, narrow strip of rump steak or fowl, especially duck, cut lengthwise or with the grain.

aillade - a French sauce made of garlic, onions, chives, leeks, herbs, spices and oil.

aïoli - a garlic mayonnaise made in Provence since the Middle Ages, usually served with fish, meat and various steamed vegetables. The name comes from the Provençal *aïoli* (*aïl*, meaning "garlic," plus *oli*, meaning "oil").

airelle - a general name for a berry shrub in the genus *Vaccinium* including bilberry and blueberry.

airelle rouge - also **canneberge.** The French name given to cranberry.

aitchbone - the rump bone of an ox or the cut of beef lying over it; also called the edgebone by false etymology. The name comes from the Middle English word *nache-bone* and the Latin *natis*, both meaning "buttock."

Aitken, Kate - see profile left.

ajam panggang - an Indonesian dish consisting of fried chicken flavored with ginger, saffron, garlic and chile peppers.

aji - also **aji amarillo.** See CHILE PEPPER.

aji-no-moto - the Japanese name for **monosodium glutamate** (MSG).

ajitsuke nori - see NORI.

ajowan - also **ajwain, bishop's weed.** The greenish-brown striped seeds of an umbelliferous plant, *Trachyspermum ammi*, related to caraway. Although the seeds appear similar to cumin or caraway seeds, they actually taste more like thyme. They are spicy and slightly bitter and can be preserved for decades. Ajowan contains great amounts of thymol in its chemical constitution, making it a powerful germicide. In India, a beverage derived from the seeds is prescribed for "traveler's tummy" and cholera. Some sources incorrectly claim that the English name for ajowan is "lovage." Although both plants belong to the same family, they are not one and the same.

ajvar - a relish made of eggplants and roasted bell or paprika peppers (can be sweet or hot, green or red), seasoned with garlic and onions and thickened with olive oil. Ajvar hails from the Balkan region of Europe and is popular there and in Greece as a condiment or side dish. It is available in jars in North America, but is a common homemade preserve in the Balkans after the autumn pepper harvest.

ajvar

akagai - see ARK SHELL.

akala - a sweet, juicy Hawaiian berry resembling a large raspberry.

akee - see ACKEE.

akni - in India, a delicate, aromatic broth used to poach or flavor either meats or fish.

aku - also **skipjack tuna.** See TUNA.

akule - also **bigeye scad.** A fish found in Hawaiian waters, usually eaten salted and dried.

akvavit - see AQUAVIT.

al - an Italian contraction meaning "at," "to" or "in the style of," used in cooking terms, such as **al dente.**

à la - a French phrase meaning "in the manner or style of," *à la mode de*. In cooking, it's used to mean that a particular dish has been prepared or garnished in a specified style. In this book, many entries for terms beginning *à la* (or *à l'*) can be found listed under the main word (for example, **à la Nesselrode** can be found at **Nesselrode**).

à la carte - a French term meaning "by the menu," indicating that each item is priced separately, as opposed to **table d'hôte** or **prix fixe,** meaning a meal of several courses offered at a fixed price.

à la diable - the French term for whole poultry split in half and grilled, then served with **diable sauce.**

alaea salt - see RED SALT.

alajú - a Spanish pastry made of sugar, nuts and ginger.

à la king - a dish of diced or cubed food (usually chicken or turkey) served in a rich cream sauce with mushrooms, green peppers and pimientos. The dish was introduced in the U.S. in the 1920s, when Foxhall P. Keene, the son of Wall Street broker James R. Keene, requested that the chef of **Delmonico's** restaurant create a chicken dish. The chef created one with pimiento and green pepper in a sherry cream sauce. He had no problem coming up with a name for it: Chicken à la Keene, which ultimately changed to Chicken à la king.

à l'américaine - a dish, usually of seafood, made with olive oil, tomatoes, wine and onions, the most popular of which is **lobster à l'américaine.**

à la mode - a French phrase meaning, literally, "in the current fashion." It originated in Paris in the late 18th century, when a restaurant hung a sign above its door to announce that only the finest beef was used in the kitchen. The sign portrayed a cow with a blue ribbon around its neck and a flower bonnet on its head. To Parisians, this suggested a fashionable cow, and the restaurant soon became known as Bœuf à la Mode. The specialty of the house was a dish of braised beef, well simmered in a stock spiked with brandy and wine, still known today as *bœuf à la mode*. Pie à la mode, meaning pie with ice cream, is strictly North American. It made its appearance circa 1920, after commercial ice cream became widely available.

a la plancha - a Spanish term meaning pan-fried or grilled, such as *calamares a la plancha* (pan-fried or grilled squid), often used in North America to describe a dish that is served sizzling on a small griddle or grill pan. *Plancha* is the Spanish word for a plate or sheet of metal.

Alaska cod - see SABLEFISH.

Alaska king crab - see CRAB.

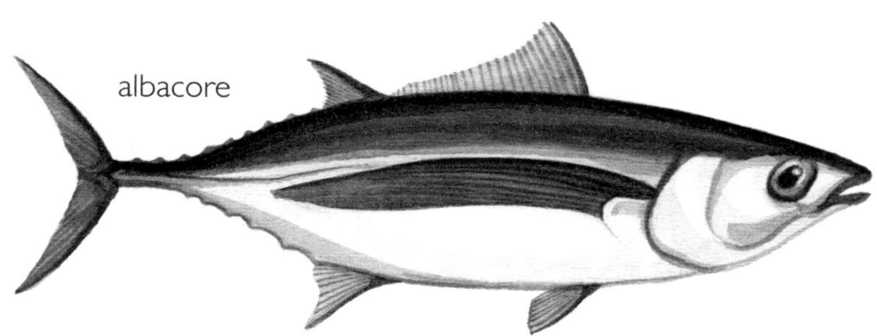

albacore - also **long-finned tuna, white-meat tuna.** A large fish, *Thunnus alalunga,* of the tuna family, one of the most prized of the tunas. Its flesh is noticeably lighter in color than that of other tuna, and is the only tuna that can be labeled "white" on cans. The name came into English via the Portuguese *albacor,* the Spanish *albacora* and the Arabic *albakurah* (from Arabic, *al* meaning "the" and *bakr* meaning "young camel").

Al-Baghdadi - see profile right.

Albany beef - in the 19th century, New York's Hudson River was abundant with sturgeon, and caviar was so plentiful that tavern owners regularly offered it under this name as a free snack.

albatross - any of various large, long-winged birds of the Diomedeidae family, which come ashore only to nest. Joseph Bank, a companion of Capt. Cook on the *Endeavour,* recorded in his diary that the crew caught some of these birds while approaching Tahiti. In his entry for February 5, 1769, he wrote, "The birds were so good that everybody commended them and eat heartily of them tho there was fresh pork upon the table."

albedo - a name given to the white inner pith of oranges and other citrus fruit.

Albert sauce - a cream sauce used in English cooking, flavored with horseradish and mustard, usually served over braised beef. It's named after Prince Albert of Saxe-Coburg-Gotha (1819–1861), husband and consort of Queen Victoria.

albóndiga - the Spanish (and Mexican) name for a spicy meatball made of pork and/or beef, served in a tomato sauce or in a beef broth.

albumen - **1.** an old-fashioned word for the white of an egg. **2.** the substance found between the skin and germ of many seeds, usually the edible part.

albumin - a class of water-soluble proteins found in egg white, milk and blood. These proteins coagulate when heated. The word comes from the Latin *albus*, meaning "white."

al burro - an Italian style of serving pasta, simply tossed with butter.

Alcatiore, Jules - see OYSTERS ROCKEFELLER.

alcohol - ethyl alcohol or ethanol, the only alcohol suitable for drinking. The word is also used as a general term for any alcoholic liquor. The term was not applied explicitly to distilled spirits until the 16th century. Although the widespread use of alcohol in cooking is relatively recent, the Egyptians may have cooked beer flavored with mandrake root, and the Greeks and the Romans may have used wine in their recipes in preference to water or as a marinade for tough and salted meats. By 300 BC, the Aztecs were brewing **pulque** from the agave cactus, but didn't learn to distill it

Al-Baghdadi (Shamseddin Ibn Al-Hassan Al-Baghdadi) (13th century) - Persian author of the first published book of Middle Eastern recipes. Culinary historians do not know much about Al-Baghdadi but they do know he was an ardent gastronome who considered food above wine, music and sex. His opus, *Kitab Al-Tabikh* (Cookbook), appeared in the 1220s. Another gastronomic text by an unknown author appeared nearly a century later, *Kitab Al-Wusla ilal-Habib fi Wasfi Al-Tayibati wal-Tib* (Book of the Bond with the Friend, or the Description of Good Dishes and Perfumes). At the time, there were only 10 handwritten copies in existence. Still, both books serve to illustrate the luxury and sophistication of 12th- and 13th-century Persian culture.

into **tequila** until taught by the conquistadors. The happy discovery of distillation is credited to the Chinese, who were probably producing a type of rice spirit by 1000 BC. The use of the **alembic** or "still" was pursued only after an Arab chemist named Geber wrote about his experiments with distillation in AD 800.

Alcohol is produced by yeast, which eats the sugar in grapes or grains, excreting alcohol and carbon dioxide in a process called fermentation. Distillation goes several steps beyond, extracting and concentrating the alcohol. "Alcohol" comes from the Arabic *al kuhl,* meaning "the kohl," because the method of distillation by vaporizing native ferment was similar to that used to produce a black powder by condensing a vapor of the metal antimony. The powder was used cosmetically, and the name survives as kohl, a black eyeliner still used in North Africa, India and the Middle East.

alcoholmetry - the percentage of **absolute alcohol** in any spirit, given either by volume or weight. Percentage by weight remains the same at all temperatures, but the percentage by volume varies with the temperature or heat of the liquid. American law requires that the alcohol content of liquor and wine must be expressed as a percentage, not just in **proof.**

aldehyde - any of a large class of organic compounds derived from alcohols through dehydrogenation (oxidation) and containing the grouping (or radical) CHO. When aldehydes are oxidized further, acid is produced. Some aldehydes contribute to the bouquet of wine.

al dente - an Italian term literally meaning "to the tooth," used to describe pasta that is not overcooked or soft, but with a bit of resistance in the bite.

ale - a fuller-flavored category of beer made with top-fermenting yeast, usually made using the simple, traditional infusion mashing method of brewing. The name is derived from the Old Norse *ol* (modern Danish and Norwegian *øl*, Swedish *öl* and Finnish *olut*). The Vikings called their favorite alcoholic barley drink *aul*, quaffing vast quantities of it before heading into battle. The Old English word for ale was *ealu*,

COMMON NORTH AMERICAN ALES

amber ale - see PALE ALE.

brown ale - gentle, good malt flavor, with notes of caramel and fruit.

pale ale - also **amber ale.** Dry, fruity, often with a pleasantly bitter aftertaste, more of a medium gold color than truly pale. India pale ale, a common subtype, was developed for British officers living in India in the 1800s. It was higher in alcohol than other pale ales, which made it more stable to transport and less likely to be ruined by the long journey at sea from England to India. Because it was shipped in large oak casks, it picked up some of the vanilla and caramel flavors in the wood, as certain wines do. Today, some brewers still age their India pale ale in oak barrels to give it that distinctive flavor.

porter - a type of dark ale that is stronger both in flavor and in alcohol content than regular ale. Its strong flavor comes from toasting the malt before the ale is brewed.

stout - an ale made with roasted malt or barley. It is stronger than regular ale. Guinness is a well-known stout.

which is derived from the Indo-European root word *alu-*, meaning something related to sorcery, magic or intoxication.

Ales are generally a bit higher in alcohol than **lager** beers. They tend to be fruitier tasting, a bit darker in color and a tad on the bitter side in some cases. To achieve their optimum flavor, ales should be drunk at a slightly higher temperature (50° to 55°F/4° to 7°C) than lagers. In North America, lager beers are more popular, but in Britain, Ireland and Belgium, ales reign supreme. There is an enormous array of ales around the world, including barleywine (a sweet, potent ale with an alcohol content similar to that of wine), bitters, brown ale, pale ale, porter, stout, Trappist ale and cloudy, yeasty wheat beers. See also BEER, NEAR BEER, SMALL ALE.

alecost - see COSTMARY.

alembic - a device used for distilling liquor, from the Arabic word *al'anbiq*, meaning "still." Made from copper, in its simplest form an alembic has two chambers connected by a tube. The mixture to be distilled is placed in the larger of the two chambers and heated until it simmers. The alcoholic steam it gives off collects on the cap of the chamber and, as it cools and condenses, runs down the tube into the smaller chamber. This pure liquor is left to cool and is then distilled again to create the richest possible balanced flavor. In more complex alembics, the tube down to the collection chamber is coiled (and called a serpentine) and runs through a container of cold water, which forces the steam to cool quickly and condense.

alemtejo - a Portuguese soft cheese typically made from ewe's milk and thistle flowers, Goat's milk is often added. It's cylindrical in form and usually made in three sizes: 2 ounces (60 g), 1 pound (500 g) and 4 pounds (2 kg).

alewife - see HERRING.

alewife caviar - found primarily in the U.S., an inexpensive caviar substitute made from processed herring roe.

alexanders

alexanders - also **black lovage, horse parsley, wild celery.** A plant of the genus *Smyrnium olusatrum*, now almost forgotten, formerly widely used in England as an herb and as a vegetable in salads, with a taste between celery and parsley. This sturdy, umbelliferous herb can reach up to 5 feet (1.5 m) in height, with yellow-green flowers and black berries. The stems can be blanched for consumption in early spring, when the plant is edible. Its French name is *persil de Macédoine* or *maceron*, and it was one of the plants Romans brought to the British Isles in their "backpacks," which carried both food and medicine. The seeds were used as an infusion for any kind of stomach problem, grippe and flatulence. From England, it traveled to America with the Pilgrims.

alfajore - caramel-filled sandwich cookies popular in South America, especially in Argentina, Chile, Uruguay and Peru. The filling is either **cajeta** or **dulce de leche.**

alfalfa - an herbaceous plant, *Medicago sativa*, known primarily as cattle feed, cultivated for livestock in Asia since prehistoric times. The Roman historian and naturalist **Pliny** mentions that alfalfa was introduced to Europe (Greece)

alfalfa

in 491 BC by the invading Persian emperor Darius. The Spanish introduced it to South America. Today, the germinated **sprouts** are eaten by humans, and sometimes the young leaves are used in infusions and herbal tea. Alfalfa sprouts can be eaten raw or added at the last minute to cooked foods. Specialty stores carry flour made from the leaves.

alfalfa honey - see HONEY.

al forno - an Italian menu term meaning "oven-baked," such as *rigatoni al forno*.

Alfredo sauce - a pasta sauce made with cream, butter and Parmesan cheese, a specialty of the Alfredo restaurant in Rome, most often served with fettuccine noodles. The original owner was Alfredo Di Lelio, who is said to have invented the dish in 1914 in the hopes of perking up his wife's appetite while she was recovering from childbirth. Di Lelio distinguished his adaptation by using triple-rich butter and only the heart of the Parmesan wheel. It became famous after film stars Mary Pickford and Douglas Fairbanks visited Rome on their honeymoon in 1927 and dined at Alfredo's every night they were there. At the end of their stay, they presented Di Lelio with a golden fork and spoon and proclaimed him "King of the Noodles." The popularity of the dish widened when the couple returned to America, although it was not well known by this name in Italy until after the Second World War.

al fresco - from the Italian for "fresh" or "cool," referring to dining outdoors on a restaurant patio, backyard terrace or picnic.

al funghetto - from the Italian *funghi*, meaning "with mushrooms," or for vegetables "cooked like mushrooms," with garlic, parsley and olive oil, a style often used for eggplant and zucchini.

alga mar - an edible and expensive seaweed of the genus *Durvillea antartica*, from Chile.

Algérienne - a French accompaniment for meat consisting of tomatoes sautéed in oil and **croquettes** of sweet potatoes.

algin - a gelatinous substance obtained from brown algae, especially the giant kelp from Asian waters, used as a thickener and emulsifier, especially in ice cream, pudding, pie filling and syrup. An **alginate** is technically a type of algin but is another name for a gum, stabilizer or emulsifier derived from brown seaweed.

alginate - see ALGIN.

alheira - a small Portuguese sausage made of chicken, turkey, beef, pork or a combination, garlic and herbs. *Alho* is Portuguese for garlic.

Ali-Bab - see BABINSKI, HENRI.

aliolo - the Spanish term for the French **aïoli,** a mayonnaise strongly flavored with garlic, generally served with seafood.

alkanna - also **alkanet.** A red or brown coloring derived from the root of two plants from the borage family, Alkanna tinctoria or A. officinalis. Used to color both food and fabric since the time of the early Arab civilizations, the dye turns red when dissolved in alcohol or oil and brown when dissolved in water. Its name is taken from the Arabic *al hinnã*, meaning "the dye," and it is still used in sausage casings and to color margarine.

alla - an Italian word like the French **à la,** meaning "in the manner or style of," indicating that a dish has been prepared in a certain style, such as *spinaci alla Fiorentina*, which means "spinach Florentine-style."

alla diavola - see DIAVOLO.

allemande sauce - also **Parisienne sauce.** A white or velouté sauce (one of the classic mother sauces outlined by 19th-century chef **Antonin Carême** in his *L'art de la cuisine française*, published in 1833) made with chicken or meat stock and thickened with egg yolk. Although the sauce is French, the name translates to "German sauce."

alliaceous - **1.** pertaining to the genus *Allium*, of the lily family, referring to garlic, onion, shallot and leek. **2.** smelling or tasting like garlic or onion.

alligator - this lizard-like reptile yields three types of meat: tender, white tail meat resembling veal; slightly tougher, pinker body meat; and dark tail meat, which is tough and used only for braising. Although eating alligator meat is a tradition in the southern U.S., especially in Louisiana, it seemed likely that this would stop when alligators were given protected status in the 1960s. However, the alligator is now farmed for human consumption, usually available only in its native regions.

alligator pear - see AVOCADO.

alligator pepper - see GRAINS OF PARADISE.

all-purpose flour - see FLOUR.

allspice - also **Jamaican pepper.** The dried, unripe berries of *Pimenta dioica*, a tree native to the West Indies and South America but grown predominantly in Jamaica. The spice is also known as pimiento or Jamaica pepper, because early Spanish explorers to Jamaica thought the berries resembled peppercorns. The use of allspice was noted in London in the early 1600s. It's widely used in North America and northern (but not usually southern) Europe. The English name refers to its flavor, which is similar to a combination of cloves, pepper, cinnamon and nutmeg.

allumette - **1.** from the French for "match." **Pommes allumettes** refers to peeled potatoes cut into matchsticks and fried. **2.** a strip of puff pastry with a sweet or savory filling or garnish, usually served as an **hors d'oeuvre.**

almonds

almond - the kernel of the fruit of the almond tree, *Prunus amygdalus*, a very close relative of the plum and peach. There are two varieties: sweet and **bitter almond.** Native to western India, the almond was mentioned frequently in the Old Testament. In Numbers 17:8, Aaron's rod, which miraculously bore flowers and fruit, was made of almond wood. Almonds were first cultivated in Europe by the Greeks, who gave us the botanical name *amygdala*. The Romans considered the almond a Greek nut, calling it *nux Graeca*. Almonds are available in a number of forms at a typical grocery store: raw (with brown skin), blanched, sliced, slivered, chopped and ground. There is no nutritional difference between blanched and raw almonds, only a textural one.

almond bracelet - see KAHK BI LOZ.

almond butter - a **nut butter** made of roasted blanched almonds. See also CASHEW BUTTER, HAZELNUT BUTTER, PEANUT BUTTER.

almondette - see CHAROLI NUT.

almond extract - a flavoring made from the oil of bitter almonds mixed with alcohol.

almond flour - a type of nut flour made by grinding the remains of nuts after they have been pressed to extract their oils (some are simply more finely ground versions of almond meal). It is dustier in texture and less oily than almond meal and can be used as a substitute for some of the regular flour in many recipes. Because almond flour lacks the gluten that helps breads rise, it cannot be substituted for all the regular flour in those recipes. Almond flour is frequently used in low-carbohydrate recipes because it contains far fewer carbohydrates than grain flours. See also ALMOND MEAL, NUT FLOUR.

almondine - see AMANDINE.

almond meal - also **ground almonds.** Blanched almonds ground until granular in appearance, used in baking to add nutty flavor, moisture and a grainier texture. It is available in some stores, but is easily made at home by grinding almonds in a nut mill or food processor fitted with a metal blade. Grinding the nuts for too long (especially easy to do in a food processor) releases the oil in the nuts and blends it with the solids to form **almond butter.** See also ALMOND FLOUR, NUT FLOUR.

almond milk - used since the Middle Ages, this beverage is made by blending one part almonds with four parts water until milky-colored and smooth. Almond milk is sometimes sweetened with a natural sweetener, such as brown rice syrup, or enhanced with a dash of vanilla. It is a popular alternative to cow's milk for vegans and people who suffer from lactose intolerance. It is also available commercially: plain, flavored, or fortified with vitamins and minerals so that it mimics the nutritional profile of cow's milk.

almond oil - an oil made by pressing sweet almonds. The nuts of these almonds contain 50 to 60 percent oil, which is used in baking and confectionery. Italy is the oil's primary producer.

almond paste - a mixture of ground blanched almonds, sugar and glycerin used in a variety of confections, both slightly more coarse and less sweet than marzipan.

aloo bukhara - a variety of dried sour plums, deep red in color, used in Pakistani cooking, thought to add tang to meat and lamb dishes.

alphabet - also **alfabeti.** See PASTA.

alpine cranberry - see LINGONBERRY.

alpine strawberry - see FRAISE DES BOIS.

Alsacienne, à l' - "in the style of Alsace," a province of northeastern France with mixed French and German heritage. It usually involves sauerkraut and sausages.

al sangue - an Italian term used for "rare" when referring to cooked meat, from *sangue*, meaning "blood."

altamura - an Italian butter-yellow bread loaf, named after its town of origin in Apulia, where it's a specialty made with local hard-wheat flour. The bread has a longer-than-average shelf life and was originally a staple taken by shepherds on their seasonal movement in search of pastures.

Altenburger - a soft, German cheese, similar to **camembert,** made from goat's milk, with a delicate white mold on the exterior and a creamy, smooth, flavorful interior.

alum - a white astringent salt (potassium aluminum sulfate) formerly used to whiten flour and to quickly clear gin, as well as to improve the color of inferior wines and as a crisping agent in some pickles.

aluminum foil - also **foil, tin foil.** A thin, pliable sheet of aluminum that can withstand both heat and cold, and is a good barrier to moisture, air and odors. It should not be allowed to come into contact with acidic foods, such as tomatoes, because the acid will eat through the foil.

amalgamer - a French word meaning to "blend" or "combine ingredients."

amandine - from the French word *amande*, meaning "almond," a term used for dishes prepared with slivered almonds (sole amandine), often anglicized, as in filet of sole almondine.

Amanita - a genus of **mushrooms,** some of which are considered a delicacy and some of which are the deadliest on earth. Best known in the deadly category is the Death Cap, *Amanita phalloides*, a yellow-green capped mushroom that contains powerful toxins that catastrophically damage the liver, leading to death. *Amanita muscaria*, a beautiful red-capped mushroom frosted with white flecks, is considered a toxic specimen, causing nasty gastrointestinal distress when eaten raw, but some dedicated mushroom aficionados claim that it is harmless when parboiled to remove the toxins.

On the edible side, *Amanita velosa*, also known as Spring Amanita, is considered a choice mushroom, with a broad, pink-to-brown cap. Though it is delicious, it may not be worth the risk, since it can easily be confused with older specimens of the deadly *Amanita ocreata*, which goes by the terrifying nickname Destroying Angel. *Amanita lanei*, also known as coccoli, is a dead ringer for the Death Cap but is also considered edible.

The most prudent approach is to avoid all *Amanita* mushrooms that have not been deemed safe by a well-qualified mycologist. It is a good idea not to harvest any mushrooms in the wild without the aid of an expert. Many poisonous mushrooms look strikingly similar to their nontoxic cousins, with variations only an expert eye can detect.

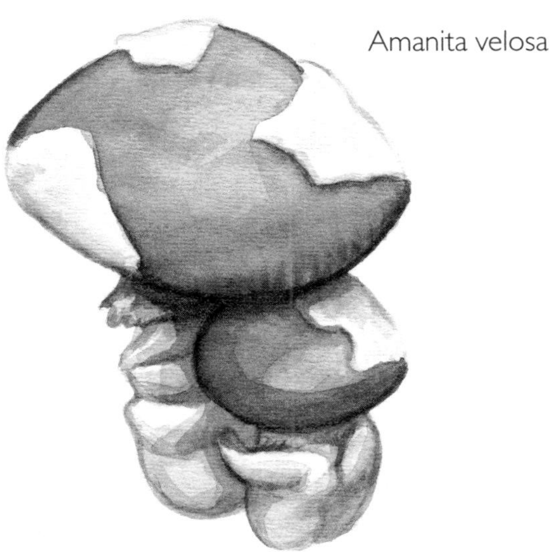

Amanita velosa

amantungula - see CARISSA.

amaranth - also **Chinese spinach** and *yin choy* in Cantonese. An annual plant once regarded as a weed in the U.S., but now seen in a more positive light. From the Greek *amarantos*, meaning "unfading," this high-protein plant is widely used in Asian cuisine, steamed, stir-fried or cooked in soups, although it can also be eaten raw. It tastes like a cross between spinach and cabbage. Amaranth seeds yield a high-protein flour with little or no gluten. Historically a staple of Aztec and Incan diets, today it is used to enrich such products as **granola** bars. In Mexico, its name is *alegría*, meaning "happiness."

amarelle - a pale-red tart cherry that has less acid and less sour taste than darker varieties and a nearly colorless juice. The best known are Early Richmond and Montmorency. See also CHERRY.

amaretti - small, round, crisp Italian macaroons flavored with bitter almond, created by **Francesco Monriondo,** a pastry chef at the court of Savoy in the mid-17th century. Italians have a special custom of making wishes with the cookies' pretty pink and blue wrappers, setting them alight, holding them high above their heads and making a secret wish as the ashes float to the ground.

amaretto - an almond-flavored liqueur made from apricot pits. A wholly unaccredited legend has it that the recipe was given to an Italian painter, Bernardino Luini, in the 16th century by an innkeeper who was the model for the Virgin Mary in his wall painting of the nativity at Saronno. As the months passed, the girl, whose name has since been forgotten, fell in love with Bernardino. To show her feelings for him, she gave him a gift of sweet almond-flavored liqueur that she had made from the trees growing in her garden. The year was 1525, and that bottle is said to have been the first Di Saronno Amaretto. It has been commercially produced since the 19th century.

amaro - pl. **amari. 1.** a type of Italian liqueur, drunk as a digestif or mixed with sparkling water as an apéritif, made by steeping herbs, spices and fruits in alcohol, usually **grappa** or plain **grain alcohol.** Amari were originally created as tonics, the herbs thought to cure a variety of ailments. Today they are drunk for their flavor and for their legendary stomach-settling properties, often alongside coffee at the end of the meal. *Amaro* is the Italian word for "bitter," which aptly describes the liqueur's bitter to bittersweet taste. Amaro is a synonym for **bitters,** a generic name for bitter herbal liqueurs of this type that are made all over the world. A number of different companies make their own well-known, unique versions of amaro, including Ramazzotti, Fernet Branca and Averna. **2.** a term often used to describe the slightly bitter undertone of some Italian dry wines and liqueurs. Traditionally, Italian palates have preferred this bitterness, making this a positive wine-tasting term.

amarone - a dry, tart, full-bodied Italian red wine made with partially dried grapes, the name meaning "very bitter." Amarone is made in the Valpolicella region of Italy, near Verona. The grapes are harvested later than regular-harvest grapes, then allowed to dry for several months before being pressed to extract their concentrated juice. The juice is then fermented, yielding a rich, full-bodied wine that is higher in alcohol than most red wine (15 or 16 percent). Amarone is often compared to **port** and is best paired with cheeses and roasted meats.

amasake - also **amazake.** Japanese for "sweet sake," a non-alcoholic, sake-like beverage made from cooked rice, flavored with ginger.

Amatriciana, all' - an Italian style of sauce traditionally served over spaghetti, bucatini or rigatoni, made with tomatoes, onions, hot chiles, **pancetta, guanciale,** bacon or ham and pecorino cheese.

amazake - see AMASAKE.

amazu shoga - a Japanese garnish of shredded or thinly sliced pink or beige pickled ginger, usually eaten with sushi. See also BENI SHOGA.

ambassadeur - a French cake consisting of a vanilla **génoise** topped with a layer of pastry cream, then a layer of candied fruit macerated in **kirsch,** although some recipes call for a layer of marmalade or jam instead of the fruit. The whole cake is then covered with a thin layer of almond paste or marzipan.

amber ale - see ALE.

ambergris - a grayish, waxy substance with a very strong musky scent. Secreted in the intestine of the sperm whale and then discharged as vomit. It's collected from the surface of tropical seas, where it's found floating, or washed up on beaches. The Chinese were the first to use ambergris as a spice. During the Middle Ages, it was used in stews, pies, custards and jams.

The French Cardinal de Richelieu, Armand Jean Du Plessis (1585–1642), was particularly fond of ambergris pastilles. Hot ambergris chocolate was a very popular drink up until the 18th century, allegedly having aphrodisiac and invigorating qualities. Today, ambergris is only used in the fabrication of perfume.

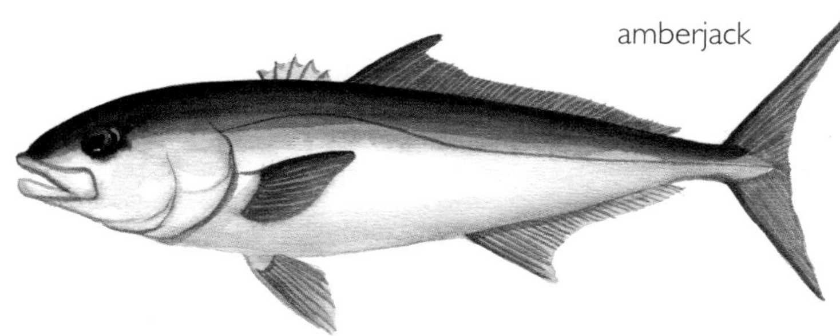
amberjack

amberjack - a lean, mild-flavored fish found along the South American coast and the Gulf of Mexico.

Ambert - see FOURME D'AMBERT.

ambrosia - from the Greek *ambrotos*, meaning "immortal." In Greek mythology, ambrosia was the food of the Gods of Olympus. The Greek poet and musician Ibicus, born in Rhegion in 600 BC, once described it as "nine times sweeter than honey." Today it's used generically to describe a particularly luscious food. The word also refers to a cold fruit dessert with coconut and, in Mexico, a sweet-scented herb whose leaves are used in cold beverages, like mint.

Ambrosia apple - see APPLE.

amchur - also **amchoor, amchor, mango powder.** A powder made from dried slices of sour, unripe mangoes, which are peeled, sliced and sun-dried, prepared in the northern parts of India. It's used in place of lemon juice to impart a sour flavor to curries, chutneys and soups and also acts as a meat tenderizer. It is always folded in at the end of cooking.

américaine - see À L'AMÉRICAINE.

American cheese - also **processed cheese.** An informal term used mostly in the United States for processed cheese slices, most commonly heard in diners when ordering a cheeseburger: "Do you want Cheddar or American cheese?"

Americano

American chop suey - what we think of as Chinese-style **chop suey** was actually invented in America, as was this fancifully named baked casserole of ground beef, pasta, peppers, onions and tomato sauce.

American cocoa powder - also **nonalkalized cocoa powder.** This cocoa powder is made from **chocolate liquor** that has been pressed to remove the **cocoa butter.** The paste that forms after the cocoa butter has been removed is left to cool, then ground into a fine powder. It is not treated with alkali like **Dutch-process cocoa powder** and therefore is lighter, less bitter and more acidic. See also CHOCOLATE.

American eggplant - see EGGPLANT.

American mustard - also **ballpark mustard.** A mild mustard made from white seeds also known as "ballpark mustard," because it is most often used on hot dogs and hamburgers at baseball games. Ironically, one of the best-selling American mustards is called French's. First made when the 19th century was turning to the 20th by Robert Timothy French and his son, George, of Ithaca, New York, this creamy, mild mustard achieves its characteristic bright yellow by the addition of turmeric. For hot-dog lovers and kids who like to paint their food, squeezable containers (introduced in the 1970s) make mustard more fun. See also MUSTARD.

Americano - an apéritif made with **Campari,** sweet vermouth, sparkling water and an orange slice, served on ice. The drink is said to have been created by Domenico Marenco of Cuneo, Italy, in 1880. It's unclear why it was named Americano, except possibly as a corruption of Marenco.

Amer Picon - a bitter French orange-flavored cordial, made with orange peel, cinchona bark (the main flavoring in **quinine water**) and gentian, usually mixed with grenadine and lime or lemon juice to make Picon punch, or mixed with soda water and served as an **apéritif.** The cordial is named after its inventor, Gaetan Picon.

amino acids - any of a group of organic compounds occurring naturally in plant and animal tissues, and forming the basic constituents of proteins.

amlou - a Moroccan nut paste or butter made with **argan oil,** ground almonds and honey, usually eaten as a dip or spread for bread or crackers. It is a traditional food of the Berber people of southwestern Morocco, to which the argan tree is native.

ammonium bicarbonate - also **baker's ammonia, hartshorn, powdered baking ammonia.** A leavening agent that is the forerunner of modern baking powder and baking soda. Ammonium bicarbonate is also called hartshorn because deer, or hart, antlers were the traditional source of ammonia before laboratories were able to extract it from other sources. Hartshorn is also the name of an ammonia preparation used as the base of smelling salts.

amontillado - see SHERRY.

amor en bolsa - see CAPE GOOSEBERRY.

amorphous sugar - melted sucrose, allowed to dry, then crystallized and made into a hard, brittle, crystal-clear mass, sometimes known as **"rock candy."**

ampelography - a science gradually developed since the times of **Pliny** to identify and classify grape varietals by the appearance of their vines, leaves and fruits. It is not an exact science, although it is excellent for telling apart major varietals; it is more problematic when trying to distinguish sub-species — often caused by natural mutations — from one another. Due to this inaccuracy, DNA testing of grapevines is becoming more common, allowing vintners to identify precisely what grapes they are growing.

amphora - a jar or vase used in ancient Rome and Greece for storing wine and oil, oval-shaped, with a narrow neck, two handles and a pointed end that used to be stuck in the earth or sand of a cellar or store. In the Roman world, while some wines were buried in the cool ground, most of them were put on the top storage tower of houses, in the apotheca, or storeroom, near the smoke pipes. Contact at a lukewarm temperature with these porous earthenware pipes gave the wine a smoky flavor that was much liked at the time. According to Columella, a Roman agronomist and writer from the 1st century AD, the best smoke came from the pipes that carried it away from the bathhouse. Many Greek and Roman wines were kept for 15 to 25 years before they were considered ready for drinking. The Gauls introduced wooden casks, and the Romans adopted these for shipping wine, but for storage they remained faithful to amphorae and used both corks and sealing wax to protect the wine. The Greek amphora held 8½ gallons (32 L), while the Roman amphora held 5½ gallons (20 L). The name comes from the Latin *amphora* and the Greek *amphoreus* (*amphy*, meaning "on both sides," and *phoreo*, "to carry," for example, by its two handles).

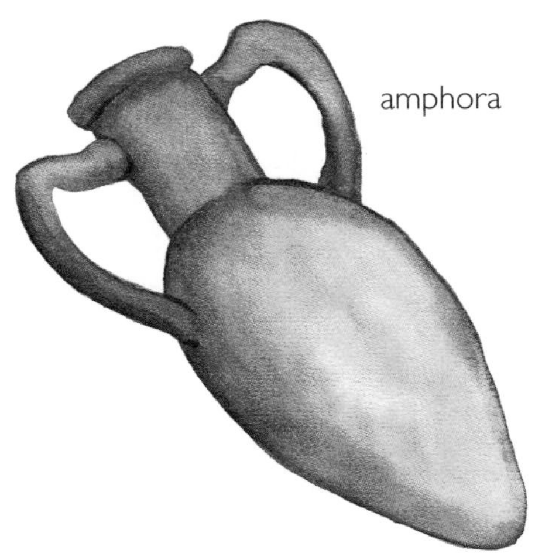
amphora

ample - a wine-tasting term used to describe a wine that has a full **mouth feel.**

amuse-bouche - also **amuse-gueule**. From the French *bouche* and *gueule*, meaning "mouth," a single-bite palate teaser served before the appetizer that amuses or tickles the taste buds.

an - also **anko.** A sweet Japanese red-bean paste made with **azuki beans** and sugar, available smooth (*koshi-an*) or chunky (*tsubushi-an*).

anadama bread - a leavened wheat and cornmeal bread flavored with molasses.

anago - the Japanese name for the **conger eel,** a name commonly seen on sushi bar menus. Anago is often eaten in the same way as **unagi,** or common eel: grilled and basted with a sweet barbecue sauce.

Anaheim chile - also **Californian chile.** A somewhat mild, green or sometimes red, chile pepper, long with a blunt end, generally used fresh or roasted. It is named after the California city where it originated. See also CHILE PEPPER.

anardana - one of the rare spices taken from a fruit, in this case the pomegranate. Anardana is used in India for chutneys and some curries. The seeds and pulp are separated from the rind of the fruit and sun-dried for 10 to 15 days, turning reddish brown. The final step is the milling process to transform the dried material into powder.

anasazi bean - also **Aztec bean, Jacob's cattle bean.** A dried bean of the family Phaseolus and a relative of the pinto bean. The bean is white with purplish red splotches, originally grown by the prehistoric Anasazi tribe, who lived in cliff dwellings in the Four Corners area of Arizona, Utah, Colorado and New Mexico. It is a relative of the **appaloosa bean.**

anchoaïde - also **anchoyade**. A specialty of Provence consisting of mashed anchovy with garlic and sometimes olive oil, usually spread on toast, eaten as an appetizer with an apéritif.

ancho chile - a large, deep-purple dried chile pepper, fruity in flavor, often used in Mexican cooking. In its fresh form, it's called a **poblano** chile. See also CHILE PEPPER.

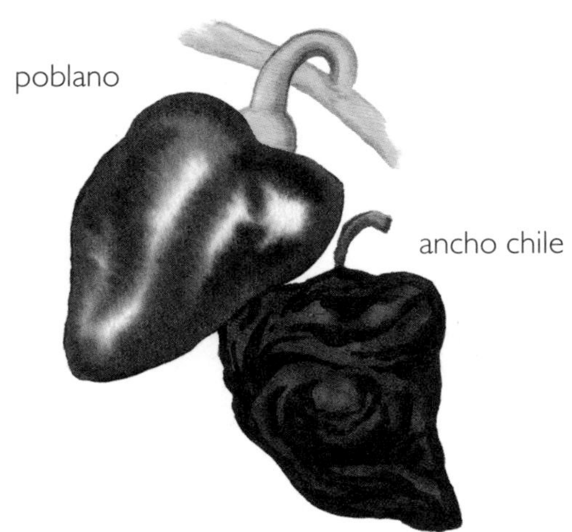

anchovy - a small fish, *Engrolis encrasicolus*, about 4½ inches (12 cm) long, weighing little more than 2 ounces (60 g). They are most often caught in the Mediterranean, but can also be found in the Black Sea and the Atlantic Ocean. Almost every country has its "anchovy," although it is not always the same fish. All, or most, are members of the Engraulidea family, and all have one thing in common: they are rarely eaten fresh, but are generally salt-**cured** and canned in oil.

anchovy paste - made from anchovies, vinegar, spices and water, sold in tubes, used in cooking or as a spread.

anchovy pear - also **river pear**. The fruit of a West Indian tree, resembling the mango in flavor, often served pickled.

ancienne, à l' - a French term designating dishes prepared "in the old style," meaning (especially of beef) braised and then simmered.

andalouse, à l' - a French term for dishes made with tomatoes, pimientos and often rice pilaf and sausage. Because Empress Eugénie, wife of Napoleon III, was a native of the Andalusia region of Spain, many dishes bearing this name are now part of classical French cuisine.

Anderson, Alexander P. - see PUFFED CEREAL.

andouille - a spicy, smoked sausage made from **chitterlings** and seasonings. The word may derive from the Latin *inductile*, meaning something drawn out "to insert." Andouilles were a great delicacy in France in the Middle Ages and are today a specialty of Cajun cooking.

andouillette - a pale French sausage made of pig intestines and cow tripe, a smaller version of the French andouille sausage, not to be confused with the spicy **andouille** sausage adored in Cajun cooking. In 2000, France banned the use of cow intestines and other internal organs in foods, such as andouillette, in an attempt to protect the public from exposure to animals infected with **mad cow disease.** Despite the ban and the risks, andouillette continues to be produced and enjoyed around the world.

anelli - see PASTA.

anesone - a clear, Italian anise-flavored liqueur, stronger and less sweet than **anisette.**

angel food cake - also **angel cake.** Known since the 1870s, this North American sponge cake is baked in a tall ring pan, made so light and airy from many egg whites, it's said to have the sublimeness of angels, hence its name.

angel hair pasta - see PASTA.

angelica - a sweet herb, *Angelica archangelica*, dies after flowering but self-seeds plentifully. Young leaves and stalks can be candied for cake decoration or cooked with tart fruits and rhubarb as a sweetener. It's still cultivated in France for the production of liqueurs (it imparts a green color). In England, it used to be sun-bleached and consumed as a salad. In Norway and some other northern countries, such as Greenland, Denmark and Sweden, the root is used as an alternative to bread by milling the dried roots to make flour.

In nearly every European language, it's linked to angels and is considered a cure against the evil eye, as well as a cure for many illnesses. There are repeated and various legends of an archangel bringing it as a cure for the plague.

Native Americans used angelica medicinally in poultices, placed on the side of the body opposite to the pain in order to relieve soreness. Rocky Mountain, Sioux and Crow Indians made decoctions and teas from angelica roots and drank them as tonics to build up strength after an illness.

angel pie - a sweet dessert pie made with a meringue or crumb crust and a light, silky filling that is bound together with gelatin or whipped cream. The name surely reflects the texture of the dessert, which is as light and heavenly as an angel.

angels on horseback - a dish of oysters baked or grilled, wrapped in bacon, served on pieces of buttered toast. See also DEVILS ON HORSEBACK.

angels' share - a term used by distillers to refer to the amount of the spirit lost to evaporation during aging in barrels.

angel's teat - see MOONSHINE.

anglaise, à l' - a French term meaning "in the English style," referring to food poached or boiled, or coated in bread crumbs and fried.

anglerfish - see MONKFISH.

Angostura bitters - the most renowned of any bitters, made by combining an infusion of herbs and gentian root with a strong rum base. Originally a medicine, this secret blend of herbs and spices is today used primarily as a flavoring ingredient in beverages and cooked dishes.

The bitters are the creation of **Dr. Johann Gottlieb Benjamin Siegert,** a German surgeon general in Simon Bolivar's army in Venezuela. The name "Angostura" comes from the town where he was based, and not for the tree of the same name as commonly thought. In 1824, using gentian blossoms along with other ingredients, he concocted a tonic for Bolivar's ailing wife. The medicine proved so effective that he began to bottle it for commercial sale. Sailors going ashore at the port found the bitters a great remedy for seasickness, and soon Angostura was a stock item in the medicine cabinets of oceangoing vessels. The sailors also found that the medicine added zip to a glass of rum.

In time, such drinks as gin-and-bitters and the ubiquitous Manhattan made Angostura a standard bar accessory. Now manufactured on the Island of Trinidad and Tobago (off the coast of Venezuela), the bitters are sold all over the world, through the direct descendants of the original creator, Dr. Siegert.

angular - a negative wine-tasting term for a wine with too much acidity and no softness or depth. It is a sour, unpleasant wine without the proper balance of acid and sugar.

aniline - a chemical by-product of petroleum, usually used as food coloring. The red color is the cheapest and the best for culinary purposes, although some questions about its safety for human consumption have been raised.

Animal Cracker - a trademarked cookie developed by the Walter Wilson Co. for the opening of the Philadelphia Zoo in 1870.

animelles - **1.** a French name for animal testicles, usually bull, pig or lamb. **2.** Italian word for **sweetbreads.** See also VARIETY MEAT.

anise - also **aniseed.** A plant, *Pimpenella anisum*, it contributes its flavor not to its green growth, but to its essential oil–rich "seeds" (properly fruits), which have a distinctive sweet licorice taste. Anise is a native of Levant (the former name for a region that now comprises Lebanon, Israel and parts of Turkey and Syria) and was known to the Greeks by the 4th century BC. Culinary use extends at least as far back as

Ancient Rome, when historian **Pliny** wrote of the seed: "Be it green or dried it's wanted for all conserves and flavorings." The Greeks, Romans and Hebrews used anise as a condiment. Today, it's most often found in desserts and liqueurs, including **anisette, ouzo** and **Pernod.** Because of the value of anise, it became one of the spices used by the Romans to pay taxes. England's King Edward I levied an import tax on the herb in 1305. But despite its popularity, it was not cultivated in England before the 16th century.

Aniseed was a favorite both with the old herbalists and the ladies of fashion, for the seed was said to be good "for affections of the diaphragm where the body is tightly laced and if suspended by the pillow for the sleeper to smell, it will give him a youthful look and prevent disagreeable dreams." **John Gerard** (1545–1612), the English herbalist, said, "Aniseed helpeth the yeoxing or hicket and should be given to young children to eat which are likely to have the falling sickness [epilepsy] or to such as have it by patrimony or succession." And finally, founders of America thought so well of it that the organizers of the colony of Virginia required every man to plant six seeds of the herb, perhaps because "the seed thereof found in a little bag or handkerchief and kept at the nose to smell to, keepeth men from dreaming and starting in their sleep and causeth them to rest quietly." Mexico is currently the largest producer of anise. See also STAR ANISE.

anise

anise basil - see BASIL.

anise extract - an **extract** made by combining **grain alcohol,** water and **anise oil.** Anise extract has a strong, sweetish licorice flavor and is commonly added to baked goods, such as cookies. Italian **pizzelle** cookies often contain a touch of anise extract.

anise oil - the oil extracted from the seeds of the anise plant, commonly used in cooking, to make **anise extract** and as an herbal remedy. Anise oil is an ancient treatment for coughs and colds and is also used to soothe symptoms of more serious pulmonary ailments, such as emphysema and pneumonia.

anisette - a clear, very sweet liqueur made with aniseeds, tasting of licorice. The most famous brand is Marie Brizard, named for the Bordelaise widow who began producing anisette commercially in the mid-1700s. She was simply following the old Mediterranean custom of flavoring alcohol with anise. Another story claims she was given the recipe by a West Indian associate.

Anjou pear - see PEAR.

anko - see AN.

Anna potatoes - also **pommes Anna.** See POTATOES ANNA.

annatto - see ACHIOTE SEED.

annatto oil - also **achiote oil.** A bright orange-red oil made by steeping one part **achiote seeds** in two parts warmed cooking oil, such as olive or vegetable oil, commonly used to color foods in the Caribbean and Latin America. Annatto oil is also used as an emollient in soaps and other topical preparations. In addition to their brilliant color, achiote seeds add their distinctive, musky, slightly bitter flavor to the oil, which is a common ingredient in Caribbean cod cakes.

anolini - see PASTA.

anpan - a Japanese sweet bun filled with **an,** the basis of the wildly popular Japanese cartoon character Anpanman.

antelope - a ruminant animal of the Bovidae family, wild in its native Africa but raised on game farms in the United States, specifically in Texas. The farms import and stock their hunting areas with black buck and nilgai antelope (two of many species), which are allowed to roam freely. Antelope sold in gourmet stores may be labeled as such or sold under the generic name of venison, which can include deer, elk, moose, caribou and **pronghorn** (a native American species similar to African antelope). The taste of antelope is similar to that of deer meat, but the flesh is leaner.

pronghorn antelope

anthocyanin - any of a variety of naturally occurring pigments in foods that produce red, blue and purple colors, present in such fruits as blueberries, cherries, cranberries and grapes. Anthocyanins are a type of flavonoid, a class of healthy plant chemicals that are credited with preventing a variety of diseases, including certain types of cancer and heart disease. Anthocyanins in blueberries and cranberries are also prized for their ability to keep the urinary tract healthy by preventing bacteria from sticking to the walls of the bladder and causing painful infections.

antioxidant - **1.** a substance that reduces the browning process of fruits and vegetables when exposed to air. **2.** a biologically active component of some plant foods that may be protective against certain diseases.

antipasto - pl. **antipasti.** An Italian term literally meaning "before the meal." An appetizer composed of an assortment of cured meats, cheeses, olives, fish and raw or marinated vegetables. In Sicily, appetizers are called *grape'u pitittu* (mouth openers).

antojito - Spanish for "little whim," Mexican **tapa,** served as an hors d'oeuvre or snack.

Anzac biscuit - from Australia and New Zealand, made with bitter golden syrup, rolled oats and coconut, named after the Australian and New Zealand Army Corps or the acronym ANZAC, which fought at Gallipoli in 1915.

AOC - see APPELLATION D'ORIGINE CONTRÔLÉE.

ao nori - also **ao noriko.** A green seaweed that is dried and either flaked (ao nori) or powdered (ao noriko) and used as a seasoning in Asian cuisine. See also NORI.

apee - the name for two different types of cookies; one made with butter and flavored with caraway seeds; the other a soft cookie made with sour cream, named for the initials of Ann Page, a famous cook in Philadelphia in the 1800s.

apéritif - any light alcoholic drink taken before a meal.

Apfelbrösi - in Germany, a bread pudding with apples and sultana raisins.

Apfel pfannkuchen - the German name for an apple pancake.

aphrodisiac - a food or other substance that is believed to increase sexual desire. In the Middle Ages, coffee was called the "black enemy of sleep and copulation." If copulation had an enemy in coffee, it has alleged allies everywhere else all throughout history. The list of foods said to increase sexual desire is almost endless. The Old Testament mentions the mandrake root, a cousin of the potato and the tomato, which sometimes resembles the human male genitalia. Its alleged powers as an aphrodisiac seem to be based more on its suggestive physical appearance than on anything else. The Chinese appreciation for ginseng root has the same foundation.

The Greeks used the carrot as "love medicine" and called it *Philtron*. They credited the leek with powers of sexual indulgence. Roman historian **Pliny** echoed the Old Testament's views on the mandrake root and also prescribed the snout and foot of the hippopotamus to increase sexual potency. Ovid listed a number of aphrodisiacs of his time: pepper, shallots, eggs, honey and nuts. Horace spoke of dried marrow and liver as the popular love foods of his era. Petronius and others of his century recommended the pith from a branch of the pomegranate tree, the testicles of an ass, the intestines of various birds and fish, assorted parts from reptiles and shellfish, snails, snails' heads in sauce, frogs, mushrooms, fava beans and even onions.

Shaykh Nefzawi, author of *The Perfumed Garden*, said, "He who boils asparagus and then fries them in fat and then pours upon them the yolks of eggs with pounded condiments and eats every day of this dish, will grow very strong for coitus and find in it stimulant for amorous desires." **Jean Anthelme Brillat-Savarin**, author of *La Physiologie du Goût* (The Physiology of Taste), wrote that truffles can "make women more tender and men more apt to love." He also recounts a story from the Crusades. The sultan Saladin supposedly locked up some celibate dervishes to test their ascetic will by feeding them meat and presenting them with "two odalisques of surpassing loveliness [but the] saints emerged from their soft ordeal as pure as the diamond of Visapoor." Saladin then put the men on a diet of fish and exposed them once again to the temptations of the flesh, "and this time the two happy cenobites succumbed most marvelously." Some ancient cults encouraged their people to eat great amounts of fish but forbade priests, who were supposed to be celibate, to eat any at all. To arouse Louis XV, Madame DuBarry was said to have used truffle, sweetbreads, venison, pheasant cooked in white wine, capon in sherry broth and various vegetables, herbs and spices.

In addition to the foods listed above, all of the following and more have been cited at one time or another as aphrodisiacs: anise, avocados, beans, raw beef, white beets (named by Pliny along with asparagus, dill, licorice and hyena eyes), **bird's nest soup,** carrots, cheeses of various kinds (notably Parmesan), chocolate and cocoa (forbidden to their women by the Aztecs and to 17th-century monks), chutneys, cloves, eels, eggs (especially raw eggs), fennel, garlic, honey, hot sauces, mushrooms (particularly morel and truffle), mutton with caraway seed, nutmeg, olives, peas, peppermints and peppermint oil (mentioned by Aristotle), pimientos, pistachio nuts, radishes, saffron, thyme, tomatoes (those dangerous "love apples") and vanilla.

Apicius - see profile below.

apio - see ARRACACHA.

à point - a French term used to describe food cooked to the perfect stage of doneness. The term is also used to describe a steak cooked medium-rare.

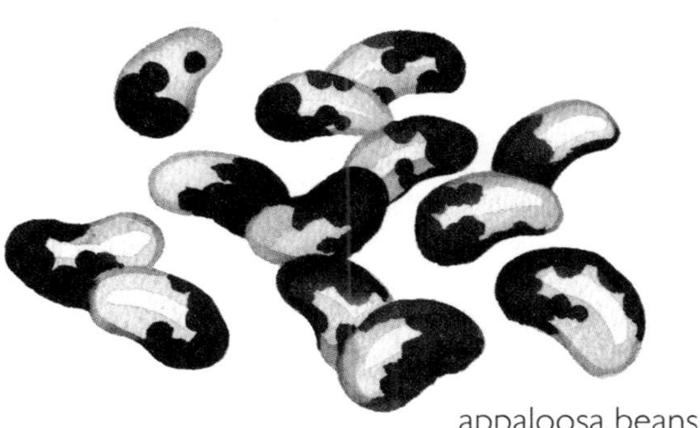

appaloosa beans

appaloosa bean - a dried legume that is white on one end with a splash of speckled brown on the other end, like the spotted coat of an Appaloosa horse.

appareil - the French name for a ready-mix, such as for cakes, for use in any cooking preparation.

Apicius (c. 1st century AD) - Roman gourmet, author of perhaps the world's oldest existing cookbook. However, there is some mystery about the exact identity of the trailblazing author. There is mention of three different Romans named Apicius who were all gourmets. We know most about Marcus Gavius Apicius (AD 14–37), who served under Augustus and Tiberius. Furthermore, there have been so many changes, additions and deletions to the original recipes over the centuries that it is impossible to know just which of the recipes in the manuscripts actually date back to the 1st century. Nevertheless, the Apicius cookbook has been studied for centuries. It was still a classic reference book as late as the 18th century, when the legendary French chef **Antonin Carême** included it among the treasures in his culinary library.

Appert, Nicolas François (c. 1750–1841) - French confectioner, chef and distiller, who paved the way for canning by inventing a technique to preserve food. Appert began experimenting when Napoleon offered a large cash prize to the inventor of a way to deliver food to his army and navy without spoiling along the way. Appert's technique — partially cooked food sealed in glass bottles and jars, and then immersed in boiling water — won the prize in 1810. He published his findings in *The Art of Preserving All Kinds of Animal and Vegetable Substances for Several Years,* which became a well-referenced book in its day. That same year in England, King George III, with his military to feed, granted **Peter Durand** a patent for preserving in vessels other than glass. Durand built on Appert's work by using metal cans, for better transport and less waste. Once he coated the iron with tin, his cans were airtight, rustproof and corrosion-free. Appert opened the world's first canning factory with his prize money, but Durand did no canning himself. In 1812, Englishmen Bryan Donkin and John Hall, using Durand's idea, set up the first commercial cannery.

Appellation d'Origine Contrôlée (AOC) - a strict, labyrinthine set of French laws initiated in 1935, designed to protect the quality of certain French wines and foods, especially cheeses. To meet AOC standards and to be allowed to carry a name that is protected under AOC regulations, the producer must comply with rigid standards that set out exactly where a food item may be grown; what crop variety is used to make a specific product; a maximum allowable yield per hectare of land for specific crops; practices that may or may not be used to cultivate the food; the amount of alcohol in the finished wine (or amount of butterfat in a finished cheese) and so on.

To carry this impressive designation, a producer must clearly label his or her product with all the salient details that show that the product is acceptable under AOC rules. In some cases, there are thousands of producers of a single type of cheese, such as **Brie,** but only a handful who have gained AOC status, a guarantee of quality and therefore sales. However, many fine cheeses and wines are produced that do not comply with AOC standards and therefore do not bear this seal of approval from the French government. Therefore, ultimately, the tastes of the consumer are often the best guide to selecting the "best" product.

In the wine world, there are other levels of quality that can be attained that are considered below those of AOC but are still quite desirable. The second best after AOC are **Vins Délimités de Qualité Supérieure (VDQS),** which allow higher yields of grapes per hectare and slightly lower levels of alcohol in the finished product. The least strict level is **Vins de Pays,** or country wines, which have much looser standards than AOC but are still excellent, depending on the producer. The Languedoc-Roussillon region is famous for the excellent Vins de Pays it produces. See also CRU.

Appenzeller - also **Appenzell.** A straw-colored Swiss cheese with holes and a brownish-yellow rind, marinated in cider or white wine before aging, then pressed into wheels 12 inches (30 cm) in diameter, weighing about 15 pounds (7 kg). More moist and creamier that **Emmental** and much more robust than **Gruyère,** Appenzeller is said to go as far back as the 8th century BC, but most certainly since the days of Charlemagne (AD 742–814).

Appert, Nicolas François - see profile above.

appetitost - a semisoft nut-flavored cheese from Denmark, made from buttermilk and, sometimes, caraway seeds.

appetizer - also **starter.** Any food served before a meal to increase the appetite or excite the palate, including both finger foods and the first course of a meal served at table.

apple - the fruit of a tree of the genus *Malus*, native to Europe and West Asia and introduced to North America in the 17th century. There is evidence that the apple was already under cultivation in the Neolithic times. The apple has long had a prominent place in Western culture as a symbol of temptation and instigation: the unnamed fruit in Genesis has traditionally been considered an apple; Paris gave Aphrodite a golden apple and thereby caused the Trojan War. Lemons, in medieval times, were "Persian apples;" dates were "finger apples;" pomegranates, "apples of Carthage." In other legends, William

Tell shot an apple off his son's head; Snow White's stepmother used an apple to poison her; and Isaac Newton's legendary inspiration was a falling apple. In white magic and esoteric cults, the apple is the feminine symbol linked with Venus. If you cut an apple vertically into two exact halves, you can see some likeness to female genitalia. If you cut it in half horizontally, you can, like the Pythagoreans, see it as a perfect five-pointed star, the pentagram, a key to occult sciences, in that it reveals the secret of the knowledge of good and evil. The fact that the Latin word for apple is *malum*, a homonym for "evil," may be a pure coincidence.

The first apples were probably small and sour, like our crab apples. Pomologists, or apple experts, believe that apples originated somewhere between the Caspian and Black seas in Southwest Asia. It's hard to pin down the time and place accurately because, by the Stone Age, apples had spread over much of Europe. Ancient Roman texts on agriculture mention 22 varieties (there were undoubtedly more) and gave instructions on grafting that are still applicable today. In the 17th century, 56 different kinds of apples were part of the menu for a banquet given by the Grand Duke Cosmo III of Tuscany. Of the more than 5,000 varieties that have existed, most were developed in the 18th and 19th centuries.

Early North Americans, most famously Johnny Appleseed, developed many different types of apples. European colonists brought native varieties to North America; the English to Virginia and New England; the Dutch to New York; and the French to Canada. Documents dated October 10, 1639, chronicle the first U.S. harvest of apples plucked from trees planted in Boston. The record mentions "ten fair pippins." Today, **pippin** refers to many varieties of apple, most of which are used for cooking, although some can be eaten either cooked or raw, such as the Newton-Pippin.

The first commercial nursery was established on Long Island about 1730. By 1823, its catalog included four varieties that are still popular: Winesap, Yellow Newton, Rhode Island Greening and Baldwin. So many varieties of apple exist because of a botanical idiosyncrasy: apple seeds from one tree do not necessarily reproduce exactly the same way. If you plant the seeds from an apple, you will end up with several apple trees that do not bear a resemblance to one another. There are dozens of different varieties on the market today, the most common of which are described below.

The grading of apples is based on many factors. The Fancy and Extra Fancy grades are judged mainly on surface color and appearance, which do not necessarily reflect the quality of the fruit inside. So, an apple with less color may taste just as good as one with more.

APPLE VARIETIES

Ambrosia - a native of British Columbia, an accidental crossbreed likely derived from **Golden Delicious** and **Starking Delicious.** It is a crisp apple with attractive gold-streaked red skin, good for snacking and for salads because it is slow to brown after being cut.

Beauty of Bath - an anomaly in the apple world because it is never found in stores. It should be eaten straight from the tree, as it rots very quickly after picking. It has a sharp but sweet, juicy flesh.

Braeburn - a crisp, juicy dessert apple that only grows in the Southern Hemisphere. This apple is easily recognizable by its smooth pale-green skin flushed with red.

Bramley - the foremost British cooking apple. Large, green, sometimes flushed with red, its flesh is sharp and juicy and is not usually eaten raw. It can be used for making apple chutney or cored, peeled and sautéed in butter to serve with bacon and sausage at breakfast, as is done in parts of England.

Cortland - a modern American variety bred partly from the McIntosh. Large with a shiny red skin, it's especially useful for fruit platters and fruit salads, because its flesh resists browning when exposed to the air.

Cox's Orange Pippin - crisp, firm and juicy, this is Britain's most popular eating apple. Also used in cooking.

continued on page 34

Crispin - see MUTSU.

Elstar - a sweet-tart variety with crunchy yellow skin and yellowy-white flesh, grown in both Canada and the U.S. but more popular in the Netherlands and Ireland. It is a cross between the **Golden Delicious** and an heirloom variety called Ingrid Marie. Elstars are particularly good for applesauce, though they are also delicious eaten out of hand. They have blushes of reddish orange on their yellow skin, while Red Elstar apples, a variant of the breed, are mostly red with blushes of yellow.

Empire - this cross between the **Red Delicious** and the **McIntosh** is sweet-tart and good for eating and for salads. It was developed in New York in 1966 and named for the state's nickname, the Empire State.

Fuji - a red-skinned apple with a yellow-green undertone and creamy-white flesh. The Fuji is firm, very sweet and quite juicy, making it ideal for eating out of hand. It also holds its shape well in baking and cooked desserts and makes excellent applesauce. This Japanese apple was developed in the 1950s and is named for the most famous mountain in Japan. It is a cross between **Red Delicious** and Ralls Janet, an heirloom variety of apple rarely seen anymore.

Fuji

Gala - also **Royal Gala.** A variegated red and yellow all-around apple, it is especially good for eating but also tasty in baking and applesauce. The Gala is a native of New Zealand. Now grown in North America, it is a cross between the **Cox's Orange Pippin and Golden Delicious**.

Golden Delicious

Golden Delicious - also **Yellow Delicious.** One of the major varieties of dessert apples in America, South Africa and England, firm and crisp when the skin is greenish, less crisp but sweeter when the skin is completely golden. Considered to be a good contrast to blue cheese, this apple first appeared around 1900.

Granny Smith - originally grown from a pip in 19th-century Australia. This apple's crunchy, hard flesh, sharp, distinctive taste and bright green skin have made it popular and easily recognizable, a worldwide choice both for cooking and eating raw.

Gravenstein - originated in northern Germany or Denmark before 1800. Large and yellow, with bright red and orange stripes, it has a rather acidic flavor.

Ida - the favorite apple of all applesauce makers, it can also be eaten raw, but more than likely you'll find it in a jar of applesauce on a grocery store shelf.

Ida Red - also **Idared.** An American apple bred in the 1940s, it is sweet, medium-size, red and yellow, cooked or eaten raw.

Jonagold - large, round, green-yellow apple and one of the most delicious. It is a hybrid of the **Jonathan** and the **Golden Delicious**.

Jonathan - small, orange-red apple with a white, faintly acidic juicy flesh that can be used both for eating or cooking. Originated in North America, but now available almost everywhere.

Katy - a crisp, sweet, very juicy apple. This hybrid was first developed in Sweden from the Worcester Pearmain variety.

Lady apple - also **Pomme d'api.** A small, tart, late-harvest apple with crisp, white flesh and yellow skin suffused with red. Some say this apple was brought to Rome by travelers returning west along the Silk Road; others credit an Etruscan monk with its development. Later, invading Romans brought it north through Europe to Britain. Often sold fresh at Christmas for use as a garnish for food, fruit baskets or wreathes, Lady apples are also available canned.

Macoun - a relatively new, midseason, hardy apple. Described as crisp, fragrant and sweet, it has the well-known **McIntosh** as one of its parents.

McIntosh - slightly tart, best eaten freshly picked, originally named for John McIntosh of Ontario, who discovered it as a chance seedling in 1811. It's a fine all-purpose winter apple, red with sometimes a tinge of green, pleasantly tart and juicy, good on its own, in salads or with meat, taking less time to cook than other varieties.

Mutsu - also **Crispin.** A late, dull-green apple of Japanese origin, eaten raw or cooked.

Mutsu

Newton-Pippin - one of the oldest commercially cultivated apples grown in North America. Green-skinned with crisp, tart flesh that's sweet enough to eat fresh, this is a good variety for apple pies and applesauce.

Northern Spy - also **Spy.** A very large, yellow-and-red-striped American apple used especially for cooking.

Northwest Greening - a large, tart and juicy apple with a tough, green skin, grown in North America for cider making and cooking.

Pippin - see NEWTON-PIPPIN

Pomme d'api - see LADY APPLE.

Red Delicious - an American variety, one of the world's best eating apples, firm and sweet. Its red skin makes it look attractive in a fruit bowl as well as served baked.

Rome - also **Rome Beauty.** A bright red-skinned, crisp-fleshed apple with a tart bite, it's best used for baking and applesauce and is delicious in pies. It is widely cultivated across North America, so named because it was discovered in Rome Township, Ohio, in the early 1800s.

Royal Gala - see GALA.

russet - a name for a group of very distinctive apples with matte brown skin. The flesh is crisp and slightly tart, and the apples keep well. Russets are used for eating and cooking.

Spartan - developed by Danes in 1926 from **McIntosh** and **Newton-Pippin** varieties, it is a firm apple with a custard-like taste, popular for eating raw and cooked. It goes well in a cold salad with onions and cured meats, the way it's served in Denmark.

Spy - see NORTHERN SPY.

Starking - also **Starking Delicious.** A crisp dessert apple from France with red streaked skin and very white, sweet flesh, best served early in the season, on its own at the end of a meal, with cheese, or as fritters, cored, sliced in rounds and fried in a sweet batter.

Stayman Winesap - see WINESAP.

Winesap - also **Stayman Winesap.** An excellent tart apple with a long shelf life, it's ideal for cider and for eating out of hand thanks to its rich, wine-like flavor. It is thought to be native to New Jersey and is one of the oldest apple varieties cultivated in North America, grown extensively since Colonial times.

Yellow Delicious - see GOLDEN DELICIOUS.

apple brandy - also **applejack, cider brandy.** A brandy distilled from apples. See also CALVADOS.

apple brown betty - see BETTY.

apple butter - a thick reddish-brown preserve made from apples, cider, sugar and spices, used like jam as a spread for bread.

apple charlotte - see CHARLOTTE.

apple cider vinegar - see CIDER VINEGAR.

apple corer - see CORER.

apple-cream pie - see MARLBOROUGH PIE.

apple crisp - see CRUMBLE.

apple crumble - see CRUMBLE.

apple dumpling - see DUMPLING.

apple fritter - see FRITTER.

apple-glazed ham - a Pennsylvanian specialty, a fully cooked boneless ham with an apple glaze, usually made of apple jelly, lemon juice and cloves.

apple green eggplant - see EGGPLANT.

apple ice wine - see ICE CIDER.

applejack - an American version of **apple brandy.** See also CALVADOS.

apple juice - juice pressed from fresh apples that is filtered and treated with heat to be shelf stable. Also available in a concentrate or frozen.

apple pandowdy - an almost-forgotten humble dish of spiced, sliced apples covered with a crust. It was a favorite of Philadelphia's founding fathers.

apple pear - see ASIAN PEAR.

apple pie spice - a ready-made mix of ground cinnamon, nutmeg and allspice (and sometimes other spices, such as ground cloves and ginger) available in grocery stores, used for baking apple pies, desserts, quick breads and cakes.

applesauce - a purée of stewed apples, smooth or chunky, often sweetened with sugar and spiced.

apple schnitz - dried apple slices, much used in Amish cooking.

apple turnover - a puff pastry stuffed with apple called *Apfel im Schlafrock*, or "apple in its bathrobe," by the Swiss. The French called them *chausson aux pommes*, or "apple socks."

apricot

apricot - the fruit of a tree, *Prunus armeniaca*, closely related to the plum, peach, cherry and almond. Apricots seem to inspire poetry and legend wherever they're grown. A Persian poet describes the fruit as the "golden seed of the sun." The Chinese, who were probably the first to have cultivated apricot trees more than 4,000 years ago, thought they had special powers and called them *zard-alu*, meaning "yellow plum." Confucius is said to have perfected his philosophies while sitting under an apricot tree. From China, apricots traveled westward to Europe. Before the days of Alexander the Great, they were being grown in the warmer Mediterranean regions. Some of the first settlers brought the apricot to North America, but the East Coast was no place for apricots. California was destined to become the apricot capital of the world, thanks to Spanish padres, who planted them in the gardens of the missions they founded during the late 1700s. Outside California, the main producers of apricots are Israel, Morocco, Japan, Australia and Spain.

Apricots have a very short growing season and a very short shelf life. The name apricot comes from the Latin word for *praecocia*, meaning "precocious," because the apricot ripens earlier than other summer fruits. The fruit's genus name, *armeniaca*, reflects the belief that the fruit originated in Armenia.

apricot brandy - brandy distilled from apricots.

apricot kernel oil - the oil pressed from the inner kernel of the apricot pit, used most often in topical preparations as an emollient, but also used sparingly for cooking and in salads for its nutty taste and healthy unsaturated fat. The kernels themselves are poisonous if eaten raw because they contain amygdalin, which can combine with digestive enzymes to form a type of deadly cyanide in the body. Apricot kernel oil, however, is not poisonous because the amygdalin does not dissolve in the oil as it is extracted and is left behind in the remaining solids. Apricot kernel oil is often substituted for almond oil or peach kernel oil and is used in confectionery as well.

aprium - see PLUOT.

aquaculture - the cultivation of fish, shellfish or aquatic plants for human consumption. Known since ancient Greece, the practice did not begin to expand rapidly until the 1980s. Species as diverse as oysters, clams, crayfish, lobsters, trout and salmon are all raised in this way.

aquavit - also **akvavit.** Made in Scandinavia since the 15th century, this grain-based spirit (sometimes using potato) is flavored with cumin, caraway or fennel. Its name comes from the Latin *aqua vitae,* meaning "water of life." In Germany, it's called **Schnapps,** in Denmark **schnaps,** while in Sweden, Norway and the Netherlands, **snaps.** The name derives from the old Nordic verb *snappen,* meaning "to snatch or seize," referring to the way one drinks it, down the throat in a single gulp.

aqua vitae - see EAU DE VIE.

arabica - considered to be one of the best coffees in the world, with complex and subtle flavors, but a low caffeine content. The principal crop is grown in Colombia, but the finest arabica comes from West Africa. The varietal was first discovered in Arabia, hence the name. See also COFFEE.

arak - also **arrack**. A liquor distilled from dates in Egypt and the Middle East, grapes and seeds in Greece, palm sap in India and sugarcane juice in Java, usually flavored with anise. It's possible that some form of arak was the first spirit. There are claims that it was first made in India about 800 BC. The name comes from *araq,* Arabic for "juice" or "sap."

arame - a long, black, shredded seaweed that's very mild and sweet, often used in salads and soups in Japanese cuisine. It is usually available dehydrated, in packets, in Asian grocery stores and requires just a few minutes of soaking to reconstitute. Arame has very few calories, but is high in vitamins and minerals.

aram sandwich - also **levant.** A sandwich made by spreading a **lavash,** a round, flat bread, with cream cheese and then layering with fillings, such as meat, cheese, vegetables, pickles, etc. The whole is then rolled up and refrigerated before being cut into thick slices.

aranciata - a carbonated beverage made with sparkling water, orange juice and sugar, from the Italian word "arancia," meaning orange, also called Italian orange soda or orangeade. See also CHINOTTO, ITALIAN SODA, LIMONATA.

arancini - Italian appetizers, balls of **Arborio rice,** peas, cheese and seasonings, often stuffed with a bit of **ricotta** cheese or meat in the center, then coated with crumbs and deep-fried. Many cooks tint the rice a light shade of orange by cooking it with a pinch of saffron. The name means "little oranges" in Italian for their shape (and color, if saffron is included).

arán prátaí - famed Irish potato bread.

arare - a small, crispy Japanese wheat cracker, sweet or savory, with soy sauce, sesame seeds or seaweed.

arbol chile - also **chile de arbol.** See CHILE PEPPER.

Arborio rice - an Italian-grown short-grain rice traditionally used in making **risotto,** because its high starch content gives the dish its characteristic creaminess. See also RICE.

Arbroath smokies - a popular Scottish dish of small haddock that has been gutted, salted, smoked, then split and broiled, often sold in pairs, usually served as an appetizer.

Arbuckle, John - see profile below.

Arbuckle, John (1838–1912) - American coffee industrialist who patented a technique for roasting coffee and a machine that could fill, seal, label and package one-pound (500 g) parcels of coffee. In 1865, Arbuckle teamed up with his younger brother, Charles, who was already in the grocery business in Pittsburgh. John patented their coffee roasting technique, which entailed coating the beans with egg and sugar. With the expertise of a draftsman and a machinist, he invented his packaging machine. The coffee became a favorite of chuck-wagon cooks, who made gallons of coffee for cowboys in their camp. Arbuckle became the world's largest importer of coffee. He also owned ships that sailed to the U.S. with South American coffee on board. In 1906, he went into the ship-salvaging business, eventually acquiring a fleet of telegraph-equipped tugboats used in rescue missions. Today, the Arbuckles' brand is a leading manufacturer of flavored coffees.

arbutus - of the genus *Arbutus unedo*, the fruit of the strawberry tree, a rather tasteless berry used mainly in preserves.

Arctic char - see CHAR.

Ardennes ham - also **jambon des Ardennes.** An air-dried, salt-cured ham similar to **prosciutto,** made in Belgium and northern France, named for the heavily forested region of Ardennes, which extends into both countries and a portion of Luxembourg. The ham is served in the same way as prosciutto, namely raw and sliced paper-thin, or sometimes sautéed briefly in butter.

areca nut - see BETEL NUT.

arepa - a thick grilled Venezuelan and Colombian flatbread made from coarsely ground cooked corn. Arepas are delicious plain, spread with butter or sprinkled with crumbled cheese. Many restaurants serve stuffed arepas, filled with meats, cheeses, eggs, vegetables or whatever else happens to be on hand.

argan oil - oil pressed from the nuts of the argan tree, *Argania spinosa*, native to the semidesert climate of southwestern Morocco and found nowhere else. The oil is high in **omega-6 fatty acids** and **antioxidants**, and has a pleasantly nutty flavor that makes it an excellent salad oil. Like **flaxseed oil,** argan oil is best used in cool or cold dishes, because its healthful components break down when exposed to high temperatures in cooking.

Argenteuil, á l' - garnished with asparagus. The name comes from the French town of Argenteuil, where, at one time, the best asparagus was thought to be grown.

arhar dal - see DAL.

ark shell - any of a number of **bivalves** of the family Arcidae, eaten in Europe, Asia and Africa, so named because the shell looks like a ship with a raised deck, like Noah's ark. Most varieties of ark shell are eaten cooked, but some are also eaten raw, such as A. *broughtonii*, which is frequently eaten in Japan as a sushi topping and is known by the name *akagai*.

armadillo - from the Dasypodidae family, a mammal related to the anteater, it originated in South America, but can now be found as far west as Colorado and as far north as Newbraska. An armadillo is edible, indeed good to eat, provided that seven glands have first been removed from its legs and back. The animal may then be cleaned and baked in its own armored shell of small bony plates, which encases both the head and the body. It was a very popular food in Texas during the Great Depression under the apt name of "Hoover hog." The name is Spanish and means "the little armed one," a diminutive of *armado*, or "armed."

Armagnac - made in southwest France, sometimes called "the other brandy," dating back to the 1400s. The difference between it and the more popular **cognac** is that cognac is made, for the most part, from the Ugni Blanc grape, while Armagnac's base wine is made from a number of varieties. Locally grown black oak casks are used for the maturation.

armavir - a sour-milk cheese of the Western Caucasus made from ewe's milk and sour buttermilk or whey. The uniqueness of the cheese is that the **affinage,** or ripening process, is done in a warm environment.

Armenian bole - a red clay, native to Armenia, once used as a color additive for food, but no longer. Historically, used as an astringent. It is also used in bookbinding for coloring.

Armenian cracker bread - see LAVASH.

Armenian flatbread - see LAVASH.

Armour, Philip Danforth - see profile right.

arm roast - **1.** a tough cut of beef from the center of the chuck section of a steer, with or without the bone included, sometimes cut into thinner arm steaks, which are often the base for **Swiss steak.** See also BEEF. **2.** a roast cut from the shoulder of a veal calf, often sold boned and rolled. **3.** a roast of

armadillo

pork cut from the top part of the picnic shoulder at the front leg of a pig. The roast may be cut into thinner arm steaks. See also PORK.

aroma - **1.** the fragrance or smell of a food or beverage. **2.** in reference to wine, the smells associated with a particular grape variety, used to refer to the smell of a young wine. See also BOUQUET.

aromatic - any of several fragrant or spicy plants used to flavor food or drink.

aromatic complexity - a term used to describe the variety of **aromas** associated with a particular wine. A wine with good aromatic complexity will offer up a number of scents at the same time; for example, a Cabernet Sauvignon with good aromatic complexity may give off scents of blackberry, plum, minerals, oak and chocolate.

aromatic rice - a term used for those varieties of rice with a nutty flavor and aroma. Among the most popular are **basmati**, Texmati, jasmine and **Wehani.** See also RICE.

aromatized wine - a wine that has some type of flavoring added, typically herbs or spices, though some may be fortified with neutral spirits or brandy as well. The most famous aromatized wine is probably **vermouth,** though **retsina** is another example.

aronia - also **black chokeberry, chokeberry.** An edible, but extremely bitter, berry from the *Aronia* genus, grown mostly in Siberia and eastern Europe where it is processed into juice. Not to be confused with chokecherry, a wild cherry.

arrabbiata - a name given to Italian dishes with a spicy sauce of tomatoes, chiles and usually pancetta, from the Italian word for "angry," originally made with penne or tortiglioni, although different types of pastas can be used.

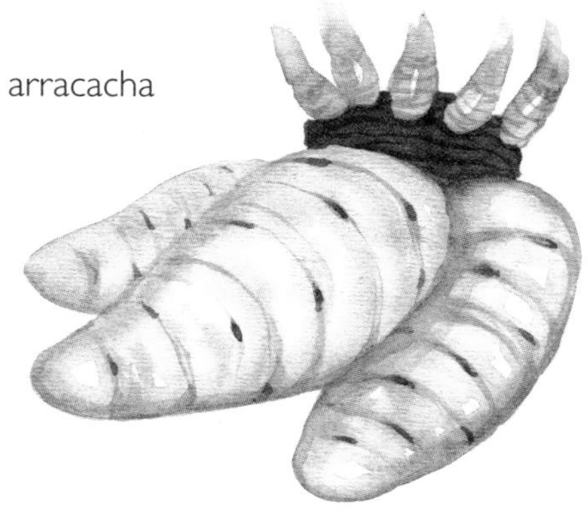
arracacha

arracacha - also **apio, Peruvian carrot, Peruvian parsnip.** A popular South American tuberous vegetable, *Arracacia xanthorrhiza,* similar to **celeriac,** with a knobby tuber and longer "fingers" that jut from the bottom. The flavor of arracacha falls somewhere between those of the carrot, **yucca** and celeriac, with the thinner "fingers" being milder and more tender than the knobby part of the vegetable. It can be cooked in the same way as the potato, yielding a starchy-textured result that is pleasant in soups, stews or simply mashed and served as a side dish. Thanks to its high starch content, it can also be ground into a coarse flour or meal for use in a variety of recipes. Arracacha is also called *apio,* which means "celery" in Spanish, for its herbal celery-like taste.

arrack - see ARAK.

arrowhead - also **Chinese potato, swamp potato, Tule potato.** A root vegetable, *Sagittaria sagittifolia,* a water plant with arrow-shaped leaves, whose roots and leaves are used in Chinese cooking.

arrowroot - also **Indian arrowroot.** A dry, chalky and nutritious starch used as food. It's made from the pith of the roots of *Maranta*

Armour, Philip Danforth (1833–1901) - American meat-processing baron who gave Henry Ford the idea for his assembly line. At 19, Armour decided to walk to California from his home state of New York — it took him six months — to seek his fortune in the gold rush. In four short years, he earned $8,000 and headed back east to go into business. He started a grain business in Wisconsin, but moved on to Chicago to found his meat-processing business in 1867. In setting up his operation, Armour made economy and efficiency paramount, bragging that he used the entire pig, "except the squeal." He sold his by-products in the form of glue, oil, fertilizer, hairbrushes, buttons, margarine and drugs. He designed his system of production based on his observation that a line of men, each carrying out a specific portion of a task repeatedly, was more productive than a man performing the full task alone. While touring the plant as Armour's guest, Ford reportedly called it "the disassembly line."

arundinacea. Arrowroot is a light, dense white powder, insipid and odorless, and will keep for many years in a dry place. It was given its name by Native Americans after the plant *araruta* ("flour root"). **Florida arrowroot** is made in Florida from the coontie plant.

arroz con leche - literally "rice with milk" in Spanish, this creamy rice pudding is popular in Spain and Latin America. It is made with rice, milk and sugar, and is often accented with cinnamon and/or lemon peel.

arroz con pollo - a simple dish of chicken and rice, customized in thousands of local ways, all over Spain and Latin America, often flavored with saffron and green peppers. The name literally means "rice with chicken" in Spanish.

artichoke - a thistle, *Cyrana scolymus,* native to the Mediterranean. Artichokes were probably known to the Greeks and were considered a delicacy in Rome, of which Roman historian **Pliny** professed to be ashamed: "Thus we turn into a corrupt feast the earth's monstrosities, those which even the animals instinctively avoid." Yet in Rome, in the 2nd century AD, no other garden vegetable fetched such a high price. The artichoke enjoyed by the Greeks and the Romans was not the globe (French) artichoke or the thistle flower head whose petal bases and "heart" we eat today. The ancient Carthaginians, as well as the Greeks and the Romans, ate the **cardoon** (*Cynara cardunculus*), whose edible portions were its young leaves and undeveloped stalks, grown in the dark to keep them white and tender. The name is a corruption, via the Italian, of the Arabic *al'qarshuf;* for some reason the Latin word *cynara* did not survive even in the Romance languages. (However, the Italians make an apéritif called **Cynar,** from artichokes.) Some believe that the word artichoke is a culinary hybrid. The true name is said to be derived from two Middle English words: *hortus* and *chokt,* literally meaning "a garden strangler."

Although artichokes have always grown like weeds in Sicily, they were first cultivated near Naples in the 15th century. Forgotten by the aristocracy during the Middle Ages, the artichoke was rediscovered and revived during the Renaissance by a certain Filippo Strozzi in Florence around 1466. Later, its fame traveled to Florence, where it became a favorite dish of the Medici family, who took artichokes to France in the 16th century, where they became very

artichoke

popular in French cooking. **Catherine de' Medici** was said to love them so much, she often fainted from eating too many. Artichokes were suspected to have powerful aphrodisiac properties, and women were regularly forbidden to eat them. This unusual vegetable is actually a very large bud, harvested before it has a chance to bloom.

It was the Italians and Spaniards who introduced artichokes to America. It was discovered that artichokes adapted well to Californian coastal regions, mainly around Castroville, often billed as the artichoke capital of the world. There are more than 50 varieties of artichokes grown worldwide. Baby artichokes are not immature artichokes but simply a small version grown lower on the plant.

Artichokes act as a diuretic and can be used as a liver tonic to invigorate the system and promote bile flow. They should never be cooked in an aluminum pot, as they tend to turn the pot gray. Add sugar, half a lemon or cider or white wine vinegar, and salt when cooking to retain color and obtain a better flavor. In Italy, where the artichoke is known as *carciofo,* women at the market stalls usually rub two together before making a selection. If the artichokes make a little squeak on contact, they are deemed fresh. If they are *muto,* "silent," the ladies simply pass them by. See also CHINESE ARTICHOKE, JERUSALEM ARTICHOKE.

artichoke bottom - the fleshy base of an artichoke, the cup-shaped section at the bottom of the leaves and heart. Artichoke bottoms are often steamed and used to hold poached eggs, stuffings, pâtés or mousses, and are available in cans in some specialty grocery stores. Artichoke bottoms are the base of the rich dish **eggs Sardou.**

artificial sweeteners - also **non-nutritive sweeteners.** These sugar substitutes are made from a variety of chemicals and naturally occurring amino acids. Some mimic the taste of sugar well and can be used in cold and hot applications, while others break down when exposed to heat or acid and therefore are not suitable for cooking. Many leave an unpleasant aftertaste or can be easily detected in foods and beverages by those who dislike them. In any case, they are low in calories, usually non-nutritive (meaning they are not broken down or changed in any way in the body and therefore excreted intact) and are suitable for people on sugar-restricted diets. However, there is substantial controversy over their long-term health effects: while the companies that produce these sweeteners claim that they are safe at low doses, there is considerable concern over the negative health effects of consuming large doses, from headaches to allergies to cancer. See also ACESULFAME POTASSIUM, ASPARTAME, SACCHARIN, SUCRALOSE.

artisanal - a word used to describe food or beverages made by hand, not by machines, using traditional techniques instead of modern industrial ones, and with only fresh, natural ingredients. Artisanal bakers and cheesemakers especially have enjoyed a large-scale comeback in Europe and increasingly in North America, thanks to a growing interest in sustainable and organic agriculture and the **Slow Food** movement, which emphasizes locally handmade foods. Artisanal foods are made in small batches and are not precisely uniform like factory-made ones, and are appreciated for their rich, honest flavors and textures, unlike mass-produced food, which sacrifices taste for the sake of shelf life and ease of packaging and transportation.

Artisanal bread contains only natural, chemical-free ingredients and is leavened with wild yeasts or traditional sourdough starters fed daily to keep them alive. The loaves are kneaded and allowed to rise slowly, then formed by hand and baked into crusty rounds, loaves and so on. They are always baked the day they are sold; they are never par-baked, or baked partially for storage until the baking can be finished (supermarkets specialize in this type of "artisanal-style bread," which is really just factory-made bread passed off as handmade and freshly baked). Because it contains no preservatives, artisanal bread must be eaten quickly before it hardens or grows mold.

Artisanal cheese is made with milk from local farms, which guarantees freshness. Because the milk is locally sourced in small batches, it has different characteristics, depending on the animals' feed and the season in which it is harvested, which can translate into intense, unique flavors that change from batch to batch. Artisanal cheesemakers use no machinery to produce their cheese — mixing, stirring, salting and forming the cheese by hand and aging it naturally over a period of days, months or years.

Farmhouse cheese, also known as farmstead cheese, is another type of artisanal cheese made by a farmer from the milk of a single herd at his or her farm. It is also made by hand using old-fashioned techniques and without mechanical processes as much as possible.

There are many other types of artisanal products that are growing in popularity. Jams, sausages, oils and vinegars are all made by artisanal producers, who perpetuate and nurture traditional food-making techniques, using fresh, natural, local ingredients.

artisanal sea salt - see SALT.

ärtsoppa - a yellow pea soup with smoked pork, traditionally served on Thursday, only during the long winter months, in Sweden.

arugula - also **Italian cress, rocket, roquette, rucola.** Arugula is an assertive salad green, *Eruca sativa,* which has a peppery taste somewhere between nasturtium and watercress, used frequently in Mediterranean dishes. The Romans utilized the leaves and seeds. Thomas Jefferson, in written instructions to his gardener at Monticello, lists it as essential for the kitchen garden. Although its leaves resemble those of the dandelion, arugula belongs to the same

arugula

family as watercress, radish and mustard and can reach about 20 inches (50 cm) in height. When young, its long, tender leaves have a pleasant peppery flavor, while mature arugula has a stronger, more assertive flavor that can be bitter. It can be eaten raw or cooked, and the seeds are used to make very potent mustard in the Mediterranean and the Middle East.

arum root - a Japanese root used to make a translucent jelly-like cake called *konnyaku* and the clear noodles called *shirataki*.

asadero cheese - also **Chihuahua cheese, Oaxaca cheese, quesilla.** A popular type of Mexican string cheese, similar to **pasta filata** cheeses, often used to make **quesadillas,** now available all over North America. Asadero means "fit for roasting" in Spanish, which describes the cooking method that best renders the cheese into its creamy, pleasantly stringy cooked texture. Asadero is also commonly known as quesilla, quesilla de Oaxaca, Oaxaca cheese or Chihuahua cheese for the region where it was developed. It is frequently eaten on sandwiches called **cemitas** and melted in recipes.

asafetida - also **asafoetida, devil's dung, stinking gum.** A resin, asafetida comes in a brown chunk or a tan-colored powder and is a spice to use in minuscule quantities. It's derived from a giant plant resembling fennel, which grows mostly in Iran and India. In powder form, it has a very unpleasant odor, which disappears when the spice is cooked; it then imparts an onion-like aroma. A variety of asafetida from Judea was known by the Romans as a garnish under the name of *silphium* or *laserpitium*. The Romans called it *inter eximia deorum dona*, "one of the gods' presents." Its English name comes from the Latin *foetidus*, meaning "fetid."

ascorbic acid - vitamin C, used as an antioxidant to slow down spoilage, especially to retain the red color of fresh and preserved meat.

as de pique - French culinary slang for "*croupion*," a fowl's rump.

aseptic packaging - a food-packaging system that allows perishable foods to be kept at room temperature without spoilage for six months or more, used widely in Europe and Asia for several decades but introduced to North America in the 1980s, slowly becoming a common sight on supermarket shelves. Unlike commercially canned foods, which are heated for several minutes in their containers, then cooled for even longer periods to ensure sterilization, aseptically packaged foods are flash-heated to an ultra-high temperature (between 195°F/90°C and 285°F/140°C) for three to 15 seconds, then flash-cooled to room temperature and packed in sterilized containers in a sterile environment. The short periods of heating and cooling ensure that fewer nutrients are lost and preserve the flavor of the food better than canning. In North America, a variety of foods come in aseptic packaging: milk, soy beverages, juices and tofu are some of the most common. In other parts of the world, these and hundreds more foods are sold in aseptic packaging, including some types of cream and even premade sauces such as hollandaise.

Ashanti pepper - a kind of pepper, *Piper guineense*, grown and used in West Africa, milder than ordinary black pepper.

ash cake - also **ash bread.** A category of breads traditionally baked in the hot ashes from a fire, such as some types of North American cornbread and Australian **damper bread.** The bread is often wrapped in leaves to add flavor and protect it from the ashes and high heat of the coals.

ashta - see KASHTA.

Asiago - a pale, smooth, yellow cheese with small "eyes" and a thin brownish rind, made in Italy from skim milk and aged for up to two years.

Asian celery - also **Chinese celery.** A highly prized vegetable in Chinese and other Asian cooking, similar to, but stronger in flavor than European or North American celery. Asian celery is invariably eaten cooked, as its flavor raw is overpowering. This juicier, thinner, darker green form of celery is used extensively in soups or stir-fried mixtures of vegetables.

Asian chili paste and sauce - blends of hot chile peppers, salt and possibly oil and garlic, which are a feature of Chinese, Korean and southeast Asian cuisines. Sometimes, such ingredients as black beans, soybeans and ginger are added. Those containing a high proportion of soybeans are known as "hot bean pastes." Some Chinese and Korean varieties are fermented. Usually, chili pastes are used in cooking, whereas the sauces are served as condiments. See also CHILE PASTE.

Asian eggplant - see EGGPLANT.

Asian noodles - made with wheat, rice, mung bean, buckwheat, seaweed, corn, arrowroot, sometimes even with flour extracted from a plant related to the arum family, called devil's tongue. They come in a variety of shapes from ribbons to strands to nests. Dried wheat noodles, made with or without eggs, are called longevity noodles because they're believed to contribute to long life. In the south of China, and particularly in Cantonese cuisine, rice noodles are more popular than wheat because this is the country's main rice-growing area. See also BIJON, CANTON NOODLE, CHOW FUN, DAN ZAI NOODLES, HARUSAME, MIKI, MISUA, RAMEN, RICE STICK NOODLE, SHIRATAKI, SOBA, SOMEN, TRANSPARENT NOODLES, UDON.

Asian okra - also **Chinese okra, loofah, silk gourd, silk melon, silk squash, sponge gourd.** Not a relative of okra at all, this is the **loofah** squash, *Luffa acutangula* or *L. cylindrica,* that most North Americans associate with their bathrooms sponges, not their kitchens. In Asian cooking, however, it is well known and used in soups or stir-fries, deep-fried or fried up in an omelet. The flesh turns a bit spongy and soft when cooked, but has a pleasantly mild flavor reminiscent of both okra and cucumber.

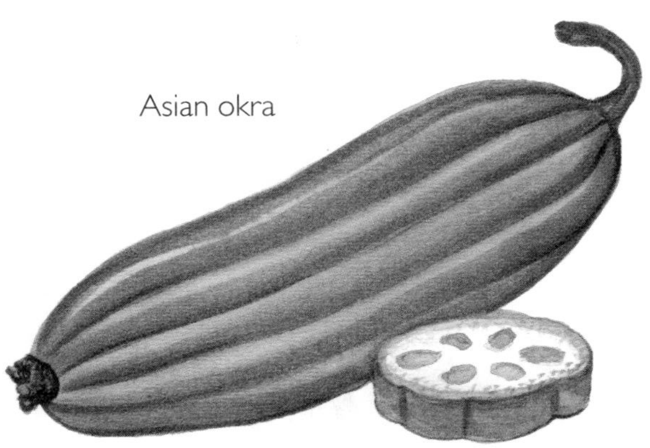
Asian okra

Asian pear - also **apple pear, Chinese pear, Japanese pear, Nashi, nijisseiki, Oriental, salad pear, sand pear.** A firm, but juicy pear that ranges from golden brown to yellow-green. It is noticeably more crunchy than European or North American varieties of pear. There are more than 100 varieties of pears, most of which

Asian pear

come from Japan. Nijisseiki, a Japanese hybrid, is one of the most popular Asian pears around the world and is now grown in North America where it is also known as "20th Century pear."

Asian radish - see DAIKON.

asopao - a soupy stew of chicken or seafood and rice, one of the most famous Puerto Rican dishes, similar in consistency to **gumbo.** There is no single recipe for asopao, and cooks tailor it to their tastes and the contents of their cupboards. The stew is seasoned with **sofrito** and is in part a descendent of the Spanish dish **paella.**

asparagus - the young shoots of an almost leafless plant, *Asparagus officinalis,* a member of the lily family. Asparagus was well known in antiquity; we find it, for example, carved in the ancient Egyptian hieroglyphics. The Egyptians were eating wild asparagus no bigger than a child's forefinger before the second pyramid was constructed at Giza, but the delicate stalks firmly resisted all efforts at cultivation along the Nile. We know that the Greeks used it as an aphrodisiac, collecting it from the wild, but never cultivating it. The Greek word *aspharos* means "as long as one's throat," a label, the pundits tell us, conferred on the long slender spears because overeager diners often consumed them whole. It was not until the Roman period that it was cultivated. The Romans enriched a form of what we now call pasta by adding creamed asparagus to the flour, thus enhancing both the texture and the taste of the pasta. Not only did the Romans eat asparagus in season, they also dried asparagus shoots for later use. Even then, asparagus was highly regarded. Julius Caesar was said to enjoy eating it with melted butter.

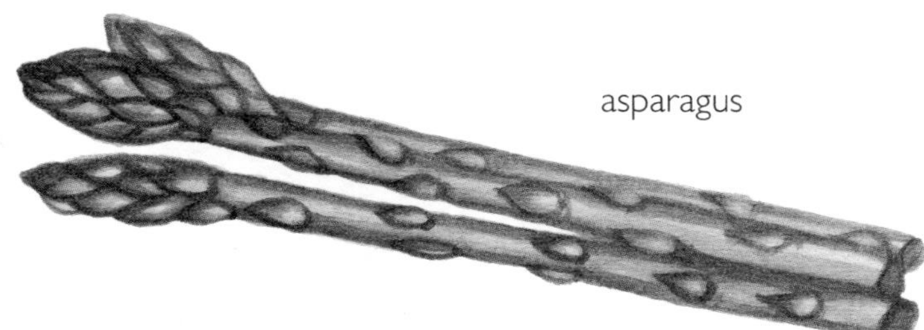

asparagus

In the 1st century AD, the Roman gastronome **Marcus Gavius Apicius,** in the first known book of recipes, instructed cooks to combine pounded asparagus tips with pepper, lovage, fresh coriander, savory, onion, wine, oil, eggs and a fish-flavored sauce, sprinkled with more pepper after baking. Romans tended to overindulge in asparagus, considering a dinner negligible unless it featured both an asparagus appetizer and main dish. Even then, chefs knew better than to overcook it. Whenever Augustus Caesar wished to terminate some unpleasant business at hand, he would proclaim, "*Velocius quam asparagi coquantur,*" meaning, "Let it be done quicker than you would cook an asparagus." During the Middle Ages, Europeans forgot about asparagus, even though it was still cultivated by the Arabs. There's little mention of asparagus being eaten in England or France until the 17th century, when Louis XIV became fond of it and put it on the plates of Europe. Before asparagus was used for food, it was considered a cure for heart trouble, dropsy and toothaches. It was even supposed to prevent bee stings. Early colonists brought it to the U.S. and often called it "sparrow grass."

One can find beautiful purple asparagus, wild asparagus, green asparagus, variegated asparagus and tender white asparagus, or *asperge blanche*, which is planted under mounds of soil to block sunlight, reducing the plant's ability to produce chlorophyll. But all varieties of asparagus have one thing in common: once picked or purchased, they should be promptly cooked, because the spear's natural sugar will quickly turn to starch, causing the asparagus to lose flavor and develop a woody texture. When you can't rush asparagus from the market to the cooking pot, slice off about 1 inch (2.5 cm) of the stalks and stand them in cool water as you would cut flowers. Refrigerate them, uncovered, and cook as soon as possible. The harvest of many other crops has been mechanized, but asparagus is still hand-cut.

Anyone who eats asparagus excretes methyl mercaptan, but not everyone may become aware of the odor. Asparagus contains a harmless sulfur compound that may cause a strange odor in urine, occurring in approximately 40 percent of the population. Asparagus is also a well-known diuretic and a source of potassium, iron, calcium, and vitamins A, B_2 and C. Its root is used as an expectorant, diuretic, nervous stimulant and tonic. As well, it's said to have a beneficial effect on the female reproductive system.

asparagus bean - also **Chinese long bean, long bean, Thai bean, yard-long bean.** An Asian green bean that grows about 12 to 18 inches (30 to 45 cm) long, with a flavor similar to but less sweet than the common green bean.

asparagus bush - a native plant of West Africa, *Dracaena manii*, the young shoots of which are cooked like asparagus. The natives of Cameroon also eat the leaves boiled, chopped and mixed with rice.

asparagus chicory - see ITALIAN DANDELION.

asparagus cooker - a tall metal-wire framework used for cooking whole spears of asparagus upright in a deep pot. The cooker is placed in a tall pot, into which is poured a small amount of water. The asparagus stalks are then arranged upright inside the cooker so that the woody ends are submerged in the water and the tips are at the top of the pot. The boiling water cooks the tough ends thoroughly as steam cooks the tender stalks and tips, yielding a perfectly cooked (not mushy) result.

asparagus cooker

asparagus lettuce - see LETTUCE.

asparagus peeler - a V-shaped kitchen utensil with two handles joined at one end. The opposite end of each handle is equipped with a two-sided blade (similar to that of a potato peeler), used for quickly and neatly peeling off the outer layer of a stalk of asparagus. Larger, thicker asparagus stalks often have a woody outer layer that is unpleasant to eat and therefore require peeling (smaller, thinner stalks do not).

asparation - see BROCCOLINI.

aspartame - an artificial sweetener that tastes very much like ordinary sugar but is 200 times sweeter. NutraSweet is a brand-name aspartame product used in beverages, yogurts and sugar-free desserts. See also ARTIFICIAL SWEETENERS.

aspic - a savory jelly made by adding gelatin to meat, fish or vegetable stock, as well as to juice, as in tomato aspic. Generally believed to be named after the asp, an Egyptian cobra, especially since the first mold was shaped like a coiled snake. Aspic was probably derived from the Latin *aspis* or *aspidis*. Etymologists disagree about exactly why aspic should conjure up images of a venomous reptile. Some argue that the name refers to the colors of aspics, which vary like a snake's skin. Others contend that its name stems from the fact that this food is cold to the touch, as in the French expression *froid come un aspic*, "cold as an asp."

aspic leaves - see ASPIC POWDER.

aspic powder - also **aspic jelly powder.** A commercial powder made with gelatin and flavored with meat or fish stock, used to quickly and easily make the base for an **aspic.** This product is also made and dried into sheets called **aspic leaves.**

ass - either of two four-legged animals, *Equus africanus* or *E. hemionus*, of the horse family. In times of emergency the ass has provided a most acceptable meat for the hungry, its flesh being very nutritious. Henry Du Pré Labouchere (1831–1912), the British politician and noted wit who gained journalistic fame with his dispatches from Paris during the siege of 1870, said that the donkey meat he had eaten was like mutton in color, firm and savory. "I can solemnly assert," he added, "that I never wish to taste a better dinner than a joint of donkey or a **ragoût** of cat, *experto crede*." In China, the wild ass was used for sport during peace and for food for troops during war.

Assam tea - see TEA.

assemblage - a French term for the process of blending a selection of **still wines** to create a complex **sparkling wine,** such as **Champagne.** The winemaker blends a variety of fine still wines, then allows them to undergo a second fermentation in the bottle, which makes them effervescent. The term means "assembly" in French. See also MÉTHODE CHAMPENOISE.

Asti Spumante - a well-known type of Italian **sparkling wine,** made primarily in the Piedmont towns of Asti and Alba. Asti Spumante is made from white **Muscat grapes** (known as *moscato bianco* in Italian) and fermented in large steel tanks, using the **Charmat method** instead of the traditional French **méthode champenoise** to create its copious bubbles. It is made in varying levels of sweetness and has a much fruitier taste than Champagne. The wine is named for both the town of Asti and for its extremely bubbly, foamy texture, called **spumante** in Italian.

astringency - characteristic of beer and wine taste mostly caused by **tannins,** oxidized tannins (phenols) and various **aldehydes,** which cause the palate to pucker.

aşure - also **ashure, asure.** A thick, sweet Middle Eastern soup or pudding made of whole grains, legumes, nuts and dried fruits, also called "Noah's pudding" for the Bible story of Noah's ark, often made with 15 or more ingredients. According to the legend, this soup was made by Noah and his family to celebrate the receding waters after the flood; the family took all the foods that were left on the ark — beans, rice, chickpeas, dried fruits, nuts, wheat — and created a celebratory meal when they disembarked. This dish is still served all over the Middle East and in the Balkan region as well, often as a dessert soup; the ingredients vary according to the local staples, availability of foods and palates of the diners. The name *aşure* is derived from the word *ashura*, or the 10th day of Muharram, the first month of the Muslim calendar, on which Noah is supposed to have landed.

ata - also **atta, chapati flour.** A very finely ground whole wheat flour from India that is low gluten and mainly used in bread.

atemoya

atemoya - from the Philippines, a heart-shaped fruit that is a cross between *ates*, Tagalog for sweetsop, and the South American **cherimoya.** The fruit is very sweet, but not overly juicy, with a pudding-like pulp containing black seeds.

Athenaeus - see profile below.

Atlantic cod - see COD.

Atlantic croaker - see DRUM.

Atlantic oyster - also **Eastern oyster.** See OYSTER.

Atlantic rosefish - see OCEAN PERCH.

atole - a thick, Mexican drink, a favorite of mission fathers and Indians, still enjoyed today, made of corn flour (**masa**) or rice flour, often with added flavorings, cooked very slowly. See also MASA HARINA.

atole flour - see MASA HARINA.

attereau - a skewer used for cooking a brochette or kebab.

aubergine - see EGGPLANT.

au bleu - an old French cooking technique for trout and other freshwater fish. The fish is plunged, alive, into a boiling **court-bouillon,** which causes the skin of the fish to take on a bluish aspect and the fish to arch in a half-moon shape.

au gratin - a term describing a dish coated with sauce, sprinkled with cheese and/or bread crumbs and browned in the oven or under the broiler.

au jus - a French term, meaning "with juice," for meats served with their natural cooking juices.

au lait - the French term meaning "with milk," used to describe any dish or drink made with milk, such as a café au lait.

au naturel - a French term for foods cooked and/or served without any additions, as close as possible to their natural state. The term is applied to vegetables cooked without any seasoning, meat or fish grilled without butter or sauce, omelets without fillings or garnishes, and fresh fruit served plain between courses or as a dessert.

Aunt Jemina - see GREEN, NANCY.

auricle - see OREILLETTE.

aurore sauce - **béchamel** with just a touch of tomato added to make it pink, like the dawn sky, or *aurore* in French.

Auslese - a German wine label term for specially selected, hand-picked, perfectly ripe grapes used to make medium- to heavy-weight wines. German grapes used for winemaking are classified and labeled according to their ripeness, not necessarily their sweetness, and by the weight, or body, of the wines they produce, from thin and light-bodied to syrupy and full-bodied. Auslese grapes may or may not have **Botrytis cinerea** on them, and the wines they produce can vary from a bit sweet to very sweet. See also BEERENAUSLESE, KABINETT, SPÄTLESE, TROCKENBEERENAUSLESE.

autolyzed yeast - yeast cells that have been broken down by their own enzymes to make smaller, simpler proteins — a process known as

Athenaeus (c. 200 AD) - Greek author of *Deipnosophistai* (The Learned Banquet), a 15-book opus of anecdotes shared at a fictional banquet by a group of characters, many modeled on historical figures. Up for discussion, not surprisingly, were food, wine and music. But the book also recorded discussions on such racier subjects as literary gossip, sex and pornography. Written in 200 AD, the book's importance lies in its mention of historical works, writers and events, which provided future scholars with information that would otherwise have been lost.

autolysis, from the Greek *auto*, meaning "self," and *lysis*, meaning "loosening." Autolyzed yeast extract is used to make yeast spreads, such as **Marmite** and **Vegemite,** and as a food additive, similar to **monosodium glutamate,** to add a savory flavor to packaged foods.

Auvergne - a blue-veined cow's milk cheese from the center of France, sometimes called **Bleu-d'Auvergne.**

aux champignon - a French term meaning "with mushrooms," for a dish made or served with mushrooms or mushroom sauce.

avgolemono - a Greek soup and sauce made from chicken broth, egg yolks, lemon juice and (in the case of the soup) rice. The name literally means "egg-lemon," from the Modern Greek *augolémono: augó*, meaning "egg," and *lemóninion*, meaning "lemon." The Arabic name is *tarbiya* and the Turkish is *terbie* — in both cases it means "treatment," as in an improvement.

avocado - a New World fruit, *Persea americana*, botanically a fruit, eaten both as a fruit or vegetable, native to Mexico, belonging to the Laureaceae family. It did not become popular in Europe until the middle of the 19th century, when modern transport allowed growers in California to market this fruit worldwide. The fruit's name comes from the Aztec *ahuacatl*, roughly translated as "testicle," which is most likely a reference to the avocado's shape. The Spanish conquistadors, obviously more prudish, censored the name: they translated the word phonetically as *abogado*, meaning "lawyer." Time distorted this to *aguacate*, meaning "green testicles," but the damage was done. Both the French and the Germans compounded the misconception. France's *poire d'avocat* and Germany's *advokatbirne* have the same meaning, "lawyer's pears." In 1527, the conquistadors returned to Spain with avocados. In 1653, Spanish priest Bernabe Cobe described three kinds of avocados — Mexican, West Indian and Guatemalan. He wrote that they come in hundreds of varieties, including round, pyriform and "necked" (like a crookneck squash), in green, purple, maroon and black, with skin textures that may be bark-like, scaly or smooth.

At 19, George Washington visited Barbados with his brother, Lawrence, who required a warm climate to recover from an illness. Young George sampled such tropical fruits as "agovado," which he notes as abundant and the most popular fruit.

Known early on as **alligator pear,** the many varieties of today's avocado range from pear-shaped to round. The two most widely marketed varieties are the **Hass,** rough-skinned and almost black; and the **Fuerte,** smooth-skinned and green. Avocados were introduced into southern Florida in 1833 by horticulturist Henry Perrine, who planted Mexican varieties on his grant of land south of Miami. While Mexicans used the fruit in avocado bread, guacamole and in other ways, the alligator pear was not be grown commercially until 1901. California planter R. B. Ord made the first commercially successful planting of avocados in that state, using Mexican trees in Santa Barbara. But it's Rudolph Hass we have to thank for the Hass variety of avocado, the only variety that is grown year-round. The mail carrier bought the seedling in 1926 from A. R. Rideout of Whittier, California, and planted it in his yard.

After planting the tree, Hass planned to graft other varieties from it, but when the grafts didn't take, he considered cutting it down. His children talked him out of it, saying they liked the taste of the avocados it produced better than any others. So, he named the variety of avocado it produced for himself, taking out a patent in 1935 and entering into an agreement with nurseryman Harold Brokaw to promote the fruit. The patent expired in 1952, the year Hass died. By then, the Hass avocado had taken off because of its taste, durability and shelf life. It passed its green rival, the Fuerte in the 1960s and now accounts for about 80 percent of consumption, bringing in about $350 million a year.

The mother tree, the one to which every Hass avocado can trace its lineage, died of root

avocado

rot in 2003 in La Habra Heights, California, at 76 years old. It was chopped down in September of that year. The black bumpy-skinned Hass is king of all avocados. Hass trees produce 95 percent of the avocados grown in California, which is the United State's top avocado-producing state, according to the California Avocado Commission. They also provide seedlings to growers worldwide.

High in vitamin C, thiamin and riboflavin, avocados are a good source of protein, with a higher fat content than most vegetables. A common half portion has 138 calories. California avocados that are picked from November to March have two-thirds less fat than those picked from September and October. They are less mature and have only two grams of fat, compared to six grams of fat. The fat in avocados is mostly monounsaturated, which is one of the fats most preferred by the body (easily digested, high in vitamins and minerals, and containing no cholesterol). Avocados will ripen quickly when placed in a brown paper bag with some flour and set in a warm place. Another method of ripening avocados is to place them in a plastic bag with a piece of banana peel or an apple.

avocado leaf - the leaf of the Mexican avocado tree, *Persea americana* var. *drymifolia,* used as a seasoning in Mexican cuisine for its delicate licorice flavor. The leaves are toasted on a **comal** or in a skillet, then added to dishes, especially black beans. Avocado leaves are usually available dried in Mexican and Latin American grocery stores in the United States. They should not be picked from just any avocado tree: the leaves of non-Mexican varieties can be toxic to humans and deadly to some animals.

avocado oil - usually extracted only from damaged fruit due to the high demand for the fruit crop. The pulp of the avocado fruit contains about 15 to 20 percent oil and a high percentage of lecithin. It is used mainly as cooking oil as it has a high **smoke point.**

avond koffie - Dutch name for evening coffee, usually served with cookies or cake.

awabi - see ABALONE.

awenda bread - an American bread usually made with hominy grits and cornmeal, named for a community on the coast of South Carolina where both Native and Africa-American traditions still intermingle.

ayran - a cool, refreshing yogurt-based drink consumed in Turkey and the Middle East. The yogurt is mixed with water and ice and blended until smooth, then seasoned simply with salt or dressed up with chopped fresh mint leaves. It is especially delicious served with shish kebabs or other grilled meats.

azarole

azarole - also **Mediterranean medlar, Naples medlar.** The fruit of the hawthorn, *Crataegus azarolus.* At home in dry hilly regions, the tree is indigenous to the Mediterranean basin through Central Asia, and has been grown for ornament and for the fruit – and traditional medicines made from it – for centuries. The small, yellow-orange haws taste of apples (apples and hawthorns both belong to the Rosaceae family). Said to ripen sweeter where it is warmer, they are eaten fresh or candied, dried or pickled, and made into jams, jellies, and syrups. See also HAWTHORN.

Aztec bean - see ANASAZI BEAN.

azuki bean - also **adzuki bean.** A bushy Eastern bean, *Vigna angularis,* closely related to the **rice bean.** Both are grown extensively in China and Japan, where they're eaten like the **French bean** when freshly picked; the dried seeds or beans are crushed and made into a kind of flour used for cakes and puddings. They originated in China and were introduced to Japan in the 3rd century. After the soybean, they are the most commonly used bean in Japanese cookery.

b
bananas

baak gwo - also **bai guo, ginkgo nut.** This Chinese fruit is the nut of the mature female ginkgo tree. The nuts are white but turn pale green when cooked. They have a mild flavor and are eaten raw, deep-fried or, often, cooked in one-pot dishes.

baba au rhum - also **baba, rum baba.** This rich, rum-soaked cake was supposedly named by King Stanislas I of Poland, an amateur cook and enthusiastic gourmet who, when dethroned in 1736, promptly fled to France, where his son-in-law, Louis XV, welcomed him as a fellow gastronome. Some accounts say that Stanislas himself whipped up the first baba in the kitchen of his château in a Paris neighborhood, but it was probably his pastry cook who actually made the cake. At least Stanislas gave it fame by naming it after his favorite fictional hero, Ali Baba of *The Arabian Nights*. While charming, this story is not entirely convincing because the shape of the cake is of Slavic origin. The 13th-century Danish chronicler Saxo Grammaticus describes a Baltic pagan harvest-festival bread as a "cake, prepared with mead, round form and standing as high as a person."

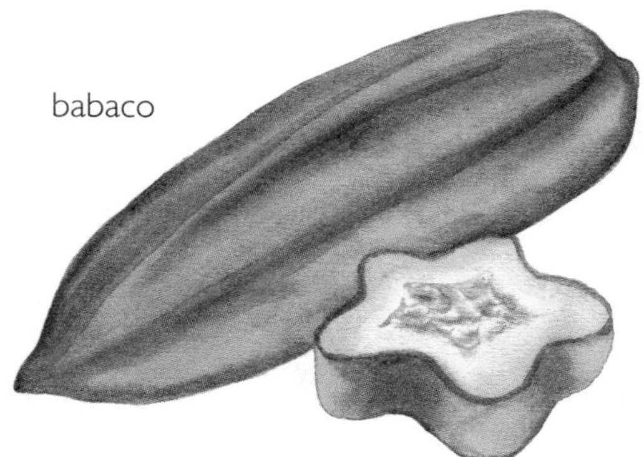
babaco

babaco - a strange fruit that looks like a bright-yellow zeppelin, with a soft rim running along the length of the fruit. This five-sided fruit is from the papaya family and is 6 to 10 inches (15 to 25 cm) long and 4 inches (10 cm) wide. The fruit has no seeds and does not need to be peeled. A slice resembles a softly shaped star and grows in clumps on heavy tree-like vines. Ecuador was the first country to cultivate the fruit because the high altitude and climate provided ideal conditions, although it's also grown in California and New Zealand.

baba ghanoush - also **baba ghanouj.** A Middle Eastern eggplant purée found in Algeria, Tunisia, Lebanon and Turkey. It's flavored with lemon, olive oil, garlic and sometimes with coriander and crushed sesame seeds.

baba mold - also **dariole mold.** A tall, metal cake pan shaped like a tapered cylinder, used for making the traditional French cake **baba au rhum.**

Babcock, Stephen Moulton - see profile below.

Babinski, Henri (Ali-Bab) - see profile right.

babka - a sweet yeasted coffee cake with a spongy, bread-like texture, common to many eastern European countries, such as Poland, Lithuania and Russia, made with flour, eggs, yeast, butter, citrus peel and raisins. The cake is often baked in a tube pan so there is a characteristic hole in the middle. Modern-day babkas come in many varieties, some flavored with rum or almonds, some with swirls of fruit filling, cinnamon or cocoa powder through the dough. The name is derived from the Russian and Polish word *baba*, meaning "old woman," for the grandmothers who traditionally baked the cakes on a weekly basis.

baby back ribs - see PORK.

baby banana - also **finger banana, lady finger banana, sugar banana.** A tiny variety of banana, no more than 3 inches (7.5 cm) long, about the length of a female finger. These short bananas have a soft flesh that is intensely sweet, good for eating out of hand or for cooking.

baby broccoli - see BROCCOLINI.

Babcock, Stephen Moulton (1843–1931) - New York biochemist who developed the "Babcock Test," a method of measuring the butterfat content of milk, in 1890. Babcock earned his PhD in Germany and then spent more than 40 years at the University of Wisconsin, where he developed the test, a discovery that brought international acclaim to the university and turned his laboratory into a center of pioneering research in nutrition and vitamin chemistry.

Babinski, Henri (Ali-Bab) (1855–1931) - author of a seminal culinary work, *Gastronomie Pratique* (Practical Gastronomy) first published in 1906 and written under the pseudonym Ali-Bab. Born in Paris, he was the son of a Polish engineer, who emigrated from Warsaw. Following in his father's profession, Babinski became a mining engineer, during the course of which he traveled widely. By all accounts he had an excellent palate, a passionate interest in eating well and a commitment to collecting recipes on his journeys, all of which wended their way into his masterpiece. A polymath, who has been called "the **Brillat-Savarin** of the 20th century," his survey of gastronomy through the ages includes personal anecdotes often of a humorous nature, such as being served beer in a teapot while traveling in the American west. His detailed and frequently footnoted recipes have been used as source material by contemporary writers, such as **Elizabeth David** and **Julia Child,** and inspired chefs, such as the colorful Jeremiah Tower, a godfather of California cuisine. Interestingly, later editions of the book include medical information on treating obesity, perhaps reflecting the change in Babinski's circumstances. He abandoned his profession and spent the last eleven years of his life caring for his older brother, Joseph, a neurologist who appears to have suffered from somewhat debilitating neuroses. Joseph studied under the famous Jean-Martin Charcot (who also mentored Freud) and is remembered for discovering the extensor plantar response, a reflex reaction useful in diagnosing certain conditions. Some who knew them believed that Henri made an invaluable contribution to his brother's career. As one of Joseph's students reflected, "Joseph Babinski lived for science, and Henri lived for his brother; without Henri Babinski, Joseph would not have accomplished that much." Sadly, neurology's gain may have been gastronomy's loss.

baby carrots - any of a number of varieties of carrot that are full-flavored and delicious when harvested tiny and tender. The darling of the **nouvelle cuisine** movement, baby carrots come in a rainbow of colors, from the usual orange to more-exotic browns and purples. The baby carrots usually seen in plastic bags in the grocery stores are not true baby carrots; they are baby-cut carrots, which are just regular-size carrots peeled, cut and shaved into a convenient two-bite size.

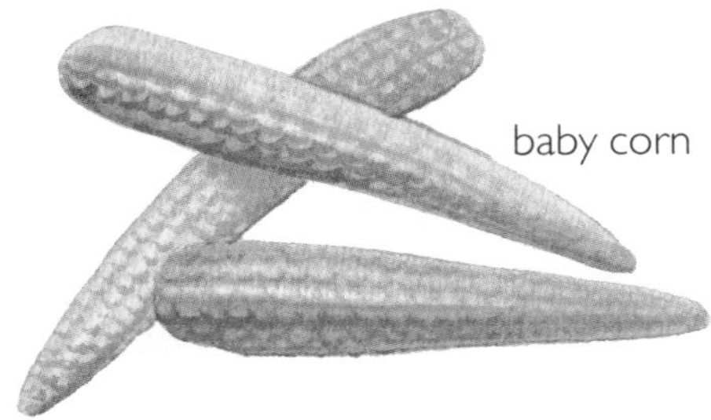

baby corn

baby corn - a tiny ear of immature corn, eaten whole, including the cob. Baby corn is commonly used in Asian cooking and is sold mainly in cans in North America.

baby eggplant - also **Italian eggplant.** See EGGPLANT.

baby lamb - see LAMB.

baby potato - see NEW POTATO.

baby vegetables - first cultivated in France, these vegetables are sometimes harvested simply by picking them in the early developmental stages. Others are genetic hybrids, bred to be true miniatures, as perfectly formed as their full-size counterparts.

baby whitefish - see CISCO.

bacalao - the Spanish name for "salt cod."

baccalà - the Italian name for "salt cod."

bacciferous - producing or bearing berries.

back bacon - see CANADIAN BACON.

backfin crabmeat - also **lump crabmeat.** See CRAB.

back of the house - a term used in hotels and restaurants referring to areas that are out of view, such as the kitchen and its staff, offices and the area where goods are received. The **front of the house** refers to the area of the establishment where there is direct contact with the public, such as the dining room and bar.

back ribs - see BEEF, PORK.

backward - a wine-tasting term that describes a wine that remains young-tasting even after aging, especially when compared to similar wines of the same vintage. This can be a negative term if the wine was expected to improve after extended cellaring.

bacon - meat from the side of a pig, both cured and smoked. This was originally the French name for pig, and its meaning in 18th-century England was pork meat of any kind.

bacon bits - crumbled cooked bacon, usually added to salads or used as a garnish. Imitation bacon bits are made from soy and artificial flavorings and colored to look vaguely similar to the real thing.

bacon grease - the fat **rendered** from bacon as it cooks, often used in the southern U.S. instead of oil or butter in recipes or to fry foods to give them a smoky flavor.

bacon press - a heavy, flat tool with a handle on top, used for holding down bacon as it cooks to prevent it from curling. A bacon press may be a small rectangle the size of a few strips or a large circle designed to hold down a whole frying pan full of bacon. These presses are usually made of cast iron or a similar heavy material to give them the weight they need to hold down the meat as it cooks.

bacteria - any of various single-cell microscopic organisms, present more or less everywhere. While some bacteria can cause food to spoil and others cause disease, some are beneficial. Two types in particular are valuable in food production: one producing lactic acid, used in making cheeses, yogurt, pickles and salami; and another producing acetic acid, which turns alcohol into vinegar.

badger - a burrowing mammal, *Taxidea taxus* or *Meles meles*, related to the weasel, native to the northern hemisphere, found frequently in North America and in Europe. The badger has a plump body, thick fur and sharp claws, with a distinctive black-and-white striped head. In Ireland and England, badgers were often eaten for food, prized for their rich, strong-flavored meat (which some compare to pork, others to mutton) and plentiful fat, which was often used for cooking. Badgers were also the targets of baiting and hunting, which was done for sport rather than for subsistence. Today, badgers are protected by strict anti-hunting laws in Britain: baiting, harming, possessing and/or killing them is met with large fines or jail time, although the practice does continue in some areas.

bael - also **Bengal quince, Indian quince.** The fruit of an Asian tree, *Aegle marmelos*, not a quince at all but related to citrus fruits, similar in appearance to a gray-yellow orange, with a refreshing pulp that is gummy and studded with seeds. Baels can be eaten fresh and are frequently made into jellies, drinks and sherbets. They are also used as a curative in India and Southeast Asia for dysentery, hepatitis, and brain and heart ailments, among other things. In India, the leaves of the bael tree are considered a sacred offering to the god Shiva.

bagel - a chewy doughnut-shaped yeast roll with a shiny crust, due to the fact that it is boiled in water before being baked. The word "bagel" was used in the U.S. for the first time, by some accounts, in 1932; it is a variation on the Yiddish *beygl* or *beigel*, and the German word *beugel*, which means "a round loaf of bread." Historically, the bagel is an Ashkenazi (central, northern or eastern European), rather than a Sephardi (Portuguese or Spanish) food. As one expert in Jewish history, Claudia Roden, explains: "Because of their shape — with no beginning and no end — bagels symbolize the eternal circle of life." Interestingly, the first discovered mention of the bagel was in 1610 in Krakow, Poland, when a piece of literature referred to it as something to give to women in labor. According to another legend, in 1683, a Jewish baker shaped dough into the form of a riding stirrup to honor King Sobieski of Poland, a skilled horseman who had saved the Austrian people from Turkish invaders.

bagel

Today, bagels are made in hundreds of flavors and incarnations. Generally speaking, there are two basic types of bagels. Water bagels are made without eggs and are chewier because they don't contain any added fat. Egg bagels are, obviously, made with eggs and are softer and more similar in texture to egg bread, such as **challah.** Montreal-style bagels are egg bagels made without salt, but with the addition of malt. They are boiled in honey-sweetened water, which gives them their characteristic sweet taste and dense texture, and topped with either sesame seeds or poppy seeds — no other fancy toppings are added to a Montreal-style bagel — then baked in a wood-fired oven. New York–style bagels contain malt and salt, come in a variety of flavors and are baked in gas or brick ovens, giving them a puffier, lighter texture.

Bagels have grown to outsell doughnuts in the United States. The Einstein/Noah Bagel Corp. sold more than 300 million bagels in 2002 (more than five million a week).

baghar - in India, a spicy butter used mainly to flavor yogurts, **dals,** vegetables, relishes and stews.

bagna cauda - also **bagna caôda, bagno caldo.** A sauce from Piedmont, Italy, made of olive oil, butter, garlic and anchovies. Its name translates literally as "hot bath." This warm antipasto is a dip for raw or cooked vegetables, usually served in the winter months, when cooks can take advantage of freshly milled olive oil.

bagoong - from the Philippines, a shrimp paste, which may also be made from small fish. They are cleaned, mixed with salt in the proportion of one part salt to three parts fish, pressed into vats and colored with dye. **Nam pla,** from Thailand, is a distant cousin.

baguette - also **French stick.** A long, stick-like French bread with a crisp crust and chewy interior, taking its name from the Latin *baculum*, meaning "stick," developed in the 1930s in Paris. The baguette's exceptional flavor comes from the soft French flour used to make it and the addition of very little yeast. The same dough recipe is used in France to make different shapes and sizes of breads, such as *flûtes*, *ficelles*, *bâtards* and *petits pains*.

baguette pan - a perforated metal baking pan designed for baking long, thin French **baguettes,** usually large enough to hold two or three loaves. The perforations help the air circulate around the dough, creating the ideal thick, crisp crust.

Bahia orange - see ORANGE.

baies roses - see PINK PEPPERCORN.

bai guo - see BAAK GWO.

bainiku - a Japanese condiment made of puréed **umeboshi**.

bain-marie - also **double boiler, water bath.** A bain-marie is a set of two pots, pans, bowls or dishes, one fitting on top of the other, designed to permit slow and even cooking or warming of food in the upper pan with steam from water in the bottom one. The name did not come from scientist Marie Curie, who may have used the technique in her laboratory, as some rumors suggest, but from the French *bain-marie*, "the lower pan," from medieval Latin *balneum Mariae*, "Marie's bath," a mistranslation of the Greek *Káminos Marias*, "Maria's furnace." In the Bible, Maria (Miriam) was Moses' sister (*Exodus* 15:20), to whom a treatise on alchemy was attributed.

bake - to cook food by exposing it to dry heat, as in an oven.

bakeapple - also **bake-apple berry, baked-apple berry.** See CLOUDBERRY.

bake blind - to bake a pastry crust (pie shell) without the filling, usually because the filling would cause the pastry to become soggy if the two were baked together. Pastry baked blind tends to rise, so it's usually weighted down during baking. The crust is lined with foil or parchment paper and filled with dried beans or peas or ceramic beans, usually removed in the last five to 10 minutes of baking.

baked Alaska - also **omelette Norvégienne.** A mound of ice cream on a cake base completely covered in **meringue** and quickly baked in the oven. Some say this dessert was created by **Delmonico's** chef Charles Ranhofer in New York in 1867 to celebrate the U.S. purchase of Alaska. Another story credits the invention to American-born physicist Benjamin Thompson, also the inventor of one of the first professional cooking ranges and the coffee percolator. In the course of his research, Thompson (known as Count von Rumford when he moved to Germany), conducted many experiments with heat, one of which possibly led to the invention of this dish. Yet another account claims that the original recipe was perfected (or rather brought back into fashion at the Hotel de Paris in Monte-Carlo) by chef Jean Giroix. However, according to the Baron Brisse in his cooking column in *La Liberté* on June 6, 1852, a chef to a Chinese delegation visiting Paris introduced this dessert to the French.

baked beans - also **Boston baked beans.** Navy beans are baked in an earthenware pot and flavored with molasses and salt pork. There are quite a few foods that originated in Boston; these baked beans are one. The Pilgrims found Indians baking beans in 1620. The Indians soaked the beans first to make them swell and soften their skins, then baked them overnight with deer fat and onions in a clay pot placed in a hole lined with stones. Since the Pilgrim women could not, for religious reasons, cook on Sunday, baked beans cooked the night before became a Sunday tradition. Later, when religious laws became less strict, a baked bean dish was a Saturday-night special, with pork replacing the deer fat of the Indians, and brown sugar and seasoning added. For years, the beans were baked by bakers, who called each Saturday morning, took the family's bean pot to a community oven and returned the baked beans with a bit of brown bread for Saturday supper or Sunday breakfast.

baker's ammonia - see AMMONIUM BICARBONATE.

baker's caramel - also **blackjack.** A natural food coloring, or browning agent, that adds a deep-brown hue to sauces, candies, breads, etc. Baker's caramel is simply dark brown to almost black caramelized sugar, so it adds its rich color plus a touch of sweetness, unlike **gravy browning,** which also includes seasonings and a fair amount of salt. See also CARAMEL COLORING.

baker's dozen - a term for 13 items sold for the price of a dozen, created as a result of a law passed in 1266 by the British Parliament that prevented bakers from short-changing their customers. The law specified a strict weight per loaf of bread, which was difficult for bakers to achieve given their non-mechanical methods of baking (they also didn't want to buy new loaf pans of a larger size to ensure the correct-weight loaves). Therefore, bakers erred on the side of caution when selling their loaves and included an extra one with every 12 to be sure that they met or exceeded the weight requirement. The term stuck and is still used today in bread, bagel and pastry shops.

baker's peel - see PEEL.

baker's pin - see ROLLING PIN.

baker's wax - see PARAFFIN WAX.

Bakewell tart - a pastry shell lined with a layer of jam and topped with almond sponge cake. This English dessert is named after the town of Bakewell in Derbyshire.

baking ammonia, powdered - see AMMONIUM BICARBONATE.

baking chocolate - see CHOCOLATE.

baking powder - a chemical leavening agent that works on the principle of carbon dioxide gas. Its ingredients include baking soda, an acid, such as cream of tartar, and something that absorbs moisture, such as cornstarch. The leavening comes from the interaction of the basic salt (baking soda) with the acid and produces a more controlled reaction than does baking soda alone. Baking powder can be bought commercially or made at home. It must have liquid added in order for the release of carbon dioxide to take place.

In North America, virtually all baking powder sold is double-acting, which means it contains two types of acid: one that activates upon contact with liquid and the other when exposed to heat in the oven. Single-acting baking powder is much harder to find and is only active immediately after being exposed to liquid, so the batter must be instantly put in a preheated oven or else the rising action is lost. Double-acting baking powder dominates the market because it turns out more reliably light and airy baked goods than the more quickly exhausted single-acting baking powder.

baking powder biscuit - see TEA BISCUIT.

baking sheet - also **cookie sheet.** A flat sheet of metal with one or more upturned edges on which cookies, etc., are baked.

baking soda - also **bicarbonate of soda.** A simple leavener used in baking that is activated when mixed with an acid, such as buttermilk or yogurt. Carbon dioxide bubbles are produced, which causes a batter or dough to rise. Baking soda begins to react immediately when wet, so it should always be mixed thoroughly with dry ingredients first.

baking stone - also **pizza stone.** A flat, heavy piece of stone placed on the lowest rack of an oven and heated with the oven, which is supposed to replicate the brick floor of a commercial pizza or bread oven. The "stone" is either porous stone or — more commonly — fired, unglazed clay. Some are now sold with racks with handles to grasp so you can lift the stones easily in and out of the oven, then set the rack on the counter to let the baking cool.

baklava

baklava - a popular, rich, Middle Eastern pastry made of several sheets of **phyllo** pastry drenched in butter and either honey or sugar water, with pistachios and almonds. It's cut into trademark diamond or triangle shapes prior to baking and separated into pieces after it's baked. It was probably first made in the Ottoman sultan's kitchen at the Topkapi palace in Istanbul and linked to the observation of Ramadan, the ninth month of the lunar Islamic calendar. According to this account, on the 15th day of Ramadan each year, the Janissary troops in Istanbul would march in full regalia to the palace, where each regiment was presented with two trays of baklava. They would suspend the offering in sheets of cloth from a pole and parade back to their quarters. This was known as *baklava alayi*, or the Baklava Procession.

bakonyi betyárleves - a very spicy Hungarian soup made of chicken, beef chunks, thin noodles, mushrooms and vegetables. It's also called **outlaw soup,** since legend has it that when outlaws escaped from authorities, they rewarded themselves with this soup as a celebration.

balachan - also **blachan.** A salty, pungent Malaysian condiment of shrimp, clams, razor clams and other seafood that have been salted and allowed to ferment in the sun. It can be purchased as a paste or powder.

balanced - a wine-tasting term used for a wine that is not dominated by any one characteristic, having the perfect proportions of sugar, acidity, fruit flavors, tannins, alcohol and so on.

Balducci, Andy - see profile below.

Bali lemon - see POMELO.

balloon - a tall-stemmed wineglass with a large, round bowl that narrows at the top, often recommended for drinking fine, vintage red wines. The wine is swirled around the bowl of the glass to release its aroma; the narrow top of the glass concentrates the aroma, so that it can be fully appreciated when the glass is raised to the nose or lips.

balloon fish - see PUFFERFISH.

Balducci, Andy (early-20th century) - American gourmet retailing pioneer who transformed his family's produce business into a renowned purveyor of fine foods. In 1915, Balducci's parents, recent immigrants from southern Italy, ran a fruit and vegetable stand in Brooklyn. It was 30 years before they crossed the river to do business as Balducci's in Greenwich Village, and it would take nearly another 25 years, in the mid-1970s, for the shop to move to a larger space and begin its gourmet transformation. "We've been selling great melons for years," Andy Balducci said to his father. "Now we're going to sell prosciutto to go with them." They carefully added cheese, other meats, fish, coffee, pastries, bread, condiments and all manner of gourmet fare. Patrons loved the variety, despite the steep prices; high-ticket items, such as truffles, sold well. Balducci eventually took over as president of the company and was very careful in his expansion. To keep an eye on quality and to ensure that his Queens commissary could continue supplying his new stores, he opened only two more: one in Westchester and another on Long Island. Balducci sold his company to the Sutton Place Gourmet grocery chain when he retired in 1999.

balloon whisk - see WHISK.

ballottine - a French term referring to a hot or cold dish consisting of poultry or meat that has been deboned, stuffed, rolled, tied in the shape of a bundle and braised or poached. The name is the diminutive of the French *ballotte*, which is derived from *balle*, meaning "bale," after the appearance of the dish. See also GALANTINE.

ballpark mustard - see AMERICAN MUSTARD, MUSTARD.

balm - see LEMON BALM.

baloney - a North American version of bologna.

balsamic vinegar - a distinctive type of vinegar, once considered so valuable that it was included in the dowries of young ladies of nobility and specifically mentioned in wills. It has been made for hundreds of years from the cooked and concentrated **must** of white grapes in the area around Modena and Reggio Emilia in Italy. The juice of local Trebbiano grapes is aged in a succession of 12 kegs, each decreasing in size, made of different aromatic woods, such as juniper, mulberry, chestnut and red oak. This process can take as long as 50 years, giving the vinegar a somewhat syrupy texture and a rich, deep-mahogany color. Stored in a light and airy attic, subject to the heat of the summer and the cold of the winter, it will age and thicken to the consistency of molasses. Bona fide balsamic vinegar (*aceto balsamico tradizionale di Modena*) is strictly controlled by law and must have been aged in wood for at least 12 years. Vinegar aged 25 years or more is called *stravecchio*. The name balsamic means "balm-like," reflecting its digestive character. Indeed, the best has a flavor so smooth and sweet that it can be drunk on its own as a *digestivo* (after-dinner drink). See also VINEGAR.

balsam pear - see BITTER MELON.

Balthazar - see WINE BOTTLES.

balut - a Filipino delicacy consisting of a boiled duck egg that has been incubated almost to the point of hatching, commonly sold by street vendors.

bamboo broom - see BAMBOO WHISK.

bamboo leaves - the leaves of certain varieties of bamboo, long and slim, used to wrap around foods that will be grilled or steamed. Although tough and basically inedible, bamboo leaves add a subtle, woody flavor to the foods wrapped inside them. Dried bamboo leaves are often available at Asian or gourmet grocery stores.

bamboo shoots - the young shoots of an edible species of bamboo plant, *Phyllostachys*, which originated in the tropical regions of Asia and has been consumed there for thousands of years. The leaves are edible, as well as the heart and the sugary sap, which is extracted by slicing the skin of the plant. The shoots are harvested as soon as they emerge from the ground. They're ivory in color because they're grown without light and are kept covered to avoid the production of chlorophyll, which would turn them green. Although many species of bamboo have edible shoots, they shouldn't be eaten raw. They contain toxins, which are destroyed by the cooking process or even a slight blanching. Winter bamboo shoots are considered more desirable because they are more tender and less fibrous.

bamboo skewer - a type of skewer made from the flesh of the bamboo plant (actually a type of woody grass, rather than a tree), sturdy and flexible, made in a variety of thicknesses. Bamboo skewers are excellent for grilling chunks of meats and vegetables, but they must be soaked in water for about 30 minutes prior to grilling to prevent them from catching fire. (The ends still tend to char, despite prolonged soaking.) The bamboo adds a bit of a woody, smoky flavor to the food as it smolders.

bamboo steamer - a round basket made of porous bamboo, often multi-tiered, with a tight-fitting lid made of woven bamboo strips, used for steaming Chinese foods, such as

bamboo steamer

dumplings, fish, vegetables or assorted tidbits for **dim sum.** The steamer basket is lined with parchment paper or cabbage leaves, or the is food placed on a plate so that the juices don't come into contact with the bamboo, making it simple to clean with just water. The steamer is then placed inside a wok or a large pot on a rack over a small amount of boiling water and steamed until the food inside is cooked through and quite moist. The absorbent bamboo lid sucks up the condensation that forms inside so that it does not drip on the food and make it soggy.

Bamboo tea - see TEA.

bamboo whisk - also **bamboo broom.** See WHISK.

bamboo yuba - see YUBA.

bami goreng - also **bahmi goreng, bami, mee goreng.** An Indonesian dish, widely available in Malaysia as well, of noodles often fried with pork, shrimp, eggs, vegetables (onions, leeks, green beans, peas, cabbage, cauliflower and celery) and seasonings, common at hawkers' stands on city streets. The name literally means "fried noodles."

bammy - a Jamaican fried bread made from grated **cassava,** often served with fried fish. The grated cassava is seasoned with salt, pressed into a pancake shape, then fried briefly. After it cools, it's soaked in coconut milk, then fried again until brown and crispy.

banana - the long, curved fruit of a tropical plant from the genus *Musa*, which turns yellow when ripe. In the tropics, bananas have been a food staple for as far back as history can be traced. They were cultivated in Southeast Asia long before other fruits were domesticated. The botanical name of one species, *Musa sapientum*, "fruit of the wise men," comes from the legend that Indian gurus sat in the shade of its large leaves while they meditated. Alexander the Great invaded India and discovered bananas growing about 300 BC. But it took the Arabs to introduce the fruit to the Near East and the Mediterranean. The fruit of the Garden of Eden, says the *Koran*, was not an apple but a banana. In the 1400s, the Portuguese took banana plants to the Canary Islands. Just a few years after Columbus' voyages, bananas traveled to the Caribbean Islands and Mexico. They spread so rapidly that later visitors thought bananas were native to the Americas.

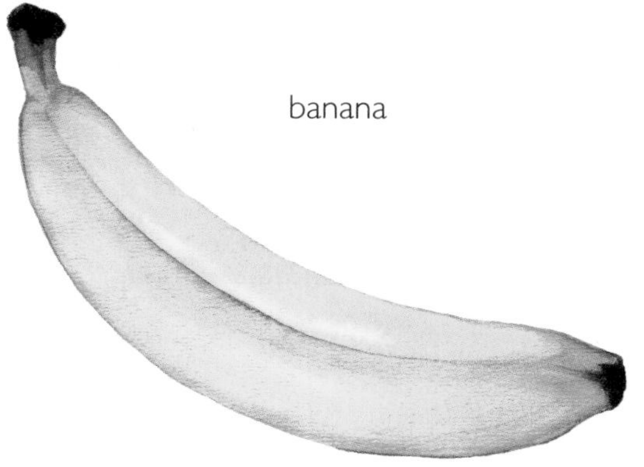

banana

Bananas contain less water than most other fruits and are part of the berry family. They grow on a huge tropical plant classified as an herb. The plant can grow up to about 30 feet (9 m) in height and is the largest herb in the world with a woody stem. Each stem or shoot from the trunk of the plant produces about 10 "hands," each with about 12 "fingers," or bananas. The entire stem, which only produces fruit once, is cut off. Bananas are one of those fruits picked prior to ripening and, like tomatoes, gassed with **ethylene** to ripen them in the van on the way to market and turn them almost instantaneously yellow.

In a world of more than 500 banana varieties, North American and European consumers are loyal to just one, the **Cavendish.** The crop, grown mostly in Latin America, is huge and unvaried. Each year, the United States alone imports more than $1 billion in bananas, almost all Cavendish. Wild bananas have full seeds and reproduce on their own, but the edible varieties contain only the remnants of seeds, so they're sterile. They are perpetuated only because farmers transplant shoots from the main stems of older plants. With no genetic mixing, the crops can't adapt to new conditions, such as disease outbreak, so banana crops are relatively vulnerable to epidemics. The Gros Michel, sweeter than the Cavendish and the probable inspiration for the old slip-on-a-banana-peel slapstick routine, was wiped out by Panama disease in the 1950s and 1960s. The Cavendish was immune and became the banana of choice. The current scourge is black Sigatoka, a fungus that attacks the leaves of the Cavendish and other banana varieties. The disease has affected crops in virtually all key banana-growing areas of the world. As people and goods travel the globe faster than ever before, banana diseases can spread more quickly, which could be devastating for millions of people living in poor regions where the banana is a diet staple.

banana flour - also **pisang starch, plantain flour.** Powdered dried bananas, used in Asia primarily as a food for invalids because it is easily digestible.

banana flower - also **banana blossom, banana bud, banana heart.** The purple flower bud that forms on the tip of a developing bunch of bananas, eaten as a vegetable in Asian cuisine. Banana flowers may be used as a garnish or sliced and eaten in salads (they should be parboiled or soaked in **acidulated water** first to remove some of their bitterness and to soften them). The sliced flowers are often simmered in coconut milk or stir-fried in highly spiced noodle dishes to balance their natural bitterness.

banana leaf - the large leaf of the banana plant, used to wrap foods to be baked or steamed.

banana pepper - also **banana chile, Hungarian hot wax pepper.** A variety of pepper available sweet or hot. It has a banana shape with pods approximately 4 to 6 inches (10 to 15 cm) long. See also CHILE PEPPER.

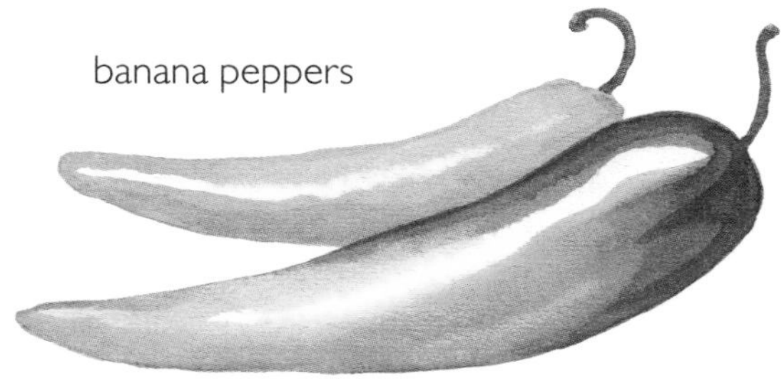
banana peppers

bananas Foster - a dessert consisting of a banana cut in half lengthwise, sautéed briefly in butter, brown sugar, spices and rum, then **flambéed** and served with its sauce and vanilla ice cream. In the early 1950s, a New Orleans chef by the name of Paul Blange made the dessert for a regular customer, Richard Foster.

banana split - a dessert consisting of a banana split in half lengthwise and served usually with three different scoops of ice cream topped with three different syrups. The whole dish is then covered in whipped cream and decorated with **maraschino** cherries.

banana squash - see SQUASH.

Banbury cake - a small, oval, flaky pastry stuffed with butter, dried fruit, sugar and spices. According to records, the cake originated in Oxfordshire, England, where one Betty White first sold it in 1638.

Bancha tea - see TEA.

B & B - a mix of equal parts Bénédictine and brandy, invented in 1937 by a bartender at the "21" Club in New York.

bang - a mixed drink of warm spiced ale, cider and whiskey.

bangbang - a Chinese dish made of cold chicken spiced with sesame seeds or sesame oil.

bangers - British sausages made of ground pork and bread crumbs. They are so named because if they're not pricked before cooking, they'll explode like a firecracker, which in England is called a banger.

bangers and mash - a dish of sausages or **bangers** served alongside mashed potatoes, often covered in gravy.

banh mi - a Vietnamese submarine sandwich consisting of a toasted roll or baguette filled with barbecued pork and/or pâté, pickled julienne vegetables (such as daikon, carrot and cucumber), fresh cilantro, sliced chiles and mayonnaise. Banh mi have recently become popular fast food options in large North American cities, such as New York and Toronto, where there are large concentrations of Asian restaurants.

banh pho - also **ho fun.** A medium-width, flat, long rice stick noodle used in Vietnamese *banh pho bo*, the classic beef noodle soup of that nation. Banh pho are also used in Thai and Chinese cuisine under the names *sen lek* in Thai and *ho fun* in Chinese. Banh pho are the ideal noodle for use in the stir-fry **pad Thai.**

banira - the Japanese name for vanilla, usually used to describe a vanilla-flavored ice cream.

banjo - see SKATE.

bankebiff - in Norway, the name given to a beefsteak browned in unsalted butter, then simmered in beef stock.

banneton - a French coiled willow basket used to hold rising bread dough. It is floured before the dough is added, and its shape imprints on the rising dough, giving the resulting loaf a beautiful striped design. In German, it is called *brotform*.

banneton

bannock - **1.** a large, round Scottish cake made of barley and/or oatmeal and baked on a griddle. The Druids are known to have made their own version and were careful to ward off bad luck by always kneading the dough clockwise. **2.** a camp bread brought to North America by British explorers and early setters. (Robert W. Service, the poet of miners and prospectors himself in the early 1900s, saluted it in his poem 'While the Bannock Bakes.') Bannock quickly became a staple for Native Americans across North America. It may be made with a simple dough of cornmeal, flour, rolled oats or wheat bran combined with water. If they're available, however, eggs, baking powder, berries, molasses, raisins, sunflower seeds, and shortening or lard, may be added. Traditionally, in lean times, bannock serves as a **famine food.**

banon - a French semisoft cheese, first dried in leaves and then dipped in a blend of brandy and **marc,** a spirit distilled from the husks of grapes after wine has been made. Finally, it's wrapped in chestnut leaves that have also been dipped into brandy.

banquet - a sumptuous feast given to celebrate some special occasion. One account of the origin of the word relates it to the French word *banc*, meaning "bench," thought to have come into use during the feudal period, when extra benches were brought to the large castle dining hall for seating the many visitors. Another account of the word dates from the 14th century and comes from the Italian *banchetto*, meaning a small bench on which guests used to sit.

bantam chicken - a dwarf or miniature breed of chicken, about one-half the size of an ordinary chicken. Bantam hens lay smaller eggs than regular hens: two bantam eggs are roughly the equivalent of one regular chicken egg. Bantams are not widely used commercially, but many small farms raise them, and bantam eggs can be found in some farmer's markets. The birds are named for the port of Bantam in Java.

Banyuls - a famous French dessert wine, a blend of grape varietals (principally Grenache Noir), often compared in color and taste to a tawny port. It has notes of ripe fruit, nuts, even melted butter, and is one of very few wines that pairs well with chocolate. Banyuls is made in the town of Banyuls-sur-Mer in France, near both the Mediterranean Sea and the Pyrenees. The wine is also made into the famous and expensive **Banyuls vinegar.**

Banyuls vinegar - vinegar made from **Banyuls** wine, aged for about five years in oak barrels, four of them outside so that they are exposed to the extremes of hot and cold. The wine is then inoculated with Banyuls vinegar from an earlier year and allowed to age another six months as it turns into a true vinegar. It has a complex flavor with notes of walnut and spices, which is prized in vinaigrettes and for deglazing pans to make rich sauces for meats, fish or mushrooms.

bao - sweet, yeast-raised, steamed Chinese buns filled with meat, vegetables or sweet bean paste.

baobab - a tropical tree, *Adansonia digitata*, chiefly found in Africa, where it's also known by the name "monkey bread tree" and in Senegal specifically by the name "the thousand year tree," because of its exceptionally long life span. The mucilaginous pulp of its oblong fruit has a pleasant if somewhat acid taste and is used chiefly to make a cooling drink. The leaves are made into powder and used in soups and stews as a condiment. The tree grows 10 to 40 feet (3 to 12 m) tall and up to 30 feet (9 m) in diameter.

bao bing - **1.** a thin Chinese pancake made from finely ground wheat flour and water, a traditional accompaniment to **Peking duck,** which is sliced thinly and wrapped inside the pancakes at the table. **2.** a Chinese dessert of

A B C D E F G H I J K L M N O P Q R S T U V W X Y Z

shaved ice served with any of a variety of sweet toppings, such as sweetened bean mixtures, sweetened condensed milk or fruit syrups.

bap - a soft yeast roll with a surface dusted with flour. Baps are traditional breakfast rolls in Scotland.

Baptist cake - also **holy poke, huff juff, hustler.** A doughnut-like cake made with a ball of yeast dough that is deep-fried by being immersed (baptized) in hot fat. It was especially popular in New England during the 1930s.

bar - **1.** a retail outlet for drinks, which were originally consumed standing up (or sitting on a bar stool) in front of a counter fitted with a copper or wooden bar as the footrest, hence the name. **2.** also **bar cookie, slice.** A baked confection made from the same ingredients as a cookie and pressed into a baking pan, rather than dropped free-form onto a cookie sheet. The result is cut into small bars, squares or triangles after it is baked and cooled. Bars can also have a crust, such as a shortbread base, and a topping or filling sprinkled over it before baking.

bara brith - a sweet, moist Welsh bread studded with currants, raisins, candied peel and spices, often served for afternoon tea and baked for holidays and special occasions. Bara brith may be leavened with yeast or baking soda, depending on the recipe. The name is Welsh for "speckled bread," referring to the bits of dried fruit throughout the loaf.

barack - a Hungarian **eau de vie** distilled from apricot juice.

Barbados cherry - see ACEROLA.

Barbados gooseberry - also **blade apple.** The edible fruit of a leafy climbing cactus, *Pereskia aculeata,* native to the West Indies and northern coastal regions of Central and South America, grown as an ornamental plant in warm coastal regions of the U.S., such as California, Hawaii and Florida. The sweet-tart, round or pear-shaped fruits have yellow to orange skin, and the juicy flesh contains a small number of soft, flat, brownish-black seeds. The fruits can be eaten raw, but are often cooked with sugar and made into jams or preserves. The fruit is often called *blade apple* because of the sharp, pointed leaves that grow out of it as it ripens (most fall out when the fruit reaches peak ripeness).

Barbados sugar - see SUGAR.

Barbaresco - a strong, dark red Italian wine from the Piedmont region of Italy, with an assertive flavor that is best paired with hearty foods, such as **risotto** or roasted meats. Barbaresco is made from Nebbiolo grapes, the same grapes used to make **Barolo** wine, and is quite high in **tannins.** It is best suited to long aging, perhaps 10 to 15 years, which tames its strong, tannic bite and renders the wine rich and mellow.

barbari - also **nan-e-barbari.** A thick, long, rectangular Iranian flatbread made of white flour, cooked in a clay oven called a *tanoor* (the Persian name for the well-known Indian **tandoor**), usually consumed at breakfast and lunch.

barbecue - also **barbeque.** A method of cooking in which meat or other foods are cooked outdoors over an open fire (either charcoal or some other fuel, such as propane or natural gas). The word can also be used for the appliance on which such cooking is done and for an informal meal at which food cooked in this way is served. The word comes from the Spanish *barbacoa,* meaning "a framework of sticks."

barbecue sauce - a sauce used for basting barbecued meat, usually made of tomatoes, onion, spices, sugar or honey and vinegar, although wine or beer may also be included.

barbeque - see BARBECUE.

Barberey - also **Troyes.** A soft French cheese similar to **Camembert,** but more pungent. A specialty of the city of Troyes.

barberry - also **Oregon grape.** A shrubby plant, *Berberis vulgaris,* bearing small acidic, astringent red berries, which are pickled or ripened and

Barbados gooseberries

barberries

made into preserves, syrup and wine. In ancient Egypt, a barberry syrup mixed with fennel seeds was taken to prevent plague. In Europe during the Middle Ages, medicines made from the plant were prescribed as antiseptics, purgatives and tonics. Native Americans prepared decoctions from the roots and the bark and drank them in teas to restore the body from general debility and to improve the appetite. The name comes from the Arabic *barbãris* and, later, the French word *berberis*, but the spelling has been modified to give the word an English appearance.

barberry honey - see HONEY.

barbina - see PASTA.

barbotine - see TANSY.

bard - to tie fat or bacon onto or around lean meats or fowl to keep them moist during cooking. The name comes from the noun "bard," an armored breastplate worn by horses.

Bardolino - a light, Italian red wine named for the town of Bardolino in the Veneto region of northern Italy, closer to pink than red in color, light-bodied, with a fruity, almost spicy flavor. Bardolino comes in a number of varieties, most of which are **still wines,** but one is a **sparkling wine** called *chiaretto,* which is usually drunk chilled in the summer.

barfi - an Indian fudge-like candy made with sweetened reduced milk, nuts, cardamom or other flavorings.

barigoule - an artichoke dish from Provence, France, that began as a peasant recipe using small and tender artichokes and other vegetables plus bacon stewed together, similar to a **ratatouille.** There is also a version where larger artichokes are stuffed, braised in white wine and served with the reduced broth.

barista - **1.** the name given in India to the crisp, fried onion shreds used in Muslim cooking. **2.** the person making espressos and other coffees in a coffee shop.

bark - a confection consisting of melted chocolate poured over nuts, dried fruits, candied fruits or peel, or even small candies, cooled and broken into bite-size chunks, named for the way it resembles the swirled, rough, bumpy bark of a tree.

Bar-le-Duc - a preserve originally made of selected whole white currants, traditionally seeded by hand and served with cheese. Today, gooseberries, strawberries or other berries are commonly used. Its name is derived from the city in France where it was first prepared in the Middle Ages.

barley - an extremely hardy ancient grain, dating back well over 4,000 years, used to make breads and other simple baked goods as well as hearty hot cereals. The grain is also converted to malt and fermented to make beer, after which it can be distilled to make whiskey. Barleycorns (the grain of the barley plant) were also used as a unit of measure. A royal decree in Tudor England standardized the inch as three barleycorns long, the foot as 39 barleycorns and the yard as 117 barleycorns. In the 16th century, Bavarian nobleman **Duke Wilhelm IV** originated the Rheinheitsgebot ("purity requirement"), the world's first consumer- protection decree, which stated that beer be made only from barley malt, hops and water. (For Barley Types, see page 62.)

barley farfel - see FARFEL.

barley flour - see FLOUR.

barley malt syrup - also **malt syrup.** See MALT EXTRACT.

barley sugar - an old-fashioned English hard candy made from boiled sugar, cooked to the hard-crack stage, spread on pans, cut into sections and twisted slightly before cooling. Although barley is not always an ingredient in the sweet these days, it was once the base of the candy. Barley water mixed with sugar, instead of

BARLEY TYPES

barley flakes - also **rolled barley.** Similar to rolled oats, rolled barley is sliced and rolled to create flat flakes that cook more quickly than pearl barley.

barley grits - barley kernels that have been toasted, then cracked to speed up cooking, similar to **bulgur** in texture.

barley groats - see WHOLE-GRAIN BARLEY.

hulled barley - see WHOLE-GRAIN BARLEY.

pearl barley - also **pearled barley.** The most common processed form of barley, it has the hull, bran and endosperm removed, so it is less nutritious, although tastier, than less-refined barley. Only the "pearl" inside the barley is left, hence its name.

pot barley - see SCOTCH BARLEY.

quick-cooking barley - an instant form of pearl barley, steamed so that the cooking time is very short. It is just as nutritious as pearl barley, even though it cooks more quickly.

rolled barley - see BARLEY FLAKES.

Scotch barley - also **pot barley.** The second-least processed form of barley, with the outermost hull and bran layer stripped off. It is still nutritious but lacks some of the fiber of whole-grain barley. It also takes a long time, up to an hour, to cook, but is more palatable than whole-grain barley.

whole-grain barley - also **barley groats, hulled barley.** This is the least processed type of barley eaten, with only the thick outermost hull removed. Because most of the bran and endosperm layers are intact, it is highly nutritious and full of fiber. It takes long, slow cooking to make it soft enough to eat.

a water-sugar combination, was boiled down, giving the candy a mild barley flavor. Today, barley sugar is often flavored with lemon juice and/or extract.

barley water - an old-fashioned, but still useful remedy for general malaise made by boiling **pearl barley** in water, then sweetening the resulting cooled liquid with sugar and flavoring it with lemon or orange.

barley wine - historically, the name given by ancient Egyptians and Greeks to wine made from barley, translated in modern English texts as barley wine. Nowadays in England, the name is used for any top-fermented beer of unusually high, wine-like (about 12 percent) alcohol content.

barm - a yeast formed on fermenting malt liquors.

barm brack - also **bairin breac, barn brack.** A sweet Irish bread containing raisins or currants, candied peel and usually some spice, such as caraway seeds, popular at Halloween.

barnacle - a crustacean related to the lobster, crab and shrimp; it is hermaphroditic, meaning that it has both male and female parts. The flesh is rather hard and can be eaten raw, with a squeeze of lemon or vinaigrette. Smaller ones can be cooked like mussels, while bigger ones can be grilled. There are approximately 1,000 species of barnacles, most fixing themselves to rocks or other hard surfaces with an adhesive, which is so strong that the attached part of the animal is still immovable 10 to 15 years after the living part has died.

Barolo - one of the world's great dry red wines. At the beginning of the 20th century, however, it used to be sweet and slightly sparkling. Today, the huge Banfi winery still makes a bubbly red in Piedmont, Italy, called Brachetto.

baron - a French word designating a cut of meat consisting of two loins or sirloins that have not been split apart from the backbone. *Baron d'agneau* ("lamb baron") is a cut consisting of both legs and both fillets of the lamb.

barquettes - pastry hors d'oeuvres shells shaped like little boats and filled with either sweet or savory fillings. The French name, etymologically, is cousin to the English "barge" and "bark."

barracuda - any of a variety of fish of the genus *Sphyraena,* up to 3 feet (1 m) long, slim, with sharp teeth that can deliver a vicious bite. The barracuda is found in the warm waters of the Pacific, Caribbean and sometimes the Atlantic, and its flesh can be highly toxic if eaten raw, due to the large amounts of toxins it absorbs and retains from the small fish it eats. Barracuda is oily and dark with a meaty, rich flavor, and its firm flesh is well suited to a variety of cooking methods. Some cooks say that it is best paired with highly fragrant spices, such as ginger and lemongrass, and not suited to recipes that call for cream or butter because it is already quite oily.

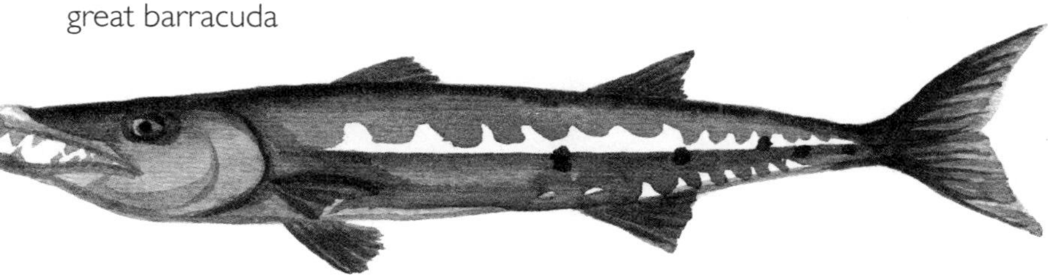
great barracuda

barramundi - also **giant perch, giant sea perch.** A saltwater fish, *Lates calcarifer,* related to **perch,** found from the Middle East to Australia, frequently eaten in Australia and India, with firm, mild, white flesh that cooks into large flakes. The barramundi can grow quite large (about 5 feet/1.5 m long) and is frequently hunted as a game fish as well as for its flesh. The barramundi is considered the king of sport fishes in Australia, doing spectacular leaps out of the water and sawing through nets with the sharp edges of its gills. The fish is popular for eating as well, so barramundi farming is a growing industry along the northern coast of Australia. The name is likely a derivative of an Australian aboriginal word, but its exact origin is unknown.

barrel - a cylindrical container made of strips of wood held together with metal hoops, used especially for aging wine and other spirits. The Gauls taught the Romans how to make barrels, not to improve the wine but to store it.

barrel-aged - a term used to describe wines, beers, liquors or liqueurs that are aged in a barrel, usually wooden. Some beverages are aged in stainless-steel barrels, which do not impart any taste to the finished product. Wooden barrels, on the other hand, impart a variety of flavors to the liquids aged in them, notably to wines. Oak barrels are commonly used to age white wines and produce a characteristic flavor reminiscent of vanilla, caramel and wood. Some types of bourbon, rum and beer are aged in charred oak barrels, giving them a dark-caramel color and a rich, toasted flavor. See also BOTTLE-AGED.

barrel proof - the term used as an indication of the strength of a whiskey to which no water has been added, bottled at the same **proof** it reached in the barrel. There may be some variation in this measurement from bottle to bottle.

Bartlett pear - see PEAR.

basbousa - also **basboosa.** In the Middle East, a semolina cake baked in the oven, often with nuts, and steeped in syrup or honey.

basella - a vine, *Basella rubra,* native to tropical Asia and Africa, with red or green leaves that are eaten cooked or raw like spinach. The red variety also yields a red juice, which is used especially in China as a food coloring.

basi - the traditional alcoholic drink of the Ilocanos of the Philippines, prepared by fermenting sugarcane juice and flavoring it with herbs.

basil - an aromatic annual plant, *Ocimum basilicum,* a member of the mint family. This herb is native to India, dear to the Provençals and the Italians, and considered a sacred herb in many cultures. Its name means "royal," from the Greek *basilikon* (perhaps indicating that the herb was reserved for the king's use), but in the Roman world, the Latin *basilicus* refers to the basilisk, a fire-breathing dragon, perhaps in the belief that the plant was a charm against the beast. Joseph Pitton de Tournefort, a 17th-century botanist, gives us the following anecdote: "A certain Gentleman from Siena being wonderfully taken and delighted with the smell of Basil, was wont very frequently to take the Powder of the dried Herb and snuff it up his Nose; but in a short Time he turn'd mad and died; and his Head being opened by Surgeons, there was found a Nest of Scorpions in his Brain."

The Hindu people worship basil, which they consider a sacred herb and dedicate to the gods Vishnu and Krishna. Sprigs of the plant at one time were laid on the breast of the dead to protect them from evil in the next world and to offer them entrance to paradise. Even today, a good Hindu is laid out with a basil leaf in his hand. During the British occupation of India, officials were looking for something sacred for Indians to swear by for courtroom oaths, and the sacred basil plant was chosen for the vow.

In ancient Greece, basil represented hate, and to hand a sprig of it to an individual was to silently convey the message "Beware, someone is plotting against you." In Roman times, women were not allowed to pick it. The priest in charge of the cutting had to purify his right hand with water from two different springs, sprinkled over the hand with an oak branch. He had to be dressed in new garments, without anything made of metal on his person, and menstruating women were forbidden to approach him. According to legend, Helena, mother of the Emperor Constantine, was told in a dream that she would find the remains of the true Christ's cross in a place where the air was scented with perfume. The dream came true when she found the cross buried in a patch of basil.

Of all annuals, basil is the most interesting, both in its many varieties and in the legends and beliefs that have sprung up around it. According to the Roman historian **Pliny,** "Basil must be sown by curses; muttered if you have near neighbors, but genuine nonetheless, and if the earth is rammed down and prayers uttered that the seeds never come up, so much the better." In Italy, it's said that a pot of basil on the window drives away flies. As it was also the custom for a young girl to set a pot of basil in the window to signal her lover that she was ready for his clandestine visit, it seems inevitable that, at times, some most disconcerting confusion must have arisen. Basil is also used to flavor the liqueur **Chartreuse.**

basilico - Italian for "basil."

Baseler leckerli - also **Basler leckerli.** see LECKERLI.

basmati rice - a narrow long-grain rice grown in the foothills of the Himalayas. It should be soaked before cooking and is the best rice to eat with Indian food. See also RICE.

bass - any of various edible freshwater and marine fish of the families Serranidae and Centrarchidae, many of which are characterized by having spiny fins. See also CHILEAN SEA BASS, SEA BASS.

bastard saffron - see SAFFLOWER.

baste - **1.** (v.) to moisten food at intervals while cooking by spooning a sauce, pan drippings, fat, butter, wine or any other liquids over it in order to prevent drying and to add flavor. **2.** (n.) see MOP.

COMMON TYPES OF BASIL

African basil - has a camphor-like scent.

anise basil - has purple leaves, with a spicy anise flavor and smell.

chocolate basil - has hints of chocolate in its scent and flavor.

cinnamon basil - has medium-size leaves, with a delicate cinnamon scent.

clove basil - has the pungency of cloves.

holy basil - mainly used in Indian cooking, it has a spicy scent.

lemon basil - has a citrus scent.

lettuce leaf basil - has a fruity scent.

purple basil

lime basil - a variation on **lemon basil,** with a strong lime scent.

opal basil - has a heavy perfume and dark purple leaves.

purple basil - has a lavender scent and dark purple leaves and is used as a red coloring in vinegar.

sweet basil - has a sweet, fruity scent.

Thai basil - similar to **anise basil,** with a pungent flavor but with less of a licorice overtone, vital to Vietnamese and Thai dishes, especially **pho.**

baster - a ladle, cup or syringe used to baste food while cooking. Perhaps the most familiar type of baster is the bulb baster, a tube topped with a rubber bulb, similar in shape and function to an eye dropper. When compressed and then released, the bulb creates suction, which draws pan juices up into the tube, so they can be squirted over cooking meat.

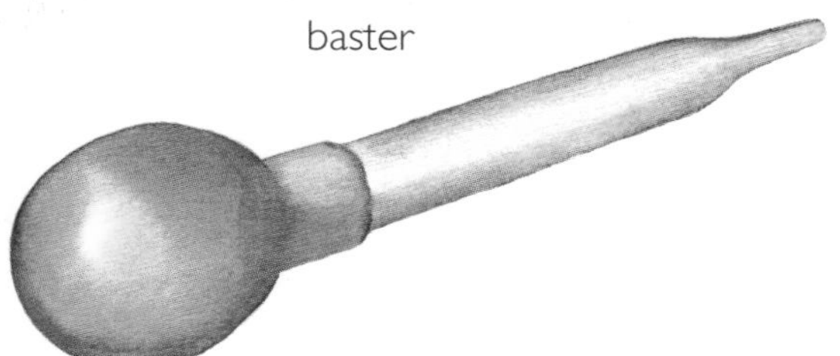
baster

bastila - also **bastela, bastilla, bestilla, b'steeya, pastilla.** A pigeon pie, a sumptuous, utterly rich and magnificent preparation made for special occasions in Morocco, such as holidays, weddings or when esteemed guests arrive. The pie is surrounded by a very thin pastry leaf called **warqa,** meaning "leaf," the top of which is sprinkled with powdered sugar and a latticework of ground cinnamon. This collection of leaves, now forming a whole thin sheet, is carefully but quickly peeled off and set side. Warqa is thinner than **phyllo**, although phyllo can be used in bastila. The name of the pie comes from *pastilla*, the Spanish word for pastry. Rudolf Grewe, a researcher of Hispano-Muslim history, found a dish called *judhaba* in an anonymous 13th-century cookbook and considered it a clear antecedent of the Moroccan bastila, beçause it was a chicken pie enclosed in many paper-thin sheets of dough.

The French made a kind of pie or cake called *pastillus*, a word that was transformed into *gastellus*, *gastiel*, *guastellus* and *wastellus*, all names of different stuffed cakes that appear in texts from 1129 to 1200 in the areas of Champagne, Ile-de-France and Picardie. It was a luxury pastry made with very fine, good-quality flour and stuffed with meat or fish, spices and fat, corresponding to the Moroccan bastila. The term crossed the English Channel, where the Scottish king William the Lion served *wastelli dominici* to Richard the Lion-Heart. It also appears in yet a different guise in Sicily as *guastedde* or *vastieddi*, a kind of spleen calzone. It still appears today in Corsica as *bastella*, a meat and vegetable pie.

bat - a name covering all flying mammals constituting the order of the Chiroptera family. In the Bible, bats are named among the unclean birds, which the Hebrews were not allowed to eat (*Deut.* 5:18), an indirect admission that some people ate bats. Nowadays the fruit-eating bats of India and some countries in Southeast Asia are widely eaten and even considered a delicacy by some. In Papua, New Guinea, bats are called flying fox, and most restaurants that serve dog often serve bat as well.

bâtard - a loaf of crusty white French bread a bit larger than a baguette.

bâtarde - a French sauce of white **roux** with water, egg yolks, butter and lemon juice. The name literally means "bastard" because of its indirect affiliation to other classic sauces.

batata - see BONIATO.

batata dulce - see BONIATO.

Batavian endive - see ESCAROLE.

Bath bun - a sugar-coated yeast bun with candied fruit and currants or raisins, said to have originated in Bath, England, during the 18th century.

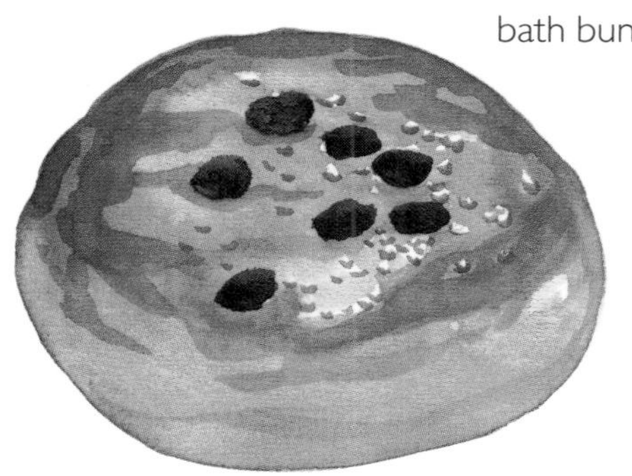
bath bun

Bath chaps - a British specialty consisting of the lower portion of a pig's jaw with its attached cheek, cured similar to bacon and cooked. The word "chap" is a variation on "chop," which in the 16th century was used to refer to the jaws and/or cheeks of an animal.

Bath cheese - a ripened, soft, English cream cheese with a delicate flavor, made in the city of Bath.

Bath Oliver biscuit - a flat, hard, crisp biscuit made of flour, butter and milk. The original biscuit was created by Dr. W. Oliver of Bath in the mid-1700s. At that time, the town was a fashionable spa resort, and the biscuit was introduced as a diet item. It's now very popular with cheese.

batido - a cold Latin American beverage combining water, ice, fruit juice, often a splash of milk and sometimes sugar. Batido is the past participle of the Spanish verb *batir*, meaning "to beat or strike," probably for the beating it gets in a blender prior to serving. See also JUGO, MERENGADA.

batiste - see BONIATO.

batoko plum - see LORI-LORI.

baton - also **batonnet.** A French term for little sticks of vegetables, most often potatoes, cut a bit larger than a **julienne.**

bâtonnage - a French winemaking term for the act of periodically stirring up the **lees** in a barrel of wine that is aging to give it a richer, more complex flavor. The winemaker stirs the wine with a long, metal rod to bring the solids at the bottom of the barrel back into suspension in the wine. Many white wines, such as Chardonnay and Sauvignon Blanc, are barrel-aged and treated to a weekly or monthly bâtonnage session. The term is derived from the French word *bâton*, meaning "stick" or "cane."

bat out - in the U.S., to flatten slices of raw meat.

Battenberg cake - a popular British cake consisting of four squares of sponge cake, two pink and two yellow, stuck together with apricot jam. The whole thing is then covered with a sheet of almond paste. When sliced, this produces a checkered cross section. The cake appears to have been named in honor of the marriage of Queen Victoria's granddaughter Victoria to Prince Louis of Battenberg (later Lord Mountbatten) in 1884.

batter - an uncooked thick or thin mixture that can be spooned or poured; for example, in making cakes, pancakes or waffles. Batter is also used to coat food, such as fish or vegetables, before deep-frying. The word batter is a derivation of beat, since all batters are formed by a steady beating motion.

batter bowl - a large, deep, wide bowl with a handle on one side and a lip on the other for pouring liquid batters, such as those for cakes or pancakes. Batter bowls come in plastic, earthenware and glass and often have a rubber ring on the bottom to prevent them from slipping as the batter is mixed vigorously inside.

batter bread - a specialty yeast bread from the southern U.S. made of white cornmeal, eggs and yeast, whose **gluten** is developed by beating rather than kneading. See also UNLEAVENED BREAD.

batter whisk - see WHISK.

battery cage - a small, wire cage in which hens on a factory farm are kept for laying eggs. Battery cage hens are kept in extremely close quarters without freedom of movement or access to outside light or fresh air. Their heads are allowed outside the cage to access their food trough, and eggs are deposited through the cage floor onto a conveyor belt below. See also FREE RANGE, FREE RUN.

Bauernfrühstuck - a typical German breakfast dish of fried potatoes topped with scrambled eggs, ham and cucumber, literally "farmers breakfast."

Bauernschmaus - an Austrian dish of sauerkraut, pork, sausages and dumplings.

Bauernsuppe - a peasant soup that originated in Germany in the Middle Ages, made of bacon, vegetables and legumes.

Bauerwurst - an uncooked German farmer's sausage made of ground pork, well spiced but mild and dark red to brown in color, often grilled and served with cabbage, especially **sauerkraut.**

Baumkuchen - a traditional German Christmas cake constructed in layers to look tall like a tree trunk and iced with chocolate to resemble bark. A similar French version is called *bûche de Noël.*

bauple nut - see MACADAMIA NUT.

Bavarian blue - a somewhat mild German blue cheese made from cow's milk, creamy yet tangy, made especially to avoid the sometimes overwhelming sharpness of French blue cheeses. It can be sliced or crumbled, the paste white with regular spots or veins of blue mold. Bavarian blue is a good stand-in for **Roquefort,** without its sharp tang, excellent crumbled over salads or in dressings. See also BLUE CHEESE.

Bavarian cream - also **bavarois.** Regardless of the name, this is a French dessert made of cold custard and gelatin with whipped cream folded in as the mixture thickens. The legendary French chef **Antonin Carême** gave us the recipe in the early 19th century and called it *fromage bavarois*. Some food historians suggest that it was brought to France by a French chef who had been working in Bavaria, but the relationship has not been proven.

bavettine - see PASTA.

bay leaves

bay leaf - also **laurel leaf.** The glossy leaf of the bay laurel tree, *Laurus nobilis*, is an evergreen native of Asia Minor that grows 50 to 60 feet (15 to 18 m) tall. Dried or fresh, the bay leaf has many culinary uses, ranging from flavoring soups and meats to enhancing puddings and custards.

In classical times, wreaths of laurel were bestowed as a symbol of honor (hence our term "laureate"). The Romans attributed great power to the plant. During storms, the fearless emperor Tiberius (42 BC–AD 37) could always be found under his bed, a laurel wreath upon his head. According to Ovid, the laurel is thus distinguished because Daphne metamorphosed herself into this tree rather than surrender herself to Phoebus, whom Cupid had wounded. Perhaps it's because laurel was venerated so vastly as a protector and a symbol of greatness and honor that the death of a tree was considered an evil omen. In fact, in 1629, the bubonic plague broke out in Padua, Italy, after the laurel trees of the city all died. Laurel was also strewn on medieval floors for its strong aroma and antiseptic properties.

Bayonne ham - also **jambon de Bayonne.** This ham is cured at Orthez, in southwestern France, in a brine of red wine, rosemary and olive oil, then wrapped in straw and smoked.

Bayrischer Bierkäse - a Bavarian cheese that is dunked in beer before eating.

bay scallop - see SCALLOP.

beach plum - a dark purple plum that grows wild in sandy soil along the Atlantic coast of the U.S. These cherry-size fruits were among the first foods eaten by the early colonists.

bead - another word for the bubbles present in **sparkling wines.** Aficionados insist that the smaller and more long-lasting the bead, the better the taste of the wine. Champagne **flutes** are said to be the best glasses for a fine sparkling wine because they preserve the bead for the longest time.

bean - the seed pod of various legumes, distinguished from both peas and lentils. Beans were a staple of the Roman and Greek diets, and several recipes for bean stews continue to exist from that era. Many beans were first brought to Italy from the Middle East, but some, like **fava,** were indigenous and used as ritual offerings to the dead. Alexander the Great brought the white bean from India and started the tradition of white bean salad in Macedonia, Greece and probably Rome, which has survived to this day. In Italy, we find mention of the first trace of bean cultivation about 1528 in the town of Belluno, where a certain humanist named Valeriano started sowing beans imported from Peru. Valeriano considered the discovery of beans similar to the discovery of a treasure, and under his influence, bean agriculture was extended to other regions of Italy.

In France, the first mention of beans was in a document dated about 1564, which related that beans were cultivated in the region surrounding the town of Vienne, having been introduced from a monastery near Lisbon, Portugal. Pietro Andrea Mattioli, a Sienese botanist, described the strange new food: "When eaten, they bloat the stomach but they generate virile seed and encourage sexual intercourse and even more so if they are eaten with long pepper, sugar and galingale." By the end of the 16th century, the cultivation and lore of beans was well established throughout Italy, France and Spain, and these regions were the basis for the further expansion of beans to other areas of the world. Beans have always been a popular peasant food, but during the Renaissance, **Catherine de' Medici** attempted to refine Italian cuisine and

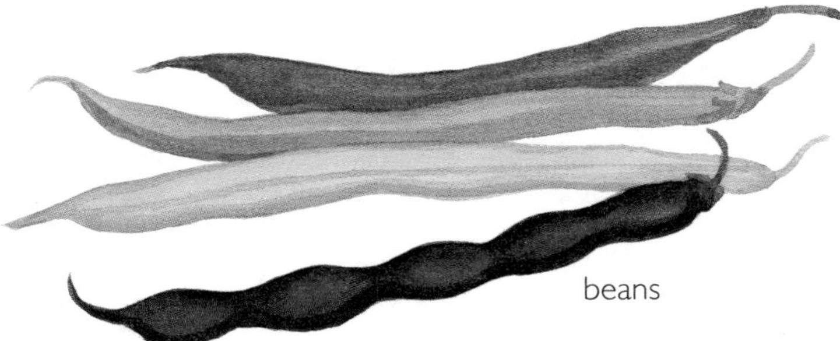

failed. Thanks to their highly nutritious and economical qualities, beans and **pulses** have once again become an important ingredient in cooking.

Whether a bean is a snap bean, pod bean, shell bean or a dry bean is determined by its stage of development and harvest. Green beans, yellow wax beans and purple wax beans are picked at a very early stage and are actually the undeveloped pods of the bean. Shell beans, such as kidney beans, long beans and cranberry beans, are the mature fresh seeds. Dried beans are the seeds that have dried in the pod.

After eating beans, some people experience the problem of flatulence. Gas is produced by the fermentation of complex sugars called raffinose sugars, which are found in beans and other vegetables. The small intestine does not have the proper enzyme to break down the sugar, so it passes into the large intestine, where bacteria break down and ferment it, producing hydrogen, methane and carbon dioxide gases. Flatulence was first studied when it became a problem for pilots (the higher the altitude, the more gas expands). At 35,000 feet (10 km), gas will expand to 5.4 times more than at sea level, causing pain.

See also AZUKI BEAN, BLACK BEAN, BLACK-EYED PEA, BLACK TURTLE BEAN, BORLOTTI BEAN, CANNELLINI BEAN, FAVA, FERMENTED BLACK BEANS, FLAGEOLET, FUL MEDAMES, HARICOT BEAN, HORTICULTURAL BEANS, KIDNEY BEAN, LIMA BEAN, MUNG BEAN, NAVY BEAN, PIGEON PEA, PINK BEAN, SOYBEAN, TONKA BEAN, WHITE BEAN.

bean curd - see TOFU.

bean flakes - dehydrated flakes of steamed legumes designed to cook quickly; can be used in recipes that call for mashed beans or added to soups as a thickener. Bean flakes are usually found in health food or camping stores and come in all kinds of varieties, such as pinto, black bean, soybean and so on.

bean flour - see FLOUR.

bean herb - see EPAZOTE.

bean pastes - also **bean sauces**. These are condiments made from fermented soybeans and used in many Asian cultures, including Chinese, Vietnamese and Korean cooking. See also MISO.

bean pot - a deep, bulbous glazed earthenware crock with a tight-fitting lid, used for making baked beans in an oven. Bean pots have wide, flat bottoms and narrow tops, with handles on either side of the opening to make lifting easy. They were a staple of the Colonial American household and are still a useful kitchen tool for making all sorts of legume dishes and stews, which need long, slow cooking.

bean slicer - a kitchen utensil consisting of a set of sharp metal blades on a barrel that turns inside a housing, used to cut regular green beans into French-style green beans. The whole beans are pushed into the top of the slicer; a crank on the outside is turned to feed the beans through the blades, which cuts them into thin, uniform ribbons. The French-style green bean is supposed to mimic the delicate taste and texture of **haricot vert.**

bean sprouts - the highly nutritious green shoots produced by allowing beans to germinate and grow for only a short time. The Chinese have been sprouting mung beans and soybeans as a food source for at least 3,000 years. See also SPROUTS.

bean stick - see YUBA.

bean thread - see HARUSAME.

bear - most popular in German and Russian cooking. The European bear (*Ursus arctus*) and the American bear (*Ursus americanus*) are occasionally enjoyed for their steaks, but the paws are considered to be the prime parts.

beard - the common name for the byssus of a bivalve mollusk, the network of silky filaments it secretes and uses to adhere to rocks. Clams, mussels and oysters need to have their beards removed before they are cooked, as they are unpleasant to eat. See also DEBEARD.

Beard, James - see profile below.

béarnaise sauce - one of the classic French sauces, made with a reduction of vinegar, wine, tarragon, shallots, egg yolks and butter. It was said to be named in honor of Henri IV of France who was known as *Le Grand Béarnais*, because he was tall and was born in the province of Béarn. The connection between the name of the sauce and the king's place of birth probably arose because béarnaise sauce was supposedly first made by Chef Jules Colette in the 1830s, in a restaurant called Le Pavillon Henri IV. However, a similar recipe appeared in *La Cuisine des Villes et des Campagnes*, published in 1818.

beat - to stir with a brisk, whipping motion, using a fork, whisk or other form of beater, which lifts a mixture over and over in order to introduce air into it and make it very smooth and light.

beaten biscuit - a hard, crisp biscuit that originated in the southern U.S. in the 19th century, made by beating (pounding) the dough vigorously for as long as 30 minutes or more before rolling it out and cutting it into small circles.

Beard, James (1903–1985) - author, television personality, newspaper columnist and cooking teacher. Born in Portland, Oregon, the only child of older parents who, he once said, "were unhappy together and managed me like a hotel," Beard had an eccentric childhood. His mother, an adventurous English expatriate, was one of the first successful women innkeepers in America, and she instilled a great appreciation for culture in her son. From a very early age, he was taken to the theatre and out to dine, developing a precocious interest in food and a selective palate while still a child. He and his mother summered on the coast, where they grew their own produce, caught salmon and dug for clams, which they sautéed for breakfast. This bounty of fabulous fresh ingredients influenced his approach to food and laid the foundation for his commitment to fostering the so-called "new American cuisine."

Becoming a food professional wasn't his dream. His first choice was acting, but he shifted gears when he realized his would be a career of supporting roles. Since cocktail parties were much in vogue, in 1937 he opened a catering company with two partners. This led to his first cookbook, *Hors d'Oeuvre and Canapés* (1940). Beard made television history in 1946 when he starred in the first television cooking show (NBC's *Elsie Presents James Beard,* named for the Borden Company's Elsie the cow). A natural and enthusiastic teacher, he opened his first cooking school in 1955.

A corpulent man with legendary appetites, Beard's great gift to food was his encyclopedic knowledge of the subject, which is documented in his many books, especially the comprehensive tome *James Beard's American Cookery* (1972). He had phenomenal recall for the tastes and the details of past meals and is fondly remembered for being an extraordinarily kind and generous man, who supported many newcomers, including **Julia Child,** when they were making their mark on the food world. Among his many accomplishments, he played a key role in developing New York's celebrated Four Seasons restaurant, which opened in 1959, based on the then radical notion of serving seasonal American cooking. Food harvested at the peak of freshness and prepared simply was what he remembered from his childhood, and no one did more to ensure that it became part of the nation's gastronomic consciousness. In fact, **Craig Claiborne** called him "the founding father of the national interest in good eating." The James Beard Foundation was founded in his honor to celebrate achievements in culinary excellence.

Beauvilliers, Antoine (1754–1817) - French chef and restaurateur, invented the soufflé in 1782. Beauvilliers opened La Grande Taverne de Londres in Paris during the early 1780s. It is considered the first "true" **restaurant** because of its rarefied décor, formal service and elaborate menu. The gregarious Beauvilliers spoke five languages and often played host in a flamboyant costume, offering advice on both what to eat and drink. In 1814, he published *L'Art du cuisinier* (The Cook's Art), the first work of its kind to include aspects of restaurant management.

Beaufort - a French cheese made in the high Alps, round and flat, similar to **Gruyère** and sometimes called Gruyère de Beaufort.

Beaujolais - a fruity, French red wine named for the ancient Château de Beaujeau, which no longer exists. There are 10 varieties of Beaujolais from 10 different villages. The trend of Beaujolais Nouveau started in the 9th century, when a small portion of Beaujolais was made into red wine for drinking when just a few weeks old. Years ago, this fruity French wine was such a local neighborhood specialty that it rarely made it into a corked bottle. Now it's an international phenomenon that makes November 15, the date on which it's released each year, the most important date on every Beaujolais Nouveau lover's calendar. The difference between Nouveau and other Beaujolais wines is that Nouveau grapes are not crushed but left whole, so that each grape undergoes fermentation individually. The result is a light, fresh wine that is best drunk almost immediately — in the late fall or early winter. This seasonal wine is better served chilled to accentuate its fruitiness and youth.

Beaumont cheese - also **Tomme de Beaumont.** A French cow's milk cheese with a nutty mild flavor.

Beauty of Bath apple - see APPLE.

Beauvilliers, Antoine - see profile above.

Beavertails - a trademarked name for a Canadian specialty consisting of a flat oval of deep-fried dough, often served dusted with sugar and cinnamon.

béchamel - a French **white sauce** made by stirring milk into a butter and flour **roux,** one of the classic "mother sauces." The thickness of the sauce varies depending on the proportions of flour and butter to milk. This cream sauce has mistakenly been said to have been invented by the French financier Louis de Béchameil, Marquis de Nointel (1630–1703), who served Louis XIV in the honorary post of Lord Steward to the Royal Household. The sauce was most likely invented by **Françoise Pierre La Varenne** and named to honor de Béchameil, prompting the jealous old Duc d'Escars to say, "That fellow Béchameil has all the luck. I was serving breast of chicken à la crème 20 years before he was born, but I have never had the chance of giving my name to even the most modest sauce." The recipe first appeared in print in La Varenne's *Le Cuisinier françois* in 1651. See also MORNAY, SOUBISE.

bêche de mer - see SEA CUCUMBER.

Beck, Simone - see CHILD, JULIA.

bee balm - see BERGAMOT.

Beecher, Catherine Esther - see profile below.

Beecher, Catherine Esther (1800–1878) - American educator and author, the first teacher of domestic science and an early advocate of higher education for women. In 1841, she published *A Treatise on Domestic Economy,* the first book to explore the science behind domestic life, establishing home economics as a discipline. She also wrote *Female Education* (1827), *The Duty of American Women to Their Country* (1845), *Miss Beecher's Receipt-Book* (1846), *Common Sense Applied to Religion* (1857), and, with her sister, Harriet Beecher Stowe, *The American Woman's Home* (1869).

beechnut oil - up to the Second World War, this oil was readily available on the market, but beechnuts are now rarely grown for oil. If one is fortunate enough to find it, do not use it on strong or pungent blends of salads because they will overpower the very delicate taste of this oil. The flavor of the nut itself is midway between hazelnut and chestnut, with a light astringency that disappears when roasted.

beef - the meat from bovine animals, such as cows, steers and bulls, more than one year old. See also CHATEAUBRIAND, HAMBURGER, KOBE BEEF, MEAT, PORTERHOUSE, SIRLOIN, SKIRT STEAK, SPARERIBS, STEAK, TEMPERATURE.

beef à la mode - see À LA MODE.

beefalo - a cross between beef cattle and buffalo that some cattle ranchers began raising in the mid-1900s. The meat is leaner and sweeter than beef and has all the characteristics of buffalo. However, it has not become a widely utilized meat.

beef jerky - see JERKY.

beef pudding - in England, a meat pie that has been boiled or steamed.

beef shin - another term for a beef **shank,** a cut of meat made from the shin on the lower leg of a

BEEF CUTS

arm roast - tough cut from the center of the **chuck** section, with or without the bone.

back ribs - what remains when the rib roast is taken off the bones, with little meat but very tender, often grilled.

brisket - under the first five ribs, best braised, used to make corned beef.

chuck - from between the neck and shoulder, usually ground. **Flatiron steak** or top blade steak is one of the two muscles that make up the external top blade area of the chuck or shoulder. When the top blade is cut horizontally into two pieces, the shape resembles an old-fashioned flatiron. It is also called book steak, butler steak, lifter steak and petit steak. **Chuck short ribs** are ribs one to five, with lots of meat and less fat than **plate ribs. Blade pot roast,** also **chuck blade roast,** is a cut that includes a variety of small muscles with pieces of the blade bone. It is suitable for long simmering or braising.

flank steak - a long, fibrous muscle from the underbelly, best quickly grilled and thinly sliced against the grain, but never past medium-rare or it will be tough and dry.

hanger steak - the part of the diaphragm that "hangs" between the last rib and the loin.

loin - the most tender and expensive cut, although not the most flavorful, the choicest being the **tenderloin,** which is very tender and lean. **Top loin** and **sirloin** are more flavorful but not as tender. **Club steak** is from the loin between the T-bone and rib section. It is firm, tender and flavorful. **T-bone steak** is a crosscut that includes parts of the tenderloin and top loin, different from the **porterhouse** only in that it has a larger portion of the tenderloin.

plate - the bottom horizontal third of the chest and belly, including the brisket, behind the front legs, and the flank, in front of the hind legs. **Plate short ribs** are ribs six to 12, although usually taken from the flat ends of ribs six to nine, cut to 2-inch (5 cm) widths, ribs 10 to 12 being fattier.

rib - tender and well-marbled, making it juicy and full of flavor. **Prime rib,** also **standing rib roast,** is cut from the upper rib section of the back of the steer, a piece cut from ribs six to the 12, the best considered to be from the 10th to 12th rib.

round - from the carcass hind, where the muscles have been well exercised, which makes the meat tough, requiring slow, moist cooking. **Bottom round** is cut from the bottom of the round and is taken from the hindquarter that borders the tip.

top round - cut from the inward-facing side of the leg it is the most tender; thick steaks, sold as London broil, are cut from this section. The rump, a triangular piece cut from the top of the round, is sold as **rump roast** (boneless, sometimes rolled) or **standing rump roast** (bone-in); it may be barbecued, braised or roasted and cut into **rump steak.**

cow. This cut is sometimes called "gravy beef" as well. It is a tough cut of meat, best suited to slow braising or stewing. See also BEEF.

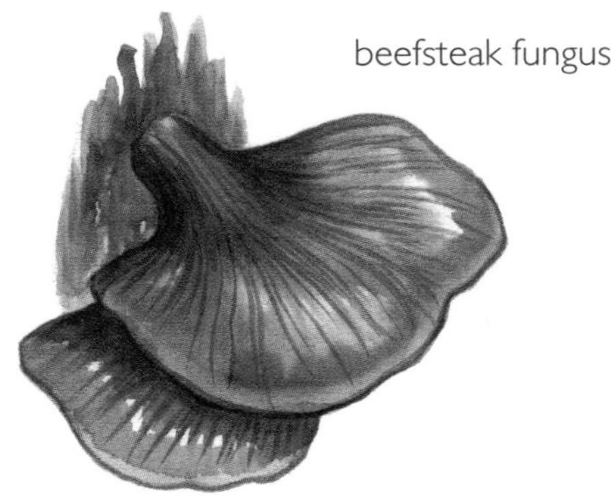

beefsteak fungus

beefsteak fungus - a mushroom, *Fistulina hepatica,* named after the beef-like appearance of its flesh, found growing on dead, or occasionally on living, trees, especially oaks.

beefsteak plant - see SHISO.

beefsteak tomato - see TOMATO.

beef Stroganoff - beef sautéed with onions, mushrooms and sour cream. Despite his years of government service, 19th-century Russian diplomat Count Paul Stroganoff is now best remembered for the dish that bears his name.

beef tartare - see STEAK TARTARE.

beef Wellington - a dish of beef fillet, goose liver **pâté** and mushroom **duxelles** wrapped in puff pastry and baked. When Napoleon Bonaparte was defeated at Waterloo by the British forces under the control of Arthur Wellesley, Duke of Wellington, the overjoyed English conveyed their gratitude by naming several items of clothing after him, including waterproof Wellington boots. This dish was also named in his honor.

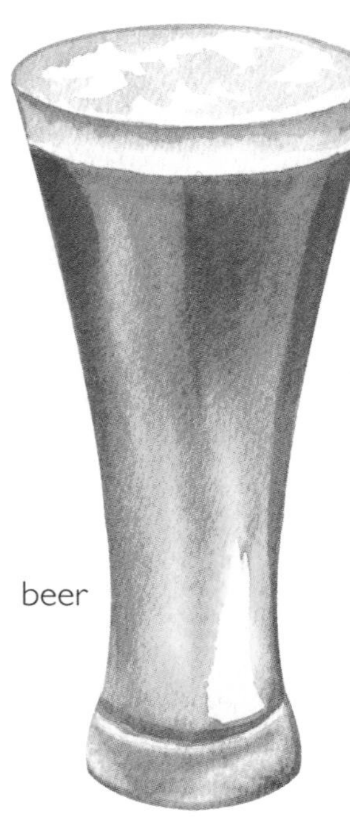

beer

beer - a fermented alcoholic beverage brewed from malt and flavored with hops. Beer is one of civilization's oldest beverages and may even have been a precursor to the invention of leavened bread. Some scholars believe that beer came before bread, with the accidental discovery of

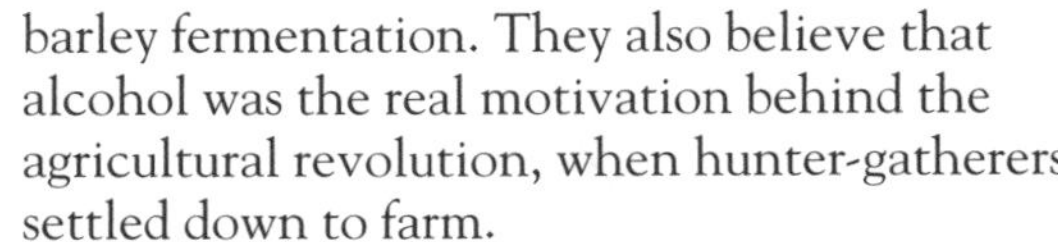

barley fermentation. They also believe that alcohol was the real motivation behind the agricultural revolution, when hunter-gatherers settled down to farm.

In biblical times, grain was the principal crop in the Middle East, not grapes, which would make beer more common than wine. As such, beer was the drink of the common folk, while the elite enjoyed wine. Egypt was a major exporter of beer to the entire Mediterranean region. Beer was drunk thousands of years before the birth of Christ. In the ancient world, beer was used as medicine, in ritual and as a beverage.

Early brewing methods have been dated as early as 10,000 BC in Sumeria. Ninkasi, the Goddess of Plenty (whose name means "the lady who fills the mouth"), and Ama-Gesting, the Earth Mother, were the two venerated deities, known also as the protectors and providers of beer. Preserved on several clay tablets is the Hymn to Ninkasi, which has a recipe for beer that is nearly 4,000 years old. It calls for mixing *bappir,* a type of bread, with water and "aromatics" and setting it to ferment in large vats before straining. At that time, priestesses were the only brewers, and one could only drink the divine beverage during religious ceremonies. As beer developed into a social drink, women became the first bar owners. The beer was fairly crude at the time: cloudy and hardly ever filtered. It was fermented and served in the same pot, and drunk through a long piece of straw or reed. Many of these bars, or "Bit Sikari," used signs and pottery with illustrations of buxom, alluring women — not very different from today's marketing. Beer was so important in ancient society that the Code of Hammurabi said that tavern owners who overcharged their customers could be put to death by drowning.

The Mesopotamians, Sumerians, Babylonians, Egyptians and Chinese all brewed beer. In ancient Babylonia, the Goddess of Beer was Nidaba; in Sumeria she was called Nin-Bi. Pa-e-bi was the name in pre-dynastic Mesopotamia (3000 BC) of the official brewer to the royal family and court; his status was that of a high priest.

In the Middle Ages, monks used hops as a flavoring and preservative, further refining the art of beer making. Louis Pasteur perfected the art with his capability to accurately control the exchange of sugar to alcohol. Germany and England became legendary for their beers because of their ability to grow barley in a cooler climate. In the U.S., Thomas Jefferson passed legislation to encourage a healthy beer industry. When Franklin D. Roosevelt became president, he abolished Prohibition. New types of American beer that came after the Second World War (mainly Pilsners) were mass-produced and generally very bland. President Jimmy Carter legalized home brewing when he held office in the late 1970s, bringing in the age of **microbreweries** and beer hobbyists.

Beer is an intricate combination of flavors and aromas created by a range of ingredients from around the world. The traditional recipe is an amalgamation of malt, hops, water and yeast with diverse additions. The end aroma and flavor of a beer depends to a great extent on the type of yeast used and the temperature at which it was fermented. See also ALE, FRUIT BEER, NEAR BEER, SMALL ALE.

MAIN YEAST VARIABLES

Ale yeasts (top-fermenting) are used at temperatures ranging from 50° to 77°F (10° to 25°C). They rise to the surface during fermentation, creating a very rich, thick yeast head with a bready aroma. These yeasts are used for brewing ales, porters, stouts and wheat beers.

Lager yeasts (bottom-fermenting) are used at temperatures ranging from 45° to 59°F (7° to 15°C). They grow more slowly than ale yeasts, with less surface foam, and have a tendency to settle near the end of the fermentation process. These yeasts are usually used for brewing lagers, Pilsners, bocks and American malt liquors.

Adjuncts are other fermentable ingredients added to, or used as a substitute for, malt or hops, generally to make the beer lighter-bodied and/or less expensive. Corn is usually the adjunct of choice for brewers, mainly in the U.S. Its quality, accessibility and composition are consistent, and it produces fermentable sugars comparable to those of malt. It has a sweet, smooth flavor, which lightens the body and clarity of a beer while stabilizing the flavor. Rice is also commonly used (particularly in the U.S.), especially in light-colored lagers. Favored because of its unaggressive taste, rice doesn't meddle with the balance of malt and hops. It does, nevertheless, provide a dry, crisp and refreshing taste familiar to traditional American Pilsners, such as Budweiser.

TYPES OF BEER

All ales and lagers are types of beer. The variety in taste is a result of how the brews are fermented and the ingredients that go into them. The basic beer recipe consists of water, barley malt, hops and yeast. To create different tastes and weights, brewers may add corn, rice or wheat, vary the temperature at which the fermentation takes place and experiment with different types of yeast. The age of the beer also contributes to its flavor.

ale - made with a type of yeast that floats to the top during fermentation. They have a full flavor and are a bit higher in alcohol content than regular beer. Ales often have a slightly fruity flavor. They are not aged.

bock - dark, sweet, full-bodied German beers traditionally brewed in the spring at the beginning of beer season. They are rich and malty, brewed with roasted malts. The name comes from the German word for the male goat, or billy goat. See also DOPPELBOCK.

lager - all the major American beers technically are lagers. Lagers are brewed with yeast fermented slowly on the bottom of the vat. They are aged from one to six weeks.

Pilsner - a pale golden beer. Light beers are Pilsner lagers that have about one-third fewer calories and 20 percent less alcohol than regular lagers.

beer bean - see EDAMAME.

beer can chicken - a whole chicken, often rubbed with a mixture of spices, impaled upright on a half-full can of beer and then roasted or barbecued over **indirect heat.** As the beer boils and evaporates during the cooking, it adds moisture to the chicken, yielding a juicy, unctuous quality to the resulting meat. The type of beer does not seem to matter, and some cooks say that the cheaper the beer, the better the chicken. The exact origin of the dish is uncertain, but cooks in the American South and Texas have been fond of the dish for years.

beer cheese - see BIERKÄSE.

Beerenauslese - a German wine label term for hand-picked slightly overripe grapes used to make heavy-weight wines. The grapes may be picked individually or by the bunch, and some or all of them may have **Botrytis cinerea.** German grapes used for winemaking are classified and labeled according to their ripeness, not necessarily their sweetness, and by the weight, or body, of the wines they produce, from thin and light-bodied to syrupy and full-bodied. Beerenauslese wines can vary from a bit sweet to very sweet. See also AUSLESE, KABINETT, SPÄTLESE, TROCKENBEERENAUSLESE.

beet - a large, firm, edible root vegetable, *Beta vulgaris*, with an edible leafy top. Beets are of three colors and kinds: red, white and yellow. The white is mostly used in producing beet sugar, the red for culinary purposes and the yellow for feeding cattle. Beets have been eaten by humans since prehistoric time and are native to a wide swath of Eurasia from Britain to India. Both the Greeks and the Romans cultivated beets, mostly to use the roots, while other Europeans ate only the green tops. Besides eating them, the Greeks also used beets for medicinal purposes, such as a remedy for constipation. In some cases, the water in which the beets were boiled was added to wine gone sour to return it to its original taste and color. Columella, the early Roman agriculturist, noted in the 1st century AD that "This curious plant owes its name, Beta vulgaris, to a physical resemblance to the second letter of the alphabet." From the 16th century, the English and Germans consumed the red beet, or garden beet, while the white beet was used as forage for animals.

The beet consists mostly of a swollen hypocotyl, or lower stem, although it's partly a root. The beets we know today were developed from a wild, slender-rooted species that was common in Southern Europe, especially in sandy soil along the sea. The beets more commonly grown now, with large, round, red roots, are fairly modern as vegetables go, and only a few varieties were available as recently as 100 years ago. The ability to metabolize the bright red pigment betacyanin (an **anthocyanin,** extremely soluble in water and the same pigment found in grapes) is controlled by a single genetic locus. Those people who have inherited two recessive genes pass the pigment in their urine. The slightly blue hue of the root before cooking makes it "bleed," meaning the purple sap of the beet starts to ooze on contact with water. This characteristic is exploited in the making of borscht, a soup originally from Eastern Europe, which can range from a fairly thin consistency to a very thick blend with the beets finely cut in order to imbue the soup with as much color as possible. When handling cooked beets, a little lemon juice will easily remove the red stain from your fingers.

In the 18th century, a white variety of beet began to be cultivated for sugar production. Up to 8 percent of its weight is sugar, an exceptional figure for a vegetable. In 1757, Andreas Sigismund Marggraf, a French chemist of Prussian origin, identified the sugar extracted from beets to be similar to the sugar extracted from sugarcane, hence the name "sugar beets." In 1793, in Berlin, François Achard perfected a process for producing sugar from beets; he

beet

revealed the process that year at Kunern, in Silesia. **Benjamin Delessert,** head of the Bank of France, saw the possibilities in beet sugar for sugar-starved France during the English blockade. He set up huge factories for producing sugar at Passy about 1810. Delessert installed modern steam engines (invented by James Watt only 40 years before) and developed ways to strain the molasses and crystallize the sugar. Napoleon Bonaparte visited the factories, honored Delessert and ordered sugar beets planted on great stretches of land in the north of France. Delessert's factories turned out more than 8 million pounds (4 million kg) of sugar in two years, but when Napoleon's empire fell at Waterloo and cane sugar came in from Martinique, Guadeloupe and Brazil, the price of sugar dropped by one-third. Beet sugar was not commercially practical again until the late 1870s, when a new production process and more efficient mills were developed. When these were demonstrated at the Paris World's Fair of 1878, almost every European country hurried to plant sugar beets and build facilities for sugar making. In terms of botany, the development of the sugar beet surpasses any other achievement of human ingenuity in food creation.

beet greens - the edible leaves of the beet, dark green with red veins and long stalks, eaten in the same way as spinach or other leafy greens. Beet greens are best eaten when young and tender, as older, larger greens have a strong flavor that can be unpleasant. They are high in the vital nutrient folate and contain some beta-carotene, iron and calcium as well.

Beeton, Mrs. Isabella - see profile below.

beetroot - the British term for beet.

beggar's button - see BURDOCK.

beggar's chicken - a famous Chinese dish from Beijing that comes to us from the old legend of a beggar, without a home or food, who stole a chicken from a farm and then cooked it in a humble manner. He covered it with mud, made a fire in a hole in the ground and baked the chicken, peeling the feathers off as he ate. It's said that, despite this tale, the people of

Beeton, Mrs. Isabella (1836–1865) - author of the *Book of Household Management* (1861), probably the bestselling cookbook of all time. Born Isabella Mary Mayson, she married publisher Samuel Beeton in 1856 and got her start as a writer penning articles for his publication *The Englishwoman's Domestic Magazine*. These articles form the basis of her huge tome, which is more than 1,000 pages in length and features 2,751 entries, ranging from recipes to practical advice on such subjects as managing servants and raising children. Encyclopedic in scope, the book is a comprehensive guide to running a household in Victorian England. Mrs. Beeton's recipes were culled from a variety of sources (the original edition describes her as the editor, rather than the author), including those of her contemporary **Eliza Acton,** from whom she is accused of plagiarizing. However, she tested and standardized the recipes and introduced a few innovations of her own, noting estimated cost, as well as the quantity produced and whether the dish could be made throughout the year or only when the ingredients were in season. The book, published when its author was a mere 25 years old, was an immediate success, selling more than 60,000 copies within a year of publication, and is still in print.

Unfortunately, Mrs. Beeton didn't fare as well in her personal life. Her feckless husband infected her with syphilis on their honeymoon, likely causing the death of their first child and subsequent miscarriages. Ironically, this paragon of domestic excellence died of puerperal fever at the age of 28 while giving birth to their fourth child, because the attending doctor didn't wash his hands. Worse still, her surviving children never enjoyed the legacy of her endeavors. Samuel was a poor money manager. Without Isabella's guidance, he went bankrupt within six months of her death and was forced to sell all rights to her work. While her family reaped few of the financial rewards of her great success, others did. Not only has her book sold millions of copies, in 1995 a manufacturer of meat pies paid £1 million for the right to call its products "Mrs. Beeton's."

Beijing think that their special chicken is too fine a preparation to carry the name "beggar" and prefer to call it *fu guai gai*, or "rich and noble chicken."

beggar's purse - an **hors d'oeuvre,** originally consisting of a small crêpe topped with caviar and **crème fraîche,** the edges of which were pulled up and tied with a fresh chive to look like a purse. Variations on the original beggar's purse are everywhere now, filled with everything from roasted duck to salsa and based on almost anything shaped like a pancake, from a crêpe to a tortilla.

begonia - any plant of the genus *Begonia*, native to South America, with edible flowers. Begonia hybrids with tuberous roots (commonly known as tuberous begonias) grow pretty white, bright yellow, orange, pink and red edible blossoms that are crisp and have a mild citrusy flavor. They are beautiful and tasty in salads. See also EDIBLE FLOWERS.

begonia

beigli - pl. **beiglik.** A flaky Hungarian yeast-leavened pastry, sometimes identified as a *strudel*, filled with poppy seeds or walnuts. The dough is made with butter and a bit of sour cream to give it a delicious tang, then rolled out until very thin. The dough is then covered with the filling and rolled up jelly roll–style and baked. When the roll has cooled, the pastry is cut into thin slices, which look like pinwheels.

beignet - a traditional crisp, puffy, deep-fried pastry resembling a doughnut, found in New Orleans, France and Quebec.

Beijing kao ya - see PEKING DUCK.

belacan - also **belachan, blacang, blachan.** The Malaysian version of **shrimp paste,** probably the most common name for this seasoning, which is called **trassi** in Indonesia and is similar to **bagoong** in the Philippines. Tiny shrimp are sun-dried and salted, then ground into a paste and fermented. The paste is then formed into cakes or bricks and dried. Small bits are broken off for use in recipes and must be cooked to mellow the flavor (and notoriously acrid smell) before they are added to other ingredients. Belacan is used sparingly in cooking to add a slight sweetness to meats, similar to the way Thai fish sauce is used to add balance to a dish. Belacan is also the basis of a typical Malaysian condiment called *sambal belacan*, which combines the cooked paste with lime juice and chiles.

Belegtes Brot - the name given in Germany to an open-faced sandwich.

Belgian endive - see ENDIVE.

Belgian waffle - a type of waffle with very deep indentations, usually served with fruit and whipped cream.

beli sir - a sourish Yugoslavian cheese, brine-ripened for about a month and pressed in rectangular molds, produced in both farmhouse and factory versions.

belle Hélène - also **poire belle-Hélène, poire Hélène.** A dessert, made of ice cream, a poached pear and chocolate sauce, named after the famous operetta by Jacques Offenbach.

Bellelay cheese - see TÊTE DE MOINE.

bellevue - a French term to describe food in **aspic,** through which it can be plainly seen.

Bellini - a cocktail made of one-third peach juice and two-thirds Champagne. The drink was concocted at Harry's Bar in Venice in the 1930s by Giuseppe Cipriani but was not given its name until 1948, in honor of the Renaissance artist Giovanni Bellini, for whom an exposition was being held that year in the city. At Harry's Bar, it's served in a slender but not very tall glass. Elsewhere, it's commonly served in a Champagne glass. According to Arrigo Cipriani (Guiseppe's son), the peach juice must be made by using a food mill to produce the pulp, which is then pushed through a fine sieve. The cocktail is made by combining fresh white peach juice (best if chilled before using) with Champagne (in Italy, with **prosecco**), poured into a chilled glass.

Bellini

bell pepper - see SWEET PEPPER.

bellyfish - see MONKFISH.

Bel Paese - a semisoft Italian cheese, one of the best-known in the U.S. and all over the world. This cheese is a baby among the Italian cheeses, having been created in the north of Italy in the early 20th century. Bel Paese is the brand name of one of a group of cheeses, generically classified as **"Italico"** cheeses, which have been made in Italy, with only slight deviation, for about 100 years. It's the best known of Italicos, and its three chief contenders in Italy (they are not imported by the U.S.) are Pastorella, Bick and Fior D'Alpe.

Its name, poetically, means "beautiful country." Petrarch used it to refer to Italy in Dante's *Inferno* and in a sonnet. Much later, *Bel Paese* was a title of a trendy book about Italy written for young people by an Italian priest, Antonio Stoppini, whose picture appears on the Bel Paese packaging. Stoppini was a friend of Italian cheese maker **Egidio Galbani,** whose hobby was mountain climbing and who spent every Sunday in the mountains at Lecco, near Lake Como. The local cheeses there impressed him, and he studied the methods used to make them. At that time — this was the beginning of the 20th century — only the poor ate native Italian cheeses; with the exclusion of **Parmesan,** wealthy Italians snubbed local cheeses and bought only French luxury cheeses. Galbani wanted to make a luxury cheese in Italy at a popular price. The recipe he developed was one of the building blocks for what was to become the Galbani empire, a conglomerate that today holds in Italy the same household recognition that Kraft enjoys in the U.S., with an export business that reaches every corner of the world.

beluga caviar - see CAVIAR.

Benedict - see EGGS BENEDICT.

Bénédictine - a cognac-based herbal liqueur developed in 1510 by Dom Bernardo Vincelli, a monk at the French Abbey of Fécamp. "Deo Optimo Maximo" ("Praise be to God, most good, most great"), he cried out on first tasting the liqueur that now bears his order's name. He reportedly poured his "elixir" for the resident monks, who sipped it as a cure for fatigue — or so the story goes. It's sold in bottles of distinctive shape and, because the label bears the initials D.O.M., Bénédictine is sometimes referred to as D.O.M. Liqueur. It's believed to be the world's oldest liqueur. What's certain is that the Normandy monastery produced it until the French Revolution in 1789, when monasteries were forcibly closed and distilling was forbidden. Bénédictine was formally banished until the 1860s, when it was revived by a descendent of the monastery's lawyer Alexander Le Grand. On finding the secret recipe in the middle of a bunch of yellowed papers, he was inspired to build a new distillery in the high Gothic style at Fécamp, and the secularized liqueur — first christened Bénédictine by Le Grand — was resurrected.

Bénédictine is a bright golden concoction of honeyed sweetness, embracing an herbalist's pantheon of medicinal plants and spices, including **hyssop.** Only three people know the exact formula at any given time, but it's thought to contain as many as 75 aromatic ingredients. The famed **B&B** liqueur, which is Bénédictine mixed with brandy, is also made in the same factory of Fécamp and was originally created at New York's "21" Club shortly after the repeal of Prohibition.

Bengal isinglass - see AGAR-AGAR.

Bengal quince - see BAEL.

beni shoga - also **gari.** A Japanese pickled or vinegared ginger whose natural color is white, although it usually has a red tint in the market. It's served as a garnish with many dishes. See also AMAZU SHOGA.

beni shoga

benne - an African-derived term for sesame, probably from the Malinke or Bantu word *bene*, meaning "sesame." The term was adopted in the American South, thanks to African slaves who brought the term with them when they were brought to America. The word is still used in some parts of the country, especially in reference to **benne wafers.**

benne wafer - a thin, crisp cookie made with sesame seeds, or **benne,** especially popular in Georgia, South Carolina and Louisiana. Legend has it that benne bring good luck, and these cookies are said to as well.

Benoît, Madame Jehane - see profile below.

bento box - also **bento.** A Japanese term referring to a boxed meal, often packed in an elaborate box with separate compartments for each food item.

bentoo no tomo - a Japanese seasoning compound consisting of dried fish, salt, soy sauce, seaweed and **monosodium glutamate,** used in Asian cooking.

berbere - an Ethiopian spice blend usually consisting of red pepper, cardamom, coriander and fenugreek, as well as other spices, used as a rub to flavor meat and fish. It can also be fried with onion and/or garlic and other spices and made into a paste, used to flavor soups and stews.

Bercy - a sauce or compound butter whose primary ingredients are wine and shallots, part of French cuisine since the early 19th century, named for the Parisian district noted to have been the largest wine market in Europe.

bereketei - a whole wheat Sabbath bread made by Ethiopian Jews, usually a simple loaf that is flavored with crushed, roasted fenugreek seeds and baked inside a shell of leaves.

bere meal - a barley meal made and used in Shetland and Orkney in Britain for making ale, barley griddle cakes, porridge and **bannocks.** Bere meal is made from a special variety of barley, which was originally called *bygg* or *bigg*. It can be hard to find outside its native area, although some online stores sell the meal outside of Orkney and Shetland. Whole-grain flour, such as whole wheat, makes an acceptable substitute in some baking recipes.

bergamot - also **bee balm, Oswego tea.** A flowering plant, *Monarda didyma*, bergamot has dark green aromatic leaves that are used in salads and as a flavoring herb. The botanical name comes from a Spanish physician, Dr. Nicholas Monardez, who was the first to describe the medicinal properties of the herb in 1577. The Oswego Indians used the leaves for tea, which is said to have been popular among

Benoît, Madame Jehane (1904–1987) - cookbook author and radio and television personality, whose encyclopedic knowledge of food, strong work ethic and folksy charm established her as a Canadian icon for almost 40 years. Born Jehane Patenaude to a prominent Montreal family, she rebelled against tradition and, at a time when higher education for women was very much an exception, persuaded her father to send her to study at the Sorbonne in Paris. In 1925, she graduated with a degree in food chemistry. Returning to Montreal, she started a cooking school, which soon became successful. In 1935, she opened a restaurant, The Salad Bar, an early purveyor of vegetarian cuisine. As a television personality, she cultivated the image of a conventional grandmother but didn't marry until 1940, when she was in her mid-30s, possibly because she had other priorities.

The author of 30 cookbooks, in French and English, Madame Benoît, as she was known professionally, published her masterpiece *The Encyclopedia of Canadian Cooking* in 1963. This tome of more than a thousand pages leaves little doubt that her grandmotherly demeanor disguised a serious social historian with an exhaustive knowledge of Canadian culinary history. As she notes in the introduction, "The entire history of civilization could be written from the standpoint of food alone." In 1973, she was awarded the Order of Canada, the country's highest honor, for her work in documenting Canada's history through the story of its food.

A B C D E F G H I J K L M N O P Q R S T U V W X Y Z

the rebellious American patriots who refused to drink English tea.

bergamot orange - a hybrid of orange, first developed in France in the late 18th century, bitter and quite acidic but with a pleasant taste. The essential oil from the rind is used in confections, as well in perfumes and pharmaceuticals and, perhaps the most famous of its uses, to provide **Earl Grey tea** with its distinctive taste. See also ORANGE.

bergamot orange

Bergkäse - a hard yellow German cheese from the Bavarian Alps.

Berlin doughnut - see BISMARCK.

Berliner Kuhkäse - a soft, German cheese made with cow's milk and covered with caraway seeds.

Berliner Pfannkuchen - the German interpretation of the jelly doughnut.

Berliner Weisse - a regional top-fermented beer from northern Germany, principally Berlin, very pale but not white. It's traditionally served in large, bowl-shaped stem glasses with a dash of green essence of **woodruff** or red raspberry syrup. Its popularity dates back to Imperial Germany, but it's mentioned in texts as early as 1572. It's also known as the "Champagne of the Spree" and was nicknamed *Champagne du Nord* by Napoleon's troops.

Bermuda onion - see ONION.

Bernade - an Italian cheese of cow's and goat's milk, flavored with saffron and brushed with coarse salt.

Berner platte - a Swiss specialty, consisting of sauerkraut and/or green beans topped with a variety of meats, such as bacon, ham, pork chops, pigs' feet, sausages, salted tongue and ribs.

berries - a name applied in common usage to various small fruits, although botanical definitions of berries differ from this popular conception. (To a botanist, a berry is any fruit with seeds scattered through pulp. This would include, for example, cranberries and grapes and also cucumbers and pears, but not strawberries and blackberries.) Since berries of all types are found the world over, it's assumed that they first grew wild and were cultivated by Europeans and Asians. When the first pilgrims came to the New World, they found Native Americans enjoying cranberries, blueberries and strawberries. Strawberries, as we know them today, were cultivated from a cross between a Chilean strawberry and wild berries native to West Virginia. The Native Americans also taught the settlers to dry blueberries to add to their winter soups and stews. Along with blueberries, cranberries are one of the truly native North American fruits.

berry sugar - a fine grind of granulated sugar, still sufficiently coarse to distinguish the individual crystals.

Berthaut, Robert - see ÉPOISSES.

Bertholle, Louisette - see CHILD, JULIA.

besan - also **chana flour, channa flour, chickpea flour, gram flour.** A pale yellow, high-protein flour made from ground chickpeas, used in East Indian cooking to make dumplings and noodles as well as for thickening sauces.

best-before date - see EXPIRATION DATE.

bestilla - see BASTILA.

beta-carotene - a nutrient found in carrots, broccoli, squash, spinach and sweet potatoes, which the liver converts to vitamin A. It's believed to be a potent antioxidant and is said to reduce the risk of cancer and heart disease.

betel leaf - also **paan.** The heart-shaped leaf of the betel pepper plant, *Piper betle*. It is used for cooking and as the base of **paan** in Asia.

betel nut - also **areca nut, pinang.** The seed of the betel palm, *Areca catechu*, grown throughout Asia and in parts of Africa, chewed (on its own, as a component of **paan,** or with tobacco) for its stimulating effect. Betel nut contains arecaine and arecoline, stimulants similar to nicotine, which suppress the appetite and are mildly intoxicating and addictive. Betel nut is chewed for about 20 minutes, then the fibrous remains of the nut are spat out. The residue is a brilliant shade of red and is a common sight on sidewalks all over India and other parts of Asia. In Taiwan, where betel nut chewing has been popular historically, scantily clad young women known as betel nut beauties sell betel nut at neon-lit roadside stands, usually to truck drivers who chew it to stay awake on long drives. In Taiwanese, betel nut beauties are called "binlang xishi," for Xi Shi, a legendary beauty of ancient China.

betony

betony - a purple-flowered plant, *Stachys officinalis*, that makes a fine substitute for regular black tea, especially when mixed with other dried herbs. It was one of the Egyptians' magical herbs, and the Romans listed it as a cure for 47 different illnesses. As late as the 17th century, a physician recorded 30 medicinal uses for betony. In the Middle Ages, it was the herb most planted in churchyards, and men and women sported good-luck charms made of it because they believed betony was a safeguard against harm and that the plant warded off evil spirits. "He has as many virtues as betony" is a centuries-old Spanish saying that demonstrates the regard people once had for this plant.

betty - a baked pudding made of layers of sugared and spiced fruit and buttered bread crumbs. The most popular type of betty is apple brown betty, made with apple slices and brown sugar.

Betty Crocker - see HUSTED, MARJORIE.

betzah - the Hebrew term for the roasted egg served at the Seder, an annual symbolic meal eaten on the Jewish holiday of Passover, which commemorates the Exodus of the Jews from Egypt. The egg represents offerings once made at the Temple in Jerusalem before it was destroyed, and symbolizes birth and the hope for a new life. The egg is placed on a plate of five symbolic foods in the center of the table.

beurre blanc - a classic French sauce made from a reduction of wine, vinegar and shallots, to which chunks of soft butter are added and then whisked until the sauce thickens and becomes smooth. It's served with poultry, seafood, eggs and vegetables.

beurre composé - French for **"compound butter."**

beurre manié - also **kneaded butter.** A mixture of equal parts butter and flour kneaded into a paste, used to thicken sauces.

beurre nantais - a different name for **beurre blanc,** meaning "butter in the style of Nantes." Some chefs prepare beurre nantais in exactly the same manner and with the same ingredients as beurre blanc, while some assert that true beurre nantais is enriched with a dollop of cream. In either case, it is considered an ideal partner for fish of any type and meat brochettes.

beurre noir - also **black butter.** A French sauce usually reserved for fish but sometimes served with offal **(variety meat).** It consists of butter cooked over high heat to the point at which the butter begins to brown, giving it a delicious hazelnut taste. It's sometimes flavored with vinegar or lemon juice, capers and parsley.

beurre noisette - also **brown butter.** A French term for butter cooked to a light noisette or hazelnut color. It is the step before **beurre noir.**

bharta - also **bartha.** An Indian dish of smoked eggplant, fried with onions, tomatoes, herbs and spices.

bhatoora - also **bhatura.** An Indian specialty of leavened dough made of white flour, yogurt and potatoes. After it has risen, it's rolled into circles and deep-fried.

bialy - a flat roll that has a depressed center and is sometimes covered with onion flakes. It's a

Yiddish word, short for Bialystoker, "of Bialystok," a city in northeastern Poland.

Bibb lettuce - see LETTUCE.

bibimbap - a Korean medley of rice, vegetables and meat served in a sizzling-hot black clay pot called a *tukbaege*. A mound of cooked medium-grain sticky rice is the first ingredient to go into the clay pot. Then toppings are added, including (but not limited to) cooked beef shreds, spinach or other greens, various types of seaweed, paper-thin cucumber slices, mung bean sprouts and fiery hot **gochu jang.** The mixture is topped with a runny fried egg, which the diner mixes with the other ingredients. Bibimbap is usually served with an assortment of side dishes, including **kimchi.**

bible leaf - see COSTMARY.

bicarbonate of soda - see BAKING SODA.

Bierkaltschale - in Germany, a cold beer soup, usually eaten in the heat of the summer months.

Bierkäse - also **beer cheese.** A semisoft German cheese that is very similar to **Limburger,** but slightly more pungent, usually melted in hot beer.

bierock - see RUNZA.

Bierplinsen - a German specialty of cooked meats or sausages dipped in a beer batter, then deep-fried.

Bierschinken - a German cooked sausage made of fresh pork and bits of ham, flavored with pistachios, large in diameter like **mortadella** and eaten in thin slices.

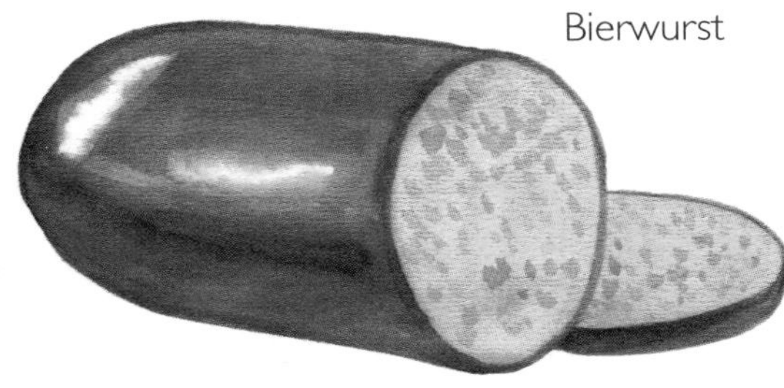

Bierwurst

Bierwurst - a German sausage made of a blend of beef and pork, usually quite spicy.

bietola - Italian for "Swiss chard."

big - a wine-tasting term used to describe a full-bodied wine with a strong taste and aroma, usually high in alcohol as well, a positive term for a wine with a good flavor and texture.

biga - a sourdough-type yeast starter used for baking Italian breads, such as **ciabatta** and **pugliese.** A combination of flour, water and a small amount of yeast are mixed together and allowed to ferment for 18 to 24 hours, sometimes even up to 48 hours. The biga gives breads a rich, deep flavor and heady, slightly sour aroma typical of traditionally made **artisanal** breads. Unlike many other sourdough starters, biga is usually made fresh for each batch of bread, rather than kept alive over a long period of time with periodic feedings of flour and water. See also SOURDOUGH, SPONGE, STARTER.

bigarade

bigarade - the French name for the bitter **Seville orange,** from the Provençal *bigarrado*, meaning "variegated."

bigarade sauce - a classic French sauce made from duck gravy, orange and lemon juice, blanched orange peel and sometimes **curaçao,** usually served with duck.

bigaro - see PERIWINKLE.

bigeye scad - see AKULE.

bigeye tuna - see AHI, TUNA.

bigoli - see PASTA.

bigos - considered by many to be the national dish of Poland, this "hunter's stew" is a combination of sauerkraut and meat simmered at length. The dish often includes wild mushrooms and sometimes calls for the addition of sausage, often **kielbasa.** The dish can feature a single type of meat or an assortment of beef, duck, ham, mutton, pork or venison — whatever is on hand or the preference of the cook. Tradition dictates that the stew be prepared a day or two ahead and reheated so that the flavor can best develop, probably because hunters traditionally made and carried this stew along with them and reheated it a number of times, creating a deeper, richer flavor with each cooking cycle.

bijol - a bright reddish orange powdered seasoning mix that contains ground **achiote seed,** ground cumin and fine corn flour. Bijol is used in Latin American cooking to season and inexpensively color foods, such as **paella, arroz con pollo** and so on, that are traditionally tinged yellow with very expensive saffron.

bijon - noodles produced commercially in Southeast Asia from corn kernels, used in soups, spring rolls, cold salads and stir-fries.

bilberry - see HUCKLEBERRY.

bilí - see HONEYBERRY.

billfish - see MARLIN.

billi-bi - also **billy-bi.** A creamy, saffron-scented French mussel soup that may be served hot or cold, traditionally with the mussels strained out. There are a variety of legends attached to the naming of this soup. The most likely is that the soup was named for William "Billy" B. Leeds, an American industrialist whose fortune was made on tin. He often dined at the famous Parisian restaurant Maxim's, where his name became associated with his favorite mussel soup.

biltong - a narrow strip of meat, dried in the sun, especially beef, venison or ostrich. The name comes from the Afrikaans word for "buttock tongue."

bind - to combine ingredients together by adding beaten egg or a thick **roux**-based sauce, so they do not come apart during cooking.

binder - see LIAISON.

Bing cherry - see CHERRY.

bioengineered foods - also **genetically engineered foods.** Foods whose natural qualities or characteristics have been modified artificially by extracting a specific gene or group of genes and replacing them with genes from another plant or animal. Bioengineered foods are altered to improve their resistance to certain pests and diseases, as well as to change their flavor, texture, perishability or appearance. For example, one type of genetically engineered corn has been given genes from *Bacillus thuringiensis* (Bt), a bacterium that produces a toxin that kills European corn borers, a pest that is the age-old enemy of corn plants and farmers. Canola, corn and soybeans are some of the most common genetically engineered crops in North America. In the U.S., it is estimated that 75 percent of the total soybean crop is grown from genetically modified seeds, as is 32 percent of the total corn crop and 51 percent of the total canola crop.

Although bioengineering sounds like a positive turn of events for agriculture, it has generated an immense amount of opposition and controversy. Many detractors assert that the long-term effects of artificial genetic modification on plants (and on the people and animals who consume them) are unknown and therefore not worth the risk. Some opponents worry about the risks of decreasing the number of species of plants that farmers grow. They worry that without natural variety, a single blight or disease heretofore unknown could decimate the majority of the world's yield of a specific crop, creating famine. These opponents advocate growing and saving **heirloom seeds** and avoiding all genetically modified plants, animals and foods.

biotin - see B VITAMINS.

birch beer - a sweet, carbonated, nonalcoholic beverage made with syrup distilled from the sap of birch trees. Birch syrup tastes similar to **wintergreen** syrup and gives birch beer its distinctive wintergreen flavor. The majority of birch syrup is made in Alaska; it takes thousands of gallons of sap to make a single bottle.

bird - see ROULADE.

birdlime - see MISTLETOE.

bird's eye chile - also **bird chile, Santaka, Thai chile.** This small chile, either red or green, is extremely hot. Tiny and elongated, it has a slightly nutty flavor. See also CHILE PEPPER.

Birdseye, Clarence - see profile right.

bird's nest soup - refers quite literally to its contents, which include the nest of an Asian bird, *Collocalia whiteheadi*, or Whitehead's Swiftlet. The nest is constructed with the bird's own gelatinous saliva (unlike other birds, which build their nests with twigs, grass and mud) after

Birdseye, Clarence (1886–1956) - American inventor of a quick-freezing method for food production, and "the father of frozen food." Brooklyn-born Birdseye was a naturalist employed by the U.S. government and stationed in the Arctic from 1912 to 1915, where he observed how the Eskimo handled their freshly caught fish. Because of the extremely low temperatures, the fish froze so quickly that ice crystals didn't have a chance to form, which left the cellular structure of the flesh intact. He also found that fish caught and frozen mid-winter tasted superior to fish caught and frozen later in the season. He moved to Massachusetts and came up with his double-belt freezer in 1925: two parallel conveyor belts were sprayed with cold brine from above the top belt and from below the bottom belt, which instantly froze the packaged foods passing between them. By 1927, Birdseye had processed one million pounds (500,000 kg) of fish and began considering quick-freezing meat and produce. In 1929, he relinquished all his patents and sold his company to General Foods, which kept his name as part of the trademark but split it into Birds Eye, the brand associated with all forms of frozen foods, from fruits and vegetables to fish, meats and family-size meals.

eating and regurgitating the seaweed **agar-agar** and is harvested, often under perilous conditions, from caves high up in cliffs of Indonesia, Malaysia, Thailand and the Philippines. The finest bring astonishing prices, depending on their quality. The best of all are those called white nests, consisting almost completely of dried spittle and resembling small white cups. Also highly valued are the blood nests, deeply colored because of the minerals consumed by the birds. White or red nests can fetch as much as $200 each. The least expensive are the black nests, because they contain bits of twigs, grasses, leaves and feathers. The Chinese call this soup *yan wo tang*, or "swift nest soup."

Birnenformige salami - a German sausage whose name means "pear-shaped," which is a perfect description of its form.

biryani - also **biriani.** An elaborate dish from India of layered basmati rice pilaf, which can be made with just about anything, from poultry to red meat to fish to vegetables.

biryani curry paste - see CURRY PASTE.

biscotte - the French term for **rusk** or **Zwieback,** a slice of bread or dough cooked until it's dry and hard, the name meaning "twice cooked."

biscotto - pl. **biscotti.** An Italian specialty from the Veneto region, it's a hard-textured sweet cookie that has been baked twice, laced with almond slivers and usually dipped in **vino santo.**

biscuit - originally a French word, meaning "twice cooked" (from *bis*, "twice," and *cuire*, "to cook"). So diverse are the foods now called biscuit in different countries of the world that one can only guess at the composition of the first biscuit. In most European countries, it refers to a sweet confection. In France, "biscuit" is a simple sponge cake or jelly roll, or it may mean ladyfingers (*biscuit à la cuillère*). In Spanish, *bizcocho* is a sponge cake. In England, a biscuit is a hard, thin, flat cookie or cracker. In North America, a biscuit is usually a quick bread, such as a baking powder biscuit or tea biscuit.

biscuit cutter - a tall-sided circle of metal similar in principle to a cookie cutter, with a smooth or wavy edge and a handle on top, used for cutting biscuit dough. This cutter has a sharp edge to cut quickly and cleanly through thick, sticky dough. A dull cutter can squash the edge of a biscuit, which may keep it from rising properly or make the end result tough.

biscuit mix - a mixture of all-purpose flour, baking powder, salt and vegetable shortening that is cut together until smooth and powdery, designed to be mixed with milk, water, eggs

biscotti

and/or other liquid ingredients to make dough for biscuits, pancakes, etc. There are a variety of packaged versions available, but biscuit mix is also easy to make at home from regular baking ingredients. Biscuit mix relies on baking powder as a leavener, which allows baked goods to rise somewhat, but not as high as yeast does.

bishop - **1.** a hot drink made of red wine simmered with a clove-studded orange. See also MULLED WINE. **2.** a modern-day cocktail made with red wine, lemon juice, orange juice and sugar. The orange juice, lemon juice and sugar are shaken until blended and poured into a cocktail glass, then ice is added and the glass is filled with red wine. Some recipes call for a small amount of rum to be floated on top of the drink.

bishop's bread - a sugared bread filled with dried fruit, said to be named when an inspired Kentucky homemaker quickly improvised a recipe for such a loaf when her local clergyman dropped in unexpectedly.

bishop's weed - see AJOWAN.

Bismarck - another name for the cocktail **Black Velvet.**

bismarck - also **Berlin doughnut, long john**. A long, thin jelly-filled doughnut.

Bismarck herring - see HERRING.

bison - also **buffalo.** The American bison, of the genus *Bison*, once existed in enormous numbers on the plains of western North America. Near extinction by the 1890s, it's now protected from hunting. While it still flourished, however, it provided almost complete sustenance to the Plains Indians. Bison are now being farmed, either on their own or bred with beef. Bison meat is much like beef, but surprisingly tender and extremely lean.

bisque - a rich, thick soup, usually made of puréed seafood (especially crayfish or lobster, although sometimes fish is used) and cream.

bissar - **1.** an Algerian dish made of couscous, chicken and vegetables. **2.** Moroccan name for dried **fava** beans.

bistro - a small café serving relatively simple food and wine. The origin of this name is obscure. It first appeared in the French language in 1884, but its etymology is often given as the Russian word *bistro* ("quick"), which the Cossacks used when demanding fast service at bars during the Russian occupation of Paris in 1815. The most likely origin is an abbreviation of the word *bistrouille*, which is used in northern France for a mixture of coffee and brandy; *bis*, meaning "twice," and *touiller*, meaning "to mix."

bitter - **1.** a British golden-brown ale flavored with hops. **2.** see FIVE BASIC TASTES.

bitter almond - see ALMOND.

bitter almond oil - oil extracted from bitter almonds, which has a high concentration of prussic acid, which is considered highly poisonous. In the countries where it's legal to use the oil, it's recommended that it be used only in very limited amounts.

bitterballen - a Dutch ball-shaped meat **croquette,** to which "bitter" does not really apply, as the dish (which is usually served as an appetizer) is rather sweet.

bitter buttons - see TANSY.

bitter herbs - also called *maror* in Yiddish, eaten during the Jewish holiday of Passover, usually horseradish but can also be romaine lettuce, endive or escarole. The ancient Hebrews used cilantro root. They are the symbols of the bitter time the Jews spent in slavery in Egypt.

bitterkoekjespudding - the Dutch version of English plum pudding, made with raisins, fruits, rum or wine and spices, with the addition of crushed macaroons.

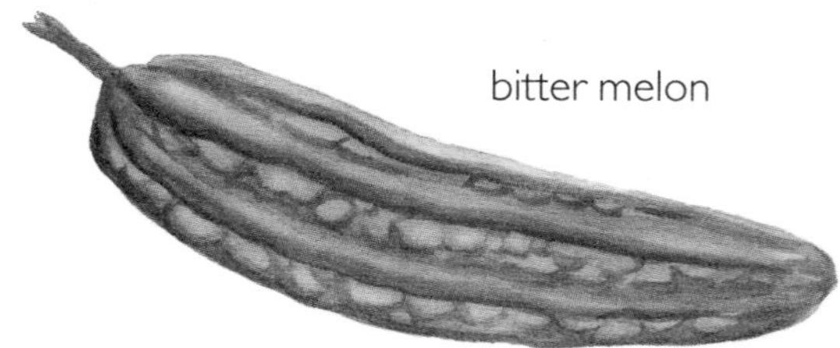

bitter melon

bitter melon - also **balsam pear.** The fruit of a perennial garden plant, *Momordica charantia*, which originated in tropical India. The bitter melon was consumed in Asia for centuries, primarily for its medicinal properties. It belongs to the same family as the pumpkin, melon and cucumber and is grown in the same fashion — on a vine that can reach more than 30 feet (9 m). The fruit itself resembles a cucumber and can grow to approximately 10 inches (25 cm) in length. The pale-greenish skin is not edible; the flesh is thick and fairly dry, with a large number of seeds. The taste is quite astringent due to the **quinine** content; consumption is somewhat limited due to its bitterness. As the fruit matures, it becomes less bitter. You can distinguish the degree of ripeness by the coloration of the skin, which turns yellow or orange with maturity. In Chinese cooking, it's often steamed and then incorporated into soup. In India, it's usually served as a marinated appetizer or incorporated into curries.

bitter orange - see ORANGE.

bitters - a liquid distilled from aromatic herbs, barks, roots and other parts of plants, used to flavor cocktails, apéritifs and foods. They have a high alcohol content and a bitter or bittersweet flavor. See also ANGOSTURA.

bittersweet chocolate - see CHOCOLATE.

bitto - a rich, medium hard cheese from the Valtellina mountain area in the Alps. It has a delicate taste when young with a few holes, within a few years of aging it becomes a good grating cheese.

bivalve - any soft-bodied mollusk that has two shells hinged together by a strong muscle. Clams, oysters and mussels are all bivalves.

bixin - a coloring agent extracted from **achiote seeds** and usually used as a dye for butter and cheese.

bizcochito - a small anise-flavored sugar or shortbread cookie, a traditional accompaniment to **Mexican chocolate.** Bizcochitos are also the official state cookie of New Mexico, adopted in 1989. They are often served at Christmastime, which is a tribute to their origin in Spain, where they were originally reserved for special occasions, such as a baptisms and weddings. The word means "small cake" or "small biscuit" in Spanish.

bizcocho borracho - a Spanish sponge cake, flavored with cinnamon and very generously enhanced with brandy and wine. *Borracho* means "drunk" in Spanish. The name literally means "drunken cake."

blaa - also **bla, blah.** A specialty bread roll from Waterford, Ireland, larger and lighter than a **bap,** dusted on top with flour. Waterford bakers believe that French Huguenots introduced the blaa in the late 17th or early 18th century, perhaps from the crescent shape of the croissant that they brought with them.

blachan - see BALACHAN.

black and tan - also **half and half.** A mixture of half stout or porter and half lager or pale ale. Often the two are simply combined in a tall beer glass, but some pickier drinkers prefer their black and tans poured carefully so that the layers stay separated in the glass, with the pale-color "tan" lager on the bottom and the "black" stout on the top. The terms "black and tan" and "half and half" are often used interchangeably, and there is a great deal of dispute over which brands of beer constitute a "true" version of either, but two classic combinations mix Guinness stout with either Harp Lager or Bass Pale Ale. See also BLACK VELVET.

black bean - also **black turtle bean, turtle bean.** A shiny, black variety of the common bean, *Phaseolus vulgaris*, black beans are tender and sweet-tasting, virtually a staple food in Central and South America.

black bean sauce - a thin, salty sauce made with fermented black beans, flavored with garlic and sometimes also with **star anise.**

blackberry - also **bramble.** A shiny black fruit, *Rubus ulmifolius*, that decorates country hedgerows in late summer and early autumn, the blackberry has been cultivated for more than 100 years in North America, although it is not considered worth the trouble anywhere else in the world. At first, it was called a brambleberry or bramble (as it still is in England) and was regarded as a nuisance, even in the colonies. Beginning in the 1830s, however, it became quite popular and went into pie and the molded

blackberries

dessert **flummery.** Eaten fresh, blackberries make a tart, refreshing dessert, but they are more often preserved as jam or jelly. Blackberries and **dewberries** (two relations of the rose and the raspberry) are virtually indistinguishable; the main differences between them being that blackberries are larger, juicier and slightly sweeter.

black bottom pie - a chilled open-faced pie, usually made with a gingersnap-crumb crust, filled with a layer of chocolate custard, then a layer of rum-flavored custard and topped with whipped cream and shaved chocolate.

black bread - a dark Eastern European, especially Russian, bread usually made with rye flour, yeast or a sourdough starter, and any of a host of other ingredients that give it its dark color and rich, earthy flavor, including chocolate or cocoa powder, beer, molasses or coffee. It is often seasoned with caraway and fennel seeds.

black bun - a traditional Scottish dark fruit cake eaten during Hogmanay (New Year's), consisting of dried and candied fruit, nuts and spices topped with in a rich pastry crust.

black butter - see BEURRE NOIR.

black cake - also **Jamaican fruitcake, rum cake.** A rich, blackish-brown fruitcake made with dark fruits (prunes, dark raisins and currants), dark rum, spices, nuts and mixed candied citrus peel. The cake is often made darker and more flavorful with the addition of dark caramel or **gravy browning.** Black cake is a common Christmas offering in many Caribbean countries and is sometimes covered with **fondant** or icing and served as a wedding cake.

black calypso bean - see CALYPSO BEAN.

black chanterelle - also **black trumpet mushroom, horn of plenty, trompette de la mort, trumpet of death.** A decidedly undeadly edible fungus (*Craterellus fallax* or *C. cornucopioides*), trumpet-shaped with frilly edges at the opening of the trumpet, dark gray to black in color. Despite its name, it is not a member of the chanterelle genus, *Cantharellus*. It has a rich, nutty flavor and can be used in everything from soups to marinades to stuffings. It is available fresh in the fall but can often be found dried in gourmet grocery stores year-round.

black cherry - **1.** a generic and wildly variable name for any variety of dark reddish-purple to black cherries, can be sweet and juicy or sour and acidic. This term is often seen in the names of jams and sweets and is not intended to indicate which particular variety is used. **2.** the fruit of the black cherry tree, *Prunus serotina*, quite acidic and bittersweet, a less-than-pleasant cherry for eating, sometimes used to make wines, jams or pies that are well sweetened.

black chokeberry - see ARONIA.

black cod - see SABLEFISH.

black Corinth grape - see CHAMPAGNE GRAPE.

black cow - any of a variety of sweet soft-drink-based beverages popular in the United States. Most frequently, it means a root beer float, but in some places a chocolate ice cream soda or even a mixture of cola and milk is called by this name.

black currant - see CURRANT.

blackened - a very spicy Cajun method of cooking fish or meat using an extremely hot cast-iron skillet. The combination of the spices rubbed on the flesh before cooking and the temperature at which it's cooked make it very crispy.

black-eyed pea - also **black-eyed bean, cowpea, southernpea.** This small bean is cream-colored, kidney-shaped and characterized by a black dot and a mild flavor. Despite the second part of its name, it's more closely related to the bean than the pea. Native to India and Iran, it is widely consumed in Africa as well. Black-eyed peas require less soaking than most dried beans. In Italy, a famous painting by

black chanterelle

Annibale Carracci (1560–1609), a Bolognese, is called the *Mangiatore di Fagioli*, "the bean eater." It depicts a *contadino*, or farmer, sitting down to eat a big bowl of *fagioli dell'occhio*, "beans with eyes," and is the first ever known painting to feature black-eyed peas.

blackfish - a confusing generic name for a variety of different freshwater fishes, including the Alaska blackfish, *Dallia pectoralis*, which is found in Alaska and the islands in the Bering Sea; the Sacramento blackfish, *Orthodon microlepidotus*, which is found in lakes and rivers in central California and frequently sold in Asian markets in San Francisco; and the black sea bass, Centropristis striata, found along the East Coast. The term blackfish is also applied to certain saltwater fishes, such as the tautog, *Tautoga onitis*, which is found in coastal waters from Nova Scotia to New York, and some small whales.

Black Forest cake - also **Black Forest torte.** A confection of layers of kirsch-flavored chocolate cake, whipped cream and sweetened sour cherries, garnished with chocolate curls and cherries. It has been suggested that it was created in the 1930s in Berlin, but firm evidence is elusive. The name in German is *Schwarzwälder Kirschtorte*.

Black Forest ham - a German smoked ham commonly found at the deli counter in North American supermarkets, traditionally dipped in beef blood and smoked over pine and fir branches to give it its characteristic black rind. The Black Forest ham in most delis these days still has the dark rind, but eschews beef blood in favor of caramel coloring to achieve it.

black forest mushroom - see SHIITAKE.

black fungus - see WOOD EAR.

black grouper - see GROUPER.

black haw - see NANNYBERRY.

blackjack - see BAKER'S CARAMEL.

black lentil - see LENTIL.

black lovage - see ALEXANDERS.

black Mike - a term used by loggers in the northern part of the U.S. for a stew of meat and vegetables.

Black Mission fig - see FIG.

black olive - see OLIVE.

black onion seeds - see NIGELLA SEEDS.

black pepper - see PEPPERCORN.

black pudding - see BLOOD SAUSAGE.

black radish

black radish - a strong-smelling and -tasting radish, *Raphanus sativus niger*, related to both radishes and horseradish, used primarily in European cooking, although it is available through specialty produce markets in North America. It looks like a large black turnip and has a crisp, white interior; its flavor can be assertively horseradish-like.

black rice - see RICE.

black rice vinegar - see RICE VINEGAR.

Black Russian - a cocktail made of two parts vodka and one part Kahlúa, shaken together and poured over ice in an **old-fashioned glass.** A **White Russian** is simply a Black Russian with cream or milk floated on top.

black sea bass - see SEA BASS.

blackstrap molasses - see MOLASSES.

black tea - see TEA.

black trumpet mushroom - see BLACK CHANTERELLE.

black turtle bean - a shiny variety of the common bean, *Phaseolus vulgaris*. Tender, with a sweet flavor, they are a staple food throughout the Caribbean, Central and South America, and Mexico. Fried black beans and rice is the national breakfast dish in Costa Rica, known as *gallo pinto*, while *feijoada completa*, mixed meats and black beans served with **cassava** meal (*farofa*), diced oranges, hot fresh pepper sauce and collard greens, is the national dish of Brazil.

Black Velvet - also **Bismarck.** A cocktail made of equal parts Champagne and stout, the heavier stout poured in first, then the light Champagne poured very carefully over the back of a spoon onto the stout, so that the two form distinct layers and don't mix, served in a Champagne flute. Legend has it that this drink was the favorite libation of German Chancellor Otto von Bismarck. According to the Guinness brewing company, which makes the world-famous Guinness stout, the drink was invented in 1861 on the morning after Prince Albert died. Apparently, Champagne was not a solemn enough breakfast beverage, so it was mixed with Irish stout to create an appropriately somber eye-opener. See also BLACK AND TAN.

black walnut - a native North American nut, *Juglans nigra,* often regarded as the national tree of the United States, although it grows only in the eastern half of the country. The nut has a thick, extremely hard shell, blackish brown in color, which is very difficult to crack without breaking up the kernel.

black walnut

blade apple - see BARBADOS GOOSEBERRY.

blade pot roast - see BEEF.

blade roast - see PORK.

blaff - a classic Caribbean fish dish usually made with a whole red snapper, marinated in a mixture of lime juice and spices, including allspice berries, garlic and chiles. The fish is removed from the marinade, which is combined with water and brought to a boil. The whole fish is then dropped into the resulting bouillon and poached until cooked. The onomatopoeic name comes from the "blaff!" sound that the fish makes when it hits the boiling bouillon.

blah - see BLAA.

blanc de blancs - a white wine made from only white grapes, once a term exclusively applied to Champagne made from Chardonnay grapes but now applied to sparkling and still wines made from any variety of white grape. The name means "white of whites" in French.

blanc de noirs - a white wine made from black grapes (also known as red grapes), whose skins are removed as early in the juicing process as possible so that their pigments do not tint the wine. Blanc de noirs Champagne is made from Pinot Noir or Pinot Meunier grapes. A still wine, such as white Zinfandel, can also be described as a blanc de noirs, although it is pale pink in color. The name means "white of blacks" in French.

blanch - to plunge food into boiling water briefly, usually followed by plunging it into cold water to stop the cooking process, used mostly for vegetables to loosen skin before peeling, to parboil and to remove strong flavors. Vegetables are blanched before freezing to help preserve color and texture. Some foods, such as sweetbreads, are blanched to make them white and firm. Bacon, salt pork, pork rinds, calves' feet, etc., are blanched to remove excess salt and other strong flavors and are often brought to a boil from cold water rather than being plunged directly into boiling water. Blanching times vary according to the type of food.

blancmange - an English molded pudding made with milk, sugar, vanilla and cornstarch, from the French *blanc manger,* meaning "white food." The original recipe, made about the 15th century, was made with chicken, ground almonds, milk, sugar and eggs. It can be traced back to the medieval Arabic kitchen, later to Spain, and then to England, France, Germany and the Nordic countries.

blanquette - a classic white French veal, chicken or lamb stew, with leeks and cream, and finished with egg yolk.

Blarney Stone - a cocktail from the 1920s, originally made with Irish whiskey, curaçao and **absinthe** and named after the famous "wishing stone" at Blarney Castle, which is believed to have been broken from the Scottish Stone of Scone.

blawn fish - a typical British technique of "aging" fish. As soon as the fish is caught, it's hung in a breezy place to get an outdoor flavor from the countryside.

blend - to mix two or more ingredients so thoroughly that each loses its identity.

blender - a small, electric, countertop kitchen appliance that uses a rapidly rotating blade to chop, purée, blend and liquefy foods. See also IMMERSION BLENDER.

blenny - any of a variety of saltwater fishes of the families Blenniidae and Clinidae, some with scales and some with a mucous coating instead of scales. Blenny is delicious fried, thanks to its mild white flesh. The name comes from the Greek *blennos*, meaning "slime," for the slimy coating on the outside of the fish.

blessed trinity - see TRINITY.

bleu - cooked (as in a steak) so rare that it's just warmed through. See also AU BLEU.

bleu cheese - see BLUE CHEESE.

Bleu-d'Auvergne - see AUVERGNE.

Bleu de Bresse - also **Bresse Bleu.** A buttery, French blue cheese made from cow's milk, white with blue pockets of mold instead of veins or streaks. It is mild for a blue cheese, like a creamy **Brie,** but with a pleasant spicy tang from the mold. Bleu de Bresse was developed in the Bresse region of France about the time of the Second World War as an alternative to strong-tasting blue cheeses, such as **Roquefort.** See also BLUE CHEESE.

Bleu des Causses - a French blue cheese made from cow's milk, similar in flavor and appearance to **Roquefort,** moist, spicy and firm-textured or even crumbly. Bleu des Causses, again like Roquefort, is aged in limestone caves, where natural moist breezes keep the cheese at the perfect temperature and circulate the natural molds needed to produce its classic blue cheese flavor. See also BLUE CHEESE.

blewit - an edible mushroom, named for its bluish-violet cast, found under deciduous trees or conifers, as well as in grassy pastures and woods. They appear from October to December and are best fried or baked.

blewit

blind pig - see SPEAKEASY.

blini - small, yeast-raised pancakes usually made with buckwheat flour and served with sour cream and caviar (or smoked salmon). The word "blini" is the plural of "blin," but in conversational English, blini can serve as both singular and plural. Blini are important to Russian cuisine and have a history that extends as far back as the Middle Ages. Blini were particularly significant during the *Maslenitsa* (butter festival), the week before Lent, when they were eaten as a treat twice a day by everyone. In the Middle Ages there were other occasions for eating blini. Three times a year, the middle and lower classes held prayers for the dead, after which they had a ceremonial meal of blini. At funerals, blini, along with boiled wheat and vodka, were consumed beside the grave, and a small offering of each was dispensed into the grave. The word comes from the Yiddish *blintzeh*, meaning "pancake."

blintz - a very thin pancake that is rolled around a sweet or savory filling, such as ricotta cheese, fruit or meat mixtures, from the Yiddish *blintzeh*, meaning "pancake."

blister - a method of removing skins from vegetables, such as peppers and eggplants. The vegetable is placed under a preheated grill (broiler) and turned frequently until the skin blisters and burns. After cooling, the skins of peppers can be rubbed off with a cloth. Eggplant skin needs to be peeled off with a sharp knife. Blistering over charcoal gives the flesh of vegetables a unique smoky flavor.

bloater - see HERRING.

blockwurst - see CERVELAT.

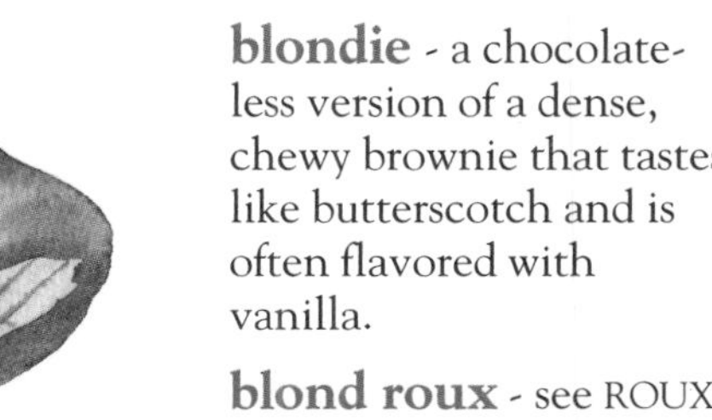

blondie - a chocolate-less version of a dense, chewy brownie that tastes like butterscotch and is often flavored with vanilla.

blond roux - see ROUX.

blood - the fluid that circulates through the veins and arteries of a vertebrate animal, carrying nourishment and oxygen to cells and organs and carrying away waste products for excretion. Blood is a source of food for many cultures, some of whom drink it as is, such as the Masai tribe in Kenya, who regularly consume cow blood in the belief that it makes them strong and powerful. In other cultures, blood is cooked with other foods and is often used as a thickener. **Blood pudding,** also known as blood sausage, is a typical example of this type of cuisine; blood is mixed with rice, meat and spices and stuffed into a casing. Other well-known blood-based sausages are **Blutwurst, boudin noir** and **boudin rouge.** Pig and cow blood are the most common types of blood consumed, but sheep and goat blood are consumed in some areas. Poultry blood is less commonly used, but more-traditional recipes for **coq au vin** call for the sauce to be thickened at the end of cooking with rooster blood. Blood, specifically ox or bull blood, was traditionally used as a **fining** agent to clarify wines, but it is no longer used in most places. Dried bull blood was officially banned as a fining agent at the peak of the **mad cow disease** crisis in Europe.

blood orange - see ORANGE.

blood peach - also **Indian blood peach, Indian cling peach.** An heirloom variety of clingstone peach with dark red skin and juicy red flesh, probably derived from the French Sanguinole variety, famously cultivated by Thomas Jefferson in his experimental garden at Monticello starting in 1807. Blood peaches are a bit tarter than white or yellow peaches, good for eating out of hand, but excellent in sauces, syrups and preserves. See also PEACH.

blood pudding - see BLOOD SAUSAGE.

blood sausage - also **black pudding, blood pudding.** A sausage made of pig's blood, suet, bread crumbs and oatmeal, usually sold precooked, almost black in color.

Bloody Caesar - also **Caesar.** A popular cocktail made with a mixture of clam and tomato juices, vodka, Worcestershire sauce and hot sauce, served in a glass rimmed with a mixture of salt and ground celery seeds and garnished with a celery stick. A fairly recent star in the cocktail galaxy, it was invented in the late 1960s by Walter Chell, a bartender who worked for the Westin hotel chain in Calgary, Alberta, to celebrate the opening of an Italian restaurant. The drink has since become so popular that some call it the national drink of Canada.

Bloody Mary - a cocktail made of tomato juice, vodka, Worcestershire sauce, Tabasco and other seasonings, first made by Pete Petiot, bartender at Harry's New York Bar in Paris in 1921. The name is said to refer to Mary Tudor, Queen of England (the older sister of Elizabeth I), known for her bloody persecution of Protestants.

bloom - **1.** the harmless grayish streaks or patches that form on improperly stored chocolate. There are two types of bloom: fat bloom and sugar bloom. Fat bloom occurs when chocolate is stored at too high a temperature and blotches of whitish cocoa butter form on the surface. Sugar bloom is caused by condensation that forms on the surface of chocolate when it goes rapidly from a cold environment to a warmer one (such as from the refrigerator to the cupboard). The moisture that forms on the surface of the chocolate as it heats up melts some of the sugar inside, which recrystallizes as the condensation evaporates. Neither form of bloom is harmful, but it does affect the appearance of the chocolate. **2.** the velvety, powdery protective coating on the outside of some varieties of grape that keeps diseases at bay and keeps the fruit moist. Bloom is harmless and can be consumed without concern.

blowfish - see PUFFERFISH.

BLT - a classic American sandwich of crisp cooked bacon, lettuce and tomato on toasted white bread spread with mayonnaise. The name is an acronym of "bacon, lettuce and tomato."

blue - see AU BLEU.

blueberry - the most widely distributed fruit in the world, blueberries grow wild in Scandinavia, the British Isles, Russia and North America. They grow in the Arctic regions and are an important part of the Inuit diet. This abundance of wild blueberries is the reason that cultivation started only recently. A New Jersey woman named Elizabeth White deserves most of the credit for "taming" the blueberry. Every year, she offered prizes for the largest wild blueberries. A Department of Agriculture botanist became interested and started crossbreeding the winners in 1909. The result was the superior berries we have today.

blueberry grunt - see GRUNT.

Blue castello - a Danish **triple-crème** soft-textured cheese made from cow's milk.

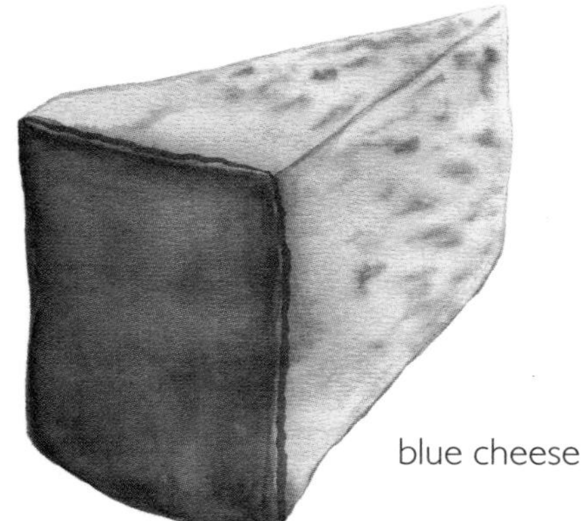
blue cheese

blue cheese - also **bleu cheese.** A class of cheeses injected with mold to form the blue veining that gives them their distinctive flavor. The spelling "bleu" may be an indication of the French imported version, rather than a domestic cheese.

blue Cheshire - a worthy rival to **Stilton,** blue Cheshire is an English semihard cheese made from cow's milk, made into cylindrical shapes. It has a rich taste and is best served as a dessert cheese.

blue corn - any of a variety of corn species that have blue kernels, sometimes so dark that they appear nearly black on the cob. Blue corn has a flavor similar to regular corn, but is slightly sweeter. It can be made into the same types of products, but yields a grainier cornmeal than yellow corn. Blue corn is infrequently seen whole in supermarkets in North America but it is commonly available in the form of blue corn tortillas or tortilla chips. It is used extensively in Mexico and the southwestern U.S., made into a variety of dishes, such as **atole** and **chicos,** and traditional flatbreads. See also CORN.

blue crab - see CRAB.

blue curaçao - see CURAÇAO.

blue Dorset - also **blue Vinney.** An aged, chalk-white cheese from England, blue Dorset is made from skimmed cow's milk and has a horizontal streak of bright blue through the center.

bluefin tuna - see TUNA.

bluefish - also related to the **pompano,** with extremely delicate flesh when eaten immediately after it's caught, fairly abundant on the Atlantic coast and easily recognized by its bluish back and silvery belly.

blue huckleberry - see TANGLEBERRY.

Blue Marlin - a cocktail created in the Bahamas that is mixed with blue curaçao, gin, lemon and pineapple juice and peach Schnapps. It's shaken together, then served over ice, garnished with an orange slice.

blue marlin – see MARLIN.

blue pea - one of the tastiest of several varieties of dried peas, *Pisum sativum*, with a floury texture, retaining its shape when cooked.

blue plate special - a menu term for a daily special, usually consisting of an entire meal at one set price.

Bluepoint oyster - also **Atlantic oyster.** See OYSTER.

blue Shropshire - a new arrival among blue cheeses, made into cylindrical shapes, not in Shropshire, England, but in Scotland.

blue Stilton - see STILTON.

blue Vinney - see BLUE DORSET.

blunt - a less-than-positive wine-tasting term for a wine that is high in alcohol, lacking a pleasant aroma and short on the palate. This type of wine is considered unbalanced, without the proper complexity of flavors, **acidity** and sugar.

blush wine - also **rosé wine.** A broad term for wines that are pink, made from red grapes; can be **dry** or sweet. To make blush wines, grapes are crushed and the skins allowed to remain in contact with the juice for a short period of time. Natural pigments called **anthocyanins** in the grape skins tint the juice (if left longer, the wine would become red) and add only a small amount of **tannins.** The term *rosé wine* is the traditional name for this type of wine, but the term *blush wine* has begun to overtake it in some circles. However, some wine experts maintain that there is a difference: blush wines are light-bodied and sweet, such as the light pink ones made from Zinfandel grapes, while rosé wines are drier and darker reddish pink. See also RED WINE, WHITE WINE.

Blutwurst - a spicy, salty, flavorful German blood sausage, usually smoked, made with pork, beef, beef blood and sometimes bits of ham. In some parts of Germany, it is made with horsemeat as well, and it's usually served with sauerkraut. The name comes from the German blut, meaning "blood," and wurst, meaning "sausage."

boar - very popular in European and Russian cooking, the European wild boar (*Sus scrofa*), although plentiful on the Continent and in some parts of America, is still best known for its medieval associations. Only the meat of the young boar is really tender; older animals need to be hung for two or three days and the flesh marinated before cooking. Domesticated boar is available in Europe and North America through gourmet purveyors, often made into **prosciutto** and sausages.

boba ice tea - see BUBBLE TEA.

bobotee - a very spicy, American pudding-like dish made of milk, bread crumbs, almonds and onions.

bobotie - a popular South African baked dish of ground beef or lamb with bread, rice or mashed potatoes, as well as onions, garlic and curry, all blended together with an egg-and-milk sauce. The dish is served cut into wedges.

bobwhite

bobwhite - any bird of the quail genus *Colinus*, the most popular being *C. virginianus*, which is the most commonly hunted type of quail in the eastern and central United States. *C. virginianus* is also traditionally hunted in Ontario, Canada, but was listed as an endangered species in 2003.

bocconcini - small, round balls of fresh mozzarella cheese, about 1 inch (2.5 cm) in diameter, from *bocca*, Italian for "mouth," into which one fits perfectly.

bock - see BEER.

Bockwurst - an uncooked, mild German sausage made with ground veal (or a mixture of veal and pork), milk and eggs and seasoned with parsley and chives, pale cream in color and highly perishable, so it must be cooked thoroughly and immediately. It can be boiled or grilled and is often served with sweet mustard.

Bocuse, Paul - see profile right.

bodega - the Spanish name for a wine store or cellar, adopted in many lands for wine bars and cellars.

body - a term applied to both food and drink to describe the fullness or richness of its flavor or texture. A full-bodied wine, for example, has a rich, complex flavor and feels pleasant on the tongue.

boeuf à la mode - see À LA MODE.

boeuf bourguignonne - see BOURGUIGNONNE, À LA.

Boiardi, Hector - see CHEF BOYARDEE.

boil - to cook foods or liquids at the boiling point, 212°F (100°C).

boiled custard - custard cooked on the top of the stove rather than baked in the oven.

boiled dinner - see NEW ENGLAND BOILED DINNER.

boiled ham - a mildly flavored, boned ham that is boiled until fully cooked, usually thinly sliced and sold in the deli section of the supermarket. Ham can certainly be boiled at home, often with herbs or spices to give it more flavor.

boiled icing - a fluffy frosting made by whipping hot sugar syrup into beaten egg whites. An Italian meringue is made in the same way.

boiled sweets - a term used in the United Kingdom for hard, translucent candies made by boiling sugar solutions.

boilermaker - a shot of whiskey followed by a cold beer chaser.

boiling firepot - see MONGOLIAN HOTPOT.

boiling-water canner - see CANNER.

Bocuse, Paul (1926–) - French chef and chief proponent of **nouvelle cuisine.** Bocuse was born just outside Lyon, into a lineage of chefs dating back to the 17th century. He began his apprenticeship in the middle of the Second World War, with an interruption in 1944, when he enlisted in the army. He was shot while in Alsace, but not so badly injured that he couldn't celebrate the war's end in Paris a year later. Bocuse then began to cook in earnest and finished his apprenticeship at La Pyramide in Vienne under **Fernand Point,** his culinary master and a mentor to a generation of acclaimed chefs. In 1959, with a solid culinary education and some life experience under his belt, Bocuse returned to the family home and took over his father's suburban café. He transformed it into L'Auberge de Collonges-au-Mont-d'Or, and in recognition of his talent and skill, Michelin awarded him a star in 1961, a second star a year later and his third in 1965. Bocuse has maintained his three-star status for more than 40 years.

During the 1970s, Bocuse became associated with what came to be called nouvelle cuisine, a term coined by *Le Nouveau Guide,* a food and wine magazine whose sensibility was inspired by a new wave of culture sweeping France. The magazine cited Bocuse and 48 other chefs of the day, as creators of a new style of noteworthy cooking, using lighter ingredients and techniques, which revealed more of the food's true flavor. French President Valéry Giscard d'Estaing awarded Bocuse the Legion of Honor in 1975. A year later, Bocuse published *La Cuisine du marché* (Market Cuisine), his best-known book.

For the next 10 years, Bocuse enjoyed both critical and commercial success. He bought a vineyard and created a line of food products, wines and spirits, which became very popular in Japan. He recorded 70 cooking programs for German television and established a school of culinary arts, and hotel and restaurant management. In 1987, he launched the Bocuse d'Or, an international chef's competition, which established a world standard of accomplishment in culinary skill and technique.

During his late 60s and into his early 70s, Bocuse opened four new restaurants in Lyon and travels the world as an ambassador for the Cuisinart brand. He likes to boast that his family has lived in the same village since 1765, emphasizing the importance of tradition and *terroir* in his life and work. He is a serious motorcycle enthusiast. As recently as 2003, when he was 77, Bocuse claimed that he never missed the annual Bike Week in Daytona, Florida.

bok choy - also **bok choi, celery mustard, Chinese chard, Chinese white cabbage, choy sum, pak choi, pak choy.** A mild leafy vegetable with crunchy stalks and tender, dark green leaves, bok choy originated in China or East Asia. Its name translates literally as "white vegetable" because of its white bulbous stalk. There are at least 33 different varieties of bok choy, most of them totally unknown in the U.S. Although consumed for thousands of years in China, it has only been known in Europe since the 18th century. Chinese workers who participated in the Gold Rush at the end of the 19th century were the first to introduce bok choy to the U.S. It can be eaten raw, cooked, fried or marinated, but overcooking will wilt the leaves and ruin this beautiful vegetable.

Bo Lei - see TEA.

boletus - also **cep, cèpe.** A superior-tasting mushroom, *Boletus edulis,* widely eaten in Europe. Found in woodland clearings in late summer and autumn, usually under coniferous trees, they are distinguished by their stout stalks, with delicate, raised white veins running toward the top and the vertical tubes underneath the

bok choy

cap, in which the brown spores are produced. See also CEP, PORCINI.

bollito misto - a dish made with a variety of meats (usually veal, chicken, beef and/or sausage, such as **cotechino**), boiled together in a flavorful broth and served with a spicy green sauce made of anchovies, parsley, garlic, capers, olive oil and vinegar. The dish is especially popular in the Piedmont, Emilia and Lombardy regions of Italy. The name is sometimes loosely translated as "mixed stew" but is closer to "mixed boil," "bollito" meaning "boiled" and "misto" meaning "mixed."

bologna - also **baloney.** This Italian sausage is a specialty of the city of Bologna. It is a fairly large, precooked sausage made of ground pork and chunks of pig fat, seasoned with coriander, pistachio and white wine. See also MORTADELLA.

bolognese - also **ragù.** The term applies to several dishes inspired by Italian cookery, especially from Bologna, served with a thick sauce based on beef or veal and vegetables. In Italy, bolognese sauce is known as *ragù*, which is a corruption of the French word **ragoût.**

Bombay duck - also **bummalo, bummalow.** This dish has nothing to do with duck whatsoever, but rather is an Indian specialty with a very misleading name. Bombay duck is actually a small, long, silvery species of fish called *bummalo*, which is scaled, gutted, split, boned, filleted and sun-dried. The fish is native to India, where it's often eaten fresh, but it's better known in its dried form, used as a flavoring in curries.

bombe - a frozen dessert consisting of layers of softened ice cream or sherbet spread into a mold and refrozen. The center of the bombe is often filled with custard and fruit, and the unmolded bombe is often served with a sauce.

bon appétit - a French phrase meaning "good appetite" or, more loosely translated, "dig in" or "enjoy your meal." The phrase was the signature sign-off of American cooking legend **Julia Child,** who introduced 1960s housewives to classical French cooking on her show *The French Chef*.

Bonbel - a brand name for a mild French cow's milk cheese with a delicate buttery flavor, sold coated with red wax. Smaller versions, under the brand name Babybel, are widely available across North America.

bonbon - the name comes from the French *bon*, meaning "good." In North America, it's a piece of candy, specifically one having a center of **fondant,** fruit or nuts and coated with chocolate. In France, a bonbon is a small, hard candy.

bonboniere - a small gift of sweets given to guests at a wedding reception. The word comes from the Italian for the delicate porcelain or silver container that traditionally held the gift of **confetti** for wedding guests. Today, the word is used interchangeably for the container or the contents, and is sometimes applied to non-food favors as well.

Bondon - a French soft cheese from Normandy made from cow's milk.

Bondost - also **Bundost.** From Sweden, this well-known firm, mellow cheese is made of cow's milk, flavored with caraway and cumin. A similar Bondost is now made in Wisconsin.

bone - also **debone.** To remove the bones from meat, fowl or fish.

bone marrow - see MARROW.

boniato - also **batata, batata dulce, batiste, camote, Cuban sweet potato, tropical sweet potato**. A tropical sweet potato, *Ipomoea batatas*, with a dark reddish peel and white flesh, something like a cross between a baking potato and a sweet potato, with a fluffy, starchy texture and a nutty flavor similar to that of chestnuts. The boniato is larger than a sweet potato but smaller than the largest yams and can often serve more than one person. It is popular in Caribbean and South American cuisine and is slowly becoming a more frequent sight on American tables, especially in south Florida, where there is a large Hispanic and Caribbean population, which favors the tuber.

boniato

boning knife - a knife with a slim 6- to 8-inch (15 to 20 cm) curved blade used for cutting raw meat away from bones. The curved tip and bottom allow the knife to move through the meat and around the bones more easily than a wide straight-edged knife.

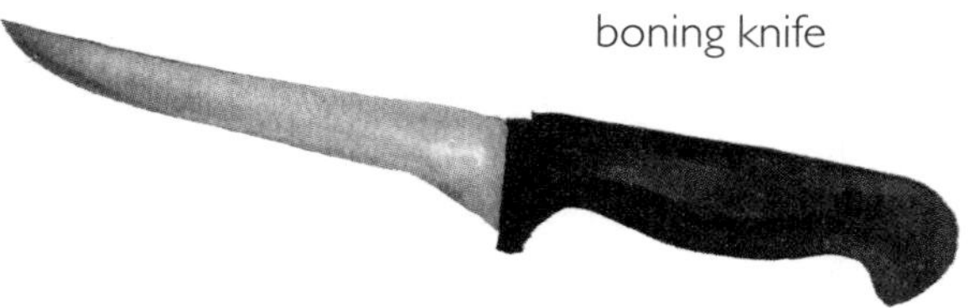
boning knife

bonito - a small, white member of the tuna family, used almost exclusively in Japanese cooking, dried, salted or flaked, used to make **dashi.**

bonnyclabber - see CLABBER.

boova shenkel - an Amish specialty that takes its roots from a centuries-old German recipe, a stew of beef and potato dumplings.

booya - also **booyah.** A Midwestern, specifically Minnesota and Wisconsin, tradition, a thick stew based on chicken, beef (often including **oxtails)** and a variety of vegetables, usually cooked outdoors in huge kettles over an open fire or an enormous gas burner for a crowd (and sometimes stirred with a canoe paddle). The word "booya" tends to describe both the stew and the party at which it's served, and rumor has it that the term is a derivative of the French verb *bouiller*, meaning "to boil," or a shortened form, **bouillabaisse**. Booya is often made for large-scale fundraisers, frequently by the local fire department, which minds the less-than-safe burners.

booze - slang for alcoholic beverages, usually liquor, as opposed to beer or wine. Booze was originally a verb, not a noun, in Middle English, meaning "to drink alcohol." The English borrowed the word directly from the Dutch *busen*, which means "to drink to excess," which the Dutch likely borrowed from the Middle High German *busen*, meaning "to carouse or revel."

borage - a European herb, *Borago officinalis*. Every bit of borage tastes like cucumber — the stems, the fuzzy greenish gray leaves, even the bright blue flowers — and it's easy to understand its medieval reputation for making people happy. The tradition a few centuries ago was to smuggle borage into the drinks of prospective husbands to give them the courage to propose. Roman historian **Pliny** called it *euphorinum* and recommended its use as an antidepressant. The Greek physician Dioscorides (AD 40–90) wrote in his *De Materia Medica* (On Medical Matters) that one should take borage to "cheer the heart and lift the depressed spirits." Romans soldiers used to say "*Ego borago gaudia semper ago*." English herbalist **John Gerard**'s translation is: "Borage always brings me courage," which is a fairly loose translation since the Latin word *gaudia* means "delight," not "bravery." Francis Bacon wrote, "The leaf of Burrage hath an excellent spirit to repress the fuliginous vapor of dusky melancholie."

Bordeaux - the red and white wines from the wine-producing region surrounding the French southwestern port city of the same name. The reds are made from Cabernet Sauvignon, Cabernet Franc, Merlot, Malbec, Petit Verdot and Carmenere grapes **varietal,** while the whites are made from Sémillon, Sauvignon Blanc and Muscadelle. The finest Bordeaux, both red and white, carry the name and label of a particular château, such as Château Ausone, Château Cheval-Blanc, Château d'Yquem, Château Haut-Brion, etc.

Bordeaux mustard - see MUSTARD.

bordelaise sauce - a French sauce made with red or white wine, brown stock, bone marrow, shallots and parsley, usually served with grilled meats.

Borden, Gail - see profile on page 96.

borage

Borden, Gail (1801–1874) - American businessman and inventor of the process used to condense milk. As a boy, Borden learned to be a surveyor while moving west with his family from their home state of New York. At 28, he went to Texas, where he farmed, raised cattle and drafted the state's first topographical map. He invented a "meat biscuit" made with dehydrated meat and flour, which he was unable to market successfully. In 1856, he patented his process and formed the New York Condensed Milk Company a year later. He finally became successful during the Civil War, where he found a ready market for his product. The company was later known as Borden Inc., an international dairy, food, chemical and packaging conglomerate. The Texas town where Borden died and its surrounding county were named after him. See also CONDENSED MILK.

borecole - a variety of kale that can grow up to 6 feet (1.8 m) high, from the Dutch *boerenkool,* meaning "peasant's cabbage."

Boré, Jean Étienne - see profile below.

börek - also **burek.** This family of Middle Eastern pastries consist of phyllo or puff pastry wrapped around a variety of fillings, including cheese, spinach, ground meat and potatoes.

borghol - see BULGUR.

borjúpaprikás - a Hungarian veal **fricassée,** with onions, red pepper, tomatoes, garlic and, of course, the beautiful Hungarian reddish paprika.

Borlaug, Norman Ernest - see profile right.

borlotti bean - also **saligia bean.** A pinkish Italian bean variety, similar in appearance to the **cranberry bean,** except that its coloring is burgundy, with similar red speckles, usually baked in spicy casseroles or served cold in salads. See also LAMON BEAN.

borlotti beans

borscht - also **borsch.** This is the national beet soup of Poland and some of the western provinces of Russia as well. There are many ways of making borscht, but two ingredients are indispensable: beets and sour cream. In Germany, it's called *Beetensuppe*.

Bosc pear - see PEAR.

Boston baked beans - see BAKED BEANS.

Boston brown bread - a rich rye bread made with molasses, often containing raisins.

Boston bun - a sweet yeast bun made with sultanas, currants and spices (such as cinnamon and nutmeg), topped with icing and pressed in desiccated coconut, a common treat in Australia and New Zealand. The frosting is frequently dyed bright pink, thanks to food coloring or, occasionally, raspberry flavoring. Served as a snack or a sweet accompaniment to a cup of tea, the bun is often split open and buttered. The origin of the name is unclear: if there is a tie to the city of Boston, it is not well documented. One source claims that the bun was created in the U.S. in the 1700s, but other sources do not corroborate the link. To add further confusion, the bun is sometimes called by the name **Sally Lunn** in New Zealand, although it is not the same as the Sally Lunns that most North Americans know.

Boré, Jean Étienne (1741–1820) - founder of the Louisiana sugar industry. Born in America into a noble French family and educated in France, Boré spent 10 years in service to Louis XV before returning to the U.S. to farm indigo in Louisiana. He switched to sugarcane when pests wiped out his indigo crops in the mid-1790s. Boré perfected the process of making granulated sugar, which made him very wealthy. He was Mayor of New Orleans from 1803 to 1804.

Boston cracker - a biscuit usually served with cheese, a little bit larger than the common cracker, thinner and slightly sweeter.

Boston cream pie - a chocolate-covered pound cake with a custard or cream filling.

Boston lettuce - see LETTUCE.

Botany Bay greens - see NEW ZEALAND SPINACH.

Botrytis cinerea - also **noble rot.** A gray mold that affects grapes on the vine. Under the right climatic conditions, the fungus causes the grapes to shrivel and concentrates their flavor and sugar. Under humid conditions, it causes the disastrous botrytis bunch rot, which can ruin an entire crop. Noble rot is called *pourriture noble* in French and *Edelfaule* in German and is responsible for the creation of some of the world's finest sweet wines, including the French **Sauternes,** the German **Beerenauslese** and **Trockenbeerenauslese** wines, and California late-harvest wines.

bottarga - a type of caviar, a silver mullet or tuna roe sack that is salted, sun-dried and pressed into a sausage shape, golden to reddish brown in color and strongly flavored. Unlike most other types of caviar, which are served loose, this pressed roe is usually sliced and served like sausage, often as an appetizer with a drizzle of olive oil and lemon juice on top of crackers or small toasts. Bottarga is a specialty of southern Italy, in particular Sicily and Sardinia. See also CAVIAR.

bottle - a glass or plastic container for storing liquids, including wine. In ancient times, wine was stored and transported in **amphorae.** The cask, supposedly invented by the Gauls, was a significant improvement. Small quantities of wine were transported in goatskins known as *boutiaux* or *boutilles* (from the medieval Latin *butticula,* meaning "small cask"), and this probably was the origin of the word "bottle." Long-term storage in glass bottles did not become prevalent until the 18th century.

bottle-aged - a term used to describe a wine that has been aged in its own bottle rather than in a large tank or barrel, giving the finished product a more complex flavor. People who cellar their wines for long periods of time are bottle-aging them, allowing them to mature and become mellower and richer as they age. See also BARREL-AGED.

Bottled-in-Bond - a term used in the U.S. on North American whiskey or bourbon labels that indicates that the liquor is 100 **proof** (50 percent alcohol), produced by a single distiller, and aged for at least four years in a bonded warehouse under the watchful eye of government agents. By aging their whiskey or bourbon in these warehouses, producers avoid paying taxes until the finished bottles are sold and shipped to a retailer.

bottle fermentation - see MÉTHODE CHAMPENOISE.

bottle gourd - also **calabash, cucuzza, upo.** Any of a number of edible gourds, *Lagenaria siceraria,* with a medium-green to yellow inedible peel, a member of the Cucurbitaceae family. The bottle gourd has mild flesh, similar to the zucchini, to which it bears a distant resemblance, and can be eaten cooked or raw. The greens of the plant are also edible, although they have a bitter undertone.

Thanks to their tough rinds, bottle gourds are often hollowed out and dried for use as

Borlaug, Norman Ernest (1914–) American agricultural scientist and developer of new strains of wheat. Three years after earning his doctorate in plant pathology from the University of Minnesota, Borlaug was appointed director of a wheat research project in Mexico, co-founded by the Mexican government and the Rockefeller Foundation. He developed a high-yield, disease-resistant wheat that increased Mexico's harvest threefold. The wheat was exported to Pakistan and India in the mid-1960s, significantly increasing yields for both countries. He later developed **triticale,** a wheat-rye hybrid, which created agricultural self-sufficiency for many developing countries. For the humanitarian benefit of advancing agricultural technology, Borlaug was awarded the Nobel Peace Prize in 1970.

containers. Because they can grow a long, slim neck, they have long been used as bottles — hence their name. Interestingly, strings or bands can be tied around the gourds as they grow, encouraging them to form curved shapes or even knots in the long necks. In Asia, bottle gourds are often used as decorations, painted intricately or formed into whimsical shapes as they grow. Perhaps the most interesting non-food use for a member of the bottle gourd family is as the only clothing item worn by Dani tribesmen in rural West Papua, New Guinea. These "modesty gourds" are grown quite long, often decorated with flowers, bells or shells, and tied on with cords around the waist so that they jut out at an angle.

The Italian cucuzza, *Lagenaria siceraria* 'Longissima', is a long, thin, curved version of the bottle gourd, the name often shortened to *suzza* or *zuzza*. The Philippine name for the gourd, *upo*, is increasingly seen in North American grocery stores.

bottle gourd

bottle opener - any of a number of differently shaped utensils used for pulling off the sealed metal caps on the tops of glass beer and soft drink bottles. Bottle openers are often combination tools, some with a sharp pointed end for piercing tin cans of condensed milk or the like and a rounded end with a small metal lip used to pry off bottle caps. They are sometimes referred to (especially in the context of drinking beer) by the humorous slang nickname "church keys."

bottle stink - an unpleasant, stale smell, often described as similar to that of rotten eggs, that some bottles of wine emit when they are uncorked. Wines, especially white wines, that are treated with sulfur dioxide to keep them slightly sweet or to preserve them, build up these smelly compounds in the air space between the wine and the bottom of the cork. Bottle stink does not reduce the quality or enjoyment of the wine, because it tends to dissipate quickly after the wine is exposed to air. It should not be confused with the bad smell emitted by a **corked** wine, which tends to get worse the longer the wine sits.

bottom round - see BEEF.

botulism - a rare but dangerous form of food poisoning caused by the bacterium *Clostridium botulinum*. Since it was first recognized in people who had endured the hardship of eating spoiled sausage, the name for this form of food poisoning comes from the Latin word for "sausage," *botulus*. The diminutive of *botulus* is *botellus*, which became the Latin word for not only a "small sausage," but also the "small intestine" used to wrap sausage. The sausage word *botellus* finally wound up, as it were, in the English word "bowels." *Botellus* also gave rise to the Old French word for "blood sausage," *boudin*, which in turn gave way to the English word "pudding," which was first applied to sausages. Later, "pudding" came to mean any of numerous dishes boiled or steamed in a sausage-shaped bag or cloth and, in time, to designate a multiplicity of soft foods.

bouchée - a small filled pastry shell, similar to **vol-au-vent,** but bite-size, as a canapé, and eaten as a finger food, from the French *bouche*, meaning "mouth."

boucher - **1.** French for "butcher." **2.** person, often a butcher, in a professional kitchen who cuts meat, bones and poultry, and may also purchase meat. See also BRIGADE SYSTEM, CHEF, ENTREMETIER, ESCOFFIER, GARDE MANGER, PASTRY CHEF, POISSONIER, RÔTISSEUR, SAUCIER, SOUS CHEF, TOURNANT.

Bouchet - see CABERNET FRANC.

boudin blanc - **1.** a fine-textured, cooked French sausage made with a paste of ground poultry, veal or lean pork mixed with cream, eggs and mild spices. Its name means "white pudding" in French, because of its pale color. **2.** also **white boudin.** A Louisiana Cajun sausage of pork, rice and onion, not as fine-textured as the French boudin blanc, thanks to the rice, which acts as a chewy filler.

boudin noir - the French name for blood sausage.

boudin rouge - a Cajun version of blood sausage, made with fresh pig blood and rice, usually quite spicy, with cayenne pepper. It is hard to find this typical Louisiana sausage because of the pig blood it contains: it must be consumed almost immediately because it does not keep well. See also BLOOD SAUSAGE.

bouillabaisse - a seafood stew originating in Provence, consisting of a mixture of fish and shellfish, onions, tomatoes, white wine, olive oil, garlic, saffron and herbs. The word is a contraction of two verbs, *bouillir* ("to boil") and *abaisser* ("to reduce"), and, in fact, bouillabaisse is more a method of rapid cooking than an actual recipe. The name first appears in the French dictionary *Littre* in 1883 as *bouillon abaissé*, literally "broth lowered." The freshwater version is called *Matelote de poisson*. Fishermen, who used a large cauldron over a wood fire to cook the fish that was least appropriate for the market, originally made bouillabaisse on the beach.

bouillabaisse

bouilli - a classic Cajun soup, a specialty of many restaurants in New Orleans, almost like a stew made with beef offal **(variety meat).**

bouillon - a French term for a clear stock made by boiling bones and meat with vegetables and herbs for one or two hours, then strained and clarified. The word comes from *bouilli*, meaning "boiled." The distinction between a bouillon and a consommé is merely that the ingredients of the latter are browned before simmering.

bouillon cube - a compressed and concentrated cube of dehydrated chicken, beef or vegetable stock that must be dissolved in hot liquid before using. **Julius Maggi,** a Swiss flour manufacturer, brought bouillon cubes to the market in 1882.

boula-boula soup - a combination of green pea soup and canned green turtle soup enriched with sherry and served with a dollop of whipped cream, legendarily served at state dinners in the White House during the Kennedy administration in the 1960s and alleged to be a personal favorite of First Lady Jacqueline Kennedy. The name of the soup was supposedly inspired by the lyrics of the Yale University fight song.

boulangerie - the French word for bakery. The term is the root of several French baking-related words, including *boulanger,* meaning "baker," and *à la boulangère*, a term for roasted or baked foods, such as meat roasted over a layer of potatoes and onions.

boule - also **miche.** A round loaf of bread, from the French *boule*, meaning "ball." **Artisanal** bakers often use this term for a dense, crusty, country-style round loaf of white bread. The term *miche* is often used interchangeably but is technically a round sourdough loaf.

boulette - the French term for a small hand-formed patty, usually of ground meat, **pâté** or puréed potatoes, often pan-fried or seared until crisp. The term is the diminutive of the French *boule*, meaning "ball."

bounce - a popular beverage in Colonial America made with rum or brandy, fruit, sugar and spices, fermented for several days or weeks. Cherry bounce was particularly popular and, in its time, was rumored to be an antidote to women's monthly "troubles."

bounceberry - a synonym for cranberry, so called because ripe cranberries bounce when dropped on a hard surface.

bouquet - the **nose** of mature wine characteristic of its maturation. The word "aroma" refers to the nose of a young wine.

bouquet garni - a bundle of herbs tied together with kitchen string (usually a few sprigs of parsley, a sprig of thyme and a bay leaf), used to flavor stocks, soups and stews. You can also tie them around a piece of celery or inside a pouch of cheesecloth, or even poke the herbs into a tea ball. The name has been used in French cooking since the 17th century. This mixture of herbs was created to move away from the use of heavy and expensive medieval spices. Author of *Le Cuisinier,* Pierre de Lune, in 1656, described a

bouquet garni

bouquet garni as "a strip of bacon, chives, thyme, cloves, chervil and parsley."

bouquetière - a garnish of vegetables that have been arranged with some flair (usually around meat), as if in a bouquet. *Bouquetière* is French, meaning "flower girl."

bouquette - a Belgian specialty of buckwheat pancakes, usually served as dessert.

bourani esfenaj - an Iranian starter of cooked spinach, fried onions and garlic mixed with yogurt.

bourbon - America's only native spirit, this whiskey was distilled in Kentucky more than 200 years ago at Elijah Craig's mill in Georgetown, Bourbon County, hence its name. It was called *Bourbon County Whiskey* at first and the name *Bourbon Whiskey* has been used ever since for whiskey distilled wholly or chiefly from corn. Bourbon is a part of the larger category of grain spirits known as whiskey. It must be made from a minimum of 51 percent corn, balanced with malted barley and either rye or wheat, then aged for a minimum of two years, only in brand-new American oak barrels that are heavily charred or toasted on the inside to a depth of about 1⁄4 inch (1 cm), which allows the spirit freer access to the vanillin and tannins in the wood. No one knows for certain where the charring practice came from, but it appears that it was the outcome of a happy accident. Contrary to popular belief, bourbon can be made in any state in the U.S., not just Kentucky.

bourguignonne, à la - a French term meaning "from or in the style of Burgundy," usually referring to meat (especially beef) braised in red wine with white onions and small mushrooms.

bourride - a Provençal version of **bouillabaisse,** thickened and flavored with **aïoli** and served with bread.

Boursault - a French triple-cream cheese with a soft, white rind and a rich, nutty flavor.

Boursin - a French triple-cream cheese, soft and delicate, which can be used as a spread. Boursin is a fairly new addition to the vast menu of cheeses. It's not an **artisanal** product but rather made in large, modern factories.

boutargue - also **Mediterranean caviar.** An expensive French delicacy from Martigues, a town on the outskirts of Marseilles. It's the intact membrane of the egg pocket of the gray mullet, pressed, salted and sun-dried. It probably originated in Tunisia, where it's still very popular; the Arabs brought it with them during their conquest of Spain, Sicily, Sardinia and Italy. In these areas, it is called *bottarga,* but in Old Provençal it's called *boutargo.* Traditionally, it's eaten over slightly toasted bread with olive oil and lemon juice.

bovine growth hormone (BGH, rBGH) - also **recombinant bovine somatotropin (rbST).** A synthetic hormone developed by the biotechnology company Monsanto, which increases the milk output of cows by 20 to 25 percent, legal for use in the U.S. but banned in Canada and Europe, as well as voluntarily by many dairy co-operatives and farmers in the United States. When the hormone was approved in the U.S. in 1993, it started a tidal wave of controversy. The U.S. Food and Drug Administration and Monsanto maintain that their studies show that milk from cows injected with BGH (known under the trade name of Posilac) is perfectly safe for human consumption. The Canadian and European governments — plus many small-scale, local farmers and dairy co-ops in the U.S. — maintain that the synthetic hormone's negative effects on the animals is too high a price to pay for the increase in milk (cows given BGH have, in some studies, been at higher risk of mastitis and lameness, leading to their early culling from dairy herds). They also maintain that the hormone's effects on consumers have not been studied for a long enough period to deem the chemical safe.

bovine spongiform encephalopathy - see MAD COW DISEASE.

Bovril - a concentrated meat broth, reduced to a thick, dark brown, salty paste or cube. Bovril is considered a British classic, but it has a French and Canadian connection. The French, at war in 1870 against the Germans, ordered millions of cans of beef to feed the troops. The contract went to a Scot named John Lawson Johnston. Undeterred by a short supply of beef in Britain, Mr. Johnston traveled to Canada to develop his new product, then known as Johnston's Fluid Beef. He returned to London in 1884 and the Bovril Company was formed in 1901. Johnston concocted the name from the first two letters of the Latin word for beef "Bōs" and "Vril," meaning "an electric fluid."

box grater - see GRATER.

boxty - an Irish potato bread made with grated raw potatoes, mashed potatoes and flour. The name likely comes from the Gaelic *bacús*, meaning "griddle" or "pan."

boysenberry - a fruit of the genus *Rubus* resembling an oversize raspberry, developed in 1923 by horticulturist Rudolphe Boysen, who crossed the raspberry, blackberry and loganberry to create this wine-red fruit.

boysenberries

braciola - pl. **braciole.** The Italian term for a **roulade.**

Bradenham - a black-skinned English ham, dry cured and then soaked in molasses (which gives it its characteristic black skin), then hung for many months to age.

Braeburn apple - see APPLE.

braendende kaerlighed - a Danish specialty of mashed potato with bacon, literally meaning "burning love."

brain - a type of **variety meat** considered a delicacy by some. Beef, lamb and pork brains are commonly available, but are extremely perishable and therefore best eaten right away. In recent years, beef or calf brains have become taboo at the table, thanks to the threat of **mad cow disease.**

braise - a cooking term meaning to first brown or sear meats or vegetables in a small amount of fat over medium heat in a skillet on the stove top or in the oven, then cook them slowly in a very small amount of liquid in a covered pan. The slow, wet cooking tenderizes, adds flavor and moisturizes the meat. The liquid remaining after cooking may be thickened or reduced to provide a tasty sauce or gravy for the meat. Common liquids to add are a good stock or broth, wine, fruit or vegetable juices or just water.

braising pan - a cooking pan with high sides, a tight-fitting lid and two handles on opposite sides of the pan used for braising meats, poultry, vegetables, etc. A braising pan can be used over direct heat on the stovetop to sear the outside of the food, as in the case of meats and poultry, then transferred directly to the oven to continue cooking slowly. Because it has a large surface area that encourages evaporation, it can also be used to reduce cooking juices into luscious sauces at the end of cooking.

bramble - see BLACKBERRY.

bramble jelly - a jelly made from crab apples and blackberries, a Pennsylvania Dutch specialty.

bramble pie - a deep-dish pie made from wild blackberries, a Pennsylvania Dutch specialty.

Bramley apple - see APPLE.

bran - the outer covering of grains, such as wheat and oats, removed during the milling process. The word "bran" springs from the Middle French word *brenno*, which means "unattested." An earlier Celtic word for bran was *bren*, which meant a broken or split coat of armor, which makes sense when you recognize that bran, in edible form, comes from a split outer cover. Until the 1980s, no one outside Asia had initiated any vital use for **rice bran** with the exception of animal food. But recently, in Louisiana's rice belt, farmers have begun cultivating many new marketable products from rice bran — particularly polyunsaturated oil, which is elevated in vitamin E and fiber and entirely allergen-free. The French call bran *son*, which means "ring," or "cover," while the Germans dub it "*Kleie*," and the Italians *crusca*, which may be translated as "rough stuff." The Spanish call it *salvado*, or "salvation," which illustrates their faith in the nutritional value of bran.

branch water - plain water, as opposed to a carbonated beverage (such as ginger ale or soda water), used as a mixer in an alcoholic mixed drink, such as a **highball.** Used primarily in the southern U.S., this term originally meant the clean, pure water from a creek or stream.

brandade - also **brandade de morue.** A cod preparation originally from Provence, but now associated with Nîmes, made of salt cod cooked on low heat with olive oil and cream or milk, stirred constantly (its consistency is like mashed potatoes) and finished with garlic, lemon and nutmeg. Originally called *branlade*, meaning "something that is pummeled," although that name has disappeared.

Brandenberger, Jacques Edwin - see profile below.

Brandkäse - a German sour-milk cheese whose curd is moistened with beer, mixed with salted butter, then pressed into bricks and afterward ripened in old beer kegs.

Brandon puff - in the U.S., a muffin made with cornmeal and flour.

brandy - a spirit distilled from wine or other fermented fruits, named for the Dutch *brandewijn* and German *Branntwein*, meaning "burnt wine." In 1300, the first brandy was distilled at the 92-year-old Montpellier University by French medical professor Arnaud de Villeneuve.

Brandy Alexander - a rich cocktail made with brandy, **crème de cacao** and cream, shaken well with ice, then poured into a chilled cocktail glass.

brandy butter - the English name for **hard sauce,** traditionally used to garnish plum pudding or mincemeat pie.

brandy extract - an extract made by distilling brandy down to a concentrated essence or by using artificial flavorings, commonly used in baking to give a pronounced brandy flavor (although it can taste obviously fake if artificial flavorings are used to make the extract). Brandy can be substituted for it in baking, but the flavor will be much subtler.

brandy snap - a British **lace cookie,** made with mostly butter and sugar and only a small amount of flour, often flavored with brandy (although not always), ginger and lemon juice. The thin dough is spooned onto a prepared baking sheet and baked until the cookies are browned, crisp and look like lace. They are then removed from the oven and rolled, while still warm, around the handle of a wooden spoon into hollow cylinders and allowed to cool.

brandy snifter - see SNIFTER.

Branston pickle - a pickled assortment of vegetables eaten in Britain with cold meat, cheese and sandwiches, a chutney-like condiment made with cauliflower, rutabaga, carrots, zucchini, dates, tomatoes and spices. Branston pickle is sweet and tangy at the same time, which makes it an excellent complement to other foods. Crosse & Blackwell (now owned by Nestlé) owns the trade name Branston, which it applies to its pickle relish, but the name is often used generically for this type of condiment, and there are a variety of recipes for similar chutneys available on the Internet.

Brandenberger, Jacques Edwin (19th–20th century) - Swiss engineer and inventor of cellophane. Sitting in a restaurant on a lunch break while working in a textile factory, Brandenberg got an idea. He was watching the waiter change a tablecloth after a customer had spilled some wine and wondered if fabric could be made waterproof. Back in the lab, he applied liquid viscose to the fabric, which made the cloth stiff, but the coating peeled off in a transparent film. In 1908, Brandenberger built the first machine for making these transparent sheets, and patented both his machine and the process. Four years later, his product was used in gas masks. In 1923, DuPont bought the North and Central American rights to make and sell cellophane. DuPont scientists made the invention waterproof in 1927.

brasserie - often confused with bistro. Both serve relatively inexpensive food, but a brasserie has greater emphasis on service, while a bistro has a less formal and definitely quicker delivery from kitchen to table. Some brasseries have very elaborate early 19th-century decoration, while others are in the Art Deco style. Another distinguishing characteristic of a brasserie is its capacity to accommodate a large number of people at the same time. The term dates to medieval times and was originally reserved for a place where beer was made, from the French word for beer maker, *brasseur*. Later, it became a term used to designate a place serving food and beer.

brassica - any of various plants of the genus *Brassica*, including cabbage, broccoli, kale, turnip and cauliflower.

Brathering - a cold, German breakfast dish of grilled or fried pickled herring.

Bratwurst - a German style of sausage, either broiled, grilled or fried, made of minced and spiced pork and/or veal.

Braunschweiger - a cooked German **Bratwurst** style of sausage, made of smoked liver and containing eggs and milk.

brawn - see HEAD CHEESE.

brazier - a small bowl filled with hot coals with a wire grate over top, used for lightly cooking or toasting food at the table, commonly seen in the center of a **pupu platter.** The word comes from the Old French brasier, meaning "fire of hot coals."

Brazilian red wine tapioca - see SAGU DE MANDIOCA.

Brazil nut - also **cream nut, para nut.** The seed of a giant tree, *Bertholletia excelsa*. For once, the common name is a good guide. The Brazil nut is native to the Amazon and attempts to cultivate the tree elsewhere have failed. Even in Brazil, there are only a few commercial plantations; most trees remain in the wild. The tree (which starts bearing fruit when 12 to 15 years old) can grow up to 150 feet (45 m) tall and 6 feet (1.8 m) in diameter and bears 12 to 20 seeds in woody pods 6 inches (15 cm) in width. The pods are gathered only after they have fallen to the ground; because they weigh about 5 pounds (2.2 kg), they can be lethal missiles, and

brazil nuts

harvesters must carry shields to protect themselves. Brazil nuts are little consumed in Brazil itself and have been exported since about 1835. Because of their size and high oil content, two Brazil nuts contain as much fat as one egg. They are also rich in sulfur-containing amino acids.

bread - **1.** (n.) a food staple made from flour, water and a leavener. Although the exact origin of bread is unknown, the earliest humans probably made a mash of crushed beechnuts and acorns, mixed it with water and left it to dry in the sun. It's interesting that a flour-and-water mixture is still our first step in bread making and that hundreds of generations have contributed only two revolutionary changes. The first was the switch from beechnuts and acorns to cereals, and the second was the discovery of the **leavening** process.

Some authorities believe leavening took place in the 7th century BC, when the slave of an Athenian magistrate made leavened bread by accident. He left some wheat dough in an earthenware pan and forgot all about it. When he found it, several days later, it had soured, and his impulse was to discard it, but his master was approaching, so he hastily mixed it with some fresh dough he had in reserve. Later, the slave was summoned to the archon, who was pleased by the bread, and he confessed what had happened. The story quickly spread all over Athens, and soon the art of making "Athenian bread" was heralded throughout Greece.

Today, Russia consumes more bread than any other country, more than a pound (500 g) of bread (*khleb*) a day being the national average (in rural areas the amount is probably even higher), although the consumption has declined slightly in recent years. About 200 kinds of bread are made today in Russia, 130 in

Moscow's central bakeries alone. There are black breads and white breads, made of wheat, barley, rye and corn flour and the flour of several other cereal grains. There are even about 20 different kinds of dietetic bread.

The idea that "bread is the staff of life" comes from an English saying that has been traced to 1638, but it's probably older. In recent times, the chief money earner in a family has been called the breadwinner; the economic depression of the 1930s produced breadlines, and in the 1960s bread found a place in the hippie vocabulary as a synonym for money. **2.** (v.) to coat a food, such as vegetables, fish or chicken strips, with flour, beaten eggs and bread crumbs or cracker crumbs before cooking.

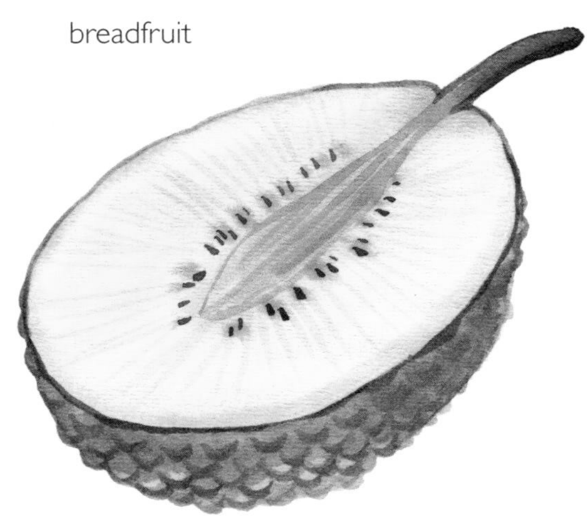

breadfruit

bread-and-butter pickles - sweet pickles made from slices of cucumber, usually pickled with onions and flavored with cloves, mustard and celery seeds, and turmeric.

bread crumbs - small bits of bread, either soft (fresh) or dried, used to coat food or as a topping.

bread dumplings - may be sweet or savory. Bavarian *knödl,* Austrian *knödel,* and the Czech *knedliky* are all made with stale bread or yeast dough. The English Norfolk dumpling falls into this category, being a boiled yeast dough that accompanies meat broths and stews, sometimes served with sugar, honey or treacle as a sweet.

bread flour - see FLOUR.

breadfruit - the large and starchy fruit of a tall tree, *Artocarpus incisa,* native to the Pacific islands, usually boiled, fried or roasted before eating. Breadfruit is also used as livestock feed. We can't think of it without thinking of Capt. William Bligh of *Mutiny on the Bounty*. Bligh had served as sailing master aboard the *Resolution* on the second expedition (1772–1774) of Capt. James Cook; he was called "Breadfruit Bligh" after he discovered the virtues of the melon-size fruit that served as a staple food in Tahiti. (Breadfruit had actually been described earlier, in 1688, by Capt. William Dampier, the English pirate-explorer-navigator, who found it growing in Guam.)

Natives of Polynesia and Malaysia had been eating breadfruit for as long as anyone could remember. *Rima,* as they called it, was often baked whole in the hot embers of a fire; its flesh, when scooped out, tasted like boiled potatoes and sweet milk. Bligh's mission on the *Bounty* in 1787 was to bring specimens of the breadfruit tree to the West Indies as a new source of food for England's colonies in the Caribbean. His purpose was foiled by the mutiny in 1789, but Bligh, although coldhearted, was also indefatigable. Set adrift in a small boat by the mutineers, he reached land after a long voyage, got back to England and, in 1791, set sail once again, this time aboard the *Providence* (accompanied by a tender aptly named *Assistant*). In 1792, Bligh once again loaded his decks with breadfruit plants in Tahiti. This time, he completed his mission, planting 10 of the saplings in St. Helena, in the South Atlantic (later the last place of exile for Napoleon), and hundreds on the islands of St. Vincent and Jamaica. The young trees had to be watered daily on the long sea voyage, even when it meant that the sailors went thirsty.

bread knife - a knife with an 8- to 10-inch (20 to 25 cm) serrated blade made to smoothly and cleanly saw back and forth through bread, without crushing or tearing the hard crust or the soft interior.

bread knife

bread machine - an electric appliance that can be used to mix, knead and bake bread dough without human intervention. Bread machines have a small, usually Teflon-coated, paddle in the bottom of a nonstick baking pan, which stirs and kneads dough according to a computerized setting. Some machines come with timers, which allow them to be set up and left for several hours before they begin the mixing cycle. Most machines also have a dough cycle, which allows the user to shape the dough and bake it in his or her regular oven. When they first arrived on the market, bread machines were only available with tall, square baking pans, so the loaves they made were awkwardly shaped and difficult to slice and use for sandwiches or in toasters. Today's bread machines come with the traditional tall loaf pans or with standard loaf-shaped baking pans for a more "normal" result.

bread pudding - a simple dessert made of chunks of bread soaked in a mixture of milk, eggs, sugar, vanilla and spices, baked and served hot or cold.

bread salad - see PANZANELLA.

bread sauce - a creamy white British sauce made of bread crumbs instead of flour, milk, onions and cream, usually seasoned with cloves, often served with game birds and other poultry.

bread stick - a stick-shaped roll of bread dough baked until crunchy, often served as an appetizer or an accompaniment to soup. Bread sticks can be short and fat or thin and delicate like **grissini.**

breakfast - the first meal of the day, eaten when one gets out of bed.

breakfast teas - see TEA.

bream - also **porgy.** A freshwater or saltwater fish. The freshwater bream, *Abramis*, is a close relative to the carp and has very little gastronomical value. The **sea bream,** also called *Pagellus centrodontus*, common in Alaska and Canada, is a very delicate fish, best from June to December. See also FISH.

breba - a fig of the first annual crop from fig tree varieties that bear fruit twice a year, from the Spanish *breva*. See also FIGS.

Brebichon - also **Brebichon Corsica.** A French sheep's milk cheese made on the island of Corsica, formed into a thick, small wheel with an edible whitish gray rind that often has a bloom of the mold *Penicillium candidum*. The interior is creamy to bright white, and the flavor is sweet and nutty at the same time.

brebis - the French word for a ewe or a sheep's milk cheese.

brèdes - another name for the famous **callaloo** of the British and French West Indies, a stew made with local greens and root vegetables. On some islands, the recipe includes the addition of fish or even pigs' feet. In Latin, the names *bliton* and *blitum* mean "green leaves eaten boiled." In French, the Latin meaning is preserved in *blette* (a name for a green of the Chinese cabbage family), as well as in Spanish, *bledo*, and in Portuguese, *bredo*. In 1998, the food publication *Chauvet* explains that Portuguese sailors, while establishing *comptoirs*, or trading outposts, on the coast of Africa and in the Indian Ocean, applied the name *bredo* to any green vegetable that was eaten boiled, and the name was later altered into regional French and **Creole.**

Bregenwurst - an elongated, thin, smoked sausage made of pig brains, onions, flour and oats, a German specialty of the Black Forest region.

brek - also **brik.** A savory, deep-fried turnover made in Tunisia, consisting of a pastry crust enclosing a filling of ground meat or canned tuna, egg, capers and spices. The egg is cracked over the filling before the pastry is sealed around it, so it cooks to the consistency of a runny fried egg in the boiling olive oil. (Small chicken eggs and quail eggs are best for these turnovers, because a smaller amount of pastry is required to enclose them.) Breks are usually served with

bream

spicy **harissa** or lemon wedges to squeeze over them. The name is a corruption of the Turkish **börek,** meaning "pie."

Bremer Kükenragout - a creamy German **ragoût** of chicken and vegetables.

bresaola - from the mountains of Piedmont in the Italian Alps, a cut of lean tenderloin of beef, dried, then cured with white wine and rubbed with a pickling solution of salt, herbs, garlic and onion. It's usually served in paper-thin slices, typically topped with olive oil, lemon juice and sometimes capers, and is very similar to the *Bündnerfleisch* of Switzerland, which is also called *viande des Grisons*, "meat from the Grisons Mountains." Traditionally, in both countries, the process is started in late autumn and completed during the long winter months.

Brési - also **Breuzi.** Dried, salted beef, smoked for several weeks or months, made in Jura in the Franche-Comté region of France, which borders Switzerland. Brési is typically served in thin slices as an appetizer, or as an accompaniment to **fondue** or **raclette.**

Bresse Bleu - see BLEU DE BRESSE.

Breuzi - see BRÉSI.

brew - **1.** (v.) to steep a solid in a liquid in order to obtain a drinkable solution, such as beer, tea or coffee. To make beer or ale, the process is taken several steps further than simple steeping. The liquid produced by combining barley, yeast, sugar and hops is heated and allowed to ferment until the amount of alcohol and flavors have developed. To brew coffee or tea, the solids (tea leaves or ground coffee) simply need to be infused in hot water to release their flavors and yield the desired beverage. The word is derived from the Middle English *brewen*, which is a descendent of the Old English word *breowan*, meaning "to brew." **2.** (n.) a beverage made by brewing.

brewer's rice - broken grains of rice, not marketable for table use, reserved for beer brewing instead.

brewer's yeast - see YEAST.

brewis - another name for hardtack, or hard bread, a traditional food still consumed in Newfoundland as an accompaniment to salt cod, the dish called simply "fish and brewis." Fish and brewis is made by soaking the cod and the brewis separately, then simmering the fish in fresh water until it is heated through. Then, the soaked brewis is added and the whole dish sprinkled with crisp, fried bits of salt pork called "scrunchions" in the local dialect. The term brewis was originally applied to bread soaked in fat or meat drippings and used as the thickener for a simple broth.

brewpub - a small-scale brewery attached to a restaurant, where most of its beer is sold, often drawn straight from the storage tanks in the brewery. A brewpub becomes a microbrewery if more than 50 percent of its output is sold offsite. Brewpub is a relatively new term, officially recognized in 1984 after the first brewpubs opened in North America.

brickbat - a British cheese made from heavy cream and fresh cow's milk, aged for a full year before being put on the market.

brick cheese - an American cheese first made in Wisconsin about 1870 by a family of German descent, known in the old country as "box cheese." There is some speculation that an actual brick was used to press the cheese into its trademark form. Brick cheese is made with whole milk, has irregular boils, or eyes, and can be considered a semisoft cheese. It's sweet and mild when young, cream-color and firm-textured, and for this short period it belongs with bland cheeses. As it ages it acquires a formidable potency.

bricotta - also **broccio.** It's been said that the chefs of Napoleon Bonaparte always carried with them this superb semisoft cheese from the emperor's native Corsica, a salty sheep's milk cheese blended with sugar (sometimes honey) and rum, usually eaten as a dessert.

bridge mix - a mix of candy, nuts and/or raisins, usually covered with chocolate, traditionally served at bridge parties or other festive occasions.

bridigini - a delicate and elegant anise-flavored cookie from Tuscany.

Brie - a mold-ripened cheese from France made from whole milk; when sliced at room temperature, it refuses to hold its shape and will start running. It's meant to be eaten as it is, center, crust and rind, following the example of Charlemagne, who reportedly enjoyed it most

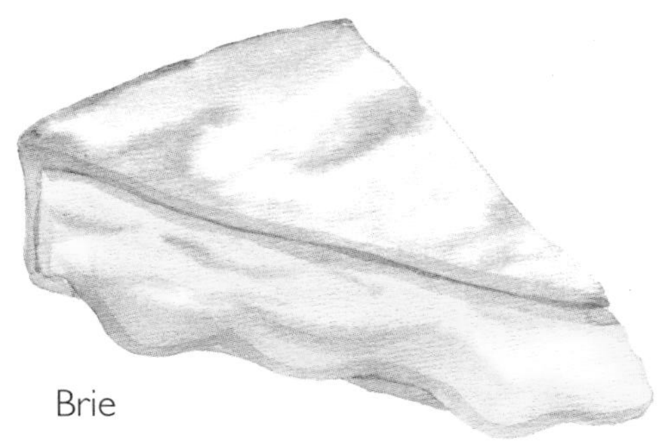
Brie

heartily. It is buttery smooth and white-crusted, as flat as a small pie, with a flavor no words can adequately describe. It's still made in France much as it has been since the 10th century. Since the Middle Ages the milk used to make the cheese was from the Frisonne-Holstein breed (which is no longer the main breed used in this part of France).

The Congress of Vienna officially recognized Brie as a "royal cheese" in 1815, when that august body was presided over by Prince Metternich, with Prince **Talleyrand** among the 30 European ambassadors casting votes in favor. Since then, the famous cheese is commonly known as *roi des fromages* and *fromages des rois* ("king of cheeses" and "cheese of kings"). The most well known is the Brie of Meaux, but the Brie of Melun, the Brie of Montereau and the Brie of Nangis are others worthy of their title.

Brie de Coulommiers - see COULOMMIERS.

brigade system - also **classical brigade.** A system of kitchen organization and hierarchy developed by French chef **Auguste Escoffier** in the late-19th century and still used today. Modeled from his military experience, Escoffier brought order to the professional kitchen, establishing rank, responsibility and the chain of command. The *chef de cuisine* lead the brigade assisted by one or more *sous chefs*, depending on the size of the kitchen, and followed by *chefs de partie*, mid-level chefs who've finished their apprenticeships and are now known as journeyman cooks. The *tournant* is the relief cook, taking a different station daily for that cook's day off. The station chefs are each responsible for specific elements of the meal: the *entremetier* (vegetables and side dishes), *garde manger* (cold food), *grillardin* (broiling), *pâtissier* (pastry), *poissonier* (fish), *rôtisseur* (roasted meats), *saucier* (sauces). The brigade system includes everyone from the *sommelier* (wine steward) to the *chef de salle* (headwaiter) to the dishwashers. See also CHEF, ENTREMETIER, GARDE MANGER, PASTRY CHEF, POISSONIER, RÔTISSEUR, SAUCIER, SOUS CHEF, TOURNANT.

brik - see BREK.

briki - see TURKISH COFFEE.

brill - a flat fish, *Scophthalmus rhombus*, closely related to the **turbot** (sometimes sold as *turbotin*, or small turbot, by unscrupulous fisherman), commonly found in northern European waters and not as delicate as the turbot.

Brillat-Savarin - a French **triple-crème cheese** made from cow's milk, sold in rounds covered with a velvety white rind, with a rich, buttery-soft yellow paste inside. The cheese is named after the famed gastronome **Jean Anthelme Brillat-Savarin.**

Brillat-Savarin, Jean Anthelme - see profile below.

brine - a strong solution of salt and water, with herbs, spices or sugar, to preserve or flavor foods, such as pickles and olives, or to impart flavor, as with corned beef. The name comes from the Anglo-Saxon *bryne*, meaning "burn," referring to its strong and burning taste. A brine mixture is also used to tenderize meat.

Brillat-Savarin, Jean Anthelme (1755–1826) - French country doctor, judge, politician, musician and gourmand, born in the town of Belley in 1755. He wrote a celebrated book about food, *La Physiologie du goût* (The Physiology of Taste), which contains many anecdotes and observations about food including, "Tell me what you eat and I will tell you what you are." He wrote that truffles "can make women tender and men more apt to love." **M.F.K. Fisher** translated the English version of the book, which also includes her commentary. One of the famous triple-créme cheeses (Brillat-Savarin) and a pastry (savarin) are named for him.

brinza - also **bryndza.** A soft, buttery cheese sometimes used as a basis for **Liptauer** spread, brinza is made in Hungary, Romania and in the Carpathian Mountains from goat or sheep's milk.

brioche - a sweet bread made with eggs and butter. *"Qu'ils mangent de la brioche,"* or "Let them eat cake," was Marie Antoinette's infamous outburst when told the people of Paris were rioting in the streets because they had no bread. Brioche was much more expensive then the daily regular bread of the common people. Her comment infuriated the populace, adding to their rage against the monarchy. The origin of the name is from the French *broyer,* meaning "to break up, to grind or to crush," referring to the extended kneading of the dough.

It probably originated in Normandy, which, since the Middle Ages, has been well known for the quality of its butter. The consumption of brioche is usually reserved for breakfast, but a toasted piece as an accompaniment to goose liver is a pure delight.

Many French towns lend their names to brioche; the only difference between them is the shape of the loaf. The best known is from Paris, called *brioche à tête*, or "brioche with a head," because of a small ball of dough on top. The brioche of Saint Pierre d'Albigny is also called *Mains de Santa Agathe*, or "Saint Agatha's hands." This rather gory allusion is to the severed hands of Saint Agatha as she tried in vain to protect her breast from being cut off. See also MINNE DI SANT' AGATA.

brioche molds

brioche mold - a fluted circular metal baking pan with a narrow bottom and a widely flared top, used to make the rich French bread **brioche.** Brioche pans come in a variety of sizes, from small individual-size to large family-size.

briquettes - see CHARCOAL.

brisket - see BEEF.

brisling - see SPRAT.

British mixed spice - see MIXED SPICE.

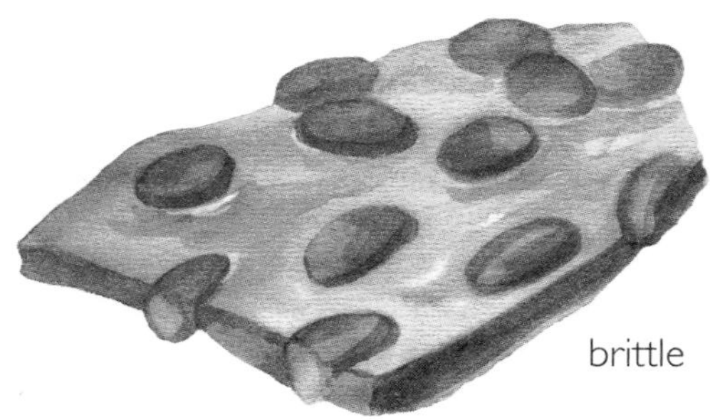

brittle

brittle - a candy made of caramelized sugar and nuts, especially peanuts; usually served powdered, crumbled or cracked. See also PRALINE.

broad bean - see FAVA.

broad-leaved endive - see ESCAROLE.

broccio - see BRICOTTA.

Broccoflower - the trademarked name for a vegetable cross between cauliflower and broccoli. It looks like a bright-green cauliflower, with a milder flavor than either of the original vegetables.

broccoli - an emerald green vegetable, the clusters of buds of *Brassica oleracea botrytis*, one of the oldest members of the cabbage family. The Greeks and the Romans were eating broccoli more than 2,000 years ago. Caesar and his court loved broccoli with such a passion that it was served up twice and sometimes even three times during a meal — apparently always to the diners' delight, although the cooking method never varied. Roman chefs simply boiled the broccoli "before bruising it" in a manner that the Roman cookbook from the 1st century AD by **Apicius** prescribed: "with a mixture of cumin and coriander seeds, chopped onion plus a few drops of oil and wine." Drusus, the oldest son of the emperor Tiberius, was so addicted to this recipe that he ate nothing but broccoli for a month. According to Roman historian **Pliny,** Drusus gave up broccoli only when his urine turned bright green and he was severely chastised by his father for "living precariously."

The word broccoli is a corruption of the Latin *brachium*, which means "strong arm" or "branch"; Roman farmers referred to this vegetable as "the five green fingers of Jupiter." Although broccoli became popular in America in the mid-20th century, it arrived a long time before. Thomas Jefferson is credited for bringing the seeds from Italy to his bountiful garden at Monticello. But aside from some Italian immigrant families who brought "broccali" seed from the Old Country to grow in their backyard gardens, this delicious vegetable was almost unknown to the American public until the 1920s. The D'Arrigo Brothers, enterprising growers in Northern California's Santa Clara Valley, started shipping sample crates back east and promoting the "new" vegetable on that narrative apparatus, the radio. The demand increased rapidly, and, by the early 1930s, broccoli was both an established crop and an accepted part of the American diet. **Calabrese** or **sprouting broccoli** is a variety of broccoli with large, tightly packed blue-green flowers and a very delicate flavor, named after Calabria in Italy.

broccoli

Broccolini - also **asparation, baby broccoli.** Trademarked name for the cross between broccoli and Chinese kale. Originally developed by the Sakata Seed Co. of Yokohama, Japan, the vegetable is sweet and delicate and much more tender and less fibrous than broccoli. The stalk does not need to be peeled before eating.

broccoli rabe - also **broccoli raab, rapini.** A bitter vegetable related to the turnip and cabbage family, which is why the leaves look like turnip greens hence another name it's often called: Italian turnip. It first appeared in the U.S. in the 1920s, brought by Italian farmers, who are fond of the bitter taste and use the vegetable in everything from salads to soups. Known and appreciated by the ancient Romans, broccoli rabe is cultivated all over the southern Mediterranean.

brochette - a skewer or small spit used to broil or roast vegetables, fish or meat, from the French *broche*, meaning "spit" or "skewer."

broil - to cook food either directly under or directly over a heat source, such as the top grill of an oven or on a barbecue. See also GRILL.

broiler - also **fryer.** The name for a young chicken, male or female, weighing no more than 3 pounds (1.4 kg).

bromated flour - low-protein flour to which potassium bromate is added, allowing it to develop stronger gluten and rise higher than if it were untreated. Bromated flour is available in much of the United States, but Europe, Canada and other countries have banned it because potassium bromate is a known carcinogen. In California, bread or other foods made with bromated flour must carry a cancer warning label, and even the U.S. Food and Drug Administration has warned consumers to avoid these products.

bromelain - an enzyme used as a meat tenderizer, which is extracted from pineapple.

brook trout - also **speckled trout.** *Salvelinus fontinalis* found in cold, freshwater brooks, streams, and lakes; some, nicknamed "salters," also survive in the saltwater river mouths along the Atlantic coastline of Canada's Maritime provinces. In the past they were so plentiful in the lakes and rivers of the U.S. Northeast that they were named the official state fish of Michigan, New Hampshire, New York, Pennsylvania, Virginia and West Virginia. Brook trout, which often evade anglers by lurking under overhanging riverbanks or rock ledges, usually reach only a foot or less (30 cm) in length during their five-year life span. A favorite of sport fishermen, they are also popular in the frying pan or on the grill. See also LAKE TROUT, TROUT.

brose - a traditional Scottish standby, a broth made by mixing uncooked oatmeal with boiling water or milk, often seasoned simply with butter and/or salt. The dish is not cooked but rather just mixed together, so it is not as thick as porridge, which is simmered until pasty. Other types of grains can also be used in a brose, including meal made from yellow peas (peasemeal) or barley. A variety of vegetables are traditionally added to brose, such as nettles, turnips and kale, and meat stocks can be substituted for the water or milk to make a more savory result. An especially well-known variation is Atholl brose, an alcoholic drink of oatmeal, honey, whiskey and water typically quaffed at Robbie Burns Day celebrations. The oatmeal is left to stand in the water for several hours, then strained and pressed to extract all the liquid, which is mixed with the honey and whiskey. Cream may be added to enrich the mixture for a special occasion. Atholl brose is said to be named after the Duke of Atholl, who, in 1475, poured this heady mixture into his enemy's well and got him so drunk that he could not fight.

brotform - see BANNETON.

broth - the name used for the clear liquid in which meat, fish or vegetables have been boiled.

Brotsuppe - a German soup made of leftover bread, flavored with nutmeg, floating in a thick meat stock.

brousse - a French cheese made from whey or skim milk.

brown - to cook food quickly over high heat so that the surface turns brown in color, but the inside stays moist. This gives food a richer flavor than it would otherwise have.

brown ale - see ALE.

brown bean sauce - also **brown bean paste.** A salty flavoring paste made from fermented soybeans, salt and flour, commonly used in Chinese cuisine. Thai versions are often available in Asian grocery stores, but they are saltier than their Chinese counterparts. Thanks to its high sodium content, the sauce can be kept indefinitely if refrigerated.

brown betty - **1.** see BETTY. **2.** in Old England, a hot or warm drink of brandy and ale served with spiced toast. **3.** a nickname for the traditional teapot used in England since the 17th century, made of dark brown glazed terra-cotta from the Bradwell Woods area of Stoke-on-Trent. The brown betty is alleged to make the finest pot of English tea, thanks to the heat-retaining red clay of which it's made and its squat, chubby shape, which allows the tea leaves to swirl and infuse perfectly as hot water is poured in.

brown bread - **1.** a Canadian term for any type of wheat bread that isn't white, usually whole wheat bread. **2.** a shortened form of **Boston brown bread,** commonly used by people in New England.

brown butter - see BEURRE NOISETTE.

brown goods - a term used to distinguish alcoholic liquors, such as whiskey, brandy, etc., that are brown in color because of aging. The antonym **white goods** applies to clear spirits, such as vodka and gin.

brownie - a rich, North American chocolate cookie, named after its deep brown color, its origin unclear. Brownies have been eaten in the U.S. since the 19th century, the first recipe appearing in print in 1897 in the Sears and Roebuck catalog. Some brownies have a fudge-like consistency, while others look and taste like cake. They are all made of flour, sugar, cocoa or unsweetened chocolate, butter, eggs and sometimes vanilla and chopped pecans or walnuts.

brown rice - the whole natural grain of the rice before it has been processed. Brown rice needs more water and a longer cooking time than white rice. See also RICE.

brown rice flour - see FLOUR.

brown rice syrup - see RICE SYRUP.

brown roux - see ROUX.

brown sauce - **1.** the name given in the U.S. to the classical French **espagnole** sauce, made with brown **roux,** brown stock, browned **mirepoix,** tomatoes and **bouquet garni,** reduced and strained. **2.** in England, a thick, bottled brown relish with a spicy flavor.

brown sherry - see SHERRY.

brown stock - any dark stock made from beef, veal or chicken bones (and sometimes meat) that have been roasted for color and additional flavor.

brown sugar - essentially a mixture of white sugar and molasses, often mistakenly thought to be healthier than white sugar, because it's believed to be less refined.

brown sugar pie - see SUGAR PIE.

Brown Turkey fig - see FIG.

bruise - to lightly crush ingredients with a mortar and pestle, or the flat of the blade of a large cook's knife. Garlic, gingerroot and herbs are bruised to release flavor and aroma. Because the bruised ingredient is not broken into pieces, it can be easily removed from the dish before serving.

brunch - a late, hearty breakfast that makes a separate lunch unnecessary. The word, like the meal itself, is a blend of breakfast and lunch.

brunello di Montalcino - an Italian red wine made in Tuscany from only Brunello grapes, a clone of the famous Tuscan **Sangiovese** grapes, the clone isolated in the 1870s by a vintner name Ferruccio Biondi-Santi. The rarest and priciest of the Tuscan reds, brunello di Montalcino is made in the town of Montalcino, south of the area where **Chianti** is made. The wine is richly flavored and redolent of berries and chocolate, complex on the palate and full-bodied. It can be aged for an extremely long time, some say up to 100 years, and still offer incredibly complex flavors and aromas. The name *brunello* means "nice dark one" in Italian, for the beautiful dark red-purple color of the grapes.

brunoise - **1.** (n.) finely diced vegetables used to flavor soups, sauces, sautés and stews. **2.** (v.) the technique of cutting vegetables into a very fine (about ⅛ inch/0.5 cm) dice.

Brunswick stew - a hearty squirrel and onion stew (or, more recently, rabbit or chicken and onion stew), which originated in Brunswick County, Virginia. Other vegetables are often added as well, including okra, corn and lima beans.

bruschetta - toasted or grilled bread rubbed with garlic, then drizzled or soaked with extra virgin olive oil, from the Italian *abbrustolire*, meaning "to toast." Often confused with **crostini,** bruschetta is a popular modern appetizer topped with chopped tomatoes, herbs and, often, cheese.

brush - to apply a liquid, such as melted butter, to the surface of a food with a brush.

Brussels sprouts - *Brassica oleracea gemmifera*, a member of the cabbage family, resembling miniature cabbages that grow in a knobby row on a long stalk. The Romans called these tender knobs *bullata gemmifera* ("diamond makers"), because consumption was alleged to increase a diner's mental dexterity. Marc Antony is said to have chewed Brussels sprouts for days before the battle of Actium. What was true about this mini-cabbage during antiquity was its rareness. Roman chefs imported them from Western Europe, where they grew wild. Because the cabbage formed a "head," early surgeons believed Brussels sprouts were a natural cure for a hangover (according to Roman historian **Pliny**).

They are said to have originated near Brussels, Belgium. The Dutch botanist Rembertus Dodonaeus made the first mention of Brussels sprouts as a variety of cabbage in 1554. Brussels sprouts have been a source of Flemish national pride for more than eight centuries. But not until 1820 was the Brussels sprout publicly recognized by the king of Belgium as the country's official green. In 1623, one botanist described some plants he had heard of (but never seen) that "bear 50 heads the size of an egg." Two hundred years later, an American botanist improved on the story by writing about a "thousand-headed cabbage." The Germans give Brussels sprouts their most romantic name: *rosenkohl*, meaning "rose cabbages," a pretty and eloquent name, as they look like small rosebuds. The French dub them *chou de Bruxelles* (literally, "the cabbage of Brussels"), and the Italians *cavolina di Brusselle* ("the little cabbage of Brussels").

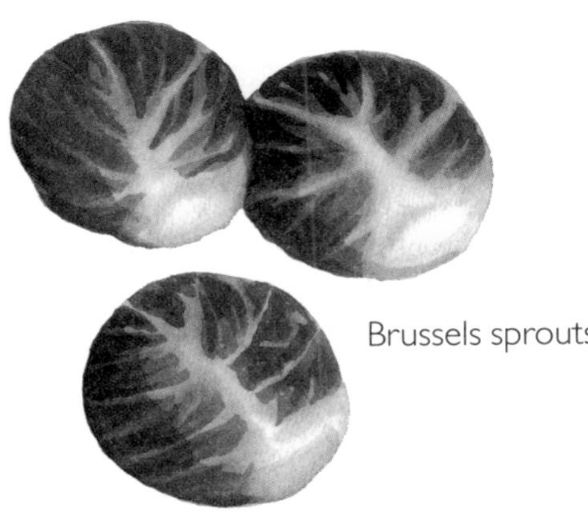

Brussels sprouts

brut - a term used to describe Champagne that is not sweet. Brut Champagne contains no or very little sugar, similar to **dry** wine. Champagne that is labeled "extra dry" is slightly sweeter than brut.

bryndza - see BRINZA.

BSE - see MAD COW DISEASE.

b'steeya - see BASTILA.

buah keras - see CANDLENUT.

bubble and squeak - a dish of British origin made of cabbage or other greens and potatoes fried together on high heat. (More than 300 years ago, the dish was traditionally employed for disposing of the remains of cold salted beef.) It's so called for the sounds made in the cooking process.

bubble tea - also **boba ice tea, pearl tea.** A sweet, cold beverage made with brewed green or black tea, a flavored syrup and **tapioca** balls, or bubbles, served with a colorful wide straw to suck up the bubbles. Some versions contain sweetened condensed milk or gelatin-based additions, such as squares of coconut or lychee jelly, instead of the bubbles.

Prototypes of the drink are said to have been developed in Taiwan in the 1980s as an after-school treat for thirsty, tired schoolchildren. The story goes that a certain tea shop began offering a combination of brewed tea and fruit flavorings, which were shaken together with ice to produce the signature tiny bubbles on the top of the drink. The trend took off, and tea purveyors began to add cooked tapioca bubbles to the drink, giving it bubbles on the bottom as well.

The chewy tapioca bubbles are typically made from **cassava,** or **yuca,** starch and can be greenish black, white or transparent. **Pearl sago** are often used as well as a substitute for tapioca. Bubble tea is also known by a variety of other names, including pearl tea, *nai cha* and QQ drink ("QQ" sounds like the word for "chewy" in Taiwanese). Another popular name is boba ice tea, boba meaning "breast" in Chinese, which refers to both the shape and the texture of the tapioca bubbles.

bucatini - see PASTA.

bûche de Noël - also **Yule log.** A **génoise** topped with **pastry cream,** flavored whipped cream or **buttercream** and rolled up, then cut at an angle and arranged to look like the intersection of two tree branches. The log is then frosted with chocolate buttercream, combed with a **cake comb** or fork to resemble bark, and decorated with meringue mushrooms, crushed pistachio "moss" and/or confectioner's sugar "snow." The name means "Yule log" in French.

Bûcheron - an aged goat cheese from the Loire Valley of France, formed into logs that are creamy and soft in the center and drier out toward the hard, edible rind. It is mild, creamy and pleasantly tangy, excellent spread on bread or crackers, often served as a dessert cheese.

buckle - a rich old-fashioned fruitcake made most often with blueberries.

buckling - see HERRING.

buckwheat - an annual, *Fagopyrum esculentum*, thought to be native to China, not a grain but rather the seed of a plant related to rhubarb. When ground, however, it behaves exactly like other cereals. It's easy to grow in harsh climates and, for this reason, is a staple for much of Northern Europe, especially the northern provinces of Poland, Prussia and the Ukraine. There, its flour is made into porridge and noodles, and its **groats** are treated like rice. Its seeds are roasted and made into flour for pancakes, **blinis, varnishkes,** crisp, thin cakes and noodles. The Japanese use buckwheat to make **soba,** thin light brown noodles that are often served cold or in broth.

Buckwheat might be a souvenir left over by the Tartars' invasion of Southern Europe in the 1400s. But more than likely, it's from the Moors. The Italians refer to it as *grano saraceno;* the Spanish as *trigo sarraceno;* and the French as *sarrasin*, or "Saracen grain." Although buckwheat is nutritionally similar to wheat, it's unrelated, and many people who cannot tolerate wheat have no trouble with buckwheat products.

buckwheat groats - see KASHA.

buckwheat honey - see HONEY.

Buddha's hand citron - also **finger citron, fingered citron.** A beautiful but bizarre-looking exotic citrus fruit, *Citrus medica* var. *sarcodactylus*, native to Asia, with long, yellow

Budda's hand citron

"fingers" protruding from a central stem. The Buddha's hand has no real pulp or juice but is used instead for its aromatic peel, which can be used fresh or candied. In Asia, the fruit is highly prized for its scent and is often hung in closets to keep them smelling sweet. See also CITRON.

buffalo - see BISON.

buffalo berry - a tart yellow fruit, *Shepherdia argentea,* the size of a currant and containing one seed, used in making pies and preserves, native to the Americas and well known to the Plains Indians.

buffalo fish - any of a number of freshwater fish of the genus Ictiobus, similar to carp, a sucker-mouthed fish found throughout the central U.S. and Canada. Buffalo fish tastes similar to **catfish,** with firm, mild, white flesh, good for many types of cooking, especially **deep-frying.**

buffalo mozzarella - an Italian cheese originally made entirely from water-buffalo milk but now more often made from partially skimmed cow's milk, although an American imitation is often made with whole milk. In Italy, unless it's made with buffalo milk, it can't be called mozzarella. (The cheese made from cow's milk is called *fior di latte.*) Apparently, Marc Antony brought water buffalo to Italy from Egypt, where he became a lover of the cheese, and sent the animal as a gift to Caesar with directions on how to make the milk into mozzarella. The breeding of the water buffalo became a craze in the area between Rome and Naples. The largest buffalo mozzarella factory in the U.S. is in Vermont, where there are 200 head of water buffalo. Water buffalo milk brings between $50 and $75 per hundredweight (100 pounds/45 kg), about five times the price of regular milk. See also MOZZARELLA.

Buffalo wings - deep-fried chicken wings coated in a spicy sauce and served with blue cheese dressing. They were invented and given that name in 1964 by the owner of the Anchor Bar in Buffalo, New York. Teresa Bellissimo found herself facing an oversupply of chicken wings and a visit from her son with numerous hungry friends. Since 1977, the city of Buffalo has declared July 29 "Chicken Wing Day."

buffet - a meal at which guests serve themselves food from dishes set out on a sideboard, table or counter.

bugne - see OREILLETTE.

bugs - the eating of bugs has an official name, entomophagy. The most commonly consumed bug the world over is the grasshopper, although chocolate-covered crickets are a Mexican specialty.

bulb baster - see BASTER.

bulb fennel - see FENNEL.

bulgogi - also **pulgogi.** An extremely popular Korean dish of marinated thinly sliced beef, often grilled at table over a charcoal brazier or gas grill. The beef is usually well marbled and marinated in a mixture of soy sauce, sugar, green onions, garlic and sesame oil for maximum flavor. The grilled slices are served with a soy-based dipping sauce, an assortment of **kimchi** and rice.

bulgur - also **borghol, burghul.** A Middle Eastern staple, the parched, steamed and dried kernels of wheat that are eaten hot or cold, for breakfast, lunch or dinner. It's used to make **tabbouleh.** Traces of bulgur have been found in Egyptian tombs, Etruscan **amphorae** and Hun saddlebags. The Romans even had a word for bulgur, *cerealis*, named after Ceres, the goddess of the harvest. The Ancient Israelites called it *dagan*, meaning "bursting kernels of grains."

bulk process - see CHARMAT METHOD.

bullhead - a type of catfish, in black, brown and yellow varieties, often caught when it weighs about 1 pound (500 g). Bullheads do not have deeply forked tail fins like other catfish, but they do have the tell-tale barbels, or whisker-like protrusions, around their mouths that identify them as catfish.

bull's eye beet - see CHIOGGIA.

Bullshot - a savory cocktail made with vodka and beef bouillon or consommé, which may also contain any combination of Worcestershire sauce, Tabasco, lemon juice, celery salt and freshly ground pepper. Developed as a hangover cure, reputedly in the 1930s, this meal in a glass may be served steaming hot, as well as cold.

bully beef - in the U.K., a term used for corned beef, especially when canned.

bulz - see MAMALIGA.

bumbleberry - a fanciful term for an assortment of berries — often blackberries, blueberries, strawberries, raspberries, cranberries and/or Saskatoon berries — combined with apple and rhubarb and used as a filling for pies. There are also recipes for bumbleberry jam and bumbleberry crisp, which are made with any number of berry-and-fruit combinations.

bummalo - also **bummalow.** See BOMBAY DUCK.

bun - **1.** any of a variety of small, usually round yeast rolls, which can be either sweet or savory. Although the source of the name for this baked good is not entirely clear, some authorities suspect it comes from an Old French word, *bugne*, meaning "a bump on the head" or "a boil." **2.** a category of dishes in Vietnamese cuisine served over **rice vermicelli,** commonly seen on restaurant menus in the U.S. Bun can come with meat, seafood, poultry or vegetarian toppings, and there are hundreds of variations on the theme, some specific to a region, a town or even a single restaurant.

Bündnerfleisch - also **Bindenfleisch.** Air-dried beef traditionally made in the Swiss canton of Grisons (known as Graubünden in German), dipped in white wine and rubbed with salt, herbs and onion before it is hung to dry. It is usually served in paper-thin slices with an oil-and-vinegar dressing. See also BILTONG, BRESAOLA.

Bundost - see BONDOST.

Bundt pan - a name for a type of tube baking pan with curved and fluted sides.

bung - the stopper used in the hole of a wine cask (called the bunghole), usually made of wood, cork or even silicone.

Bunter Hans - a large bread dumpling from Germany, cooked in a towel to hold its shape, then served with an accompaniment of vegetables and stewed fruits.

buñuelo - a Mexican fritter-like pastry, fried in fat and usually powdered with cinnamon and sugar or covered with syrup. *Buñuelo de viento*, meaning "of the air," refers to a version of this pastry, whose airy pockets are filled with cream.

burbot - the only freshwater fish, *Lota lota*, of the cod family having lean, white flesh and a delicate flavor, found throughout North America and continental Eurasia, one of the few freshwater fish to spawn under ice from January to March. Burbot have firm tasty flesh, the liver is reputedly a delicacy, and the eggs are sold as a form of "caviar" in some places.

burdock - also **beggar's button, gobo.** A wild, thistle-like plant, *Arctium lappa*, common to the Northern Hemisphere. The young leaves and stems are used in salads, and the lengthy, slim root is praised for its crispy texture. Japan is the only country where it's eaten on a large scale, although it enjoys some popularity in Hawaii, where the Japanese introduced it. In Japan, a distinction is made between two forms, one with green stalks, the other with purplish stalks. The varieties that are most esteemed are Ouragobo, from Oura, near Tokyo, and Horikawagobo, an old favorite from Horikawa, near Kyoto.

burdock

burek - see BÖREK.

burghul - see BULGUR.

burgoo - a stew made with a mixture of meats and vegetables. The origin of its name is obscure, but it possibly comes from Kentucky during the frontier days, for a community get-together called a burgoo. A stew, to which neighbors contributed the various ingredients, was prepared in a huge iron pot (also called a burgoo). Originally, however, it was a sailor's name for oatmeal pudding. See also MULLIGAN STEW, RAGOÛT.

Burgundy - **1.** one of the main wine-producing regions of France, located in the central part of the country. It is known for the wines produced from its two main grape varieties: Pinot Noir and Chardonnay. Its cool climate is ideal for these two varieties under good conditions, but it can pose problems when there is a particularly sunless and moist year, which can produce crops of less flavorful grapes and therefore less flavorful wines. The wines that Burgundy produces in its good years are considered some of the most complex and flavorful made in France. **2.** a wine produced in the Burgundy region of France. Wines from this region fall into two broad categories: white burgundies and red burgundies. White burgundies are made primarily from the region's abundant **Chardonnay** grapes. Red burgundies are produced from **Pinot Noir** grapes with few exceptions. (Beaujolais, a sub-region of Burgundy, produces a wide variety of wines made from **Gamay** grapes and is considered a separate creature altogether.) Burgundy wines are almost never blended, and they never combine Chardonnay and Pinot Noir.

The Côte d'Or area of Burgundy, in the north near the city of Dijon, produces the most renowned wines of the region, from basic table wines to the finest Premier **Crus** or Grand Crus. The majority of the hundreds of different wines produced are red, but the southern half of the area is also planted with Chardonnay grapes, yielding fine white wines. **Chablis** is another well-known area of Burgundy, famed for its crisp, tart wines produced from Chardonnay grapes. Just south of Côte d'Or is the less-well-known Côte Chalonnaise, an area that produces good-quality, usually cheaper, whites and reds. The Mâconnais is the southernmost wine-producing area of the region, known for its fine white wines. The village of Pouilly-Fuissé is located in the Mâconnais, and produces fine but expensive whites that are considered overrated by some critics.

buridda - the Italian name for a fish stew similar to the Provençal **bourride** and similar to **bouillabaisse.** Buridda is a specialty of Liguria and often contains **stockfish** or a combination of seafood, such as octopus, squid and **cuttlefish.** The seafood, tomatoes, anchovies, garlic and herbs are traditionally layered in a casserole dish and cooked until thick and steaming hot, then ladled over slices of toasted bread rubbed with garlic.

burnet - see SALAD BURNET.

burnt cream - the English name for crème brûlée, a direct translation from the French.

burnt ends - a delicacy in American barbecue circles, the burnt trimmings from a smoked **beef brisket,** often added to other dishes, such as baked beans, to lend them a rich, smoky flavor. Barbecue restaurants in the American South and Kansas City also serve burnt ends as a dish unto itself for the patron to mix with barbecue sauce and eat alongside other dishes.

burrata - a southern Italian pulled-curd cheese, a version of the well-known, well-loved **mozzarella,** traditionally made from buffalo milk but nowadays usually made from cow's milk. Burrata is stretched and pulled in the same way as mozzarella, then formed into balls that surround a liquidy center of cream mixed with finely chopped mozzarella curds. When you bite into a ball of the cheese, cream oozes out of the center. Burrata is highly perishable, thanks to the fresh cream in the center, so it must be refrigerated and is best eaten with a day or two of purchase. The name comes from the Italian word for butter, *burro*.

burrito - a Mexican-American staple whose name means "little donkey," a tortilla stuffed, rolled and cooked on a griddle, probably so named because it resembles the back of a donkey, laden like a beast of burden with its many ingredients. If fried, it's known as a **chimichanga.** The modern burrito originated in the dusty borderlands between Tucson and Los Angeles. The word *burrito* first saw print in America in 1934, and they were sold at Los Angeles's famed El Cholo Spanish Cafe during the 1930s. Burritos entered Mexican-American cuisine in other parts of the Southwest in the 1950s and went nationwide a decade later.

burro banana - also **orinico banana.** The name given in Mexico to a variety of a flat, almost square banana whose flavor is a mix of banana and lemon.

bush nut - see MACADAMIA NUT.

butanoic acid - see BUTYRIC ACID.

butcher block - also **chopping block.** A table-style cutting board made from maple or other hardwoods, used for heavy-duty chopping in the kitchen. Butcher blocks are built with thick, sturdy legs that can withstand the force of a cleaver used to chop the largest cuts of meat. There are also butcher-block-style countertops and cutting boards that look and behave like this old-fashioned kitchen table but aren't stand-alone pieces of furniture.

butcher knife - a knife with a long thick blade, usually between 7 and 10 inches (17.5 and 25 cm) in length, that narrows to a curved tip for easy cutting and trimming of meat, especially larger cuts.

butcher's steel - see SHARPENING STEEL.

butcher steak - see HANGER STEAK.

butiffara - a Spanish firm-textured sausage, generally of pork, white wine, seasonings and spices, boiled and air-dried, which may be eaten cold. It's featured in the Catalonian cooked dish *cazuela a la catalana*.

butt - the name for the lean upper cut of the pork shoulder or the large end cut of a beef loin.

butter - a fatty spread made by churning cream until it reaches a semisolid state. The origin of the name is a combination of the Greek *bous*, or "cow," and *turos*, "cheese." The origin of butter goes back to the earliest nomadic people, who used to churn the milk of the cows, goats, ewes, asses, mares and camels that were following them in their wanderings. The Aryans brought the knowledge of butter to India, where it soon became a sacred food. In Indian mythology, the Salmala is a river of butter that winds about the world. (For Butter Grades see below.)

butter bean - see LIMA BEAN.

butter cake - the standard all-purpose cake with a delicate, tender **crumb,** often lightly scented with vanilla, made with butter as its main fat. Butter cake is the most basic and malleable cake in the baker's repertoire and can be embellished with any number of flavorings, such as almond or chocolate. It can be baked in square, rectangular, round or even cupcake pans and frosted with any flavor of icing.

butter clam - a hard-shell clam, *Saxidomus giganteus*, native to the Pacific Northwest and often harvested in Puget Sound in Washington State. The butter clam is abundant in the region and is harvested in great quantities, both for commercial canning and for sale fresh in seafood markets. It has a sweet, butter-like flavor and is delicious in soups and pasta sauces as well as steamed or broiled on its own.

BUTTER GRADES

The U.S. Department of Agriculture divides butter, unsalted or salted, into three quality grades. Butter quality is based on taste and smell tests conducted by a USDA inspector.

Grade AA - the finest, sweetest butter flavor and scent, with just the right amount of salt (if salted). It may have only half a point deducted for a fault, unlike lesser grades.

Grade A - butter with a good taste and scent, can have one point deducted for a fault. Grade A butter may be just slightly acidic, bitter or flat-tasting, or it could be just a bit too salty.

Grade B - fair butter flavor and smell, can have 1½ points deducted for faults. Grade B butter may be very slightly musty, vegetal, scorched or metallic, but is allowed to have a pronounced acidity, bitterness or aged smell.

The Canadian government only allows producers to sell Grade I butter (not to be confused with the Grade A rating in the U.S.) to the public. To achieve Grade I status, the butter must have a regular, desirable butter flavor, smooth texture, even moisture throughout and uniform color. If the butter is salted, the salt must be completely dissolved. **Cultured butter** is allowed to have a tangy, acidic flavor.

butter cookies - a broad class of cookies, made with butter instead of any other fats, usually a relatively large amount of butter in relation to the other ingredients, giving the cookies a short, rich, crumbly texture. Butter cookies are popular in many cultures, especially in Scandinavia, where they are often delicately flavored with cardamom or topped with sliced almonds. Danish butter cookies are well known around the world, piped into wreaths and cut into a variety of shapes, usually sold in nicely decorated tins for gift giving at the holidays.

buttercream - a very rich mixture of butter, sugar and egg yolk used either to ice cakes or as a filling.

buttercrunch lettuce - see LETTUCE.

buttercup squash - see SQUASH.

butter curler

butter curler - a kitchen utensil, often made of stainless steel, with a serrated hook at one end, drawn along the top of a stick of chilled butter to make attractive curls or scalloped balls.

buttered eggs - **1.** an old-fashioned Irish method of preserving freshly laid chickens' eggs, done by rolling the warm eggs in butter between the palms of the hands. The warm shell soaks up the butter quickly, forming a hard, shiny protective barrier against bacteria and air. The egg inside soaks up some of the butter's flavor, which it retains when it is cooked. Buttered eggs can be kept without refrigeration for up to six months. **2.** an antiquated term for scrambled eggs, immortalized in many of the "cookery books" of the 19th and early 20th century, such as those from **Fannie Merritt Farmer** and **Mrs. Isabella Beeton.**

butterfat - also **milk fat.** The natural fat of milk and the chief component of butter.

butterfish - also **dollarfish.** An oily, rich-tasting fish usually found in the Atlantic, although a relative called the **Pacific pompano** is often also identified under this name. Butterfish has dark, sweet flesh and is usually sold whole, or gutted and with the head cut off, for pan-frying. Its name comes from its rich, buttery flesh.

butterfly - a culinary term for cutting into fish or meat but not fully through, then opening up the flesh to resemble the shape of a butterfly.

butterhead lettuce - see LETTUCE.

butterhorn

butterhorn - also **Schnecken, snail. 1.** a rich, buttery cookie, sometimes topped with a filling of nuts, spices or jam, made in the same manner as butterhorn rolls. Butterhorns are basically the same as **Kipfel** or **rugelach.** They are called Schnecken in Austria and Germany. Each cookie resembles a curved horn or curled shell. **2.** a rich, buttery yeast roll made by rolling out a large circle of dough, cutting it into wedges and rolling up each wedge to form a crescent shape.

butter knife - traditionally, a small knife with a dull, curved blade that ends in a rounded tip or an upturned point, used for serving butter at a formal meal. In a formal table setting, each diner has a butter knife laid out near his or her bread-and-butter plate. However, some hosts offer a butter knife only on the butter dish. In that case, the butter knife should be used to transfer some butter onto the bread-and-butter plate, then the regular dinner knife can be used to spread it. Of course, in most homes, where dining is informal, the term *butter knife* has become synonymous with any dull-bladed dinner knife.

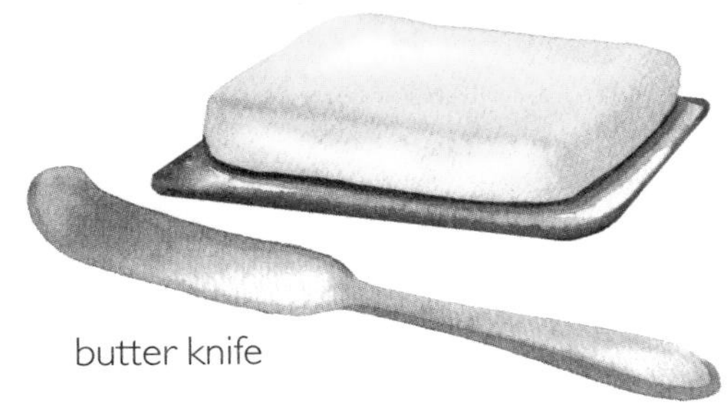

butter knife

buttermilk - originally, the sour milk left over from butter making. Today, buttermilk is usually made from pasteurized skim milk with an added culture for thickening. It's used as a drink, in baking and confectionery, and as a milk substitute. See also MILK.

buttermilk pie - a popular open-faced dessert pie in the American South, made with butter, sugar, eggs, vanilla, nutmeg and buttermilk, which gives the pie its characteristic sweet-tart flavor. It is similar to **chess pie,** another Southern favorite.

butter mold - an old-fashioned kitchen tool used to make butter into various shapes, traditionally made of wood with a design carved into the bottom, which was impressed upon the finished butter. Soft, freshly made butter was spooned into the mold, then left to firm up into the shape of the mold. Many molds have a plunger, which pushes the finished butter out of the hopper. Antique butter molds are highly collectible and are available with beautiful carvings of natural motifs, such as stars, cows and wheat sheaves. Modern butter molds, which are actually harder to find than antique ones, can be made of plastic or metal as well.

butter muslin - the British term for cheesecloth.

butternut - also **oilnut, white walnut.** The edible nut of the native North American white walnut tree, *Juglans cinerea,* with a dark brown, deeply grooved shell and rich oily meat, grown from southern Quebec to Georgia and from eastern Minnesota to the eastern coast of the United States. Native Americans pressed butternuts for their rich oil, which was used ceremonially and for cooking. Because of their high oil content, the nuts go rancid quickly and must be used soon after they are harvested.

butternut squash - see SQUASH.

butter paddle - an old-fashioned kitchen tool used to form and shape butter into decorative balls, either smooth or ridged depending on the desired result. Two paddles are used simultaneously to work cool butter into balls (using the hands to mold the butter would cause it to melt from the heat of the skin). Antique butter paddles are a popular collector's item and are versatile too: the ridged version can be used to impress designs on dough before baking and can be handy for pressing the characteristic ridges into the tops of **gnocchi.**

butterscotch - a candy or flavoring made by boiling together brown sugar, butter, corn syrup and water.

butter stamp - similar in purpose to a **butter mold,** a butter stamp is an old-fashioned wooden kitchen utensil used to press a decorative design onto a portion of butter. The stamp has a short handle and a disk on the bottom with a design carved into it. Typically, the designs are pastoral in nature, featuring cows, sheaves of wheat or flowers, such as thistles. Butter makers often used these decorative stamps to impress their mark on their butter, similar to the way a trademarked design is used today to identify a particular brand. Antique butter stamps are in high demand today among antique collectors, but there are also modern kitchenware companies that offer a limited selection of new butter stamps.

butter substitutes - any of a variety of products that mimic the flavor (and possibly texture) of butter without the fat and/or milk ingredients that are present in butter. Margarine is a butter substitute that tries (but usually fails) to mimic the taste of real butter — some versions even contain a small amount of cream or milk to give them "authentic flavor." Regular high-fat margarine comes closer to the texture of butter and can be used in many recipes that call for butter, although its faux flavor usually gives it away in the finished dish. It can be a satisfactory substitute in some baking, but lower-fat versions contain more water than butter does, which can leave baked goods waterlogged. There are also butter substitutes that come in granule or powder form, which are designed to be sprinkled over foods to give them a buttery flavor with almost zero calories or fat and no cholesterol. These substitutes are often made from a corn derivative called maltodextrin, as well as salt, butter flavoring and coloring. There are also liquid forms, many in spray bottles, which can be used to mist certain foods, such as popcorn.

butter tart - a Canadian pastry with a filling of butter, eggs, brown sugar and usually raisins.

buttery - a wine-tasting term for a wine that gives the impression of butter flavor on the palate, used to describe certain **Chardonnays.** A buttery flavor is often the result of malolactic fermentation, a natural or winemaker-initiated process in which beneficial bacteria in the wine convert the sharp malic acid in the grapes to softer-tasting lactic acid. The result is a smoother, less crisp wine.

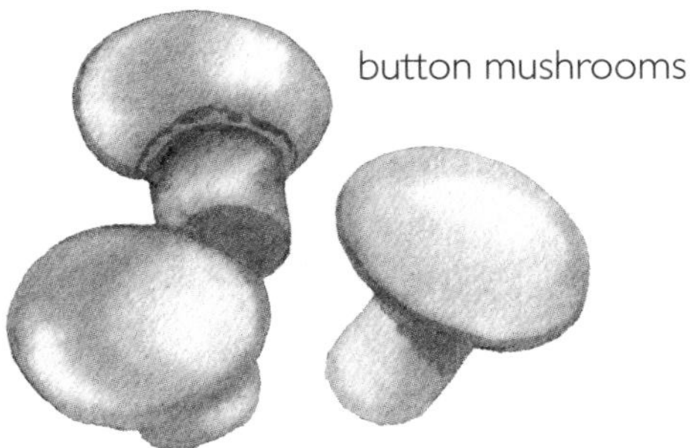

button mushroom - also **button head mushroom.** A variety of cultivated mushroom with nearly pure white flesh and a round, silky, half-ball-shaped head.

button onion - see PEARL ONION.

butyric acid - also **butanoic acid.** A naturally occurring fatty acid that gives butter its distinctive flavor and that, when present in larger amounts, creates the foul smell associated with rancid butter. It is also found in small amounts in some fruits. Butyric acid is also made into synthetic flavoring agents for foods.

B vitamins - a complex of eight water-soluble vitamins: thiamin (B_1), riboflavin (B_2), niacin (B_3), pantothenic acid (B_5), pyridoxine (B_6), cyanocobalamin (B_{12}), folacin and biotin. The most fundamental job of the B vitamins as a whole is to help the body covert fat, protein and carbohydrates into energy. They are also considered anti-stress vitamins, so many people take B-complex supplements or eat B-vitamin-rich foods to help them stay calm and fight off daily tensions. While only small amounts are necessary for good health, B vitamins are considered essential nutrients because the body will not function properly without them (deficiencies can cause everything from panic attacks to heart malfunctions to uncontrollable cravings for sweets). They are fairly easy to consume in foods and are found in a wide variety of plant and animal products. Because they are water-soluble, any excess B vitamins ingested are excreted in the urine.

THE EIGHT B VITAMINS

thiamin - also **thiamine, vitamin B_1.** Found in a wide variety of foods, including whole grains, wheat germ, nuts, legumes and pork. Thiamin promotes a healthy appetite, keeps the nervous system and the heart functioning properly, aids digestion, keeps the brain healthy and mood lifted, and can even prevent motion sickness. A severe deficiency of thiamin is called beriberi, and is commonly seen in people who subsist on unenriched white flour and white rice, because the thiamin that occurs naturally in the outer coatings of the grain have been stripped away. Switching to enriched white flour and converted rice (which has been boiled before husking, locking the vitamin into the grains) can prevent this deficiency from occurring.

riboflavin - also **vitamin B_2.** Found in higher amounts in dairy products, almonds, meat, poultry, fish, whole grains, leafy greens and eggs. Riboflavin works with the other B vitamins to break down proteins, carbohydrates and fats into usable energy. It is essential for reproduction, helps the adrenal glands produce hormones and works with other chemicals to fight off toxins and keep all the systems in the body healthy. It is also a key player in eye health. Riboflavin deficiency usually occurs in conjunction with other B-vitamin deficiencies, causing, among other things, scales to form at the corner of the mouth and excess blood vessels to form on the surface of the cornea.

niacin - also **vitamin B_3.** Found in fish, lean meats, poultry, legumes, whole grains and many fortified foods. Niacin is essential for healthy skin and helps the body digest carbohydrates, fats and proteins. It is also important for proper blood clotting and for the production of an assortment of hormones, including estrogen and testosterone. A severe niacin deficiency is called pellagra, a common disease in people who live on a corn-based diet. The only exceptions are Mexico and Central America, where corn is typically cooked or soaked in limewater, a solution of calcium hydroxide, which releases the niacin in the corn protein so that it can be absorbed in the body. Pellagra causes "the four Ds": dementia, diarrhea, dermatitis and (if untreated) death, so it is vital to treat any signs of a deficiency immediately.

pantothenic acid - also **vitamin B_5.** Found in a wide variety of foods, but in the largest amounts in dairy products, liver, kidney, avocados, eggs, some vegetables and legumes. Pantothenic acid is important for the digestion of proteins, carbohydrates and fats, and aids in the body's production of hemoglobin and acetylcholine, an important neurotransmitter. Pantothenic acid also helps the body produce antibodies, fats, cholesterol (which is a component in the formation of cells) and steroid hormones, all vital for good health. It is rare for a deficiency of this vitamin to occur, but when it does, the hallmark symptoms are burning pain in the feet, cramps, headache and insomnia.

pyridoxine - also **vitamin B_6.** Found in fish, poultry, bananas, potatoes and spinach. Vitamin B_6 is essential for the production of cells, enzymes and red blood cells. It is also essential for maintaining a healthy immune system and for proper nerve cell function (although an excess of the vitamin can damage the nerves it is intended to protect). Without the proper amount of this essential nutrient, the immune system can become severely depressed, allowing serious infections, especially in people with already-depressed immune function, such as the elderly and people with AIDS.

cyanocobalamin - also **vitamin B_{12}.** Found in animal foods, including shellfish, fish, meat, poultry, eggs and dairy products. Vitamin B_{12} is necessary to keep brain tissue and nerve cells healthy, for the formation of red blood and to help the body use certain amino and fatty acids. A severe deficiency of the vitamin can cause permanent nerve damage and a type of anemia caused by the incomplete maturation of red blood cells. People over the age of 60 are susceptible to vitamin B_{12} deficiency, because the body's ability to absorb B_{12} diminishes with age. **Vegans** are also susceptible to this type of deficiency due to the lack of naturally occurring B_{12} in the vegan diet. Vegans and vegetarians who consume inadequate amounts of dairy products or eggs are advised to take a B_{12} supplement to avoid this.

folacin - found naturally in leafy greens, vegetables, orange juice and legumes, as well as in synthesized form in many fortified foods. Folacin is the current official name of this B vitamin, although many people still call it by the names **folic acid** and **folate.** Folate is accepted as a generic term for both natural folacin, which is found in foods, and synthesized folic acid, which is found in supplements and fortified foods. The nutrient is responsible for helping the body form red blood cells and for fighting off stress, as well as keeping levels of homocysteine in check (an amino acid that, at high levels in the body, can be a contributing factor to heart disease). Although the body can store a small amount of folacin for several months (unlike other B vitamins), deficiencies are quite common. In women of childbearing age, this is particularly problematic because folacin helps prevent neural tube defects, such as spina bifida, in growing fetuses. Although consuming a diet rich in folacin is possible, it is often easier to take a multivitamin that contains the optimal dose of folic acid to maintain the body's stores of this essential nutrient.

biotin - found in many foods, including liver, egg yolks, yeast and wheat bran. Biotin's largest role is in metabolizing fatty acids and sugars consumed in food. Biotin can be synthesized in the intestines, so dietary intake is not as crucial as it is for other B vitamins. Interestingly, biotin is a vital nutrient during periods of fasting or starvation because it helps the body convert certain acids into glucose for energy when food energy is unavailable. A deficiency of biotin can result in eye infections and can reduce immune system function, allowing diseases to take hold. Symptoms of a deficiency include brittle nails; red, scaly skin; and thinning hair. A severe lack of the nutrient has been linked to developmental delays in infants.

Byrrh - the brand name of a bitter French apéritif similar to **Dubonnet,** made by blending red wine with quinine, often mixed to make cocktails, such as Byrrh cassis, a mixture of Byrrh, **crème de cassis** and soda water.

byssus - see BEARD.

C
cabbage

cabaret - a restaurant where dancers and singers entertain. Before the 17th century, there was a clear distinction in France between the *taverne* and the *cabaret*. Originally, the novelty of the cabaret consisted of selling wine *à l'assiette*, for instance serving it at a table where the customer could sit and possibly have something to eat. If the cabaret proprietor did not have the necessary license to do this, the wine was sold *au pot*, or by the jug.

cabbage

cabbage - a vegetable, *Brassica oleracea capitata*, with a large, usually spherical head of tightly packed leaves, from the Old French word *caboche*, meaning "head." Germans call it *kohl*, and early Britons dubbed it *cole* (hence "coleslaw," meaning "sliced cabbage"). The plant's Latin name is *caulia*, meaning "stem" or, more accurately, "a very thick stalk." No one knows for sure when cabbage became more rounded, but when Caesar invaded Britain, he brought spherical cabbages as food for the troops; they're mentioned in his dairies as *capitalae*, "with heads."

Cabbage has a long and varied history, cultivated in the West since at least 400 BC and seen as a valuable medicine. It has been used since Greek physician Dioscorides' time (AD 40–90) as a digestive remedy and a joint tonic, and for skin problems and fever. Known as *colewort* in folk medicine, cabbage was a standby cure for all manner of family ills. During the Boxer uprising in China, scrolls from 1000 BC were discovered detailing the prescription of white cabbage as the only cure for infertility in males of advanced age. The Egyptians raised altars to it, and the Greeks and the Romans believed that cabbage cured every disease from paralysis to pleurisy. Aristotle, among others, followed the Egyptian practice of eating cabbage before banquets in belief it would keep the wine from fuddling his prudent academic head.

Cabbage was an important food during the Dark Ages, and by the Middle Ages, it was abundant, as we can see when we study the paintings of that period. The French, Germans and English traveled to America with cabbage seeds, and both the settlers and the Indians began planting and eating this vegetable. They boiled fresh cabbage with corned beef and onions, which evolved into a New England specialty. One of the most notable fans of *Brassica* was Thomas Jefferson, who campaigned for this vegetable's acceptance by his fellow Americans all his life. In his incredible garden at Monticello, Jefferson raised more than 22 different varieties of cabbage imported from all over the world. One of Jefferson's prides was the **savoy cabbage.**

Cabbage contains a harmful chemical called thioglucoside, which may adversely affect the thyroid gland, but is destroyed by cooking. Cabbage tends to release strong-smelling ammonias and hydrogen sulfide chemical compounds during cooking, a problem that can be reduced by steaming or cooking it in a small amount of water as quickly as possible, or by adding a few pieces of white bread to the cooking water.

The National Cancer Institute has designated cabbage a food with high cancer-fighting power. Two particularly potent cancer-fighting phytochemicals are available in cabbage: indoles, which help to metabolize estrogen thus protecting against breast cancer; and isothiocyanates, which help the body to detoxify carcinogens. Also, people who consume large quantities of cabbage have been shown to have low rates of colon cancer.

cabbage roll - a ubiquitous Eastern European and Russian dish of blanched cabbage leaves wrapped around a filling, usually of spiced ground meat combined with rice, typically simmered in a tomato-based sauce. These rolls are a staple in many countries and are often identified by their names in different languages: in Polish, *golabki;* in Ukrainian, *golubtsi or holubtsi;* in Russian, *galuptze;* and in Yiddish, **holishkes.** Each country or culture customizes the dish to regional tastes, using local staples. Polish cabbage rolls can be quite peppery or even a touch sweet, while Ukrainian versions may have grains other than rice, such as kasha or millet, or omit meat altogether in the filling.

cabbage turnip - see KOHLRABI.

Cabécou - this tiny goat cheese has a delicate, slightly sweet flavor with little salt and faint acidity; made in small flat disks, often wrapped in chestnut leaves. In the *langue d'Oc*, the old language of the south of France, a *cabécou* is the generic name for small goat cheese. See also CHABICHOU.

cabello de ángel - a sweet, popular, Spanish squash pudding, meaning "angel's hair."

Cabernet Franc - a red grape of the *Vitis vinifera* species, one of the parent grapes (along with **Sauvignon Blanc**) of **Cabernet Sauvignon,** important for winemaking, especially in the Loire Valley and Bordeaux regions of France, also grown in California, New York and Washington State in the U.S. Cabernet Franc grapes are thinner-skinned than Cabernet Sauvignon grapes and not quite as acidic. They create fairly full-bodied, tannic red wines but don't have quite the tannic bite of a Cabernet Sauvignon, making them good for blending. Their flavor is often described as spicy and **herbacious,** with notes of plum and berry. They are more tolerant of cold weather than other reds, which makes them well suited to the cold winters in New York and Washington State. Cabernet Franc is also known under the French names *Bouchet* and *Gros Bouchet*.

Cabernet Sauvignon - one of the classic red grape varieties, along with **Merlot, Pinot Noir** and **Syrah,** grown in most wine-growing regions of the world but especially well loved in the Bordeaux and Languedoc-Roussillon regions of France and in California. The wines produced from Cabernet Sauvignon grapes can vary wildly in their flavors and complexity. When they are of high quality, they have excellent tannins and lush flavors of black currant, cassis, plum and berries. Because of their tannin content, they are excellent wines for cellaring, improving each year and becoming progressively silkier, more complex and more flavorful. A poorly made Cabernet Sauvignon, on the other hand, can taste **vegetal,** like green peppers or boiled cabbage, or emit a whiff of wet dog.

Cabernet Sauvignon

cabezone - also **cabezon.** The name is derived from the Spanish *cabezón*, meaning "large head," augmentative of *cabeza*, "head," for a large, green-fleshed sculpin found in North American Pacific coastal waters.

cabinet pudding - also **diplomat pudding.** A classic English dessert that comes in many varieties, the most common consisting of layers of dried fruit, ladyfingers or sponge cake and custard (or gelatin), usually flavored with some type of liqueur and served with a sauce.

caboc - a Scottish **double-crème cheese** (60-percent fat content) made from cow's milk, shaped into small logs or cylinder shapes and rolled in toasted oatmeal. It has a fairly sweet flavor and goes well with fresh fruit.

caboose - from the Old Danish *kabuis*, or a "little hut, room or cabin." Today, it refers to the kitchen of a ship or to the last car of a freight train.

Cabrales - traditionally a goat's milk cheese (although there are now ewe's milk varieties) from the mountainous region of northern Spain. Formed into a log, Cabrales has blue-brown veins and a strong, pronounced taste.

cabreiro - an old-fashioned cheese from Portugal made of a mixture of ewe's and goat's milk. The cheese can be appreciated either young, with a delicate flavor, or aged, with a very sharp and pungent taste. The name comes from the Portuguese *cabra*, meaning "goat."

cabrito al pastor - a northern Mexican dish of kid (baby goat) grilled on a spit outdoors over a hot fire, often made with fragrant woods, such as mesquite, to give the meat a delicious smoky flavor. The succulent roasted kid is served with typical Mexican side dishes, such as guacamole, frijoles, chopped tomatoes and/or salsa, onions, etc. The name is Spanish for "shepherd-style kid," which evokes the open-fire cooking method a shepherd would employ when out in the field with his herd.

cacao - the dried, fatty, partially fermented seeds of the cacao tree, *Theobroma cacao*, used for the production of chocolate, cocoa and cocoa butter. See also CHOCOLATE.

cacciatore - also **cacciatora.** Italian for "in the style of the hunter," a sauce made with onions, garlic, tomato, herbs and wine, most often served with chicken.

cacciatorini - see SALAMI.

cachaça - also **pinga.** Brandy made from sugarcane in Brazil, the base for the popular Brazilian drink **Caipirinha.**

cachat - a strongly flavored French goat-cheese spread that's popular in Provence, traditionally made by mashing together leftover pieces of goat cheese, cream, herbs, garlic and brandy and aging the mixture in a crock.

caciocavallo - a mild, slightly salty Italian cheese made from cow's milk, often with sheep's or goat's milk added, formed into gourd shapes, hung by their "necks" to dry in pairs. Like **provolone,** it's a **pasta filata,** or "draw curd" cheese, softened by hot water so that it can be easily shaped by hand, as opposed to **grana** cheese, like padano, whose curd takes the form of rolled pellets. Translated loosely as "cheese on horseback," caciocavallo was originally made from mare's milk and stamped with the figure of a horse, the seal of Naples. The best is said to come from Sorrento, although the same cheese is also made in Abruzzi, Molise and Apulia.

caciotta - pl. **caciotte.** The generic name for a wide variety of small, **artisanal** semisoft cheeses made in Italy, the only common denominators between them being their size, rounded disk shape and fairly mild flavor. Caciotte may be made with goat's, sheep's or cow's milk (or a combination of them) and are often identified by the region in which they are made; for example, one made in Tuscany would be labeled *caciotta toscana.* Some are flavored with herbs or other seasonings, probably the most decadent being one flavored with truffles, called *caciotta al tartufo.*

cactus (prickly pear)

cactus - a flowering succulent plant with needles, or spines, that prevent the overevaporation of moisture, allowing the plant to thrive in dry conditions. There are 1,500 to 1,800 species, only some of which bear fruit. The pads, or stems, known as **nopales** in Spanish, have long been a distinctive part of Mexican cuisine, although the health food movement has begun promoting them for their nutritional value. Native to Mexico, the cactus has been naturalized in Southern California and Arizona, and also grows in Israel under the name *sabras cactus,* cultivated specifically for its fruit. Cactus fruit is known by a number of names, the most common being **prickly pear,** *Opuntia ficus indica,* also known as **Indian fig, tuna** and **mission cactus.** *Hylocereus undatus,* also known as **dragon fruit, pitahaya, pitaya** and **strawberry pear**. These pink oval fruits have moist, white pulp studded with tiny, black edible seeds. See also NOPALES.

Caerphilly - a cow's milk cheese from Wales with a mild, slightly sour taste and a slightly crumbly texture, usually formed into a log.

Caesar - also **Bloody Caesar.** A popular drink made with a mixture of clam and tomato juices, vodka, Worcestershire sauce and hot sauce, served in a glass rimmed with a mixture of salt and ground celery seeds and garnished with a celery stick. A fairly recent star in the cocktail galaxy, it was invented in the late 1960s by Walter Chell, a bartender who worked for the Westin hotel chain in Calgary, Alberta, to celebrate the opening of an Italian restaurant. The drink has since become so popular that some call it the national drink of Canada.

Caesar salad - a salad originally consisting of romaine lettuce, garlic, croutons, grated Parmesan, coddled eggs, olive oil, Worcestershire sauce and sometimes anchovies. The standard story of the salad's creation credits the recipe to **Caesar Cardini,** who was born in Italy in 1896. He and his brother, Alex, and their partner, Paul Maggiora, emigrated to the U.S. after the First World War, living in San Diego but operating a restaurant or hotel in Tijuana to dodge Prohibition. Rosa Cardini, Caesar's daughter, claimed that her father tossed the first salad on the evening of July 4, 1924. Livio Santini, an elderly resident of Tijuana, claims that he made the salad from his mother's recipe in the kitchen of Caesar's restaurant when he was 18 years old, in 1925, and that Caesar took the recipe from him. Maggiora claimed to have tossed the first Caesar salad in 1927 for American airmen from San Diego and called it an "aviator's salad." Before his death in 1975, Alex claimed that he had developed the salad and also allegedly called it "aviator's salad." In any case, in 1948, Caesar and Rosa began to commercially bottle the dressing, although because the term Caesar salad was in the public domain (which suggests it was pretty well known), they could trademark only "Original Caesar's" and "Cardini" for the dressing's name. Caesar was said to be against the addition of anchovies in the preparation, as the anchovies in the Worcestershire sauce itself were a sufficient source of this distinctive flavor.

café - **1.** a restaurant or coffeehouse that serves a light bill of fare at inexpensive prices. **2.** French for "coffee."

café au lait - a French beverage consisting of equal parts strong coffee and scalded milk.

café brûlot - a strong, dark coffee made with liquor and spices, a specialty of New Orleans, customarily prepared tableside and served in a tall, narrow cup.

café frappé - iced coffee.

café liégeois - an after-dinner coffee served with ice cream and whipped cream, not originally from Belgium but rather Vienna, where it was called *café Viennois*. It was popular all over Europe, but the name was altered during the Second World War. The two drinks were originally the same, but today café liégeois is served with vanilla ice cream and sprinkled with liqueur coffee beans, while café Viennois is served cold with heavy cream, topped with whipped cream.

cafeteria - a combination of *café* and *teria*, meaning "shop." Today, it refers to a restaurant where the customer lines up at a counter and collects their food with a tray, or a school lunchroom. The word "café" is the descendent of the old **coffeehouse,** though it now refers to a small restaurant or bar.

cafézinho - a very small cup of extra-strong coffee from Brazil.

caffè Americano - a shot of **espresso** diluted with hot water. Some espresso bars say that the dilution should be no more than a 1:1 ratio, whereas some use two to three times the amount of water versus espresso. See also CAFÉ LUNGO.

caffè correto - a cup of espresso "corrected" with a shot of **grappa,** an Italian specialty, served for breakfast in some regions. Some North American restaurants interpret the drink loosely and serve caffé correto with any type of liquors from Irish cream to Kahlúa liqueurs.

caffeine - the bitter alkaloid found in coffee, tea and kola nuts in particular, from the German word *Kaffein*, from *Kaffee*, and the French word *caféine*, from *café*.

caffé latte - a hot beverage of espresso mixed with foamed steamed milk. When foam-topped coffees, such as café latte and cappuccino, became common take-aways, domed disposable plastic lids were created to accommodate their airy peaks.

caffè lungo - another name for **caffè Americano,** or an espresso diluted with water. The name means "long coffee."

caffè macchiato - also **cafè macchiato.** Italian for "stained coffee," an espresso whose color has changed with the addition of half-and-half cream or a dollop of hot foamed milk.

caffè ristretto - an espresso made with the normal amount of coffee but with half the water, yielding an extra potent half-shot. The name is Italian, meaning "condensed coffee."

Caipirinha - a Brazilian cocktail made with a lime, sugar, ice and **cachaça.** A traditional drink during Carnival, it's made by quartering the lime, then putting it in a glass and pressing, or **muddling** it, to release the juices. The sugar, ice and cachaça are then added and stirred.

Caipirinha

cajeta - a thick, dark brown syrup or paste made from sugar and goat's milk boiled down to a thick, concentrated caramel, popular in Mexico and across South America. Versions made with cow's milk or a combination of goat and cow's milk are also available under the name "cajeta," but, technically, all-cow's milk versions are really **dulce de leche.** Cajeta comes in several different flavors, including plain (also called caramel or *quemada*, meaning "burnt" in Spanish), vanilla and wine. It is a decadent dessert on its own, but is also frequently used as a topping for fruit or ice cream. It is also the filling used to make the South American version of **alfajores.**

Cajun - a Louisiana-born style of cooking inspired by French roots. The French Acadians immigrated to Nova Scotia, mostly from the South of France, in the early 1600s and settled a colony, which they called Acadia. The British later drove them out, and many settled in Louisiana, where they found a home within the existing French culture. Thus, Cajun cooking has its origins in old-fashioned French country cooking, but has been adapted according to location and the availability of certain new foods.

Most of the dishes use crawfish, chicken, pork and seasonal game. Cajun seasonings include **filé,** parsley, bay leaves, cayenne pepper and a variety of blended hot peppers. Typical Cajun dishes are crawfish **étouffée, gumbo** and **jambalaya.** Cajun cooking is often confused with Creole cooking, which originated in New Orleans from a mixture of many ethnic traditions, not only the French but also the Carib Indian, Spanish, Italian, African and American Indian.

Cajun popcorn - a well-loved snack or appetizer in Louisiana, Cajun popcorn is shelled **crayfish** tails dipped in a seasoned batter and deep-fried until crisp. The batter invariably gets its spicy kick from cayenne pepper, a key ingredient in Cajun cooking.

Cajun seasoning - also **Creole seasoning.** A ready-made seasoning mix of salt, red pepper, paprika, onion and garlic (and often a variety of other spices), used to flavor Cajun dishes, such as **blackened** fish.

cake - usually a sweet, baked batter with or without frosting, although pancakes and coffee cakes are quick breads, and potato and fish cakes are savory preparations. Fruitcakes were popular in Egypt during the time of the Pharaohs; cheesecakes were the subjects of poetry in classical Greece. But in ancient times, a cake was never the towering, feather-light concoction that is the goal of today's North American bakers. Not until the technique of beating air into egg whites was discovered did cakes reach their present light texture. The origin of the word "cake" is obscure. Some believe it to be a derivation of the Old French *gâter*, meaning "to spoil," although unless this meant the recipients were overindulged, the connection is difficult to understand. The Old Norse word *Kaka* referred to a sweet pastry. So does *Kuchen* in German, but it is not much like a North American cake: some Kuchen have a butter-rich crust with a cream or fruit filling, more like a pie; others are made with a yeast dough (like *Zwiebelkuchen*, or "onion cake"). The feather-light German cake is more likely to be called a torte. *Gâteau* is French for "cake" and includes everything from buttery-crisp pastries to yeast-raised sweet cakes (like **baba au rhum**) to the delicate **génoise.**

cake comb - a metal or plastic utensil with notches cut into the edge, used to make decorative swirls and patterns in the icing on a cake. Some cake combs are small and triangular with different-height serrations cut on each side for a variety of design options. Others are long pieces of metal or plastic with serrations on one or both sides, available in a number of depths to make different types of patterns.

cake flour - see FLOUR.

cake pans - pans typically made of metal (usually aluminum or steel), although some are made of glass, used for baking cakes, available in all sorts of shapes and sizes, from traditional square, rectangular and round pans to fanciful ones made in the shapes of cartoon characters, animals, hearts and so on. Metal cake pans have shiny or dark finishes; some are coated with Teflon or other nonstick coatings to ensure clean removal of the finished cake. There are also numerous special cake pans usually known under their specific names, including: springform pans, tube pans, baba molds and Bundt pans.

cake tester - a kitchen gadget designed for checking the doneness of baked goods; a long metal rod or thick wire with a handle at the top, inserted into the center of a baked item to see if it is fully cooked. Cakes are usually done when the tester comes out clean. Brownies are usually done when a few moist crumbs cling to the tester (if it comes out clean, they are probably overdone). Before fancy store-bought cake testers came on the market, there were several other items commonly used to test cakes: a clean broom straw, a leftover turkey skewer or a toothpick, which all work just as well.

cala - a Creole **fritter** made with cooked rice, an Afro-Caribbean-influenced breakfast food served frequently in New Orleans, similar to a **beignet.** Cooked rice is stirred into a sweet vanilla-flavored batter leavened with baking powder, then spoonfuls of the batter are dropped into hot fat and fried until golden and crisp. Calas are served dusted with powdered sugar or drizzled with honey or cane syrup.

calabash - see BOTTLE GOURD.

calabaza - also **Cuban pumpkin, Cuban squash, West Indian pumpkin, zapallo.** Any of a variety of Latin American winter squash, *Cucurbita moschata*, especially well known and loved in Cuban and other West Indian cuisine, round and either mottled green or striped yellow, with a flavor similar to that of other winter squash. The flesh is often cooked in soups or baked, usually nicely spiced to complement its natural sweetness.

calabrese - see BROCCOLI.

calabrese salami - see SALAMI.

calalu - see CALLALOO.

calamansi - see CALAMONDIN.

calamarata - **1.** see PASTA. **2.** an Italian pasta dish made with rings of calamari (squid) and calamarata pasta, which is shaped like squid rings. The dish is served topped with tomato and white wine sauce, which disguises the similarly shaped squid and pasta, leaving the diner wondering which he is getting with each forkful.

calamari - the Italian name for squid, *Loligo vulgaris*. This cephalopod has a long body with swimming fins at the rear, two tentacles and eight arms. The name comes from the Medieval Latin *calamarium*, meaning "pen case," and the Latin *calamus*, "reed pen," because of the inky liquid excreted by the squid and used in pastas and sauces. Calamari are eaten throughout Italy, often dredged in flour and deep-fried, especially the small ones, called *calamaretti*. Medium-size squid may be stuffed with bread crumbs, garlic and herbs and sautéed in olive oil.

calamata olive - see KALAMATA OLIVE.

calamondin - also **calamansi, China orange, Panama orange.** A small citrus fruit resembling a tangerine, very popular throughout Southeast Asia, especially the Philippines. It has a very sour taste. In Asia the juice is used to baste fish, fowl and pork. See also KALAMANSI.

Calcagno - a hard, Italian grating cheese from Sicily, made from ewe's milk.

calcium - an essential mineral necessary for building and maintaining bones and teeth, found especially in dairy products and green leafy vegetables, such as broccoli and spinach.

calabaza

caldo verde - a Portuguese term meaning "green broth," a soup made of a purée of potatoes and greens, often with the addition of smoked sausage. In Portugal, caldo verde is made from finely shredded leaves of a large cabbage named *couve*.

calendula (marigold)

calendula - any of various plants of the genus *Calendula*, including the marigold. The flowers can be dried and ground into a powder that usually substitutes for saffron. The flower dye is used mainly to color butter, custards and liqueurs. The Romans gave the name to the plant after they observed that the flowers were in bloom on the first day, or *calends*, of every month. They used the extracted juice of the plant to treat scorpion bites, but also cultivated the flowers for their beauty. In the Middle Ages, a woman who could not choose between two prospective husbands was directed to macerate a fine powder of dried calendula petals mixed with marjoram and thyme in a combination of honey and white wine. She would then rub the mixture all over her body, lie down and say three times, "St. Luke, St. Luke, be kind to me: in dreams let me my true love see!" Then, in her dreams, she would see her husband to be. In Elizabethan times, the powder or the flower itself was widely used and mixed with almost every cooked vegetable. The first European settlers to North America brought the plant with them; and during the American Civil War, it was used to stop bleeding and to sustain the healing of wounds. See also EDIBLE FLOWERS.

calf - the offspring of a cow, its meat known as **veal,** a word introduced to England with the Norman Conquest, derived originally from the Latin *vitellus*, meaning "little cow." The word "calf" is from the Old English *cealf*.

calf's foot jelly - an **aspic** made by boiling calves' feet to extract the gelatin, then seasoned with wine and spices, and possibly sweetened.

calico bean - also **Christmas lima bean.** An heirloom variety of lima bean, white with a swirly maroon pattern over top, with a mild flavor reminiscent of chestnuts. Calico bean soup is not necessarily made with these beans; it is merely a soup made with a mixture of different colored beans, like the multicolored flowers on calico cloth. Calico bean salad is much the same.

California chile - see ANAHEIM CHILE.

California roll - a type of maki-zushi, or rolled sushi, commonly served in North America, with a filling of crab-style **surimi,** sliced avocado and sliced cucumber. The rolls are made by spreading a sheet of **nori** with seasoned sushi rice, then turning it over and placing the filling on the nori side. The sheet is then rolled up tightly with the rice on the outside. The roll is cut into bite-size slices (usually six) and sprinkled with toasted sesame seeds and sometimes **flying fish** roe. The avocado is what makes this type of sushi California-style.

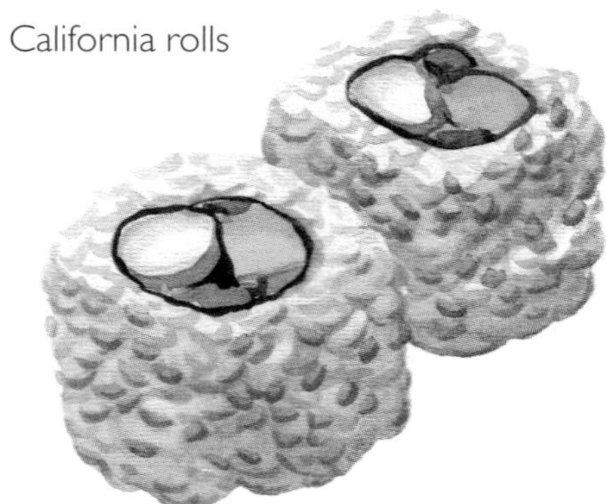
California rolls

California sole - see ENGLISH SOLE.

Calimyrna fig - see FIG.

callaloo - also **calalu. 1.** bitter green leaves from the **taro** plant most often cooked in a soup or stew. **2.** a soup or stew made in the West Indies, its ingredients varying from island to island, but most often using taro root, amaranth, okra, eggplant, tomato, onions, garlic, chiles, cloves, herbs and meat, often pigs' feet or fish.

callibogus - a beer made by boiling tender, young spruce shoots in water, mixed with rum and molasses; a specialty from Newfoundland, Canada.

calorie - a unit expressing the heat-producing or energy-producing value in food when oxidized in the body.

Calrose rice - see RICE.

calumpang nut - see CHAROLI NUT.

Calvados - a dry apple brandy from Calvados, in the Normandy region of northern France.

calypso bean - also **black calypso bean, orca bean, yin-yang bean.** A dried bean, half white and half black, with a black dot on the white part that makes it look like the Chinese yin-yang symbol or an orca whale. The calypso bean turns brownish as it cooks and has a very mild flavor.

calzone - a half-moon-shaped stuffed pizza filled with a variety of fillings, originally from Naples. Its name comes from the Italian for "trouser leg."

Cambozola - a German cheese with a soft, downy rind and a blue-veined interior, tasting like a cross between **Camembert** and **Gorgonzola.**

cambric tea - also **nursery tea.** A milky beverage made of a mixture of hot water, milk, sugar and a dash of tea served to children. The tea is thin and white just like the cambric linen from the city of Cambrai in France, from which the drink is named.

Cambridge cheese - also **York's cheese.** An English cheese made of cow's milk, made by a fast coagulation of the curd; needs to be eaten when very fresh.

Cambridge sauce - a British specialty named after the city of the same name, a cold mayonnaise-based sauce of sieved hard-boiled egg yolks, anchovies, capers, chives, chervil and spices, usually served with cold cuts.

Cambridge sausage - an English sausage of pork, herbs and spices.

camel - the chief beast of burden in western Asia and northern Africa, much too valuable to be slaughtered for food. In biblical times, when there were many more camels than there are now, they were greatly valued for the table. Aristotle placed the flesh of the camel above all other delicate viands; it was also valued by the Persians and Egyptians, but not by the Romans. The Jews were forbidden from eating it. The best part of the camel was said to be the hump. There are two types of camels: the Bactrian or Asiatic camel, *Camelus bactrianus*, with two humps, and the dromedary or Arabian camel, *Camelus dromedarius*, with one.

Camembert - made from whole cow's milk, this cheese has been known since the 12th century. In 1680, a French document refers to Camembert as "a very good cheese, well suited to aid digestion after a meal washed down with good wine." In 1791, Camembert was reputably reinvented by a French farmer's wife named Marie Harel (née Fontain), then 30 years old, near Vimoutiers in Lower Normandy. By one account, she learned the secret of its manufacture from a priest, whom she had hidden on her farm to protect from the revolutionaries in Paris. She is sometimes confused with another Marie Harel, born in 1779, who, at age 12, is said to have invented the cheese on her farm near Camembert. Others claim that it was Napoleon III who named the cheese after having been presented with some by Marie Harel's daughter, Marie Harel Paynel, when he went to Vimoutiers for the inauguration of the Paris Grand Railroad. Still others claim that the emperor did not pass through Vimoutiers but rather stopped at Surdon, where he received the cheese from Thomas Paynel, who married the second Marie Harel.

The well-known light, rounded, wooden box used for packing Camembert was invented in 1890 by M. Eugène Ridel. This permitted the fragile cheese to be shipped abroad and achieve worldwide fame. In 1910, *Penicillium candidum* was added to the cheese, a bacterium that gives the cheese its characteristic white-dusted outside layer.

Camerani - a garnish for fowl or **sweetbreads** consisting of goose liver, truffles, beef tongue and a **suprême sauce,** served in a small tartlet. It takes its name from the famous mid-19th-century Italian comedian Roberto Camerani.

camomile - see CHAMOMILE.

camote - see BONIATO.

campanelle - see PASTA.

Campari - an apéritif, brilliant rose-red in color, made from herbs, **quinine** bark and orange peel, introduced in 1892 by Italian entrepreneur Davide Campari, whose father, Gaspare, opened a café in Milan's Galleria Vittorio Emanuele in

1867. The younger Campari acquired a factory at Sesto San Giovanni to produce the apéritif after studying the art of distilling in France.

can - to preserve food by hermetically sealing it in either glass containers (at home) or in metal cans (commercially). The principle at work is an airtight seal that keeps microorganisms from spoiling the food.

Canadian bacon - also **back bacon.** Cut from the boned, lean muscle of a pork loin, previously cured, then smoked, fully cooked and sliced. It's meatier than ordinary bacon. Canadian bacon is a must in eggs Benedict.

Canadian whisky - see WHISKEY.

canapé - a French term literally meaning "couch," used as a bed or base for bite-size portions of savory foods, usually bread or toast covered with minces or pastes. Anything spread on crustless toast, or bread that has been cut into shapes, qualifies as a canapé. The linguistic history of the word "canapé" begins with the Greek term *konops*, meaning "gnat" or "mosquito." *Konops* comes from the Greek *konopion*, "a bed or couch surrounded by curtains to keep away mosquitoes." Over the centuries, this word came to mean, in various languages, the see-through mosquito netting around beds and couches.

canard - see DUCK.

canard à la presse - see PRESSED DUCK.

Canary melon - also **Juan Canary melon.** An ovoid melon with a bright yellow rind, and very pale green to white flesh that is soft, sweet and quite fragrant. Its name pays tribute to the Canary Islands of Spain, where the melon originated.

candied chestnut - see MARRON GLACÉ.

candied flowers - also **crystallized flowers.** Fresh, edible flowers, such as violets, rose petals or scented geraniums, that have been painted with a mixture of egg white and water, then sprinkled with sugar. The sugared flowers are then left to dry until firm, at which point they are basically nonperishable and can be kept at room temperature for quite a while. The sugar gives the flowers a frosted appearance and preserves their form for use on cakes and fancy desserts.

candied fruit - a method of preserving fruit by slow cooking it in a sugar-water solution. The fruit's water content is replaced with sugar, turning it into candy. After the fruit is dried on a rack, the sugar forms a crystallized coating.

candied ginger - also **crystallized ginger.** Slices or chunks of peeled fresh gingerroot that have been boiled in a sugar syrup, then rolled in fine or coarsely granulated sugar to coat. Candied ginger can be used in savory or sweet dishes and is sometimes eaten on its own or coated with chocolate as a confection.

candlefish - see SMELT.

candlenut - also **buah keras, Indian walnut, Tahitian walnut.** A rich, oily nut often used in Asian cooking, especially Indonesian, Thai, Malaysian and Indian cuisine. It has a cream color and is similar in flavor and texture to a macadamia nut. Candlenuts must be roasted before they are consumed because they contain a toxic substance that can only be destroyed by thorough cooking. The roasted nuts are often ground and added to stews and curries to give them a deliciously nutty flavor and a thick, rich texture. They are more widely available in their native Asian countries, but are available in some Indian and Asian markets in North America. The name comes from the nut's one-time use as a source for oil to make candles. In Malaysia, these nuts are known by their Malay name, *buah keras*.

candy - **1.** (n.) any of various confections with a high sugar content, from the Arabic *qand*, "sugar." **2.** (v.) to coat fruits, flowers, peel, etc. in sugar, usually by dipping or cooking the food in a sugar syrup. See also TEMPERATURE.

candy apple - also **candied apple, taffy apple, toffee apple.** Similar to a caramel apple, this treat is a tart apple, such as Granny Smith, that has been impaled on a wooden stick and dipped

candied flowers

in a thick-colored sugar syrup to form a sweet, hard, candy coating. Candy apples are invariably dyed a bright shade of crimson and are eaten in the fall, usually at Halloween.

candy cane - a hard red-and-white striped rod made of a boiled sugar mixture flavored with peppermint, bent at the top into the shape of a cane, a ubiquitous candy at Christmastime in North America.

candy-cane beet - also **candy-stripe beet.** See CHIOGGIA.

candy coating - see CONFECTIONERY COATING.

candy floss - see COTTON CANDY.

candy thermometer - see THERMOMETER.

canestrato - a sharply flavored, hard cheese traditionally made in the Puglia region of Italy. This cylindrical, **artisanal** or "farmhouse" cheese is made using fresh milk (the ewe's are milked twice a day) and **rennin** paste, and may be aged from two to 10 months. Its name and the characteristic texture of its yellow rind are earned when the cheese is pressed into locally woven reed baskets, called "*canestro*."

canestrini - see PASTA.

cane syrup - the brown, filtered and concentrated juice extracted from sugarcane, similar to molasses, widely used in Caribbean and East Asian cuisine. See also SUGARCANE.

cane vinegar - see VINEGAR.

canistel - see MAMEY SAPOTA.

cannaroni - see PASTA.

canneberge - see AIRELLE ROUGE.

cannelle knife - also **channel knife.** French for "channel," because it cuts channels through fruit or vegetable skin, leaving behind the rind or peel in a long, thin strip, this tool is used by bartenders to make "twists" from citrus fruits for cocktails and by cooks to flavor sauces or to make decorative garnishes.

cannellini bean - a creamy, white kidney bean, *Phaseolus vulgaris*, slightly larger than the navy bean and with a fluffier texture, used mostly in Italian cooking, often with tuna in *tonno e fagioli*.

cannelloni - see PASTA.

cannelon - hollow tube of pasta or puff pastry made by wrapping strips of dough around a piece of pipe or tubing, then either baking or frying it. The pipe is then removed and the cavity filled with **forcemeat,** cream or preserves.

canner - a large pot used to hermetically seal cans of homemade preserves and protect them against bacteria and spoilage. Special canning jars, lids and rings are required for the proper seal. A **boiling-water canner** is a large porcelain-coated steel or aluminum pot with a tight-fitting lid. Filled cans are placed in a rack and lowered into boiling water and boiled at 212°F (100°C) for several minutes to ensure a good seal and to kill all bacteria.

A boiling-water canner is recommended for foods that are relatively high in acid or that have an adequate amount of an acid, such as citrus juice or vinegar, added to them. Fruits, jams, jellies, tomatoes and pickled vegetables can all be canned in a boiling-water canner.

A **steam-pressure canner** is a large pot with a lid that securely clamps into place, and a dial or weighted gauge on the top that measures the pressure inside the pot as steam builds up inside it. Filled cans are placed on a rack inside the canner, then the lid is placed on top and sealed shut. The pot is then heated until the air pressure inside reaches a specific number of pounds per square inch. The steam inside the pot circulates around the cans, bringing them up to 240°F (115°C), the temperature at which all bacteria are killed. Meat, poultry, seafood and foods that are low in acid, such as vegetables, must be processed in a steam-pressure canner to ensure that they are free from dangerous bacteria and therefore safe to store.

canning salt - also **canning and pickling salt.** See PICKLING SALT, SALT.

cannelle knife

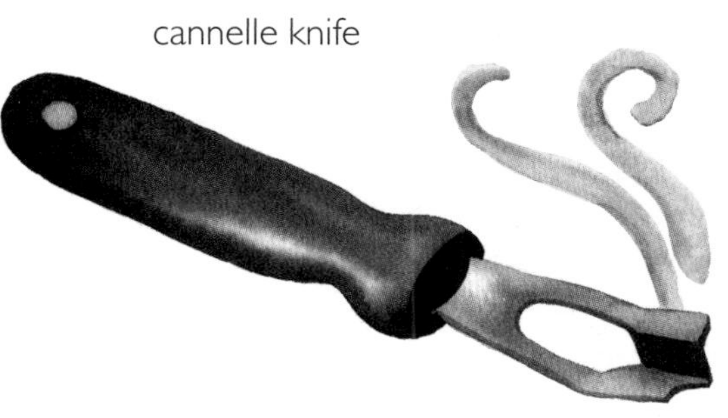

cannoli - an Italian confection of Sicilian origin consisting of deep-fried pastry tubes filled with whipped cream or ricotta cheese, nuts and other flavorings. From the Italian *cannello*, meaning "tube."

canola oil - from "can" for "Canadian" and "ola," from the Latin *oleum*, for "oil," this oil is made from rapeseeds, which are high in monounsaturated fats and low in cholesterol, good for both cooking and in salad dressings. Canadian farmers first planted the crop during the Second World War, and canola oil is now one of Canada's largest cash crops, sometimes surpassing wheat.

Cantal - a French semifirm cow's milk cheese, dating back 2,000 years and protected by an **Appellation d'Origine Contrôllée,** from Cantal in the Auvergne region, originally formed in wooden cylinders called *fromage*, the source of the French word for "cheese."

cantaloupe - a melon, *Cucumis melo,* with a delicately aromatic orange flesh and a netted rind; originally a wild variety native to the region stretching from Egypt to northwest India. First cultivated by Italians outside Rome at Cantalupo, a papal summer holiday home popular in the 15th century.

Canton noodle - a noodle, produced commercially in Southeast Asia, made from wheat flour, and sometimes eggs, salt and vegetable oil. See also ASIAN NOODLES.

cantucci - a sweet, hard Italian cookie made with slivers or pieces of almonds. In different regions of Italy, it's also known as *cantuccini* or *biscotti di prato*.

cape capensis - also **cape hake, cape whiting, South African hake.** The name of two varieties of saltwater fish, *Merluccius capensis* and *Merluccius paradoxus*, found off the coast of South Africa; both members of the **hake** family. Cape capensis is eaten in Europe and the U.S. The flesh is mild, firm and white, and is well suited to many different cooking methods, including frying, baking and poaching.

cape gooseberry - also **amor en bolsa, golden berry.** A yellow fruit, *Physalis peruviana*, similar to a **ground cherry,** which originated in South America can be eaten raw but is more likely to be made into preserves. The colorful Chilean name for this fruit is *amor en bolsa*, which means "love in a bag," because the pretty orangey-yellow fruit is encased inside the papery bag-like husk.

cape gooseberries

capelli d'angelo - see PASTA.

capellini - see PASTA.

caper - the pickled bud of the *Capparis spinosa* plant, a low, prickly, flowering bush, seldom consumed fresh except in Provence, where it's sautéed in olive oil. Elsewhere, they're cured in salt, vinegar or brine. The largest capers have the strongest flavor, and the smallest (called *nonpareil*) are the most subtle. In certain parts of France, caper shrubs are set out on special sun-drenched terraces, and the buds are harvested every two days to guarantee that they will be plucked when they are most tender. They're found primarily along the Mediterranean coastline and are common in the cuisine of this region.

The caper has been known since classical Greek and Roman times, when it was called by its Greek name, *kapparis*. The Greeks introduced the caper to France circa 600 BC. Tender young shoots, including immature small leaves, may also be eaten as a vegetable or pickled. More rarely, mature and semimature fruits are eaten as a cooked vegetable. Ash from burned caper roots has been used as a source of salt.

caperberry - the semimature fruit of the caper bush, *Capparis spinosa,* usually pickled with its stem attached. Common in Mediterranean cuisine, the caperberry is green, the size and shape of an olive, with pale white stripes and a distinct, sharp flavor that's a little milder than that of a caper. See also CAPER.

Cape Shark - the new name given to the spiny dogfish by the USDA to improve its image. Once considered a **trash fish,** it is now hunted

Cape Shark
(aka spiny dogfish)

for both sport and culinary purposes. The flesh is firm, good for kabobs or grilling. Cape Sharks are often overfished in their native areas, so it pays to know who caught the fish and how the fishery in the area is managed to avoid depleting the breeding stock. It's known as rock salmon in Great Britain. See also DOGFISH.

capicollo - an aged, cured pork shoulder butt, mildly seasoned, available hot or "sweet," sliced very thin for antipasto or sandwiches.

capon - a fattened castrated rooster, slaughtered when six months old. The practice originated in 162 BC, when Roman law forbade the eating of fattened hens as a way to save grain. Breeders castrated the cocks, which caused the birds to grow to twice their normal size and easily gain weight. Capons figured on the bill of fare of all great medieval feasts given in Italy, England and France. There are frequent mentions of capons in Shakespeare's plays, such as "The justice in fair round belly with good capon lin'd" (*As You Like It, II.7*), an allusion to corrupt magistrates who accepted fat capons as bribes. Capons can range from 6 to 10 pounds (3 to 5 kg) in weight and are noted for their tenderness and high proportion of white meat to dark. They're usually roasted. It's no longer legal to raise capons in Britain. The name comes from a Saxon word, which has passed into culinary French as *chapon*.

caponata - a Sicilian dish of eggplant, onions, tomatoes, anchovies, olives, pine nuts, capers and vinegar, usually served at room temperature.

cappelletti - see PASTA.

cappon magro - an elaborate Italian salad of cooked vegetables, anchovies, fish, crab, lobster and garlic-rubbed toasted bread.

cappuccino - an Italian coffee made by combining espresso with foamed steamed milk. The name is to commemorate the dull gray or brown hooded garb worn by the austere order of monks known as Capuchins. In Italian, *cappuccio* means "hood." In Italy, a cappuccino is drunk only before midday.

caprese salad - see INSALATA CAPRESE.

caprino Romano - see ROMANO.

capsaicin - the chemical compound found mostly in the seeds and membranes of some chiles that makes them hot. See also SCOVILLE UNITS.

capsicum - refers to members of the pepper family, whether sweet or hot (chiles). See also Scouville units.

carafe - a decorative glass or terra-cotta container for beverages; a French word from the Arabic *gharrafah* or *gharafa*, meaning "to dip up water."

carambola - see STARFRUIT.

caramel - **1.** made by cooking sugar in a third of its weight in water. The sugar will dissolve and then boil vigorously, its temperature increasing rapidly, reaching 350°F (180°C) and turning the liquid golden brown. Caramel is used to line ramekins for crème caramel and becomes the hard crust of crème brûlée when a layer of sugar is exposed to direct heat. **2.** a chewy candy made from sugar, butter, corn syrup and cream.

caramel apple - a favorite at summer fairs and carnivals, this sweet is a whole tart apple, such as Granny Smith, dipped in hot caramel and sometimes chopped peanuts. The caramel firms up as it cools but retains a chewy, gooey texture. The apple is impaled through its stem, so that the maker can dip it easily and the eater can access the entire apple without ending up with sticky hands. See also CANDY APPLE.

caramel coloring - a light brown food coloring made from caramelized sugar and water. Caramel coloring adds sweetness as well as a brown tint to baked goods, sauces, soft drinks and liquors, among other things. See also BAKER'S CARAMEL.

caramelize - to cook food to achieve a golden brown color, a result of the breaking down of the natural sugars found in vegetables and in the amino acids of meats. See also BROWN, SEAR.

caraway

caraway - a delicate plant, *Carum carvi,* used chiefly for its aromatic seeds, although the root and leaves are also edible. Caraway seeds have been around since the Stone Age, when they were used to flavor food. They were found in Switzerland 8,000 years ago, and were well known to the Greeks, Romans and Egyptian priest-physicians from before the writing of the book of Exodus. Caraway is mentioned in ancient Arab and Byzantine writings, as well as in texts from the Middle Ages, mostly extolling the virtues of its positive medicinal effect on digestion, flatulence and the internal organs. **Nicholas Culpeper,** the 17th-century English botanist, says of it, "Caraway comfits once only dipped in sugar syrup and a spoonful of them eaten in the morning fasting and as many after meals, is a most admirable remedy for those that are troubled by wind."

The folklore of caraway claims it to have the gift of retention, preventing the theft of any object that contains it, holding the thief in custody within the invaded house. Similarly, it was thought to keep lovers from proving fickle (forming an ingredient in "love potions") and also to prevent fowls from straying. At the time of Henry VIII, it was called *Herba-barona,* because it was used to flavor the huge barons of beef. The leaves flavor soups and stews, the roots can be cooked as a vegetable, and the strongly flavored seeds are used in cakes and breads, or to spice cabbage, cheese, sausages and sauerkraut. Chewing the digestive seeds helps ease heartburn and, if infused, reduce colic.

carbohydrate - a very broad grouping of sugars, starches and fibers from which the body derives energy (as glucose).

carbonado - an Argentine stew made of beef, apples, pears, potatoes, onions and tomatoes.

carbonara, alla - an Italian pasta sauce made of cream, bacon or **pancetta,** eggs and Parmesan cheese. The name may come indirectly from the Italian word *carbonara* or "coal miner's wife."

carbonation - the process of injecting beverages, such as soft drinks, with pressurized carbon dioxide gas or **dry ice** to make them fizzy. When soft drinks are carbonated, they become slightly acidic, which enhances their flavor and gives them their characteristic tang. Natural ingredients can also cause carbonation, such as champagne yeasts, which ferment and create bubbles.

carbonnade - a French method of braising meat, originally referring to meats grilled over charcoal (*carbon*). *Carbonnade à la Flamande* is the French name for a rich Belgian stew whose key ingredient is beer. Carbonnade probably derives from the Spanish *carbonada,* meaning "broiled meat," yet the recipe today calls for searing rather than broiling. It's believed that *carbonada* moved to Flanders from Spain when Queen Isabella's daughter Juana married Philip, a Habsurg Prince and Prince of the Netherlands (of which Flanders was part), who resided there. *Al flamenco,* the Spanish word for "in the style of Flanders," was among the many cultural exchanges made between those two countries at that time.

Carborundum stone - the trademarked name of an artificial stone used for sharpening kitchen knives. The stone is made of different abrasives, often silicon carbide (a common ingredient in sandpaper), pressed into a brick. Several drops of mineral oil are placed down the center of the stone and the blade of the knife drawn across the stone at a 10- to 20-degree angle. A Carborundum stone often has a coarse side and a fine side, and the blade is roughly honed on the coarse side first, then finished on the fine side.

carciofo - Italian for "artichoke."

cardamom - tropical plant, *Eletaria cardamomum Maton,* from the ginger family, an important part of the Greek trade with the East as early as the 4th century BC and probably the most popular spice in Rome at that time. Cardamom is said to have grown in the Hanging

Carême, Antonin (1783–1833) - 19th-century French chef who is credited with being the founder of **haute cuisine.** Born into a large and impoverished family, he went to work in a tavern at the age of 10. By the time he was 16, he had acquired enough skill to be apprenticed to Sylvain Bailly, one of the best pastry cooks in Paris, whose specialty was cream tarts. While there, he was encouraged to learn and spent long hours in the Bibliotheque Nationale, reading cookbooks and studying architectural prints to use as models for pastries. Flamboyant table decorations in the form of structures, such as temples or bridges, carefully rendered in edibles, such as marzipan or pork fat, were popular at the time, and Carême's sense of himself as a chef was very much linked with his skills as a draftsman. "Of the five fine arts," he once said, "the fifth is architecture, whose main branch is confectionery."

Carême's time at Bailly's introduced him to the firm's clients, who were members of the French aristocracy. In those days, prior to the advent of restaurants, the best cooking was practised and displayed in the great houses, and an excellent table could play a significant role in social and political success. Few understood this better than **Charles Maurice de Talleyrand-Périgord,** diplomat and statesman, who immediately recognized Carême's talent and hired him as his chef. By all accounts, it was a happy relationship. "M. Talleyrand understands the genius of a cook," Carême wrote. "He respects it...and his expenditure is both great and wise at the same time."

Hard-working and ambitious, over the course of his career Carême was employed in many of Europe's great houses. He worked for the Prince Regent of England (later King George IV), Prince Metternich of Austria, the Russian Czar Alexander I and, finally, Baron de Rothschild, among others. A true artist, he remained dedicated to advancing his knowledge of cookery and often turned down lucrative job offers so that he could study instead. His commitment to culinary excellence distinguishes the five cookbooks he wrote, although his message is somewhat dulled by his mangled prose and a pompous tone, for which he is often criticized. But he was passionate about his work, and slackers incurred his wrath. He devoted an entire chapter in one of his books to exposing sloppy or dishonest cookbook authors who plagiarized the recipes of others. He died in Paris at the age of 48. Legend has it that, on his deathbed, he chastised the cook of his last meal. The **quenelles** of sole were good, he apparently said, "but prepared too hastily. You must shake the saucepan lightly — see, like this..." And just like that he died.

Gardens of Babylon in 720 BC. It's most often encountered today in the cuisine of the Indian subcontinent and in Baltic and Scandinavian baked goods and in the cardamom-flavored coffee that is so popular in the Arab countries. Cardamom seeds are the third most expensive spice, after saffron and vanilla, and are produced primarily in India and Sri Lanka.

Cardinal pears - see POIRES CARDINAL.

Cardini, Caesar - see CAESAR SALAD.

cardoon - a celery look-alike, *Cynara cardunculus*, is actually related to artichokes, because it belongs to the thistle-lily family. Cardoon is an Italian favorite highly prized since the height of the Roman Empire. It's also a staple in the households of southern France during the winter holidays. Immigrants from the Mediterranean brought cardoons to America, and they're now grown in northern California. It can be prepared like celery or asparagus and is delicious **au gratin,** but not edible raw. It should be blanched with the addition of a little lemon or vinegar to avoid discoloration.

cardamom

Carême, Antonin - see profile above.

cargo rice - see RICE.

caribou - a species of deer found in Canada's far north, past the Boreal Forest, a lean and nutritious Inuit staple for millennia. Since 2000, wild caribou has been hunted to supply restaurants in North

America and Europe as part of an Inuit entrepreneurial initiative, although it's also farmed. Caribou is said to have a flavor distinct among game and, in the case of the loin, is best cooked rare or medium-rare to prevent dryness and toughness, or in the case of other cuts, stewed long and slowly.

carissa - also **amantungula, Natal plum.** The small oval or round berrylike fruit of the South African tree of the same name, *Carissa macrocarpa* or *C. grandiflora*, similar in taste and texture to a plum but a bit more sour. When fully ripe, the skin is bright red with streaks of dark red, and the flesh is a deep red, sometimes flecked with white; it can be eaten raw or cooked to make jam. Carissas are frequently grown in the warm tropical climate of South Florida, usually in backyard gardens rather than commercially. They are sometimes available at specialty produce markets.

carmine - see COCHINEAL.

carnaroli rice - see RICE.

carnation - the common name for double-petaled varieties of *Dianthus caryophyllus* (also known as pinks or **clove pinks**), grown both for its beauty and for its edible clove-scented and -flavored petals. See also EDIBLE FLOWERS.

carne adovada - also **carne adobada**. A specialty of the state of New Mexico, a dish of pork marinated and cooked in chili-laden **adobo sauce,** the name meaning "marinated meat" in Spanish. Carne adovada can be used as a filling for burritos or **sopaipillas,** served over rice or served with tortillas to soak up the zesty sauce. It is often accompanied by beans or **posole.**

carne asada - thin slices of beef marinated in a combination of lime juice, garlic, onions and black pepper, or any number of other spices, and grilled quickly over a hot fire. Carne asada is a popular, well-loved Mexican dish found all over the southwestern U.S. and Southern California. The name means "grilled meat" in Spanish and can be served on its own, in tacos or wrapped in tortillas.

carne guisada - a Mexican-style beef stew flavored with tomatoes and traditional Mexican spices, often made in Texas and the Southwestern U.S., closely resembling chili con carne but with large chunks of beef instead of ground meat. The name is Spanish for "stewed meat," referring to the long, slow simmering required to cook the beef until it is tender and falling apart. Carne guisada is a loose term, roughly the equivalent of "beef stew" in English, so there are a plethora of variations on the dish in Spanish-speaking countries.

carne machaca - also **machaca.** Shredded slow-cooked beef seasoned with tomatoes, onions, garlic and chiles, often scrambled with eggs as well, served in Mexican and Southwestern cuisine as a burrito or enchilada filling. The name is Spanish for "mashed meat."

carne seca - sun-dried salted beef, used frequently in Mexican and Latin American cuisine. Sun-drying and salting is a traditional and convenient manner of preserving beef, because it can be stored at room temperature for a significant period of time. The strips of meat can be eaten as is or cut into shreds for use in recipes or as a main dish with beans, tortillas, salsa, etc. The name is Spanish for "dry meat."

carnitas - a dish of seasoned pork butt or shoulder that is simmered until tender, then shredded and baked until nicely browned. Carnitas are served on their own as an appetizer; in a warm corn or flour tortilla with salsa, rice and beans; or as a filling for tacos, burritos or tamales. This traditional Mexican dish is well known across the southwestern U.S. and Southern California, the name meaning "little meats" in Spanish.

carnival - derived from the Latin for "a removal of meat." Carnival is specifically the evening of the first day of Lent (Ash Wednesday), which begins the 40 days during which Christians are supposed to go without eating meat. The final spree came to be known as Mardi Gras ("Fat Tuesday"). As time went on, the word "carnival" came to refer to a whole season of wintertime festivities, and later was applied still further to more general types of festivities. The word "carnival" belongs to a fleshy linguistic family that includes: carnal, carnage, carnivore and chili con carne.

carnival fritters - see OREILLETTE.

carnival squash - a small, multicolored, pumpkin-shaped winter squash, a cross between an acorn squash and a sweet dumpling squash, with a yellow-and-orange striped rind dotted with patches of white and deep green. The dark yellow flesh of the carnival squash is sweet and mild, suited to baking, boiling and stuffing.

carob - also **locust bean, St. John's bread.** Bean that yields the well-known chocolate substitute for people who cannot tolerate the real thing. A tree legume, *Ceratonia siliqua,* it is native to Syria and has been cultivated in Mediterranean countries for centuries. Carob beans served as forage for the cavalry of the Duke of Wellington in his Peninsula Campaign and for Sir Edmund Allenby's cavalry in Palestine. The beans were imported to the U.S. to flavor chewing tobacco and dog biscuits, as a chocolate substitute and as a thickener and additive for foods.

The name came out of a confusion about the English translation of passages in the gospels of Matthew and Mark, which note that while living in the wilderness, John the Baptist survived on "locusts and wild honey," making some believe that the prophet made repast of swarming insects. It's said that he was actually eating the more appealing carob bean, also known as "locust." Etymologically, the name comes from the Arabic *karrūba*.

Carolina rice - see RICE.

carom - see AJOWAN.

carotenoid - any of a variety of naturally occurring pigments, usually red, orange or yellow, such as **beta-carotene** and **lycopene,** found in such foods as carrots, tomatoes and corn. They are a prime source of vitamin A in the human diet (beta-carotene is converted by the body into this important vitamin) and are powerful antioxidants that protect against a variety of cancers and heart disease. They also help to prevent eye diseases and vision degeneration.

carnival squash

carp - a freshwater fish that probably originated in China, where it's steamed or baked, often with a sweet-and-sour sauce; in Europe, it's stuffed and jellied.

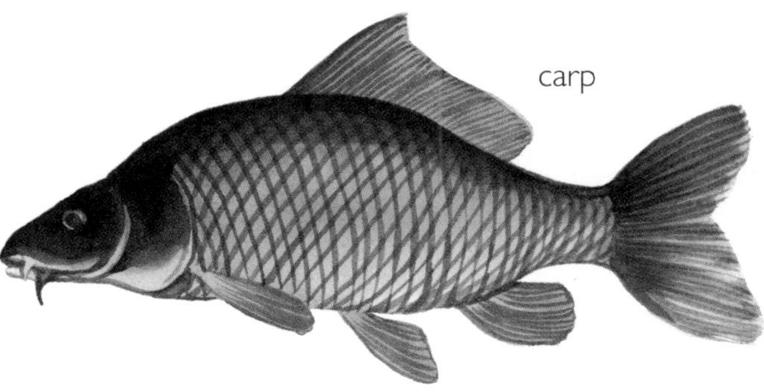

carp

carpaccio - an Italian dish of thinly sliced raw beef drizzled with olive oil and lemon juice, often garnished with Parmesan shavings. Giuseppe Cipriani, the founder of Harry's Bar in Venice (not connected with the famous American bar in Paris), first prepared the dish for a customer who could not eat cooked beef, naming the dish in honor of the Italian Renaissance painter Vittore Carpaccio, whose works were being exhibited in Venice at that time. The painter was well known for his use of carmine colors.

carpetbag steak - usually identified as an Australian dish but almost certainly of American origin; a carpetbag steak is a thick steak sliced along one side to form a pocket. The pocket is stuffed with oysters that have been seasoned or sautéed in butter, then the pocket is skewered shut and the steak is grilled. Some say that the dish was created around the end of the American Civil War and named after northern "carpetbaggers," who migrated to the war-destroyed American South to exploit its people and resources. Steak and oysters were indeed popular partners on opulent restaurant menus at the end of the 19th century, but food historians discredit this claim because there is no written history of the dish until the 20th century. The dish was first mentioned in print in the 1941 cookbook *Cooking à la Ritz* by Louis Diat and was a popular dish on the menu of Chasen's restaurant in Los Angeles, which didn't open until 1936. It's more likely that the name came from the resemblance the steak

Carré, Ferdinand (1824–1900) - French engineer who was granted a U.S. patent in 1860 for inventing the ammonia vapor-compression system used for refrigeration. Building on **Dr. John Gorrie**'s model, patented nine years earlier, Carré used ammonia, instead of air. Ammonia expands at a faster rate and liquefies at a much lower temperature than water, which allows it to absorb more heat, which made the process more efficient. The invention was the first to find a practical commercial application, but it was too large and heavy to adapt for shipping perishables. With further refinement, Carré developed a system to ship frozen meat from Argentina to France by creating the world's first refrigerated ship.

bears to a carpetbag, a popular type of suitcase carried by travelers in the late 1800s. The bulging pocket below and the tightly closed top resemble a packed carpetbag.

carrageen - also **Irish moss.** This seaweed, hand-raked on the coast of northern Europe, New England and the Maritime provinces of Canada, is reddish purple but turns white when dried. Fibers and gums extracted from the seaweed are used to make **carrageenan,** a commercial **emulsifier** and thickener similar to **agar-agar,** which is an exceptional source of vegetable-based gelatin. As a vegetable, carrageen is similar to spinach and can be eaten in salads, either fresh or dried.

carré - French for "square," also used to describe a square cheese.

Carré, Ferdinand - see profile above.

carrot - a root vegetable, *Daucus carota*; no one seems to know exactly where carrots came from or when they were domesticated from wild plants. It's believed that the carrot originated in the country known today as Afghanistan, where it's thought to have been cultivated for millennia. The carrot is a biennial, which was bred to become an annual. The ancestor of the carrot we know today was a deep purple color, almost black. In Egypt, they still grow carrots with small, purple roots. Although already known in ancient times by the Romans, Greeks, Germans and Slavs and mentioned in texts as early as 500 BC, the carrot received very little notice in history and did not reach England until about the time of Queen Elizabeth I. The carrot is not even mentioned among the 90 edible plants in *De Villis*, which registered the names of plants in the gardens of the Emperor Charlemagne, even though the ancient Greeks and Romans used the wild carrot primarily for medicinal purposes.

The carrot was little appreciated as a food for centuries because, up until the Renaissance, it was yellow and tough with a woody heart. Little by little, its texture and taste improved, and even its appearance brightened with the emergence of orange coloration in the middle of the 19th century, thanks to the intervention of some French agronomists. When carrots traveled from Holland to England during the Elizabethan age, they became popular immediately. Shakespeare mentions the carrot in *The Merry Wives of Windsor.* And they were not just used as food. During the reign of James I, it was the fashion for ladies to wear carrot leaves as a headdress — the ladies thought the feathery, fern-like carrot leaves were so pretty that they used them for decoration in their hair.

There are more than 100 varieties of carrots today. They can be as small as a fingertip or as long as 3 feet (90 cm) and up to 2½ inches (6 cm) in diameter. Carrots come in orange, white, yellow,

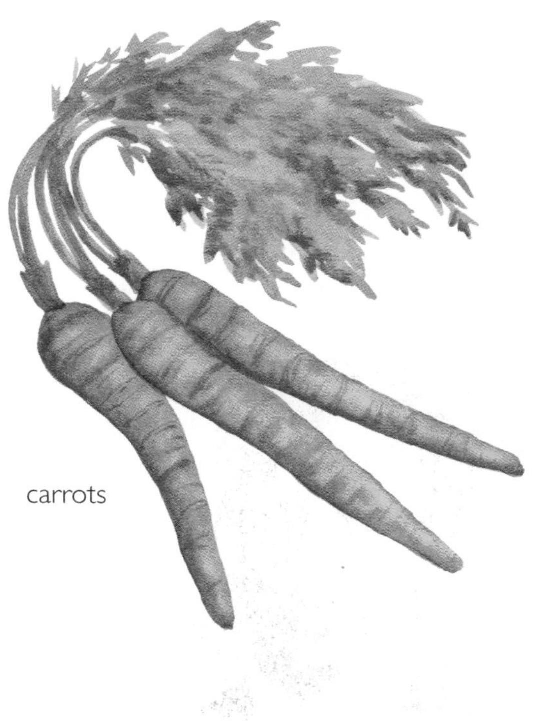

carrots

mauve, purple and black and have unlimited uses, from appetizers to desserts. Carrot greens are very much appreciated by gourmets. According to the United States Department of Agriculture (USDA), scientists improved carrots to such a degree that they now have twice as much **beta-carotene** as they did in 1950.

carrot halva - see HALVA.

Caruso, Enrico - see SPAGHETTI ALLA CARUSO.

carve - to cut a large piece of roasted meat, such as a whole turkey or a roast of beef, into slices for serving. The meat is usually allowed to rest for a short period of time, from 10 to 30 minutes, to make it easier to cut it into even, attractive slices without the meat falling apart. To carve properly, you need a very sharp carving knife and a carving fork.

Carver, George Washington - see profile below.

carving board - a wooden cutting board with a channel around the edge, used for carving roasts. The channel catches the delicious juices of the meat as it's carved, which can then be served at the table if desired.

carving fork - a fork with two long tines, used to steady a large cut of meat as it is carved.

carving knife - a knife with a long, sturdy blade and a pointed or curved tip, used for **carving** roasted meat. Wider versions are better for slicing sturdy large roasts, such as roast beef or ham, while thinner ones are better for slicing more delicate poultry, such as turkey or chicken.

casaba - a variety of winter melon with a yellow rind and sweet, whitish flesh, named for Kasaba (now Turgutlu), a city in western Turkey, where the melon was introduced.

casareccia - see PASTA.

cascabel - a small, round, dried, fairly hot chile pepper from Mexico with a reddish brown skin. The name comes from the Spanish *cascabel*, meaning "rattle" or "little bell," an allusion to the sound of the seeds rattling inside the dried chile.

cascara sagrada - Spanish for "sacred bark," a buckthorn, *Rhamnus purshiana,* of western North America. An extract of the plant is used to flavor liqueurs, soft drinks, ice cream and some baked goods, and the fruit may be eaten cooked or raw. Its main use is from the bark's extract, known for thousands of years in the New World as a natural laxative. *Cascara sagrada* was named by the conquistadors,

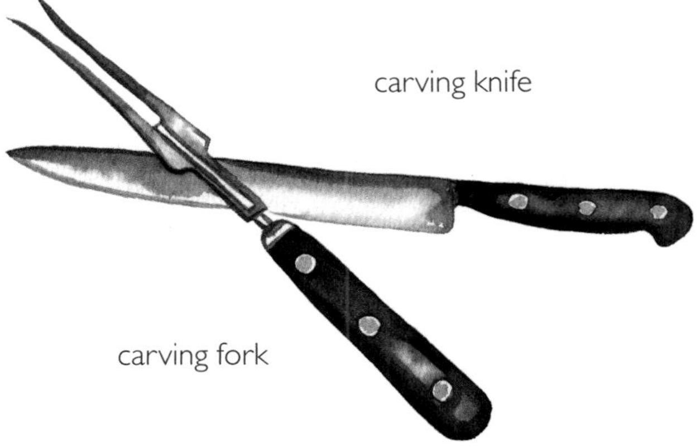

Carver, George Washington (1861–1943) - American botanist, educator, agricultural chemist and inventor. Thanks to Carver's discoveries and inventions, previously noncommercial crops became agricultural industries, including 325 products from peanuts, 108 applications for sweet potatoes and 75 products from pecans. Carver encouraged farmers to plant these crops, and he developed a method of crop rotation that relieved the South's dependence on cotton, a crop that caused soil exhaustion and was vulnerable to pests.

Carver was born to slave parents in Missouri. At 14, he left his community in search of an education, working odd jobs while attending grade schools in Missouri and Kansas. He became a homesteader in 1885, when he was refused admission to a college because of his race, but eventually won admittance to an Iowa college when he was 29. In 1897, he was invited to join the faculty of Tuskegee Negro Normal Institute, later known as Tuskegee University, where he stayed 47 years.

suggesting that the native peoples used the bark for medicinal and religious purposes.

casein - the main protein in milk, occurring when **rennet** turns milk to curd during cheese making; used also for making edible cheese labels embedded into the crust and various plastic products.

case-knife bean - see RUNNER BEAN.

Cashel Blue - an **artisanal** Irish blue cheese made from pasteurized cow's milk; moist, firm and crumbly when young, but quite soft and spicy when aged. At its peak, the cheese collapses in the center and has a pungent, rich flavor from the blue mold pockets throughout the paste. Created in 1984 by Jane and Louis Grubb in Tipperary, Ireland, Cashel Blue is a newcomer in the world of blue cheese, available in specialty cheese shops around the globe. See also BLUE CHEESE.

cashew butter - a nut butter made of roasted cashews. See also ALMOND BUTTER, HAZELNUT BUTTER, PEANUT BUTTER.

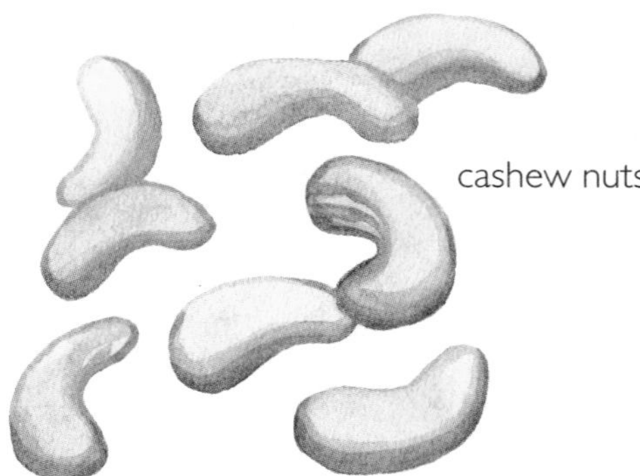

cashew nuts

cashew nut - the fruit of a tropical tree, *Anacardium occidentale,* native to America, usually sold shelled and salted. The cashew grows as a single, hard protuberance beneath a fleshy, apple-like fruit. Both the soft covering and the kernel are edible, but there is a toxic oil in the nut's shell that can be destroyed by roasting before eating. **Kajú** is a liquor made from the fruit. While the cashew is used as a savory ingredient in Asian and North African cooking and in desserts, it is often served with cocktails. *Cajú* is Portuguese for cashew.

casing - a natural or synthetic membranous case used for sausage. Natural casings are usually taken from the small intestine of animals, such as pigs.

cask - from the Spanish *casco,* meaning "helmet," a general term for a closed, leak-proof vessel containing liquor. Casks of varying shapes and sizes are used for different wines, but they're usually smaller than a barrel.

cassabanana - also **musk cucumber, sikana.** A vine, *Sicana odorifera,* sometimes grown for ornamentation, popular for its fruit, notably in Cuba, Puerto Rico and Mexico. It can be eaten raw, but is mostly made into jam. Unripe fruit is used in soups and stews. Some like to store it with their linen, because its fragrance is believed to repel moths.

cassareep - a syrupy, West Indian condiment made from the juice of the **cassava** plant boiled with brown sugar and spices.

cassata - **1.** a sumptuous Sicilian cake, often brick-shaped, filled with ricotta and candied fruit and coated on all sides with marzipan, usually served at celebrations, such as weddings and Easter. The word *cassata* may be derived from the Latin *caseus,* meaning "cheese," and *capsa,* meaning "box" or "coffer." It may also have roots in the Arabic word *qas'at,* referring to the deep, sloping dish in which such cakes were made. **2.** a round ice cream dessert often with a cake center, layers of different flavored ice creams, candied or dried fruits, coated with nuts. See also TARTUFO.

cassava - also **manioc, yuca, yucca.** Originating in Brazil and Mexico, this tuber from a small bush, either bitter cassava, *Manihot esculenta,* or sweet cassava, *Manihot dulcis,* grows to about 8 inches (20 cm) in length and about 2 inches (5 cm) in diameter. It's cultivated in tropical and subtropical regions and is the main food staple in parts of Africa, Asia and South and Central America. Cassava is white, yellow or red, covered with a brown skin, and resembles a sweet potato when young. In some African countries, it's sometimes left in the ground for as many as six years, in case of famine, reaching a weight of more than 50 pounds (23 kg). However, it becomes extremely hard and fibrous at that age and weight. There are several varieties of cassava, all of which contain some cyanide, which is eliminated by the cooking process. Bitter cassava is used to make **tapioca.**

cassava beer - also **manioc beer.** An alcoholic beverage made from the *manihot* plant. The first description of such a beer, produced by the

Tupinamba cannibal tribes of coastal regions of Brazil, dates back to Hans Staden. The Tupi tribes were annihilated in the 16th and 17th century, but manioc beer is still the daily and sacred beverage in Amazonia and the favorite drink of the Jivaros.

cassava flour - see TAPIOCA.

casserole - any of a wide variety of foods cooked in the same dish they're served in, containing meat, vegetables, rice, pasta, beans or whatever the cook wishes to add. The name is a diminutive of the Old French *casse*, meaning "ladle" or "pan," and was first introduced into English as the word for a kind of stew pan. Only later did casserole come to denote the pan's contents.

cassia - see CINNAMON.

cassis - French for "black currant," a liqueur made from the same.

cassolette - **1.** a small individual baking dish. **2.** the food baked in a cassolette dish.

cassoulet - a French slow-cooked dish of white beans, pork, sausages or duck, depending on the region, originally from Languedoc. The name is derived from *cassole d'Issel,* a type of earthenware pot made in that area.

cassoulet dish - a rustic-looking, glazed earthenware dish, usually wide and deep and flared at the top, used for making the traditional French bean stew **cassoulet.**

caster sugar - also **castor sugar.** See SUGAR.

cast-iron cookware - heavy pots and pans made of iron that has been cast, or melted and poured into molds to form a particular shape. Cast-iron cookware is either plain or coated with enamel to make enamelware. Cast iron conducts and holds heat well, so it is good for a wide range of cooking techniques, although it is not recommended for sauce making, because it retains heat too well and can scorch delicate foods. A cast-iron pan must be seasoned with oil, which forms a coating on the surface of the metal to prevent foods from sticking. Once seasoned, it only has to be wiped clean with a damp towel (when washed with soap, the oil is scrubbed off and the pan must be reseasoned). Cast-iron cookware also offers a unique nutritional benefit that other pans do not: it adds a large amount of iron to the diet, because this important mineral leaches out into the food as it cooks.

castle pudding - a type of sponge pudding made in ramekins, **dariole** molds or castle-pudding molds. When they are turned out of their molds, the puddings looks like sandcastles, hence their name.

cataplana - a clam-shaped pan made of metal (the most attractive ones are made of hammered copper), used for cooking a variety of Portuguese stews, hinged at the back like a clam with two round "shells."

cataplana

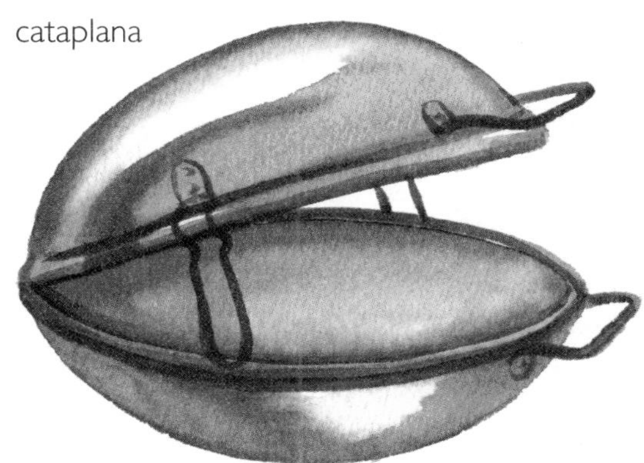

Catawba grape - a reddish purple grape, *Vitis labrusca* 'Catawba', used to make dessert wines, jellies and jams, often by commercial producers, but also found in some markets as a table grape. It makes excellent juice for drinking because of its strong, rich flavor. Catawba grapes are also frequently pressed to make sparkling pink nonalcoholic "wines."

catchup - see KETCHUP.

catfish - the name given to a number of unrelated fish that have in common long whisker-like barbels, or feelers, that hang down from the mouth. Catfish have a very tough skin, removed before cooking, and are popular in Cajun cuisine.

Catherine de' Medici - See MEDICI, CATHERINE DE'.

catnip - also **catmint.** An herb, *Nepeta cataria*, from the mint family and a useful leafy edging plant; it's loved by cats, who are quickly stimulated by its scent. Its leaves are too strongly aromatic for use in food, but its very small, young shoots are acceptable in small quantities in green salads and some stews.

Cato, Marcus Porcius - see profile below.

cat's tongue - a thin, crisp cookie made in the shape of a rounded hourglass, resembling a cat's tongue, called *langue-de-chat* in French and *lingua di gatto* in Italian. The dough, which can be flavored with vanilla, chocolate, extracts or citrus zest, is pressed through a pastry bag onto a cookie sheet or spread into a **cat's tongue pan** to create the cookie's characteristic shape. Cats' tongues can be served as is, dipped in chocolate or with jam sandwiched between them.

cat's tongue pan - a metal cookie pan with several hourglass-shaped depressions, used to make cats' tongues.

catsup - see KETCHUP.

caudière - also **caudrée.** A thick seafood soup or stew, created in France, with chunks of fish, whole mussels and onions. The name "caudière" is the same as the French word for a cauldron or large cooking pot, descended from the Latin root word "calere," meaning "to be warm."

caudle - an English beverage made from ale or sometimes wine, thickened with bread crumbs, oatmeal or egg yolks, and usually sweetened with sugar.

caul - a thin, fatty, lacy membrane from the small intestine of pigs and lambs, resembling a net, used to cover and contain pâtés or some roasts. It melts during cooking.

cauliflower - a variety of cabbage, *Caulis brassica*, with a large, white head. Cauliflower is a native of the Mediterranean and Asia Minor and has been cultivated in that area since at least 600 BC. It's thought to have originated in China and then traveled to the Middle East. The English called it "Cyprus colewort" because it reached them from the island of Cyprus. The Moors introduced it to Spain in the 12th century, and from there it found its way to Europe and England via established trading routes by Flemish weavers fleeing the persecution of Spain's Philip II.

cauliflower

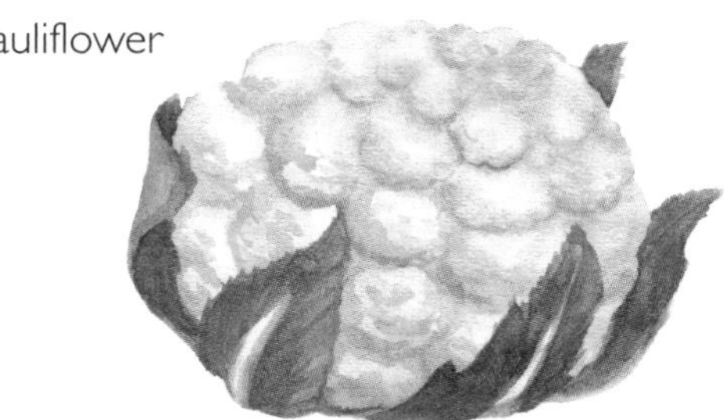

The early cauliflower was the size of a tennis ball, but it has since been cultivated to the size we see today. Ironically, baby cauliflower is now fashionable. Mark Twain once famously said, "Cauliflower is a cabbage with a college education," and even its name means "cabbage flower." Due to certain chemicals in cauliflower, it's best not to cook it in aluminum or iron pots. Contact with the metal will turn the cauliflower yellow, brown or blue-green.

cava - the Spanish version of **Champagne,** a sparkling wine made using the **méthode champenoise.** Cava is produced in the Penedés region of Spain in Catalonia, near Barcelona. It is made mostly from three types of Spanish white grapes — Xarel-lo, Macabeo and Parellada — although other grapes, such as Chardonnay and Garnacha, are added to create complexity in the finished wine. Like Champagne, cava comes in a variety of sweetness levels, from **brut** to **doux.**

cavatappi - see PASTA.

cavatelli - see PASTA.

Cavendish banana - see BANANA.

caviar - salted sturgeon roe (the roe of mullet, cod, salmon and lumpfish are not caviar), the *ne plus ultra* of foods and the priciest. Historically, fishermen were the only consumers of caviar, removing the roe before selling the fish. Caviar

Cato, Marcus Porcius (234–149 BC) - Roman statesman and author of *De re rustica* or *De agri cultura* (On Farming), written circa 160 BC, a text about daily agricultural life in Ancient Rome. This practical treatise includes techniques for building a threshing floor, curing hams, growing cabbage and asparagus, and advice on treating sick cattle. Cato is often cited as having made the first known reference to pizza, in his mention of "flat, round of dough, dressed with olive oil, herbs, and honey, baked on stones."

MAIN TYPES OF CAVIAR

beluga - the largest and therefore most fragile, taken from the largest of the white sturgeon species *Acipenser huso.* The prefix *bel* means "white" in Russian. An average 33 pounds (15 kg) of eggs are taken from each fish, and the color varies from light to dark gray. Considered to be the finest, beluga is the most expensive, although gourmets and connoisseurs don't all agree that it's the best.

osetra - smaller and firmer than beluga and less perishable, ranging in color from dark brown to gold and sometimes slate gray. It has a distinct, almost nutty taste. Many connoisseurs consider this to be the best caviar.

sevruga - the smallest, dark gray in color, with a strong taste of iodine, so delicate that they burst open quickly when eaten, releasing their fine flavor.

pressed caviar - made from damaged eggs of all three sturgeon caviars, pressed together into a stiff licorice-color concentrated mass. It takes 5 pounds (2.2 kg) of regular caviar to produce 1 pound (500 g) of pressed caviar. The essence of caviar flavor abounds, but the price is around half that of the other caviars.

first appeared in texts by Diphilius of Siphnos in the 4th century BC, who made the distinction between fresh and salted caviar. References by other authors reveal that caviar, like the meat of the sturgeon itself, was already extremely popular in Ancient Greece, so much so that it was imported from the Black Sea. The emperor Severus was famous for having caviar served up on a bed of roses, to the sound of flutes and drums. During the Roman era, sturgeon was considered the finest fish in the world, but caviar fell into oblivion for several centuries.

From 11th century trading registers and 12th century Greek poems, we learn about a refined dish called *kabiari*, found in Constantinople, on the shores of the Black Sea, honored and considered a luxury item. It gradually returned to Western tables in the 14th century, probably due to Genovese and Venetian merchants, who controlled most of the seagoing trade when caviar first appeared in Italy.

The first trace of the word *caviari* appears in a Latin text dated 1319. The origin of the word is uncertain, but probably comes from the Turkish *havyar or khavyar* meaning not just any fish's egg, but those of the sturgeon. The Greeks, however, offer another explanation: they claim it comes from the ancient Greek word *avyarion*, from the root word *avyon*, meaning "egg." In France, the word appeared for the first time in 1432 as *cavyaire*. When Czar Peter the Great's ambassador ceremoniously presented the young Louis XV with a spoonful of the priceless caviar, he promptly spat it out, disgusted, on the carpet of Versailles. During the Czarist era, the first sturgeon caught were considered to be the Czar's by right. Later, the same right was transferred to the Shah of Iran. Since the Russian Revolution, the premier supplier of Russian caviar has been the Petrossian family, who introduced it to post-First World War Paris. In 2006, the United Nations, alarmed by the plunging number of sturgeon in the Caspian Sea, banned the global trade of caviar in the hope that the ban will help save the endangered fish and stop illegal poaching. The ban does not apply to farmed sturgeon. See also MALOSSOL CAVIAR.

cayenne chile - a bright red, very hot chile, usually sold dried, used in soups and sauces. See also CHILE PEPPER.

cayenne pepper - a hot, pungent, peppery powder made from various ground dried chiles blended with salt.

cazuela - a deep, round terra-cotta dish used often in Spanish and Latin American cuisine for long, slow cooking. The interior of the dish is glazed, which makes it easy to clean, while the exterior is unglazed, allowing it to soak up and retain heat well. It is most often used for baking or braising foods in an oven, but is also well suited to the microwave or heating directly on the burners of a stove.

cebiche - see SEVICHE.

Cebrero - also **Cebreira.** An aged cheese, soft to cured, made mainly from cow's milk from Puertos del Cebreiro in Spain.

ceci - Italian for "chickpea."

celeriac - also **celery root, knob celery.** A garden plant, celeriac, *Apium graveolens* var. *rapaceum*, from the Mediterranean region, is a highly nutritious root from certain types of celery. Like cultivated celery, it is derived from the wild celery that originated in Europe and the Middle East. It is said to have been introduced to Britain from Alexandria in the early 18th century. During Greek and Roman times, it was used to purify the blood. While used in Europe for many centuries and, to some extent, in Asia and North America, celeriac is relatively unknown in South America and Australia.

Celeriac has an irregular shape and can reach about 4 inches (10 cm) in diameter and weigh as much as 1½ pounds (750 g), the size of a large turnip. The brownish skin is rough and thick; the flesh is crunchy and cream-colored and tastes like celery, only stronger and slightly tangy. Easier to grow than celery, it can be easily preserved, which keeps it handy during winter. Celeriac is usually eaten raw, cut in julienne strips, cubed or grated, often mixed with a mayonnaise or mustard to create *céleri rémoulade*.

celery - a garden plant, *Apium graveolens*, consisting of a bunch of petioles, or leaf stalks, rather than a main stem. Cultivated or wild, this plant got its start in the Mediterranean. Although first cultivated for its medicinal properties, celery was long considered to have aphrodisiac properties. The Greeks called it *selinon*, and it's mentioned in Homer's *Odyssey*, which dates it from about 850 BC. Before the Christian era, the Greeks used celery leaves as a crown for their athletes, who were also given celery wine. The Romans used to flavor their foods with the seeds, and later on, during the Middle Ages, added it to a paregoric that was used to fight arthritis and help digestion.

Celery is really the cultivated variety of a common European weed called smallage, the English name for wild celery, which Italian gardeners improved beyond recognition during the 17th century. Up until very recently, celery was used medicinally only, as it was considered to be too bitter to eat even as late as the 16th century. It was first recorded as a food plant in France in 1623. The first stalks of celery were grown in America 16 years after the Declaration of Independence. The seedlings, sent for by Thomas Jefferson's gardeners, were meant to grace the herb garden at Monticello. However, the plants vanished in the Virginia climate. A Dutch immigrant who came to Kalamazoo, Michigan, with a sack of celery seeds is responsible for celery's triumph in the U.S. The first plant was harvested in 1874, and today it's the third largest agricultural industry in the country (after potatoes and tomatoes).

Celery contains the chemical *furocoumarin psoralens*, an essential oil known to cause contact dermatitis and skin sensitivity to light in some individuals. This chemical is also found in other foods, such as dill, caraway seeds and the peelings of lemons and limes. Photosensitivity has also been a problem for workers who handle celery daily with bare hands.

celery cabbage - see NAPA CABBAGE.

celery mustard - see BOK CHOY.

celery root - see CELERIAC.

celery salt - a seasoning made from ground celery seeds and refined salt, used in any savory dish where the taste of celery is desired.

celery seed - the seeds not of the edible vegetable celery but of the herb smallage, also known as wild celery, used in pickling and as a flavoring.

Celeste fig - see FIG.

cellentani - see PASTA.

cellophane noodles - see HARUSAME.

Celsius - also **centigrade.** Named for Swedish astronomer Anders Celsius, this 100-point temperature scale devised in 1742 established the freezing point at 0°C and the boiling point at 100°C. See also FAHRENHEIT.

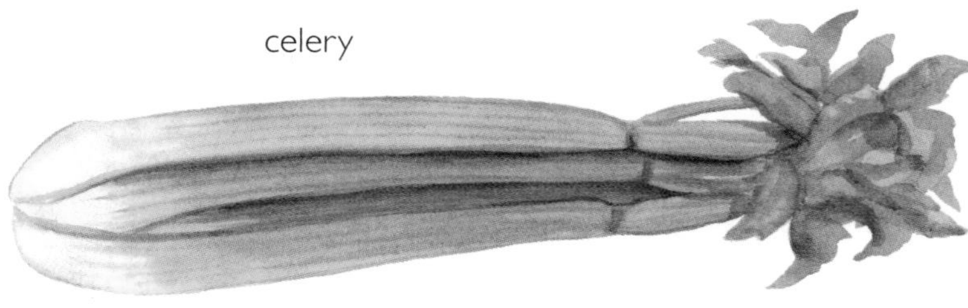
celery

Celtic gray salt - see SALT.

celtuce - also **asparagus lettuce, Chinese lettuce, stem lettuce.** A variety of lettuce with an edible thick stalk, some say tasting like celery or artichoke. Its name is a combination of celery and lettuce. See also LETTUCE.

cemita

cemita - a Mexican version of a submarine sandwich, a crusty, round roll piled with layers of meats, cheeses (usually mild white **quesilla**) and chiles. They are different from Mexican **tortas** because they are served on round, chewy cemita rolls and seasoned with **papalo leaves,** which give them a distinctly citrusy, herbal note. Cemitas are easy to find in Southern California and have recently been growing in popularity in New York, but they can be hard to find outside neighborhoods with large Mexican-American populations.

cencioni - see PASTA.

cendré - in France, the name given to cheeses traditionally coated with ash from burnt grapevine roots, but today usually covered with a mix of industrially powdered charcoal and salt. *Cendre* is French for "ash."

century eggs - see HUNDRED-YEAR-OLD EGGS.

cep - also **boletus, cèpe, porcini.** An edible wild mushroom with a smooth cap and fat stalk. Ceps, like certain other edible fungi (such as chanterelles and truffles), exchange nutrients through their filamentous root systems with tree roots. The origin of the name is from the Gascon word *cèpe*, meaning "tree trunk." Cep has sometimes been used as a synonym for the general term "boletus," which covers a large group of fungi, very popular in both France and Italy, where they're called porcini. They are also called Penny Buns, because their light brown color and large heads make them look like freshly baked bread.

cephalopod - any marine mollusk of the class *Cephalopoda*, including octopus, squid and cuttlefish, which moves by shooting water from a tube-like siphon in its head. Cephalopods have tentacles and sucker-covered arms for apprehending their prey, plus an ink sac, which releases a brownish black cloud of ink that can conceal them when they are attacked. Cephalopods also have very good eyes and usually a sharp beak with which to tear their prey apart. Humans eat all manner and all parts of cephalopods, from the tentacles up to the head. The origin of the name is Greek, from *kefale*, meaning "head," and *pod*, meaning foot, which is appropriate because cephalopods' feet are attached directly to their heads.

cereal - the name widely used for any edible starchy grain or seed, such as wheat, corn, rice or oats, or for products prepared from such grains, such as oatmeal or cornflakes. Cereals are made from different grains left whole, cracked, rolled, or coarsely or finely ground. The word comes from the Latin *cerealis*, "of grain" from Ceres, the Roman goddess of grain.

ceriman - see MONSTERA.

cervelas - a fresh French sausage — sometimes, but not always, lightly smoked — made from finely minced pork or a combination of pork and beef, seasoned with garlic and spices; it is sometimes confused with some forms of the similarly named German sausage **cervelat.** An English version of this sausage is called **saveloy.** The name comes from the French word *cervelle*, meaning "brains," a traditional ingredient in the sausage that is no longer used.

cervelat - also **cervelatwurst.** A smoked German sausage made of finely minced pork and beef seasoned with garlic and spices, similar to salami but with a finer texture and less spice; may be large or small in diameter. There are many types of cervelat, some of which are spreadable and some of which are made for slicing. This, along with the similarity in name and sometimes form to the French sausage **cervelas,** creates confusion about what constitutes "real" cervelat. In North America, the names are often used interchangeably, despite whatever differences there are between the two types of sausage. Some large smoked sausages of fine texture fall under the cervelat category but are called by other names, such as **blockwurst.**

ceviche - see SEVICHE.

Ceylon moss - see AGAR-AGAR.

Ceylon tea - see TEA.

cezve - see TURKISH COFFEE.

cha - the Chinese, Japanese and Korean word for tea, commonly seen as part of the name of certain green tea types, such as **matcha** and **sencha.** See also TEA.

Chabichou - a French goat cheese with a delicate and slightly sweet flavor, with little salt and a faint acidity. According to French tradition, Chabichou should be on the table from Easter to All Saints Day in November, but it also ages well. It's also one of the oldest recorded cheeses. In the 18th century, the Saracens were repelled at Poitiers, the region where **Cabécou** is made. The Saracens were originally Arabs who settled in the south of Spain but gradually moved into France. When they were expelled, they left behind not only goats but also the recipes for making cheese from their milk. See also CABÉCOU.

Chablis - a village in eastern central France in the Burgundy wine-growing region, as well as the name of the white wines produced in the region. Chablis is made from Chardonnay grapes but has a very different character from the Chardonnay wines made in California, to which many North Americans are accustomed. Chablis wines often exhibit a high level of acidity, which some call crisp and others call unpleasantly tart. The wine also picks up a high level of mineral flavor from the limestone and clay soil the grapes grow in, perfectly described by the wine-tasting term "gunflint," which means a metallic taste on the palate. And because most Chablis wines are not aged in oak barrels, the way California Chardonnays are, they lack the vanilla flavors that most people associated with wines made from Chardonnay grapes.

chafing dish - used to cook food and keep it warm for serving, held in a metal container filled with hot water, positioned over a heat source, such as a candle or electric element.

chai - Indian name for "tea." See also MASALA CHAI, MATKA CHAI.

chalaza - pl. **chalazae.** One of the two rope-like strings in the white of a bird's egg that help keep the yolk suspended in the center of the egg white. Each chalazae attaches at one end to the yolk and at the other to the membrane that lines the inside of the shell. Chalazae are completely edible, although some recipes, particularly those for custards, call for them to be removed for a smoother consistency. The size of the chalazae is an indication of the freshness of the egg: the larger they are, the fresher the egg.

challah - also **hallah.** A kosher bread, sometimes colored golden brown with saffron, challah is traditionally served on the Sabbath. The bread is braided or twisted, glazed with beaten egg and sprinkled with sesame or poppy seeds. Two loaves are served at each of the three Sabbath meals, as a remembrance of the double portion of **manna** that fell for the Israelites in the wilderness. For certain festivals, such as Rosh Hashanah and Yom Kippur, challah may be rounded, rather than braided, and decorated with a dove wing or ladder made from excess dough. When challah is prepared, a small piece of the dough is pinched off and put in the oven to burn as a symbolic offering to the priesthood. In Hebrew, challah means "the priest's share" or "portion." Claudia Roden in *The Book of Jewish Food* says: "It is derived from the Hebrew word used for 'portion' in the Biblical commandment 'Of the first of your dough you shall give unto the Lord a portion for a gift throughout your generation.'"

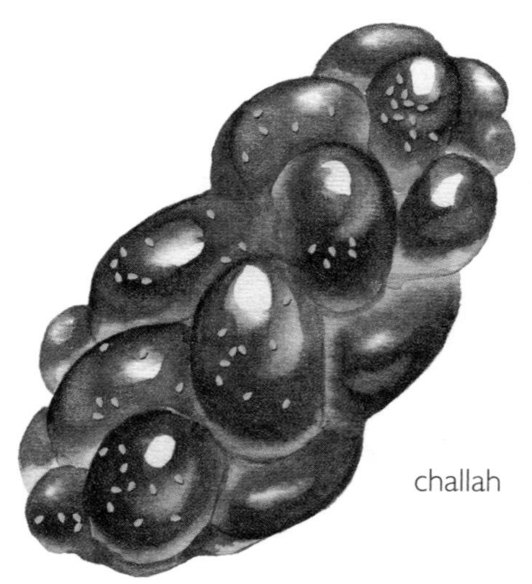

challah

chalupa - from the Spanish word for "boat," a fried corn tortilla shaped into a hull and then stuffed with vegetables, cheese or meat.

Chambord - the brand name of a French black raspberry liqueur, made from black raspberries steeped in cognac, then combined with red raspberry, currant and blackberry extracts. **Acacia** honey, herbs and spices are also added to give the deep purple liqueur its heady flavor and exquisite sweetness. The liqueur is packaged in an instantly recognizable orb-shaped bottle with a crown on top.

chamin - see CHOLENT.

chamomile - also **camomile.** A perennial plant, *Chamaemelum nobile*, with a daisy-like flower. The ancient Egyptians revered the many virtues of this herb, above all its ability to cure ague, a stage of malaria, and dedicated it to their gods. The Greeks called it *kamai melos*, meaning "ground apple," referring to its scent; the Spanish call it *manzanilla*, "little apple." The sherry called **manzanilla** was long ago flavored with chamomile. During the Tudor era, the plant was used in decorative lawns to suppress weeds and keep insects away. For centuries, it was also referred to as "the plant physician," to aid in digestion, stimulate the appetite and treat colic, flatulence and heartburn. The famous herb tea is highly recommended to induce sleep, prevent nightmares, settle nervous disorders and cleanse the blood. It can be used to make beer, but is today primarily used to make **tisanes,** hair rinses, eye lotions, cosmetics and perfumes. Its essential oil is also said to revive cut flowers.

champ - an Irish dish made of mashed potatoes beaten to a light, foamy consistency and combined with cabbage, onions and various mixed vegetables. The dish is served with a giant dollop of melting butter in the center.

Champagne - a sparkling wine specifically made in the French region of the same name, using a traditional process that makes the wine effervescent due to the release of carbonic acid gas during a secondary fermentation in the bottle, a technique known as **méthode champenoise.** The bottles are placed neck first, sloping down, in special racks, and turned by hand in calculated degrees on a specific schedule known as *rémuage*, allowing sediment to collect at the cork. They're then opened, releasing the sediment in its carbonated spray, then topped up, recorked and sent to market. In the early 1970s, the Spanish winemaker Freixenet invented the gyropalette, sometimes called a *girasol*, Spanish for "sunflower," a spherical steel frame that mimics *remuage*, finally mechanizing the centuries-old costly and time-consuming practice. A gyropalette can hold about 500 bottles of sparkling wine, and the entire frame is tilted and rotated incrementally by computer. They're now widely used in Spain, California and France.

The first reference to any "wine of Champagne" dates back to 1493, when it was only a still wine and tawny in color, owing to the slow, manual pressing that kept the **must** in contact with the skin and seeds for a prolonged period of time. Champagne is made exclusively with Chardonnay, Pinot Noir and/or Pinot Meunier grapes, and it's illegal in Europe to use the word Champagne for sparkling wines not made in its region using its method. Some U.S. wineries still appropriate the name for their sparkling wines, but to a lesser degree than before. Although it's impossible to credit Champagne's development with any one person, the 17th-century French Benedictine monk **Dom Perignon** is often credited with its creation.

champagne grape - also **Black Corinth grape, miniature currant grape, Zante grape.** A tiny, sweet grape used mainly for garnish and for eating out of hand, recently resurrected from relative obscurity during the 1980s, when miniature fruits and vegetables became popular. One of the oldest grape varieties known to humans, these tiny grapes were used to make raisins and wine, especially in ancient Greece, where they were prized. Originally grown on the island of Zante off the coast of Greece and named for the city of Corinth, the fresh grapes are known under the variety name Black Corinth; when dried, they are known as black currants or Zante currants. Despite their name, champagne grapes are not used to make Champagne.

champignon - see MUSHROOM.

chana flour - also **channa flour.** See BESAN.

channa dal - see DAL.

channel knife - see CANNELLE KNIFE.

chanterelle

chanterelle - also **egg mushroom, girolle.** An edible mushroom, *Cantharellus cibarius*, commonly found in beech and oak woods from summer to midwinter, the chanterelle is popular throughout Europe and North America. It smells faintly of apricots and, when cooked, tastes slightly peppery, with a delicate perfume. Its firm flesh requires longer cooking than other fungi. Chanterelles cannot be artificially cultivated but are available dried or canned. The name derives from the Latin *cantharella*, meaning "little cup," alluding to its shape. See also MUSHROOM.

chantilly cream - also **Chiboust cream, crème chantilly.** Named for its inventor, a French pastry chef in the late 19th century; a lightly sweetened whipped cream, sometimes flavored with vanilla, used as a topping for desserts.

Chaource - a French cheese from the Champagne region, soft and creamy, like **Camembert,** that melts in the mouth like snow. Not all cheese needs to mature for a long time; Chaource is a young cheese, **artisanal** in its production, ready to eat in only two weeks.

chapati - also **chapatti, chappati.** A thin, crisp, unleavened Indian bread that has been deep-fried in oil, from the Hindi *capati* and Sanskrit *carpati*, meaning "thin cake." Also called *phulka*.

chapati flour - see ATA.

chap chae - see JAP CHAE.

chaptalization - the practice of adding sugar to fermenting grape juice. It was named after Dr. Jean-Antoine Chaptal, a professor at the Montpellier University and later Napoleon's minister of agriculture, who proficiently exposed and legalized the process. It has been practiced in cooler regions of France for centuries.

char - also **Arctic Char, charr.** A fish from the salmon family found in deep European lakes and rivers and Alaskan waters. It resembles trout but has finer scales and teeth, black spots on the sides, and its flesh is more delicate than salmon.

character - a term used to describe the overall impression a food or beverage gives, often used to describe wines, liquors and cheeses. Character is determined by numerous variables, such as the characteristics of the base ingredients, the particular flavors and aromas associated with a particular year's harvest, the flavors and aromas drawn from the soil where the fruits are grown (or the influence of a particular type of feed on the flavor of the milk of an animal), etc. A food or beverage that is described as having "fine character" is distinctive and complex in flavor and aroma, making it stand out from the crowd.

charbroil - to broil over hot charcoal. The term comes from the words "charcoal" and "broil."

charcoal - a black form of carbon produced by partially burning wood or other organic matter and used as a fuel. In the 1920s, Henry Ford, with the help of his friend Charles Kingsford, invented the briquettes of charcoal used today. At that time, a great deal of wood was used to make automobiles and, because the sawed-off pieces were going to waste, Ford decided to sell them as charcoal. The oddly shaped charcoal, however, proved difficult to transport, so he ordered it ground and compressed into uniform shapes that burned longer, provided a more concentrated form of fuel and gave off more heat. Ford's briquettes did not find a market at the time, but were rediscovered several decades later when backyard barbecuing came into fashion.

charcoal biscuit - a biscuit made of powered charcoal, flour, butter, sugar and eggs, first made in England in the early 19th century, originally as an antidote to flatulence and stomach trouble.

charcuterie - a place where sausages are made and where one can find what is referred to in the United States as cold cuts. Also prevalent in charcuteries are **pâtés** of all types, cooked and uncooked, such as **rillettes** (a smooth, rich pâté of pork preserved in its own fat), **jambon persillé** (a jellied mold of pieces of cooked ham with parsley) and **jambonneau** (cured small ham, cooked and rolled in crumbs). The name is derived from the French *char cuite*, meaning "cooked flesh."

chard - also **silver beet, Swiss chard.** An older member of the beet family, it never develops the large, fleshy, red root we associate with beets. Chard is grown for its succulent stems and leaves and is very similar to that grown in prehistoric times in the Near East, Asia Minor and the Mediterranean regions. Aristotle wrote about red chard in the 4th century BC; light and dark green varieties were developed later, and a Swiss botanist described its yellow form in the 16th century.

chard

Chardonnay - **1.** a widely grown grape variety used for winemaking, considered one of the five classic white varieties, along with **Chenin Blanc, Riesling, Sauvignon Blanc** and **Sémillon.** Chardonnay grapes are grown around the world and produce some of the finest white wines in France, the United States, Italy, Argentina, Chile, Australia, New Zealand and South Africa. **2.** a wine produced from Chardonnay grapes alone, made all over the world, usually **full-bodied,** lushly flavored and dry. Most Chardonnays are aged in oak barrels, which gives them extra depth of flavor and complexity, adding soft butter and vanilla notes to complement the fruity undertones. An exception is **Chablis,** produced in the village of the same name in the Burgundy region of France, which is usually aged in stainless-steel tanks or non-oak barrels, creating a crisp, highly acidic wine that lacks the toasty flavors of Chardonnays produced in North America and beyond.

Charentais melon - a French variety of cantaloupe, orange, sugary and with a fragrant flesh that makes it popular both as a dessert or a first course. Available year-round in many places, it keeps well when stored in a cool, dry place, and ripens after several days in a warm room. When ripe, it's fragrant even before being cut.

charger - a large serving platter.

chargrill - a term identical to charbroil, meaning to grill a food over hot charcoal, a blend of "charcoal" and "grill."

charlock - also **wild mustard.** An uncultivated kind of mustard (or field mustard), *Sinapsis arvensis* or *Brassica kaber,* that can be used as a substitute for other types of mustard, although it's better not to encourage it in the garden, as it soon becomes a troublesome weed.

charlotte - a dessert with several versions, including one baked, the other unbaked. **Apple charlotte** is a baked dessert made by lining a mold with buttered bread, then filling it with stewed apples and topping it with more bread. It is served warm. It first appeared in the late-18th century in Britain and may have been named in honor of Queen Charlotte, wife of King George III.

Charlotte russe is an unbaked dessert that consists of a mold lined with sponge fingers or ladyfingers and filled with Bavarian cream. It is served cold. It first appeared in the early-19th century. Its invention is often credited to **Antonin Carême,** who likely discovered the original charlotte when he worked for the Prince Regent of England (the son of King George III) and named his version in honor of his Russian employer Czar Alexander I.

Charlotte may be a corruption of the Old English word *charlyt*, meaning a dish of custard, or it could have been derived from the Yiddish name for an apple pudding called *shalet*, a variation of the word **cholent.**

charlotte mold - a bucket-shaped, smooth metal pan with two handles used for making **charlottes, aspics,** custards and puddings.

Charmat method - also **bulk process.** An inexpensive method for making **sparkling wine,** much less time- and labor-intensive than the **méthode champenoise,** which involves fermenting wine individually in bottles. A blend of still wines is placed in a gigantic steel tank and combined with sugar and yeasts. The mixture is then pressurized, speeding up the fermentation and creation of carbon dioxide by the yeasts in the wine. The wine is then separated from the solids and bottled while still under pressure, ensuring that the carbon dioxide remains dissolved in the wine and that the bottle yields plenty of bubbles when uncorked. Because the entire process is done mechanically, and enormous batches can be made at one time, the cost of the resulting sparkling wine is much lower than hand-produced Champagnes.

charoli nut - also **almondette, calumpang nut, chirauli nut, chironji nut, cuddapa almond.** The central seed inside the fruit of a tree of the *Buchanania* genus, commonly used in Asian, especially Indian, cooking. Charoli nuts are often roasted, chopped and used as a garnish on desserts for their subtle almond-nutmeg flavor. They go by a variety of names on the Indian subcontinent, including *charoli*, *chirauli*, *chironji* and *cuddapa almond*. In Malay, the nut is known as *calumpang*. In some countries, the name *almondette* is used because of the nut's similarity to the more familiar species.

charoseth - also **haroset.** A traditional mixture of chopped nuts and apples combined with a little wine, served during the Jewish Seder meal at Passover to symbolize the mortar used by the slaves in Egypt.

charr - see CHAR.

Chartreuse - **1.** a liqueur made by the Carthusian monks at their monastery named Grande Chartreuse near Grenoble, where in 1084 St. Bruno started the monastery with his first six followers. Chartreuse is a brandy flavored with herbs according to the monks' secret recipe (the exact formula is known only to three people at any given time), although we know **hyssop** and basil are included. Unlike **Bénédictine,** Chartreuse is still made by monks. They were banned from France at the time of the French Revolution, and the order was allowed back into the country after the defeat of Napoleon. The original version is dated from 1605 and was called simply "Elixir." **2.** as a cookery term, a French word applied to a molded mixture of chopped vegetables or fruits in **aspic,** or to minced game or poultry baked in custard cups and garnished with mushrooms or truffles. However, Chartreuse of partridge is made of chopped partridge meat rolled up in cabbage leaves and braised, served with a rich brown sauce.

chaser - a drink swallowed immediately after another drink, usually alcoholic in both cases.

chasseur sauce - a brown sauce made with mushrooms, shallots and white wine, from the French word for "hunter."

Châteaubriand - originally a method of cooking meat, created for French author and statesman François René, Vicomte de Châteaubriand, by his chef, Montmireil, who discovered that the tenderness of the meat could be preserved if two pieces of lesser meat were cooked surrounding it. Today, Châteaubriand most often refers to a cut of meat, specifically a 2- to 2½-inch (5 to 6 cm) thick, tender center-cut of the tenderloin, cooked so that it is well browned on the outside but still quite rare in the center, traditionally served with a **béarnaise** sauce.

Châteauneuf-du-Pape - a town in the southern part of the wine-producing Rhône region of France, which produces some of the best-known red wines of the region. To bear the Châteauneuf-du-Pape name, wines must meet a strict set of criteria determined under French **Appellation d'Origine Contrôlée** laws. They can only be produced from 13 approved grape varieties. On the red side (in order of importance), they are: **Grenache** Noir, **Syrah,** Mourvèdre, Cinsaut, Muscardin, Counoise, Vaccarèse and Terret Noir, of which the first four figure most prominently. On the white side (again, in order of importance), they are: Grenache Blanc, Clairette, Bourboulenc, Roussanne, Picpoul and Picardan. Most Châteauneuf-du-Pape reds are full-bodied, earthy, berry-flavored, with hints of minerals and undertones of leather and tar, ideal for matching with salty, earthy Mediterranean cuisine. The whites and rosés of Châteauneuf-du-Pape only account for about 10 percent of the area's production, some of which are excellent and some of which are less-than-memorable. The name of the town means "new castle of the Pope," for the summer castle built in the 14th century by Pope John XXII, who resided there instead of in Rome, following the lead of his predecessor, Clement V, who shifted the papal residence to the town of Avignon, just south of where the summer castle would be built.

chaud-froid - cooked meat, poultry or game covered with a glaze and served cold. The dish was said to have been an accidental discovery by the Maréchal de Luxembourg in 1759, who was entertaining company at dinner when he was handed a message from the king demanding his immediate presence. Forced to leave his dinner party, he returned later so hungry that he ate the leftover chicken in its sauce without reheating it and found the sauce tasted even more delicious cold than hot. For the next party, he demanded that his chefs prepare the same dish to be served cold, but as this was a day when all banquet food had to be elaborate, his chefs turned the chicken into an **aspic** with the cream sauce coating the outside, set with truffles and other garnishes. The name literally means "hot cold" in French.

chaudière - see CHOWDER.

chaurice - a spicy, Creole pork sausage often eaten in Louisiana, flavored with chopped fresh herbs, onion, garlic and plenty of ground red chiles. Chaurice is frequently sliced, fried and eaten with white or red beans, and it is a common component in gumbo and jambalaya. The name and seasonings are similar to those of Spanish **chorizo,** which was likely its inspiration.

chaya - also **tree spinach.** The edible green leaves of a Central American shrub, *Cnidoscolus chayamansa*, frequently used in Central American and Mexican cooking. Chaya is often praised for its high nutrient content. It provides vitamins A and C, niacin, riboflavin, thiamin, calcium, iron and phosphorus, and is a good source of protein. Chaya is picked young and cooked in the same way as spinach. It cannot be eaten raw or when mature, because the leaves develop hairs on them that sting the tongue and skin. Chaya is also used as a medicinal plant to treat such varied ailments as diabetes, kidney stones, hemorrhoids and acne.

chayote - also **christophene, mirliton, vegetable pear.** A pear-shaped fruit, *Sechium edule*, native to Mexico and Central America and embraced by Asia, the chayote has a pale green skin, white flesh and a single seed. It can be prepared in the same way as any summer squash. The entire plant is edible: the young shoots can be boiled and served like asparagus; the delicious leaves can made as one prepares any other green; and the fruit has a refreshing, mild taste reminiscent of cucumber.

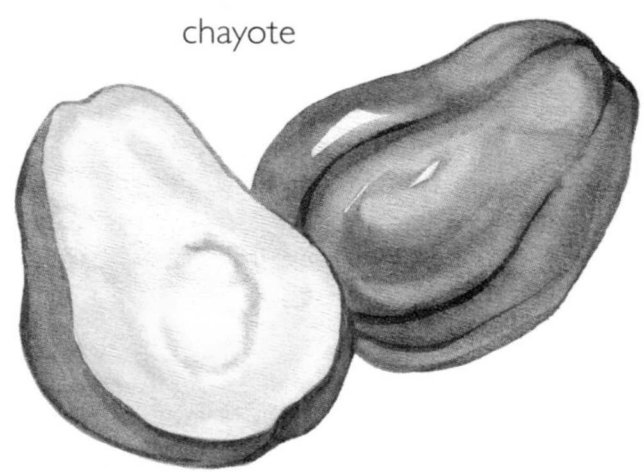
chayote

Cheddar - the best-known cheese in the English-speaking world, named after a small village called Cheddar in the English county of Somerset. It gained its fame in the 17th century when, thanks to the pooling of milk from individual farmers, whose cows grazed on the warm, fertile soil south of the Mendip Hills in Somersetshire, huge cheeses weighing from 20 to 120 pounds (9 to 55 kg) were produced. They were aged from two to five years, until the cheese was flaky, sharp and mellow, as only a fully mature cheese can be. A Cheddar weighing 1,100 pounds (500 kg) — a striking thing to behold — produced as a bridal gift for Queen Victoria was made from the milk of 780 cows. Victoria herself never had so much as a wedge of it; the farmers who made it were so proud of their creation, they wanted it put on exhibit. Afterward, the queen permitted them to keep it, but the farmers quarreled as to who should have it. The ownership controversy ended in court, and the final disposition of the cheese remains a mystery.

Large as Victoria's bridal Cheddar was, it was dwarfed by comparison by a Wisconsin Cheddar produced especially for the 1964–65 New York World's Fair. Weighing more than 17 tons (15 tonnes) — 34,951 pounds (16,000 kg) to be exact — the cheese was 6½ feet (2 m) wide, 5½ feet (1.6 m) high and 14½ feet (4.4 m) long. A crew of 20 worked in round-the-clock shifts for 43 hours to produce it, using 367,000 pounds (167,000 kg) of milk. Altogether, this represented the daily milk production of 16,000 cows. The cheese was so huge that a special trailer truck with glass sides, appropriately called the "Cheesemobile," was built to transport it to the fair. Although free samples of the cheese were handed out to fair visitors, there was still enough of the cheese left at the end of the fair to bring it back to Wisconsin, where it was cut into thousands of 2-pound (1 kg) souvenirs.

In 1860, a cattle disease that struck England and Wales caused such a shortage of milk that the English started importing Cheddar from North American factories, and even today a very large portion of the Cheddar consumed in England is made in North America.

cheeks - see BATH CHAPS, VARIETY MEAT.

cheese - a dairy product made from milk curds that have been separated from the whey, with countless varieties from all parts of the world. The first real evidence of cheese is in ancient Sumerian writings from about 3000 BC, which refer to nearly 20 types of soft cheese. There is some evidence of cheese making found in the residues in Egyptian clay pots, dating from 2300 BC. Egyptian wall paintings depict workers making both butter and cheese and show milk stored in bags made of animal skin.

The first cheese was probably the result of prolonged bacterial action beyond the point at which a homogenous, yogurt-like texture is reached. It makes sense that the **rennet,** an extract from the fourth, or true stomach, of a milk-fed calf would have been discovered as an especially efficient curdling agent after the organ had been used as a bag to carry milk. It is not known when this discovery was made.

According to one historian, the Greeks ate cheese at the end of the meal, but it was in order to renew their thirst for wine. The Greeks of the Golden Age made much of cheesecake, with each city-state boasting its own special recipe for this delicacy. To this day, at least a dozen kinds of **tiropita** (which literally translates as "cheese pie" or "cheese pastry") are made in Greece. Cheese was also one of the foods for athletes competing in the original Olympic games. The Greeks used fig-tree branches as a rennet substitute to bring about coagulation of the milk, and the Romans added seeds and spices to their cheeses. Cheese was a subject of fascination to Roman gourmets in the days of the great Caesars, and over the roads of the Roman Empire many wagons carried wheels of cheese to be sold in the Imperial City. **Pliny,** the Roman historian, in his 10-volume *Natural History,* wrote of *caseus helveticus,* a Swiss cheese that was in great demand in Rome. He described the cheese as hard enough to grate into powder. Cheese experts believe it was the original of what is now called **Sbrinz,** or it may have been the forerunner of **Saanen,** the cheese said to have remained edible for 100 years. The Romans also imported cheeses from France, England and the Dalmatian coast.

Besides the sheep cheese of Nîmes mentioned by Pliny, a cheese from Toulouse was highly rated by Roman gastronomes, including the Emperor Augustus, who liked it on black bread, accompanied by figs and fried little fishes. **Cantal** cheese from the Haute-Auvergne was another French cheese singled out by Pliny — and this golden, savory cheese is still produced today in France, much as it was 2,000 years ago. When the Romans reached England, they were so impressed by the excellence of **Cheshire** cheese that they built a wall around the city of Chester to protect the cheese-making industry. Very likely, sheep cheeses from biblical lands were also served at Roman tables, for many references to cheese appear in the Bible. Semiramis, Queen to Ninus, the legendary founder of Nineveh, was said to have been nurtured on cheese brought by birds when she was a child, and Pliny reports that the prophet Zoroaster lived on a single cheese in the wilderness for 20 years. It must have been the cheese of the same mammoth size as those that David took to the armies of Saul, for David carried only 10 cheeses to feed 1,000 men.

cheeses

With the rise of Christianity in Western Europe, some of the cheeses were produced by monks, and the many French cheeses named for saints attest to the devout faith of the friars who, when they succeeded in producing especially fine cheeses, recognized that much of their success was due to divine providence. It would appear that, during the Dark Ages, the appreciation of cheese was preserved in the religious houses (as was true of so many other aspects of civilized life).

The Latin word for cheese, *caseus*, became German *Käse* and English "cheese," as well as Spanish *queso* and *queijo* in Portuguese. The Italian *formaggio* and the French *fromage* also derive from Latin, although the root of these words is in the Greek *formos*, the Cyclops' wicker basket. (Homer's *Odyssey* tells how Ulysses and his men hid in the Cyclops' cavern while the one-eyed giant milked his ewes and goats, then curdled half the milk, drained the curds and set them aside in wicker baskets.)

Some cheeses are coated in order to prevent moisture loss, spoilage and physical damage. Cloth, wax, fat, foil and plastic are all used for this purpose. Some of them have also been artificially colored for centuries with dyes, which are added to the milk along with the starter bacteria, or rennet. Carrot juice and marigold petals were among the first materials used, and annatto, or **achiote,** the crushed seed of a tropical tree, has colored **Leicester, Cheshire** and **Cheddar** cheeses for 200 years (the Spanish found the Mexicans reddening their chocolate beverage with it in the 16th century).

Because of its high protein and fat content, a small piece of cheese can curb a large hunger. The principle difference between cheese and other cultured milk products is the extent to which curdling and fermentation are allowed to proceed. Cheese is about one-tenth the volume of its original milk and, because it's drier and more acidic, it's much more resistant to spoilage. See also ADMIRALS, AETTEKEES, ALEMTEJO, ALTENBURGER, AMBERT, APPELLATION D'ORIGINE CONTRÔLÉE (AOC), APPENZELLER, APPETITOST, ARMAVIR, ARTISANAL, ASADERO, ASIAGO, AUVERGNE, BANON, BARBEREY, BATH CHEESE, BATTELMAT, BAVARIAN BLUE, BAYRISCHER BIERKÄSE, BEAUFORT, BELI SIR, BEL PAESE, BERGKÄSE, BERLINER KUHKÄSE, BERNADE, BIERKÄSE, BITTO, BLEU DE BRESSE, BLEU DES CAUSSES, BLUE CASTELLO, BLUE CHEESE, BLUE CHESHIRE, BLUE DORSET, BLUE SHROPSHIRE, BOCCONCINI, BONBEL, BONDANE, BONDOST, BOURSAULT, BOURSIN, BRANDKÄSE, BREBICHON, BREBIS, BRENZA, BRICKBAT, BRICK CHEESE, BRICOTTA, BRIE, BRILLAT-SAVARIN, BROUSSE, BÛCHERON, CABÉCOU, CABOC, CABRALES, CABREIRO, CACHAT, CACIOCAVALLO, CAERPHILLY, CALACAGNO, CAMBOZOLA, CAMBRIDGE CHEESE, CAMEMBERT, CANESTRATO, CANTAL, CAPRINO FORMAGGIO, CASHEL BLUE, CEBRERO, CHABICHOU, CHAIVARI, CHAOURCE, CHEDDAR, CHENNA, CHESHIRE, CHÈVRE, COLWICK, COTHERSTONE, COTTAGE CHEESE, COTTENHAM, CREAM CHEESE, COULOMMIERS, CREMA DANIA, CRESCENZA, CROTTIN, DANBO CHEESE, DANISH BLUE, DERBY CHEESE, DOLCELATTE, DOUBLE-CRÈME CHEESE, DOUBLE GLOUCESTER, DRY JACK, DUNLOP, EDAM, EMMENTAL, ÉPOISSES, ESROM, EXPLORATEUR, FARMER'S CHEESE, FETA CHEESE, FONTINA, FOURME D'AMBERT, FROMAGE BLANC, GAMONEDO, GJETOST, GOAT CHEESE, GORGONZOLA, GOUDA, GRABETTO, HALOUMI, HANDKÄSE, HAVARTI, HERVE, HOOP CHEESE, JARLSBERG, KASSERI CHEESE, KEFALOTYRI, LANCASHIRE, LAPPI, LEICESTER, LEYDEN, LIEDERKRANZ, LIMBURGER, LIPTAUER, MANCHEGO, MAROILLES, MASCARPONE, MAYTAG BLUE, MIMOLETTE, MONK'S HEAD, MONTEREY JACK, MONTRACHET CHEESE, MOZZARELLA, MUNSTER, MYCELLA, MYSOST, MYZITHRA, NÖKKELOST CHEESE, OKA, PANEER, PARMESAN, PECORINO, PEPPER JACK, PETIT-SUISSE,

CHEESE TYPES AND THEIR DISTINGUISHING FEATURES

fresh cheese - unripened curd eaten shortly after it's made.

soft cheese - briefly ripened, easy to spread, containing a high percentage of moisture and fat.

semihard cheese - matured with less moisture (may contain a high percentage of fat), easy to cut.

hard cheese - long-matured with low moisture content but may contain up to 50 percent fat; a good grating cheese but difficult to cut.

PLYMOUTH CHEESE, PONT-L'EVEQUE, PORT SALUT, POT CHEESE, PROVOLONE, QUARK, QUESO ANEJADO, QUESO BLANCO, QUESO FRESCO, RACLETTE, REBLOCHON, RICOTTA, RICOTTA SALATA, ROMANO, ROQUEFORT, SAANEN, SAGA BLUE, SAGE CHEESE, SAPSAGO, SBRINZ, SCAMORZA, SHROPSHIRE BLUE, SONOMA JACK, STEPPE CHEESE, STILTON, STRACCHINO, STRING CHEESE, SWISS CHEESE, TÊTE DE MOINE, TILSIT, TOMME CHEESE, TRIPLE-CRÈME CHEESE, TYBO, UNRIPENED CHEESE, VACHERIN, VALENÇAY, WENSLEYDALE, WHEY CHEESE, YARG.

cheese ball - mashed cheese mixed with herbs or liqueurs and reshaped into a ball, which may then be rolled in nuts, herbs or other garnishes, usually served as an **hors d'oeuvre.**

cheeseburger - a hamburger topped with a slice of cheese.

cheesecake - a dessert made by combining cream cheese (and sometimes cottage cheese or ricotta) with sugar, eggs and flavorings, usually baked and topped with a fruit compote or other garnishes relating to the flavor of the cake. It was popular in ancient Greece, but the Greeks used the term generically to include many different concoctions, including "fried cheesecakes," a pastry shell with a soft cheese filling and molded fresh cheese chilled in snow.

cheesecloth - a fine, lightweight cotton cloth used for draining and straining sauces to give them a fine consistency. A sieve or strainer is lined with cheesecloth and then the sauce (or any liquid) is slowly poured and passed through. Cheesecloth is also sometimes used for lining cheese drainers and wrapping herb and spice sachets to drop into soups or sauces.

cheese curds - fresh, unaged curds made when milk is combined with **rennet** and salt to make cheese, left in their natural shape, rather than pressed and molded into blocks or rounds. Cheese curds in North America are usually young Cheddar cheese, in some places called "squeaky cheese" or "squeaks" for the sound they make when chewed. Cheese curds are milder in flavor than aged cheese and are used in a number of dishes, notably the Canadian favorite **poutine.** In Wisconsin, where much of the U.S.'s excellent Cheddar cheese is made, cheese curds are often served battered and fried.

cheese drainer - a small mold used to drain off whey from curd cheese. Sometimes lined and/or covered with cheesecloth, cheese drainers are made of china, earthenware and metal (mostly aluminum).

cheese dream - the original name for a grilled cheese sandwich, made fashionable during the Depression as a frugal but tasty Sunday supper dish for company. Cheese dreams are also a kitschy appetizer, a type of open-faced grilled cheese made of bread topped with slice of cheese, then bacon, and broiled until the cheese is melted and the bacon is crisp.

cheese grater - see GRATER.

cheese iron - a small, metal corer for removing a plug from the interior of a cheese to test the aroma, flavor and texture.

cheese knives - any of a variety of specialized knives used for cutting different types of cheese.

CHEESE KNIVES

cheese plane - shaped like a spatula with a razor-sharp slot cut in the center, made for planing thin slices off a block or wedge of cheese.

double-handled cheese knife - works well for slicing large wheels or blocks of cheese that an ordinary knife would not get through in a single pass.

cheese plane

Gorgonzola knife - with a wide, dull-blade, excellent for cutting and spreading soft, crumbly cheeses, such as blue.

offset cheese knife - with a 5-inch (12.5 cm) blade, good for many different cheeses, especially sticky semisoft ones, which won't adhere to the perforated or indented sides of the blade.

Parmesan knife - round with a pointed tip, perfect for cutting hard cheeses.

Parmesan knife

Chef Boyardee (Hector Boiardi) (1897–1985) - Italian-American chef whose eponymous brand sparked a national fascination with Italian food in the 1920s. Hector Boiardi arrived in New York City at the age of 18 and cooked at the Plaza Hotel, where his brother, who worked there, helped him find work. Hector went on to cook at the Ritz Carlton and then moved to Cleveland to become chef at the Hotel Winton. Boiardi opened his first restaurant in 1924, serving Italian food so popular that guests would buy sauce to take home. The demand was so great that he opened a production kitchen and began selling dinner kits of dry pasta, tomato sauce and Parmesan cheese, all for 60 cents, and the first of his products was born. To make it easier for Americans to pronounce his name and tackle it phonetically, he became Chef Boyardee and, in the process, created an enduring brand. By 1928, he moved his take-out business into assembly-line production and he spent the 1930s developing the sales and distribution of his packaged meals. Because of the economy of his products, Boiardi did well during the Depression and also benefited from military contracts. After the war, American Home Foods paid handsomely for Boiardi's company. He stayed on as an advisor until his death at the age of 87.

cheesemonger - an English dealer of cheese.

cheese plane - see CHEESE KNIVES.

cheese rennet - any plant whose leaves, sap or flowers can curdle milk in the cheese-making process.

cheese scraper - another name for a *girolle*, used to scrape lovely rosettes from **tête de moine** cheese. It can be used on any wheel of firm or hard cheese to make flowers or curls.

cheese steak - also **Philadelphia cheese steak, Philly cheese steak.** An American sandwich consisting of a bun topped with thinly sliced beef, sautéed onions and cheese.

cheese straw - a strip of pastry, especially puff pastry, sprinkled with cheese (or with cheese mixed into the dough) that is twisted and baked until puffed and golden, served as an appetizer.

cheeseweed - see MALLOW.

cheese wire - a long piece of fine wire with a thin, cylindrical handle attached to each end, used for cutting wheels of cheese that a knife would not be long enough to cut. This tool is also useful for cutting large cakes, such as a wedding cake, into layers.

chef - a title given to a person in charge of a professional kitchen and adept at preparing food. The chef's duties can include everything from creating menus and ordering the food to coordinating the kitchen staff and managing costs. He or she is the executive chef in what French chef **Auguste Escoffier** called the "brigade system," which he developed in the late-19th century based on his military experience. He created a hierarchy of cooks from the chef to the *sous chef* to the *saucier* etc. See also BRIGADE SYSTEM, ENTREMETIER, GARDE MANGER, PASTRY CHEF, POISSONIER, RÔTISSEUR, SAUCIER, SOUS CHEF, TOURNANT.

Chef Boyardee (Hector Boiardi) - see profile above.

chefs de partie - see BRIGADE SYSTEM.

chef's knife - also **cook's knife, French knife.** An all-purpose knife appropriate for a number of cutting jobs, including chopping, mincing and slicing. It has a sturdy, heavy handle and a tapered blade that measures between 8 and 14 inches (35 cm) long. The term "cook's knife" is considered less off-putting by some, since it implies that anyone, not just someone with specialized knowledge, can use it.

chef's salad - a salad of tossed greens with cold **julienned** meats and cheeses, sliced vegetables and hard-boiled eggs, topped with a dressing, usually served as an entrée.

Chelsea bun - a sweet bun made by tightly coiling a strip of egg-enriched bread dough flavored with lemon zest around a filling of currants, cinnamon and sugar. The buns are then packed into a baking pan and allowed to rise side-by-side so that, when baked and cut apart, they come out square. The buns are often sprinkled with coarse sugar or glazed. Chelsea buns were named for the Bun House of Chelsea in London, where they were originally made in the 18th century.

chemical leavener - a chemical, such as baking soda or baking powder, that is added to a dough or batter to make it rise, using the carbon dioxide gas produced when the leavener comes into contact with liquid. See also LEAVENING.

chemisé - also **en chemise.** A gastronomic term for food that is coated with a sauce or wrapped in a covering, such as a crêpe or a layer of pastry. The term means "in a shirt," from the French "chemise," meaning "shirt."

Chenin Blanc - one of the classic white grape varieties grown around the world, along with **Chardonnay, Riesling, Sauvignon Blanc** and **Sémillon.** Chenin Blanc is widely grown in the Loire Valley in France and in California, and is the main grape grown in South Africa, where it is known by the name Steen. It creates wines that can be everything from dry to sweet, usually full-bodied, with lovely fruit flavors, often reminiscent of melon, apple and pears.

chenna - also **channa.** A soft, very mild, unripened cheese made in India, usually from cow's milk, and used extensively in cooking, from savory main dishes to desserts. Chenna is a fresher, less dried form of **paneer,** which is pressed and drained to remove more of the whey.

cherimoya - the fruit of *Annona cherimola*, a tree native to the mountains of Peru and Ecuador, where archeologists have dug up prehistoric terra-cotta vases depicting the tree. Sheltered in a green alligator-like skin, the heart-shaped cherimoya is about the same size as a fist. The name comes from the Spanish *chirimuya*, meaning "cold seeds," presumably an allusion to the wet freshness of the fruit and the seeds it contains. Despite the fact that the outer appearance is not very glamorous, when absolutely ripe, this fruit, which was a favorite of Mark Twain, is one of heaven's great contributions. The texture is close to custard, which is why cherimoyas are more often called "custard apples." The ancient Peruvians cultivated cherimoyas, and the cherimoyas from Huánuco still are famous in that country.

cherimoya

cherries jubilee - a dessert consisting of pitted dark red cherries that have been sautéed with sugar, and brandy or **Kirsch,** flambéed and served over vanilla ice cream. They were invented by the great French chef **Auguste Escoffier** in 1887 for Queen Victoria's Golden Jubilee. They were first called "jubilee cherries."

cherry - a small, stoned fruit of the genus *Prunus*. Cherry pits have been found in the earliest human habitations. **Theophrastus,** the Greek "Father of Botany," described cherries in a book written about 300 BC, and **Pliny,** the Roman historian, mentioned 10 kinds of cherries favored by his countrymen. The ancient Chinese first cultivated cherries, but it was the Greeks and Romans who perfected the fruit. Grafting of cherry trees to develop superior fruit was a practice known in 50 BC. Cherry pie was first introduced in England during the reign of Queen Elizabeth I, and it has remained a favorite sweet with the English ever since, as it has in all other English-speaking countries.

Cherry trees were probably cultivated first in Asia Minor near the town of Cerasus, which loans its name to the cherry, or *cerise*. Cherries are grown on large trees with heavy foliage. Picking them is difficult because not all the fruit ripens at the same time. Japanese cherry trees do not produce the sweet variety found in produce markets but are grown for their beautiful blossoms. According to legend, a 5th-century Japanese emperor came to be in awe of the cherry blossoms when they floated into his sake cup while he was boating on a lake. He decided to enjoy his sake underneath the cherry trees every day after that. Even today, the Japanese annually rejoice at the arrival of spring in the blossoming cherry orchards.

Cherries are categorized into three groups: sweet for eating, sour for cooking, and hybrids for both eating and cooking, such as Dukes and

Royals. In the U.S., the most popular sweet cherry is the Bing. It developed as a chance seedling from an older variety called the Republican, carried to Oregon in a covered wagon by a family of horticulturists named Lewelling. They named the Bing after a Chinese worker in their orchards. Some other varieties of cherries available are: Amarelle, Black Tartarian, Damasca or Ameresca, Early Richmond, Early Rivers, Maraschino, Montmorency, Morello and Royal Ann.

cherry bomb - see CHERRY PEPPER.

cherry cake - see POUND CAKE.

cherry pepper - also **cherry bomb, Creole cherry pepper, hot cherry pepper, Hungarian cherry pepper, wiri-wiri.** A sweet to medium-hot red chile pepper shaped like a plump cherry, used fresh but more often used for pickling. It looks similar to a **cascabel** chile, but is never dried like the cascabel because of its thick, moist flesh. It is called wiri-wiri in the Caribbean. See also CHILE PEPPER.

cherry pitter - also **cherry stoner.** A kitchen utensil created in a variety of shapes and sizes in the 19th century, now a small hand-held device with a long, thin prong that pushes the cherry pit out through the bottom of the fruit as it sits in the perforated holder. It is essentially the same device as an olive pitter, which works in much the same way.

cherrystone clam - a quahog, or hard-shell clam, in middle growth. See also CLAM.

cherry tomato - see TOMATO.

chervil - a mild-flavored relative of parsley (similar, but more delicate) from western Asia and the Balkans. The Latin name, given by Roman historian **Pliny** himself, is *cerefolium*, meaning "waxen-leaved." The dainty chervil was known to the Ancient Greeks, and, in Rome, the foliage was eaten in salads and the roots used as a vegetable. Charlemagne grew it in his gardens, and Pliny recommended chervil seeds soaked in vinegar as the best cure for hiccups. The great English herbalist **John Gerard** remarked, "Chervil root boiled and after dressed as the cunning cook knoweth how better than myself is very good for old people that are dull and without courage."

chervil

The flavor and aroma are very similar to the myrrh brought by the Magi to the baby Jesus. Because of this and because chervil is considered a symbol of new life, it became customary to serve chervil soup on Holy Thursday. Lacy chervil leaves, one of the most delicate of herbs, render a mild anise flavor. This member of the **fines herbes** quartet should be used fresh, since the dry herb has little flavor. Today, it's far more popular in France than in the United States. Hemlock, a wild plant that resembles chervil, is poisonous and should be avoided.

Cheshire - one of England's oldest and finest cheeses, it was even mentioned in the *Domesday Book* in the 11th century; it is appealing to the eye, as it can range from red to white and can also be blue-veined. When the Roman legions landed in England, they discovered the cheese that would later became part of their daily ration. In the 1930s, more than 400 farms produced Cheshire cheese, but today there are less than a handful. Cheshire derives its distinct character from the salt marshes on which local cattle graze. Most of the Cheshire produced now is factory-made. However, there is a growing demand for traditionally made Cheshire.

chess pie - a classic open-faced dessert pie native to the American South, made with a very simple filling of butter, sugar, eggs and vanilla, similar to the filling of a butter tart. Some chess pie recipes also call for the addition of lemon juice, vinegar or cornmeal for added flavor and/or texture.

chester pudding - an egg custard with almonds, lemon rind and butter spread in a pastry shell and topped with a stiffly beaten egg white. Lemon meringue pie derives from this pudding.

chestnut - a starchy and sweet, roughly spherical nut with a shiny brown husk enclosing crunchy, ivory-colored flesh which softens when cooked. Produced by temperate-zone species including the American chestnut, *Castanea dentata,* the Chinese chestnut, *C. mollissima,* and the European or Spanish chestnut, *C. sativa,* chestnuts were eaten by Native Americans, and early Greeks and Romans. Collected from both wild and cultivated species, they remained an everyday staple, subsistence food and common livestock fodder on both sides of the Atlantic until the early 20th century.

Often eaten whole, chestnuts were also ground into flour or meal that earned them the nickname "bread of the mountains." The meal was used in the original Italian polenta; the flour is still used in bread and other baked goods, particularly in southern Europe. Candied for the famous French confection, **marrons glacés,** the nuts are cooked and sieved for the classic **Mont Blanc** and **Nesselrode** puddings. Contemporary cooks use sliced or whole chestnuts in hors d'oeuvres, pilafs, salads, soups, stews and stuffing, and puréed in dips and pesto, as well.

Dubbed "the king of the forest" and growing to a height of more than 100 feet (30 m) and a girth of more than 8 feet (2.4 m), the American chestnut once covered 9 million acres (4.75 million hectares) of Carolinian woodlands from southern Ontario to northern Florida. Across the Appalachians, where the abundance of chestnut blossoms gave the peaks a snowy appearance in the spring, the nuts — a significant source of cash for local families — were gathered in the fall. Shipped to large eastern cities, they were a popular snack in the chilly weather (served hot from the portable roasters of sidewalk vendors), and a favorite Christmas treat at home (roasted over the fire or added to poultry stuffing). But an Asian fungus began killing this native species early in the 1900s. Virtually wiped out by the 1950s, it is now considered a threatened species by the World Wildlife Fund. The American Chestnut Foundation and The Canadian Chestnut Council, work for its restoration. Since the 1700s, several varieties of chestnut species (including the bushy, blight-resistant, Chinese chestnut) have been introduced to North America.

To prevent stomach upsets, chestnuts should not be eaten raw. Before cooking, the meat may be removed by halving each one using clean secateurs, then roasting, steaming or microwaving the nuts until the flesh falls easily from the shells. Whole chestnuts can be boiled, roasted on an open fire or baked in the oven by first piercing a small slit or scoring an X in the shell of each one to prevent it bursting in the heat (specialty knives are sold for this purpose). Dried, frozen and vacuum-packed chestnuts are available throughout the year; fresh ones from October to February, mostly imported from Italy and Portugal.

chestnut cream - a sweet, creamy mélange of puréed chestnuts, sugar and vanilla, used in chestnut cakes, truffle fillings, ice creams and even as a spread for toast. It can be hard to find outside of gourmet shops, where it may also be sold under its French name, *crème de marrons*. It is sweeter and creamier than **chestnut purée.**

chestnut knife - a special knife with a short, fat, hooked blade designed to score the tough skin of a chestnut before it is roasted. As it roasts, the skin curls back, allowing it to be peeled more easily. A chestnut knife is also helpful for scratching off stubborn pieces of skin that roasting has not quite softened.

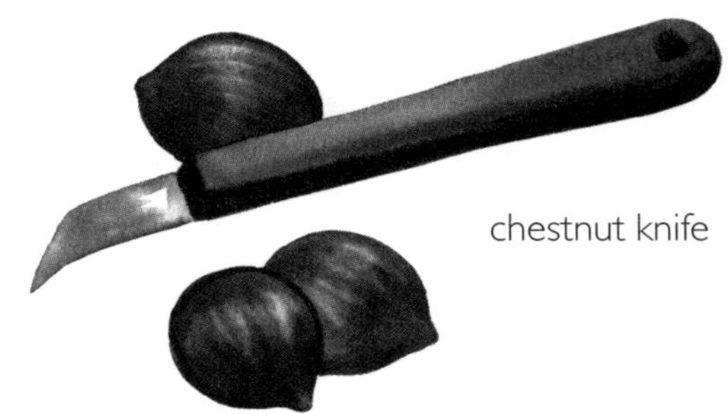
chestnut knife

chestnut purée - chestnuts ground, then cooked until thick and pasty, available in cans and jars for use in everything from soup to desserts, such as **Mont Blanc.** Chestnut purée may be sweetened or unsweetened, or flavored with orange or vanilla. It is much less sweet than **chestnut cream.**

chèvre - the French name for nanny goat, or goat's milk cheese.

chewing gum - a range of gums, resins and plant latexes that have been chewed for thousands of years. The oldest known gum was found in 1993 in what is now western Sweden.

It was a 9,000-year-old piece of resin sweetened with honey, and unsurprisingly bore the tooth marks of a teenager. Commercial chewing gum as we know it today was first created in Bangor, Maine, in 1848 by John Baron Curtis, with only a middling outcome. However, in 1869, a New Yorker by the name of Thomas Adams used **chicle,** the dried latex material from a Central American sapodilla tree. In 1871, Adams received a patent for chicle gum. In 1885, William J. White of Cleveland further refined and improved gum by adding syrup and peppermint. Chicagoan **William Wrigley** invented Juicy Fruit and Spearmint gums in 1893; in 1900, Frank Fleer of Philadelphia placed a hard shell on the gum and called it Chiclets, and 28 years later, Fleer invented bubble gum.

chewy - a wine-tasting term for a wine, often a tannic red, that has a viscous texture and is so full-bodied that it feels as if it could be chewed, instead of drunk.

Chianti - a full-bodied Italian red wine, probably the most famous wine of Tuscany, once the clichéd companion to all Italian meals in North America and served in a straw-covered bottle. Although Chianti had a reputation for poor quality in the 1970s and 1980s, today's regulated Chianti Classico wines are a different matter. Chianti Classico's main grape is the **Sangiovese,** blended with a variety of different reds, such as Cabernet Sauvignon, Canaiolo and Merlot. By law, it can also contain a small percentage of white grapes, such as Trebbiano and Malvasia, for added acidity and zest, but most producers of fine Chianti omit these in favor of a blend of balanced reds. A good Chianti is richly flavored, with notes of plum and cherry, a bit spicy with a hint of saltiness (though it contains no salt at all). Chianti enjoyed a surge in popularity, at least in name, in 1991, thanks to the movie *The Silence of the Lambs,* in which cannibalistic serial killer Hannibal Lecter says: "A census taker once tried to test me," he says. "I ate his liver with some fava beans and a nice Chianti."

chia seeds - the tiny, black seeds of the chia plant, *Salvia hispanica,* eaten frequently in their native Mexico, a traditional staple of the native peoples of the American Southwest and Mexico. Chia seeds retain an enormous amount of water (they form a thick, mucilaginous substance when mixed with water), and so are excellent at keeping the body hydrated. The seeds were known as an endurance food, eaten before battles or long marches, by cultures as ancient as the Aztecs. Chia seeds are more familiar to North Americans as the green sprouts growing from the tops of Chia Pet planters, but they are gaining ground as a health food, praised for their **omega-3 fatty acids,** large amount of soluble fiber and variety of vitamins and minerals. Chia sprouts are especially popular, eaten in salads and on sandwiches. In Mexico, chia seeds are ground and mixed with water and lime juice to make a refreshing, if slightly gelatinous, drink called *chia fresca.*

Chiavari - an Italian sour-milk cheese made from whole cow's milk.

Chiboust cream - see CHANTILLY CREAM.

chicharrón - pl. **chicharrones.** A deep-fried square or strip of pork skin, a wildly popular Latin American version of **cracklings.**

chicken - a barnyard fowl that could rightly be called the best of all birds named poultry. Among domesticated fowl, it's the single most important source of food the entire world over. There are many hundreds of varieties of hens: the White Cornish and the White Rock in America; the Light Sussex in England; the Faverolles and Bresse in France. The way that breeds have been developed is a closely guarded secret. Birds are rated by how many days it takes

chicken

to reach a certain weight. In five weeks, the American Cobb 500 will reach 4½ pounds (2 kg) and Britain's Ross 1 can reach a thumping 5 pounds (2.2 kg). See also CAPON, LAYING HEN, TEMPERATURE.

CHICKEN TYPES

Chickens are also sold under different names, normally according to their age and weight:

broilers or fryers - weigh between 2 to 3 pounds (1 to 1.4 kg) and are mostly used for frying or broiling.

poussins - French for "baby chickens" that are four to six weeks old and weigh up to 2 pounds (1 kg). They are most popular in England and parts of Europe.

roasters - weigh about 3½ to 6 pounds (1.6 to 3 kg) and are ideal for roasting, barbecuing or frying; hens, fowl or stewing chickens, upwards of 2½ pounds (1.25 kg) require long, slow cooking.

Rock Cornish game hens - a cross between Cornish and White Rock hens and weigh up to 1½ pounds (750 g). They are most popular in North America and used for baking, broiling and roasting.

chicken à la king - see À LA KING.

chicken cacciatore - see CACCIATORE.

chicken cordon bleu - see CORDON BLEU.

chicken-fried steak - a dish from the American Midwest and South, consisting of a thin piece of steak pounded and coated in a milk-egg mixture and seasoned flour, then fried until crisp and brown, usually served with **country gravy** or **milk gravy.**

chicken fryer - a special, typically American sauté pan used for deep-frying chicken, often made of heavy cast iron for good heat retention and a steady temperature, usually with a lip on one side for pouring off oil.

chicken Kiev - a boned chicken breast wrapped around a piece of herbed butter, breaded and then deep-fried.

chicken lobster - the smallest size live lobster available for sale, weighing from 1 to 1¼ pounds (500 to 625 grams).

chicken Marengo - supposedly created during the Battle of Marengo in Piedmont, Italy, in 1800 by Dunand, Napoleon's famous chef. The emperor never ate anything before battle. When it came time to prepare Napoleon's post-battle meal, the only things the chef could find after a thorough search, were three eggs, a couple of tomatoes, a small hen, some garlic, a few crayfish, some oil and a spartan ration of bread. Dunand used the bread for **panada** (a paste made of several ingredients, including dried bread crumbs), broke up the hen into quarters, sautéed the tomatoes and the garlic in oil and fried the eggs. He then took the liberty of using some of the emperor's cognac, poured it over the dish and steamed the crayfish on top. Napoleon was so pleased with the meal that he requested to be fed this way after every battle. Others say the dish was served originally at the home of French statesman **Charles Maurice de Talleyrand-Périgord** or that it was originally created at Marengo in Algeria.

chicken pot pie - a **pot pie** made with diced cooked chicken.

chicken Tetrazzini - a dish of cooked spaghetti and strips of chicken in a sherried Parmesan cheese sauce, created especially for the opera singer Luisa Tetrazzini (1871–1940). The dish originated in San Francisco, the city the soprano visited most often.

chickpea - also **garbanzo bean.** This buff-colored seed is a plant native to the Mediterranean. Its Latin name, *Cicer arietinum,* found its way into Old French as *chiche*. Speakers of Middle English adopted this name for the legume and tacked on a redundant "pea" at the end. Not long afterward, the resulting compound transformed into "chickpea." An ancestor of the greatest orator of ancient Rome, Cicero, supposedly had a chickpea-like wart at the end of his nose, thus the family name.

Chickpeas are one of the oldest cultivated foods in the world. They were grown in Neolithic times in what is now Sicily. During the Roman Empire, they were shipped in jars from Sicily to the rest of Italy, where they are called *ceci.* The chickpea is said to have resulted in the massacre of Charles I and his French soldiers in 1282, when Sicilian rebels identified the foreigners by asking them to pronounce the word *ceci* correctly. Those who did not were killed.

In India, chickpeas are known as *gram*; in Spain as *garbanzos*; in France as *pois chiche*. At one time, they were commonly used in Turkey to feed horses, and more than likely to feed camels, too, because the Turkish name translates to "camel corn."

chickpea flour - see BESAN.

chickpea noodles - see SEVIAN NOODLES.

chickweed - a troublesome and despised weed, *Stellaria media*, in times of plenty, but one that's quite acceptable as human food in times of scarcity. It can be cooked like spinach. The French call it *mouron blanc*.

chicle - see CHEWING GUM.

chicory - a plant, related to **endive,** with long, white, tightly folded leaves and a slightly bitter taste, which probably originated in the Mediterranean region. First used by the Greeks and Romans as a medicinal plant, it became a consumable vegetable in the 14th century. The plant's name may be derived from its Egyptian name, because it was cultivated there about 5,000 years ago. The Greek physician Dioscorides mentioned it, and Charlemagne listed it among the 75 herbs to be grown in his garden. In the mid 17th century, the British herbalist **Nicholas Culpeper** recommended chicory extract "for nurses' breasts that are pained by the abundance of milk."

Chicory flowers are a beautiful blue, likened to astonishing blue eyes, and they close as if asleep at night. Chicory roots can also be roasted and used as a coffee substitute.

chicos - dry-roasted corn kernels, a traditional food of New Mexico, served as a snack and made into a spicy pork stew of the same name. Chicos are often dried in traditional wood-fired ovens, which gives them a smoky flavor.

chifferi - see PASTA.

chiffon - a fluffy mixture, usually containing stiffly beaten egg whites, used, for example, as a filling for a pie.

chiffonade - a term used to describe salad vegetables and herbs that are cut into fine strips. Lettuce, spinach, basil and sorrel are most often cut into chiffonade, so that their tender leaves are not bruised, as they would in a mince. The name comes from the French *chiffon*, meaning "rag."

chicory

chiffon cake - a light, sponge-like cake containing oil, rather than solid shortening, and stiffly beaten egg whites.

chigae - a rich, flavorful, spicy Korean stew, different from *kuk*, or soups, which are lighter and contain more water. Korean cuisine offers a wide variety of different chigae dishes, including *kimchi chigae*, a fiery dish made of **kimchi** and pork; *soon-dubu chigae*, a spicy tofu stew; and *dwen-jang chigae*, a stew of fermented bean paste, clams and vegetables.

Chihuahua cheese - see ASADERO.

chilaca - see CHILE.

chilaquiles - a Mexican dish born out of thriftiness, chilaquiles is a mixture of leftover tortillas cut into strips (or broken into pieces, if hard and stale), then mixed with whatever is on hand, such as chorizo, scrambled eggs, beans, chiles, cheese and/or a tomato sauce. Chilaquiles are normally eaten for breakfast in Mexico and can either be an informal tossed mixture of ingredients or a layered, baked dish. Legend has it that the name comes from the Nahuatl *chil-a-quilitl*, which means "greens with chili" or "broken-up old sombrero," which the hard tortilla strips resemble.

Child, Julia - see profile on page 162.

Chilean lentil - see LENTIL.

Chilean sea bass - not a sea bass at all, its real name is Patagonian toothfish, for its large, pointed teeth, renamed as part of a marketing initiative that succeeded in making the fish extremely popular. It's a rich, oily fish, with softer flesh than that of sea bass.

chile bean paste - also **chili bean paste, dou ban jiang, hot bean paste, toban djan.** A chunky, fiery hot Chinese seasoning paste made of ground red chiles, fava beans or soybeans, garlic, salt and water. Chile bean paste is used to

Child, Julia (1912–2004) - cookbook author and television personality, who is credited with introducing French cooking to America. Born in Pasadena, California, to a family with a cook, the Smith College graduate couldn't do much more than boil water when she met her food-loving husband, Paul, while both were working abroad during the Second World War. Returning to the U.S., she enrolled in cooking school to ensure she would win his heart. Years later, when he was posted to the American embassy in Paris, she signed up for courses at the Cordon Bleu. Louisette Bertholle and Simone Beck, who had written a book on French cooking, were part of the couple's social circle, and the three women decided to write a book that would demystify French cuisine for Americans. Louisette soon took a minor role, but Julia and "Simca", as Simone was known, threw themselves wholeheartedly into the project, which involved 10 years of diligent work.

In 1961, Knopf published *Mastering the Art of French Cooking, Volume One*. Originally, the book had been contracted to Houghton Mifflin, who turned it down, saying it would be "too expensive to publish," but Child felt that their female editor's enthusiasm had been overruled by men at the company. After listening to Houghton Mifflin's reasons for preferring another book on their publishing list, she concluded they would have preferred recipes that were fast and easy, probably made with a mix and often containing marshmallows.

The book was an immediate success. **Craig Claiborne**, food editor of *The New York Times*, called the recipes "glorious," and others praised the attention to detail and the "commonsense approach to French cuisine." The first printing of 10,000 immediately sold out, and within a year of publication 100,000 copies had been shipped. When she made a guest appearance on public television in Boston, Child's next career was born. The phones rang off the hook, and the station was deluged with letters requesting her return. Viewers were enchanted by her distinctive warble, lack of pretense and great sense of fun. She was offered her own show, *The French Chef*, which first aired in 1963 and was an immediate hit.

By all accounts, an extraordinarily warm and generous woman, who was highly regarded by just about everyone, Julia Child went on to become an American icon. She wrote 16 more cookbooks including *Mastering the Art of French Cooking, Volume Two* and *The French Chef Cookbook*, and starred in seven additional television series, including *In Julia's Kitchen with Master Chefs*, filmed when she was in her 80s, and *Julia and Jacques Cooking at Home* with **Jacques Pépin.** Her numerous broadcasting awards included two Emmys and the Peabody Award. She was no stranger to civil awards as well: in 1991, she received the French Legion of Honor and, in 2003, the Presidential Medal of Freedom, America's highest civilian award. To celebrate her 90th birthday, the Smithsonian National Museum of American History deemed her a national treasure, dismantled the kitchen in her recently sold Cambridge, Massachusetts, home and reassembled it at the museum for all to share. She died in her sleep, just two days short of her 92nd birthday.

season many Chinese dishes, especially the spicy tofu dish **ma po tofu.** The Korean version of chile bean paste is called **gochu jang.** See also CHILE PASTE.

chile de arbol - see CHILE PEPPER.

chile paste - also **chili paste.** A paste made of ground hot red chiles and other ingredients, common to many cultures, with many variations. Though North Africa offers the well-known fiery **harissa,** chile paste is often associated with Asian cuisine. In China, this seasoning is made with chiles, oil and vinegar, often seasoned with garlic. Thai chile paste is called *nam prik pao*, made with chiles, sugar, onions, oil, dried shrimp or shrimp paste and often tamarind paste. In Malaysia and Indonesia, **sambal oelek** (thinner, only seasoned with vinegar and salt) and sambal bajak (thick and pasty, flavored with a variety of spices) are the local fiery chile pastes. See also ASIAN CHILE PASTE AND SAUCE, CHILE BEAN PASTE.

chile pepper - also **chili, chilli, hot pepper.** Mexicans refer to all peppers as chiles, but North Americans reserve the word for hot peppers. There are more than 100 varieties, many of them indigenous to Mexico. Sweet or hot, they're all members of the Capsicum family and play a featured role on the world's menus.

The Native Americans burned chile peppers when they were fighting off the invading English. The fumes apparently kept the English at bay. Chiles are one of the foods Christopher Columbus "discovered" in the Americas and hence have been part of the diet in most other countries for only the past few hundred years. Now, they have found their way into Hungarian as well as African cooking; they're part of the **kung pao** recipe of China, and the chili dog in America. Three decades ago, pharmacologist Wilbur Scoville devised a unit to measure the hotness of spice, now called **Scoville units** (SU). The higher the unit, the hotter the spice.

The general rule of thumb in regard to chiles: the smaller the pepper, the bigger the burn. A slice of sweet pepper is a kiss on the cheek compared to a speck of Scotch bonnet, which can blister your lips. It's not the flesh that is so incendiary, but what lurks inside. **Capsaicin,** the compound that gives chiles their heat, is found primarily in the fleshy vein-like membrane and seeds; the flesh can be hot as well, but never as much. To mitigate a chile's burn, seed and devein it before cooking and use rubber gloves; the chile's "oil" can burn eyes and skin on contact, a condition known as "Hunan hand," referring to the chile-rich province in southern China. If pepper burns your skin, you can get relief by washing the area with white vinegar.

chile peppers

CHILE PEPPER VARIETIES

aji - also **aji amarillo.** Hot with a fragrant, fruity undertone, thin-fleshed, yellow to orange-red skin, grown and eaten extensively in Peru and other parts of South America, commonly used in **seviche,** good in sauces, stews and marinades; 30,000 to 50,000 SU.

Anaheim chile - a mild, green or red chile; 500 to 1,500 su.

ancho chile - a dried **poblano** chile, round rather than long. It looks very much like a dried **mulato** chile, to which it is genetically related. Ancho is deep purple with a fruity flavor, often used in Mexican cooking.

arbol chile - also **chile de arbol.** Hot, slim, 2 to 3 inches (5 to 7.5 cm) long, bright red even when dried, good for salsas, soups and chilies; the name *arbol* means "tree" in Spanish; 15,0000 to 30,000 SU.

banana pepper - see HUNGARIAN.

bird's eye chile - also **bird chile, Santaka, Thai,** tiny and thin-skinned; 40,000 to 60,000 SU.

cayenne - thin, bright red, fiery sweet, 4 to 6 inches (10 to 15 cm) long, most often dried and ground into powder or used in making hot sauces, such as Tabasco; 10,000 to 50,000 SU.

chilaca - the fresh form of the **pasilla** chile, sometimes available in Mexican or farmer's markets but harder to find than the dried version; blackish green when immature and dark brown when fully ripe; thin and anywhere from 6 to 12 inches (15 to 30 cm) long, often used in fresh salsas; 1,000 to 1,500 SU.

chile de arbol - see ARBOL CHILE.

chiltepín - also **chiltecpín, tepín.** Red, the size and shape of a cranberry, sharp-tasting and extremely hot; *chiltecpin*, meaning "flea chili" in Nahuatl; known as the mother of all peppers because it is thought to be the oldest of the *Capsicum* genus; 50,000 to 100,000 SU.

chipotle - see JALAPEÑO.

Fresno - cone-shaped, only 2 to 3 inches (5 to 7.5 cm) long, green when immature and red when ripe, with thick flesh but not as thick as the similar **jalapeño,** good in salsas and cooking, named for the city in California where it was first grown; 5,000 to 10,000 SU.

guajillo - mild to moderately hot, dark red-brown and leathery, usually dried whole, although some companies make guajillo chile powder; excellent toasted on a **comal** and used in chili, soup or salsa; 2,500 to 5,000 SU.

habanero - meaning "from Havana," fruity, they look like tiny green and orange jack-o'-lanterns; related to **Scotch bonnet;** 100,000 to 500,000 SU.

hot wax - see HUNGARIAN.

Hungarian - also **banana pepper, hot wax pepper,** a small, shiny, yellow pepper, often pickled; 5,000 to 50,000 SU.

jalapeño - the state pepper of Texas, thick-skinned, green and medium-hot, about 1½ inches (4 cm) in length; called **chipotle** when dried and smoked; 5,000 to 10,000 SU.

mulato chile - genetically similar to the **poblano** chile, it is about 4 inches (10 cm) long, and is mild to medium-hot. Flat, wide, wrinkled and the color of dark chocolate, mulato chiles are also available ground. They are used in salsa, sauces, soups, stews and **mole.**

New Mexico - somewhat mild, green or red, 4 to 6 inches (10 to 15 cm) long; 500 to 1,000 SU.

pasilla - Spanish for "little raisin" because of its mild, chewy sweetness, purplish black, used dried, about 5 inches (12.5 cm) in length, the chile of choice for **mole;** 1,000 to 1,500 SU.

pepperoncino - small, fleshy, mild, green or red globes, mostly pickled, often served on antipasto plates; 100 to 500 SU.

pequín - also **piquin.** A 1-inch (2.5 cm) tapered orange chile, used dried, similar to cayenne in flavor but much hotter; 50,000 to 100,000 SU.

pimiento - also **pimento.** Red, heart-shaped, fleshy, mild and sweet pepper, mostly roasted and bottled and used to stuff green olives, or dried and ground to make paprika; 500 SU or less.

poblano - green to red, with a mild, smoky-sweet flavor and thick walls ideal for stuffing, always used in **chiles rellenos;** fresh version of **ancho chile,** *ancho*, meaning "wide"; 1,000 to 1,500 SU.

Santaka - see THAI.

Scotch bonnet - related to **habanero,** widely used in Yucatan and Caribbean cuisines, one of the world's hottest chiles; 200,000 to 300,000 SU.

serrano - Spanish for "mountain," smaller, thinner and hotter than the **jalapeño;** 10,000 to 25,000 SU.

tepín - see CHILTEPÍN.

Thai - see BIRD'S EYE CHILE.

New Mexico chiles

When dining out, remember that cuisines that use lots of hot peppers, such as Mexican, Thai and Indian, invariably provide a complimentary food or beverage to cool you down. Starches, such as rice and tortillas, absorb chile oils in the mouth, while sour cream, yogurt and milk neutralize chile's oils and cool the burn. Sweet drinks, especially those with ice, can serve to distract from pepper's punishment. Water and beer, however, offer little relief. Water doesn't cut the oils and offers nothing in the way of flavor, while beer's bubbles seem to intensify the pain, rather than alleviate it.

Researchers are studying chile peppers for their ability to fight heart attacks and strokes. As well, the peppers are a good source of vitamin C and beat-carotene, antioxidants that provide good support for the immune system. New Mexico has one of the lowest incidences of heart disease, which may be due to the high consumption of chile peppers, which are widely grown there. More than 55,000 tons (50,000 tonnes) are eaten annually in New Mexico. See also ANAHEIM CHILE, ANCHO CHILE, CAYENNE CHILE, CHIPOTLE CHILE, PEPPERCORN, PIRI-PIRI, SWEET PEPPER.

chiles rellenos - mild green chiles, usually poblano, stuffed with cheese, battered and deep-fried, Spanish for "stuffed peppers."

chili con carne - also **chili.** A dish of ground beef and chiles or chili powder or both; beans, especially red kidney beans, are sometimes added as well. Rumor has it that it was William Gebhardt, a German immigrant in New Braunfels, Texas, who originated modern chili dishes by finding a way, in about 1902, to extract the pulp from chile pods and mix it with the right spices to create **chili powder.** Gebhardt built a successful chili con carne canning business in San Antonio. Originally called carne con chili (*con carne* is Spanish for "with meat"), the dish was, by some other accounts, invented by nuns in Mexico, using minced meat, beans and chiles. Today, it's known as the state dish of Texas, which has an International Chili Appreciation Society. Aficionados, called "chili heads," have included Will Rogers, who judged a town by the quality of its chili, and Jesse James, who refused to rob a bank in McKinney, Texas, because that was where his favorite chili parlor was located. See also TEX-MEX.

chilindrón - a Spanish dish of sweet red peppers, onions, tomatoes, garlic and chicken or lamb.

chili oil - a vegetable oil in which hot red chiles have been steeped, frequently used in Chinese cooking.

chili powder - an American innovation, first introduced in Texas early in the 20th century, a blended spice that combines ground hot red peppers (chile peppers), ground cumin, oregano and garlic powder. Commercial chili powder may also include paprika, cayenne, black pepper, salt and occasionally coriander and cloves. See also CHILI CON CARNE.

chili sauce - a spicy, sweet condiment made from tomatoes, chiles or chili powder, onions, green peppers, sugar, vinegar and spices, usually served as an accompaniment to meat.

chill - to make a food or beverage cold, but not frozen, by placing it in the refrigerator at between 30° and 40°F (–1° and 4°C).

chiltepín - see CHILE PEPPER.

chimichanga - the name of a deep-fried burrito, with either a savory or sweet filling, said to have been invented when a cook accidentally dropped a burrito into the fryer. The origin of the name is much debated, but the interesting possibility is rather cryptically that, in Spanish, the word *changa* means "female monkey" and *chimenea* means "chimney or hearth." See also TEX-MEX.

chimichurri - an all-purpose herb sauce, marinade or condiment from Argentina, made with parsley, oregano and sometimes thyme, as well as onion, garlic, olive oil, lemon juice or vinegar.

China orange - see CALAMONDIN.

chine - the bony piece, or backbone, adhering to the fillet, usually removed before cooking. To chine (in culinary parlance) is to remove the backbone or ribs from meat, from the French word *échine*, meaning "spine."

Chinese amaranth - the "spinach of the East," *Amaranthus gangeticus*, a branching annual native to China, also grown in India and most warm parts of Asia, where it is one of the most widely used green-leafed vegetables. See also AMARANTH.

Chinese artichoke - also **chorogi, Japanese artichoke, knotroot.** An Eastern perennial, *Stachys affinis*, grown for its white, crispy-fleshed tubers, cooked or eaten raw. The tubers, or rhizomes, are not affected by frost and may be left in the ground all winter, pulled up as needed and used immediately; once out of the ground, they rapidly shrivel and lose their flavor. They're very well known in France, where they're called *Crosne du Japon*. They were first introduced in Europe in 1882 by M. Pailleux of Crosne (hence their French name), who was sent them by a doctor in service to the Russian Ambassador in Beijing.

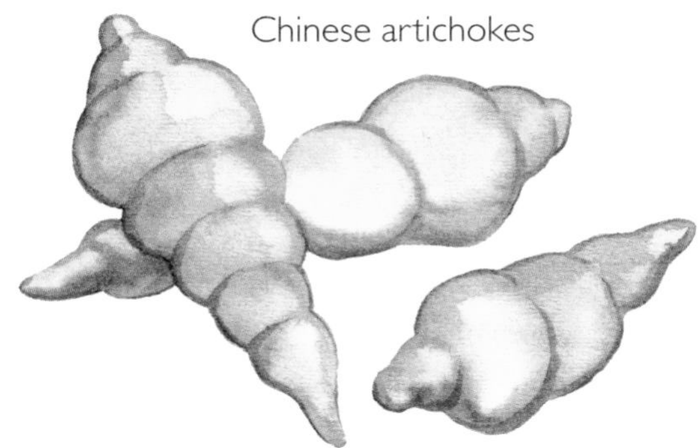
Chinese artichokes

Chinese black beans - see FERMENTED BLACK BEANS.

Chinese broccoli - see GAI LAN.

Chinese cabbage - also **Chinese white cabbage.** A generic name used in North America for different Asian members of the *Brassica* genus, generally cabbages that are elongated instead of round, such as **napa cabbage, bok choy** and **po tsai.** There are hundreds of varieties of Asian cabbages, many of which are called by the wrong names in North America or lumped together under this generic term.

Chinese chard - see BOK CHOY.

Chinese chives - see GARLIC CHIVES.

Chinese cleaver - the all-purpose knife of choice in Chinese kitchens, prized in North American ones as well, with a long, tall rectangular blade that can be used to slice, mince, chop, shred or dice. The wide, blunt back of the blade can be used as a meat pounder, and when turned on its side, the blade easily crushes ginger or garlic. Chinese cleavers were traditionally made of carbon steel, but many are now made of rustproof stainless steel. They come in several sizes for different cutting tasks and in light and heavy weights in each size. Although they look like Western meat cleavers, they are not tough enough to chop bones and can chip if they strike something hard.

Chinese cleaver

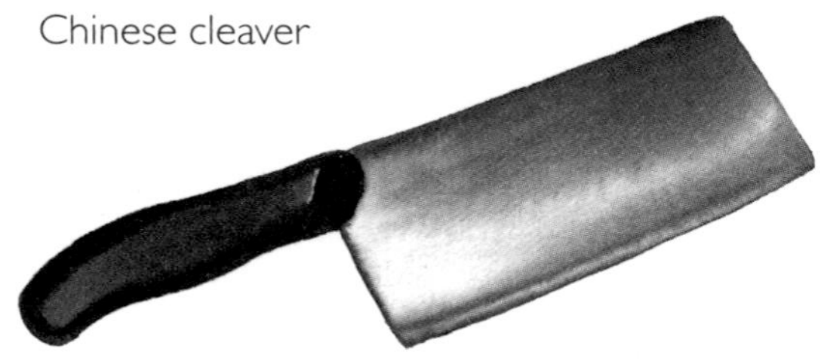

Chinese date - see JUJUBE.

Chinese eggplant - see EGGPLANT.

Chinese firepot - see MONGOLIAN HOTPOT.

Chinese five-spice powder - also **five spices.** This distinct flavor combination is comprised of equal amounts of ground Szechwan peppercorns, cloves, cinnamon, fennel seeds and star anise.

Chinese garlic stems - also **garlic flower stems, green garlic.** The tall, thin flower stalks of Chinese garlic, a variety of *Allium sativum*, cut from the young, tender garlic bulbs when soft and green, not to be confused with either **garlic chives** or **garlic scapes.** These edible stems have a strong garlic flavor and are often a bit too strong to use raw. They are better after cooking, when they become softer and mellower. The stems are usually 12 to 18 inches (30 to 45 cm) long, pliable and solid (not hollow in the center as green onions are), about the diameter of thin asparagus or a pencil. They are often sold in bunches in Asian grocery stores.

Chinese ginger - see FINGERROOT.

Chinese gooseberry - see KIWIFRUIT.

Chinese grapefruit - see POMELO.

Chinese kale - see GAI LAN.

Chinese key - see FINGERROOT.

Chinese leaf - see PO TSAI.

Chinese long bean - see ASPARAGUS BEAN.

Chinese mustard - see WRAPPED HEART MUSTARD.

Chinese mustard cabbage - see GAI CHOY.

Chinese okra - see ASIAN OKRA.

Chinese pancake - see MANDARIN PANCAKE.

Chinese parsley - see CILANTRO.

Chinese pea pod - see SUGAR SNAP PEA.

Chinese pear - see ASIAN PEAR.

Chinese pepper - see SZECHWAN PEPPER.

Chinese potato - see ARROWHEAD.

Chinese sausage - see LAP CHEONG.

Chinese spinach - see AMARANTH.

Chinese vinegar - see RICE VINEGAR.

Chinese white cabbage - see CHINESE CABBAGE.

Chinese wolfberry - see GOJI BERRY.

chinois - **1.** a conical strainer with a fine stainless or wire mesh, used mostly for straining sauces to make them perfectly smooth. Swedish stainless-steel conical sieves are the most

chinois

practical to clean and have a hook opposite the handle to grip onto the lip of a bowl or pot. **2.** a fruit similar to the tangerine.

chinook - see SALMON.

chinotto - **1.** an orange, *Citrus aurantium* 'Chinotto,' related to the **Seville orange,** grown mostly as an ornamental fruit in North America but grown for candying and cooking in Europe. Chinotto oranges are also called myrtle-leaf oranges. **2.** A bittersweet Italian carbonated beverage made with the essence of the chinotto orange.

chinquapin - the Native American name for pine nut.

chioggia - also **bull's eye beet, candy-cane beet, candy-stripe beet**. An Italian **heirloom** variety of beet usually found at farmers' markets and specialty produce stores, although it can easily be grown in a home garden. When sliced, a chioggia has beautiful concentric circles of white and red inside, although the stripes may turn to red and pink when cooked. Chioggias don't bleed their color the way that regular red beets do, so they are excellent for cooking with other vegetables or foods.

chipolata - a small, spicy pork sausage, popular in France, of Italian origin. The name derives from the Italian *cipollata*, meaning "with onion" and *cipolla*, "onion," although mysteriously the sausage often doesn't contain onion.

chipotle chile - the name for a smoked, dried jalapeño chile. Its flavor is sweet and almost chocolaty. See also CHILE PEPPER.

chipped beef - see CREAMED CHIPPED BEEF.

chips - **1.** any of various thinly sliced, deep-fried foods, such as tortilla chips or potato chips, usually eaten as snacks. **2.** a name used outside the U.S. for french fries.

chirashi-zushi - see SUSHI.

chirauli nut - also **chironji nut.** See CHAROLI NUT.

chitarra - see PASTA.

chitlins - see CHITTERLINGS.

chitterlings - also **chitlings, chitlins.** The cleaned and scraped small intestines of pigs (usually fried), chitterlings are famous in the southern U.S., where they're served with collard greens. The name of this dish is generally pronounced "chitlins" and comes from the Middle English *chitirling*, meaning "body organs."

chive - a member of the Alliaceae family, the smallest bulb of the onion family, native to Europe and Asia. The ancient Greek was a heavy consumer of fresh chives. The Chinese, or garlic, chive, *Allium tuberosum*, has been cultivated in China for more than 2,000 years. It has been part of Chinese cuisine since 3000 BC and was also valued as an antidote to poison and a medication to stop bleeding. The Chinese variety is a little bit stronger than the European varieties.

Nobody seems to know why, but the Romans used chives to tell fortunes. In the Middle Ages, it was thought that chives could ward off diseases and evil powers, and it was common practice for people to suspend bunches of them in their dwellings. Chives seem to have been popular with everyone except that skeptical

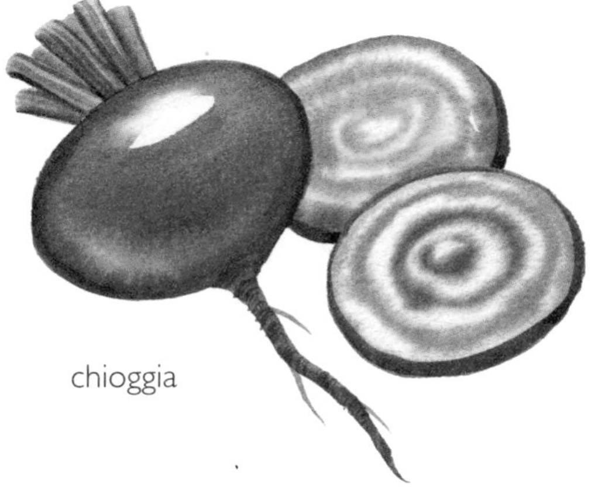
chioggia

17th century herbalist **Nicholas Culpeper**, who warns, "If eaten raw they send up very harmful vapors to the brain, causing troublesome sleep and spoiling the eyesight."

The plant grows very easily, either wild or cultivated, and is now found on all continents. In the early days, the Dutch settlers planted chives in their pastures; they used to call it "the Little Brother of the Onion") so that their cows would give chive-flavored milk. When the plant starts flowering, it produces only two colors, either white or purple. The leaves are hollow and are harvested very close to the ground, so that they will grow back rapidly.

chive blossom - the edible flower of the chive plant, delicate pinkish purple and infused with a light, oniony flavor. The petals can be stripped off the flower head or the whole flowers can be added to salads or used as a garnish. See also EDIBLE FLOWERS.

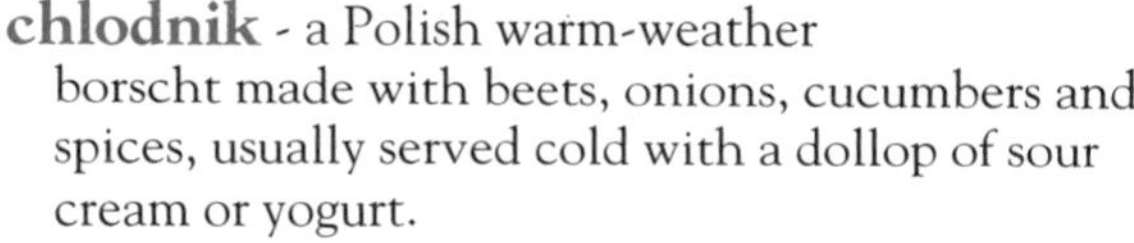

chive blossom

Ch'l - see TEA.

chlodnik - a Polish warm-weather borscht made with beets, onions, cucumbers and spices, usually served cold with a dollop of sour cream or yogurt.

chlorophyll - the blue-green pigment present in plants (especially the leaves) that allows photosynthesis to occur, the process by which the plant uses energy from the sun for growth and maintenance. Chlorophyll is touted as a health-enhancing nutrient, credited with preventing the body from absorbing toxins (especially metals), cleansing the blood, increasing hemoglobin in the blood (and therefore the ability of the cells to take in oxygen) and purifying the liver. There are numerous sources of concentrated chlorophyll that humans take as dietary supplements, including green algae (spirulina and chlorella), which is often taken in pill or powder form, and wheat grass, which is often juiced and drunk.

chocolate - the roasted, ground and refined beans of the **cacao** plant, used as a flavoring, beverage or confection. It was not the Aztecs (as it is generally believed) but the Olmecs who first cultivated the tree 3,000 years ago. The Mayans called the tree *cacahuaquchtl*, meaning "tree," because as far as they were concerned, there was no other tree worth naming. They believed the cacao pods were a gift from the gods to man and considered them a symbol of life and fertility. It was Christopher Columbus (not Ferdinand Cortés) who, in his fourth and final trip to the Caribbean in 1502, first recorded the name as *tchocolatl* or *xocolat* from the Aztec name.

Three factors are important in describing chocolate: the bean variety, origin and the percentage of cacao. Most chocolate is made from a blend of cacao beans from all over the world. **Forastero,** the base bean of most blends, is grown in Africa, Brazil and Asia; it makes up 90 percent of the world's cocoa supply. Other varieties include **Criollo,** a prized bean from South and Central America and Southeast Asia; and **Trinitario** (a hybrid of Criollo and Forastero) from Trinidad, but nowadays grown in other regions, such as Venezuela, Ecuador and Colombia.

Switzerland is recognized for its chocolate. Swiss chocolate dates back to 1819, when François-Louis Cailler opened a mechanized chocolate factory near Lake Geneva. At the time, chocolate was brittle, rough-surfaced and bitter. In 1867, the first milk chocolate was produced when Daniel Peter, a Swiss manufacturer, managed to combine chocolate with milk. The real breakthrough came in 1879, when Rodolphe Lindt hit upon the idea of adding cocoa butter to smooth out the texture in a shell-shaped machine called a *conche*, which churned and turned the mixture for three days.

The percentage of cacao specifies the amount of cocoa mass (or chocolate liquor) plus cocoa butter (natural fat in the cacao bean). The cocoa mass itself is made up of roughly half cocoa butter and half dry cocoa solids, but since the ratio varies amongst beans, two brands labeled 70 percent cacao may not have the same percentage of cocoa butter. One consistent factor is that most of the residual content is sugar, so the higher the cacao percentage, the less sugar in the chocolate. See also MEXICAN CHOCOLATE, PHENYLETHYLAMINE, TEMPERING.

chocolate basil - see BASIL.

chocolate chip cookie - see TOLL HOUSE COOKIE.

chocolate éclair - see ÉCLAIR.

CHOCOLATE VARIETIES

baking chocolate - see UNSWEETENED CHOCOLATE.

bittersweet chocolate - frequently called **dark chocolate,** it must have at least 35 percent chocolate liquor, but many brands now go beyond that; these chocolates (mostly in the 60 to 75 percent range) have a concentrated flavor and, as the name implies, are not very sweet.

cocoa powder - partially defatted liquor treated with flavor-robbing alkali, for cooking only or with water or milk added for drinking.

couverture - has a high percentage (at least 35 percent) of cocoa butter, used for candy making and cooking only.

dark chocolate - see BITTERSWEET CHOCOLATE.

milk chocolate - invented in Switzerland in 1876, a combination of at least 10 percent chocolate liquor, cocoa butter, milk and flavoring.

semisweet chocolate - often labeled dark, sweet chocolate. FDA classification standards don't distinguish between bittersweet and semisweet chocolate, but usually semisweet is to some extent sweeter and has a little less intense chocolate flavor than bittersweet.

sweet chocolate - about 15 percent liquor, for cooking and eating.

unsweetened chocolate - also **baking chocolate.** A pure chocolate liquor that is cooled and molded; 53 percent cocoa butter, used for cooking.

white chocolate - technically not a real chocolate because it doesn't contain any chocolate liquor. Contains a combination of cocoa butter, milk, sugar, lecithin and usually vanilla flavor, for eating or cooking.

chocolate fondue - a dessert using melted chocolate instead of cheese in a fondue pot, and fruit and cake instead of bread for dipping. See also FONDUE.

chocolate fondue

chocolate liquor - also **cocoa mass.** A sticky paste extracted by grinding the nib found in the core of the cacao bean. Chocolate liquor contains 53 percent **cocoa butter.** See also CHOCOLATE.

chocolate Mexicano - see MEXICAN CHOCOLATE.

chocolate milk - a childhood favorite in North America, this is a mixture of fluid milk and sweet chocolate syrup. Chocolate milk can be made with whole, 2 or 1 percent milk, and offers the same nutrition as plain milk, except for a slightly higher amount of sugar and, consequently, more calories.

chocolate pot - a tall, porcelain pot, often elaborately painted, traditionally used for making and serving hot chocolate when it was a luxury for the wealthy in the 17th and 18th centuries. While it is shaped like a tall coffee pot, a chocolate pot can be distinguished by its small, stout pouring lip at the top. It does not have a long spout that starts at the base, like a teapot or coffee pot. Old-fashioned hot chocolate was made by mixing milk with sugar and a solid bar of chocolate, so a long wooden **chocolate spoon** was required to stir the beverage until it reached a smooth, drinkable consistency.

chocolate sauce - usually made with melted chocolate, cocoa, sugar, milk and/or water, and sometimes corn syrup in commercially prepared products.

chocolate syrup - usually made using corn syrup and/or molasses, with chocolate liquor as its base.

chokeberry - see ARONIA.

chokecherry - a small, North American dark red to purple berry, *Prunus virginiana*, from a deciduous tree whose white blooms appear from May to June and whose fruit is ready for picking between July and October.

choko - an Australian vegetable, *Sechium edule*, known as **chayote** in North America.

cholent - also **chamin.** A Central European Jewish dish consisting of beans and sometimes meat and other ingredients, baked for a long time in a slow oven. Religious Jews, who do not believe in working on the Sabbath, prepare the dish on Friday and slip it into the oven just before sundown. Twenty-four hours later, when the Sabbath is over, the dish is removed from the oven. Chamin is the Sephardic name. See also DAFINA.

cholesterol - a compound necessary for the proper working of the digestive and nervous systems, but which promotes arteriosclerosis if present in high concentrations in the blood.

chop - **1.** (n.) a cut of meat from the rack or the loin, such as pork, veal, lamb or mutton chops. **2.** (v.) to cut into fine pieces.

chopped egg - chopped hard-boiled eggs, used as a garnish in salads and as a flavoring in **chopped liver** at Jewish delicatessens. See also EGG SALAD.

chopped liver - a mixture of chicken livers and onions cooked in **schmaltz,** seasoned with salt and pepper, mixed with chopped egg, and mashed or blended to a spreadable consistency. Chopped liver is used as a sandwich filling in Jewish delicatessens and is the nosh behind the timeless comeback "What am I, chopped liver?" The phrase apparently doesn't come from Yiddish but is an American invention. The theory is that chopped liver was originally served as a side dish, never a main course. So, if you're just "chopped liver" to someone, you're insignificant — just a side dish to something or someone else more important. The phrase expresses anger or hurt over being treated as something dispensable.

chopping block - see BUTCHER BLOCK.

chopsticks

chopsticks - long, slender sticks, Chinese and Japanese eating utensils, traditionally made of bamboo or wood. The word chopsticks comes from the Chinese *kuai tzu*, meaning "quick ones." The light, Japanese type are called *hashi*, meaning "bridge" to transport the food from bowl to mouth. See also OHASHI.

chop suey - the name is from the Cantonese *jaahp seui*, "odds and ends," and it was invented, by some accounts, in New York in 1896 by one of the cooks serving Chinese goodwill emissary Li Hongzhang, who had grown tired of American fare at banquets. Other reports credit the invention to a San Francisco cook, who served a mixture of leftover meat and vegetables late at night to a group of drunken miners. At least one authority traces the origin of *tsap seui*, or the Mandarin *tsa sui* (both names meaning "miscellaneous scraps") to Toisan, a rural county near Guangzhou, which is the home of most of the early immigrants from China to California. More authentically American-invented "Chinese" dishes include: chow mein (from the Cantonese *chaau mihn*, "fried noodles"); **egg foo yong;** and, of course, fortune cookies.

chorizo - a Spanish (and Latin American) sausage with many variations but always including pork and some kind of chile pepper, usually in narrow casings. Some chorizos are fresh, but most are dried and smoked. *Chouriço* is a Portuguese version.

chorogi - see CHINESE ARTICHOKE.

Choron sauce - a variation on the classic French **béarnaise** or **hollandaise** sauce, made pink with the addition of tomato purée, created by the chef of the same name, who worked at the famous Voisin restaurant in Paris in the late 1800s. Choron is best known for serving gourmet meals made from zoo animals during the Siege of 1871 in Paris, when food was incredibly scarce.

choucroute garnie - an Alsatian version of sauerkraut "garnished" with a variety of sausages, meats and potatoes. Choucroute is sweeter and less acidic than German sauerkraut because it is rinsed before cooking, then simmered in wine. It is also heavily spiced with juniper berries, peppercorns, cloves, allspice and bay leaves, or any number of other seeds, such as coriander, caraway or cumin, depending on the cook's preference.

choux pastry - also **choux paste, pâte à choux.** A classic French pastry dough used for making **cream puffs, profiteroles** and **éclairs** by adding flour and butter to boiling water, cooking it briefly on the stove and then adding eggs. The dough is piped into desired shapes and baked. The technique causes them to rise and nearly hollow out, perfect for fillings of whipped cream, **pastry cream** or ice cream.

chow - an American colloquialism for food, especially in the military, a variation of pidgin Chinese *chowchow*.

chowchow - also **chow-chow.** A relish of chopped mixed vegetables. Originally, it was a Chinese dish with orange peel, ginger and other ingredients in a sweet syrup. The modern version is strongly flavored with mustard.

chowder - a thick soup, frequently but not always made with seafood, from the French *chaudière*, meaning pot or cauldron, in which (according to one story) marooned French sailors on the Maine coast made a stew out of clams dug up on the beach, with salvaged pork, onions, potatoes and ship's crackers. Another more credible story has it that when the French Acadians fled Canada's territories to settle in Florida, they showed this cooking technique to the people they encountered during their long trip south.

chowder clam - see CLAM.

chow fun - a Chinese wide, flat rice noodle. See also ASIAN NOODLES.

chow mein - a Chinese dish of vegetables and meat or fish served with crisp, fried noodles, as opposed to **lo mein,** in which the noodles are soft and not fried.

choy sum - see BOK CHOY.

Christmas lima bean - see CALICO BEAN.

Christmas melon - see SANTA CLAUS MELON.

Christmas pudding - see PLUM PUDDING.

christophene - see CHAYOTE.

chromium - a nutrient consumed in common foods, a trace mineral that is alleged to help the body properly convert glucose in foods into energy. The theory is that chromium prevents diabetes by helping the body use insulin efficiently to metabolize sugars. Animal tests have found a link between the two, but whether this is true for humans as well is still under debate. Some natural sources of chromium are whole grains, meats, brewer's yeast and nuts.

chrysanthemum leaves - bright green and very fragrant, used as a vegetable or in a stir-fried dish.

chub - see CISCO.

chuck - see BEEF.

chuck blade roast - see BEEF.

chufa - also **earth almond, earthnut, rush nut, tigernut.** This tiny tuber from an African plant, *Cyperus esculentus*, with a nut-like texture, is fairly popular in Europe. When ground, it's used in the Spanish drink *horchata de chufa*. It is also eaten as a snack food. Called "earth almond" because of its almond taste.

chukandar - the Hindi word for "beetroot." Eaten baked and boiled, added to chutney and soup, and served with yogurt in salads, chukandar is also used as a food coloring.

chukar partridge - an Eurasian partridge, *Alectoris chukar*, introduced to western North America in the late 1800s and successfully established in the dry, rugged terrain stretching from British Columbia to Colorado by the 1930s. Imported as a game bird, it is also farmed for its eggs and smooth-textured, strong-flavored meat.

chukar partridge

chuka soba - long, curly Japanese wheat-flour noodles, low in fat, usually white but sometimes colored yellow, often used in soups. Chuka soba is not fried, but rather dried in blocks before it is packaged for sale. These noodles are an excellent low-fat alternative to **ramen** noodles, which are deep-fried. Chuka soba is easy to find in most North American grocery stores, as well as Asian markets.

churn - to agitate cream, so that the fat separates from the liquid and forms butter.

churrasco - **1.** a dish of thickly sliced grilled beef, a specialty of many Latin American nations and especially prized in the native lands of the gauchos, the cowboys who work in the grasslands of Brazil and Argentina. In Brazil, the succulent slices are served with a hot, spicy sauce, and in Argentina, with herbal **chimichurri** sauce. Churrasco is popular in many other countries, such as Nicaragua and Cuba, each with its own regional variation on the grilled-meat theme. **2.** Portuguese for "barbecue," used in Portugal and many former Portuguese colonies to describe dishes cooked on a grill or over an open flame. Spicy churrasco chicken is a frequent sight in Portuguese neighborhoods in North America.

churro - a Spanish and Mexican deep-fried pastry, rolled in cinnamon sugar while still hot or dipped in chocolate.

chutney - also **chutnee.** A tangy relish made from a mixture of fruits (and sometimes vegetables), herbs, spices, sugar and vinegar, which originated in India and takes its name from the Hindi word, "*catni*," which means "to be liked" or "to be tasted." In its home country, chutney may be slightly lumpy and usually has a sharp, sweet-sour flavor. Recipes range from region to region, but Indian chutneys are often made with chopped or whole fruit (mango is especially popular), sugar, vinegar and seasonings, such as ground chile peppers and ginger, and minced coriander, garlic and mint. Other ingredients include chopped carrots, cherries, limes, peaches, plums, pumpkin, tomatoes (ripe or unripe) and walnuts, or shredded coconut. Indian chutneys liven up bland dishes, such as dal and rice. The colonial British helped export chutney around the globe, but their versions usually look more like jam and taste sweeter than the originals. North American cooks often serve chutney as a condiment alongside hot or cold meat, or in sandwiches, alone or spread onto sliced cheese or lunchmeat.

cider

ciabatta - from the Italian for "slipper," a loaf of bread about 8 inches (20 cm) long, with a light, thin, floury crust. Its contours do look a lot like an ordinary slipper.

cibreo - an Italian dish going back to the Middle Ages, made of cockscombs and sweetbreads, served with a vegetable **timbale.** A French dish as ancient as the Italian offering is called *crêtes de coq à l'ancienne*, meaning "cockscombs the old-fashioned way."

cicely - also **sweet cicely.** A licorice-tasting herb related to parsley, a flavoring agent used since early Roman times. Its stems, leaves and seeds can be used in salads or in a **bouquet garni.** Cicely is also used in the making of liqueurs, most notably **Chartreuse.**

cider - the juice expressed from fruit, usually apples, for drinking or to make other products, such as applejack or cider vinegar. Fresh cider is often referred to as **sweet cider. Hard cider** is fermented in sealed bottles to make it alcoholic and sparkling.

cider brandy - also **cider spirits, cider whiskey.** See APPLE BRANDY.

cider vinegar - also **apple cider vinegar.** This vinegar is made from apple pulp, whose sugar is converted to alcohol and then to acetic acid, just as with all vinegars. Homemade cider vinegar is cloudy, while commercial types are crystal clear, due to filtering. It's used for general cooking purposes and also makes an excellent substitute for rice vinegar in Chinese cooking. See also VINEGAR.

ciecamarito - a thick, tasty soup from Puglia, Italy, made from leftover bread cut into cubes and simmered together with vegetables. The term means "blind husbands," referring to how it will fool them into thinking it's difficult to make when it's not.

cilantro - see CORIANDER.

ciliegini - tiny balls of fresh mozzarella cheese, smaller than **bocconcini,** about the size of a cherry. The name comes from the Italian word for cherry, *ciliegia*.

Cimarron onion - see ONION.

cinchona - the bark of the cinchona tree of the genus *Cinchona*, which contains quinine, the primary ingredient in tonic. It was named for the Countess of Chinchón, wife of a Peruvian viceroy. It's also used to make **Dubonnet,** a fortified wine infused with the botanical bark and experiences an additional fermentation. Dubonnet is now made in New Jersey.

Cincinnati chili - a well-loved chili particular to Cincinnati, Ohio, served in one of five ways. One way is just chili. The second is spaghetti topped with chili. The third way is spaghetti topped with chili, then shredded Cheddar cheese. The fourth is the third version, further topped with chopped onions. The fifth adds a layer of beans to the bottom of the fourth version. All are eaten with **oyster crackers** sprinkled over top. See also CONEY.

cinghiale - Italian for "wild boar." See also BOAR.

cinnamon - a spice that comes from the inner bark of two related evergreen trees from the laurel family. True, or Ceylon, cinnamon is taken from a white-flowered shrub, *Cinnamomum zeylanicum*. The paler cinnamon is the better quality, since pale bark comes from the young shoots, and the strips of bark, or "quills," should be thin and delicate. The second of the two trees, which has a bark that is more strongly scented, is called **cassia.** Today, most of the "cinnamon" sold in the United States is actually cassia imported from Vietnam. The two are most easily distinguished by color: true cinnamon is tan, while cassia is a darker, reddish brown. The trees are native to Asia, and cinnamon was among the first commodities regularly traded from the East to the Mediterranean, at first along arduous routes and then by barge.

There is evidence that cinnamon was used in Egypt about 3000 BC, and it's often mentioned in the Old Testament. In Exodus, for example, God has Moses consecrate the temple with a mixture of myrrh, cinnamon, cassia and olive

cinnamon

oil. Cassia was found in China in 2500 BC; was known in Egypt by 1600 BC; and gradually headed for Europe. During the Middle Ages, cinnamon was second in popularity only to black pepper. In the Far East, cinnamon is the traditional emblem of good luck, and in Indonesia, a drink flavored with cassia buds is always given to newlyweds.

Ground cinnamon soon goes stale, so it should be bought in small quantities. Cinnamon also contains a chemical compound called eugenol, the same one that gives cloves their distinctive aroma.

cinnamon basil - see BASIL.

cinnamon cap - see NAMEKO MUSHROOM.

cinnamon oil - oil extracted from the pods of the cinnamon tree, whose bark is made into cinnamon sticks and ground cinnamon. It can be used as a flavoring in candies and baked goods, but is quite concentrated and spicy. Cinnamon oil is also touted as an effective natural mosquito repellent and curative for a number of disorders, although it is quite strong and must be diluted for most applications.

Cinzano - the brand name for vermouth made by the Campari Group of beverage producers in Italy. Cinzano Rosso (red) was the first variety made, starting in 1786, and is now accompanied by five other flavored vermouths, including ones enhanced with lemon, orange and even rose. Large umbrellas bearing the Cinzano logo are ubiquitous on the patios of European bars and restaurants.

cioppino - an Italian-American stew originating in San Francisco, made with tomatoes and a variety of fish and shellfish.

cipaille - see SEA PIE.

cipollini - a small, squat, disk-like Italian onion, with an unique, sharp flavor. They were once only available as an heirloom variety in the Mediterranean, but now are widely grown by specialty producers throughout Canada and the U.S. They are also sold in jars of olive oil or pickled in balsamic vinegar, which complements their mild bitterness very well.

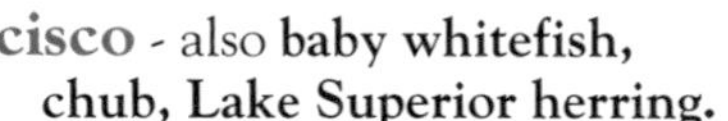

cipollini

cisco - also **baby whitefish, chub, Lake Superior herring.** A number of small freshwater fish native to the northern United States and southern Canada. Frequently cured with smoke in the same manner as whitefish, it's used often in Jewish cooking. Cisco may also be cooked whole, like trout.

citric acid - an additive that adds a pronounced sour flavor wherever it is used, although it has none of the complexity of lemon or other citrus fruits.

citron - fruit, *Citrus medica,* which originated in China. It's very sour and not eaten raw, but its thick peel is candied and used in baking. In Egypt, it was cultivated as far back as the 3rd century BC. In the Jewish religion, it's believed that the **etrog citron** (a smaller version) is the fruit of knowledge from which Adam took a bite. Today, the cultivation of the fruit is more or less restricted to Mediterranean countries, such as Greece, Italy, Corsica and Israel. Citron is the name for lemon in many countries. See also BUDDHA'S HAND CITRON.

citrus - first cultivated in India (the word "orange" comes from Hindi), China and Japan. With the exception of the grapefruit and other recent hybrids, the members of the citrus family are native to Southeast Asia. The **citron,** now known only in candied form, was brought back to Europe by Alexander the Great in the 3rd century BC, but it wasn't until the Middle Ages that the lemon and, in the 15th century, the orange, made it to the West, where they were initially treated as ornamentals and spice plants. The seedless navel orange was known along the Mediterranean by the 17th century, and the loose-skinned mandarin or tangerine species had been long cultivated in China and Japan before Europeans found them in the 19th century. The grapefruit was born in the West Indies in the 18th century as a cross between the orange and the **pomelo,** a large citrus fruit that had been brought to the New World a few decades earlier. The Ruby variety, with its bright red flesh, was discovered as a chance "bud sport," or mutation, on a Texas farm in 1929.

The original lime, variously called West Indian, Mexican and Key, was displaced in the U.S. by the Persian or Tahitian lime, apparently a hybrid of the lime and the citron, about 1920. The Key lime still predominates in the rest of the world. While the lemon-shaped Persian lime bears larger fruit and is more resistant to cold and pests, it's said that the small, round Key lime is more flavorful. Other notable citrus hybrids are the **temple orange,** a cross between mandarin and orange, and the **tangelo,** a mandarin crossed with grapefruit.

Citrus fruits are, of course, valued for their vitamin C content. This vitamin is more highly concentrated in the peel and pith (the white layer just under the peel) than in the flesh. The juice of an orange contains only a quarter of the vitamin C in the whole fruit, and grapefruit juice holds an even smaller proportion.

Citrus trees planted from seed take about 15 years before they bear much fruit, and they're thorny. Budded trees have practically no thorns and start bearing fruit after five years. Most Florida orange trees have lemon-tree roots. Almost all California lemon trees have orange-tree roots. One citrus tree, in fact, can, with a botanist's help, have lemons, limes, oranges, tangerines, kumquats and grapefruit growing on its branches at the same time.

citrus trumpet - a handy kitchen utensil usually made of nonreactive stainless steel, used for juicing citrus fruits, with a small, threaded cylinder with a hollow center and a flared spout at the top. The trumpet is screwed or pressed through the peel and into the flesh of the whole fruit. The fruit is then squeezed, and the juice collects in the hollow center and dribbles out the spout. The fruit can then be refrigerated with the trumpet still in it, until more juice is needed.

city chicken - a Michigan dish of veal and/or pork kabobs or patties of ground veal and/or pork formed to look like chicken legs. Apparently, the dish got its name at the beginning of the 20th century, when chicken was comparatively expensive in the United States. Veal and pork were more readily available at a reasonable price, so they were "dressed up" to emulate the more expensive poultry. Some city chicken recipes call for the meats to be breaded and deep-fried, while others are marinated and grilled or broiled.

city ham - a ham, usually mass-produced, bone-in or boneless, that has been cured before smoking or air-drying, using the **wet cure** method. A wet cure means that the ham has been soaked in **brine** rather than rubbed with a salt mixture, the way a country ham is.

civet - a **ragoût** or **fricassée** of game (sometimes also poultry) cooked in wine and the blood of the freshly killed animal. The name, which has nothing to do with the almost wholly inedible civet cat, comes from the Old French *civette*, now *ciboulette*, meaning "chive," the savory herb that used to be the distinguishing flavor of this dish.

clabber - unpasteurized milk that has gone sour and thickened, but not to the point at which the solid curds separate from the liquid whey. Clabber is similar to buttermilk but is thicker and tangier. Clabber is created spontaneously by bacteria that are naturally present in the milk, unlike buttermilk, which is made by adding specific bacteria to milk to begin the souring process. The term is short for "bonnyclabber," an English word adopted from the Irish term for a thick, sour, curdled milk dish.

clafouti - a French country dessert consisting of a mixture of fresh fruit and a pancake-like batter, which is baked. It's served hot or cold, most commonly using cherries, but plums and peaches can also be used.

Claiborne, Craig - see profile below.

clam - any of a large group of bivalve mollusks found in salty coastal waters around the world. New England prides itself on its **quahogs,** *Venus mercenaria,* which are also known as hard-shell

Claiborne, Craig (1920–2000) - cookbook author, food editor and critic, born in Sunflower, Mississippi. Because his father wasn't a good provider, his mother, Kathleen, took in lodgers and her considerable skills as a cook played a significant role in the family's survival. Claiborne learned how to cook helping her in the kitchen, and his interest in food developed early. After graduating in journalism from the University of Missouri in 1942, he served in the military, then used GI funding to attend a prestigious hotel school in Switzerland, earning a certificate in classic French cuisine. He began his career as a receptionist at *Gourmet* magazine and, in 1957 fulfilled his dream of becoming food editor at *The New York Times,* the first male to hold the position.

He published the first of many cookbooks, *The New York Times Cookbook*, in 1961. It quickly became a household staple, eventually selling 3 million copies. More of a collector and populizer than a documentarian or creator, Claiborne was often criticized by purists, who accused him of promoting branded products and fast food. Yet, there is no doubt that he played a significant role in the development of American cuisine. Among his accomplishments was the introduction of the four-star restaurant rating system, based on multiple visits by an anonymous reviewer. **Peter Kump,** founder of the eponymous cooking school, credited him with being one of four people who revolutionized American cooking in the 20th century. The other three were **James Beard,** Henri Soulé, chef at the legendary restaurant Le Pavillon, and **Julia Child.**

Remembered as a true gentleman by most who knew him, he became the center of controversy in 1975, when he bid for a dream dinner at a charity auction and ran up a $4,000 tab dining at Chez Denis in Paris. In response to his article about the experience, *The New York Times* received thousands of outraged letters denouncing his extravagance. In 1982, he published his autobiography *A Feast Made for Laughter*, which dealt candidly with some of his experiences as a homosexual.

CLAM VARIETIES

There are hundreds of species of clam, ranging from the aptly named giant clam, which can grow to a length of slightly more than 4 feet (1.2 m) to the tiny pebble-like Venus and littleneck clams, which are less than 2 inches (5 cm).

chowder clam - see QUAHOG.

hard-shell clam - one of two varieties of clam, distinguished from soft-shell clams by their ability to completely close their shells. See also QUAHOG.

littleneck clam - see QUAHOG.

long-neck clam - see SOFT-SHELL CLAM.

quahog - also **chowder clam, hard-shell clam, large clam, littleneck clam.** A round hard-shell clam from the U.S. Atlantic coast, living in somewhat deep waters, gathered by raking, not digging; from the Algonquian name *poquauhock*. Clams from the U. S. west coast are called **Pacific littleneck clams.**

soft-shell clam - also **long-neck clam.** Inappropriately named, because they actually have a thin, brittle shell, clams of this kind cannot completely close their shells due to their long neck.

clams; cherrystones when they're at middle growth; and littlenecks when very young. **Littlenecks** and **cherrystones** are eaten on the half shell, but when older and larger, they go into chowders. One edge of the quahog shell is usually deep purple, and there are sometimes splotches of purple elsewhere. The Lenape, Powhatan and Renápe Indians used the purple parts to make bead money, or wampum. Purple wampum was worth twice the value of white, which was made from conch shells. See also PACIFIC LITTLENECK CLAM, RAZOR CLAM.

clambake - originally a gathering of neighbors, family and friends for a feast of clams on the beach in New England. Nowadays, it's the process of steaming an assortment of foods, such as clams, lobsters, crabs, chicken, unhusked corn and baked potatoes, in a pit dug in the seashore sand, layered with hot rocks and covered with seaweed.

clam chowder - clam chowder is a perennial favorite in the Northeastern United States. While people usually only acknowledge two types of clam chowder, there are actually three: **New England clam chowder** is cream- or milk-based; **Manhattan clam chowder** is tomato-based; and **Rhode Island clam chowder** is made with a clear base of clam broth. See also CHOWDER.

clam juice - the broth created when clams are steamed or boiled, often found bottled in grocery stores (but easy to make at home), used as a base for soups and pasta sauces. Clam juice is also a feature in some cocktails, such as the Bloody Caesar.

clam knife - a short, thick, round-ended knife used to open live clams. An **oyster knife** is often more pointed than a clam knife, but the two are very similar in size and shape.

clam knife

clams casino - clams on the half-shell stuffed with a layer of sautéed green pepper or pimiento, garlic, bread crumbs and butter, topped with a slice of bacon, and baked or broiled until the clams are cooked through and the bacon is crisp. It is usually served as an appetizer and was a staple in 1950s American entertaining.

clapshot - a Scottish specialty of leeks and mashed potatoes and turnips, with chopped chives, and butter or bacon fat.

claret - a British term for red **Bordeaux,** from the Middle Ages, derived from the French word *clairet*, used to distinguish the light style red Bordeaux wines from the more robust reds of Portugal and Spain. Today, claret refers to all red Bordeaux wines, while *clairet* now refers to the rosé style wines of the region.

clarified butter - also **drawn butter, ghee.** Used in cooking because it can sustain high temperatures without burning, clarified butter is made by slowly melting unsalted butter, allowing the water to evaporate and the milk solids to settle. See also BEURRE NOISETTE.

clarify - to remove impurities, either by straining or by adding something, such as egg whites, that will attract particles from the liquid. Clarifying the butter — as, for example, when making ghee — destroys the normal bacteria in it and removes the milk solids from it, which greatly lengthens its shelf life. This may be one reason why ghee is so popular in India, where refrigeration still remains a luxury for many. See also CONSOMMÉ.

clary - an herb, *Salvia sclarea,* with dull gray, furred leaves, tasting slightly like sage. The English name comes from the Latin *sclarea,* which in turn comes from *clarus,* meaning "clear." Centuries ago, it was believed that a decoction of the seeds, when used as an eyewash, would cleanse the eyes and improve vision. In 16th-century Germany, wine merchants used to fool the taste buds of their customers by infusing clary with elder flowers and mixing it with Rhine wines, converting the wine to a Muscatel-like taste and aroma. Clary can be used in any recipe calling for sage, and its essential oil is used to flavor beverages, baked goods, candies and liqueurs.

classical brigade - see BRIGADE SYSTEM.

Clause, Jean-Pierre - see profile below.

clay baker - also **clay roaster.** A baking dish made of terra-cotta with a tight-fitting lid, used for roasting meats, poultry, fish or vegetables in their own juices in the oven. The inside of a clay baker is sometimes glazed to keep it from absorbing food juices and odors, but otherwise the pan is unglazed. First, the pan is soaked in water until it is thoroughly moistened, then the food is put in, usually without the addition of fat or oil. The liquid that runs out of the food as it heats boils and steam-cooks the food, creating a moist, tender result.

cleaver - a large, heavy, nearly rectangular knife that can cut through bone as well as meat. Its large, flat blade can also be used for pounding meat and crushing garlic.

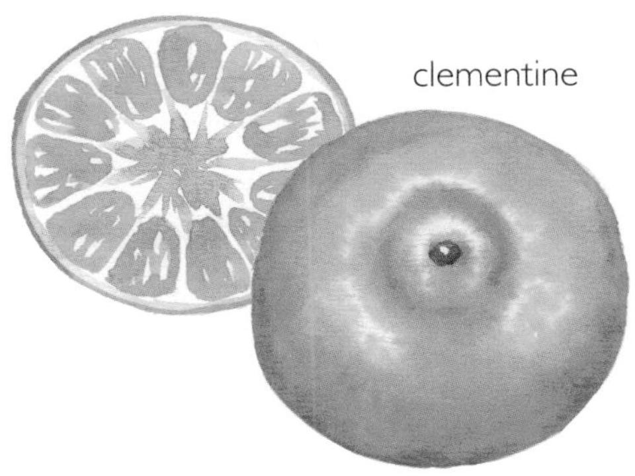
clementine

clementine - a seedless North African orange, regarded by some as a cross between the mandarin orange and the tangerine and by others as a variety of tangerine. It has an orange skin that is easily removed and a refreshingly tangy, juicy flesh. **Father Clément Rodier,** a French missionary, developed it in Algeria in 1902.

Clements, Mrs. - see MUSTARD.

cling film - see PLASTIC WRAP.

clingstone - see PEACH.

closed crumb - see CRUMB.

closed date - see EXPIRATION DATE.

clotted cream - also **Devon cream, Devonshire cream.** This thick English cream from Devon is made by slowly heating whole milk, allowing a layer of cream to rise to the top and ferment. When cool, the thickened cream

Clause, Jean-Pierre (18th century) - French chef from Lorraine, inventor of *pâté de fois gras* in Strasbourg, some time between 1778 and 1784. In service to the Marquis de Contades, Clause was asked to prepare a grand banquet with some new dishes. He devised a new method of preparing fois gras, or fattened goose liver, during a sleepless night before the event. He added bacon fat and baked it in a crust, christening it *pâté en Contades,* after his employer, although today it is known *as pâté de fois gras en croute,* meaning "in pastry."

is skimmed and served as part of the classic English **cream tea** with scones and jam. While the terms "clotted cream" and "Devon cream" are often used interchangeably, there is a technical difference. Traditional clotted cream contains about 55 percent milk fat and has a thick, butter-like texture. It's often used as a spread on its own for scones or as a topping for pies or fresh fruit. Devon cream is slightly lower in milk fat at 48 percent and is easier to spoon than clotted cream. It is used on its own as a spread or topping and also as a component in many recipes.

cloudberry - also **bakeapple, bake-apple berry, baked-apple berry, mountain berry, yellow berry.** A small, tart, gold-color fruit, *Rubus chamaemorus*, that grows wild in large areas of open moorland, especially in parts of Scotland and Ireland, but also in Scandinavia, Siberia, the western U.S. and Canada, where it is known as bakeapple berry. It is a distant relative of the raspberry. It ripens slowly, allowing the flavor to develop to an extraordinary intensity and sweetness, making it perfect for desserts, jams or fruit soups.

cloud ear - see WOOD EAR.

clove - **1.** a single segment of a bulb, such as garlic. **2.** the unopened flower bud of the tall evergreen clove tree, *Eugenia aromatica*, which originated in the Spice Islands, Molucca Islands, Zanzibar and Madagascar, and is now grown in many areas of Southeast Asia. The name comes from the Latin *clavus* and the French *clou*, meaning "nail," and that's just what the spice looks like: a tiny nail. Chinese courtiers used the clove to sweeten their breath in the presence of the emperor about 300 BC, and the ancient Chinese name for it, *ki she kiang*, can be translated either as "bird tongue spice" or "chicken tongue spice." It was used by the Egyptians in the 2nd century AD and was known throughout Europe by the 8th century. The Emperor Constantine sent the Bishop of Rome gold and silver vessels filled with cloves, which was considered the ultimate in munificent gifts.

The monopoly on the clove trade was held by the Portuguese, who discovered the Moluccas while searching for cloves, and then the Dutch. In 1770, the monopoly was broken by the French, when a diplomat named Pierre Poivre (which translates as "Peter Pepper") managed to smuggle some seedlings into the French colonies of Isle de France and Bourbon. A single tree survived, and from it descended the entire plantation in Africa and the Americas. Today, half of the world's output (Tanzania is the largest producer) is consumed in Indonesia, where tobacco is smoked with cloves.

It has been known for centuries that eugenol, the main constituent of clove oil, has local anesthetic properties, used to alleviate toothaches. The oil is also used in perfumes, bath salts and in some brands of mouthwash.

clove basil - see BASIL.

clove pink - also **gilly flower.** Known to the Greeks and Romans, this edible flower comes from the carnation family, Dianthus caryophyllus. The Romans believed that placing petals of clove pink in their wine would delay inebriation.

clover honey - see HONEY.

cloverleaf roll - a yeast roll, popular in the U.S., made by putting three small balls of the same size of dough in a muffin tin, with the resulting shape like that of a cloverleaf.

club cheese - a processed cheese made by heating and blending ground Cheddar and other cheeses, water, condiments and seasonings.

club sandwich - also **clubhouse sandwich.** This tiered sandwich consists of three slices of bread or toast, filled with chicken or turkey, bacon, tomato, lettuce and mayonnaise.

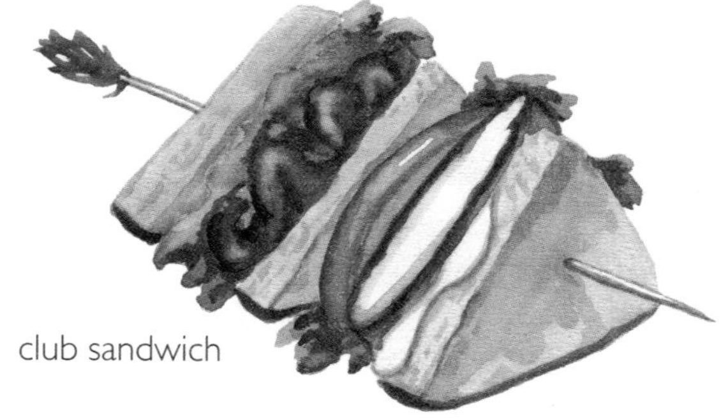
club sandwich

club soda - see SODA WATER.

club steak - see BEEF.

cluster eggplant - see EGGPLANT.

coagulant - a substance that causes a liquid to curdle, such as **nigari** or **gypsum,** which is used

A B C D E F G H I J K L M N O P Q R S T U V W X Y Z

to make tofu from soy milk, and **rennet,** which transforms milk into cheese.

coarse sugar - also **crystal sugar.** See SUGAR.

coat - to cover a food with an outer layer or coating, such as bread crumbs, batter, flour, seasonings, etc.

coated ginger - in commercial terms, unpeeled ginger. Peeled ginger is known commercially as uncoated ginger.

cobbler - a baked dessert consisting of a layer of fruit covered with a thick biscuit crust sprinkled with sugar.

Cobb salad - created in 1936 by Robert Cobb, the owner of the Brown Derby restaurant in Hollywood. According to Walter Scharfe, later president of the Brown Derby Restaurants, "Its origin was quite by accident. One evening, Robert H. Cobb went to the icebox and found an avocado, which he chopped with lettuce, celery, tomatoes and strips of bacon. Later, he embellished it with breast of chicken, chives, hard-boiled egg, watercress and a wedge of Roquefort cheese for dressing." The Cobb salad and the **Caesar salad** were the first "main-course salads." Up until that time (the 1920s and 1930s), salads were side dishes composed of greens with a simple dressing of oil, vinegar and salt.

cockle

cobnut - see HAZELNUT.

cochineal - a red pigment obtained from the cochineal beetle, *Dactylopius coccus*, found in Central and South American living as a parasite on the pads of certain cactus such as prickly pear, used as a food coloring called carmine.

cochin ginger - a very short, red-gray variety of ginger.

cocido - a rich Spanish stew, often called *cocido madrileño* because it is a specialty of Madrid, consisting of a single pot filled with chickpeas, assorted meats (such as chicken, pork and sausages), vegetables and spices. The dish is simmered for several hours until all the elements have been cooked through and have infused the broth with their flavor. The broth is then strained out of the pot, and short vermicelli noodles are added and cooked until soft. Meanwhile, the meats and vegetables are cut into serving-size pieces and arranged along with the chickpeas on a platter. Both dishes are served at the same time along with crusty loaves of bread to sop up the richly flavored broth. The dish can be altered by adding whatever ingredients are on hand. The name is the past participle of the Spanish verb *cocer*, meaning "to cook." See also OLLA PODRIDA, PUCHERO.

cock - a male chicken too old to roast, usually used for chicken soup or stock. The famous French **coq au vin,** or cock in wine sauce, can't be better than when a cock is used.

cock-a-leekie - also **cockie-leekie, cocky-leeky.** A Scottish soup of chicken and leeks cooked in chicken broth, sometimes thickened with oatmeal or cream. The English claim that the dish originated in England in the 14th century and was "borrowed" by the Scots.

cockle - bivalve mollusks of the genus *Cardium*, recognizable by their cockleshell, which is heart-shaped and ribbed. Like many other bivalves that fall within the general category of clams, cockles come in dozens of varieties. Although they are associated with England, the North American coastline boasts several species, including the spiny, prickly and giant Atlantic cockles (one of the best in the world). Unfortunately, cockles, which were sold on street corners in London just a century ago, have lost their popularity and are seen only rarely in North American fish markets.

cocktail - a drink made with one or more alcoholic beverages combined with a non-alcoholic mixer, usually consumed before a meal. By some accounts, the cocktail was invented in 1776 at an Elmsford, New York, tavern when barmaid Betsy Flanagan decorated her bar, Halls Corner, with poultry feathers. An inebriated guest demanded that she bring him "a glass of those cocktails," and she served him a mixed drink garnished with a feather.

The word "cocktail" appeared in print for the first time in 1806 in a Hudson, New York, newspaper; it was described as "a stimulating liquor, composed of spirits of any kind, sugar, water and bitters." There are several other stories for the origin of the word, including that it refers to the color in a cock's tail. Or it may be derived from the French *coquetier,* meaning "eggcups," which came about in New Orleans in 1838 (not 1793, as often reported). The story may be true but happened too late to be the origin of the word): apothecary Antoine Amédée Peychaud, the inventor of Peychaud bitters, served a beverage of cognac and bitters in eggcups to his customers. The English-speaking clientele pronounced *coquetier* as "cocktail." Another story also claims a French origin for the word, from *coquetel,* a drink from the Bordeaux region introduced to Americans by French officers during the American Revolution. It is a drink that will "cock your tail."

One story claimed the word is of English origin, from the popular 17th-century English drink cock-ale, a mixture of ale, raisins, spices and a boiled cock, which is left to brew for a week or more. The American journalist H.L. Mencken found many etymological references for the word, including cock-bread-ale, a mixture of stale bread, ale and bitters fed to fighting cocks. There is also a possibility that it came from the practice of toasting the victor in a cockfight by placing the number of feathers left in the cock's tail in the drinks.

Finally, cocktail may come from the word "cocktailings," which are the dregs of various casks, drained out of the cocks or spigots, mixed together and sold as a cheap drink.

cocktail glass - a tall, footed glass, usually the same shape as a **Martini glass** (with a narrow bottom and a widely flared rim) but sometimes with a simple rounded or straight-sided bowl, used for serving chilled cocktails, such as **Martinis, Daiquiris** and **Manhattans.**

cocktail onion - a tiny, pickled onion, can be sweet or sour depending on the maker; the garnish that turns a **Martini** into a **Gibson.**

cocktail sauce - made of ketchup and prepared horseradish, usually with lemon juice and often Tabasco, served with shrimp and other seafood.

cocktail wieners - also **cocktail franks, cocktail weenies.** Small hotdogs, about 2 to 3 inches (5 to 7.5 cm) long, often served skewered on toothpicks at cocktail parties as a playful appetizer. A cocktail frank is a close cousin to the Vienna sausage, often used to make **pigs in a blanket.**

cocoa - see COCOA POWDER, HOT CHOCOLATE.

cocoa butter - a natural fat removed from cocoa beans during the process of making chocolate and cocoa powder. It's used to make chocolate, white chocolate, and some soaps and cosmetics.

cocoa mass - see CHOCOLATE LIQUOR.

cocoa mix - see INSTANT COCOA.

cocoa powder - also **cocoa.** Used as a flavoring, this unsweetened powder is made by hulling and crushing cocoa beans and extracting most of the cocoa butter.

coconut

coconut - the fruit of a tropical palm tree, *Cocos nucifera.* Coconuts, which contain "milk" but are also a fruit, grow between the palm fronds at the crown of the tree, probably among the oldest and most useful of plants. Dried coconut pulp can be pressed for its oil for use in cooking and soap making. Coconut shells, wood and leaves are used in furniture making, hut walls and roofs, and tools and flooring materials. The tree's roots are ground to make tea.

Coquitos, or baby coconuts, are cultivated in Chile, sold without their husks, having smooth, dark brown shells the size of acorns. The stem end, or base, of the coconut has three spots that form a monkey-like face; *coco* is Portuguese for "grinning face."

coconut cream - a coconut-flavored liquid made in the same manner as coconut milk but using less water, so that the resulting liquid is thicker and more flavorful.

coconut milk - a coconut-flavored liquid made by pouring boiling water over shredded coconut, which is then cooled and strained.

coconut oil - an oil pressed from **copra,** the name for dried coconut meat. It contains natural lecithin; is one of the few saturated fats that doesn't come from animals; and is excellent for frying.

coconut water - the clear or cloudy liquid contained in the shell of a fresh coconut.

cocotte - a general term used to describe any round or oval cooking vessel, from a large casserole to individual dishes, in which food is both cooked and served. Large cocottes are usually made of cast iron or earthenware, with a handle on each side for easy lifting, and a close-fitting lid. They're used for the same purpose as a casserole. Smaller cocottes, also called "ramekins," are generally made of fireproof china, porcelain or earthenware. The term *en cocotte* means a dish cooked in a cocotte.

cocoyam - see TARO.

cocozelle - also **Italian vegetable marrow.** An Italian variety of summer squash that falls under the zucchini umbrella, with green skin striped with light green or yellow. Cocozelle are commonly eaten in southern Europe, but are also grown and sold in North America.

cod - popular saltwater fish, once the staple of the North Atlantic, doubly valuable because it could be salted and dried, allowing it to be caught far offshore and kept for months before using. Cape Cod was named after it, and a wooden cod hangs above the entry to the Massachusetts State House in Boston. No food was more important, and it was so plentiful that the air bladders of the fish (called cod sounds) were stewed in milk as a popular breakfast item. Now, however, the true **Atlantic cod,** *Gadus morhua,* while not an endangered species, is what the experts call a "depleted fishery" and can no longer be profitably caught and sold for widespread distribution. Today, Atlantic cod comes mainly from Icelandic waters, which that nation began strictly managing in the 1950s. Haddock, *Melanogrammus merluccius,* often sold as cod, is not much more plentiful. Hake, *Merluccius virens,* and whiting, *Merlangus merlangus,* are abundant on both coasts and good substitutes for cod in most recipes. See also SALT COD.

cod

coddes - a Maryland specialty of deep-fried breaded codfish cakes.

coddle - to simmer gently and briefly in a liquid below the boiling point.

cod's roe - roe that is washed and dry-salted for six to eight hours, then rewashed, dipped in boiling water to rehydrate, then smoked. Among the Japanese preserved roes are *hontarako,* a salted and dried cod's roe, *karasumi,* made from gray mullet or tuna roe, salted, pressed and dried; and *tarako* or *momojiko,* salted Alaskan Pollock roe.

cod tongues - the tongues of codfish, a traditional delicacy in Newfoundland, often served fried or baked.

coeur à la crème - a pretty French dessert consisting of **fromage blanc,** sweetened and combined with **meringue,** sour cream and/or whipping cream, spooned into individual perforated heart-shaped molds and chilled until most of the whey has drained off. The cheese mixture is then unmolded onto a plate and served topped with berries. The name means "heart with cream" in French.

coffee - from the Arabic *qahwah,* via the Turkish *kahveh, café* in French and Spanish, *caffe* in Italian and *Kaffee* in German, all remarkably alike. The Arabic word originally designated any stimulating drink. Coffee was discovered in AD 850, according to legend, by the Arab goatherd Kaidi in southern Ethiopia, who noticed that his goat became frisky after chewing the berries from certain tall evergreen shrubs. Coffee originated in Ethiopia, where *Coffea arabica,* one of the three main species, grows wild. The others, *robusta* and *liberica,* were later found in the Congo and Liberia respectively. The coffee tree requires a hot, moist climate and rich soil. While *arabica* grows best at a high altitude — from 2,000 to 6,000 feet (600 to 1,800 m) above sea level — the other species grow better at altitudes below 2,000 feet (600 m).

Originally, coffee was known as food by some African tribes, who would crush the ripened berries (called cherries), mix them with animal fat and form the resulting paste into balls. It was usually eaten before battles to enhance strength and vigor. Coffee was served as a drink much later, not as we know it today, but as a wine from the fermented juices of the cherries. It was not until AD 1000 that the Arabs learned to boil the burned beans and drink it as a hot beverage.

By 1454, coffee was introduced to Constantinople by the Ottoman Turks. The beverage is popular in the Middle East, although many Muslim authorities disapprove, observing that Mohammed did not drink coffee.

Coffee is marketed under the name of the locality in which it is grown or the shipping port. Brazilian coffees are chiefly Rios and Santos. Mocha is the highest quality of Arabian coffee. Java and East Indian are also high-grade coffees, and Kona is the fine grade of mild coffee produced in Hawaii. Low-grade Rios are the cheapest coffees on the market (the United States is the biggest consumer). Maracaibo, Bogota and Sumatra are the other well-known varieties. Usually, the varieties of coffee are no longer obtainable separately but are blended to advertise brands.

The content of caffeine in an espresso coffee is less than a regular cup of coffee, due to the length of roasting of the beans. Strangely enough, the exact identity of the flavor of coffee has never been established. The term "caffeoyl" has for many years been applied to the substance or the group of substances developed by roasting, which are thought to be responsible for aroma and bouquet. Caffeoyl has been described as an essential oil, yet coffee contains no essential oil. Flavor substances (at least a part of them) are known to be water-soluble, a property not possessed by any true oil. Whether the flavor substances are held in some oils or fats of coffee and released by hot water has never been clear. Too long a heating process at too high a temperature may remove or destroy all characteristic flavor and bouquet.

In June 2003, the journal *Nature* reported that, at last, science might have solved one of the most vexing problems of the modern age: how to make a cup of decaf coffee that tastes good. By altering the genes of the coffee plant, Japanese scientists have found they can reduce the caffeine content by 70 percent. Scientists say it will take a few more years before they have a product ready to market. Currently, coffee beans go through a punishing ordeal to remove their caffeine. They are soaked in solvents or scraped in machines, losing not only their caffeine, but also many of the compounds that make coffee smell and taste so good to millions of people. Bad as most decaf tastes, it still accounts for about 20 percent of American coffee sales. If the new technology works as hoped, genetically engineered decaf will taste

COFFEE BEAN VARIETIES

Colombian - a full-bodied coffee bean with little acidity.

Costa Rican - a mild-tasting bluish green arabica bean with slight acidity.

Jamaican - a large, yellow bean with a delicate flavor, the most famous variety being Blue Mountain coffee, very popular in Japan.

Kenyan - the pale green African arabica bean, with a rich, sharp-tasting liquor when roasted.

Mocha - an arabica type, originally from the old port of Mocha in Yemen, one of the world's finest coffees. Production is limited, so the label "mocha" can mean a blend, such as Ethiopian, real Mocha, Honduras and Nicaraguan coffee.

Mysore - East Indian arabica, a bluish gray bean, its liquor a fine, strong taste.

Santos - a green-yellow bean with a smooth, mellow-tasting liquor with no acidity.

Turkish - not a blend but a pulverized coffee, made mostly in Cyprus, traditionally from Mocha but now mostly from Brazilian beans. A typical blend might be one-third each Santos, Rio and Victoria, all Brazilian arabicas.

more like full-strength coffee. Unlike more controversial genetic engineering feats, in which genes from one species are added to another, these coffee beans will simply have an existing gene turned off. See also ARABICA.

coffee cake - a rich cake-like bread usually flavored with nuts, fruit or spices, topped with a glaze or **streusel,** most often served at breakfast or brunch. Known as *Kaffekuchen* in Germany.

coffee cream - see CREAM.

coffee gelatin - a dessert made from hot brewed coffee, unflavored gelatin and cream. The ingredients are stirred together until the gelatin is melted, then poured into a large mold or individual molds and refrigerated until set. The dessert, which is popular in New England, is served topped with whipped cream.

coffee grinder - see GRIND.

coffeehouse - a commercial establishment serving coffee and other, usually nonalcoholic, beverages, along with light snacks and entertainment, that has traditionally functioned as a gathering place for artists, poets, plotters, political activists and neighborhood gossips, and provided a spot for a quiet game of chess or backgammon. Males-only-allowed, the first coffeehouses opened their doors in Persia in the 16th century. They arrived in England and Europe, along with their namesake drink about 100 years later (in a 1664 diary entry, the ever-curious Samuel Pepys himself reports visiting one to drink a "jocolatte" and, no doubt, catch up on the latest doings). Within a decade, Boston had one, too. Today, big-name coffee companies offer their own brand of coffeehouse, designed more for the contented than the contentious.

coffee press - see FRENCH PRESS.

coffee whitener - a nondairy product used as a cream or milk substitute, usually made with corn syrup and other ingredients.

coffin - **1.** an old-fashioned term for a pastry case or crust surrounding a filling, such as for a pie. The term is often seen in cookbooks printed before the early 19th century, usually in the form of an instruction to pour the filling into a coffin. The term derives from the Greek word *kophinos*, meaning "basket." The current use of the word, as a box for burial of a corpse, did not emerge until the 16th century, but it did eventually overshadow the culinary meaning. **2.** an equally old-fashioned term for a pie plate.

cognac - considered to be one of the most valued grape-based spirits in the world. Ugni Blanc grapes from the town of Cognac, in the Charentes region, are made into a light white wine and then distilled twice to create **eau de vie** ("water of life"), a brandy aged in oak casks, becoming more concentrated from natural evaporation, for as long as 80 years. These oak casks are still made entirely by hand: works of art that have been cautiously cut and fitted without nails, so that the cognac never has contact with metal.

In the 12th century, the invading Moors introduced the pot still, in which cognac is still distilled today. Paradoxically, centuries ago, the grapes were boiled down or distilled as a means to save space on ships as well as taxes, since wine was taxed by volume. The thought was to reconstitute the concentrated wine by adding water. Little did these frugal souls know that they were generating the prototype of what we know today as cognac. Quite a few countries make brandy, but only the French can call it cognac. There are diverse and distinctive ranks of cognac, from the most basic VS (Very Special), to VSOP (Very Superior Old Pale), where minimum aging standards are used. Then, there are the superior grades, such as Napoleon, Extra and XO, and vintage cognacs that separate the ordinary from the extraordinary. In addition, producers permit their cognac to age longer in wooden casks for the ultimate in smoothness, since once the cognac is bottled, it won't age further.

coho salmon - see SALMON.

cohune oil - a semisolid fat used in cooking and for some cosmetic preparations, from the nuts of the cohune palm, a Central American tree found in tropical rainforests and coastal southern Mexico.

coil whisk - see WHISK.

Cointreau - a clear, orange-flavored French liqueur, launched in 1849 by the Cointreau brothers, Edouard and Adolphe, and initially sold under the brand name Triple Sec White Curaçao. So many other proprietary Curaçaos began to be sold as Triple Sec that the family decided to give it their own name instead. Up to the mid-1980s, Cointreau used to buy part of its bitter-orange harvest from the Grand Marnier plantations in Haiti.

cola - a sweet, dark, carbonated soft drink flavored with cola nuts, caramel, sugar and other ingredients. An extract of coca leaves from the cocaine plant used to be used as well, but this practice stopped in the 1920s.

colander - a perforated bowl-shaped container used for draining liquids from solids.

cola nut - also **kola nut.** The fragrant reddish seeds of the kola tree, *Cola acuminata* and *Cola nitida*, native to tropical Africa. They are the main flavoring ingredient in cola and contains caffeine.

Colbert sauce - a French sauce named after Louis XIV's chief minister, made from **demi-glace** flavored with butter, shallots, wine, lemon juice and tarragon, often served with game or grilled meats.

Colby - a popular mild American cheese with a slightly granular texture, originally from Colby, Wisconsin. Made in various shapes, it's a washed-curd cheese (if the curds are washed thoroughly in cold water, the moisture content of the cheese is increased, making it mature more quickly).

colcannon - an Irish peasant specialty of mashed potatoes with milk, butter, finely chopped cooked onions, and kale or cabbage.

cold cuts - thin slices of various meats, such as ham, beef, salami and turkey, served cold, especially for making sandwiches.

cold pasteurization - see IRRADIATION.

cold pressing - see OLIVE OIL.

cold smoking - see SMOKED FOODS, SMOKED SALMON.

coleslaw - made with shredded cabbage and various other vegetables, usually dressed with mayonnaise. It came to the American colonies with the Dutch and went through many transformations before arriving at the more or less standard recipe that we know today. In 1905, Mrs. John E. Cooke of New Castle, Pennsylvania, was rewarded with a $100 sewing machine and long-lasting gastronomic notoriety after winning the first prize for a dressing for coleslaw. The name comes from the Dutch *kool sla*, meaning "cabbage salad."

collards

collards - also **collard, collard greens.** Like kale, collards are primitive members of the cabbage family that don't form heads. The name comes from the Anglo-Saxon *colewarts*, meaning "cabbage plants." Grown since prehistoric times, their exact origin remains uncertain, although it was probably in Asia Minor or around the Mediterranean. The Greeks grew collards, and so did the Romans, who introduced them to France and Britain. For almost 2,000 years, they were the chief vegetable in England. By 1669 and maybe even earlier, these greens were being grown in the colonies.

collation - the term applied to a simple, light, but nourishing snack, originally some food offered to children between breakfast and lunch. The name comes from the Latin *collatio*, in remembrance of the light meal monks ate after vespers.

Collins glass - see HIGHBALL GLASS.

colocasia leaf - see PATRA LEAF.

Colombian coffee bean - see COFFEE.

colombo - a West Indian spice mixture imported to the Caribbean in the 19th century by Sri Lankan immigrants and named after Colombo, Sri Lanka's capital. Known as the curry powder of the West Indies, it likely consists of turmeric, coriander, allspice and a variety of other spices, such as garlic and cinnamon. Colombo is also used to describe stews seasoned with the mixture, such as lamb Colombo, chicken Colombo or pork Colombo, the latter being traditionally served on Christmas Eve in Guadeloupe.

Colonel Sanders - see SANDERS, COLONEL HARLAND.

colored sugar - see SUGAR.

Colwick - a traditional English cow's milk cheese usually made into cylinders, with a "dished" or concave upper surface, which can be filled with cream and fruit. The cheese is usually sold unsalted, to be served as a dessert, but can also be salted and eaten as a savory cheese.

comal - a Mexican stovetop griddle, traditionally made of a slightly concave circle of unglazed earthenware, but now often made of cast iron, used for making tortillas or roasting sweet or hot peppers over charcoal or, nowadays, a gas burner.

comfort food - food that is traditional or prepared in a homey style, designed to evoke feelings of nostalgia for times past. Macaroni and cheese is likely one of the most popular comfort foods. Stews and hearty soups, mashed potatoes, casseroles, meat loaf, old-fashioned tapioca pudding, any food that evokes warm feelings of home, protection and love can be a comfort food.

comfrey - a medicinal herb, *Symphytum officinale*, used to make tea. The fresh, young leaves have also been eaten for centuries, generally in small doses, in salads or cooked as greens. The word derives from the Latin *conferta*, meaning "grow together," and the Greek word for the generic name of the plant *Symphytum*, meaning "coming together." The Roman historian and naturalist **Pliny,** on experimenting with comfrey roots, remarked that they were so sticky that, when pieces of meat were cooked with them they would all become glued together in one lump. Consequently, for hundreds of years, people were convinced that comfrey could close wounds and knit broken limbs. One has to be careful not to consume it on a regular basis; in 1978, a study revealed that the leaves contain an alkaloid that could cause kidney and liver damage and that laboratory animals who were fed comfrey regularly developed some forms of liver cancer.

Comice pear - see PEAR.

complete protein - a **complete protein** is one made up of the proper amounts of the nine essential amino acids needed for the human body to sustain itself: tryptophan, threonine, isoleucine, valine, histidine, lysine, methionine, phenylalinine and leucine. An **incomplete protein** is one that is missing one or more of the essential amino acids. Because humans cannot synthesize these amino acids, they must consume them in foods. Meat and other animal foods are considered sources of complete protein, while vegetables, fruits and grains are sources of incomplete protein. However, vegetables, fruits and grains can be eaten in combinations that yield the same results as consuming animal products. The good news is that each meal does not have to contain all of the amino acids in a strict balance, so careful food combining, once considered a must for vegetarians, is not necessary. Nutrition researchers have determined that eating a variety of plant-based foods over the course of the day can yield sufficient amounts of amino acids to ensure good health. See also PROTEIN.

composed salad - a salad in which the ingredients are attractively arranged on the serving plate, rather than tossed together. The dressing is drizzled over the ingredients once they are arranged. The French name for this type of salad is *salade composée*. **Salade Niçoise** is a classic composed salad.

composed salad

compote - fresh or dried fruit slow cooked in a sugar syrup, sometimes with liqueur or flavorings added, served cold. Dried fruits, such as prunes and apricots, are soaked in cold water first. Compote can also refer to chicken, pigeon or partridge that has been cooked for a long time. *Compotier* is a deep dish on a stem used to serve compote.

compound butter - softened butter creamed with other ingredients, such as chopped herbs, spices, garlic or shallots, then often formed into a cylinder and refrigerated until firm. Slices of the compound butter are placed on top of hot foods, such as grilled meats, and allowed to melt and add flavor to the dish. The French name for compound butter is *beurre composé*.

compound chocolate - see CONFECTIONERY COATING.

Comté - also **Gruyère de Comté.** See GRUYÈRE.

concassé - to chop roughly or to crush a mixture, quite often referring to tomatoes.

conch - a very large marine mollusk, related to the whelk, that has a distinctive spiral shell with a series of knobs, and a pointed end. The conch is an endangered species, so harvesting from the wild is tightly controlled. The best-quality conchs come from the Bahamas and Turks and Caicos, where in Providenciales, conchs are harvested at the Caicos Conch Farm, the only commercial conch farm in the world. Collectors prize the spiral shell for its lovely shades of pink; musicians use it as a trumpet. High-priced cameos from Naples dating as far back as the mid-15th century were made of conch shells.

conch

conche - see CONCHING.

conchiglie - see PASTA.

conchigliette - see PASTA.

conchiglioni - see PASTA.

conching - a commercial process for enhancing the flavor of chocolate and making it smooth for use in confectionery, achieved by slowly churning warm chocolate paste (called chocolate mass) or liquid chocolate in large vats with rotating blades, thus removing excess moisture and volatile acids from the mixture. **Rodolphe Lindt,** a famous Swiss chocolatier, invented the **conche** in 1879. It consisted of a heated stone trough and a large roller, which slowly and rhythmically pressed the chocolate back and forth, exposing it to air and allowing excess water to evaporate, then pressing the fat particles out of the cocoa butter and smoothly incorporating them into the other ingredients. The mass may be kneaded at a steady, warm temperature for several hours or for up to a week to achieve the proper texture, at which point flavorings, such as vanilla, orange oil or mint extract, are incorporated if desired. The result is highly stable chocolate that gives the impression of silk on the tongue. Today, conches consist of enormous metal vats and steel blades that turn, kneading the chocolate mixture, but the result is the same. The conche got its name from the curved ends of the stone trough, which resemble the shell of a **conch.**

Concord grape - see GRAPE.

Condé - the term applied to numerous culinary preparations, including Condé, a pastry made of leftover puff pastry; potage Condé, puréed red beans and croutons; eggs à la Condé, fried eggs served on potage Condé; Condé glace, also called **glace Royale,** egg whites, almonds and powered sugar used in pastry; and riz à la Condé, a kind of rice pudding usually served with apricots and Kirsch. All these dishes were named for the illustrious house of Louis I de Bourbon (1530–1569) and his son, the Grand Condé.

condensed milk - sweetened cow's milk that has had 60 percent of its water removed by evaporation. Sugar accounts for 40 to 45 percent of the total volume before evaporation. The mixture is very sticky and sweet and is typically canned. Often used in baked goods and desserts. A patent was issued for the product in the United States in 1856 to **Gail Borden,** a businessman from Norwich, New York, who formed the New York Condensed Milk Company, later known as Borden Inc. Prior to Mr. Borden's development, milk could only be kept fresh for a few days. An unopened can of condensed milk can keep for months, if not years. By 1858, Borden's milk, sold as Eagle Brand, had gained a reputation for purity, durability and economy. Condensed milk proved a godsend to the shattered South after the Civil War, a conflict in which both sides made wide use of canned foods. As well, the availability of condensed milk lowered the infant mortality rate in North America at that time. Not to be confused with evaporated milk, which undergoes a more complex process and which is not sweetened. See also MILK.

condensed soup - a commercially produced, canned soup base made by removing much of the water from a soup, reducing its volume by about 50 percent. Condensed soups are reconstituted with an equal amount of water or milk. The

Campbell Soup Co. pioneered this technology in 1897 and has remained one of the largest producers of this type of soup in the world. By condensing their soups, the company was able to save on transportation and packaging costs and provide them at a much lower cost to the American public, which embraced them wholeheartedly — and still does today.

condiment - an aromatic, acidic, sweet, salty or spicy flavoring agent used to enhance the taste of food. Ketchup, mustard and mayonnaise are some of the most popular North American condiments.

coney - a favorite dish of residents of Cincinnati, Ohio, consisting of a hot dog topped with mustard, onions, chili and shredded Cheddar cheese. The hot dog used for a coney is usually a bit smaller and shorter than a regular one to accommodate the bulky toppings in the bun. See also CINCINNATI CHILI.

confection - a general term for any candy or other sweet preparation.

confectioner's custard - see PASTRY CREAM.

confectioner's sugar - also **icing sugar, powdered sugar.** Used to make meringues, cakes, cake frosting and other confections, this is an even finer version of granulated sugar, with the addition of tricalcium phosphate, the chemical name for cornstarch, to prevent dampening, which causes the sugar to go lumpy or to solidify.

confectionery coating - also **candy coating, compound chocolate, summer coating.** A mixture of vegetable shortening, sugar, coloring and flavoring (vanilla or chocolate) that is pressed into disks or tablets, melted and used as a coating for candies. Confectionery-coating disks usually come in white and chocolate varieties, but some colored versions are available. If not, the white disks can be tinted and flavored with flavoring oils or extracts if desired. The chocolate versions contain cocoa powder to give them their flavor and color, but they do not contain cocoa butter, so they are not real chocolate and therefore cannot be used in its place in recipes.

confetti - not colored pieces of paper, but sugarcoated almonds tossed at festivals and weddings for good luck, originated in the Abruzzo region of Italy. See also DRAGÉE, JORDAN ALMONDS.

confit - a French culinary term used to describe meat and poultry (especially duck) cooked and preserved in its own fat, or fruits or vegetables cooked and preserved in brandy or liquor syrup.

confit d'oie - a type of **confit** made by cooking pieces of goose meat slowly in clarified goose fat and lard, then transferring them to a **cassoulet** dish, where they are covered with the fat which they were cooked in. The fat protects the meat and preserves it. The name is French for "prepared goose."

confiture - a French term often seen in North America, meaning "preserves," usually used to refer to a jelly, jam, preserve or marmalade made from fruit. Although the term is normally used for fruit preserves, it is sometimes applied to those made from savory ingredients, such as onions.

congeal - changing a liquid into a solid by lowering the temperature, such as in the case of olive oil, or sauces high in natural gelatin, such as concentrated meat stocks.

congee - a thin watery **gruel,** an Asian (especially Chinese) rice porridge, usually served for breakfast.

congeners - the impurities in spirits produced during fermentation, giving the spirit its color, aroma and flavor. Also present, although in much lower concentrations, in wine.

conger eel - the common name for a number of different saltwater scaleless fish related to the common **eel,** including Atlantic and Mediterranean conger eels (such as *Conger oceanicus* and *Conger conger*) and the Pacific conger eel (*Conger myriaster*). The Atlantic

conger eel

and Mediterranean species can grow to enormous proportions (up to 200 pounds/90 kg), while the Pacific species is rarely larger than a few pounds. The rich, white flesh is excellent in soups or smoked. Conger eel is often seen on sushi menus in Japanese restaurants in North America under the name **anago.**

Congo pepper - the Trinidadian name for the fiery hot **habanero** chile pepper, the name also often used as a synonym for the **Scotch bonnet** pepper. Congo peppers are a vital component in spicy Trinidadian cuisine.

conserve - jam-like product made of a mixture of fruits, which may also contain nuts, raisins or coconut.

consommé - from the French, meaning "consumed or boiled down," a clear soup made of rich meat (beef, chicken, duck, caribou or veal) or vegetable stock, or both, and clarified with what's called a **raft.** As the liquid heats, a mixture of added egg whites, ground vegetables and meats, and aromatics begins to rise, collecting the particles that make the stock cloudy, lifting them to the top, forming the raft, which is tipped to reveal the clear soup below. A distinction must be made between consommé and bouillon: the meat for a consommé is browned before simmering.

continental breakfast - consisting of some kind of bread (toast, rolls, croissants, etc.) and a beverage, such as coffee, tea or juice. See also ENGLISH BREAKFAST.

continental lentil - see LENTIL.

convection oven - powered by gas or electricity, with an interior fan to circulate heat evenly.

converted rice - see RICE.

cook - from the Latin *coquus*, meaning "a cook" and *coquere*, "to cook."

cookie - from the Dutch *koekje*, meaning "little cake," a small flat confection, usually classified by its distinctive ingredient or by the way in which it is prepared. It is believed that the first batches of cookies were made in Persia in the 17th century, probably because Persia was one of the first countries to cultivate sugar. See also PRESSED COOKIE, SPRINGERLE.

cookie cutters

cookie cutter - a tool made in an endless number of different designs for cutting rolled cookie dough into fanciful shapes. A shaped cookie cutter is often made from molded plastic or, more traditionally, a continuous strip of stainless steel or other metal, such as copper, which is bent into the desired shape and riveted together. The cutter is pressed down onto the dough to cut out the desired shape. Rolling cookie cutters are made from plastic or metal and have a continuous raised design or a variety of shaped cutters attached to a rolling barrel. The cutter is rolled over the dough to make a number of cutouts in one pass with very little wasted dough between shapes.

cookie mold - a form made of wood or ceramic into which cookie dough is pressed to shape it and/or impress a design onto it. Such cookies as **Springerle, ma'amoul, shortbread** and **speculaas** are made using cookie molds, often with intricately carved designs.

cookie press - also **cookie gun.** A kitchen tool used to make **spritz** cookies, consisting of a large cylinder-shaped barrel with a trigger at one end and an opening at the opposite end, over which any of a number of different decorative perforated plates can be affixed. The soft, buttery spritz dough is spooned into the barrel, then pumped through the perforated plate onto a cookie sheet to make any of an enormous variety of shapes.

cookie sheet - see BAKING SHEET.

cooking spray - also **nonstick cooking spray, vegetable oil spray.** Oil, such as canola or olive, packed into a pressurized aerosol container and released using a propellant, used to grease

Cooper, Peter (1791–1883) - American chemical engineer and inventor who was granted the first U.S. patent for making **gelatin** desserts in 1845. Gelatin was first mentioned in 1682 in the published findings of French scientist Denis Papin, who experimented with releasing the glutinous material from animal bones by boiling them. Cooper's gelatin was attractively packaged, but didn't sell. The idea of gelatin desserts languished for 50 years, until businessman **Pearle Wait** bought Cooper's patent. Wait flavored the gelatin, and his wife, May, named it Jell-O. The Waits were unsuccessful in selling the new product. Wait's neighbor, Orator F. Woodward, bought the Jello-O name for $450 in 1899 and then sold it the next year to the Genesee Pure Food Company, which put on an advertising campaign that produced $250,000 in Jell-O sales only two years later.

baking sheets, grill grates and pans to prevent foods from sticking to them as they cook. Cooking spray is excellent for people who are watching their fat intake, as a quick spray of this oil usually amounts to much less than the amount typically applied by hand to grease a pan. The only caution is that the spray can be dangerous in certain situations — a cloud of spray can quickly ignite if sprayed near an open flame.

cooking tongs - see TONGS.

cooking wine - also **cooking sherry.** An inexpensive, often lower-grade wine or sherry, mixed with salt, for use in cooking. The salt acts as a preservative, keeping the wine fresh enough to use for up to a year — and it also makes the wine utterly undrinkable. Most chefs recommend that you avoid cooking wine and use a wine that you would normally drink (the flavor is much better), but cooking wine is handy to have on hand in a pinch.

cook's knife - see CHEF'S KNIFE.

cooler - see HIGHBALL GLASS.

cooling rack - a platform made of wire mesh or a pattern of thick, crisscrossed metal wires for cooling baked goods, such as cookies or cakes. Cooling racks are usually raised up on small legs, so that air can circulate around baked goods as they cool, allowing steam and moisture to escape and preventing them from getting soggy.

coon - **1.** a sharp, crumbly, American Cheddar-type cheese made by a patented process that includes scalding. It is also aged at a higher temperature than normal. **2.** an oyster native to Florida waters.

Cooper, Peter - see profile above.

copha - solidified coconut oil, a type of shortening used for baking, especially in Australia, where it is extremely popular. Copha adds a delicate coconut flavor to baked goods and is used frequently to make cookies and sweets. It is hard to substitute any other type of shortening for copha, because of the unique flavor it adds. See also COCONUT OIL, COPRA.

coppa - **1.** also **coppa crudo.** A mild, Italian sausage made from pork loin, flavored with red wine and garlic, pressed into a large casing and dry-cured. It is tender and highly esteemed, often confused with **capicollo,** although less spicy. **2.** also **coppa cotto.** A spiced Italian pork product made from the remnants of a pork carcass, similar to **head cheese.**

copra - the dried kernel of the coconut, from which an oil is extracted. See also COCONUT OIL, COPHA.

coq au vin - a French dish of pieces of chicken cooked in red wine with mushrooms, onions, bacon or salt pork, and herbs. See also COCK.

coquilles St. Jacques - a dish of scallops in a creamy wine sauce served in a scallop shell, topped with bread crumbs and/or cheese and browned. See also SCALLOP.

coquitos - see COCONUT.

coral - the name given to the red, firm substance, or roe (eggs), found inside the shell of lobster and scallop, used in French cooking to impart a brilliant reddish color to butter and sauces. From the Latin *corallium*, a translation of the Greek *korallion*, meaning a "reddish color."

cordial - a sweet, flavorful, distilled drink, usually a liqueur, often taken after a meal, first made during the Middle Ages. At that time, they were spiced, flavored with herbs and considered to be restoratives. By the 14th century, they were widely consumed in Italy and taken to France by **Catherine de Medici,** where their popularity quickly spread.

cordon bleu - **1.** French for "blue ribbon," used to describe the honor given to chefs of the highest excellence, taken from the name of a cooking school founded in 1880 at the Palais Royal in Paris, by cooking teacher Marthe Distel. The Grand Diplôme awarded by the new school to its best pupils is the highest credential a chef can have. **2.** a dish of thin, boneless chicken breasts or veal scallops topped with thin slices of ham and cheese, then breaded and sautéed.

core - **1.** (v.) to cut out the center of a fruit or vegetable in order to remove the seeds or inedible parts. **2.** (n.) the tough or seeded center of a fruit or vegetable that does not contain a single large pit or stone.

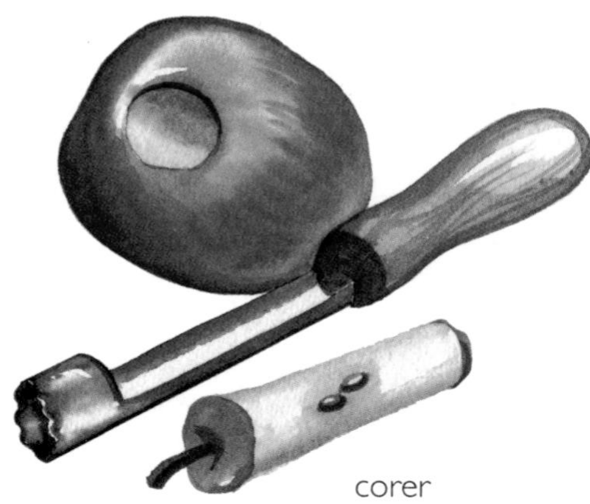

corer

corer - a tool for removing the core of a fruit or vegetable. A fruit corer has a short tube at the end of a handle and is pushed down through the center of the fruit to neatly extract the core. A fruit corer, especially one designed for apples, can also be shaped like a wagon wheel, with flat spokes radiating from a circle in the center to the edge. It cuts an apple into even slices as it cuts out the core. There are also specialty corers specifically made for certain foods, such as zucchini corers (long and thin) and pineapple corers (large and round).

coriander - a plant, *Coriandrum sativum*, from which the spice coriander and the herb **cilantro** are derived. The leaves, stems and root of the plant are usually called cilantro (although they are sometimes, confusingly, referred to as fresh coriander or Chinese parsley); the seeds are dried and ground and always referred to as coriander. The plant is native to southern Europe and the Middle East.

The word "coriander" purportedly refers to a likeness to the odor of bedbugs, but this refers to the leaves, not the seeds. That, in any case, was the conviction of the ancient writers, who pointed out a tie between the spice's Greek name, *koriandron*, and *koris*, the Greek word for "bedbug." If true, this would also make coriander a linguistic relative of the flower coreopsis, whose name literally means "bedbug-like," since the minuscule, horned seeds of this yellow flower look like little bugs with antennae — which is why this flower also goes by the name tickseed.

Coriander was listed in the *Ebers Papyrus*, a treatise that was contemporary with Moses. The leaves, mentioned by almost all writers of antiquity, have one of the longest recorded histories of any herb and were compared to the **manna** eaten by the children of Israel. Coriander seeds have been found among funeral offerings in Egyptian tombs. From the land of the Pharaohs, in all probability, the herb came into use by the ancient Hebrews, who made it one of the bitter herbs involved in the ritual of Passover. Even today, the Chinese believe that coriander seeds can grant immortality; they have been using the plant as far back as the Han dynasty (207 BC–AD 220). The leaves of this plant are now thought of as typical of Arab, Chinese, South American and Indian cookery, but it has been forgotten that they were a favorite herb among the Hebrew, Greek and Roman people. The ancients recommended that the seeds be eaten by expectant mothers to produce ingenious and witty offspring. William Turner warns, "Coriander taken out of season doth trouble a man's witt with great jeopardy of madness," but since he neglects to say what the season is, we have to take our chances. Many others cultures developed coriander concoctions out of their belief that it aroused passion. This rumor may well have commenced with *The Arabian Nights*, the Arabian fantasy in which coriander was referred to as an aphrodisiac. It became popular in 17th-century Paris, where it was the principal ingredient in *eau de carnes*, a

cilantro leaves (coriander)

concoction that could be used either as a liqueur or as a cologne. The leaves are also used in making liqueurs, and the writers of antiquity claimed that they made wine stronger and more exhilarating. Coriander is thought to have many medicinal virtues, as a stimulant, a digestive, a carminative and a bactericide.

corkage - the fee charged by a restaurant when a patron brings in his or her own bottle of wine to consume with dinner. Corkage fees vary widely, from just a few dollars to upwards of $100 per bottle in more expensive restaurants with extensive wine lists. Some restaurants even vary their fees depending on the type of wine (the fee is usually lower if the wine is not offered on the wine list). Corkage is purportedly charged in order to cover the cost of the sommelier opening and serving the wine, and the cost of providing and washing the glasses. In fact, it is designed to discourage diners from decreasing the restaurant's wine sales.

So why pay corkage fees? Sometimes, it may actually save money. A customer may want to bring in a fine wine that he has been saving for years — perhaps he bought it 10 years ago for $25, and the bottle now fetches $100 in the restaurant. If a $25 corkage fee applies, he's still only paying half of what he would if he purchased the wine from the house. Sadly, this is usually the exception rather than the rule, and corkage can end up costing the diner twice the price of a particular bottle purchased in the restaurant. The best bet is to inquire about corkage fees before sitting down to dinner.

corked - a negative wine-tasting term for a wine that has been infected by bacteria embedded in the cork, making it smell like a wet dog or a damp, musty basement. Though unpleasant, this does not make the wine dangerous or harmful to drink. Wines of any vintage or quality can be affected, so it cannot be avoided by selecting a particular variety.

corkscrew - a tool with a sharp-ended metal spiral, used to remove the cork from a bottle of wine. Corkscrews come in a variety of shapes: some with a handle that is perpendicular to the screw, and some with "ears" that rise up as the screw is twisted into the cork and then pulled down to pop it out of the bottle. A popular corkscrew is the brand-name Rabbit corkscrew, which uses a single lever to twist the screw into the cork and then pull it back out, all in one smooth movement.

corkscrews

cormorant - a large seabird, *Phalacrocorax carbo*, thriving in practically all latitudes. If the Hebrews had not been forbidden to eat cormorant (*Deut.* 14:17), nobody would have thought that anyone ever wished to eat the rank, dark flesh of this glutton among fish eaters. Yet, it is on record that the "squabs," or cormorant chicks, are highly valued in Norway, Sweden and Denmark and that, as one islander has said, "Sometimes young cormorants are used, instead of young pigeons, for squab pies, but in this case the birds have to be skinned before being used." Cormorant squabs are said to taste rather like roast hare.

corn - the word used throughout Europe to describe cereal grains. Throughout North America today, however, the word refers to what Europeans call maize, *zea mays*. Corn originated in South America and had enormous significance to the population of the entire continent, which was said to live and die by corn. The people referred to it as their "first mother and father, the source of life," by far their most important food. Corn was also used for other purposes, such as for shelter, fencing, clothing and decoration. The Aztecs had corn-planting ceremonies, which included human sacrifices, and other tribes had similar customs to appease the corn god. Corn is woven into a multitude of myths, each tribe telling a slightly different story, but each with similar themes of planting or harvesting.

For anthropologists and historians, corn is a compelling study. As early as 2700 BC, maize and common beans were cultivated in what later would be Mexico. In 1492, as Columbus disembarked on the island now called Cuba, he was met by Carib Indians offering gifts of hospitality: one was tobacco and the other something called *mais*, which was later described as "well tasted, bak'd, dry'd and made into flour." Unknown to Columbus, at least 700 varieties of maize grew in the Western Hemisphere. He brought maize seeds back to Spain, where it was called **"Indian corn"** and grown in gardens as a curiosity.

In 1515, the Portuguese planted maize in China, where it was adopted more quickly and more widely than in Europe, Africa or other parts of the world. In 1529, vast fields of maize from America were grown in Turkey, from where the grain went to England as "Turkey corn." In 1749, pellagra, a vitamin-deficiency disease caused by a lack of niacin, also known as "corn sickness," was first recorded in Italy, where polenta made of cornmeal was a dietary staple in some areas. The name comes from the Italian words *pelle agra*. Symptoms included diarrhea, dementia and, ultimately, death. Although corn contains niacin, it is bound to other molecules that cannot be digested in the digestive tract of humans. Centuries ago, the Aztecs and Incas, whose diets were high in corn, did not suffer from this disease because they learned to presoak their maize in limestone, lye or wood ashes prior to cooking, which broke the chemical bond, thus freeing the niacin for absorption by the body and protecting against pellagra — something the Anglo-Saxons did not follow. By the end of the next century, Egypt and other African countries where peasants lived mainly on cornmeal had suffered pellagra epidemics.

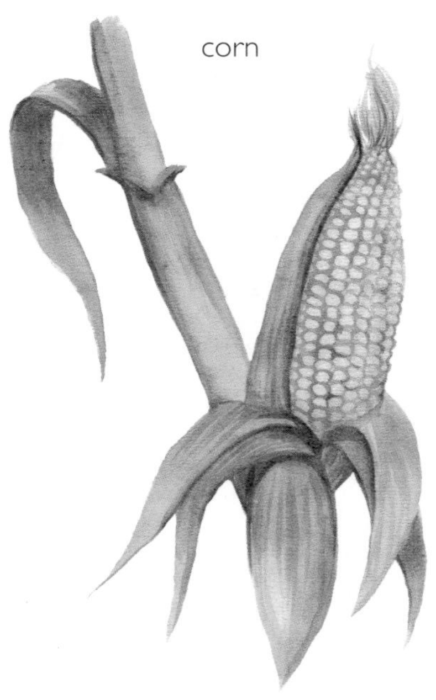
corn

Corn was believed by Europeans to have unearthly powers (it rises to heaven as it grows) ever since Columbus brought the first samples back to Spain from the Caribbean in 1496. Early Spanish churchmen, for example, assumed that the intake of raw kernels would cure souls troubled by the devil. Martyrs suspected of shameful associations were often force-fed a mixture of corn and water, and made to sit naked in the hot sun until the mixture, which expanded inside them in the heat, either flushed out their sins or ripped them open.

Until hybrids were developed in the 1920s, the corn grown in the U.S. Corn Belt was what was known as **"dent corn,"** with orange, yellow, red or white kernels, each with a dent or dimple on top, its ears and kernels larger than any other corn. The corn the Indians grew was the same corn grown by the Pilgrims, mostly soft, flour corn, its kernels generally white, the major variety in the South until hybrid corn was introduced. Sweet corn was unknown until 1779, when Richard Bagnal, an officer in General John Sullivan's expedition against the Iroquois, found it grown by Indians along the Susquehanna River in western New York. Bagnal carried seeds of it back East, but it was not until the 1850s that sweet corn began to replace field corn on North American tables. Corn is one of the least nutritionally complete grains. See also FLINT CORN, POPCORN.

cornbread - a **quick bread** that uses cornmeal as a dominant dry ingredient in addition to flour. It can be flavored or plain.

corn chips - a snack food made by dropping bits of cornmeal-based dough into hot oil and frying them until crisp. Corn chips are the same as corn tortilla chips, made from ground corn and fried (although some are now baked to reduce the amount of fat they contain).

corn chowder - a milk- or cream-based soup that contains corn, chunks of potatoes and spices, often flavored with bits of bacon as well, a typical New England soup. See also CHOWDER.

corn dodger - also **corn dab.** A type of cornbread, usually formed into ovals and baked, boiled or fried, principally seen in the southern U.S. Fried corn dodgers are often cooked in bacon fat to give them a deliciously crisp exterior and a smoky flavor.

corn dog - a frankfurter on a stick, dipped in cornmeal batter and fried until crisp on the outside, called **Pogo** in Canada.

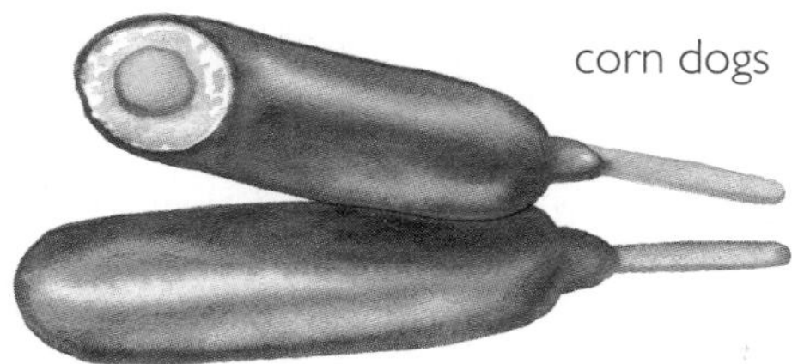
corn dogs

corned beef - cuts of beef, such as the plate, chuck, brisket or round, that are boned, trimmed, seasoned with bay leaves and whole peppercorns, and cured in brine. The name comes from the English use of "corn" to mean a small particle; in this case, salt. It is available uncooked for boiling and serving hot, or sold cooked, along with other cold meats at deli counters. Corned-beef sandwiches made with rye bread or bagels with sweet dill pickles are a staple of Jewish-American deli cuisine. In Britain, corned beef is used wholly for compressed canned pieces of salt beef, which is typically used for sandwiches and salads.

Cornell bread - a high-protein bread developed by researchers at Cornell University in the 1930s, made by substituting part of the unbleached white flour with soy flour, wheat germ and nonfat milk.

cornet - any of various horn-shaped items, such as ice cream cones and paper cones filled with candy or used for decorating, from the French *cornet,* diminutive of "cone."

corn-fed chicken - a chicken fed a diet of exclusively or mostly yellow corn, rather than other grains, making its flesh and skin yellow, instead of the usual pale pink. Some say the flavor of the meat is enhanced by the all-corn diet, while others maintain that the flesh tastes like regular chicken. Some corn-fed chickens are raised on simple, natural, dried corn, while others are fed a mixture of corn and pigments that enhance the natural yellowing effect of the corn on the skin and meat. See also CHICKEN.

cornflakes - toasted breakfastcereal flakes made from a mixture of milled corn, sugar, malt flavoring, vitamins and minerals, invented by brothers **John Harvey and W.K. Kellogg** in 1894, when a cooking experiment went wrong. The Kelloggs were working on new foods that would improve the health of patients in the Battle Creek Sanitarium, a facility that treated health-conscious, vegetarian Seventh Day Adventists. A boiled wheat mixture was left overnight by accident, and the brothers, who were on a very tight budget, decided to roll out the mixture in the hopes of creating long sheets of dough. The mixture broke up into flakes, and the Kelloggs decided to toast the flakes and see if their patients liked them anyway. They did, and the brothers' experiments with developing nutritious grain-based cereals continued. Prototypes of cornflakes were made with whole kernels of corn, but were scrapped in favor of a version made with milled corn and malt flavoring, two of the main ingredients in today's cornflakes. Today, the cereal is used not only as a main morning meal but also crushed as a coating to make crispy, deep-fried or baked foods. Kelloggs refers to its cornflakes as Kellogg's Corn Flakes®.

corn flour - a very finely ground cornmeal used in baked goods and for breading. In Britain, "corn flour" is another name for cornstarch.

corn holder - a small eating utensil designed to hold a hot ear of corn on the cob as it is eaten. Corn holders have one or two thick metal spikes protruding from a decorative handle, the most common ones are made of yellow plastic molded in the shape of an ear of corn. The spikes are driven into the ends of the cob (one for each end), and the diner is free to bite off the buttered kernels without burning his or her fingers.

corn husk - the papery outer layers of an ear of corn, usually sold dried in Latin American markets, used as a wrapper for a variety of foods, such as **tamales.** Corn husks make good packages for steamed food, softening and adding their delicate flavor to the foods cooked inside them. The dried variety must be soaked before use to make the husks pliable enough to bend around the filling.

cornhusker - a soft Cheddar-type cheese made in Nebraska from cow's milk.

cornichon - see GHERKIN.

CorningWare - the brand name for ceramic baking and serving dishes originally made by the Corning Glass Works of upstate New York, now owned by World Kitchen. CorningWare comes in a myriad of sizes, shapes and designs.

Cornish hen - see ROCK CORNISH GAME HEN.

Cornish pasty - also **pasty.** A savory turnover made of short-crust pastry wrapped around a filling of meat and potatoes. They take their name from Cornwall in England, where in the 18th and 19th centuries they were a standard lunch for tin miners and fishermen. The food followed the miners and their wives who moved to North America to work in the copper, gold and iron mines of Michigan's Upper Peninsula, for example, where the half-moon turnovers are still a regional favorite simply called "pasties."

cornmeal - white or yellow corn that has been cleaned and ground to a fine, medium or coarse texture; it contains very little fat and not more than 15 percent moisture.

cornmeal mush - also **corn mush.** A porridge made from cornmeal, salt and water, a southern U.S. version of polenta, often eaten topped with sorghum syrup, molasses, milk, gravy or maple syrup. It can also be cooled, then cut up and fried into cornbread cakes, such as **johnnycakes.**

corn nuts - a popular snack food made by parching or roasting corn kernels until they are browned and quite crunchy, usually sold salted or flavored.

corn oil - one of the numerous polyunsaturated oils that find great favor with dieters, a good frying oil because of its high **smoke point,** but some find it too heavy for salads. It's been extracted from corn since the 1960s. Quite a lot of corn is needed to make the oil, since corn germ, when fully grown, makes up only 8 percent of the grain's weight, and only half of that is oil. It takes 10 to 14 ears of corn to produce one tablespoon (15 mL) of corn oil.

corn pone - a flatbread specialty of New Mexico, made of cornmeal dough that's fried or baked.

corn salad - see MÂCHE.

corn smut - see HUITLACOCHE.

cornstarch - a finely milled starch obtained from corn by removing the germ and grinding what remains of the kernels. Unlike white flour, cornstarch is not treated with chemicals to alter its color or cooking properties. It's used primarily as a thickening agent, leaving sauces less starchy than sauces thickened with flour. The British call it corn flour.

corn sugar - a crystallized dextrose-glucose obtained by the hydrolyzation of cornstarch with acid.

corn syrup - a thick, sweet syrup obtained from cornstarch and composed of dextrose, maltose and glucose. In the U.S., corn syrup is sold in two forms: light and dark. **Light corn syrup** has had all the color removed to make it crystal clear, and it has virtually no taste unless it has been flavored with vanilla. **Dark corn syrup** is made by adding caramel coloring and a touch of refiner's syrup (a type of molasses) to corn syrup, giving it a much stronger flavor and dark brown color. In Canada, **golden corn syrup** is also available and preferred by many for its sweet, rich-but-not-assertive flavor and golden color.

Corson, Juliet - see profile right.

Cortland apple - see APPLE.

corzetti - see PASTA.

cos lettuce - see LETTUCE.

Cosmopolitan - a cocktail made with vodka, orange-flavored liqueur (such as Cointreau or Triple Sec), cranberry juice and lime juice, shaken with ice and poured into a chilled **Martini glass.**

Corson, Juliet (1841–1897) - American cooking teacher and author. A self-taught librarian, Corson was working at a New York City women's training school when she began offering cooking classes, bringing in a trained chef to demonstrate while she lectured. Two years later, she established the New York Cooking School, which put her in great demand as a touring lecturer. She wrote *Fifteen-Cent Dinners for Families of Six* (1877), *Twenty-Five Cent Dinners for Families of Six* (1878), *Juliet Corson's New Family Cook Book* (1885), *Miss Corson's Practical American Cookery* (1886) and *Family Living on $500 a Year* (1887).

Costa Rican coffee bean - see COFFEE.

costmary - also **alecost, bible leaf, mint geranium.** *Chrysanthemum balsamita*, or the ancient botanical name of *Tanacetum balsamita*. "Cost" comes from *costum* or *costis*, meaning "Oriental herb" or "spicy herb," while "Mary" comes from the plant's association with the Virgin Mary. Very few herbs have had as many names as costmary; it is still called, in some parts of the world, "Our Lady's herb," as well as "mace," "Mary's mace," "Mary-mint," "sage o' Bedlam" (for Bethlehem), "sweet sage" and "goose tongue" (for the shape of its leaves). Early Americans called it "Bible leaves," because of the custom of using it as a bookmark in the family Bible. The herb has strong, aromatic foliage, planted as a potherb as well as a salad green, and enjoyed considerable popularity up to the late 19th century. It was introduced in England in the 16th century and was used extensively not only to flavor dishes, but also to perfume linens and strew on floors.

costmary

cotechino - a large, Italian pork sausage made with white wine and spices, often served with beans. In Italy, it is made fresh, but a partly cured, precooked variety is commercially distributed and exported. The fresh sausage needs several hours to cook; the commercial sausage, about 30 minutes only.

Côtes-du-Rhône - red, rosé and white wines produced in the Rhône River Valley of southeastern France, near the Alps, most of them from the southern part of the valley. Côtes-du-Rhône wines are often blends of a number of different varieties. To make reds, producers mainly use **Grenache** Noir, **Syrah,** Mourvèdre, Cinsaut and Carignan. To make whites, the most widely used are Grenache Blanc, Clairette, Bourbolenc, Roussanne and Voignier. The wines produced in this region are generally well priced, although quality can vary.

Cotherstone - An English blue-veined cow's milk cheese made in Yorkshire, Cotherstone has an ivory interior and crumbly texture.

cotija - see QUESO ANEJADO.

cottage bacon - a type of bacon made from the shoulder of the pig, rather than the side or belly, less fatty than regular bacon, cut into lightly fat-streaked slices similar to **back bacon.** The slices make excellent fillings for sandwiches, such as BLTs, because they are wider than regular bacon strips. See also BACON.

cottage cheese - an unripened cheese made from skim milk, fresh or dried, plus salt and a lactic bacterium that brings about the curdling. The old name was "cottager's cheese" because it was almost always made at home. Some manufacturers use acid, however (such as phosphoric or hydrochloric acid) to bring about the separation of the milk, a method unsuited to the consumer who prefers a natural method. Those brands that employ acid say "directly set" or "curd set by acidification" on the label. Every milk-producing country in the world has its own version of cottage cheese, known by various names: in France, it's *fromage blanc;* in Germany, *Quarkkäse*, in Italy, *ricotta;* in England, *pot cheese*, and in Scotland, *Aberdeen Crowdie*.

cottage fries - see HOME FRIES.

cottage roll - also **cottage ham.** An oval, usually boneless, cut of pork from the shoulder butt, brined and often smoked. The brine for this type of ham is usually a little on the sweet side, but it complements the saltiness of the meat. Cottage rolls are usually slow-cooked in moist heat to make them tender and to melt away some of their fat. They usually come packaged in netting or are vacuum-packed, available in the meat aisle of the grocery store.

Cottenham - an English, semisoft **double-crème cheese,** blue-veined, like Stilton but with a creamier texture and richer flavor.

cotton candy - also **candy floss.** A confection made by wrapping long, flavored, colored strands of spun sugar around a paper cone.

cotton candy

cottonseed flour - mainly used to enrich breads, with a much higher protein content than wheat.

cottonseed oil - obtained by crushing cottonseeds, which yield 20 percent of their weight, an excellent edible oil, usually hydrogenated to make shortening and margarine.

couche couche - a New Orleans specialty, a typical Cajun fried corn dough, usually served with preserves or cane syrup.

coulibiac - a classic Russian fish pie with layers of mushrooms, **duxelles,** and herbs or greens, usually made with pike, turbot, perch or, as in France, salmon.

coulis - **1.** a thick sauce or purée of fruits or vegetables. An 18th-century recipe calls for bacon, veal, ham, carrots, onions, celery, butter, flour and parsley cooked until almost dry; water is added, and it is cooked again until yellowish, then strained. **2.** a thick shellfish soup.

Coulommiers - a soft, French cheese made from unpasteurized cow's milk, related to **Brie** but formed into smaller wheels, hence its other names, *Petit Brie* and *Brie de Coulommiers*. It has a bloomy white rind and a creamy interior, which starts out mild and becomes more flavorful as the cheese ages. The name comes from the town where it originated, in the Ile-de-France region.

country captain - a Southern curried chicken stew made with tomatoes, onions, green peppers, celery, currants and a variety of spices, including curry powder. The dish is served over rice, topped with a sprinkle of toasted almonds. There is considerable debate over the origin of the stew's name. Some say it's named for a captain in the British army, who brought the recipe back with him after an extended tour of duty in India. Others claim it was the legacy of a sea captain working the spice routes to India. Still others say that "country captain" is a nickname for a **capon,** which is particularly delicious as the base ingredient in the curry.

country gravy - made from pan drippings and milk and thickened with flour, often served with chicken-fried steak.

country ham - also **country-cured ham.** A **dry-cured** bone-in ham that is smoked, then aged for up to a year until it is flavorful and firm, quite salty and smoky. **Virginia ham** and **Kentucky ham** are two well-known examples of country hams. A true country ham is one produced using these methods in a rural area in the southern United States, but many "country-style" hams are made in more populated areas outside the south with good results. See also CITY HAM, HAM, WET CURE.

country-style ribs - see PORK.

coupe - the French term for a simple dessert of ice cream, sorbet or sherbet topped with any of a variety of garnishes, usually fruit and a touch of whipped cream, although rich sauces and even candied chestnuts make appearances atop some coupes. *Coupe normande*, for example, is a coupe from the Normandy region of France, consisting of a scoop of apple sorbet drizzled with **Calvados.** The name can also refer to a dish of vanilla ice cream topped with apples and Calvados. *Normande* is a shortened form of **à la normande,** or "in the style of Normandy," so named for the apples and Calvados, which are typical products of that region. The term also applies to the short, footed, wide-mouth bowl in which the dessert is served.

courgette - see ZUCCHINI.

courgette flowers - see ZUCCHINI BLOSSOMS.

court-bouillon - a stock acidulated with lemon juice or vinegar, used for poaching fish and seafood. Sometimes, meat and vegetables are also poached in a court-bouillon.

couscous - **1.** a North African grain, granular semolina. **2.** a dish made in Algeria and Morocco with semolina or barley, and in Tunisia with green wheat. The name is derived from the Arabic *kouskous*. There's some doubt about the meaning of the word. Some experts believe "couscous" meant food in a bird's beak used to feed its young. Another possible origin is from the Gallic form of *rac keskes* (meaning, "to pound until small") or phonetically from the words *koskos*, *keuscass*, *koskosou* and *kouskous*, used in different parts of North Africa to describe a cooking pot in which semolina is prepared.

couscoussière - a special pot used for making African couscous dishes, consisting of two parts: a large, often bulbous cooking pot on the bottom and a smaller straight-sided pot with a perforated bottom that fits securely on top. The large bottom pot is used for making a flavorful stew. When the stew is nearing completion, the smaller pot containing the tiny pellets of dried couscous is placed on top of the stew pot, so that the steam from the stew can cook them through. The resulting fluffy couscous is then served topped with, or alongside, the stew.

couscoussière

couverture - see CHOCOLATE.

cowberry - see LINGONBERRY.

cowboy caviar - see PRAIRIE OYSTER.

cowpea - see BLACK-EYED PEA.

Cox's Orange Pippin apple - see APPLE.

crab - any of various crustaceans with 10 legs, the front two of which have pincers. (For Crab Varieties, see page 198.) See also LUMP CRABMEAT.

crab apple - a small, sour, bright red apple of the species *Malus*, which probably came originally from Siberia, northern China and Manchuria, but has been cultivated for its fruit and flowers in China and Japan for centuries. Variations of the flowers in particular (but also the plant, fruit, color and size) have been cultivated, in almost all cases, to double and become more dramatic. The Siberian crab apple is the hardiest of the fruit trees; it grows with great rapidity, thrives in many soils and bears fruit year after year with increasing abundance. The fruit is most often used for making jams, jellies and preserves. See also APPLE.

crab boil - also **shrimp boil, shrimp spice.** A ready-made seasoning mix of whole spices, such as mustard seeds, peppercorns, coriander seeds, hot red peppers, bay leaves, dill seeds, allspice and cloves (or another mixture of similar savory spices), used to season boiled or steamed crab, shrimp, lobster or crayfish. The bag of spices is added to the boiling water and allowed to permeate the seafood as it cooks.

crab cake - a mixture of crabmeat with bread crumbs, milk, egg and seasonings, shaped into small cakes and fried.

crab imperial - a mixture of crabmeat and mayonnaise (or cream sauce flavored with sherry) that is packed into an empty blue-crab or scallop shell, topped with Parmesan cheese and/or bread crumbs and baked until hot and golden. The rich filling is then spooned out of the shell as an entrée. Crab imperial is a common sight in Maryland, where crabs are abundant.

crab Louis - a cold dish of crabmeat garnished with a dressing of mayonnaise, chili sauce, scallions, green pepper and lemon juice, served on a bed of lettuce. The dish originated in San Francisco and Portland in the early 1900s and has been tremendously popular everywhere since.

CRAB VARIETIES

blue crab - a medium-size crab, *Callinectes sapidus,* with a gray body and brilliant blue claws and legs, found in the Gulf of Mexico and off the Atlantic coast of North America, mainly in the Chesapeake Bay region. The blue crab is prized for its tender, sweet, snow-white meat, which comes mainly from the body, not the legs or claws. The genus and species names are poetic and appropriately descriptive: Callinectes means "beautiful swimmer," and sapidus means "delicious."

blue crab

Dungeness crab - is a famous West Coast delicacy harvested in the Pacific Ocean from Mexico to Alaska, *Cancer magister,* with a large, wide body and long claws and legs. Their tender flesh, which can be culled from the body, legs and claws, is excellent on its own or in any dish that calls for crab.

Jonah crab - a large crab, *Cancer borealis,* found off the eastern coast of Canada and the U.S., from Nova Scotia to South Carolina. Jonah crabs can grow up to 7 inches (17.5 cm) across, excluding their legs, and have large claws, which are prized for their fine white meat. Jonah crabs are usually caught by lobstermen and sold whole for their claw meat, which can quickly deplete stocks. But some fishermen are now making the most of the crab's talent for replacing missing appendages. The fishermen catch the crabs, break off one of the claws and throw back the crabs. The crabs soon regrow the claws, and the population is not depleted.

oyster crab - also **pea crab.** A pale pink soft-bodied crab, *Pinnotheres ostreum,* about the diameter of a penny, which lives inside bivalves, such as clams, cockles, mussels, oysters and scallops, in both the Atlantic and the Pacific, siphoning off some of their incoming food. Considered a delicacy and relatively scarce, they are sought-after by foodies.

soft-shell crab - caught when it has just molted its first hard shell and before the next shell has hardened, from late spring through August; especially the **blue crab,** common along the Atlantic and Gulf coasts. The cleaned crab, with its lungs and tail removed, is usually floured, sautéed and eaten whole.

stone crab - also **Florida stone crab.** A palm-size, reddish brown crab that lives in the warm waters of the Caribbean and the Florida Gulf up the Atlantic coast to the Carolinas and feeds mainly on oysters, other small mollusks and sea grass. Only the claw meat of *Menippe mercenaria* is used, so just the larger so-called "crusher claw" is removed at a joint, then the crab is returned to its habitat; within a year or two, a new, even larger claw will have grown in its place. Stone crabs are hand-picked and caught in traps and pots. To protect the stocks, American jurisdictions have a minimum claw-size required for harvest. Since the raw meat adheres to the shell when chilled, iced or frozen, the claws are cooked before sale, immediately after harvest.

Jonah crab

cracked olive - see OLIVE.

cracked wheat - whole wheat grains that are crushed into coarse fragments.

cracker - a brittle, dry, unsweetened, usually salted flatbread, which first appeared in North America in the 18th century, named for the sound it makes when broken, often eaten with cheese.

cranberries

crackling - the crisp rind of pork after it has been roasted.

craft beer - also **craft-brewed beer.** A term used to describe beers brewed exclusively from malt made from barley, wheat or rye, unlike beers made by many major large-scale North American breweries, which use cheaper rice, corn and sugar adjuncts to round out their recipes. Craft-brewed beers are made at **microbreweries** and **brewpubs** (but can also be made by microbreweries that have outgrown the definition and produce more than 15,000 barrels per year). These producers favor high-quality ingredients and old-fashioned, less industrial methods for making beer. Craft brews can be ales, pilsners, porters, stouts or any other type of beer, and are distinguished from mass-market beers by their rich, interesting flavors, beautiful colors and wonderful aromas.

cranberry - a shiny, tart, red berry, grown in bogs on trailing vines, *Vaccinium macrocarpon*, in the Ericaceae family. The cranberry is a very important part of traditional North American Thanksgiving and Christmas feasts. When the Pilgrims first tasted cranberries, they found them very sour; had it not been for the assurances of the friendly Indians, the Pilgrims might never have used them. Thankfully, they did; the berry protected the first New Englanders from scurvy.

The fruit was initially referred to as "crane berry," because the plant's slender stem and downward-hanging blossoms resemble the neck, head and bill of a Sandhill crane. Others say the Pilgrims named them "crane berry" because they noticed the cranes wading in the bogs where the cranberries grew. The Indians, who called the berries *I bimi*, mashed them into a paste mixed with dry meat to make **pemmican.** They also used the juice of the berries for a poultice to prevent blood poisoning from arrow wounds. The berries also provided a beautiful red dye.

The cranberry is one of only a handful of fruits native to North America, the Concord grape and blueberry being the others. Cranberries are rich in vitamin C and contain **anthocyanin,** a flavonoid with anti-inflammatory properties.

cranberry bean - also **romano bean.** Named for its red streaks and specks, the cranberry bean has a pleasant, nutty flavor but loses its coloring once cooked.

crapaudine - from *crapaud*, French for "toad", referring to a technique and sauce used for a small bird, such as a spring chicken, squab, quail, partridge, etc. The bird is split down the back, trussed like a frog, broiled and served with crapaudine sauce, made with vinegar, capers and herbs in a red wine reduction.

crayfish - also **crawdad, crawfish, mudbug.** Freshwater crustaceans that resemble small lobsters, from the Old French *crevis* and *crevice*, which survives in today's French word for crayfish, *écrevisse*. The word "crawfish" appeared in the U.S. in the 19th century and is still used, mainly in Louisiana. They are also referred to as "crawdads" in certain regions of the U.S. Since they are found on the muddy bottoms of bayous, lakes, streams and swamps, crayfish, with their insect-like antennae, exoskeletons and eyestalks, are also called "mudbugs."

crayfish

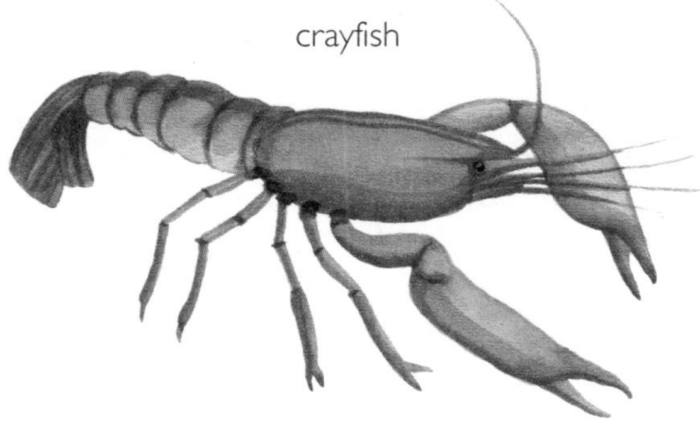

cream - **1.** (n.) a component of milk in which the fat globules have become more concentrated than usual. For general purposes, cream is classified as coffee or whipping cream, depending on fat content. **Coffee cream** or **table cream** usually contains 18 percent fat and is sometimes known as **light cream** in the U.S. In Canada, light cream refers to a cream with just 5 percent fat. **Whipping cream** contains approximately 35 percent fat. In the U.S., there is also a light whipping cream that contains 30 to 36 percent fat. **Half-and-half** is a mixture of equal parts milk and cream and is 10 to 12 percent fat. See also DOUBLE CREAM, HEAVY CREAM. **2.** (v.) to mix and beat one or more foods (such as butter, or butter and sugar) for a cake or cookies by hand or with a spoon, fork or other mechanical tool until soft and fluffy.

cream cheese - a fresh, unripened cheese that is soft and spreadable, made from cow's milk and cream. Cream cheese originated in the U.S. in 1872 when a dairyman in Chester, New York, developed a rich cheese made from cream and whole milk. Then in 1880, a New York cheese distributor, A.L. Reynolds, began distributing cream cheese wrapped in tin foil wrappers, calling it Philadelphia Brand. Neufchâtel cheese is similar to cream cheese, with a slightly lower fat content. There is also a French **Neufchâtel.** Cream cheese is often combined with other ingredients, such as herbs, pepper or garlic, giving it extra flavors that range from mild to spicy. Cream cheese has the highest water content of all cheese varieties, more than 80 percent. See also AETTEKEES, BATH CHEESE, BOURSAULT, BOURSIN, CABOC, COTTENHAM, EXPLORATEUR, MASCARPONE, PETIT-SUISSE.

creamed chipped beef - a homey, old-fashioned dish of dried salted beef (called **chipped beef** or **dried beef**), cooked in a creamy roux-thickened sauce, usually served on toast. Chipped beef was a staple food in the early part of the 20th century, especially in wartime, when meat was rationed. The thinly sliced meat is still sold in cans, jars and pouches in grocery stores and is a staple in some remote locations, where fresh groceries are hard to come by. Creamed chipped beef on toast was a dish commonly served to soldiers and sailors, often for breakfast, which they often referred to by the humorous nickname "shit on a shingle." Some purists insist that "shit on a shingle" was actually made with ground beef and more closely resembled what we call "sloppy joes" today, but the term is used interchangeably for both concoctions.

creamed honey - see HONEY.

creamer - also **nondairy creamer.** A powdered or liquid milk substitute used to lighten coffee. Creamers contain mostly sugars and vegetable oils combined with chemicals, which reduce coffee acidity and keep the fats in the creamer from separating. They also contain natural or artificial colorings and artificial flavorings. They do not contain lactose, although some products do contain milk derivatives, such as sodium caseinate, so they can be a good choice for people who suffer from lactose intolerance.

creamer potato - see NEW POTATO.

cream nut - see BRAZIL NUT.

cream of coconut - a thick, homogenized mixture of coconut, sugar, water and stabilizers, used as the base of piña coladas and other cocktails. It is not the same as coconut cream because it has added sugar, which makes it much sweeter.

cream of tartar - potassium bitartrate, a powdery white substance commonly used to stabilize beaten egg whites; also a by-product of winemaking. Cream of tartar was once a common leavening agent for breads made without yeast.

cream puff - a small, hollow pastry (**choux pastry**) filled with whipped cream or sometimes custard.

cream sauce - a **béchamel** made with milk or cream and used as a base for various dishes, or whipping (35 percent) cream added to a flavored wine reduction and then reduced again and strained.

cream puff

cream sherry - see SHERRY.

cream soda - a carbonated beverage flavored with vanilla and sometimes honey, naturally clear; it may contain added food coloring, which makes it pale golden or even pink.

cream soup - 1. a soup made by adding cream, usually toward the end of cooking to prevent it from curdling, sometimes applied to soups made with lighter dairy products, such as whole milk or condensed milk. **2.** a soup made with silky, puréed vegetables and thickeners, with or without the addition of cream, using a base of chicken, fish or vegetable stock.

cream tea - see AFTERNOON TEA.

Crécy, à la - a French term referring to dishes cooked or garnished with carrots. Two towns in France, Crécy-en Brie in Picardie and Crécy en Ponthieu, take credit for a creamy carrot soup called Potage Crécy. Both towns claim to grow the finest carrots in France.

crema - Italian for "cream," it's the beautiful, silky froth that forms on the top of a perfectly brewed espresso. **Baristas** claim they can tell whether a cup of espresso has been perfectly brewed by the color of the crema. Crema that is more white than brown shows that the water has not been in contact with the coffee long enough, and crema that is too dark in the center means that the water has been in contact with the coffee for too long. A perfect cup will be an even brownish cream color.

crema agria - also **crema mexicana agria.** A thick, rich sour cream popular in Mexican cooking, stiff and quite tangy. Crema agria is usually used as a topping for tostadas, tacos, enchiladas and other savory dishes. The name means simply "sour cream" in Spanish. See also CREMA MEXICANA.

crema catalana - a Spanish version of the French **crème brûlée,** flavored with lemon zest and cinnamon, typical of the northeast region of Cataluña, of which Barcelona is the capital. The name means "Catalan custard."

crema cotta - see PANNA COTTA.

Crema Dania - also **Crema Danica.** A Danish **double-crème cheese** made from cow's milk, with a white rind and a rich, buttery interior. It is often served as a dessert cheese.

crema mexicana - a mild, almost sweet, thick cream, similar to **crème fraîche** or **Devon cream,** used as a topping for Mexican dishes, usually desserts, and as a thickener in sauces. The name is Spanish for "Mexican cream." See also CREMA AGRIA.

crème anglaise - a custard sauce made with milk, egg yolks and sugar, cooked gently until the mixture thickens to form a light cream, so named because there is no word in French to match the English term "custard."

crème brûlée - a rich, baked custard that's given a hard crust of melted sugar by caramelizing it under a broiler, although today, often by using a blowtorch. The dessert is so popular that gourmet shops now sell kitchen-size torches specifically for crème brûlée. French for "burnt cream," this dessert is not even French, but rather a very old English specialty. In the 18th century, the name was made French most likely by the great French food lover Thomas Jefferson. René Verdon, the last French chef in the White House, served it to the Kennedy family as originally made, with real vanilla beans. According to a 2002 poll by *Bon Appétit* magazine, the crunchy sugar–topped custard is America's favorite dessert, followed by cheesecake, cobbler and ice cream.

crème caramel - custard baked in a caramel-lined dish; when inverted after the custard has cooled, the custard reveals a gold trim left by the caramel, as well as giving the dessert its own caramel glaze.

crème chantilly - see CHANTILLY CREAM.

crème de - a prefix meaning "cream of," for a complete array of liqueurs that have nothing to do with cream liqueurs, virtually always consisting of the one prevailing flavor indicated in the name, such as **crème de cassis;** often, but not always, a fruit and usually colored. Originally, the term *crème* was used to indicate that they were sweetened, as distinct from dry spirits, such as cognac or **Calvados**.

crème de cacao - a liqueur flavored with chocolate and vanilla beans, available in dark and white versions, which taste exactly the same.

crème de cassis - a liqueur made from black currants, vital for making the drink **kir.**

crème de marrons - see CHESTNUT CREAM.

crème de menthe - a liqueur flavored with peppermint leaves, may be clear or tinted with green, yellow or red food coloring.

crème de violette - also **liqueur de violette.** A liqueur traditionally made by steeping violet petals in either brandy or grain alcohol, though some versions are made with violet extracts or artificial flavoring. It can be quite difficult to find in North America and is increasingly so in France as well, where much of the world's supply is made. Some specialty liquor stores or Internet sites may be able to order it from overseas.

crème fraîche - a cultured cream product similar to sour cream, but thinner and richer.

crème pâtissière - see PASTRY CREAM.

cremino - pl. **cremini.** A mushroom that is closely related to the common white mushroom, with a light brown color, firmer texture and fuller flavor. Cremini, also known as **crimini** and **Roman mushroom,** mature to become **portobello mushrooms.**

Crenshaw melon - a hybrid of Persian and Casaba melons, brought to market in the 1940s.

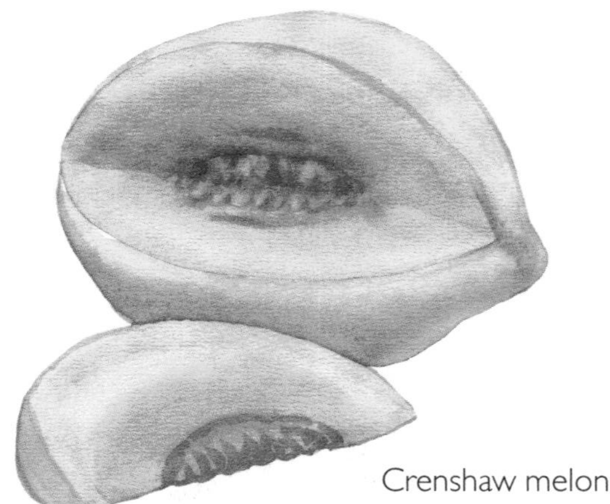

Crenshaw melon

Creole - a person born in the Americas of French and/or Spanish ancestry. The word is a French derivation of the Spanish *criollo*, meaning a Spaniard born in the Americas. As a culinary term, Creole most frequently is used in connection with the cuisine of New Orleans.

Creole bread pudding - see NEW ORLEANS BREAD PUDDING.

Creole cherry pepper - see CHERRY PEPPER.

Creole coffee - also **New Orleans coffee.** A brew made from a mixture of ground coffee and ground roasted **chicory** root. Creole coffee is a specialty in Louisiana and is especially well loved in New Orleans.

Creole seasoning - see CAJUN SEASONING.

crêpe - a very thin, unleavened pancake made with a thin egg batter cooked on a very hot pan, usually filled with sweet or savory fillings.

crêpe pan - a heavy, shallow metal skillet, usually with a long handle, used for making crêpes. The best crêpe pans are made from metal that conducts heat well and evenly, such as heavy-duty steel or aluminum, so that the crêpes cook quickly without burning or sticking.

crêpes Suzette - a very thin pancake dessert often made with Grand Marnier, orange and lemon rinds, orange juice and butter, and usually flambéed tableside.

An invention that some say can be credited to chef Jean Redoux, who, in 1667, named the dish possibly for Suzette, Princesse De Carignan, who lived in the Château de Juvisy near Fontainebleau. Another account claims that, in 1895, the dessert was invented in Monte Carlo's Café de Paris by assistant waiter Henri Charpentier, who was not quite 16. Charpentier apprenticed under the great French chef **Auguste Escoffier** and claimed to have prepared the dish of thin pancakes with liquor and sauce at a luncheon given by the visiting Prince of Wales, whose party included a girl named Suzette, the young daughter of one of the prince's guests. Charpentier insisted until his death in 1962 that he was the originator and that the flaming sauce caught fire by accident. But it was later proven that Charpentier falsely claimed to have invented the dessert, because he had not been old enough at the time to be a waiter serving the prince. However, back in United States as Rockefeller's chef, Charpentier did introduce the fashion for flaming the dessert.

Still another story claims that the original crêpes Suzette were pioneered by M. Joseph in 1897, while running the Marivaux restaurant in Paris. There was a play at the Comédie Française in which the actress Suzanne Reichenberg played a maid, who was required to eat pancakes; these were supplied by the restaurant Marivaux. Joseph's creation included dipping his pancakes into a sizzling mixture of butter, sugar and orange juice. Joseph came to London and introduced his version of the dessert to London society at the Savoy. Soon after Joseph's invention at the Marivaux, in 1898, the Parisian restaurant Marie became well known for its pancakes called Suzette.

crépinette - a small, flat sausage made of ground pork (or sometimes veal, lamb or chicken), wrapped in pig's **caul** instead of a regular casing. Crépinettes are usually well spiced and often contain specks of **truffle.** Their name comes from the French word *crépine*, meaning "caul."

crescenza - also **crescenza stracchino.** An Italian cheese of the **stracchino** family, made from whole cow's milk, mild but tart, with a creamy, soft interior. Crescenza is an uncooked cheese, so it is perishable and must be kept refrigerated and eaten soon after it is made. Made in the Lombardy region of Italy, this cheese is formed into large cubes with little or no rind.

cress - any of a variety of plants of the genus *Lepidium*, related to the cabbage family and having small, dark leaves, thin stems and a peppery flavor. Watercress is the most popular of the cresses, which also includes garden cress, broadleaf cress (or cressida), garden cress, mustard cress and peppergrass (or curly cress).

creste di galli - see PASTA.

crevette - the French word for shrimp.

crimp - to give a shell-like edge to pastry.

crinkle cutter - a kitchen utensil with a U-shaped handle and a wavy blade for cutting decorative slices of carrots, zucchinis, cucumbers and other firm vegetables and fruit.

Criollo bean - see CHOCOLATE.

crisp - **1.** see CRUMBLE. **2.** (v.) to soak vegetables in ice water to refresh them. so that they are crisp again. **3.** a wine-tasting term used to describe a wine with pleasant, refreshing acidity, possibly a bit on the tart side, but in a positive way.

crispbread - also **knäckerbröd.** An unleavened flatbread usually made of rye flour, baked until dry and crisp, hence its name. Crispbread was created in Scandinavia and is still a popular snack there, although it has been widely adopted in North America in recent years, because most versions are high in fiber and quite low in calories. Crispbread can be eaten plain, although it is much tastier topped with traditional cracker or sandwich toppings.

crisphead lettuce - see LETTUCE.

Crispin apple - see APPLE.

croaker - see DRUM.

Crock-Pot - see SLOW COOKER.

crocodile - any of a variety of aquatic reptiles of the genus *Crocodylus*, native to Africa, the Americas and Asia, eaten in some places for its sweet, delicately flavored flesh, which tastes like chicken with a hint of fish. Crocodile meat is an increasingly popular alternative to other meats, as it is high in protein and low in fat.

Overhunting of crocodiles for their skins has led to hunting bans and stiff penalties in many countries, and the Convention on International Trade in Endangered Species of Wild Fauna and Flora (CITES), a multinational trade agreement, has instituted a worldwide ban on all products harvested from wild crocodiles. Today, the crocodile that makes it onto plates is farmed, much of it raised in Africa, Asia, Australia and New Zealand.

The tail meat is reputed to be the most tender, with the leg meat following a close second. The body meat is edible, but can be tough. Long, slow, moist cooking, such as braising and stewing, is excellent for crocodile meat. Tail steaks can also be pan-fried, grilled or broiled in the same way as beef steaks.

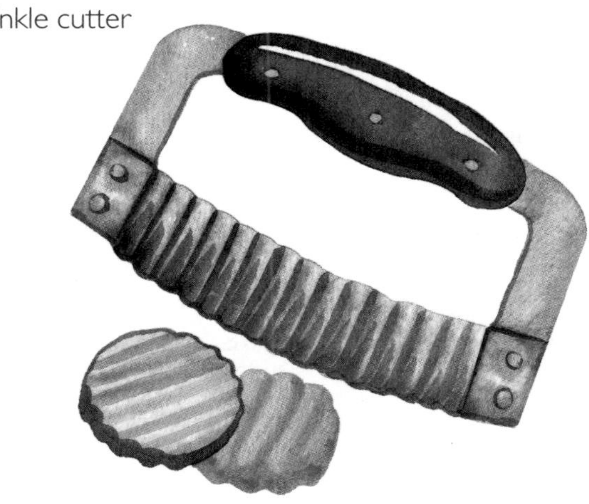
crinkle cutter

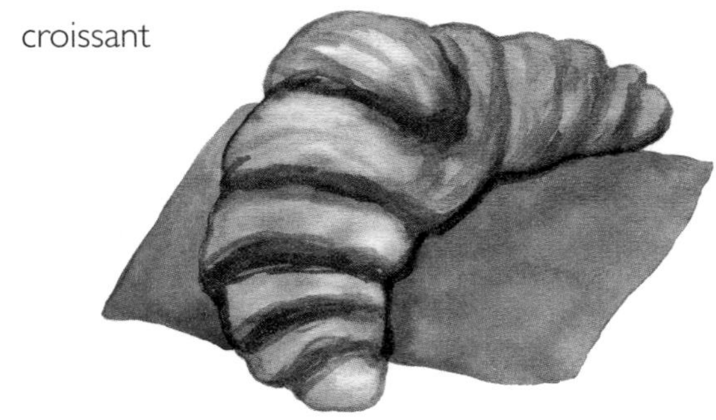
croissant

croissant - French for "crescent," a flaky pastry whose legendary origins are often disputed. The often-told tale has croissants being invented in Budapest in 1686 by bakers who overheard the invading Turks tunneling under the city just before dawn, attempting a surprise attack. The bakers were up and alert and in the middle of their workday. They were able to notify the army in time to foil the assault. The pastry's shape mirrors the crescent moon of the Turkish flag, a reminder of the historic defeat. The French are credited with giving croissants their **mille-feuille** quality by using puff pastry–style dough.

croissant cutter - a gracefully shaped tool for cutting a single rectangle of croissant dough into a series of perfect triangles with no waste. The cutter has two handles, similar in design to a rolling pin, with two circles at the end of each handle, into which are inserted several sharp curved blades that cut perfect side-by-side triangles when rolled over the dough. Croissant cutters come in different widths: some one triangle-wide, perfect for the home cook; while others are two or three triangles-wide, ideal for the professional baker who needs to make a large number of pastries in very little time.

cromesky - see KROMESKY.

crookneck squash - see SQUASH.

croque madame - a **croque monsieur** made with chicken, instead of ham, or served with a fried egg on top.

croquembouche - an elaborate French pastry in which small, individual cream puffs are dipped in caramel, so that they will stick while being carefully arranged in gradually decreasing concentric circles to form a cone, usually decorated with spun sugar.

croque monsieur - a grilled ham and cheese sandwich dipped in beaten egg and fried.

croquette - a savory mixture, often bound with a thick **béchamel** sauce, rolled into a cylindrical shape, coated with egg and bread crumbs, then deep-fried. See also DAUPHINE.

crossing the bridge noodle soup - a traditional Chinese soup consisting of boneless pork loin, shrimp and rice noodles mixed together and boiled in stock, from the Hangzhou province. In China, it's called *guor kiu mai fun tong*. Legend has it that, long ago, a scholar studying for his advancement in the imperial court's inner circle moved away from his home, his wife and his family, so that he wouldn't be distracted. For him, to be away was to be "across a bridge." His wife would make this soup and bring it to him, hence the name.

crostata - pl. **crostate.** The Italian term for a pie or tart, derived from the Italian word *crosta*, meaning "crust." Often these tarts have a shortbread-like pastry crust and simple toppings. Two classic *crostate* are *crostata di marmellata*, which is topped with a layer of thick jam or marmalade, and *crostata di frutta*, which is covered with a layer of pastry cream, then fresh fruit glazed with a sugar syrup to make it shiny, much the same as a fruit **flan.**

crostata

crostini - the Italian name for **canapés** or **croutons**, such as fried cubes of bread to garnish soups, or fried or toasted pieces of bread used as a base for canapés. Another type of crostini very popular in Italy is made with a slice of firm polenta, instead of bread. See also BRUSCHETTA.

crottin - a generic term for French goat cheeses made in small flattened rounds, the name meaning "horse dung" or "horse droppings" for their distinctive thick, patty shape. Crottin cheeses are often baked or grilled inside their rinds and served atop salads. One of the most famous examples is **Crottin de Chavignol.**

Crottin de Chavignol - a goat cheese from the Loire Valley region of France, with a natural, slightly wrinkled rind that may or may not have faint spots of blue or white mold. The interior is white, moist and fine-textured, mild when freshly made and increasingly nutty, creamy, flavorful and dense as it ages. This goat cheese has been produced since the 16th century in the French town of Chavignol.

croustade - a container made of bread, sliced potatoes or apples, fried dough, etc. that holds stews, creamed mixtures or any other thick liquid mixture. The softened croustade is eaten after its contents are spooned out.

croûte - a round or triangle of crustless bread, either toasted, or fried until crisp and golden in butter, or equal parts butter and oil. Croûtes are used as a base for hors d'oeuvres and as a garnish. Food baked in a pastry case is described as *en croûte*.

crouton - diminutive of *croûte*, French for "crust," a small cube or piece of bread either toasted or fried until crisp and golden, used to garnish soups or salads, sometimes cut into decorative shapes. See also SIPPET.

crown roast - also **crown rack.** See LAMB, PORK.

cru - the French term for a vineyard or estate that produces wine, literally translated as "growth." In France, winemakers in each region are ranked, and bottles are labeled to reflect the rankings of their producers. Generally speaking, in regions that do not have their own labyrinthine classification systems, fine wines fall into such rankings as: *Premier Crus* (1st growths, or the top-rated wines), *Grand Crus* (great growths, or the next-best quality) and so on. Bordeaux likely takes the prize for having the most complex regional classification system, with the Médoc area of the region alone divided into five different ranks: *Premier Crus* (1st growths), *Deuxièmes Crus* (2nd growths), *Troisièmes Crus* (3rd growths), *Quatrièmes Crus* (4th growths) and *Cinquièmes Crus* (5th growths).

This ranking system was first put into place (and nearly carved in stone for eternity) with the 1855 Classification, which ranked wines according to their price, not necessarily their level of quality. In that year, the eternally famous Premier Crus were determined: Château Margaux, Château Haut-Brion, Châteaux Latour and Château Lafite-Rothschild. These exclusive ranks remained closed until 1973, when Baron Philippe de Rothschild finally won a *Premier Cru* designation for his formerly *Deuxième Cru* Châteaux Mouton-Rothschild after 20 fruitless years of petitioning the government.

First-growth wines are made on the most desirable land in the region and tend to be two to three times the price of a regular, just-plain-good Bordeaux wine. The classification system for different crus, although helpful in identifying the general quality of the wines they produce, is not always the best indicator of value. Many châteaux that produce excellent wines are not ranked at all, because they were built after the classification system was created, and many lower-rated châteaux produce finer wines now than they did when they were initially classified. A drinker's preferences are still the best guide to determining which wine is "best."

cruet

crudités - raw vegetables served as an appetizer, usually accompanied by a dip.

cruet - a glass container, often with a stopper or lid and a pouring lip on one side, used to hold vinaigrette, oil or vinegar at the table. The word is the diminutive of the Old French *crue*, meaning "flask."

cruller - a type of doughnut made from a twisted oblong of dough, usually glazed or sprinkled with sugar after frying, from *krulle*, Dutch for "twisted cake."

crumb - **1.** a small flake or morsel of food, such as bread. Bread crumbs, cookie crumbs and cracker crumbs are all commonly used in recipes. **2.** the interior texture of a bread or cake. An **open crumb,** such as in sourdough bread, is airy and holey, whereas a **closed crumb,** such as in traditional white bread or cake, is fine and much denser.

Crumb, George - see POTATO CHIPS.

crumble - **1.** (n.) also **crisp.** A dessert, most often made with apples, similar to a cobbler, but made instead with a crumb topping. **2.** (v.) to break up food into small pieces.

crumpet - a griddle-cooked bread, from the Middle English word *crumpen*, meaning "to curl up," as the original version tended to do.

crumpet ring - see ENGLISH MUFFIN RING.

crush - to reduce a food to the finest texture possible. Foods with a high moisture content can be crushed to a liquid or paste, whereas dry foods can be crushed to crumbs or powder.

crust - a variable term that can mean the cooked outer layer of a food, such as the dough used to enclose or cover a pie filling; the crisp, cooked bread base of a pizza; or the hard, outermost layer of a loaf of bread. A crust can also form on the outside of a cooked piece of meat that has been rubbed with spices, flour or cornmeal. It is also a term for the sediment that forms inside wine bottles when they are aged for a long time.

crustacean - aquatic arthropods, such as lobsters, shrimps, crabs and barnacles, from the Latin *crustacea*, meaning "shell," their distinguishing feature being that their skeleton (carapace) is on the outside, concealing a soft and delicious flesh.

Cryovac - see SOUS VIDE.

crystal fold - a Chinese dish of meat, often pork but sometimes seafood or even **Peking duck,** stir-fried with various seasonings and chopped vegetables, served with fresh lettuce leaves for wrapping around the filling. The name likely comes from the crystal-like sheen of the lettuce as it is folded around the hot filling.

crystallized flowers - see CANDIED FLOWERS.

crystallized ginger - see CANDIED GINGER.

crystal sugar - see SUGAR.

Crystal Wax onion - a white Bermuda onion. See also ONION.

csipetke - Hungarian egg and flour dumplings made from scraps of dough, dropped into boiling water and served with soups and goulash.

Cuba libre - a **cocktail** made by pouring a shot of rum over ice in a tall glass and topping the glass up with cola, served with a wedge of lime to squeeze into the drink. A happy result of the Spanish-American War, the "Cuba libre" was named for the cry of the Rough Riders: *Cuba libre* means "Free Cuba." These American soldiers, who steamed into Cuba to help the islanders end Spanish colonial rule, brought their beloved Coca-Cola with them, which they mixed with Cuban rum and a squeeze of lime juice to toast the newly independent country.

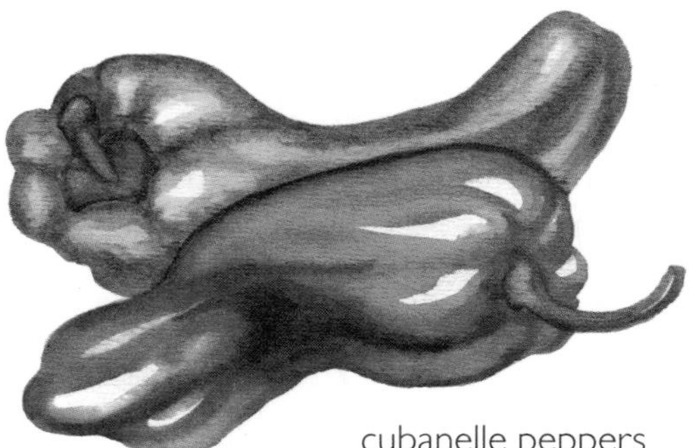

cubanelle peppers

cubanelle pepper - a long, tapered sweet pepper, yellow to light green when immature and bright red when fully ripe. It is sweet and mild, and can be stuffed or used in almost any recipe that calls for a sweet pepper.

Cuban oregano - see JAMAICAN THYME.

Cuban pumpkin - also **Cuban squash.** See CALABAZA.

Cuban sandwich - also **cubano, sandwich mixto.** A hot grilled sandwich made with layers of sweet ham, roast pork, Swiss cheese, sliced dill pickles and mustard (never mayonnaise in an authentic one), a popular meal in Florida based on a traditional recipe from Cuba. The recipe calls for Cuban bread, which is similar to French bread, although wider and flatter than a baguette. The sandwich is buttered and grilled in a sandwich press called a *plancha* ("iron" in Spanish), which melts the cheese and toasts the bread while compressing the delicious layers together. A *medianoche* sandwich is a variation on the Cuban sandwich, basically the same but made on smaller pieces of light, fluffy egg bread. Its name means "midnight" in Spanish, so called because it is a popular midnight snack, usually eaten cold.

Cuban sweet potato - see BONIATO.

cube steak - also **minute steak.** A tough piece of round steak run through a commercial tenderizing machine, which pokes hundreds of holes in it (or cubes it) to make it tender enough to eat. Cube steaks cook quickly, are quite flavorful and are inexpensive, because they are made from a less-tender part of the cow. However, it's wise to check what you're getting, because cube-steak machines can also knit two undesirable pieces of meat into what looks like one solid piece of steak.

cucumber - a long, green fruit, *Cucumis sativus*, one of the oldest vegetables known to humans. Cucumbers and hot weather seem to go together. These relatives of the muskmelon originated in the valleys of India, between the Bay of Bengal and the Himalayas. Long before history was recorded, cucumbers spread westward. They are one of the few vegetables mentioned in the Old Testament, where we learn that the cucumber was cultivated in Egypt. The Greeks and Romans enjoyed them too. The ancient Romans treasured cucumbers, and their enthusiasm for the vegetable spread throughout Europe. The Roman historian and naturalist **Pliny** described how cucumbers were forced to grow out of season for the Emperor Tiberius, who demanded they be available every day of the year (he consumed at least 10 a day year-round). Columbus took cucumber seeds, along with other vegetable seeds, to Haiti in 1494. Very soon, French, English and Spanish explorers reported that Indians were growing them from Florida and up into Canada.

The first vital review of cucumbers in Europe took place in France during the reign of Pépin the Short at the end of the 8th century. According to his gardener's record books, Pépin ordered that *concombres* be planted in triple rows adjacent to his vineyards, to protect the precious grapes from boll weevils, borers and cutworms. It took an additional 50 years before his son, Charlemagne, was permitted to eat a cucumber simply for enjoyment. It must have pleased his fancy, for Charlemagne declared at once that the cucumber was his favorite "fruit." He ate them only as dessert, in sweet tarts and custards.

Cucumbers require a humid environment, which is why you see them on market shelves coated with a thin wax coating to preserve the moisture content and enhance appearance. There are about 40 different kinds of cucumbers. Unusual varieties are now appearing in the U.S. One is a burpless cucumber, developed in Europe and enjoyed there for centuries; another is a lemon cucumber that looks more like a tennis ball than a vegetable. The British have developed a variety of seedless cucumber, which is grown in a greenhouse without the need for bee pollination. This next fact about cucumbers is really surprising, and some think it is just another old wives' tale, but it actually works: the next time you purchase a standard cucumber (not the long, skinny English variety), cut about 1 inch (2.5 cm) off the end and rub the two exposed areas together in a circular motion while occasionally pulling them apart. This creates enough suction to release a substance that causes some cucumbers to have a bitter taste. Then, discard the small end you used to release the bitterness.

cucumber chutney - a sweet-tasting mixture of cucumbers, mustard seed, sugar, vinegar, onions, peppers and spices, which goes well with cold meats, cheeses and grilled foods.

cucuzza - pl. **cucuzze.** The Italian name for a popular type of **bottle gourd.** It is a long, thin, curved squash, medium green to yellow in color, a member of the Cucurbitaceae family of gourds. The cucuzza, *Lagenaria siceraria* 'Longissima', has mild flesh, similar to the zucchini, to which it bears a distant resemblance, and can be eaten cooked or raw. The greens of the plant are also edible, although they have a bitter undertone.

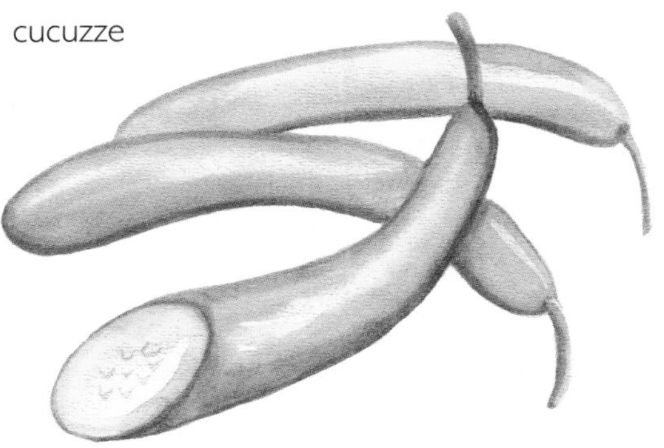
cucuzze

cuddapa almond - also **cudapah almond.** See CHAROLI NUT.

cuisine - the French word for "kitchen," used to describe the style, manner or principles of cooking of a particular culture or group, such as "Cantonese cuisine." It can also be used as a noun for the actual food cooked by a devotee of a specific type of cuisine. See also CUISINE BOURGEOISE, CUISINE MAIGRE, CUISINE MINCEUR, HAUTE CUISINE, NOUVELLE CUISINE.

cuisine bourgeoise - French for "middle class cooking," it is a sophisticated type of home cooking that includes some of the rich sauces and complex techniques of traditional French **haute cuisine,** but simplified for the everyday kitchen. It is not peasant cooking, which is much simpler and focused on regional specialties and seasonal ingredients.

cuisine maigre - a French term that literally means "meager cooking" or "light cooking," a low-fat style of French cooking that uses no meat.

cuisine minceur - a lightened-up style of French cooking developed in the 1970s by Michel Guérard and still practiced at his restaurant and spa, Les Prés d'Eugénie in the village of Eugénie-les-Bains in southern France. Cuisine minceur features less cream and butter than traditional French cooking, lighter sauces, lean cuts of meat and poultry, and more vegetables and vegetable-based sauces.

cuitlacoche - see HUITLACOCHE.

culantro - also **fitweed.** An herb, *Eryngium foetidum*, native to Latin America and the Caribbean, similar in flavor to cilantro; so much so that it is frequently called "false cilantro," "long cilantro" or "spiny cilantro." The long, saw-toothed green leaves of the plant are used often in Puerto Rican, Mexican, Thai and Vietnamese cuisine for their pungent cilantro-like flavor.

culatello - an expensive cured Italian ham, salted and soaked in dry white wine before curing, then stuffed into a covering (traditionally a clean pig's bladder) and trussed with string into its characteristic pear shape. Culatello is allowed to dry in a more humid environment than other Italian cured hams. The lean meat turns a lovely bright red as it cures. Culatello is usually shaved thin, like **prosciutto,** and eaten raw with an assortment of antipasti. The name means "little backside," because it is taken from the rear muscles of the hind legs of the pig.

cullen skink - a traditional Scottish soup made of smoked haddock (better known as **finnan haddie**) and mashed potatoes. This milk-based chowder is often served at Robbie Burns Day celebrations and is named for the fishing village of Cullen, near the North Sea coast in Scotland. See also BROSE.

Culpeper, Nicholas - see profile below.

cultivated mushroom - *Agaricus bisporus*, traditionally grown from spawn on stable manure. It comes in three sizes: the smallest, or button; the medium-size, or cup; and the largest, or open (flat) mushroom. A "wild" version is the field mushroom, *Agaricus campestris*.

cultured butter - a type of butter used frequently in Europe, made from cream in which the naturally occurring lactic acid bacteria are allowed to multiply, changing the flavor and texture of the cream and making butter that is tangy and higher in fat than regular North American sweet cream butter. The butter is churned from the cultured cream and the buttermilk removed, getting rid of the majority of the lactic acid bacteria, which, if left in the butter, would make it sour. North American dairies are catching on to the appeal of this European staple, making their own versions with milk from local dairies.

Cumberland sauce - an English sauce served with game, made with red currant jelly, port, orange and/or lemon zest, mustard and other seasonings.

Culpeper, Nicholas (1616–1654) - English herbalist, botanist, physician and writer best known for *The English Physitian: or an Astrologo-Physical Discourse of the Vulgar Herbs of this Nation* (1652), a study of herbs and their medicinal and astrological properties, also used extensively as a botanical reference source by food historians. Culpeper was born to a noble Surrey family, who expected him to become a minister, but from childhood he was captivated by nature, the stars and the functioning of the human body. While at Cambridge, he decided to elope, but his betrothed was killed on her way to meet him when her coach was struck by lightning. After recovering from his grief, he abandoned Cambridge and his plans to study medicine, and apprenticed with an apothecary instead. He began treating the poor using local herbs and astrology, charging very little and seeing as many as 40 patients a day.

Cumberland sausage - a coarse-textured English sausage consisting of roughly chopped pork and black pepper.

cumin - a fragrant and versatile spice of Egyptian origin, mentioned several times in the Old and New Testaments, as well as in some very early English records. Cumin seeds are listed in the *Ebers Papyrus* (1500 BC) as a medicinal plant grown in Egypt. The name derives from the Hebrew *kamon*, a word of Babylonian origin, and *kuminon* in Greek. The Romans used a huge amount of cumin both as a flavoring agent and as a medicine. The seeds were the symbol of a miser, due to their tiny size. Marcus Aurelius was nicknamed "Cumin" because he was greedy. Roman historian and naturalist **Pliny** declared cumin to be the best appetizer of all condiments. Greek author **Theophrastus,** in 4th century BC, said, "One must curse and abuse it while sowing the crop if it is to be fair and abundant." The seeds are taken from a low-growing border plant, which blossoms with lavender flowers in the spring. Crushed into powder, cumin lends an aromatic sweetness to any dish and can be used in either sweet or savory recipes.

cupcake - a small individually sized cake made in a muffin pan and usually iced.

cupcakes

curaçao - a white rum-based liqueur, first invented by the Dutch, flavored with the peel of bitter oranges found by the settlers on the island of the same name. Strangely enough, the liqueur has never been subject to any **appellation** regulations. In addition to naturally clear white curaçao, many companies make colored versions in red, orange, green and blue. They add the same flavor to cocktails, but give them a shot of vibrant color as well.

curcuma - see TURMERIC.

curd - **1.** the coagulated fats and other solids produced from milk by the addition of **rennet** and natural ripening. **2.** a sweet preserve made with sugar, water, eggs, butter, cream, pectin and a fruit flavoring (often citrus juice and/or zest). Lemon and lime curd are two of the most popular types, used as a spread on bread or baked goods or as a filling for pies or tarts.

curd cheese - the general name given to all unripened cheeses made from the separated curds of cow's or goat's milk. Curd cheese is slightly acidic and is used in cheesecakes, and sweet or savory fillings. It is also a popular base for dips and spreads.

curdle - to transform from a liquid into a thickened, coagulated solid, often because of spoiling, as with milk, or from heat, as in cheese making.

cure - when applied to meat, simply means that meat is cured of its propensity to putrefaction or preserved from spoiling quickly. In the past, dry salting was often unsatisfactory, because salt was coarse and unrefined and could produce uneven results. Sugar, which helps soften the meat and adds flavor, was used only by the few who could afford it. Meat was thus dry, hard and very salty, but in the late 18th century, some attempt was finally made to refine curing techniques. Early Mesopotamians may have been the first to discover that meat could be cured with salt. According to legend, a wounded pig ran squealing into the waters of what we now call the Persian Gulf. As he died of his wounds, he was washed with brine. Someone noticed that this somehow kept the meat fresh and edible for much longer than usual. The legend may be invention passed on from generation to generation, but it was certainly through accidents like this that most such discoveries were made.

curing salt - a ready-made mixture used for curing meats, a combination of salt and sodium nitrite, sometimes with sodium nitrate, sugar and/or flavorings added. Curing salt is usually dyed pink to make it easily distinguishable from table salt in the cupboard. It can be either rubbed directly onto the meat or dissolved in water to make a brine.

curly chicory - also **curly endive.** See FRISÉE.

curly parsley - a common North American type of parsley, *Petroselinum crispum,* used frequently as a garnish and a seasoning in foods. It has a strong, grassy parsley flavor that is considered harsh by some and interesting by others. See also ITALIAN PARSLEY, PARSLEY.

currants

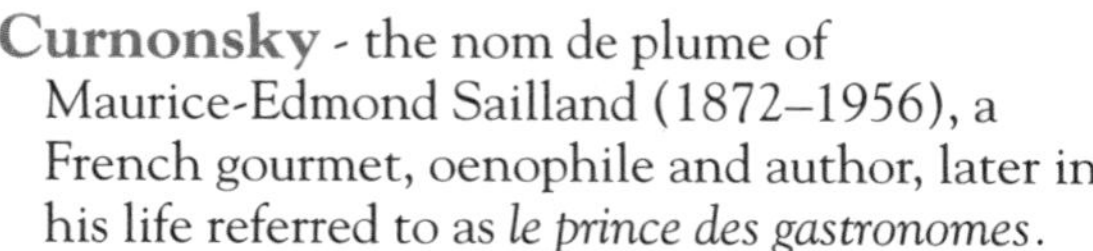

Curnonsky - the nom de plume of Maurice-Edmond Sailland (1872–1956), a French gourmet, oenophile and author, later in his life referred to as *le prince des gastronomes*.

currant - **1.** the red, black or golden (called white) berries from a shrub of the genus *Ribes*. They are rather tart for eating raw, but have many other uses: they make a sparkling jelly, excellent with roast lamb, poultry and game, and beautiful jams; they're delicious, added to a summer salad of tossed and grated raw vegetables; and they can be dipped by the bunch in egg whites and "frosted" with fine sugar. The Greeks and Romans considered red currants to be a refreshing medicinal essence. **2.** dried **Zante grapes** (resembling tiny, purple raisins, but slightly more tart) used in baked goods, puddings and sweets. The name "currant" comes from the French *raisins de Corinthe*, since currants were originally imported from Corinth, Greece.

currant tomato - see TOMATO.

curry - any of various hot and spicy Indian or Caribbean meat and/or vegetable stews flavored with **curry powder,** usually served with rice.

curry leaves - a component of some **curry powders;** small, shiny green leaves from the curry plant. They have a citrus scent, similar to that of lemongrass, and a pungent bittersweet flavor.

curry paste - a blend of spices, usually curry powder, coriander seeds, cumin, fenugreek,

CURRY PASTE TYPES

biryani curry paste - a medium-spicy Indian curry paste that combines coriander, cumin, ginger, garlic and other spices, used to flavor **biryani,** a dish of rice with meat or fish.

green curry paste - a mild Thai blend of green chiles, garlic, lime leaves, coriander leaves and lemongrass, used frequently for chicken and fish dishes.

korma curry paste - a mild, creamy Indian curry paste made with spices, such as turmeric, paprika and ginger, usually mixed with a creamy base to make a smooth, gentle curry.

Madras curry paste - hot and spicy Indian curry paste, with strong notes of ground coriander and cumin, used in Madras-style vegetable, legume, meat or seafood curries and soups.

red curry paste - a fiery Thai curry paste made with ground, dried red chiles, galangal, lemongrass, garlic and shrimp paste, often used in pork and beef curries.

tandoori curry paste - a mild Indian curry paste consisting of tamarind, spices and acids (such as lemon juice) for tenderizing and marinating meats or fish before cooking them in a **tandoor,** typically colored a glowing shade of red to enhance the finished look of the food.

tikka curry paste - a mild Indian curry paste flavored primarily with tamarind, ginger and ground coriander, used to combine with yogurt as a tenderizing marinade for grilled chicken and fish.

vindaloo curry paste - a spicy, sour Indian curry paste typical of Goa in southwestern India, containing a variety of spices, tamarind and vinegar, often used to season chicken or fish dishes.

yellow curry paste - a medium-spicy Thai curry paste flavored with garlic, lemongrass, dried red chiles, galangal, cumin, cinnamon, anise, turmeric, lime zest and ground coriander, frequently used in soups.

chiles, etc., depending on the desired style of cuisine, mixed with **ghee,** other oils or water, usually with a mortar and pestle. Curry paste can be used as the base for curries, sauces, marinades or as a flavoring agent. It's also available prepared commercially.

curry powder - from *kari,* the South Indian word for "sauce," a blend of many spices as unique as the person blending them. Commercial curry powder generally contains cayenne, cinnamon, coriander, cloves, cumin, fennel seeds, fenugreek, ground mustard, black pepper, turmeric and more. The distinct color comes from the turmeric, and the heat level ranges from mild to spicy; hotter blends are generally labeled *Madras*. Indian cooks, in their remarkable curries, don't use prepared powder. They choose their preferred individual spices and toast, grind and combine them in amounts suitable to a particular palate or dish. In using commercial powder, one can improve the flavor of raw spices by sautéing them slightly before use.

cusk - a North Atlantic coldwater fish related to cod, *Brosme brosme,* found off the coast of northern New England and the eastern coast of Canada. The cusk has a long body and a large mouth, with a single barbel on the underside of the chin. It can range from greenish brown to reddish brown, with a white or cream-color belly. The flesh is lean and white, delicately flavored and suited to a variety of cooking methods. It is one of the many cod-like fish used to make salt fish (often labeled **salt cod**). Like cod and other major commercial fish species, its stocks have been depleted significantly in the U.S. and Canada, so it faces endangerment.

custard - a blend of milk and eggs, baked or boiled. Although probably derived from a Middle English word, the term resembles *croustade,* the French word for "pie." Custard mixtures have been used as pie fillings for centuries. One of the cheesecake recipes described by **Athenaeus** in the early 3rd century sounds amazingly like a custard pie.

custard apple - a term for a group of fruits that includes the **cherimoya, sweetsop** and **soursop.** They are tropical fruits that rarely appear in temperate-zone markets. The cherimoya has a pineapple flavor, while the sweetsop, particularly popular in the West Indies, has a sweet, custard-like flesh. The flesh of the soursop is white and the most acidic of the group.

custard cup - a glass or ceramic cup, similar to a **ramekin** but flared instead of straight-sided, with a volume of between 6 and 10 ounces (175 and 300 mL), used for making baked custards, such as a flan and **pot de crème.**

custard cups

cut in - to incorporate cold fat, such as butter, lard or shortening, into a flour mixture, breaking it up into distinguishable small pieces, usually accomplished using a pastry blender, a fork or two knives. Proper cutting in coats the fat pieces with flour, allowing them to be incorporated whole into a pastry dough, where they will melt when exposed to heat in the oven. As the fat melts, it creates steam and puffs up the flour particles, yielding a light, flaky result. Fat can be cut in with the fingers, but it must be done quickly (with cool hands), using a finger-snapping motion, so that the heat of the skin does not prematurely melt the fat, creating tough, chewy pastry. The metal blade of a food processor can also cut in fat quite well if it is pulsed quickly and not allowed to overmix the ingredients.

cutlet - a thin, tender cut of meat taken from the rib or leg, from *cotellette,* a French descendant of *costa,* Latin for "rib." This makes "cutlet" an etymological relative of quite a few other words related to ribs, flanks, sides and ribbed. For instance, the English cooking apple is known as a *costard,* and the *entrecôte* steak is cut from "between the ribs."

cutting board - a wooden, rubber or plastic board on which food can be chopped, minced or sliced, designed to protect countertops from damage; made of materials that receive the blows of a sharp knife edge without dulling it excessively. Wooden cutting boards are a traditional favorite for their knife-cushioning powers, beauty and resilience. There is considerable controversy surrounding the germ-spreading capabilities of the different materials from which cutting boards are made. Some say that wood is the more sanitary choice, citing studies that show wood does not allow bacteria to be transferred from it to other surfaces, thanks to natural compounds in the wood. Others recommend using plastic or rubber cutting boards instead of wood, because they are often treated with antibacterial chemicals. In either case, the safest way to prevent the spread of germs in the kitchen is to wash any cutting board well with hot, soapy water or, better yet, sanitize it by running it through the dishwasher at 140° to 160°F (60° to 71°C).

cuttlefish - a cephalopod of the genus *Sepia,* a relative of the squid and the octopus, with eight arms and two tentacles for grabbing prey, often used in Asian and Mediterranean cuisine. Cuttlefish are caught in the wild, but are also extensively farmed in countries such as Thailand. They can be cooked fresh, dried and reconstituted in water for cooking; or dried and seasoned, as for the snack food **surume.** Their flesh tends to be sweeter and less chewy than that of squid or octopus. Cuttlefish also have an ink sack, which produces a natural brown-black ink once used by artists, who called it "sepia" for the cuttlefish's genus name. Cuttlefish use their ink as a type of cloaking device when threatened: they squirt a jet of ink at their opponent and then flee while the opponent is blinded by the dark ink. Today, cuttlefish ink is used in Mediterranean cooking as a flavoring and coloring for dishes, usually ones that involve rice, such as the Italian *risotto nero,* or black risotto, as well as pasta.

cyanocobalamin - see B VITAMINS.

Cynar - a dark brown, extremely bitter Italian apéritif, with an alcohol content of 17 percent, made from artichokes. Too bitter to consume on its own, it is typically served over ice or mixed with soda water.

d
dragon fruit

dab - see PLAICE.

dacquoise - a layer cake originating in, and named for, Dax, a town on the southwestern coast of France, made of layers of baked nut meringue filled with butter cream.

dafina - also **adafina.** The Sephardic version of **cholent,** or Sabbath stew, made in Morocco, North Africa and southern Spain, baked a day ahead in a slow oven, so that observant Jews do not have to do any cooking once the Sabbath begins. When the Jews were expelled from Spain by the Moors in 1492, they took their recipes for *hamin* or *chamin* (the Sephardic equivalent of the Ashkenazi Jewish term cholent) with them and adapted them to local flavors and staples in their new homes. Dafina sometimes includes lamb or mutton instead of the beef used in Eastern European cholent, and includes chickpeas instead of beans. The spicing of the dish also reflects North African tastes, including hot red peppers, cumin, cinnamon, allspice, turmeric, saffron and/or coriander seeds. The dish is often served with dumplings called *kouclas*, and contains hard-boiled eggs called *huevos haminados*. Whole eggs in their shells are submerged in the stew, where the gravy permeates them, penetrating the shells and turning them dark brown, hard-cooking the white and yolk and infusing them with the flavors of the stew. The name "dafina" comes from the Arabic word meaning "covered," in reference to the covered dish the stew was cooked in.

Dagwood - a many-layered sandwich containing several different meats, cheeses and condiments, named after Dagwood Bumstead, a character from the comic strip *Blondie*, who made a habit of making and eating such a sandwich.

daikon - also **Asian radish, Oriental radish.** From the Japanese *dai*, meaning "large," and *kon*, meaning "root," this large, cucumber-shaped radish is available in three varieties, all of which may be eaten raw or cooked. The Korean daikon is about 8 inches (20 cm) long and cone-shaped with a green coloration at the top; the Chinese is a similar size and shape but completely white; and the Japanese is the same size but more cylindrical than conical.

dainty - a small cake, cookie or confection, usually used in the plural form, "dainties," to describe any type of bite-size, sweet baked goods.

Daiquiri - a simple cocktail of rum, lime juice and sugar shaken with ice and strained into a chilled glass rimmed with sugar. Versions made with fruit juices and blended with crushed ice are called **Frozen Daiquiri.**

daisy - the common name for flowers of both the *Bellis* and *Chrysanthemum* genera, with edible petals. If small enough, daisies can be eaten whole, but the petals of larger flowers are better stripped off the flower heads and sprinkled over salads or other dishes. See also EDIBLE FLOWERS.

dal - also **dhal.** The Hindi word for any of a wide variety of split dried pulses, such as beans, peas and lentils, and the dishes made with these pulses. These dishes may be spicy or mild, and are often puréed. In their whole form, these pulses are known as *gram*.

POPULAR TYPES OF DAL

channa dal - split chickpeas.

masoor - also **masur dal.** Split red lentils.

moong dal - also **mung dal.** A split **mung bean.**

toor - also **arhar dal, tur.** Split pigeon peas.

urad - also **urd dal.** The split pulse of a bean plant, *Vigna mungo,* native to southern India.

dallé - see DARNE.

dalo - see TARO.

damper bread - an Australian non-yeast bread traditionally baked in the ashes of a fire or inside a Dutch oven, a creation of the first

Korean daikon

British settlers to arrive in Australia in the late 1700s and probably inspired by Irish soda bread. Damper bread tends to be flattish, sometimes like a large cracker, and has a texture and flavor rather like **naan.** Modern-day recipes tend to call for **self-rising flour,** which contains baking powder to give the dough a slight rise. Some recipes suggest cooking the bread over a fire or adding gum leaves to a regular oven to give the bread the classic smoky flavor it absorbs from being baked in ashes.

Dampfnudel - pl. **Dampfnudeln.** A sweet German dumpling made with a raised yeast dough, filled with puréed prunes or served plain with melted butter, fruit or a vanilla-scented sauce. The dumplings are simmered in water or steamed until cooked through. In Bavaria, Dampfnudeln are small, baked cakes, similar to French **brioche,** usually served warm, covered in a rich caramel or vanilla sauce. The word translates into English literally as "steamed noodle," but its meaning is really "steamed dumpling."

damson plum - see PLUM.

Danbo cheese - also **King Christian.** A popular Danish semisoft cow's milk cheese with a pale yellow, slightly stretchy interior punctuated with small holes. It is a mildly flavored cheese and comes plain or enhanced with pungent caraway seeds, often in wax-covered rectangular blocks. Danbo is also known as King Christian cheese, named for King Christian IX of Denmark, who reigned from 1863 to 1906.

Dancy orange - see MANDARIN ORANGE.

dandelion - a perennial flowering plant, *Taraxacum officinale*, common to all temperate regions, with the greatest varieties native to Europe and Asia. It has occasionally been cultivated on a small scale and has been used as a novelty and in emergencies as a green vegetable, probably since prehistory. The leaves can be eaten raw in salads or cooked like spinach. Dandelion wine is made from the flowers. The roots can be roasted to make a coffee substitute (it was fairly popular in France during the Second World War); they're used in Japanese cuisine and give a magenta dye (the leaves can produce a brown dye as well).

The botanical name is clouded by two opposing theories. Some believe that *Taraxacum* comes from the Persian *tark hashgun*, meaning "wild endives," while others believe that the name is derived from the Greek *taraxos*, meaning "disorder," and *akos*, meaning "remedy." The common name is derived from the French *dent-de-lion*, meaning "lion's tooth," referring to its saw-toothed leaves. In France, it's also called *pissenlit* ("wet the bed"), a reference to its supposed diuretic properties. The plant name first appeared in the 10th-century medical journals of Arabian physicians. By the 16th century, British apothecaries, who called the plant *herba taraxacon* or *herba urinara* (for its diuretic ability), considered dandelion an important and valuable drug.

dandelion chicory - see ITALIAN DANDELION.

danger zone - see FERMENTATION, TEMPERATURE.

dangleberry - see TANGLEBERRY.

Danish - also **Danish pastry.** Made from a buttery, flaky yeast dough, filled with fruit or cheese and often glazed, it is usually served at breakfast. The Danes refer to what we call a Danish as *Wienerbrød*, meaning "Vienna bread."

Danish blue - also **Danablu, Jutland blue.** A Danish blue cheese made from cow's milk, created as an alternative to expensive **Roquefort,** although milder in flavor. Its taste is sometimes described as metallic, but its creamy, sharp, salty flavor is prized by devotees. It is semisoft at its peak and can be spread or crumbled easily.

Danish lobster - see PRAWN.

Danish Port Salut - see ESROM.

dandelions

Das, Nabin Chandra (1846–unknown) - Indian confectioner, inventor of **rasgulla** (also *rosogolla* or *rasagolla*), a sweet whose popularity swept Eastern India during its 19th-century cultural renaissance. Das came from a family with considerable holdings in sugar, but at the time of his birth, the fortune had nearly disappeared. At the urging of his mother, he opened a sweet shop in Calcutta, but it failed. He opened a second shop in 1866 and began thinking about developing an alternative to **sondesh,** the popular sweet of the time. He disliked it, because it always left the mouth too dry as it dissolved. His experiments resulted in a confection made with milk protein, shaped into balls and soaked in syrup, which he called *rasgulla*, from *rasa,* meaning "syrup," and *golla,* meaning "round object." It didn't catch on until a wealthy businessman, stopping by the shop one day with his son, tasted the sweet and was so impressed with its flavor that he began to spread the word. Das's son, Krishna Chandra, carried on the legacy by opening his own shop in 1930, with his son, Sarada Charan.

Danish salami - made of a mixture of pork, beef or veal, spices and sometimes garlic.

dan zai noodles - a specialty from Taiwan, thin noodles made of wheat flour or translucent rice flour (*mi fen*), topped with juicy beef, shrimp, minced garlic and parsley, with a shrimp-flavored broth. The noodles are named after the *dan*, the shoulder pole used by street vendors to carry the noodles.

Danzi Goldwasser - see GOLDWASSER.

dariole - **1.** a baked or steamed, molded dish of creamy dessert custard in a puff pastry. There are also savory versions of cheese, meat, seafood or vegetable mixture. Classic versions are sweet, but those first served in 14th-century Britain, were small puddings of minced herbs, meat and spices. **2.** a cylindrical mold which flares outward from base to rim. Modern nonstick metal and plastic versions (available large and small) are used to mold cakes, **castle puddings,** appetizers and individual Christmas puddings.

dariole mold - see BABA MOLD.

Darjeeling tea - see TEA.

Dark and Stormy - a famous Bermudian drink of dark rum mixed with ginger beer, served over ice in a tall glass.

dark chocolate - see CHOCOLATE.

dark corn syrup - see CORN SYRUP.

dark meat - the meat found in the legs of cooked poultry, such as the thighs and drumsticks, darker in color and higher in fat and calories than **white meat.**

dark raisin - a raisin made from a variety of different dark-skinned grapes, such as Thompson seedless or Muscat, usually sun-dried until almost black and leathery. See also GOLDEN RAISIN, RAISIN.

dark roux - see ROUX.

dark rum - see RUM.

dark syrup - a blend of golden syrup and **treacle** used primarily in baking. It adds a darker color to foods than golden syrup and is slightly less sweet because of the treacle.

darne - a French term for any thick slice of fish. A thinner slice is called a *dallé*.

dash - an imprecise measure of seasoning added to a dish, often less than 1/8 teaspoon (0.5 mL).

dasheen - see TARO.

dashi - from the Japanese for "broth," a broth or soup stock made from seaweed (**kombu**) and dried flakes of **bonito** (**katsuobushi**).

Das, Nabin Chandra - see profile above.

date - a fruit that grows in clusters on a palm tree, *Phoenix dactylifera,* native to the Middle East and Mediterranean. The fruit has a thin skin, which, when ripe, becomes yellow, brown, black or even reddish. For centuries, it was the food of nomads and desert travelers. Dates were cultivated in the Middle East as early as 3500 BC. To the ancients, palm trees provided more than just a nutritious and delicious staple fruit; every part of the tree was used. The leaves were used as roofing and woven into mats, baskets or any number of other useful household items. The fibers could be carved into needles. Date enthusiasts say that there were more than 365 different uses for the tree. Muslims consider the date palm to be the

DATE VARIETIES

There are hundreds of date varieties across the globe. The Middle East produces and sells the majority of the world's dates, but California is the primary producer in North America. Date palms are also cultivated extensively across North Africa and on the Indian subcontinent. The following varieties are commonly seen in grocery stores across North America:

Deglet Noor - introduced into California in 1900, this variety constitutes about 75 percent of the state's date crop today. It is still one of the most popular types grown in Tunisia and Algeria, where it is grown in inland oases. It is not as sweet as other varieties, with a semidry texture, but keeps well and is ideal for transporting, good for cooking.

Halawy - also **Halawi.** A small, soft, moist date brought to California from its native Iraq. Halawy means "sweet," which describes the flavor of the date perfectly; good for eating out of hand.

Halawy

Khadrawy - also **Khadrawi.** A variety grown in California and Arizona but much more popular in Iraq and Saudi Arabia. A soft, very dark date that is considered to be among the best in flavor and texture for eating fresh. It is perfectly, not overly, sweet, and richly flavored, but it does not keep well and should be eaten quickly.

Medjool

Medjool - also **Medjul.** Introduced into California in 1927 from Morocco, now a popular "deluxe" date with soft, sweet flesh and very little fibrous texture inside. It is excellent for eating fresh, very moist, and ships well.

Zahidi - the oldest type of date palm grown. It is extremely popular in the Middle East, especially Iraq, where it is the main variety sold. Introduced into California in the earliest years of the 20th century, it can be sold soft, medium or dry and is good for almost any application. Light golden brown, extremely sweet and sugary, it keeps well and is excellent to have on hand for baking.

tree of life, because they believed it was created from the dust leftover from the creation of man. The prophet Mohammed often fasted on a diet of water and dates.

Date palms, which are grown in coastal areas that offer sufficient moisture, are abundant producers. Up to several hundred pounds (up to 100 kg) of dates can be harvested from a single tree. Dates are usually pasteurized to prevent mold. Corn syrup is frequently added to keep them from drying out, even though they're very high in natural sugar.

The Ancient Romans referred to the flat of a human hand as *palma* and later applied the same word to the tree whose leaves resembled an oversize version of the same. Like the Romans, the Greeks also noticed a resemblance between their own fingers and the date palm's smooth, brown elongated fruit, which they called *daktulos*, or "finger."

date square - a dessert consisting of two layers of rolled oat mixture with a date filling in the middle. Known as **matrimonial cake** in the Prairies.

date sugar - a powdered natural sweetener made from ground dried dates. Date sugar can be stirred into drinks, although it doesn't dissolve like real sugar, used in baking or substituted for sugar in other recipes. Date sugar is considered a healthier alternative than processed white table sugar, because it retains the naturally occurring vitamins, minerals and fiber that are present in whole dates. It is usually sold at health food stores, although it is quite simple to grind your own at home.

date syrup - also **dibis, halek.** A sweet syrup made by boiling down dates with water and straining the thick liquid; used as a sweetener in many countries, especially in the Middle East and India. In the Middle East, the syrup is called *dibis*; in India, *halek*.

daube - a French term to describe a dish of meat (usually beef) braised in wine and herbs.

dau miu - also **dou miao, dow miao, dow miu.** See PEA SHOOTS.

daun pandan - see PANDAN.

dauphine - also **pommes dauphine.** Named for Marie Antoinette (1755–1793) when she was Dauphine of France; deep-fried **croquettes** made from a potato purée to which **choux pastry** has been added.

dauphinoise potatoes - also **pommes à la dauphinoise.** A baked dish of thinly sliced potatoes combined with cream or **crème fraîche,**

David, Elizabeth (1913–1992) - food writer who documented French, Italian, English and Mediterranean cooking. Her work is responsible for changing the way that British people cook and think about food. Born on Boxing Day, 1913, to a prominent Sussex family, David didn't discover the pleasures of food until she was in her late teens, when she was sent to France to study at the Sorbonne. While there, she boarded with Mme Barette, who served delicious food, unlike any she had eaten in England, "not...elaborate sauces or sensational puddings,...but beautifully prepared vegetables like *salsifis a la crème* and *pommes mousseline,*" David later recalled.

An adventurous young woman, she pursued a career as an actress, fell in love and boated around the Mediterranean with her lover. Their idyll was cut short by the onset of war, but they spent time in Greece, Italy and France, where David, under the tutelage of Norman Douglas (a well-known travel writer and gourmand whom the couple had met), began to think seriously about food. In 1941, she ended up in Cairo, where she learned how to cook from her talented cook, Suleiman, and married Tony David, an army officer, whom she divorced in 1958 after a long separation.

During her time abroad, David collected recipes. Returning to England after the war, she worked on the manuscript for *A Book of Mediterranean Food,* published in 1950. She also began to write articles for the British edition of *Harper's Bazaar*. Other books, such as *French Country Cooking* (1951), *Italian Food* (1954), *Summer Cooking* (1955) and *French Provincial Cooking* (1960), followed in fairly rapid succession. Over time, her influence became apparent. In the swinging '60s, Britain's smart set gave dinner parties using her recipes, and the ingredients she trumpeted, such as aubergines, figs, pine nuts and olive oil, gradually crept into English shops. In 1966, concerned about the lack of quality cookware in England (at the time, most people bought cooking utensils at hardware stores), she opened a chic kitchen shop, Elizabeth David Ltd., which also stocked foodstuffs, such as olive oil and wine.

Always an avid reader, she researched extensively and was noted for her graceful writing and evocative style, which conveyed the tastes, textures and aromas of food. David's recipes were intended to inspire, more than instruct. She was keen to place a dish in context; providing precise instructions on execution took a secondary role. She received numerous awards, but the one that pleased her most, because it recognized her skills as a writer, was being made a fellow of the Royal Society of Literature in 1982. She died of complications following a stroke in 1992. Her memorial service was held in London's St. Martin-in-the-Fields; afterward, friends and food professionals whose careers she had inspired produced an elegant picnic in her honor, featuring the kinds of food she loved.

nutmeg, garlic and often cheese (usually Gruyère), named for the Alpine region of Dauphiné in France. This type of gratin dish is typical of the region and has been widely embraced in North America, sometimes under its French name but more often under its English name, "scalloped potatoes."

David, Elizabeth - see profile left.

Davidson, Alan Eaton - see profile below.

daylily - a plant, *Hemerocallis fulva,* cultivated for its showy, edible, trumpet-shaped orange flowers, which bloom for a single day before dying. All parts of the daylily are edible and are often cooked, with a flavor similar to a cross between asparagus and zucchini. See also EDIBLE FLOWERS.

deba - see JAPANESE KNIVES.

debeard - to remove the stringy, unpleasant-to-eat **beard** of a bivalve mollusk, such as a clam, before cooking.

debone - see BONE.

de Bonnefons, Nicolas - see profile on page 220.

decaffeination - the process of chemically or mechanically removing the water-soluble caffeine from unroasted coffee beans. Legally, coffee labeled "decaffeinated" must meet strict standards for caffeine content. In Canada and Europe, this means the coffee beans can only contain 0.08 percent residual caffeine. In the U.S., the standard is stricter at 0.032 percent residual caffeine. This translates to about 5 milligrams of caffeine per cup, compared with

daylily

Davidson, Alan Eaton (1924–2003) - diplomat, publisher, food writer and editor. Born in Northern Ireland, Davidson joined the British Foreign Office after he had graduated from Oxford and served in the Royal Navy during the war. His career as a food writer began in the early 1960s when he was posted to Tunis and his wife asked him to find her a book explaining how to cook the local fish. Coincidentally, the world authority on Mediterranean fish, Professor Giorgio Bini, was visiting Tunis at the time, and so Davidson enlisted him as co-author of *Seafish of Tunisia and the Central Mediterranean,* which he self-published in 1963. Through the assistance of **Elizabeth David,** who reviewed the original pamphlet, a book-length version, *Mediterranean Seafood,* was published in 1972. While serving as ambassador to Laos in the 1970s, Davidson published three books on Lao cooking before deciding to retire from diplomacy and make writing his career. With his wife, Jane, and their daughters, he returned to London, where his natural enthusiasm and charming eccentricity enlivened the culinary scene.

A man of boundless intellectual energy and restless curiosity, he embarked almost immediately on a series of projects. In 1979, with the help of his wife, Jane, **Elizabeth David, Richard Olney** and book editor, Jill Norman, he founded *Petits Propos Culinaires,* an eclectic journal devoted to gastronomy. Next, he set up a publishing company, Prospect Books, to publish idiosyncratic books on food-related subjects. A fellowship at the University of Oxford to study science in the kitchen led to the Oxford Symposium on Food, which he launched in 1981 and established as an annual event. Throughout this period, he was writing *The Oxford Companion to Food,* a massive work containing 2,650 entries, which took him 20 years to complete. Published in 1999, it won numerous awards. *The New York Times Book Review* called it "the publishing event of the year, if not the decade," and the *New Statesman* said it was "the best food reference work ever to appear in the English language."

de Bonnefons, Nicolas (17th century) - French writer and valet at the court of Louis XIV. With the 1654 publication of *Les Delices de la campagne* (Delights of the Countryside), de Bonnefons introduced a modernized cuisine that promoted simplicity in flavor and presentation, when the vogue was a heavy use of seasoning and complicated adornment. He is also lauded by wine historians as having included in the book a description of French winemaking that is considered to be unique. It is the only one of its kind in the 17th century and created a historical record of wines produced at that time in the Parisian basin. However, he was not a fan. He described the wines as *"toujours bon à garder, jamais bon à boir"* ("always good to keep, but never good to drink").

the 60 to 180 milligrams in a cup of regular coffee.

Methylene chloride is the chemical solvent used in **regular decaffeination** and can be used directly or indirectly. In the direct method, the chemical is added to a heated mixture of coffee beans and water, where it absorbs the caffeine in the beans. The beans are drained, steamed to remove the excess solvent, then dried and roasted. In the indirect method, the beans are soaked to leach their caffeine and flavorful oils into the water. The liquid is then combined with methylene chloride, which binds with the caffeine, and heated to evaporate the caffeine-solvent combination away. The beans are combined with the water and left to reabsorb their flavorful oils, then dried and roasted. **Natural decaffeination** uses the naturally occurring compound ethyl acetate, which is found in fruit, to bind with and absorb the caffeine in coffee beans. The chemical is used in the same way as methylene chloride in the indirect method. Although the chemical is found in a variety of fruits, companies usually use synthesized ethyl acetate, so the label "natural" is a bit of a misnomer. **Swiss water decaffeination** process is a trademarked name for the generic water process of removing caffeine from coffee beans. The water process begins by soaking a batch of coffee beans in pure water to extract their caffeine and flavorful oils; the beans are discarded and the water run through a charcoal filter to remove the caffeine. The flavored water is then combined with a new batch of beans, so that they can absorb natural coffee flavor as they release their caffeine into the water, which is drained off, filtered and used for the subsequent batch. The beans are then dried and roasted. A less widely used, solvent-free method is **carbon dioxide decaffeination**, in which CO_2 gas is used to dissolve the caffeine in the beans without added solvents or by-products. It is an expensive process used by some large-scale coffee producers and is said to produce the tastiest decaffeinated coffee.

There has been a considerable amount of controversy over the safety of solvent-based decaffeination methods. Studies have shown that only minuscule amounts of the solvents are left behind (especially during the indirect method of decaffeination), and therefore any health risks associated with decaf consumption are low. One 2005 study at Harvard University went even further by showing a link between regular consumption of decaffeinated coffee and a reduced risk of rectal cancer. There is no conclusive evidence, although the popularity of water-process and "naturally" decaffeinated coffees remains high.

decant - to pour a liquid, usually aged red wine, from its original bottle into another, usually a **decanter,** to separate the sediment from the drinking wine, leaving it behind at the bottom of the bottle. Decanting also oxygenates the liquid.

decanter - see DECANT.

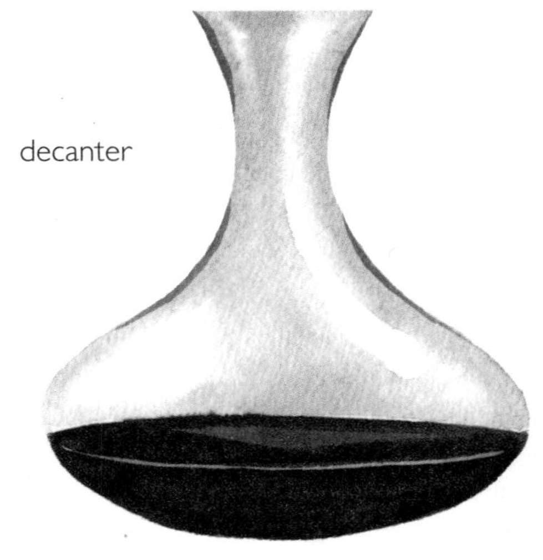
decanter

deckle - the thick layer of fat and tough muscle that joins the brisket (the pectoral muscle of the animal) to the ribs; can be used to refer to beef or lamb. The term is often mistakenly used as a synonym for the brisket point: the tough, well-marbled piece of meat attached to the top part of a beef brisket by a thick piece of fat. Beef briskets used for long, slow, Southern-style barbecuing are often labeled "deckle-off" to signal that only the flat and point parts of the brisket are being used.

deconstructed dishes - dishes made using a culinary technique that involves breaking a traditional dish down into its basic ingredients and serving them separately or in a different and more interesting combination in order to stimulate the mind and the palate. For example, deconstructed **oysters Rockefeller** would consists of all the elements of the dish (oysters, spinach, bacon, etc.), only arranged differently: perhaps cooked oysters set atop a bed of spinach with a garnish of bacon and an anise-butter sauce drizzled over the whole creation. The idea is that, while the dish is served in a completely different form, its flavors will blend together to give the overall taste of the original. Deconstructed dishes often feature one or more of the base ingredients of the original dish made into a variety of sauces, foams and the like, which give the same flavor but change the texture and appearance of the dish dramatically.

decorating sugar - also **decorator's sugar.** See SUGAR.

de Cussy, Marquis Louis - see profile below.

deep-dish pie - a pie made in a 3-inch (7.5 cm) deep pie plate, compared with the usual 1½-inch (4 cm) deep pie plate, usually with only a single crust.

deep-dish pizza - the so-called "Chicago-style" pizza baked in a rimmed pan (often dusted with cornmeal) to create a crust with a tall, chewy edge. It was offered first when Chicago's Pizzeria Uno opened its doors in 1943. The airy, thick crust with its deep edges provided the perfect base for cheese (laid on first, unlike most other pizza), followed by chunky tomato sauce with lots of extras — usually sliced Italian sausage, mushrooms, onions and sweet peppers.

deep-dish pizza

deep-fry - to cook food in hot oil at a temperature of 350°F (180°C). The food should be completely submerged in the oil and is normally coated in a batter or breading before frying.

deep fryer - also **deep-fat fryer.** A heavy-duty pan used on the stove or an electric appliance used to deep-fry foods. The classic version is simply a heavy cast-iron pot, wide and deep, with a basket insert that can be lowered into the bubbling fat and removed quickly to efficiently drain excess grease from fried foods. More complex electric fryers are based on the same design, but have built-in thermostats to ensure that the correct cooking temperature is maintained. Some even have a rotary basket that slowly moves and shifts the food as it fries to ensure an evenly crisp result.

deer - the name of many different members of the Cervidae family, ruminant quadrupeds distinct from others because of their branching horns or antlers, which they lose at molting

de Cussy, Marquis Louis (1766–1837) - French chef and author, chief steward to both Napoleon and Louis XVIII. In 1843, he published *Les Classiques de la table* (Classics of the Table), a history of gastronomy, in which he wrote that the **saucier,** the chef responsible for sauce making, is an "enlightened chemist, the creative genius and the cornerstone of the edifice of superlative cookery."

time and then replace soon after. From the gastronome's point of view, the best deer is the roe deer; followed, in order of merit, by the fallow deer, the red deer or elk, the moose and the reindeer. The meat is called **venison,** a word that derives from the Latin *venari*, "to hunt." At one time, all game was "venison," but deer was the prize of the hunt. The best meat is taken from the buck in its second year, and the most popular cut is the haunch, although the loin is also very good. Deer, in general, are eaten for their meat and liver.

deer

deglaze - to pick up and dissolve the sediments and cooking juices in roasting pans and skillets after cooking meat, poultry and game. The pan is placed over high heat and wine, brandy, stock or water is added. It's then stirred to scrape up the residue, or caramelized bits, adhering to the bottom of the pan, extracting the concentrated flavors to make a liquid that's used to make an accompanying sauce to serve with the meat.

Deglet Noor dates - see DATES.

dégorgement - see MÉTHODE CHAMPENOISE.

degrease - to remove fat from the surface of foods to make them palatable. Liquids are degreased before serving by drawing a skimmer or slotted spoon over them. If casseroles, soups, stocks, etc., are left to cool, the fat will rise to the surface of the liquid and solidify and can then be lifted off easily. Fried foods can be partially degreased by draining on paper towels.

degreasing pitcher - see FAT SEPARATOR.

dehydrate - to remove the natural water from a food by drying it slowly, assisted only by air or sunlight.

dehydrated garlic - see GARLIC.

dehydrated onions - see ONIONS.

Delaware grape - a small, red grape with a mild, sweet flavor, named after Delaware, Ohio. It can be eaten out of hand and is often used for wine and juice making.

Delessert, Benjamin - see BEET.

delicata squash - see SQUASH.

Delicious apple - see APPLE.

deli meats - see COLD CUTS.

Della rice - see RICE.

Delmonico potatoes - sliced potatoes baked in cream sauce with butter and chives. Originally made by Lorenzo Delmonico (1813–1881) in his restaurant Delmonico's in New York City.

Delmonico's - opened in New York City in 1827 as the first upscale restaurant where the clientele could order **à la carte,** as opposed to having whatever the kitchen was offering that day. Delmonico's created the standard for American fine dining, with a number of classic French dishes as part of its repertoire and the cachet of a menu printed in both English and French. The restaurant is also credited with creating such American classics as **eggs Benedict, lobster Newburg, Delmonico steak** and **Delmonico potatoes.**

Delmonico steak - offered for the first time in 1850 at the famous Delmonico's restaurant. Over the years, it's been known as club steak, boneless rib eye, New York steak and Kansas City strip steak.

Demerara rum - a strong, flavorful, dark rum distilled from the sugarcane grown along the Demerara River in Guyana. Demerara rum may be aged for up to 21 years, concentrating its flavor and making it quite smooth.

Demerara sugar - see SUGAR.

demi-glace - a rich **brown sauce** or **espagnole sauce** reduced from a meat stock, usually beef or veal, until it becomes a glaze, classically flavored with Madeira.

deviled eggs

demi-sec - a term used to describe Champagne that is medium-sweet. See also SEC.

demitasse - **1.** a tiny handled cup used for drinking espresso. A French word, *demitasse* means "half cup" for its diminutive size. **2.** the coffee served in a demitasse cup.

density thermometer - see THERMOMETER.

dent corn - see CORN.

Denver sandwich - see WESTERN SANDWICH.

Derby cheese - a semifirm cow's milk cheese from England, similar to Cheddar, sometimes flavored with sage, known as Sage Derby.

derma - a natural sausage casing made from animal intestines, the term possibly derived from the Yiddish word *gederem*, meaning "intestines." Beef or fowl derma are often used to make the Jewish sausage **kishke,** which is also commonly called "stuffed derma."

desalt - to remove excess salt from food, usually by soaking in water. Salty ham and bacon are desalted by soaking in cold water overnight, then draining. Canned anchovies are desalted by soaking in milk.

dessert - the final, and usually sweet, course of a meal, from the French, *desservir,* meaning "to clear the table."

dessert wine - any of various sweet wines, including port, sherry and Madeira, that go well with dessert.

devein - to remove the intestinal vein from shrimp or prawn.

devil - to combine or cook a food with spicy seasonings, such as cayenne pepper or hot sauce.

deviled egg - a hard-boiled egg cut in half, with the yolk removed and mixed with mayonnaise and spices, usually hot, and put back into the white.

deviled ham - a sandwich spread made of ground cooked ham mixed with spices, available in small cans in supermarkets across North America. The Underwood Co. of Boston created this canned seasoned ham and patented their Underwood Devil logo in 1870. The logo still appears on their cans today and is the oldest logo in continuous use in the United States. Although most people think of the iconic canned Underwood deviled ham, there are plenty of recipes available for homemade versions, as well as other brands, including some made from tasty **Smithfield hams.**

devilfish - see OCTOPUS.

devil's dung - see ASAFETIDA.

devil's food cake - an American invention that first appeared about 1900, some 20 years after the emergence of the **angel food cake.** The name suggests both its sinful richness and the disparity between its dark chocolate color and that of its angelic counterpart.

devils on horseback - a broiled canapé consisting either of oysters seasoned with red pepper or hot pepper sauce and wrapped in bacon; or prunes stuffed with whole almonds and mango chutney and wrapped in bacon. They are served on toast points, which is toast cut into triangles, having "points," or toothpicks. See also ANGELS ON HORSEBACK.

Devon cream - see CLOTTED CREAM.

Devonshire cream - see CLOTTED CREAM.

dewberry - small, sweet, dark purple berry of various *Rubus* species used in baking, preserves and liqueurs. The low brambles, *R. canadensis*

dewberries

(smooth dewberry) and *R. ursinus* (California dewberry) are indigenous to North America and were eaten either fresh, cooked or dried by native Americans (as well as bears). Imported for cultivation, their upright European relative, *R. caesius*, has become invasive.

dextrose - a naturally occurring form of glucose.

dhal - see DAL.

diable sauce - a French sauce based on the classic **espagnole sauce,** to which is added a reduction of white wine, vinegar, shallots, thyme, bay leaf and black pepper, often served with poultry or meat and garnished with chopped fresh parsley. See also À LA DIABLE.

dianthus - see CLOVE PINKS.

Diat, Louis - see VICHYSSOISE.

diavolo - also **alla diavola, fra diavolo.** An Italian style of preparation that uses a liberal amount of crushed hot peppers to create a spicy flavor. Foods served *alla diavola* ("in the style of the devil") or *fra diavolo* ("brother devil") are often served with a tomato-based sauce to evoke the devil's signature color.

dibis - see DATE SYRUP.

dibs - a sweet syrup of Middle Eastern origin made from concentrated grapes, pomegranates, dates or figs.

dice - to cut into very small cubes.

dietary fiber - a substance found in plant-based foods, divided into two types, soluble and insoluble. Soluble fiber dissolves in water and is present in fruits, vegetables, beans and oats. Studies of soluble fiber have shown it to reduce cholesterol levels and offer protection against heart disease. Foods with insoluble fiber include whole grains, wheat bran and some vegetables and fruits. This type of fiber doesn't dissolve in water, but it does have a high capacity for retaining water and aids in digestion and promotes regularity by adding bulk to the stool.

digestif - a French term referring to a drink (such as brandy) taken after a meal to aid digestion.

digestive biscuit - a slightly sweet biscuit made of whole-grain wheat flour, commonly eaten in Britain as a snack with tea. Digestive biscuits got their name because they are fairly plain and supposedly easy to digest, and they contain a fairly large amount of baking soda, which is a known digestive aid. Digestive biscuits come in several varieties: one variety is plain, another has one side of the biscuit dipped in chocolate, and a third is topped with chocolate and caramel.

digestive enzymes - natural **enzymes** found in foods that have been distilled into capsule or liquid form, taken to prevent stomach upsets and flatulence by helping the body break down foods more effectively. Some digestive enzyme supplements contain a variety of enzymes, such as **papain** (from papayas) and **bromelain** (from pineapples), two types of proteases, which break down proteins; lipases, which break down fat; and amylases, which break down starches, such as those in dried beans. Another easy-to-find digestive enzyme supplement is an amylase-based liquid that can be taken to ward off flatulence caused by beans and legumes. The complex sugars in beans and cruciferous vegetables can be hard for the body to digest and therefore ferment in the intestines, causing gas to build up. The liquid enzyme, taken with the food, helps the body break the sugars down into a simpler form, which the body can easily absorb and digest.

digital thermometer - see THERMOMETER.

Dijon mustard - an ochre-color mustard originally made in the Dijon region of France from mustard seeds blended with salt, white wine or **verjuice,** and spices. See also MUSTARD.

dill - a tall herb, *Anethum graveolens*, with feathery green leaves, which originated in Central Asia and belongs to the same family as

dill

parsley. The Romans praised it for its fortifying qualities, and food given to the gladiators was covered with it. The Romans brought it to Great Britain, and it then made its way to Gaul and the rest of the Roman Empire. Dill was one of the herbs used by magicians in spells and charms against witchcraft. It was the plant believed to be most hated by witches, and to be rid of them one had only to hang a bunch of it in the doorway. Dill is especially popular in India and Scandinavia. The name comes from the Saxon word *dilla,* meaning "to lull" (the seeds were first used to soothe babies to sleep). The leaves of the plant, often called "dillweed," are used either fresh or dried as an herb, often added to hot dishes at the last minute to preserve their delicate flavor. Dill seeds, which have a strong flavor similar to those of aniseed or caraway seeds, may be used whole or ground as a spice, and are especially good at imparting their flavor to dill pickles. Because their flavors are so different, dillweed and dill seeds are not good substitutes for each other.

dill head - the cluster of unopened flower buds on the dill plant, cut with a short length of stem and used whole in pickling, especially in dill pickles.

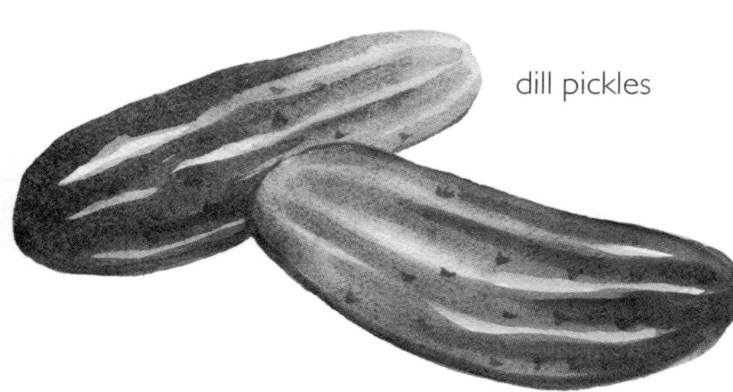

dill pickles

dill pickle - a small, whole, immature cucumber (or a slightly larger cucumber cut into wedges), preserved in a brine made with vinegar, salt and **dill heads** or seeds, often with added garlic, mustard seeds, onions and/or hot pepper. The mixture can be left to ferment for a number of weeks at room temperature or it can be cooked, then transferred to canning jars and processed in a **boiling-water canner.** Dill pickles are also widely available commercially, and their unique taste is a popular flavoring for potato chips and rice cakes in Canada.

dill water - see GRIPE WATER.

dilute - to add extra liquid to a mixture to make it thinner or weaker-tasting.

dim sum - a Cantonese term meaning "small center," from *dim*, "dot" or "speck," and *sam*, "heart." *Dim sum* is a traditional Chinese meal consisting of a variety of items served in small portions as a light meal, mostly steamed or fried, usually with a filling, sometimes considered a Chinese version of **tapas.**

diner - an inexpensive restaurant, usually one that serves home-style foods, as opposed to fancier kinds of food.

dinner - the main meal of the day, now more commonly eaten at night than at noon.

dip - a thick, semi-liquid mixture of smooth or puréed ingredients — often including a fatty, creamy component, such as sour cream, yogurt or mayonnaise — served with bread, crackers, vegetables, etc. for dipping. Dips are usually served as **hors d'oeuvres** and are common to most cultures. Some of the most popular exotic dips today are **baba ghanoush, hummus** and **taramasalata.**

diplomat pudding - see CABINET PUDDING.

diplomat sauce - also **riche sauce.** A sauce made to accompany delicate fish, such as sole or turbot, made with lobster butter, truffles and lobster meat. In French cuisine, any dish made with the combination of lobster and truffles is called *à la diplomate* to evoke the rich foods a diplomat would likely have on his menu.

direct food additive - see INTENTIONAL FOOD ADDITIVE.

dirty Martini - a **Martini** made with either gin or vodka, dry vermouth and a splash of the brine from a jar of green olives, garnished with olives. The olive juice makes the drink slightly cloudy, hence the appellation "dirty."

dirty rice - a Cajun dish of rice mixed with minced cooked chicken **giblets** and pieces, such as livers, gizzards, necks and wings. It's called "dirty" because the brown bits of meat "dirty" the white rice. It's seasoned with traditional Cajun spices and herbs, including cayenne pepper, thyme, black pepper and paprika, as well as onion, garlic and green pepper.

discoloration - the process of turning brown or black when certain pale-fleshed fruits and vegetables, such as apples, pears, bananas, artichokes, fennel and avocados, are peeled and/or sliced, exposing the inner flesh. A sprinkle of lemon juice will stop discoloration if done immediately after cutting. Lettuces also discolor, especially romaine and iceberg, if left cut more than 24 hours, but they "rust," turning red at their cut edges.

disher - a small, spring-loaded scoop, similar to an ice cream scoop, used to portion out cookie dough, **ganache** for truffles, muffin batter, etc., so that each portion is the same size and shape, which ensures even baking in the case of cookies and muffins. Dishers come in a range of sizes, from 8 (the largest, which holds about ½ cup/125 mL)) to 140 (the smallest, which holds about 1 tsp/5 mL). The number comes from the number of scoops you can make from one quart of ice cream.

dishrag gourd - see LOOFAH.

disjoint - see JOINT.

dissolve - to stir a solid with a liquid until the solid becomes an indistinguishable part of the mixture, such as a gelatin leaf in warm water for use in a pudding, or cornstarch in cold water or wine for use as a thickening agent in a stew.

distillate - the product of **distillation.**

distillation - from the Latin *distillare*, *de* plus *stillare*, meaning "to drip," and *stilla*, meaning "drop." It is the procedure of evaporating or boiling a liquid and condensing its vapor. Alcohol has a lower boiling point than water (about 173.3°F/78°C, compared with 212°F/100°C), so when a fermented drink is heated, the alcohol vaporizes some time before the water is driven off as steam. When the alcohol vapor hits a cool surface, it condenses and reverts to a fluid with a much higher percentage of alcohol than the original liquid. In the 4th century BC, the Greek philosopher Aristotle, described distillation as a means of purifying seawater to make it potable. He comments that the same handling can be given to wine, which is reduced, as a result, to a sort of "water." He was close to a breakthrough, but the experiment did no more than prove for him that wine is a form of tailored water and that, while the final product will be clear as water, the original flavor and perfume will be retained. Distilled beverages are actually fermented beverages that have been concentrated, having a higher concentration of alcohol.

distilled vinegar - although any vinegar can be distilled, malt vinegar is the usual choice. Distilled vinegars are colorless and very strong, simply because distillation has increased their percentage of **acetic acid.** It's because of their strength and their slowness to deteriorate that they're used for pickling, particularly onions. Manufacturers also use them in bottled sauces.

distilled water - water that has been purified through **distillation** so that it is free of minerals, impurities and flavor. Distilled water has been periodically touted as a healthy alternative to tap and filtered water, because it is free of any contaminants and totally pure. Health experts agree, however, that it is of no benefit to humans to drink distilled water. It may even be harmful because distilled water contains none of the helpful minerals the body needs to function properly and may actually leach them out of tissues. Some cooks swear by distilled water in soups or other liquid dishes that require a neutral base, but it is not necessary, and the minerals in good well or spring water can actually yield a tastier product.

ditali - also **ditalini.** See PASTA.

divinity - a white fudge-like candy made with beaten egg whites, sugar and nuts. It's called **seafoam** when brown sugar is substituted for the granulated sugar.

Dobos torte - a torte made of six to eight layers of sponge cake filled with chocolate buttercream and topped with a caramel glaze, created in the 1920s by the Hungarian pastry chef József Dobos.

dock - **1.** (v.) the technique of pricking dough to keep it flat and prevent it from puffing or bubbling up during baking. Professional kitchens use a tool called a docker to make multiple perforations in dough, giving crackers and pre-made pizza crusts their characteristic holes. **2.** (n.) see SORREL.

dog - although no member of the International Wine and Food Society could possibly entertain for a moment the thought of eating dog, it's on record that Hippocrates recommended dog's flesh as being of light digestion and excellent taste. The ancient Greeks were very partial to it; however, in ancient Rome, the patricians left dogs to be eaten by the poor. In China, dogs have long been specially fattened for human consumption and are a highly esteemed article of diet in some parts of the country. Whether Henry Du Pre Labouchere (1831–1912), the British politician and journalist, meant it or merely wished to shock his friends, he wrote that when he was in Paris during the siege of 1870, he enjoyed various breeds of dog and gave them the following critique: "Spaniel, like lamb; Poodle, by far the best; and Bulldog, coarse and tasteless."

dogfish - also **smooth dogfish, spiny dogfish, spur dog.** Any of a variety of small sharks, usually of the families Squalidae (spiny dogfish, now known as **Cape Shark**) and Triakidae (smooth dogfish). They are long and slim and weigh, on average, 25 pounds (11 kg). They are found in the waters of the Atlantic, Pacific and Mediterranean. The flesh is firm, white to pink, with a fairly rich flavor, boneless, like other sharks, so there is very little waste. Dogfish can be fried, baked or broiled. See also NURSEHOUND.

doggie bag - a bag or container offered in a restaurant for transporting leftovers home, presumably for the family dog to eat.

dogs in a blanket - see PIGS IN A BLANKET.

Dolcelatte - also **Gorgonzola dolce.** Italian for "sweet milk," a style of Gorgonzola cheese, but sweeter, creamier and milder than its original, as the name suggests, and a little more difficult to find.

dollarfish - see BUTTERFISH.

Dolly Varden - also **Dolly Varden char, Dolly Varden trout.** A fish, *Salvelinus malma* Waldbaum, related to trout and char, found in both saltwater and freshwater habitats in northeastern Asia and the Pacific Northwest area of the U.S. and Canada, related to the bull trout and often misidentified as such. It has flaky, mild, white flesh, like other trout and char, and is good baked, fried, broiled, etc. The name of the fish comes from a character in Charles Dickens' novel *Barnaby Rudge*, for the colorful dotted pattern on its skin, which imitates the flashy, colorful dress of the character.

dolma - pl. **dolmades.** Any of a variety of fruits, vegetables or leaves (especially grape leaves) stuffed with a savory filling and baked. The name comes from the Turkish word *dolmak*, meaning "to fill or be filled."

dolo - a type of millet beer made in Africa, it's brewed locally and varies considerably from one region to another and sometimes even within the same region. Neither hopped nor filtered, it's flavored with various bitter plants, such as sisal, castor oil, bean, cassia and sometimes pimiento and tobacco leaves. The sugary pulp of cassia is added to increase its alcoholic strength.

dolphin - also **dolphin fish.** See MAHI-MAHI.

Dom Pierre Pérignon - see profile on page 228.

donburi - the Japanese name for a bowl of cooked rice topped with any of a number of stir-fried, grilled or deep-fried foods. One of the most popular types of donburi is *oyako donburi*, which is topped with a mixture of cooked chicken and softly set scrambled egg (in Japanese, "oyako" means "parent and child," for the chicken and egg). Other *donburi* commonly found on Japanese menus are: *gyudon* (short for *gyu donburi*), topped with a mixture of stir-fried sliced beef, greens and pickled ginger; *tendon* (short for *tempura donburi*), topped with **tempura** shrimp and/or vegetables; and **katsudon** (short for *tonkatsu donburi*), topped with **tonkatsu.**

Dolly Varden

Dom Pierre Pérignon (1638–1715) - French Benedictine monk said to have "invented" champagne. Dom Pérignon was considered a specialist in winemaking, which is why the Catholic Church sent him to the Hautvillers Abbey in the Champagne region. The church owned most of the region's vineyards, and a powerful climate change during the 1490s had all but ruined the wines. The colder temperatures cut the primary fermentation short, and in the spring, a second fermentation made the wines effervescent, which was not considered a good attribute at the time. It was Dom Pérignon's assignment to rid the wine of its bubbles. In England, in the meantime, Charles II had begun to express his enjoyment of sparkling wine, and French taste followed suit almost immediately, which changed Dom Pérignon's orders abruptly. He was then asked to add *more* bubbles to the wine. One hundred years after Dom Pérignon's death, the Chandon family bought the Hautvillers Abbey and married into the Moët family, which owned the adjacent vineyard. Moët & Chandon became the world-renowned champagne producer; the company introduced Cuvée Dom Pérignon in 1936, marketed as the first prestige champagne.

doneness, steak - When you order a steak in a restaurant and the waiter asks how you want it cooked, there are accepted terms you can use to describe the degrees of doneness (see below). An easier and more convenient way to test for doneness than temperature is the touch test. The feel of the flesh at the base of your thumb is similar to that of cooked steak. With an open palm, the flesh at the base of the thumb feels like a steak done blue rare to rare. By touching the thumb to the index finger, it feels like a medium-rare steak. Next, by touching the thumb to the middle finger, the flesh feels like a steak cooked medium. By touching the thumb to the ring finger, it feels like a medium-well steak. And by touching the thumb to the pinkie, it feels like a well-done steak.

DEGREES OF DONENESS

blue rare - seared just on the outside and completely red on the inside, tending toward bluish red in the center, 130°F (54°C).

rare - seared more deeply than blue rare, but still red 75 percent of the way through, 130° to 140°F (54° to 60°C).

medium-rare - seared on the outside, with only 50 percent of the interior red, 140° to 145°F (60° to 63°C).

medium - seared on the outside and 25 percent pink inside, 145° to 150°F (63° to 66°C).

medium-well - cooked all the way through, with only a hint of pink in the center, 150° to 160°F (66° to 71°C).

well-done - cooked all the way through to an even brown, 160° to 170°F (71° to 77°C).

doner kebab - a Turkish version of the **shawarma.**

done to a turn - a synonym for the French term **à point,** meaning cooked to the perfect degree of doneness. The phrase was first recorded in the late 1700s, undoubtedly from the method of cooking meat over an open fire on a spit. The meat was placed on the spit and turned by hand over the fire hundreds of times over the course of several hours. When it was fully cooked and ready to eat, it was said to be "done to a turn." That meant the cook had turned the roast the exact number of times needed to cook it perfectly. Although this is an old-fashioned term, considering that most people don't own spits anymore, let alone cook meat over an open fire, it is still commonly used today to describe any food cooked perfectly to the tastes of the diner.

donut - see DOUGHNUT.

Doppelbock - a German beer much stronger than a simple **bock,** but not necessarily double the strength, as the German adjective *doppel*, meaning "double," implies. In Bavaria, the Italian monks of the St. Francis of Paula order brewed the original of this style in the 17th century, named Salvator, after the Savior. They were granted permission to sell their product by the court of Bavaria in 1780.

dorado - see MAHI-MAHI.

dosa - also **dosai.** A crêpe or pancake eaten in India for breakfast or as a side dish, crisp outside with a soft interior, slightly sour to the taste. Dosas are usually made from a combination of rice, lentils, water and fenugreek that is fermented, usually overnight, and then ground into a batter. The batter is then poured onto a hot griddle or pan and fried until crisp. There are many varieties of dosa, the most common of which is probably masala dosa, which is a dosa rolled around a savory vegetable curry or spiced potatoes.

dosage - see MÉTHODE CHAMPENOISE.

dot - to drop tiny bits of an ingredient all over the surface of a mixture, such as dropping small bits of butter on top of apple pie filling or scalloped potatoes. The butter melts into the other ingredients as the food cooks; covering the top with tiny dots ensures that there is butter flavor throughout the dish, rather than just here and there.

dou ban jiang - see CHILE BEAN PASTE.

double boiler - see BAIN-MARIE.

double cream - a thick, spoonable, extra-rich form of cream available in Britain. It contains 48 percent butterfat, compared with the standard 35 percent of North American whipping cream.

double-crème cheese - also **double-cream cheese.** A soft or semisoft cheese that contains 60 to 74 percent butterfat, more than regular cheeses but less than **triple-crème cheeses,** which contain 75 percent or higher butterfat. Examples of double-crème cheeses are **Havarti, blue castello** and **Petit Suisse.** Examples of triple-crème cheeses are **mascarpone, Boursault** and **Explorateur.**

double-double - a Canadian term for a cup of coffee with double cream and double sugar, commonly used when ordering in coffee shops. The term is a fairly recent invention and was only incorporated into the *Canadian Oxford Dictionary* in 2004.

double fillet - see FILLET.

double Gloucester - see GLOUCESTER.

double-smoked bacon - a large slab of bacon that has been smoked twice (or for an extra-long time) to give it a deep, rich, smoky flavor. Double-smoked bacon is excellent in **roulade** and German potato salad.

dough - a mixture made of flour and other ingredients, as in baking or the making of noodles, pliable and often worked by hand, as opposed to batter, which can be poured.

doughnut - also **donut.** A small, round or ring-shaped deep-fried cake of sweetened and leavened dough. Dutch housewives fried what they called *olykoeks* ("oil cakes"), but these were round or ball-shaped, without holes. The name "doughnut" was in use long before the invention of the hole, for Washington Irving described "a large dish of balls of sweetened dough fried in hog's fat and called dough nuts or *oly koeks*" in his book *Knickerbocker's History of New York*, published in 1809 (under the pseudonym of Dietrich Knickerbocker). It was a Maine sea captain, **Hanson Gregory,** who invented the doughnut with a hole. Because his mother's round doughnuts came out of the frying kettle still soft and uncooked in the center, he suggested removing the centers before the "nuts" were cooked. The resulting fried cakes were so much better that he began selling his mother's sugared and lifesaver-shaped doughnuts, and soon other New England cooks began cutting their dough the same way. Doughnuts were traditionally tossed in the air for children to catch on Mardi Gras, the day before Lent begins.

doughnut peach - also **donut peach.** A round, flattened variety of peach shaped like a doughnut with a depression in the middle where the stem is, sweet and white-fleshed. It is the descendent of a Chinese variety of flat peaches called Peento and often sold under the names "saucer peach," "Saturn peach" or "galaxy

doughnut peach

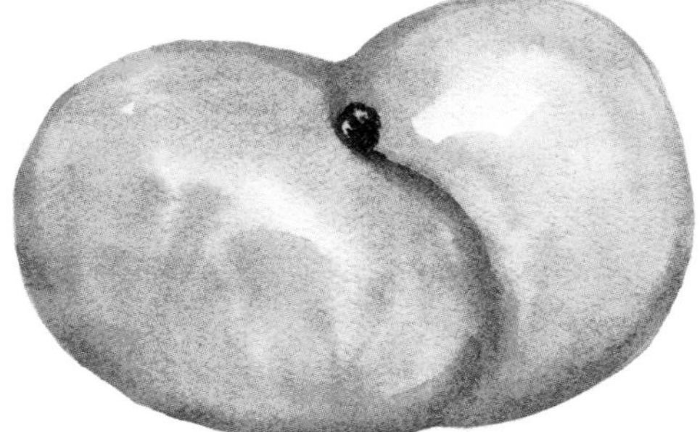

peach," because it's shaped like a UFO, the ringed planet or the Milky Way galaxy, respectively.

doux - a term used to describe Champagne that is quite sweet. The word means "sweet" in French. See also BRUT, DEMI-SEC, SEC.

dove - another, more genteel, name for a pigeon, sometimes used in recipe language, especially in fancy recipes that call for the bird.

Dover sole - see SOLE.

draft beer - also **draught beer, tap beer.** Drawn from a keg or cask, most draft beer is not pasteurized during brewing, unlike bottled or canned beers. See also BEER.

dragée - **1.** sugarcoated almonds, from the Latin *tragemata*, meaning "sweetmeats." See also CONFETTI, JORDAN ALMOND. 2. small candies, usually silver-colored, used for decorating cakes.

dragon and phoenix - any of a number of Chinese dishes that feature a combination of lobster and chicken, invariably served at Chinese weddings to symbolize the balance between the male (dragon) and female (phoenix) roles in marriage. In Chinese, the word for lobster literally means "dragon shrimp," and chicken are frequently referred to as "phoenix" on restaurant menus, such as the popular Chinese dish of "phoenix feet," or chicken feet. The dragon and phoenix are a popular theme for many of the foods and items at a Chinese wedding, and many couples choose wedding cakes or sweets with dragon and phoenix designs to represent the balanced, yin-yang nature of the marriage relationship.

dragon fruit - also **pitahaya, pitaya, strawberry pear.** The sweet, ovoid fruit of the tall, Central American cactus *Hylocereus undatus*. Also called strawberry pear, it develops from spectacular white flowers that bloom at night. The pink fruit sports pointed, leaf-like green scales; inside, juicy, white flesh is scattered with small black seeds. It is made into juice or syrup or eaten, chilled, as a fresh fruit. See also CACTUS.

dragon's eye - see LONGAN.

dragon tongue bean - a kind of snap bean, similar to a regular green bean but with a mottled purplish red and white pod that loses most of its color when cooked. Dragon tongue beans can be cooked and eaten in the same way as green beans.

Dragon Well tea - see TEA.

drain - **1.** to extract the liquid from a mixture by allowing it to run off, usually by placing the food in a sieve or colander. **2.** to place a greasy or oily food, such as cooked bacon or fried fish, on absorbent paper or paper towels to remove some of the excess fat.

drake - a male duck. See DUCK.

dram - technically, an amount of liquid equal to $\frac{1}{8}$ ounce (3.7 mL), but colloquially used to mean a small amount of liquid to drink. The term is frequently used when referring to alcohol, especially in Scotland, where one might be offered "a wee dram of Scotch."

Drambuie - a Scotch-based liqueur whose name comes from the Gaelic expression *an dram buidheach*, meaning "the drink that satisfies." Its formula is the property of the MacKinnon family, who keeps it a secret; they registered the name in 1892 and only launched the drink commercially in 1906. Bonnie Prince Charlie supposedly gave the recipe to Capt. John MacKinnon in 1746, when MacKinnon sheltered him on the Isle of Skye after his defeat by the English at the Battle of Culloden. All that is known for certain is that the liquor contains Scotch whiskey and heather honey.

draught beer - see DRAFT BEER.

draw - **1.** to heat butter until it is melted and the solids separate from the oil, at which point the butter oil is drained off and called

dragon fruit

clarified butter. 2. also **eviscerate.** To pull out or otherwise remove the entrails of an animal to be cooked, such as poultry or fish.

drawn butter - see CLARIFIED BUTTER.

drawn poultry - see DRESSED POULTRY.

dredge - to coat food with flour, bread crumbs, etc., especially before frying.

dredger - a shaker with a fine screen on top or a perforated lid, used for dusting foods with a dry, powdery ingredient, such as flour, cocoa powder, ground cinnamon or confectioner's sugar.

dregs - see LEES.

dress - **1.** to drizzle and/or toss with a dressing, as in a salad. **2.** to prepare meat, poultry, fish or game for cooking by **drawing,** scaling, skinning, plucking and/or trimming it.

dressed poultry - poultry from which the feathers and blood have been removed after slaughter. The term **drawn poultry** applies to a dressed bird with head, feet and entrails removed.

dressing - **1.** a usually cold sauce used on salads. See also SALAD DRESSING. **2.** also **stuffing**. A mixture often containing bread crumbs or cubes, forcemeat, oats, potatoes or rice, along with seasonings and dried or fresh fruit, herbs and nuts, used to stuff meat, seafood (such as squid), poultry or vegetables.

dried baker's yeast - also **active dry yeast.** Bakers' yeast is used for the same purposes as fresh yeast, but keeps for a much longer period. It is manufactured in factories and is almost always based in a solution of molasses and water. See also YEAST.

dried beef - see CREAMED CHIPPED BEEF.

dried fruit - fruit that has been preserved by removing all natural moisture. See also FRUIT LEATHER.

drippings - the liquid left in the bottom of a roasting pan after roasting a large cut of meat, such as a whole turkey or a beef roast. This combination of juices and fat is often used to make a gravy or sauce to go with the meat. In the case of a traditional English roast beef, the drippings are used to cook **Yorkshire pudding.**

drisheen - a specialty of Cork, in southwestern Ireland, a kind of sausage made from sheep's blood mixed with milk and seasonings. The name comes from the Gaelic *drisin*.

drizzle - to slowly pour a liquid in a fine stream.

drop cookie - made by dropping spoonfuls of batter or dough onto a baking sheet, as opposed to cutting cookie dough from a roll or shaping them by hand.

drum - any of several fish related to the **croaker** that make a drumming noise, especially in the mating season, such as the saltwater black drum and redfish, and the freshwater sheephead.

drumstick - the meaty lower half of a turkey or chicken leg, so named because it resembles a mallet used to beat a drum.

drupe fruits

drupe fruit - a term used to describe a category of fruits, those that have a thick, fleshy layer surrounding a single pit or stone, all covered with a layer of skin. Most drupe fruits, such as cherries, peaches, nectarines, plums and apricots, have thin, pliable skins and soft, juicy flesh surrounding the pit, which is not edible. Others, such as almonds or coconuts, have fibrous or tough flesh and a hard shell, and the almond's pit is an edible nut. Smaller drupe fruits, such as raspberries and blackberries, are called drupelets or **aggregate fruits.**

dry - a term used to describe **still wine** that is not sweet. A fully dry wine contains no residual sugar. The French word for dry is *sec*. See also OFF-DRY, SEMIDRY.

dry cure - to rub a piece of meat, usually a ham, with salt, sugar, sodium nitrate (and/or sodium nitrite) and seasonings and let it stand for a number of days, so that the flesh cures, preventing the formation of harmful bacteria and concentrating the flavor of the meat. As the ham stands, the dry mixture mixes with the juices of the meat to penetrate it all the way through. The ham is then washed to remove the salty coating before it is air-dried or smoked. See also COUNTRY HAM, HAM, WET CURE.

dry-cured olive - see OLIVE.

dry ice - frozen carbon dioxide, often used as a packing material for shipping highly perishable foods, such as meat. Because dry ice is frozen at –109.3°F (–78.5°C), it has twice the cooling power of ice made from water. It is also more convenient than regular ice, because it disappears into carbon dioxide gas as it degrades, rather than melting into a pool of water. Dry ice can also extend the life of regular ice by keeping it colder longer. There are food-grade forms of dry ice available that can be added to drinks to make them bubble and give off clouds of fog. This is especially popular at Halloween, when people make punches that bubble and steam like a cauldron of witches' brew.

Dry Jack - an aged **Monterey Jack** cheese, a firm, yellow cow's milk cheese with a sharp, full flavor, unlike the mild mass-produced Monterey Jack found in supermarkets. Dry Jack is an excellent grating cheese, like Parmesan, and is delicious served with bread, dried dates and sherry. See also SONOMA JACK.

dry measure - a measuring cup made of metal or plastic with a sturdy handle on the side, used for measuring dry or solid ingredients, such as flour, sugar, grains, solid butter, etc. Dry measures come in graduated sets or in a variety of yields, such as $\frac{1}{4}$ cup (50 mL), $\frac{1}{3}$ cup (75 mL), $\frac{1}{2}$ cup (125 mL) and 1 cup (250 mL). It's especially handy to have a set that includes extra cups for $\frac{1}{8}$ cup (25 mL), $\frac{2}{3}$ cup (150 mL) and $\frac{3}{4}$ cup (175 mL). A dry measure should not be used for liquid ingredients because liquids do not fill the space the same way, and the yield will be different. To fill the cup with the proper amount of a granular dry ingredient, such as flour or sugar, dip the cup into the ingredient, then level off the top with the flat back of a knife blade. Alternatively, spoon the ingredient into the cup until it is overflowing, then sweep off the excess with the back of the knife. See also LIQUID MEASURE.

dry milk - also **dried milk.** See POWDERED MILK.

dry mustard - see MUSTARD.

dry rub - see RUB.

dry sausage - a sausage that has been air-dried and is considered ready to eat; may be smoked or unsmoked. Unlike raw, fresh sausages, dry sausages need no further cooking to make them edible. Some rely on lactic acid bacteria to cure them, leaving them with a tangy flavor, while others do not. As they air-dry, these sausages progressively lose more moisture, resulting in more concentrated meat inside the casing. A semidry sausage weighs only about 70 percent of its original, or "green," weight after drying, and a fully dried sausage will weigh about 60 percent of its original weight at the end of the process. Some well-known examples of dry sausage are **chorizo, frizzes, pepperoni** and Genoa **salami.** Well-known semidry sausages are **cervelat, mortadella** and **summer sausage.**

Du Barry - the name given to any dishes with cauliflower as a main ingredient, named after the Comtesse du Barry (born Jeanne Bécu, 1746–1793), who was one of the mistresses of King Louis XV of France.

Dublin Bay prawn - also **langoustine.** A relative of the lobster that looks like a miniature version of its larger cousin, cooked in much the same way as a lobster: steamed or boiled, then stuffed and made into a variety of dishes. See also PRAWN.

dry measure

Ducasse, Alain (1956–) - French chef and architect of a hospitality empire studded with Michelin stars. Ducasse was born in the southwest of France and began his career by apprenticing in his native region. Next, he forced his way into Michel Guérard's kitchen, where positions were always in demand, but openings were rare. In 1977, Ducasse began working with Roger Vergé at Moulin de Mougins, and a year later under Alain Chapel, who became his mentor and "spiritual master." In 1980, Alain Ducasse came back to Mougins and Vergé, who put him in charge of one of his restaurants, a public vote of confidence for his abilities as a cook and a leader. This led to Ducasse's appointment as chef of La Terrasse, where he won his first two Michelin stars in 1984. In 1987, he was asked to take on the Louis XV restaurant in Monaco's Hôtel de Paris; in just under three years, he won three stars, the first time Michelin awarded a hotel restaurant. In 1995, Ducasse restored a 12-bedroom country inn in Provence, which garnered a Michelin star. A year later, Ducasse opened his first namesake restaurant in Paris, which was awarded three stars, just eight months after opening. At 40, he became the first six-star chef in history, with his two restaurants 588 miles (946 km) apart.

In Paris in December 1998, he opened Spoon, Food & Wine, his first concept restaurant (which he would later adapt for Mauritius in 1999, London in 2000, Saint Tropez in 2002, and Hong Kong and Gstaad in 2003). In the 12-month period beginning January 1999, Ducasse accomplished what few of the most successful of his contemporaries were able to do in a lifetime. In February, he took over as President of the Château & Hôtels de France chain. By midyear, he debuted Bar & Boeuf in Monte Carlo, his second concept restaurant. In November, he opened ADF, a state-of-the-art international training center for chefs and hospitality professionals. In December 1999, he took on his second hotel project, an 18th-century 10-bedroom mansion in Provence.

The first year of the new millennium was similarly prodigious. In New York City that June, he opened his second eponymous restaurant. In Paris, he opened two new venues: in September, he moved his eponymous Parisian restaurant to the Hôtel Plaza Athénée and, in December, opened a restaurant called 59 Poincare. North Americans who had followed his European accomplishments watched the New York City restaurant closely, convinced it wouldn't succeed. The restaurant was an over-the-top luxurious room of only 65 seats, with a single seating per night. White-gloved waiters cut tea leaves at the table for a pot of tea; purse benches keep women's handbags off the table and the floor; and the mineral water sommelier makes discerning recommendations for high-end waters. Both Alain Ducasse New York and Plaza Athénée were awarded three stars. He is now the world?s first nine-star chef.

Ducasse continues to develop hotels and restaurant ventures (from the most traditional, such as bistro Aux Lyonnais, to the most modern, such as the bakery-grocery store named BE, both in Paris). In 2005, he opened his second restaurant in Tokyo: Benoit, after the successful opening a year before of his fourth signature restaurant in partnership with Chanel Tokyo called Beige, Coco Chanel's favorite color.

Dubonnet - a "tonic apéritif" introduced to Paris in 1846, made with either red or white wine (for red or white Dubonnet) infused with **cinchona** bark during a second fermentation. Cinchona bark contains **quinine,** the primary ingredient in tonic. The red variety is the more popular of the two. Dubonnet is now also made in New Jersey.

Ducasse, Alain - see profile above.

duchess potatoes - a purée of cooked potatoes, egg yolks and butter, which can be eaten as is or formed into small shapes and baked until golden.

duchess soup - a rich, old-fashioned soup, popular in the 19th century and early 20th century, made of milk, onions, eggs, flour and cheese, seasoned simply with salt and pepper. After the onions are cooked, they are pressed through a sieve, making the final soup relatively smooth and creamy. Some recipes call for the addition of finely diced carrots and celery and a pinch of **mace** for extra flavor.

duck (mallard)

duck - wild or domestic web-footed birds. All ducks can swim, but it makes all the difference to the gastronome whether they swim (and still more where they feed) in freshwater or saltwater.

The Chinese domesticated ducks 4,000 years ago, by taming wild species or hatching eggs. In China, the gratification of eating duck is strengthened by the poetic and symbolic association of the bird (for instance, it represents conjugal fidelity). The Egyptians tamed ducks that swam on the Nile.

In North America, the most common and best of the wild ducks is the **mallard,** the ancestor of the majority of breeds of domesticated ducks. Some farmers still produce mallards on a small scale: duck lovers rear the Long Island, Aylesbury and Peking types. The most famous breed of duck in America is certainly the Long Island duckling, first brought to New York from China by a New York merchant in 1873. There are several other types, including teal, widgeon, shoveler, pochard and scaup. They have a moderately thick layer of fat underneath the skin, but the flesh itself is not particularly fatty. In culinary terms, the male is called a drake, while the female is a duck; in French, the masculine forms, *canard* and *caneton*, are always used for duck and duckling, whether male or female, and the feminine forms, *cane* and *canette*, are seldom used on menus.

duck à l'orange - a classic French dish of whole duck roasted with a combination of orange juice and spices. Some recipes call for orange juice concentrate, orange marmalade or orange liqueur instead of the juice. The orange is thought to offset the greasiness of the rich, dark duck meat. In French, it is known as *canard à l'orange*.

duck confit - see DUCK FAT.

duck egg - see BALUT.

duck fat - the semifirm yellowish fat **rendered** from duck skin or made from the drippings of a roast duck, a popular gourmet cooking fat in Europe, especially France. Duck fat has a rich flavor that enhances both meat and vegetable dishes. It is a primary component of the popular French dish **duck confit.** The fat is easy to render at home, but there are now tinned or packaged varieties available in gourmet stores. Mixed with garlic, the fat is transformed into **Gascony butter,** a flavoring used to enhance soups, stews and **cassoulet.** See also GOOSE FAT, SCHMALTZ.

duck press - an elaborate tableside tool essential for making the classic French dish **pressed duck** or *canard à la presse*, a tall cylinder with a spigot at the bottom mounted underneath a pressing plate that can be lowered by turning a screw at the top of the device. The succulent breasts and legs of the very rare roasted duck are removed, then the remaining carcass is placed inside the cylinder. The legs go back into the oven to continue cooking, and the breasts are sliced thinly. The pressing plate is lowered onto the carcass and incrementally screwed down to squeeze out all the duck's juices. The juices are added to a red wine reduction that is simmering on a hot plate nearby and cooked briefly. The sauce is enriched with butter and cognac, cooked until smooth and thickened, then served over the slices of duck breast and the crisp legs.

duck sauce - see PLUM SAUCE.

duff - a boiled or steamed pudding that contains flour, eggs, spices and fruits, either dried (such as figs) or fresh (such as plums or peaches). The mixture is either steamed in a pudding mold or boiled in a white muslin pudding bag. Duffs are extremely popular fare in Newfoundland, Canada.

du jour - a menu term meaning "of the day," as in *soup du jour*.

dukkah - a traditional Egyptian specialty composed of roasted or grilled nuts and spices crushed together. Usually eaten with pita bread dipped first in olive oil, it is popular as an appetizer or snack and may be sold in paper cones as a street food, to be sprinkled over bread. It may also be used as a coating for poultry or fish. Although dukkah mixtures are highly individual, they often contain hazelnuts and cumin and sesame seeds.

dulce de leche - a rich, very sweet caramel made from milk and sugar, boiled down until thick and sticky, often used as a dessert on its own but also popular as a topping for ice cream or as a filling for **alfajores** in South America. It is similar to the Mexican caramel **cajeta,** but is made with cow's milk instead of goat's milk. Its name means "sweet made of milk" and is sometimes called by the name "milk jam."

dulse - a coarse seaweed that is rose or purplish when fresh and dark brown when dry, harvested along the coast of the British Isles, Iceland and in Canada's Atlantic provinces. Usually sold dried, it can be cooked like spinach or chewed like candy or gum. The name comes from the Irish and Gaelic word *duileasg*.

Dumas, Alexandre - see profile below.

dumpling - **1.** loosely shaped balls of dough cooked by being dropped into liquids, such as soups or stews. **2.** a dough-wrapped parcel of savory filling, common in Asian cuisine, usually boiled separately and added to soups, or boiled and then fried, to be eaten as an appetizer or side dish. **3.** a baked dessert made by wrapping fruit in a sweet pastry dough, often served with a sauce, cream or ice cream.

dumpling wrappers - squares or circles of thinly rolled dough, used for wrapping around savory fillings to make Asian-style dumplings, such as **gyoza, potstickers** or **wontons.** Dumpling wrappers are usually made of nothing more than flour and water, but some contain eggs to give them a golden hue and chewier texture. Rice flour or wheat flour may be used, depending on the desired texture of the finished wrapper and the traditional staples of a particular cuisine; for example, Chinese wrappers are usually made with wheat flour, whereas Thai wrappers are often made from rice flour. See also GYOZA SKINS, WONTON WRAPPERS.

Dundee cake - a traditional, rich fruitcake from Dundee, Scotland, usually served at Christmastime in Britain. Dundee cake is a light-color fruitcake made with candied citrus peel and dried fruits, such as currants and sultanas, and sometimes a generous soaking of whiskey or rum. The top is covered with blanched almonds, often arranged in distinctive concentric circles.

Dundee marmalade - first made by Scottish grocer James Keiller in the town of Dundee in the 1700s. A Spanish ship had left a cargo of Seville oranges at Tayside's dock for sale at a very cheap price, and Keiller took home a cartload, but they were too bitter to eat, so Keiller's wife, Janet, a kitchen worker, turned the fruit and the rind into jam. Marmalade in Scotland had been made from quince and other fruits for centuries, but Keiller's was the first commercial marmalade. He sold his first batch in a few hours, bought some more of the bitter oranges and soon after began to market his product in white stone pots as "Keiller's Marmelade." See also MARMALADE.

Dungeness crab - see CRAB.

Dunlop - a Scottish Cheddar-style cheese made from cow's milk, with a rather bland, buttery taste, often eaten with buttered oatcakes.

durable-life declaration - SEE EXPIRATION DATE.

durian - a very large fruit, *Durio zibethinus*, native to southeast Asia. Probably one of the biggest fruits in the world, it can weigh up to more than 10 pounds (5 kg), and the tree itself can climb to 130 feet (40 m), belonging to the same family as the baobab and the cotton tree. The fruit is entirely covered with sharp prickles, and its soft, cream-color pulp is delicious, but

Dumas, Alexandre (1802–1870) - famous French novelist, author of *The Three Musketeers* and *The Count of Monte Cristo*; he also wrote a book on cookery, *Le Grand dictionnaire de cuisine* (The Great Dictionary of Cuisine), which was published after his death.

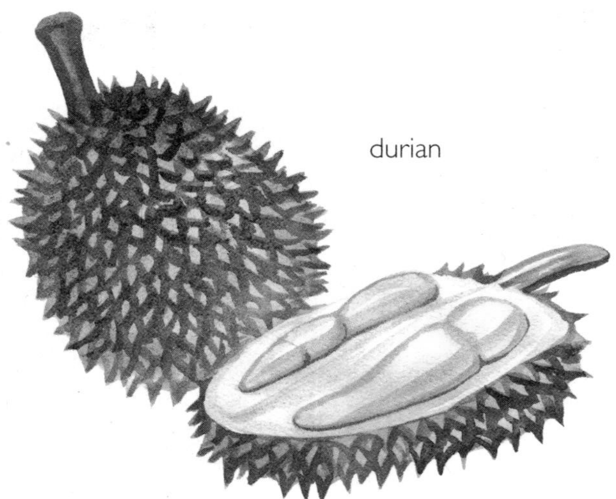

its smell is always very strong and becomes putrid when the fruit is overripe. The seeds can also be roasted and eaten like chestnuts.

durum - a very hard wheat used in making **semolina,** from the Latin *durus*, meaning "hard."

Dusseldorf mustard - see MUSTARD.

dust - to lightly coat a food with a powder, such as flour or confectioner's sugar.

dust balls - see MEXICAN WEDDING CAKES.

Dutchie - a flat, square, glazed doughnut studded with raisins, invented by Tim Horton, a Canadian hockey player who started the ubiquitous Canadian coffee and doughnut franchise of the same name in 1964. The Dutchie is still on Tim Hortons menu and has popped up on other doughnut shop menus as well.

Dutch loaf - also **old-fashioned loaf.** A mixture of coarsely ground beef and pork seasoned with a blend of spices, fashioned into a large loaf, smoked, and sliced thinly.

Dutch oven - a large, heavy pot, especially one made of cast iron, with a tight-fitting lid used for stewing and braising, dating back to American colonial days.

Dutch-process cocoa powder - also **European-process cocoa powder.** This cocoa powder is made by extracting the cocoa butter from chocolate liquor, which is then treated with alkaline substances, including sodium carbonate, sodium hydroxide, potassium or magnesium, to make it soluble (a process also called solubilization). The alkalized chocolate liquor is then pressed and ground in the same way as American cocoa powder. See also CHOCOLATE.

duxelles - a mixture of finely chopped mushrooms, shallots and herbs sautéed in butter. The derivation of the word is disputed: some claim that the name "duxelles" was created at Uzel, a small town in the Côtes-du-Nord, in France. Others attribute it to Louis Chalon du Blé, Marquis d'Uxelle, a renowned gourmet who lived in the latter part of the 17th century. His chef and attendant, **François Pierre La Varenne,** the influential cookbook author and one of the founders of classical French cooking, may have invented it.

e
eggs

Earl Grey tea - black tea flavored with oil of **bergamot.** The English Earl **Charles Grey** served as Prime Minister under William IV and left a political legacy that included helping to end slavery all over the British Empire. According to folklore, the earl received the recipe for the blending of the brew in the 1830s as a gift from a Chinese government official whose life had been saved by a British diplomat.

earth almond - also **earthnut.** See CHUFA.

earthenware - cookware made from natural clay and fired until hard and heatproof; can be glazed or unglazed. Earthenware retains heat well, although it takes a long time to heat up at first, and is suitable for dishes that need prolonged cooking, such as slow-cooked stews or baked beans (traditionally made in earthenware **bean pots**). Glazed earthenware is nonporous and cleans up nicely without retaining any odors, making it suitable for a variety of foods. Unglazed earthenware is often used to make **clay bakers** and must be soaked prior to use. It will absorb odors and flavors, so it is best used for the same types of dishes over and over.

easter egg radishes

Easter egg radish - a variety of spring radish harvested when small, the rounded roots tinted brilliant shades of red, pink, purple and white. Easter egg radishes are crisp and have a mild radish flavor, making them a perfect colorful addition to salads. See also RADISH.

Eastern oyster - see OYSTER.

Eastern sandwich - a sandwich containing an omelet made with diced onions, peppers and cheese. See also WESTERN SANDWICH.

eat crow - a phrase meaning to suffer a humiliating, humbling defeat in front of others, with the connotation that one has to swallow one's pride and admit the mistake. Because crows are carnivores, often carrion eaters, their flesh is foul-tasting and rank, much like the experience of accepting humiliation in front of others. The phrase was not recorded until the middle of the 19th century, and it then took the form of "eat boiled crow." An equivalent expression in Britain is "eat **humble pie**."

eau de vie - also **aqua vitae, fruit brandy.** French for "water of life," a highly prized colorless, **dry** alcohol made from whole fruit, not just fruit juice, with no added flavorings, colorings or sweeteners. Eau de vie should not be confused with liqueur, which is sweetened, fruit-flavored brandy or a plain neutral spirit with added sweetener, fruit flavor and coloring. See also BARACK, CALVADOS, FRAMBOISE, GRAPPA, KIRSCH, SLIVOVITZ.

ebelskiver iron - see AEBLESKIVE.

Eccles cake - small and round like a **Banbury cake,** made of puff pastry filled with currants, dried fruit, sugar, butter and spices.

éclair - a small cream-filled pastry made with **choux pastry,** appearing for the first time during the 16th century. The batter used to make the delicious finger-like shell is called *pâte à choux*. It was not until the 19th century, however, that variations appeared in French and English pastry shops. The French version, *éclair au chocolat,* is filled with chocolate-flavored pastry cream and topped with chocolate **fondant** icing. The English version is filled with vanilla whipped cream and finished with melted chocolate. The name is a literal translation of "lightning flash." No one knows exactly why, but some assume that it refers to the shine of its icing or the baker's scolding that these pastries be yanked from the oven and served "in a flash." The name may also refer to the lightning speed at which they're consumed.

E. coli - the abbreviation and common name for hundreds of different strains of the bacterium *Escherichia coli.* Most strains of this bacterium are harmless, living in the intestines of healthy animals (and humans), but the strain *E. coli* 0157:H7 can be deadly to humans, who usually ingest it in contaminated meats (especially ground beef) and unpasteurized milk. *E. coli* 0157:H7 is a major cause of food-borne illness, causing severe bloody diarrhea, abdominal cramps and dehydration. It is deadliest in infants and the elderly, whose immune systems are weaker than those of healthy adults.

Two to 7 percent of all cases of *E. coli* 0157:H7 poisoning lead to an illness called hemolytic uremic syndrome, in which red blood cells are destroyed and the kidneys fail. People with this syndrome must be treated immediately in an intensive care unit of a hospital; about 3 to 5 percent of people treated will die, despite efforts to save them.

The best ways to prevent *E. coli* 0157:H7 poisoning is to cook all meats (especially ground meats) thoroughly; avoid unpasteurized dairy products, juice and cider; wash all produce thoroughly; and immediately disinfect all surfaces that come into contact with raw food, especially meat. Hamburgers are a common culprit, leading to *E. coli* 0157:H7 poisoning being called "hamburger disease." The safest way to ensure that a hamburger is cooked all the way through, killing this bacteria, is to insert a digital thermometer into the thickest part and make sure that it reads 160°F (75°C). If it does not, it needs to be cooked further until all bacteria are destroyed.

Edam - a famous Dutch cheese made from partially skimmed cow's milk and sold in a ball shape coated with red wax.

edamame - also **beer bean, edible soybean, garden soybean, green soybean, immature soybean, vegetable soybean.** Japanese name for green soybeans. Edamame are often called "beer beans" because they are a favorite hot-weather dish in Japan, boiled and salted and served with a cold glass of beer.

Edelfaule - see BOTRYTIS CINEREA.

edible flowers - safe for consumption only when grown organically and pesticide-free. They can be used to add flavor and as a garnish in salads, soups, desserts and beverages. The most popular include **begonias, calendula, chive blossoms, daisies, geranium leaves, Johnny-jump-ups, lavender, marigolds, nasturtiums, pansies, roses, squash blossoms** and **violets.** The Roman emperor Nero spent the equivalent of $16,000 on roses for a single banquet celebrating Rosalia, the Roman festival of roses. His guests ate rose puddings, breathed air scented with rose oil and reclined on pillows stuffed with rose petals.

Louis XIV of France developed a staggering appetite for flowers. During the 1672 season alone, 10,000 tuberoses were grown in Avignon and transported to Versailles. Columbines, carnations, pinks, irises, lilies and peonies were shipped in from all over Europe to please his fancy.

edible soybean - see EDAMAME.

Edinburgh rock - a powdery-textured Scottish candy shaped into short, thick sticks, available in pastel hues and various (usually fruity) flavors. This popular sweet is sold to millions of tourists every year at Edinburgh Castle in Scotland and is named for the imposing rock on which the castle stands.

EDTA - the less tongue-twisting abbreviation of ethylenediaminetetraacetic acid, a preservative used to prolong the shelf life of certain perishable foods, such as mayonnaise and salad dressings. This chemical prevents metals that come into contact with the food during processing from reacting with components in the food and causing it to go rancid. It also binds with trace amounts of metals in the food to remove any metallic taste. EDTA is also used as a treatment for lead poisoning, as it binds with lead molecules in the body, allowing them to be excreted safely.

eel - a snake-like fish of the genus *Anguilla*, popular in Europe and Japan, with a long, slender body, poorly developed fins and rich, firm, sweet flesh. See also ELVER.

effervescent - a word used to describe beverages that release bubbles of carbon dioxide when they are exposed to air. Champagne and other sparkling wines are naturally effervescent as a result of the natural fermentation of yeasts, whereas soft drinks are often **carbonated** artificially with pressurized carbon dioxide to make them fizzy.

egg - the oval-shaped reproductive body of birds. Long before Christianity, the Hebrews, Assyrians, Egyptians, Persians, Greeks, Romans and others used eggs on occasions of pomp and

EGG SIZES AND GRADES

In the U.S., eggs are sold by weight per dozen. Eggs are graded AA, A, B and dirty, depending on the quality of their shell, the size of their air cell and yolk and the firmness of their whites. Only grade AA, A and B eggs make it to supermarket shelves. They fall into the following size categories.

peewee - 15 ounces per dozen

small - 18 ounces per dozen

medium - 21 ounces per dozen

large - 24 ounces per dozen

extra-large - 27 ounces per dozen

jumbo - 30 ounces per dozen

In Canada, eggs are also sold by weight, but each egg is weighed individually in its shell, with specific weights sold under specific names. The eggs are graded A, B or C, using the same parameters as the U.S. Grade A eggs are the highest quality and the type sold in grocery stores.

peewee - less than 42 grams

small - 42 to 48 grams

medium - 49 to 55 grams

large - 56 to 62 grams

extra-large - 63 to 69 grams

jumbo - 70 grams or more

ceremony. To them, the egg symbolized the universe and was presented to their gods as an offering. The outer shell represented the limitless sky, the inner layer of skin the air, the white of the egg the waters and the yolk the earth. At one time, in ancient Rome, it was forbidden to eat eggs; the egg was regarded as a potential chicken and therefore too valuable to be eaten. Fortunately, the Romans eventually discarded their proscription and enjoyed eggs with everything from rose petals to fowl's brain. Starting early in the Christian era, the symbol of coloring eggs at Easter meant that the salvation of the world was bought with the blood of Christ. In the 9th century, the church banned the eating of eggs during Lent, during which time the eggs were collected and decorated and saved until Easter.

The consumer who pays a premium for a certain color of shell is wasting money. The color of the shell is in no way related to quality of the egg. Nor do brown eggs have darker yolks, as many people believe. The color of the yolk is influenced chiefly, if not entirely, by feed. Egg producers usually feed sufficient grains to give a yolk a medium intensity of color; if not, the yolk will be dark and watery. Most egg experts insist that newly laid eggs are the hardest to peel, so you can take comfort in the fact that your eggs are fresh if you struggle with the shell. When separating eggs, make sure that the egg whites are free of fat. If there is any egg yolk in the whites, they will not beat to the maximum volume. Also note that egg whites whip better at room temperature.

The **egg white,** also called **albumen**, is the thick, clear liquid surrounding the yolk. It contains about half of the protein in the egg and a large amount of water. The **egg yolk** is the yellow orb of liquid in the center of the egg, which contains the balance of the protein, much less water and a large amount of fat. It is also highly nutritious because it contains a variety of vitamins and minerals, including vitamins A, B_{12}, C, D and E; calcium; folate; and iron.

egg barley - see FARFEL.

egg beater - see ROTARY MIXER.

egg coddler - a small, lidded porcelain cup used to **coddle** a combination of egg, cream and seasonings, often placed in a pan filled with hot water so that the food inside cooks slowly and gently. An egg coddler is sometimes called by the old-fashioned name "pipkin," the name for a small, lidded earthenware jar, often with a handle on the side.

egg cream - originally produced in New York, a soda fountain beverage, whose foam-covered head and rich consistency suggest it holds both eggs and cream, although it actually contains neither. It was first invented at the turn of the century, when eggs were fairly costly; an egg cream is made from chocolate syrup, ice-cold milk and a smidgen of seltzer water.

egg cups

egg cup - a tiny, footed cup designed to hold a soft-boiled egg. The top of the egg is sliced off with **egg scissors** and the soft interior scooped out with a spoon and eaten with toast.

egg drop soup - a Chinese specialty made from chicken broth, with chicken or pork, dried shiitake mushrooms and other ingredients. Just before serving, beaten egg is added to the hot soup.

egg foo yong - also **egg foo yung, egg fu yung.** A classic Chinese-American recipe, a pancake-shaped omelet, made by combining eggs with various foods, such as bean sprouts, water chestnuts and chicken, beef, pork or shrimp and then pouring into a skillet and frying until golden brown. It's similar to a Cantonese dish of the same name, which is cooked in a ladle to give it a deflated spherical shape and served in a gravy-like brown sauce.

eggfruit - see MAMEY SAPOTA.

egg in a basket - see TOAD IN THE HOLE.

egg mushroom - see CHANTERELLE.

eggnog - a classic Christmas-season beverage of beaten egg yolks and sugar, spiced with nutmeg and spiked with spirits (often rum, but also bourbon, brandy, rye whiskey or sherry). It may have evolved from English **posset;** but Americans can claim eggnog as their own. Records show it first being served in a Philadelphia tavern in 1796. Ever the generalist, George Washington added brandy, rum, rye and sherry to his. See also TOM AND JERRY.

egg noodles - see NOODLES.

egg piercer - a kitchen gadget with a hole in the center that encloses a sharp metal spike, used for piercing the shell of an egg before boiling. The wide end of the egg is placed over the hole and pushed down onto the spike so that it pierces the shell. This tiny "pinpoint" hole allows the escape of tiny bubbles that form inside the egg as it boils, which would otherwise force their way out by cracking the shell.

eggplant - also **aubergine.** Botanically a fruit, *Solanum melongena*, a member of the nightshade family, but most often used as a vegetable; comes in purple, green, white, lavender and pink. Cooks everywhere disagree about whether or not an eggplant should be peeled. But it's important to note that an overripe eggplant, or one that has been stored for a long time, will have a tough skin that won't soften during cooking, so it is generally a good idea to peel it. There is also disagreement about salting eggplants. Once done to rid them of their bitterness, modern farming methods have just about eliminated that problem. It's true, however, that salting eggplants before cooking will reduce the amount of oil absorbed during frying.

The first mention of its cultivation was in China in 5 BC, and it's thought to have been eaten in India long before that time. The Moors introduced the eggplant to Spain some 1,200 years ago, and it was grown in Andalusia. It's likely the Moors also introduced it to Italy and, possibly from there, to other parts of southern

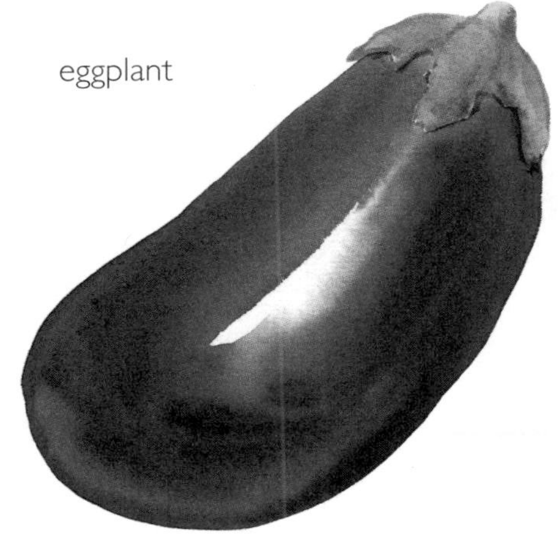
eggplant

EGGPLANT VARIETIES

American eggplant - see WESTERN EGGPLANT.

apple green eggplant - a newer American variety developed in the 1960s, round and bright green, about the size of a baseball.

Asian eggplant - also **Chinese eggplant, Japanese eggplant, Oriental eggplant.** Narrow and long, with pinkish, white, striped purple and white or all-purple skin, tender and sweet. The lighter-color varieties tend to fall under the Chinese name, while the darker purple ones are often labeled Japanese.

baby eggplant - see ITALIAN EGGPLANT.

Chinese eggplant - see ASIAN EGGPLANT.

cluster eggplant - see PEA EGGPLANT.

Filipino eggplant - pale to deep green, long and thin or small and oval, with mild, creamy flesh.

globe eggplant - see WESTERN EGGPLANT.

Italian eggplant - also **baby eggplant.** A smaller version of **Western eggplant,** deep purple and pear-shaped, with delicate skin and flavor.

Japanese eggplant - see ASIAN EGGPLANT.

Oriental eggplant - see ASIAN EGGPLANT.

pea eggplant - also **cluster eggplant.** A tiny, green Thai variety the size of a cherry, usually sold in bunches on the branches on which they grow, frequently used whole in curries.

striped European eggplant - a catchall term for a number of different varieties from Italy and Spain, such as Rosa Bianca and Listada de Gandia, rounded with thick, striped pinkish or purple and white skin and creamy flesh.

Thai eggplant - round, grape- to golf-ball-size, lime green to yellow in color (often striped), with mild, sweet flesh containing a large number of seeds.

Western eggplant - also **American eggplant, globe eggplant.** Typical North American supermarket eggplant, large and shiny, lavender to blackish purple, in a plump, rounded pear shape.

white eggplant - another type of Asian eggplant, can be long and thin or small and egg-shaped, usually dense-fleshed with thick skin.

Europe. It was introduced to England in 1597. Eggplant's name came about through a series of misunderstandings. In the 6th century in China, it was noted that raw eggplants caused much intestinal distress, so they were named *ch'ieh-pzu*, meaning "poison." When eggplant reached the Mediterranean a millennium later, it became known as *mala insana*, or "bad egg," which may have come from *melanzane*, Italian for eggplant, or *mela*, Italian for apple. In Italy, eggplants are known as mad apples. Another possibility for the name is that the first ones to reach England were white and egg-shaped, hence the name eggplant. By the time this much-maligned fruit reached France, it was named *aubergine*. Traced back to the Arabic *albadingen*, an adaptation of the Persian *badingen*, "aubergine" derives ultimately from the plant's Sanskrit name, *vatimgana*.

egg replacer - any of a variety of substances made from non-animal ingredients that take the place of eggs in **vegan** cooking and baking, such as ground **flaxseed, arrowroot** powder, **tofu** or powdered egg replacers. These substitutes mimic the binding and emulsifying actions of eggs, keeping baked goods moist and helping ingredients stay suspended in a cooked mixture. Powdered egg replacers are made from a blend of natural starches and gums, and can be found in most health food stores.

egg ring - similar to an **English muffin ring,** this metal ring, usually between 3 and 4 inches (7.5 and 10 cm) in diameter with a ½- to 1-inch (1 to 2.5 cm) high side, is used to fry or poach eggs, so that they come out in perfect circles. Most egg rings, unlike English muffin rings, have a handle, so that they can be easily lifted away from the egg when it is done cooking.

egg roll - a thin square of dough wrapped around a filling of minced vegetables and/or chicken, shrimp or beef and either deep-fried or steamed. See also SPRING ROLL.

egg roll wrapper - also **egg roll skin.** A thin square of dough used to wrap around any of a variety of fillings to make egg rolls. Traditional egg roll dough is quite heavy and may contain eggs, but many egg rolls today are often made with thinner, lighter spring roll wrappers, which are made from flour and water and rolled out a bit thinner, so that they are quite delicate when deep-fried.

egg salad - a mixture of chopped hard-boiled egg, mayonnaise and seasonings, used as a sandwich filling or served on its own on a bed of lettuce. Jewish delicatessen menus invariably offer egg salad, not only because it's delicious but also because it's **pareve** (a Jewish cookery term describing a neutral food that includes neither animal nor dairy products), so that it can be combined with either a meat or a dairy dish, depending on the diner's dietary requirements. See also CHOPPED EGG.

eggs Benedict - a creation, in the late 1920s, of New York City's **Delmonico's** restaurant, in response to two patrons, Mr. and Mrs. LeGrand Benedict, who complained that there was nothing new on the lunch menu. The chef, the manager and the maître d' collaborated to please their clients' palates, and the result was a poached egg and ham or Canadian bacon on a toasted English muffin, topped with hollandaise sauce. The dish is often confused with eggs Benedictine, a French specialty of cod topped with eggs.

egg scissors - also **egg topper.** A kitchen gadget with a ring at one end and scissors-style handles at the other. The ring is placed over the top of a soft-boiled egg sitting in an egg cup, then the handles are deployed, and a set of sharp teeth or a razor-sharp blade cuts off the top portion of the egg, so that the inside can be eaten tidily with a spoon.

egg separator - a small, cup-like utensil with a slot running midway around the bottom of its perimeter, so that the egg white runs through while the yolk stays in the center.

egg slicer - a small, squarish kitchen utensil with a slotted egg-shaped depression on the bottom and a row of wires or blades on a hinged top that can be lowered down onto a hard-boiled egg to cut it into neat, even slices.

eggs mimosa - see MIMOSA.

eggs Sardou - an acclaimed dish of the famous New Orleans restaurant Antoine's, consisting of poached eggs served atop steamed **artichoke bottoms,** topped with anchovies, truffles, ham and hollandaise sauce. This exquisite, rich dish was named in honor of the French playwright Victorien Sardou (1831–1908), who was known for his melodramas, in which actress Sarah Bernhardt starred repeatedly. Sardou also wrote the play *La Tosca,* which became the basis of Giacomo Puccini's opera *Tosca*.

egg substitute - also **egg alternative.** A ready-made mixture of egg whites, vitamins and minerals, which mimics the look and (to some extent) the taste of whole eggs without using the yolks. The vitamins and minerals added to the egg whites allow them to offer the same nutrition as whole eggs, without the fat and cholesterol in the yolks. A nice visual benefit of vitamin fortification is that many egg replacers are dyed yellow by the beta-carotene that is added to them, so they look a little more natural when used to make scrambled eggs or omelets. Like **egg replacers,** they can easily be used in baking as a substitute for whole eggs, but they are not acceptable for **vegans.**

egg timer - any of a number of differently designed miniature count-down clocks or hourglasses used to monitor the cooking time of eggs or other foods.

egg topper - see EGG SCISSORS.

egg wash - a mixture of beaten whole eggs, yolks or whites, with either milk or water, brushed over breads and pastry dough before being placed in the oven, to give them both color and a glossy finish.

egg white - see EGG.

egg yolk - see EGG.

egusi seed - a mutant seed of the watermelon variety *Citrullus lanatus* var. *lanatus*, cultivated in large numbers in Nigeria and sold dried, usually ground into flour or meal and added to soups and stews as a thickener and an additional source of protein and carbohydrates. The flesh of this particular type of watermelon is not edible, so it is cultivated specifically for its seeds. Egusi seeds can be hard to find in North America, but are usually sold in stores that specialize in African foods.

Eisai - also **Myoan Yosai** (1141–1215). Japanese monk credited with introducing **shojin ryori,** a Zen Buddhist form of cooking and eating. To supplement his religious studies at home, Eisai traveled to China twice and, on returning from his second trip in 1168, he established the first Japanese Zen temple, as well as his own sect. In keeping with the first tenet of Buddhism ("Thou shalt not kill"), meals were vegetarian, based on two foundation stocks — mushroom and kelp — which represented the earth and sea. The preparation of the meal, the ingredients and the cooking methods were all revered as part of the ceremonial worship, not unlike the Buddhist tea ceremonies that would become widespread three centuries later. Historians attribute Eisai with creating a grand tradition of cooking and dining alongside religious enlightenment.

Egyptian onion - see TREE ONION.

eight-jewel duck - a dish of symbolism from China that consists of freshly killed duck that must be stuffed with eight ingredients. These ingredients represent the eight auspicious signs of Buddha, the eight immortals of Taoism, the eight famous horses of Mu Wang of the Chou dynasty and the eight paths to everlasting happiness. They are rice, lotus seeds, ginger, shrimp, dark soy sauce, chestnuts, mushrooms and bamboo shoots, using rice vinegar and chicken stock for broth.

86 - a term used by bartenders to indicate that a guest will not be served more alcohol and is no longer welcome, due to an unacceptable level of inebriation. In restaurant parlance, 86 means that the kitchen is out of a certain item, so it can no longer be offered. A few differing stories are current among restaurant and bar workers regarding the origin of the term. In the 1930s in New York City, the end of the subway line was 86th Street, and the conductor would yell out to his passengers: "86th Street, end of the line, no more service!" How this term leaped from the subway into bars and restaurants is a mystery. Another story has it that in the Wild West, bartenders used to serve drinks of 110-proof alcohol; however when one of the guests was becoming a bit too drunk, his next glass would be cut to 86-proof.

Eisai - see profile above.

Eisbock - see ICE BEER.

eishta - see KASHTA.

Eiswein - see ICE WINE.

elbow macaroni - see PASTA.

elderberry - the fruit of the elder tree of the genus *Sambucus*, commonly scattered throughout Europe and North America, bearing bunches of white flowers and a small black berry, both of which are used in making wine. The flowers impart a muscatel flavor much more potent than that of the best Muscat grapes, and the berries furnish a deep-carmine color. **Sambuca** is flavored with elder. The berries are made into chutney; and elderflowers are used to make tea, vinegar and cocktails, such as the elderflower Martini. They can also be deep-fried for a succulent treat.

The Greeks and Romans used elder for both food and medicine, and as one of the earliest recorded insecticides (a decoction of the plant was sprinkled over plants and flowers to discourage pests). The Roman historian and naturalist **Pliny** wrote of the use of the wood to make musical instruments. Small boys in Roman times made popguns from the stems. A contemporary of Pliny wrote, "Needless to write any description of the elder, since every boy that plays with a popgun will not mistake another tree for the elder." Legends from all over the world cited that wherever the elder grows, evil lurks. A gypsy tradition forbade them to burn elder in their campfires. Another ancient legend

elderberries

is that Judas hung himself on the branch of the elder tree, and it's said that the cross of Christ was made of elder wood. The Sicilians believed that a piece of wood from the tree will kill serpents and keep robbers away. The name "elder" comes from the Anglo-Saxon *aeld*, meaning "fire," because a pipe made of a hollowed branch was used in antiquity to blow on the embers to stir up a fire.

electric skillet - also **electric frying pan.** A type of skillet that can be plugged directly into an outlet and heated independent of the stovetop. It is less versatile than a traditional skillet, because its temperature is steadier and can't be increased or decreased as quickly as a regular skillet over a burner, but it is a convenient as an extra cooking surface when the stove is crowded with pots and pans. Most electric skillets have a removable plug and thermostat, which can be taken off completely, so that the pan can be immersed when it is washed.

electrolytes - naturally occurring substances, such as sodium, potassium, chloride, calcium and magnesium, that dissolve in the blood and form positively and negatively charged ions, which allow the body to conduct electricity. Electrolytes help nerves transmit messages, keep the pH level of the body in check (not too acid, not too base), keep the heart beating rhythmically, and maintain the correct balance of fluid inside and outside cells. The body loses electrolytes through sweat and excretion (particularly during bouts of diarrhea), so it's vital to get enough of them through food and beverages. People who exercise heavily need to make sure they get enough of these substances to prevent exhaustion, muscle fatigue or even serious risks to the heart and nerves. Special hydrating drinks made with electrolytes, such as Gatorade, are helpful.

elephant ear - **1.** see TARO. **2.** see WOOD EAR. **3.** see PALMIER.

elephant garlic - see GARLIC.

elephant trunk clam - see GEODUCK.

elevenses - the colloquial British term for a light snack eaten at about 11:00 a.m., between breakfast and lunch, not the same as brunch, which is a large meal designed to stand in for both the morning and midday meals. Elevenses tends to feature sweet, not savory foods, such as biscuits and breads, similar to the foods served at **afternoon tea.** This morning snack is a favorite of the ever-hungry hobbits in J.R.R. Tolkien's *Lord of the Rings* series. In *The Fellowship of the Ring*, it's mentioned in a conversation between Merry and Pippin, two famished hobbits on an adventure that doesn't seem to include their regular mealtimes. When told by Aragorn that he's already had his breakfast, Pippin asks his friend Merry, "What about elevenses? Luncheon? Afternoon tea? Dinner? Supper? He knows about them, doesn't he?" To which Merry replies, "I wouldn't count on it."

elicoidali - see PASTA.

elk - a large deer of the Cervidae family that is both hunted and farmed in North America for its meat, native to the northern regions of North America, Europe and Asia. European elk, *Alces alces*, is known as "moose" in North America; North American elk, *Cervus elaphus*, is a different genus altogether and quite a bit larger than a moose, and also goes by the name **"red deer"** or **"wapiti."** It is found in North America, Europe and Asia. Generally speaking, elk meat is similar to **venison** and is lean, low in fat and cholesterol, with a fine flavor and texture if cooked properly. It has a tendency to dry out if overcooked and so is best for braising and quick searing (such as grilling or pan-frying).

Elstar - see APPLE.

elver - also **glass eel.** The name for a baby eel, eaten whole for its sweet, tender flesh, considered a great delicacy in many cultures. These tiny eels are nearly colorless and are often harvested by hand in small nets, so yields are low and prices in the hundreds of dollars per pound. They are prized in Asian, as well as many European, cuisines. In Spain, they are known as *angulas*, and are considered a special dish in the northern Basque region of the country.

Emmental - also **Emmentaler, Emmenthal, Emmenthaler.** A Swiss cheese made from skim cow's milk, Emmental means "valley of Emme," after the river running through Switzerland. Cutting open the 250-pound (113-kg) wheel reveals large holes, or "eyes." The cheese has a natural rind and is softer and much milder than **Gruyère,** often used to make fondue.

empanada - a Spanish or Mexican turnover with a pastry crust filled with chopped meat, vegetables, and sometimes cooked egg, olives and currants. It can also be filled with fruit for a dessert. The dish takes its name from *empanar*, meaning "to bake in pastry."

emperor fish - several species, including *Lethrinus chrysostomus* (called sweetlip emperor in Australia), and *L. laticaudis* (called grass emperor in the Solomon Islands), found mainly in warm Indo-Pacific waters.

emperor's fish - a Chinese dish made by scoring the sides of a cleaned fish, inserting sliced mushroom and ham into the cuts, then marinating it in rice vinegar and wine, seasoned with ginger, peanut oil and soy sauce. It is then steamed and served with coriander, scallions and sweet red pepper.

Empire apple - see APPLE.

emu - a large flightless bird of the family Dromaiidae, Dromaius novaehollandiae, similar to, but smaller than an ostrich and larger than a **rhea;** farm-raised in its native Australia and now in North America for its oil, eggs and meat, which is low in fat and cholesterol and high in iron. Emu meat is similar to that of the ostrich and rhea and tastes more like beef or lamb than poultry. It is cooked is the same way as ostrich meat, and is often seen in steak form on restaurant menus.

emulsifier - a binder, such as egg yolks or **xanthan gum,** added to foods to make normally unmixable ingredients come together. Even mustard can be an emulsifier, as it is in some vinaigrettes, where it temporarily holds vinegar and oil in a suspension.

emulsify - to slowly whisk together two normally unblendable ingredients, such as oil and vinegar, with an emulsifier, such as egg yolks, until they become a thick, smooth emulsion.

emulsion - describes sauces, such as mayonnaise and hollandaise, in which oil or butter is held in a thick, creamy suspension by egg yolks, because the fat becomes distributed evenly throughout the sauce by vigorous whipping, either by hand or mechanical tool. When sauces curdle and separate, or "break," the globules of fat have not emulsified.

enamelware - cookware made of enamel-coated metals, such as heavy cast iron or cast steel. Enamelware made of cast iron retains heat well, and the enamel coating is **nonreactive,** so it's well suited to long-simmering acidic sauces, such as tomato sauce or acidic fruits, such as rhubarb. It's not as good for sautéing or browning, because the coating doesn't allow a crisp crust to form or deep browning to occur on foods.

en chemise - see CHEMISÉ.

enchilada - a dish of Mexican origin consisting of a tortilla spread with chili-flavored tomato sauce, stuffed with a mixture of meat (generally chicken), rolled up and covered with more sauce. The name is Americanized Spanish meaning "to season with chili."

en cocotte - see COCOTTE.

en croûte - see CROÛTE.

endive - a leafy vegetable of the Asteraceae family, one of the largest plant families. Belgian endive (*Cichorium endivia*), also known as French endive, has long, pointy tightly furled white leaves, produced by depriving the plant of light. Their slightly bitter taste is often used for stuffing or in a **composed salad. Witloof** is another name for Belgian endive, from Middle Dutch *wit*, meaning "white," and *loof*, meaning "leaf." Curly endive (*Cichorium intybus*) is also known as curly chicory and **frisée.** It has long, frilly spiky leaves, which are often used in **mesclun** mixes. **Escarole,** of the same family, has broad, slightly curved leaves that are milder than Belgian or curly endive and are best used in salads when young.

endosperm - the interior layer of a kernel of grain, inside the outer covering of bran and surrounding the germ in the center. The endosperm is rich in starch and protein, but not high in vitamins and minerals. All-purpose flour is ground from the endosperm of wheat kernels and does not contain the germ or the bran.

English bean - see FAVA.

English breakfast - a full, hearty breakfast of fruit, eggs, sausages and/or bacon, toast, and perhaps fish, potatoes and mushrooms. See also CONTINENTAL BREAKFAST.

English breakfast tea - see TEA.

English cucumber - see CUCUMBER.

English honey - see HONEY.

English muffin - a small, round bread made with yeast dough, baked on a griddle. Because of how it's cooked, it's flat on the top and bottom and splits easily with a fork. It's usually served toasted and buttered, sometimes with jam.

English muffin ring - also **crumpet ring.** A metal ring, usually about 4 inches (10 cm) in diameter and 1 inch (2.5 cm) deep, used to give English muffins and crumpets their perfectly round shape as they cook on a griddle. An English muffin ring is similar to an **egg ring** and can easily be used as a substitute.

English mustard - see MUSTARD.

English sole - also **California sole, lemon sole.** *Parophrys vetulus*, commercially trawled along the west coast of North America from Alaska to Mexico. Frequently sold labeled only as "filet of sole," this Pacific flounder has fine-textured, lean white flesh. After hatching, the young require from two to four years to mature in near-shore waters; in addition to predation from large marine birds, fish and mammals, both immature and full-grown English sole are susceptible to industrial pollutants, given their proximity to human habitat.

English toffee - see TOFFEE.

English walnut - see PERSIAN WALNUT.

English whole grain mustard - see MUSTARD.

enhanced meat - meat, such as pork or poultry, that has been injected with a solution that includes flavoring, salt, preservatives and/or coloring to enhance its taste, texture or appearance. Pork and poultry are commonly injected with a salty brine to prevent them from drying out as they cook. Pork is also enhanced to add flavor, which can be lacking in the extra-lean flesh that is commonly bred for market today. Enhanced meats, by law, must be labeled with the ingredients that have been added to them.

enoki - also **enokitake, golden mushroom, golden needle mushroom, velvet stem mushroom.** A mushroom, *Flammulina velutipes*, native to Japan, with a long, thin stem and a tiny, white or orange cap. It has a crisp texture and mild flavor; heat tends to make it tough.

enoki

enologist - also **oenologist.** A wine chemist who analyzes samples of juice and wine and gives advice to winemakers. An oenophile is an aficionado of wine.

en papillote - see PAPILLOTE.

enrich - to add vitamins or minerals to a food to make it more nutritious. Flours, which are made into pastas, cereals and breads, are enriched with iron, niacin, riboflavin, thiamin and folic acid to replace the nutrients that are removed when the grains are milled. Many vegetarian soy foods and dairy-free beverages, such as soy milk, rice milk and almond milk, are enriched with calcium and vitamin B_{12}, both difficult to get in a strict vegetarian diet.

ensaïmada - a sweet pastry made from lard, sugar, flour, yeast and eggs, which originated on Majorca, one of the Balearic Islands off the coast of Spain, made either plain with a dusting of icing sugar on top or filled with jam, cream or custard. An ensaïmada is shaped a bit like a turban, which some say could be a tribute to the bun's possible Moorish heritage. The name is derived from the Majorcan word *saïm*, which means "lard," the main ingredient in the buns. Ensaïmadas are also frequently found in the Philippines, a former Spanish colony, where they are made with butter instead of lard, and the spelling changes to *ensaymada*.

entomophagy - see BUGS.

entrecôte - the French name for a steak cut from between the ninth and 11th ribs of a side of beef, the name meaning "between the ribs."

entrée - a term with a confusing meaning: originally in French cooking, the entrée was the course served after the fish and before the main course of meat, but now it's come to mean the main course itself. To further complicate the issue, in Australia, the entrée is the appetizer, or first course, of a meal.

entremetier - cook in a professional kitchen who prepares vegetables, appetizers, soups, eggs and side dishes, one of the positions in the brigade system created by French chef **Auguste Escoffier** in the late-19th century. See also BRIGADE SYSTEM, CHEF, GARDE MANGER, PASTRY CHEF, POISSONIER, RÔTISSEUR, SAUCIER, SOUS CHEF, TOURNANT.

entremets - originally a side dish served in addition to the main course of a meal, but later used to mean a dish served between the roast and the dessert. Today, it's a dessert served after the cheese and before the fruit. At one time, the word was even used to describe the entertainment that came in the middle of the meal. The word comes from the French *entre*, meaning "between," and *mets*, "dishes."

enzymes - naturally occurring proteins formed by cells in living organisms that act as catalysts for specific reactions. Enzymes are commonly used in the preparation of foods; for example, rennin, the enzyme component of **rennet,** is used to coagulate milk to form curds for cheese making. The rennet begins the reaction that allows the fats and solids suspended in liquid milk to precipitate, forming curds and leaving the watery **whey** behind. Enzymes are also present in the human gut, allowing us to digest the vast array of foods we consume. **Digestive enzymes** can even be purchased in supplement form to aid in the digestion of problematic foods, such as beans and cruciferous vegetables. See also BROMELAIN, FICIN, PAPAIN.

epazote - also **bean herb, Mexican tea, pigweed, wormseed, worm weed.** A popular Mexican herb, *Chenopodium ambrosioides*, with a strong odor and pungent but pleasantly bitter flavor. Epazote is frequently added to bean dishes in Mexico, because it is a traditional remedy for flatulence. It's also added to **moles** and **quesadilla**, and the dried leaves are steeped for tea. Toxic if consumed in large quantities, it was used as a medicinal herb by the Aztecs.

epazote

épices fines - also **fines épices.** See SPICE PARISIENNE.

epicure - currently refers to someone with discriminating taste dedicated to the sensual enjoyment of food and drink, or one who cultivates refined taste for the pleasures of the table (synonymous with gourmet). The term refers to Epicurus, the ancient Greek philosopher, who praised the delights of food. He founded Epicureanism, a popular school of Hellenistic philosophy. Despite what his name means today, Epicurus argued that when eating, you should not eat too richly for it could lead to dissatisfaction later when you realize that you might not be able to afford such delicacies. The first citing of an epicure is found in the Plato's *Republic* (circa 360 BC), in which he compares himself to "an epicure who snatches a taste of every dish which is successively brought to table before he has fairly enjoyed the one before."

épigramme - a French culinary term describing one kind of meat served two ways on the same dish, such as two chops, one breaded and fried, the other broiled. The name comes from an 18th-century marquise, who in a literary conversation, mistook the word "epigram" for a new dish and instructed her chef to prepare it. The chef's ingenious creation is still known by the malapropism.

Époisses - also **Époisses de Bourgogne.** A strong-smelling and strong-flavored French cow's milk cheese, with an reddish orange rind that is washed with **marc,** and a runny, creamy interior. Époisses has been made in the village of the same name in the Côte d'Or region of Burgundy (Bourgogne) since the 16th century, and all but disappeared after the Second World War. In 1950, cheesemaker Robert Berthaut revived the industry, and his brand is still considered the finest example of the cheese. Époisses is especially nice paired with white wine or sweet wine, such as **Sauternes**, and the nearly liquid interior must be accompanied by bread to adequately sop it up. It counts among its fans Napoleon and **Jean Anthelme Brillat-Savarin,** the famed French gastronome, who dubbed it "the king of cheeses."

escabeche - also **escabèche, escovitch, scavece.** A dish of fried fish that is covered with a hot, well-spiced vinegar-based marinade and allowed to cool, usually served cold. Escabeche has its origin in Spain, where the sweet-and-sour vinegar-based marinade was traditionally used to preserve fish when refrigeration was not available. This method of preparation is popular in a variety of countries other than Spain where fish is a common staple, including Italy (*scavece* or *scapece*), France (*escabèche*) and Jamaica (*escovitch*).

escalope - a French word used to designate a thin slice of meat without any bone on it. The name is most often used in connection with narrow strips of veal cut from the loin, which need to be flattened before cooking. This cut is known as "scallop" in North America.

escargot - French word for edible snails. **Apicius,** the Roman author from the 1st century AD, includes a recipe for snails in his cookbook. The Romans cultivated them in "snaileries." Roman historian and naturalist **Pliny** wrote that they were eaten as a snack, grilled and served with a wine sauce, as an appetizer or even after a meal. The Gauls enjoyed them for dessert. In the Middle Ages, during Lent, the church authorized their consumption. They came back into fashion in the 17th century, when legendary French chef **Antonin Carême** made some for dinner for the czar of Russia.

True escargot devotees can enjoy this delicacy more easily with the help of some clever specialized tools. **Escargot tongs** have a perfectly snail-shaped set of jaws that help grip the shell as the diner teases out the meaty snail with a slim two-tined fork designed especially for negotiating the tight space inside the shell. For those who prefer their escargot without a fight, a special escargot dish with several deep depressions neatly holds snails and garlic butter together and can be popped into the oven to keep the dish warm.

escarole - also **Batavian endive, broad-leaved endive.** A type of endive and part of the same botanical family Composite as chicory and endive. Escarole has broad, slightly curved, pale green leaves. It is milder than Belgian or curly endive. The name derives from the Latin *esca*, which simply means "food." See also ENDIVE.

Escoffier, Auguste - see profile on page 250.

escovitch - see ESCABECHE.

Eskimo pie - originally known as the "I-scream bar," chocolate-covered ice cream on a stick, patented by Danish-born schoolteacher and candy-store proprietor Christian Nelson of Onawa, Iowa, in 1920. In 1921, it became Eskimo pie when chocolate maker Russell Stover teamed up with Nelson to sell franchises for the manufacture and sale of the bars.

espagnole sauce - a classical **brown sauce,** one of the French "mother sauces," which is the foundation for numerous other sauces.

espresso - made by forcing steam through finely ground coffee to make a strong brew, served in a demitasse. There are several stories about its origin. Probably because the word is Italian for "express," many say it was first made at a Milan train

espresso

Escoffier, Auguste (1846–1935) - French chef and author of the enormously successful *Le Guide culinaire* (1903), published in English as *A Guide to Modern Cookery,* and the 20th century's first "celebrity chef." Born in the village of Villeneuve-Loubet, he followed his father's orders and became a cook. On his 13th birthday, he was taken to his uncle's restaurant in Nice and put to work as an apprentice. As he later commented, "There was nothing I could do but obey."

Ambitious and hardworking, he may have been an overachiever to compensate for his diminutive stature: as a young man, he wore elevated shoes to raise himself over the stoves. His career progressed steadily until he met **César Ritz,** a brilliant hotelier, who understood that luxury hotels should offer fine cooking in addition to opulent appointments and who hired Escoffier as *chef de cuisine* at the Monte Carlo Grande Hotel. It was the beginning of a productive partnership. In 1890, the theatrical impresario Richard D'Oyly Carte hired them to run his fledging Savoy Hotel in London. The Savoy quickly became a hub for the city's sophisticates, offering such innovations as rapid service for those attending the theatre as well as opportunities for more leisurely meals and, perhaps most significantly, a climate of the utmost discretion. The Prince of Wales and his mistress Lillie Langtry were regular patrons, and the hotel gracefully flaunted convention, making it respectable for women to dine in public. However, Escoffier's professional success came with a price. His wife, Delphine, whom he had married in 1878, hated London. Shortly after their arrival, she returned to Monte Carlo taking their two children with her and giving birth to their daughter, Germaine, in France. Escoffier and his wife spent most of their remaining years apart. However, separation from his family allowed him to throw himself into his work. He and Ritz went on to open a string of illustrious establishments.

Escoffier once said, "My success comes from the fact that my best dishes were created for ladies" — the most famous being **peach Melba,** invented for the Australian singer Nellie Melba. But rumors swirled about his relationships with other women, most spectacularly the actress Sarah Bernhardt, whom he had known as a young chef in Paris. When she stayed at the Savoy later in her career, he often cooked dinner for her and dined with her in her suite, setting tongues wagging. He also spent a great deal of time with Rosa Lewis, owner of the Cavendish Hotel. Beautiful and outgoing but famously discreet, the former kitchen maid and favorite of the Prince of Wales kept a photograph of Escoffier in her parlor for some 40 years.

Aside from his writing, most of Escoffier's contributions to gastronomy took place in commercial kitchens. He is credited with streamlining the extravagant dishes of the 19th century (the towering architectural monuments refined by **Antonin Carême**) and instituting reforms in the kitchen including the **brigade system,** which organized professional kitchens into strict positions or stations with well-defined responsibilities, still used today. He also seems to have had a promotional bent and marketed sauces and pickles under his name. He died after a lingering illness on February 12, 1935, interestingly, only six days after Delphine passed away.

station as people boarded the express trains, an idea supported by the fact that it's usually taken standing and drunk quickly for a flavorful boost of energy. The coffee maker was called *macchina a vapore*, or "steam machine," invented in Naples in 1901.

espresso macchiato - see CAFFÈ MACCHIATO.

Esrom - also **Danish Port Salut.** A Danish cheese similar to **Port Salut,** made from pasteurized cow's milk, with a brownish yellow rind and a light yellow, mildly flavored interior when young. The cheese has a smattering of tiny holes throughout the stretchy interior. As it ages, it can become quite pungent and full-flavored. The cheese gets its name from Esrom, the town whose monastery the cheese originated in. It is good with beer or dark red wine, as well as strongly flavored foods, such as rye bread, sardines and onions.

essence - a concentrated, usually oily, liquid made from a herb, flower, spice or fish, used in small amounts as a flavoring. See also EXTRACT.

estouffade - a French term for a dish in which meat is first browned in some type of fat, then moistened with a liquid (wine and/or stock are common additions) and allowed to slowly stew, covered, in the oven or over low heat for several hours. The term looks similar to the name of the popular Cajun dish **étouffée** because both come from the same origin, although they have evolved into different dishes using different cooking methods. Although *étouffé* is also related to the French word *étouffer,* meaning "to smother," it and *estouffade* are also related to the term *à l'étouffé*, meaning a dish cooked with a small amount of liquid in a tightly sealed casserole dish.

ethanol - see ALCOHOL.

Ethiopian flatbread - see INJERA

ethyl alcohol - see ALCOHOL, GRAIN ALCOHOL.

ethylene ripening - the use of ethylene gas to speed up the ripening of fruits through a general stimulation of cell metabolism, allowing farmers to pick fruit while it's still green. The gas is now used extensively to ripen lemon, oranges, tomatoes, bananas, dates and persimmons.

étouffée - **1.** a style of cooking over low heat in a covered pan, so that the resulting captured steam allows flavors to develop more quickly and keep the contents moist, from the French for "smothered." **2.** a Cajun specialty of seafood, especially crayfish and shrimp, cooked in this style with vegetables, using dark **roux,** and usually served with rice.

etrog citron -see CITRON.

ettekees - see AETTEKEES.

eucalyptus honey - see HONEY.

eulachon - see SMELT.

European-process cocoa powder - see DUTCH-PROCESS COCOA POWDER.

evaporated milk - milk produced by the removal of water from fresh whole milk, that is then pasteurized, homogenized, concentrated, left unsweetened and usually fortified with vitamin D. It's similar to **condensed milk,** but more perishable because it has no sugar. Once opened, it should be stored and treated like fresh milk. See also MILK.

eviscerate - see DRAW.

expansive - a wine-tasting term used to describe a wine that is richly flavored and complex, often used for a wine that has an excellent blend of flavor notes and aromas.

expiration date - also **expiry date.** Simply speaking, the date printed on a packaged food by which it should be consumed. Two types of dates are generally printed on a package. A **closed date** is a numerical code stamped on the package by the manufacturer, retailer or distributor, which allows them to determine the age of a product and whether it should be pulled from the shelves. Closed dates tend to appear on cans, jars and boxes of unrefrigerated foods. With a closed date, the onus is on the seller to remove products past their prime to ensure food safety and palatability for consumers. An **open date** is a calendar date stamped on a package that allows both the retailer and the consumer to monitor the food's freshness. This is primarily used on perishable foods, such as eggs, dairy products and meat. The date represents the last day on which the product is considered at its peak freshness — not necessarily the day upon which the food spoils or becomes dangerous. Many products are still edible past their expiration date, but it is probably safest to accept this date as the last day a food should be consumed.

In the United States, there is no federal law that designates which foods must be dated or how the process should be carried out. About half the states require some form of open dating, but some states require only certain items to be dated, and still others don't require any dating at all, leaving the choice up to the producer.

When open dates are printed, they fall into three broad categories. The first is the **sell-by date**, which indicates the date by which a store should sell a product. It's up to the consumer to determine how long the product should be kept at home before consumption. The second falls under the name **best if used by (or before).** This date indicates when a product's quality and flavor will begin to decline, not when it becomes dangerous to consume. The third is the manufacturer-determined **use-by date,** the last day on which a product is considered to be at its peak flavor, freshness and safety. It should, ideally, be discarded after that date.

Certain shelf-stable foods, such as baby-formula powder or baby food, are labeled with a use-by date, even though they are not considered perishable. This is because the nutrient content of the formula begins to diminish after that date. To ensure proper nutrition, the formula or food must be consumed by the use-by date.

In Canada, many of the same general principles apply to food dating. However, most products that have a shelf life of less than 90 days are required by federal law to have a **durable-life declaration** printed on the package or on a poster next to the item in the store. The durable life of a food is simply the number of days that it remains at its peak freshness, nutritional quality and taste after it is packaged and before it is opened (it must be stored under the proper conditions, which are also stated on the label). Foods that have been packaged in a store, such as meat, poultry and fish, must also carry the date on which they were packaged, so that the consumer can tell when the food is past its prime. A **best-before date** is another way of expressing this durable-life information and is considered an acceptable alternative. The terms **expiry date** and **expiration date** are only used for drugs and natural-health products, never food.

Explorateur - a rich, French **triple-crème cheese** made from cow's milk and containing 75 percent butterfat, often served as a snack or after-dinner cheese paired with spicy red or crisp white wines. Wheels of Explorateur are covered with a bloomy white rind and have firm, butter-colored interior that offers a creamy, mushroomy flavor. The cheese was developed in honor of, and named for, the first U.S. satellite, *Explorer*, which was launched in January 1958.

extract - a concentrated flavoring obtained from a plant or other food in a two-step process: producing a solution from the soluble portion of the substance and reducing it through evaporation or distillation to the desired consistency. See also ESSENCE.

extra virgin olive oil - see OLIVE OIL.

Extrawurst - a pale German sausage made from a mixture of beef and pork or bacon fat, smooth in texture and easily sliced.

eye - a term used to designate a hole in cheese.

eyeballs - eyeballs, particularly sheep eyes, are considered a great delicacy in the Middle East, usually removed from the head after roasting or boiling and eaten straight away, with or without a sauce or seasoning.

eye of the dragon - see LONGAN.

f
figs

faba - see FAVA.

fabada - also **fabada asturiana.** A thick Spanish stew hailing from the northern region of Asturias, made of **fava** beans, ham, bacon, **chorizo** and **morcilla.** The name "fabada" comes from the Asturian word *fabes*, meaning "broad beans."

fagara - see SZECHWAN PEPPER.

fagioli - Italian for "beans."

faggot - a fresh, rustic British sausage patty made of minced pork (often including **variety meats,** such as **lights,** liver and heart), spices and bread crumbs, wrapped in **caul** fat, similar to the French **crépinette.** The patties are baked and often served hot with gravy, although they can also be eaten cold. The name "faggot" means "bundle," from the traditional English term for a bundle of sticks used to build a fire. The name of these patties became particularly appropriate in 1666, when a batch was left too long in a downtown baker's oven, allegedly starting the Great Fire of London.

Fahrenheit - devised by German-Dutch physicist Gabriel Daniel Fahrenheit in 1724, a temperature scale using a range of 180 degrees to separate the melting and boiling points of water, with freezing at 32°F and boiling at 212°F. See also CELSIUS.

fair-trade - a descriptor used for a food or craft item that is produced by a small business or cooperative, which is paid a fair wage for its products. Unlike some large corporations, which work hard to maximize profits by paying below-minimum wages to small producers and using giant economies of scale to pay shareholders large dividends, fair-trade organizations (FTOs) have the interests of the small producer at heart. FTOs work to decrease the number of middlemen between the producer and the consumer, thus increasing the amount of money that can go directly to the producer. FTOs work with farmers' and artisans' cooperatives that provide decent, living wages to workers, as well as health-care benefits, child care and low-interest business loans. They also try to keep more jobs in the country where the goods are produced, creating processing and packaging facilities in the country of origin, so that the majority of the money produced by the industry stays there. In North America, fair-trade coffee and tea are common sights, as well as fair-trade crafts, textiles and home furnishings. In Europe, fair-trade crafts are not as large a market, but coffee, tea and food commodities, such as bananas, are commonplace.

fajita - a dish of marinated strips of beef or chicken, grilled or boiled, rolled in a flour tortilla and garnished with grated cheese, guacamole, sour cream and salsa. Its name means "little belt," referring to the strips of meat. See also TEX-MEX.

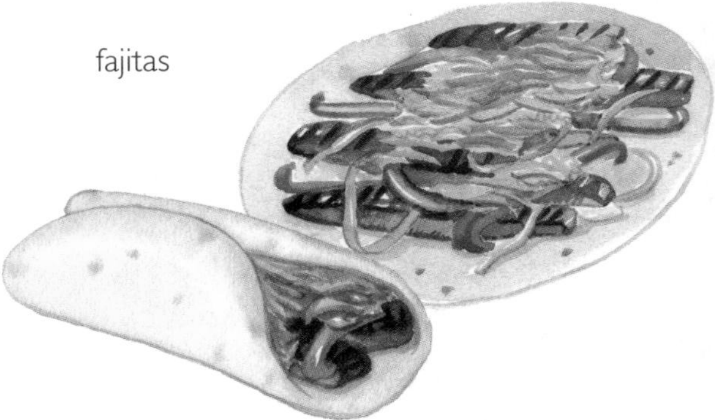
fajitas

falafel - also **felafel.** Small, fried patties or balls made of ground chickpeas and spices, a Middle Eastern specialty; often placed inside pita pockets and topped with **tahini.**

Falernum - a flavoring syrup from Barbados made with cane syrup and hints of lime juice, ginger and almonds, used to make rum-based cocktails. Falernum used to be always slightly alcoholic, but in recent years nonalcoholic versions have popped up and become easier to find.

fallow deer - see DEER.

famine food - also **survival food.** Edible animals, marine life and plants, including indigenous wild plants and tulip bulbs, and domestic pets, as well as animal fodder — usually avoided as food for reasons of taste or tender feelings, but eaten during famines caused by such events as crop failure, drought, forced migration of peoples and war. In extremis, people may resort to eating indigestible material, such as bark, cornhusks and grass, as famine food.

farce - a term for a stuffing or **forcemeat** that is stuffed into something else and cooked, originally a French term that has worked its way into the English language. The origin of the word is the Latin word *farcire*, which means "to stuff."

farfalle - see PASTA.

farfel - also **barley farfel, egg barley. 1.** A traditional pasta used in Jewish cooking, the dough shaped into barley-size bits by hand, by chopping or by grating the dough through the large hole on a grater. Farfel can be added to soups, deep-fried to make it crunchy or baked in any number of dishes. Farfel is often eaten at the Jewish New Year, Rosh Hashanah, because its round shape represents an abundant harvest in the new year. The word comes from the Yiddish "farfl," which is derived from the Middle High German word "varveln," meaning "noodles." **2.** another word for crumbs or pieces, such as matzo farfel, used in such dishes as kugel.

farina - a fine flour or meal made from wheat, nuts or vegetables, often used to make cereal or pudding.

farinata - a traditional, Italian pancake-like flatbread from Liguria, made of chickpea flour, water and olive oil, usually seasoned simply with rosemary and sea salt, and baked over a hot fire or in the oven. Farinata is a well-loved and common food eaten at any meal of the day or as a snack.

Farmer, Fannie Merritt - see profile on page 256.

farmer's cheese - also **farmer cheese.** A type of cottage cheese, pressed into blocks, made from cow's milk. See also HOOP CHEESE.

farmhouse cheese - also **farmstead cheese.** See ARTISANAL.

faro - see LAMBIC BEER.

farro - a wheat-like grain, *Triticum dicoccum*, with a hearty flavor and a chewy, creamy texture, popular during the golden days of ancient Rome. It has recently enjoyed a revival, first in Italy, and is now starting to show up in Italian delicatessens and natural food stores in the U.S. It makes a delicious alternative to cracked wheat, rice and similar carbohydrates.

Fastnacht - also **Fasnacht.** A potato-based pastry, deep-fried like a doughnut. A Pennsylvania Dutch tradition, eaten on Fastnacht Day or Shrove Tuesday, the day before Lent begins, similar to **Pancake Day** in Britain. The pastries are a way of using up all the butter and fat in the home forbidden during Lent.

fatback - the strip of pure fat carved from the back of a hog, usually used fresh, but sometimes cured with salt and dried. Fatback is often confused with salt pork, but is pure fat and does not contain any traces of lean meat, as salt pork does.

fat choy - also **black moss, hair seaweed.** An edible, furry, blue-green algae, its name comes from the Cantonese *fat tsai*, meaning "hair vegetable."

fat mop - also **grease mop.** A kitchen tool that looks like a small string mop, used to absorb excess fat or grease off the top of cooked foods. A fat mop can be dragged across the surface of soups or stocks as they cool to soak up and remove floating fat, or dabbed over the top of greasy foods, such as bacon or pizza, to soak up grease.

fat rascal - a sweet tea cake made in Britain, specifically a specialty of Yorkshire, a fruity, nutty scone traditionally made with almonds, cherries and citrus peel, but now often made with just currants.

fats - saturated or unsaturated, the latter either mono- or polyunsaturated, referring to single or multiple hydrogen atoms within its chemical makeup. Saturated fats are solid at room temperature, usually animal products but not exclusively, and associated with health risks, heart disease among them. Unsaturated fats are usually liquids from plant sources, associated with lowering LDL, or "bad," cholesterol, monounsaturates more so than polyunsaturates. See also HYDROGENATION.

TYPES OF FATS

saturates - butter, lard, margarine, suet, vegetable shortening, coconut and palm oils.

monounsaturates - canola, olive and peanut oils.

polyunsaturates - corn, safflower, sesame and soybean oils.

Farmer, Fannie Merritt (1857–1915) - cookbook author and domestic scientist. Born in Boston, Farmer suffered two strokes as a child, which left her with a permanent limp and prevented her from attending college. At the age of 30, she enrolled in the Boston Cooking School, one of the first schools teaching the emerging discipline of domestic science, which encompassed such matters as nutrition and how to run an efficient and tidy kitchen. In 1884, Mary Lincoln, the school's principal, produced the first edition of *The Boston Cooking-School Cook Book,* aimed at professional cooks. By 1894, Mrs. Lincoln had resigned from the school; Farmer was principal and assumed editorship of the new edition which was released in 1896. Although she wasn't an originator of recipes, she tested and retested recipes from a variety of sources to ensure more predictable results and directed her work toward novice as well as experienced cooks. Conventional wisdom suggests that Farmer invented precise measurements by volume, rather than weight, but in fact others, including her predecessor, Mary Lincoln, contributed far more to techniques for measuring accurately. She did, however, promote the cause and helped to ensure that the concept of the level measure (a level, rather than a rounded, teaspoon or cup) became generally accepted. Farmer's approach to cooking was sensible, rather than imaginative, believing as she did that "cooking should and could be a precise and standardized procedure." While she appreciated the elegance of French cuisine and included recipes for some representative dishes, her heart was in more down-to-earth fare, such as pot roasts and dumplings. As the poet Elizabeth Bishop wrote in her 1971 poem *Lines Written in the Fannie Farmer Cookbook*, "You won't become a gourmet cook/By studying our Fannie's book."

Even so, the book was an immediate success and soon established itself as "the Bible of the American kitchen". Writing in *The New York Review of Books,* critic Michael Field called it one of "the culinary trinity upon which, for better or worse, the gospel of American cooking has been built." (The other two cited were *The Joy of Cooking* and *The Settlement Cook Book*.) Since Farmer's death, the book has been revised numerous times, selling about 4 million copies in its various editions. The name "Fanny Farmer" has become a brand, symbolizing quality and wholesomeness in food preparation, which, in addition to the cookbook, is now associated mainly with the chain of candy shops that bear her name.

fat separator - also **degreasing pitcher, gravy separator.** A glass or plastic pitcher with a long spout that begins at the base of the container, used to separate the fat from gravy or other liquids. Gravy or drippings are poured into the pitcher and allowed to stand for several minutes until the fat rises to the top (fat is lighter than other liquids and floats in a non-emulsified mixture). Then, the heavier gravy or flavorful liquids in the drippings are poured out through the spout, leaving the fat behind.

fattoush - a Middle Eastern mixed green salad topped with crumbled, toasted pita breads, very popular in Lebanon and Syria. Fattoush often contains the green **purslane,** as well as an assortment of other greens and chopped vegetables, and is seasoned with ground **sumac** and chopped fresh mint. The word "fattoush" means "moistened bread."

fava - **1.** also **broad bean, English bean, faba, horse bean, Windsor bean.** The Latin word *faba* means "broad bean," making it redundant to call them "fava beans," as we commonly do. They were the only beans available in Europe until the 16th century. The fava supposedly originated in North Africa. However, some Chinese writing indicates that it was cultivated in China more than 5,000 years ago. The fava was also cultivated in biblical times by the Hebrews and later by the Egyptians. The Greeks used it as a ballot and believed that the soul would be reincarnated in a fava. In ancient Rome, the bean was used as a token for the lottery, to designate the king of Saturnalia, a festival of uninhibited feasting and merrymaking. Pythagoras, the famed 6th century BC philosopher and mathematician, is known for insisting his disciples avoid the fava. His edict

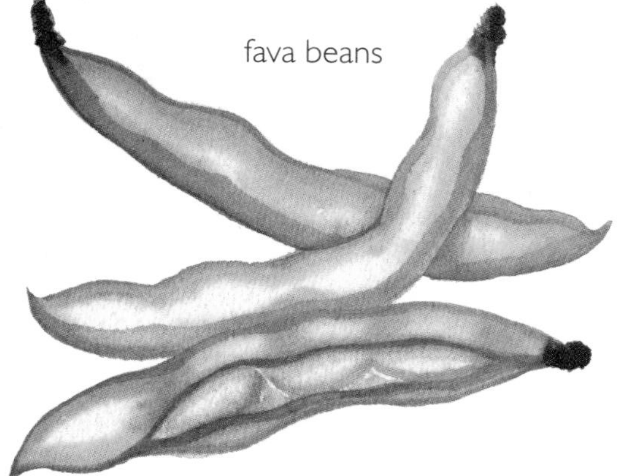

against the bean has intrigued cooks and historians for centuries. An ancient story tells of a group of Pythagoreans, pursued by their enemies, refusing to cross a field of favas. Rather than disobey the master's dictates and flee through the field, they were slaughtered. Scientists today believe Pythagoras had a fatal sensitivity to the bean. For some people the fava can be poisonous. Sensitive individuals, whose red blood cells lack the enzymes needed to break down the peptide glutathione in favas, may suffer hemolytic anemia within a few minutes of exposure to the pollen of the fava plant or a few hours of eating the beans. Symptoms include jaundice and high fever, and, in severe cases, death may occur within one or two days. **2.** a Greek spread made from mashed, cooked yellow split peas, seasoned with lemon juice, onion or garlic, and sometimes oregano, made smooth and rich with the addition of olive oil. Fava is usually served with a variety of other **mezedes** and crusty bread.

fedelini - see PASTA.

feijoa - also **pineapple guava.** The fruit of a small evergreen tree, *Feijoa sellowiana,* originating in South America, bearing magnificent bright red flowers. It belongs to the same family (Myrtaceae) as the guava, clove and eucalyptus, and was named for the Spanish botanist Don da Silva Feijoa. The fruit combines the taste of pineapple, guava, berries, pineapple and mint, and has edible seeds. See also GUAVA.

feijoada - the Brazilian national dish, feijoada comes in all kinds of regional variations, but is always a black bean stew served with an assortment of side dishes. Normally, the dish includes a selection of sliced pork products, such as sausages, pig's ears, feet and even tail; rice; fried collard greens; roasted **manioc** flour (called "farofa" in Portuguese); and sliced orange, which is alleged to counteract the fattiness of the pork. The history of the dish goes back several hundred years to the slaves who worked on Brazilian farms. The cheap by-products of pork processing, such as salt pork and various **variety meats,** were given to the slaves, who combined them with other inexpensive staples, such as rice and manioc flour. This slave staple then began to grow in popularity among the working classes and eventually found its way onto menus at even the most exclusive restaurants. Traditionally, a **caipirinha** is the recommended beverage partner to feijoada.

felafel - see FALAFEL.

felino - a delicate, Italian pork salami from the city of Parma, made with a little salt, peppercorns and wine.

fell - see LAMB.

fennel - also **bulb fennel.** A plant that is known for its tasty bulb and aromatic leaves and for the seeds harvested from mature plants, *Foeniculum vulgare dulce,* or Florence fennel. *Foeniculum* is the Roman word for "fragrant hay."

Bulb fennel, however, has only been popular in the U.S. for the last 10 or so years, although it's had a long history of cultivation. The Egyptians, Greeks and Romans used it. Europeans and Asians have known it for the past thousand years. But before that, inhabitants

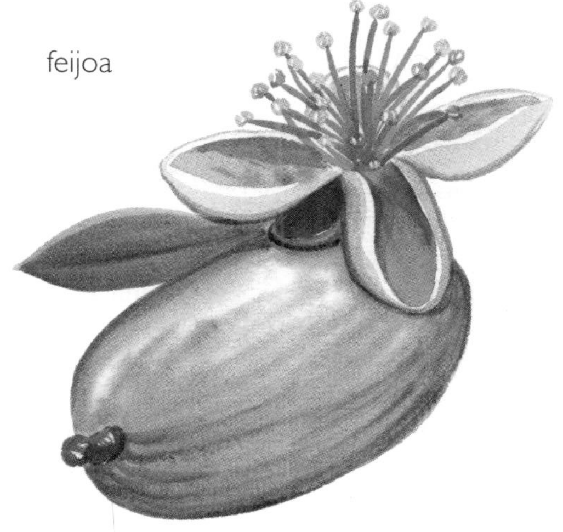

of Mohenjo-Daro (4,000 years before the birth of Christ) believed that the Gods transmitted knowledge to humanity in the form of fire in the lacy branches of fennel. For this reason, the roots, seeds and even the fragile fronds of the plant were scorched and roasted until they turned to fine ash, and the powder used to season most of their food.

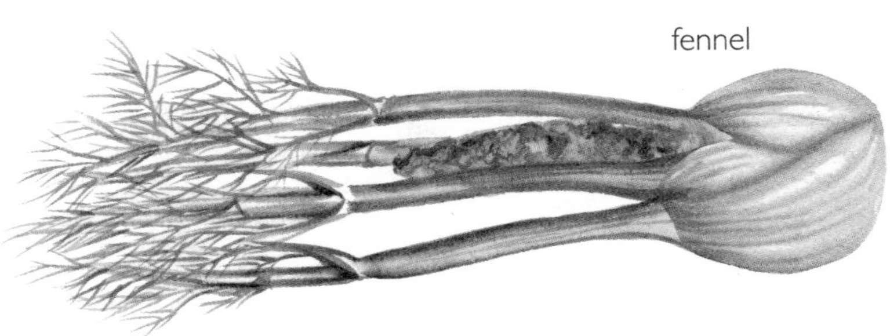

The Greeks referred to fennel as "marathon," after the celebrated battle of Marathon in 490 BC was fought on a field of fennel. Socrates recommended a stalk of fennel and a glass of water as the lone cure for a night of overindulgence. The Romans grew it for its fragrant, herb-like green leaves to use for seasoning. They also believed that serpents sucked the plant's juice to improve their eyesight, and Roman historian and naturalist **Pliny** recommended the herb for "dimness of the human vision."

The plant was in the garden of Charlemagne, who was responsible for its introduction in Europe. In the Middle Ages, chewing the seeds was a favorite way to stop gastric rumbles during church sermons. Fennel was also one of the nine sacred Anglo-Saxon herbs.

In 17th century Italy, fennel was often served at the end of the meal, sprinkled with salt. It's been known in Italy for several centuries and all over the Mediterranean countries.

Fennel is known as *fenouil* in France, *fenchel* in Germany, *finocchio* in Italy and *hinijo* in Spain. Mistakenly called "sweet anise," fennel has a mild anise, or licorice, flavor, although not a sweet one. Fennel bulbs look similar to celery, with a white bulbous base that extends into celery-like stems.

fennel seed - from the familiar plant native to southern Europe, grown primarily for its bulbous stalk. Although they come from two different plants, fennel and aniseeds are similar in appearance and taste and can often be used almost interchangeably. Seeds from Florence fennel have a mild anise flavor. Aniseeds, which come from a member of the parsley family, are native to the Middle East and taste stronger than fennel seeds.

fenugreek - also **methi.** A seed of a legumous plant native to southern Europe and western Asia. Its botanical name *Trigonella foenum-graecum* comes from the Latin *trigonella*, referring to the flowers triangular shape, and *foenum-graecum*, meaning "Greek hay," the Roman name for it. One of the oldest cultivated plants, it was used by the Egyptians in embalming and encouraged for cultivation in central Europe by emperor Charlemagne in AD 812.The largest producers today are India, Egypt, Lebanon and Argentina. Because it's a seed and a legume, fenugreek is rich in protein, and in some countries it's an important food, not just a spice. Fenugreek is the principal flavoring in imitation maple syrup. Brown fenugreek seeds are bitter. Lightly toasting them removes some of the bitterness. The seeds are an ingredient in **sambar** powder, a seasoning mix from South India. The leaves are also used in Indian cuisine. The young, tender, bitter leaves are used both as a flavoring for breads or savory fritters and as a vegetable, often cooked in the same manner as spinach. Fenugreek leaves are also used in Yemeni and Ethiopian cooking, often as a flavoring in sauces. The fresh leaves can be harder to find in North America, but the dried version, found in Indian grocery stores, is an acceptable substitute.

fermentation - a chemical process that breaks down carbohydrates and glucose in food, producing effervescence, alcohol or decomposition. Beer and wine are perhaps the best-known products of fermentation. Liquid foods, such as soups, sauces or stews, will bubble, as if cooking, when they're decomposing. If left too long in the **danger zone** (40° to 140°F/4° to 60°C, the temperature at which bacteria feasts on the natural sugars in food and multiplies) all food will spoil and become unsafe to eat.

fermented black beans - also **Chinese black beans, salty black beans.** Small, black, salt-preserved soybeans with a very strong flavor, used in China since the 2nd century BC, where they're called *chi*; fermented black beans require soaking in water before use, most often made into black bean sauces for meat, fish and some vegetables.

fermented milk drinks - a number of sour-milk variations from different parts of Asia and the Middle East.

FERMENTED MILK DRINKS

dough - yogurt beaten with salt and water, popular in Iran, available bottled as a soft drink.

kaelder - a traditional Scandinavian fermented milk beverage akin to **kefir.**

kefir - popular in Eastern Europe, made from fermented camel's milk.

koumiss - from Russia, made from mare's milk.

kyringa - a gassy, alcoholic sour milk from Central Asia.

laban - yogurt drink from the Middle East.

lassi - yogurt drink from India.

mazoum - popular Armenian yogurt product.

skula - from the Carpathian region of Central Europe.

skyr - a yogurt-type drink made in Iceland, sometimes served with fruit.

fermented tofu - see TOFU.

Fernet-Branca - a bitter Italian apéritif, an **amaro** created in 1845 by Bernardino Branca. The secret recipe contains 27 herbs and other ingredients such as rhubarb, myrrh and red cinchona bark.

feta cheese - made with fresh curd set in a concentrated salt solution, made from either goat's or sheep's milk. All brands are chemical-free. The name comes from the Modern Greek *tyri pheta* (*tyri,* meaning "cheese," and *pheta,* meaning "slice") and the Italian *fetta,* meaning "slice." Originally from Greece but today made in many countries, feta is used in numerous Greek recipes.

fetticus - see MÂCHE.

fettuccine - also **fettuccini.** See PASTA.

fettuccine Alfredo - see ALFREDO SAUCE.

fiber - see DIETARY FIBER.

ficelle - an extra-thin loaf of French bread, similar in shape to a baguette, but much thinner. The name means "string" in French to describe its long, skinny shape.

ficin - from the Latin *ficus*, meaning "fig," a proteolytic **enzyme** acquired from the latex of certain fig trees and used as a protein digestive, notably as a curding agent for milk in the making of cheese. It is also used as a tenderizer for meat and poultry. See also BROMELAIN, PAPAIN.

fiddlehead - the coiled tip of a young fern, with a wonderful, delicate flavor, somewhere between that of asparagus and wild mushrooms. Introduced to European settlers in North America by Native Americans, fiddleheads are also popular throughout Asia; called *pohole* in Maui, they are considered a delicacy in Hawaii. Commonly available fiddleheads are the Ostrich and the Cinnamon. The Bracken fern is toxic and is not recommended. Sold fresh in the spring, frozen fiddleheads are available year-round. After food-borne illness, perhaps due to a natural toxin, hit several people who had eaten raw fiddleheads, health agencies in Canada and the U.S. now recommend that

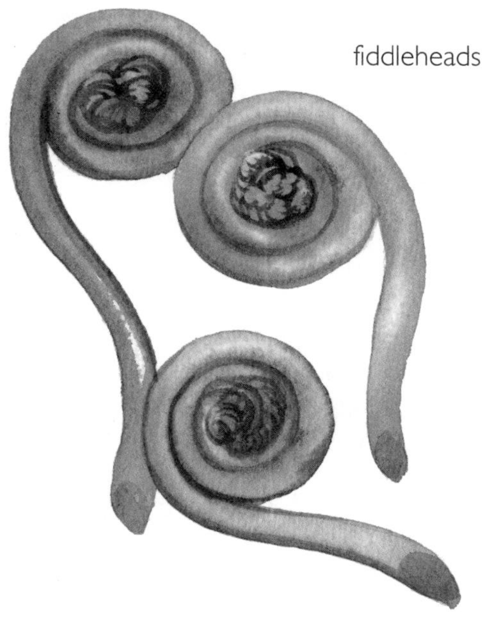
fiddleheads

fiddleheads be washed in several changes of water, then thoroughly boiled or steamed until tender. Do not pick this delicacy on your own, as several types of wild fiddleheads are poisonous.

fidelini - see PASTA.

field greens - see MESCLUN.

field lettuce - see MÂCHE.

field pea - see PEA.

field mushroom - *Agaricus vaporarius*, one of the many varieties of wild mushrooms found in meadows and pastures in summer and autumn. Now developed commercially, the well-known white cap of the field mushroom is abundant in food stores throughout the world. See also MUSHROOM.

field salad - see MÂCHE.

fig - probably the world's oldest fruit, *Ficus carica*, according to biblical references. Figs were said to grow in the Garden of Eden, and when Adam ate the apple and discovered his nakedness, it took a handy fig leaf to restore his dignity. Historians tell us that figs most likely existed in the Stone Age. In fact, figs probably originated in Asia Minor, although the oldest fig tree in the world is reputed to be growing in Palermo, Sicily. The ancient Greeks and Romans certainly enjoyed figs, which are still as highly prized today. During some periods of history, the leaf of the fig tree seems to have been more important than the fruit. And during the Dark Ages, artistic censors were kept busy protecting the public by strategic placement of fig leaves on the scandalously naked gods and goddesses. Both the Greeks and the Romans appreciated the fruit itself. The Greeks valued it so highly that Solon, the ruler of Attica, forbade its export. **Theophrastus,** an ancient Greek botanist, even describes caprification, the process used to "set" the fruit, or cut the flow of sap to the cluster, so that it matures on the tree, a technique still used today.

Botanically speaking, a fig is not a fruit, but simply a sweet receptacle designed to hold the seeds, or "fruits," inside. Since the seeds can't be pollinated, because they're hiding protectively

COMMON FIG VARIETIES

Adriatic - green skin covering sweet pink to purple flesh, excellent fresh, called Verdone in Italy.

Adriatic

Black Mission or **Mission** - deep purple, almost black, exterior with red fruit inside.

Brown Turkey - brown to black skin covering beautiful pink flesh, eaten fresh because it does not dry well.

Calimyrna fig - golden skin with pinkish-white flesh, the name given to the **Smyrna** fig from Turkey when grown in California. The name comes from a blending of "California" and "Smyrna".

Celeste - purple-brown skin covering pink flesh, pear-shaped, very sweet and well suited to drying.

Kadota - thick, yellow-green skin covering a golden interior when ripe, almost seedless, excellent fresh or dried, the American version of the Italian Dottato variety.

Mission - see BLACK MISSION.

Smyrna - see CALIMYRNA FIG.

Black Mission

inside the fruit, the tree does not blossom. Cultivated throughout the world, fig trees flourish in arid, semi-desert regions and are harvested all year long. Figs contain the chemical **ficin,** a proteolytic enzyme capable of breaking down proteins with an action similar to that of papain (found in papayas) or bromelain (found in pineapples). Ficin is effective in temperatures ranging from 140° to 160°F (60° to 70°C), the temperature range for simmering stews. If fresh figs are added to the stew, they will help tenderize the meat and impart excellent flavor. Canned figs will not work, because they're heated to very high temperatures during the sterilization process. Figs are also used to ease constipation. Figs can be bought fresh, dried or canned, and are often used in preserves. See also BREBA.

Figaro sauce - named for the 18th-century opera protagonist, a tomato hollandaise sauce finished with parsley.

filbert - see HAZELNUT.

filé - also **filé powder, gumbo filé.** Used to thicken and flavor soups, stews and gumbos, filé consists of dried **sassafras** leaves that have been reduced to a powder. The Louisiana cook who coined the term used a variation on the French verb *filer* (meaning "to spin thread"). Filé is usually added at the end of cooking or after the dish is taken off the heat, since stirring it into boiling liquid can cause it to become unappetizingly stringy, like the spun threads of its name.

filet mignon - an expensive, very tender and lean slice of beef cut from the wide portion of the tenderloin, usually about 1 inch (2.5 cm) thick. See also BEEF.

Filipino eggplant - see EGGPLANT.

filled milk - milk or milk beverage, or cream (condensed, dried, evaporated and powdered) in which natural fats have been replaced with vegetable fats or oils, altering the taste and texture. To protect consumers, regulations in Canada and the United States govern such preparations. Products constituted primarily of edible oils, such as some liquid coffee whiteners, are exempt however.

fillet - also **filet.** From the French *filet*, a diminutive of *fil*, meaning "thread," fillet is the term for a boneless strip or piece of meat or fish. Fillet is the style both for the verb and the noun. In fish terms, a **single fillet** is one side of the fish; a **double fillet,** also called a butterfly fillet, is both sides of the fish, with a small piece of the flesh and the belly skin holding them together on one side.

filleting knife - also **fillet knife.** Any of a variety of knives similar in size and shape to a **boning knife,** sometimes with a more sharply pointed tip or a slightly thinner, more curved blade, ideal for slicing meat off bones and into fillets. The size, strength and flexibility of the blade should be proportional to the size of the animal: a small fish calls for a short, thin, flexible filleting knife, while a large cut of beef requires a longer, sturdier, rigid blade.

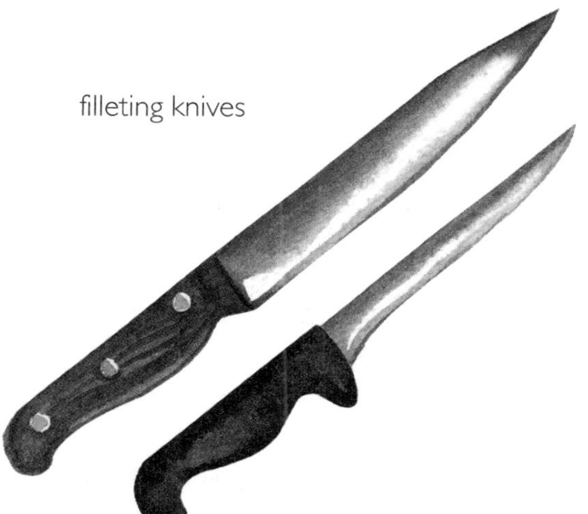
filleting knives

filo - see PHYLLO.

filter - to strain through very fine paper or cheesecloth to remove all solids from a liquid.

financier - also **friand.** A French sponge-like tea cake, similar to a **Madeleine** (both are baked in special molds), made with **beurre noisette** (brown butter), which creates a rich nutty flavor, and ground almonds or almond flour, eggs whites and confectioner's sugar. The traditional molds are rectangular (the finished product is said to resemble bars of gold, hence the name "financier"). The alternate name friand, means "tasty."

financière, à la - the French term for a dish served with a rich ragoût of Madeira wine, chicken **quenelles,** mushrooms and truffles. The thick sauce is a classic garnish for meats, such as sweetbreads or veal, and is frequently used as a filling for pies or **vol-au-vents.** The name means "in the style of a financier" to denote the richness of the ingredients in the dish, foods only a wealthy financier could afford.

fine bouche - literally French for "sensitive mouth," referring to someone with a discerning palate and olfactory sense.

fines herbes - the classic herb combination of equal parts finely chopped fresh chervil, parsley, tarragon and chives.

finger banana - see BABY BANANA.

finger bowl - a small silver, crystal or fine china bowl filled with warm water and often a slice of lemon or flower petals, used for cleaning the fingers at a formal dinner often before the dessert course. A waiter brings the filled finger bowl to the table and places it on top of a doily atop the dessert plate. The diner then gently dips the fingers of one hand in the finger bowl, wipes them on his napkin, and repeats the process on the other side. When finished, he places the finger bowl and the doily at the upper left side of the place setting for the waiter to remove before dessert is served.

finger citron - also **fingered citron.** See BUDDHA'S HAND CITRON.

finger food - a small snack or **hors d'oeuvre** that is eaten with the fingers, instead of silverware.

fingerling potato - also **finger potato.** As its name implies, this is a finger-shaped potato, usually only 2 to 3 inches (5 to 7.5 cm) long, which comes in a large number of varieties and colors and is generally lower in starch. Fingerling potatoes are considered very flavorful and can be prepared in any number of ways, from roasting to grilling to boiling.

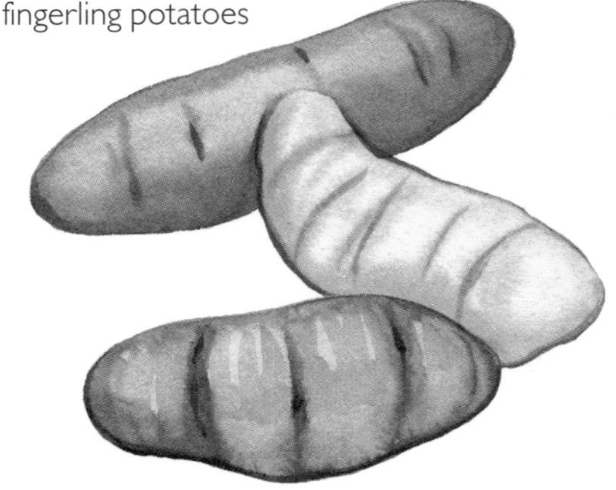
fingerling potatoes

fingerroot - also **Chinese ginger, Chinese key, ka chai, kra chai, krachai.** A relative of ginger and **galangal,** with a similar flavor but a pungent, aromatic scent all its own, used frequently in Thai cooking. The fingerroot, *Boesenbergia pandurata,* looks like long, slim, brown-skinned fingers protruding from the rhizome of the plant. It is often peeled and cut into slivers for use in fish dishes, as well as soups and curries.

finger sandwich - also **tea sandwich.** A bite-size or small sandwich, often cut into strips or shapes (such as stars or circles) or rolled into pinwheels, designed to be served at a fancy luncheon or tea party and picked up and eaten with the fingers. Finger sandwiches are made of tiny rolls or delicate white bread (usually with the crusts cut off) and frequently contain soft, spreadable fillings, such as egg salad, chicken salad, seafood salad or soft cheeses. Finger sandwiches are also called "tea sandwiches" because they are served at **afternoon tea.**

fining - the process of removing fine particles in wine or beer to make the liquid clear, accomplished by adding one or more of the following: **isinglass,** activated charcoal, gelatin, egg whites, diatomaceous earth or bentonite clay. The fining agents carry a positive or negative electrical charge, attracting the suspended particles, which are also electrically charged, and settle to the bottom of the container, allowing the clear beer or wine to be siphoned off the top. Fining must be done carefully and judiciously, so that the added matter does not diminish the flavor or texture of the liquid. Too much fining can result in a lackluster beer or wine.

finish - also **length.** A wine-tasting term used to describe the taste and feel of a wine that lingers after it is swallowed, often described in terms of duration (a long finish) or taste (a tart finish, for a wine with strong acidity). A fine wine should have an extremely long finish, with no one flavor or characteristic edging out the others.

Finnan haddie - see SMOKED HADDOCK.

fino - see SHERRY.

finocchio - see FENNEL.

Fisher, Abby (1832–unknown) - African-American cook, entrepreneur and author of one of the first published African-American cookbooks. Fisher was born in South Carolina in 1832. She moved to Alabama, where she met her husband, Alexander C. Fisher, and gave birth to 11 children. In 1879, they moved to California, where she won medals for her preserves at the Sacramento State Fair. With her husband's help, Fisher built a successful preserves business. Fisher never learned to read or write; with the help of an editor, she published *What Mrs. Fisher Knows About Old Southern Cooking* in 1881. She included a long list of clients at the back of the book, which revealed that as a cook and caterer she served a high level of California society.

fire point - see FLASH POINT.

firewater - a slang term coined in the 18th century for a strong alcoholic drink, usually whiskey. The name is the translation of the Ojibwa word for whiskey, *ishkodewaaboo*, undoubtedly from the burning intensity of the liquor as it goes down the throat.

firm tofu - see TOFU.

fish - aquatic cold-blooded vertebrate with a two-chambered heart that oxygenates blood through thoracic gills. There are 25,000 recognized species of fish, and 200 to 300 new species are discovered each year. The earliest record of Homo sapiens eating fish is from 380,000 years ago, and the first recorded recipe was Chinese, dated 1300 BC, for a salad of marinated carp. The Catholic Church is credited with boosting fish consumption beginning in the Middle Ages, ordering 166 days of fasting each year, during which fish was permitted. Worldwide, 98 million tons (89 million tonnes) of fish are caught every year, 84 percent of which are from saltwater and the remainder from freshwater.

Flatfish is a 500-species category of lean, sweet-fleshed fish, with eyes on the upper side of its slender, horizontal body, making it compatible with its habitat on the Atlantic and Pacific ocean floor; includes sole, flounder and halibut. **Roundfish** is a general term referring to fish with eyes on either side of their head, as opposed to flatfish. Roundfish is also the name for a plentiful freshwater whitefish, *Coregonus quadrilateralis*, found in Britain, the U.S. and Alaska. **Shellfish** are aquatic shelled invertebrates, categorized either as mollusks or crustaceans. See also AKULE, ALBACORE, ALEWIFE, AMBERJACK, ANCHOVY, AQUACULTURE, BASS, BLAWN FISH, BLUEFISH, BREAM, BRILL, BURBOT, CABEZONE, CARP, CATFISH, CHAR, CISCO, COD, CRAYFISH, DRUM, EEL, GRAYLING, HADDOCK, HAKE, HALIBUT, HERRING, JOHN DORY, LAMPREY, MACKEREL, MENHADEN, MONKFISH, PERCH, PICKEREL, POLLACK, POMPANO, PORGY, POUTINE, PRAHOC, PUFFERFISH, RED MULLET, SALMON, SALT COD, SARDINE, SCROD, SHAD, SMELT, SOLE, SPRAT, TAUTOG, TURBOT.

fish and chips - a pub or fast-food dish consisting of deep-fried fish fillets and chips, or french fries. Wildly popular all over Britain, Australia and New Zealand, they are served (at chip shops, or "chippies," as they're known in England, and "fish shops" in Australia) in a traditional cone of white paper and newspaper to keep them warm and soak up excess grease. In Britain, fish and chips are usually served with salt and malt vinegar, whereas they are served with tartar sauce and lemon for the fish and ketchup for the chips in the U.S. Canadians enjoy their fish and chips with any or all of these condiments, and often with white vinegar instead of malt vinegar. Almost any type of white fish can be used; some popular choices are cod, halibut, haddock and pollock.

fish cake - see KAMABOKO.

Fisher, Abby - see profile above.

Fisher, Mary Frances Kennedy - see profile on page 264.

fish eyes and glue - a rather gruesome childhood nickname for tapioca pudding made with pea-size tapioca.

fish poacher - also **fish kettle.** A long, deep pan with a tight-fitting lid, used for cooking a whole fish, with a rack inside that allows the fish to be poached or steamed. The typical fish poacher will accommodate a fairly long, large fish, but there are also special ones designed for cooking flatfish (specifically turbot), called "turbot poachers" or, in French, *turbotière*.

Fisher, Mary Frances Kennedy (1908–1992) - food writer, who also wrote fiction and a screenplay and translated **Jean Anthelme Brillat-Savarin**'s *The Physiology of Taste*; known for her elegant and evocative prose. Born in Albion, Michigan, Fisher grew up in Whittier, California, where her father owned and edited the local newspaper. Her awareness of food as a subject developed early; it was rooted in familial tension between her resident grandmother, who scorned sensual pleasure, and the other members of her family, who enjoyed good food and dined well whenever the matriarch was away.

Fisher began writing about food in the early 1930s, while living in Dijon, France, with her first husband, Albert Fisher. By 1937, when she published her first book, *Serve It Forth*, a collection of musings on a broad assortment of culinary subjects, she was deeply involved in a passionate affair with the painter Dillwyn Parrish, whom she married in 1939. The great love of her life, he committed suicide in 1941 after an extraordinarily painful and debilitating illness. Tragically, her brother also died by his own hand not long afterward.

Perhaps not surprisingly, Fisher's work, while ostensibly about food, betrays a profound longing for security and love, driven by relentless hunger. Although her life appeared very glamorous — she was considered a beauty, had many lovers and was, for instance, the subject of an article in *Look* magazine on the new breed of 1940s career women — her biographer, Joan Reardon, has documented many cracks in the polished veneer. In 1943, Fisher announced she was going away on a secret assignment. In fact, she was living incommunicado in a boarding house in Altadena, California, where she gave birth to a daughter, Anne, whom she identified as an "adopted" child and raised as a single parent. Interestingly, while awaiting the birth, she wrote *The Gastronomical Me*, a reflection on her life to date, which is generally considered the best of her books. She also had another daughter, Kennedy, from her marriage to publisher and literary agent Donald Friede.

A prolific writer whose career spanned more than 60 years, Fisher produced hundreds of stories for *The New Yorker* magazine and 15 books of essays, in addition to other work. Hired as a writer on the Time-Life series, *Foods of the World*, she met and became lifelong friends with **Julia Child.** In 1963, the esteemed poet W.H. Auden called her America's greatest prose writer and compared her to the French writer Colette. Even so, she felt her work was not taken seriously because it was "women's stuff." However, in 1991, she was elected to the American Academy and Institute of Arts and Letters, becoming the first culinary writer to be so honored. Although she enjoyed extended stays in France, she spent most of her life in California and died there in 1992, after a long battle with Parkinson's disease.

fish sauce - a strong-flavored, salty liquid popular in Southeast Asia, used as both a substitute for salt and as a flavoring. There is good evidence that fish sauce came to Asia from the Roman Empire, where it was known as **garum.** In the Philippines it is called **patis,** in Japan **shottsuru,** in Thailand **nam pla,** in Vietnam **nuoc nam.** See also KETCHUP, PADEK.

fish slice - a British term for a wide, slotted metal spatula used for turning or serving fish.

fishsticks - lengths of white fish meat, breaded and usually frozen, made popular as part of the boom in frozen prepared foods.

fitweed - see CULANTRO.

five basic tastes - Even though we perceive the taste of food as more complex, the thousands of taste buds on the human tongue respond to only five basic tastes: sweet, sour, bitter, salty and **umami.** Saltiness is sensed in foods that contain sodium chloride, or salt; sweetness in foods that contain any type of sugar; sourness in foods that contain an acid, such as vinegar or lemon juice; bitterness in foods that contain alkaloids and other chemicals; and umami, or savoriness, in foods that contain glutamates, which are often found in fermented or aged foods, and in **monosodium glutamate** (MSG). Umami is the newest addition to the list; it's a Japanese word that means "delicious flavor." It is a common concept in Asian cooking, especially Chinese and Japanese cuisine, but is now gaining ground in the West as a way of describing the savory flavor of fermented foods, some vegetables, seafood, meats and cheeses.

five-second rule - the age-old rule that allows you to pick up and dust off any food (within reason) that has been dropped on the floor as long as it's been there for five seconds or less. (The time limit is sometimes changed to three, 10 or even 15 seconds, depending on whom you ask.) Sadly, for kitchen klutzes everywhere, a Chicago high school student named Jillian Clarke disproved the theory once and for all in 2003. Her experiments showed that *E. coli* and other similarly nasty disease-causing bacteria can attach to foods as soon as they hit the floor. The safest bet is to discard anything you drop.

five spices - see CHINESE FIVE-SPICE POWDER.

fizz - a type of **cocktail** made primarily with liquor, lemon or lime juice and fizzy soda water, which gives the drink its name. All the ingredients except the soda water are shaken with ice and strained into a tall, ice-filled glass, then topped with soda water. The most popular type of fizz is the gin fizz, which comes in myriad variations, but fizzes can be made with almost any liquor, from brandy to rum to whiskey.

flabby - a negative wine-tasting term used to describe a wine that is lacking in character, usually due to a dearth of acidity; the opposite of **crisp.**

flageolet - a small, green variety of common bean (haricot), *Phaseolus vulgaris*, native to the Americas. It can be eaten fresh or dried, and is also available precooked and canned. In France, it's traditionally eaten with roast lamb.

flake - to use a fork to break up a food into bits or flakes, or to separate its natural layers from each other, such as those of cooked fish.

flaky - a term used to describe pastry that breaks apart into flat crumbs shaped like flakes; usually applied to pastries made with a fairly high ratio of fat to flour. When fat is cut into a flour mixture, it is broken up into small lumps that become coated with, but not fully incorporated into, the flour mixture (sometimes the lumps can be as large as peas, sometimes as small as bread crumbs). These flour-coated lumps of fat melt and create steam as they bake, creating fine air pockets between the layers of flour, which makes the pastry crumbly and tender when it is dry and fully baked. Overmixing the fat and flour mixture makes the fat melt before it goes into the oven and yields a tougher pastry, because mixing develops the **gluten** in the dough, which becomes more elastic the more the dough is handled. Therefore, pastry should be handled and rolled as briefly as possible to yield a tender, flaky result.

flambé - a French term meaning "flamed" or "flaming," used to describe dishes that have been doused with warmed liquor and set aflame. This technique is quite dramatic and is often used to create a splash of excitement at the table. Crêpes Suzette and cherries jubilee are two desserts that use the technique.

flambé pan - a round, shallow version of the skillet, often with a long handle, used for **flambéing** a variety of dishes, both savory and sweet, over an open flame. Flambé pans are often made of copper or tin-lined copper for both excellent heat conduction and beauty.

flameproof - a term used to describe pots or cookware that can be used over open flames on the stovetop and/or baked in the oven without damage from the flames or high heat. Recipes that call for flameproof casseroles or dishes often start out with a sautéing step on the stovetop, then transfer the dish to the oven for a long braising or baking step.

flan - **1.** a shallow, uncovered, pastry-lined tart filled with a fruit, cream or savory mixture. **2.** a Spanish egg custard, often caramel-flavored, made in a mold, turned out and served cold. From the Latin *flado* to Old French *flaon*, meaning "a flat cake," flans have been known since the 6th century; they were mentioned by Latin poet Fortunatus and were featured in medieval cooking.

fruit flan

flanken - also **short ribs. 1.** a cut of beef from the chuck side of the short ribs, including sections of the bones; fatty and tough, but flavorful and delicious when cooked slowly in moist heat, such as braising. Flanken should not be confused with boneless **flank steak,** which is a long, lean, tough piece of meat taken from farther back, between the rib and the hip of the cow. *Flanken* is Yiddish for "flank" or "side." **2.** any of a number of Jewish boiled or stewed dishes that have flanken as their central ingredient, often served with horseradish.

flank steak - a cut of meat taken from the fleshy part of the side between the rib and the hip of a cow. See also BEEF.

flannel cake - see PANCAKE.

flan ring - also **tart ring.** A simple circle of stainless steel, about 3/4 to 2 inches (2 to 5 cm) high, used to form the edge of a baked flan or tart. The ring is centered on a parchment-paper-lined baking sheet, then the dough is rolled out and fitted into the bottom and up the side of the ring to form the crust. After the flan is filled and baked, the ring is lifted away to leave a freestanding, easy-to-cut dessert.

flapjack - see PANCAKE.

flash point - also **fire point.** In cooking, the flash point refers to the lowest temperature at which cooking oil ignites, between 600° and 700°F (315° and 370°C). Although there seems to be a marked jump in temperature from the **smoke point,** the flash point is still considered a warning, because heat is conducted very efficiently from the pan to its contents.

flat - **1.** a wine-tasting term used to describe a wine that lacks flavor and tastes dull, usually because it does not have enough acidity. **2.** a tasting term used to describe carbonated beverages, such as sparkling wine, beer or soft drinks, that have lost their characteristic bubbles due to improper storage or serving techniques.

flatbread - **1.** a catch-all term for any bread that is thin and flat, leavened with yeast or not, of any texture, from chewy and soft to crisp. Flatbreads are becoming more and more common on North American tables, thanks to the influx of foreign cuisines. It is not uncommon for a supermarket to carry a varied assortment of ethnic flatbreads, including focaccia, lavash, naan, pitas and tortillas. **2.** a thin, dry-type wafer of Scandinavian origin made of rye flour dough.

flatfish - see FISH.

flathead catfish - see GOUJON.

flatiron steak - see BEEF.

flat-leaf parsley - see ITALIAN PARSLEY.

flat whisk - see WHISK.

flauta - a tortilla rolled around a meat filling and then fried in oil, so named because of its resemblance to a flute.

flavonoids - a class of more than 4,000 plant compounds, broken into five main categories: flavonols, flavanones, flavones, catechins and **anthocyanins.** Flavonoids are present in brightly colored fruits and vegetables and concentrated in many foods derived from plants; green tea, onions, beer, wine and soybeans are particularly rich sources of these beneficial nutrients. Like **carotenoids** and certain vitamins, these compounds act as **antioxidants,** vacuuming up harmful **free radicals** and preventing damage to the cells in the body. People who consume large amounts of flavonoids have a lower risk of heart disease, according to studies, due to their cholesterol-lowering effect. Flavonoids are also linked to lower incidence of certain types of cancer, particularly soy **isoflavones** in relation to breast cancer, although there is substantial controversy over whether an overabundance of this compound could actually increase the incidence of the disease in certain women. Flavonoids are also credited with a host of other beneficial effects, including reducing inflammation, preventing age-related vision problems (such as macular degeneration and cataracts) and fighting off viruses and bacteria that cause illness.

flavored sugar - see SUGAR.

flaxseed - also **linseed.** The seeds of the flax plant, *Linum usitatissimum*, used in cooking for their nutty flavor and healthful nutrients. Flaxseeds are reddish brown to brown and slightly larger than sesame seeds, teardrop-shaped with one pointed end. They are rich in polyunsaturated fat and high in alpha-linolenic acid, an **omega-3 fatty acid** credited with lowering heart disease risk. Flaxseed is also rich in fiber, especially soluble fiber, and lignans, plant chemicals that are thought to have a protective effect against cancer. Flaxseeds are often used in baked goods, in both ground and whole form. Ground flaxseeds can also be used as an egg substitute in vegan baking, because the mucilaginous compounds in the seeds bind with water to make a powerful **emulsifier.**

flaxseed oil - also **flax oil, linseed oil.** The oil extracted from flaxseeds, used as a salad oil or supplement. Like flaxseed, flaxseed oil is high in alpha-linolenic acid, one of the heart-healthy **omega-3 fatty acids.** It is best suited for use in cool or cold dishes, because it is particularly sensitive to high heat and will break down if used in cooking at all but the lowest heat.

fleshy - a wine-tasting term used to describe a wine with a rich, smooth, full **mouth feel.** A fleshy wine is supposed to evoke the sensation of biting into a fragrant, fleshy fruit at its peak of ripeness.

fleur de sel - see SALT.

fleuron - a small, crescent-shaped piece of puff or flaky pastry, used to garnish fish dishes and sometimes pies.

flexitarian - a sometime vegetarian, mainly for health or practical rather than moral concerns, who is flexible enough to occasionally eat dairy, fish and seafood, meat and poultry products, but usually eats four or more meatless meals weekly. The term came into usage in the late 20th century. See also PESCATARIAN, VEGETARIAN.

frikadeller - see MEATBALL.

flint corn - also **flint maize, Indian corn.** This variety of corn has a hard outer shell and small kernels that range from white to red colors, often used as livestock feed or to make processed food.

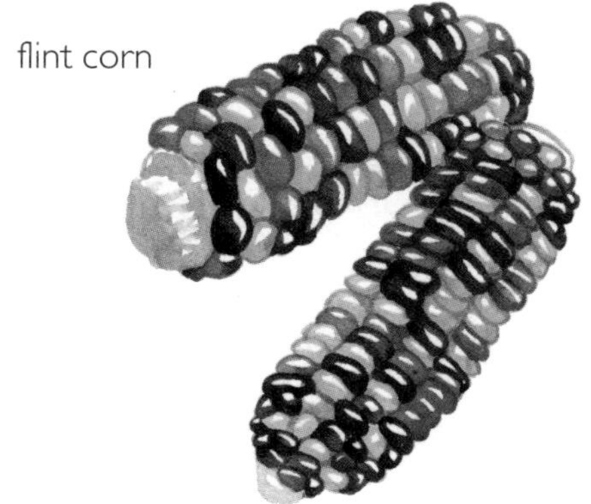
flint corn

flip - an alcoholic beverage made with liquor or wine, an egg, sugar and spices, and shaken with ice until frothy. The original flip was a well-loved Colonial American drink made with strong beer, sugar or molasses and a shot of rum. The drink was made sizzling hot by thrusting a red-hot iron fireplace poker into it and swizzling it around the cup. Some tavern keepers specialized in rich flips made with eggs and cream, which evolved into the present-day flip.

flitch - a half pig, also known as a flitch of bacon. It has represented marital felicity since medieval England: during the Dunmow Flitch ceremony (which takes place on Whitmonday at Dunmow in Essex), a couple who can swear that they have neither quarreled nor repented of their marriage for a year and a day may claim a flitch of Dunmow bacon.

float - **1.** a sweet, cold beverage made by topping a tall glass filled with a soft drink, commonly root beer or cola, with a scoop of ice cream. Floats are commonly on the menu at ice cream shops and old-fashioned soda fountains. See also BLACK COW, ICE CREAM SODA. **2.** a small amount of liquor poured very gently on top of a cocktail, so that it does not mix in, such as the **Galliano** float atop a **Harvey Wallbanger.** The best way to ensure that the float liquor doesn't mix in is to slowly pour it over the back of a spoon over the drink.

floating island - also **île flottante.** According to the annals of French classical cuisine, this dessert is constructed with stale sponge cake cut into thin slices, steeped in **Kirsch** and **Maraschino liqueurs,** spread with apricot jam and sprinkled with blanched almonds and currants. The layers are then put back together to re-form a cake, iced with sweet, vanilla-flavored whipped cream and decorated with almonds, chopped pistachios and currants, finished with berry coulis or vanilla custard poured over top. This dessert is often confused with **oeufs à la neige, quenelles** of meringue poached in milk served on a pool of custard. Modern chefs, including French chefs loyal to the traditions of classical cuisine, continue to take liberty with this dish, making variations of *oeufs à la neige,* with or without poaching the meringues, and calling them "floating islands."

flor de calabaza - see SQUASH BLOSSOM.

florentine - a chewy, nut-based cookie that combines chopped almonds and candied citrus peel, partially cooked on the stovetop before being dropped onto cookie sheets and baked. The finished cookie is then spread with a thin layer of chocolate on one side.

Florentine, à la - the French term for a dish served on a bed of spinach or made with spinach and **Mornay** sauce, such as *oeufs à la florentine* (better known as eggs Florentine in English). The name means "in the style of Florence," the city where spinach was purportedly used for the first time in French cooking in the 16th century.

floret - a small, tree-shaped portion of a cruciferous vegetable, such as broccoli or cauliflower, actually a cluster of tiny, unopened flower buds. The name comes from the Middle French *flouret*, the diminutive form of the word for "flower."

Florida arrowroot - see ARROWROOT.

Florida mustard - see MUSTARD.

Florida stone crab - see CRAB.

flounder - any of a variety of flatfish of the order *Pleuronectiformes*, with eyes on one side of the body (usually on the right side, but there are some species with eyes on the left). Different species of flounder are found in the Atlantic, Pacific and Indian oceans; plaice, dab and sole are all types of flounder, although they are sold under these other names. Flounder is mild in flavor and well suited to a variety of cooking methods.

flour - 1. (n.) the milled and finely ground starch product of cereal grains or vegetables. In modern usage, unless it's otherwise identified, the word refers to wheat flour, although there's also flour made of rice, rye, buckwheat, corn and potato.

The word is derived from the French *fleur de farine*, meaning "flower [or the best part] of the wheat." Chemicals, such as chlorine dioxide, benzoyl peroxide or acetone peroxide, are used to bleach flour, which destroys most of its vitamins. Government regulations require that vitamins be added to produce enriched flour. **Gluten** is the starch element of wheat, also known as essential or vital gluten, which is extracted from the wheat during a washing and rinsing process and used mainly as an additive to dough. **Wheat germ** is the isolated highly nutritious core, or germ, of the grain, which spoils very quickly if not refrigerated. **Wheat bran** is the outer layer of the wheat kernel and is very high in carbohydrates, calcium and fiber.

2. (v.) to dust a greased cake pan with flour in order to prevent the cake from sticking to the side of the pan; this allows the cake to release easily when it is done. Flour also means to dip a food into flour (then usually into beaten eggs, then bread crumbs) as a preparation for frying, or to dust a work surface, your hands, a utensil or a piece of dough with flour to prevent it from sticking to another object that touches it.

COMMON TYPES OF FLOUR

all-purpose flour - a blend of hard and soft wheat, with a gluten content of 9 to 11 percent, which can be bought bleached or unbleached.

bread flour - also **hard flour.** Made from hard, red winter wheat, with a very high gluten content, between 12.5 and 14 percent.

cake flour - a bleached soft flour with about 8 percent gluten. The chlorination turns the flour pure white and contributes to making a thicker batter.

hard flour - see BREAD FLOUR.

pastry flour - about 9 percent gluten, usually available only from commercial suppliers.

self-rising flour - a mixture of all-purpose flour, salt and baking powder designed for baking certain types of breads and cakes. Although self-rising flour is available commercially, it is easy to make at home.

soy flour - made from milled soybeans, high in protein and full of a host of vitamins and minerals. As a rule, soy flour is deodorized to neutralize its strong odor.

white wheat flour - with the bran and germ removed during the milling, also known as unbleached white flour.

whole wheat flour - also known as **whole meal flour** in Britain and Australia, made by milling the entire grain of wheat, specifically including the bran and germ.

OTHER FLOUR TYPES

barley flour - ground from whole-grain barley, higher in fiber than whole wheat flour but easy for most people to digest. Barley flour can be substituted for regular flour in some baking, but its gluten is weaker than that of wheat flour, so breads made with it won't rise as well. It is also a good thickener for soups and stews.

bean flour - made from finely ground soy, romano or garbanzo beans (chickpeas).

brown rice flour - flour ground from whole-grain brown rice, used for baking, cooking and to make gluten-free pastas. It has a nutty flavor and is high in fiber. Because the natural oils in the bran layer of the brown rice are included, the flour does not have as long a shelf life as more-processed flours. However, storing it in the refrigerator or freezer can extend its life. Some rice flours on the market are made from parboiled rice, which can keep the oil from going rancid during storage.

gluten flour - also **high-gluten flour.** Hard-wheat flour treated to remove much of the starch, leaving a high amount of protein (often 40 to 80 percent), used for adding extra rising power to bread recipes that call for a large amount of lower-gluten flour, such as rye. It is considered too high in protein to be used on its own in bread recipes.

graham flour - when first devised in the 1840s, a coarse whole wheat flour made by removing the germ and the bran, then adding back the bran in a higher-than-usual proportion. Today, graham flour may also be a blend of whole wheat flour and rye flour.

gravy flour - see INSTANT-BLENDING FLOUR.

high-gluten flour - see GLUTEN FLOUR.

instant-blending flour - also **gravy flour.** A bleached soft flour with an 8 to 10 percent gluten content.

semolina - a variety of **durum** wheat that has been relatively coarsely ground, then sifted to remove the fine flour.

southern flour - a bleached, extra-soft flour milled from very soft winter wheat, often labeled plain flour, with a gluten content of about 7 to 8 percent.

flowering chives - see GARLIC CHIVES.

flowering kale - also **ornamental kale.** Any of a variety of brightly colored kale plants, with dark green, frilly outer leaves on colored stems and bright white or purple center leaves, usually grown in home gardens as an ornamental and used as a garnish. Flowering kale is not just a pretty face: it is just as edible as common green varieties, although it can be rather tough if prepared in the usual manner. Flowering kale is best salted before eating raw (the younger the leaves, the better) or steamed to make it tender and tasty. See also KALE.

flower pepper - see SZECHWAN PEPPER.

flowers, edible - see EDIBLE FLOWERS.

Fluffernutter - a classic American children's sandwich made with white bread, Marshmallow Fluff and peanut butter. Marshmallow Fluff is the trade name for a thick, gooey, white marshmallow spread, which is also used to make certain types of fudge and confections. Marshmallow Fluff was invented in the 1920s by H. Allan Durkee and Fred L. Mower, two Massachusetts men who peddled their homemade product door-to-door for several years before starting up their first factory. In the 1930s, Marshmallow Fluff became a household name across New England, thanks to the inventors' sponsorship of the weekly *Flufferettes* radio show. See also MARSHMALLOW CREAM.

flowering kale

fluke - also **summer flounder.** A **flatfish** belonging to the **flounder** family, actually a variety of left-eye flounder, meaning both of its eyes are on the left side of the head; found in the waters off the east coast of the U.S., from the mid-Atlantic states to New England. Flukes are especially abundant in New Jersey, and are some of the most widely available flatfish in that state. Flukes have mottled gray-brown skin and sweet, mild, white flesh that is especially delicious pan-fried in butter. The name "fluke" is often mistakenly applied to other Atlantic flounders, especially when they are caught young or small, but this is a misnomer.

flummery - **1.** an old-fashioned, nearly extinct British dessert, a pudding made with finely ground oatmeal (or even just oat bran, in some cases), cooked until thick and gelatinous, sweetened and enriched with milk or cream. The name is also applied to a molded dessert custard made with cream and sometimes finely ground almonds, thickened with gelatin, such as from **calves' feet** or **isinglass.** Flummery was often further flavored with wine, such as Madeira or sherry. **2.** an American dessert made by cooking berries, then thickening the juicy mixture with cornstarch or arrowroot. This type of flummery is often served cold, topped with fresh cream or whipped cream.

flute - **1.** (n.) a tall, thin, stemmed wineglass used for serving Champagne. The small surface area on the top conserves the carbonation in the Champagne, keeping it bubbly and fresh longer. This narrow glass is also supposed to force the Champagne to hit the front of your tongue, where you taste sweetness, for better appreciation of its flavor. **2.** (v.) to crimp the edge of a piece of pastry, such as for a pie, to make an attractive, decorative finish. Fluting is done by folding under any overhanging pastry and pressing the raised edge against the pie-plate edge, then pressing down and pinching the dough with the thumbs and/or forefingers at evenly spaced intervals to make a peak-and-valley type of finished edge. **3.** (v.) to carve decorative patterns or grooves into fruits and vegetables, such as mushrooms, to make garnishes. The delicate cuts that fluting produces are best made with an extremely sharp, pointed fluting knife, the tiny cousin of the paring knife. **4.** (n.) a long, thin loaf of crusty French bread, a thinner version of the baguette. In France, the word is spelled *flûte*, but many North American bakeries omit the circumflex. **5.** (n.) a thin, crisp wafer cookie, rolled while still warm to form a thin cylinder, often served with pudding or ice cream.

flying fish - any of a number of fishes of the family Exocoetidae that have wing-like pectoral fins that allow them to glide as if flying, when they jump out of the water. They can often be found in warm waters in the Atlantic, Pacific and Caribbean, and have a mild flavor that is appropriate in many different dishes. Flying-fish roe is well regarded, especially in Japan, where it is known by the name **tobiko.** This roe comes in several varieties — unseasoned or seasoned with wasabi, ginger, hot chiles or even squid ink — but is usually used unseasoned as a main ingredient in or garnish for sushi.

flying fish

foam - a frothy mass of bubbles that forms on the surface of a liquid, made by furiously beating the liquid or injecting it with steam, such as the bubbles atop steamed milk, which are spooned onto the top of a cappuccino. Foams are popular for adding flavors to dishes without adding bulk or extra calories. They give the impression of an ingredient without having to include whole pieces of it in the dish. For example, a smooth, silky seafood bisque may be topped with a foam of fish roe and cognac to give the impression of both flavors without disturbing the texture or flavor of the soup. Foams can be made using the steam nozzle on a cappuccino maker, a French press coffee maker, a whisk or an immersion blender. The Catalán chef **Ferrán Adrià** is well-known for his many dishes accompanied with foam.

focaccia - from the Latin *focus*, meaning "hearth," differing from pizza because it goes through a second rising. Focaccia is, to a large extent, thicker than pizza, often with toppings of little more than sea salt, olive oil and fresh herbs. "Dimpling" the dough before it's baked traps tasty little pools of oil.

focaccia

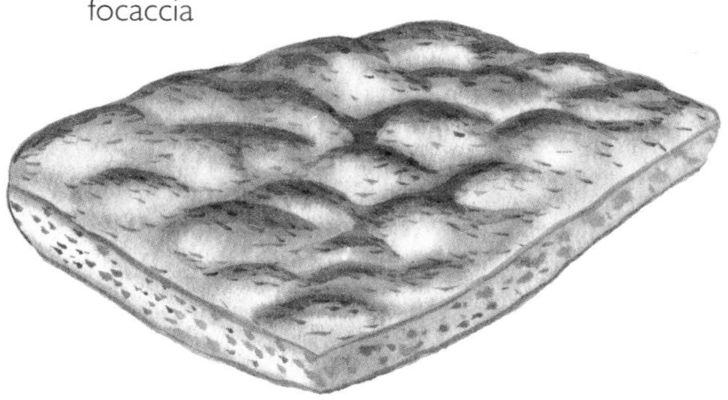

foie gras - goose or duck liver that has been enlarged by force-feeding, often with a diet of figs, known to the ancient Egyptians and popular among rich and noble Romans. As we know from **Apicius**, the Roman author from the 1st century AD, it was to become a great delicacy. Roman lovers of good food came to revel in "goose liver fattened with figs."

foil - see ALUMINUM FOIL.

folacin - also **folate, folic acid.** See B VITAMINS.

folding - a method of lightly combining beaten egg whites or whipped cream with another heavier mixture in such a way that the air cells are not broken down and the batter doesn't deflate. The technique calls for a gentle downward cutting motion of the spoon, then lifting it slowly in a gentle vertical motion, as opposed to stirring.

fond - meat or fish stock, most often prepared either of two ways: as a white stock (*fond blanc*) by placing the ingredients directly into the cooking liquid, or a brown stock (*fond brun*), in which the ingredients are first browned in the oven.

fondant - a sugar icing mixture that may be prepared with or without cooking, used as a coating or filling for pastries and confections. Fondant is usually made into a thick paste, which is kneaded and rolled, then draped and shaped over cakes. Fondant can also be cooked and thinned to a pourable consistency for use over a variety of different cakes, especially **petits fours.**

fondue - French for "melted" and the name given most often to the classic Swiss specialty of two or more melted cheeses — Emmental and Gruyère are de rigueur — combined with Kirsch, white wine and a little flour, nutmeg, pepper and salt (a way for thrifty peasants, so the story goes, to use up hardened cheese and stale loaves). Using long, two-tined forks, diners dip chunks of crusty bread into the communal fondue pot, kept hot at the table. To the dismay of the Swiss, the famous French chef, **Jean Anthelme Brillat-Savarin,** included eggs in his version which was later popularized in **Isabella Beeton's** *Book of Household Management*. Today's cooks can create the dish from scratch or buy ready-to-melt fondue mix. "Fondue" is also used to describe a course in which chunks of meat, seafood or vegetables are cooked in a pot of hot oil and served with savory dipping sauces (an example, with beef, is the French *fondue Bourguignonne*), or a dessert in which pieces of cake or fruit are dipped into melted chocolate or white chocolate. See also KAASDOOP.

fondue pot - also **fondue set.** A small, round-bottomed pot set on a stand over a short candle or alcohol burner, used for heating fondue to the correct temperature and consistency at the table. Fondue sets come with long-handled, slim forks for spearing bread or other delicate bites to dip in the melted cheese. Each fork usually has a different colored dot at the end, so that diners don't mix up their utensils.

fonduta - the Italian version (from Piedmont) of the French fondue, consisting of melted cheese (usually Fontina) butter, milk or cream, egg yolks and sliced white truffles.

fonio - the seeds of a West African crabgrass, used as a cereal.

Fontina - a cheese first made more than 500 years ago, according to the dairy bible *Summa Lacticiniorum* in 1477 by Pantaleone da Confienza, an Italian physician. Although Italian law specifies that Fontina cheese (more properly called Fontina Val d'Aosta) can only be made in the Val d'Aosta region in the north, this buttery cheese with a nutty flavor is extensively copied outside Italy. The French version, known as Fontal, is softer, sweeter and more buttery, while Danish Fontina is tart, and Swedish Fontina has a fuller, yet less complex flavor. One easy way to spot the Italian original, considered by many to be the best of the bunch, is the rind, which ranges in color from light to dark brown; the others sport red rinds. Fontina d'Aosta is traditionally used to make **fonduta,** a fondue topped with white truffles.

food additives - any of the various 2,000 legal chemical additives found in our food, added intentionally to give food specific qualities. Some food additives help keep food fresh; others add nutritional value; and others make food look, smell or taste more appetizing. The earliest chemical alteration of food was in 1859, when Sir William Henry Perkins discovered that coal-tar oil could be used to change the color of food to make it more appealing to the consumer. But, in 1906, it was banned by the Food and Drug Act passed by U.S. President Theodore Roosevelt. The long-range effects of consuming the chemical additives found in our food are still unclear. Laws regarding which food additives are allowed and how these must be listed on packages vary greatly from one country to another.

food coloring - a dye, pigment or substance used to impart color to food, all of which are regulated for safety. The Food and Drug Administration certifies nine synthetic color additives, and there are 22 color additives exempt from certification because they're from natural sources (animal, vegetable or mineral) or they are man-made derivatives of natural sources.

food mill - a kitchen tool used for puréeing foods, such as apples or tomatoes, a standard kitchen utensil before the advent of the electric food processor or blender, still used today to produce purées that are silky and not as liquid as the ones produced in a blender. A food mill is basically a perforated bowl with a handle that houses a hand-turned blade, which presses food against the perforations to purée it. The glory of a food mill lies in its all-in-one-operation efficiency: it can purée whole, unpeeled, uncored foods, leaving all traces of skins, seeds and fiber behind in the bowl.

food processor - an electrical appliance that consists of a hard, plastic bowl, a tight-fitting top with a feed tube, and a cutting blade placed over the motor shaft, used to slice, chop, mince or purée foods. Food processors also come with plastic dough blades for kneading bread dough and making pastry, and cutting disks, which can shred or grate foods pushed through the feed tube.

foo-foo - also **foofoo, fufu.** A bread-like paste from West Africa made from mashed boiled yams, cassava root or plantain.

fool - a dessert of fruit or berries mixed with whipped cream, from the French *fouler,* meaning "to crush."

foo yong - see EGG FOO YONG.

Forastero bean - see CHOCOLATE.

forcemeat - a mixture of finely ground meat, poultry, fish, vegetables or fruit and seasonings, bound with eggs or bread crumbs and used as a stuffing or made into **quenelles.**

Forelle pear - see PEAR.

forequarter - the front part of the lateral half of a carcass cut between the 12th and 13th rib.

fork - a utensil, usually metal, containing two or more tines with a long handle. Early forks were very large often with two prongs used for stabilizing meat while carving. The ancient Egyptians used a two-pronged massive fork made of bronze to lift sacrificial food during religious ceremonies. The first evidence that forks were used for eating is about the 7th century at royal courts in the Middle East. In the 10th century, a smaller version was used by the wealthy in Byzantium. The table fork

food mill

eventually traveled to Italy in the 11th century, brought there by a Byzantine wife of a Venetian Doge, Domenico Selvo. The Italians, however, were slow to adopt its use and were, along with the clergy, outraged by the Doge's wife refusal to eat with her hands. "God in his wisdom has provided man with natural forks — his fingers," said one church leader. It wasn't until several hundred years later in 1518 that the fork was first observed being used at a banquet in Venice. Jacques Le Saige, a French silk merchant, wrote, "These seigneurs, when they want to eat, take the meat up with a silver fork." When **Catherine de' Medici** came from Italy to France in 1533 to marry the future king Henry II, she brought with her, along with her many chefs and exotic foods, the fork. Again, as in Italy, the French did not embrace the utensil.

In his 1570 book, *Cooking Secrets of Pope Pius V,* **Bartolomeo Scappi** included the first picture of a fork, a two-tined implement evidently made of silver. In 1611, the Englishman Thomas Coryat wrote, after visiting Venice, that the Italians "do alwayes at their meales use a forke…" Coryat's neighbors back in Somersetshire ridiculed his foppish affectation in using a fork at the table and called him "furcifer," meaning "fork bearer."

In 1616, in the theater production *The Devil is an Ass*, by English playwright Ben Jonson, one character asks another what forks are, the reply being, "The laudable use of forks, brought into custom here, as they're in Italy, to the sparing of napkins." *The Queen of Corinth*, by English playwright John Fletcher, satirizes Thomas Coryat as "the fork-carving traveler."

Anne of Austria, who in 1615 married France's King Louis XIII, never used a fork, instead she plunged her hands into the serving dish as had been common in medieval times. Use of the fork would become firmly entrenched at the court of France and among the aristocracy in the reign of Anne's son Louis XIV, who was the first European host to provide a complete table setting for his guests. See also CARVING FORK, PIE FORK, SNAIL FORK, SPORK.

formaggio caprino - an Italian goat's milk cheese.

fortified wine - a wine fortified with neutral grape spirits or brandy, either to stop the fermentation process and create a sweet wine with high residual sugar, or to add extra alcohol and strength to the final product after it has fully fermented. Vermouth and sherry are two well-known types of fortified wine.

fortune cookie - a round, thin, crisp and golden cookie folded into a crescent, while still warm, around a strip of paper printed with a wise saying or lucky prediction. Invented in early-20th century California, it soon became the obligatory finish to Chinese-restaurant meals served anywhere in North America. Today's gourmet versions, such as chocolate, ginger and strawberry, may also deliver advertising or public-service messages. In New York, the largest U.S. producer now makes four million a day. A Cantonese Chinese-American in Los Angeles, David Jung, and a Japanese-American of San Francisco, Makoto Hagiwara, are competitive claimants as the cookie's sole inventor.

fouace - also **fouasse, fougasse.** A yeast-leavened French flatbread, basically the same as Italian **focaccia,** often seasoned with salt, but sometimes made with candied fruits, frequently eaten as a treat at Christmastime.

fougasse - a flatbread, the French version of Italian focaccia.

Fourme d'Ambert - a tall, cylindrical, firm blue cheese from France, made with cow's milk, with uneven patches of blue mold throughout the paste of the cheese. Fourme d'Ambert has a wrinkly, natural rind covered with a fine dusting of white-gray mold. It is a bit spicy, quite creamy and assertive, without the saltiness of other blue cheeses. Fourme d'Ambert has been made in France for thousands of years, since the period when the Romans ruled the Gauls. See also BLUE CHEESE.

four mendiants - see QUATRE MENDIANTS.

four spices - see QUATRE ÉPICES.

fowl - a general term for a variety of wild and domesticated birds used as food, including chicken, turkey and guinea fowl. It is often used more specifically to refer to an adult female chicken that is 10 months to $1\frac{1}{2}$ years old, sometimes called a "boiling fowl", "stewing hen" or "baking hen" in English or "*poule*" in French. This type of fowl needs long, slow cooking, such as braising, to make it tender enough to eat. See also CHICKEN.

Foyot (19th century) - French chef to King Louis Philippe and creator of the famed Parisian restaurant Chez Foyot, which outlasted him. Although sauce Foyot, a **béarnaise** with demi-glaze, was named for him, it's also known as sauce Valois. During the 1950s, just over 100 years after his royal tenure in the king's kitchen, Chez Foyot became a favorite of the literary world, the leisured class and political dignitaries in Paris. The restaurant is mentioned in Ernest Hemingway's *The Sun Also Rises* and plays a key role in *The Luncheon*, a short story by Somerset Maugham, in which the protagonist has been asked by the object of his affections to take her to Foyot's for lunch.

foxberry - see LINGONBERRY.

foxy - a usually negative wine-tasting term used to describe the musky "grape jelly" flavor of a wine, usually associated with wines that are made from *Vitis labrusca* variety grapes, such as Concord. Legend has it that European settlers called these native American grapes "fox grapes" for Aesop's fable, *The Fox and the Grapes*.

Foyot - see profile above.

fra diavolo - see DIAVOLO.

fraise des bois - **1.** also **alpine strawberry, woodland strawberry.** A variety of tiny wild strawberries, *Fragaria vesca*, known worldwide for its intense, fragrant, strawberry flavor, grown in many different temperate countries, but made famous by the French, who have adored the berries for centuries. The name is French, meaning "strawberry of the woods" for the berry's natural habitat. The ancient Romans cultivated fraises des bois in their kitchen gardens, often for their medicinal properties: they are credited as a curative for urinary tract infections and dysentery. **2.** an **eau de vie** or liqueur made from wild strawberries.

fraise des bois

framboise - a clear, unsweetened brandy, or **eau de vie,** made with raspberries. The name is literally "raspberry" in French. There is also a sweetened framboise liqueur, but true framboise has no added sugar.

Francatelli, Charles Elmé - see profile right.

Franconia potatoes - sliced potatoes browned and cooked with a roast and basted with drippings, taking its name from the German *Franken;* Franconia was the former duchy of southern Germany, where the dish originated.

Franey, Pierre - see profile right.

Frangelico - a famous brand-name hazelnut liqueur with notes of cocoa and vanilla. The Frangelico bottle is iconic, made in the shape of a monk's robe, complete with the traditional corded belt around the middle, for the Christian monks who first brewed the beverage in the hilly Piedmont region of Italy. The name is said to be a contraction of Fra Angelico, a legendary hermit monk who lived in the area during the 17th century.

frangipane - also **frangipani. 1.** a mixture of crushed almonds, sugar, flour, butter, eggs, milk and vanilla used in pastry making. One account attributes the confection to the Franciscan friar Frangipani, who concocted a pastry with these ingredients in Rome in 1532. A more likely source of the name comes from a 16th-century Italian nobleman, the Marquis Muzio Frangipani, who lived in Paris and developed a perfume for scenting gloves based on bitter almonds, inspiring pastry cooks of the time to make an almond-flavored cream they named *frangipane*. **2.** a mixture of flour, egg yolk, butter and milk prepared like a **choux pastry,** used in poultry and fish **forcemeat.**

frankfurter - an ancestor of the ubiquitous hot dog. The genuine frankfurter is made of lean pork and salted bacon fat blended into a paste

Francatelli, Charles Elmé (1805–1876) - Anglo-Italian royal chef and ice-confection innovator, known for his elaborate designs, but also for being the first chef to use conical wafers to hold ice cream. Francatelli was born in London and learned to cook in France. He spent most of his career in service to the aristocracy, most famously to Queen Victoria. He also wrote three books. *The Modern Cook* (1845) became a 19th century classic, reprinted many times. *A Plain Cookery Book for the Working Classes* (1861) presented humbler fare, with curious recipes for Baked Bullocks Hearts, Sheep Pluck and Cow Meal Broth. Francatelli is best known for his ice puddings or ice desserts, which were molded ice confections, using frozen creams, fresh fruit, dried fruit and sometimes flowers, arranged in elaborate designs. Ice puddings were logistically challenging, since chefs worked without benefit of refrigeration. **Antonin Carème** had been making them for years, and his **Nesselrode** ice pudding was a court favorite. It was Francatelli's ice-pudding designs, considered to be the century's most spectacular, that set him apart from his contemporaries. His Victoria pudding, which appeared on the cover of his 1864 book, *The Royal Confectioner,* had a built-in cooling system, a sculpted piece of ice that functioned as its stand. For another pudding, he used wafer cones filled with ice cream as a theme and for garnish. Francatelli's notes on this design are the first English record of the ice cream cone.

and smoked, but there are now many variations in ingredients, as well as in size and shape. Often the ingredients include beef and pork trimmings, tripe and pig hearts. American frankfurters contain beef and pork. Vienna sausage is a small "cocktail" frankfurter. **Knackwurst** is a small, plump, lean-meat frankfurter containing beef and pork. See also HOT DOG.

franks and beans - a homey dish of hot dogs and baked beans, sometimes found in old-school diners, the hot dogs often chopped and mixed with the beans. The name is short for "frankfurters and baked beans."

frappé - **1.** the French word for "iced," used frequently to describe iced desserts made with fruit and cream. **2.** an alcoholic drink, especially a liqueur, served poured over crushed ice. **3.** New England milkshake.

freegan - a person who consumes a diet that is partially or totally composed of food deemed to be waste. So-called "dumpster divers" are freegans by necessity, but others choose this lifestyle to protest the excesses of the conventional economy and to limit their consumption and impact on the environment. Some have formed communal distribution groups, which collect and exchange foods that would otherwise be thrown away.

free radicals - atoms or groups of atoms inside the human body that carry one or more extra negatively charged electrons, the by-product of many normal metabolic processes, stress and exposure to toxins in the environment or food. When these negatively charged atoms come into contact with DNA or cell membranes, they can cause damage or cell death, which can stimulate the development of cancers and other

Franey, Pierre (1921–1996) - French chef who established the first U.S. world-class French restaurant, Le Pavillon, in New York City. Franey was born in Burgundy and apprenticed in good restaurants in Paris. He went to New York in 1939 to cook in France's pavilion at the World's Fair. When war broke out, he was recruited to cook for General Douglas MacArthur but declined, choosing instead to serve as a machine gunner in the U.S. army. Franey presided over Le Pavillon's kitchen for 15 years. Long-time friend **Craig Claiborne,** who was then *The New York Times'* food critic, encouraged Franey to write a column for the paper. Franey's *60-Minute Gourmet* became popular and launched his writing career. He published 14 books, including his memoir, *A Chef's Tale.* He also hosted three cooking series for PBS: *Cuisine Rapide, Cooking in America* and *Cooking in France.* Franey died at the age of 75, still working, doing cooking demonstrations on the ocean liner *Queen Elizabeth 2.*

diseases. Antioxidants, such as **carotenoids,** vitamins C and E, and the trace mineral selenium, circulate through the body, bonding with these free radicals, effectively "mopping" them up and rendering them harmless. Preventing free radical damage is a primary benefit of consuming a varied diet rich in **antioxidants** and vitamins, many of them found in whole natural foods, such as vegetables, fruits and whole grains.

free range - also **free roaming.** Chickens that have been given access from their coops to the outdoors are considered free range by the United States Department of Agriculture. The agency doesn't specify, however, how much time the fowl is required to spend outside.

free run - chickens, usually those used for laying eggs, that are kept in large, open-concept barns, rather than **battery cages,** and allowed to walk around. They are not allowed to go outdoors, as **free range** chickens are.

freestone - the term applied to any fruit, such as cherry, peach, plum or prune, having a stone to which the flesh doesn't cling, its antonym being clingstone, in which the pulp adheres to the pit. See also PEACH.

freeze - to expose a food to a temperature of less than 32°F (0°C) for a long enough period that the liquid inside it turns to a solid. Foods are frozen to preserve them or to change their texture. Most foods can be frozen and later thawed successfully if they are wrapped properly to prevent freezer burn, but eggs, sauces that contain eggs, cream sauces or mixtures, and lettuce do not return to their former glory when they are thawed. Most types of liquor will not freeze in a home freezer because the ethyl alcohol in them requires much colder temperatures to solidify than other liquids. That's why Martini aficionados can keep their vodka in the freezer, at the ready, to make an ice-cold drink. See also FREEZER BURN.

freeze-dried tofu - see TOFU.

freeze-dry - a controlled version of freezer burn. Moisture is removed through sublimation, the transformation of ice directly into water vapor. We think of freeze-drying as a very recent novelty, but it actually goes back at least to the pre-Columbian Andes, where the Peruvian Indians would trample on potatoes during the day to squeeze out water and then leave them outside to freeze overnight. Today, freeze-dried vegetables are pretty much limited to use in instant soup mixes, emergency rations and camping foods. Coffee has had the most successful application of this technique.

freezer burn - the white or gray spots that appear on food that has been improperly wrapped and stored in the freezer. The cold air of the freezer dehydrates the exposed food, causing it to lose flavor along with its moisture. Freezer burn does not make a food unsafe to eat, but it does make it unpalatable. The spots can be cut off so that the remaining undamaged food can be consumed.

French beans - refers to dried kidney beans, flageolets and haricot beans, originated in South and Central America. The beans have been cultivated in that part of the world since ancient times and were brought to Europe after the Spanish conquest in the 16th century.

French bread - a general term used in North America for a loaf of white bread with a thick, crisp crust and an airy, holey interior. French-style baguettes and round **boules** are two standard types of French bread found in grocery stores and many bakeries, but the growing number of **artisanal** bakers have expanded North Americans' tastes for other types of French bread, such as **pain au levain.**

French-Canadian pea soup - see PEA SOUP.

French dressing - a simple, classic salad dressing, also known as vinaigrette, made with three or four parts oil to one part vinegar or citrus juice, and seasoned with salt and pepper. Some recipes also add a variety of minced fresh herbs, mustard or garlic to the mix. In North America, commercial French dressing is a standard offering at restaurants and on supermarket shelves, but it bears little resemblance to the original: it is creamier, sweeter and reddish orange, thanks to the addition of tomato paste.

french fries - deep-fried potato strips that are not named because they're French, but because they have been cut into long strips, using the technique to french. They probably originated in Belgium in the 19th century and only later spread to France, where they're called *pommes frites*.

French ice cream - a U.S. product that has a greater percentage of egg solid and cream.

French knife - see CHEF'S KNIFE.

French onion soup - a rich soup of beef stock (sometimes chicken stock is used, but beef is traditional) and deeply **caramelized** onions, usually served in an ovenproof crock topped with a **croûte** and cheese, then broiled until the cheese is melted and the croûte is crisp around the edges. The traditional cheese of choice is Gruyère, but the dish can be garnished with mozzarella, which is also excellent melted. The broth may also be enriched with white wine, beer or even brandy.

French press - also **coffee press, plunger pot, press pot.** A manual coffee maker with a plunger in the cap that acts as a filter. Ground coffee is placed in the pot and the pot filled with hot water. The coffee is left to steep for a few minutes, then the plunger is depressed slowly, corralling the coffee grounds in the bottom of the pot, so that the coffee can be poured free of sediment. Java junkies claim that the French press yields a more flavorful cup of coffee.

French press

French 75 - a cocktail of gin, lemon juice and sugar, shaken with ice and poured into a Champagne glass, then topped up with Champagne. Some recipes call for the addition of Cointreau, and some substitute brandy or cognac for the gin. The drink is named for the French 75, a 75-millimeter field gun supplied to American National Guard troops when they entered the First World War in 1917. This French gun was revolutionary, because it rarely jammed, unlike many other field guns of the era, operating smoothly and precisely under the intense conditions of battle. Legend has it that the French 75 cocktail was served to officers to stiffen their resolve prior to a battle, while the troops received more-pedestrian rations of rum. In any case, the drink was christened for its potent alcoholic kickback, much like the gun's powerful physical kickback.

French spice - see SPICE PARISIENNE.

French stick - see BAGUETTE.

french, to - a technique of cutting food lengthwise into long strips or cutting meat away from a bone, as in rack of lamb.

French toast - dry bread soaked with egg and fried in butter, usually served at breakfast. Originally called German toast, but renamed French by the Americans after the First World War. In France, this dipping of bread into egg is more commonly called *pain perdu*, meaning "lost bread."

French whisk - also **sauce whisk.** See WHISK.

fresh ham - the name for the fresh, unprocessed meat taken from the hind leg of a pig. Once it has been processed in any way, it is called cured ham. A fresh ham roast will taste like a pork loin roast or pork chops, rather than a smoky ham. See also HAM.

Fresno chile - see CHILE PEPPER.

Frey, Emil - see LIEDERKRANZ.

friand - see FINANCIER.

fricassée - meat (usually chicken or veal) that has been cut into pieces and stewed in a gravy.

frico - a small, round Italian wafer made by dropping spoonfuls of grated cheese, such as Montasio, Asiago or Parmesan, into a skillet and cooking them until melted and lacy in appearance, then cooling until firm and crisp. The warm wafers of melted cheese can be left flat, draped over different shapes to make cups, or rolled into cones that can be filled for hors d'oeuvres. The cheese may also be seasoned with any of a variety of fresh or dried herbs.

fried rice - a ubiquitous dish in Chinese restaurants across North America, a stir-fried combination of cooked rice, oil, flavorings (such as soy sauce or garlic), perhaps a lightly scrambled egg, and bits of meat, seafood and/or vegetables. Most restaurants carry a variety of these dishes, including pork fried rice (with diced, Chinese barbecued pork), shrimp fried rice, chicken fried rice or vegetable fried rice. While it is primarily thought of as a Chinese dish, most Asian cultures have some form of fried rice in their culinary repertoire.

fries - **1.** the shortened form of french fries, often heard in North America. **2.** a type of **variety meat.** See PRAIRIE OYSTERS.

frijol - pl. **frijoles.** The Spanish word for kidney beans, used in Mexico to refer to beans in general, often the pinto bean, which is used throughout Mexican cuisine.

frijoles refritos - see REFRIED BEANS.

frill - a small, feathery paper cover for an exposed bone on a roast, such as a crown roast.

frisée - also **curly chicory, curly endive.** *Cichorium intybus* has long, slender, spiky pale green leaves attached to a central core by thick, white stems. Its bitter, delicate, frilly leaves are widely used as a salad green, especially in **mesclun** mixes. The chicory and endive families are so closely related that they are often confused and their names used interchangeably, hence frisée's other names: *curly chicory* and *curly endive*. The name "frisée" is a shortened form of the French name for the plant, *chicorée frisée*, meaning "curly chicory."

frisée

frittata - an Italian omelet that incorporates the eggs with other ingredients rather than folding as a French omelet, then flipped to cook on both sides and served flat. From the Italian *fritto*, meaning "fried."

fritter - a sweet or savory food dipped in batter and deep-fried, usually fruit (apple is a popular choice) but also meats, fish and vegetables, best served hot.

fritto misto - Italian for "mixed fry," morsels of meat, seafood or vegetables dipped in batter and deep-fried.

frizzante - see PROSECCO.

frizzes - an unsmoked, Italian **dry sausage** made of coarsely chopped pork and/or beef, flavored with garlic and aniseed, similar to pepperoni. The spicy version is tied with a red cord, while the mild version is tied with a blue string for easy identification. It can be eaten on its own or used in cooking. Like pepperoni, it is an excellent pizza topping.

frizzle - to fry or bake until crisp and curled at the edges.

frog - any of a number of edible amphibian animals of the genus *Rana*, especially *Rana esculenta* (common European frog), *Rana clamitans* (green frog), *Rana pipiens* (leopard frog) and *Rana palustris* (pickerel frog). The bullfrog, *Rana catesbeiana*, is also edible, plentiful in North America and a common species raised for food. Frogs are usually considered a delicacy specific to French cuisine, but they are eaten all over the world. Only the large, muscular hind legs are eaten, because they have more meat than the smaller front legs and the inedible body. The meat is white, mildly flavored and often compared to chicken.

frogfish - see MONKFISH.

fromage - the French word for "cheese." A cheese shop is a *fromagerie* and a cheesemonger is a *fromager*.

fromage blanc - a fresh French cheese made from cow's milk, similar to cream cheese and Neufchâtel, but creamier and more akin to thick yogurt in texture. It is excellent for eating straight or making herbed spreads or desserts, such as **coeur à la crème.**

fromagerie - French for "cheese dairy," also used for a cheese boutique.

front of the house - a term used in hotels and restaurants referring to the area of the establishment where there is direct contact with the public, such as the dining room and bar. The **back of the house** refers to areas that are out of view, such as the kitchen, offices and the area where goods are received.

frost - **1.** to cover a cake, cupcake or other dessert with frosting. **2.** to chill a cocktail glass, so that it has an opaque coating of ice or frozen mist. Frosted glasses are often rimmed with sugar for sweet drinks. **3.** to coat a food in egg white and dip it in sugar, such as frosted fruit, to preserve it and give it a sparkly, shiny finish.

frosting - also **icing.** Used to decorate baked goods, frosting can be made in a variety of ways. Some are cooked and are also known as boiled frostings. Frostings can be as simple as a mixture of confectioner's sugar and water, or a little more complex, involving pouring a heated sugar syrup into stiffly beaten egg whites and then, once cooled, beating in softened butter. Modern **buttercream** frostings are generally made from sugar, butter, water and eggs.

froth - **1.** (n.) see FOAM. **2.** (v.) to quickly and vigorously beat a liquid, such as egg whites, to form a generous layer of fine-textured air bubbles on the surface. Liquids are usually frothed with a whisk.

frozen custard - a dense, sweet, ice cream–like frozen treat, which originated on Coney Island in New York, especially popular in the Midwest and central United States. It's made using the same basic ingredients as ice cream, but there are a couple of differences: egg yolks are always added to frozen custard to make a richer base, and less air is stirred into the mix as it's frozen, resulting in a richer, creamier product. It usually clocks in at more than 10 percent milk fat, making it as rich and fatty as most premium ice creams.

Frozen Daiquiri - at its most basic, a cocktail made of rum, lime juice, sugar and crushed ice, blended until the ice and liquids form grainy crystals, with a texture similar to that of a **slush** or **granita.** There are thousands of variations, flavored with all manner of fruit juices, fruit liqueurs and whole, sliced or puréed fruit. A Frozen Daiquiri is often served in a tall glass, such as a **hurricane glass,** with a garnish of fruit and a tiny paper umbrella.

Frozen Daiquiri

frozen yogurt - a dessert similar to ice cream, which uses yogurt as its base instead of fluid milk or cream. Frozen yogurt comes in a wide variety of flavors and fat percentages, and can be sold in a firmer form in tubs or boxes or extruded by a soft-serve machine, as it is at the numerous frozen yogurt stands in malls and shopping centers across North America.

fructose - also **levulose.** A very sweet form of sugar found in fruit and honey, fructose is often extracted from its source to make a sweetener.

fruitarian - see VEGETARIAN.

fruit beer - any of a wide variety of beers that are flavored with fruit, such as cherries, peaches or raspberries. The fruits are seeded and crushed or macerated before they are added to the fermenting liquid and allowed to steep, releasing their flavors and aromas into the mixture. Fruit beers are popular in Europe and have made their way to North America, thanks to small-scale craft breweries, which are more likely to experiment with flavored beverages than large-scale beer producers. See also BEER.

fruit brandy - see EAU DE VIE.

fruit butter - a sweet spread made by cooking fruit pulp with sugar to a thick consistency and often spiced.

fruitcake - a sweet, dense cake made with dried fruits, spices, and brandy or rum. The earliest version was made in ancient Rome. Honey and additional spices were added during the Middle Ages. During the 18th century in Europe, fruitcake was made following the nut harvest and saved until the following year, when it was eaten to herald another good harvest. It became a Christmas favorite during the same century, when the use of dried fruits was restricted to Christmas, Easter, weddings and funerals. Dark fruitcake is made with dark-color ingredients, such as brown sugar, dark corn syrup, molasses, brown liquors (such as bourbon), walnuts, raisins and currants. Light fruitcake is made with light-color ingredients, such as granulated sugar, light corn syrup, colorless liquors (such as rum), blanched almonds, dried apricots and golden raisins. Many fruitcake haters have only tried the dark versions of the cake and are surprised to find that the lighter versions are extremely tasty and not as heavy as their dark counterparts.

fruit cocktail - a mixture of fruits served as a cold salad or an appetizer. In North America, the term is more often applied to the canned variety, and the term "fruit salad" used for a combination of fresh fruits. Homemade fruit cocktail can contain any type of fruit, such as cubed melon, fresh berries, sliced apples or pears, orange or grapefruit sections, and cubed tropical fruit, such as mango or pineapple. To give the cocktail added flavor and zing, a dash of Champagne or liqueur may be added. The canned version of fruit cocktail usually contains chopped pears and peaches and the ubiquitous and less-than-flavorful grapes and pitted cherries, all floating in a sugary syrup or fruit juice.

fruit cocktail

fruit corer - see CORER.

fruit leather - puréed fruit spread thinly on a baking sheet or large pan and left to dry and form a chewy, leathery solid. The sheet of dried fruit is then cut into rectangles or long strips and eaten as a snack. Fruit leather is a popular snack for children and can be found in many forms at the grocery store. More-natural versions (without added sugar, colorings or flavorings) are easy to find in natural food stores and can also be made at home (with or without a mechanical dehydrator).

fruit salad - see FRUIT COCKTAIL.

fruits and vegetables - the definitions of fruits and vegetables reveal some of our hidden attitudes toward them. "Fruit" originally meant any plant used as food and eventually came to mean the edible layer that surrounds the seeds. In the 18th century, as the meticulous science of botany emerged, the term became more technical, its definition still in force today: a fruit is the organ derived from the ovary and surrounding the seeds. Plant anatomy replaced edibility as the decisive factor. Also in the 18th century, and perhaps as a result of the narrowed range allowed to fruit, "vegetable" made its first appearance as a word meaning "plant food eaten along with meat or other parts of the meal." Originally, it meant simply a plant, as opposed to an animal or inanimate object. Of course, the technical definition is not commonly in force today. Green beans, eggplants, cucumbers and even corn kernels are all fruits anatomically, but we call them vegetables.

Common usage is based not on plant anatomy, but culinary custom: we use apples and orange in one way, corn and eggplants in another. No less an authority than the U.S. Supreme Court has based a decision on this consideration: late in the 19th century, a New York food importer had claimed duty-free status for a shipment of tomatoes from the West Indies. He argued that tomatoes were fruits and so, under the regulations of the time, not subject to import fees. The customs agent disagreed and imposed a 10 percent duty on the shipment he defined as vegetables. Constitution and statute offered no guidance on this question, so the Court decided on the grounds of linguistic custom. Tomatoes, held the majority, are "usually served at dinner in, with or after the soup, fish or meat, which constitute the principal part of the repast and not, like fruits, generally eaten at dessert." Therefore, the tomato is a vegetable and the importer had to pay the duty.

The etymology of the terms reflects the special status of fruit. "Vegetable" comes from the Latin verb *vegere*, meaning "to animate or enliven." "Fruit," on the other hand, comes from *frui*, meaning "to enjoy." This root is largely evaluative and attributes desirability to its object. So, both etymology and their equivalent figures of speech implicate fruit with pleasure and support the judgment of most children and probably not a few adults: vegetables may be good for us, but it's fruit that tastes good.

fruits de mer - the French term for seafood in general, used for dishes that feature a mix of seafood, especially shellfish. The term means "fruits of the sea." *Frutti di mare* is the equivalent in Italian.

fruit sugar - **1.** see FRUCTOSE. **2.** another term for superfine sugar, sometimes called instant dissolving fruit/berry sugar.

fruity - a term used to describe a liquid that has the subtle or pronounced flavor of ripe fruit. Many liquids can be described as fruity: wines, beers and even certain types of olive oil can all have fruity flavors.

frutti di mare - see FRUITS DE MER.

fry - **1.** to cook using a small amount of fat in a shallow pan. See also DEEP-FRY. **2.** a party or social occasion where fried food is served, such as a fish fry. The "World's Biggest Fish Fry" has been held every April since 1961 in the town of Paris, Tennessee, and features 12,500 pounds (5,680 kg) of catfish cooked in traditional Southern style, battered and coated with cornmeal and served with **hush puppies** and beans. **3.** baby fish that have recently hatched or tiny adult fishes, sometimes used as food in dried or fresh form.

fry bread - a deep-fried quick bread of Native American origin.

frying - See FRY.

frying pan - see SKILLET.

fu - a Japanese protein source similar to **seitan.** Fu is made in the same way as seitan (flour is kneaded with water to form a dough, which is then washed to remove the starch, leaving only the stringy gluten), except that the resulting gluten is then kneaded with whole wheat or unbleached flour to make a marbled mixture. The fu is then rolled or stretched until fairly thin and toasted to create a brown outer layer and a soft, puffy interior. Fu comes in a number of varieties, shapes and colors (sometimes beautifully formed into delicately colored flowers) and can be added to soups, stews and vegetable dishes.

fudge - a confection of sugar, milk and butter, originating in the 19th century from an error made during the manufacture of toffee, when the sugar recrystallized.

Fuerte avocado - see AVOCADO.

fufu - see FOO-FOO.

fugu - see PUFFERFISH.

Fuji apple - see APPLE.

ful - dried yellowish beans, *Lathurus sativatus*, popular in the Middle East, where they originated; used to make the national dish of Egypt, *ful medames*, which uses these beans baked with eggs, cumin and garlic. Their white counterparts are called *ful nabel*.

full-bodied - a wine-tasting term used to describe a wine with a heavy, full **mouth feel,** usually perceived when a wine contains a relatively high amount of alcohol. A full-bodied wine might feel more like cream on the tongue than a light-bodied wine, which might feel more like milk or even water.

ful medames - see FUL.

Fumé Blanc - see SAUVIGNON BLANC.

fumet - a stock of fish or vegetables, stewed with wine and aromatics and gently reduced.

funazushi - see MATSUHISA, NOBUYUKI.

funeral pie - see RAISIN PIE.

funghi - the Italian word for mushrooms, seen frequently on restaurant menus.

fungus - pl. **fungi.** A vast group of plant-like organisms that do not use chlorophyll for photosynthesis, but rather feed on dead or decaying matter. Fungi can be of almost any size, from single-celled yeasts or molds to enormous mushrooms, and are common in the everyday cooking of virtually all people. Yeasts are responsible for leavening breads and making alcoholic drinks; molds are responsible for the varied and luscious flavors of many cheeses. Mushrooms are commonly used in cuisines on every continent. See also BLUE CHEESE, MUSHROOM, YEAST.

funistrada - documented in 1991 by Bill Bryson, a made-up word used by the U.S. Army in 1974 to survey soldiers' dietary preferences.

Although no such food existed, "funistrada" was selected by more soldiers in the survey than lima beans and eggplant.

funnel cake - a deep-fried pastry made popular by the Pennsylvania Dutch, made with a thin, sweet, pancake-like batter poured through a funnel into hot oil to form a lacy circle. Funnel cakes are served hot, topped with any of a variety of toppings, often a dusting of confectioner's sugar or maple syrup.

fusilli - see PASTA.

fusion cooking - a style of cooking that incorporates ingredients and methods from a variety of different ethnic cuisines, without regard to fitting into one category or another. It is especially common to hear the term used in reference to a combination of Eastern and Western foods and cooking techniques. Chef Wolfgang Puck was a pioneer of fusion cooking in California, beginning in the 1970s and continuing today, blending the most seemingly incompatible ingredients into delicious and artistically presented combinations. Fusion cooking is not considered avant-garde today, but rather the natural result of an increasingly global marketplace.

futomaki - see SUSHI.

fuzzy gourd - also **fuzzy melon, hairy gourd, hairy melon, hairy squash, little winter melon.**

fuzzy gourd

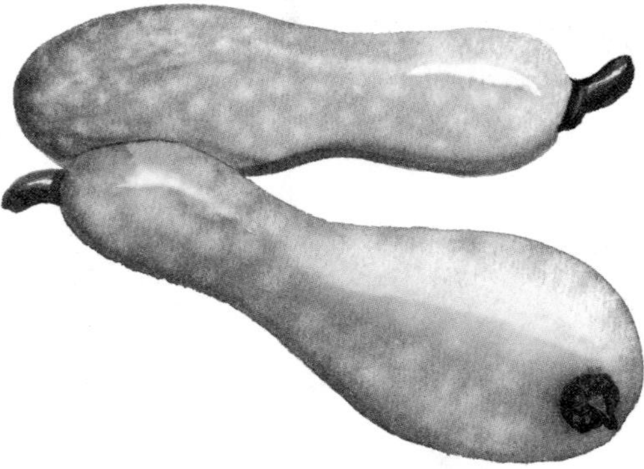

A cylindrical, mottled, green Asian squash with small, white hairs all over its skin, similar in flavor to cucumber and zucchini, with a light citrusy undertone; must be peeled before using. It is often served in Asian cuisine, seeded, stuffed with pork and steamed; stir-fried with oyster sauce or meat; or steamed and eaten plain. Fuzzy gourds are also frequently pickled when young and tender.

Fuzzy Navel - a cocktail made with peach Schnapps and orange juice, usually served over ice in a highball glass. A hairy navel calls for the addition of a shot of vodka. The name is inspired by the ingredients: "fuzzy" for the peach, and "navel" for the orange in the drink.

g
gingerroot

gado gado - also **gado-gado.** An Indonesian platter of vegetables (fresh and/or cooked), served with spicy peanut sauce infused with coconut milk. The platter is often garnished with hard-boiled eggs and fried onions.

gai choy

gai choy - also **Chinese mustard cabbage, kai choy.** An Asian member of the *Brassica* genus, similar in appearance to many varieties of **bok choy,** but with broader leaves and a more-pungent mustard flavor. Gai choy can be cooked and eaten in the same way as bok choy or **napa cabbage,** and is often salt-pickled, such as for **kimchi.** In Japanese markets, it is known by the name *takana.*

gai lan - also **Chinese broccoli, Chinese kale.** A leafy, green vegetable of the *Brassica* genus that is neither broccoli nor kale, but looks like a cross between the two, with wide, rounded, deep green leaves atop stalks reminiscent of thin broccoli stems, topped with white flower buds. Gai lan has a taste similar to that of collard greens and is usually blanched and/or stir-fried until the stems are tender-crisp. It can be used in any recipe that calls for broccoli or rapini.

Gala apple - also **Royal Gala.** See APPLE.

galaktoboureko - a traditional Greek dessert, a semolina-based custard inside a top and bottom crust of crisp phyllo, soaked with a sweet sugar syrup. Galaktoboureko is cut into squares or diamonds and served in the same manner as **baklava.** The name is sometimes translated into English as "milk pie." The word comes from the Greek *gala*, which means "milk" and *bourekia*, which means "stuffed phyllo pastries."

galam - see SHEA BUTTER.

galangal - also **galanga root, galingale, Laos ginger, Siamese ginger, Thai ginger.** A plant of the ginger family, grown for its aromatic saffron-color root, sold fresh, dried or ground, used extensively in Thai cooking, known by Marco Polo and widely used in the Middle Ages. See also LAOS POWDER.

galangal powder - see LAOS POWDER.

galantine - boned and stuffed poultry, pressed to make a symmetrical shape, poached in stock and served cold, sliced, sometimes with **aspic.** The French borrowed the word from the English, who served the popular *galyntynes* throughout the Middle Ages, a stuffing-like accompaniment to meat or fish. A man named Prevost, Parisian chef to the Marquis De Brancas until 1789, introduced the modern galantine. See also BALLOTINE.

Galbani, Egidio - see BEL PAESE.

galbi - see KALBI.

galette - a flat, sweet or savory cake, such as a potato galette or one filled with fruits, free-formed with surrounding dough. A party galette, or *galette des rois*, is a festive cake traditionally baked on Twelfth Night (the Feast of the Epiphany on January 6), made of flaky pastry or yeast dough. A hidden bean is baked into the dough, and whoever discovers the bean in his or her portion is dubbed king or queen for the evening.

galia melon - also **gallia melon.** A small, sweet, round melon, *Cucumis melo*, developed in Israel, now grown throughout the southern U.S. and Costa Rica. It has a netted, bark-like rind that turns from green to golden yellow when ripe.

Galliano - a liqueur whose secret formula is said to be based on 80 herbs, roots, berries and flowers, named by its inventor, Tuscan distiller Arturo Vaccari, after Major Giuseppe Galliano who, in 1895, held out under siege in Ethiopia for 44 days against greatly superior Abyssinian forces.

Gamay - a red grape variety grown primarily in the Beaujolais area of the Burgundy region of France, used to make the famous fruity, light-bodied reds of the same name. Gamay lacks the natural tannins of most red grapes, making it much less acidic and therefore tastier when served slightly chilled, unlike most red wines. Other winemaking regions of the world have varieties that fall under the Gamay name, but they are not true variants of this grape. California's Napa Gamay is actually a grape known as Valdiguié, and its Gamay Beaujolais is actually a clone of the **Pinot Noir** grape. Both are used to make red wines and sweet blush wines that are similar to **White Zinfandel.**

game - undomesticated birds and animals hunted for food. Game is generally leaner and less tender than farm-raised meat, because the animals fend for themselves in the wild, rather than have their food presented to them daily. Game tastes best marinated to sweeten the gamey flavor, and cooked very slowly in moist heat to keep the meat succulent, since it has so little inherent fat. **Larding, barding** and **basting** also help keep the meat moist. Pheasant, partridge, grouse, woodcock, rabbit, hare, deer, elk, caribou, bison and moose are typical types of game eaten in North America and Europe. Zebra, lion, camel, boar and kangaroo are also considered game. Each country has legislation that protects game by restricting the hunt to specific seasons. See also GAMY.

gammon - an uncooked cured ham cut from the upper part of the hind leg of a pig, usually sold in larger steaks or thick slices. It tastes similar to ham and can be used in any recipe that calls for ham or bacon. The name comes from the Old French word *gambe*, meaning "leg."

galia melons

Gamonedo - a Spanish blue cheese that hails from the northern region of Asturias, made from a blend of cow's, goat's and sheep's milk, lightly smoked before it is aged in natural caves for three to four months. Because Gamonedo is lightly pressed when it is molded, it has a fine, closed texture (smooth, with no holes) that is pleasantly crumbly. The flavor is often described as buttery but sharp, with an aftertaste reminiscent of hazelnuts. Gamonedo is excellent crumbled over salads and melts well in sauces. See also BLUE CHEESE.

gamy - a term used to describe the strong, musky taste of wild game animals or birds, often used to describe a meaty flavor that is just shy of being tainted. There is no one single flavor common to game animals and birds, but specific foods in an animal's diet can affect the flavor of its flesh, as can the slaughtering and butchering methods used to preserve it. If a bird or animal is hung for several days after it is killed (a common practice with venison and game birds), the flesh can take on a more pronounced flavor, which some hunters and connoisseurs find highly desirable. See also GAME.

ganache - an icing or filling made with equal parts **couverture** and whipping cream, used as a base for truffles and to cover cakes and pastries, among many other applications. It is said to have been invented in the mid-1800s in Paris at the Patisserie Siraudin.

gandule - see PIGEON PEA.

garam masala - a mixture of aromatic spices (its name means "warm mixture" in Hindi) used in Indian cooking. It can include up to 12 spices, including a traditional mix of coriander seeds, cumin seeds, peppercorns, cinnamon, cardamom pods and cloves. Garam masala is generally added at the end of cooking, so that the inviting aroma remains strong when the dish is served.

garbanzo bean - see CHICKPEA

garbure - a thick vegetable broth or soup from the Béarn region of France, always served with a thick slice of bread floating on top.

garde manger - **1.** French for "icebox" or "pantry." In a professional kitchen it is a well-ventilated food station where cold dishes, such as hors d'oeuvres, buffet items, salads, **pâtés, terrines** and **chaud-froids,** are prepared and stored. **2.** the cook who is charge of cold food production in a professional kitchen is known as a chef garde manger, one of the positions in the brigade system created by French chef **Auguste Escoffier** in the late-19th century to bring order to the professional kitchen. See also BRIGADE SYSTEM, CHEF, ENTREMETIER, PASTRY CHEF, POISSONIER, RÔTISSEUR, SAUCIER, SOUS CHEF, TOURNANT.

garden bunting - see ORTOLAN.

garden soybean - see EDAMAME.

garganelli - a type of hand-rolled fresh pasta made with eggs that looks like a ridged quill, similar in shape to penne, but with ridges that run across the width of the tube, not the length. A square of fresh pasta is rolled from corner to corner over a ridged board and sealed to make this shape, which is excellent for soaking up everything from delicate cream sauces to rich, chunky, vegetable-based tomato sauces. The name comes from the Latin *gargala*, meaning "trachea," which is similar in appearance to the horizontally ridged tubes of pasta. See also PASTA.

gari - **1.** a delicious condiment of pickled ginger root used to clear the palate between bites of sushi. See also AMAZU SHOGA, BENI SHOGA. **2.** also **garri.** A flour made from **cassava,** commonly used as a grain-like staple in West African cuisine. Gari is made by grating cassava and allowing it to ferment slightly as it dries. Once dried, it is fried in a dry skillet or roasted to give it extra flavor and to remove any leftover moisture, so that it can be stored until needed. It then only has to be moistened with liquid to make it ready for the table. Gari is a breakfast and lunch staple, often served with beans and a tomato sauce. Sometimes a drop or two of palm oil is added to give the cassava mixture color and flavor. Ready-made dried gari is available in some African markets in North America.

Garibaldi - a British cookie with a layer of red currants, named after the 19th-century Italian nationalist and revolutionary leader Giuseppe Garibaldi, whose followers wore a red shirt as a sign of partisanship.

garlic

garlic - an aromatic and strong-flavored bulb, *Allium sativum*, a member of the lily family, known to have been cultivated by the Egyptians about 3200 BC. An Islamic legend claims that when Satan stepped out of the Garden of Eden after the fall of man, garlic sprang up on the spot where he placed his left foot and onion from where his right foot touched. For protection against the spells of Circe, Odysseus gave Hermes moly, a magic herb with milky, white flowers and black roots, known to us today as yellow garlic, *Allium moly*. The Greeks and Romans both believed garlic to have magical qualities. Gods were appeased with gifts of garlic, and cloves of garlic were secured around the necks of babies to protect against evil.

Symbols and models of garlic found in the pyramids of ancient Egypt bear witness to the fact that garlic was not only an important foodstuff, but that it had ritual significance as well. The Egyptians swore on a clove of garlic when they took a solemn oath. It was the main component in the diet of the slaves who built the pyramids, since it was thought to prevent heat prostration.

Hungarian jockeys used to carry garlic believing that it prevented another horse and rider from getting in front of them. In India, garlic is worn for protection against evil spirits and spells. And, of course, garlic was said to repel vampires, providing it was more than one month old, made into a necklace and worn around the neck, each head of garlic separated by no more than 2 inches (5 cm).

The Greeks and the Romans also used garlic for its therapeutic qualities. It was believed to be an aphrodisiac and also believed to be a remedy for eczema, toothache and snakebites. Garlic is found all over Europe (vats of butter strongly flavored with garlic, which date to 200–300 BC, have been found by archaeologists in Ireland). Garlic was grown in Charlemagne's gardens during the 7th century and was used in England even before the Roman Conquest. Once called the "stinking rose," garlic holds much greater culinary status now than it did in ancient Roman times. Then, the patricians gave it to their laborers to keep up their strength; the wealthy citizens considered garlic too pungent for their own taste, but included it in soldiers' rations to make them strong and heroic.

During the First and Second World Wars, the plant was credited with saving thousands of lives. Garlic was used as an antiseptic to disinfect open wounds and prevent gangrene because penicillin and other drugs were scarce.

Garlic has a sulfur-containing compound, allicin, which is believed to do good even though it's what makes garlic smell bad. Claims have been made that garlic not only has antibacterial and antioxidant properties, but that it is an effective expectorant. It is also said to boost the immune system, discourge intestinal parasites, inhibit tumor growth, lower blood pressure, prevent blood clots, promote heart health and reduce cholesterol. For decades, scientists have been conducting human trials, using various garlic preparations, to test these hypotheses. In the absence of proof, the faithful dose themselves with deoderized tablets and garlic oil sold by health food stores.

Throughout 5,000 years of flavorful history, it seems that garlic has been used as a cure-all for everything from depression to deadly epidemics.

TYPES OF GARLIC

dehydrated garlic - see GARLIC FLAKES.

elephant garlic - one of the various forms of *Allium ampeloprasum,* also called giant or Levant garlic. It's more closely related to the leek than to the garlic. One cultivar bears the official name "Elephant"; it can produce heads weighing as much as 1 pound (500 g) each. The plant originated in the Levant (the former name for a region that is now comprised of Lebanon, Israel and parts of Turkey and Syria) and can be grown in the same conditions as garlic.

garlic flakes - also **dehydrated garlic.** A seasoning made of freeze-dried minced garlic.

garlic salt - a seasoning made of refined salt crystals pounded and mixed with garlic.

powdered garlic - a seasoning made of powdered, freeze-dried garlic that often has MSG and salt added.

In the culinary world, the least understood fact about garlic is that the longer you cook it, the milder and sweeter it becomes. When peeling garlic, try rinsing it in hot water first; the skin will come off more easily. The name comes from the Old English word *garleac, gar,* meaning "spear" and *leac*, referring to its resemblance to the leek. Some of the more common varieties are white, pink and purple garlic (only the outside skin is colored). Rocambole garlic, or Spanish garlic, *A. scorodoprasum*, is the sweetest of any garlic. There are two subtypes of garlic: **softneck** and **hardneck.** Softneck is the most common type found in stores in North America. It has soft center leaves that can, if left long, be easily bent and used in garlic braids. It does not produce a tall seed stalk like hardneck garlic. Softneck garlic has more protective outer layers of papery skin, which makes it last longer on store shelves. Hardneck garlic has a hard central seed stalk called a "scape" and fewer, larger cloves than softneck garlic. Because it lacks many outer layers of skin, it tends to go bad more quickly than softneck garlic, hence its absence in many grocery stores. See also ROASTED GARLIC.

garlic bread - slices of French or Italian bread spread with garlic butter, then broiled or baked until golden and crusty. Garlic bread is often served with pasta in Italian restaurants and sometimes as a dinner accompaniment in Greek restaurants.

garlic butter - a mixture of softened butter and minced garlic, used to flavor garlic bread, **escargots** and grilled meats. It is simple to make, but can often be found premade in grocery stores.

garlic chives - also **Chinese chives, flowering chives, ku chai, nira.** A tall, spiky green herb, similar botanically and in appearance to chives but with larger, flatter leaves and a garlic-like flavor. They are very common in Asian cooking, particularly in China, where they are called "ku chai," and Japan, where they are called "nira." There are two main varieties: a larger one, whose leaves are used for cooking; and a smaller one, grown for its flowers, which are used as a garnish or flavoring.

garlic flower stems - see CHINESE GARLIC STEMS.

garlic oil - a flavored oil made by steeping fresh garlic cloves in a neutral-tasting oil, such as canola, vegetable or olive oil. Supplements are also made from garlic oil, and much research suggests that they help lower cholesterol levels and prevent cancer. Homemade garlic oil is delicious, but it can be dangerous if kept too long, as spores of *Clostridium botulinum*, a deadly food-borne toxin, can easily multiply in the oxygen-starved atmosphere of the oil. The oil itself is not the problem; any minute amount of soil left on the garlic cloves can be contaminated with the toxin and make its way into the oil. The safest way to prevent botulism while still enjoying garlic-infused oil is to add 1 tablespoon (15 mL) of acid, such as lemon juice or vinegar, for every cup (250 mL) of oil as it is prepared (adding it later has no protective effect). The mixture should be kept in the refrigerator for no more than a week.

garlic peeler - a kitchen utensil used to quickly and easily strip the skin from a clove of fresh garlic; the most common kind being a small rubber tube. The two ends are trimmed off the garlic clove, then the clove is placed inside the tube and rolled back and forth on the work surface. The papery garlic skin adheres to the sticky rubber wall of the tube, and the cleanly peeled clove of garlic is dropped out of one end.

garlic pepper - a ready-made seasoning mix of powdered garlic and ground black pepper, sometimes mixed with other spices and/or sugar.

garlic press - a useful gadget in which whole garlic cloves can be pressed to a pulp when squeezed through a perforated chamber by tightly pressing together two handles.

garlic scapes

garlic scape - the tall seed stalk that grows up from the center of a bulb of **hardneck garlic**, a by-product of garlic production, which is edible, fibrous and chewy, with a pleasant garlicky flavor. Garlic farmers often remove the scape to force the plant to concentrate more energy in the growing cloves, yielding larger heads. Scapes can be sliced and added to salads or cooked to make them tender and release their aromatic flavor.

garlion - a cross between garlic and onion, this hybrid vegetable was developed in the 1980s.

Garnacha - see GRENACHE.

garnish - from the French *garniture*, food used not only to decorate a dish when it's served, but also to add to its enjoyment. The color and flavor were chosen to complement, combine with and assist the color and flavor of the dish itself.

garum - the original fish sauce, with origins in ancient Rome, where it was used as a seasoning, similar to salt. Garum was made by pressing salted fish, especially mackerel, to yield its drippings. It was put into little pots, and each guest flavored it to his or her liking, either with vinegar, water or oil.

Gascony butter - see DUCK FAT.

gas mark - a temperature scale used in Britain and some Commonwealth countries to measure the heat generated by a gas oven. The gas mark is indicated by a number, such as "gas mark 5," and is standardized to a specific temperature in Fahrenheit and Celsius.

Gas Mark	Fahrenheit	Celsius
gas mark ¼	225°F	110°C
gas mark ½	250°F	120°C
gas mark 1	275°F	140°C
gas mark 2	300°F	150°C
gas mark 3	325°F	160°C
gas mark 4	350°F	180°C
gas mark 5	375°F	190°C
gas mark 6	400°F	200°C
gas mark 7	425°F	220°C
gas mark 8	450°F	230°C
gas mark 9	475°F	240°C
gas mark 10	500°F	250°C

Gasparini - see profile above.

gastrique - a sauce of sugar and vinegar **reduced** to a syrupy consistency and added to savory

Gasparini (18th century) - Swiss pastry chef attributed with the invention of **meringue.** Gasparini is said to have devised the egg white confection in 1720 and named it for the town of Meiringen, where he lived. But the contention has been refuted, primarily because "meringue" appeared in a dictionary that predates the alleged invention by nearly 20 years. Still, residents of Meiringen refused to give up the legend. They claimed to have found documentation proving their claim, but it was destroyed in a town fire. Further evidence resurfaced at the beginning of the 20th century in the Frankfurt Culinary Museum but, sadly, bombs destroyed the building during the Second World War.

dishes that feature fruit to complement their sweetness with a touch of acidity. Some gastriques also call for the addition of wine.

gastronome - a person who loves to eat good food, a devotee of the art of **gastronomy.** See also EPICURE.

gastronomy - the art of good eating, derived from the Greek *gastros* ("stomach") and *nomos* ("law"). The word came into general use in France in 1801 and, in 1835, the Academie Française officially entered the word *gastronomie* in the dictionary.

gastropod - a mollusk of the class *Gastropoda*, with a single shell or no shell at all, and a head with sensory organs. There are many gastropods commonly eaten by humans, including a variety of snails (known more often by their more appetizing French name, **escargot**), **abalone** and **periwinkles.** The name "gastropod" means "stomach foot" in Latin, because these creatures move with a single large muscle that runs along their underside, near their stomach.

gâteau - a rich, but delicate cake. The word comes from the Old French *guastrel*, which turned into "wastrel" in medieval England, where it meant flour that was used to make breads and cakes.

gâteau Saint-Honoré - see SAINT-HONORÉ.

gau cake - eaten on Chinese New Year, a round pudding or cake made of steamed sweet mochi rice flour, sugar, sesame seeds and red dates. Like many Asian foods, gau has a number of symbolic connotations. The round shape stands for the unity of the family; the sticky rice for cohesiveness; the sugar for the sweetness of life; the sesame seeds for fertility of the women in the family; and the red dates for good fortune.

gaufrette - an oblong or fan-shaped crisp waffle cookie used as a garnish for ice cream or ices, or served alongside wine in France. Gaufrettes (which means "little waffles" in French) are made from a thin, pourable dough made of melted butter, beaten egg whites, flour, sugar, salt and vanilla. The dough is spooned onto the center of a preheated **gaufrette iron** and cooked on the stovetop until crisp and golden. Gaufrettes can be served as is, or rolled into cylinders or cones and stuffed with a variety of fillings, including flavored whipped cream or ice cream.

gaufrette iron - a metal pan with waffle-patterned surfaces used to make thin, crisp **gaufrettes.** A gaufrette iron is usually oblong, with two identical sides joined together by a hinge, and long handles on the side of the pan opposite the hinge.

Gault, Henri André Paul Victor - see profile on page 290.

gazpacho - a cold soup, Spanish in origin, usually made from finely chopped cucumber, tomato, onion and red pepper, seasoned with olive oil and garlic. There is also a "white" gazpacho made with almonds or pine nuts. Strangely enough, Mary Randolph, in her classic *The Virginia Housewife* (1836), classified "gaspacho" as a salad, which makes some sense considering the ingredients. The mystery of how gazpacho made its way from Spain to the American South still remains unsolved.

gefilte fish - a traditional Jewish dish of fish patties or balls simmered in a savory fish stock, made from ground whitefish, onions and carrots, seasoned and mixed with eggs and matzo meal to hold the patties together. The fish patties are chilled and served with the jellied stock the next day, accompanied by tangy prepared horseradish, mustard and/or pickles. Gefilte (from the German for "stuffed") fish is said to have originated as a frugal way of stretching fish when it was in limited supply; because the preparation is done a day ahead and the dish is

Gault, Henri André Paul Victor (1929–2000) - French food critic who, with partner **Christian Millau,** coined the term **nouvelle cuisine** in 1973 in their magazine, *Le Nouveau Guide.* Influenced by the time's new wave of culture, most noticeably in filmmaking and how it was being reported in *Cahiers du Cinema*, Gault and Millau began writing about a new style of cooking in the hands of such chefs as **Paul Bocuse, Jacques Pépin,** Michel Guérard, Louis Outhier and Alain Senderens, the decade's representatives of modern French cuisines. The *Guide Gault-Millau* was later established as a modern alternative to the Michelin Guide, with a rating system of chef toques instead of stars. Although Gault split with Millau in 1985, their *Guide* continues to thrive.

served chilled, it is the perfect meal for the Sabbath, when cooking is not allowed. The Polish version of gefilte fish tends to be rather sweet, while the Russian version is more savory, with a hot note of black pepper.

gelatin - an organic substance derived from animal connective tissue found in bones, tendons, ligaments and cartilage, processed into brittle, transparent, colorless, odorless sheets (known as **leaf gelatin**), although it is also available in powdered form. Gelatin is also extracted from certain algae, as is the case with **agar-agar, carrageenan, gum tragacanth** and **Irish moss.** Dissolved in water, gelatin swells and becomes an elastic, transparent mass. It's used in fruit drinks, in confectionery, to set mousses and jellies, and in ice cream.

gelatin desserts - gelatin desserts began to be popular in the 1890s. Charles B. Knox, a salesman in Johnston, New York, watched his wife make calf's foot jelly and remembered hearing about powdered gelatin, which would make her job easier. Knox packaged the powder in easy-to-use envelopes and, at his wife's suggestion, had salesmen go from door to door to show women how easily the gelatin could be dissolved in water to make **aspics,** molds and desserts. **Peter Cooper,** the inventor of the "Tom Thumb" locomotive, had invented a mixture of powdered gelatin, sugar and artificial fruit flavors as far back as the 1840s. However, it wasn't until Jell-O came along, half a century later, that people were ready for a shortcut dessert.

gelato - Italian for "ice cream." Generally, gelato tends to have a more intense flavor than North American ice cream, because less air is introduced during production. Also, gelato is made with milk, putting its fat content at 3 to 10 percent, whereas North American ice cream is made with heavy cream, giving it a fat content of 16 to 30 percent.

Gelbwurst - a fresh, large-diameter sausage known as "diet bologna" in its native Germany, made from veal and pork, spiced with nutmeg, white pepper and ginger. Gelbwurst is pale cream in color, low in salt and fat, free of nitrites and preservatives, very mild and touted to be good for children and adults who have trouble digesting regular fatty cold cuts. Gelbwurst must be kept refrigerated and is delicious sliced on sandwiches or pan-fried. The name means "yellow sausage" in German for its bright yellow casing.

gemelli - see PASTA.

gem pan - an old-fashioned term for a mini-muffin pan, named for the tiny cakes or quick breads once called gems. The cups in a gem pan hold about 2 tablespoon (25 mL) of batter, compared with the $\frac{1}{2}$ cup (125 mL) held by the cups of a standard muffin pan. See also MUFFIN PAN.

gelato and gaufrette

General Tso's chicken - also **General Chow's chicken, General Tsao's chicken.** A Chinese restaurant dish of deep-fried chunks of dark meat chicken topped with a sweet, hot, chile-infused sauce flavored with ginger, garlic and sesame oil. Exactly who created the dish and named it remains a matter of debate, but historians agree that it was named in honor of the Chinese general Tso Tsung-t'ang (nowadays spelled Zuo Zongtang), who lived from 1812 to 1885. General Tso was a fearsome military leader responsible for crushing a number of rebellions in the 19th century, leaving some to posit whether it was his slicing and dicing of enemies that inspired his link to this dish.

genetically engineered food - see BIOENGINEEERED FOOD.

genevoise - a sauce served with fish poached in **court-bouillon.** This classic French sauce begins with a combination of **mirepoix, espagnole** sauce, fish **fumet** and red wine, which is cooked down, then strained. Then, the mixture is enriched and finished with anchovy paste, finely chopped mushrooms and butter.

genip - see HONEYBERRY.

genmai miso- see MISO.

Genoa salami - see SALAMI.

génoise - a versatile sponge cake that originated in Genoa, adopted by the French, hence its name.

gentleman's relish - see PATUM PEPERIUM.

geoduck - also **elephant trunk clam, gweduck.** An enormous Pacific Coast clam, *Panopea abrupta*, which can weigh up to 8 pounds (3.6 kg), eaten sliced (not whole) in dishes that call for clams, especially raw as a type of sushi, and in soups. The neck grows so long that it cannot be withdrawn into the shell and hangs out the side. Because the long brown wrinkly neck resembles an elephant's trunk, the Chinese name for the geoduck is "elephant trunk clam." The name comes from the Nisqually Indian word *gwe-duk*, meaning "dig deep."

geranium leaves - see EDIBLE FLOWERS.

Gerard, John - see profile below.

germ - the nucleus or center of a kernel of grain, tucked inside the **endosperm** and the outer covering of bran. The germ is high in oils, vitamins and minerals and is therefore of high nutritional value in whole grains and whole grain products, such as flours and cereals. Wheat germ is particularly well known as a stand-alone ingredient made exclusively from the germ of the wheat kernel. It is rich in B vitamins as well as the antioxidant vitamin E and a host of essential minerals and healthy plant chemicals. It can be added to baking recipes or sprinkled over foods to give them a boost of nutrition.

German chocolate cake - a study in how deceptive names can be. With its characteristic frosting of coconut and pecans, this cake comes from a recipe published in a Texas newspaper in 1957. It called for Baker's Sweet Chocolate, referring to Dr. James Baker, the financier of the country's first chocolate factory, and not the fact that the component was a favorite among bakers. The German refers to Samuel German, the employee credited with developing the sweet chocolate.

German mustard - see MUSTARD.

German potato salad - cooked potatoes dressed with a hot vinaigrette made with bacon fat, usually served over vegetables. See also POTATO SALAD.

Gerard, John - English herbalist (1545–1612), who started his career as a surgeon and later wrote *Herball or Generall Historie of Plantes* in 1597, cataloguing herbs and plants of his day. As well as commenting on the plants' "vertues," Gerard offered colorful and informative advice on health and cooking for everything from **borage** to strawberries, newly fashionable at the time. About chervil he had this to say: "Chervil root boiled and after dressed as the cunning cook knoweth how better than myself is very good for old people that are dull and without courage." The poor tomato, introduced to England in 1597, did not fair well. He found the tomato "of a ranke and stinking savour," but admired the fruit for its ornamental possibilities, which helped make the tomato a popular garden adornment. He recommended yarrow to relieve "swelling of those secret parts."

Gesundheitskuchen - a type of German pound cake, often flavored with a bit of lemon and dusted with confectioner's sugar. This cake was often seen in the early part of the 20th century in North America, baked by Jewish women of German descent and brought as a gift to the mother of a newborn baby as a wish for good health. The word *gesundheit* translates from the German as "health" and is often used in North America to wish good health to someone who has just sneezed.

Gewurztraminer - also **Gewürztraminer.** A **dry,** intensely fruity white wine of the Alsace region of France, made from grapes of the same name. The best examples are naturally low in acid, but still balanced enough to prevent them from becoming **flabby.** Unlike other white wines, Gewurztraminer ages fairly well, increasing its fruity flavors and aromas of vanilla, ginger, minerals, lychee nuts and even honeysuckle. In Alsace, the name is spelled without the umlaut over the *u*, but versions produced outside the region (usually in Germany) are crowned with the umlaut, making it easy to spot their provenance on the label.

ghee - see CLARIFIED BUTTER.

gherkin - a very young cucumber, picked unripe, preserved in vinegar and served as a condiment. In French, they are called *cornichon*, meaning "little horn."

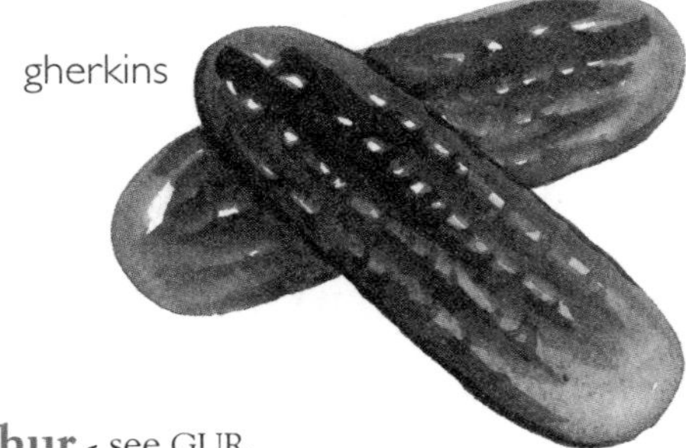
gherkins

ghur - see GUR.

gianduja - a type of chocolate made with ground hazelnut paste in Piedmont, Italy, originally invented during the Napoleonic wars, when the British naval blockade created a European cocoa shortage. The makers used the hazelnut paste to extend whatever cocoa they could get their hands on, and a delicious sweet was born. The European chocolate hazelnut spreads that have become increasingly popular in North America in recent years are happy descendents of gianduja.

giant garlic - see ROCAMBOLE, SAND LEEK.

giant perch - also **giant sea perch.** See BARRAMUNDI.

giant puffball mushroom - a large mushroom, *Lycoperdon giganteum*, found in woods and meadows from August to October, eaten only when young, firm and white.

giant sea bass - see GOLIATH GROUPER.

giant sea kelp - see KELP.

giardiniera - see JARDINIÈRE.

giblets - the **gizzard,** liver and heart of a fowl, often sold packaged inside the cleaned bird in North American supermarkets. Some birds also come with the cleaned neck inside the giblets package. Giblets are often boiled to make a base for gravy, especially to go with turkey at a traditional North American Thanksgiving feast. See also VARIETY MEAT.

Gibson - see MARTINI.

gigli - see PASTA.

gigot - a French name for a leg of mutton or lamb.

gilly flower - see CLOVEPINK.

Gimlet - a cocktail made of gin stirred with **lime juice cordial** and ice, strained into a cocktail glass. The typical ratio is four parts gin to one part cordial. Many bartenders and aficionados say the key to a good Gimlet is the thorough, proper stirring of the ingredients with the ice.

gin - a clear, colorless spirit, flavored with juniper oil, created as a medicine, in 1650, by Dr. Franciscus Sylvius, a physician in the Netherlands. Christened *genever* (a variation of the French for "juniper"), it became known as gin, Dutch courage, mother's ruin and Old Tom after it crossed the Channel. By 1665, it was commercially produced from corn or grain, sweetened and sold cheaply to the urban poor. Gin was so popular that an early version of the vending machine was created to dispense it: many establishments mounted a black wooden cat (hence the "Old Tom") on their storefronts; customers could simply insert a coin into a built-in slot, then wait for the bartender to send a shot of gin down a funnel that emerged between the cat's paws and served as a drinking straw. A century later, Londoners were drinking 11 million gallons of gin a year (not necessarily through Old Tom). A neutral grain spirit, gin has a final distillation that adds the flavor of juniper and botanicals, such as anise, angelica root, cardamom, cassia bark, cinnamon, coriander seed and orange peel. Different styles that are available include Genever (from Belgium and Holland), London Dry (a Martini must), Plymouth Dry (also a brand name) and "bathtub gin" (only a household name). See also FIZZ, TOM COLLINS, TONIC WATER.

gingerroot

ginger - also **gingerroot.** Ginger comes from a tropical plant in the Zingiberaceae family, about 3 feet (90 cm) tall with large, lance-shaped leaves and thorns, and chubby, yellow red-rimmed flowers. The part used in cooking is the rhizome, a thick underground horizontal stem that sprouts new roots and shoots.

Ginger originated in Southeast Asia. The Chinese were using ginger in the 6th century BC. When the Persian trade missions sent Darius to India in the 5th century BC, he brought back ginger. The Indians used it copiously, but it had only limited success in Greece and Rome. Roman gastronome **Marcus Gavius Apicius** scarcely mentions it in his 1st-century recipes, or at least not in the manuscripts we have. Dioscorides and Galen thought it was the root of the pepper plant, but Roman historian and naturalist **Pliny** described ginger as a small plant with a white root.

Arab traders brought ginger to the Mediterranean sometime before the 1st century AD. Ginger became one of the more prominent spices in the cuisine of the Middle Ages; practically every sauce recipe included it.

One of the wonders that Marco Polo found in Cathay in the 13th century was ginger — he mentioned seeing vast plantations devoted to growing it. Nostradamus mentioned a "tonic" confection of sweet almonds, egg white, sugar and ginger pounded together as "excellent and very useful." The Spaniards brought ginger to the Western Hemisphere in the 16th century.

It is believed that ginger took is name from Gingi, near Pondicherry in southern India, where it's thought to have originated. The word came into Latin as *zingiber*, and French as *gingibre* in the 12th century and *gingembre* in the 14th century. Italian *gengiovo* became *zenzero*, and Old English *gingiber* became "ginger."

For centuries, the Chinese have used ginger to subdue nausea; more recently, ginger ale became a common home remedy served to stomach-flu sufferers. Following tradition, today's herbalists still use ginger to treat arthritis, bronchitis, colitis and menstrual cramps, as well.

ginger ale - a carbonated soft drink developed in 1903 in Bennettsville, South Carolina, by Dr. C. R. May, who devised the drink after encouraging his patients to drink local mineral-rich well water for stomach ailments. He added Jamaican ginger to make the drink more palatable, and a business was born.

ginger beer - a sweet nonalcoholic carbonated beverage flavored with ginger and lemon, much spicier than ginger ale, very popular in the Caribbean islands and in West Africa, also the base of the classic Bermudian cocktail **Dark and Stormy.**

ginger biscuit - see GINGERSNAP.

gingerbread man

gingerbread - a sweet cookie or cake made with ginger and molasses, popular since the Middle Ages, when it was made primarily with bread crumbs, honey and spices. Gingerbread cookies are made from a stiff dough, rolled out and cut with festive-shaped cookie cutters (such as gingerbread men, the traditional favorite), then decorated with **royal icing** and candies for

Christmas. The moist, dense cake version of gingerbread is baked in a pan and cut into squares, usually served topped with whipped cream or lemon sauce.

ginger grater - see GRATER.

ginger paste - a thick paste of equal parts grated fresh gingerroot and water, sometimes combined with other flavorings, such as garlic, often available ready-made in Indian and Asian grocery stores. Ginger paste is a convenient way to add the taste of freshly grated ginger to recipes when fresh gingerroot is unavailable. It is easy to make from scratch at home if the jarred variety is not easy to find, and keeps well in the refrigerator or freezer.

gingerroot - see GINGER.

gingersnap - also **ginger biscuit.** A crisp, brittle cookie flavored with ginger and molasses. The name is likely inspired by the sound the cookie makes when broken. Also called "ginger nuts" in Britain.

ginkgo nut - see BAAK GWO.

ginseng - a plant whose roots are valued by the Chinese and Koreans as a cure-all, often made into teas or commercially prepared tonics. According to one legend, ginseng began as a divine gift to a deserving young wife. She had no children after three years of marriage and became frantic because Chinese custom permitted her husband to take a concubine if his marriage hadn't produced children during this time. She had a dream about an old man in the mountains, who could give her an herbal remedy, so she went out to find him, took the remedy and bore a child. When she later journeyed back to see him, she thanked him so graciously that he (who, of course, was a deity in disguise) filled the woods with this miraculous plant.

A centuries-old esteem for the plant's root has provoked incredible market demand, astronomical prices, over-harvesting, largely ill-fated schemes and a lingering curiosity. The greatest value is placed upon the root, whose trunk and extremities look like arms and legs. The shape prompted the Asiatic species of *Panax* to be named *schinseng*, meaning "man-shaped."

The legendary Chinese emperor and physician, Shen Nung, who lived around 2300 BC wrote, "Ginseng is a tonic to the five viscera, quieting the animal spirits, stabilizing the soul, preventing fear, expelling the vicious energies, brightening the eye and improving vision, opening up the heart benefiting the understanding, and if taken for some time will invigorate the body and prolong life." Moreover, it's regarded as an aphrodisiac. One Chinese emperor declared himself the sole ginseng dealer, buying all that was harvested, keeping the best for himself and selling the remainder at a fat profit. When its reputation as an aphrodisiac took hold, both the Chinese and the Tartars wanted the plants enough to kill for them; wars broke out over good ginseng territory. Storage areas had to have armed guards, and smuggling the root was punishable by death.

In early America, it was a commodity traded on the frontier along with furs. Thomas Jefferson lists it in his inventory of native plant resources. Ginseng and Virginia snakeroot (a perennial plant also used in teas) made up most of Virginia's medicinal exports. In 1773, a sloop out of Boston took 55 tons (50 tonnes) of ginseng to China, where it was sold for $330,000. Philadelphia records show that Daniel Boone sold ginseng to a company in the city.

girolle - **1.** see CHANTERELLE. **2.** see CHEESE SCRAPER.

gizzard - a muscular sac that forms the lower part of the stomach of a domestic fowl, usually containing stones or sand to help the bird grind its food up for proper digestion. The gizzard is considered a **variety meat** and is eaten in many cultures, but it is tough and needs long boiling or slow braising to make it tender enough to chew.

gjetost - a Norwegian goat cheese (*gje* for "goat" and *tost* for "cheese"). Genuine (*ekte*) gjetost is still made in limited quantities. See also MYSOST.

glace - French for "ice" or "glaze." In cooking, a glace, or glaze, is meat or fish stock that has been reduced to the consistency of syrup. It's sometimes used as the sauce itself, as in **demi-glace,** used as the base for a sauce, as in **bordelaise,** or added to a dish or another sauce for added body and/or flavorful richness. See also GLAZE.

glace de viande - French for "meat glaze." See also GLAZE.

glacé fruit - also **fruit glacé.** See CANDIED FRUIT.

glace Royal - see CONDÉ.

glass eel - see ELVER.

glass noodles - see HARUSAME.

glassware - See BALLOON, COCKTAIL GLASS, FLUTE, HIGHBALL GLASS, HURRICANE GLASS, MARTINI GLASS, OLD-FASHIONED GLASS, PILSNER GLASS, SNIFTER, STEIN, STIRRUP CUP, TANKARD.

glasswort - see SAMPHIRE.

Glayva - a Scotch whisky–based liqueur flavored with spices, herbs and a hint of honey and orange, created by an Edinburgh wine and spirit expert. Named after the Gaelic words *Glé mhath* (pronounced "Glay-va"), meaning "very good," which seemed the perfect name for the smooth-tasting drink.

glaze - **1.** (n.) a sweet or savory sauce used to glaze food, also a reduction of meat or fish stock. A glaze for a cake is a liquidy sugar-based sauce or melted chocolate poured over the top and allowed to drip down the side. The glaze hardens to a shiny, smooth surface. **2.** (v.) to give food a sheen. In baking, egg, milk and sometimes sugar are used to glaze breads, pies and pastry before baking. Diluted jams are brushed onto flans and sweet tarts to glaze them after baking. Vegetables are glazed by sautéing with butter and sugar; meats, such as a roast ham, are brushed with their glaze throughout their cooking. See also GLACE.

globe artichoke - see ARTICHOKE.

globe eggplant - see EGGPLANT.

globefish - see PUFFERFISH.

globe squash - a summer squash, a type of gourmet zucchini, actually an **heirloom** variety, small and round with a mottled green exterior. The flesh is like a meatier version of regular zucchini, with tiny, edible seeds. It can be cooked and eaten in the same way as regular zucchini or sliced and used in the same way as eggplant in some casseroles. Globe squashes are usually available at specialty produce markets. See also SQUASH, ZUCCHINI.

glögg - a Swedish mulled-wine punch, made with red wine, brandy or **aquavit,** sweet spices (such as cinnamon, cloves and cardamom) and citrus peel. Glögg is a traditional drink served throughout Advent and on Christmas in Sweden, as well as in Finland and Denmark; it is always served steaming, ladled over almonds and raisins in a mug or glass.

Gloucester - an old-fashioned, British aged cow's milk cheese with a smooth, semifirm texture. **Double Gloucester** is made from whole cow's milk and is rich and buttery with a flaky texture, made since the 16th century in Gloucestershire, England, traditionally from the milk of Old Gloucester cows, which are now all but extinct. **Single Gloucester** is made from skimmed milk and is not as rich or as aged as double Gloucester, but has a lovely flavor all its own.

glucose - a simple sugar containing six carbon atoms. It is the body's principal source of energy and is normally the only sugar found in the blood. Digestion causes carbohydrates, such as corn, rice, wheat or potato, to break down into glucose. The natural form of glucose is also referred to as **dextrose,** especially in the food industry. Glucose is also a product of photosynthesis in plants. It can be found in fruits, vegetables and honey.

gluten - a protein blend found in certain grains, especially wheat, that makes dough elastic; it is developed during kneading and allows bread to rise by trapping the gases created by the yeast. See also WHEAT GLUTEN.

gluten flour - see FLOUR, WHEAT GLUTEN.

glutinous rice - also **sticky rice, sweet rice.** See RICE.

globe squash

glutton - one who eats and drinks excessively.

glycerin - also **glycerine, glycerol.** A clear, sweet, viscous syrup, actually a type of alcohol derived from fats, used in confectionery and in non-food applications, such as cosmetics, soaps and moisturizers. Glycerin adds sweetness to foods as well as moisture, keeping them from drying out. It is used as a thickener, especially in chocolate when it is being piped onto cakes, and to add shine and malleability to rolled **fondant** icing. The name is derived from the Greek word *glykeros*, meaning "sweet."

gnocchi - **1.** eaten like pasta as a first course or a side dish, but, unlike pasta, require no special equipment to prepare — not even a rolling pin. Indeed, they're no more difficult to make than a batch of cookies. The dough can be formed from a base of potatoes, flour, cornmeal or bread crumbs, and a variety of gnocchi abounds all over Italy. In the Val d'Aosta region, for instance, gnocchi are made from buckwheat flour and served with melted **Fontina** cheese. Saffron colors the tiny gnocchi of Sardinia, and pumpkin is favored in Lombardy. In the Alto Aldige region, gnocchi are made with rye bread crumbs. In the mountainous Abruzzo region, gnocchi are served **carbonara**-style, with an egg and pancetta sauce. North of Venice in Friuli, sweet gnocchi, flavored with raisins, cocoa and cinnamon, are a traditional Christmas treat. **2.** a dried pasta that is shaped like a hollow ridged shell, similar to the domed top of a soft, doughy gnocchi. See also PASTA.

goa bean - see WINGED BEAN.

goat - a ruminant mammal, *Capra hircus*, raised for both its meat and its milk, native to Asia and widely used in Europe since the Neolithic period; a close relative of the sheep. Goat meat is a favorite food in a wide variety of cultures. Roasted baby goat (kid) is regularly served in the Balkans, the Mediterranean region and the Middle East. Curried goat stew is a favorite in the Caribbean, especially Jamaica. There are also a number of well-loved goat dishes in Latin America and Asia. Goat meat is comparable to lamb in flavor, slightly gamy and a bit greasier, and can be used in many recipes that call for lamb or mutton. The tastiest, mildest goat meat comes from kids under 6 months of age; the flesh of adult goats gets progressively tougher and stronger-tasting as it ages. See also GOAT MILK.

goat

goat cheese - also **chèvre.** A soft cheese, although more crumbly than smooth, with an earthy, tart flavor. It's extremely versatile, sold fresh, dry, aged and flavored. *Chèvre* is French for "goat."

goatfish - see RED MULLET.

goat milk - a lower-lactose alternative to cow's milk, goat milk also contains proteins and fats that are more easily digestible than those in cow's milk. Goat milk has a distinctive, creamy flavor, and the small fat globules in the milk create smooth, creamy goat cheeses with tiny curds. Goat milk is much more widely available than it once was, nowadays often available in health food stores and in the natural foods or dairy sections of supermarkets.

gobo - see BURDOCK.

gochu jang - a hot, fermented Korean chili paste that lends a spicy taste and beautiful red color to many dishes, from the Korean *gochu*, meaning "chili," and *jang*, meaning a flavoring sauce made with salt. It is used both as a cooking ingredient and as a condiment for virtually every Korean dish. Traditionally, gochu jang was prepared on a yearly basis by every household. On March 3, a traditional day of good luck, glutinous rice was cooked to a sticky paste, then seasoned with red chiles, a fermented soybean cake, salt and malt syrup. The mixture was then transferred to a black earthenware jar and placed on the roof of the home (a tradition still seen today on the roofs of some Korean houses). The mixture was then allowed to ferment for at least three months, sometimes with the lid off during the day, so that the sun could beat down on the mixture and speed up the fermentation. The final product was a much reduced, very sticky paste with a fiery kick and a mildly sweet-salty flavor.

Goetheglatzen - German for "bald Goethe," a ficticious cookie made famous by German comedian Heinz Erhardt (1909–1979); he joked it was a flat cookie, sugarcoated on one side and rounded on the top, to honor the bald, beloved German author Johann Wolfgang von Goethe.

goetta - a type of fresh German-style sausage typical of Cincinnati, Ohio, made of ground pork, ground beef, steel-cut oats and spices, packed into pans or casings and refrigerated. It is then cut into slices and fried in oil or butter and served with eggs and toast for breakfast, used as a sandwich filling or added to other dishes. Goetta is similar to the Pennsylvania Dutch specialty **scrapple.**

goji berry - also **Chinese wolfberry**. A tiny reddish berry from the Matrimony vine, *Lycium barbarum*, edible raw or cooked and native to the Himalaya region, but now grown all over the world. The fruit is preserved by drying and tastes much like raisins. Goji berries have been used in traditional Asian medicine for thousands of years. They are a very rich source of vitamins and minerals, especially in vitamins A, C and E, **flavonoids** and other bioactive compounds.

golabki - see CABBAGE ROLL.

golden berry - see CAPE GOOSEBERRY.

golden Cadillac - a cocktail made with **Galliano,** white **crème de cacao** and cream, shaken with ice, then strained into a Champagne flute. The drink gets its name from its golden color (from the Galliano) and its rich ingredients, like a luxurious Cadillac car.

golden corn syrup - see CORN SYRUP.

Golden Delicious apple - see APPLE.

golden mushroom - also **golden needle mushroom.** See ENOKI.

golden needles - see LILY BUDS.

golden nugget squash - a small, orange-fleshed winter squash, similar in flavor to pumpkin, with a thick, dull orange rind and relatively little flesh in comparison to rind and seeds. It is delicious and sweet when baked, like an acorn squash, and can be boiled or steamed as well. The pumpkin-shaped golden nugget squash starts out with a shiny skin, which dulls as it ripens, so that the dullest versions, despite their unattractive appearance, are the best tasting. See also SQUASH.

golden nugget squash

golden oak mushroom - see SHIITAKE.

golden pepper - see PEPPERONCINI.

golden raisin - a raisin made from seedless white grapes, sometimes treated with sulfur dioxide and dried using artificial heat, so that it stays moist, light golden and plumper than a **dark raisin.** See also RAISIN.

golden raspberry - see RASPBERRY.

golden syrup - also **light treacle.** A syrupy amber-colored liquid sweetener made by evaporating sugarcane juice until it's thick and sticky like molasses, or **treacle.** This sweetener is popular in Britain, Australia and the West Indies, where it's used in baked treacle tarts, steamed puddings and pancakes, and as a topping for porridge.

gold leaf - see VARAK.

Goldschläger - the brand name of a spicy, cinnamon-flavored **Schnapps** with tiny flecks of gold suspended in it. It should not be confused with **Goldwasser,** which, although identical in appearance, does not taste the same. Goldschläger can be sipped straight or used as an ingredient in cocktails.

Goldwasser - also **Danzig Goldwasser, Danziger Goldwasser.** A trademarked liqueur flavored with citrus peel, herbs and spices. German for "gold water," the French called it *Liqueur d'or,* referring to the tiny flecks of 22K gold that are suspended in the drink, which are harmless to ingest. It was originally produced in 1598 in Danzig, Poland, at Der Lachs, a German distillery.

Goliath grouper - also **giant sea bass.** The new, less offensive name for the well-known jewfish, *Epinephelus itajara*, endangered in the early 1990s but now often found in the waters off the coast of Florida and in the Caribbean. It is a favorite of spear fisherman and prized for its mild, firm white flesh.

goma - Japanese for sesame seeds. **Shiro goma** is unhulled sesame seeds.

gomashio - also **goma shio, goma-shio.** A ready-made mixture of toasted black sesame seeds and sea salt, used as a condiment or seasoning in Japanese cuisine. It is commonly found in Asian grocery stores in North America, but can be made from scratch. The name means "sesame salt" in Japanese.

goober - also **goober peas.** A name used in the American South for the peanut, from "nguba," an African word for peanut. The name has been immortalized in the well-known Southern campfire song, *Goober Peas*.

good King Henry - see GOOSEFOOT.

goose - one of the most valuable of our barnyard fowls; fatty, with a mildly gamy flavor. In English, the adult male is called a "gander," but in culinary parlance, both the adult male and female are called "geese." And for their first six months, they're called "goslings."

Goose is traditional at Christmas, conveniently so because it hatches in the spring and is at its prime eight to nine months later. Any older and it will not be a success roasted; at this stage, it's best braised. Among the Cree of northern Canada, roast goose is the meat of choice at every wedding feast. Goose-hunting season is a festive time, and special cooking areas are set up for the duration. There are many varieties, including the Emden goose, originating in Germany and the Netherlands; the Chinese goose; the Roman and Brecon Buff — all of which are reared for Christmas and Michaelmas. The French Toulouse goose is bred for its contribution to *pâté de foie gras*, and the Strasbourg for *confit d'oie* (pieces of goose preserved in goose fat). By and large, while table geese are expensive and yield much less meat compared with turkeys, they are considered by many to be the better of the two.

gooseberry - a summer fruit, *Ribes grossularia*, with a growing season that lasts only a few weeks, known and enjoyed in Europe since the Middle Ages. Sweet varieties are delicious eaten raw, while tart ones make an excellent preserve and can be used in many desserts.

goose fat - a popular cooking fat in Europe since the Middle Ages; fine, flavorful and soft like butter, hence its English country nickname of "goose grease." The fat is made by roasting a goose and straining out the pan drippings or by **rendering** the fat out of the skin and meat. Goose fat can be made at home or purchased in tins or packages at gourmet stores. It is excellent for basting meats or cooking vegetables or potatoes, as well as for making the signature French dish **confit d'oie.** See also DUCK FAT, SCHMALTZ.

goosefish - see MONKFISH.

goosefoot - also **good King Henry, mountain spinach, orach.** A plant named for the shape of its triangular leaves, which are used in a similar way to spinach, for which goosefoot is often substituted: as a cooked green, fresh in salads, to color pasta or as an herb in egg dishes, soups and stews. A native of Europe and the Mediterranean region, *Atriplex hortensis* has naturalized in parts of North America.

goosefoot

goose liver - see FOIE GRAS.

goose tongue - see ACHILÉE.

Goosnargh cakes - a sweetened shortbread with caraway seeds, named after in a village in Lancashire, England, where they have been

A B C D E F G H I J K L M N O P Q R S T U V W X Y Z

made for centuries and can still be purchased in local shops.

gordita - a thick Mexican corn **tortilla** with a raised lip around the edge, made with **masa,** lard or shortening, and water, often made into an open-faced "sandwich" or folded up around fried crumbled **chorizo,** refried beans or other typical taco or burrito fillings. The gordita is first baked on a heated **comal** or griddle, then fried in oil to give it the proper chewy-crisp texture. The name is a term of endearment in Spanish meaning "little fat one."

Gorgonzola - one of the earliest of all veined cheeses. Named after a village near Milan, it was introduced to the Po Valley in the 9th century, with the green-blue mold developing accidentally sometime around the 11th century. It is traditionally made with cow's milk, although it's sometimes made from a mixture of cow's and goat's milk.

Gorgonzola is likely an evolution of type of Cacio cheese that Ansperto da Biassono, the Archbishop of Milan, mentions in his testament of 881. There are many legends surrounding the distinctive veining of this cheese. One story has it that a cheese maker forgot his equipment and left the curds out all night long in the open air, finding them covered in mold the next morning. According to another story, Gorgonzola was initially an uncured and unveined cheese made by farmers who sold it at a market close to the town tavern. Those who did not have enough money to pay for their wine used to give the tavern keeper cheese as a substitute, and he accrued so many that they had to be stored in the cellar, where they ultimately developed a green mold.

Along with English **Stilton** and French **Roquefort,** Gorgonzola is considered one of the top three blue cheeses in the world, although the characteristic veining of the celebrated cheese is actually more green than blue.

Originally, Gorgonzola was made through natural contact with spores of *Penicillium glaucum* in the air, causing blue striations of mold called *erborinati* (from a dialect word of Lombardy for "parsley"), and then aged in caves. Today, it's commercially produced by inserting steel or copper needles into the cheese, allowing in oxygen and the penetration of chemically made bacterium.

Gorgonzola dolce - see DOLCELATTE.

Gorgonzola knife - see CHEESE KNIVES.

goro - a Norwegian cookie scented with cardamom and lemon, similar to a **krumkake,** rectangular in shape and cooked on a two-handled iron, which impresses a design on the cookie as it bakes. The name likely comes from the Norwegian *god råd,* meaning "affluent," because the rich ingredients (eggs, heavy cream, sugar and butter) in the cookie were once only available to the wealthy.

GORP - an acronym for "good old raisins and peanuts" or "granola, oats, raisins and peanuts," often called by the name **"trail mix."** It's a mixture of calorie-dense nonperishable foods, usually nuts, seeds, chocolate, grains and dried fruits, created for hikers, who need lightweight, filling snacks to eat as they walk.

Gorrie, Dr. John - see profile below.

Gouda - a Dutch cheese almost identical in mellow flavor and handling to **Edam,** except that Gouda is made with whole cow's milk and so has a higher fat content; can be eaten fresh or aged.

gougère - a type of savory **choux pastry** flavored with shredded **Gruyère** cheese, piped into rounds (or wreaths of rounds) on a baking sheet and baked until golden, crisp and puffed.

goujon - **1.** also **goujonette.** The French term for small strips of mild fish cut from a fillet, usually

Gorrie, Dr. John (1803–1855) - American physician and inventor of the air-cooling device that was granted the first U.S. patent for mechanical refrigeration in 1851. Gorrie was treating yellow fever in Florida and theorized that colder temperatures would cure the illness. At the time, ice was available, even in the southern states. It was cut midwinter from frozen lakes in the north and sent south by boat, arriving at the Florida Keys by midsummer. With an epidemic at hand, Gorrie invented a device whose basic principle is still used in refrigeration today: a compressed gas is cooled through radiating coils and then expanded, to reduce the temperature further. See also CARRÉ, FERDINAND.

battered and deep-fried to look like small, whole fish, the upscale cousin of the mass-produced fish stick (also known as "fish finger" in Britain). The name is also used for a dish made with these fried strips of fish. **2.** also **flathead catfish.** A North American freshwater catfish, *Pylodictis olivaris*, native to the area around the southern Mississippi River, but now common in the central U.S. and Texas, with a long, flattened head and jutting lower jaw. They are considered an invasive species, because they have wiped out a fair number of indigenous catfish species once common to the central U.S. Goujons are often hunted by sport fishermen for their flesh and as a trophies.

goulash - a stew of meat and vegetables, highly seasoned with paprika, taking its name from the Hungarian word *gulyas*, meaning "herdsman" or "cowboy."

gourd - a generic term for members of the Cucurbitaceae family, which includes squash, melons and cucumbers. The term is most often applied to the inedible fruits of some of these plants, rather than the edible members of the family, although fruits such as **bottle gourds** are edible. Gourds are often used as table decorations, or hollowed out and used as tools or containers.

gourmand - one who is fond of good eating, often indiscriminately and to excess.

gourmandise - a sweet, mild French cheese spread flavored with cherry juice or **Kirsch,** or with walnuts or walnut paste, usually sold in foil-wrapped wedges or rounds for spreading on bread or crackers.

gourmet - one who is a connoisseur of good food and drink; an **epicure** or epicurean.

gowdie - see GURNARD.

goyave - see GUAVA.

Grabetto - a hard, Australian goat's milk cheese, usually a fresh **farmhouse cheese,** but also available aged. As Grabetto ages, it gets harder and harder, with an almost flaky texture and a tangy, sharp flavor. Formed into a pyramid shape, these cheeses may or may not be covered in a layer of ash.

graham cracker - a crumbly, rectangular cracker made from **graham flour** and sweetened with honey, invented as a health food in the 1830s by **Sylvester Graham,** an early pioneer of vegetarianism and whole-grain diets, whose name the cracker and the flour bear. Graham believed in the supreme healthfulness of unsifted whole wheat flour, which was the main ingredient in his "Graham bread." He also asserted that his whole wheat graham crackers reduced carnal urges, which he believed to be the scourge of his era. Nowadays, graham crackers are made with more refined flour than graham flour, and often with more sugar than the original recipe, plus a touch of cinnamon. They are a popular snack food for children and adults alike, and are often crushed and used to make crusts for pies and cheesecakes.

graham flour - see FLOUR.

Graham, Sylvester - see profile below.

grain alcohol - also **grain spirits, neutral spirits.** Flavorless **ethyl alcohol** distilled from grain, 190 proof (95 percent pure alcohol), used as a base for a variety of flavored liqueurs or as an additive to other distilled liquors. Grain alcohol can also be used in drinks and punches, but it is incredibly strong and can be irritating to the throat and stomach if drunk straight.

grains - the seed or fruit of any of a variety of cereal grasses, such as barley, corn, millet, oats, quinoa, rice, rye, sorghum, spelt, teff, triticale,

Graham, Sylvester (1794–1851) - American minister, dietary health advocate and inventor of the **graham cracker** in 1829. Although Graham was ordained a Presbyterian minister in 1826, his preaching focused primarily on diet and health. He advocated vegetarianism, chastity, temperance, loose clothing, vigorous exercise, cold showers, sleeping on hard mattresses in open-windowed rooms, eating homemade bread made with whole wheat flour and avoiding all stimulants. His most vocal crusade was for the use of unsifted, coarse-ground wheat flour, which became known as graham flour, which he used in his invention of the graham cracker in 1829. He inspired a movement whose followers called themselves Grahamites.

wheat and wild rice. These seeds or fruits can be cooked and eaten whole or, in most cases, ground, rolled or pressed into other forms for use in cooking. They are often called cereals; this name derived from the Roman goddess Ceres, the goddess of agriculture.

grains of paradise - also **alligator pepper, Guinea grains, Guinea pepper, melegueta pepper.** The seeds of *Aframomum melegueta*, a rhizomatous, reed-like plant related to cardamom and ginger. This spice also shares their peppery, pungent flavors. Harvested from West-African countries along the Gold Coast, the whole seeds may be bloomed in a skillet or crushed into pieces or powder to release their flavor. In the Middle Ages, caravans brought melegueta pepper overland into Europe; by the mid-1300s, ships did the job. Despite its popularity, however, it became less used over time and almost disappeared from European cookery by the mid-1800s. Used mainly in African and Moroccan dishes, such as **ras el hanout,** melegueta pepper is still uncommon in North America, perhaps because there is no large-scale commercial cultivation of it.

gram flour - see BESAN.

gramigna - see PASTA.

grana - a cheese-making technique in which the curd is scalded at 120° to 130°F (48° to 54°C), then mechanically stirred, as opposed to the **pasta filata** technique, in which the curds undergo a mechanical stretching process. The best-known cheese in this style is **Grana Padano,** which is very similar to **Parmigiano-Reggiano,** although not as expensive. **Emmental** and **Gruyère** are also grana cheeses.

granadilla - a large, orange-skinned fruit of the **passion fruit** family, similar in flavor but less fragrant than smaller dark colored passion fruit.

granadilla

Grana Padano - see PARMESAN.

Grand Marnier - an amber, aromatic, cognac-based liqueur flavored with bitter orange peel (namely, *Citrus bigaradia*), aged in oak, then enjoyed neat, over ice, in mixed drinks and in **crêpes Suzette.** It was created in 1880 at the Lapostolle family distillery in Neauphle-le-Château near Paris when Louis-Alexandre Marnier (grandson-in-law of the firm's founder) had the grand idea of flavoring their cognac with orange. An immediate fan, famous hotelier **César Ritz** helped introduce the new drink to the right people.

granita - Italian for a cool and refreshing water-based ice, frozen into grainy crystals. Some historians say that granita was enjoyed by the ancient Romans, who sent runners to the nearby mountains for snow, which they flavored with honey, wine, fruit syrups or herbs.

granité - French for "granita."

Granny Smith apple - see APPLE.

granola - a cereal whose primary ingredients are rolled oats, oat bran, honey, dried fruit and nuts, although numerous varieties are sold on the market today. Originally developed by **John Harvey Kellogg** in 1876 as part of a vegetarian regime focused on whole grains, its original name was Granula, which wasn't actually original. It belonged to a whole grain product developed a decade earlier. On being sued, Kellogg changed the name to granola, but it never really caught on. Kellogg and his brother, William Keith, are best known for inventing Cornflakes in 1902, but it wasn't until the 1960s that granola reappeared, with the addition of dried fruits and nuts, responding to a burgeoning health food craze.

Granton-edge blade - see HOLLOW-EDGE BLADE.

granulated sugar - see SUGAR.

grape - one of the oldest fruits known to humankind and the most cultivated, yet its origin is uncertain. More than likely, grapes emerged from Asia Minor, around the Caspian Sea, or Armenia. Grapes were grown in Asia more than 7,000 years ago. Some grape residues were discovered in Egyptian tombs dating back to 375 BC. The Greeks and the Romans used to drink it in abundance and wrote a great deal about its salutary influence under the cults of Dionysus, Bacchus and Osiris for the Egyptians. At the fall of the Roman Empire, the Gauls took over the cultivation of grapes, and even later the monasteries took over.

The grape family includes three main varieties. *Vitis vinifera* is the European variety, the most cultivated (95 percent of grapes are from this variety), with about 1,000 subvarieties. The North American variety is split into two subvarieties, the *Vitis labrusca* and the *Vitis rondundifolia*. The black Concord grape, the green Niagara grape and the red Catawba grape are varieties of V. *labrusca*, and the Delaware (red) is a cross between V. *inifera* and V. *labrusca*. The third group is known as the French Hybrids, which originally came from the *Vitis vinifera*. In 1863, the *Vitis vinifera* suffered a deadly attack of a louse (*Phylloxera vastatrix*) that feeds on the roots of the vines and destroys them completely. The American V. *labrusca* was immune to the disease, and the European vineyards were saved thanks to the grafting of the two species. Very few countries are immune to the **phylloxera;** the ones that are include Chile, Cyprus, South Australia and some parts of Hungary and Austria, as well as a few acres in Oregon. The largest producers of grapes in the world are Italy, France and Spain.

The fruits are erroneously called grains, but they're actually berries. A cluster of grapes can hold from six to 300 berries, depending on the variety, and every berry will have between one and four seeds, unless they're from a seedless variety.

grapefruit - a plant, *Citrus paradisi*, probably originating in the West Indies, but its origin is obscure. Some sources say the Spanish introduced grapefruit to the West Indies. We know for certain that the English called grapefruit "shaddock" for many years, confusing it with another fruit taken from the East Indies to Barbados by a Captain Shaddock in 1693. In the 18th century, merchant ships are said to have used shaddock for ballast and for cleaning their decks. By 1820, the French botanist, the Chevalier de Tussac, wrote that the fruit was no larger than a good orange, borne in bunches like grapes and designated by the English in Jamaica as "Forbidden Fruit" or "smaller shaddock." Indisputably, this was a grapefruit, but botanists cannot decide whether it was a mutation of the pomelo or a cross between it and an orange.

grapefruit

Philippe Odet, a former surgeon of Napoleon's army, planted some in Florida about the same time the fruit was first recorded in the West Indies. Not only was this the start of Florida's commercial grapefruit industry, but these trees also became the parent trees for all grapefruit varieties grown today. Pink grapefruit was developed mainly in the Rio Grande Valley of Texas. The main varieties are Pink Marsh, also called Thompson and Ruby, which has the distinction of being the first citrus fruit ever patented. Although some food historians attribute the grapefruit's name to the grape-like clusters in which it grows, others insist that it originated with an early recorder of horticultural finds in the West Indies who likened the grapefruit's taste to that of a grape.

grapefruit knife - a knife with a thin, pliable blade with serrations on both edges and a curved tip, used to cut between the pulp and the membrane of grapefruit sections to release the fruit. There's also a grapefruit spoon with a pointed tip and serrations on both edges.

grapefruit knife

grape leaves - see DOLMA.

grapeseed oil - grape seeds contain between 6 and 20 percent oil, which is used in salads and for making margarine.

grape tomato - see TOMATO.

grappa - a type of brandy (very similar in taste and smell to the French **marc**), the traditional

Italian spirit obtained from the pomace, the debris remaining after the final pressing of grapes in wine making. The Nonino family distillery in Venice is famous for its highly sophisticated single-vineyard grappa and fruit liqueurs. In the last 10 years, California became a major producer of grappa, with some remarkable results considered by purists to be exceptional examples of the genre.

Grasshopper - an ultra-sweet, chocolaty, minty cocktail made with white **crème de cacao,** green **crème de menthe** and cream or milk, the color of a green grasshopper. The ingredients are shaken with ice and strained into a cocktail glass.

grasshopper pie - a gelatin-based pie made to taste like a **grasshopper** cocktail, flavored with **crème de cacao** and **crème de menthe,** with a creamy filling made light and airy by gently folding in whipped cream. The pie is usually made with a crust made from crushed graham crackers or chocolate wafer cookies.

grassy - a wine-tasting term, positive or negative depending on the taster's preference, for a wine that has flavor notes of freshly cut grass or hay. Wines made from **Sauvignon Blanc** grapes are most often identified as grassy. Wines that have this flavor are often described as **green** as well.

grate - to pass a hard food, such as Parmesan cheese or carrots, over razor-sharp holes or a coarse, burred surface to make small particles or shreds. See also MICROPLANE GRATER, SHRED.

grater - a kitchen utensil used to shred or crumble foods, can have a single type of cutting surface, such as sharp round holes or burred perforations, or a variety of them on a single

GRATER VARIETIES

box grater - has four sides, each with a different type of cutting surface, usually a coarse and a fine shredding side and a coarse and a fine grating side. Food is passed over the outside, and the shredded or grated food emerges in the center of the box. Box graters have some sort of handle on the top, so that they can be held still while pressure is applied to the side of the grater.

box grater

cheese grater - usually contains a grating wheel or barrel inside a housing with a crank on the side for grating or shredding hard cheeses over pasta or salads. They work well with chocolate, too, creating soft shreds to sprinkle over desserts. Cheese graters often come with different cutting wheels for a variety of textures; the French brand **Mouli** makes a fine stainless-steel version with a variety of cutting wheels.

ginger grater - an Asian kitchen tool usually made of porcelain, a small bowl with a nubbly raised center, used for grating fresh gingerroot. Some ginger graters are made in fun shapes, such as fish, or designed to look like tiny washboards with several rows of bumps running down the center. Grating ginger with this tool grinds the fibrous root into tiny, fine shreds and releases the spicy, aromatic juices, so that they are better incorporated into recipes.

nutmeg grater - a small grater shaped like a cone, with one flat side and burred perforations on the rounded side. It is perfect for grating whole nutmeg or other small, hard foods, and usually comes with a lid so that extra or leftover whole nutmegs can be stored inside.

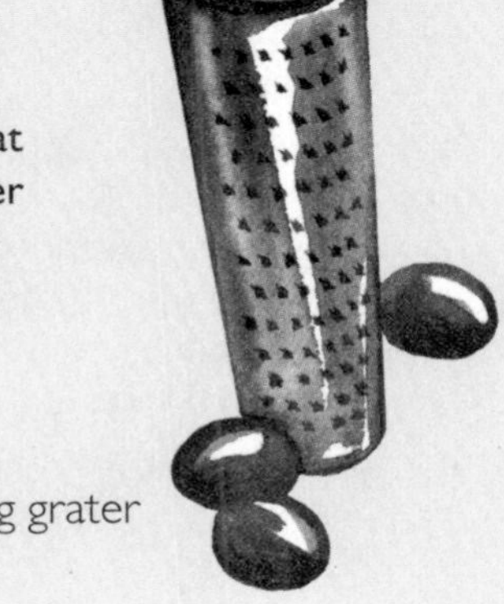

nutmeg grater

tool. Some graters are stationary, so that food must be passed over them by hand, while others are contained inside a housing that turns with a handle for extremely fast results. In either case, a grater cuts food into thin or tiny uniform pieces more quickly and accurately than could be done by hand. See also MICROPLANE GRATER.

gratin dish - a shallow round or oval dish with two handles, used for making and serving **au gratin** dishes. Gratin dishes can be made from any of a variety of materials, such as stainless steel, enameled cast iron, porcelain or even copper.

gratiner - to give a crisp, golden brown finish to a dish. See also AU GRATIN.

Gravenstein apple - see APPLE.

gravlax - also **gravadlax, gravlaks.** Raw salmon fillets cured with salt, sugar, pepper and fresh dill, sometimes flavored with additions, such as crushed juniper berries, gin, cognac or aquavit. The name comes from the Swedish *grava*, meaning "to bury," and *lax*, meaning "salmon," which alludes to the original method of curing gravlax underground. While the fish is never cooked over heat, the salt-sugar mixture chemically "cooks" and preserves the fish. Gravlax is usually served in paper-thin slices on dark, grainy rye bread with a dill-mustard sauce, either as an appetizer or as an open-faced sandwich. It's a typical component of the Swedish **smorgasbord.** See also LOX.

gravy - a sauce made with meat juices and thickened with cornstarch or flour.

gravy boat - also **sauce boat.** A squat, elongated pitcher used for serving gravy or sauce at the table, usually accompanied by a matching plate, which sits under the boat-shaped pitcher to catch drips from the spout.

gravy browning - a coloring agent that enhances the appearance of brown sauces and gravies, its composition simply being caramel, salt and water. It should be used with caution and added drop by drop until the desired color is obtained. Sometimes flavors are added, such as **hydrolyzed vegetable protein** and MSG. The mixture is boiled and filtered before bottling.

gravy flour - see FLOUR.

gravy powder - concentrated extracts, dehydrated into powder, blended with a thickening agent and then reconstituted to make gravy.

gravy separator - see FAT SEPARATOR.

grayling - a beautiful, silvery fish with a thyme-like scent, hence its Latin name, *Thymallus*, a freshwater fish of the salmon family.

grease - **1.** to brush or wipe a pan with oil or a solid fat, such as butter or shortening, to prevent food from sticking to the pan as it cooks.
2. rendered fat, especially that of an animal.

grease mop - see FAT MOP.

greaseproof paper - what the British call "waxed paper."

great Northern bean - a plump, mild-tasting, dried white bean often used in soups, stews and baked bean dishes for its delicate flavor.

Greek coffee - see TURKISH COFFEE.

Greek honey - see HONEY.

Greek lasagna - see PASTITSIO.

Greek olive - see OLIVE.

Greek seasoning - a ready-made blend of herbs and spices, including dried oregano, dried mint, garlic and onion, which can be added to dishes to give them a hint of some of the classic Greek flavors.

green - a wine-tasting term for a wine that has undertones of grass, moss or vegetables. If a wine is made with grapes that are not fully ripened, it may end up tasting green. White wines, such as **Sauvignon Blanc, Riesling** and **Gewurztraminer,** can be a bit green and still taste good, but greenness in red wines is usually considered a negative characteristic.

green bean - also **snap bean, string bean.** A long, thin green pod containing seeds; both the pod and seeds are edible. At one time a tough thin string ran down the center of the bean that had to be removed before eating, thus the name "string bean." Today, most green beans available in the market are stringless. The "snap" refers to the sound the fresh beans make when broken in two. See also ASPARAGUS BEAN, BEAN, HARICOT BEAN, HARICOT VERT, RUNNER BEAN.

Green, Nancy (Aunt Jemima) (1834–1923) - African-American cook who "became" Aunt Jemima to market a new pancake mix, which made her advertising's first living trademark. Green was born a Kentucky slave and was cooking in the home of a Chicago judge in the mid-1890s. At the time, a popular vaudeville character named Aunt Jemima sang a song that was on everyone's lips. To capitalize on the song's success, the Pearl Milling Co. decided to name their newly developed pancake mix Aunt Jemima, and chose Green, who was 59 at the time, to play Aunt Jemima and help sell their new product. She was naturally affable and proved to be an excellent choice. Introducing the product at the World's Columbian Exposition in Chicago in 1893, she made and served thousands of pancakes all day, while regaling the crowd with her storytelling. She was so effective that 50,000 orders for the new mix were placed that day. She was signed to a lifetime contract and went on a national tour. She enjoyed many years of travel, celebrity and prosperity, but died suddenly, at the age of 89, when she was hit by a car on a street in the South Side of Chicago.

green bell pepper - see SWEET PEPPER.

green cheese - refers to a cheese that has not been fully ripened. The old saying, "The moon is made of green cheese," may have come about because the drained or pressed curd, while lying in curing cellars, often has a mottled look, much like the surface of the moon. See also SAGE CHEESE, SAPSAGO.

green chile sauce - see RED CHILE SAUCE.

green curaçao - see CURAÇAO.

green curry paste - see CURRY PASTE.

green garlic - see CHINESE GARLIC STEMS.

green goddess dressing - a creamy mayonnaise-based salad dressing flavored with tarragon vinegar, fresh tarragon, anchovies, parsley, green onions, chives and garlic. It is named not just for the lovely shade of green lent to it by the chopped fresh herbs, but also for the play *The Green Goddess*, by William Archer. The dressing was invented at the historic Palace Hotel in San Francisco in the 1920s, when Archer's play was a hit in the city.

green lentil - see LENTIL.

Green, Nancy (Aunt Jemima) - see profile above.

green olive - see OLIVE.

green onion - a young onion that has not developed into a bulb, also known as scallion.

greens - a term used for leafy greens that have a strong, bitter flavor; used cooked as often as raw. Collards, mustard greens, kale and turnip greens fall into this category. All these spicy greens have their past in ancient history, as they were important foods for the wandering tribes in India, China, the Mediterranean and Asia.

green soybean - see EDAMAME.

green tea - see TEA.

green tomato - an unripe tomato, used often in Southern cooking for its rich tomato flavor and high acidity. Green tomatoes are often used to make jams and preserves and one of the most well-known Southern treats: fried green tomatoes, made by dipping sliced green tomatoes in cornmeal and frying them in bacon fat or oil.

Gregory, Hanson - see DOUGHNUT.

gremolata - also **gremolada.** A mixture of finely chopped parsley, lemon peel and garlic, added fresh and raw after a dish is cooked. It is the classic garnish for **osso buco,** although it can be used for meat, fish or vegetables.

Grenache - also **Garnacha.** A Spanish variety of red grape (called *Garnacha* in Spanish,

Grenache

Grenache in French, often *Grenache Noir* in English), used for winemaking. Grenache is vital for making **Châteauneuf-du-Pape** wine and is usually a major ingredient in **Côtes-du-Rhône** wines. It is also used to make the sweet, fortified wine **Banyuls.** The white form of this variety is called Grenache Blanc and is used as a component in a variety of blended wines in the Languedoc-Roussillon, Provence and southern Rhône regions of France. Two other colors are also available: Grenache Gris and Grenache Rose, some used to make delicious **rosé wines.** Grenache grapes produce medium- to **full-bodied** wines that are a bit spicy and definitely on the fruity side; they are excellent blended with other varieties.

grenadine - a bright red cloyingly sweet syrup, traditionally made from pomegranate juice and sugar. Modern grenadine is sometimes made with the real juice, but is more often than not just a combination of water, sugar and artificial color and flavoring. Grenadine is added to mixed drinks to give them color and sweetness. It's the featured ingredient in the nonalcoholic kiddie cocktails **Shirley Temple** and **Roy Rogers.**

Grey, Charles - see EARL GREY TEA.

Grey Poupon - a brand name reflecting the partnership between Maurice Grey, who had a recipe for making mustard, and a financier named Poupon, who invented an automated steam-operated method of producing the mustard, first introduced in Dijon, France, in 1777. The region has strict regulations on making mustard, which go as far back as 1634, requiring, among other things, that only workers wearing "clean and modest clothes" make mustard. Later rules required that mustard be made only from brown and black mustard seeds and seasoned with wine or vinegar, spices and herbs. Grey Poupon is now also made in New Jersey.

gribbenes - also **gribenes, grieven, griven.** The Yiddish word for chicken skin cracklings, a by-product of rendering chicken fat into **schmaltz.** These crunchy bits of onion-scented skin can be eaten as is or added to dishes, including stuffing, chopped liver, mashed potatoes or **kasha varnishkes.**

griddle - a heavy, flat, smooth metal pan with just a tiny lip around the edge, which is used for cooking foods, such as pancakes or bacon, with little or no added fat. A griddle can be as simple as a metal plate or pan that sits on the stovetop, or as elaborate as the gas- or electric-powered stand-alone griddles used in commercial kitchens. Griddles are usually made of heavy cast iron or cast aluminum, and many are coated with a nonstick finish.

griddle cake - see PANCAKE.

Grigson, Jane - see profile right.

grill - to broil using a grill, as with a barbecue, or to cook on a griddle. North Americans consider grilling to refer to the source of heat below the food, leaving char markings from the hot iron of the grill; they consider broiling to be done in a closed oven, with the source of heat above the food. In England, "grilling" is what North American's call "broiling." See also BROIL.

grill basket - a long-handled basket made of thick, crisscrossing metal wires that locks together to contain delicate foods, such as vegetables, as they are grilled. Grill baskets come in a variety of shapes and sizes, from small, square baskets that hold sliced vegetables to large, oblong baskets that hold whole fish. The basket is placed atop the grill and turned as the food cooks, keeping it off the grill grate, where it might stick and fall apart or fall through.

grill pan - a heavy-duty skillet-style pan with raised ridges along the bottom, used to grill foods indoors on the stove, instead of on an outdoor gas or charcoal grill. The ridges hold the food away from the bottom of the pan, creating lovely grill marks, but the pans can't replicate the smoky flavor that true grilling imparts to food. The ridges also prevent the food from sticking to the bottom of the pan without the addition of lots of oil, making the grill pan a cooking tool of choice in low-fat kitchens.

grill pan

Grigson, Jane (1928–1990) - English cookbook author, journalist and translator, noted for the high literary quality of her work. Born in Gloucester, she grew up in Sunderland. After attending Cambridge University, she worked in book publishing and, during this time, met her husband, the distinguished poet and author Geoffrey Grigson. Her early work as a translator from the Italian was considered outstanding; in 1963, she shared the John Florio Prize, awarded annually for the best English translation of a full-length Italian work.

Food captured her interest as a subject when her family, with baby Sophie in tow, began to vacation in France. Shopping for food, she became fascinated by the varied French methods for preparing pork; she started researching the subject and, after much diligent work, produced *Charcuterie and French Pork Cookery*. Prior to publication in 1967, her publisher sent the manuscript to **Elizabeth David** for comments. She loved it! As David later recalled, "Here was a writer who could combine a delightful quote from Chaucer on the subject of a pike galantine with a careful recipe for a modern chicken and pork version of the same ancient dish, and who could do so without pedantry or a hint of preciousness." Several months later, the *Observer* asked David to replace their food writer. She was too busy with other projects, but suggested Jane Grigson for the job.

Grigson went on to write 10 more cookbooks, many of which have become classics, including *Good Things* (1971), *English Food* (1974), *Jane Grigson's Vegetable Book* (1978) and *Jane Grigson's Fruit Book* (1982). Not only do her recipes work, they are as much fun to read as they are to cook. She wrote as though the study of food were an exploration of human history. She once said, "Although I love food and I love cooking, in a way that's not what really interests me. But by learning about food, I've also learned more about art, architecture and literature of the past." She shared this experience with her husband, whose formidable erudition certainly inspired and influenced her work. He passed away in 1985, and five years later she succumbed to cancer. In her later years, she was very proud to know that the torch had been passed to their daughter, now one of Britain's most highly regarded food writers.

Grimod de la Reyniére, Alexandre Balthazar Laurent - see profile on page 308.

grind - to mechanically break into tiny granules or reduce to powder. Old-fashioned manual grinders are turned by hand and use a rotating screw inside a hopper to force foods against a sharp grinding plate and reduce it to the desired texture. Modern grinders use the same mechanism but are powered by an electric motor. Food processors or mini-choppers can also grind food, but use a sharp metal blade that rotates at high speed to grind food inside the work bowl. There are also small electric **coffee grinders** for grinding whole coffee beans and **spice grinders** for grinding whole spices. Both work on the same principal as the food processor, but with much smaller blades and bowls.

grinder - **1.** see GRIND. **2.** the New England name for a submarine sandwich.

gripe water - a combination of natural herbal essential oils, such as dill, fennel and/or anise, and water, a traditional British treatment for colicky infants still used today, commonly seen in stores in North America. Gripe water, also simply called **dill water** when it contains dill oil alone, is considered a safe treatment for hiccups, upset stomach and gas in infants. *Gripe* is an old-fashioned term for stomach pain or spasms.

grissini - thin, crunchy bread sticks made in Italy and now available in most North American supermarkets. The singular form is *grissino*, although it is rarely heard in North America, where the plural is usually used interchangeably as singular and plural, as it is for another popular Italian term: **biscotti.**

gristle - tough, fibrous, inedible pieces of cooked meat, usually consisting of sinews and cartilage, considered extremely unpleasant and unpalatable and not consumed by choice.

grits - coarsely ground grain, usually corn, separated from the hull, served as a breakfast cereal or side dish, especially in the Southern U.S.

groats - crushed oats from which the husk has been removed. Buckwheat and barley can also be used.

Grimod de la Reyniére, Alexandre Balthazar Laurent (1758–1838) - French lawyer, theatre critic, gastronome, creator of the new literary genre of food criticism during the late 18th and early 19th centuries. Grimod was introduced to gastronomy by the Abbot in the Lorraine where he'd been banished by his parents for throwing lavish banquets while they were away. He liked to boast that he came from a long line of gastronomes, with his declaration, "One of my ancestors died in the field of honor choked by a fatty liver pâté." When his father died, Grimod inherited his father's fortune and continued to throw his theatrical banquets, including the staging of his own mock funeral. He wrote critiques of Parisian cafés, restaurants and shops, which were published as *L'Almanach des gourmands* between 1803 and 1812. He founded a society of food critics to which restaurateurs presented their fare for approval and promotion. The poignant irony of Grimod's life was that he was born with deformed hands, and the two loves of his life — writing and gastronomy — were heavily dependent on the free use of one's hands. Still, in 1808 he published *Manuel des Amphitryons* (A Handbook for Hosts), where he writes, "A host who can neither carve or serve is like the owner of a fine library who cannot read." Later in life, he married the actress with whom he had lived for 20 years. He died in 1837, at the age of 80, following a Christmas midnight dinner.

grog - an alcoholic drink usually made with rum, hot water and lemon juice, named by Royal Navy sailors after it was decreed that their daily ration of rum should be diluted with an equal amount of water. The unpopular order came from Vice Admiral Edward Vernon (1684–1757), nicknamed "Old Grog" by the sailors, because of the grogram cloak he wore on deck.

Gros Bouchet - see CABERNET FRANC.

ground almonds - see ALMOND MEAL, NUT FLOUR.

ground beef - see HAMBURGER, TEMPERATURE.

ground cherry - a sweet, but slightly acidic fruit of the genus *Physalis*, enclosed in a lantern-shaped husk, usually made into preserves, but can also be eaten raw. See also CAPE GOOSEBERRY.

groundhog - also **woodchuck.** Historically very popular, groundhog is an excellent table meat, which is easily found throughout the countryside in open grassy areas and farmers' fields. When tanned, the hide is extremely durable. It's believed that, when our forefathers first came to North America, they where introduced to the groundhog as a food staple by North American Indians.

groundnut - 1. also **Apios, bog potato, Indian potato, potato bean, wild bean.** The starchy tuber of a leguminous plant, *Apios americana* or *Apios tuberosa*, native to North America, with twining vines and showy, fragrant flowers. A traditional food of native hunter-gatherers, the tuber can be dug out of the earth and stored for prolonged periods. The starchy flesh has a texture similar to that of potatoes and can be prepared in the same way. The tubers can also be ground into flour and used as a thickener in soups and stews. Though it shares the same nickname, this groundnut is not the same as the peanut, though both are legumes. It is also not the same as apio or **arracacha**. 2. see PEANUT.

ground nuts - see NUT FLOUR.

groundsel - a yellow-flowered plant from the sunflower family, Asteraceae, brought to the U.S. in the early 17th century by the Pilgrims. The leaves can be eaten in salads; the roots are used in pharmacopoeia; and the seeds are used in pet food, especially for canaries.

groundsel

ground shark - see SAND SHARK.

ground turkey - see TURKEY.

grouper - the name for a wide variety of saltwater fishes of the genus *Epinephelus*, including the **Nassau grouper, red grouper** and **black grouper,** found in warm waters across the globe. Groupers tend to be sold in the 3- to 5-pound (1.4 to 2.2 kg) range in fish markets, but can grow to gargantuan proportions, sometimes upwards of 1,000 pounds (450 kg). Grouper has strong-smelling skin that can taint the flesh inside, so it must be removed before cooking. The flesh is firm and lobster-like in texture, snow white and tasty, well suited to almost any method of cooking, from frying to broiling to simmering in chowders or soups.

grouse - the common name of a number of rasorial birds, ones that scratch the ground for food; with mottled plumage. There are many varieties of this protected bird: the red grouse of Scotland; the ruffled grouse of northern Nevada; the black grouse, also called blackcock; and the capercaillie or ptarmignan of northern Europe. Several American game birds bear the name grouse — the sage grouse, the ruffled grouse, the **prairie chicken** — but they're not related to the family. As with other game birds, grouse's availability is limited to hunting season. Young birds are suitable for roasting, broiling or grilling; older birds are best braised.

growing zone - also **USDA plant-hardiness zone.** A numbered region indicating the climatic conditions to which any plants cultivated outdoors in that region will be subject. Growing-zone numbers are shown on plant tags at nurseries, in seed catalogues and on maps in gardening books. On a herb tag, for example, they indicate, whether it can be grown in a garden plot as a perennial or should be planted in a pot set outside over the summer, then brought indoors to overwinter. In North America, two numbering systems are used, but in either case, the higher the number, the more benign the growing conditions. The United States Department of Agriculture (USDA) bases its numbers on temperature alone. On Canadian maps, the growing zones are based on multiple factors: elevation, length of frost-free period, maximum temperature and wind speed, minimum winter temperature, summer rainfall, January rainfall and snow cover. When consulting publications such as this one that list USDA growing-zone numbers, the rule of thumb is to add one for the Canadian equivalent.

gruel - a thin, watery form of porridge, often oatmeal-based in the West or rice-based in the East. Gruel is frequently used to feed people with digestive problems, as is the case with *okayu,* or Japanese rice porridge, a traditional food for the elderly or the infirm.

grunt - also **slump.** The grunt is a type of cobbler first developed in the late 1700s in America. It was most often made with berries, topped with biscuit dough and then steamed in a covered kettle that hung over an open fire. Water was added to the fruit; as it steamed, sugar formed syrup on top of the fruit. The name "grunt" comes from the sound that the fruit makes as it releases steam. Grunts are still popular in New England, where they're served with ice cream.

Gruyère - a Swiss cheese, with variations widely produced in France as well. France and Switzerland argued over the right to the name, which was finally granted to both by the Convention of Stresa in 1951. Swiss Gruyère has a smooth, uniform paste, or body, with only a few pea-size holes and a natural dark brown rind. Some confusion arises with the French Gruyères: the paste of the *Gruyère de Comté* has larger holes, while *Gruyère de Montagne*, or *Beaufort* is similar to the Swiss type. Gruyère is a fine dessert cheese and very versatile in savory cooking.

guacamole - an uncooked **mole** made from mashed avocado pulp, and chopped chile, coriander, onion and tomato (lime juice is often added to prevent browning). The Aztec ate the first version called *ahuaca-mulli* from the Aztec *ahuacatl*, meaning "avocado" and *mulli*, meaning "sauce." As a sauce, it moved from Mexico into mainstream America in the early 1900s, then became a ready-made dip in the 1960s when corn chips were introduced.

guajillo - see CHILE PEPPER.

guanabana - see SOURSOP.

guanciale - an Italian salt-cured pork made from the cheeks and jowls of the pig, from *guancia,* meaning "cheek." It is often seasoned with pepper, spices and/or chiles, and is not cooked, but rather cured for several months. Guanciale is leaner than other forms of cured pork, such as bacon or pancetta, and is usually served cooked in pasta dishes, such as pasta **all'Amatriciana.**

guard of honour - a traditional roasted meat dish consisting of two **frenched** racks of lamb or pork pressed together, so that the bones interlock and form a crisscross pattern, similar to the crossed swords of soldiers at a military ceremony. The racks are then tied together with butcher's twine and roasted.

guar gum - a thickener or **stabilizer** made from the ground endosperm of the seeds of the guar plant, *Cyamopsis tetragonoloba*, a type of drought-resistant legume grown in dry climates for food and processing. When dissolved in water, guar gum forms a thick, viscous paste, which manufacturers use to bind ingredients together in packaged foods. Guar gum is often found in store-bought breads, dairy products and sauces. See also GUM ARABIC, GUM TRAGACANTH, XANTHAN GUM.

guava - a sweet tropical fruit, *Psidium spp.*, often confused with the **feljoa.** Even though both the guava and feljoa come from the same botanical family and are often thought to be identical tropical fruits, they actually represent two different species. Part of the confusion stems from the fact that feljoas are also called "pineapple guavas," when they're not guavas at all. However, the two fruits are compatible in recipes, being close in size, with tart skins and a similar tropical fruit flavor. Both fruits are left to ripen on the tree until they literally drop to the ground. So, you are likely to find the fruits at their flavor peak in markets, unlike many domestic fruits today. Feijoas flourish in New Zealand and Brazil. Guavas are from the same family as cinnamon, clove and eucalyptus. They were intensively cultivated by the Incas and are still widely consumed in South America. Guavas are grown in any tropical or subtropical region, notably in Africa, Australia, India, Mexico, the U.S. (Hawaii, Florida and California), Brazil and Taiwan. Guavas are often identified under their French name, *goyave*, or their Spanish name, *guayaba*.

guava

guava paste - also **guava cheese, pasta de guayaba.** A stiff, sweet paste made with guava flesh, water and sugar. The mixture is simmered until thick and pasty, then turned out into a pan and allowed to air-dry or sun-dry until firm and sliceable. Guava paste is often eaten as a complement to cheeses or used as an ingredient in Latin American and Spanish desserts.

güero - a hot, yellow chile pepper. See also CHILE PEPPER.

Gueuze - a style of beer made only in Belgium by blending one-, two- and three-year-old **lambic beers** together in a second fermentation in the bottle, similar to **méthode champenoise,** to create a somewhat fruity, sweet-tart beer. This sparkling, **artisanal** brew is bottled with a Champagne-style cork. Visitors to *Le Musée Bruxellois de la Gueuze*, a family brewery in Brussels, can still see it being made the traditional way. A long-keeping beer, Gueuze is good even at 20 years old.

gugelhopf - also **gugelhupf.** See KUGELHOPF.

guinea fowl - related to the pheasant and once considered a game bird. Now, however, it's bred for the table and is regarded as poultry, although, like game, it's best hung for two to three days before plucking, dressing and cooking. Originally believed to have come from Guinea, West Africa, it has been domesticated for centuries in many parts of the world, and in England since the 15th century. It was called a "turkey," named for what was believed to be its country of origin, long before the bird we know today as turkey had ever been seen in Europe. When Shakespeare spoke of turkey, he meant guinea fowl. Guinea fowl, or hens, are bred on

guinea fowl

a large scale in France and are suitable for roasting, casseroles, braising and, in general, in any recipe suitable for pheasant.

Guinea grains - also **Guinea pepper.** See GRAINS OF PARADISE.

gulab jamun - a much-loved Indian sweet often served at celebratory occasions, a deep-fried ball of milk-based dough soaked in a sweet syrup flavored with **rosewater,** which is called *gulab* in Hindi.

gum arabic - a product from the *Acacia senegal* tree, grown in Africa and India, that acts as a thickener and emulsifier in candy, such as wine gums, and as a stabilizer in marshmallows, and an ingredient in soft drink syrups. See also GUAR GUM, GUM TRAGACANTH, XANTHAN GUM.

gumbo - a soup or stew influenced by Indian, French, Spanish and African cultures, one of the best-known foods of Louisiana, with as many recipes as there are cooks. Gumbo is an African word for **okra,** considered a key, but not absolutely necessary ingredient. Okra's gelatinous interior acts as a thickener and can be replaced by **filé.** Using okra and filé together is considered a cardinal sin. Gumbo typically consists of one or more meats, usually chicken, duck, sausage, pork, **tasso** or ham. Seafood gumbos often also contain meat.

Chef **Paul Prudhomme** is responsible for inventing the famous Gumbo Ya Ya in the 1970s at K-Paul's, his legendary New Orleans eatery. It contains everything that runs, swims or crawls and is so called, he says, because it makes you say, "Ya ya." *Gumbo "z'herbes,"* in characteristic Louisiana French, also known as "green gumbo," is made with herbs and at least seven greens (for good luck), including spinach, mustard and collard greens; it is usually made on Holy Thursday and eaten on Good Friday.

gumbo filé - see FILÉ.

gumdrop - a small, brightly colored, domed candy set with **gelatin** or **gum arabic,** made in a variety of flavors, often coated in sparkly granulated sugar. The first gumdrops were likely used as a means for delivering herbal medicines, such as licorice, eucalyptus or honey, for a sore throat or cough.

gum paste - a mixture of sugar, glucose, gelatin, water and some form of strengthening gum, such as **gum tragacanth.** The mixture is kneaded until smooth and pliable, then molded and painted to make stunningly lifelike decorations for special-occasion cakes, such as wedding cakes. Gum paste is often used to make beautiful, intricate flowers because it is easily modeled, like clay, and can be painted any color. It is technically edible, because it is made with natural ingredients, but it is unpleasantly hard when it dries, so it is rarely consumed.

gum tragacanth - a vegetable gum from the *Astragalus gummifer* tree in western Asia used as a thickener and to make **pastillage gum paste,** a stiff icing for cake decorating. See also GUAR GUM, GUM ARABIC, XANTHAN GUM.

Gunpowder tea - see TEA.

gur - also **ghur.** An unrefined, dark, flavorful **palm sugar** made by boiling down the sap of the date palm. Gur is used in India and in Southeast Asia, and is sticky and crumbly in texture, similar to brown sugar. See also JAGGERY.

gurnard - also **gowdie, gurnet, piper, sea robin.** Any of a variety of fish of the Triglidae family, with spiny, finger-like protrusions beside their dorsal fins, which help them find food as they creep along the ocean floor; found in the Mediterranean as well as the Atlantic and Pacific oceans. Their flesh is bony and mild tasting, best used in soups and fish stocks, but also good fried, baked or poached if the fish is large enough. The gurnard is named for the grunting sound it makes when removed from the water, from the French verb *grogner*, meaning "to grunt."

gweduck - see GEODUCK.

gymnosperm - from the Greek, *gymnos*, meaning "naked" or "exposed," and *sperma*, or "seed," the name for all plants that produce seeds not enclosed in an ovary.

gyoza - a savory Japanese dumpling filled with a mixture of ground pork, green onion, garlic or **nira,** and cabbage; pan-fried on one side until crisp, then steamed until cooked through and soft on the other side. They are similar to Chinese **pot stickers** and are usually served as an appetizer with a soy-based dipping sauce.

gyoza skin - also **gyoza wrapper.** A paper-thin circle of dough similar in flavor and appearance to a **wonton wrapper,** made from wheat flour and water for wrapping around the savory fillings of **gyoza.** Gyoza skins are usually about 4 inches (10 cm) in diameter and are sold prepackaged and frozen in many Asian grocery stores.

gypsum - the naturally occurring mineral calcium sulfate, used as a **coagulant** to transform liquid soy milk into solid tofu. It is naturally high in calcium, so tofu made with gypsum contains much more calcium than that made with **nigari.**

gyro - the Greek version of the Middle Eastern **shawarma,** a sandwich of sliced lamb or chicken that has been marinated and grilled on a rotating spit, shaved thin and served in a thick toasted pita with sliced tomato, onions and **tzatziki.**

h
hazelnuts

habanero chile - a small, extremely hot chile, light green when immature and orange when ripe, used especially in making sauces. See also CHILE PEPPER.

habicheula rosada - Spanish for "**pink bean.**"

habitant soup - see PEA SOUP.

hachis - a French word, meaning "to mince or chop," referring to a finely chopped concoction, seen often as hachis **parmentier,** a dish of minced beef, with a potato topping, similar to Shepherd's Pie, although it's traditionally made with mutton or lamb.

haddock - a saltwater fish similar to cod but smaller, with a dark spot on each side just behind the head. The name is derived from the Old French *hadot* or *hadou* and the Irish *cadog*. See also FINNAN HADDIE.

haddock

haggis - one of the national dishes of Scotland, made of sheep's heart, lungs and liver, hashed or finely minced, and mixed with suet, onions, oatmeal, salt and pepper. The whole is usually sewn up in a bag made from the stomach of the sheep and then boiled. It's traditionally served wrapped up in a stiff, starched napkin to cover the bare look of the sheep's stomach. Neat whiskey is the drink of choice with haggis. The name likely comes from Old English *haggen*, meaning to "to hack."

haidai - see KELP.

hair of the dog - the shortened form of the colloquial phrase "the hair of the dog that bit you," a slang term for having a drink of alcohol to counteract the effects of a hangover, used as early as the 16th century and still used today. The premise behind the phrase is the same as the one behind the practice of homeopathy, namely, that whatever makes you sick, when administered in small doses, can cure you. The idea is to have a little bit of the same alcohol that made you feel so wretched, in order to make your hangover go away. The concept comes from the ancient practice of treating dog bites by applying a few strands of the offending dog's hair to the wound in order to help it heal.

hair seaweed - see FAT CHOY.

hair sieve - a fine-mesh sieve used for straining lumps from custards, residue from stock, etc.

hairy dangleberry - see TANGLEBERRY.

hairy gourd - also **hairy melon, hairy squash.** See FUZZY GOURD.

hairy lychee - see RAMBUTAN.

hake - a fish of the cod family, with a delicately flavored white meat. Its name comes from the Old Provençal *hake*, meaning "hook," referring to the fish's hook-shaped jaw.

hakusai - see NAPA CABBAGE.

halal - a term for meat slaughtered according to Islamic law.

Halawy dates - see DATES.

halbtrocken - a German wine term equal to the English term **semidry.** See also TROCKEN.

haleem - also **halim, harissa.** A Middle Eastern porridge of meat, barley or wheat, and water, originally from the area that encompasses both Iran and Afghanistan; now commonly seen in many Arab countries and those with large Muslim populations. Each country where this smooth, soup-like dish is served has its own variation on the theme: some use lamb, some chicken, and some add a pinch of sugar, ground cloves or cumin. In almost every one, however, it is customary to serve the dish with oil or melted butter to drizzle over top. The dish is often eaten as a warming breakfast in the morning.

halek - see DATE SYRUP.

Halen Môn - see SALT.

half-and-half - see CREAM.

half and half - see BLACK AND TAN.

half-bottle - see WINE BOTTLES.

half-dry - see OFF-DRY.

halibut - the largest flatfish in the North Atlantic. Halibut, *Hippoglossus hippoglossus*, is obtainable year-round, but is at its best from April to August. It can weigh as much as 200 pounds (90 kg), but is best very young, weighing no more than 3 pounds (1.5 kg). "Chicken halibut," as it's known at this size, is at its prime from March to October. The name "halibut" was formed by adding the Middle English *butte* or *but,* meaning "flounder or flatfish," to *haly,* meaning "holy," because it was eaten on Lent and other holy days.

hallacas - a Colombian and Venezuelan specialty, similar to **tamale,** consisting of ground meat (beef, pork or chicken) mixed with cheese, olives or raisins, then coated in a corn dough, wrapped in banana leaves and steamed.

hallah - see CHALLAH.

haloumi - a sheep's milk cheese used for cooking in Greece and the Middle East, a special favorite of the island of Cyprus, quite salty but mild in flavor. Haloumi is excellent melted in recipes, and makes a particularly delicious appetizer when lightly floured and fried in olive oil.

halva - also **halvah, halwa.** The name for a wide variety of sweets that originated in the Middle East, many of them made from a base of cooked semolina. In North America and Western Europe, halva (frequently spelled "halvah") is a firm, nougat-like confection often associated with Jewish cooking, made from ground sesame seeds and honey, sometimes enriched with whole pistachios or almonds, dried fruit or chocolate. It is formed into individual bars, or large wheels or blocks from which smaller pieces may be cut to size.

In India, the Middle East and Central Asia, the name also applies to a confection made from sweetened spiced semolina or wheat flour cooked to a paste, then dried and cut into moist, golden bars, often scented with rosewater and/or studded with nuts. In some places, mashed cooked carrots, coconut or dried fruits are added to give the bars extra flavor. In Iraq, a semolina-free version, made by kneading together chopped dates, almonds and walnuts, is quite popular.

Confusingly, in India, halva (often spelled "halwa") is also the name of a soft dessert pudding made by cooking **semolina** with **ghee,** nuts, spices, sugar syrup, dried fruits and sometimes vegetables and/or legumes, until soft and fluffy. The resulting thick paste is frequently served warm, scented with typically Indian flavorings, such as cardamom, rosewater or coconut. Some versions omit the semolina, favoring a combination of legumes (such as lentils or mung beans) as the base. Others omit the semolina and combine vegetables, such as carrots, winter melons or squashes, with cream, cooking them down to a thick, pasty pudding. In the Middle East, especially Syria, the semolina pudding **ma'mounia** is a close cousin of these warm Indian versions of halva.

In Greece and Turkey, halva may be made from semolina, but can also be created by cooking eggs with sugar syrup. The liquid is invariably combined with nuts, and sometimes candied or dried fruit as well. The resulting sweetmeat is similar to the European or North American sesame version.

No matter where this sweet dessert comes from today, the name, in all cases, is derived from the Arabic word, *hulw,* meaning "sweet."

ham - a cut of pork from the hind leg, usually cured or smoked. Ham is either dry cured or wet cured. Dry curing involves rubbing the meat with salt, sugar, sodium nitrate and/or sodium nitrite and seasonings. It stands for a number of days so that the flesh cures, preventing the formation of harmful bacteria. As the ham stands, the dry mixture mixes with the juices

ham

of the meat to penetrate it all the way through. The ham is then washed to remove the salty coating before it is air-dried or smoked. In wet curing, the ham is soaked or injected with a brine of salt, sodium nitrite and/or sodium nitrate, sugar and seasonings. The brine quickly penetrates the flesh, shortening the curing time, an asset for most large-scale ham manufacturers. A wet-cured ham is usually lightly smoked, but it can be air-dried if desired.

The word comes from the Old English word *hamm*, meaning, "bend of the knee." **Kentucky ham** is a famous cooked and cured country ham, dry-salted and smoked with both hickory and apple wood, a process that imparts a subtle, distinctive flavor. See also ARDENNES HAM, BAYONNE HAM, BRADENHAM, CITY HAM, COUNTRY HAM, CULATELLO, DRY CURE, FRESH HAM, GAMMON, IRISH HAM, JAMÓN IBÉRICO, JAMÓN SERRANO, PARMA HAM, PICNIC HAM, PROSCIUTTO, SEAGER HAM, SUFFOLK HAM, VIRGINIA HAM, WESTPHALIAN HAM, WET CURE, YORK HAM, YUNNAN HAM.

hamantasch - pl. **hamantaschen.** A three-cornered yeast-raised pastry with a poppy seed, prune or other filling, traditionally served in Jewish homes during the festival of Purim. The shape is intended to resemble the hat of the villain Haman from the biblical *Book of Esther*.

hamburger - **1.** a patty made of ground beef, usually served on a bun with a variety of condiments, such as ketchup, mustard, relish, onions, tomatoes, etc. The hamburger was said to be invented in Seymour, Wisconsin, in 1885, where Outgamie County Fair concessionaire Charles Nagreen, 15, realizing his meatballs weren't selling because people wanted to walk around and enjoy the fair, flattened the meatball, placed it between bread slices and called it a "hamburger." By another account, the sandwich was invented in 1892 in Akron, Ohio, by Akron County Fair concessionaire Frank Menches who, when running out of sausage, ground up the meat he had left and served it as a meat patty. The hamburger got its first widespread attention in 1904 at the St. Louis World's Fair. The most plausible account is that the hamburger had its origins in the seagoing practice of grinding tough, hard, salted beef to tenderize it, then mixing it with onions and soaked bread crumbs and frying it as patties or ersatz steaks. Many immigrants first encountered this dish on the Hamburg-American liners that brought so many of them to the U.S. in the late 19th century. When they landed in America, the newcomers kept their taste for this hamburger steak. In 1837, the first printed American menu was issued by New York's **Delmonico's** restaurant and listed, as one of its most expensive dishes, "hamburger steak." A French-German-English dictionary of food published in 1899 under the title *Blueher's Rechtschreibung* noted that "Chopped beefsteak is called hamburger steak in America." **2.** ground beef.

hamburger bun - a round, slightly domed yeast roll, usually made with all-purpose flour, but sometimes from whole wheat flour or other grains, split in half horizontally for serving sandwiched around a hamburger. Traditional hamburger buns are often soft, spongy and absorbent, the perfect foil for the ketchup, mustard, relish and other condiments typically slathered over a burger. Some are flavored with herbs or onions, and many come topped with sesame or poppy seeds.

Hamburg parsley - see PARSLEY ROOT.

ham hock - see HOCK.

ham steak - a thick slice of ham cut straight through the center of the leg, with a slice of marrow-filled bone in the middle, often broiled or grilled and served with a mustard sauce.

handkäse - also **hand cheese.** A German cow's milk cheese made from sour skimmed milk, usually low in fat, with a washed rind and a powerful, sharp, pungent flavor that is best paired with beer and strongly flavored foods. The name "handkäse" means "hand cheese" in German because it is traditionally molded by hand into logs or rounds.

hand-held mixer - see MIXER.

hand roll - also **temaki-zushi.** See SUSHI.

hanger steak - also **butcher steak, hanging tenderloin.** The darling of the true French bistro, where it's called *onglet*, a 1- to 2-pound (500 g to 1 kg) strip of thick muscle of which 1½ to 2 inches (4 to 5 cm) is attached to and supports the diaphragm. It "hangs" between the last rib and the loin. There is only one hanger steak per animal. It's best served rare to medium-rare and sliced against the grain, otherwise it will be too tough to eat. Hanger steak was, and still is, called **butcher steak** because it's not easy to find — traditionally, the butcher would take it home. See also BEEF.

hangiri tub - the traditional wide, shallow, wooden tub used for making seasoned sushi rice. Hot, freshly cooked rice, vinegar, salt and sugar are combined in the tub and fanned as they are gently stirred continuously. This process gives the rice a beautiful glossy sheen and makes it the perfect texture for pressing or molding into sushi. The tub is wide and shallow to give the rice maximum surface area, so that it cools rapidly, and the wood, which is dampened before use, absorbs some of the moisture in the cooked rice as it cools to prevent it from becoming overly sticky. Hangiri tubs are often sold in Asian grocery stores in North America.

Hangtown fry oysters - a dish of breaded, fried oysters with eggs and bacon. Legend has it that this way of frying oysters comes from the "last breakfast" in a frontier town, Hangtown, named because of its frequent hangings (now Placerville, California) of a man who was about to be hanged, who wanted to combine all his favorite foods in one last meal.

happy family - a Chinese stir-fry dish frequently served at restaurants. It contains a medley of meats and seafood with vegetables in a sweet-salty sauce. The name is likely derived from the combination of seemingly disparate ingredients all in one dish, held together with the sauce, much like a family is held together by a common bond. It could also be that the varied ingredients ensure that there's something for everyone in the dish, which promotes harmony around the dinner table.

Haraszthy de Mokcsa, Count Agoston - see profile below.

hard-ball stage - see TEMPERATURE.

hard biscuit - see HARDTACK.

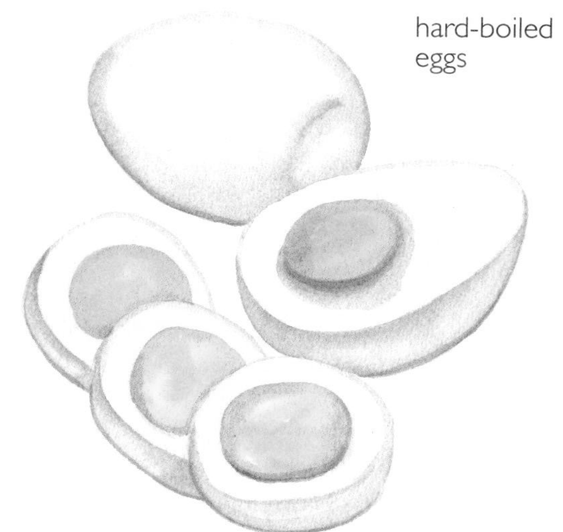

hard-boiled eggs

hard-boiled egg - also **hard-cooked egg.** An egg in its shell that has been boiled in water until the white and the yolk transform from liquid to solid. The traditional method is to cook the egg for 12 to 15 minutes at a full rolling boil, but some cooks advocate bringing the eggs to a boil, then removing them from the heat and allowing them to stand for up to 20 minutes in the hot water. If a hard-boiled egg is cooked for too long or not cooled quickly enough after cooking, iron and sulfur inside combine to form a green or gray ring around the yolk. A discolored egg is still edible and tastes no different from a properly cooked hard-boiled egg. To prevent this ring from forming, it's best to cook the eggs for the shortest time necessary

Haraszthy de Mokcsa, Count Agoston (1812–1869) - Hungarian founder of the California wine industry. Haraszthy left Europe in 1840 and traveled throughout America before settling in California in 1848. He planted vineyards, having learned plant cultivation from his family, who were famous for their fruit orchards. He formed a lasting friendship with General Mariano Vallejo, who founded the Sonoma region and was also a successful winemaker. Although the two were industrial competitors (Vallejo's wines consistently won top state awards until Haraszthy's wines surpassed them in 1858), they remained good friends. Haraszthy's two oldest sons married Vallejo's twin daughters in a dual ceremony. In 1861, the California Legislature commissioned Haraszthy to do a year-long study of European viticulture, from which he brought back 100,000 French, German, Italian and Spanish cuttings. Some say Haraszthy died when he fell into the water while inspecting a boat and was eaten by an alligator.

to harden the yolks and whites, then cool them under cold running water immediately.

hard cider - see CIDER.

hard-cooked egg - see HARD-BOILED EGG.

hard-crack stage - see TEMPERATURE.

hard flour - also **bread flour.** See FLOUR.

hardneck garlic - see GARLIC.

hard roe - see ROE.

hard salami - see SALAMI.

hard sauce - also **brandy butter.** A mixture of butter, sugar and flavorings beaten together until creamy, then spooned into a mold and refrigerated until hard. The sauce is then sliced and used on top of traditional dessert puddings, such as plum pudding or **Indian pudding.** Hard sauce can be made with any type of sugar, from confectioner's to brown sugar, and is usually flavored with a spirit, such as rum or brandy. The sauce is called brandy butter in the U.K.

hard-shell clam - see CLAM.

hardtack - **1.** also **hard biscuit, pilot's bread, sea biscuit, ship biscuit.** A dried, unleavened cracker-like biscuit made of flour, water and sometimes salt, which has been a staple for sailors, soldiers and explorers since time immemorial. When dried properly, hardtack becomes shelf-stable for months or even years. It is also cheap to make, nutritious, filling and very light to carry, making it the perfect choice for anyone who is moving great distances on foot or with limited storage space. Hardtack was often so hard that soldiers had to smash it and dip it in liquid, such as coffee or soup, to make it even remotely palatable. **2.** see BREWIS.

hard water - containing larger-than-usual quantities of calcium and magnesium.

hard wheat - wheat with a high amount of protein in the kernel, excellent for developing strong **gluten** strands, so therefore good for use in yeast-leavened breads. Soft wheat has a low amount of protein in the kernel, so it does not develop gluten as well as hard wheat, making it better for delicate, tender baked goods, such as cakes. See also WHEAT.

hare - any of various animals of the genus *Lepus*, a larger relative of the rabbit, not usually domesticated. Hunting season restricts the availability of hares. They can be roasted or cooked in casseroles, stews and terrines. Older hares are usually **jugged,** an 18th-century recipe that, at that time, referred to a method of cooking in which the blood and meat were placed in a jug and cooked in a large kettle of water. The modern version refers to hare cooked in a casserole with a sauce of port or claret, red currant jelly and the blood and meat. Many classic French dishes call for the back or saddle (*râble*) or the saddle and hind legs (*train*) only. The word comes from the Old English word *hara*.

haricot bean - a term referring to any of a number of dried beans that come from varieties of the green bean, including the red kidney bean and the navy bean. See also BEAN.

haricot vert - the French name for delicate, green string beans that are slim and quite young, best eaten when only 2½ to 3 inches (6 to 7.5 cm) long.

haricot vert

harira - a well-spiced chickpea and/or lentil soup from Morocco that is served with fresh milk and dates to break the all-day fast each evening during the Muslim holy month of Ramadan.

harissa - **1.** a fiery paste made all over North Africa, from Algeria to Somalia, usually eaten with couscous, but also used as a condiment for meat, fish, salads, soups and stews. The main ingredients are: cayenne pepper, coriander, cumin, mint, garlic, caraway seeds and olive oil. The name comes from the Arabic *harasa*, meaning "to crush or pound," which is just what's done when making the sauce. **2.** see HALEEM.

haroset - see CHAROSETH.

hartshorn - see AMMONIUM BICARBONATE.

harusame - also **bean thread, cellophane noodles, glass noodles, Japanese vermicelli, transparent noodles.** Made from mung beans, soybeans, rice flour or potato flour, *harusame* is Japanese for "spring rain," a noodle rarely eaten on its own, but rather with fish or meat, especially pork.

Harvard beets - a side dish of beets cooked with sugar and vinegar. There are several versions of how they got their name. One version claims that a Harvard student invented them. Others say the dish is the same color as Harvard's official school colors. And, finally, another version claims the recipe originated at an English pub named Harwood's: a Russian immigrant opened a restaurant in Boston with that name and began serving Harwood's famous beets, but because his English was flawed, the dish sounded more like "Harvard beets" than "Harwood's beets," and the name stuck.

Harvey Wallbanger - one of the consummate cocktails of the 1970s, this drink is a screwdriver, a combination of vodka and orange juice stirred with ice, topped with a **float** of **Galliano.** No one is completely sure of the origin of this cocktail's name, but the most colorful story claims that it comes from a surfer named Harvey who frequented a bar near the beach in California. Legend has it that Harvey liked his screwdrivers with a touch of Galliano on the top, and that one night, after a few too many, tried to leave the bar but kept bumping into the bar and the walls on his way out.

haschich fudge - see TOKLAS, ALICE BABETTE.

Hasenpfeffer - a highly spiced, peppery German stew made with marinated rabbit meat, from the German *hase*, meaning "hare," and *pfeffer*, meaning "pepper." The name is surprisingly familiar to many North Americans, thanks to the 1962 Looney Tunes cartoon *Shishkabugs*, which featured chef Yosemite Sam trying desperately to turn Bugs Bunny into hasenpfeffer for an increasingly irate king. The word is also heard in the theme song to the popular 1970s American sitcom *Laverne & Shirley*.

hash - a dish of chopped meat (usually beef and especially corned beef), potatoes and sometimes other vegetables, such as onions and green peppers, all fried together until they brown. The word comes from the French *hacher*, meaning "to chop up."

hash browns - a golden brown fried cake of grated potatoes most often served at breakfast. Hash browns can also be sautéed boiled potatoes, sometimes roughly mashed while frying to form loose golden brown cakes, but these versions are often identified as **home fries.**

hashi - see OHASHI.

Hass avocado - see AVOCADO.

hasty pudding - a Colonial staple, a combination of water or milk, salt and yellow cornmeal, sweetened with molasses, honey or maple syrup and served either at breakfast or as a filling dessert. It was named "hasty" because it only took 10 minutes to make, which, in terms of early cooking, was very fast. See also INDIAN PUDDING.

hatcho miso - see MISO.

hato mugi - see JOB'S TEARS.

haute cuisine - sophisticated food presented in an ornate manner, prepared with a high level of expertise. See also CARÊME, ANTONIN.

Havarti - a Tilsit-type semisoft Danish cheese with an open (no crust), lace-like paste and a natural or washed rind, meaning it has been brushed repeatedly with a hard brush dipped in a solution of either lime or milk residue. The dry rind gives Havarti a sourish taste; the flora on the washed rind make it taste sharper. Havarti is named after the farm where cheesemaker Hanne Nielsen developed this type of cheese in the mid-1800s.

Hawaiian bread - also **Hawaiian sweet bread.** See PORTUGUESE SWEET BREAD.

Hawaiian pink bean soup - see KAU KAU.

Hawaiian salt - see RED SALT, SALT.

Hawaiian sun fish - see TILAPIA.

hawayij - also **hawaij.** A Middle Eastern mixture of ground spices, similar to **garam masala** or curry powder, which includes black peppercorns, cumin and/or caraway seeds, cardamom seeds, ground turmeric and saffron. The mixture is ground together and used to season a wide variety of dishes, predominantly in Jewish cuisine in Yemen, although it has become popular in other countries as well.

hawthorn - more than 200 species of thorny trees bearing small fruits called "haws." These can be made into preserves, but most are so bitter they are eaten only as **famine food.** The sweeter spring flower buds, however, were once considered a treat. See also AZAROLE.

Hazan, Marcella - see profile below.

hazelnut - also **cobnut, filbert.** A fruit of the hazel tree of the genus *Corylus*. The most important variety of hazelnut is the Barcelona, introduced in the U.S. in 1885; it is the most extensively grown variety there. The nuts are large, thick-shelled, round and broad-shouldered, with a blunt point and a rich chestnut-brown color. The name "filbert," *Corylus avellana*, most often used in England for a cultivated hazelnut, takes its name from St. Philibert, a 7th-century Frankish abbot whose feast day on August 22 coincides with the nuts' ripening time. Native to the Mediterranean region but now grown all over Europe, hazelnuts can be eaten on their own or used in desserts and confectionery.

hazelnuts

hazelnut butter - a **nut butter** made of roasted skinned hazelnuts. See also ALMOND BUTTER, CASHEW BUTTER, PEANUT BUTTER.

hazelnut flour - see NUT FLOUR.

hazelnut oil - an oil pressed from hazelnuts, with a delicate flavor, extremely good on salads and in baking, easy to digest.

hazelnut paste - a sumptuous filling for cakes, pastries and chocolates, made from ground roasted hazelnuts, egg whites, sugar and hazelnut liqueur. In Italian, it is called *pasta nocciola* and is often found in Italian grocery stores under this name. While packaged versions are excellent, it is easy to make at home with a food processor.

hazenblosen - a type of German Jewish cookie made by deep-frying pieces of sweet cookie dough. The dough is rolled paper-thin and cut

Hazan, Marcella (1924 –) - Italian culinary teacher and author, and matriarch of Italian cooking in North America. Born in Emiglia-Romagna, on the Adriatic coast, Hazan earned a doctorate in biology at the University of Ferrara and only began cooking in 1955, when she married her husband, Victor, a wine and food writer. Her beginnings as a teacher were completely unplanned. She was enrolled in some Chinese cooking classes and, when her instructor went on sabbatical, her classmates asked her to teach them Italian cooking. She caught the attention of **Craig Claiborne,** who encouraged her to write a book, which she originally refused to do. Yet, by the time she turned 80 in 2004, she had released *Marcella Says…*, her sixth book. Her first, *The Classic Italian Cook Book: The Art of Italian Cooking and the Italian Art of Eating* (1973), was an instant critical success. She also wrote *More Classic Italian Cooking* (1978), *Marcella's Italian Kitchen* (1986), *Essentials of Classic Italian Cooking* (1992), a reissue of her first two books in one volume, and *Marcella Cucina* (1996). She and her husband have also conducted cooking and wine classes from their home in the Veneto, but they retired to Florida in the late 1990s, near their son, Giuliano, who now teaches Italian cooking seasonally at his parents' former home; he has published two food books and was a 1994 James Beard Award nominee. Of her favorite dish — rapini sautéed with garlic, anchovy and chiles, and tossed with pasta — Hazan writes, "I hope never to become so feeble that I am unable to respond to the potent call of this dish."

into rectangles, which are split partway up the center. As the dough fries, it puffs up, giving the cookies their characteristic shape and name, which translates as "blown-up little pants." The cookies are then dusted with confectioner's sugar.

head cheese - a sausage, not a cheese, made from the meat of a calf's or pig's head that has been cooked in a broth, cooled in a mold, chopped up and set in **aspic** made from the gelatinous stock and served cold, thinly sliced. Its traditional English name is **brawn.**

head lettuce - see LETTUCE.

heart - very nutritious part of an animal, with very little waste, requiring slow cooking. Lamb hearts have the finest taste; pork hearts are larger and slightly coarser; and beef hearts are the least tender of all.

hearts of palm - also **palm heart, palmita.** The crunchy, sweet, white core cut from the growing tips of various palm trees, used fresh (or, in North America, most often from a can) and cooked or raw in antipasto, **lumpia,** pie, pizza and salads, or pickled. The heart is cut out of the terminal bud from which new fronds emerge. When taken from coconut or royal palm trees (often growing wild), the operation kills them. Growing concerns about killing great numbers of wild palms in such countries as Brazil has led to more interest in the *Guilielma gasipaes* or **peach palm.** When mature, peach palms produce secondary buds from which the hearts can be harvested, leaving the tree to regenerate. Cultivation of the peach palm in Costa Rica, Florida and Hawaii is starting to provide much of the hearts of palm consumed in North America. Small farmers in South American who presently grow coca (from which cocaine is derived) are being encouraged to switch to peach palms as a viable alternative cash crop. See also SWAMP CABBAGE.

heather honey - see HONEY.

heavy cream - an American term for whipping cream that contains 35 to 40 percent butterfat. There is also a light whipping cream available in the U.S., but not Canada, that contains 30 to 35 percent butterfat, which is what Canadians refer to as whipping cream. See also CREAM.

Heering, Peter Frederik - see PETER HEERING.

heirloom crops - crops grown from natural, non-hybrid seeds that are open-pollinated (that is, pollinated by other plants of the same variety). Today, many seed companies and most large-scale farms used hybrid seeds, which are crosses between different — sometimes vastly different — varieties of plants that are not naturally compatible. Hybrids are fairly reliable for the first year that they are grown, producing uniform results that are supermarket-friendly. The disadvantage of using them is that they do not reproduce the same way as old-fashioned heirloom seeds do. Seeds saved from a hybrid plant, when planted the next year, are often sterile and will not grow, or else produce unreliable plants that are different than expected.

The widespread use of fewer varieties of seeds and more sterile hybrid varieties leaves the food supply open to failure on a massive scale. Without seed banks and the careful cultivation of heirloom varieties of familiar foods, if the few hybrids commonly used were to fail because of susceptibility to a particular disease, there would be no alternatives and the food supply would diminish rapidly. A movement to save and exchange heirloom seeds is gaining support across North America and Europe. Heirloom seed banks encourage farmers and gardeners to grow an array of plants (and save their seeds) to make the plant population stronger and more diverse, and therefore less susceptible to damage by a single blight or disease. See also BEANS, TOMATO.

heirloom tomato - see TOMATO.

hen of the woods - a rather large and fan-shaped mushroom with white to grayish skin, grows at the base of deciduous trees, such as oak, edible only when cooked.

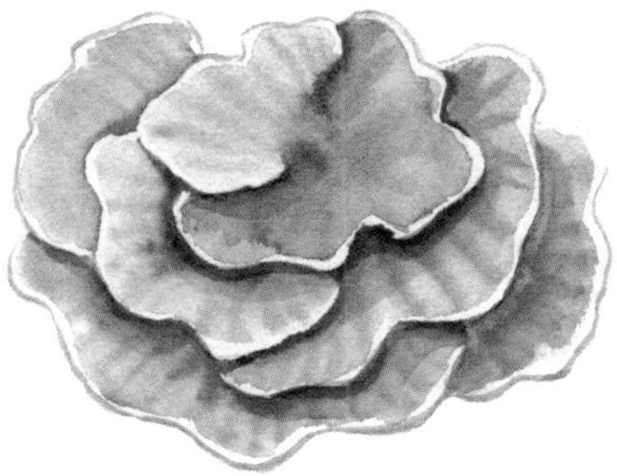

hen of the woods

Henson, Steve - see RANCH DRESSING.

herbaceous - also **herbal.** A food- and wine-tasting term used to describe something with the pronounced flavor of herbs. It can be a negative term for those who don't enjoy herbs, but it is usually a positive term, implying a pleasantly strong herbal flavor, unlike **vegetal,** which is used to describe a wine with a too-pronounced vegetable or herbal quality, which makes it smell rank. Wines made from **Sauvignon Blanc, Cabernet Franc, Cabernet Sauvignon** and **Merlot** grapes are sometimes described as herbaceous or even herbal, which implies a softer herb flavor.

herbal tea - also **tisane.** A beverage made by **infusing** herb leaves and/or flowers in boiling water, not a true tea because it contains no leaves from the tea plant. Herbal teas have been consumed both medicinally and simply for enjoyment for thousands of years. Some of the most popular are mint, chamomile, rose hip, ginger and ginseng, all purported to have positive effects on health. The French word *tisaine* passed into English as "tisane" to describe these types of drinks, originally from the ancient Greek *ptisane*, meaning "crushed barley," for the pestle used to crush that grain before making it into **barley water.**

herbal vinegars - see VINEGAR.

herbes de Provence - the famous dried herb mixture from southern France, which can include thyme, savory, rosemary, marjoram, sage, lavender, bay leaves, basil and, despite its name, fennel seeds, which are actually a spice. In commercial preparations, ingredients and proportions vary tremendously.

herbes salées - see SALTED HERBS.

herb Louisa - see LEMON VERBENA.

herb of the cross - see LEMON VERBENA.

herbs - any of a large group of annual and perennial plants whose stems, leaves or flowers are used as a flavoring. The scent and folklore of fresh herbs have permeated nearly 5,000 years of history. From savory to sweet, ambrosial to pungent, herbs have their culinary use as well as medicinal properties. Through the centuries, herbs have been used for love potions, protection against baldness, prevention against vitamin deficiencies, decorative foliage and as symbols of wealth and goodwill toward the gods. During the Middle Ages, herbs became important in a culinary sense and were used broadly in sauces, conserves, pastries, puddings, teas and especially wines.

Far from being a modern occurrence, collecting aromatic herbs can be traced back as far as ancient Egypt. About 1500 BC, Queen Hatshepsut ordered the mass felling of fig trees in her kingdom to build rafts, which were poled hundreds of miles up the Nile River to seek out exotic trees and aromatic herbs for the royal gardens. Sennacherib, son of Sargon II of Assyria, erected magnificent gardens and planted them with myrrh and other aromatic shrubs collected from the land of the Hittites. The earliest scientific works on herbs were Greek writer **Theophrastus'** *History of Plants* and *Causes of Plants* (c. 300 BC) and the seminal texts of the Middle Ages, Avienna's *Canon Medicinea* (c. 1020) and the Anglo-Saxon *Leech Book of Bald* (c. 950). See also ACHILÉE, ALEXANDERS, ALFALFA, ANGELICA, ANISE, BASIL, BERGAMOT, BETONY, BORAGE, BURNET, CATNIP, CHAMOMILE, CHERVIL, CHICORY, CHIVE, CICELY, CLARY, COMFREY, COSTMARY, DILL, EPAZOTE, FINES HERBES, HERBES DE PROVENCE, HOREHOUND, HORSERADISH, HYSSOP, LAVENDER, LEMON BALM, LEMONGRASS, LEMON VERBENA, LOVAGE, MARJORAM, MINT, OREGANO, PARSLEY, ROSEMARY, SAGE, SAMPHIRE, SAVORY, SHISO, SORREL, SPICES, TANSY, TARRAGON, THYME, VERVAIN, WOODRUFF, WORMWOOD, YARROW, ZA'ATAR.

Herbsaint - a brand-name anise-flavored liqueur, created in New Orleans in the 1850s as a cheaper alternative to expensive French **absinthe.** Although it was more like **pastis,** due to its similarity to absinthe, Herbsaint was taken off the market in 1912 when absinthe was banned in the U.S. It was later re-released (unlike absinthe, it does not contain the ingredient wormwood, which contains the neurotoxin thujone) and is still made today in Louisiana according to its secret original recipe. Herbsaint is used in a small range of cocktails and is a key ingredient in the famed New Orleans dish **oysters Rockefeller.**

hermetically sealed - a term applied to a container (usually a sterile one used for packaging foods) that is sealed completely so that it is impervious to air. Hermetically sealed packages keep foods fresh and don't allow them to come into contact with bacteria, contaminants or air, which can cause the food to spoil. A hermetic seal can also be created to lock in the steam and juices of a stew by sealing a pot's lid to its rim with bread dough or a paste made of flour and water. The word *hermetic* comes from Hermes Trismegistus, a legendary writer (or writers, some historians say it was a group of people who all worked on the hermetic writings), who is credited with producing books on magic, alchemy and astrology, and with inventing a magical seal that kept containers airtight.

hermit - a spicy, chewy cookie made with chopped fruit and nuts, and brown sugar or molasses. The name is said to come from the fact that the cookie is better after several days and kept hidden away like a hermit.

hero sandwich - see SUBMARINE SANDWICH.

herring - any of a very large family of small saltwater fish, *Clupea harengus*, found in the North Atlantic and Pacific oceans. These fish generally have long, silvery-blue bodies and strong-flavored flesh. While fresh herring can be purchased during the spring, it's more often sold canned, smoked (as kippers) or pickled. The name is German, from *heer,* meaning "an army," because they like to swim in very large schools. See also BRATHERING, CISCO, SARDINE, SPRAT.

HERRING VARIETIES

alewife - a small fish, *Alosa pseudoharengus,* found off the Atlantic coast of North America as well as in the Great Lakes.

Bismarck herring - filleted herring marinated in vinegar and spices, served with raw onion and lemon, named for the 19th-century German prince Otto von Bismarck. A **rollmop** is a herring fillet, usually Bismarck, wrapped around a gherkin or onion.

bloater - in England, a large, fat, salted herring, usually prepared with the head on and ungutted, cold-smoked to the point of golden color, then scaled and gutted just before serving.

Buckling - considered one of the best versions of smoked herring. Originally from Germany, it's also prepared in Britain, the Netherlands and Norway.

kipper - the most common form of smoked herring. It should be plump, juicy and properly smoked, not dyed to disguise inadequate treatment, as is often the case. Kippers are sold whole, usually in pairs, or as individual fillets, which are often available frozen. They can be used to make **pâté,** or broiled or grilled. They're famously part of a traditional English breakfast.

marinated herring - see PICKLED HERRING.

matjes - young **herring** caught in spring and early summer that is filleted, then marinated for at least two days in a mixture of onions, salt, sugar and vinegar, and herbs, such as dill. Popular throughout northern Europe and Scandinavia, it is usually served with sour cream and boiled, in-season, new potatoes.

menhaden - a saltwater herring, abundant near the shores of New England. It was named after a Algonquian word. Menhaden is now used mainly for oil and fertilizer.

alewife

pickled herring - also **marinated herring.** A broad category of herring preparations, many of which have a sweet taste, such as Danish pickled herrings, which are often enhanced with mustard sauces. Pickled herring is often sold in jars, some with a sour cream-based sauce, some made with salted herring, some pickled in a sauce that contains wine.

rollmop - spicy, marinated fillet of herring wrapped around a gherkin or onion and rolled on a stick, from the German *rollen,* meaning "to roll," and *mops,* meaning "pug dog."

schmaltz herring - mature, fattier herring, covered in coarse salt and weighted on top for several days. Salt must be removed before eating.

shad - a North American fish, the largest of the herring family, living in salt water but spawning in fresh, found exclusively on the eastern seaboard until 1871, when 10,000 fry were introduced into the Sacramento and Columbia rivers, with 800,000 following during the next 10 years. Shad prospered, and its roe became one of the great delicacies of spring, its Latin name, *Sapidissima,* meaning "most delicious." To the original inhabitants of New York, shad was known as *elft,* "the 11 fish," because the first shad in the Hudson was traditionally caught on the 11th of March. Shad was considered poor-man's salmon and not particularly highly regarded until the 18th century. Baked shad was one of George Washington's favorite dishes and, in the early days of the republic, congressmen sailed down the Potomac to enjoy great feasts of freshly caught shad in the spring.

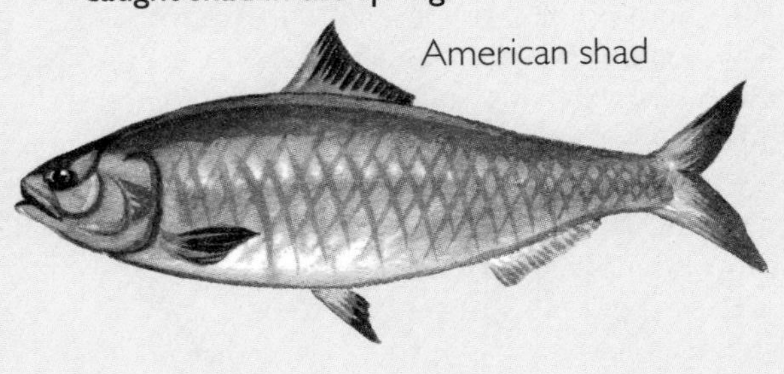
American shad

Herve - a pungent Belgian cow's milk cheese similar in flavor (and odor) to **Limburger,** with a soft, pale yellow interior surrounded by an orange-yellow crust. Herve is sold either plain or flavored with herbs, and can be much less strongly flavored if it has not been aged a long time. The cheese is named for the town in Belgium where it originated.

hibachi - a small, portable grill fueled with charcoal, used for grilling foods, from a Japanese word meaning "fire bowl." Some Japanese and Korean restaurants use this term for tables with gas grills used for cooking meats and seafood at the table.

hibiscus tea - made from the dark red petals of the hibiscus flower, a popular drink in the Middle East, where it's served hot or cold, and Mexico, where it's known as **jamaica,** served as a sweetened ice tea.

hickory nut - a broad term for any of a variety of nuts produced by trees of the genus *Carya,* including **pecans,** shellbark hickory nuts, shagbark hickory nuts and mockernuts. Hickories are relatives of the walnut and produce rich-tasting, meaty nuts with tough outer shells. The **shagbark** is named for the scruffy bark of the tree and tastes similar to the pecan, with a craggy shell that makes it looks like a cross between a chestnut and a walnut. The **shellbark** has an ovoid outer shell, like the pecan, which encloses a pleasantly sweet-tasting nut. The **mockernut** has an incredibly thick shell, which gave it its name: *mokker* is the Dutch word for hammer, which is the tool needed to crack the nuts out of their shells.

hickory smoked - see SMOKED FOODS.

hierba santa - see HOJA SANTA.

high altitude cooking - at higher altitudes, starting at about 3,000 feet (914 m) above sea level, foods must be prepared and cooked differently, and recipes adjusted, to compensate for lower air pressure. As the altitude increases,

hibiscus

the weight of the air pressing down on the earth decreases, allowing water to boil at lower temperatures, because there is not as much resistance from the air pressing down upon it. This means that water, which boils at 212°F (100°C) at sea level, boils at 208°F (98°C) at 2,000 feet (609 m) above sea level; at 203°F (95°C) at 5,000 feet (1,524 m) above sea level; at 198°F (92°C) at 7,500 feet (2,286 m) above sea level; and at 194°F (90°C) at 10,000 feet (3,048 m) above sea level. At these lower temperatures, food takes longer to cook and is less hot to the touch at the boiling point. This also makes a difference when canning foods; foods processed in a boiling-water canner must be processed longer to render them safe, and foods prepared in a steam-pressure canner must be brought up to a higher pressure to achieve the proper temperature to ensure sterilization.

At higher altitudes, the gases produced by **chemical leaveners** that make cakes and other baked goods rise expand more than they do at sea level. This means that the amount of baking soda or baking powder in a recipe must be decreased. Starting at 3,000 feet (914 m), water and liquids evaporate more quickly, so the amount of liquid is also decreased, as is the amount of sugar, to accommodate the increased evaporation of liquids, which can leave baked goods overly sweet and can lead to weaker structure, causing cakes to collapse. To compensate for all these variables, it is also a good idea to set the oven temperature 15° to 25°F (5° to 10°C) higher to "set" the batter, preventing the overexpansion of the leavening gases.

Other common cooking methods must also be adjusted to compensate for decreased air pressure at high altitudes. When deep-fat frying, the temperature of the oil must be reduced to prevent the foods from over-browning before they are cooked through. The water in the foods boils at a lower temperature, so the outside can crisp far too quickly if cooked at the normal temperature for sea level. Likewise, because water evaporates much more quickly, it's advisable to cook syrups, candies and jellies to a lower final temperature to prevent burning or excessive thickening.

highball - a cocktail served over ice in a tall glass. It's generally made of liquor and a mixer (either water or a soft drink).

highball glass - also **Collins glass, cooler.** A tall, straight-sided glass that can hold eight to 14 ounces of liquid, used for serving highballs or large mixed drinks, such as the **Tom Collins.** A cooler is an extra-large highball glass that can hold up to a whopping 21 ounces of liquid, such as for extra-large **mint juleps** or fruity rum drinks.

high-ratio cake - a professional baker's term for a cake that is made with more sugar by weight than flour, and sometimes more eggs or fat than a regular cake. This larger ratio of sugar to flour makes a light cake with a fine **crumb.**

high tea - also **meat tea.** A British late-afternoon or early-evening meal, usually consisting of various meat or fish dishes accompanied by crumpets or scones and jam, cakes and pastries, and tea. See also AFTERNOON TEA.

hijiki - also **hiziki**. A cooked, dried, shredded brownish seaweed, commonly eaten in Japanese cuisine, usually in salads and soups but not sushi. The food safety agencies in many countries, including Canada, Britain and New Zealand, have cautioned people not to consume hijiki because it contains high levels of inorganic arsenic, a carcinogen. Other types of seaweed commonly eaten in North America, including kelp (kombu), nori and dulse, do not contain inorganic arsenic and are considered safe to eat.

hippocras - one of the most popular forms of aromatized and spiced wines from the Middle Ages and even long afterward. There is every reason to believe that the basis of hippocras (once prepared for medicinal purposes) was sour wine. There must have been an embarrassingly large quantity of such wine because it was kept in ullage, referring to casks that are no longer full (a dangerous condition for any wine if left for any length of time) or in ill-stoppered bottles before the use of corks. Such wine was sweetened and spiced and then filtered through a woolen bag, known as a Hippocrates sleeve (not named after the physician but from the apothecary name for a strainer or sieve). This accounts for the name "hippocras," which was often written in medieval books as Ipocras or Ypocras.

Hires, Charles - see ROOT BEER.

hiyamugi - medium-thin white wheat noodles used in Japanese cooking, thicker than hair-thin **somen** and thinner than fat **udon** noodles. Hiyamugi are often used in cold dishes, but can also be served in soups.

hiziki - see HIJIKI.

hoagie - also **hoagy.** A term for a **submarine sandwich,** used mainly in Philadelphia and New Jersey. There's no clear origin of the term, although most stories place the coinage of the word in the 1920s to 1930s (some as early as the 1910s). The best-known and most likely stories agree that the sandwiches were discovered, or invented, in the Hog Island part of Philadelphia, which was home to a naval shipyard. One version says that Italian immigrants who worked in the shipyards were seen eating huge, homemade cold cut sandwiches, which the other workers called "hoggies" (which evolved into "hoagies"). Another version says that an enterprising man named Al DePalma invented the sandwich when he saw shipyard workers at Hog Island hungrily devouring huge sandwiches on their lunch break. Legend has it that he thought they looked like hogs slopping down their lunch, then decided to capitalize on their appetites by selling large "hoggie" (later "hoagie") sandwiches outside the gates of the shipyard.

hochepot - see POTÉE.

hock - **1.** a cut of meat from the lower leg of an animal, just above the foot, such as a **ham hock,** which is the lower portion of a pig's leg. **2.** the British name for Rhine wine, in reference to the village of Hochheim in the Rheingau. At first, "hock" implied a wine from Hochheim; later, it came to mean any Rheingau wine; and later still, any Rhine wine.

hodgepodge - see HOTCHPOTCH.

hoe cake - also **hoecake.** See JOHNNYCAKE.

ho fun - see BANH PHO.

hogfish - the common name for a number of different fishes, including the tautog, *Tautoga onitis*, an East Coast saltwater fish often identified by the generic name "blackfish"; the hog snapper, *Lachnolaimus maximus*, a fish of the wrasse family of the Eastern Atlantic; and fishes of the genus *Bodianus*, many of which are commonly found in pet stores as aquarium denizens.

hog jowl - a cut of pork from the cheeks of a pig, carved into blocks and usually smoked, similar in flavor to bacon. Hog jowls can be diced or sliced and fried for use in a variety of Southern dishes, and are especially delicious paired with black-eyed peas. See also PORK.

hog maw - the stomach of a pig, also a sausage-like dish stuffed and cooked inside a pig stomach, similar to **haggis.** Hog maw was a common dish of the Pennsylvania Dutch and of the South, often stuffed with a combination of sausage, potatoes, onions and seasonings, tied and simmered and/or baked until browned and cooked through.

hoisin sauce - also **Peking sauce.** A thick, sweet, brown sauce made with soybeans, garlic, sugar and chiles, widely used in Chinese cuisine.

hoja de aguacate - see AVOCADO LEAF.

hoja santa

hoja santa - also **hierba santa, root beer plant, yerba santa.** The leaf of the hoja santa plant, *Piper auritum sanctum*, native to Mexico and used often in the country's cuisine. The large, dinner-plate-size leaves are used in different types of **mole,** cooked with fish and frequently used as wrappers around grilled or baked foods, imparting their flavor to the food within. The leaves, which are more often available in dried form north of Mexico, have a unique taste, which is often described as similar to licorice or **sarsaparilla** (hence why hoja santa is often called "root beer plant"). The name means "sacred leaf" in Spanish.

hoka squash - see KOBACHA SQUASH.

Hokkien noodles - fresh Chinese egg noodles made with wheat flour; long and thin like spaghetti and yellow from the egg yolks they are made with. Hokkien noodles are used in saucy recipes and stir-fries, because they soak up liquids well and have a soft, pleasant texture that complements tender-crisp vegetables. Look for them in the refrigerated section of Asian grocery stores or in vacuum-sealed packages. Hokkien is the name for the southern Chinese province of Fujian in the Min-nan dialect.

holishkes - a Jewish dish of blanched cabbage leaves wrapped around a filling of spiced ground beef and rice, simmered in a thin tomato sauce. The rolls are served on the Jewish harvest holiday of Sukkot, their plump, stuffed shapes signifying abundance. See also CABBAGE ROLL.

hollandaise - a French sauce made with butter, egg yolks and lemon juice. According to some culinary historians, hollandaise sauce was originally called *sauce Isigny* (from the butter-producing town in Normandy). When butter was in limited supply during the First World War, it was imported from Holland, hence the current name. See also SAUCE.

hollow-edge blade - also **Granton-edge blade.** A knife blade made with a series of indentations along the side, so that cut food does not stick to it. **Chef's knives** and **santoku** knives are often made with hollow-edge blades.

hollyhock - a plant, *Alcea rosea,* grown as an ornamental, with edible, brightly colored flowers. The blossoms have a very mild, slightly bitter flavor, which is pleasant as a garnish for foods. The cup-shaped flower also makes an attractive container (inside a supportive bowl) for dips. See also EDIBLE FLOWERS.

holy basil - see BASIL.

holy poke - see BAPTIST CAKE.

holy trinity - see TRINITY.

home fries - also **cottage fries, cottage-fried potatoes, home-fried potatoes.** Diced or sliced potatoes pan-fried with onions, spices and sometimes peppers, often served as an accompaniment to a traditional hearty breakfast of eggs, bacon and toast. Most cooks boil their potatoes first to make the cooking time shorter and to make sure the potatoes are cooked through, but some leave them uncooked and fry them over lower heat for an extended period of time. Home fries and hash browns are often confused and their names used interchangeably.

hom ha - a soft, spoonable version of shrimp paste used in Hong Kong as a condiment and a seasoning; grayish pink and semi-liquid, instead of thick and pasty. When used as a condiment, it is mixed with water, lime juice, sliced onions and chiles for dipping. As a seasoning, it is added to marinades, stir-fries or pork that is to be steamed. It is similar in flavor to **bagoong** and **patis.** See also SHRIMP PASTE.

hominy - also **hulled corn, posole, pozole.** A staple of the American South, hominy is whole-kernel yellow or white corn that has had the germ removed and has been soaked in lye. In Mexico, where it's known as **nixtamal,** it's used to make *masa,* the meal used to make tortillas. Ground, it's called "hominy grits." The name comes from the Algonquian word *rockahominy*.

homogenization - a process of forcing milk at high pressure through a very small nozzle onto a hard surface, which breaks up the fat into more uniform particles about a quarter of their original size, keeping the fat evenly distributed throughout the milk, rather than separating and rising to the top. Developed in France about 1900, homogenization produces milk that is whiter, blander, less stable over heat and more sensitive to spoilage by light than unhomogenized milk. See also MILK.

honey - the natural nectar of a flower converted to a rich, golden syrup by hordes of hardworking bees. Centuries before sugar became widely available, honey was used to enhance the palatability of foods. Prehistoric paintings depict early man gathering wild honey in

honey

much the same manner as it's done today.

Honey was also one of the few preservatives known to the ancients and was considered a powerful source of resurrection magic. Pagan tribes in the Mediterranean once placed their dead in a fetal position and embalmed them with a jar of honey, so that they could await rebirth in heaven. Some Christian mythology claims that bees have their origin in the tears Christ shed during the Crucifixion. An ancient Egyptian scroll listed more than 500 recipes that included honey as one of the ingredients. The Greeks and Romans were particularly fond of honey and used it for everything, including flavoring wine. Honey is part of many christening, matrimonial and funerary rites in every civilization. In ancient Egypt, the bride would supply honey to the groom's parents in a yearly gift for the duration of her marriage. The ancient Hindus anointed the bride's forehead, lips, eyelids and earlobes with honey. Honey has always been associated with stimulated erotic

TYPES OF HONEY

acacia - light and delicate, made from the flowers of the acacia tree.

alfalfa - mellow-flavored, made from alfalfa blossoms.

barberry - amber, from barberry flowers.

buckwheat - dark and more robust than other honey, from the buckwheat flower.

clover - light and delicate, perhaps the most common and most popular honey in Europe.

creamed honey - honey that has been whipped or allowed to crystallize in a controlled manner to form a smooth, spreadable paste.

English - a blend of honeys gathered from a variety of English blossoms, also available creamed, essential for a "proper" afternoon tea.

eucalyptus - a creamy Australian honey that can be light or dark, and medium to very sweet, depending on the variety of eucalyptus nectar from which it's made. There are about 500 varieties of this honey, all native to Australia. Flavors range from the delicate Eucalyptus *albaros* variety to the extra-light but sweet and cloying *melliodora* and the dark, strong *tereticoruis.*

Greek - rich, sweet and soothing, sometimes mildly medicinal in flavor because the bees have been fed on thyme, as is most honey imported from Greece.

heather - extremely popular in Britain and Europe, from Ling, *Calluna vulgaris*, or Bell, *Erica cinera,* heather varieties.

Hungarian acacia - mildly flavored, tending to remain a liquid, mostly produced in Romania, France and Italy, from *Robinia pseudoacacia.*

Hymetus - flavored with thyme, marjoram and other herbal blossoms growing on Mt. Hymetus in Greece since antiquity, dark, clear and slightly thick. It's a perfect complement to tart natural yogurt and excellent for making **baklava.**

Irish - thick, rich, yet milky, its characteristic flavor being heather.

lavender - one of the most delicate of all honeys, a specialty in the south of France and certain parts of Italy.

Manuka - a thick, dark, rich-tasting creamed honey flavored by the New Zealand tea tree, *Leptospermum scorparium,* also called "ti," ideal for cooking.

orange blossom - produced mostly in Spain but also in California, Mexico, South Africa and Israel, a light, delicate citrus-tasting honey that's especially good in custards.

pohutukawa - a rare New Zealand honey with a unique, salty flavor, from the pohutukawa tree, *Metrosideros excelsa.*

sunflower - produced mainly in Greece, Turkey and southern Russia, with a beautiful fragrance, very sensitive to heat.

Tasmanian leatherwood - rich, light-color, creamy Australian honey, with a distinctive taste, high in glucose, considered to be the world's finest. If necessary, it can be put in warm water for 30 minutes to make it clear and is used for general cooking.

powers and, for centuries, all love potions and elixirs included honey as an ingredient. Still in Morocco today, the groom retires alone to eat honey to enhance his performance before his first nuptial night. Honey has also been used for colds, coughs, fever, allergic rhinitis, skin infections and in a poultice for splinters.

The flavor of honey depends on what the bees have been feeding, and can vary greatly in different parts of the world. Blended honeys are usually the least expensive and distinctive.

honeyberry - also **limoncillo, mamoncillo, Spanish lime.** The sweet edible fruit from the genip tree (*Melicoccus bijugatus*) is native to South America. The juicy yellow pulp is usually popped from the leathery green rind. The fruit is used to make jam, jelly and a liquor called **bilí.**

honey bun - see STICKY BUN.

honey butter - unlike fruit butters, which contain no butter and are cooked down to a spreadable consistency, this spread is made from a combination of softened butter and honey, whipped together until smooth and creamy. It may or may not be enhanced with spices, such as cinnamon, or other flavorings, such as grated orange zest. It is a deliciously sweet topping for toast, muffins and waffles.

honeydew melon - a large, slightly ovoid muskmelon with a smooth, creamy, yellow rind and sweet, juicy, pale green flesh.

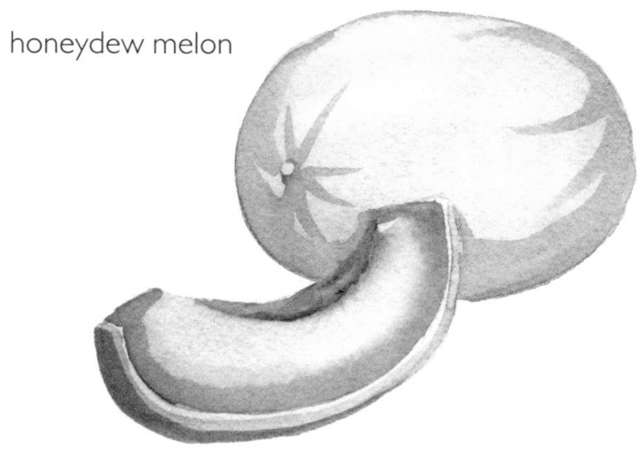
honeydew melon

honey mustard - see MUSTARD.

honey tangerine - also **Murcott.** A popular type of tangerine grown in Florida, medium-size, with a reddish to yellowish orange peel and sweet, seedy flesh. The fruit is usually found under the name *honey tangerine* in supermarkets, but its official name is *Murcott*, for Charles Murcott Smith, a South Florida nurseryman who had a number of the trees. Their origin is unclear, but it's thought that the honey tangerine was originally a cross between a tangerine and an orange, created in the U.S. in the early part of the 1900s.

hong yo chao shou - a Taiwanese boiled pork dumpling.

honyaki - see JAPANESE KNIVES.

Hoodless, Adelaide Hunter - see profile on page 330.

hoop cheese - a hard-to-find, old-fashioned cheese made from cow's milk, similar to **farmer's cheese** or pressed cottage cheese (although some versions are firmer), mild in flavor and good on crackers. In the 19th century, hoop cheese was a staple at most country stores, a large wheel of it set on the counter at the ready to be served up with crackers for a quick snack or lunch. Large wheels of the cheese were set in a contraption called a hoop cheese cutter: a lazy Susan wheel on the bottom with a sharp blade affixed over the top. The clerk would swing the wheel of cheese around and quickly slide the blade down to cleanly cut off the desired-size chunk. The name comes from the hoop-shaped mold used to form the cheese.

hootch - American slang, popular during Prohibition for illegally produced liquor, a colloquialism for cheap liquor. The word originated in Alaska during the late 19th century, where a small Tlingit tribe, the Hutsnuwu Indians, living on Admiralty Island, were distilling their own alcoholic liquor from molasses; it became known as *hoot-chinoo*, *hooch* or *hootch*. In *Report on the Population of Alaska*, published in the 1890 U.S. census, the authors wrote that the cause of "nearly all the trouble in this country" was hootch.

Hopfenkäse - a German cow's milk semisoft cheese. During processing, the cheese is layered between hop leaves, which lend their slightly sour flavor to the finished product. It may also be spiced with caraway seeds or cumin. Hopfenkäse and its similar German cousin, Nieheimer, are said to be best washed down with German beer.

Hoodless, Adelaide Hunter (1857–1910) - domestic science pioneer and founder of the Women's Institutes. Born in St. George, Ontario, she married John Hoodless, a prosperous Hamilton businessman in 1881. Her interests in social reform stemmed from the death of their 14-month-old son, apparently of an intestinal infection caused by drinking contaminated milk. The tragedy sparked her interest in domestic hygiene, and she campaigned for pasteurizing milk. Subsequently, through her involvement as a founder of the local YWCA and her husband's position as Chairman of the Board of Education, her perspective broadened. Possibly blaming herself for not being knowledgeable enough to prevent her son's death, she came to understand how society might improve, if girls received a better education in the domestic arts.

A relatively recent concept at the time, domestic science, which Mrs. Hoodless described as "the application of scientific principles to the management of the home," was also seen as a way of raising the status of women's work by aligning it with professionalism. Her active involvement in many organizations — for instance, in 1893 she was a delegate to the International Congress of Women at the Chicago World's Fair — gave her visibility and a platform. By the end of the century, she had succeeded in having domestic science added to the curriculum in Ontario's schools, and in 1898 she co-wrote a textbook, *Public School Domestic Science.*

Speaking at a conference organized by the Farmers' Institute in 1896, she was made aware that rural women had unique needs in the realm of domestic education. One stormy night in February of the following year, she asked her son, Bernard, to hitch up her favorite horse and drive her to Stoney Creek, where she addressed the Wentworth County Farmers' Institute. Some of the farmers' wives were present as guests, and they agreed to form a separate organization for women. The following week, the first meeting of the Women's Institute was held. Before the decade was out, there were more than 500 chapters across Canada. Today, this organization has chapters around the world and a membership of millions. "The education of women and girls has been my life's work," Mrs. Hoodless once said, and she died in its service. On the eve of her 53rd birthday, while speaking in Toronto on the need for university level schools of household science, her heart gave out.

hoppin' John - a dish of black-eyed peas and rice, and often meat, such as salt pork or ham hock. In the South, it's served as often as you wish, but always on New Year's Day, in which case it's said to bring good luck. The name is said to come from the fact that the children were so fond of this dish that they would hop about the kitchen, waiting for it to cook.

hops - from the Anglo-Saxon *hoopan*, meaning "to climb," the female flowering cones of a perennial vine, *Humulus lupulus*, used in beer making to impart a distinctive tart flavor, as well as to balance the sweetness of the malt. Their distinctive bitterness comes from lupulin, a sticky yellow powder found in the cones. Hops also have a preservative effect, act as a natural filter to clarify beer and contribute to better head retention.

The origin of the hops genus, *Humulus*, is considered doubtful, although it has been assumed by some writers that it is derived from humus, the rich, moist ground in which the plant grows. The specific name *lupulus* is derived from the Latin *lupus* ("wolf"), because, as Roman historian and naturalist **Pliny** explains, hops grew wild among willows like a wolf in the forest. Pliny also tells us that the Romans ate young hops shoots in spring, but in most hops growing regions it's the tough male flowers that are eaten as a vegetable. An infusion of hops has long been considered very helpful for rheumatism. Nordic countries make paper and fine cloth from the fibrous stems, which require soaking for an entire year before processing.

horchata - a cold beverage made of grains, nuts or **chufas** that have been steeped in water for a number of hours until soft, then sweetened, seasoned with ground cinnamon and blended until smooth. In Mexico, horchata is usually made with a combination of almonds and rice, flavored with cinnamon and lime or lemon zest. In Spain, *horchata de chufa* is the standard, made with chufas and flavored with cinnamon.

horehound - **1.** a plant, *Marrubium vulgare*, and member of the mint family, used as a tea and to flavor confections and candy. Its medicinal properties were known to the Egyptians, whose priests considered the plant to be under the protection of the god Horus, god of sky and light. In ancient Greece, the herb was credited with curing the bite of mad dogs. Today, we use a sprinkle in salads. In England, it's still occasionally used to flavor ales. **2.** an old-fashioned hard candy made with the extract of the horehound plant, minty with a bitter undertone.

horned melon - see KIWANO.

horn of plenty - see BLACK CHANTERELLE.

hors d'oeuvre - a small portion of savory food served usually as an appetizer, either hot or cold.

horse bean - see FAVA.

horse gram - also **kulith, kulthi.** A small, oval pulse grown in rural India for cattle fodder and for human consumption. Considered peasant or poor people's food, the legumes require prolonged cooking to be edible. They are eaten alone as a side dish or mixed with other ingredients to make a main dish. Boiled sprouted horse gram is also used for such dishes as *usal* (the sprouts are cooked in oil with chopped chile, garlic and tomatoes, seasoned with mustard seed and turmeric, then garnished with chopped coriander, **garam masala** and grated coconut).

horse meat - very red in color, with a slightly strong but sweet taste, not commonly eaten in North America or England, but more commonly found in France, Belgium, Sweden, China and Japan.

horse mushroom - a wild edible mushroom, *Agaricus arvensis*, similar to a **field mushroom,** with a white cap that yellows with age and white to pinkish gills when young, with a distinctive aniseed smell. It grows in fields, often in fairy rings. See also MUSHROOM.

horse parsley - see ALEXANDERS.

horseradish - a coarse, very strong radish, *Raphanus sativus* var. *niger*, a hardy perennial plant. A distant relative of mustard, horseradish grows wild in many parts of the world, including the eastern U.S. It can be from 2 to 3 inches (5 to 7.5 cm) in diameter and up to 6 to 8 inches (15 to 20 cm) long, weighing about 1 pound (500 g). The skin is rough and cream-color, often blackened from dirt that collects in all its crevices. The flesh is firm and white, much less juicy than the common red radish and very rarely consumed uncooked, because it has a pungent bite when raw. It's usually chopped and pickled in vinegar, as an accompaniment for roast beef, or with a seasoning of shallots and sour cream, in salad.

Horseradish was much appreciated by the ancient Greeks and Romans as well as the Asians, and is extremely popular in Eastern European countries. It's among the "five bitter herbs" eaten by Jews at Passover. In the early 1500s, it was known throughout England as red cole, or *Raphanus rusticanus*, growing wild in several parts of the country. Elizabethan herbalist John Gerard noted, "The horse Radish stamped with a little vinegar put thereto, is commonly used among the Germans for sauce to eate fish with and such like meats as we do mustarde." Not until the 1600s did horseradish become an acceptable condiment in England — and even then, it was only for "country people and strong labouring men," according to John Parkinson, an herbalist of the time, who added, "It's too strong for tender and gentle stomaches." The early settlers brought it to America and, by 1806, included it in the list of common edible American plants. When cooked, its taste can be compared to that of rutabaga. If overcooked, it becomes a sticky, tasteless gruel.

horse mushrooms

horseradish sauce - see RAIFORT SAUCE.

horsetail kelp - see KELP.

horticultural beans - beans that are harvested when the seeds inside the pods are fully ripe, not left on the stalk to dry. At this stage of development, the pod is too tough to eat in the manner of green beans, so the beans inside are shelled and cooked on their own, similar to lima beans. **Cranberry beans** and **borlotti beans** are two examples of horticultural beans, although cranberry beans may be left to dry on the stalk for use in soups, stews, etc. Horticultural beans may be brightly colored, striped or speckled when fresh, but usually turn a bland shade of brown when cooked, no matter what color they started out.

hosomaki - see SUSHI.

hot-and-sour - any of various Chinese soups or sauces flavored with chiles, chili oil, sesame oil, ginger, garlic and scallions.

hot bean paste - see CHILE BEAN PASTE.

hotcake - see PANCAKE.

hot cherry pepper - see CHERRY PEPPER.

hot chocolate - also **cocoa, hot cocoa.** A hot beverage made with cocoa powder, milk and sugar, often served as a treat for children on cold winter days. The term is used interchangeably with *hot cocoa,* but hot chocolate was traditionally made by melting squares of chocolate with hot milk and sugar, yielding a thicker, richer result. The drink was a European adaptation of the original **Mexican chocolate** consumed by the Aztecs, which was more of a bitter, savory concoction. Nowadays, Mexican chocolate is closer to its rich, sweet European and North American cousins, but is spiced with a touch of cinnamon.

hotchpotch - also **hodgepodge.** A thick soup or stew of meat, vegetables and potatoes made with mutton in Scotland, often also with beef. In England, it's called hot pot, the best known version being **Lancashire hot pot,** consisting of layers of browned lamb, sliced potatoes and onions (and, in former times, oysters). In France and Belgium, it's called *hochepot* and has pigs' ears and feet, along with a variety of other meats. The Dutch call it *hutspot* and make it with beef.

hot cross bun - a sweet yeast bun traditionally eaten on Good Friday, usually made with raisins and/or candied fruit; their tops are marked with a sugar-glaze cross.

hot dog - an American culinary archetype, not so named until 1906, when cartoonist T.A. "Tad" Dorgan drew a dachshund inside an elongated bun. Frankfurter and wiener both refer to the sausage itself, and both are Germanic in origin. Another name for a hot dog is **"tube steak."**

Some accounts claim it came to the U.S. from Frankfurt by way of a Bavarian immigrant, Antoine Feuchtwanger, who introduced it to St. Louis in the 1880s. He sold hot "franks" along with cotton gloves, so customers would not burn their fingers. Some other sources credited the introduction of the hot dog to Charles Feltman, another immigrant, who brought back the frankfurter after a visit to his German homeland at about the turn of the century and opened an establishment on Coney Island, New York. An employee, Nathan Handwerker, broke away from Feltman in 1916 and, with his wife, Ida, started Nathan's Famous, Inc., which now calls itself the world's greatest hot dog purveyor. See also FRANKFURTER.

hot dog bun - a long, yeast roll split down one side (almost, but not quite all the way through), used to sandwich a hot dog. A New England hot dog bun is cooked in a special individual pan, so that it is rectangular and has no crust on the sides, which allows it to be toasted on both sides until crisp. The bun comes pre-split down the center of the top and condiments are drizzled down the center of the hot dog after it's placed in the bun. These buns are also the essential basis of other popular New England sandwiches, such as the clam roll (a bun filled with fried clams) and the lobster roll (a bun filled with lobster salad).

hot fudge - a rich, thick sauce made from chocolate, butter, sugar and cream, poured hot over ice cream or desserts.

hot fudge sundae - an ice cream sundae topped with hot fudge. The classic recipe calls for a dab of hot fudge sauce in the bottom of a footed sundae glass, then a scoop of ice cream (traditionally vanilla), then a large scoop of hot fudge. The sundae is topped with a sprinkle of chopped peanuts, a dollop of whipped cream and a maraschino cherry. When the hot topping comes into contact with the cold ice cream, it hardens slightly into a chewy, taffy-like texture, while the top layer of ice cream melts into a pool at the bottom of the glass.

hot oven - a relative term for oven temperature, usually considered to be between 400° and 425°F (200° and 220°C), or gas mark 6 or 7. A very hot oven is in the range of 450° to 475°F (230° to 240°C), or gas mark 8 or 9. An oven set at 500° (250°C), or gas mark 10, is considered extremely hot. See also GAS MARK, MODERATE OVEN, SLOW OVEN.

hot pepper - see CHILE PEPPER.

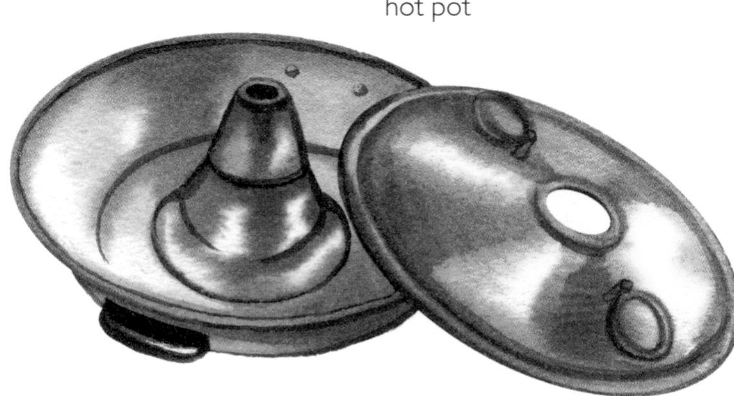
hot pot

hot pot - a lidded, metal pot with a central chimney that extends from the base to above the rim, held on a metal stand over a fuel source. Since the pot was originally placed over the coals of an open fire at a communal meal, the funnel-shaped center functioned as a real chimney and let the smoke escape; nowadays, it just helps heat the broth inside. For quick cooking, dumplings and chunks of marinated fish, meat (traditionally lamb), poultry, seafood and vegetables are dipped into the hot broth by each diner. Piquant pickles and sauces are served on the side. With noodles added, the flavorful cooking broth is often shared out to finish the meal. See also HOTCH POTCH, MONGOLIAN HOTPOT.

hot sauce - also **hot pepper sauce.** A condiment or seasoning made of ground hot chile peppers, salt and vinegar. More complex versions flavored with spices, herbs and fruit purées (such as mango) are also available, as are brand-name versions, such as Tabasco.

hot smoking - see SMOKED FOODS, SMOKED SALMON.

hot water bath - **1.** another term for a boiling-water **canner,** seen often in recipe directions, such as: "Process cans in hot water bath for 10 minutes." **2.** the technique of cooking a delicate food, such as a custard or cheesecake, in a pan that is placed inside a larger pan filled with water. The hot water keeps the heat around the inner dish low and consistent for even cooking, preventing overheating and cracking of the surface of the food.

hot wax pepper - see CHILE PEPPER.

hua moa - a short, fat Tahitian banana variety often grown in Hawaii, closer in texture and taste to a plantain than a banana. The starchy hua moa is a common breakfast food in Hawaii and is usually cooked, often baked, and served with brown sugar and cinnamon. It can be eaten fresh as well, although it is best when it is quite ripe. The skin is yellowy green, but the flesh is pinkish golden, and the fruit only grows about 3 inches (7.5 cm) long. It is available in some California produce markets and is easily obtainable in Hawaii. The name is Polynesian for "chicken egg," for the fruit's squat, slightly oval shape.

hua moa

hubbard squash - see SQUASH.

huckleberry - also **bilberry, whortleberry.** A wild berry, *Vaccinium myrtillus*, that resembles the blueberry, but is very acidic when raw; used mainly in desserts and confectionery; available canned or fresh during summer months. In Central Europe, it's also made into wine both for drinking and medicinal purposes.

huevos rancheros - Spanish for "rancher's eggs," a Mexican-American breakfast of fried eggs, corn tortillas, tomato-chile salsa and, sometimes, ground beef.

huff juff - see BAPTIST CAKE.

huitlacoche - also **corn smut, cuitlacoche, maize mushroom, Mexican truffle.** A fungus, *Ustilago maydis*, that grows on ears of corn, enlarging and turning the kernels black or gray as they fill up with the mushroom spores, considered a delicacy in Mexican cuisine, but a scourge on American and Canadian corn crops. This wild mushroom has been prized as a food for centuries in Mexico, originally by the Aztecs and Mayans, who considered it similar in importance to meat in their diet. Americans and Canadians, on the other hand, have considered it a plague and traditionally destroyed any corn crops that came down with a case of this fungus. This attitude is slowly changing with the growing availability of canned huitlacoche (although farmers are still resistant to the idea of actually cultivating it). It has a smoky, earthy flavor that is somewhere between corn and mushrooms, and can be used in the same manner as regular mushrooms in a wide variety of dishes, including omelets, quesadillas and soups. The root of the word is the Nahuatl word *cuitlatl*, meaning "dung," probably for the ugly, blackish appearance of the mushroom.

hull - **1.** (n.) the outer coating of a fruit, seed or nut. **2.** (v.) to remove hulls, or in the case of strawberries, to remove the persistent calyx, the tough, fibrous area just below the stem, at the top of the berry.

hulled barley - also **whole-grain barley.** See BARLEY.

hulled corn - see HOMINY.

humble pie - historically, an English dish using the inner and less choice parts (the humbles or umbles) of a deer or other animal, usually given to the servants at hunting feasts while the gentry feasted on the better cuts. When people "eat humble pie," they swallow their pride and make humble apologies.

humbug - a hard candy made of pulled sugar, usually flavored with mint, with a slightly twisted shape.

hummus - a Middle Eastern sauce or dip made of ground chickpeas, lemon juice, garlic and olive oil, usually served with pita.

hundreds and thousands - tiny, colored sugar sprinkles or **nonpareils,** used for decorating cakes and cookies. This term is often used in the United Kingdom, but is occasionally seen in North America.

hundred-year egg - also **century egg, Ming Dynasty egg, thousand-year egg.** A Chinese preserved-egg specialty. A chicken, duck or goose egg is coated in a paste of ashes, lime and salt, moistened with tea, sometimes wrapped in rice husks or tea leaves, then buried for100 days. Unearthed, the crusty, blackened shell opens to reveal an amber, gelatin-like white and a creamy, green yolk. Minced gingerroot, pickled vegetables and soy-based sauce are the usual accompaniments for this popular appetizer. Cut into wedges, hundred-year eggs may also be served with rice porridge.

Hungarian acacia honey - see HONEY.

Hungarian cherry pepper - see CHERRY PEPPER.

Hungarian chile pepper - see CHILE PEPPER.

Hungarian salami - see SALAMI.

Huntsman cheese - an English layered cow's milk cheese consisting of layers of **double Gloucester** and **Stilton** cheese. The firm, milder double Gloucester complements the sharp tang of the softer blue-veined Stilton. It is often served as a dessert cheese, excellent with dried fruits, or with a glass of port or beer.

Hurricane - a cocktail made with light and dark rum, passion fruit juice or syrup, and lime juice, shaken with ice and served in — what else? — a **hurricane glass.** Some versions also call for the addition of orange, grapefruit or pineapple juice, sugar and/or **grenadine,** with a maraschino cherry or pineapple garnish.

hurricane glass - a tall, footed, hourglass-shaped glass commonly used for serving blended tropical drinks, including, as the name implies,

Husted, Marjorie (1892–1986) - the voice of Betty Crocker, the enduring brand and trademark that personified idealism in homemaking. Betty Crocker was concocted to sell flour in 1921 in Minneapolis by the Washburn Crosby Co., which later became General Mills. Three years later, Husted was hired to play Betty Crocker on a radio program called *Betty Crocker Cooking School of the Air,* which she scripted and performed for more than 10 years. The program was eventually picked up by NBC and ran nationally for 24 years.

Hurricanes. The name of this glass also comes from the resemblance it bears to the hurricane glasses traditionally used to keep candles from blowing out in a high wind.

hush puppy - a deep-fried, cornmeal dumpling flavored with scallions or onion, popular in the American South. The name is said to derive from the fact that bits of cornmeal batter were once cooked in the pan along with the fish frying for dinner, then tossed to the hounds that yelped when they caught the enticing scent of the meal cooking.

husk - **1.** (n.) the outermost layer of a fruit, vegetable or seed, often fibrous or papery and easy to peel off. **2.** (v.) to remove the husk of a fruit, vegetable or seed, used particularly often in reference to peeling the outer skin off an ear of corn.

husk tomato - see TOMATILLO.

huss - a British term for the edible flesh of the **dogfish.**

Husted, Marjorie - see profile above.

hustler - see BAPTIST CAKE.

Hu Szu-Hui - see profile below.

huzarensla salad - a Dutch meat and potato salad, also made with apples, beets, hard-boiled eggs and bound with mayonnaise. Also called "hussar's salad."

hydrogenation - a chemical process that forces hydrogen into unsaturated fats, making them saturated. Hydrogenation is best illustrated in how it converts vegetable oil into solid and semisolid fats, such as vegetable shortening and margarine, long preferred for commercially prepared goods because of their long shelf life. Hydrogenation creates **trans fatty acids,** which have been linked to heart disease, although small amounts of trans fats occur naturally in dairy products, some meat and other animal-based foods.

hydrolyzed plant protein - also **hydrolyzed vegetable protein.** Obtained from various plants (including soybeans, corn and wheat), broken down into amino acids and used as a flavor enhancer in some processed foods.

Hu Szu-Hui (13th century) - Chinese dietary physician to several imperial courts of the Yuan Dynasty during the 13th century, most notably to Kublai Khan. Hu wrote *Yin-shan Cheng-yao* (Proper and Essential Things for the Emperor's Food and Drink), considered to be the first Chinese cookbook. Since its publication in 1330, the text continues to fascinate historians. As recently as 2000, a scholarly text about the book ignited new discussions about Chinese cultural history. Oxford historian Elisabeth Hsu called the work "the epitome of multiculturalism," putting to rest the historical debate about China's rejection of foreign cultural influences at that time. Hu's recommended diet was a mix of Chinese foundation ingredients, such as ginger, orange peel, cabbage, soybean sauce and bean paste noodles, with the Mongolian technique of boiling food in a cauldron, like soup, using lamb, wild camel hump, offal and wild goose fat. The spicing was unmistakably Turko-Islamic in its use of fenugreek, saffron, turmeric, black pepper, cardamom and cinnamon. Hu's reference in his book to glutinous rice powder offers historians a glimpse into early food processing.

hydromel - from the Greek *hydro*, meaning "water," and *meli*, meaning "honey," a beverage made from the fermentation of honey and water, consumed in large quantities by the Romans and Greeks, and through to the Middle Ages. Hydromel is still produced by a few European countries.

hydroponics - a method of growing plants in enriched water, rather than soil.

Hymetus honey - see HONEY.

hyssop - a plant, *Hyssopus officinalis*, of the mint family, with a history of use as a cleansing herb, because of its strong camphor-like odor. There are some early references to the plant in the 7th century, when it was strewn about the floors of sickrooms and used to improve the smell of kitchens and outhouses. The name is from the Greek *azob*, meaning "holy herb," because it was often used to clean temples and other sacred places. Hyssop was used by the Egyptians to wash lepers, and the herb is often mentioned in the Bible as a purifier. An essential oil derived from the green parts of the plant is used to makes perfumes, especially English and German eau de colognes. Hyssop's minty leaves and flowers are used to flavor green and fruit salads, and the dried leaves and flowers are used for teas. It was, and still is, used in the preparation of some liqueurs, including **Bénédictine** and **Chartreuse.** The recipe book written in 1723 by John Nott, a cook for the Duke of Bolton, recommends hyssop water for a good complexion. He calls for six spoonfuls of hyssop juice in ale every morning.

hyssop

i
ice cream

Iberico ham - see JAMÓN IBÉRICO.

ibrik - see TURKISH COFFEE.

ice - 1. (n.) to cover a confection with frosting. See also GRANITA. **2.** (v.) to chill a food or beverage, usually in ice or ice water or on top of a bed of crushed ice.

ice beer - a beer that is fermented at low temperature, then semi-frozen, so that the ice crystals can be removed, resulting in a more flavorful brew that is higher in alcohol than regular beer. North American ice beers tend to be crisp and dry, unlike their predecessors, German **Eisbocks,** which are thick and sweet. Legend has it that Eisbock is a happy accident of a very cold Oktoberfest, when thick, rich **Doppelbock** beers were accidentally frozen. Drinkers apparently loved the strong, concentrated beer that formed when the water in the mixture was frozen and removed, and a tradition was born. See also ICE WINE.

iceberg lettuce - see LETTUCE.

icebox cookie - **also refrigerator cookie.** A type of cookie made from dough that is rolled into a log and refrigerated until firm enough to slice. The dough is then cut into rounds and baked. Logs of icebox cookie dough can often be frozen for later use, too.

ice cider - also **apple ice wine.** A rare apple wine made exclusively in Quebec, Canada, using a similar process to the one used to make ice wine from grapes. Apples are left on the tree until after a hard frost and picked in sub-zero temperatures, when they are frozen (some producers freeze apples or their juice after they are harvested, but this must be declared on the label). The apples are immediately pressed to extract their juice, which is concentrated, because so much of the water is left behind in the form of ice. The juice is then fermented for about seven months until it becomes a sweet, nectarous wine. Ice cider is expensive, because so many apples are needed to make a single bottle. It is available mainly in Canada, but also in the U.S., Scandinavia and some Asian countries through high-end importers.

ice cream - a frozen confection made usually with some combination of cream, milk and sugar, and a wide variety of flavorings. **Soft-serve** is a popular form of ice cream, especially when extruded into cones on a hot summer day. It is the same as regular hard ice cream, except that it is served in a semi-frozen state. Soft-serve machines keep the ice cream at a higher temperature than a commercial freezer, which allows it to maintain this unctuous state. If a soft-serve mixture were placed in a freezer, it would turn into regular ice cream in a short time.

Exactly where and how ice cream got its start is unclear. The Arabs were the first to develop a kind of fruit ice, but the Chinese seem to have invented milk-based ice, which Marco Polo described on his return from the Orient. Nero is supposed to have served cream frozen in snow at Roman banquets.

Some historians say **Catherine de' Medici,** a Florentine who married Henry II of France in the mid-1500s, introduced a variety of iced desserts (frozen thanks to icehouses, which were storage spaces, sometimes crude pits, for ice that was harvested). Bernardo Buontalenti was one of the 50 Italian chefs she brought with her, and he is credited with the invention.

In the 1660s, a Sicilian opened a café in Paris specializing in sherbets. They soon became the rage and, in due course, ice creams followed. Soon, there were about 250 shops and restaurants in Paris that were officially licensed to make and sell ice cream and water ices. Thomas Jefferson brought the recipe for ice cream to the U.S., when he returned home after serving as the first ambassador to France. Governor Francis Fauquier of Virginia wrote his brother that, in July 1758, a hailstorm provided a supply of ice that he used to cool wine and freeze cream. The Philadelphians claim it was introduced to their city in July 1782, served at a party given by the French envoy, with General George Washington in attendance. Washington became hooked and soon began making ice cream himself. In May 1784, his diary recorded that he spent 1 pound, 13 shillings and 4 pence on a "cream machine for ice."

In 1846, an American named **Nancy Johnson** invented the hand-cranked freezer that is still used in many homes today. Her sketch, which was patented two years later by William G. Young, employed a simple and steady mechanical action to keep the mixture moving, cooling it evenly, preventing the growth of large ice crystals and incorporating some air. The second historic advance for the frozen treat came in 1851, when Jacob Fussel, a Baltimore milk dealer, decided to use up all his surplus milk by freezing it into ice cream, hence becoming the first large-scale manufacturer.

ice cream cone - a thin, edible sugar wafer formed into a cone shape or cup for holding ice cream. One historical account claims it was invented at the 1904 St. Louis World's Fair. A concession vendor named Ernest A. Hamwi was selling waffle pastries called *zalabi*. A neighboring vendor was selling ice cream cups, but ran out one day. The waffle vendor came to his rescue by making a cone-shaped waffle that would hold the ice cream. The cone, called World's Fair Cornucopia, was the food sensation of the fair.

ice cream soda

ice cream float - see FLOAT.

ice cream maker - a manual or electric machine used to freeze and churn ice cream to the proper consistency. An American, **Nancy Johnson,** invented the hand-cranked freezer in 1846. All ice cream makers have a paddle, also called a dasher, which continuously turns as the cream mixture freezes to ensure that the proper amount of air is incorporated and to prevent any large, unpleasant ice crystals from forming. The dasher in a manual ice cream maker is turned by hand, and the ice cream mixture is poured into a metal canister inside a larger bucket filled with ice and rock salt, which creates the proper temperature to freeze the cream mixture. Electric ice cream makers come in a wide variety of size and styles, but all use an electric motor to turn the dasher. Some contain small refrigeration units to chill the bowl inside, and others have a removable bowl that must be frozen in the freezer prior to use.

ice cream scoop - a specially shaped spoon with a deep, wide, circular bowl, used for creating perfectly round scoops of ice cream, ideal for making ice cream cones. Ice cream scoops come in a variety of styles, some with a temperature-sensitive gel inside the handle and the bowl, which warms up when grasped, so that the scoops of ice cream easily slip out of the bowl without sticking. Some have a plunger or a scraper inside the bowl that can be activated with a lever to neatly and quickly deposit a ball of ice cream into a dish or onto a cone. These scoops are also useful for measuring muffin batter neatly and evenly into baking cups or for dropping large scoops of dough onto cookie sheets for even-sized cookies. See also DISHER.

ice cream scoop

ice cream soda - a cold beverage made from soda water, ice cream and flavored syrup, sometimes served topped with whipped cream, invented in Philadelphia at the 1876 Centennial Exposition. See also BLACK COW.

iced tea - came about, according to an oft-told tale, in 1904, when an English tea salesman, Richard Blechynden, was promoting his wares at the St. Louis World's Fair, the same Louisiana Purchase centennial celebration that saw the birth of the ice cream cone. Blechynden's steaming hot tea received little interest from the sweltering July fair-goers. In desperation, he put a chunk of ice in the tea urn and created a sensation, partly because most cold drinks at the time were alcoholic, and the temperance movement was booming in the Midwest.

ice milk - a frozen dessert nearly identical to ice cream, except that it contains no cream (only milk) and therefore less fat. By law, ice cream must contain 10 percent milk fat or higher (unless it contains chocolate, cocoa, nuts or other confections, in which case it can contain as little as 8 percent milk fat). In Canada, ice milk must contain between 3 and 5 percent milk fat. In the United States, the term "ice milk" has dropped out of favor: in 1995, the United States Department of Agriculture dropped the label term "ice milk" in favor of "low-fat ice cream," which must contain no more than 3 grams of fat per 4-ounce (125 g) serving. See also GELATO, SHERBET.

ice wine - also **Eiswein.** A sweet dessert wine originally made in Germany, but now made in Luxembourg, Austria, Belgium, Canada and upstate New York. It is traditionally made with Riesling or a hybrid of Vidal grapes, which are left to overripen on the vine and freeze during a winter night when the temperature is at its lowest. When the frozen berries are harvested, they are taken off the grape cluster and then immediately pressed so the ice particles are removed and the sweet, concentrated juice runs free. A few wineries in Canada and New York State have tried to fool the grapes by artificially freezing them, which by law must be indicated on the label. So favorable is the environment in Canada for making ice wine that it has become the leading world practitioner of this frozen art. The whole process is so labor-intensive that the end result is quite expensive, and, most of the time, only half-bottles are available on the market.

ichimi togarashi - see TOGARASHI.

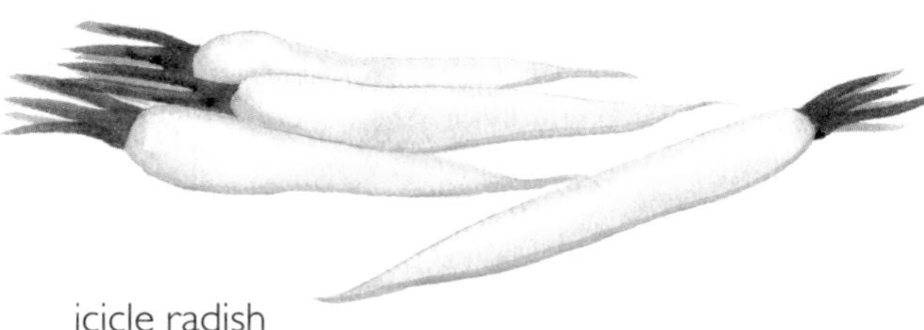

icicle radish

icicle radish - a small, thin, elongated type of spring radish, mild in flavor and quite juicy, can be white-, red- or pink-skinned, depending on the variety. Icicle radishes make excellent appetizers and additions to salads, sliced or eaten whole in the manner of baby carrots. Gourmet stores, farmer's markets and specialty produce shops are the usual purveyors of this type of radish. See also RADISH.

icing - see FROSTING.

icing sugar - see CONFECTIONER'S SUGAR.

Ida apple - see APPLE.

Idaho potato - also **russet.** See POTATO.

Ida Red apple - see APPLE.

idli - a small, Indian steamed cake or dumpling made from a dough of water, ground rice and pale yellow **urad dal,** which is fermented overnight to give the cakes their distinctive flavor. The dough is formed into rounds and steamed in a special perforated steamer "tree," a series of metal disks hung on a central pole, each disk containing several round indentations in which the patties sit over the boiling water. Idli are often eaten for breakfast, especially in South India, where they are extremely popular, usually with thick lentil soup and coconut chutney. Idli are often savory, flavored with spices or garlic, but there are sweet versions that substitute semolina for the urad dal and add **jaggery** to the dough. Sweet idli are often spiced with cardamom or nutmeg and may be stuffed with nuts, dried fruits or sweetened coconut.

île flottante - see FLOATING ISLAND.

imam bayildi - a well-known dish in the Middle East that originated in Turkey, consisting of roasted eggplant stuffed with tomatoes, onions, garlic, pine nuts and peppers, always drizzled with a generous amount of olive oil. The name of the dish means "the imam fainted." Legend has it that the dish was served to an imam (the Muslim equivalent of a priest in Christian cultures), and the flavors were so rich and delightful that he fainted dead away after the first bite. Another story alleges that this same mythical imam fainted at the realization of the amount of expensive olive oil his wife had used to make the eggplant taste so good. Either way, the dish caught on and remains ones of the most popular ways to serve eggplant in the Middle East.

immature soybean - see EDAMAME.

immersion blender - a handheld blender with a rotary blade at one end that can be immersed into a pot or beverage to purée or blend the contents.

immersion freezing - a commercial technique for freezing food, such as poultry, by spraying it with a supercooled liquid (usually liquid nitrogen) for several seconds. This method is often used to start the freezing process after a food is cooked. The frigid nitrogen causes the outermost layers of the food to freeze quickly, stopping the cooking process and sealing in juices. The food is then frozen solid, using any of a variety of other methods. See also IMPINGEMENT FREEZING, INDIVIDUAL QUICK FREEZING.

impingement freezing - a commercial technique for freezing foods incredibly quickly, so that small ice crystals form, resulting in a tastier, better-textured product that is not mushy when defrosted. Foods are placed on a conveyer belt and run through a tunnel or a spiral chamber, where they are blasted on either side with supercooled air, liquid nitrogen or carbon dioxide. This removes the warm air, or thermal barrier, surrounding the food, allowing it to freeze quickly and without drying out or losing flavor, texture or color. See also INDIVIDUAL QUICK FREEZING.

inari zushi - a type of sushi made by wrapping a deep-fried tofu pocket around seasoned sushi rice studded with toasted black sesame seeds. The tofu pocket is cooked in a sugary soy sauce mixture, making this a more sweet, than savory snack. The name comes from the name for the Shinto god of rice, Inari. In Japan, foxes are the animals most closely associated with Inari, and legend has it that the sweet, deep-fried tofu pockets are their favorite food.

incidental food additive - also **accidental food additive, indirect food additive.** A food additive that is not added on purpose, one that is a result of the growing, harvesting, processing or packaging of the food. For example, a food that is packaged may contain trace amounts of the packaging material, which will likely not be noticeable to the consumer. As long as the amount is minuscule and within accepted limits, the government agency that regulates food additives (such as the Food and Drug Administration in the United States) declares the food safe for human consumption. See also INTENTIONAL FOOD ADDITIVE.

incomplete protein - see COMPLETE PROTEIN.

Indian arrowroot - see ARROWROOT.

Indian blood peach - see BLOOD PEACH.

Indian borage - see JAMAICAN THYME.

Indian candy - see SMOKED SALMON

Indian cling peach - see BLOOD PEACH.

Indian corn - see CORN, FLINT CORN.

Indian cress - see NASTURTIUM.

Indian-cure salmon - see SMOKED SALMON.

Indian date - see TAMARIND.

Indian fig - see CACTUS.

Indian pudding - a baked dessert, similar to rice pudding or bread pudding, made of cornmeal, molasses, eggs, milk and spices. It is often served with whipped cream, ice cream or **hard sauce.** Indian pudding is so named because its main ingredient, cornmeal, was called "Indian meal" by European settlers, who encountered it for the first time in the New World as a staple of the Native American diet. See also HASTY PUDDING.

Indian quince - see BAEL.

Indian-smoked salmon - see SMOKED SALMON.

Indian walnut - see CANDLENUT.

Indica rice - see RICE.

indirect food additive - see INCIDENTAL FOOD ADDITIVE.

indirect grilling - a technique for barbecuing larger cuts of meat or poultry that need a long cooking time, but that would burn if grilled over direct heat. In barbecue circles, this technique involves placing the meat, such as a beef roast or whole chicken, over the unlit burners of a gas grill or beside, but not over, the glowing coals of a charcoal barbecue. The heat from the flames or the coals circulates inside the covered grill, roasting the meat slowly, instead of searing it quickly. The meat takes on the delicious, slightly smoky flavor of the grill, but remains juicy and tender. **Beer can chicken** is a prime example of a popular indirectly grilled dish.

individual quick freezing - also **IQF.** The technique of rapidly freezing fruits, vegetables, seafood, etc., that creates small ice crystals in the food and prevents the cells from rupturing and making the food mushy when it is defrosted. Foods that are frozen slowly at standard temperatures form larger ice crystals, which can leave them with an undesirable texture. As their name implies, IQF foods are also frozen so that each piece is separate from the other, instead of in a block or clump. This means that IQF foods can be packed in containers without sticking together, making it easier to remove and defrost only as much as is needed at a given time. IQF foods are often placed on a conveyer belt and frozen using the **impingement freezing** method.

Indonesian bay leaf - see SALAM LEAF.

infornate - see OLIVE.

infuse - to extract flavor from an ingredient by steeping it in a hot liquid. Milk for making **béchamel** sauce is infused with onion, bay leaf, nutmeg, salt and pepper. For sweet dishes, such as custards, milk is infused with a vanilla bean, cinnamon stick, orange or lemon peel; wine for cooking can be infused with mushroom or truffle peelings.

infusion - a solution made by steeping herbs, spices or other substances in liquid (often hot water), so that they release their essential oils and flavors. Herbal teas are a type of infusion. Garlic and shallots are another — often infused in oil, which is then used to flavor dishes.

injection curing - see WET CURE.

injera - also **Ethiopian flatbread.** A slightly sour, spongy Ethiopian flatbread made from a fermented mixture of **teff** flour and water, used as both a platter and an eating utensil for traditional Ethiopian stews. At a typical Ethiopian meal, a large circle of injera is laid out, then an array of meat and vegetable stews are spooned on top of it. More injera is served on the side, and diners tear off pieces to scoop up bite-size portions of stew. The meal is not considered finished until the bottom layer of injera, now soaked with the delicious juices from the stews, is gobbled up.

inkfish - see CUTTLEFISH.

insalata caprese - a classic summer dish from the island of Capri, hence its name, which means "salad of Capri." This simple Italian salad is made with sliced fresh tomatoes, sliced mozzarella cheese (preferably **buffalo mozzarella**) and fresh basil, seasoned with salt and pepper, then drizzled with flavorful olive oil. Because of its simple, honest ingredients, this salad is best made only when tomatoes and basil are in season.

insalata caprese

instant-blending flour - see FLOUR.

instant cocoa - a mixture of cocoa powder, sugar and powdered milk designed to be mixed with hot or cold water to make a chocolaty drink. Store-bought mixtures may contain other additives, and many versions include tiny, dried marshmallows, which rehydrate when mixed with hot liquid. See also HOT CHOCOLATE.

instant coffee - brewed coffee that has had all its water evaporated off, forming crystals or a powder that can be reconstituted in hot water. Instant coffee can be freeze-dried or spray-dried; both processes involve no chemicals or additives, so the resulting crystals or powder are pure coffee. Freeze-drying involves freezing a concentrated coffee solution until the water forms ice crystals. The ice crystals are removed, and the solids that remain are the dried coffee granules. Spray-drying starts with the same strong coffee solution, which is sprayed from the top of a tower into a chamber of hot air. As the spray falls, the heated air evaporates the remaining water, and the powdered coffee solids fall to the bottom of the chamber, where they are collected and packaged. Because spray-drying involves so much heat, the oils in the coffee are affected and some of the taste is lost. Freeze-drying yields a more flavorful result, although not nearly as flavorful as a cup of freshly brewed coffee. Instant coffee is excellent for baking, especially because it is nonperishable and easy to keep on hand.

instant pudding - a powdered mixture of sugar, cornstarch and flavorings that can be mixed with milk and shaken until the proper thick pudding consistency is achieved. It is "instant" because it doesn't require a long period of cooking, unlike traditional milk-and-cornstarch-based puddings. The first Jell-O instant pudding was marketed in 1953 in chocolate, vanilla and butterscotch, three of the most popular flavors still on the market today.

instant-read thermometer - see THERMOMETER.

instant rice - see RICE.

integrale - the Italian term for a food made from whole wheat, such as *pane integrale* (whole wheat bread) or *farina integrale* (whole wheat flour).

intentional food additive - also **direct food additive.** A food additive that is added on purpose in order to change a food's color, texture, nutrition, shelf life, etc. **Xanthan gum,** food colorings and preservatives are all examples of intentional food additives. These substances are regulated by the government (such as the Food and Drug Administration in the United States) and are generally listed on the ingredients list on the package. See also INCIDENTAL FOOD ADDITIVE.

invert sugar - also **inverted sugar.** Sucrose, processed common sugar, is first separated into its two component sugars, fructose and glucose, then "inverted" by adding a diluting acid, usually sulfuric acid, equally to each component, modifying their molecular structure. This process prevents crystallization and results in a smoother product.

involtini - any of a variety of Italian dishes of thinly sliced foods, such as meats or vegetables, wrapped around a filling and cooked. Involtini are the same thing as **braciole.** The word is usually seen in the plural ("involtino" is the singular) and is the diminutive of the Italian word *involto*, meaning "bundle."

iodized salt - finely granulated table salt fortified with the mineral iodine, an important addition to the North American diet, because it is traditionally poor in iodine-rich foods, such as seaweed. Among other things, iodine encourages healthy thyroid function and prevents goiter, or an enlargement of the thyroid gland, which is often caused by insufficient intake of iodine in foods. In 1924, the Michigan State Medical Society began to use iodized salt in its experiments to prevent thyroid disease and mental retardation caused by iodine deficiency. The program was wildly successful, and the use of this enriched seasoning became standard in the majority of North American households by the middle of the century. Today, iodized salt is still one of the best-selling types of salt, although gourmet unfortified salts are increasing in popularity for their softer, mellower levels of saltiness.

iriko - see SEA CUCUMBER.

Irish bacon - also **rashers.** Slices of bacon cut from the loin of a pig, similar in looks and taste to Canadian bacon, but with streaks of fat through it like American bacon. Irish bacon is traditionally eaten boiled with cabbage on St. Patrick's Day, a precursor to what most North Americans think of as the consummate Irish boiled dinner: corned beef and cabbage.

Irish breakfast tea - see TEA.

Irish coffee - a cocktail of whiskey, hot coffee, sugar and whipped cream, enjoyed by the Irish for a century or more; brought to North American attention in the 1940s by Irish bartender Joe Sheridan, who served them at Foynes Airport in County Limerick, where Atlantic flights refueled before their ocean crossing.

Irish cream liqueur - a creamy, unctuous liqueur made by combining Irish whiskey and cream, used as the basis of many cocktails and as a flavoring for coffee. The alcohol in the whiskey acts as a natural preservative for the cream, making the liqueur shelf stable for up to two years.

Irish ham - the cured leg of a pig, sometimes pickled or brined and smoked over a peat fire, as in Belfast, or smoked over a fire of juniper branches, as in Limerick. Irish ham is available through some butchers and specialty stores in North America, and is sold as a cooking ham, because it is not fully cooked in the curing process.

Irish honey - see HONEY.

Irish moss - see CARRAGEEN.

Irish oats - see STEEL-CUT OATS.

Irish soda bread - see SODA BREAD.

Irish stew - a traditional stew consisting of lamb or mutton, potato and onion.

Iron Goddess - see TEA.

ironware - see CAST-IRON COOKWARE.

irradiation - the use of radiation on food, without making the food radioactive, to sterilize, control insects, reduce the likelihood of food poisoning and provide a longer shelf life, especially with fruit. The process is also known as cold, electronic or energy pasteurization, as well as ionization. Since 1986, the U.S. Food and Drug Administration has made it mandatory that irradiated food be labeled, either with an internationally recognized logo (a flower named "radura") or with text indicating that the item has been irradiated.

isinglass - a very pure form of gelatin acquired from the bladders of sturgeon and other cold-water ocean fish. Although it was very popular in the beginning of the 1900s for sweet and savory jellies and aspics, it fell out of favor with the introduction of more easily obtained, and conveniently used, forms of gelatin and is rarely used today.

isoflavone - a type of phytoestrogen, or natural plant chemical that, when consumed in larger amounts, mimics the activities of the human hormone estrogen. Isoflavones are found primarily in soy-based foods in the human diet and for a long time had been credited with decreasing the unpleasant symptoms associated with menopause and with lowering cholesterol levels and heart disease risk. However, a 2006 study from the American Heart Association found no evidence to prove these claims. The jury is still out on whether they can lower the risk of hormone-dependent cancers, such as breast and prostate cancer. There is significant debate over the effects of high isoflavone consumption and whether it may have negative effects on the body as well, but more studies are needed to prove definitively whether isoflavones are curative or causative agents in disease.

Italian bread - a generic name in North America for a crusty loaf of white bread with an airy, holey interior, almost the same as French bread, but flatter and wider. There are many fine varieties of traditional Italian breads known by other names, including **focaccia** and **ciabatta.**

Italian chicory - see ITALIAN DANDELION.

Italian cress - see ARUGULA.

Italian dandelion - also **asparagus chicory, dandelion chicory, Italian chicory.** Not actually a dandelion, but quite similar in appearance to one, this plant produces long, dark green sawtooth leaves, which are excellent in salads when young or braised when older and tougher. Italian dandelion is a member of the chicory family and is similarly bitter and refreshing.

Italian dressing - a tangy salad dressing of olive oil, vinegar, garlic and spices. It is similar to traditional French dressing, but with an extra-spicy zing from the garlic and usually the inclusion of the typical Italian spices basil and oregano.

Italian eggplant - see EGGPLANT.

Italian flat bean - also **Roma bean, Romano bean.** A flat, broad type of green snap bean, mild in flavor, good as a cooked vegetable on its own or as a component of another dish. Although it bears the same name, this is not the same as the pink-striped romano bean, or cranberry bean.

Italian herb seasoning - a ready-made blend of typical Italian dried herbs, such as basil, oregano, thyme, sage and rosemary, which can be used in Italian-American style dishes, such as spaghetti or pizza.

Italian ice - another term for a **granita,** an icy, flavored frozen slush made with water and no dairy products.

Italian olive - see OLIVE.

Italian parsley - also **flat-leaf parsley.** This parsley, *Petroselinum crispum* var. *Neapolitanu*, has flat, dark green leaves, succulent stems and a strong flavor. See also CURLY PARSLEY, PARSLEY.

Italian sausage - a generic term in North America for an uncooked pork sausage made in the Italian style with coarsely ground meat and flavored with typical Italian seasonings, including fennel seed and garlic. The sausage comes in sweet (mild) and hot varieties, the hot ones flavored with crushed red pepper flakes, which give them their characteristic pinkish red color. Italian sausage is often served on its own grilled (in or out of a bun with typical hotdog toppings); used in pasta sauces or stews; or sliced as a topping for pizza.

Italian soda - a carbonated beverage made by adding a sweet flavored syrup to soda water. Italian syrups come in a staggering variety of flavors, from fruit to coffee to nuts, and can be used in almost any beverage. They are popular additions to fancy coffees served at coffeehouses, and are ordered by the shot.

Italian vegetable marrow - see COCOZELLE.

Italian wedding soup - a combination of chicken stock, small pasta, such as orzo or **acini di pepe,** escarole or spinach, and tiny meatballs. As its name implies, it is a traditional Italian soup that is sometimes served at weddings, but that use came later and mostly at Italian-American nuptials. Food historians say the English name is a misunderstood, a too literal translation of its Italian name, *minestra maritata*. "Minestra" certainly means "soup," but "maritata" can mean "married" or simply "well paired." The meat and greens in the soup are considered an ideal match, so they are "*maritata.*" In Italy, the soup is much more complicated than its North American counterpart, involving a variety of meats and greens, and is served as a one-pot meal, rather than as a starter course.

Italico cheese - see BEL PAESE.

jelly beans

jaboticaba - the fruit of a plant of the species *Myrciaria cauliflora*, native to Brazil, similar in appearance to a large, dark purple or black grape, but with a thicker, tart skin. Jaboticabas taste similar to grapes, especially those of the muscadine family, with a slight pine undertone. They are available in North America through some specialty produce growers, and the trees can be grown in the warm climate of the Southern U.S. Jaboticabas are often eaten plain, but are also used in jams, jellies and salads.

jack - see NORTHERN PIKE.

Jack cheese - see DRY JACK, MONTEREY JACK, SONOMA JACK.

jackfruit - also **jakfruit.** A variety of breadfruit, *Artocarpus heterophyllus* or A. *integrifolia*, common in the tropics, considered to be the biggest fruit in the world, able to grow to more than 50 pounds (23 kg). It can be eaten raw or cooked, and the seeds can be roasted or boiled like chestnuts.

jackknife clam - see RAZOR CLAM.

Jacob's cattle bean - see ANASAZI BEAN.

Jaffrey, Madhur - see profile below.

Jägermeister - a bitter, strong herb liqueur made by macerating 56 different herbs, fruits, roots and barks in a mixture of alcohol and water, made since 1878 by the Mast family in Wolfenbüttel, Germany. The secret recipe was developed by Curt Mast and is still a family secret;, however, the company has revealed that cinnamon, bitter oranges, gingerroot, red sandalwood and blueberries all figure somewhere in the mix. The spiced liquid is blended, then aged in oak barrels for a year. After it is aged, it is filtered, sweetened with sugar and caramel, then filtered again before bottling. Jägermeister is used in some mixed drinks, but is especially popular in North America as a shot, notably with university students. The name means "hunt master" in German and is symbolized by a deer head on the product's logo.

jaggery - an unrefined, dark, flavorful palm sugar or cane sugar used across the Indian subcontinent and in parts of Southeast Asia. Jaggery comes in loaves or cakes and is yellowish tan in color. It should be sticky and crumbly in texture, similar to brown sugar. See also GUR.

jagging wheel - see PASTRY WHEEL.

jakfruit - see JACKFRUIT.

jalapeño pepper - see CHILE PEPPER.

jalousie - a small, flaky pastry filled with almond paste and topped with a layer of jam, then a lattice top. The cake looks like, and is named for, a type of louvered glass door or venetian blind: the jam "peeks" through the slats of pastry. The word is taken from the French, meaning "jealous."

jam - a thick, sweet spread made by cooking crushed or chopped fruits with sugar. Jam tends to hold its shape, but is generally less firm than jelly.

Jaffrey, Madhur (1933–) - Indian-born actor and prolific cookbook author. Jaffrey left Delhi in the 1950s to study at the Royal Academy of Dramatic Arts in London. After graduating, she moved to New York City and married Indian film actor Saeed Jaffrey, with whom she has three daughters. The Jaffreys take credit for having introduced the late Ismail Merchant to James Ivory, the acclaimed and prolific producer-director team who made *Shakespeare Walla,* Madhur's first major film, for which she won Best Actress at the 1965 Berlin Festival. She didn't begin writing cookbooks until after her divorce, when she was in financial straits. Her first, *An Invitation to Indian Cooking,* appeared in 1973. Then, beginning in 1981, she published a string of eponymous titles issued at a rate of about one a year. Among her books are a culinary memoir, *Climbing the Mango Trees* (2005), and a book about Eastern mythology, *Seasons of Splendour* (1984). In the meantime, she continued acting, including some projects with Merchant and Ivory. Not counting television roles and cooking programs, she has appeared in 21 films. In 2004, the British Foreign Office named her an honorary Commander of the Order of the British Empire for her services to drama and Indian culture and cuisine.

A B C D E F G H I J K L M N O P Q R S T U V W X Y Z

jamaica - the Mexican name for dried hibiscus flowers, which are frequently made into a sweetened iced tea, called *agua de jamaica* in Spanish, sold in Mexican restaurants in Southern California, the Southwestern U.S. and Texas. See also HIBISCUS TEA.

Jamaican coffee bean - see COFFEE.

Jamaican fruitcake - see BLACK CAKE.

Jamaican patty - a highly spiced, savory turnover common all over the island of Jamaica and in many parts of North America, a mixture of minced or ground beef and spices enclosed in a flaky pastry crust. The crust is often colored with **annatto** or turmeric to make it the characteristic saffron yellow. In Jamaica, patties are the fast food of choice, similar to hamburgers in North America.

Jamaican pepper - see ALLSPICE.

Jamaican pepper pot soup - see PEPPER POT.

Jamaican sorrel - see ROSELLE.

Jamaican thyme - also **Cuban oregano, Indian borage.** An herb, *Coleus amboinicus*, grown in Africa, Asia, South America and the West Indies, often used as a flavoring for Caribbean fish dishes and stews; also used in India as an ingredient in cooking, as well as herbal teas and medicines.

jambalaya

jambalaya - the famed New Orleans rice dish containing chopped ham, bacon or pork, shrimp or crabmeat, green pepper, chopped tomato and onion. Originally, like so many dishes that have become classics, jambalaya was designed to use up leftovers. The dish stands in that great tradition of frugal cooks with profound respect for food, who could not afford to throw away leftovers. The name is a nod to its Spanish influence: **paella,** made with sausage, shellfish, rice and tomato, among other ingredients, and *jamón*, meaning "ham."

jamberry - see TOMATILLO.

jambon - French for "ham."

jambon de Bayonne - see BAYONNE HAM.

jambon des Ardennes - see ARDENNES HAM.

jambonneau - see CHARCUTERIE.

jambon persillé - see CHARCUTERIE.

jammy - a wine-tasting term used to describe a wine that has a strong berry flavor, usually tasting of cooked berries, rather than fresh ones, reminiscent of jam.

jamón ibérico - also **Iberico ham, pata negra.** The cured leg of the *ibérico* pig of western Spain, with purplish pink flesh streaked with yellow fat, often called *pata negra* in Spanish because of the pig's black hooves. The ham gets its distinctive, nutty flavor from the pigs' diet of wild acorns. Each ibérico pig is allowed a six-month period of wild foraging called the *montanera*, during which time it gorges itself on these acorns. When it has reached its ideal weight, the pig is slaughtered, and the leg is cured, using a combination of salt and air-drying. In the early stages of the curing process, a gray mold is allowed to form on the outside of the ham to infuse it with its earthy aroma. When it is fully aged, the consumer buys the whole leg, setting it in a special stand at room temperature and cutting it down, slice by slice, until it is gone. One of the most expensive hams in the world, jamón ibérico is a well-loved staple in Spanish cuisine, but was not approved for sale in the United States until recently because slaughterhouses in Spain do not comply with USDA regulations. Thanks to the construction of a USDA-compliant abattoir in Córdoba, the hams are slowly beginning to make their way to North America.

jamón serrano - also **serrano ham.** A Spanish dry-cured ham similar to **Virginia ham** but much less salty, aged for up to one year, usually sold in Spain as a whole leg, including the hoof. Because it is a kind of national obsession, special jamón serrano stands are used all over Spain, in homes and bars alike, to hold a ham as it is sliced and used over a period of weeks or months. It is also a common sight to see legs of jamón serrano hanging in vast quantities from the ceilings of bars, restaurants and even some coffee shops. Jamón serrano is usually carved into paper-thin slices and enjoyed with bread or alone for its rich, melt-in-the-mouth flavor and texture. The name means "mountain ham" in Spanish for the cool mountain air that is ideal for curing it.

Japanese artichoke - see CHINESE ARTICHOKE.

Japanese black mushroom - see SHIITAKE.

Japanese bread crumbs - see PANKO.

Japanese eggplant - see EGGPLANT.

Japanese horseradish - see WASABI.

Japanese knives - the traditional knives used in Japan for centuries, highly prized by chefs and home cooks in the West as well. Unlike many Western knives, they are honed on one side only, typically on the right side for right-handed users (left-handed users need to request a left-handed knife when purchasing one). The knives fall into two broad categories, which reflect the length of time their edges stay sharp without honing: **honyaki** are the hardest steel and therefore the best at staying sharp for a long time, also the most expensive, brittle and difficult to sharpen; and **kasumi** are more moderately priced, not as hard as honyaki and easier to sharpen.

Japanese medlar - see LOQUAT.

Japanese moss - see AGAR-AGAR.

Japanese pumpkin - see KOBACHA SQUASH.

Japanese vermicelli - see HARUSAME.

jap chae - also **chap chae.** A Korean stir-fry of cellophane noodles, marinated sliced beef, mushrooms and vegetables (usually spinach, carrots and onions), seasoned with a sauce made of soy sauce, sugar, garlic, green onions, pepper and sesame oil. The dish is often served over rice, in which case it is called jap chae bap.

jardinière

Japonica rice - see RICE.

jardinière - **1.** a French term for a dish, usually meat, served with diced cooked vegetables, such as boeuf à la jardinière, which literally means "beef in the style of the gardener" in French. **2.** a pickled combination of vegetables that often contains cauliflower, carrots, and sweet or hot peppers, often served in North America as part of an antipasto tray. This pickle is called *giardiniera* in Italian.

COMMON JAPANESE KNIVES

There are four common Japanese knife shapes, each of which fulfills a specific duty in the kitchen.

deba - similar in shape to a Western **chef's knife,** but the blade curves upward to a pointed tip. It is designed for efficiently boning and filleting fish, although it is useful for a variety of cutting tasks.

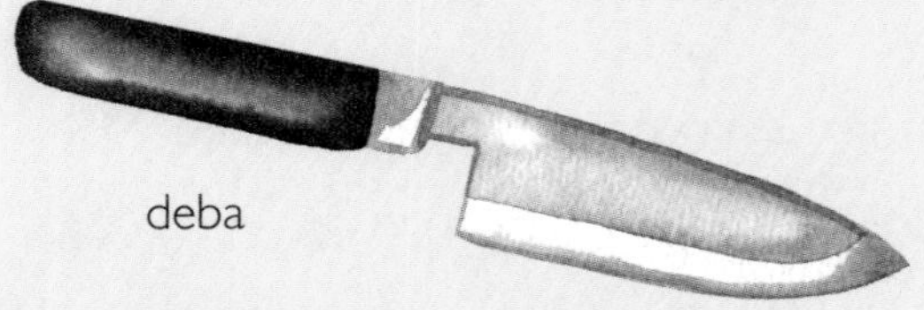

deba

santoku - a later invention than the deba, usuba and yanagi; its stout, flat-edged blade with indentations along its length makes it an excellent all-purpose knife, good for cubing, slicing, mincing and dicing all types of foods. The indentations keep wet or sticky foods from adhering to the blade. The santoku has taken the United States by storm in recent years, thanks to the popularity of TV cooking show host Rachael Ray, who familiarized her viewers with the cutting implement.

usuba - has a square blade, shaped like a small, narrow cleaver, and is used for chopping vegetables.

yanagi - looks like a long, narrow **slicing knife** with a sharply pointed tip. It is used for slicing meat or raw fish into perfect, neat slices for sashimi, hence its English name, sashimi knife.

yanagi

Jarlsberg - a Norwegian cow's milk cheese, firm and buttery, with a mild nutty taste, white to light yellow in color, with large holes scattered throughout. It's covered with a thick rind and a yellow wax, commonly used in *landgang*, the Norwegian version of a **hero sandwich.**

jasmine rice - see RICE.

jasmine tea - see TEA.

Java almond - see PILI NUT.

javelina - see PECCARY.

jawbreaker - an extremely hard, round candy made by whirling a sugary center together with a variety of different-colored and/or flavored sugar solutions until the candy is built up to the proper diameter. Jawbreakers got their name because they are so hard they can't be bitten through. They must be sucked slowly until each colored layer dissolves to reveal the next one underneath. Because they contain so many layers and must dry between coatings, jawbreakers can take weeks to make.

jee choy - see LAVER.

jell - to congeal, set or take on the consistency of jelly. See also GELATIN.

jellied eels - a traditional Cockney dish served in the East End of London, consisting of thick slices of eel boiled in an herbed vinegar marinade, then left to cool until the marinade jells. The lightly pickled eels are served with a parsley gravy called liquor (although it's not alcoholic). Jellies eels are often sold frozen and in cans, but were once exclusively the domain of street stalls and "pie and mash" shops, which sold the common man's staple of beef pies and mashed potatoes. They're also easy to make at home, so recipes abound.

Jell-O - see COOPER, PETER; GELATIN DESSERTS.

jelly - **1.** usually made by cooking fruit juice with sugar. (Some are made without cooking, using special uncooked jelly recipes.) A good jelly is clear and firm enough to hold its shape when turned out of the container. The natural pectin of the fruit or added gelatin is key in making a well-formed jelly. **2.** a British and Australian term for gelatin or gelatin-based desserts. The term "jelly powder" is the equivalent of the North American "gelatin powder," usually used to describe store-bought powders used to make flavored gelatin desserts. **3.** the British generic term for any gelatin-based candy, such as a gumdrop.

jelly bag - an open-topped fine-mesh bag used for draining the juice from crushed or cooked fruit to make jelly. The bag is anchored at the top to a metal ring, which stands atop several feet that fit over the lip of a bowl. The fruit is crushed or cooked without peeling or seeding, then spooned into the jelly bag and allowed to drip until all the liquid is extracted. Allowing the juice to drip freely, without squeezing the bag, yields the least cloudy juice possible for making crystal-clear jellies.

jelly bean - a small, colorful, chewy candy made with sugar, corn syrup and flavorings and coated with a glaze to give it a firm outer shell. Traditional jelly beans are larger than their gourmet counterparts and contain flavor only in the outside layers. They tend to stick to the traditional flavors: lemon, cherry, orange and licorice among them. Gourmet jelly beans have flavorings both in the center and in the coating to give them a richer taste, and they come in an array of exotic flavors, such as coconut, buttered popcorn, root beer, cappuccino and even jalapeño. The theory is that jelly beans are descendents of the sweet, chewy candy **Turkish delight.** They have become exceptionally popular at Easter, because they are shaped like eggs, a symbol associated with Easter and rebirth. Children often receive jelly beans in their Easter baskets, which are filled with candies made in the shapes of springtime symbols, such as rabbits, chicks and eggs.

jelly doughnut - a raised doughnut without a hole in the middle, filled with jam or jelly, commonly coated with confectioner's sugar. These doughnuts can be round or elongated, like **Berlin doughnuts.** Small, round jelly doughnuts called **sufganiyot** in Hebrew are a common Hanukkah treat in Israel and Jewish communities in North America.

jellyfish - any of a variety of invertebrate sea creatures related to coral and sea anemones, with a nearly transparent umbrella-shaped body and long, dangling tentacles. Although many jellyfish are poisonous and can deliver a vicious sting, some are edible, especially *Rhopilema esculenta*, a well-loved species eaten throughout Asia, especially in China and Japan. Strips are cut from the body and parboiled before being salted. The salted strips must be soaked prior to use to make them more palatable and decrease their high sodium content. They are often served in cold seafood salads, dressed with soy sauce, sesame oil, sugar and vinegar, and have a crunchy texture and very mild flavor. Although jellyfish is a widespread delicacy in Asia, it is rarely eaten in North America outside of Asian restaurants. However, packages of heavily salted, dried jellyfish strips can be found in Asian grocery stores.

jelly melon - see KIWANO.

jelly roll - a thin, rectangular sponge cake baked on a baking or cookie sheet spread with a filling, often a jam or jelly and sometimes cream, and rolled into a log to be sliced into rounds. It's known as **roulade** in France, where meat is often rolled around a savory filling; and **Swiss roll** in England, where the sponge is thicker and rolled less tightly.

jelly rolls

jelly roll pan - a shallow, rectangular, metal cake pan used to make large, thin sponge or sheet cakes, as for jelly rolls or **bûche de Noël.**

jerk - a Caribbean spice mix containing allspice, pepper, ginger, brown sugar, cinnamon, thyme, garlic and Scotch bonnet pepper, handed down from West Africans taken to Jamaica as slaves during the 17th century. Rubbed and marinated with the spice mix, the meat, most often pork or chicken, is cooked in large, stone-lined barbecue pits, covered with green pimiento wood, which smokes easily, imparting another characteristic flavor. Today, in Jamaica, jerk meats are sold by roadside vendors, who cook in vertically halved oil drums, most often using dry pimiento wood.

jerky - from *charqui,* the Spanish appropriation of a native Indian word, referring to meat dried using a technique taught to early settlers by the Indians, so that they could take nourishment with them when away from home. See also PIPIKAULA, SMOKED SALMON.

Jerusalem artichoke - also **sunchoke.** A tuber, *Helianthus tuberosus*, native to North America, first cultivated by Champlain in 1606 in Massachusetts, where settlers observed Huron Indians growing "sunchokes" and began trading for them. They were introduced to France in 1607, first called *pomme de terre,* then *topinambour,* after an exhibit of the Topinambur tribe brought back to Paris by Claude Delaunay from his journey of discovery to Brazil. From France, they went to Holland and were cultivated at Ter Neusen by Pastor Petrus Hondius, who gave specimens to his friends abroad, including some in London. The name comes from the Italian *girasole articiocco,* meaning "sunflower artichoke."

jewfish - see GOLIATH GROUPER.

jicama - also **Mexican potato.** A round tuber with a thin, beige skin and crisp, white flesh, tasting like a cross between an apple, turnip and water chestnut, a staple in Central American cuisine, usually eaten raw.

jigger - also **shot glass. 1.** a small flared glass that is supposed to hold a standard $1\frac{1}{2}$ ounces of liquor, although there are more generous versions that hold 2 ounces and stingier ones that hold only 1 ounce. It is the standard measuring glass at bars for mixing cocktails. A jigger can also be found on one side of a double-ended measuring jigger, a bar tool with a long handle and an hourglass-shaped set of two measuring cups on the end. A **pony** is the smaller side of the two. **2.** the amount of liquor container in a jigger, as in "a jigger of gin."

Jiggs' dinner - the Newfoundland equivalent of **New England boiled dinner,** a combination of salted beef or salt pork, turnips, potatoes, cabbage and carrots boiled together with water in a large pot. A pudding bag filled with soaked split peas is often added to the water to make a **pease pudding** while the rest of the dinner cooks. A boiled **figgy duff** is the typical dessert served after (or sometimes with) the meal. The meal is named after the comic strip character Jiggs from the cartoon *Bringing Up Father*, created by George McManus in 1913. The strip follows the adventures of a long-suffering Irish fellow named Jiggs, whose social-climbing wife, Maggie, won't let him hang around with his regular friends when he wins the lottery. Jiggs' greatest desire is to act like he always has, go down to his local pub on a regular basis and eat his beloved humble dinner of boiled corned beef and cabbage.

jimmies - see SPRINKLES.

Job's tears - also **hato mugi.** The seeds of an Asian grass, often found in Asian markets, a nutritious whole grain that can be used in the same way as rice or barley in a number of dishes. Although more botanically similar to rice, Job's tears is commonly misidentified as a type of barley, thanks to its Japanese name, which means "dove barley" and is often translated as "pearl barley." Japanese naturopathic doctors recommend eating this grain for its purported ability to strengthen the stomach and the nervous system and purify the blood.

John Dory - a golden yellow fish, *Zeus faber,* with a dark spot, like the haddock, on either side of its body. It was called St. Peter by the English, French and Italians because it was thought to be the fish mentioned in a passage from *Matthew 17:27,* in which Jesus tells Peter, "Go to the sea and cast a hook and take the first fish that bites and when you open its mouth you will find a shekel." The fish's marks are said to have been made by the saint's thumb and forefinger while he retrieved the coin from its mouth. Simply named "Dory" for centuries, from the French *doré,* meaning "gilded," "John" was added in the 1700s, after a fashionable song about a French pirate of that name.

johnnycake - also **hoe cake.** A flat, dry bread made with cornmeal, salt and water, baked on hot stones, which was a staple of the early American frontier. The name is believed to be a derivation of "journey cake," because it was easy to slip into a backpack or pocket, although another account claims it was originally called "Shawnee cake" because its technique was learned from the Shawnee Indians. The Indian word for johnnycake is *joniken.* Hoe cakes were so named because they were often cooked on the blade of a hoe over a fire.

Johnny-jump-up - a type of **violet** also related to the **pansy,** commonly grown in North American gardens for its delicate, colored blossoms, usually purple and yellow, which are edible. The flowers have a sweet violet-like flavor, which is stronger than that of violets of the *Viola odorata* variety. They are often used as a garnish or in salads. See also EDIBLE FLOWERS.

joi gai - referred to as "drunken chicken" in Shanghai, where it's steamed and cooked whole in Shao-Hsing wine.

joint - also **disjoint.** To separate meat, such as a whole chicken, at the joints, using a sharp knife to cut cleanly through the sockets.

Johnson, Nancy - see ICE CREAM, ICE CREAM MAKER.

jollof rice - a well-loved West African dish similar to pilaf; a mixture of rice and a variety of other tidbits, such as meat, seafood or vegetables, spiced with any of a variety of spices, always colored red with palm oil or tomato paste, and, in many places, spicy and hot from the addition of chiles or ground hot red peppers. Jollof rice is often served in North America at Kwanzaa celebrations in December.

Jonagold apple - see APPLE.

Jonah crab - see CRAB.

Jonathan apple - see APPLE.

Jordan almonds - large almonds covered with a smooth, hard, candy coating in pastel colors. As the legend goes, these candies were created as a celebration of marriage, mixing the bitter and the sweet together in one delicious bite. They do not come from Jordan, but from Malaga, Spain. The name derives from *almaund,* Old French for "almond," and *jardin,* meaning "garden." The name once described a variety of almonds called *jardin almaund,* but English speakers soon anglicized it in spite of the possibility of geographical confusion. See also CONFETTI, DRAGÉE.

jostaberry - sweet-tasting reddish black berry, a cross between a gooseberry and black currant, which originated in Germany and became widely available in 1977 when the cultivar was released to the public (and North American growers) by the German plant breeder who had been working on it for several decades.

Juan Canary melon - see CANARY MELON.

Judas' ear mushroom - see WOOD EAR.

jugged hare - a 700-year-old technique for cooking hare in an earthenware pot, its most important ingredient being blood, which tenderizes the meat and thickens the sauce. Known to the French as *civet de lièvre,* it has many variations, including *civet Mère Jean,* with cream, classically accompanied with fried bread and **ceps** cooked with garlic. The dish is also an English favorite, mentioned by Winston Churchill in a discussion of politics at the outbreak of the Second World War. "First catch the hare," he is reported to have said, meaning that the hare must be caught before the cooking can begin, referring to the need to capture Hitler before further discussion of world politics could continue. Modern versions of the recipe often substitute port or red wine for the blood, but purists would strenuously object.

jugo - the Spanish word for "juice," this Latin American beverage is either straight juice or a mixture of ice, water, juice and sometimes sugar. See also BATIDO, MERENGADA.

juicer

juicer - an electric or manual kitchen appliance used to squeeze the juice out of fruits and/or vegetables. A manual juicer can be a small bowl with a ridged **reamer**-style top used for pressing the juice out of halved citrus fruits, or a larger mechanical device with a long handle, which exerts more force than a hand juicer. Electric juicers come in a variety of styles and can handle almost any type of fruit. Many are designed to juice vegetables, leaving their tough pulp behind, which is nearly impossible to do by hand.

jujube - **1.** a small, fruit-flavored candy with a gelatinous texture. In the 19th and early 20th centuries, they often contained cough medication. **2.** a fruit, also misnamed "Chinese date" because it looks like one, with gleaming, reddish brown skin, crisp texture, the flavor of a mild, sweet apple and a large pit relative to the size of the fruit. China is credited for cultivating the fruit, even though it probably originated in Syria. Europeans eat them with honey, while the Chinese use them in pastries, preserves and mincemeat. Jujubes were brought to California, Texas and Mexico as part of the Spanish migration to the New World.

Julekaka - a traditional Norwegian yeast bread flavored with raisins, candied fruit and cardamom, available at Scandinavian bakeries in North America. Its name means "Christmas cake" in Norwegian.

julep - from the Persian *gulab*, meaning "rose water," a sweet drink. The most well-known is the cocktail, **Mint Julep,** made with bourbon, sugar, crushed ice and mint leaves.

Julien brothers - see SAVARIN.

julienne - **1.** (n.) a term used to describe food sliced into thin, long or short **matchstick** strips. Julienned citrus peel, firm cheese, cooked fish, poultry or meat, pickles or raw fruits or vegetables may be used as a garnish for salad or soup. Foods, such as potatoes, are often julienned before cooking (straw potatoes are an example). Aside from the pleasing texture this creates, it also speeds up the cooking. **2.** (v.) a technique of slicing foods into thin, long or short strips, usually using a knife or **mandoline.**

June berry - see SASKATOON BERRY.

juniper - a tree, *Juniperus communis*, producing aromatic berries used to flavor gin, game, sauerkraut, pâté and salads. Historically, juniper was regarded as a magic shrub to protect against devils, evil spirits and wild animals. The Bible mentions juniper as a symbol of protection. Legend has it that juniper planted beside the front door will keep out witches; the only way for a witch to get past the plant is by correctly counting its needles. The Dutch were the first to flavor their gin with juniper berries in the 18th century, and juniper berries are said to stimulate the appetite.

junket - a type of pudding made of milk, sugar, flavorings and **rennet,** formerly "junkate," from the Italian *giuncata*, a cream cheese.

jus - French for "juice," the natural meat juices produced during cooking.

jus lié - a sauce for roast beef made by lightly thickening the **jus** from the beef with a **slurry** of arrowroot or cornstarch and water. The name means "connected juice" or "bound juice."

Jutland blue - see DANISH BLUE.

k
kale

kaa-he-he - see STEVIA.

kaasdoop - a combination of the Dutch words for "cheese" (*kaas*) and "baptism" (*doop*), commonly translated as "cheese dip." Kaasdoop is a **Gouda**-based Dutch **fondue,** flavored with brandy and nutmeg, into which chunks of brown or dark rye bread are dunked.

kabanos - a Polish sausage made of minced pork.

Kabinett - a German class of good-quality wines, often Rieslings, that are light, dry (no sugar is added) and reasonably priced.

kabob - also **kebab.** See SHISH KEBAB.

ka chai - see FINGERROOT.

kachori - also **kachauri.** An Indian delicacy, balls of **poori** dough usually stuffed with a spiced, savory filling of mashed, cooked green peas or potatoes (but sometimes stuffed with a sweet filling of shredded coconut or chopped nuts and dried fruits), and deep-fried in **ghee** or oil until golden and crisp. Perfect for portable snacks or appetizers, savory kachori are often served with chutney. Ready-to-cook frozen versions are available at Indian food stores.

kadaif - also **kataifi, knafeh. 1.** a Mediterranean pastry made of thin strands of phyllo, wrapped around a cinnamon-spiced filling of chopped almonds and walnuts, which is baked, then topped with a thick, sweet syrup and allowed to cool. **2.** the shredded phyllo, which resembles angel hair pasta, available frozen or refrigerated from Greek and Middle Eastern food stores.

kadhai - also **karhai. 1.** a broad, two-handled Indian pan, similar to a wok, used for stir-fried dishes and curries, which the cook usually starts by heating oil in the kadhai. The traditional kadhai was iron; now brass, enamelware, nonstick aluminum and stainless-steel versions are available. **2.** an adjective applied to the dishes, such as murg kadhai, that are cooked in this pan, and **3.** the spice mix added to them.

Kadota fig - see FIG.

Kaffekuchen - German for "coffee cake." See COFFEE CAKE.

kaffir - the fragrant leaves, peel and intensely flavored juice of the kaffir lime, native to Southeast Asia and now grown in California. The fruit has green, knobby skin and is slightly pointed at the stem end. An integral part of Thai cuisine, the kaffir lime is prized primarily for it leaves; its Thai name is **makrut.**

kafta - Lebanese meatballs. See also KOFTA.

kahk - a usually sweet Middle Eastern bread, shaped into a ring, named "kahk" after the Arabic word for "bracelet." It may have spices, such as allspice, anise, coriander, cumin and **mahleb,** added, and is often given an egg wash then sprinkled with sesame seeds before it is baked.

kahk bi loz - also **almond bracelet.** A ring of baked, bead-shaped cookies that is served in Egypt at engagement parties and weddings. A soft dough of egg white, ground almonds, orange-flower water and sugar is shaped into "beads," then laid end-to-end on a baking sheet; as they bake, they swell and the circle closes.

Kahlúa - a coffee-flavored liqueur imported to the U.S. from Mexico in 1959 by Jules Berman. The oldest bottle on record is dated 1937, depicting a man wearing a turban and smoking a cigar, fueling the impression that Kahlúa is Arabic in origin. Following its export, the label showed a Mexican wearing a large sombrero. Although some of the liqueur is still made in Mexico using homegrown coffee beans, the Danish company Peter Heering also makes it under license in Europe.

kaiseki ryori - a traditional Japanese haute cuisine meal centered around the foods of a particular season, featuring a series of courses, all arranged artistically, so that the eyes as well as the taste buds are stimulated. A kaiseki meal consists of a variety of dishes, each reflecting a different flavor and/or traditional cooking method, perfectly balanced so that each course complements the next in flavor, color and texture. A true, high-drama kaiseki meal can last for hours, each exquisite course consisting of only a mouthful or two of beautiful food perfectly arranged on a gorgeous dish, which complements the color and texture of the food.

The meal starts with **sake** and ends with rice to complete the circle, because sake is considered the very essence of rice. In between, the diner is served a number of the following traditional Japanese foods: *suimono* (clear soups), *nimono* (simmered dishes), *aemono* (dressed foods, such as salads), *sunomono* (vinegared dishes), *mushimono* (steamed dishes, such as the popular savory custard dish, *chawan mushi*), *yakimono* (grilled dishes) and *agemono* (fried dishes). The menu reflects the foods of the season, such as pumpkin in the fall or asparagus in the spring.

This style of haute cuisine is derived from *chakaiseki ryori*, or "tea ceremony cuisine," the small portions of simple, attractive food offered to prime the stomach before a traditional Japanese tea ceremony. The ritual of preparing and serving the foods, and of accepting the hospitality of the host, are as important as the foods themselves.

kaiser roll - also **Vienna roll.** A large, crusty roll popular for deli sandwiches, purportedly invented in Vienna and thought to have been named to honor Emperor Franz Josef.

kaiware - also **radish sprouts.** Japanese name for the young sprouts of the **daikon** radish. Kaiware add crunch and a sharp, peppery taste to **maki rolls, sashimi** and sushi. In North America, they are becoming a common addition to salads and sandwiches. Like most sprouts they are grown hydroponically, so they are available year-round.

kajú - see CASHEW.

kaki age - Japanese dish of chopped seafood and vegetables deep-fried in **tempura** batter.

kalamansi - also **kalamondin.** A very sour lemon or lime-like fruit, a cross between a lemon and a mandarin orange. See also CALAMONDIN.

kalamata olive - also **calamata.** Greek aubergine-color olives, usually packed in brine, with a rich, fruity flavor, widely used in Greek salads. See also OLIVE.

kalbi - also **galbi.** Korean grilled marinated beef rib steak with a portion of the rib bone attached, popular at outdoor barbecues and restaurants that feature grilling tables, where patrons can cook their meat to their liking. Kalbi is marinated in a soy-based marinade the same way as **bulgogi.**

kale - a member of the cabbage family, thought to be one of the first cultivated brassicas, the family of vegetables that includes broccoli and cauliflower. Colewort, its wild ancestor, still grows along the coast of Western Europe. In 1773, Thomas Jefferson experimented with European foods, and one of them was German kale.

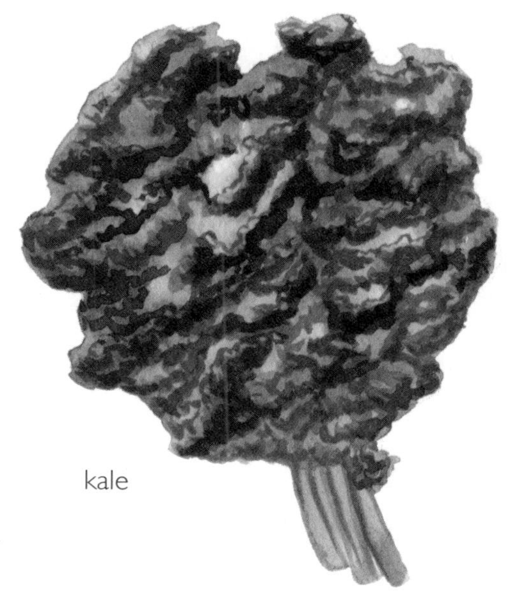

kale

Kale's moniker in other languages is highly descriptive: the French call it *chou frisé* (curly cabbage), the Germans *Krauskohl* (crispy cabbage), the Italians *cavolo arricciato* (curled cabbage), the Spanish *col rizada* (curly cabbage) and the Dutch *boerenkool* (farm cabbage). The Irish considered the plant to have supernatural powers and said that fairies rode kale stalks during the new moon. It has been said that when an Irish farmer finds the curly leaves in disorder at first light, it means his crops will all flourish and grow tall.

kalua pua - a Hawaiian specialty, pig roasted in an earthen pit at a luau, from *kalua*, meaning "to bake in the ground," and *pua*, meaning "pig."

kamaboko - also **fish cake.** A Japanese steamed fish paste cake, made by mashing delicately flavored white fish, then mixing it with egg and cornstarch to make a sticky, smooth paste. The paste is then molded into a log or half-log and steamed until cooked through and it has a solid, rubbery texture. Kamaboko can be sliced and used in a variety of dishes, including **ramen** and **oden,** or chilled and eaten on its own as an appetizer. Ready-made kamaboko is easy to find in Japanese and Asian grocery stores and comes in plain white or with a layer of vibrant color, such as pink or green, on the outside. There are many types of specialty kamaboko. *Chikuwa*, which is shaped like a bamboo pole, with a hole

kamaboko

running through the center, and *narutomaki,* which is white with a pink swirl pattern, are just two of the many varieties.

kampyo - strands shaved from **bottle gourds** (most often by machine), then dried and usually packaged in cellophane (they resemble broad egg noodles), for Japanese cuisine. Softened by boiling or soaking first, they are used to stuff roll-ups wrapped in **nori**, in cooked dishes or as edible ties for food packets. The chewy strips readily absorb other flavors.

kamut - the ancient Egyptian word for "wheat" and the ancestor of our modern strains of this grain. Kamut was a dominant crop from 4000 BC until the late Roman Empire and was called "grain of the pharaohs." It fell out of favor, however, when the Greeks and Romans developed the close relatives of our durum wheat.

kangaroo - **1.** an Australian indigenous, herbivorous marsupial mammal (the term is also used generically to include wallaby and wallaroo). Following the example of the Aboriginals (who ate kangaroo, usually gutting it, then separating the feet and tail and roasting it in a fire pit) colonists hunted the animal for food and sport. Some began keeping fenced herds, but cattle and sheep soon became the norm. In the late 20th century, kangaroo began to become popular as an appealing, healthy option. The lean, low-cholesterol meat, popular in Europe, can be cut into steaks or ground, grilled, roasted and smoked, or made into a traditional kangaroo-tail soup or a "steamer" (kangaroo and salt pork, simmered together for hours). Kangaroo has also been promoted as farm livestock that is less demanding than hoofed animals on the continent's native grasses and soils, but some Aussies are said to be loath to consume their country's living symbol. **2.** see MARTINI.

Kansas City strip steak - see DELMONICO STEAK.

kanten - the Japanese name for **agar-agar.**

kaoliang - a Chinese fermented beverage made of sorghum during the Song dynasty (AD 960–1278). *Kaoliang* is also the word for **sorghum,** which was cultivated predominantly in Szechwan province.

kapi - see SHRIMP PASTE.

kapusta - a name given to various Eastern European dishes that contain cabbage. In Poland, classic kapusta (often called Polish sauerkraut) consists of sliced onions and shredded cabbage, sautéed in butter and seasoned with caraway seeds, salt and pepper, then served with egg noodles and sour cream. In Russia or the Ukraine, however, kapusta could be a soup or stew containing cabbage, carrots and onions, beef or pork, mushrooms and tomatoes — and maybe noodles.

kara age - a Japanese method of dusting cut-up or whole fish, meat, seafood or vegetables with cornstarch, flour or **kuzu,** then deep-frying them.

karhai - see KADHAI.

karhi - a creamy, Indian buttermilk or, more usually, yogurt-based, hot spicy soup often served with dumplings or **pakora.**

karite - see SHEA BUTTER.

kasha - also **buckwheat groats. 1.** toasted and crushed hulled buckwheat seeds that have a nutty texture and taste. Available in fine to coarse grinds, kasha is quick to cook. Only buckwheat groats are called kasha in North America, but in Europe and Russia the term is also used for other types of groats, as well. **2.** a name given to various dishes, many Polish or Russian, that contain kasha. These include porridge and pudding (often sweet and containing dried fruit, nuts and spices), pilaf, soup and stew. Kasha is also mixed with chopped meat and vegetables, then stuffed into cabbage or peppers and roasted.

kashi - see OKASHI.

kashruth - also **kashrut.** Denotes the Jewish dietary laws defining **kosher** ingredients, production methods and consumption practices. Many non-Jews also prefer to purchase kosher food. Some believe it is safer; others, such as Seventh Day Adventists and vegetarians, choose it for religious or philosophical reasons. As a result of this increasing consumer demand, many brand-name products, such as Heinz Tomato Ketchup, have sought and obtained kosher certification.

kashta - also **ashta, eishta, kishta.** A thick, Lebanese clotted cream, the equivalent of the Turkish **kaymak,** made by heating cream or whole milk, then letting it stand until a skin forms on top and it is thick enough to spoon. Kashta is commonly eaten with breakfast or used as a topping or filling for sweets.

kasnudin - a variety of Austrian ravioli, made savory, filled with cheese or meat, or sweet, filled with fruit and spices.

kasseri cheese - a creamy, unsalted Greek pasta filata–type cheese made from ewe's milk (or a mixture of ewe's and goat's milk). Mild and semisoft, it can be eaten on its own, fried in slices in the classic Greek dish, **saganaki,** used to top pizza or as an ingredient in various savory and sweet foods.

kasumi - see JAPANESE KNIVES.

kasutera - a sweet Japanese sponge cake brought to Nagasaki — the only Japanese port open from about 1600 to the mid-1800s — by Portuguese sailing ships. A specialty of the city, it is made with eggs, sugar and white wheat flour and may be flavored with chocolate, honey or green tea.

kataifi - see KADAIF.

katayef - a small, sweet pancake filled with soft, mild cheese or cream and nuts, usually with sweet syrup over top, served as a dessert at the *iftar,* the meal a family shares at nightfall to break the daily fast during the Muslim holy month of Ramadan.

Katenrauchwurst - a firm, dark-skinned German sausage made with coarsely cut smoked pork. *Katen,* which means "peasant huts," is also the name of the German village where it was originally made, hung in the chimneys to be naturally smoked.

kathi roll - also **kathi roll of nizam.** A popular Indian fast food sold by street vendors in such cities as Mumbai (Bombay) and Calcutta, this roll-up, featuring **paratha** bread wrapped around hot, spicy mixtures of chicken, lamb, potato or other vegetables, is now a popular order in North American restaurants as well.

katsu - also **tonkatsu.** Said to be a derivation of the Japanese pronunciation of "cutlet," *katsu* refers to a crunchy slice of something breaded. The term is also used in Hawaii, where boneless chicken is used. **Tonkatsu** is specifically breaded fried pork.

katsudon - see DONBURI.

katsuobushi - shaved dried **bonito,** used in all manner of Japanese dishes, especially as a garnish and as the base for **dashi.**

Katy apple - see APPLE.

kau kau - also **Hawaiian pink bean soup, Portuguese bean soup.** Brought to many Pacific islands by passing sailors, this hearty soup is made with **pink beans,** carrots, chicken stock, **chorizo,** onion, potato and turnip. The name "kau kau" is also a local pidgin term for "food."

kava - Polynesian tree of the pepper family and the name of a beverage made from it, with no relation to coffee, despite the common misconception. It was made from the roots of a giant tree called *Piper methysticum,* but is now illegal on many of the islands because of its hallucinogen content.

kaymak - a Middle Eastern clotted-cream spread made of goat or water buffalo milk. (It is also made in Afghanistan and India.) The milk is simmered until it is covered with a thick layer of clotted cream (the kaymak), which is removed, cooled, then used in baked goods and confections.

kebab - also **kabob.** See SHISH KEBAB.

kecap manis - also **ketjap manis.** A Javanese dense, soy-based, deep brown sauce flavored with garlic and star anise, and sweetened with palm sugar, used in Indonesian cuisine as a basting sauce, condiment, dip, marinade and seasoning. *Kecap,* a designation for various Asian and Indonesian sauces, is the precursor of the word "ketchup." See also KETCHUP.

kedgeree - see SMOKED HADDOCK.

keema - see KHEEMA.

kefalotyri - a pale yellow unpasteurized Greek ewe's or goat's milk "farmhouse" cheese, made since the Byzantine era. Traditionally, the first cheese of the season, it is made with full-cream milk in the spring, just after the young goats or lambs are weaned. Salty and sharp-smelling, it ripens hard enough to grate.

kefir - a fermented, curdled liquid made from cow's, ewe's or goat's milk, originally made from camel milk in the mountains of the Caucasus. With a consistency of drinkable yogurt or soft custard, kefir is a refreshing, if thick sip that contains beneficial **probiotic** bacteria and up to about 2 percent alcohol to boot. Slightly fizzy and sour, it is traditionally flavored with fruit, fruit juice or spices as a drink. It also makes a perfect base for dressings and dips. See also FERMENTED MILK DRINKS.

kefta - also **kefte, kufta.** See KOFTA.

keftedes - see MEATBALL.

Kellogg, Ella Eaton - see profile below.

Kellogg, John Harvey and W.K. - see CORNFLAKES, GRANOLA.

kelp - also **giant sea kelp, haidai, horsetail kelp, kombu. 1.** long-fronded, edible brown seaweed. The two most important types are *Alaria esculenta* and *Laminariaceae*. *Alaria esculenta* (found along cold-water shorelines from New England to Iceland to the Faroes) is used to make candies, jellies and puddings; the ribs, fresh or marinated, are used in salads. The *Laminariaceae* family of giant sea kelp found in the Pacific is harvested by the Chinese (who call it **haidai)** and the Japanese (who call it **kombu**). It is used dried, fresh or marinated, and cooked in stir-fries, soups and stews.

A Buddhist monk is credited with starting the cultivation of kelp off the coast of Japan in the early 1700s. From there to Russia, giant sea kelp, which can grow up to 100 feet (30 m) long, is now farmed along the shoreline on floating rafts and on reefs, where it grows during the winter months. Such a strong market exists that some North American jurisdictions, such as British Columbia, are studying the viability of commercial cultivation as well. Kelp is rich in vitamin C. **2.** the ash obtained by burning the kelp, traditionally used to make iodine and potash. See also KOMBU.

Kendal mint cake - a cake of crystalline candy invented in 1869 by **Joseph Wiper,** a candy maker in Kendal, in England's Lake District. After a moment's inattention by Wiper during the cooking, a clear mixture turned cloudy. The rest is history. Pressed into slabs, this hard peppermint and sugar treat was sold as the original power bar. Nicknamed the "best-traveled candy," it accompanied Earnest Shackleton to the Antarctic in 1914 and climbed up Mount Everest with Edmund Hillary and Tensing Norgay in 1953. Nowadays, white, brown and chocolate-covered versions are available.

Kellogg, Ella Eaton (1853–1920) - American nurse, teacher, author, dietician and home economist, who brought palatability to the Kellogg dietary regime. Kellogg was born in New York State and was the youngest person to graduate with a bachelor's degree from Alfred University in 1872. She met her future husband, Dr. John Harvey Kellogg, in Battle Creek, Michigan, during a family trip, when her sister contracted typhoid fever and was sent to the doctor's famous sanitarium for care. She married him in 1879 and joined him in his health reform movement, taking on the challenge of making his austere diet more flavorful. She studied cooking and spent the next 10 years researching her book, *Science in the Kitchen: A Scientific Treatise on Food Substances and their Dietetic Properties, Together with a Practical Explanation of the Principles of Healthful Cookery, and a large Number of Original, Palatable, and Wholesome Recipes*. She opened a cooking school, which later became the Battle Creek Sanitarium School of Home Economics, where she taught dietetics to nurses. She also wrote *Every-day Dishes and Every-day Work* (1900) and *Studies in Character Building* (1905).

Kennedy, Diana Southwood (early 20th-century–   ) - cooking teacher and cookbook author, who introduced authentic Mexican cooking to the English-speaking world. Born and raised in England, she served in the Women's Timber Corps during the Second World War. While serving in Wales, she remembers savoring the farm fresh food, an experience that triggered her interest in serious eating. While visiting Haiti in 1957, she met and soon married Paul Kennedy, *The New York Times* correspondent for Central America, Mexico and the Caribbean. Their home in Mexico City soon became a mecca for interesting people who arrived for the conversation and left raving about Diana's glorious Mexican food.

She was introduced to the pleasures of Mexican cooking by various members of the household staff, who could cook traditional dishes and taught her the practical skills. A natural researcher, Kennedy began collecting cookbooks, befriended the country's foremost authority on Mexican cuisine and spent many hours poring through his extensive library. When her husband became ill with cancer, they returned to New York. After his death in 1967, **Craig Claiborne,** a visitor to their Mexican home, suggested she open a school to teach Mexican cuisine. She did so and published her first book, *The Cuisines of Mexico*, in 1972.

Linked with the work of **Elizabeth David** and **Jane Grigson,** the book quickly became the definitive work on Mexican cuisine, clearly drawing the line between authentic dishes and the "Tex-Mex" imitations Americans had come to know as Mexican food. A competent writer, Kennedy's real strength is as a culinary anthropologist, who painstakingly documents the ingredients and methods of traditional dishes, as well as the tools and vessels used to make them. She travels around Mexico, identifying the best cooks of particular dishes in every region. Obtaining an invitation into their home, she carefully documents their recipes, gradually building a collection of the country's culinary history. Often criticized for being a purist, she responds, "I make no excuse for being a traditionalist. We have got to know the original recipes as far as we can."

Her five books have been credited with documenting a vital aspect of Mexican culture which otherwise would have been lost. For this she was awarded the Order of the Aztec Eagle, the highest honor bestowed on foreigners by the Mexican government. She has received numerous awards from her peers in the food world, including a 2003 Lifetime Achievement Award from the International Association of Culinary Professionals.

The environment is another of her passions, and her primary residence is an ecologically sustainable abode house surrounded by seven acres of organic gardens in the village of San Francisco Coatepec de Morelos in the province of Michoacan. In 2003, the British government awarded her an MBE (Member of the Order of the British Empire) for her services to the environment, as well as for fostering cultural understanding between Mexico and the United Kingdom.

Kennedy, Diana Southwood - see profile above.

Kentucky burgoo - a grab-bag stew of the American South, usually eaten at an outdoor get-together. Early settlers would have thrown chicken, pork, rabbit and squirrel, along with root vegetables, into the pot; today's cooks may make it with beef, chicken, mutton, pork or veal, and top up the root vegetables with beans, corn, okra, onions and peppers. A **roux** is usually added partway through cooking. Owensboro, Kentucky, called the "center of the burgoo universe," hosts just one of the area's festivals, at which burgoo is sold by the cup or the gallon and served up with slices of bread. See also BURGOO.

Kentucky fire - see MOONSHINE.

Kentucky ham - a famous cooked and cured country ham, made from pigs fattened on acorns, beans, clover and grain. It is dry-salted and smoked with hickory and apple wood, a process that imparts a subtle, distinctive flavor. The ham is left to age for a year after curing. See also COUNTRY HAM, HAM, VIRGINIA HAM.

Kentucky Hot Brown - an open-faced sandwich of slices of bacon, pimientos and turkey arranged on toast, then topped with **Mornay** sauce and broiled. Chef Fred Schmidt created the sandwich for the midnight dinner served to more than 1,000 guests who danced the nights away at the Brown Hotel in Louisville, Kentucky, in the 1920s. The original has spawned versions with asparagus, Cheddar, ham, Parmesan and even gravy.

Kenyan coffee bean - see COFFEE.

kernel - the germ of a seed that may comprise the entire seed of a cereal, such as corn, for example, or the soft core of a fruit, nut or seed that is enclosed by a husk, hull or shell.

Kerner, Justinus - see profile below.

Kerr, Graham - see profile right.

ketchup - also **catchup, catsup.** The ubiquitous, predominantly North American condiment with exotic origins; its name comes from the ancient Chinese sauce called *ke-tsiap;* in many Eastern countries, one can find sauces called *keo-siap, kitjap* or *ketjap*. In the 1800s, English cooks recreated a Malaysian fish sauce and called it *ki chop*. The first known recipe for tomato ketchup was published by immigrant American cook James Mease, who supported the British in the American Revolution and who moved to Nova Scotia. He called the condiment, which he had made in New Jersey prior to 1782, "love apple," which is an affectionate nickname for the tomato or "tomato ketchup." Previous recipes for "ketchup," or "catchup" (from the Malay *kechap*), had been for an unstrained, spicy, soy sauce–based fish sauce. *Cook's Oracle*, a cookbook by London physician William Kitchiner (1775–1827), gives a recipe for "tomata" ketchup, which he called "Wow-Wow Sauce," containing anchovies and strained tomato pulp. The earliest maker of ketchup in the U.S., and certainly now the most well known, was Henry John Heinz, who made the first bottle of Heinz Tomato Ketchup in 1869.

ketjap manis - see KECAP MANIS.

kewra - see PANDAN.

Key lime - small, round, acidic lime named after the Florida Keys, where these limes were first produced circa 1913. Mostly grown in Central America and Mexico now, as well as California and Texas, the Key lime, *Citrus aurantifolia*, is less tart and has a more yellow skin than *C. latifolia*, the so-called Persian or Tahiti lime, which is its main commercial competitor. See also LIME.

Key lime pie - a Key-lime curd pie similar to a lemon meringue pie, but with a graham-cracker crust; it is topped with a swirl of whipped cream.

Khadrawy dates - see DATES.

khandsari - a golden brown Indian sugar made from crystallized, boiled sugarcane juice that is similar to **jaggery,** used by candy makers, bakers

Kerner, Justinus (1786–1862) - German physician and poet who classified 13 cases of food poisoning in 1815 as botulism. Kerner's patients were sick because they ate spoiled sausages, which is why he took the Latin for sausages, *botulus,* as the root of his name for the disease. The number of botulism cases rose dramatically at the beginning of the 19th century, due to poverty and unhygienic food preparation following the Napoleonic wars. In 1817, Kerner published the first report on botulism poisoning. In 1895, Belgian microbiologist Emile Van Ermengem became the first to identify and isolate the toxic bacterium in botulism and name it *Clostridium botulinum*; he had been studying 23 local cases caused by contaminated preserved ham.

The botulinum toxin is the most poisonous substance known to humans. One gram in its crystalline form is toxic enough to kill one million people. It has been a biological weapon since the 1930s, when the Japanese fed it to their prisoners. But just as Kerner predicted in his original report, the toxin has therapeutic uses. Nearly a century later, the toxin was being used to treat muscle hyperactivity disorders. In the U.S. in the 1970s, Dr. Alan Scott tested the toxin to treat crossed or twitching eyes. Dr. Jean Carruthers, a Canadian ophthalmologist, was using Scott's technique in similar therapeutic use when she noticed that the patient's frown lines were greatly reduced. Her dermatologist husband, Dr. Alastair Carruthers, volunteered to have his frown lines and crow's feet injected as part of an experiment to prove that the toxin had cosmetic applications. Carruthers published her findings in 1990, and Botox, the therapeutic toxin's proper name, is now approved for therapeutic and cosmetic use in more than 70 countries.

Kerr, Graham (1934–) - London-born gourmet and television cooking show pioneer. Produced in Ottawa and broadcast for the first time in 1969, Kerr's milestone program was called *The Galloping Gourmet*, named for his exuberant personality and performance style. He liked to enjoy a glass of wine while cooking, and his signature close to the program was a romp into the audience to pull someone onto the set to enjoy the finished meal with him at a table for two. At its peak, the show had an audience of 200 million viewers in 38 countries and was produced by his wife, Treena, his childhood sweetheart. A near-fatal car accident in 1972 marked a religious awakening for Kerr and led to a change in his culinary focus. He began veering away from the rich and decadent preparations that were his trademark, exploring instead healthy, low-fat cooking, which became the focus of his current programs for Christian television.

and home cooks, and to make molasses. It is available, plastic-bagged, in Indian food stores.

kheema - also **keema.** Indian ground meat that may be used as a filling for vegetables, such as onions, or specialties, such as **samosa**s and **biryani.** One of its most common uses is as an ingredient in curry.

kheer - also **khir.** An Indian dessert pudding of rice, milk or cream, sugar, and almonds or pistachios, much the same as North American rice pudding, only creamier in texture and scented with cardamom or rose water.

khubz - Arabic for "bread." See also LAVASH, PITA.

kibbeh - also **kibbee, kibbi, kibee.** A Middle Eastern paste made of pounded **bulgur,** onions, pine nuts and meat (often lamb), which is formed into patties or sausage-like cylinders. It is cooked in different ways, depending on what part of the world it is served in, be it Lebanon, Syria, Egypt, Israel, Iraq or southern Turkey (it also has as many different names). Some countries serve it raw as a sign of good-quality meat and hospitality, while others stew, poach, deep-fry or bake it.

kichel - a traditional Jewish cookie. The simple dough of eggs, flour and sugar is rolled out and cut into diamonds, squares or strips, and sometimes dusted with sugar before baking, during which they puff up like **hanzenblosen.** Kichels vary with their bakers: dough strips may be twisted in the center to make "bow-tie kichel." Poppy seeds may be added to make "moon kichel" (from the German word, *mohn* for "poppy"). "Haman's ears" are kichel dipped in sugar syrup, flavored with cinnamon and rose water, served during the Jewish holiday Purim. "Kichelkies" denotes "little kichel."

kickshaw - a fancy or elegant food; from the French *quelque chose*, meaning "something."

kick-up - see PUNT.

kidney - the fat-coated, curved organ that removes waste from the bloodstream and, along with water, excretes it as urine. Kidneys occur in pairs and may have one or more lobes each; they darken with age and acquire a tougher texture and a stronger smell and taste. Classed as **variety meat,** kidneys from cattle, pigs, poultry, rabbit and sheep are eaten; calves' liver is considered a delicacy. They should be eaten almost immediately after they are purchased. Usually soaked in water first to minimize any odor, then trimmed of fat if necessary, kidneys are cooked slowly by braising, broiling or simmering in pies or stews. They may also be sliced and stir-fried in China, grilled for a full breakfast in England, served on skewers in the Middle East or added to soup in Poland.

kidney bean - a kidney-shaped legume, *Phaseolus vulgaris*, in a variety of colors, ranging from white to light red to dark red, usually dried. Grows in an elongated, straight or slightly curved pod. Originating in Peru, the bean spread throughout South and Central America by migrating Indian traders. The English first used the name "kidney bean" in 1551 to distinguish this New World bean from Old World types. Kidney beans that are white in color are known as **cannellini beans**.

kielbasa - a Polish sausage of ground pork and beef that is garlicky and well seasoned.

kikuna - the edible leaves of a Japanese chrysanthemum, with a distinct fragrance and light, astringent taste.

kikurage - see WOOD EAR.

killed lettuce - see WILTED SALAD.

kimchi - also **kimchee, kim chi.** This spicy, extremely pungent, relish is a common Korean staple. There are two versions: winter kimchi, which is usually made with **Chinese cabbage,** salt, chili and garlic and is allowed to ferment packed into earthenware pots; and summer kimchi, which is made with **daikon,** cucumber and **ogo,** among other vegetables, and is sweeter and not fermented.

kinako - a protein-rich Japanese soy flour made from toasted soy beans, used as a thickener and in baked goods and sweets. See also FLOUR.

King Christian - see DANBO.

kingfish - see WAHOO.

kinoko - a Japanese mushroom, meaning "child of a tree," with a woody fragrance and delicate flavor, usually eaten fresh, but can be dried or canned.

kinoko

kinome - hot, minty and peppery, fresh leaves of the ash tree from which **Szechwan pepper** is harvested, used in Japanese cooking. The whole leaves are also available pickled.

kipfel - traditional European cookie made with dough that usually contains cottage cheese, cream cheese or sour cream. The dough is rolled flat, cut into shapes (most often into triangles) and then a filling, such as apricot preserve, or a mixture of brown sugar, cinnamon and chopped walnuts, is spooned on and the dough is rolled into a crescent and baked.

kipper - **1.** (n.) see HERRING. **2.** (v.) a method of curing herring by slicing it open, then salting and drying or smoking it.

kippered black cod - see SABLEFISH.

kippered salmon - see SMOKED SALMON.

Kir - a cocktail of white wine with a drop of crème de cassis, known as kir royal if made with Champagne. When the Germans occupied France during the Second World War, they confiscated all the red wine available (they preferred the red, because their own country produced mostly white wine). Faced with an overabundance of white wine once the war ended, the mayor of Dijon renovated a popular drink that had previously been made with red wine, promoting its virtues but made with white wine instead. His name was Felix Kir, a monk and hero of the French Resistance.

Kirby cucumber - also **pickling cucumber.** A short cucumber, usually between 3 and 6 inches (7.5 and 15 cm) long, used for pickling and slicing fresh. Unlike larger field cucumbers, the Kirby has waxless skin, so it can be scrubbed and eaten with the peel on, if preferred. It also has soft, small seeds, similar to an English cucumber, so it is an excellent choice for sushi rolls or salads. See also CUCUMBER.

Kirsch - also **kirsch, kirschwasser.** A colorless brandy distilled from cherries, usually aged in a paraffin-lined cask to prevent it from taking on the color of the wood, Kirsch is also another name for cherry **Schnapps,** from German *Kirs* or *Kirsche*, meaning "cherry," and *Wasser*, meaning "water."

kishimen - a Japanese wheat-flour noodle that is a ribbon-type, broad and flat. It is often served in miso broth.

kishka - also **kishke.** A sausage, a Jewish specialty, made with ground meat, flour, onions and matzo meal, stuffed into a casing made from beef intestine. *Kishka* is Yiddish for "intestine." See also DERMA.

kissel - the Polish name for the dessert of red fruits that Germans call **rote Grütze.**

kisses - **1.** small meringues, served in pairs. The more romantic French version, *baiser* (French for "kiss") links the two meringues with buttercream, cream or ice cream. **2.** macaroons, such as the Italian *baci d'Alassio* (Alassio kiss), a chocolate-hazelnut cookie. **3.** a generic term for small, round toffees or boiled hard candies. **4.** the trademarked, teardrop chocolate Hershey Kisses that are wrapped in foil.

kitchen bridage system - see BRIDAGE SYSTEM.

kitchen shears - general-purpose scissors with heavy-duty, often toothed blades, and handles that may incorporate bottle and jar openers. The blades are sharp enough to cut through fine herbs, parchment paper or twine, and sturdy enough to slice through small bones. Specialized versions, such as lobster and poultry shears, are also available.

kiwano

kiwano - also **African horned cucumber, African horned melon, jelly melon.** Brilliant red-orange fruit, shaped like a hand grenade with menacing thorns, the kiwano is bright kelly green inside, with jelly-like pulp evocative of banana and lime and seeds resembling those of a cucumber. Originally grown in the deserts of southwest Africa, they became popular with New Zealand growers just over 60 years ago. Today, Florida is also a popular growing region. New Zealanders consider kiwano pulp to be the ultimate thirst quencher.

kiwifruit - also **Chinese gooseberry.** This sour, egg-size, brown fruit, *Actinidia chinensis*, has hairy skin, lime green pulp and tiny black seeds,

kiwifruit

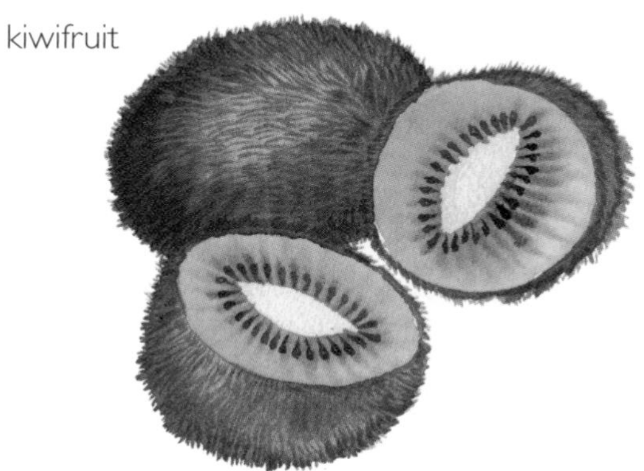

and is available from midsummer to winter. In the courts of the great khans of southern China, they called it *yang tao* and held it in high esteem. In the 19th century, the British cultivated it under the name "Chinese gooseberry," having brought the fruit vines to New Zealand, where they tried to sell it, unsuccessfully, under that name. In the late 1960s, the fruit was named after New Zealand's native bird, the apteryx, whose nickname was "kiwi," but only after considering the following names: monkey peach, sheep peach, yang tao and Ichang gooseberry. An American GI stationed Down Under during the Second World War grew fond of the fuzzy brown fruit and took it back with him to the U.S., and it wasn't long before kiwifruit became a major crop for California, and now Florida and Texas as well. Modern yellow varieties have recently been marketed in North America.

Klopse - see MEATBALL.

kluski - narrow, but thick Polish egg noodles, 1 to 4 inches (2.5 to 10 cm) long, commonly used in **kapusta.**

knäckerbröd - see CRISPBREAD.

Knackwurst - also **Knockwurst.** From the German *Knacken*, meaning "to crackle," Knackwurst is a highly seasoned sausage usually made short and thick. See also FRANKFURTER.

knafeh - see KADAIF.

knaidel - see MATZO BALL.

knead - a method of pressing, folding and stretching dough to develop the flour's **gluten,** which, along with yeast and other leavening agents, causes dough to rise.

kneaded butter - see BEURRE MANIÉ.

knife - first used in Palestine about 10,000 BC in the form of a reaping knife with a flint blade. The knife had its beginning as a tool and weapon and was not used as an eating utensil until man discovered how to make fire. In the Middle Ages, people brought their own utensils to the table. Early knives were like daggers, with two sharp edges for cutting and a sharp point for spearing food and bringing it to the mouth. In the 17th century, King Louis XIV of France, wanting to discourage violence while dining, decreed it illegal for anyone to carry a pointed dinner knife, for cutlers to make them or for innkeepers to serve them. The king also ordered that all table knives be made with rounded ends. Others say it was the French religious and political leader Cardinal de Richelieu, who, in the same century, was responsible for the knife's new design because he couldn't stand the sight of a frequent guest picking his teeth with the sharp end. See also BONING KNIFE, BREAD KNIFE, BUTCHER KNIFE, BUTTER KNIFE, CANNELLE KNIFE, CARVING KNIFE, CHEESE KNIVES, CHEF'S KNIFE, CHESTNUT KNIFE, CLAM KNIFE, FILLETING KNIFE, GRAPEFRUIT KNIFE, JAPANESE KNIVES, PARING KNIFE, SERRATED KNIFE.

knish - a Jewish pastry, a little dumpling filled with a variety of fillings including chicken livers, mashed potatoes, **kasha,** cabbage and ground beef. In the U.S., the pastry is potato or egg-based, while in France, where it's known as **pirozhski,** the dough is often made with yeast or a puff pastry.

knob celery - see CELERIAC.

Knoblauchwurst - a strong, German garlic sausage made with fat and lean pork.

knockwurst - see KNACKWURST.

knotroot - see CHINESE ARTICHOKE.

Kobe beef - named for the port from which they were once shipped, although they've never been raised there. This exclusive beef is very expensive and exquisitely tender, because the beef is raised without exercise (so the muscles don't toughen), in darkness, given hot feed in winter, usually beer mash, and massaged daily to distribute the weight and give the flesh perfect marbling. The cattle used for Kobe beef are from the Japanese **Wagyu** breed, but even costlier are the Wadakin and Matsuzaka breeds, which are very rare. They are raised in Mie Prefecture in Japan, about 1½ hours from Mount Fuji.

kobacha squash - also **hoka squash, Japanese pumpkin, kabocha squash.** A spherical dark green squash mottled with lighter green, which is usually harvested when it's between 3 and 4 pounds (1.4 to 2 kg). A longtime staple in Japanese kitchens, it is eaten at the winter solstice (called *toji*) to ensure good health in the coming year. The firm and sweet golden flesh is good simply baked, simmered or steamed. It can also be added to soups or stews, or puréed for sweet breads, cakes and pies. Uncut and stored in a cool place, kobocha squash can be kept for about two months.

kobucha - a Japanese tea made by steeping powdered, dried **kombu,** a type of edible **kelp.** Kobucha may be homemade or prepared with a ready-made mix.

kofta - also **kafta, kefta, kefte, kufte.** Meatballs made from several cultures, notably India, Afghanistan, Pakistan and the Middle East. The term may have come from the Persian word *koffteh*, meaning ground meat. The seasoning, binder and cooking style varies among cultures. Kofta may be deep-fried, grilled on a skewer, braised, poached in a curry or tomato sauce, sautéed in oil or steamed. Occasionally, balls made from ground fish or vegetables, such as potatoes or chickpeas, are identified as "kofta," but this is not traditional. In the Middle East, a sticky mixture of egg, chopped mint and ground lamb (spiced with allspice, cinnamon, chili powder, cumin and turmeric) may be formed around a skewer. In Azarbaijan, soccerball-size *koofteh Tabrizi* may be shaped around a center of dried fruit and nuts. In India, they are called *kofta nargisi*. Egg yolk, ground meat and minced onion spiced with **garam masala,** ground cloves, cumin, ginger and turmeric may be mixed into a paste with **besan** and yogurt, then shaped into balls around hard-boiled eggs. The cooked meatballs open to reveal the white and yellow "narcissus" at the center, for which they are named.

kohana fu - crisp, slightly spongy, air-dried Japanese wheat-gluten dough, formed into tiny, flower shapes and sometimes tinted with color. They can be added to soups, stews and vegetable dishes. Kohana fu are sold by themselves in plastic bags or included in instant soup mixes.

kohlrabi - German for "cabbage turnip." It takes its name from the Greek *kohl*, "kale" and the Latin *rapa*, or "turnips" and aptly so because it is a crossbreed of these two vegetables, a favorite

kohlrabi

of Eastern Europeans, Germans and Asians. It's also a newcomer as far as vegetables go, less than 500 years old, and also one of the few that originated in northern Europe. Rumor has it that kohlrabi came from Asia with Attila the Hun. It was first described in 1554, and by the end of the 1500s was known in Germany, England, Italy and Spain. Records of its cultivation in the U.S. go back to 1806. It's not a root, but actually a swollen rhizome, like ginger that is globe-shaped with green stems and leaves that jut out on all sides. They may be green or red, like beets, with red-veined leaves. In the garden, one of the most amazing things — and one of the motives for growing kohlrabi — is that a few plants of the fragrant blooms discourage more garden pests than a pint of malathion (a common chemical found in nurseries to eliminate garden pests). In France, it's called *chou-rave*, in Italy *cavalo rapa*, in Spain *colinabo*, in Russia *kohlrabbe*, in Denmark, *kaalrabi*, and in Portugal, *cove rabano*.

koji - a Japanese yeast-like starter used to ferment **miso, sake** and soy sauce, among other things. Koji is made by combining a steamed grain or legume with *Aspergillus oryzae* mold and allowing it to ferment for a number of days. The koji is then added to other ingredients, where it begins the fermentation necessary to produce the finished product. The type of grain or legume used in the koji depends on the product it will be used to create: sake koji is made with rice; miso koji is made with rice, barley or soybeans; and soy sauce koji is made from a combination of ground roasted wheat and soybeans.

kola nut - see COLA NUT.

kombu - a popular Japanese dried kelp that, along with **bonito,** is a key ingredient in **dashi,** a soup stock, or to infuse for a tea-like drink. Because it's a seaweed, it must be washed before using to remove the saltiness and to soften it.

kome miso - see MISO.

konnyaku - see ARUM ROOT.

kopi luwak - the most expensive kind of coffee in the world (hundreds of dollars per pound) and a recent fad among well-heeled coffee aficionados, this is a whole coffee cherry that has been eaten and passed undigested through the digestive tract of the common palm civet, a small furry animal that lives on the coffee plantations in Sumatra, Java and Sulawesi in Indonesia. The coffee cherry emerges in the animal's excrement with the majority of the inner layers of the cherry protecting the bean inside, which is then extracted and roasted. Connoisseurs of the brew claim that the digestive enzymes in the civet's gut ferment the coffee bean, giving it a unique, rich flavor with notes of caramel and chocolate (called "musty" and "earthy" by its detractors). The name comes from the Indonesian words for coffee (*kopi*) and civet (*luwak*).

korma - also **kurmah. 1.** an Indian technique for braising. In a heavy pot with a tight-fitting lid, meat is braised over very low heat in a minimum amount of liquid (water, stock, yogurt, cream or any combination thereof may be used). Traditionally, the pot is sealed with a flour and water paste and is shaken several times during cooking to ensure that the ingredients are adequately basted. Upon completion, the meat is removed, and the sauce is embellished with a mixture or *bhogar* of ghee and complementary aromatics. Vegetables may also be prepared using this method. **2.** dish cooked by the korma method, consisting of meat and/or vegetables, aromatics and a small amount of liquid.

korma curry paste - see CURRY PASTE.

Kroc, Ray (1902–1984) - American entrepreneur and founder of McDonald's Corporation, the world's largest quick-service restaurant company. When he met Earl Prince, the inventor of the five-spindled milkshake mixer, Kroc was a paper cup salesman and Prince was one of his customers. Seeing an opportunity, Kroc bought exclusive marketing rights to sell the Multimixer across the country, which he did for 34 years. In his travels, Kroc met Dick and Mac, the McDonald brothers, who bought eight mixers. They ran a busy walk-up restaurant in San Bernardino, California, at a time when the fashion was to be served at your car in the parking lot. Kroc was impressed with the restaurant's economy and the idea of serving a limited menu at the lowest possible price. In 1954, at 52, Kroc became the brother's National Franchise Agent, and a year later created McDonald's System, Inc., the predecessor of McDonald's Corporation, and in 1961, bought out the brothers.

kosher - from the Hebrew *kasher,* meaning "pure," referring to the strict Jewish dietary laws known as *Kashruth*, which govern the selection, butchery, preparation and consumption of food. The law permits the eating of poultry, fish with scales and the flesh from the forequarters of quadrupeds that chew their cud and have cloven feet, such as sheep and cattle. Pork and shellfish are forbidden. Slaughter must be carried out by a certified kosher butcher, called a *shochet*, in a special ritual involving prayer. Meat and dairy must be prepared separately, using separate cookware and utensils, eaten on separate tableware and never at the same meal.

kosher salt - see SALT

koumiss - also **kumiss.** A mildly alcoholic beverage that originated in Mongolia, reportedly drunk by Genghis Khan, made at that time with camel's milk, now made with mare's. See also FERMENTED MILK DRINKS.

koya-dofu - also **freeze-dried tofu.** See TOFU.

kra chai - also **krachai.** See FINGERROOT.

kreplach - a small Jewish dumpling with a savory filling, often served in soup. They are traditionally eaten on Purim, Rosh Hashanah and the day before Yom Kippur.

kringel - a traditional Estonian or Latvian cake, made with saffron and often shaped as a pretzel, served on special family occasions.

Kroc, Ray - see profile above.

kroepoek - also **krupuk.** See SHRIMP CHIP.

kromesky - also **cromesky.** A sort of fritter made from a **salpicon** or **croquette** mixture of fish, game or fowl, shaped into corks, then either rolled in thin pastry or battered and then fried. An oyster kromesky is an oyster dried with a cloth, wrapped with a thin slice of bacon, pinned with a toothpick, dipped in batter and fried.

krumkake - also **krumcake.** A thin, Scandinavian cookie, sometimes spiced with cardamom, that is baked in a krumkake iron (similar to an Italian **pizelle** maker), which impresses it with an intricate, embossed design. While still warm, the krumkake is rolled into a cone around a special krumkake pin, traditionally made of wood.

krupnik - also **krupnick. 1.** a thick Polish soup, often made with chicken stock and garnished with sour cream. It may include chunks of chicken, turkey giblets, smoked meat, white beans, cabbage, carrots, potatoes or zucchini, but it will always include lots of grain (usually barley, buckwheat or oatmeal). **2.** a Polish drink served warm in the winter and popular since the 1300s, made from wild-bee honey, vodka or whiskey, spices (usually cinnamon, cloves and nutmeg) and citrus zest. **3.** a brand-name liqueur produced in Poland, flavored with honey and spices.

krupuk gendar - ready-to-cook, Indonesian or Malaysian rice crackers.

krupuk udang - a Malaysian or Indonesian shrimp-flavored cracker made with tapioca flour that puffs up when deep-fried, eaten as a snack or served with rice or stir-fries. See also SHRIMP CHIP.

ku chai - see GARLIC CHIVES.

Kuchen - German for "cake." See also CAKE.

kudzu - also **mile-a-minute plant.** The Chinese have known this vine, *Pueraria lobat*, for more than 2,000 years, using every part of it: for human consumption, livestock feed and paper production. Kudzu roots yield a starch that can substitute for arrowroot and used like gelatin in confections; they are also an exceptional fertilizer, due to their high nitrogen content. The tender leaves are eaten like spinach. The plant was first introduced to the U.S. by the Japanese in 1883, at the New Orleans exposition, and was adopted very rapidly, first as a shade plant and soon after as a cattle food and in confectionery. Before long, the name was changed to "mile-a-minute plant," because it can grow more than a foot a day. In Japan, a decoction made from the roots is used as a powerful and efficient remedy for hangover.

kufta - See KOFTA.

kugel - German for "ball," "bowl" and "orb," kugel denotes pudding in Jewish cookery. Savory versions, made with eggs, onions and potatoes or rice (and sometimes cheese, chicken fat or sour cream) are a typical Sabbath dish. Sweet kugels, made with eggs, egg noodles, and fresh or dried fruit, nuts and spices, are served as desserts.

kugelhopf - also **gugelhopf, gugelhupf, kugelhupf.** An airy, rich yeast cake, with lemon zest, raisins (some cooks soak them in rum first) and maybe candied fruit and nuts. Baked in a tall **ring mold,** it is turned out and sprinkled with icing sugar. In Alsace, considered its birthplace, this cake is baked on Saturday to eat at Sunday breakfast, but is also enjoyed with afternoon coffee or tea throughout Europe.

kuih - a generic term for sweet, Malaysian cakes.

kulfi - Indian ice cream made with milk and cream that have been cooked down until thickened and significantly reduced (rather than being thickened with eggs like North American ice cream), usually poured into cone-shaped molds and frozen, rather than churned in an ice cream maker. At its most traditional, kulfi is flavored with saffron and pistachio nuts, sometimes with a pinch of cardamom added for heady fragrance and taste. Another well-loved, common flavor is mango, often seen in Indian restaurants in North America.

kulich - a tall Russian Easter cake, containing candied fruits, nuts and saffron — rich treats that celebrate the end of Lent. Baked in a container, such as a coffee tin, the cake rises up and over the rim; the rounded top is often cut off and centered on a platter, then slices of the cake are arranged around it. It is served with **paskha,** a molded, sweet cheese mixture, and hard-boiled eggs. Traditionally, the kulich and paskha were carried to church to be blessed by the priest.

kulith - see HORSE GRAM.

kuminost - see NÖKKELOST CHEESE.

kumiss - see KOUMISS.

kümmel - a homemade or ready-made clear liqueur flavored with caraway seeds. Bottled versions — made in France, Germany, Holland (where it originated) and Russia — may also be flavored with additional spices, such as anise, cloves, cumin and fennel, and usually have a **grain-alcohol** base (homemade versions often use vodka).

Kump, Peter - see profile on page 368.

kumquat - similar to a miniature orange, but not a citrus fruit, of the genus *Fortunella,* orange and oval, the size of an olive. Kumquats are sour tasting, but are edible including the rind. The shrubby kumquat tree is native to China and is valued there because it is resistant to cold and grows farther north than any other citrus-like tree. Also grown in Japan and the U.S. The name comes from the Cantonese *chin kan,* meaning "golden mandarin." Probably because

kumquat

Kump, Peter (1938–1995) - American cooking teacher who founded his own cooking school in New York City in 1975. Kump was born and raised on a ranch in Fresno, California, and was introduced to fine cuisine at 15, when he moved with his family to Switzerland. He returned to the U.S. to study speech and drama at Stanford University, and earned a master's degree in drama at Carnegie Mellon, which was also, coincidentally, where **James Beard** studied drama. Kump had financed his education by teaching Evelyn Wood's speed-reading technique, and in the late 1960s, Wood's company made Kump national director in New York City. One of his first assignments was to teach speed-reading to Richard Nixon's White House staff, some of whom would later be indicted for their involvement in the Watergate scandal. Around this time, Kump took a class with James Beard and found that he had natural abilities. Like Beard, who became a lifelong friend, Kump gave classes from his home and officially opened Peter Kump's New York Cooking School in 1975. He developed a professional program for aspiring chefs in 1983, inviting his own esteemed teachers to give classes, including Beard, **Marcella Hazan** and **Diana Kennedy.** He became the founding president of the James Beard Foundation, established in Beard's honor to celebrate achievements in culinary excellence, which Kump promoted tirelessly throughout his life.

of its funny name, W.C. Fields used it in one of his most infamous lines: "How about a kumquat, my little chickadee?" See also CALAMONDIN.

kung pao - also **kung pao ming ha.** A literal translation for "crown prince," this traditional dish from Shanghai is made of chicken or shrimp, horse beans, chili sauce, sugar and crushed Szechwan peppercorns, named by the prince in whose honor the dish was made while he traveled through the region.

kuro goma - the Japanese term for whole, black sesame seed. See also GOMA, SESAME.

kutya - a traditional Christmas Eve dish long enjoyed in Russia and the Ukraine, consisting of a **wheat-berry mush** cooked with honey and poppy seeds, then served cool with sherry and sliced candied cherries and almonds. The wheat berries symbolize hope and long life; the honey lends happiness. A spoonful of kutya is flung at the ceiling; if it sticks, the household can expect the next harvest to be generous.

kuzu - the starch derived from the tuberous roots of **kudzu** vines, which are native to Japan. Used to thicken sauces, soups and stews, it adds luster as well. It is also an ingredient in a type of Japanese noodle.

kvas - a fermented beverage made by the Proto-Slavs as early as 2,000 years ago. The basic recipe calls for mixing dried bread crumbs with hot water and then adding a sugar solution and yeast for fermentation, during which it's flavored with raisins, mint, juniper, wormwood, honey and, although rarely, hops. For a more upscale market, kvas was flavored with bilberries, Morello cherries, currants, apples, lemons, pears, raspberries and loganberries. Kvas is still produced in northern Russia, using rye bread crumbs, and is usually delivered in cistern trucks, from which people buy it directly on street corners or in markets.

1
lime

Lachance, Fernand - see POUTINE.

La Chapelle, Vincent - see profile below.

lactic acid - produced in milk products when certain kinds of bacteria react to the milk's **lactose,** the acid partially responsible for the sour taste of yogurt; also used in the production of pickles and sauerkraut.

lactic curd cheese - see ACID CURD CHEESE.

lactose - also **milk sugar.** The least sweet of all sugars, occurring naturally in milk. It is difficult to digest by people whose systems lack the lactase enzyme. See also MILK.

lacto vegetarian - see VEGETARIAN.

laddu - also **ladoo.** A festive Indian sweet. **Besan** or coarsely ground wheat flour or rice flour is cooked in **ghee,** then mixed with sugar, spices and, sometimes, grated coconut or ground nuts, and shaped into balls, which may be rolled in poppy or sesame seeds. Enjoyed on special occasions, laddu are also given as dowry gifts to the groom's family and prepared as offerings to the Hindu god Ganesha.

ladle - **1.** (n.) a spoon with a long handle and a generous bowl. Small versions are used with gravies and sauces. Glass or clear plastic ladles are used to portion out eggnog or punch. Large ladles, with handles attached straight up from their bowls, are designed to dip into deep stockpots and serve up soups or stews; some have angled handle tips, which hook over the pot rims. **2.** (v.) to serve food using a ladle.

ladle

ladoo - see LADDU.

Lady apple - see APPLE.

Lady Baltimore cake - an airy, multi-layered white cake, lightened with five egg whites. It is filled with a rich mixture of frosting and chopped figs, pecans, raisins and orange zest, and topped with frothy white icing. Named after a fictional heroine, the cake first appeared in Owen Wister's 1906 novel, *Lady Baltimore*, set after the Civil War in the South. A recipe for the cake was developed post-novel, and the Lady Baltimore became a favorite Southern wedding cake. See also LORD BALTIMORE CAKE.

ladyfinger - a small, light, delicate sponge biscuit, approximately 3 inches (7.5 cm) long and 1 inch (2.5 cm) wide, often used in making desserts, such as **charlottes** or **tiramisu.** In France, a biscuit that is a simple sponge cake or jelly roll, known as *biscuit à la cuillère*, may sometimes be referred to as a ladyfinger. In Italy, they are called *savoiardi*, but they are twice as thick. In England, okra is also known as ladyfinger.

lady finger banana - see BABY BANANA.

lager - a light, golden type of beer very popular in North America, brewed at lower temperatures than ale, so that the bottom-fermenting yeasts grow slowly. These beers were originally put in casks for one to three months and aged (lagered), but now can be made faster using modern refrigeration methods. See also BEER.

lagniappe - also **lagnappe.** A term used in Louisiana and other Gulf states to describe a complimentary "little something extra" given to the diner or customer by a server or shopkeeper, or, conversely, an extra gratuity given by the customer to the server. The word derives from the Spanish *la nãpa*, meaning "the gift," and came originally from the word *yapay*, meaning "to give more" from the Quechua Indian language of South America.

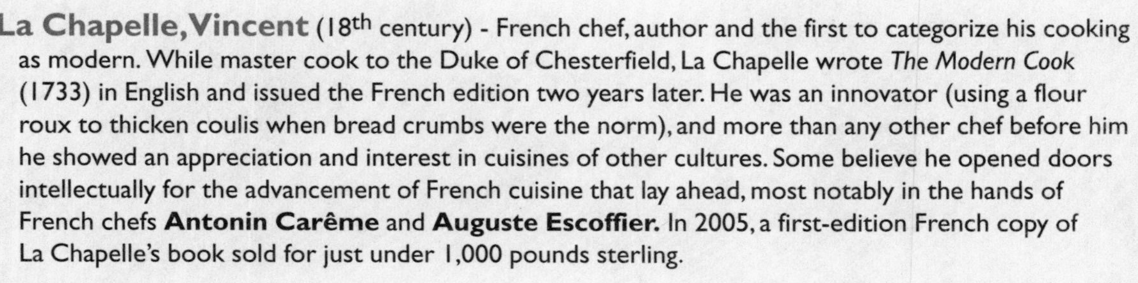

La Chapelle, Vincent (18th century) - French chef, author and the first to categorize his cooking as modern. While master cook to the Duke of Chesterfield, La Chapelle wrote *The Modern Cook* (1733) in English and issued the French edition two years later. He was an innovator (using a flour roux to thicken coulis when bread crumbs were the norm), and more than any other chef before him he showed an appreciation and interest in cuisines of other cultures. Some believe he opened doors intellectually for the advancement of French cuisine that lay ahead, most notably in the hands of French chefs **Antonin Carême** and **Auguste Escoffier.** In 2005, a first-edition French copy of La Chapelle's book sold for just under 1,000 pounds sterling.

lahvosh - see LAVASH.

lait - French for "milk."

lake sturgeon - see STURGEON.

Lake Superior herring - see CISCO.

lake trout - also **Mackinaw trout, salmon trout.** The largest trout, *Salvelinus namaycush*. This predatory fish is native to the Great Lakes and other cold, northern fresh waters. Considered a good catch — commercially and for sport — lake trout is so popular with anglers, as well as diners, that it was introduced into California's Lake Tahoe in the 1880s. A so-called "fat lake trout," known as a "siscowet," can be caught in the deepest water of Lake Superior; it is eaten only after it is smoked.

laksa - a popular Southeast Asian noodle soup that features seafood or chicken, fiery red chiles, a fragrant spice paste of garlic, lemongrass, ginger, turmeric and cilantro, and rich coconut milk. It is a popular street food, and every vendor has his own version of the soup. The name comes from the Persian *lakhsha*, meaning "slippery." It is thought that the slippery noodles used in the soup originated in Persia, and that they and their name migrated to Southeast Asia along trade routes from the Middle East.

laksa leaf - see VIETNAMESE MINT.

lamb - sheep graded according to age: **baby lamb** is milk-fed and 6 to 8 weeks old; **spring lamb,** also milk-fed, is 3 to 5 months old; **lamb** is 5 to 12 months old; **yearlings** are between 1 and 2 years old; **mutton** is any sheep slaughtered after 2 years of age. Young lamb is favored for its sweet, pink flesh, which darkens in color and strengthens in flavor with age. Teeth are also used to gage a lamb's age. Young lambs have not yet grown their first two incisors, also known as nippers, while yearlings have grown these first two permanent teeth. Lamb is best roasted or broiled, because of its high fat content, which provides a tremendous amount of flavor, adding to the distinctive taste of the meat. (For Cuts of Lamb see below.) See also TEMPERATURE.

Lambert cherry

Lambert cherry - a black-fleshed, heart-shaped, sweet cherry, best eaten fresh, but also used in cooking. It was developed in 1875 by Oregon grower Seth Lewelling (the same man responsible for the **Bing cherry**). Still grown in Oregon, it is also cultivated throughout other northwestern states, particularly in Washington. Trees take about six years to start producing, but can continue to do so for decades. See also CHERRY.

CUTS OF LAMB

breast - a long cut including ribs from the foresection, sometimes sold boneless and served stuffed.

breast riblets - long cuts from the breast, including ribs, usually braised.

crown rack - also **crown roast.** The entire rib section tied into a ring, the bones from the chops giving the appearance of a crown.

leg - the sirloin section with the hipbone, shank and round bone, with a covering of **fell,** a thin white membrane that must be removed before cooking.

leg shank half - the sirloin half removed, leaving the lower half of the leg and the round bone.

leg sirloin chop - the backbone and some hipbone.

loin chop - part of the backbone, can also be pan-fried.

rack lamb roast - see RIB ROAST.

rack of lamb - also **rib chop, rack lamb chop.** The backbone and sometimes rib bone.

rib roast - also **rack lamb roast.** Includes the ribs and backbone.

shank - a cut from the foreleg or shoulder containing the leg bone and a section of the shoulder bone, usually braised.

shoulder arm chop - the cross section of the front round bone and rib bones, usually braised.

Lambic beer - a dry, fruity wheat beer made exclusively in the Senne Valley, just west of Brussels, spontaneously fermented by the wild indigenous yeasts, *Brettanomyces bruxellensis* and *B. lambicus*, unique to the area's grain. The beer is "young" until its first birthday and "old" after no less than "two summers." Young lambic is often sour and flat but, in time, will mellow and become carbonated from a secondary fermentation in the bottle. **Gueuze** lambics are a legally regulated blend of two parts young lambic to one part old lambic, with the ability to age well for up to two years. **Faro** lambics have been sweetened with sugar or caramel. See also BEER.

lambrusco - **1.** A type of light, often sparkling Italian wine grown in the Emilia-Romagna region in the north. *Amabile* (sweet) or *secco* (dry), wines are available in red, rosé and white, and are usually enjoyed at a tender age. Some connoisseurs say that producers switched from quality to quantity in the late 1900s, in their rush to satisfy a surging North American appetite for lambrusco wines; these wineries are now rebuilding their reputations. **2.** the grape variety from which lambrusco wines are made.

lamb's lettuce - see MÂCHE.

Lamington - a small square of sponge cake dipped in melted chocolate and rolled in coconut, a typical treat in Australia, usually served with afternoon tea. In the city of Victoria, Australia, Lamingtons are often made with a layer of raspberry or plum jam. So popular are these tiny treats that Australian schools and women's organizations often have Lamington drives to raise money.

The origin of the Lamington is a topic of some debate. Among those claiming credit are the Scots, who say that a sheep shearer's wife in the village of Lamington first made this cake for a group of itinerant sheep shearers. New Zealanders also claim credit for inventing the tiny cakes, citing their town of Leamington as the source. And, of course, the Australians also lay claim to the Lamington, attributing it to Charles Wallace Baillie, Lord Lamington, the governor of Queensland from 1895 to 1901. Lord Lamington was known for wearing a hat that looked like the cake, which may have inspired its invention. During Lord Lamington's tenure, the cakes were often served at formal state occasions in Queensland, much to the governor's chagrin. He hated them and frequently referred to them as "those bloody, poofy, woolly biscuits." Other sources say that Lamingtons were created simply to disguise stale sponge cake.

lamon bean - a thin-skinned tender bean, a large variety of **borlotti,** grown in the Lamon plateau of Italy's Veneto region, their production safeguarded by a number of mountain communities who oversee their seeding. The lamon bean was, among other things, part of **Catherine de' Medici**'s dowry in her marriage to Henry II.

Lampong peppercorns - see PEPPERCORNS.

lamprey - a scaleless, eel-like fish, with a suctorial mouth, inhabiting both fresh and salt water, considered a delicacy, getting its name from the Latin *lambro*, meaning "to lick," and *petra*, meaning "stone."

Lancashire - a white, softy, crumbly English cheese made from milled, salted and pressed curd, ripened between two and three months. It's similar to white Cheshire, and Cheshire is sometimes sold as Lancashire.

Lancashire hot pot - see HOTCHPOTCH.

landgang - see JARLSBERG.

landjager - a Bavarian-style pressed, smoked and dried sausage, containing beef, pork and seasonings, such as caraway seeds, coriander and nutmeg, usually stuffed inside a **natural casing.** It is also produced and popular in North America, especially in the Midwest. Unopened, it needs no refrigeration, so it's a good take-along food for campers, backpackers, hikers and hunters.

Lane cake - a four-tiered white cake made with eight eggs. The egg whites go into the cake batter; the yolks combine with sugar, butter and pecans, and chopped candied and dried fruits (along with a dash of bourbon) to make the filling between the layers. Emma Rylander Lane from Clayton, Alabama, created the cake, which won a contest at the state fair. Lane published the recipe in her 1898 cookbook *Some Good Things to Eat* calling it "Prize Cake."

langostino - Spanish for "prawn." See also LANGOUSTINE.

langouste - see LOBSTER.

langoustine - also **Dublin Bay prawn, Norwegian lobster, scampi.** The French name for *Nephrops norvegicus*. These pink prawns are an important commercial species to Europe, especially in the northeastern Atlantic fisheries. The meat tastes like that of lobster and is concentrated in the tail section (the claws contain almost none); it is usually cooked quickly and can be prepared **en papillote,** grilled, poached or in paella. In Britain, the breaded tails are famous as "scampi." Some chefs scoop out the contents of the head to make a sauce. Out of water, this prawn doesn't keep well, so it's often cooked before it's sold. Whether it's fresh or frozen, uncooked langoustine is best used soon after it's purchased. Its sustained popularity has swollen its harvest by large trawlers, which has led to concerns for the stock and conservation efforts to limit the damage caused to the seabed.

langue-de-chat - see CAT'S TONGUE.

Laos ginger - see GALANGAL.

Laos powder - a ready-made seasoning of finely ground, dried galangal, used mainly in Asian, Indonesian, Malaysian and Thai dishes, such as marinades, sauces, soups, stews and stir-fries. See also GALANGAL.

lap cheong - also **Chinese sausage, lap chong, lap chung.** Coarse-textured, thin, red Chinese pork sausage, usually air-dried rather than smoked, which resembles pepperoni but tastes sweeter. Traditionally, these are made with cinnamon, sugar, soy sauce and, sometimes, Chinese wine.

lapin - French for "rabbit."

Lappi - a Finnish semisoft, sweet cheese, peppered with small holes, which is named after its place of origin, Lapland. A good "melting cheese," it's creamy and delicious in a fondue pot.

Lapsang Souchong - see TEA.

larb - a spicy, Thai meat salad. Minced beef, chicken, duck or pork (an exotic Australian version is made with kangaroo) is stir-fried and cooled, then tossed with such ingredients as chile paste, fish sauce and lime juice, chopped fresh chile pepper, garlic, onion, coriander and mint leaves. The mixture is served on a bed of rice, usually with a fresh green, such as shredded cabbage, on the side.

langoustine

lard - firm, pure-white clarified fat rendered from pork fat, which is often used for deep-frying and as an ingredient in baked goods. **Leaf lard,** derived from fat in the abdominal cavity and particularly surrounding the kidneys, is considered the highest quality. To lower their dietary fat, some bakers use butter (or half butter, half lard) in their pastry; others, who are vegetarian or keep a kosher kitchen, use shortening (a vegetable fat) instead of lard. Many still swear, however, that lard makes the flakiest pastry. See also SHORTENING.

larding - to sew long, thin strips of pork fat, called **lardons** or lardoons, into lean pieces of meat to keep them succulent and flavorful during cooking, giving them an attractive marbling effect. The technique is most frequently used for fillet of beef or veal, and for venison. The lardons are sewn, evenly spaced, into the meat, using a **larding needle.**

larding needle - also **lardoire.** A long, hollow metal skewer with a pointed tip. Thin strips of fat or bacon, called **lardon,** are threaded through the needle, then the needle is pushed through lean meat or fowl to insert the fat.

lardoire - see LARDING NEEDLE.

lardon - also **lardoon. 1.** thin strips of fat used for larding, generally about 1½ inches (4 cm) long and ¼ inch (1 cm) wide. **2.** bacon cut into short strips, blanched and then fried, often used in stews, casseroles and salads.

large clam - also **quahog.** See CLAM.

lasagna - pl. **lasagne.** A noodle and a dish of these flat noodles made with cheese, tomato sauce and sometimes meat and vegetables, called *lasanum* by the ancient Romans, consisting, at that time, of strips of dough baked on a flat surface. Since lasagna requires an oven, which for most of Italian history was found only in the kitchens of the wealthy, the dish was considered to be lavish and for special occasions. By the 19th century, lasagna became widely popular in Italy as well as in America. However, the name's origin is not too appetizing: in ancient Greece, *lasanon* was a "chamber pot" or, as one Greek lexicon puts it, a "night chair." The Romans picked up on this word and later jokingly applied their version of it, *lasanum*, to a large cooking pot, which eventually give way to the modern Italian name for this hearty dish. See also PASTA.

lassi - see FERMENTED MILK DRINKS.

late harvest - a term used to describe apples, grapes (and the wines made from them) or other produce picked late in the season. Late-harvest apples, such as Granny Smith and Golden Delicious, take until autumn to ripen and are almost always firm-fleshed and good keepers; while russet apples are considered best picked after they have been mellowed by a hard frost. Late-harvest white wines are made from grapes affected by **noble rot** (the mold *Botrytis cinerea)*. Slightly shriveled by the time they are harvested, these grapes are sweet, and so are their wines.

latke - a crisp, golden "pancake" made from matzo meal, coarsely grated onions and potatoes tossed with beaten eggs, then fried in oil. Usually latkes are simply seasoned with salt and pepper. A tradition for the Jewish holiday Hanukkah, they arrive at the table piping hot, with applesauce and sour cream served on the side.

latte - Italian for "milk" and a common short-form name for the relatively new term "caffé latte." If you had ordered "latte" 30 years ago in a café or restaurant, you might simply have been served a glass of milk.

latte macchiato - hot, frothed milk with a splash of espresso "staining" it. The opposite of a **caffè macchiato.**

lattice cutter - **1.** a series of notched, revolving, circular blades, mounted side by side on an axle, the ends of which are joined to a handle. Rolled across a sheet of pastry dough, this tool cuts out staggered rows of elongated ellipses. The resulting sheet of dough — which resembles the net-like pattern of a string bag rather than the square, cross-hatched pattern seen on lattice tops woven from single strips of dough — is used to top pastries, such as fruit pies. Classic models have metal axle, blades and housing, and a wooden handle, but sturdy all-plastic versions are also available. **2.** a set of two plastic pieces: a solid base and a cutting disk perforated with diamond-shaped holes. Fitted together, these are laid on the work surface, the sheet of rolled-out dough is laid on top, then rolled again, over the cutting disk, to create a latticework which can be turned onto a pie.

laurel leaf - see BAY LEAF.

La Varenne, François Pierre - see profile below.

lavash - also **lahvosh, lavosh.** This flat, round bread, also called Armenian cracker bread or Armenian flatbread, which can be kept a month without losing its freshness, probably originated in the Caucasus. Although it looks like **matzo,** it differs a great deal from it because lavash has both leavening and salt, while matzo has neither. In Armenia, it's cooked in an oven in the ground or in the floor of the house. A fire is built in a brick-lined pit, and when the right temperature has been reached, the coals are removed and the bread is put in.

lavender - from the Latin *lavare*, meaning "to wash," a plant of the genus *Lavandula*, whose evocative scent has been loved for centuries.

La Varenne, François Pierre (1618–1678) - influential 17th-century European cookbook author, chef and founder of classical French cooking. His *Le Cuisinier françois,* published in 1651, was the first major new collection of French recipes published since the 1500s. La Varenne was a court chef for King Louis XIV and likely creator of **béchamel** sauce, which he dedicated to the French financier Louis De Béchameil, who held an honorary post for the king. La Varenne later worked for Louis Chalon du Blé, Marquis d'Uxelle, and is said to have created **duxelles,** a mixture of chopped mushrooms, shallots and herbs sautéed in butter, in his honor.

All over North Africa, where the Romans established their protectorates, they took with them the habit of perfuming their baths and themselves with lavender, practices that soon spread among the locals. In the Middle Ages, lavender was thought to be an herb of love that worked both ways; although it was considered an aphrodisiac, a sprinkle of lavender water on the head would keep you chaste. Superstition persisted that the asp made his nest in lavender bushes, which was useful to herb dealers because it drove up its price. Branches of lavender were strewn on medieval floors to counteract unpleasant odors and deter insects, while dried lavender was, and still is, used in bunches or sachets to keep moths from linens. Queen Elizabeth I was partial to a conserve made of pears, honey and lavender flowers; and up until the last century, English cookbooks included "lavender snow," a heavy cream froth of lavender flowers steeped in sugar and egg whites, served on lavender twigs.

Lavender is used in many imaginative ways in modern cuisine: lavender sweet bread, shortbread, sorbet, ice cream, crème brûlé and even a Provençal-inspired lavender marinade for lamb. Often an ingredient in **herbes de Provence**, lavender has a light, eucalyptus-like flavor. Until the Second World War, the plant was used as a disinfectant for wounds. See also EDIBLE FLOWERS.

lavender gem - also **pink tangelo, tangelolo, wekiwa.** A miniature tangelo-grapefruit hybrid, deep pink with a hint of blue inside.

lavender honey - see HONEY.

laver - also **jee choy.** Any of several red seaweeds that have been gathered along the coasts of Britain, Ireland and Wales for centuries. One type is called sea lettuce; it is used in salads, sauces and soups and also mashed and boiled into laver bread. The Japanese laver, *Porphyra tenera*, is gathered and dried into a thin, flexible, dark brown sheet called hoshi **nori** and askusa nori. It's used in soups and vinegared rice dishes. The Chinese name for this seaweed is *jee choy*, or "purple vegetable."

layer cake - assembled from graduated or same-size layers of cake with a moist filling, such as whipped cream, frosting or macerated fruit, sandwiched in between, and often frosted.

laying hen - a female chicken kept to produce eggs for consumption. Known as a **pullet** when she is less than 12 months old and as a hen when she is 1 year or older, she usually lays eggs from 6 to 18 months of age, after which she is sold as a stewing hen. See also CHICKEN.

lazy Susan - see TURNTABLE.

leaf gelatin - see GELATIN.

leaf lard - see LARD.

leaf mustard - see MUSTARD GREENS.

lear oil - an acronym for low erucic acid rapeseed. See CANOLA OIL.

leathers - see FRUIT LEATHERS.

leaven - to add an ingredient, such as baking powder, baking soda, beaten egg whites, sourdough starter or yeast (all **leavening** agents), to a batter or dough to make it rise.

leavening - also **leavener.** A substance or technique used to lighten the texture and increase the volume of batters and baked goods. The most common leavening agents are baking powder, baking soda and yeast. The former two become activated when they come into contact with liquid, producing carbon dioxide, which creates pockets of air. Yeast leavens due to its inherent live culture, which is activated with warm water. This creates the environment the yeast needs to grow, and sugar, the food that sustains its growth. Leavening agents work both before cooking, as in batters for pancakes, fritters and batter-fried foods, and during cooking, as in breads and cakes. Stiffly beaten egg whites take the place of leavening in some recipes. They must be very carefully handled to avoid deflation. The leavening of puff pastry is the result of the multiple folding during its preparation, adding numerous layers of its butter-flour-water mixture so that, during baking, the water steams and expands between the layers of the dough, and the butter melts into the flour to create its characteristic flavor. The leavening of **choux pastry** for **profiteroles** or éclairs is the result of egg yolks beaten into a warm mixture of butter, water and flour. As in a bread **starter,** flour in warm water will form natural yeast, encouraged to grow because of warm temperatures and fed by the flour's natural sugars, which are part of its carbohydrate composition.

Leberkäse - a mild, fine-textured Bavarian sausage made from pork, or sometimes veal, flavored with garlic, herbs and onion. It is usually served warm (sliced and fried or steamed). In Vienna, it's a popular hot snack available at sausage stands on the street.

Lebkuchen - a German spiced cookie from Nuremberg usually served at Christmastime, traditionally made in carved wooden Lebkuchen molds and baked in festive shapes, similar to the technique used to make **speculaas.** These cookies are direct descendants of traditional European honey cakes, and are usually made chewy and rich with the addition of honey. They are flavored with nuts and a variety of spices, including ground cloves, cinnamon, allspice and black pepper. The origin of the word is not clear, although the second half of the word, *kuchen,* means "cake" in German. Some linguists think *leb* is derived from the Latin word *libum,* meaning "flatbread," or the German word *Laib,* meaning "loaf." One folksy explanation is that it comes from the German word *Leben,* which means "life," although linguists disagree. However, this doesn't stop many Germans from eating this "life cake" in the winter to stave off depression and ill health.

leche - Spanish for "milk."

lecithin - a fat-like substance present in egg yolks and beans (especially soybeans), used as an **emulsifier** in foods. Commercial lecithin, derived from soybeans, is used as a preservative and emulsifier, as well as to maintain moisture in some packaged foods.

leckerli - also **Baseler leckerli.** A chewy, Swiss spice cookie, originally from the city of Basel, often made at Christmas (the name comes from the German word *lecker,* meaning "luscious"). Ground cinnamon, cloves and nutmeg are heated in a pan with honey and sugar, then removed from the heat; candied lemon and orange zest and ground almonds are stirred in. This mixture is added to a plain dough, flavored with **Kirsch,** then rolled out and baked. Frosted while still warm, then cut into cookies while in the pan and allowed to cool.

leek - a plant of the genus *Allium* and, with onions and garlic, a member of the lily family. Leeks were well known to both the Greeks and Romans. Nero often kept a leek in his mouth because he believed it would add timbre to his voice and, for this reason, was nicknamed *Porrophagus,* from *porrum,* meaning "leek" and *phagus,* meaning "to eat." Roman historian and naturalist **Pliny** tells the story of Mela, a government official whom Tiberius criticized for poor administration and who took his own life by drinking three silver denarii's weight in leek juice, expiring instantly without the slightest symptom of pain. During biblical times, leeks were widely consumed in Egypt as well as in other lands bordering the Mediterranean.

There are references to leeks in England as far back as the Dark Ages, but during the Middle Ages, they were rarely mentioned. Many superstitions are centered on leeks, most notably as a guard against fires, lightening and sorcery, which is why Charlemagne ordered them planted on housetops. During the 16th, 17th and 18th centuries, the aristocracy didn't eat leeks, because they were unfashionable and considered "poor man's asparagus."

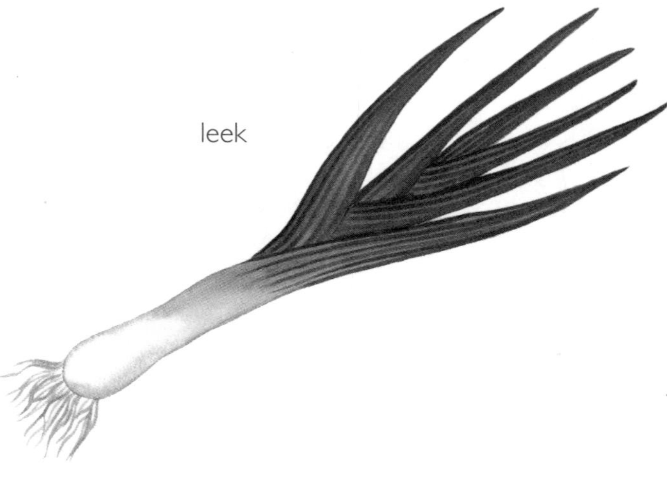
leek

Phoenician traders introduced the leek to Wales, where it has been the national emblem since AD 640, when the Welsh scored a victory over the Saxons wearing leeks pinned to their hats for identification. It's still traditional in Wales to wear a leek on March 1 to celebrate St. David's Day — for the influential religious leader and patron saint of Wales — and serve leek broth (*cawl cennin*) and chicken and leek pie. (All 10 monasteries founded by St. David were vegetarian.) The Scottish make **cock-a-leekie** soup and consume even more leeks than the Welsh.

lees - also **dregs, sediment.** The sediment, such as dead yeast and fruit material, that settles in a cask or other container during the fermentation process of an alcoholic beverage. Some wines are aged "on the lees" (called *sur lie,* in French) to achieve a more complex aroma and flavor. Before bottling, the wine is drawn off, leaving the lees at "the bottom of the barrel."

lefse - Norwegian **flatbread** that has mashed or riced potatoes and flour as its main ingredients. The dough is formed into a long rope, sliced, then rolled into thin, flat rounds. Cooked to be crisp or soft, one side at a time, these griddle cakes can be used to make **roll-ups,** served plain with dishes, such as **lutefisk,** or spread with butter and cinnamon sugar and eaten as a sweet.

legume - from the Latin *lego,* meaning "to gather," referring to how they are harvested. Even though "legume" translates as "vegetable" in French, the word has a much stricter definition in English. It refers to a plant that bears fruit in the form of pods that split along both sides when ripe, with nitrogen-rich fruits and roots. Their absorption of nitrogen from the air makes them rich in protein and very useful in maintaining the fertility of the soil. Peas, soybeans, lentils, peanuts, chickpeas, cowpeas, lima beans, green beans, kidney beans — in fact, all beans — are legumes that are suitable for human consumption. Alfalfa and clover, however, are known as forage legumes and are most often used as animal fodder. Dried seeds of a legume are **pulses.**

Leicester - a firm, mild English cheese distinguished by its bright orange color, due to the addition of **annatto** dye; shaped into a cylinder.

Leiden - see LEYDEN.

lekvar - also **prune butter, prune jam.** A thick paste of puréed simmered prunes or dried apricots, used to fill traditional European baked goods, such as **hamantaschen** and **kipfel.** It can be made at home or bought, in jars, at most grocery stores.

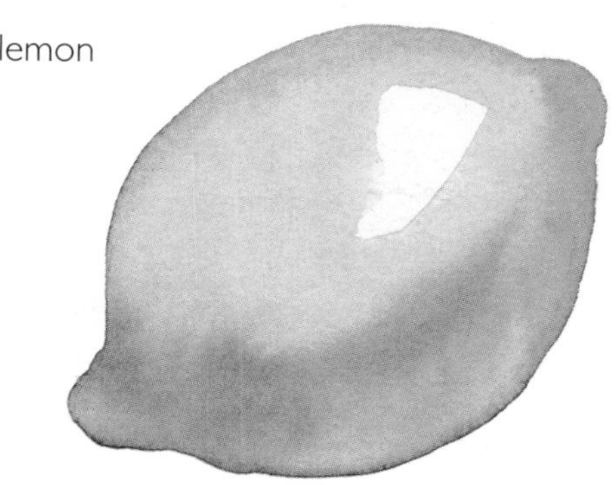
lemon

lemon - a citrus fruit, pale yellow and thick-skinned, said to have originated in the Indus Valley during the Bronze Age (about 2500 to 1700 BC). In 1493, Christopher Columbus introduced lemons to the New World and by the mid-1700s they were cultivated in California. Lemons, *Citrus limon,* are cold-sensitive. With warmth, sun and irrigation, lemon trees thrive in soil types ranging from clay to sand — even poor soil — as long as it's well drained, so the steep, rocky and apparently inhospitable slope of the Mediterranean coast have proven perfect for their culture. Sicily produces 90 percent of all lemons, and southern California produces 80 percent of the American crop but, in the Western Hemisphere, significant commercial crops — which must be handpicked — are also harvested in Arizona, Florida, southern Mexico and parts of Central and South America.

The acidic juice enhances the taste of soft fruits, fish, seafood and tea; flavors fillings, pies and puddings; adds pectin to jams and jellies; and is used in mayonnaise, sauces and salad dressings (often as a substitute for vinegar). Coated in lemon juice, cut fruits, such as apples, won't brown in the air. Sometimes dried for cattle fodder, the aromatic rind is candied or pickled for human consumption. Scraped from the skin, the **zest** is used fresh or dried in savory and sweet dishes, baked goods and confections. Fragrant oil, pressed from the rind, is used in perfume. In Indian, lemons are preserved in mustard oil; in Morocco, they are salted and kept in their own juice to serve with **tagine.**

For centuries, lemon juice has been used in remedies that bleach freckles, reduce fevers, ward off colds and promote "regularity" to name a few. The fruit's most famous medical role, perhaps, is the prevention of scurvy in sailors of the British Navy, which instigated regular rationing of lemons in the early 1800s, several decades after a study by Naval Surgeon James Lind had shown their efficacy. See also MEYER LEMON.

lemonade - see ADE.

lemon balm - an herb, *Melissa officinalis*, with wrinkled, green leaves resembling mint, and a fresh lemony flavor. In the Middle Ages, it was used to make "scholar tea," as mentioned in the 1300s by Arnaud de Villeneuve, known for his research on distillation, who gave it to his students at the University of Montpellier on the eve of examinations as a memory aid. The practice continued for centuries afterward, under the name *eau de melisse*, so named because *melissa* is the Greek word for "bee"; lemon balm was planted near beehives to guide bees back to their home and to attract them from other hives.

The French Carmelite nuns used lemon balm to make "a digestive drink, a remedy for headaches and neuralgia as well as cheering up the despondent," a tonic that Emperor Charles V was said to enjoy daily. Before the appearance of lemons, lemon balm was used in just about everything now flavored with citrus. The Medicis had a recipe for duck stuffed with lemon balm. Shakespeare mentions it in *The Merry Wives of Windsor* as a strewing herb, to make the house smell more festive and inviting for guests. Today, lemon balm is often used in salads and as a flavoring agent with cooked meats.

lemon balm

lemon basil - see BASIL.

lemon bush - see ROSELLE.

lemon curd - lemon juice (and sometimes **zest**), combined with butter, egg yolks and sugar, and cooked in a nonreactive double boiler or saucepan. The thickened, cooled mixture is used as a filling for cakes and tarts or, especially in England, as a spread on toast or scones at breakfast or tea.

lemon drop - **1.** a cookie flavored with lemon juice and zest, often dusted with sugar, glazed or frosted. **2.** a traditional lemon-flavored hard candy. **3.** a cocktail most often made with citron vodka as its base and sometimes flavored with other spirits, such as **Galliano** or **triple sec;** the flaming version features a sugar-coated lemon wedge that is soaked with rum and set alight before serving.

lemon extract - liquid flavoring that tastes of lemon rind (not the juice) used especially in desserts and sweets, available pure and artificial.

lemongrass - also **sereh.** A tall, tropical grass, *Cymbopogon citratus*, whose stalk and leaves are used in Thai and Vietnamese cuisine. In India, it's used in blends of curry powder. Lemongrass contains citral, an essential oil used in perfumes and the substance found in the outer rinds of lemons. It is now grown extensively in Florida and California, brought there by Vietnamese immigrants. It can be purchased fresh or dried and is believed to relieve flatulence.

lemonleaf - see SALAL.

lemon liqueur - a brand-name or homemade liqueur, such as the Italian **limoncello,** flavored with lemon.

lemon meringue pie - a light, tart, **lemon curd** pie with a precooked pastry crust and topped with stiff peaks of meringue (the assembled pie is baked until their tips turn gold). Egg yolks are used in the custard, the whites in the meringue. Light and sweet, this pie is claimed by the American South, but culinary-history buffs credit baker Elizabeth Coane Goodfellow with introducing it in her Philadelphia pastry shops late in the 1700s. The pie was so popular that, about 100 years later, **Fannie Merritt Farmer** included a recipe for it in her famous cookbook. It's still a favorite these days, but many cooks make the curd from a mix; alas, most mixes contain artificial lemon color and flavor.

lemonnaise - mayonnaise that is tarted up with extra lemon juice. A popular sauce on artichokes, it can be made at home (some recipes start with a tofu base) or bought, ready-made, at grocery stores.

lemon oil - a fragrant, golden oil extracted from the skin of the lemon, often used in dressings and dips.

lemon pepper - also **lemon pepper seasoning.** A ready-made mix of dried lemon zest and black pepper, which is used primarily on chicken, fish and vegetables. Depending on the manufacturer, lemon pepper may or may not include other ingredients, such as celery seed, coriander, chiles, garlic, **MSG** and salt.

lemon sole - see ENGLISH SOLE.

lemon verbena - also **herb of the cross, Spanish thyme, verbena.** A small, fragrant, flavorful herb native to South America, available dried and sometimes, although rarely, fresh. It was introduced to England in the 18th century. English cookbooks of this period call it "herb Louisa." It's is also referred to as "herb Luisa," presumably because the Spaniards are credited with bringing it across the sea. It is also known as "herb of the cross" and "Spanish thyme."

Lemon verbena became a common culinary and medicinal herb throughout Europe, used to season fish and fruit dishes, jams and preserves, stuffings and puddings and, of course, to make tea. In the countryside, bunches of dried verbena were hung over doorways to ward off evil spirits." Thomas Jefferson, well known for his love of sorbets, wrote about "lemon sorbet," actually referring to a sorbet made with lemon verbena. Today, it is used in confections and as a favorite herbal tea. Despite its common names, lemon verbena — or, scientifically, *Aloysia triphylla* — is not a true member of the *Verbena* family. Dried and kept in an airtight container, this herb stores well for up to two years.

length - see FINISH.

lentil - an annual, *Lens culinaris*, with edible round, flat seeds, believed to have originated in Central Asia. Archaeological findings in the Middle East date the lentil back 8,000 years. According to Roman historian and naturalist **Pliny,** lentils were not only a Roman staple, but were also used (almost 3 million Roman pounds of them) as ballast in the specially built ship that transported the Egyptian obelisk to Rome, where it still sits in St. Peter's Basilica.

Lentils are mentioned in the *Book of Genesis* and were introduced to India before the birth of Christ. The "mess of pottage" for which Esau sold his birthright was supposedly a lentil stew. Lentils have the most protein (25 percent) of any edible plant. They can be brown, green, black, yellow, orange or red, sold whole or skinned, and, after germination, can be milled into flour. Canada and the U.S. are the two chief producers of lentils for export, with two main varieties: the **Chilean,** with a solid tan-color coat and yellow interior; and the **red chief,** with a light tan coat and pale reddish orange interior. See also PULSE, PUY LENTIL.

LENTIL VARIETIES

brown - also **continental.** Most readily available, can get mushy if overcooked.

coral - see PINK.

green - flavorful lentil, holds its shape well after cooking.

orange - used in Middle Eastern and Indian dishes, very mild in flavor.

pink - also **coral.** From the Middle East and northern Africa, fast-cooking and bland.

Puy - also **French green lentil.** The most cultivated variety in France, strong in flavor; doesn't easily disintegrate during cooking.

red split - used in making dal (they are second only to rice in traditional Indian cooking). In Turkey, they are used to make the traditional red lentil soup called *mercimek corbasi.*

lettuce - from the genus *Lactuca*, a common plant whose leaves are eaten in salads. More than 4,000 years ago, lettuce was cultivated not only for its leaves, but also for the oil contained in its seeds. Wild or cultivated, leaf lettuce was known all over the ancient world bordering the Mediterranean and even China. Lettuce was served on the tables of Persian kings in the 6th century BC, but Romans evidently waited until the 1st century AD to eat lettuce, one variety of which they named after themselves (romaine).

Lettuce was valued for its assumed medicinal qualities. There's a story that Caesar called an astrologer when his physician was unable to treat him; the astrologer decided on the emperor's prescription while lying in the lettuce patch: Caesar was to eat only lettuce. When he recovered, Caesar erected a statue and altar to show his gratitude. The ancient Egyptians considered lettuce sacred, using it in ceremonies as an offering to the fertility goddess, since it was believed to be an aphrodisiac, which is amusing when we consider that, during the Middle Ages, monks were fed a daily ration of lettuce to help them preserve their chastity. The Greeks and Romans found other virtues and medicinal qualities in lettuce, such as eating lettuce to end insomnia.

lettuce leaf basil - see BASIL.

LETTUCE VARIETIES

There are five distinct types of lettuce: butterhead and crisphead (two varieties of **head lettuce,** so called because they grow tightly clustered in a compact round head); leaf (also called loose-leaf lettuce); romaine or cos; and stem (also called asparagus lettuce).

asparagus - see STEM.

butterhead - also **buttercrunch.** Variety of head lettuce whose name suggests its buttery texture and flavor. It has lovely, crisp, curly, red-purple to green leaves. Their heads are looser and smaller than crisphead (the other variety of head lettuce) and can look a little like an open rose. The best-known varieties are **Boston,** with a medium-large head and very tender, dark green outer leaves, and **Bibb,** with a small head and tender, dark green leaves. Limestone is a Bibb lettuce grown in limestone soil, mainly in Kentucky and Indiana.

celtuce - see STEM.

cos - see ROMAINE.

crisphead - variety of head lettuce, including Great Lakes, **iceberg** and Ithaca, that look like a small soccer ball, consisting of layers of folded, tightly packed, crisp, juicy leaves. The outer leaves are much darker than the inner ones, which are a pale greenish white to almost white. Iceberg is the most popular, so called because it was covered with ice during transportation in the beginning of the last century. Other varieties, such as Imperial, Yatesdale and Target, have reddish leaves that are tinged with green and plain, or scalloped or frilly edges.

leaf - also **loose-leaf.** A variety of lettuce whose heads are looser and smaller than crisphead and can look a little like an open rose. Varieties include oak leaf, green leaf and red leaf. They have thin, soft, floppy leaves with a delicate buttery flavor. See also LOLLO ROSO.

romaine - also **cos.** A tall, cylindrical lettuce with long, upright, narrow leaves and a crisp, sweet taste. Their leaves, which can be dark green to a dark red-brown, are crisper and coarser than the crisphead lettuces. Also known as cos, named after the Aegean island where it was first grown. According to legend, Venus hid Adonis in a bed of cos lettuce, where he was killed by a foraging wild boar; hence, lettuce was eaten by the Greeks and Romans at funeral repasts.

stem - also **asparagus lettuce, celtuce, Chinese lettuce.** This lettuce is not very well known in the U.S. but relished in Asia, where the thick stalk, which grows to about 12 inches (30 cm) in length, can be eaten raw and is said to taste similar to celery or artichoke. (Its name is a combination of celery and lettuce.) The stem must be peeled first to remove the bitter skin, then cut or shredded and used in salads or stir-fries. The leaves, which look similar to romaine, are also bitter and are best eaten when young.

Lewis, Edna (1916–2006) - chef and cookbook author, who pioneered the interest in Southern cooking and African-American food. The granddaughter of slaves, she was born in Freetown, Virginia, a farming community; the seasonal rhythm of rural life defined her approach to food. She came of age in a self-sufficient community accustomed to living off the land, and by the time she left home to make her own way in the world she knew enough about cooking to support herself as a chef. Arriving in New York City in the 1930s, she became politically active and, for a time, worked at the left-wing *Daily Worker* newspaper. In 1948, with a partner, she opened her first restaurant, Café Nicholson, on Manhattan's East Side. Serving country cooking at its best — such dishes as succulent roast chicken and pork chops with cranberries — the restaurant soon acquired a devoted clientele, which included such celebrities as William Faulkner and Greta Garbo. A fortuitous accident sparked her transition to food writing. When she broke her leg and was unable to work, she finally had time to jot down her recipes. *The Edna Lewis Cookbook*, written with the help of Evangeline Peterson and published in 1972, was her introduction to a wider audience and the first step toward becoming what *Gourmet* magazine called "the dean of Southern cooks."

In 1976, she published her masterpiece, *The Taste of Country Cooking.* Lewis turned 60 the year the book was published, and it is very much a memoir of an idyllic rural childhood told through recipes and menus, such as "A Spring Breakfast When the Shad Were Running" and "Making Ice Cream on a Summer Afternoon." She retired as a chef in 1992 and entered a new chapter of her life, moving to Decatur, Georgia. Four years later, she set up house with Scott Peacock, a young chef whom she met in 1988, when he cooked at the Georgia governor's mansion. The two shared a common commitment to inspiring others with their love of rural American food from the Deep South and jointly wrote *The Gift of Southern Cooking,* which was published in 2003. Lewis won numerous awards, including being named the Grande Dame of Les Dames d'Escoffier International in 1999. She died in her sleep in February, 2006, at her home in Decatur, Scott Peacock by her side.

levant - see ARAM SANDWICH.

le virtù - meaning "the virtues," an Italian soup of meat and vegetables, a specialty of Teramo in Abruzzo, traditionally served on May 1, in which the remains of the winter food supply are mixed with the first of the spring crop.

levulose - see FRUCTOSE.

Lewis, Edna - see profile above.

Leyden - also **Leiden.** A Dutch semihard cheese covered with a dark yellow rind and then red wax. It's made from whole or skimmed cow's milk, with caraway and cumin seeds, and shaped into cylinders.

liaison - a thickening and binding agent for soups and sauces, made of egg yolk and cream, from the Latin *ligare*, meaning "to bind."

libation - an ancient religious ritual in which wine, milk, oil or blood were sprinkled on the ground or on the altar to honor the gods. A libation was made while standing, with cup in hand, looking up in the direction of the heavens. A few drops of liquid were sprinkled and a short prayer spoken with the arms extended toward the sky, and then the offering was drunk. In ancient times, no one would dream of eating a meal without first performing a libation. As well as being a display of deference to a divine being, a libation was also intended to enlist help in times of need, especially before a battle or a journey. It was also used to seal a cease-fire or a treaty. Today, the term "libation" refers, often humorously, to an alcoholic drink.

lichee - also **lichi.** See LYCHEE.

licorice - a plant in the legume family, its botanical name *Glycyrrhiza glabra*, comes from the Greek *glykyrrhiza*, meaning "sweet roots." The medieval name was *gliquiricia*, from which the name "licorice" or "liquorice" is obtained. This popular flavoring dates back to the

Assyrians; it is native to the Middle East and was used in Egypt 4,000 years ago for medicinal purposes. A Roman papyrus makes reference to the therapeutic value of licorice, and the roots were mentioned in the first Chinese herbal book *Shen Nong Ben Cao Jing* in the 1st century AD. It was used in Chinese prescriptions for coughs, sore throats, asthma, gastric and duodenal ulcers, and as a "mediator" of potentially toxic ingredients. All the ancients, from Greek physician Hippocrates to Greek writer **Theophrastus** and Roman naturalist **Pliny,** made reference to it.

However, licorice was not introduced to Europe until the 15th century, during the last Crusades, at a Black Friars' monastery in Pontefract, which is also the origin of Yorkshire's still-world-renowned Pontefract sweet. The Blackfoot Indians used wild licorice as an infusion to treat earaches, while other Indian tribes ate it fresh.

Today, it's a popular ice cream flavor in Europe. The Chinese use it in particular to flavor fish. The roots are used in candy and to flavor and color a variety of foods and beverages, including beer. But by far the greatest quantity of the licorice imported by the U.S., perhaps as much as 90 percent, ends up in tobacco, where it's used to sweeten and to moisten the leaves. Licorice extract is made by boiling the plant's yellow roots and allowing the excess liquid to evaporate. The remaining black substance has two important components: the essential oil, called anethole, which licorice shares with anise and fennel (which is why they share this characteristic flavor); and glycyrrhetic acid, which is what makes licorice sweet. Glycyrrhizin, a component in the raw root, is 50 times sweeter than table sugar. Before the advent of cheap sugar, licorice root was often cut into strips and chewed on its own, which is perhaps why modern licorice candy is sold in long strips.

licorice liqueur - a brand-name or homemade liqueur flavored with anise or licorice root. Famous brand names include the French **Pernod** and the Italian **Sambuca.** Well-know generic names for these liqueurs include anisette and ouzo.

Liebfraumilch - a sweet German white wine, meaning "milk of the Blessed Mother," probably so named because of its sweetness. The wine originated in the vineyards surrounding Liebfrauenkirche ("Ch urch of Our Lady"), founded by the Capuchin monks in 1296. It is made from a blend of any combination of Müller-Thurgau, Riesling, Silvaner and Kerner grapes, plus no more than 30 percent other grapes.

Liebig, Justus, Baron von (1803–1873) - German organic chemist, who made meat extract as an economical alternative to meat, which later became known as Oxo. At 21, Liebig was already a professor of chemistry in Giessen and began teaching at the University of Munich in 1852. Specializing in organic chemistry and the classification of food, Liebig proved that plants feed off the nitrogen and carbon monoxide in the air, and invented a nitrogen-based fertilizer. He developed his meat extract in 1840; established the Liebig Extract of Meat Co. and its headquarters in London in 1865; and set up a factory in Uruguay a year later, using cattle that had, up until then, been slated for destruction once their hides had been harvested for other industries. The extract became known as Oxo in 1899. Although Liebig had intended the extract for the poor, it became a staple in middle-class European homes, as well as part of a soldier's rations during the Second World War.

Liebig, Justus, Baron von - see profile left.

Liederkranz - an American cheese, now extinct, similar to **Limburger,** the strong-smelling Belgian cheese. Liederkranz is mild, very soft, and has a washed rind with a characteristic red smear of corynebacteria. The cheese was developed by an apprentice, **Emil Frey,** in Monroe, New York, in 1892. Frey did not name the cheese for a German town, but rather for a local singing society, with whom his employer sang. *Liederkranz,* which was also the name of the hall on East 58th Street where the society met, is German for "wreath of song."

light corn syrup - see CORN SYRUP.

light cream - see CREAM.

lights - the name given to an animal's lungs, which in Britain and America are generally reserved for pet foods, but are cooked for the table in other countries. Not very substantial in themselves, they're either served with a sauce or added to stews.

light treacle - an amber-colored, sweet syrup produced in the first boiling of sugarcane during sugar refining (blackstrap molasses is produced by later boiling). An ingredient in many confections and baked goods, light treacle is also used as a honey substitute by vegans. See also GOLDEN SYRUP, MOLASSES.

lilikoi - also **yellow passion fruit.** A yellow-skinned, *Passiflora edulis*, introduced to Hawaii. The vine is now considered an unpopular pest plant on the islands, but the fruit is popular for its juice, pulp and edible seeds. The blossoms last less than a day and ripen into fruit, which is used to flavor everything from cheesecake to **mahi-mahi** sauce. The flesh may be cut up, battered and deep-fried. See also PASSION FRUIT.

Lillet - a classic French red or white apéritif, made in the Bordeaux region for more than a century. It consists of 85 percent red or white wine and 15 percent fruit liqueur, which are combined, then aged in oak casks for six to 12 months. Bitter, green and sweet oranges and peel, and **quinine** are just some of the ingredients of the fruit liqueur, which itself is aged for four to six months. Usually served chilled, over ice, with a slice of lemon, lime or orange, Lillet is also used in cocktails and cooking.

lily buds - also **golden needles.** *Hemerocallis* buds, from the tiger lily, picked when they are between 3 to 5 inches (7.5 to 12.5 cm) long; they retain their yellow color when dried. Before use, they are soaked in water to soften them; then, the chewy buds are chopped, scored or knotted to release their gentle floral, fruity flavor. Called golden needles, the dried buds, symbols of gold and wealth, are familiar ingredients in dishes, such as **hot-and-sour** soup. They are also mixed into various foods for good luck during celebrations of the Chinese New Year.

lily bulb - a Chinese specialty available either dried or fresh. They look like garlic bulbs without their skins, and can be peeled like petals from a flower. The best bulbs traditionally come from Lanzhou and were once regarded as worthy to serve in tribute to the imperial court.

lima bean - also **butter bean, Madagascar bean.** The fruit of an herbaceous plant, *Phaseolus lunatus*; the lima bean originated in South America, with evidence of its existence found in Peru, dated 7,000 years ago. They were cultivated in the Caribbean and in Central America well before the discovery of the continent by Columbus; later, the Spanish introduced them to Europe. The lima bean plant is a vine, which can grown up to 60 feet (18 m) long in a great range of colors: white, red, purple, brown, black, plain or spotted. Some varieties contain toxic substances, which disappear during cooking.

Limburger - once Belgian, but now made in Germany, a piquant and strongly pungent cheese. The rind is washed with corynebacteria, and the cheese is ripened for three to four weeks.

lime - the fruit of a small evergreen, *Citrus Latifolia*, originally native to Asia. The nickname "limeys" was given to British sailors almost 200 years ago and comes from their daily ration of citrus fruit. Sailors from other countries may have laughed at the practice, but it accomplished its purpose: it wiped out scurvy, common on long voyages when the diet consisted of hardtack and **bully beef** (dry biscuits and corned beef). Today, of course, we know that vitamin C in limes helps to prevent scurvy. Limes flourish in a hot, humid climate and were quite at home in Egypt, when Arab traders brought them there. The crusaders were

limes

the first Europeans to see limes and carried them to Europe. Limes crossed the Atlantic with Columbus on his second voyage in 1493 and were grown wherever the Spaniards settled and where climate was favorable. See also CITRUS, KEY LIME.

limeade - a lime drink to which, if effervescence is deemed desirable, club soda can be added. See ADE.

lime basil - see BASIL.

lime cordial - also **lime-juice cordial.** A non-alcoholic, sweet-tart light syrup, made with lime juice and sugar, used in cocktails, such as the **Gimlet.** The well-known Rose's brand was created by a Scotsman of the same name, who introduced it in Edinburgh in the 1870s. The Royal Navy is given credit for familiarizing his brand around the globe.

lime flowers - also **lime blossoms, linden flowers.** Fresh or dried flowers harvested from some of the long-lived, deciduous *Tilia* or linden trees — commonly referred to as "lime trees" in Britain — which are native to temperate Asia, Europe and North America. The flowers have traditionally been used to make teas and tinctures to treat disorders as varied as colds, hysteria and indigestion. Since the fragrant tea is enjoyed even by the healthy, the dried flowers are sold in health food stores; ready-made teas, which may combine lime flowers with another ingredient, such as chamomile, are also available. Unpicked, the nectar-rich flowers are a favorite of honeybees and, consequently, their keepers; as a result, linden trees have been protected by law in some countries.

lime-juice cordial - see LIME CORDIAL.

lime rickey - a generic term used for several drinks that include lime juice, an alcoholic spirit (such as gin or rum) and, usually, simple syrup.

limonata - a carbonated beverage made with sparkling water, lemon juice and sugar, from the Italian word *limone*, meaning "lemon," also called "Italian bitter lemon soda" or "lemonade." See also ARANCIATA.

limoncello - a cold, Italian beverage made by immersing carefully grated lemon zest (so no pith is attached) in 100-proof vodka and aging it for up to 40 days in the dark, at room temperature. Sugar and water, simmered into a syrup — or simple syrup — is then added, and the mixture is strained into jars (to remove the zest) and frozen until use. The thawed lemon yellow–tinted liquid is enjoyed over ice, straight up or poured over desserts or fresh fruit, preferably while the drinker or diner sits in the sun, overlooking the Mediterranean.

limoncillo - see HONEYBERRY.

limpa bread - also **Swedish limpa.** A rich, moist, sweet, Swedish rye bread made with molasses. Usually flavored with orange zest, it may also be spiced with one or more of anise, caraway, cumin and fennel.

limpet - also **opihi.** An edible gastropod familiar to beachcombers by its broadly conical, ridged shell with a pearlescent interior. When the tide recedes, each limpet clings to a rock face, on which it has ground out a shallow, circular trough that fits the toothed edge of its shell and improves the adhesion of its "foot." Although archeologists have found evidence in Britain that limpets have been consumed by humans since Mesolithic times, their toughness ensures that they are eaten in Europe only occasionally as **famine food,** or used as fish bait. An exception is Hawaii, where limpets are called **opihi** and considered a delicacy; there, they may be eaten raw — alone or mixed with edible seaweeds — or grilled.

limu - an edible seaweed, the most common of which is **ogo,** a term that originally referred to any plant that could grow in water. Once harvested from reefs, limu is now an important farmed Hawaiian species, which serves as a link among Hawaii's many Asian ethnic groups, who brought with them an appreciation of edible sea vegetables from China, Korea and Japan. Limu is used in salads, **kimchi** and even in a sesame candy.

Lincoln, Mary Johnson Bailey - see profile below.

linden flowers - see LIME FLOWERS.

linden-flower tea - see LIME FLOWERS.

Lindt, Rodolphe - see CONCHING.

ling - of the genus *Molva molva*, closely related to cod, usually salted or smoked.

lingonberry - also **cowberry, foxberry, mountain cranberry.** A tart, red berry from the genus *Vaccinium*, whose Latin root, *vacca*, means "cow," which provided its English name, cowberry, and reflects the berry's popularity with bovines. The lingonberry, related to the cranberry, has almost as many names as it has homes: foxberry, red whortleberry, mountain cranberry, rock cranberry, moss cranberry, alpine cranberry and partridgeberry. In North America, it is indigenous to most of Canada and the northern U.S. Available fresh or frozen, the berries are used to make candy, jam, jelly, juice, syrup and wine. Occasionally, they are pickled.

linguine - see PASTA.

linseed oil - a flaxseed oil, powerfully flavored and not to everyone's taste, often blended with other oils to diminish its potency, best suited to hearty green salads. Only the cold-pressed variety is for human consumption; the hot-pressed is used industrially in the making of linoleum and added to paints and inks to make them dry faster.

Linzertorte - see TORTE.

Liptauer - a Hungarian cheese spread made from sheep's and cow's milk, a factory product based on a sheep's milk cheese called *liptó*. Common variations of this spread are made with the addition of butter, capers, onions, mustard and spices.

liqueur - an alcoholic beverage, most often sweet, distilled or infused with flavorings, originally produced for medicinal purposes.

liquid measure

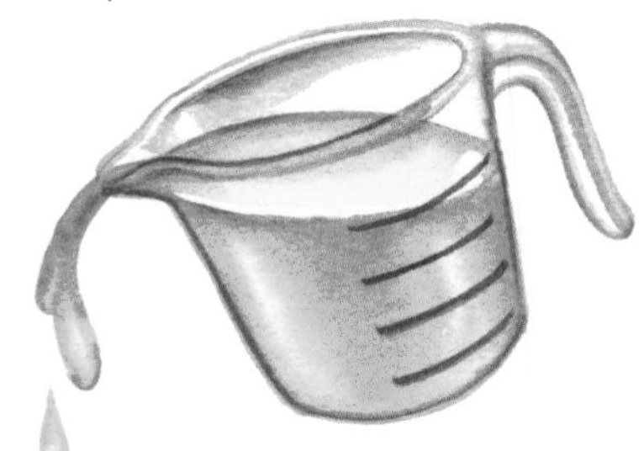

liqueur de violette - see CRÈME DE VIOLETTE.

liquid measure - liquid measuring containers are available in glass, plastic and stainless steel in a range of sizes from 1 cup (250 mL) to 8 cups (2 L) with a convenient pouring spout. The measurements, often available in both metric and imperial, are labeled on the outside of the container. The liquid is poured

Lincoln, Mary Johnson Bailey (1844–1921) - American cook, writer and teacher who wrote the Boston Cooking School's first cookbook and two of its official texts. Lincoln was born in Massachusetts and taught school before marrying in 1865. When her husband became ill, she took over the responsibility for the household's earnings. She was hired at the Boston Cooking School in 1879 and became its first principal that same year. In 1883, she published *Boston Cooking School Cook Book,* which was reprinted with a new introduction in 1884 as *The Boston Cooking-School Cook Book*. Despite what the title may imply, **Fannie Merritt Farmer**'s *Original Boston Cooking-School Cook Book* didn't appear until 1896, 13 years later; Farmer graduated from the school in 1889. Lincoln is also noted for being the first to indicate specific measurements for a recipe, and to list ingredients and amounts at the start of a recipe. She was also a natural businesswoman. She owned and edited *American Kitchen Magazine* and founded a baking powder company. She became so well known and highly regarded that she was often asked to endorse products with publications or recipes. She also wrote *Peerless Cook Book* and *Carving and Serving,* both published in 1886, and, in 1904, *What to Have for Luncheon*.

in to the desired level. To get an accurate reading, do not hold the cup up to eye level — make sure the container is on a flat, level surface and then bend down to read it. There are also angled measuring cups available, which allow you to view the measurement by looking down into the cup. A **dry measure** should not be used for liquid ingredients because liquids do not fill the space the same way, and the yield will be different.

liquid smoke - a ready-made liquid flavoring, derived from the condensed smoke of burning chips of hardwood (primarily hickory, but also beech, maple and oak), used in marinades or as a brush-on sauce to give foods a barbecued-over-the-fire taste.

liquor - **1.** (n.) a distilled alcoholic liquid, a spirit. Distilled spirits are often referred to as "hard liquor" to differentiate them from fermented spirits, such as beer and wine. From the 15th century on, Europeans began keeping their delectable and somewhat dangerous spirits locked away in a special liquor cabinet. In colonial American, portable cabinets, known as cellarettes, were common in many homes. Later, in Prohibition times, liquor cabinets were disguised as innocent bookshelves or drop-leaf tables. **2.** a nonalcoholic liquid, or syrup, such as "fruit liquor" (a liquid in which fruit has been steeped or simmered). **3.** (v.) to get or make drunk with an alcoholic spirit.

listeria - the shortened name for *Lysteria monocytogenes*, food-borne bacteria that can cause serious illness (called "listeriosis") in pregnant women, the elderly, small children and people with compromised immune systems. This pathogen is commonly found in unpasteurized milk (and products made from it, such as soft cheeses); cold cuts; raw or undercooked meat, poultry, fish or eggs; and sometimes unwashed fruits or vegetables. When contaminated food is consumed, the listeria bacteria enter the bloodstream quickly but can take days or weeks to incubate and cause symptoms. Listeria usually causes common flu-like aches, coughs and fevers, so it can easily be misdiagnosed, leading to meningitis and, if untreated with antibiotics, possibly even death. For susceptible people, it is best to wash and cook foods thoroughly and avoid such foods as cold cuts, soft cheeses and sushi.

litchi - see LYCHEE.

littleneck clam - see CLAM.

little winter melon - see FUZZY GOURD.

liver - an iron-rich glandular organ that filters external chemicals and naturally produced toxins. Young liver is best, because it's tender and has a lighter flavor than that of an older animal. Liver is usually soaked in milk or cream before cooking to draw out some of its blood and to soften the taste. It toughens easily if overcooked, which is why it's often served medium-rare for more juiciness. See also VARIETY MEAT.

liverwurst - originally from Germany, a smooth mixture of ground pork, liver, onions and seasoning.

loaf - **1.** a mass of baked bread in its entirety. Although loaves may be shaped into cylinders, ovals, rounds or squares, commercially baked loaves often conform to standard sizes or weights. **2.** a mass of molded foodstuff, such as a cheese or a meat mixture.

lo bok - also **Chinese white radish, loh bak.** A large, white radish similar to daikon, but with a stretched-out oval shape that is plumper in the middle than a daikon. This Asian radish is usually the same creamy color as a daikon, but some varieties have a green-tinged top. Available year-round at many produce markets or Asian grocery stores, lo bok harvested in the spring and summer is spicier but less flavorful than that harvested in the fall and winter. Lo bok can be eaten raw (although it is a bit too pungent on its own for some), but is at its best as an accompaniment to other vegetables or as a component of **kimchi.**

lo bok

lobster - from the genus *Homarus*, a crustacean whose edible, sweet flesh is found in the claws, knuckles and tail, its name derived from the Old English *loppe*, meaning "spider," referring to how the 10-legged creature moves. Like other crustaceans, lobsters turn red when cooked because of the pigment astaxanthin, which is released with heat. Like fowl, male and female lobsters are known as cock and hen, respectively. The "lady" is another name for the stomach, a small, white pouch found between its stalked eyes, which contains the lobster's teeth. The "coral" is the female's edible, delicious roe, greenish black and runny when raw and early in its development; coral color and firm when mature. The "tomalley" is the green-color liver and pancreas, often added to sauces or butters, once considered a delicacy but not recommended for regular consumption today, because these organs naturally filter and therefore collect environmental contaminants. It takes five to seven years for a lobster to reach its minimum legal harvest size, during which time it will molt about 25 times, discarding its shell and growing a new one each time to accommodate its growth. Similarly, if a lobster loses a claw, which it often does, usually in a fight, it will grow a new one. Despite its popularity, lobster wasn't embraced until the middle of the 19th century, probably because of its formidable physical characteristics, although records indicate that it made its way to the American table two centuries earlier.

LOBSTER VARIETIES

American lobster - see MAINE LOBSTER.

langouste - see SPINY LOBSTER.

Maine lobster - also **American lobster.** Found off the Atlantic coast of Canada and the Northern U.S., has two strong front claws, which contain lots of meat. Maine's catch of lobster accounts for more than half of all U.S. lobster.

rock lobster - see SPINY LOBSTER.

sea crayfish - see SPINY LOBSTER.

spiny lobster - also **langouste, rock lobster, sea crayfish.** From the southern Atlantic and California coastal waters, with small claws, most of the meat being in the tail; the shell is covered with sharp spines and long antennae. The spiny lobster can live for 25 to 50 years, but the finest for cooking are 4 to 5 years old.

lobster à l'américaine - cooked with garlic, shallots, onion, olive oil and tomatoes, said to have been invented in Paris in 1867 for three late-arriving Americans. With most of his pantry exhausted, the chef promptly improvised with a lobster that had already been poached. His guests were delighted, and he named the dish in their honor. The tale has been challenged often. Even the great French chef **Auguste Escoffier** thought the dish had been exported to America by a chef from Nice. *Lobster à l'armoricaine* is the result of creative spelling that stuck. Some recipes that use this name come from Brittany and Languedoc and appear to be freely reinterpreted versions of the dish, using cream.

lobsterette - see PRAWN.

lobster Newburg - chunks of cooked lobster in a sherried cream sauce finished with egg yolk. Created by a chef at **Delmonico's** restaurant in the 1860s, it was originally called Lobster Wenberg after the customer for whom it was prepared. When Wenberg shamed himself one night by engaging in a drunken brawl at the elegant restaurant, the chef took the dish off the menu. His customers raised such a fuss that he returned it to the menu, but reversed the first three letters of Wenberg's name and changed "berg" to "burg."

lobster Thermidor - a dish of cooked lobster meat combined with a rich cream sauce, placed back in the shell, sprinkled with cheese and browned. Some say this recipe was created at the Paris restaurant Maire on January 24, 1894, to honor the opening of Victorien Sardou's play *Thermidor*. Others say the dish was first tasted by Napoleon during Thermidor, the 11th month of the calendar devised during the French Revolution, the period between July 19 and August 17.

locust - strictly speaking, a grasshopper, *Schistocerca gregaria*, in a phase of its metamorphosis, considered a delicacy in ancient Mesopotamia. The Greeks ate roasted grasshoppers. The ancient Jews, who would eat no shellfish, ate several kinds of insects. Moses named four of them in his list of animals that the tribes of Israel were permitted to eat (*Lev. 11:21–22*). In St. Jerome's Latin translation, these were *locusta*, *bruchus*, *ophimachus* and *attacus*, the last three translated as "bald locust," "cricket" and "grasshopper." Muslims may not eat pork, but locusts are quite permissible. Mohammed is said to have received trays of them as gifts from his wives. The Greeks also ate cicadas (which Americans sometimes call locusts, although locusts are quite different insects).

locust bean - see CAROB.

loganberry - the edible raspberry-blackberry hybrid, *Rubus loganobaccus*, introduced in the U.S. in 1881 by California Judge J. H. Logan, used as a dessert fruit, for tarts and in pies, jams and preserves.

loin - see BEEF, PORK.

lola rosa - see LOLLO ROSSO.

lollipop - from "lolly," meaning "tongue" in northern English dialect, or "loll," which means to stick out one's tongue in Old English. The "pop" came from the sound made when the candy is pulled from sucking lips. Or (a more likely source) from "pap," meaning an infant's food.

lollo rosso - also **lola rosa. A** type of **loose-leaf lettuce** with crisp, wrinkled, curly-edged leaves that are bright green at their base, shading to coppery red at their tips.

lo mein - a Chinese dish of cooked, long, wheat noodles (similar to vermicelli), stir-fried with bits of meat, seafood and/or vegetables and tossed with a savory soy-based sauce. It's the noodle-based cousin of fried rice.

London broil - originally a flank steak in a pungent marinade, which was then grilled and sliced against the grain. Today, however, London broil can mean any lean and less tender steak from the top round, sirloin or even the shoulder.

longan - a small round fruit with a shell that turns a medium brown shortly after harvesting, available only from late May to mid-August. The fruit originated in Malaysia, but China is now the biggest producer. It's known all over Asia under the Cantonese name *long-ngan*, meaning "dragon's eye," for the white eye-shaped spot on the black pit inside the fruit.

long bean - see ASPARAGUS BEAN.

long-finned tuna - see ALBACORE.

Long Island duck - a popular breed of domesticated duck, produced for consumption in North America, which has dark, juicy flesh. See also DUCK.

Long Island Iced Tea - a cocktail that packs a powerful punch. Belying its genteel name, the basic version is mixed with equal parts of gin, rum, tequila, triple sec and vodka, topped off with a dash of cola. Some bartenders dress it up with lemon wedges, sour mix (a syrup of lemon juice, sugar and water) or a shot of vermouth. Legend has it that this cocktail came into being during Prohibition (so its name was a necessary subterfuge), but most people credit a Long Islander named Robert "Rosebud" Butt with inventing the drink half a century later. Surprisingly, happy drinkers swear it actually tastes like tea.

Long John - see BISMARCK.

long-life - foods, such as milk and cream, heated at high temperatures to provide a longer shelf life. See also ASEPTIC PACKAGING.

long-neck clam - see CLAM.

loofah - also **dishrag gourd, luffa, sponge gourd.** Any of several edible gourds of the *Curcurbitaceae* family, including *Luffa acutangula* and *L. cylindrica*. Native to tropical Africa and Asia, these gourds are now cultivated around the globe. Grown as annuals in North America, they are rampant vines; given heat and sunshine, they will grow

longan

30 feet (9 m) in a season. Left to mature, the long gourds, resembling English cucumbers with one clubbed end, can reach 2 feet (60 cm) in length and about 6 inches (15 cm) in diameter. But cooks harvest and use only young ones less than 6 inches (15 cm) long. These can be served shredded, sliced or whole as a boiled or steamed vegetable, in soups and stir-fries, and are a popular ingredient in Asian cooking. The mature gourds become a springy, tough mass of fibers; skinned, seeded and dried, these are familiar as back scrubbers in the bathtub and pot scrubbers in the kitchen. The seeds are pressed to extract edible oil.

loose-leaf lettuce - see LETTUCE.

loose-skinned orange - see ORANGE.

loquat - also **Japanese medlar, mayapple, Nispero.** This Chinese and Japanese evergreen, *Eriobotrya japonica,* bears a slightly tart fruit, about the size of an apricot, with a large stone. It can be eaten fresh or stewed and is also made into jam.

Lord Baltimore cake - a rich, multi-layered golden cake, tinted with five egg yolks, probably named after Lord Baltimore, one of the early colonizers of Maryland. It is filled with a mixture of frosting, crumbled macaroons, chopped almonds, candied cherries and pecans, and lemon juice, orange extract and sherry, then iced with white frosting. In her famous cookbook, **Fannie Merritt Farmer** recommends a garnish of candied-cherry halves and diamond-shaped cutouts of **angelica.** See also LADY BALTIMORE CAKE.

lori-lori - also **batoko plum, louvi.** A small, sour, round and red tropical fruit, *Flacourtia inermis*, grown mainly in Australia, Indonesia and Malaysia, where it is used to make jam, jelly and syrup. The small shrubs have been introduced to subtropical and tropical parts of the United States; it has naturalized there and is now considered an invasive alien.

lotte - see MONKFISH.

lotus - a sacred plant, *Nelumbo nucifera,* from India and China, used extensively in the cooking of the Far East. The lotus flower, an edible water lily, is considered a great delicacy in many Asian countries. The **lotus leaf** and **lotus seed** are also eaten. But the plant's most commonly eaten part is the **lotus root** or stem, a series of plump links resembling a light brown sausage.

The lotus grows in muddy ponds and yet produces beautiful flowers, making it a sacred plant to Buddhists, who see it as a representation of what can be achieved from humble beginnings. The name, mentioned often in *The Odyssey,* was vaguely applied to a number of different plants famous in mythology, especially a tree whose fruit was fabled among the ancient Greeks to have the power to make people forget their country and friends and to remain idle.

lotus leaf - harvested from the Asian lotus, *Nelumbo nucifera.* Known as the "sacred lotus," it grows in muddy pools, but holds its flowers and foliage, clean, above the water. Tender, young leaves are chopped and added to foods. Mature leaves, about the size of dinner plates, are dried for sale; after soaking to restore their pliability, the fragrant leaves are used to wrap dim sum dumplings, fish, savory and sweet sticky-rice mixtures, and meat and vegetable dishes into packets for boiling or steaming. Today, twine has largely replaced the traditional "strings" of bamboo, raffia or straw used to tie them, but fresh lotus blossoms are still used to garnish the cooked, leaf-wrapped packets.

lotus nut - see LOTUS SEED.

lotus root - also known as **renkon.** The firm, rhizomatous underwater stem of the Asian lotus is strung together like sausages. The long, reddish brown rhizomes are separated, peeled and sliced to reveal off-white flesh with a pretty, symmetrical pattern of holes. They can be candied, canned, deep-fried, pickled, steamed, stir-fried, cooked in soups and stews or added fresh to salads. The entire root is sometimes sliced open, stuffed and cooked. Fresh or cooked, they have a gentle flavor and slight crunch.

lotus seed - also **lotus nut, shi lian zu.** Light brown, peanut-size seeds produced by the Asian lotus plant. Throughout Asia, these are eaten fresh or dried as a snack; sugared, they are enjoyed at Chinese New Year. Lotus seeds are also candied, pickled, dried for later use in savory soups and stews, and ground into a starchy powder for use as a **thickening agent** in cooking. After simmering in sweet syrup, the ground seeds are also made into a paste to fill **mooncakes,** pastries and sweets. The dried seeds are also strung together as prayer beads. Emerging from a plant held sacred across this region, lotus seeds are believed to have special, life-giving properties: used as a tonic in traditional Chinese medicine, for example, they also figure prominently in Chinese and Hindu legends and play a seminal role in the Buddhist creation story. They are sold, bagged in plastic, in Asian grocery stores.

loukanika sausage - a fresh, Greek lamb and pork sausage, traditionally made when the pigs were slaughtered after harvest. It may be seasoned with allspice or coriander, cloves and **marjoram,** but always contains orange zest.

loup - the name for **bass** in France.

louvi - see LORI-LORI.

lovage - an herb, *Levisticum officinale*, native to the Balkans and the Mediterranean, introduced to much of Europe and Great Britain by the Romans. Both the Greeks and Romans had medicinal uses for the herb. In the Middle Ages, lovage was a cultivated sweet herb as well as a cure-all. In Central Europe, women wore lovage around their neck when meeting their lover, because the herb was thought to guarantee everlasting devotion, which is why it was often the main ingredient of love potions.

The roots, leaves and seeds of this herb all have either medicinal or culinary applications. Its dark green leaves taste like celery (lovage is a relative), with a distinctive spiciness all its own, often used to flavor broths. Lovage can grow

lovage

4 to 6 feet (1.2 to 1.8 m) tall, and its hollow stems, which are often candied, like angelica, are eaten cooked or raw; they can also be cut and used as straws or swizzle sticks. In rural England, a drink called "lovage" is still made from a centuries-old recipe, which involves a maceration process in which the leaves, stalks and roots are used.

love apple - see TOMATO.

love-in-a-cage - see PHYSALIS.

lox - brine-cured salmon, sometimes smoked, from the German *lachs*, meaning "salmon." Its North American roots as a Jewish favorite began before refrigeration, when salmon arrived from Alaska in brine. New York delicatessens would refresh it with a rinse to remove some of the salt and sell it sliced, calling it "lox." A higher grade of lox is known as **Nova,** for Nova Scotia salmon that has been salt-cured with brown sugar and then smoked.

Slicing is the test of good-quality lox; it must maintain its shape when sliced transparently thin. Recipes for lox are closely guarded secrets, but there is a common general procedure. Filleted salmon is heavily seasoned with a sugar-salt mixture, sometimes spiced and splashed with alcohol, depending on the desired flavor, and left to cure for about 12 hours. It's then put into a brine for another 12 hours; then removed, rinsed (or "refreshed"), "painted" with desired flavors, such as rum and brown sugar, and smoked, if desired.

luau - an Hawaiian feast, often held outdoors, which almost always features a pig roasted in a pit lined with lava rocks, and other *ono*

(Hawaiian for "delicious") island foods. Lots of flowers and music are also on the menu. A modern luau may celebrate a baby, a birthday, a graduation, promotion, wedding or retirement.

Lucia buns - see LUSSEKATTER.

luffa - see LOOFAH.

luganega - also **luganeghe.** An Italian pork sausage that is made into links, similar to **kielbasa.**

Luk On - see TEA.

lulo fruit - see NARANJILLA.

lumache - see PASTA.

lump crabmeat - also **backfin crabmeat.** Pieces of tender meat from the body of the crab (not including the claws), removed from the shell. Sold canned, fresh or frozen, it is used mainly in chowder, crab cakes, salads and sandwiches.

lumpia - an Philippine version of a roll-up, consisting of a thin, crepe-like wrapper (made with an egg, rice flour and water dough), sometimes lined with a lettuce leaf, that is rolled around a mixture of chopped chicken, meat, seafood and/or vegetables, then usually fried. A common Philippine version contains shrimp, pork and *ubod* (heart of palm). These are often served topped with chopped peanuts, with a sweet or sweet-and-sour dipping sauce and chopped garlic on the side. Popular as a main dish or snack, lumpia are fast becoming a global favorite; ready-made lumpia wrappers are now available in many North American food stores.

lump sugar - made in two varieties. Yellow lump sugar consists of large, golden crystals, it is very popular with Chinese cooks and is used in desserts and drinks. Dark lump sugar comes in dark brown concentrated blocks and is used in many Chinese and Indian dishes.

lunch - **1.** (n.) a casual, light meal eaten midday. The word "luncheon," from which it derived, is now rarely used and refers to a noon or early-afternoon buffet or meal served on more formal occasions. **2.** (n.) the food prepared and served at the meal. For those away from home during the day, lunches have long been simple and portable — a hunk of cheese or meat, sandwiched between two pieces of bread. Nowadays, an array of packaged instant soups, microwavable stews and the like are sold for take-to-work meals. **3.** (v.) the eating of lunch by the humble or the well-heeled, as in "to lunch" (for the latter, listen to Stephen Sondheim's biting, but hilarious song *The Ladies Who Lunch*).

lunch meat - cooked, prepared meat mixtures, such as **macaroni and cheese loaf** (containing ground beef and pork) or Spam, often sold sliced for sandwiches. One such lunch meat, baloney, may be fried for either breakfast, lunch or dinner in Newfoundland — and, in a pinch, a large loaf or roll can stand in for Sunday roast.

lupine - also **lupin, lupini bean, tremoco.** The leguminous fruit of an herbaceous plant of the genus *Lupinus*. Some varieties of lupines originated in the Mediterranean region, where they're called "tremoco," and others in North and South America. Lupines have been cultivated for their edible seed in Europe for more than 2,000 years. While the Greeks and Romans cultivated it extensively, the Romans considered it food for paupers: during holidays and religious festivities, great quantities were given to the poor. While lupines are now widely grown for their colorful flowers, the consumption of the lupine seed is usually confined to Italy, the Middle East, North Africa and South America.

There are about 100 varieties of lupine, some of which contain a highly toxic substance that disappears after the plant has been cooked for at least two hours or soaked for 12 to 15 hours in fresh water. Since the 1930s, some low-alkaloid varieties have been developed that can be safely consumed without pre-treating the seeds. The Andean lupine, or *tarwi*, with a 50 percent protein content, is toasted, salted and eaten as a highly nutritious snack or appetizer. Lupines are delicious blanched and splashed with a little bit of lemon juice or olive oil. Roasted and ground, the seed serves as a coffee substitute. Lupine flour can be milled and used to make bread (a method often used in the Middle East) or pasta.

lussekatter - also **Lucia buns, St. Lucy's buns.** Golden Swedish yeast buns, colored with **saffron,** studded with two currant "eyes" and glossed with an egg wash, celebrate the life of St. Lucia of Sicily, patron saint of blindness. Associated, as is her name, with light and lucidity, this 4th-century saint is said to have worn a circle of candles on her head to light her way into the catacombs, where Christians lived in hiding; in time, she was put to death for her beliefs and her help to the poor and persecuted. In the Swedish tradition, the eldest daughter of the household arises and makes the lussekatter and coffee, then dons a red sash and a wreath with candles set into it, and serves breakfast to her family to begin the Christmas season.

lutefisk - a Norwegian and Swedish specialty, **stockfish** that has been soaked in water for five or six days (changing the water daily), then in a lye solution for two more days, then in water (again, changing it often) for another four to six days to leach out the lye. The soaked, expanded fish is then boiled briefly until it reaches the desired gelatinous texture. Lutefisk is served garnished with ground allspice and pepper and often with white sauce or butter, with a host of other side dishes, such as potatoes or **lefse** and a glass or two of **aquavit.**

lutein - a member of the **carotenoid** class of plant pigments, responsible for the deep green color of leafy vegetables, such as spinach and kale, and the yellow color of corn kernels and egg yolks. It is an **antioxidant** nutrient, which helps mop up **free radicals** and prevent disease. Lutein is especially important in maintaining good eyesight and preventing macular degeneration, an eye disease that commonly occurs in the elderly and can cause blindness.

lychee - also **lichee, lichi, litchi.** The most popular of Chinese fruits, *Lychee chinensis*; its tree can reach 65 feet (20 m) in height and can produce up to 300 pounds (150 kg) of fruit a year. They have been cultivated in China for more than 2,000 years, and they're one of the fruits given as a good luck charm to celebrate Chinese New Year. It's said that an ancient Chinese poet bragged about his lychee habit, claiming to eat a minimum of 300 every day and as many as 1,000 in one day. The first book about the cultivation of the fruit was written in AD 1056.

lycopene - a member of the **carotenoid** class of plant pigments, responsible for the deep red color of tomatoes, as well as the pink hues of red grapefruit and watermelon. It is an **antioxidant** nutrient credited with reducing **free radicals** and preventing a number of serious diseases. Lycopene is most often praised for the protective role it plays against prostate cancer and heart disease. Lycopene in tomatoes is best absorbed if the tomatoes are well cooked (such as those in tomato paste), although quickly cooking fresh tomatoes with a small amount of oil significantly increases the body's absorption of the nutrient.

Lyonnaise - generally, a term for a dish that features onions, such as potatoes Lyonnaise, and, specifically, a French sauce with onions, white wine and **demi-glace,** invented by Duke Philippe de Mornay, the leader of the Huguenots, in the late 1500s. See also MORNAY.

lychee

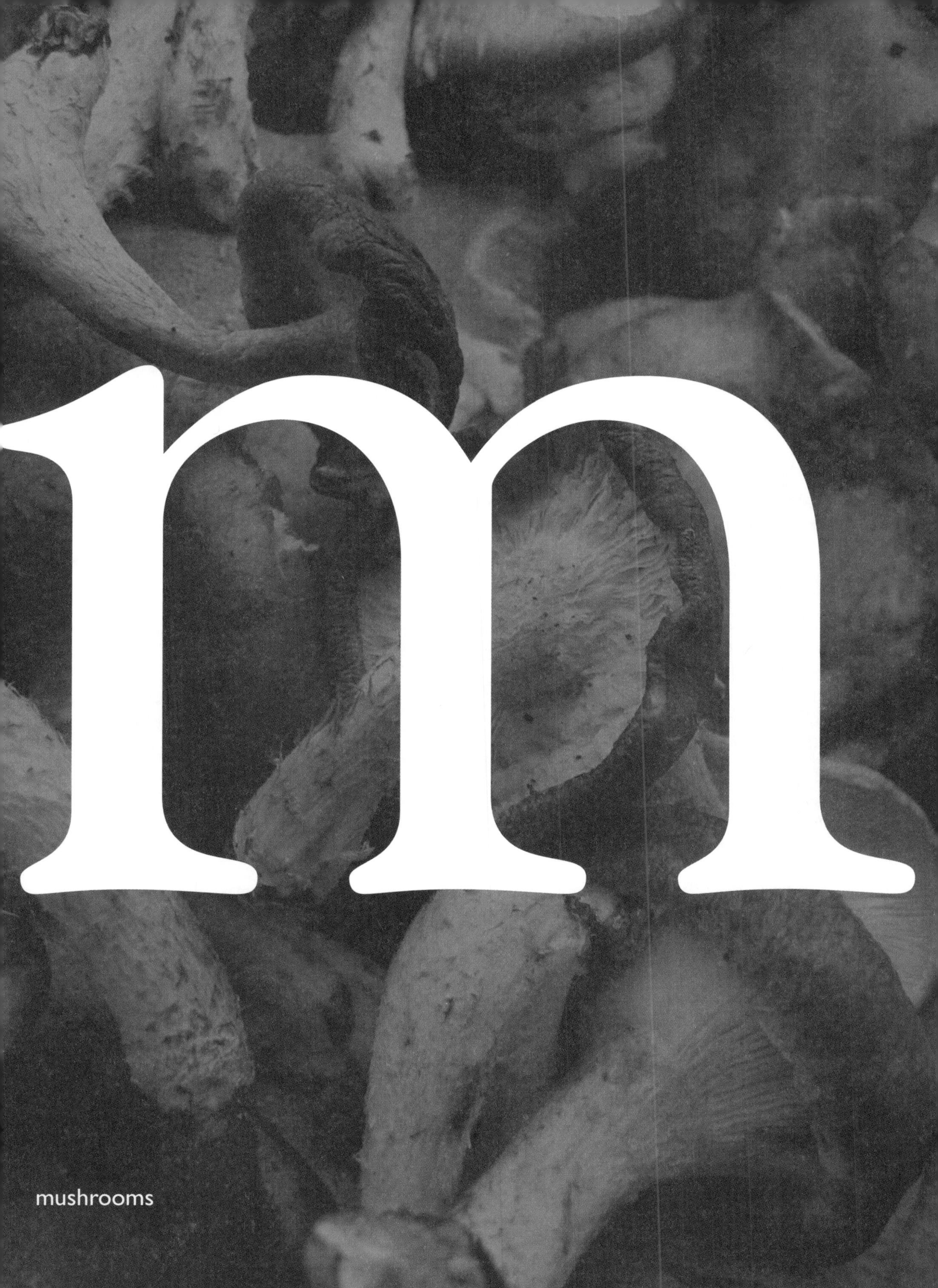
m
mushrooms

ma'amoul - a filled cookie made from **semolina,** often served as a celebratory dessert at the Muslim celebration of Eidul-Fitr, which marks the end of the somber holy month of Ramadan. The filling is typically made from puréed dates and/or chopped nuts, such as walnuts or pistachios, and scented with orange flower water and rose water. Traditionally, a ball of the buttery semolina dough is pressed into the bowl of a decoratively carved wooden spoon. The filling is dropped into the center, and the edges are pulled up around the filling and sealed to form the bottom of the cookie. The ma'amoul is then dropped out of the carved spoon, which has formed it into a beautiful geometric shape. The cookies can also be formed by hand and pressed with the tines of a fork to create a decorative finish. The popularity of ma'amoul has spread all over the Middle East, and the cookies are a particular favorite in Israel as well. They are often served as an Easter treat in Christian households in Lebanon and Syria.

maca - also **mace, pepperweed.** A biennial, low-growing Peruvian plant, *Lepidium meyenii*, which has been cultivated for at least 2,000 years high in the Andes for its sweet, radish-like root. The roots, which range in color from white to gray to red to purple, grow to about 2 inches (5 cm) in diameter. After harvesting, they are laid in the sun for at least five days, then stored, dry. For human consumption, they are roasted, whole in fire pits between glowing coals. Touted as an aphrodisiac, fertility aid and general tonic (some proponents claim Inca warriors consumed maca to boost their battle-readiness) concentrated forms of the root are available in health food stores as dried powder, gel or tablets. It's also available as a tincture and added to fruit juices and smoothies in health food restaurants and juice bars.

macadamia nut - also **bauple nut, bush nut, Queensland nut.** A creamy white, tender nut from the macadamia tree, *Macadamia ternifolia*, originating in Queensland, Australia. Its nuts were eaten by the Aborigines long before the Europeans came to the continent. It was not until after 1850 that European settlers discovered that the nuts were edible. The tree was named in honor of the Australian naturalist John Macadam, but today it's most often associated with Hawaii, where it was introduced in the 1890s.

mac and cheese - the colloquial term for macaroni and cheese.

macaroni - see PASTA.

macaroni and cheese loaf - a cooked, prepared **lunch meat** of finely ground beef and pork (some manufacturers also include chicken) and seasonings, embedded with Cheddar cheese and macaroni noodles, which may be sold whole or sliced.

macaroni pie - a favorite of Thomas Jefferson, who served it both at his home, Monticello, and at formal parties in Washington. Jefferson became fond of this dish while in Italy, but when he made it in the U.S., he used American cheese, which is how macaroni and cheese is said to have come about.

macaroon - a cookie made with ground almonds and/or coconut.

maccheroni - Italian for "macaroni" and used to describe various shapes and sizes of pasta, not just the type North Americans call macaroni. See also PASTA.

macchiato - see CAFFÈ MACCHIATO, LATTE MACCHIATO.

mace

mace - **1.** the aril, or bright red lacy covering, of the nutmeg, which is the seed of an evergreen, *Myristica fragrans*, native to Indonesia. Nutmeg and mace were brought to the Mediterranean by Arab traders in the 12th century and later became a lucrative monopoly along with cloves. In the brief period when they controlled the Moluccas, the British introduced the nutmeg tree to Singapore and the West Indies. The trees reach about 40 feet (12 m) in height and have smooth, dark green leaves and small flowers. Any recipe calling for nutmeg can use mace as a substitute, which is similar in flavor, but more

MacElhone, Harry (20th century) - Expatriate Scottish bartender and founder of Harry's Bar in Paris (not to be confused with Harry's Bar in Venice). Before taking over the bar that would bear his name and become replicated throughout Europe, MacElhone tended bar in London. He went to Paris in 1923 to run what was then called the New York Bar, in the Opera District. It would become known as Harry's New York Bar and later Harry's Bar, attracting a famous literary and theatrical clientele, among them Ernest Hemingway, Jean-Paul Sartre, Marlene Dietrich and Noel Coward. At one time, there were Harry's Bars in Florence, Berlin, Munich, Montreux and Hanover. Numerous famous drinks were said to have been invented at Harry's Bar, the most famous being the Bloody Mary.

subtle and much more expensive. See also NUTMEG. **2.** a popular name for **maca.**

macédoine - an assortment of diced fruits and vegetables, believed to have been named for the Macedonian archipelago, presumably because the diced foods are reminiscent of the group of small, scattered islands. From classical French cuisine, the name is given to a pickled side dish of small white onions, cauliflower, French beans, artichoke bottoms and small pimientos.

MacElhone, Harry - see profile above.

macerate - to soak a food, usually fruit, in liquid to soften and flavor it, most often using sugar syrup and alcohol.

machaca - see CARNE MACHACA.

mâche - also **corn salad, fetticus, field lettuce, field salad, lamb's lettuce.** A perennial plant, *Valerianella olitoria*, probably from the Mediterranean region. It has no relation to corn or lamb, but is a relative of catnip, cultivated and consumed like a lettuce, with a high tolerance for frost. Appreciated since Roman times because of the delicate flavor of its tender leaves, mâche is best eaten young, because it can become bitter with age. Some varieties have a slight hazelnut flavor.

mackerel - *Scomber scombrus*, high-fat fish, available smoked and fresh. The one drawback of mackerel is that it will spoil more quickly than almost any other fish, a fact that gained it the privilege of being the only fish in Elizabethan times to be hawked in the streets on Sunday in London. Scomber is the true mackerel caught in the Atlantic and the Mediterranean, although there are several species, including the **chub**, or "Spanish mackerel," and the scad, or "horse mackerel." Others include the **amberjack**, jack mackerel and **pompano** of American and Southeast Asian waters.

Mackinaw trout - see LAKE TROUT.

Macoun apple - see APPLE.

Madagascar bean - see LIMA BEAN.

mad cow disease - also **bovine spongiform encephalopathy, BSE,** a fatal disease that afflicts cattle and destroys their nervous system. Humans who eat meat contaminated with BSE can develop Creutzfeldt-Jakob disease, a fatal brain illness. Exposure to specific parts of the cow, including the brain, spinal cord, vertebrae and ileum (part of the intestines), increases the risk considerably, so many people avoid consuming these parts, some of which are considered delicacies. Sausages, such as **andouillette,** that are made with some of these riskier cuts of meat are technically outlawed in Europe to reduce consumers' exposure to the disease, but they are still widely available illegally.

Madeira - a Portuguese island in the Atlantic off the northern coast of Africa, which produces a unique fortified wine of the same name. In 1420, Prince Henry of Portugal, then 26, planted grapevines on the island, and wine makers promptly turned these grapes into wine right after picking. For some reason, this strong, smoky wine improved when barrel-aged in the equatorial sun. Most wine is delicate and suffers during long voyages. Madeira only got better. A 100-year-old Madeira is not only drinkable, it's exceptional. The wine was very popular in the U.S. during the Revolutionary War, and the

Madeira trade was an important part of the young nation's economy. Madeira is available sweet or dry: the former having brandy added during fermentation, leaving the wine very sweet, and with a high alcohol content; and the latter left to ferment entirely before adding brandy, which keeps it very dry. Today, only the sweet Malmsey Madeira is aged in the sun; the rest are heated in stoves. Sercial is the driest; Verdelho is just a bit sweeter; and Rainwater is a blend of the two. Any of these three makes a good apéritif. Malmsey and Boal, which are dark and sweet, can be served in place of port.

Madeira cake - a rich cake, similar to pound cake, topped with candied citron or lemon **zest** and traditionally served with a sweet **Madeira** wine.

madeleine - a little cake or cookie made with equal parts flour, butter, sugar and eggs in special scallop-shaped molds. Several chefs have tried to claim credit for its invention. One legend attributes its creation to Madeleine Palmier, a 19th-century French chef. Further back, another legend claims that Stanislas Leczinsky, the king of Poland, a great gourmet and Louis XV's father-in-law, introduced these little cakes to the Versailles court around 1730, where they quickly became fashionable. Others give credit to the 19th century pastry cook, Avice, chef to Prince Talleyrand, presumably because it had the approval of **Antonin Carême,** but many authorities believe the madeleine is much older than that. **Marcel Proust** made madeleines popular in his book *Remembrance of Things Past*. See also FINANCIER.

made mustard - see PREPARED MUSTARD.

maderized - also **sherrified.** A term given to wines spoiled by exposure to air or heat. Maderized wines have a telltale dull, brown tinge, and a flat, stale, nutty smell and taste that have been likened to an inexpensive, sweet **Madeira** or sherry (later still, they taste frankly of vinegar). Old or uncorked, wines may oxidize; corked wines can maderize by "cooking" in the bottle at high temperatures during shipment or in storage.

Madras curry paste - see CURRY PASTE.

madrilène - a soup made from poultry stock slightly thickened with tomato juice or puréed pulp (a dish associated with Madrid, as this French term indicates,) which is served cold, hot or chilled and jellied, often garnished with a slice of lemon.

mafalda - see PASTA.

magdalena - a classic, light Spanish sponge cake, usually baked as a cupcake with a characteristic pointed, golden brown peak, and served unfrosted in its pleated paper cup. The simple recipe calls for baking powder, eggs, flour, superfine sugar, and equal portions of milk and olive oil. In Spain, they are often enjoyed with coffee at breakfast.

Maggi, Julius - see profile below.

magnesium - an essential mineral for at least 300 biochemical processes in the body, the proper functioning of the heart and muscles, and a healthy immune system and strong bones. In an adult human, there are about 25 grams of magnesium present: about 60 percent in bones and 30 percent in muscle. Dietary magnesium is absorbed through the small intestine. Many foods, such as some dairy products, fish and legumes, green vegetables, nuts, seeds, soy products and whole grains, are good sources of magnesium, as is **hard water.**

Maggi, Julius (1846–1912) - Swiss flour manufacturer credited with the invention of the **bouillon cube,** which was first made commercially in 1882. Maggi was born in the Thurgau region of Switzerland and took over his father's mill in 1869. Bouillon cubes, which followed the development of seasoning liquids, arose from Maggi's interest in how the industrialization of the day was changing European culture. At the time, more women were becoming factory workers and had less time to prepare traditional meals, which needed lengthy cooking. Maggi was so well known for his dietary proclamations, such as the value of eating more legumes, that the Public Welfare Society commissioned him to conduct a study of the national diet, which led him to develop his commercially successful pea and bean soup powders. He continued to advance new food products and remained with the business until his death at the age of 66. Nestlé bought Maggi & Company in 1947.

magnolia - more than 100 species of trees native to parts of Asia and North and South America, often grown for their showy blooms. Used in traditional Chinese medicines for centuries, the powdered, dried bark is now sold as a remedy for everything from asthma to menopausal complaints. Named after the French botanist Pierre Magnol (1638–1715), magnolias are now the state flowers of Louisiana and Mississippi.

magnum - see WINE BOTTLES.

magret - also **maigret.** The deboned breast of a goose (sometimes a goose raised for **foie gras**) or a **moulard duck** prized, especially by French chefs, for its lean, richly flavored meat.

maguey - see AGAVE.

mahi-mahi - also **dolphin fish, dorado.** *Coryphaena hippurus*, found in the semitropical and tropical waters of the Atlantic, Pacific and Indian oceans. Thought to live about five years at most, mahi-mahi may attain a length of about 78 inches (2 m). A popular commercial catch, it has flavorful flesh that browns when it's cooked; grilling, frying and steaming are the usual methods.

mahleb - also **mahalab, mahlab.** Dried seeds of sour black cherries used ground or whole in Armenian, Middle Eastern and Turkish baked goods to lend a distinctive floral, but bittersweet taste. Although it's available whole or ground, most experts recommend grinding this spice just before use for the best flavor.

mahshi - a Middle Eastern term meaning "stuffed," used to denote a leaf or vegetable, such as an artichoke, bell pepper, cabbage leaf, eggplant, onion, tomato or zucchini, filled with spiced fish, meat or vegetables. One example is *filfil mahshi* (stuffed green pepper), which is filled with a mixture of currants, lemon juice, mint, olive oil, pine nuts and rice.

mai bowle - see MAY WINE.

maid of honor - also **maids of honor.** Small tarts filled with white curd delicately flavored with almond and lemon or, very occasionally, filled with jam. Legend has it that Anne Boleyn baked these first (while she was still a maid, with her honor and her wits about her), and that Henry VIII christened them.

maigret - see MAGRET.

main course - see ENTRÉE.

Maine lobster - see LOBSTER.

maïs - French for "**maize**," on or off the cob.

maison - French for "house." When seen on a restaurant's menu, it usually denotes a specialty of that establishment or its chef.

Mai Tai - a classic cocktail made with both dark and light rum, orange liqueur, sweet-and-sour mix, sometimes Grenadine or **orgeat,** and one or more fruit juices (lemon, lime, orange, pineapple). It's usually poured over crushed ice in a Collins glass. Victor Bergeron, of the famous California watering hole, Trader Vic's, is credited with its creation in 1944.

maître d' - short for *maître d'hôtel*, literally "master of the hotel," a French term for a restaurant's host, in charge of greeting and seating guests, managing the waitstaff and setting the tone for an establishment's ambience and style of service.

maître d'hôtel butter - a creamy or solid mixture of butter, lemon juice and parsley (sometimes other seasonings are also added), served with fish, meat, poultry or cooked vegetables.

maiwein - see MAY WINE.

maíz - Spanish for "maize."

maize - from *zea mays*, the name given to corn by the Swedish botanist Carolus Linnaeus. *Zea* is Greek for "cereal or grain," but when it becomes a verb (*zeo*), it translates as "to live." From earliest times, any cereal that could be ground into flour to make bread has been called "corn"; therefore, since corn was the cereal of the Indians, the first white settlers called it either "maize" or "Indian corn."

maize mushroom - see HUITLACOCHE.

maize oil - see CORN OIL.

maki roll - a Japanese roll-up of seasoned rice with vegetables, or seafood and vegetables, rolled up in **nori.** Some North American restaurants also offer maki rolls filled with chopped fresh fruit or cooked eggs. See also SUSHI.

maki-zushi - see SUSHI.

makrut - see KAFFIR.

Malabar peppercorns - see PEPPERCORNS.

malanga - also **tannia, yautia.** Plants native to tropical regions of the Americas and the West Indies belonging to the *Xanthosoma* genus, which have edible leaves and long, stubby yellow-brown corms. Belonging to the same family as **taro,** these starchy corms may be boiled or baked, or used in the same way as yams; the leaves are a common ingredient in **callaloo** soup. Known as *malanga* in Cuba, *yautia* in Puerto Rico and *tannia* by anglophones in the West Indies, it has been introduced as a food plant in Africa.

Maldon salt - see SALT.

malic acid - a tart, fruity-flavored organic acid, found in fruits, such as apples, bananas, cherries, grapes, pears and tomatoes. It is used as a flavor enhancer in many beverages, particularly citrus drinks. During the winemaking process, too-high concentrations of malic acid, which naturally occurs in grapes, can be converted to the milder lactic acid through malolactic fermentation, mellowing its sharpness.

mallard - see DUCK.

mallet - see MEAT TENDERIZER.

Mallon, Mary (Typhoid Mary) - see profile below.

mallow - also **cheeseweed, musk mallow.** One of various flowering annuals and short-lived perennials of the Malvaceae family. Indigenous to Eurasia, they were brought to North America by early settlers, who appreciated their culinary, medicinal and ornamental uses. Hardy to zone 5, they have now naturalized throughout much of the continent and bloom all summer. The single, frilly mauve, pink or white flowers can be used fresh in salads; dried, along with the dried leaves, the flowers can be steeped to produce an herbal tea considered by some to be effective against cough and sore throat. Fresh or cooked,

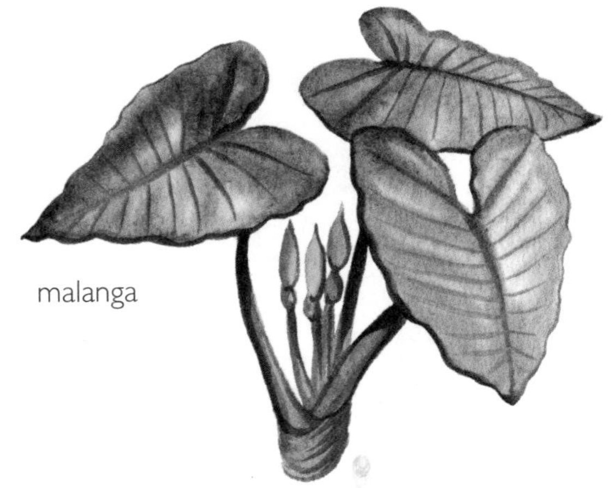

malanga

Mallon, Mary (Typhoid Mary) (1870–1938) - American domestic cook responsible for spreading typhoid where she worked. Mallon didn't know she was immune to typhoid fever, nor that she carried the disease and was responsible when her employers and members of their households began getting sick. A 1907 investigation delving into her employment past uncovered that she had infected 47 people in the New York City area between 1904 and 1914, three of whom died. Several attempts to cure her failed. She was put on trial and quarantined on North Brother Island in the East River at Riverside Hospital, which specialized in infectious diseases. At one point, she fled health authorities and took another job, but was eventually returned to her confinement, which lasted 26 years.

the leaves can be eaten as greens. Removed from their flat capsules, the seeds — similar to cheese in texture — can be roasted or eaten raw.

malossol caviar - a designation for Russian **caviar** that has been lightly salted.

Malpeque oyster - see OYSTER.

malt - **1.** (n.) germinated barley, used to make beer, distilled spirits, vinegar and an additive for foods. Malt is fired in a kiln to roast and dry, then ground into a sweet powder. **2.** (n.) an abbreviated name for a whiskey made with malt. **3.** (n.) an abbreviated name for a malted milk. **4.** (v.) to convert grain, such as barley, into malt.

Maltaise sauce - also **Maltese sauce.** A sauce based on the classic French hollandaise sauce, flavored with the juice and zest of an orange, often served over cooked vegetables, considered particularly complementary to asparagus.

malt bread - a bread made with dough to which naturally sweet, milled malt has been added. The malt adds flavor and acts as a leavening agent. Slightly sticky, brown cylindrical malt loaves (often baked in lidded tube pans with evenly spaced "slice" ridges) are a common sight at grocery stores.

malted milk - originally a beverage made from evaporated malted barley, wheat flour and whole milk; the 1869 invention of two English-born brothers, James and William Horlick, in Racine, Wisconsin. It started out as a nutritional supplement for infants, used to treat digestive disorders, but it also found niche uses as emergency or expedition rations. The drink has an honored place in Americana. Until 1922, "malted milk" drinks were made by mixing milk, chocolate syrup and malt powder. The "malted milkshake" is said to have been the invention of Ivar "Pop" Coulson, a Walgreens soda jerk in Chicago, who decided the basic mixture would taste good with ice cream added.

malted milk powder - a dry, powdered mixture of barley malt, milk, salt and wheat, used as a sweetener in baked goods and also in the "malteds" or "malted milkshakes" invented and served in North American soda shops of the 1920s. Commercial preparations, such as Horlicks and Ovaltine (which also contains cocoa powder), have long been sold as nutrition boosters (when combined with milk) for kids and are also recommended for people with appetite-suppressing illnesses. See also MALTED MILK.

malt extract - also **barley malt syrup, malt syrup.** Malt extract is made by soaking powdered malt in water, then heating and reducing the mixture to a syrup or paste. It is used in brewing and distilling, in the manufacture of breakfast cereals, as a coffee substitute, and in baking. Malt is hygroscopic, which means it retains moisture and thus gives a moist texture to brown bread. It also liberates carbon dioxide during leavening and baking, which helps dough rise, while imparting a sweet flavor.

malt liquor - **1.** a type of beer that has a higher alcohol content (from 4.5 to 8 percent alcohol by weight) than lager or regular beer. **2.** an alcoholic beverage made from fermented barley malt.

maltose - also **malt sugar.** An easily digestible crystalline sugar, used in infant formulas and beer making.

malt syrup - a thick, brown liquid made from a mash of dried, germinated malt that is filtered and evaporated. The syrup, sometimes made with other germinated, cereal grains added to the malt, is used as a sweetener. See also MALT EXTRACT.

malt vinegar - a vinegar made from malted barley. The barley is mashed, heated with water and fermented into a crude type of beer, which is then fed into vats filled with beech shavings, producing bacteria. The mixture is left for several weeks until acetic acid is formed. The vinegar is then filtered, matured and colored with caramel. Malt vinegar is used for pickling (particularly walnuts) and in the well-known Worcestershire sauce. See also VINEGAR.

malt whiskey - whiskey made from malted barley. See also WHISKEY.

mamaliga - the Romanian version of polenta. Cornmeal is simmered slowly in salted water to make a thick mush, then poured out onto a board (or sometimes into a bowl), shaped and allowed to set. Sliced, cooled mamaliga may be eaten with cottage cheese, sour cream or yogurt, or used in foods, such as *bulz*, a baked dish of mamaliga slices layered with grated cheese and butter. See also POLENTA.

mamey sapota - also **canistel, eggfruit, mammee sapota, yellow sapote.** Round or ovoid fruit with a pointed tip, glossy, yellow skin and smooth flesh, which softens toward a center formed by up to four stones. Indigenous to Central America, where it is now cultivated, *Pouteria campechiana*, a small, subtropical and tropical tree (also called a canistel tree), was introduced in Hawaii and the Philippines in the 1920s, and currently grows in the Bahamas, Cuba and throughout the Caribbean, and in southern Florida as well. Likened to cooked sweet potato or pumpkin in flavor, the flesh has the smooth firmness of a hard-boiled egg (hence one of its common names, "eggfruit"). It is eaten fresh or baked, sprinkled with lemon or lime juice, salt and pepper. Puréed, the flesh is added to blender drinks or shakes, custards, ice cream and jams. The fruit can be harvested, then allowed to ripen (it takes up to 10 days); fallen to the ground, it ferments quickly, earning it the Mexican nickname *zapote borrocho* ("drunken fruit").

mamey sapota

mamoncilla - see HONEYBERRY.

ma'mounia - a sweet Middle Eastern pudding, usually made with semolina, butter, almonds and honey, probably named after the 10th-century caliph Ma'moun. The pudding is the texture of polenta or oatmeal and is eaten hot in a bowl with cream on top.

mamra - see MURMURA.

mam tom - a popular Vietnamese condiment. See SHRIMP PASTE.

manchamanteles - a Mexican sauce, originating in Puebla, made with plantains and pineapple, but mostly red pepper; its name means "tablecloth stainer," referring to its red color.

Manchego - a semifirm Spanish strong-tasting cheese, made from the milk of Manchego sheep raised in the La Mancha region. One of Spain's most famous cheeses, author Miguel de Cervantes mentions it in *Don Quixote*.

Manchester pudding - a classic British dessert (popularized by **Mrs. Isabella Beeton**'s mid-Victorian tome, the *Book of Household Management*), consisting of a thick layer of raspberry or strawberry jam, covered by a simmered custard mixture (made of brandy, bread crumbs, eggs, lemon zest, milk, sugar and vanilla), covered, in turn, with a **short-crust pastry** lid, and baked. Some versions use puff pastry or place the pastry on the bottom, instead. Some are topped by meringue, flaked coconut or slivered nuts.

manchet bread - the name given by English bakers since the 14th century to white bread made from fine-quality wheat flour.

Mandarin cuisine - a cosmopolitan cooking style characteristic of Beijing, in northern China. For centuries, the capital pulled chefs from the far-flung provinces to prepare new dishes for the delectation of the royal family, the imperial court and the government officials known as mandarins. **Chinese cabbage, Peking duck, hot-and-sour soup, moo shu** and **pot stickers** are just some of the foods associated with Mandarin cuisine, as is the use of wheat, rather than rice. Vegetable garnishes, elaborately carved into animals and flowers, are elegant hallmarks of this cuisine.

Mandarine Napoléon - cognac flavored with mandarin peel, first released in 1892 by Belgian distiller Louis Schmidt. The origin of the name derives from the drinking inclination of the emperor Napoleon I. When the mandarin first arrived from China (hence the name) at the end of the 18th century, there was something of a rage for it. The fashion was to steep mandarin peels in cognac after eating the fruit. A French chemist, Antoine-François de Fourcroy, apparently crafted a recipe or formula that found favor with Napoleon Bonaparte, which Schmidt stumbled across while doing some chemical research. The mandarins used in this liqueur come exclusively from Sicily.

Mandarin liqueur - a strong, sweet spirit made with brandy, herbs and macerated mandarin orange peels. It is served over ice as an apéritif or **neat** as a warming pick-me-up. It is also used in cocktails, filled chocolates and desserts.

Mandarin orange - a group name for a class of small oranges with thin, easily peeled skin, *Citrus reticulata*. Tangerine is the most common mandarin found in North America. It was named for the Moroccan seaport of Tangiers. The fruit's nomenclature is often confusing because "tangerine" is often used interchangeably with "mandarin," and all tangerines are mandarins (including the tangelo and the clementine), but not all mandarins are tangerines. They both originated under the same mandarin classification, but as hybrids, tangerines developed darker skins, which, in the end, is their only difference.

Mandarins were named for the color of the robes worn by Chinese mandarins, high-level civic officials. Mandarins have been grown and eaten in China and Japan from very early times. Mediterranean cultures were enjoying them by the middle of the 19th century. They arrived in the U.S. in the 1840s, when the Italian Consul planted them in the Consulate garden in New Orleans.

The first commercial crops were grown in Florida. The most popular tangerine is called **Dancy,** after an early Florida grower (Colonel G.L. Dancy), who nicknamed the fruit "kid-glove orange," because the rind peeled so easily. **Satsuma** is a small, Japanese almost-seedless orange. See also CLEMENTINE, SATSUMA, TANGELO.

Mandarin pancake - also **Chinese pancake.** A crispy, thin pancake usually made with a simple water-and-wheat flour dough. The dough is kneaded until smooth, then allowed to rest; cut up, it is rolled into circles. Placed one on top of the other, with a little sesame oil brushed in between, two circles are firmly rolled together to make each pancake. After frying, the pancakes may be used to wrap fillings, such as pork (for **moo shu**) or **Peking duck.** They may also be refrigerated, then reheated in a steamer before use.

mandelbrot - a classic Jewish cookie flavored with almonds, similar to Italian biscotti because it is baked twice. Its name means "almond bread" in Yiddish and comes directly from the German "mandel," meaning "almond" and "brot," meaning "bread." Despite its name, the cookie is not made with bread dough. The name comes from the fact that it is sliced like bread and toasted and often made in a loaf pan.

mandoline - a countertop hand-powered slicer. Held by hand or fixed to a pusher, firm fruits and vegetables are driven against the adjustable blades to produce slices or sticks of consistent size. A traditional tool, wooden mandolines were once the norm; today's models are made of stainless steel or sturdy plastic, and some have slide-on trays underneath to catch the cut food.

mandrake root - the taproot of *Mandragora officinarum*, a sun-loving native of dry, rocky areas in the Balkans, Greece, Italy and Turkey. Containing narcotic alkaloids, the plant was used as an anesthetic as early as 200 BC. The fleshy root, with its eerie resemblance to the naked human form, has been a mainstay in magic rituals. Pulled from their earthy home, mandrake roots were said to scream in agony, "that living mortals, hearing them, run mad" — as Shakespeare wrote in *Romeo and Juliet* (Act IV, Scene III) — or even die.

mandu - a savory Korean dumpling filled with a mixture of minced beef, tofu, cabbage or **kimchi,** chives and seasonings. The dumplings are deep-fried or steam-fried (like Japanese **gyoza**) and served with a soy-based dipping sauce, or boiled and added to soup to make the traditional dish *mandu-kuk*.

mange-tout - another word for snow pea, French for "eat it all," referring to how the peas and pod are both edible.

mango - the fruit, *Mangifera indica*, of a tall tree bearing yellow flowers, one of the most commonly eaten fruits in the tropical areas of the world. India alone produces 10.5 million tons (9.5 million tonnes) of mangoes each year. Mangoes probably originated in the Himalayan region of India and Burma, where they've been

mango

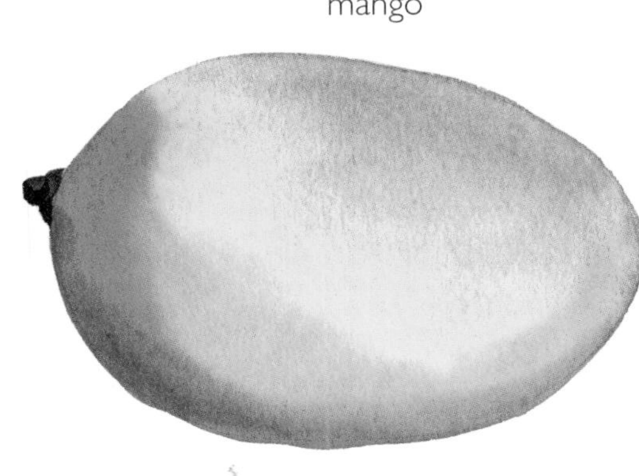

cultivated for more than 6,000 years. In the 14th century, a poet named Amir Khusrau wrote, "The mango is the pride of the garden, the choicest fruit of the Hindustan. The other fruits we are content to eat when ripe, but the mango is good at all stages of growth." In Thailand and some South American countries, the mango is eaten green. The Portuguese introduced it to Brazil in the 17th century and referred to it as *manga*, a transformation of *man-kay* or *man-gay*, which in Tamil, the language of southern India and northern Sri Lanka, means "unripe mango fruit."

In India, Hanuman, the Hindu monkey god, is often depicted holding a mango. Emotional arguments are common in Indian families over the "right" mango to use in whichever recipe handed down from prior generations. There are hundreds of varieties of mangoes, ranging in size from that of a large plum to 7 pounds (3.2 kg) or larger. The mango belongs to the same family as the pistachio and the mahogany. Mangoes were growing in Florida in 1825, but not until 1889, when the Department of Agriculture began experiments in grafting, did anyone consider the fruit a feasible commercial crop. The Hayden (also Haden), from Florida, is one of the most widely distributed varieties in the U.S. Another popular variety is the Malgoba, deep yellow with red on one side, weighing from 8 ounces to 1 pound (250 to 500 g). Some other varieties include Bennet, Sandersha, Paheri, Kent and Manila. Because the mango is a distant cousin of poison oak and poison ivy, some people have allergic reactions to its skin. Mangoes can range in color from yellow or green with a red blush to greenish yellow. They have a sweet pulp that tastes like peach. They're eaten raw or made into salsas, chutneys and preserves, available fresh from midwinter to autumn, but also available canned.

mango chutney - a mild, sweet chutney, a popular complement to spicy curries.

mango ginger - *Curcuma mangga*, belonging to the ginger family. In Asia, the tender rhizomes and shoots, said to smell like unripe mangoes, may be eaten fresh or poached in coconut milk.

mango pickle - a spicy mixture of mangoes, chiles, spices and vinegar, it can be eaten with any bland foods.

mango powder - see AMCHUR.

mangosteen

mangosteen - the fruit, *Garcinia mangostana*, of an evergreen that originated in Malaysia, the Philippines and Indonesia, cultivated for thousands of years not only for its fruit, but also for its magnificent pink flowers. The mangosteen was introduced to the Caribbean in the middle of the 19th century. Its rind is very thick, tough and inedible, but because of its high tannin content, it's used to tan hides. To reach the delicate fruit inside, the rind must be cut with a sharp knife, revealing a white flesh, which makes up only one-quarter of the weight of the fruit. The flesh is split into five to seven segments, similar in appearance to a mandarin, with very small edible seeds. The texture has been described as somewhere between a well-ripened plum and ice cream, with an incomparably delicious flavor.

Manhattan - a cocktail made with whiskey or bourbon, sweet vermouth and a dash of bitters, stirred with ice, then strained into a cocktail glass and garnished with a stemmed maraschino cherry. The most popular story has it that the drink was created at, and named for, the Manhattan Club in New York City to celebrate the election of the state's new governor, Samuel J. Tilden, in 1874. Another tale claims that the cocktail was created, again at the Manhattan Club in New York, in the late 1800s, at the behest of Supreme Court Justice Charles Henry Truax, who requested a less-fattening alternative to the Martinis he regularly drank.

Manhattan clam chowder - see CLAM CHOWDER.

manicotti - see PASTA.

Manila bean - see WINGED BEAN.

manioc - see CASSAVA.

manioc beer - see CASSAVA BEER.

manju - a Japanese sweet rice cake, made from pounded **glutinous rice** and filled with the sweet bean paste called **an.** If the sweet is not filled with *an*, it is called **mochi.** Manju are considered an excellent companion to green tea, as their sweetness is a good foil for the bitterness of the tea.

manna - **1.** the name given to the sticky, sweet liquid seasonally exuded by various trees (such as ash and tamarisk) and shrubs (such as camel's thorn) in southern Europe and the Middle East. Collected locally, it is used as an ingredient for traditional foods and medicines. **2.** a desert lichen, *Lecanora esculenta,* which easily blows loose from the rocks on which it grows and winds into tumbleweeds that are collected in African and Arab countries. It is considered a **"famine food,"** in areas where subsistence crops too often fail. Some literal-minded scholars believe this is the actual "manna from heaven." **3.** the biblical manna or spiritual nourishment given by God that guarantees life everlasting "He who feeds on this bread will live forever." (*John* 6:58) and satisfies a hunger that surpasses the physical "that he might make thee know that man doth not live by bread only, but by every word that proceedeth out of the mouth of the Lord doth man live." (*Deuteronomy* 8:3). **4.** a generic term for various no-fat, unrisen, baked or griddle-fried breads.

mannitol - a mildly laxative, sweetening and thickening agent produced from the **manna** of the deciduous flowering ash, *Fraxinus ornus*, which is indigenous to the Mediterranean and the Middle East. In Sicily, for example, the manna is harvested from ash plantations. In the summer, vertical incisions are made in the tree trunks; the sap seeps out and, exposed to the air and heat, solidifies almost immediately. When enough accumulates, it is scraped away, using special tools, and sold for processing.

manqué - a French cake that, like many creations, came into being by accident. A famous Parisian pastry chef was preparing a cake with lumpy and badly whisked egg whites. *"Le gâteau est manqué!"* screamed his boss, meaning that it was a failure. But the frugal baker refused to give up on his cake and turned it into a success by adding butter and topping it with **praline.** A customer bought it right away, loved it and returned a couple of days later to order another.

manteca - **1.** Spanish for "lard." **2.** an Italian, usually pear-shaped, **pasta-filata** cheese with a center of butter.

mantecadito - a buttery, shortbread cookie, which is a must-have Christmas sweet in Puerto Rico. Flavored with almond extract and simply spiced with a little nutmeg, the dough is rolled into balls, then pressed onto cookie sheets and topped with a sliver of red maraschino cherry. Loyal to their island's most lucrative export, many bakers include rum in their cookie recipe.

Manuka honey - see HONEY.

manzanilla - see CHAMOMILE, SHERRY.

manzanilla olive - a small- to medium-size olive from Spain, brine-cured while still green, often sold pitted and stuffed with pimiento in North America, although it is frequently seen whole in Spain. Manzanilla olives are also a source of fruity, dark green olive oil, although it can be expensive, because manzanillas contain less oil than other varieties. See also OLIVE.

manzanita - a tiny berry from the Ericaceae family, related to the blueberry and cranberry, from the Spanish word meaning "little apple," because it looks like a miniature apple.

maple butter - a creamy, soft spread made by heating maple syrup to 230° to 232°F (110° to 111°C), then cooling it quickly and stirring until it reaches the desired consistency. It should be refrigerated and can be frozen for longer-term storage.

maple honey - also **maple molasses.** Maple syrup boiled until it thickens to the consistency of molasses.

maple molasses - see MAPLE HONEY.

maple sugar - a granulated sugar made from the crystals left when maple sap is boiled past the syrup stage until nearly dry. The resulting moist mixture is left to dry further, then granulated so that it resembles regular table sugar. Maple sugar is intensely sweet, with the characteristic flavor of maple syrup.

maple syrup - a liquid sweetener made by boiling down the sap of the maple tree (usually the sugar or black maple, although almost any type of maple tree can be tapped) until thick and sticky. About 85 percent of the maple syrup produced in the world is made in Canada (more than 90 percent of that comes from the province of Quebec), but it is also widely produced in New England and New York State in the U.S. Maple syrup is a traditional topping for pancakes, waffles and French toast and is the main ingredient in the classic Quebec dessert *tarte au sirop d'erable*, or maple syrup pie. (For Maple Syrup Grades see below.)

maple walnut - a longtime favorite flavor, in such treats as cookies, fudge, ice cream and squares, achieved by adding maple syrup or imitation or pure maple extract, and chopped walnuts.

ma po dou fu - a Chinese specialty from Szechwan province consisting of bean curd in a hot chili sauce. The dish was created by an old Szechwan woman whose face was scarred by smallpox. It became so famous that people journeyed great distances to her restaurant to enjoy her invention. Although she didn't name it, the dish was named by her patrons, who called it "the pockmarked grandmother's bean curd."

maraschino cherry - a cherry **macerated** in sugar syrup, almond oil and sometimes alcohol, used as a garnish for desserts and cocktails. Historically, only the small European wild Marasca cherries from Croatia's Dalmatian area and parts of Italy that had been preserved in **maraschino liqueur** could be labeled as a maraschino cherry. Eventually, by the turn of the century in the U.S., the cherries were made with the Royal Ann variety and came to mean a cherry that had been dyed red, marinated in sugar syrup with almond oil and the alcohol eliminated.

maraschino liqueur - a clear, dry liqueur made with Marasca cherries and pure cane syrup. See also ZARA.

marble cake - a cake composed of two separately mixed batters: one a white batter, the other chocolate. The batters are alternately spooned into the baking pan, then a knife is pushed down into it and drawn across the pan, two or three times, to create swirls of light and dark. After baking, the top is simply dusted with icing sugar.

marbling - thin lines or small spots of naturally occurring fat in meat, which resemble the veins in marble. The fat keeps the meat moist and tender during cooking. Too-lean meat or poultry can be "marbled" by the cook, with **lardon** and a **larding needle.**

marc - **1.** see POMACE. **2.** a generic term for brandy or other spirit, such as Italian grappa, made from grape **pomace**.

marchand de vin - French for "merchant of wine." A term given to a type of flavored butter (often served with grilled steak) or a thick, glazing sauce (often served with poached fish), that have reduced red wine and chopped shallots as the main ingredients.

MAPLE SYRUP GRADES

The governments of Canada and the U.S. each have a unique classification system for the different grades of maple syrup. Although not identical in their label terms, the systems are similar and are based on color (which is measured by the percentage of light transmitted through the syrup). To add confusion to the matter, some provinces and states have adopted their own labeling terms, but they are based on the same five levels of light transmittance. Flavor is not considered in the grading system (unless there is an undesirable flavor, which makes the syrup unusable). The lower grades are more flavorful than the higher grades, which are quite delicate.

Light Transmittance	Canada	United States
75% or higher	No. I Extra Light	Grade A Light Amber
60.5 to 74.9%	No. I Light	Grade A Medium Amber
44 to 60.4%	No. I Medium	Grade A Dark Amber
27 to 43.9%	No. 2 Amber	Grade B
Less than 27%	No. 3 Dark	Substandard

marchpane - an old-fashioned English term for marzipan, an anglicization of the Italian *marzapane*.

Marechal Foch - **1.** a cold-hardy grape hybridized by Eugene Kuhlmann in the Alsace region of France, used to make **Beaujolais**-type red wines. It is named after the famous French marshal Ferdinand Foch, who assumed command for the Allied forces of America, Britain and France in First World War in 1918 and eventually accepted the German surrender. **2.** a type of wine made from the Marechal Foch grape. The wine ages better, perhaps, that some of its namesake's beliefs; the marshal once opined that "the airplane is an interesting toy, but of no military value."

Marengo - see CHICKEN MARENGO.

margarine - a **hydrogenated** butter substitute made of 80 percent fat (usually vegetable oils, such as soybean, cottonseed and corn, and, in some brands, a small amount of animal and/or dairy fats); the remaining 20 percent comprised of milk, water, flavoring and usually vitamins A and D.

It was named through a minor scientific error. French chemist Michel Chevreul, whose investigations of color influenced the painter Georges Seurat, isolated a substance from animal fat in 1813 that formed pearly drops and was thought to be a new fatty acid. He named it "margaric acid," from the Greek *margaron*, meaning "pearl," even though his discovery was later proven false. In 1867, French chemist Hippolyte Mège-Mouriès, then 50 years old, began developing a synthetic butter at the request of Emperor Napoleon III. Mège-Mouriès used an extract of animal fat that was thought to contain a large amount of this "acid," inspiring him to name his product "margarine," which was patented in England under the name "butterine." Mège-Mouriès worked with suet, chopped cows' udders and warm milk. He began a revolution in the butter industry with the first commercial margarine, produced in 1869.

Margarine caught on quickly in both Europe and the U.S., where patents began multiplying. But it was two Dutch companies, Van den Bergh and Juergens, that made margarine a commercial success, after the Franco-Prussian War. In 1871, 50 factories were producing the "butter of the poor" in dairy-rich Holland. By 1883, Juergens, Europe's biggest butter dealer, was shipping 40,000 tons (36,000 tonnes) of margarine to England, its biggest customer. Juergens later teamed up with Van den Bergh, its biggest competitor, and Lever Brothers, a soap manufacturing company from England to form Unilever. Lord Leverhulme, an industrialist who formed Lever Brothers with his brother James, said, in 1918, that his company had "drifted" into the margarine business "because of its close connection with oil and fats for the soap kettle."

In 1937, Unilever bought the Newfoundland Butter Co., which mainly produced margarine. It was a stroke of good timing, because wartime shortages boosted margarine sales. But no butter-colored margarine could be sold in North America (some say in surrender to the dairy lobby, others say in support of the consumer who might have been fooled by butter look-alikes) from the late 1800s until the late 1900s. By law, margarine had to be left white, its natural color, but some manufacturers did include a bright yellow colorant that could be mixed in at home. Continent-wide, the laws have changed, with the exception of Quebec; despite a court challenge from food giant Unilever, in 2005, margarine produced inside its borders remains white.

Margarita

Margarita - a cocktail usually made with three parts tequila, two parts orange liqueur and one part fresh lime juice. The rim of the glass is usually rubbed with lime and then dipped in salt. There are four conflicting stories, still debated, about how the drink originated. One story says it was first made in 1930 at a Tijuana racetrack bar. Another says it was the result of a request by a showgirl, in 1938, for a tequila cocktail, subsequently named for her, although her name was Marjorie. Another suggests it was the concoction of a Mexican bartender who had been asked to make a "magnolia," but didn't know the ingredients and made something he called a "margarita" instead. Finally, another says that it was the invention of Texas socialite Margarita Sames, who came up with the cocktail while entertaining friends at her Acapulco vacation home.

Margherita - a style of pizza named for Queen Margherita, of the Italian royal house of Savoy, who was first presented with it in 1889 at the Royal Palace of Capodimonte in Naples. The pizza has tomato sauce, mozzarella and basil: the red, white and green of the Italian flag.

Marguery sauce - a hollandaise-type sauce named for its creator, Nicholas Marguery, who began by washing dishes in one Paris restaurant and worked his way up to owning another, The Marguery, in the 1880s. A specialty of the house was this sauce, served over sole. The poaching liquid from the fish is reduced, then slightly cooled; egg yolks and butter are whisked in, and salt and pepper added. The sauce is poured over the fish and quickly glazed in the oven. Now, in North American restaurants, Marguery sauce is often made and served with trout.

Maria biscuit - also **Maria cookie.** A biscuit, similar to a **digestive biscuit,** created in England in 1874 to celebrate the wedding of Grand Duchess Maria of Russia to the Duke of Edinburgh. It is very popular in Spain, where it is sometimes served with **natillas,** a pourable custard. The biscuit is easily recognizable by the delicate imprint "Maria" on the top.

marigold - an annual plant, *Calendula officinalis*, native to Asia and southern Europe, an ancient potherb used chiefly to hide the bad smell or taste of meat that wasn't fresh. Its French name is *souci*. Today, the petals are used, either fresh or dried, as an herb and a food dye. See also EDIBLE FLOWERS.

marinade - a liquid in which fish, meat or poultry (and sometimes vegetables) are steeped to enhance taste and tenderness. An acid ingredient, such as lemon or lime juice, vinegar or wine, is present in most marinades as a tenderizer; herbs, spices, minced garlic, ginger and onion, and olive oil are also common constituents. The length of time required to marinate meat, for example, depends on the cut. For grilling or roasting, the marinade may also be used as a basting sauce. See also MARINATE.

marinara - an Italian seafood sauce. As a North American term, it takes its name from the Italian *marinaio*, meaning "sailor" — not for what a sailor would fish out of the sea and cook, but rather what would remain fresh for a long journey and could be prepared with the minimum amount of fire aboard wooden ships. A modern marinara is a light, vegetarian sauce of tomato, onion, garlic, basil and oregano, and is often used on pasta and meat.

marinate - to soak food, such as fish or meat, in a wet, seasoned mixture, called a marinade, to enhance taste and tenderness. Marinating times vary from a few hours to several days, depending on the type of food, cut of meat and the desired flavor effect. See also MACERATE, MARINADE, SEVICHE.

marinière - **1.** a French cooking term denoting mussels cooked in white wine with shallots, or other seafood or shellfish cooked in the same way, garnished with mussels. *Marinière* is French for "mariner." **2.** the name of a **Bercy**-type sauce made with butter, chopped shallots, white wine and mussel stock. In New Orleans restaurants, for example, diners find *crevettes* and *moules marinière* on the menu.

marjolaine - **1.** French for "marjoram." **2.** a **dacquoise**-style cake containing ground almond and hazelnuts, usually filled with chocolate buttercream and occasionally topped with creamy, praline-flavored frosting.

marigold

marjoram - from the same family as oregano, an ancient herb, *Origanum marjorana*, a Greek symbol of joy and happiness; its name from the Greek *oros*, meaning "mountain," and *ganos*, meaning "joy." Marjoram is either sweet, the more common variety, or wild, which has a more delicate flavor. It was such a good little plant, legend has it, that no one who had sold himself to the devil could abide it, which may have come from the belief that if marjoram grew well upon a tomb, the deceased was happy. A Latin myth about Venus wandering on Mount Ida, picking wild marjoram to heal Aeneas' wounds, led to the fashion of using the herb for cosmetic purposes. It was also believed that marjoram was a transfiguration of a handsome youth once in the service of King Cinyrus of Cyprus. One day, he dropped a vessel of sweet perfume. In terror of displeasing the king, he swooned into unconsciousness and changed into a sweet marjoram plant, which graced the palace thereafter. Another myth professed that, if you anointed yourself with marjoram before going to sleep, you would dream of your future spouse. Marjoram was used in Colonial America as a tea, a seasoning, a snuff and to dye woolens purple and linens reddish brown. See also OREGANO.

marjoram

market price - a term seen on restaurant menus (usually for items of a seasonal nature, such as lobster), which indicates that the price fluctuates, depending on availability.

Marlborough pie - also **apple-cream pie, Marlborough pudding.** A classic New England single-crust pie, with an applesauce-and-egg custard filling flavored with nutmeg and sherry. Massachusetts boasts a town called Marlborough, which was incorporated in the mid-1600s. This was just about the time that the first Duke of Marlborough, John Churchill, was named; however, the colonial town is reputed to be named in recognition of an old English town in Wiltshire also named Marlborough. It's a good bet that the American pie is named after the American town. Both cultivated and wild apples were a reliable source of fruit for colonists; in 1796, Amelia Simmons' book, *American Cookery*, included a recipe for Marlborough pudding. Whatever the lineage of its name, in Massachusetts, this pie is a Thanksgiving tradition.

marlin - also **billfish, spearfish.** Large food and sport fish from the genus *Makaira* and *Tetrapturus*, found in the open, warm waters of the Atlantic (as far north as Long Island), Indian and Pacific oceans. Marlin are easily recognized by their bill-like or spear-like upper jar and weights that reach 500 pounds (250 kg). An important commercial catch along the Mexican Pacific coast, they are an important sport fish in California, as well as the waters around Florida. Readers will remember the great marlin caught in Ernest Hemingway's *The Old Man and the Sea*. Nevertheless, the major threat to their existence is chalked up to "incidental" catches by large commercial fishing vessels; marlins are now pegged at dangerously low population levels. Various types are known as blue marlin, striped marlin and white marlin. The firm, mild-flavored flesh is good baked, broiled, fried or grilled, or served raw, in sushi.

marmalade - a jam-like preserve made from bitter oranges, usually Sevilles. It was created, according to one fanciful account, by a physician who treated Mary, Queen of Scots, for seasickness after a voyage from Calais to Leith in 1561. He is said to have served her orange and crushed sugar and remarked to someone, "*Marie est malade*." This is one version of how the word "marmalade" is said to have come about. A more likely suggestion is that it is a derivation from *marmelo*, Portuguese for "quince" (the first fruit used to make the preserve), which in turn was from the Greek *melimelon*, Latin *melimelum*, meaning "honey apple." See also DUNDEE MARMALADE.

Marmite - the English brand name for yeast extract, which is produced by autolysis, the breaking down of cells by its own enzymes; the resulting liquid is then drawn off and evaporated. A popular English spread for toast, very high in B vitamins. See also VEGEMITE.

marmite - a French tall-sided cooking pot, often lidded, used to slow-cook dishes.

Maroilles - also **Marolles.** A soft, strong-smelling and tasting cheese, made in the village of Maroilles, affectionately known to French gastronomes as *vieux puant* or "old stinker." Monks at the Abbey of Maroilles first made this cheese about AD 960.

maror - see BITTER HERBS.

marraquetas - a chewy South American white bread, made in small loaves from a simple dough of flour, salt, sugar, yeast and shortening, often enjoyed at breakfast.

marron - **1.** French for "chestnut." **2.** one of the three largest crayfish. Native to Australia, the sweet-fleshed marron, or *Cherax tenuimanus*, is now being farmed around the world in such countries as Africa, China, Japan and the United States.

marron glacé - also **candied chestnut.** A fresh chestnut poached in a vanilla-scented sugar syrup until it is candied. *Marron* means "chestnut" in French, and *glacé* means "glazed" or "candied." This French sweet dates back to the reign of Louis XIV and can be enjoyed on its own or, chopped, added to baked goods, confections and desserts. They are an expensive delicacy, often found packed in jars in North American gourmet shops. See also CANDIED FRUIT.

marrow - the soft, fatty tissue inside bones; extremely rich in calories and high in cholesterol. It is a delicacy that is usually cooked in the bone and served on its own with specially designed **marrow spoons,** but it is also the key or finishing ingredient in numerous classic French sauces.

marrow bean - a dried, small, plump and oval white bean, common in Italian kitchens, which is rehydrated before adding to soups and stews.

marrow bone - usually the long leg bone from a cow or steer, with a large, longitudinal cavity filled with marrow. Simmered for hearty soups (such as borscht) and stews (such as **pot-au-feu**), marrow bones make flavorful, nutritious, rich stock. In the 19th century, marrow bones were roasted, then the marrow was scooped out and spread on toast. Up-market restaurants have revived this fashion, serving steaming hot bones, a **marrow spoon** and toast to the diner.

marrowfat pea - a field-dried, mature, large pea, which is rehydrated before cooking. See also MUSHY PEAS.

marrow spoon - a long and slender, straight spoon with an elongated, shallow bowl, used at the dinner table to scrape marrow out of a bone; usually the narrower handle is also hollowed out along the top to form another, even slimmer scoop. Thought to have been in common use from about 1700, marrow spoons were often made of horn, pewter or sterling. See also MARROW.

marrow squash - see ZUCCHINI.

Marsala - a Sicilian fortified wine made from local grapes, available dry (*secco*), semidry (*semisecco*) and sweet (*dolce*). There are four grades: *Fine*, aged for at least one year; *Superiore*, aged for at least two years; *Superiore Riserva*, aged for four years; and *Vergine Soleras*, aged for at least five years. The label will indicate what type of grape was used: *oro* (golden) or *ambra* (amber) for white grapes; *rubino* (ruby) for red grapes.

Wine merchant **John Woodhouse** created Marsala for the English market in 1773, after he discovered that fortifying the wine with grape spirit kept it from spoiling during its passage to England. Marsala became very popular in 1798, when Lord Nelson made it the British fleet's onboard beverage of choice.

marshmallow - a perennial shrub, *Althaea officinalis*, which grows in salt marshes, common in the eastern U.S.; sometimes referred to as "the mortification plant," because the gooey substance extracted from the roots, called mucilage, was used by morticians. Known for thousands of years in many cultures for its medicinal uses, marshmallow was even a human staple during famines. The Greek physician Hippocrates paid tribute to its value in treating open wounds. Another Greek, Dioscorides, prescribed it in a vinegar infusion for toothaches and insect stings. The Roman poet Horace advertised the use of the roots and leaves as a strong laxative. The Egyptians used it for confections that they flavored with honey. Renaissance apothecaries dispensed it for urinary ailments, gonorrhea and any mouth infection. The roots can be blanched and then fried, and they're used in the inventive French confection *pâte de guimauve*. The plant's sap was used to make marshmallow candy until the mid-1800s.

Modern marshmallows are a mixture of corn syrup or sugar, gelatin, gum arabic and flavoring. In 1948, Alex Doumak, a marshmallow manufacturer, found a way to pipe the candy, so that it could be cut into the small "tubes" that children push onto the end of sticks and roast over a campfire.

marshmallow cream - also **marshmallow crème.** A fluffy, sticky whipped marshmallow spread, which is sold in jars for use as a topping or filling for baked goods and confections. See also FLUFFERNUTTER.

Martha Washington pie - actually a white layer cake named after the wife of the first president of the United States. It is filled with raspberry jam — to recreate the red-and-white stripes of Old Glory, perhaps? — and sprinkled with icing sugar.

Martini - a cocktail classically made with $2\frac{1}{2}$ ounces of gin and $\frac{1}{2}$ ounce dry vermouth, stirred with crushed ice and poured into a chilled glass, then garnished with an olive or twist of lemon. If garnished with a pickled onion, the drink is called a **Gibson.** Substituting vodka for gin creates a **"kangaroo,"** although it's best known simply as a "vodka Martini." Believed to be the invention of Martini di Arma di Taggia, the bartender of New York's Knickerbocker Hotel in 1911, it was first made with equal parts gin and dry vermouth, splashed with orange bitters. The Martini's popularity has inspired chefs to make "food Martinis," served in the characteristic glass, containing innumerable variations, such as little seafood salads and savory mousses, a nod to the shrimp cocktail popular a few decades ago. See also DIRTY MARTINI.

Martini glass - a glass with a tall stem and a cone-shaped bowl, used for Martinis and other shaken cocktails. The theory is that the sloped sides keep the shaken mixture from separating.

marzipan - a confection made of honey and crushed almonds, flavored with rose water, with origins in ancient Egypt and a grand tradition in sculpted candy making. The word is a German spelling of *marzapane*, an Italian term from the Renaissance meaning a "little box for candies"; however, in the Middle Ages, it referred to a "small container for coins." The word may derive from the Latin *marci pan* or *Marco panis*, meaning the bread of Saint Mark, who has always been associated with bread.

masa - Spanish for "dough." Corn masa is made with dried field corn cooked in calcium oxide (also known as pickling), mason's or powdered lime or lye to break down its tough outer skin, then rinsed thoroughly in water and ground into a paste. Anthropologists have dated the household equipment for the nixtamalization, as the process is called, to 1200 BC. A very fine paste is used to make tortillas, and a coarser grind is used to make tamales. See also MASA HARINA.

masa harina - also **atole flour.** Spanish for "dough flour," an industrially produced corn flour that can be made into masa by simply adding water, used to make tortillas; also a brand name — Masa Harina de Maiz — used by the Quaker Oats Co. for its corn flour. Since masa harina is gluten-free, it is a popular baking ingredient for people with celiac disease. See also MASA.

masala - an Indian spice blend, meaning "a mixture of spices." Some are referred to as "wet," meaning a blend of spices that have been ground into a paste with herbs, other seasonings and liquids, such as water, vinegar or yogurt. The most well-known "dry" spice blend is **garam masala,** meaning "warm mixture" in Hindi. It can include up to 12 spices, including a traditional mix of coriander seeds, cumin seeds, peppercorns, cinnamon, cardamom pods and cloves, and is generally added at the end of cooking, to enhance the other ingredients.

masala chai - Indian spiced tea (*masala* means "spiced," and *chai* means "tea" in Hindi) made by simmering spices, such as anise, bay leaves, black peppercorns, cinnamon sticks, cloves, freshly grated gingerroot, green cardamom pods and whole nutmeg, in water, then adding black tea and milk; some tea brewers begin with all the ingredients in the pot, including the milk. It is usually enjoyed very sweet, with added honey or sugar. A beverage drunk throughout the day, masala chai is an essential, with small snacks, at teatime.

masarica - ready-made, Latin American "instant" corn-dough mix, used to make biscuits, bread and other baked goods; also used as a thickener in chili and stews.

mascarpone - a delicately flavored **triple-crème cheese** from Lombardy, too rich to eat on its own but ideal for desserts, particularly in **tiramisu.** Mascarpone is made from the cream of curdled cow's milk and is 90 percent fat. Unlike many other cheeses, it takes only 24 hours to make.

mash - **1.** (n.) materials, such as barley malt, that are ground, then soaked and cooked in water to convert the starches into sugar to encourage fermentation in the making of alcoholic beverages. **2.** (v.) to crush or pound fruits or vegetables to a smooth mixture.

mashed potatoes - potatoes, usually peeled, that are boiled, drained and puréed into a smooth mixture, using an electric beater, a hand-held potato masher, fork or whisk, or a blender, usually with a small amount of cream or milk, and butter or oil. Seasonings, such as bacon bits, grated cheese, sour cream, and minced chipotle pepper, garlic, herbs and onions, are often added (more than one manufacturer offers ready-made seasoning mixes just for this). While mashed potatoes are one of the Western world's most popular side dishes (especially in Germany, North America and the United Kingdom), they are also used as a topping for dishes, such as shepherd's pie; mixed with egg yolks for **duchess potatoes;** or fried with eggs for breakfast. Many "instant" varieties are available.

maskinonge - see MUSKELLUNGE.

maslin pan - a large-capacity preserving kettle. This broad, deep pot has a thick bottom, which holds heat evenly across the base while preventing the contents from burning; the angled sides and wide mouth allow maximum evaporation when making jams, marmalade and preserves. Available in different versions, such as stainless steel or copper lined with stainless steel, all have a hinged carrying handle. A spout at one side of the rim with a "helper handle" on the opposite side enable neat, safe pouring.

mason jars

Mason jar - a wide-mouthed glass canning jar with a two-piece lid, used for home canning and preserving. The name comes from the jar's inventor, John L. Mason, who patented his zinc-topped invention in 1858. The Mason jar greatly improved the safety of home canning when it was invented, sealing out bacteria better than previous sealing methods, such as paraffin wax or cork stoppers. The current version has a two-piece metal lid (no longer made of zinc), consisting of a flat lid coated with a sealing compound around the edge and a metal ring that screws onto the jar and lid to form a tight, safe seal.

masoor dal - also **masur dal.** See DAL.

Matcha tea - see TEA.

matchsticks - **julienned** food that resembles wooden matchsticks in shape and size.

Matsuhisa, Nobuyuki (Nobu) (1948–) - Japanese-born chef and restaurateur. Trained in classical sushi making by top Tokyo chefs, the peripatetic Nobu has covered the globe, opening restaurants at almost every stop. His first was a sushi bar in Lima, Peru. He opened another restaurant in Buenos Aires, Argentina. After returning to travel throughout his native Japan, he went to Anchorage, Alaska, where he opened another. When he decided to settle down in the U.S., in the late 1980s, he divided his time between Los Angeles and New York. Nobu is best known as an innovator. His famous **funazushi** is a dish of freshwater trout that has been buried in rice for a year. His twist on an old standard, called "new-style sashimi," is seared fish that remains raw at the center, which he then marinates in olive oil and garlic. He has received many accolades, among them, in 1995, three stars from *The New York Times*. That same year, the **James Beard** Foundation gave him the Best New Restaurant Award and went on to nominate Nobu for Outstanding Chef in 1997, 1999, 2000, 2001, 2002, 2003 and 2004. He was given his first Michelin star in 1997 and his second in 2006. Nobu oversees operations in restaurants in Tokyo, Las Vegas, Malibu, Dallas, Miami Beach and Milan, with three more in London and three in New York, one of which he opened with actor Robert DeNiro. He has written two cookbooks, his first, *Nobu: The Cookbook,* is a collection of his favorite seafood recipes. His most recent, *Nobu Now*, was released in 2005.

maté - see YERBA MATÉ.

matelote - **1.** a fragrant and flavorful French eel or fish stew or thick chowder. Although *matelote* is French for "sailor," the main ingredients are traditionally freshwater, not saltwater creatures. Made with lots of seasonings, stock and wine, the dish may be garnished with croutons, mushrooms, small whole onions and, sometimes, crayfish. North American versions may be made with pike, salmon or trout. **2.** a rich, dark brown sauce made of minced shallots sautéed in butter, with flour, red wine, sugar and salt and pepper added as it cooks.

matjes - see HERRING.

matka chai - Indian masala tea (*chai*), sold by vendors on city streets and railway platforms, and served in a disposable, handmade clay cup (*matka*). The biodegradable cup can simply be tossed away after use. See also MASALA CHAI.

matrimonial cake - a dessert, the Prairie bakers' name for date squares, consisting of two layers of rolled oat mixture with a date filling in the middle. The name, which has been around since at least the 1940s, may refer to the two separate layers married by dates.

Matrimonial vine - see GOGI BERRY.

Matsuhisa, Nobuyuki (Nobu) - see profile above.

matsutake - also **pine mushroom.** A large, brown, meaty mushroom, with an intense flavor and a fragrance that combines notes of cinnamon and pine, used by Japanese cooks in broth, **sukiyaki**, sushi and tempura. An expensive delicacy in Japan, these are increasingly popular in North America, where they are wild-harvested from forests along the northwest coast of the Pacific in the fall. Since matsutake are also a food source for insects and other mammals — and are beneficial for the health of the forest itself — scientists in Oregon and Washington states are now studying the effect of this harvesting in local national forests.

matzo - also **matzoh.** The thin, unleavened bread, referring to the bread the Jews took with them in their flight from Egypt and slavery. There was no time to let the bread rise properly, because the exodus took place furtively, in haste and in the middle of the night. Remembered each year at Passover, when matzo is a meaningful part of the ritual ceremonies, this humble, unsalted cracker, sometimes called "the bread of affliction," represents a highly significant chapter in Jewish history.

The Hebrew name for Passover is *Pesah,* from which the English "paschal" is derived, bringing together Passover and Christian Easter as important religious celebrations that always fall close to each other on the calendar. Passover begins with Seder, the ceremonial dinner eaten on the first or second night of Passover, during which matzo plays an honored role. In fact, for the eight days of Passover, observant Jews don't eat any leavened bread or foods containing yeast. Some interpret the flat bread as a symbol of man's lowly position before God, and that the parallel lines in the surface of the matzo — created by rows of perforations through which steam escapes during baking — are a visual echo of the Red Sea, through which the Jews passed as they escaped from the pharaoh's pursuing army.

matzo ball - also **knaidel.** A spherical, seasoned dumpling made with chicken fat, eggs and **matzo meal.** A standard addition to chicken soup, matzo balls can be made from scratch or from boxed mixes.

matzo brei - a fried egg and **matzo** dish. For each serving, one matzo wafer is broken up and softened in water; after the excess water is squeezed out, the matzo bits are mixed with one beaten egg and fried in oil. Sweet versions, with brown sugar and cinnamon, are served with honey or syrup. Savory versions, which may contain asparagus tips, or chopped onion or red pepper, are served with sour cream.

matzo meal - **matzo** crushed into a fine powder and used to make fritters and pancakes, for example, as a thickener in soups and stews, and in the mixture for breading fried foods. It is available in fine and more coarsely ground types.

Maui onion - see ONION.

mayapple - **1.** also **American mandrake.** *Podophyllum peltatum*, a low-growing North American native of meadows and woodlands. Under umbrella-like leaves, white spring flowers mature into sweet, glossy yellow fruits. Edible only when ripe, the fruit pulp was a common ingredient in colonial kitchens. Although toxic, other parts of the plant have historically been used in folk-medicine laxatives, salves, tonics and wart-removing ointments. **2.** see LOQUAT.

mayonnaise - a thick, creamy sauce or dressing made of oil, egg yolks and lemon juice or vinegar. The story of the origin of mayonnaise is one of the most disputed in French culinary history. The most commonly circulated story involves Vigneron du Plessis, Duke de Richelieu (the great-great-nephew of the famed Bishop Louis-François Armand), born in Paris in 1696. He became Maréchal de France after the battle of Fontenoy in 1745. Eleven years later, he was party to the siege of Fort-Mahon, Minorca Island's capital and an English possession. After seizing Fort St-Philippe at Mahon, there was no butter or cream available, so his chef had to make a dressing from eggs and oil. When they returned to the mainland, the concoction became known as *sauce mahonnaise*. Besides enjoying status as a skillful military leader, the duke was also generally known as a bon vivant with the odd habit of inviting his guests to dine in the nude. Others believe that the sauce was known as *Bayonnaise*, from the French town of Bayonne, later changed to "mayonnaise." The legendary French chef **Antonin Carême** claimed that the word came from the French verb *manier*, meaning "to stir," and referred to the sauce as *magnonnaise* or *magnionnaise* in his writings. **Prosper Montagne,** the French chef and author who spent his life writing about food, suggested that the word was "a popular corruption of *moyeunaise*, derived from the Old French *moyeu*, meaning 'egg yolk,' which is, with oil, the base of mayonnaise."

Maytag blue - an aged, artisanal, blue cow's milk cheese made in Iowa since 1941 (yes, the original producer was the son of that other famous Maytag), following a process developed by the Iowa State University. Crumbly and pungent, it is usually eaten atop a cracker, on a salad or in a dip.

May wine - also **mai bowle, maiwein.** A German punch made to celebrate May Day. Traditionally, a special day for Europeans, the first day of May has also been a workers' holiday in Germany since 1919. **Woodruff,** called *waldmeister* in German, is steeped in a dry, still Moselle or Rhine wine to flavor it and then discarded. Champagne, seltzer or soda water is then added to the wine, along with slices of fruits, such as orange or pineapple, and a few sprigs of woodruff as garnish. May wine can be homemade or purchased ready-made.

maza - also **meze, mezze.** Persian for "taste." An array of up to several dozen types of small finger foods, served in Mediterranean, Middle Eastern and North African countries. In Greece, where it's called *meze*, this is often an appetizer course;

in Arabic countries, it may be a leisurely meal in itself. The foods may include cheeses, **dolma,** falafel, hummus, kebab, **kibbeh** balls, nuts and spiced olives.

McDonald, Dick and Mac - see KROC, RAY.

McGee, Harold - see profile below.

McIntosh apple - see APPLE.

mead - from the Greek *methy*, meaning "wine," and the Sanskrit *madhu*, meaning "honey," a fermented, mildly alcoholic liquor made from honey, water, herbs and spices; the drink of choice during the Middle Ages and whose popularity endured long after. It was the favorite tipple of Queen Elizabeth I. Mead is made by boiling the ingredients together, then letting the mixture stand for three months before bottling. It is considered ready to drink six weeks later. Other medieval drinks include **posset** (hot milk curdled with ale or wine, often spiced and sweetened) and **panch,** an Indian word meaning "five," for the number of ingredients in this punch, made of **arak** (a distilled liquor), tea, lemon juice, water and sugar or honey.

meal - **1.** finely ground grain, nut or **pulse,** or crushed, crisp food, such as **matzo meal. 2.** a generic term for a repast, such as breakfast, lunch and supper. **3.** the food itself.

mealy - denotes a dry, powdery, meal-like texture.

measuring cup - see DRY MEASURE.

measuring spoons

measuring spoon - a ceramic or metal spoon, usually found in a nesting set of several, different-size spoons used for measuring small amounts of dry or liquid ingredients, such as spices or vanilla. Commonly available in aluminum, ceramic, plastic and stainless steel, most sets include measures for $\frac{1}{4}$ teaspoon (1 mL), $\frac{1}{2}$ teaspoon (2 mL), 1 teaspoon (5 mL), $\frac{1}{2}$ tablespoon (7 mL) and 1 tablespoon (15 mL). Some have elongated bowls designed to slip easily into small spice bottles. Most have relatively long handles, which allow the spoons to be dipped into deep jars, with the size permanently impressed or embossed on each. Because they are dishwasher-safe, resistant to dents and won't melt, stainless-steel versions are considered the best. There is also a measuring spoon available that comes as a long and narrow scoop with measurements marked along the long edges and a sliding dam, parallel to the short ends, which can be moved to change the scoop or spoon size.

McGee, Harold (mid-20th century–) - American food-science writer and international expert on the chemistry of cooking. McGee's course of academic study began with a Bachelor of Science degree in literature from the California Institute of Technology, where he studied physics and chemistry. He earned his doctorate of literature from Yale University, where he taught writing for many years. His first book, the 680-page *On Food and Cooking: The Science and Lore of the Kitchen* (1984), became a bible of food science and is now required reading in Advanced Culinary Principles classes at the Culinary Institute of America. Six years later, McGee published *The Curious Cook: More Kitchen Science and Lore.* In 2004, he released the second edition of the award-winning *On Food and Cooking,* revised, updated and considerably larger at almost 900 pages. He was able to include the latest neuroscientific and chemical research, such as the discovery that the fruity esters created in dry-cured ham are the same as those that occur naturally in melon, which may explain why these two foods are considered an excellent pairing of flavors. In 1995, he was named to the **James Beard** Foundation's Who's Who in American Food.

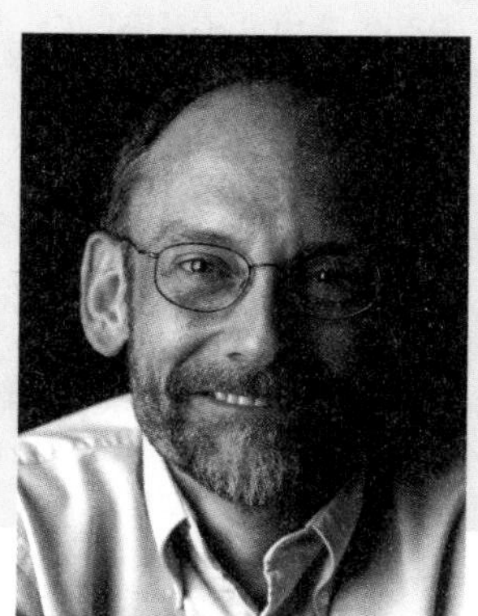

Medici, Catherine de' (1519–1589) - Italian aristocrat and Queen consort to Henry II of France. She changed the course of culinary history in the mid-16th century, when she introduced her brigade of Florentine chefs to the French court. Trained in the sophisticated art of Renaissance cooking, they transformed the noble French repertoire by introducing aspics, sweetbreads, artichoke hearts, truffles, macaroons, ice cream and zabagliones. Catherine was said to love artichokes so much, she often fainted from eating too many. Because of Catherine's influence, women were always invited to the royal table, rather than only on special occasions.

meat - Humans have been carnivores since at least 9000 BC, when they began eating sheep and goats. Pork wasn't consumed for another 2,000 years, with the husbandry of cattle beginning about 6500 BC. Today, however, there's been a reappraisal of the dietary importance of meat: for some, health concerns, such as high cholesterol levels, and environmental ethics may far outweigh meat's value as a source of protein. Regional preferences, religion and climate greatly influence a culture's cuisine. The consumption of horse, goat, reindeer, rabbit, reptiles and insects can be traced specifically back to culture and geography. National and regional preferences have been evolving for millennia, leaving us with the current preponderance of pork consumed in China, mutton and lamb in the Middle East, goat in the Caribbean and beef in Europe and America.

Modern cattle, sheep and pigs are well fleshed compared with their forebears of a couple of centuries ago. Animals have only been reared exclusively for food since the late 1800s. Before that time, beef and mutton were tough, fatty, expensive and probably strongly flavored. Candles were made from beef and mutton fat, another reason to keep the animals plump. Moreover, sheep were bred primarily for their leather and wool, slaughtered only after they were no longer able to provide these, at which point they'd become mutton. Cattle or oxen were originally raised primarily as beasts of burden.

According to a 2002 study from the University of Arkansas, meat consumption has increased 32 percent over the last 40 years. In that year, consumers ate more meat than in any other year in history: the total annual consumption per capita in the U.S. of red meat and poultry was about 219 pounds (99 kg).

meatball - a small ball made of a mixture of seasoned minced poultry or meat and a filler, such as bread crumbs, along with an ingredient, such as beaten egg or sour cream, that helps to hold it together. Meatballs may be hand-formed or shaped with a **meat baller.** Almost every cuisine has its own version. A short sampling includes the Danish *frikadeller*, the German *Klopse*, the Greek *keftedes* and the Spanish *albóndiga*. Meatballs may be cooked on a stovetop or in the oven, then eaten unadorned or added to soups, stews and pasta dishes. See also HAMBURGER, KOFTA.

meat baller - scissor-type tongs with a half-hemispherical scoop at the working end of each criss-crossed arm and a looped handle at the other. The open tongs are scooped into the meatball mixture, then closed until the rims of the scoops meet (any excess mixture is forced out a small hole at the center of each scoop) to press the mixture together.

meat fork - see CARVING FORK.

meat loaf - a baked loaf made of ground meat (beef, veal, pork, poultry or a combination), which is mixed thoroughly with bread crumbs, eggs and seasonings and then pressed into a loaf pan or mounded on a greased baking sheet. When fully cooked, the loaf is cut into thick slices and is often served with tomato sauce, gravy or ketchup.

meat mallet - see MEAT TENDERIZER.

meat tea - see HIGH TEA.

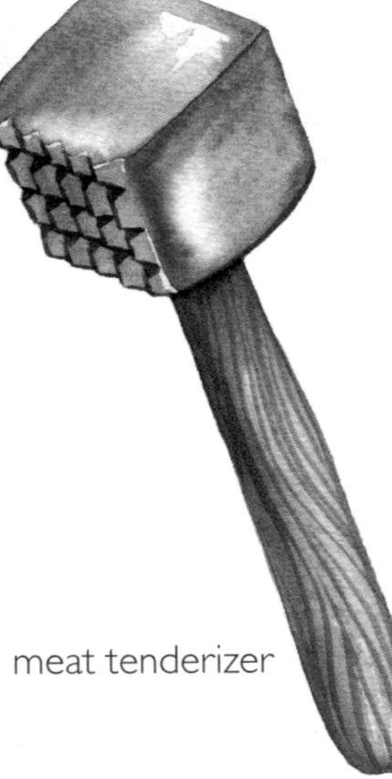

meat tenderizer

meat tenderizer - **1.** a substance used to soften meat by breaking down the fibers that make it tough.

Commercial powders contain enzymes, such as **papain,** a papaya extract, that do the job. Acid ingredients, such as lemon juice, vinegar and wine, in marinades function in the same way. **2.** a **mallet** or **meat mallet,** usually made of metal, sturdy plastic or wood. At least one surface of the head has a grid of protruding points, which break down tough fibers as it pounds the meat.

mechouia - a classic Tunisian dish of charred (broiled or grilled) green and red bell peppers, tomatoes (and sometimes, garlic and onion as well), chopped and combined on a platter, sprinkled with crumbled hard-boiled egg and flaked tuna, then drizzled with olive oil and lemon juice. Some cooks add capers, or minced mint or oregano to the toppings.

medallion - round or oval cuts of meat, poultry or fish, or sometimes even vegetables.

medianoche - see CUBAN SANDWICH.

Medici, Catherine de' - see profile left.

Mediterranean caviar - see BOUTARGUE.

Mediterranean medlar - see AZAROLE.

medium-dry - see OFF-DRY.

Medjool dates - see DATES.

medlar - the fruit of the hardy medlar, or mespil, tree, *Mespilus germanica,* a native of Europe introduced to Louisiana by the Jesuits, thriving today in most of the southern U.S., cultivated as far north as New England, although its fruit has never become popular with Americans. The medlar is apple-shaped, distinguished by the way it puckers suggestively at one end, and can be eaten raw, but only once it has started to spot, a sign of its maturity. The leaves can be stir-fried or used as a wine- or port-flavoring agent.

medlar

mee krob - a Thai dish of crispy, deep-fried rice noodles and cubed tofu, cooked until golden brown, then removed from the wok while other ingredients, such as sliced pickled garlic, pork and shrimp, are cooked. Mixed together, the dish is garnished with chile peppers and green onion and served with sweet-and-sour sauce, often as a snack or side dish.

mee siam - a Thai dish of stir-fried rice vermicelli, sprouts and shrimp, usually garnished with Chinese chives and green onions, and served with dried bean curd, wedges of hard-boiled egg, lime, soy nuts and tamarind. Now eaten throughout Asia and India, it is a popular street food in Singapore.

mein - see MIAN.

Mei, Yuan - see profile below.

mekabu - the sporophyll or spore-bearing leaf of the **wakame** plant, a Japanese brown algae. Traditionally made into a medicinal tea, mekabu is said to be nourishing because it contains a gooey component called fucoidan, an ingredient believed to fight **free radicals.** See also WAKAME.

mélange classique - see SPICE PARISIENNE.

Melba sauce - a homemade or ready-made sauce of fresh black and red raspberries and sometimes cornstarch, fresh currants and sugar, puréed then strained through a fine sieve to

Mei, Yuan (1716–1798) - Chinese poet and author of *Menu from the Garden of Leisure,* the first text to define local Chinese cooking and to summarize ancient gastronomic writing. Beginning at the age of 34, Mei traveled the country for 40 years, tasting food and gathering information for his book. Mei's description of one chef at work provides a vivid image of how cooking was conducted in his day, with the chef, "a general commanding his army." (More than a century later, **Auguste Escoffier** would also suggest the military when he developed his kitchen brigade system.) Mei went on to explain how the chef directed the stoker demanding a raging fire one minute to sear and cook quickly, and a low simmering fire the next. Mei is remembered as a talented, innovative and prolific poet, and also for his ghost stories.

remove the seeds. An essential sauce for the famous **peach Melba,** it may also serve as an ingredient for **Cumberland sauce,** a simple topping for ice cream, sorbet and yogurt, or a drizzle for cake.

Melba toast - created in 1894 by the great French chef **Auguste Escoffier** while he was chef at the London's Savoy Hotel, named for the opera singer Dame Nellie Melba; thinly sliced toast that he grilled, then split down the middle and grilled a second time. Escoffier also created Poularde Tosca (chicken stuffed with rice and served with braised fennel) to celebrate Melba's title role in the 1900 Puccini opera. **Peach Melba** was also created by Escoffier for the opera singer.

melegueta pepper - see GRAINS OF PARADISE.

melon - a fruit divided into two categories — *Cucumis melo* (muskmelon, which includes cantaloupe and honeydew) and *Citrullus lanatus* (watermelon) — both belonging to the Cucurbitaceae family (the same family that includes gourds, such as squash). Although most fruits have a high water content, melons have some of the highest. Tropical areas of Africa, Asia and the Middle East have cultivated this fruit for thousands of years. Cantaloupes and watermelons have the longest history, while other types of melons, such as honeydew, Charentais, Gala and Ogen (from Israel), are fairly recent crossbreeds.

Melons were popular in Rome, especially cantaloupes, honeydews, casabas and Persian melons, which are all sweet melons, sometimes called "muskmelons" because of their beautiful fragrance. The word "musk," like the melons themselves, is of Persian origin. Many muskmelons have skin covered with a raised, textured network (cantaloupe and Santa Claus melons are examples of these so-called netted melons); others have smooth skins (casaba and honeydew melons are examples). From the Near East, they spread to Europe. Muskmelons were known to the Greeks in the 3rd century BC; described as something new in the 1st century AD by Roman naturalist Pliny; but discovered in Egyptian hieroglyphics in 2400 BC.

The Greek physician Galen wrote of the melon's medicinal virtues in the 2nd century AD, and Romans of the 3rd century used his directions for growing them. The Roman emperor Tiberius was apparently so fond of them he built the world's first greenhouse so he could enjoy them year-round. Centuries later, Christopher Columbus, also a fan of the melon, planted them in the New World in 1494. See also CANTALOUPE, MUSKMELON, WATERMELON.

melon baller

melon baller - a stainless-steel, bowl-shaped spoon with a short handle. It is used to scoop balls out of melons and other soft fruits, even butter.

melone - Italian for "melon."

melt - **1.** an open-faced sandwich topped with cheese and grilled or broiled until the cheese is melted, such as a tuna melt or a patty melt (made with a hamburger). **2.** (v.) to transform a solid food, such as butter or chocolate, into a liquid by heating it. Butter can be melted in a saucepan over direct heat on the stove or in the microwave. Chocolate, while it can be melted over direct heat (like butter), is often safer melted in a **bain-marie,** which helps prevent it from **seizing** or burning. **3.** the spleen of an animal. Although cooked for the table, they're often sold in

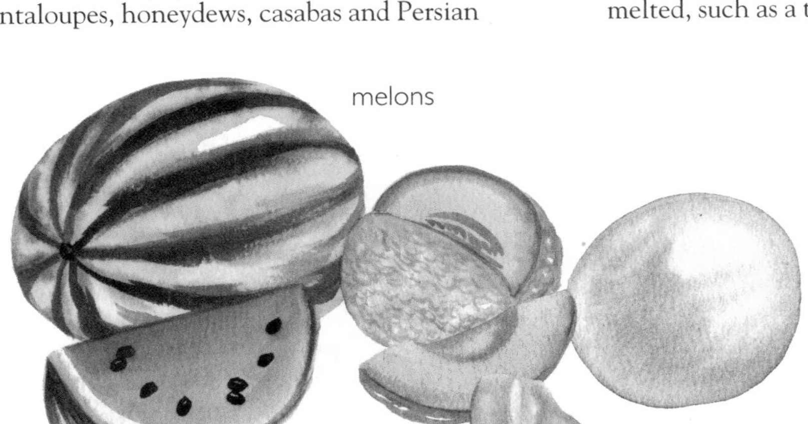

melons

Western society for pet food. Generally not highly regarded by gourmets, they're used either in sausages or, with the heart and lungs, incorporated into stews. See also VARIETY MEAT.

menhaden - see HERRING.

meniscus - the slight curvature of liquid adhering to a glass object caused by surface tension. Wine aficionados humorously call them "legs," which give an indication of alcohol content.

menu - a French term, originally from the Latin *minutus*, meaning "small," or "detailed." The oldest menu on record is a Sumerian clay tablet from about 3000 BC, which lists, in cuneiform (one of the earliest writing systems invented), a proper meal for the gods. The Roman general Lucullus always demanded that his kitchen staff present a menu to him in advance of a banquet. Although the word "menu" dates back to 1718, the custom is much older. During the Renaissance, the *escriteau* or *écriteau* (as the word is written today), or bill of fare, for ceremonial meals was displayed on the wall to let the cooks know the order in which dishes should be served. However, the modern restaurant menu, containing a large selection of foods available for ordering by customers, did not come into existence until the 18th century in France, when public **restaurants** became fashionably elegant places in which to dine.

menudo - a rich, Mexican soup that is almost a stew. Thought to have originated during the Mexican Civil War, when most of the beef was dried and sent off to the soldiers, its main ingredients are beef stock, beef **tripe** and **pigs' feet.** Chiles, garlic, onions and spices, such as anise, cinnamon and cumin seeds, are added, then it's stewed for hours. Served with cooked **posole** or tortillas, it is traditionally dished up in Mexico as a restorative on New Year's Day, served as the Sunday midday meal or sold at roadside stands to farm workers. Ready-made menudo spice mix is available.

mer - French for "sea." A word seen on French restaurant menus, for example, "mer et terre," the equivalent (in opposite order) of "surf and turf."

mère de vinaigre - see MOTHER OF VINEGAR.

merengada - a Latin American variation on the milkshake, made with fruit juice, milk or ice cream, ice and sometimes sugar. In Spain, **leche** merengada is a frequent summer treat, but is not the same as a Latin American merengada. The Spanish version is a combination of lemon zest, milk, beaten egg whites, ice and sugar, chilled until thick and cold. The word *merengada* translates as "whipped," from the Spanish. See also BATIDO, JUGO.

merguez - a North African, particularly Tunisian and Algerian, sausage made with lamb, beef, mutton or goat and seasoned with **harissa,** which gives the sausage its fiery flavor and red hue. Merguez is usually eaten grilled, often as a partner to couscous, and is one of the few sausages made in Muslim countries (most sausage is made with pork, which cannot be consumed under Islamic dietary law). Merguez is also a popular treat in France (thanks to its long colonial occupation of North Africa) and now North America.

meringue - said to have been created when Napoleon visited the Swiss town of Meiringen by **Gasparini,** a local pastry chef. He had created a cookie made with sugar, cinnamon, nuts and egg yolks; in order to not waste the leftover egg whites, he whipped them with sugar and then slow-baked small, puffy mounds of this new concoction until they became dry and crispy. He served them to the emperor with sweet cream, and Napoleon is said to have preferred the second creation best, naming them after the town. Also, unrelated to food, Meiringen is situated at the foot of the Reichenbach Falls, made famous as the location where Sherlock Holmes and Professor Moriarty fell to their deaths.

For more than two centuries now, a quiet culinary tradition has specified that copper utensils be used when making meringues. One early record of this practice is a 1771 illustration in a French encyclopedia, showing egg whites being beaten in a copper bowl. It must have been a matter of common professional knowledge, since it appears to have gone unmentioned in all French cookbooks until Henri-Paul Pellaprat's 1936 book, *L'Art culinaire moderne*, directed the cook to put the whites in a copper bowl. Today, it tends to be the fancier books that call for copper; most recipes settle for the cheaper, expedient **cream of tartar.** Only recently have people tried to explain why copper bowls should be used and

METHODS FOR MAKING MERINGUE

Here are three methods for making meringue.

French method - egg whites and sugar are beaten together until soft, or until stiff, glossy peaks form (depending on the desired result). This type of meringue separates, or "weeps," as it stands, but is fairly stable and works well for desserts, such as lemon meringue pie, baked Alaska or cookies. (French meringue is safest when used in recipes that call for baking, which kills any salmonella in the raw egg whites.)

Swiss method - egg whites and sugar are beaten in the top of a **bain-marie** until the mixture reaches 110° to 120°F (43° to 49°C). The mixture is then removed from the heat and beaten until medium, or stiff, glossy peaks form. This stable meringue is good for piping and baking into cookies or layers for rich meringue-based cakes, such as **dacquoise**.

Italian method - as egg whites are beaten a slow stream of hot sugar syrup is added. The meringue is beaten until it is cooled (it can't be overbeaten, like French meringue, which can begin to separate if beaten too long). The sugar syrup, which is boiled until it reaches the **soft-ball stage,** helps make Italian meringue superbly stable, so that it does not weep. This makes it ideal for use as a topping for pies, flans or tarts and as a component in a variety of **boiled icings** for cakes.

what exactly they do for meringues. A side-by-side comparison demonstrates that copper does indeed make a difference. It brings egg whites to their perfect state of frothiness faster and produces a creamier, yellowish foam that is harder to overbeat (to turn it to lumps and liquid) than the snowy-white, drier foam made in ceramic or stainless-steel bowls. Like cream of tartar, copper stabilizes the foam and gives the cook more leeway in the beating. On account of the similarity in effect, some cookbook writers have suggested that copper imparts an "acidity" to the whites, while others claim that the metal helps set up an electric field that somehow affects the proteins. Neither of these ideas seem likely, and attempts to find even a drop of acid in the pH of albumen or a voltage between bowl and whisk have failed.

meringue powder - a dried egg-white mix, which may also contain cornstarch, **cream of tartar, gum arabic** and sugar. Water is added, then the mixture is beaten to form stiff peaks. Since the egg whites are pasteurized, the risk of salmonella (which may be present in raw egg whites) is eliminated.

meritage - a modern term applied to blended California wines (Bordeaux-type red and white) that fall below the percentage of a named grape variety required to earn the **varietal** classification. The term was coined by combining the words "merit" and "heritage;" together, they conjure up a rather aristocratic name and lineage.

Merlot - a red wine and the grape used to make it, named in the 12th century by Cistercian monks after *merles*, French for "blackbirds," which would feast on the seeds, because the grape ripens sooner than other varieties. Merlot is considered a close cousin to **Cabernet Sauvignon,** although it matures sooner and is lower in tannins.

mesclun - also **field greens.** A very well known mixture of leaves, which originated in Nice. The term comes from *mesclumo*, a Provençal word for "mix." Originally, the leaves were from wild greens. Today, mesclun often includes dandelion, arugula, oak leaf lettuce, lamb's lettuce, chervil, **groundsel, salsify** and more.

mesentery - a membrane, part of the peritoneum, that attaches the small intestine and other abdominal organs to the back of the abdomen wall. Calf's mesentery is a sausage ingredient, but may also be fried or prepared in the same way as tripe.

mesquite - any one of several deciduous, thorny, small shrubs or trees in the dry southwestern U.S. and northern Mexico. The bane of ranchers, this invasive leguminous plant develops sweet, pulpy pods up to 6 inches (15 cm) long. They

mesquite

provide food and habitat for wildlife and were a staple in the diet of indigenous peoples, who cooked the pods whole, or used them to make syrup, tea or **pinole.** The aromatic, aged wood is commonly used (sometimes with wood from apple or pecan trees) for grilling beef, fish, pork and poultry, and smoking jerky, ham and sausages.

Metaxa - a richly flavored Greek brandy-based liqueur, made from a twice-distilled mixture of grapes combined with aged muscat wine and a blend of herbs and spices, including rose petals. Metaxa comes in three types in North America: three-star (aged at least three years in oak casks), five-star (aged at least five years), and seven-star (aged at least seven years). In Greece, there is an even finer grade called private reserve, which is aged for at least 20 years. The spirit is named for its creator, Spyros Metaxa.

methi - see FENUGREEK.

méthode champenoise - also **bottle fermentation.** The traditional labor-intensive method by which **Champagne** is made. The first step in the process is for the winemaker to transform three types of grapes — Chardonnay, Pinot Noir and Pinot Meunier — into a wide variety of still wines, sometimes up to 60 wines in total. Only Chardonnay grapes are white, so the two remaining red varieties must be harvested and pressed very gently in order to prevent the coloring in their skins from transferring to the juice and tinting it pink. These still wines are fermented in large steel vats (although some vintners still use wooden casks), and generally emerge from their first fermentation high in acid, low in alcohol and lacking in rich flavor.

The next step, and one of the secrets to good Champagne, is the **assemblage,** or the careful blending of these still wines to create the proper rich, desired flavor and balance. Some of the still wine is reserved for another year, and some is saved to be added to the finished Champagne to give it extra flavor and depth.

The next, and most characteristic, step in Champagne production is the **second fermentation** of the blended wine. The blended still wines are combined with a **dosage,** or *liqueur de tirage* (a combination of sugar and wine), and Champagne yeasts, then bottled and corked. The bottles are then set aside and allowed to ferment, the yeasts consuming the sugar in the *liqueur de tirage* and emitting carbon dioxide, which cannot escape the bottle (thanks to the cork) and dissolves in the wine. This dissolved gas, when the cork is later popped, fizzes out of the wine and creates the beloved bubbles in a glass of Champagne.

During the second fermentation, the bottles rest for about one year, allowing the yeasts to do their work. As the fermenting action of the yeast cells is exhausted and the cells begin to die, they gather at the bottom of the bottle, creating a layer of cloudy sediment called the "**lees.**" By sitting "on the lees," the Champagne gains flavor and complexity as the yeast cells go through autolysis, meaning that the enzymes in the yeast cells slowly break the yeast down into smaller, and more flavorful, proteins.

Once this step is completed, the Champagne is cloudy, with a layer of sediment on the bottom. The bottles then go through a process called **riddling,** or *rémuage* in French. They are set, neck tilted down, into A-frame structures called *pupitres*. Every few days, the bottles are turned slightly, and their angle slightly increased so that, at the end of the riddling stage, they are sitting completely upside down, with all the yeast cells and solids resting on the cork, and the clear Champagne floating on top of them. Although some traditional producers still hand-riddle their bottles, many use large machines to turn them periodically.

The final step is called *dégorgement* in French, "disgorging" in English, and is the point at which the solids are removed, leaving clear, sparkling wine nearly ready for consumption.

The bottle is carefully placed, neck down, in a frigid brine solution, which causes all the wine and the solids in the neck of the bottle to freeze solid. The bottle is then quickly turned upright and uncorked, causing the solid plug of yeast to shoot out. This leaves a clear, sparkling wine and just enough space to add another dosage (or *liqueur d'expedition*), a combination of reserved still wine and sugar, which mixes with the dry Champagne and creates the desired level of sweetness, from **brut** to **doux.** The bottle is then corked and ready to drink.

metric system - a decimal-based system of weights and measures, with a centimeter composed of 100 millimeters, 1,000 of which make a meter, and a kilogram composed of 1,000 grams. The U.S. was the first country to implement a decimal currency (one dollar composed of 100 cents) in 1792. The French adopted the metric measure three years later, although the conversion was interrupted briefly with a ban by Napoleon. In 1875, 17 nations signed a treaty at the historic Metric Convention to standardize weights and measures, and since then, the yard, pound etc. have been measured according to the metric system. In 1975, the U.S. congress passed the Metric Conversion Act, but the funding was cancelled in 1982 by then-president Ronald Reagan. The U.S., Myanmar and Liberia are the only three countries in the world still using the imperial system of measurement.

Mettwurst - also **Metwurst.** A German sausage made of beef and pork, soft enough to spread, available fine or very coarse.

meunière, à la - French for "in the style of the miller's wife," for dishes, usually fish, that are dredged in flour and sautéed in butter, then finished with lemon juice and fresh parsley. Most popularly applied to trout, *truite meunière* in French, and *trota alla mugnaia* in Italian.

Mexican breadfruit - see MONSTERA.

Mexican chocolate - also **chocolate Mexicano.** Dark chocolate usually combined with sugar, vanilla and ground nuts (such as almonds) and spices (such as cinnamon, cloves and nutmeg). Part of the culture of the Mayans, then the Aztecs, cocoa beans and chocolate were given special status as an almost sacred food and often used as ritual offerings. The beans — and the mixture — were traditionally crushed in a warmed mortar and pestle, but Mexican chocolate is now sold in cakes, disks or as a syrup. Used in the Mexican hot chocolate drink, *chocolate Mexicano*, the beverage dubbed "the national drink of Mexico," Mexican chocolate is also used in other hot and cold drinks, such as **atole,** *champurrado* (a special hot chocolate thickened with **masa)** and *tejate* (a traditional Oaxacan drink). It's also used in baked goods, and in moles, such as *mole poblano*, a spicy Mexican dish made with turkey, chiles, nut, spices and chocolate. See also MOLE, MOLINILLO.

Mexican potato - see JICAMA.

Mexican rice - see SOPA SECA.

Mexican steak - flank steak, marinated in a mixture of lemon or lime juice with minced chile pepper, garlic and oregano, that is grilled, then sliced against the grain.

Mexican tea - see EPAZOTE.

Mexican truffle - see HUITLACOCHE.

Mexican wedding cakes - also **dust balls, polvorones, Russian tea cakes, snowball cookies.** Crumbly spherical cookies made of buttery dough containing finely chopped almonds, hazelnuts or pecans and a dash of vanilla; while still warm, they are rolled in confectioner's sugar.

Meyer lemon - a hybrid discovered by Frank Meyer in 1908, who imported it from China, believed to be a cross between a lemon and a mandarin orange, as implied by its rounder shape, yellow-orange color and sweet floral bouquet.

mezcal - also **mescal.** A potent clear liquor made from the nectar of the agave plant, one of the ancient beverages of Mexico. Mezcal can be made from any species of agave, whereas **tequila** (a type of mezcal) is made from only the blue agave plant. The sweet nectar of the plant, called *aguamiel* ("honey water" in English) is extracted from the heart, which is called the *piña* in Spanish (meaning "pineapple" in English). The piñas are baked in a charcoal-fired underground oven, then shredded and pressed to extract the juices. The charcoal oven gives mezcal its distinctive smoky flavor.

Mezcal is notorious outside of Mexico, thanks to clever packaging: some bottles come to market with a maguey worm in the bottom. High-quality mezcals, as a rule, do not contain a worm. One story has it that the worm demonstrates the high proof of mezcal: if it remains intact that means that the percentage of alcohol in the liquor is high enough to pickle the worm and keep it from disintegrating. Another story has it that, in the 1940s, Jacobo Lozano Páez started a mezcal bottling operation and discovered, while tasting his product, that the worms that are endemic in some agave crops gave his mezcal an interesting flavor. Lozano Páez decided that this was the marketing gimmick he needed to make his mezcal a success. He added a worm to each bottle and sold it with a bag of salt seasoned with some more of the ground dehydrated worms.

Depending on the color of the worm, these mezcals are labeled *gusano de oro* ("golden worm") or *gusano rojo* ("red worm"). Legend has it that consuming the worm makes you strong and brave — a legend that fraternity pledges try to prove year in and year out. One brand has begun to push the bravery envelope and includes a scorpion, instead of a worm, for the most macho of drinkers. See also AGAVE, TEQUILA.

meze - also **mezze.** See MAZA.

mezzaluna - an Italian chopping device shaped like a *mezzaluna,* Italian for "half-moon," with a knob attached to each end as a handle for rocking the blade back and forth in its characteristic cutting motion. It's also one of the most practical culinary tools, and many prefer it to a chef's knife.

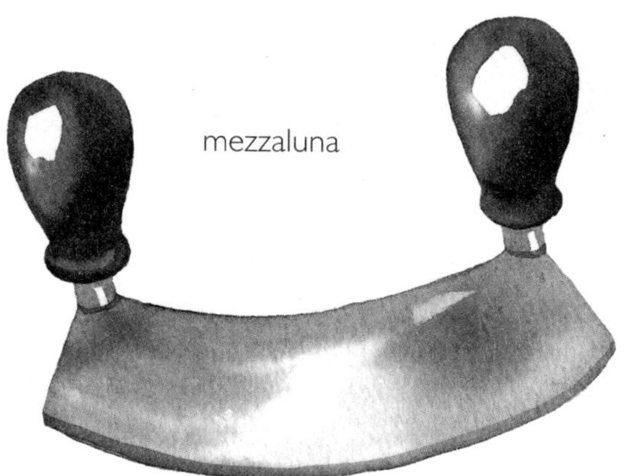
mezzaluna

mi - also **bahmi, bami, mee.** The Indonesian and Malaysian word for noodles, the base of many dishes. See also BAMI GORENG.

mian - also **mein.** Noodles made from ground barley or wheat, sometimes enriched with egg, originally from northern China. Often sold as dried bundles in North America, they are also available fresh and frozen in some stores. Strand sizes range from thread-like to ropy. Mian may be used in soups (*tan mein*), stir-fries (*chow mein*), tossed with sauce (*lo mein*), or braised, fried into a type of pancake, or shaped into nests and deep-fried.

miche - see BOULE.

microbrewery - according to the American Homebrewers Association, a microbrewery is a brewery that makes less than 15,000 barrels (17,600 hectoliters) of beer per year. Microbreweries produce a variety of more traditional **craft beers,** and their products are usually closely identified with the area where they are produced. This local pride allows each microbrewery to promote its unique product, rather than trying to fit into the homogenous landscape of similar brews produced by the major mass-markets breweries that once had an exclusive stranglehold on the North American beer scene. Today, thousands of cities and towns boast their own microbreweries, and the beer consumer has far more choice than ever before.

microorganism - a living bacteria, fungi or virus so small that it can only be seen under magnification. Beneficial microorganisms are used in the production of a host of beverages and foods, such as beer, cheese, **miso** and vinegar; consumed in **probiotic** foods, beneficial microorganisms also enhance the healthy functioning of the digestive system. Harmful microorganisms, on the other hand, cause foods to spoil and spread food-borne illnesses, such as botulism, hepatitis and salmonella.

Microplane grater - a type of rasp originally used as a woodworking tool, now widely available as a kitchen utensil for shredding or grating a wide variety of foods, including cheese, citrus zest, fresh ginger and spices. Microplanes come in a range of sizes, shapes and degrees of coarseness, and all have a perforated metal surface covered with tiny, sharp fins, which shred or grate food into tiny, delicate ribbons. See also GRATER.

microwave oven - developed in 1942 by **Dr. Percy Spencer,** an engineer for Raytheon Laboratories in Waltham, Massachusetts, while working with a magnetron tube, which produces microwaves. When he reached for a candy bar that he'd left in his pocket, he found it had melted without any obvious source of heat. To test a theory that it could have been the magnetron tube, he placed some popcorn near the tube, and it popped instantly. He then focused the beam through a box at an egg, which caused it to explode. He immediately filed a patent for the use of microwaves in cooking, and 25 years later, in 1967, the first microwave oven for home use was introduced to the market. Microwave ovens became very popular in the 1970s, probably due to the familiarity of microwaves already established in communication, navigation and diathermy, the deep treatment of bursitis and arthritis.

Midori - a bright green, brand-name Japanese melon liqueur. Introduced to North America in 1978, its honeydew-melon flavor is now common in Margaritas, Martinis, punch and shooters. Midori can also be used in cakes, cheesecakes, pies and puddings.

miele d'Abruzzo - see ACACIA.

mignardises - an assortment of small, sweet baked goods served at the end of a meal, often with coffee or after-dinner drinks. The word derives from *mignon*, French for "darling" or "cute," which reflects the appearance and scale of these one- or two-bite treats. Typical mignardises include **éclairs,** tartlets, small cookies and cream puffs.

mignonette - **1.** from the French word for "dainty," mignonette denotes a coin-shaped piece of meat, also known as a **medallion** or **noisette. 2.** a small sachet of seasoning (peppercorns and cloves), traditionally cooked in a soup or stew. **3.** coarsely ground (usually white) peppercorns, called *poivre mignonette*.

miki - commercially produced noodles from Southeast Asia, made with wheat flour, eggs and soda ash, usually served with such typical dishes as **laksa,** a soup made with fish or chicken and coconut milk.

mile-a-minute plant - see KUDZU.

milfoil - see ACHILÉE.

mil hojas - Spanish for "thousand leaves (or petals)." **1.** a layered cake from South America. Rich buttery dough, made with egg yolks, flour and milk, is rolled into several circles or sheets, which are baked, separately, until golden brown. Meanwhile, sweetened condensed milk is boiled, in the can, for several hours to caramelize it. Brushed with a brandy-and-water mixture, the cake layers are stacked up, each topped with the cooked, condensed milk sprinkled with chopped walnuts. **2.** a term used to describe meat, seafood or poultry mixtures wrapped in puff pastry (*mille-feuille* to the French) and baked.

milk - a white, opaque liquid secreted by the mammary glands of female mammals for the nourishment of their young. Milk is 87 percent water; milk fat naturally carries vitamins A, D, E and K, fat-soluble vitamins that are added to lower-fat milks because they are lost during processing. Most U.S. milk comes from Holstein cows, but Jersey and Guernsey cows are also key producers. Humans consume the milk and eat milk products of cows, donkeys, goats, sheep, reindeer, horses and camels.See also BUTTERMILK, CONDENSED MILK, EVAPORATED MILK, PASTEURIZED MILK, POWDERED MILK, SOUR MILK, SWEETENED CONDENSED MILK.

TYPES OF MILK

homogenized - milk with about 3 percent milk fat.

lactose-free, lactose-reduced - milk from which **lactose** (a type of sugar that causes bothersome, but non-dangerous digestive upsets in the lactose-intolerant) has been eliminated or reduced. Lactose intolerance usually only develops after age 5; many adults have it to some degree.

pasteurized milk - milk that has been heated to 145°F (63°C) for 30 minutes and then quickly cooled down, which destroys bacteria, but protects the flavor and nutrient value.

raw milk - unpasteurized milk.

skim milk - milk from which as much cream as possible has been removed, leaving less than 0.5 percent milk fat.

milk chocolate - see CHOCOLATE.

milk fat - see BUTTERFAT.

milk gravy - another name for **country gravy,** a southern U.S. sauce often served with **chicken-fried steak** or **cornmeal mush,** started by whisking pan drippings with flour to make a **roux.** Milk is then whisked into the roux and cooked until thickened and creamy, then seasoned with salt and lots of black pepper.

milk powder - see POWDERED MILK.

milk pudding - a generic term for bland, **nursery-food** puddings made with milk, such as the rice and tapioca varieties.

milkshake - also **shake.** A smooth, thick and frothy drink made by blending or whipping together ice cream, flavoring syrup and milk immediately before serving. Stephen J. Poplawski is credited with inventing the first electric blender to make milkshakes faster, without having to shake them by hand, in 1922. After soda fountains died out, drive-in and fast food joints began to mix and serve the shakes.

milkshake

milk sugar - see LACTOSE.

milk toast - a bland nursery or sickroom dish of dry or buttered toast in a sauce of scalded milk, often thickened with butter and flour and sometimes sprinkled with sugar and cinnamon. In the 1950s, American cartoonist H.T. Webster dressed up the term to name his meek and mild comic-strip character, Caspar Milquetoast. The noun, "milquetoast," is still used to describe a bland, timid person.

Millau, Christian - see GAULT, HENRI ANDRÉ PAUL VICTOR.

mille-feuille - see PUFF PASTRY.

millet - the tiny yellow seed of cereal grass, *Panicum miliaceum*, from the Latin *millium*, meaning "to grind." A nutritious gluten-free whole grain, millet is high in fiber and B vitamins and easy to digest.

No one seems to know when man first cultivated millet, but there's general agreement that it originated in either Asia or Africa. The first official reference to millet is in the Fran Shen-Chiu Shu, the rural edict gathered in 2800 BC, making it one of the five sacred crops of China (the others being soybean, rice, wheat and barley). Millet swayed from the top of the hanging gardens of Babylon. (Herodotus wrote that the millet was so tall, he would not reveal its true height for fear of being taken as a liar.) At the foot of the Colossus in Rhodes, millet grew so thick, it obscured the base of the statue. In the Old Testament, millet was called "the gruel of endurance," not for its weather resistance but because of its nutritional benefits. In many ancient, diverse cultures — Roman, Greek, Gallic, Persian, Etruscan, Assyrian, Tartar and Visigoth — millet was consumed as a porridge, not only for its nutritional value but especially because of the common belief that millet protected the body and mind from "a mischievous world."

In North America, almost the entire crop is used as the main ingredient in birdseed, and only a tiny portion of the harvest is allocated for humans, but some cultures consume it as commonly as rice or barley, as in Mauritania, Egypt and Ethiopia.

millionaire salad - **1.** a rich dish containing chunks of fruit and nuts suspended in a creamy base, served cold. Various versions start with cooked or uncooked mixtures (such as a cooked combination of beaten eggs, sugar and marshmallows, or an uncooked mixture of condensed milk and lemon juice or cream cheese and mayonnaise) with a wealth of nuts (such as almonds or pecans) and chunks of fruit (such as bananas, grapes, maraschino cherries, mandarin oranges and pineapple) folded in before it's chilled. **2.** heart of palm, nicknamed "millionaire salad" because of its high price.

milt - **1.** also **soft roe.** The creamy sperm or **roe** of fish, particularly herring, used cooked or raw in hors d'oeuvres, salads or sauces. **2.** see SPLEEN.

mimolette - a French cheese produced in the same manner as Dutch **Edam,** with a dark orange interior, its name derived from *mi-mou*, meaning "half-soft." Some claim it originated in Holland, while others maintain that the two countries developed the technique independently. What is probably true is that,

during a 17th-century embargo of foreign goods, the French minister Colbert forbade the import of foreign goods, including cheese, and the French began making mimolette themselves.

mimosa - **1.** a minced, hard-boiled egg yolk used as a garnish atop anchovies or fish, salad or fresh or cooked vegetables, such as asparagus and spinach. The bright yellow color mimics the flowers of the *Acacia* plant, commonly known as "mimosa" or "wattle." See also ACACIA. **2.** a refreshing cocktail made with orange juice and chilled champagne. **3.** a gelatin salad made by arranging orange sections in a ring mold, then pouring in a chilled mixture of gelatin powder, champagne or soda water, and orange juice. It's then refrigerated until set. The salad is unmolded onto a bed of salad greens, then the center is filled with strawberries. The result resembles a flower surrounded by leaves.

mince - to cut into tiny pieces or flecks, smaller than chopped food. See also CHOP.

mincemeat - a sweet mixture of dried fruits and nuts, baked into pies and tarts for Thanksgiving and Christmas, no longer containing meat. It was originally made during the medieval era as a way to preserve, extend and use up meat. It was also made throughout the Middle Ages and into the Renaissance. Meat was still prominent in its list of ingredients well into the 19th century, according to Peter Cassell's *Dictionary of Cookery*, published in London in 1875. His recipe for "old-fashioned mincemeat" called for beef, apples, suet, sugar, currants, candied lemon or orange peel, citrus, spices, salt, finely chopped lemon rinds and brandy or wine to taste. Apart from the meat, suet and perhaps the citron, these are the general ingredients of modern mincemeat.

mineral water - water from an underground source, such as an aquifer or artesian well, that contains minerals, salts and trace elements (referred to as Total Dissolved Salts, or TDS) and may contain some gases. A bottled variety may be sparkling or still, but must have a consistent composition of TDS; to be labeled "mineral water" in the U.S., for example, it must contain a minimum of 250 parts per million TDS. (Currently, no such standards exist in Canada.) In Europe, where the required level of TDS is lower, mineral waters have traditionally been regarded as healthful to drink or to bath in, at such popular spas as Baden-Baden in Germany. Although there is no conclusive science to prove health claims, the consumption of mineral waters is increasing, particularly in North America, where some people prefer it to chlorinated, fluoridated tap water or enjoy it, with a twist of lemon or lime, as a trendy, nonalcoholic drink.

minestra - Italian for "soup."

minestrone - an Italian vegetable soup, from the Latin *ministrare*, meaning "to serve," and *minestra*, meaning "soup." The ingredients vary from region to region, often even from cook to cook, but the most common ingredients are onions, beans, carrots, celery, potatoes and tomatoes.

Ming Dynasty egg - see HUNDRED-YEAR EGG.

miniature currant grapes - see CHAMPAGNE GRAPE.

minni di Sant' Agata - an Italian breast-shaped cookie. In English, it is called "Saint Agatha's nipples," which recalls the gruesome saga of Agatha, a Sicilian who endured sexual persecution at the hands of a government bureaucrat. When she resisted his advances, the official threatened to expose her as a Christian, at a time when the followers of this faith were ruthlessly victimized. When the warning failed, he sent her off to a house of ill repute, hoping to corrupt her. Even there, however, Agatha remained faithfully virtuous. Sadly, things went from bad to worse, and Agatha underwent a string of ordeals, the most famed of which was the slicing off of her breasts. Throughout Western art, Saint Agatha is illustrated holding a tray containing her cut-off breasts, similar to Salome with the head of St. John the Baptist.

mint - a fragrant plant of the *Mentha* genus, used as a medicinal herb in China as far back as 5,000 years ago. The Greeks liked to rub their arms with mint after bathing. In Greek mythology, Menthe was a gorgeous nymph and a daughter of the river god. When Hades saw her gently splashing her feet in the river, he instantly fell in love with her, which enraged his wife, Persephone, who swiftly changed the nymph into a mint plant, so that she would be trampled underfoot. Legend also has it that Zeus and Hermes would disguise themselves to test

mint

people for their sense of hospitality, and when they dined with Philemon and Baucis, they found that the wooden table had been rubbed with mint. Although sweet, some biblical scholars claim that mint was one of the bitter herbs of Passover.

Mint was held in such high esteem and value that it was used in tithing. In medieval times, mint was thought to symbolize wisdom and virtue and was a famous monastery nostrum; huge clumps of the round-leafed variety may be found among monastery ruins. The monks also used it to relieve the languor that followed epilepsy and to bring patients out of melancholia. Once used on medieval floors to repel ants, mint has a reputation (especially the pennyroyal species) for keeping ants out of food cupboards. The famous mint sauce so cherished by the British was actually an import from the Romans, who invented it in the 3rd century. There are at least 2,000 varieties of mint currently on record, and at least five types of mint growing wild. With the single exception of sweet basil, which is indigenous to tropical Africa and Asia, all the herb plants in the mint family are natives of the Mediterranean region.

The only native American mint, *Mentha canadensis*, was once used for its cooling effect on fevers. Spearmint was brought to American shores very early and was growing wild by 1672. Peppermint, on the other hand, was unknown until the end of the 17th century. Cultivated mint is usually peppermint or spearmint. The name "spearmint" came from "Spiremint," referring to the tall spires of its blooms in late summer. To prevent milk from curdling or turning, just add a leaf of mint. It is impossible to make cheese from the milk of a cow that has been eating the herb, because it will not curdle.

mint extract - a concentrated, green liquid flavoring extracted from peppermint and spearmint, which is often added to baked goods, particularly those with chocolate.

mint geranium - see COSTMARY.

mint jelly - an English recipe that originally used the pectin derived from fresh apples as a gelling base, combined with mint leaves, water, vinegar or lemon juice and sugar, giving the finished product a golden color. The modern-day commercial version of mint jelly is colored green with vegetable food dye and the apple pectin has been replaced with gelatin. Most often served with lamb.

Mint Julep - a cocktail of bourbon and sugar poured over crushed ice and garnished with fresh mint. It's thought to have been invented in 1809 at White Sulfur Springs, a West Virginia spa, and is the official drink of the Kentucky Derby (apparently because of the legend that mint was planted outside the clubhouse for the very first race in 1875). More than 80,000 Mint Juleps are served during the annual two-day event. The first Mint Julep was made with rum, because it was popular and easy to get, at the time. The switch to Kentucky bourbon didn't occur until the late 19th century. The word "julep" derives from the Persian *gulab* and the Arabic *julab*, meaning "rose water."

mint sauce - a simple preparation of finely chopped mint leaves, sugar and cider or malt vinegar, a traditionally English accompaniment to lamb.

minute steak - a piece of beefsteak sliced so thin, it can be cooked very quickly, within a minute per side, typically scored to prevent curling and to ensure the rapidity of the cooking process.

mirabelle - a small, round yellow plum used primarily for baking, preserving, syrup making and fermenting into **eau de vie** and liqueur. In the Lorraine region of France, which produces about 70 percent of the mirabelles grown worldwide, harvesters traditionally shook off the ripe fruit onto sheets of canvas laid under the

mirabelles

trees. To be labeled "Mirabelles de Lorraine," today's crop is subject to stringent standards of cultivation and collection methods, sugar content and size.

miraculous fruit - the berry, *Synsepalum dulcificum*, of a tropical African tree, owing its name to the fact that, without being particularly sweet itself, it has the property of sweetening, or neutralizing the acidity of sour fruits or drinks. When consumed fresh, the fruit coats the palate and alters the taste buds, so that everything eaten afterward tastes sweet for at least an hour or two.

mirepoix - a mixture of diced carrots, onions and celery, which, along with garlic, herbs and peppercorns, are the universal and invaluable aromatics used when making stocks. Mirepoix was created by the personal cook of the Duke de Levis-Mirepoix (1699–1757), a French field marshal and ambassador of Louis XV.

mirin - a sweet, pale yellow Japanese cooking wine made from glutinous rice, similar to **sake,** but low in alcohol, used extensively in Japanese cuisine as a common flavoring agent.

mirliton - see CHAYOTE.

mise en place - a French culinary term meaning "to put in place," or to have all equipment and ingredients assembled before you begin to cook a dish. Frequently, cookware shops and catalogues sell sets of tempered glass bowls in a variety of sizes under the name "mise en place bowls."

miso - a fermented soybean paste whose Chinese origins can be traced back to the 3rd century BC. It was known as *hisio* and wasn't imported to Japan until the 6th century, when it became a necessary part of the samurai diet. To make miso, soybeans are boiled and cooled, then grain is added, usually rice, barley or wheat, to initiate fermentation, which can last from weeks to years. Miso soup was not seen in Japan until the 20th century; the Chinese never used miso in soup.

MAIN MISO VARIETIES

genmai - whole soybeans and brown rice.

hatcho - dark, very thick and salty.

kome - a combination of fermented soybeans and white rice.

mugi - whole soybeans and pearl barley fermented in wood for at least 18 months.

sendai - reddish brown, salty and pungent.

shinshu - golden, salty and mellow.

mission cactus - see CACTUS.

Mission fig - also **Black Mission.** See FIG.

Mission olive - see OLIVE.

Mississippi mud pie - an American original, which comes in many crusts and fillings. Usually assembled in a chocolate-wafer or graham-cracker shell, this pie is layered with alternate dark and lighter brown layers, such as chocolate custard or pudding with vanilla or coffee-flavored custard; chocolate and coffee-flavored cream cheese mixtures or coffee-flavored ice cream spread with a chocolate mixture. With toppings, such as chopped nuts, toffee or whipped cream, this mud pie is a dieter's quicksand.

Miss Society onion - see ONION.

mistletoe - also **birdlime.** The only food-related use of this parasitic plant, *Viscum album*, is in the making of a tonic to stimulate the appetite. But the dried leaves and young twigs, collected before the berries sprout, have been used since before Christ as an antispasmodic and narcotic, especially for the treatment of epilepsy and nervous disorders. The Druids worshipped mistletoe: at the commencement of the new year and according to certain phases of the moon, the priests collected it with a golden sickle. Along with the oak tree that is its host, mistletoe became known as a shield against all evils. After the harvest, branches were given to the faithful and hooked on the doors to their homes. The origin of kissing under the mistletoe comes from Norse mythology. An arrow made of mistletoe wood killed Balder, the god of peace, but all the gods in concert brought him back to life and put mistletoe under the protection of the goddess of love, ordaining that anyone passing under it should receive a kiss. One of the French names for the plant is *herbe de la croix*; legend claims that, once it became a tree, mistletoe was used to make Christ's cross, cursing it, denying it a place on earth, and this is why it became a parasite.

misto - Italian for "mixture" which is used for "stew." See also BOLLITO MISTO.

misua - also **miswa.** A fine wheat noodle produced commercially in the Philippines.

mithai - small, Indian "sweet foods" exchanged at Diwali, the Hindu Festival of Lights, or served at weddings and other celebrations. They are molded from spiced pastes of cooked, puréed fruit, nuts and/or dal or rice mixed with a sticky ingredient, such as condensed milk, ghee or jaggery syrup. They may be deep-fried as well.

mitzithra - see MYZITHRA.

mixed drink - see COCKTAIL.

mixed grill - traditional British meal of various meats, usually bacon, kidneys, lamb chops and livers, sausage and steak, that are barbecued, broiled or grilled along with mushrooms and tomatoes. The modern mixed grill may include a broader range of items, such as chicken, eggplant, ribs, salmon, shrimp and tofu.

mixed spice - also **British mixed spice, pudding spice.** A ready-made or homemade English spice mixture, usually containing allspice, cinnamon, cloves, coriander, ginger, mace and nutmeg, used in traditional custards, fruitcakes, hot cross buns and steamed puddings. The similar North American **pumpkin pie spice** can be used instead, in a pinch.

mixer - **1.** electric stationary or hand-held kitchen appliance with paired or single attachments, such as rotating dough hooks, beaters, paddles or whisks, which beat, mix or whip food at variable speeds. While the beater or beaters rotate, the bowl, on a stationary or **stand mixer,** may also rotate. In rotary-action mixers, the beater is fixed at the center of the bowl, and the food that's being mixed needs to be scraped from the side; in a planetary-action mixer, the rotating beater orbits inside the bowl, keeping the side clean and mixing the food more evenly. Most stand mixers come with their own set of two or three deep, heatproof mixing bowls. Some stand mixers are sturdy and powerful enough to knead dough. A portable, **hand-held mixer** must be light enough to be held comfortably for 10 to 15 minutes at a time, and is therefore less suited to heavy jobs. **2.** a beverage, juice or water, often carbonated, added to alcohol in cocktails or mixed drinks. **3.** an informal party held to let people get acquainted.

mixer bowl - a deep, straight-sided, nonporous heatproof glass or metal bowl, designed for use with a stand mixer. The side curves into the base to fit the shape of the beater or beaters, so that all the food gets picked up and mixed in, and makes the bowl easy to scrape clean.

mixing bowl - a nonporous bowl used for mixing or whisking food by hand. Some ceramic versions, such as the familiar tan-outside, white-inside traditional English Gripstand bowls, have a flattened surface near the base on the outside, so that the bowl is stable when it's set on an easier angle for stirring. Mixing bowls of heatproof glass and metal, such as stainless steel, have their own advantages: they can be used to melt chocolate, for example, over a pan of simmering water before other ingredients are stirred in. For **meringue,** copper bowls are preferred for whisking the egg whites; the reaction of the copper with the egg whites eliminates the need to add **cream of tartar** to achieve the desired frothiness. These mixing

mixing bowls

bowls also have rounded bottoms, inside, to make them easy to scrape clean, and most are rimmed to make them easy to grasp. Some have handles, and some have spouts.

mizuame - a clear, colorless Japanese syrup made by converting a starch into sugar. The two main sources are rice (which is mixed with malt) or potatoes (which are mixed with an acid, such as sulfuric acid). Sticky, sweet and glossy, mizuame may be used in the same manner as honey, added to cooked foods to give them sweetness and sheen, or as the main ingredient in the Japanese candies called *wagashi*.

mizuna

mizuna - a delicate, feathery salad green of the *Brassica* genus (of which cabbage and mustard are also members), with deep saw-toothed edges, used in salads, soups and stir-fries for its delicate, peppery, mustard-cabbage flavor.

mocha - **1.** a type of coffee grown and processed in Yemen, specifically through the port city of Mocha (*al-Mokka*) on the Red Sea, probably the first Arabian coffee Europeans ever tasted in the 1500s. The small, round mocha coffee beans are air-dried, often on the tree before they are picked, and are a pale greenish yellow color. They produce a rich, winy, acidic coffee that is prized by coffee aficionados. See also COFFEE. **2.** a beverage that combines espresso or coffee with chocolate or cocoa. **3.** any combination of chocolate and coffee, whether in beverages, baked goods or desserts.

mochi - a Japanese sweet or unflavored rice cake made by pounding **glutinous rice** until it is a thick, sticky paste. The paste is then formed into shapes, from circles to cubes to flowers. Mochi can be sweetened, flavored, colored, painted with soy sauce and grilled, or sprinkled with roasted soybean flour. It is also a key ingredient in the Japanese New Year's soup **ozoni.**

mochiko - a Japanese flour made from **mochi rice.** Popular throughout Asia and an important ingredient in many Hawaiian dishes, it is used for breading chicken and pork, for thickening sauces and soups, and in baked goods, dumplings and puddings.

mochi rice - also **sticky rice, sweet rice.** A Japanese short-grain rice, mochi is usually steamed, often pounded to make rice cakes, popular in East and Southeast Asia and commonly used for *sekihan* (cooked mochi rice with red beans). The Japanese believe that mochi is a gift from heaven and leave rice as an offering at shrines and eat it on festive occasions, especially New Year's Day. See also RICE.

mock chopped liver - also **string bean paté.** A puréed mixture that stands in for the real thing. Usually made with a green bean or lentil base, along with cashews or walnuts, mushrooms, onions and spices, it replicates the taste and texture of chopped liver. Some versions contain chopped egg, crackers and eggplant. A longtime favorite of vegetarians — including the writer Isaac Bashevis Singer, who ate it for health reasons ("the health of the chicken," he's supposed to have said) — mock chopped liver is gaining popularity and respect as a low-calorie, low-cholesterol choice.

mock maple syrup - see PANCAKE SYRUP.

mocktail - a nonalcoholic cocktail of the type made famous by the **Roy Rogers** and the **Shirley Temple** versions for kids, or the variations on standard drinks — the alcoholic **Bloody Mary** becomes the unspirited Virgin Mary — for adults. Gussied up and given names just like real drinks, mocktails are offered at bars, and, for safety's sake, increasingly promoted at private and public social events. On campus, Students Against Drunk Driving raises awareness by serving up mocktails.

mock turtle soup - an English soup made to recreate the color and flavor of turtle soup. Devised in the mid-1700s as a cheaper alternative to the then-fashionable dish made with imported West Indian turtles, this version was made by simmering a calf's head to make the stock, then adding pieces of the meat (said to resemble turtle meat) along with spices and, sometimes, bits of the brains. If we can believe the Mock Turtle in Lewis Carroll's *Alice's Adventures in Wonderland*, the dish was a success. Between sighs and sobs, he sings eloquently: "Beautiful Soup, so rich and green, Waiting in a hot tureen! Who for such dainties would not stoop? Soup of the evening, beautiful Soup!"

Mojito

moderate oven - a recipe term referring to an oven temperature of about 325° to 375°F (160° to 190°C). Dating from the time when cooks used wood stoves with nonexistent or unreliable thermostats, a moderate oven was one in which the cook's hand could tolerate the heat for 45 seconds. See also HOT OVEN, SLOW OVEN.

Moette Punch - a popular "pink champagne" **mocktail** likely named after the famous Moët Champagne. Typically, a combination of pineapple and white grape juices are fizzed up with club soda or ginger ale, then raspberry sherbet puts this punch in the pink.

mohinga - a dish of fine noodles (made from fermented rice flour), cooked in a thin broth usually containing banana-palm hearts, coconut, curry and fish; served with chiles, fritters, hard-boiled eggs, onions and patties made with beans or shrimp. In Myanmar, mohinga is considered the national dish, enjoyed in the morning and frequently bought from street vendors.

mohn - a poppy seed filling used in baked goods, such as yeast breads, **hamantaschen** and tortes. The poppy seeds are simmered in milk, then butter, honey, lemon zest and minced raisins and walnuts are added, cooked briefly and cooled to make a thick, sweet mixture.

moisten - to add or apply a small amount of liquid to a food mixture or surface in order to dampen, but not saturate it (for example, a mixture of dry ingredients moistened to create an elastic dough rather, than a runny batter, or the edges of an **empanada** moistened to promote adhesion, before they are pressed together).

moist sugar - see SUGAR.

Mojito - a Cuban cocktail made with rum, lime juice, sugar or simple syrup, fresh mint leaves and club soda. First, the mint leaves are **muddled** with the lime juice and sugar in the bottom of a tall glass. Then, rum and ice cubes are added, and the glass topped up with club soda.

mojo - an all-purpose marinade of Cuban origin, based on citrus juice (in Cuba in particular, the juice of sour oranges), seasoned with garlic, onions, herbs, cumin, salt and red pepper. Some versions of mojo made specifically for meat also contain oil to prevent the meat from charring on the grill. The popularity of mojo has spread from Cuba throughout the majority of Latin America, where it is used on everything from chicken to beef to seafood to add a tropical flavor and tang. The word derives from the Spanish verb *mojar*, meaning "to moisten."

mojo chicken - a Caribbean dish of chicken, marinated in a mixture of **adobo sauce**, chipotle pepper, citrus juice and zest, garlic, oil and vinegar, then grilled.

molasses - the syrup remaining after sucrose has been crystallized from the juice of sugarcane. Crystallization is carried out three times, producing three grades, the final being blackstrap, from the Dutch *stroop*, meaning "syrup," whose very dark color is the result of extreme caramelization from boiling repeatedly at high temperatures. Some molasses has had sulfur dioxide added to help clarify and lighten the color of cane juice, but it imparts a distinctive smell. To make premium molasses, clarified cane syrups are added to syrups that have undergone only one crystallization. Molasses is high in B vitamins, calcium, phosphorus and iron.

molcajete y tejolote - see MORTAR AND PESTLE.

mold - **1.** (n.) a concave container used to shape foods. A smooth or fine-textured liquid or soft food, such as ice cream, butter, cheese, cake dough, chocolate or pâté, is poured or pressed into a mold. It is then baked in the oven, steamed on the stovetop or cooled in the refrigerator and allowed to set. Turned out, it retains the shape of the mold. Intricate copper

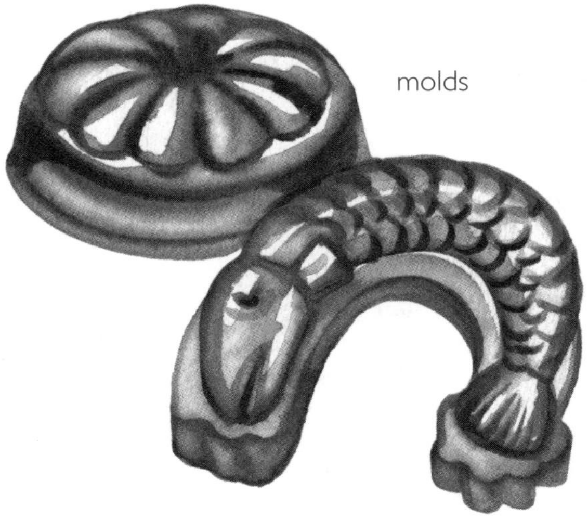

molds, shaped like fish, shells or other seafood and detailed with claws, fins, gills and scales, are traditional for aspics and savory mousses, for example, while classic shortbread is pressed into ceramic or wooden molds (carved with designs that transfer to the cookies), for baking. Some molds, such as **charlotte** or pudding molds, have lids. **2.** (n.) a dish made in a mold. **3.** (n.) various furry fungi that grow on foods, such as dairy products, fruits and vegetables and meat, and thrive in moist, warm, well-ventilated environments. Some molds spoil when improperly stored; others are used to produce blue-veined cheeses (*Penicillium*), fermented bean curd (*Mucor*) or fine wines (*Botrytis*). **4.** (v.) to shape foods by hand or using a mold.

molded cookie - **1.** a cookie formed into a ball, crescent or spiral, by hand. **2.** a cookie pressed into a patterned, textured mold (often ceramic or wood), then baked. Classic shortbread and **speculaas** are made this way.

mole - from the Aztec *molli*, meaning "concoction," "stew" or "sauce," a Mexican sauce containing chile peppers, spices and aromatics in which ingredients, such as meat, are usually cooked. Guacamole, an avocado-based mole, is one of the few that are uncooked. There are many different kinds of mole: green (with **tomatillo** or pumpkin seeds), orange, red, *mole poblano de guajolote* (with turkey) and *mole de olla*, Mexico's famous "peasant soup." Mole can be simple or complex. One of the most famous, *mole poblano*, a turkey mole invented in Puebla, is credited with introducing chocolate into the mix.

There are numerous legends about the origin of mole. One credits its invention to Fray Pascual, who accidentally created the recipe when a tray of spices and roasted cacao beans was knocked over into the pot in which dinner was being prepared. Another dates from the 1680s, when the nuns of the poor Santa Rosa Convent in Puebla de Los Angeles, Mexico, received instructions from the bishop to create a special dish for the visiting Viceroy of New Spain. The nuns mixed chocolate and peanuts with more than 100 other ingredients and blended them all into a sauce for a turkey dish. Some say it was divine intervention that impelled the nuns to include chocolate, while others say a willful draft blew the seasonings into the pot.

molinillo - a wooden pinwheel or swizzle stick, rotated between the palms to whisk and froth hot chocolate, a beverage that is ubiquitous in Latin America and Spain. Invented in the 1700s by an early Spanish colonist in Mexico, the tool became such a favorite that it and the drink were exported back to a thankful Spanish king. Handmade molinillos are still sold in Mexican street markets and also online, where one-of-a-kind antique versions are hot collectibles. See also MEXICAN CHOCOLATE.

mollete - a soft sweet, Spanish bread that resembles a small, plump pancake. The Arabs are credited with bringing the bread to the Iberian Peninsula hundreds of years ago, where it has become a staple on Andulasian breakfast tables, but mollete with savory toppings are also served as **tapas.** On some restaurant menus in Texas, however, a mollete is a roll stuffed with refried beans and melted cheese; in the Florida Keys, it may mean a roll stuffed with chopped olives and ground beef.

mollusk - a term denoting a soft, invertebrate animal. Many have shells, and many are **seafood.** They may be bivalves, which have two separate opening shells hinged together (oysters for example); **cephalopods,** which may or may not have a shell (squid, for example); or gastropods, which have one spiraling shell (land snails and sea snails are examples). While some cultures, notably the French and the Japanese, eat mollusks with enthusiasm, many cultures avoid them.

molten chocolate cake - a small warm chocolate cake that, when cut, oozes a river of melted chocolate. Its origin is unclear, but the cake was probably developed in France and imported by top-level chefs plying their trade in the New World. A variety of famous chefs have taken credit for creating the rich, **ganache**-based cakes, but there is no clear-cut creator. Some chefs admit to having created it by accident: serving the gooey, molten-centered cake to clients who clamored for more of the confection.

momo - a Tibetan dumpling with gingery, spiced minced beef or lamb filling (called *sha momo*) or vegetable filling (called *tsel momo*). Given Tibet's harsh climate and geography, meat fillings were traditional; now, greenhouses make fresh vegetables available. The fillings are placed on rounds of dough, which are then gathered at the top, or folded over like a **Cornish pasty,** and pinched together to seal them. After dipping in oil, the dumplings are steamed, then served with hot sauce. In Tibet, inedible "luck-telling" momos made at New Year (and stuffed with fillings, such as Buddhist scriptures, grass, salt, wool and even yak dung) carry messages about the future. In North America, the edible variety is becoming a familiar menu item, as more Tibetans settle here.

Mongolian grill - a style of restaurant at which the diners select their own dumplings, fish, meat, vegetables and sauces, then usually watch the chef stir-fry their meal in a **Mongolian hotpot** filled with hot broth. At some restaurants, diners actually assemble and cook their own ingredients in deep spoons with wire-basket bowls, which are dipped into the broth at a tabletop hotpot.

Mongolian hotpot - also **boiling firepot, Chinese firepot, Mongolian firepot.** A type of **fondue** well known in Chinese cuisine, consisting of a large communal bowl of boiling broth set over the open flame of a gas ring, into which are dipped a variety of raw meats, seafood, vegetables and dumplings. Diners dip their preferred foods into the boiling broth to cook them, then eat them with any of a variety of condiments or dipping sauces. At the end of the meal, the now-concentrated broth is served, often with the addition of noodles or more fresh vegetables. See also SHABU-SHABU.

monkey bread - **1.** a savory or sweet yeast bread made of individual balls of dough placed side by side, in several layers, in a pan. During baking, the dough swells and sticks together. Afterward, this "pull-apart bread" can be pulled easily into separate servings. Additions, such as cheese, herbs and sun-dried tomatoes, may be added to savory versions; chopped nuts, cinnamon, raisins and sugar may be added to sweet versions. **2.** the fruit of the tropical **baobab** or "bottle" tree. After the flowers on these solitary and strange-looking trees are pollinated by bats, the gourd-like fruits (which contain starchy, edible pulp) develop.

monkfish - also **anglerfish, bellyfish, frogfish, goosefish, lotte.** So named because of its unusually heavy and oddly shaped head, thought to resemble a fish wearing a monk's cowl. It's sometimes called **"poor man's lobster,"** due to the texture of its flesh. It is one of the ugliest fish on the market: French fishermen used to cut off its head at sea for fear of frightening land dwellers. The monkfish is also known by the name "anglerfish," because it lures its prey in front of its mouth with a spiny protrusion that dangles out from between its eyes, like an angler lures a fish with a piece of bait on his line.

monk's head - also **Bellelay cheese.** See TÊTE DE MOINE.

monosodium glutamate - also **MSG.** The sodium salt of glutamic acid, a common amino acid, has been an ingredient in Japanese cooking for a very long time, but was not actually produced as a flavoring agent until 1909. (It's known as *aji-no-moto* in Japan.) In 1908, Kikunae Ikeda, a Japanese scientist, was intent on isolating a basic taste substance that was neither sweet, salty, sour or bitter. While studying a particular kind of kelp, a seaweed traditionally used to make soup, he isolated the glutamate ion and found it to have its own taste, which he described as "savory," or **umami,** with the ability to alter the tastes of other foods in an appetizing way. Initially, MSG was manufactured from wheat proteins, which are rich in glutamic acid. In the 1950s, a bacterium was isolated that synthesizes and excretes glutamic acid when fed an excess of ammonium ions, which supply the necessary nitrogen. Today, nearly all MSG is produced by the fermentation technique that discovery made possible. World production now stands at about

Montagné, Prosper (1865–1948) - French chef and author, best known as creator of *Larousse Gastronomique*, the world's best-known culinary reference book, whose first edition appeared in 1938. Montagné was born 1865 and wanted to become an architect, but his father pushed him toward a culinary education, to which, it turns out, he was very well suited. He worked his way through the **brigade system** of numerous distinguished French kitchens and, during the First World War, ran the army's central kitchen. On his return to Paris after the war, he opened a delicatessen but, despite its popularity, closed the shop 10 years later. Montagné decided to leave cooking behind in 1907 to devote himself exclusively to writing. His first culinary work, *La Grande Cuisine illustrée* (Great Cuisine Illustrated), published in 1900, was written with collaborator Prosper Salles. Before his death in 1948, Montagné produced several more books on his own, most notably *La Cuisine fine* in 1913 (Fine Cuisine), *Le Festin occitan* (The Occitan Feast) and *Le Grande Livre de la cuisine* (The Grand Book of Cooking), both published in 1929.

250,000 tons (227,000 tonnes) annually. The Japanese use MSG to coat table salt, thereby preventing it from caking and expanding its contribution of flavor.

MSG is somewhat mysterious in that its ability (or that of several other compounds called "nucleotides") to "improve" or "enhance" flavors is not clearly understood. Whether it acts at the receptor site, in the taste cell, or at the junction of taste cell and nerve (or whether it increases receptor sensitivity or alters the pattern of electrical signals) are questions still unanswered. In the late 1960s, MSG was named as the culprit in the so-called "Chinese Restaurant Syndrome." Signaled by temporary burning or tingling sensations, headache or a feeling of pressure behind the forehead and eyes, chest pain or weakness, it can suddenly afflict sensitive people after consumption of foods to which MSG has been added, such as those commonly found in Chinese restaurants. Glutamates also occur naturally in foods (tomatoes and some cheeses are examples) not only in manufactured MSG, and studies have shown that the human body metabolizes and reacts to both types the same way. The syndrome (also know as MSG symptom complex) is not clearly understood despite several studies. Since testing of susceptible individuals has not shown MSG to trigger the syndrome all of the time, there have been suggestions that another factor, such as a high level of salt in the food, may be the cause. Because glutamic acid is found in especially large concentrations in the nervous tissue and plays a role in the transmission of nerve impulses, it has been theorized that temporary dietary excess may disrupt parts of the nervous system. Claims are also made that MSG aggravates the symptoms or conditions as wide ranging as asthma and fibromyalgia. Such claims, as well as the existence of MSG symptom complex itself, still remain controversial. As an additive or ingredient, MGS is listed on food labels in Canada and the U.S.

monounsaturated fat - see FATS.

Monriondo, Francesco - see AMARETTI.

monstera fruit

monstera - also **ceriman, Mexican breadfruit.** This Central American and Caribbean plant, *Monstera deliciosa,* is more widely cultivated as an ornamental plant than as fruit, but its edible qualities are well known. All parts of it, except the ripe fruit, are toxic. The monstera is commonly known as the "split-leaf philodendron," which has a cucumber-shaped fruit enclosed within tiny hexagonal platelets, which fall off when ripe. The soft, juicy flesh tastes like a cross between pineapple and banana. It can be eaten raw and is often made into chutney.

Montagné, Prosper - see profile above.

Montana tendergroins - see PRAIRIE OYSTER.

Montasio - an artisanal cooked cheese from the Italian Alps, which has been in production since Benedictine monks first began making it, some time around the 15th century. Originally made from ewe's milk, it is now a cow's milk cheese, aged anywhere from four to 18 months to create three separate types, ranging from semisoft to hard: fresh (aged four or five months); partially aged (aged five to 10 months); and aged (aged 19 months). The first two are considered table cheese, the latter for grating. Made in large cylinders, the cheese has a smooth, yellow interior pierced with small holes and is surrounded by a brown rind, which darkens with time. Montasio adds a fruity flavor (similar to a delicate pineapple taste) to cooked foods, such as eggplant casseroles and pasta dishes.

Mont Blanc - a French dessert, also called *Mont Blanc aux marrons*, made with creamy, puréed chestnuts flavored with vanilla. Tall, cold and white like its namesake mountain in the French Alps, this dish is topped with snowy drifts of **chantilly cream** or whipped cream. Some chefs set a ring of chestnut cream on meringue or **sablé** pastry, instead, then fill the center with chantilly cream or whipped cream.

monte cristo - a sandwich containing cheese (most often Swiss), sliced, cooked chicken or turkey and sometimes ham, dipped into beaten egg and fried or grilled. It may be sprinkled with confectioner's sugar and served with jam on the side. Reputed to have been a favorite of Elvis Presley, a bacon, banana, peanut butter and raisin bread version, eaten often enough, is guaranteed to pop the rhinestone buttons off anyone's sequined suit.

monter - a French culinary term meaning to add body or volume. A single ingredient, such as egg white, may be whisked to incorporate air and increase volume, for example. Or two or more ingredients, such as egg yolk and oil, may be whisked together to incorporate air and emulsify the mixture. See also MONTER AU BEURRE.

monter au beurre - a French culinary term meaning to swirl butter into a sauce near the end of cooking to bind the sauce and give it body and shine.

Monterey Jack - also **California Jack, Jack.** An American semisoft cheese, named after David Jacks, who started importing the cheese in the late 1880s (some say 1916) from its namesake city in California, although it's now made throughout the U.S. Available aged and unaged (**Dry Jack**). See also SONOMA JACK.

Montiño, Francisco Martínez - see profile below.

Montrachet cheese - a creamy, tangy and pure white goat's milk cheese made in Burgundy, France, that is often coated with salted ash. Best eaten fresh, it's often used for appetizers, or simply consumed with crackers or crusty bread.

moo goo gai pan - a Chinese stir-fried dish of sliced chicken and mushrooms, commonly seen on restaurant menus in North America. The dish is flavored with garlic, ginger, soy sauce, sherry and sesame oil and often includes other vegetables as well. A glossy sauce is made at the end of cooking, after the vegetables and meat have been stir-fried, using the pan juices and cornstarch as a thickener. The name means "fresh mushrooms with sliced chicken" in Chinese.

Montiño, Francisco Martínez (16th–17th century) - Spanish royal chef and author who recorded Spain's Christian interpretation of its Persian culinary roots. Montiño was chef to Felipe II, III and IV. In 1611, he published his opus, *Arte de Cocina, Pasteleria, Vizcocheria, y Conserveria* (The Art of Cooking, Cake Making, Biscuit Making and Conserving). The comprehensive 500-page book offered recipes, presentations and discussions of food, from raw ingredients to decorative arrangements, freely displaying his Muslim, Italian and French influences. In the only other book he appears to have published, about Christmas foods and celebration, he tells of a meal prepared for a visiting Japanese dignitary, to whom Montiño presented *turrón* (nougat), the traditional Christmas sweet. Thinking he was offering something completely new, Montiño was surprised to learn that the specialty had made its way around the world and that the dignitary had eaten it before. It was already a Christmas favorite in Japan.

mooli - see DAIKON.

mooncake - round pastry shells, filled with mounded, glazed savory or sweet mixtures, used to celebrate the Chinese Moon Festival, *Zhong Qui Jie*. Chinese families gather on the night of the 15th day of the eighth month on their lunar calendar to look at the bright harvest moon, drink tea, and tell their children (who are given lanterns to carry) the legend of Chang-Er, the lady in the moon; they are also called "reunion cakes," since they bring families together for the celebration. Mooncakes are traditionally shaped by hand, with puréed bean, date, lotus-seed or, sometimes, meat fillings, then imprinted with a chrysanthemum pattern, for example, or the insignia of the baker. (Cantonese cakes are made with wooden molds, which impress the designs.) Mooncakes may also contain a duck-egg yolk, which represents the full moon. Elaborate and complicated to make, mooncakes are now also produced commercially; Häagen Daz even sells an ice cream version.

moonfish - also **bluntnose, dollar fish, opah, shiner.** The small silvery fish, shaped like a slender, elongated disk, *Vomer setapinnis*, found in warm Atlantic waters from Uruguay as far north as Cape Code and, occasionally, Nova Scotia.

moong dal - also **mung dal.** See DAL, MUNG BEAN.

MoonPie - a regional bakery novelty from Chattanooga, Tennessee, consisting of marshmallow between two graham cookies, the largest five-cent snack of its time. In the early 1900s, Earl Mitchell had a store that catered to miners, who wanted a solid, filling snack for their lunch pails. When Mitchell asked the miners how big this snack should be, one looked at the rising moon and said, "about that big." MoonPies quickly caught on nationally, and the company has sold more than two billion since its creation in 1917. They're still manufactured today by the same bakery on King Street, which produces 300,000 of them every week.

moonshine - also **angel's teat, Kentucky fire, white lightning.** An illicit liquor; originally, "moonshine" meant illegally obtained, smuggled liquor. After the late 1800s, however, it came to mean illegally produced liquor, often distilled behind the barn or in a quiet spot in the back 40, especially in the rural American South of the Prohibition years. Most often a corn-based liquor, moonshine can be made with anything starchy, sweet and handy. Berries, potatoes, pumpkins and even hog feed have been used. The result is a harsh, clear and colorless spirit that is certainly intoxicating and, depending on the distiller, quite possibly dirty, poisonous and death-inducing.

Moors and Christians - a classic Cuban dish of black beans and rice, named for the Spanish festival of *Moros y Christianos*. Celebrated in more than 150 locations throughout Spain, this colorful festival, which may involve elaborate preparations and complicated staging, reenacts the Moorish conquest of Spain in 1276 and its subsequent reclamation in 1492 by the Spanish under Queen Isabella and King Ferdinand.

moose - large, herbivorous land mammal, *Alces alces*, of northern-hemisphere boreal forests. Unable to sweat and intolerant of heat, moose are usually found foraging in and around wetlands. Named for the Algonquian word meaning "eater of twigs" in North America, moose are known elsewhere as European "elk" from the Greek *alke*, meaning "strength." With males often weighing more than 1,300 pounds (590 kg), standing about 10 feet (3 m) tall and sporting broad antlers spanning 7 feet (2 m) from side to side, the moose was a generous source of meat for food, hides for clothing and bones for tool making for indigenous peoples. Mainly hunted for sport now, moose are occasionally farmed in Russia and Scandinavia.

moose

moo shu - also **moo shoo, mu shu.** A classic Chinese **roll-up** consisting of a thin pancake wrapped around a scrambled-egg mixture, usually containing onion, tiger-lily bud, **wood ear** mushroom and seasoned, shredded pork, often served with hoisin sauce. Vegetarian versions are also becoming popular.

mop - also **baste, sop.** A basting sauce painted on meat that is being smoked or barbecued to keep it moist as it cooks, a term widely used by aficionados of Southern barbecue. A mop can be made of almost anything commonly added to a marinade or barbecue sauce.

Moravian cookie - a classic, crunchy Bohemian spice cookie that is a Christmas tradition. Dough darkened with brown sugar and molasses, and spiced with allspice, cinnamon, cloves, ginger and nutmeg, is mixed then left at room temperature overnight for the flavors to blend. Rolled paper-thin, it is cut into seasonal shapes, then baked. Some North American versions of the cookie are frosted.

morcilla - the Spanish version of blood sausage, used in **fabada,** a dish that includes chorizo and bacon.

morel - an edible mushroom of the genus *Morchella*, dark, hollow, cone-shaped and covered with honeycomb-like pits, considered a delicacy. Available in the spring, the black morel (M. *angusticeps*) and yellow morel (M. *esculenta*) are the varieties most commonly consumed. Poisonous morels include the "wrinkled thimble cap" and the "false morel." Morels are found in a wide variety of habitants including open woodlands and among shrubs. Attempts to farm morels have not been very successful but dried morels are widely available year-round; it takes 8 pounds (4 kg) of fresh ones to make 1 pound (500 g) of dried. See also MUSHROOM.

morels

Morello cherry - a sour cherry *(Prunus cerasus)* with a dark red skin and flesh. It's unsuitable for eating raw, but the juice is used in liqueurs and brandies. The fruit can be found dried or canned, packed in syrup.

Morimoto, Masaharu - see profile below.

Mornay - a French sauce, essentially **béchamel** with cheese. There are many conflicting accounts about its origin. Some credit Duke Philippe de Mornay (1549–1623), who is also credited with inventing **chasseur sauce** and **Lyonnaise sauce.** A much later story credits Joseph Voiron, chef of the 19th-century Durand restaurant, who was thought to have dedicated it to his son, Mornay, himself a cook.

Moroccan olive - see OLIVE.

mortadella - a specialty sausage of Bologna, Italy, made of finely ground pork, larded, flavored with peppercorns, coriander and sometimes pistachio; some are smoked and then aged for two months. Some say the name derives from *mortaio*, meaning "a mortar," referring to the pounding of the meat to a fine

Morimoto, Masaharu (1955–) - Japanese chef and restaurateur. In 1980, at 25, Morimoto opened his first restaurant in his hometown of Hiroshima, where he'd done extensive training in traditional Japanese cooking, and distinguished himself by infusing Western ingredients and techniques into his cuisine. He left Japan five years later, selling his restaurant and embarking on a worldwide trip to see other cuisines. He traveled no farther than Manhattan, where he cooked in numerous high-end Japanese restaurants, most notably with fellow Japanese expatriate chef **Nobu Matsuhisa.** In 1998, he earned the title of Japanese Iron Chef from the popular Japanese cooking competition show, and three years later opened Morimoto in Philadelphia with Stephen Starr, theater impresario-turned-restaurateur, an ideal match given Morimoto's favorite adage: "Cooking is entertainment."

texture. However, it mostly likely comes from *mytrus* (*mirto* or *mortella* in Italian), or "myrtle," because mortadella is sometimes seasoned with myrtle berries.

mortar and pestle

mortar and pestle - still used in many kitchens, although blenders, food processors and grinders have now taken its place for many tasks. The mortar (or bowl) often has a rough texture and can be made of wood or glass, although porcelain and solid brass are more efficient. The pestle, a club-shaped implement, is useful for pounding, crushing and grinding small amounts of spices and nuts, and is still thought of as the best utensil for crushing garlic. The name "pesto" derives from the preparation of the sauce with a mortar and pestle. In Mexico, the *molcajete y tejolote*, a mortar and pestle made from volcanic rock, is considered essential, particularly when preparing uncooked sauce.

morue - the French term for **salt cod.**

Mosimann, Anton - see profile below.

moss cranberry - see LINGONBERRY.

mostaccioli - **1.** see PASTA. **2.** also **nzudda.** A specialty biscuit from Calabria, Italy, originally of Arabian origin, sweetened with honey and aniseed liqueur. The biscuits are often cut into shapes, such as hearts, animals and letters.

mostarda - also **mostarda di Cremona, mostarda di frutta.** A sweet-and-tart condiment made of simmered fruits, such as apricots, cherries, oranges, pears and quince. Mixed with vinegar or wine, and honey or sugar, the thickened mixture is perked up with a generous amount of ground mustard seed. An early version, made with turnip, was enjoyed by the early Romans. Today's mostarda, which can be homemade or purchased ready-made, is especially common in northern Italy as an accompaniment to boiled meats.

mosto cotto - Italian for "cooked **must.**" See VINO COTTO.

mother of vinegar - also **mère de vinaigre.** A clear, viscous bacterial culture or starter that transforms an alcoholic liquid, such as cider, beer or wine, into vinegar. Homemade vinegar is usually produced in a crock or vat over a period of months, often using leftover wines (which must be good-quality, untainted and unfortified). A thick, and frankly unattractive, coating of the mother bacteria forms on the surface and should be left undisturbed during the process; when the vinegar is poured out, pieces of the coating can be reused with new

Mosimann, Anton (1947–) Swiss-born chef, best known for his signature style of lean cooking, as set out in his 1985 landmark book, *Cuisine Naturelle.* Mosimann began his career working throughout Europe, the Far East, Japan and in Canada. The culinary world took note when he was named executive chef of London's Dorchester Hotel at the age of 28. He stayed there for 13 years and earned two Michelin stars for the hotel. As well as opening a private London dining club in 1988 in an early 19th-century church, he embarked on a number of enterprises, like many successful chefs, including a culinary academy, recruitment agency, party service, a line of wine and food products, and three television series, one focusing specifically on Swiss cuisine for broadcast in Switzerland. Mosimann has published 12 books, most notably *A New Style of Cooking* (1983), *The Art of Anton Mosimann* (1989), *Essential Mosimann* (1993) and *Mosimann's World* (1996).

liquid to start another batch or passed on to another vinegar maker.

mother sauces - see SAUCE.

Mother Superior cabbage salad - an easy, economical salad of grated cabbage and chopped, unpeeled red apples and minced onion, tossed with a mixture of sour cream seasoned with salt, granulated sugar, black pepper and vinegar. Madame **Jehane Benoit,** the popular French-Canadian chef and TV cooking-show host of the mid-20th century, popularized this simple recipe, explaining that it was often served in small village convents when guests came to dinner, hence the name.

moulard duck - a cross between a male **muscovy** and a female **Peking duck.** Most of them are raised for **foie gras.**

moule - French for "mussel." See also MARINIÈRE.

Mouli grater - see GRATER.

mountain berry - see CLOUDBERRY.

mountain cranberry - LINGONBERRY.

mountain oysters - see PRAIRIE OYSTER.

mountain spinach - see GOOSEFOOT.

Mount Athos - see OLIVE.

moussaka - also **mousaka, musaka.** Most familiar to North Americans as a baked dish of sliced eggplant layered with ground lamb and, perhaps, tomatoes, moussaka can be made many ways. In Greece, it usually has **béchamel** sauce or beaten eggs poured on before it's baked. In Arab countries, zucchini usually replace the eggplant and, in the Balkans, the dish may contain cabbage, celery, cheese, ground beef, noodles, sauerkraut, spinach, potatoes or rice.

mousse - a light, airy, creamy, sweet or savory mixture sometimes set with gelatin. Classical chocolate mousse gets its lightness from the use of a **sabayon** as part of its base, providing richness and body, and its airiness from the lengthy, strenuous whipping of egg yolks during its cooking. Modern seafood mousses not set with gelatin get their airiness from the mechanical aeration of being whipped in a food processor, with the addition of heavy cream and sometimes egg whites. Fruit mousses most often need gelatin, because of a high water content and therefore greater instability.

mousseline - a term used to depict a mixture that has whipped cream added to it. Sauces in particular are described in this way; hollandaise mousseline is the best known. Mousseline can also refer to small moulds or aspics made from a paste or purée of fish, poultry, vegetables or game, enhanced with cream and cooked in a bain-marie.

moutarde - French for "mustard."

moutarde de Meaux - see MUSTARD.

mouth feel - a term used frequently by wine and beer tasters and commercial food developers alike to describe the way a beverage or food feels in the mouth. It might be described as oily, creamy, smooth, astringent, fleshy, green or even "suede" (to describe a wine that feels in the mouth the way suede feels, when you run your fingers across it). Mouth feel can be subjective, as each person might describe these tactile sensations in very different terms.

mozzarella - a soft, delicate, mild cheese, traditionally made from buffalo milk but now made from cow's milk (known as *fior de latte*). No one is quite sure when water buffalo were brought to Italy from India. The Greeks or the early Christians may have introduced them. Certainly, by the 16th century, they had become a feature of southern Italian agricultural life. At this time, farmers began to use buffalo milk to make mozzarella. Its popularity soon reached the northern regions, where cheese makers started to produce inferior versions made from cow's milk.

The word "mozzarella" is the diminutive form of *mozza,* a cheese, which mozzarella was originally called. *Mozza* derives from *mozzare,* meaning "to cut off" or "dock" (as in docking a dog's tail), which probably refers to the making of the cheese: the cheese maker removes big portions of the cheese from the whey liquid and breaks or cuts off the pieces by hand. See also BUFFALO MOZZARELLA.

MSG - see MONOSODIUM GLUTAMATE.

mudbug - see CRAYFISH.

muddle - to crush an ingredient, such as an herb or a wedge of citrus fruit, to release its juices and/or essential oils for incorporation into a mixed drink. Mint leaves, for example, are muddled with sugar to make a **Mint Julep** or a **Mojito,** and lime wedges are muddled to make a

Caipirinha. Ingredients can be muddled with a spoon or a muddler, a bar utensil made of wood and shaped like a miniature baseball bat, with a rounded end.

muesli - a breakfast cereal of rolled oats, dried fruit, nuts, honey and spices, very similar to **granola,** although its oats are toasted. Muesli is also considered to be European granola. The invention of Swiss physician and nutritionist Maximilian Bircher-Benner, a proponent of eating raw foods for maximum health, muesli was originally a mixture of grated apple, lemon juice, milk and nuts.

muffin - a sweet quick bread made in individual-serving molds in an infinite variety of flavors and styles. Thought to be derived from the French *moufflet,* meaning soft bread, or the German *Muffe,* meaning a type of cake, the American muffin differs from the English muffin, which is yeast-risen and cooked on a griddle, because it's chemically leavened with either baking soda or baking powder.

muffuletta - also **muffaletta.** A distinctly New Orleans sandwich, the muffuletta is made with layered salami, capicollo, provolone, mozzarella and an olive salad (olives, shallots, garlic, parsley and olive oil) on a large, round, crusty Italian roll. The sandwich is said to have originated in 1906 at the Central Grocery, which is still open, although it was forced to close for awhile in 2005 due to Hurricane Katrina. It's still making "muffs," as they're also known. Although New Orleans doesn't have an Italian quarter per se, it has a large Italian immigrant population. The name is from the Sicilian *muffulatte,* a dialect word meaning "soft roll." The muffuletta's popularity is second only to that of the **poor boy.**

mugi miso - see MISO.

mugwort - also **old woman, sailor's tobacco.** *Artemisia vulgaris,* an aromatic, perennial herb related to wormwood, which is native to temperate Asia and Europe. In the days before hops were added to beer, mugwort was used to flavor it. When tobacco was scarce, the dried leaves of the herb were smoked instead. These days, the leaves are used to flavor fish, meat and poultry (in Germany, mugwort is a customary seasoning for the Christmas goose). The gray of its flower stalks and linings of its leaves perhaps earned it the nickname "old woman." Some Wiccans drink mugwort tea before bed to encourage their astral voyages, while butterfly larvae, which will eventually attain flight unassisted, like to eat the flowers. A hardy import, mugwort is now considered a noxious weed throughout much of North America.

mugwumps - a down-home Canadian comfort food made from cooked carrots and potatoes, mashed together, then mixed with fried, chopped onion and cubed bacon, and served hot. *Mugwumps,* an Algonquian word for "great chief," belies the unpretentious nature of the dish.

muhallabia - a creamy, simmered pudding popular throughout the Middle East. Muhallabia is made with milk, rice flour (or a combination of corn flour and ground rice), orange flower water or rose water flavoring, salt and sugar; in some recipes, ground almonds stand in for a portion of the flour. When it's cooled and set, the pudding is often drizzled with liquid honey before it's topped with the chopped almonds and pistachios, which are de rigueur. Prepared muhallabia mixes are available.

muhammara paste - a classic Mediterranean and Middle Eastern condiment and spread made from roasted red bell peppers and walnuts, olive oil and honey or pomegranate molasses, and seasonings, such as garlic, cloves, cumin and hot chile pepper. Other ingredients, such as whole wheat bread crumbs, may be added to the mixture. The paste may be served with pita bread or spread on grilled chicken, fish or tofu, pilaf or vegetable dishes.

muki goma - the Japanese term for hulled, white sesame seeds. See also GOMA, SESAME.

mugwort

mulato chile - see CHILE PEPPER.

mulberry - the three varieties of this berry are the white mulberry (*Morus alba*), the black (*Morus Nigra*) and the red mulberry or American mulberry (*Morus rubra*), the only one native to the U.S. The berries are generally eaten fresh, or used in jams, desserts and mulberry wine, and also to make a mildly astringent syrup.

mulberries

mulled wine - a wine, usually red, that is heated with sugar, citrus fruits and spices, such as clove and cinnamon.

mullet - bony fish of the Mugilidae family, which live in the tropical and warm, temperate waters of the Black and Mediterranean seas, the Atlantic and Pacific oceans, and the Gulf of Mexico and are now being commercially farmed. A saltwater fish, mullet also successfully migrate into freshwater estuaries and rivers. Prized for their soft, white flesh, gray, silver and striped mullet are usually poached in **court-bouillon,** baked or grilled. Off the Florida coast, pelican and shark enjoy their share of mullet, as well. Roe from the gray mullet has long been the first choice for making **taramosalata.** See also RED MULLET.

mulligan stew - a North American anything-goes stew, which first made its appearance during the Klondike Gold Rush, as the 19th century ended. Cooked in one pot, using odds and ends of whatever fish, fowl, game, meat and vegetables were available, it was a perfect dish for the miners and prospectors who lived rough and cooked over campfires. For the same reasons, it was popular with the hoboes and tramps of the Depression; anyone who contributed an ingredient or collected firewood for the stew earned a share. See also BURGOO.

mulligatawny - a rich curry soup that became popular among the British colonialists living in India, who brought the recipe back to England with them. The name is a Tamil word meaning "pepper water," peppers being an original primary ingredient. The dish soon evolved to cater to Western tastes, but its basic ingredients are chicken or vegetable stock, pieces of chicken, curry, coconut milk or cream, onions, celery, apples and almonds.

munchies - a colloquial term for "snacks."

mung bean - also **moong dal, mung dal.** Widely cultivated in India and China since time immemorial, mung beans, *Phaseolus aureus*, are available whole, split and skinless and are probably best known in the form of bean sprouts. Mung beans are widely used in China, where they're sprouted for their sweet, tender shoots and processed to make *fen tiao* noodles, and in India, where they're curried. The dried beans are also ground into flour to make noodles and other dishes. See also SPROUTS.

mung dal - also **moong dal.** See DAL, MUNG BEAN.

Munster - not counting the unrelated American Munster, there are two cheeses by the same name. French Munster from Alsace (near the German border) and Münster from Germany are similar in taste and size. The origin of the cheese is attributed to an Irish monk who settled in Alsace in the 7th century; the name has the same roots as "monastery." The cheese in both countries is made of whole milk; the **Appellation d'Origine Contrôlée** will only label a cheese Munster if it is made purely from the milk of the Old Vosgienne breed of cow. In the United States, one of the bestselling cheeses in the supermarket is called American Munster (or Muenster); despite its name, this cheese is not related to the European Munster. The typical characteristics of this domestic cheese are its mildness and its almost complete absence of aroma. Some Munster cheese comes covered with caraway seeds, which may give the pleasant illusion of eating a good sour rye bread.

Muntok peppercorns - see PEPPERCORNS.

Murcott - see HONEY TANGERINE.

murmura - also **mamra, puffed rice.** A crunchy, puffed rice used in Indian confections and snack foods. It may be eaten right out of the package or fried in oil seasoned with spices, such as ground chile, cumin, fennel and turmeric, and whole mustard seed, then combined with shredded coconut, nuts, **sev** and raisins. Variations of this snack, served in paper cones, are commonly sold by street vendors in Bombay. Murmura may also be mixed with melted **jaggery,** then cooled to make brittle. And it's often tossed into the air over the bride and groom at an Indian wedding.

musaka - see MOUSSAKA.

muscadine - a grape, *Vitis rotundifolia,* native to the southern U.S., which produces small clusters (not bunches) of thick-skinned blackish or purplish red grapes. See also SCUPPERNONG.

muscatel - an old-fashioned term for a sweet dessert wine made from a mixture of white and black **Muscat grapes,** from pale yellow to amber-tinted red in color, very rich and heavily perfumed with the musky scent of the grape. These wines are often seen labeled with the Italian name for the Muscat grape, *moscato,* or simply "muscat wine." It is not the same as the dry white wine Muscadet.

Muscat grape - any of more than 200 varieties of white or black grapes, with a perfumy, nectarous flavor. It is considered one of the finest table grapes, also used extensively worldwide to make rich, sweet dessert wines, such as **muscatel;** sparkling wines, such as Asti Spumanti; and brandies, such as **Metaxa** or **grappa.** Probably the oldest grape variety in continuous cultivation, the Muscat has been grown for thousands of years for its musky scent and flavor. It originated in Arabia, specifically in the sultanate of Muscat, which is part of Oman. It is now grown all over the world, from North America to South America to Europe to Australia. The fruits also make excellent raisins.

muscovado sugar - also **Barbados sugar, moist sugar.** See SUGAR.

muscovy duck - also **pato real, royal duck.** A large duck native to South America, *Cairina moschata*; it is now farmed in Europe and Central and North America for its high meat-to-bone ratio, lean, non-greasy meat and plump breasts. A drake can reach up to 15 pounds (7.5 kg), his female counterpart, 10 pounds (5 kg). Easily identified by their bright red eye patches, muscovy ducks are not only comfortable on water, but nest in trees rather than along shorelines, often occupying the abandoned aeries of eagles and other large birds. As livestock, muscovy ducks are commonly bred with domesticated ducks to produce the **moulard duck.** Similar to mules, moulard ducks are sterile; they are raised for **foie gras** and meat. See also DUCK.

muscovy duck

mush - **1.** (n.) a thick, boiled porridge of cornmeal and milk or water. Served hot for breakfast, it may be topped with brown sugar, butter, milk or sweet syrup. Allowed to cool, it can be sliced to eat cold or to fry and serve with gravy. Variations of cornmeal mush were consumed by Native Americans and introduced to Europeans as they arrived. Along the eastern seaboard, mush was sometimes enriched with wild-collected fruits and nuts, and often sweetened with maple syrup. Colonials developed their own mush, dubbed **Indian Pudding,** and sweetened it with molasses shipped from the Caribbean. The indigenous people of Mexico drank a mush called **atole** and, after cornmeal traveled across the Atlantic, the Italians created **polenta,** a thicker version that is still popular in many guises on plates around the globe. **2.** (n.) a generic term for a thick porridge made of grains or meals, such as barley, flour, oats or **sago.** See also HASTY PUDDING. **3.** (v.) a colloquial term for mashing food into a soft mass, as in: "Mush up them taters, will ya, darlin'." See also KUTYA.

mushimono - a Japanese culinary term, used to describe "steamed dishes," such as the popular savory custard dish, *chawan mushi.*

mushroom - a fungus that has no seeds or flowers, but propagates through its spores, the word possibly from Old French *mousseron* by way of Latin *muscus,* meaning "moss." **Champignon** is French for mushroom. Mushrooms and myths seem to go together. For one thing, mushrooms seem to grow like magic, springing up overnight from nowhere, and some contain enough phosphorus to glow in the dark. Combine this with the fact that they often grow in rings, and you have the origin of myths about "fairy rings" as well as stools (or umbrellas) for leprechauns. The pharaohs, who were considered gods as well as kings, declared mushrooms sacred and reserved them for their own consumption. The Romans called them food of the gods, too, but allowed anyone to eat them on holy days and holidays. The Romans enjoyed many mushrooms, including *Amanita Caesarea* (Caesar's mushroom), which was popular with the emperor Claudius and ultimately led to his downfall: his wife, Agrippina, poisoned him by adding deadly *Amanita phalloides* (the fittingly named "death cap") to a dish of his favorite mushrooms.

It's speculated that various hallucinogenic mushrooms were the legendary "ambrosia" of the gods, forbidden to mortals for their own good; that the feasts of Dionysus, divine half-brother of Hercules, were mushroom orgies rather than drinking bouts. Alexander the Great may have died of mushroom poisoning. The Greek dramatist Euripides lost his wife, daughter and two sons to the deadly *Amanita*. The Roman emperors Tiberius and Claudius are both said to have succumbed to mushroom poisoning. Pope Clement VII and France's Charles V were also victims of the fungi.

Commercial cultivation probably started in France during the reign of Louis the XIV. Ignorance about the growth and life cycle of mushrooms was widespread until the French botanist Marchant demonstrated, in 1678, that mushrooms grew from spawn, appearing on a lace-like structure, the mycelium, just beneath the surface of the soil. Market gardeners in Paris swiftly put theory into practice and transplanted the "roots" of the wild mushroom into a bed of horse manure and thus bred the ancestors of a remarkably successful product. In the 1890s, French scientists finally consolidated their long monopoly by developing a pasteurized spawn and, therefore, more dependable crops. One French cave contained 20 miles (32 km) of mushroom beds. American growers, who had first raised mushrooms in New York City and Long Island, adopted the French technique in the late 19th century. The U.S. mushroom industry started about 1891 in Kennett Square, Pennsylvania, which is still the mushroom capital of the U.S.

The cultivated mushroom, *Agaricus bisporus*, is usually harvested young, either as a "button" mushroom, with pale pink gills, or as a "cup" mushroom, where the cap, or pileus, has partially opened. The mature, or "flat," mushroom has dark brown gills. Most modern growers use stable manure that has been machine-mixed with gypsum and cottonseed or barley, made rich with nitrogenous compounds. The compost is pasteurized by steaming and laid in a controlled environment to receive the spawn. A layer of "casing" soil then covers the spawn, which is left for about three weeks at 65°F (18°C), while the compost is regularly kept moist. Mushrooms appear after the first month and continue to yield crops for three or four months. One-third of a grower's crop will be sold fresh; one-third used for canning; and the remainder used for soup. Mycologists are mushroom foragers and experts; mycophaogists are mushroom eaters.

Poisonous mushrooms used to be called "toadstools," but this dates back to when people thought they could tell safe mushrooms from poisonous mushroom by folk methods now known to be old wives' tales. Poisonous mushrooms may or may not tarnish silverware; do not turn dark in a saltwater solution; and do not turn milky in vinegar. Whether a mushroom is easy or hard to peel has nothing to do with whether or not it's poisonous. Contrary to popular belief, there is no home test that can distinguish between edible and poisonous varieties. Some mushrooms are edible when fresh and young and become poisonous when old or hit by frost; some are poisonous in one part of the country and not in another. Some can be poisonous to animals and not to humans and vice versa. Only a trained mycologist can identify wild mushrooms; in France, for example, mushroom hunters can bring their finds to a pharmacist for identification free of charge. See also AGARIC, AMANITA, BEEFSTEAK FUNGUS, BLACK CHANTERELLE, BLEWIT, BOLETUS, BUTTON MUSHROOM, CEP, CHANTERELLE, CREMINI, CULTIVATED MUSHROOM, ENOKI, FIELD MUSHROOM, FUNGHI, FUNGUS, GIANT PUFFBALL MUSHROOM, HEN OF THE WOODS, HORSE MUSHROOM, HUITALACOCHE, KINOKO, MATSUTAKE, MOREL, NAMEKO MUSHROOM,

OYSTER MUSHROOM, PARASOL MUSHROOM, PORCINI, PUFFBALL MUSHROOM, SHIITAKE, STRAW MUSHROOM, TREE MUSHROOM, WOOD EAR.

mushroom brush - a brush with very soft bristles, used to clean mushrooms without bruising or cutting their delicate flesh. Common circular versions, with easy-to-hold domed handles, resemble the mushrooms they're designed to clean.

mu shu - see MOO SHU.

mushy peas - **1.** a favorite British comfort food, traditionally made from marrowfat peas, cooked with mint, then mashed, buttered and eaten alone or alongside fish and chips or meat pie. British chef Jamie Oliver and others suggest that using frozen green peas are a good, quick alternative. **2.** the colloquial name for marrowfat peas. In the past, they were allowed to dry (often right on the plants in the cook's backyard vegetable plot), then rehydrated before cooking. "No soak" versions are now available, packaged in plastic or tinned.

musk cucumber - see CASSABANANA.

muskellunge - also **maskinonge, muskie.** A large fish, *Esox masquinongy*, found in less than 1 percent of the world's fresh waters, including lakes in eastern Canada and the U.S. Muskies are caught commercially, but prized as trophy fish. Long, strong and with a big mouth full of teeth, the muskelluge is dubbed the "barracuda of the North" and, in Ontario and Quebec, "the maskinonge." Wisconsin named it its official state fish in 1955, and that state still holds the record for the largest ever reeled in: 69 pounds, 11 ounces. Smaller fish are more tender and tasty, and may be safer to eat, too. Great Lakes muskies, for example, can live to about 30 years old and, as they age and swallow smaller fish, they accumulate environmental toxins. Governments on both sides of the border have issued safe-consumption guidelines.

musk hog - see PECCARY.

muskie - see MUSKELLUNGE.

musk mallow - see MALLOW.

muskmelon - also **netted melon, nutmeg melon.** The muskmelon is a type of edible, fragrant, sweet-fleshed melon. Many have skins covered with a raised, textured network (cantaloupe and **Santa Claus melons** are examples of these so-called netted melons); others have smooth skins (**casaba** and honeydew melons are examples). All have stringy centers containing seeds.

muskrat - a mammal weighing approximately 2 pounds (1 kg). The muskrat and beaver are very similar: they adapt well to aquatic life because of their scaly, flattened tails and their valves, or flaps, which prevent water from entering their nose, mouth and ears. Muskrat was a staple of the American Indian diet and is still considered a delicacy by many people, with the much-anticipated trapping season yielding both the delicious meat and the highly useful hide.

mussel - a marine and freshwater bivalve, which feeds on plankton, usually found living high on the shore, clumped together as a form of protection; most abundant in cooler waters and found all over the world. The two varieties most commonly found on the market are: the blue mussel, *Mytilus edulis*, also called the black or Mediterranean mussel, found along the Atlantic coast; and the New Zealand green-lipped mussel, *Perna canaliculus*, which is also known as the green or green-shelled mussel. Cultivated mussels have darker, thinner shells than wild mussels, grow five times faster and yield three times more meat.

mussels

must - unfermented wine or juice pressed from the grape, from the Latin *mustum*, meaning "new wine," and *mustus*, meaning "new, fresh."

mustard - from the Latin *mustus*, the new wine with which the Romans mixed their beloved pounded mustard seeds, and *ardeus*, meaning "burning," referring to its spiciness. From the Cruciferae family, the mustard plant produces yellow flowers with pods full of tiny seeds. The color of the seeds provides the name of the type of mustard: *Sinapis alba* produces white (or yellow) mustard; *Brassica nigra* produces black mustard; and *Brassica juncea* produces brown mustard (sometimes called black and used more often than the *nigra* variety). Crushed mustard seeds were not mixed with **must** until the Middle Ages. Until then, the powdered seeds were mixed with honey and formed into balls. Later, in Italy, the practice was to add powdered dried lemon or orange peel.

Mustard was acclaimed by Roman naturalist **Pliny** for its ability "to surmount lassitude in females." It was used as a treatment for epilepsy, lethargy and "all deep-seated pains in any part of the body." In around AD 42, the Roman agricultural writer Columella records a method for making mustard that's very similar to today's preparation. The recipe recorded by the 4th-century Roman author Palladius, a specialist on agriculture, is merely a mixture of the seeds crushed with honey, oil and strong vinegar. Modern mustard is made in much the same way, with sugar replacing the honey. Pliny also recommended a cough mixture made by boiling coarsely powdered mustard seed and dried figs in strong ale. British naturalist **Nicholas Culpeper,** as usual, came up with a fascinating conglomeration of cures: "It's good for snake poison if taken in time; the powdered seed mixed with honey into balls and taken every morning, fasting will clear the voice; the decoction of the seeds will resist the malignity of mushrooms; chewed in the mouth it often helps toothache and," he adds, "it helps also the crick in the neck."

Mrs. Clements of Durham, England, invented the modern way of making mustard powder in the 18th century, by milling the seeds to make flour; she traveled from town to town, promoting her invention, which eventually found favor with the royal court and made her

MUSTARD VARIETIES

American - also called **ballpark mustard,** because it is most often used on hot dogs and hamburgers at baseball games. It is mild, made from white seeds.

Bordeaux - a strong, aromatic, dark brown mustard made from black seeds and blended with unfermented wine. Often flavored with tarragon.

Dijon - from the city of that name in the heart of Burgundy, considered to be the mustard capital of the world. The same basic recipe has been used since the 13th century. The most famous Dijon mustard was made in 1777 by Maurice Grey. All Dijon mustards are made with the strongest mustard seeds. After they have been ground and the hulls removed, the seeds are blended with white wine or vinegar, with an addition of cloves, cinnamon and herbs. See also GREY POUPON.

Dusseldorf - mild, the most popular German type, similar in style to **Bordeaux,** popular with spicy food.

English - very hot, made with black and white seeds, along with wheat flour and turmeric, also available as a powder.

English whole grain - hot, pungent, made from whole mustard seeds, white wine, allspice and black pepper, a great complement to mildly flavored foods.

Florida - mild, usually made with white wine from the Champagne region, best with spicy food.

German - sweet and sour, lighter than most, made with herbs, spices and caramel.

honey mustard - prepared mustard sweetened with honey, ubiquitous in North America as a condiment and as a flavoring in dressings and sauces.

moutarde de Meaux - made since the 13th century, with whole black seeds, in the Dijon style, fairly hot, best with bland foods. Also called *moutarde à l'ancienne* or "traditional-style mustard," it is a truly original product with a unique flavor. Meaux mustard is the only mustard produced with visible, partially ground seeds, 98 percent of which are imported from Canada. The most well-known Meaux mustard is **Pommery,** made since 1760.

a fortune. Experimenting with mustard seeds in the 19th century, Jeremiah Colman used plants growing near the city of Norwich, which is now the center of the Colman Mustard industry, putting British mustards on the world map. Today, this powdered, dried form of mustard is found all over the world in the spice aisles of grocery stores, under the name "dry mustard." See also MUSTARD POWDER, PREPARED MUSTARD.

mustard cabbage - see GAI CHOY.

mustard greens - also **mustard spinach.** The green or red leaves of the mustard plant, which are used fresh in salads, boiled, sautéed or steamed as a side dish or added to soups, stews or stir-fries. Mustard greens may be sold canned, fresh or frozen. Blanching in salted water mellows the peppery, sharp flavor of fresh leaves.

mustard oil - an oil extracted from the mustard plants that are indigenous to India, used for deep-frying and stir-frying. It is recommended that mustard oil be heated to its smoking point before adding the food to be cooked; this releases its flavor and fragrance, which is then imparted to the cooking food.

mustard powder - ground, dried, hulled mustard seed. Jeremiah Colman, a Briton now famous for his product, produced his original packaged mustard powder in 1804. It was a mixture of powder from both black and white seeds, along with flour (to improve the texture) and turmeric (to improve the color). Encouraged by its popularity, he opened a factory in Toronto in 1830 to supply his mustard powder to North Americans. Today's version of mustard powder is made only from white seeds. See also MUSTARD.

mustard seed - the shiny, round seed of the mustard plant, said to have been used by the ancient Egyptians and Greeks for both culinary and medicinal purposes. This spice is still going strong. It's found (usually whole) in pickle brines, salads, sauces, savory spice rubs, soups and stews. The brown seeds are the most flavorful; the black the most pungent; and the pale yellow or white ones the mildest. To enhance their flavor, Indian cooks fry the seeds in oil until they pop, before adding them to a dish. Thanks to more than one biblical parable, such as that in *Matthew 13:31*, which likens heaven to a mustard seed sown by man, this tiny, but powerful seed became a lucky charm and a symbol of hope for Christians. See also TARKA.

mustard spinach - see MUSTARD GREENS.

Mutsu apple - see APPLE.

mutton - see LAMB.

muttonfish - also **ocean pout. 1.** a saltwater fish, most common in the Pacific Ocean. *Macrozoarces americanus* has sweet, white flesh and few bones. **2.** the Australian name for **abalone. 3.** a name sometimes used for the mutton snapper. See also SNAPPER.

mycella - a mild, creamy Danish blue cheese made from cow's milk, named after the blue mold, *Penicillium mycelium*, that is used to make it.

Mysore coffee bean - see COFFEE.

mysost - also **myseost.** A popular Norwegian breakfast cheese created by caramelizing cow's, and sometimes goat's, milk whey, which gives the cheese a sweetish taste and firm consistency. Mysost comes from *myse* for "whey," and *ost* for "cheese." See also GJETOST.

myzithra - also **mitzithra.** A classic, white Greek cheese made from the whey left over from making **feta** or **kefalotyri** cheeses. It comes in two types: a creamy, soft, fresh version; or a more pungent version, which is aged for about six to nine months until it is firm enough to grate. Traditionally, the myzithra was hung in cheesecloth to age. It still looks the same: about the size and shape of an ostrich egg. It can be eaten on its own (wine is the recommended drink with the young cheese; coffee or **ouzo** with the old), with dried or fresh fruit and nuts, or cut into chunks or grated over pasta dishes or salads.

n
noodles

naan - also **nan.** A chewy, semileavened Indian flatbread made with white flour and a sourdough starter, traditionally baked in a **tandoor** oven. Naan is just one of several types of Indian breads, including **paratha, roti, poori** and **chapati.**

nabemono - a Japanese term for any of a variety of one-pot meals. The meal may be served in one pot in the middle of the table, while everyone helps himself, or, like a fondue, with individual diners cooking their own food in a pot of oil or other hot liquid. **Shabu-shabu** and **sukiyaki** are two examples.

nacho - a crisp, tortilla chip topped with melted cheese and salsa or chopped chiles, usually served either as a snack or as an appetizer; the 1943 creation of Ignacio Anaya, the headwaiter at the Victory Club in Piedras Negras, Mexico. One night, a group of American officers' wives from the nearby Fort Duncan Air Base traveled across the border for dinner. When the cook was nowhere to be found, Ignacio jumped into the kitchen, picked up some **tostadas,** grated some Wisconsin cheese over top, put them under the broiler and topped them with jalapeño slices. Soon after, club owner Rudolfo De Los Santos put them on the menu, calling them Nacho's Especiales, "Nacho" being short for Ignacio. In 1977, Frank Liberto from Arlington, Texas, started selling his own version of the nachos we enjoy today. He used soft cheese and tortilla chips. See also TEX-MEX.

nameko mushroom - also **cinnamon cap.** A diminutive, brown-topped mushroom, with a slippery cap and a slightly curved, slim white stem, used in Japanese cooking. Said to be second only to **shiitake** in popularity, *Pholiota nameko* mushrooms are used in simmered dishes, soups and on tofu. Sold fresh in the winter, nameko are available in cans year-round, and kits, for ambitious home growers, can be found in specialty stores.

nameko mushrooms

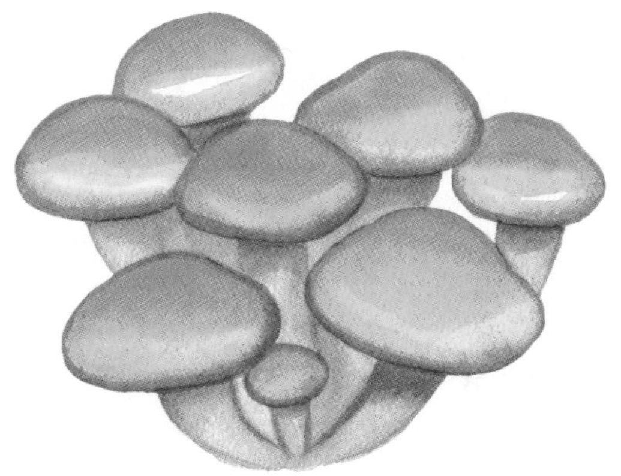

nam pla - a popular Thai fish sauce. The name translates as "fish water" (*nam* for "water" and *pla* for "fish"). It is used in the same way that the Chinese use soy sauce and has no substitute in Thai cooking. See also FISH SAUCE.

nam prik - a generic term embracing a variety of homemade or ready-made, cooked or uncooked Thai dips and sauces, which are spicy, sweet, pungent and hot. Ingredients may include chiles, dried fish flakes, small eggplant, garlic, green mango, lime juice, sugar, shrimp paste and **trassi.** Traditionally, these would have been pounded together into a paste. Still sold as a paste in cans (before use, water is added to achieve the desired consistency), it is also sold, bottled, as sauce. Nam prik is usually served with fish, rice and vegetable dishes.

nan - see NAAN.

Nanaimo bar - a Canadian dessert made with cocoa, chopped almonds, custard, butter and semisweet chocolate, its origin hotly debated, each legend still unconfirmed. Three recipes with this name were said to have been published about 1958, one in Nanaimo, British Columbia, one in an undisclosed B.C. city and another in Welland, Ontario, all three with a nearly identical ingredient list. Some claim that the dessert was originally from northern England, introduced to Canada in the 1930s by miners who had been sent the sweet from home, while others credit its introduction in Canada to Dutch settlers in the early 1900s. A similar recipe for a sweet called Chocolate Fridge Cake was published in a Vancouver newspaper in 1930. This sweet, chocolate creation is also known in the U.S. as New York Slice.

nanami togarashi - see TOGARASHI.

nan-e-barbari - see BARBARI.

nannyberry - also **black haw, sheepberry.** A deciduous, indigenous North American suckering shrub, *Viburnum lentago*, which produces edible, thick-skinned stone fruit. A traditional food of Native Americans, the juicy, sweet berries ripen to blue-black. Picked before they are too dark or eaten by birds, they make good jams and jellies. The wet-wool nanny-goat smell of fruit left to rot earned this shrub its common name.

Nantua - a classic French sauce, named for the small town in the Bugey region of France that has been famous, for centuries, for its **quenelles** served with the sauce. Red-footed crayfish caught in nearby lakes were traditionally used to make Nantua sauce and tinted it a characteristic pink. To make it, cooking liquor from crayfish is added to **béchamel sauce,** along with cream; while this mixture boils and reduces, brandy, cayenne pepper and crayfish butter are added to create the sauce. It's also used for other egg, fish and seafood dishes, especially crayfish, often paired with truffles, which are given the *Nantua* label.

nap - to thinly and evenly spoon a sauce over a prepared dish, from the French *nappe,* meaning "tablecloth" or "cover."

napa cabbage - also **celery cabbage, hakusai.** A tall, Asian cabbage with tightly packed, curly, pale yellow-green leaves, with wide, white ribs down the middle. Napa cabbage has a very delicate flavor and is prized in Asian cooking, used extensively in stir-fries, soups and dumplings. See also BOK CHOY, CHINESE CABBAGE.

napa cabbage

Naples medlar - see AZAROLE.

Napoleon - a dessert made of sheets of puff pastry layered with pastry cream, usually made in small, rectangular, single-serving portions. This darling of the French pastry world has nothing to do with the emperor and is not even French. The horizontal layering is characteristic of Naples, and its name is a corruption of "Neapolitan." The French call this pastry a *mille-feuille*, meaning "a thousand leaves," referring to the many layers of puff pastry. The smaller version of the pastry is called Josephine, named after Napoleon's wife. Of late, savory Napoleons have been cropping up on restaurant menus, featuring the same delicious pastry, sandwiched between all sorts of savory fillings, such as cheese, mushrooms and vegetables.

Napoleon cherry - see ROYAL ANN CHERRY.

naranjilla

naranjilla - also **lulo fruit.** Large, spreading *Solanum* shrubs (*S. angulatum* and *S. quitoense*) native to Colombia, Ecuador and Peru, related to nightshade; they produce fruits nicknamed "little oranges." Seeds were sent to the United States early in the 20th century. Samples of both the fruit and juice were offered at the New York World's Fair in 1939; afterward, growing trials continued in Florida and California and started in such likely spots as Australia, the Caribbean, Central America, Costa Rica and Hawaii. Fragrant flowers develop into round fruits about the size of small plums. The fruits are covered in brown fur, but, when they are fully ripe, this coat rubs off easily, exposing the shiny, orangy-yellow skin. Inside, the pulp is juicy and sweet; the taste is a combination of lemon and pineapple. At warm temperatures, the fruit softens and ferments quickly; under proper storage conditions, however, it can keep for up to two months. Eaten out of hand, a naranjilla is usually cut in half, then the pulp (seeds and all)

A B C D E F G H I J K L M **N** O P Q R S T U V W X Y Z

is squeezed into the mouth, and the leathery skin is discarded. The pulp is used to make jelly, sauces, sherbet, wine and various desserts and sweets, but most commercially grown naranjillas are harvested for juice making.

naseberry - see SAPODILLA.

nasi - the word for cooked rice, common to the Malaysian, Indonesian and Balinese languages, the base for a multitude of Southeast Asian dishes. See also NASI GORENG, NASI LEMAK.

nasi goreng - an Indonesian dish, literally meaning "fried rice," ingredients may vary depending on availability but rice is always included (in Indonesia, any dish with the word *nasi* before it means that it is prepared or served with rice). Other ingredients may include shrimp, chicken, eggs, vegetables, garlic or peanuts. If the dish is made with noodles, it's called **bami goreng.**

nasi lemak - a Malaysian specialty often considered the country's national dish, consisting of a plate of coconut rice surrounded by fried anchovies (called *ikan bilis*), fried peanuts, sliced hard-boiled egg, cucumber, a fiery **sambal** and some sort of curry (often prawn). The term comes from the Bahasa Malaysia words for rice (*nasi*) and coconut (*lemak*). The rice is simmered in coconut milk and is sometimes flavored with spices, such as pandan leaves, ginger or lemongrass.

Nassau grouper - see GROUPER.

nasturtium - also **Indian cress.** An ornamental plant, *Tropaeolum majus*, from South America, whose flowers, buds, leaves and roots are all edible. It was originally called "Indian cress," because its peppery flavor is reminiscent of watercress, and early explorers believed that the Americas were part of India. Its name comes from the Latin *nasus tortus*, meaning "convulsed nose," because of the pungent nose-clearing smell of the plant. Nasturtiums came originally from Peru and were brought to Europe by Jesuits in the 16th century. In the nasturtium, they saw a "trophy of arms," with the buds as spears, the leaves as helmets and the flowers as caltrops. There are more than 100 varieties of nasturtium; the largest can reach more than 12 feet (3.6 m) in height. Nasturtium buds can be pickled like capers. See also EDIBLE FLOWERS.

Natal plum - see CARISSA.

natillas - a pourable custard made in Spain and Mexico, usually garnished with ground cinnamon or nutmeg, often served with simple cookies, such as **Maria biscuits.** The name derives from the Spanish word *nata*, meaning "cream," to describe the thick, silky, liquid texture of the strained custard.

natto - see SOY PASTE.

navarin - a French lamb stew, usually made with the shoulder, turnips, onions, potatoes and carrots. Supposedly named after the Battle of Navarino in the Peloponnesus in 1827, when British, French and Russian troops destroyed the allied Turkish and Egyptian fleets. It's more likely that this dish was named after the French word *navet*, meaning "turnip," because the dish originally contained turnip as its main ingredient.

navel orange - see ORANGE.

navy bean - also **pea bean, Yankee bean.** This small white legume was so called because it has been a major part of the United States Navy's food rations since the 19th century. The navy bean is the state bean of Massachusetts, and in 1993, the state Legislature determined that the navy bean had been the original bean in the famous Boston baked beans recipe. See also BEAN.

Neapolitan - a three-layered brick of ice cream made with vanilla, chocolate and strawberry, named after Naples, where ices made with sweetened milk first appeared. Neapolitan is a

nasturtiums

variant on **spumone,** a cherry, chocolate and pistachio ice cream introduced to the U.S. in the 1890s.

near beer - also **nonalcoholic beer.** A malt-liquor beverage containing half of 1 percent or less of alcohol. Introduced as "cereal beverages" in the United States during Prohibition, these drinks were quickly dubbed "near beer." Brand names of these healthful brews included Bevo, Barlo, Graino and Mother's Malt. The production and sale of millions of gallons of the beverages by the early 1920s ensured that familiar American breweries, such as Miller, Pabst and Schlitz, could stay alive and liquid through Prohibition's dry spell. Today, near beers (also termed "nonalcoholic beer") are still marketed to consumers with health concerns or religious scruples.

neat - also **straight up.** A term denoting an alcoholic liquor poured into a glass and served, undiluted by ice, mixer or water.

Nebbiolo - an Italian red grape and wine appellation, named for the fog (*nebbia*) that drapes the Piemontese hills in the fall; used in making Barbaresco, Barolo and Gattinara wines. The first Italian record of it appears in 1235, although the grape was known to the Romans.

Nebuchadnezzar - see WINE BOTTLES.

nectar - **1.** the thick, diluted, puréed pulp of certain fruits, especially peach and apricot, drunk as a beverage as opposed to being used as a sauce. In Greek mythology, it was the drink of the gods of Olympus (ambrosia being their food), thought to grant immortal life. In the Homeric poems, nectar is described as the same color as red wine, served to the gods by Hebe, the divine cupbearer (perhaps the first female sommelier).

"The gods were seated near to Zeus in council, upon a golden floor. Graciously Hebe served them nectar, as with cups of gold they toasted one another, looking down toward the stronghold of Ilion." (*The Iliad, Book IV, 1–5*)
2. the sweet liquid in the center of flowers that bees use to make honey.

nectarine - a close relative of the peach, with a smooth skin and firm flesh. Nectarines are often erroneously thought to be a peach-plum cross or an especially cultivated fuzzless peach. In reality, the fruit was discovered growing wild in Asia

nectarine

more than 2,000 years ago. In 1819, the great English poet John Keats wrote to a friend, "Talking of Pleasure, this moment I was writing with one hand and with the other holding to my Mouth, a nectarine, good God how fine it went down soft, pulpy, slushy, oozy."

neep - Scottish name for "turnip" and the basis for such dishes as **bashed neeps** (the longtime companion of **haggis**), tatties and neeps (boiled potatoes and turnip, mashed together) and neep bree (turnip cooked with butter and ginger, then puréed with milk). See also TURNIP.

Negroni - a cocktail made with **Campari,** gin and sweet vermouth, said to be named after Count Camillo Negroni, who asked his favorite bartender to concoct the drink in the 1920s at the Casoni Bar in Florence.

Negus - an old English beverage made of wine or port, hot water, sugar, nutmeg and lemon juice. The drink takes its name from a certain Colonel Negus, who died in 1732. There's a recipe for Negus in **Isabella Beeton**'s *Book of Household Management*, from 1861, where it's oddly noted that the beverage was "more usually drunk at children's parties than at any other." See also MULLED WINE.

neroli oil - extracted from the blossoms of the bitter orange tree, discovered by Anna Maria de la Tremoille, Princess of Nerola, who used the extremely expensive essence to scent her gloves. In addition to its use in some culinary and pastry confections, neroli oil also has antidepressant qualities.

Nesselrode - a preparation, either for a sauce or as a dessert, made with chestnut purée, candied fruit and raisins. Count Karl Nesselrode was a Russian statesman and a figure in the army of Czar Alexander I, who helped liberate France from Napoleon. The pudding that bears his name is really the creation of the great French chef **Antonin Carême**. It was first served in Paris in 1814.

netted melon - see MUSKMELON.

nettle - also **stinging nettle.** Any of several plants of the genus *Urtica;* the one most commonly used in cooking is *Urtica dioica*. The ancient Greeks, according to Aristophanes, harvested nettles before the arrival of the swallows (migratory birds that came back every year at the same time and were thought to bring good omens) and considered them a delicacy. While nettles are no longer found in markets, one has to be careful when picking them in the wild, as they have a very bad sting, as painful as poison ivy, to which some people are allergic. While the best use of nettles is in soup, they're also used to make beer and tea. Due to their high chlorophyll content, nettles retain their dark, rich, green color after cooking. A perennial plant, which is found worldwide, nettle is considered a leaf vegetable and, like sorrel and spinach, can be cooked and puréed.

nettle

Neufchâtel - a French creamy white cow's milk cheese from the Normandy area, available in various different shapes from square to cylindrical. It is mild when young but becomes more pungent as it ages. There is also an American version of Neufchâtel. See also CREAM CHEESE.

neutral spirit - a nonflavored, high-proof ethyl alcohol (190 proof or higher), used to blend other spirits, such as gin, liqueur or whiskey.

Newburg - see LOBSTER NEWBURG.

New England boiled dinner - also **boiled dinner.** A traditional American one-pot dish, originally made with salted or cured beef but now more often made with corned beef or ham, this boiled dinner calls for cooking the meat with potatoes, onions, parsnips, carrots and cabbage. It is usually served with mustard and horseradish.

New England clam chowder - see CLAM CHOWDER.

Newfoundland pea soup - see PEA SOUP.

New Mexico chile pepper - see CHILE PEPPER.

New Orleans bread pudding - also **Creole bread pudding.** In this classic Creole dessert, small cubes of French bread are tossed with beaten eggs, brown sugar, chopped pecans, cinnamon, nutmeg, raisins and vanilla (some versions throw in chunks of apple and peaches, as well), then baked. Topped with a rich, simmered sauce of bourbon, brown sugar, butter, cream and egg, the pudding is served warm.

New Orleans coffee - see CREOLE COFFEE.

New Orleans king cakes - braided yeast rings, iced and decorated with sugar colored purple, green and gold, colors representing justice, faith and power. A New Orleans tradition, the cakes are available from January 6 (Three Kings' Day) until Fat Tuesday (Mardi Gras, the day before Ash Wednesday). During these five or six weeks, New Orleans bakeries produce more than 250,000 king cakes, each with a bean, small ceramic figure or tiny plastic baby hidden inside. For some cultures, the figure represents the Christ child. For others, the finder must portray one of the kings at the traditional king cake party, and custom has it that the person who finds the baby in his or her piece of cake is obligated to host the next king cake party.

new potato - also **baby potato, creamer potato.** A young potato that has not fully matured and therefore has a waxy texture and thin, papery skin, which does not need to be peeled before cooking. New potatoes are harvested in the

new potatoes

spring and early summer and can come in a number of colors: red, gold and white are the most common. They are excellent in salads, boiled, baked, mashed or creamed. See also POTATO.

Newton-Pippin apple - see APPLE

New York steak - see DELMONICO STEAK.

New York–style ice cream - see PHILADELPHIA-STYLE ICE CREAM.

New Zealand spinach - also **Botany Bay greens.** A herbaceous spreading plant, *Tetragonia tetragonoides*, grown as an annual in North America for its tender leaves and shoots, which have a mild, spinach-like flavor. British botanist and plant collector Sir Joseph Banks is credited with "discovering" this popular green, which is not actually a spinach at all, during a South Seas voyage with Captain Cook in the 1770s. Before it had a botanist to help, the plant migrated successfully to alien shores throughout the Pacific by means of its floating seed pods.

niacin - see B VITAMINS.

Niagara grape - a North American hybrid created by two Niagara County, New York, growers in the mid-1800s. B.W. Clark and C.L. Hoag crossed Cassady and Concord grapes to create this fragrant, golden green, sweet-tart grape, which can be eaten fresh or used in white grape juice or wine. First sold in 1882, it is still under commercial cultivation in the Niagara region, on both sides of the border, and as far away as Michigan, Ohio and Washington states.

niboshi - dried, small, whole sardines used in Japanese cooking, especially in the preparation of **dashi** (soup stock) for **miso** (after pinching off the heads and pulling out the guts). Also eaten as a snack, niboshi are sold in packages in Japanese markets; ready-made *niboshi dashi* is also available.

Niçoise - also **à la Niçoise.** A French culinary term meaning "of Nice" or "in the style of Nice." It is usually applied to dishes prepared with anchovies, black olives, garlic, oil, onions and tomatoes — all easily available in this city on the Riviera, which is surrounded by hills of olive trees on one side and the Mediterranean on the other.

Niçoise olive - see OLIVE.

Niçoise salade - see SALADE NIÇOISE.

nigari - the Japanese name for magnesium chloride, a traditional coagulant used to make **tofu** from **soy milk** in both Japan and China. Nigari is a natural component of seawater and, today, is usually refined through an ion-exchange process or through cooking, bleaching and filtering. Traditionally, extracted nigari often has impurities, so most modern tofu producers use the refined version to ensure a good-quality product. In the United States, a synthetic form of nigari is used, made from a chemical reaction between hydrochloric acid and magnesium. See also GYPSUM.

New Zealand spinach

nigella seeds - also **black onion seeds.** These tiny, black, slightly triangular seeds have been used since antiquity by herbalists in Asia and by cooks in Rome. They're crunchy, peppery and slightly bitter, and in Europe are sometimes used as a substitute for pepper. Nigella seeds are used extensively and most often in Indian and Middle Eastern cuisine and are often mistakenly called "black cumin seeds."

nigiri-zushi - see SUSHI.

nijisseiki - see ASIAN PEAR, PEAR.

nimono - in Japanese cuisine, nimono are simmered dishes and can be anything from meat to seafood to vegetables to seaweed simmered in a broth. Nimono is a traditional course in a formal multi-course Japanese meal, and the ingredients are not repeated from course to course. For example, if a fish dish has been served in a previous course, the nimono will feature a complementary food, such as vegetables or meat.

nira - the Japanese name for **garlic chives,** the pungent herbal ingredient that makes **gyoza** deliciously garlicky.

Nispero - see LOQUAT.

niter kibe - also **niter kibbeh.** This spiced clarified butter is used in Ethiopian cooking. The butter is melted in a pan, then the dry ingredients (toasted, freshly ground cardamom, cinnamon, cloves, **fenugreek,** nutmeg and turmeric) are stirred in; the mixture is brought to a boil, then the other ingredients (freshly grated ginger along with minced garlic and onion) are added. The mixture is simmered for 30 to 60 minutes. The clear liquid is strained into a container, leaving the milk solids behind, and refrigerated until use.

nitrate - also **nitrite.** An organic compound or salt derived from nitric acid, which is used as a preservative in cured and processed meats, such as bacon and hot dogs. Nitrates prevent the growth of bacteria, extend the shelf life of foodstuff and also enhance color and flavor. Their use remains controversial, however, with concerns about health problems ranging from headaches to cancer. Vegetables grown in soils fed with fertilizer containing nitrates, as well as beverages including some beers and tap waters, are other sources of nitrates in the human diet.

nixtamal - also **nixtamalado.** Cleaned, dried, white field corn, simmered in water and slaked lime (traditionally, wood ashes were used), soaked in the pot liquor for several hours, rinsed and rubbed in a colander to remove any lime and loose hulls, then ground. The nixtamal **masa** is used for making tamales and tortillas, for example, and is added to **menudo** and other dishes.

noble rot - see BOTRYTIS CINEREA.

Nobu - see MATSUHISA, NOBUYUKI.

nocino - an Italian liqueur, or **amaro,** made with immature or green walnuts, steeped in alcohol for almost two months. *Noce* is Italian for "walnut."

nockerl - classic Austrian dumplings made in two versions for either savory or sweet dishes. To serve with soups, stews and traditional dishes, such as Lungenbraten (beef tenderloin stuffed with goose liver in a cream sauce), nockerl is made with a simple mixture of egg, flour, milk, oil and salt, kneaded lightly, then boiled in salted water for about five minutes and tossed with butter. Packaged, ready-mixed dry ingredients, which need only butter and egg added, are available. For sweet dishes, Salzburger nockerl is made using a lighter dough made with stiffly beaten egg whites, vanilla and less flour. Shaped into three small "hills" in an oval dish, the nockerl puff up like soufflés when they are baked, and are then dusted with confectioner's sugar before serving.

no-eyed pea - see PIGEON PEA.

nog - **1.** short for **eggnog. 2.** a drink made with beaten eggs, cream or milk and, usually, spirits. **3.** in England, an East Anglian word for strong beer.

noisette - **1.** a French term used to describe a "nut" or round of meat that has been boned, rolled and tied into an individual portion, most commonly made with fillet or leg of lamb, although beef and veal fillet are also prepared in this way. **2.** French for "hazelnut." **3. beurre noisette** is butter cooked until it turns a hazelnut color and develops a beautiful, nutty flavor.

nökkelost cheese - also **kuminost.** A traditional, semisoft, pale yellow Scandinavian cheese, made with cow's milk and usually flavored with cloves and cumin or caraway seeds; it may be contained in its own rind or, sometimes, a wax rind. Dark breads, such as pumpernickel, and beer are considered the perfect accompaniments, but nökkelost is also a good "melting" cheese for hot dishes.

nonalcoholic beer - see NEAR BEER.

nondairy creamer - a product designed primarily for use with coffee that lightens the color and strength of the brew. Available in frozen, liquid or powdered form, it is often high in fat. Most nondairy creamers contain emulsifiers, sweeteners, vegetable oils and, despite their name, a milk protein called casein or caseinate. Fancy homemade or ready-made creamers, flavored with hazelnut, toffee or vanilla, can also be purchased.

non-nutritive sweeteners - see ARTIFICIAL SWEETENERS.

nonpareil - **1.** a French term meaning "without equal," used to describe, among other things, high-quality pickled capers that are between 5 and 7 mm in diameter, especially those from the South of France, which are considered excellent. **2.** tiny colored balls of sugar used to decorate cakes, cookies and confectionery. **3.** a flat chocolate drop covered with nonpareils, often all white ones.

nonreactive cookware - cookware made from anodized aluminum, enameled cast iron and stainless steel, or coated with a **nonstick finish,** which do not react with the chemicals, particularly acids, in some foods. The acid in fruit, tomatoes and vinegar, for instance, reacts with aluminum, cast-iron and copper pots. This reaction can discolor the food and taint the taste.

nonstick cooking spray - see COOKING SPRAY.

nonstick finish - a coating, often only on the inside surface, of pans, pots and bakeware, that stops foods from sticking and allows cooking with little or no added fat or oil, and easy cleaning. Teflon is perhaps the best known of the bunch. Depending on the finish and the way it is applied, some scratch more easily than others; to prevent this, plastic or wooden spoons, scrapers and spatulas are recommended. A well-seasoned cast-iron or enameled pot, a purist might point out, has its own nonstick finish.

nonstick whisk - see WHISK.

nonvintage - a wine that is blended from more than one year's harvest of grapes. Champagne and many sparkling wines, as well as port and sherry, are usually nonvintage; although Champagne is an obvious exception, many nonvintage wines are less expensive than their vintage counterparts. Nonvintage wines also have some advantages for their producers, who can reserve wines from year to year, then blend their own consistent and distinctive final product, less threatened by the effects of unpredictable weather on the current year's harvest. See also VINTAGE.

noodles - a dough made with flour, eggs and water, then cut into strips of various lengths and widths. They can be used fresh or dried. See also ASIAN NOODLES, PASTA.

Noonday onion - see ONION.

nopal - also **nopales, nopals.** The Spanish name for the fleshy leaves, also known as pads or paddles, of the **prickly pear cactus,** a native of the American Southwest, Central America and Mexico, and the state plant of Texas. Used as a food source by the Aztecs, the cactus was taken back to Spain by returning conquistadors. Today, it grows around the Mediterranean in gardens, in the wild (where it is becoming a weed) and in large commercial plantations (true to its roots, its Italian name is *figadindi* or Indian fig). Back home, nopal is increasingly popular for its delicate, tart flavor. With the spines removed and cut into **nopalitos,** it is used in many traditional dishes, but new ways to enjoy it (in fruit jelly, **Margaritas** and sorbet) are always being created.

nopalitos - the name of diced small pieces or sliced strips cut from **nopales.** They may be candied, canned or pickled, or added fresh or cooked to chili con carne, egg and fish dishes, salads and soups.

nori - an edible **laver** seaweed, which is sold pressed into sheets and dried, usually toasted. The color can range from dark green to purple to black. It's mainly used to wrap sushi and sometimes as a garnish for other dishes. *Ajitsuke nori* is a type of nori flavored with soy sauce, often cut into strips for eating with steamed rice. *Yakinori* is toasted seaweed.

Normande - also **à la Normande.** A French culinary term meaning "of Normandy" or "in the style of Normandy," and usually applied to dishes, such as **Normandy-style pork,** prepared with the apples and cider, **Calvados,** butter, cream and seafood produced in this region.

A B C D E F G H I J K L M N O P Q R S T U V W X Y Z

Normandy-style pork - a classic French dish of sliced pork tenderloin, apple and onion, in a creamy **Calvados** sauce.

norteño - Spanish for "northern," a term denoting the cooking style of northern Mexico, which has influenced Southwest and Tex-Mex cuisine.

northern pike

northern pike - also **jack, pickerel, pike.** A freshwater fish, *Esox lucieus*, common in the Great Lakes and regarded as a good catch by sport fishermen. Once hooked, a northern pike can put up a good fight; a mature fish can be 30 inches (75 cm) long and weigh 8 pounds (4 kg). It grows so big because it eats almost anything it can get between its toothy jaws: birds, crayfish, fish, frogs, even small mammals (in Europe, the predatory northern pike was once called "the great water wolf"). Northern pike may be baked, braised, grilled, pickled, poached or used in soups and stews.

Northern Spy apple - see APPLE.

Northwest Greening - see APPLE.

Norway haddock - see OCEAN PERCH.

Norwegian lobster - see LANGOUSTINE.

nose - the smell of a wine, best noted following a swirl in the glass, which permits the oxygen to mix with the wine and release the **bouquet.**

nosh - from the German word *nachen*, meaning "to eat on the sly." **1.** (n.) a small meal or snack. **2.** (v.) to nibble, munch or snack.

Nostradamus - see profile right.

note - a term used to describe components or elements of a taste; the overall flavor of the food or drink being the symphony, as it were.

nougat - from the Latin *nux*, meaning "nut," a confection usually made with almonds, honey and sugar, although pistachios and hazelnuts are also used, made since ancient Greece and Rome. The French city of Montélimar is the "capital of nougat." A popular legend claims that nougat got its name when an excellent candy maker gave her confection to her nieces, Lisa and Nina, who would say, "*Tante Manon, tu nous gâtes*," meaning "Auntie Manon, you're spoiling us." Another legend tells of a pastry chef from Montélimar who was madly in love with a young princess. One day, he combined honey, which reminded him of her hair color, some almonds as beautiful as her eyes and some sugar as sweet as her personality, and nougat was born. The Italians call nougat **torrone,** a traditional Christmas sweet.

nouvelle cuisine - a style of cooking, meaning "new cooking" in French, that first emerged in the early 1970s with such chefs as **Paul Bocuse,** with a fresh-market approach, smaller portions and lighter sauces, served artistically on oversize plates — a stark change from the rich, heavy sauces, multi-course meals and complex preparations of classical French cuisine. It was first discussed in print and the name coined by *Le Nouveau Guide*, a food and wine magazine whose sensibility was inspired by a new wave of culture sweeping France.

Nova lox - see LOX.

Nova Scotia salmon - see LOX.

noyaux - also **noyau.** A liqueur flavored with the stones of apricots, cherries and peaches, which results in a taste of almonds. See aslo RATAFIA.

nuoc nam - a Vietnamese condiment, meaning "fish sauce," which is used as a seasoning and dipping sauce, with a cheesy smell and salty taste. It's prepared from small fish, such as clupeids (herring and sprat), with seasonings, such as red chiles, garlic, lime juice, ginger and sugar. The whole fishes are pressed in tubs, salted, tightly sealed and left for about 12 weeks, at which point the liquid is drained off.

Nostradamus (1503–1566) - French physician, astrologer and author. Nostradamus started practicing medicine in 1529 and became renowned for his innovative ways of treating the plague during the mid-16th century. It was at this time that he began making prophecies, which he published in 1555 under the title *Centuries Astrologiques*. Three years earlier, he had released *Excellent et Moult utile opuscule* (An Excellent and Most Useful Little Work Essential), his lesser-known prescriptive book about food.

Strangely enough, nuoc nam is closest of any food additives to the **garum** sauce of the Roman Empire. *Nuoc nam an chay* is vegetarian fish sauce. See also FISH SAUCE.

nursehound - also **spotted dogfish.** A medium-size spotted shark, long harvested from the Mediterranean and the northeast Atlantic for food (and for use in cosmetic, pharmaceutical and other products). Once a **trash fish** to North Americans, nursehound, *Scyliorhinus stellaris*, now shows up on restaurant menus on this side of the Atlantic. See also DOGFISH.

nursery food - a British term that embraces the bland, soft and warm foods, such as scrambled eggs, porridge and rice pudding, that are often served to children, which become their favorite **comfort foods** in later life.

nursery tea - see CAMBRIC TEA.

nut - botanically, a dry, single-seeded, hard-shelled fruit that has to be cracked open. "Nut" also refers to any seed or fruit with an edible kernel in a hard or brittle shell, such as almonds, walnuts and coconuts.

Since the earliest times, nuts have been used as a source of food and oil. They were collected by food-gathering peoples before the birth of agriculture, used extensively by the Greeks, and cultivated by the Romans. There's evidence that, as early as the 2nd century BC, the Romans distributed sugared almonds on such occasions as birthdays and weddings. Nuts are also an important feature of Middle Eastern cookery. In fact, medieval Europe learned to use nuts in cooking from the Arabs, who used them not only in sauces with meat and poultry but also in marzipan, nougat and other sweetmeats. Spain, occupied for almost eight centuries by the Moors, also adopted the use of nuts in cooking and took the technique to the Americas, but the Spanish found the Aztecs already using pumpkin seeds, peanuts and probably pecans as thickeners for poultry, fish and shellfish sauces. Almonds are used extensively in Scandinavian cooking — it's said that whoever finds the almonds in the Swedish Christmas Eve rice pudding will be the next to marry. Almonds are also important in Indonesian, Far Eastern and African cooking. Cashews are the only nuts never sold in the shell because of the toxic oil in its shell.

nutburger - a meatless burger made of a mixture of finely chopped nuts, a filler, such as rice or wheat germ, minced herbs and onions, and seasonings, held together with a beaten egg and often shredded cheese. It is formed into patties, then broiled, fried or grilled.

nut butter - **1.** a spreadable paste, such as peanut butter or **tahini,** made of puréed raw or roasted nuts. Some contain only the nuts; others have oil, salt and other ingredients added to improve the taste or texture. **2.** softened butter mixed with minced nuts, such as almonds or cashews, and served with fish.

nutcracker - an implement used to crack nuts, available in wood, metal and cast aluminum. A typical nutcracker consists of two hinged metal levers or arms. The nut is placed in a special area with teeth-like grooves that help create pressure around it, and then the two

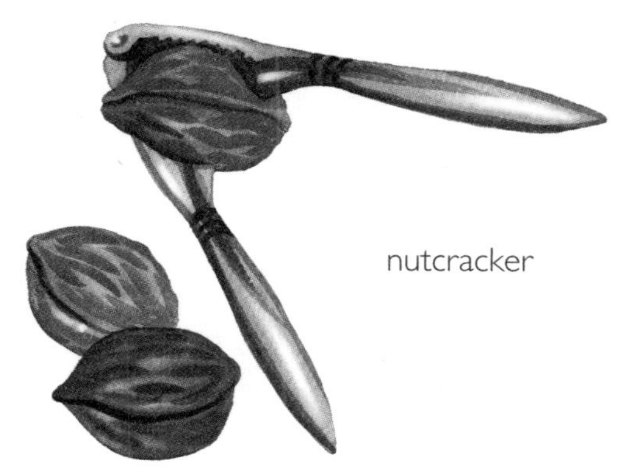

nutcracker

arms are squeezed to crack the hard outer shell. Nutcrackers are also available with special traps to collect the broken shells and also cute shapes such as squirrels, where the nut is placed in the squirrel's mouth and the tail is pressed to crack the nut.

nut flour - also **ground nuts, nut meal.** Finely ground, toasted or untoasted nuts or the finely ground cake of nutmeat left after oil has been pressed out, used to make bread, cake, cookies, confections and pastries, and in breading mixtures for chicken and fish. Nut meal is a slightly coarser grind than commercial nut flour, similar to cornmeal in texture, available in health food or low-carb grocery stores. Almond, hazelnut, pecan and walnut flours are just a few popular versions.

nut meal - see NUT FLOUR.

nutmeg - the seed of a large, tropical evergreen native to the Moluccas, with small yellow flowers and large, very fragrant leaves, surrounded by a red, fleshy casing, which is **mace,** a spice with its own distinct characteristics, more delicate and subtle than nutmeg. Nutmeg is thought to be the last of the exotic spices to become known in Europe, although it has been documented among the spices and aromatics left inside Egyptian tombs. There's still controversy as to whether the Greeks and Romans were truly familiar with nutmeg and mace. The first authenticated identification of nutmeg was thought to have been at the Byzantine court in the 6th century, brought by Arab traders from Asia. A component of its oil, myristicin, is a hallucinogen, and nutmeg has been used as an inebriant since 1576, despite unpleasant side effects when taken in large doses, such as nausea, vomiting and dry mouth. See also MACE.

nutmeg grater - see GRATER.

nutmeg melon - see MUSKMELON.

NutraSweet - the brand name under which aspartame is used as a non-nutritive additive in beverages and foods. About 200 times sweeter than sugar, NutraSweet breaks down under high heat so is not a common ingredient in baked goods. See also ARTIFICIAL SWEETENERS, ASPARTAME.

nutritional yeast - a dietary supplement rich in B vitamins that is often used in vegan and vegetarian cooking to add nutrients not easily found in that type of diet, and as a seasoning because of its cheese-like flavor. Nutritional yeast comes in flake or powder form and can be sprinkled on pretty much any food, sometimes as a nutritive non-animal substitute for cheese, such as Parmesan, that is used as a flavorful garnish. Most nutritional yeast products do not contain the essential vitamin B_{12}, which is rarely present in non-animal foods. However, there are certain brands that are fortified with it. Nutritional yeast is different from baking yeast and **autolysed** yeast, which is found in spreads such as **Marmite** and **Vegemite.**

nzudda - see MOSTACCIOLI.

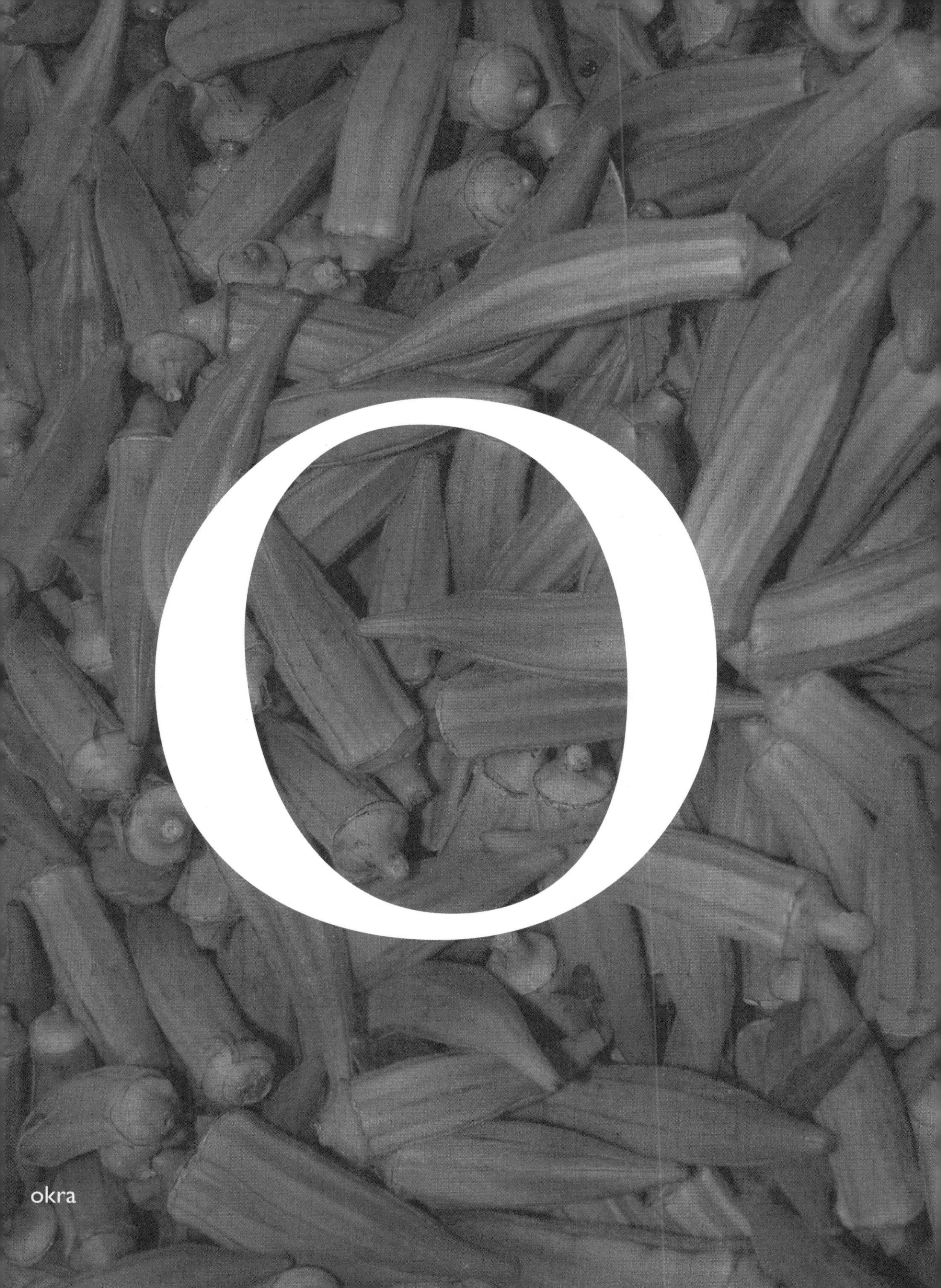
O
okra

oat - the highly nutritious grain kernel of a cereal grass, *Avena sativa,* used as horse and cattle feed since the early Bronze Age. Alexander the Great fed only oats to his legendary horse, Bucephalus, because he believed that the grain, which thrived in the south wind, passed on the swiftness of the sirocco to his horse. But, when offered a swill of oat-and-honey *kykeon,* a hallucinogenic mixture of oats or barley combined with mint, Alexander stubbornly declined to taste even a drop of it. "I preferred neither to outrun nor to out-copulate my horse," he stated. The crusaders took the grain with them to their native countries, because it was easy to carry in a saddlebag; could be cooked easily over an open fire; and provided a soldier with enough nutrients for battle. Oats have the dubious honor of being, in modern times, the lone whole grain consumed to any extent by North Americans. In most oat products, all three parts of the grain are used: the bran, the germ and the endosperm. "Oatmeal" can mean the cooked cereal or the oats themselves. See also BRAN, GROATS, OLD-FASHIONED OATS, PORRIDGE, ROLLED OATS, STEEL-CUT OATS.

oatflakes - see ROLLED OATS.

Oaxaca cheese - see ASADERO.

O'Brien potatoes - cubed, cooked potatoes, fried together with finely chopped onion, sweet pepper and pimientos. Some New Yorkers claim the dish as their own and say it showed up in the city's restaurants, along with a wave of Irish immigrants, about 1900. These days, food stores stock frozen O'Briens, and cookbooks offer recipes for spicy **jicama** variations.

oca - *Oxalis tuberosus,* an indigenous plant of the Andes, now commercially cultivated in Mexico and New Zealand as well as South America. Grown for its tubers, which resemble fat, wrinkled carrots in colors ranging from white to yellow to purple, oca is traditionally sun-dried, then boiled or roasted, often with meat, in a pit oven, dug into the earth.

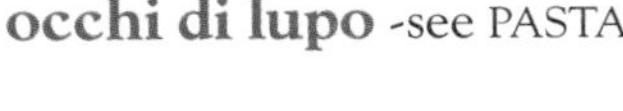

occhi di lupo -see PASTA.

occhi di passeri - see PASTA.

ocean barracuda - see WAHOO.

oceanic bonito - also **skipjack tuna**. See TUNA.

ocean perch - also **Atlantic rosefish, Norway haddock, redfish.** A commercially important, midsize fish that include *Sebastes marinus* and *S. viviparus*. Ocean perch, which are actually rockfish, not perch, are harvested by freezer-trawlers from deep waters throughout the North Atlantic and are found from Labrador to Maine and across to Scandinavia. Beneath its orangey-red skin, its rosy flesh is good eaten fresh or broiled, sautéed, steamed, grilled or poached, or salted.

ocean pout - see MUTTONFISH.

ochazuke - a Japanese dish of plain white rice with toppings, such as pickled vegetables, **nori, wasabi** and thinly sliced eel or fish, over which hot green tea is poured. It is often served at the end of a meal or put together as a quick snack; ochazuke can be made even faster using commercial packets of prepared toppings.

octopus - also **devilfish, water ghost.** Any one of a number of **cephalopods** belonging to the **mollusk** family with, as the name indicates, eight "arms," each with two rows of suction cups. Some of the smallest and largest examples are found in the Pacific ocean off the North American coastline; the *Octopus dofleini* reaches up to 30 feet (9 m) long, while the *Octopus micropyrsus* is about $\frac{1}{2}$ inch (1 cm) long. Mediterranean countries and Japan have the greatest appetite for octopus. Since this sea creature prefers to live in enclosed spaces, Italian and Japanese fishermen lower pots onto the seabed; once the octopuses set up house inside, the pots are hauled up with the catch. The eyes and viscera are removed before the chewy flesh of the arms and body are cut into chunks and eaten cold, hot or pickled, usually after tenderizing and lengthy cooking, but baby octopuses can be simply and briefly boiled or fried. The blue-black ink expelled as a defense

octopus

by a fleeing octopus is often removed from the ink sac and used as a colorant in the preparation of various dishes.

oden - a well-loved type of Japanese **nabemono,** or simmered food, consisting of **kamaboko,** deep-fried tofu patties, boiled eggs, slices of **konnyaku, daikon** radish, potatoes and carrots simmered in a salty-sweet **dashi**-based broth. Oden is a favorite winter dish in Japan, frequently served with hot sake to warm up the body on a cold night. It is also a common sight at Japanese convenience stores and street stalls in winter, where tired workers can stop for a bite to warm them up on their way home.

oenologist - see ENOLOGIST.

oeuf - French for "egg."

oeufs à la neige - see FLOATING ISLAND.

offal - see VARIETY MEAT.

off-dry - also **half-dry, medium-dry.** A term used to describe **still wine** that is between **dry** and sweet and has a medium amount of residual sugar. See also SEMIDRY.

ogen melon - a small, round hybrid named after the Israeli kibbutz where it was first cultivated; popular for its sweet succulence, available from spring to midwinter.

ogo - an edible red seaweed used in Hawaiian, Japanese and Korean foods.

ohashi - also **hashi.** The Japanese term for "chopsticks." Perfect for picking up the bite-size morsels common to Japanese cuisine, chopsticks should be laid flat, side by side, when not in use. At formal dinners especially, the business end of chopsticks are often rested on a small stand called a *hashioki*. The stands may be made of ceramic, glass, stone or wood, and, with designs that range from the fanciful to the elegant. **Saibashi** are longer chopsticks used mostly for cooking.

oil - as essential as a food ingredient as it was a source of light. The ancient Egyptians expressed

COMMON VARIETIES OF OIL

canola oil - made from rapeseed, good for both cooked and raw foods, especially in salad dressings, very low in saturated fat.

coconut oil - made from coconut flesh, solid at room temperature, very high in saturated fat, most commonly used to make margarine (except in tropical countries, where it's used for frying).

corn oil - also **maize oil.** One of the most popular vegetable oils, made from the corn kernel, very high in polyunsaturated fat, can be used at very high temperatures without smoking. Some chefs find its flavor too strong to use in salad dressings.

cottonseed oil - a pale yellow viscous oil extracted from cottonseed, used for salads and in cooking. Also used in shortenings and margarine.

grapeseed oil - a by-product of the wine-making process, good for cooking and frying and exceptionally good for marinated meats.

maize oil - see CORN OIL.

olive oil - a flavorful oil pressed from tree-ripened olives, a monounsaturated fat, used in cooking and salad dressings. See also OLIVE OIL.

palm oil - reddish orange and very pungent, the main cooking fat in West Africa, Central and South America, and the Caribbean, high in saturated fat and usually exported for soap making.

peanut oil - mild, pleasantly flavored and practically odorless, with a high-smoke point, made from pressed steam-cooked peanuts. Used for cooking, in salads and in the making of margarine.

safflower oil - extracted from the seeds of the safflower, polyunsaturated and a good source of linoleic acid, an essential fatty acid.

sesame oil - made from pressed sesame seeds, high in polyunsaturated fat. A light variety is made from raw (not toasted) seeds, usually used for frying; a dark variety is used in Asian cooking, mainly as a flavoring agent.

sunflower oil - extracted from sunflower seeds, very versatile, high in polyunsaturated fat and low in saturated fat.

oil from the radish, while the Hittites are said to have preferred almond oil. Other historical sources of oil include sesame seeds in the Middle East, poppies in Europe, and olives in Crete and Palestine. Many varieties (see box on previous page) are used for cooking and to dress raw foods, such as salads.

oilnut - see BUTTERNUT.

Oka - a monastery cheese made in Oka, Quebec, that owes its unique flavor to a special brining process invented in 1893 by Brother Alphonse Juin, who learned to make cheese in Port-du-Salut, France. See also PORT SALUT.

okara - the shredded-looking white and nutritious residue left after soy milk is pressed from the beans to make tofu. Found in Asian markets, packaged in plastic and refrigerated, okara is added to salads, soups and stir-fries.

okashi - also **kashi.** A generic Japanese term for sweets or savory snacks. A sweet version is *owa okashi*, made with roasted rice, spiced with black sesame seeds and formed into bars with barley sugar. See also WAGASHI.

okayu - see GRUEL.

okolehao - also **oke.** An ancient Hawaiian rum-like liquor, made by distilling the root of the sacred ti plant in an underground oven, creating a type of molasses that can be fermented. The name *okolehao*, meaning "iron bottom" in Hawaiian, refers to the rounded pots used to make the liquor.

okonomiyaki - a Japanese savory pancake made with any of a variety of additions, including shellfish, meat and vegetables, hence the name, which means "cooked as you like." The pancake batter is made with flour, water, salt and shredded cabbage; then, the additions are either stirred into the batter or scattered on top of a circle of the batter after it has been placed on a hot griddle. The dish is infinitely variable, and regional variations abound. Perhaps the most famous is Hiroshima-style okonomiyaki (*Hiroshima-yaki*), which is served on top of or with yakisoba, or fried noodles, and sometimes with a fried egg on top. Some restaurants have okonomiyaki cooking tables, where patrons mix and customize their pancakes themselves. No matter how it's cooked, okonomiyaki is served with a selection of toppings: mayonnaise, sweet-salty okonomiyaki sauce, **katsuobushi** and **ao nori.** Because the pancake is topped with so many things, it is sometimes referred to as "Japanese pizza."

okra - the seedpod of a tropical Asian, possibly African, plant, *Abelmoschus esculentus*, much used by the Greeks and cultivated by the Egyptians in the 12th century BC, but not mentioned in any ancient Western texts. In the 16th century, when Africans were enslaved by the Spanish and brought to the New World, they brought with them the few things they could, including the plants and seeds from home-dried peas, yams, **ackee** and okra. By the 19th century, when the slave trade was finally abolished, okra was an important part of the cuisine of the Caribbean and the southern U.S. In and around New Orleans, the Creoles, American descendants of the European settlers, adopted a popular American dish called **gumbo**, which is very close to *gombo*, the Portuguese word for okra, gumbo's most important ingredient. Native Americans used **filé** powder (the dried pounded leaves of the sassafras tree) to thicken sauce, but okra was welcomed as a more satisfactory alternative.

A relative of the hibiscus, okra is a lantern-shaped pod or capsule, usually from 2 to 4 inches (5 to 10 cm) long, containing rows of seeds; when cooked, it oozes a mucilaginous liquid. Okra is usually harvested and eaten unripe, about two or three days after the first appearance of the pods, when they're at their most tender and flavorful stage of development. In full maturity, the pods become hard and fibrous. Okra is a staple in the American South, but for Arabs, it's a delicacy reserved for special occasions.

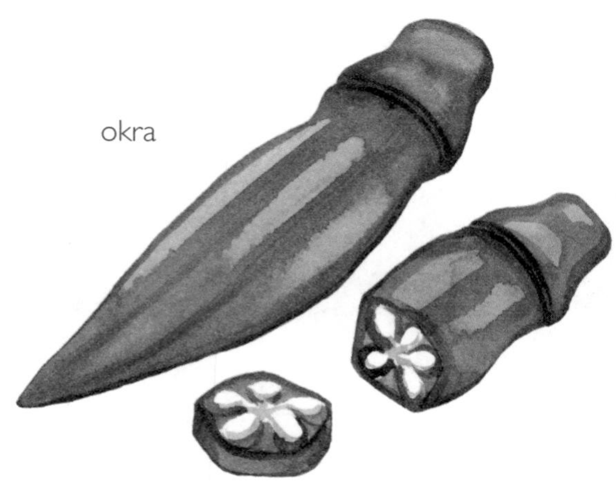
okra

A B C D E F G H I J K L M N O P Q R S T U V W X Y Z

It's best not to wash okra until it's ready for use, because it removes the protective coating that keeps the pods from becoming viscous. Okra is not much used in any European country except Greece, where it is used most famously in a delicious stew of lamb and okra. In England, okra is known as ladyfinger or lady's finger.

okra soup - see GUMBO.

olallieberry - a vigorous *Rubus* hybrid created by crossing the loganberry with the youngberry, which produces large, long shiny blackberries. Introduced in 1950, it is grown predominantly along the west coast of the United States, particularly in California, where it thrives in the milder climate. When it's not eaten fresh, the juicy fruit is a favorite for making pies, preserves and wine.

Old Bay Seasoning - a brand-name dry seasoning mix made by McCormick & Company of Baltimore, Maryland, used traditionally as a garnish or flavoring for steamed Chesapeake Bay crabs and seafood. It's a well-guarded secret blend of more than 12 spices and herbs, but the company does reveal that it includes celery seeds, bay leaves, dry mustard, red pepper and ginger.

Old Fashioned - a classic cocktail made with bitters and a sugar cube, crushed and stirred together first with a long-handled spoon, then adding ice and whiskey (some bartenders use blended whiskey, some bourbon, some Canadian). Garnished with a maraschino cherry and a slice each of lemon and orange, it is served with the spoon or a swizzle stick.

old-fashioned glass - also **rocks glass.** A short, stout glass with straight or flared sides, holds eight to 10 ounces (250 to 300 mL) of liquid, used for liquor or mixed drinks served **on the rocks** and shots that contain fruit juices. A **Black Russian** or **White Russian** is commonly served in an old-fashioned glass.

old-fashioned loaf - see DUTCH LOAF.

old-fashioned oats - steamed, whole, hulled oat kernels (groats) that have been rolled to flatten them into flakes. See also ROLLED OATS.

old marble eyes - see WALLEYE.

Old Milwaukee rye - a classic sourdough or yeast bread made with caraway seeds, molasses and rye. It's named after the city of Milwaukee, which was settled by German immigrants, who brought along their favorite bread and beverage, beer. A Friday night dinner of beer-battered cod with coleslaw, potatoes and Old Milwaukee rye bread is still something of a tradition there.

old woman - see MUGWORT.

oleomargarine - also **oleo.** Another name for margarine.

Olestra - an artificial, noncaloric fat substitute created by Procter & Gamble; used in products, such as potato chips, since the mid-1990s. By design, Olestra contains fatty acids and sucrose, which are not easily absorbed by the body.

olivada - also **olive paste.** An Italian mixture of black pepper, olive oil and puréed Mediterranean black olives (and sometimes garlic, as well), which is used as a spread on crackers or fresh or toasted bread for appetizers or sandwiches. It may also be used as an ingredient in salads, sauces and pasta dishes.

olive - the fruit of a tree, *Olea europaea,* native to the Mediterranean, one of the most ancient of cultivated fruits. Nobody seems to know exactly when the wild olive tree, which has exceptional longevity, was first cultivated, but archeologists have found evidence of cultivated olive groves dating as far back as 3000 BC on the island of Crete. The olive then spread to the Middle East, southern France and Spain.

The olive tree is intertwined with the history of the Mediterranean. One legend says that the first olive tree grew on Adam's tomb. The ancient Greeks believed that the goddess Athena planted the first olive tree among the rocks of the Acropolis. Today, in Spain, peasant women still keep an olive branch purposefully hidden in the house in the belief that it will keep their husbands faithful.

The Portuguese and Spaniards brought the olive tree to the Americas, providing fruit and oil to entire populations, as both a food staple and lighting fuel. The fruit cannot be eaten as picked; it must to go through treatments that vary according to the region. Olives are usually harvested between the months of November and March, hand-picked by workers on ladders or shaken or struck from the trees, with the olives falling into large nets laid out on the ground below. **Green olives** are picked when they are not yet ripe; **purple olives** when they're just ripe; and **black olives** when they're overripe

OLIVE VARIETIES

calamata - see KALAMATA.

dry-cured - strong-flavored and wrinkled from being packed in salt to remove most of their moisture.

infornate - black, medium-size, wrinkled, oven-dried and cured in oil, from the Italian *forno,* meaning "oven."

Italian and Greek - dark purple, soft and juicy, picked when fully tree-ripened, rock-salted in tight containers for several months before being packed in olive oil.

kalamata - also **calamata.** Popular dark purple Greek olive, made into oil, marinated or packed in brine.

kalamata olives

Manzanilla - a small- to medium-size olive from Spain, brine-cured while still green, often sold pitted and stuffed with pimiento in North America, although it is frequently seen whole in Spain. Manzanilla olives are also a source of fruity, dark green olive oil.

Mission - the common black California olive found in supermarkets, named for the Franciscan missionaries who originally planted them. The majority of the California production is used for oil, but the rest are brined or salt-cured and usually packed in olive oil or in a vinegar solution.

Moroccan - black, medium-size, soft, dry-cured, strongly flavored, often sold marinated with rosemary, garlic and red pepper flakes.

Mount Athos - the plump green olive stuffed with pimiento that's a must-have for a Martini.

Niçoise - tiny, purple, with an intense, earthy flavor, difficult to pit, a French variety named for the Provençal town of Nice.

Spanish - from Catalonia to Andalusia, hand-picked when young and green, soaked in lye, then fermented in brine for six to 12 months. The majority of the production is used to make high-quality oil, and the rest is usually bottled in weak brine and sold whole, pitted or stuffed.

Manzanilla olives

(a dark, blackish purple color). Regardless of their color, all olives are bitter when fresh and go through a four-step process after picking. They are first separated, according to color and size. Then, they're dunked in lye or wood ash. Next, they're cured in either dry salt, brine (wet salt) or in oil, or even through dry roasting. Finally, they're packed in oil or vinegar. Olives are often **cracked,** their flesh cut manually or mechanically to allow a marinade of oils and/or herbs and spices to penetrate easily and add flavor; also referred to as slit or split olives. Spain, Italy, Greece and France are the world's main olive-producing countries.

olive loaf - **1.** a **luncheon meat** embedded with pimiento-stuffed olives. The finely textured meat resembles bologna and, depending on the manufacturer, may contain beef, chicken, pork and/or turkey. **2.** an artisanal, often homemade, bread, common in Italy, that contains whole olives mixed into the dough before baking. Grated cheese, herbs and sun-dried tomatoes may also be added.

olive oil - the flavorful product of the fruit of the olive tree, *Olea europaea,* the only oil that can be consumed immediately after extraction from its source. Olives have their beginning in Greek mythology. Poseidon and Athena were competing to see which one would name the newly built city near Attica, and they agreed that the winner would be the one with the better gift for its citizens. Poseidon stuck his trident into a rock and, because he was the god of the sea, saltwater flowed. When Athena, the goddess of peace and wisdom, pierced the ground with her spear, it turned into an olive tree, which is how Athens got its name and why the olive branch is a symbol of peace. Homer called olive oil "liquid gold," and wrote that the olive tree had been thriving in Greece for more than 10,000 years.

The olive harvest can last from November to March. Olives are usually collected in nets, strewn on the ground to catch what's fallen from the trees at their most perfectly ripe, and then processed within 24 hours. For lower grades of olive oil, the trees are shaken to encourage more olives to fall, or the fruit is actually hand- or mechanically picked. Historically, olives were crushed by hand in large stone basins. Today, producers use mechanical, stainless-steel grindstones to crush olives and then a centrifuge to separate the oil from the paste, producing the **first** or **cold pressing,** to which no heat or chemicals have been added. In this form, the oil is at its optimal in color, flavor and nutritional value. It then undergoes a gentle filtering to remove sediment and becomes **extra virgin olive oil.** Like wine, the flavor of olive oil is heavily dependent on soil, climate, variety, age and processing. Unsurprisingly, its flavor characteristics — delicate, mild, spicy, nutty, floral, fruity — resemble the terms one hears used when discussing wine.

GRADES OF OLIVE OIL

extra virgin - made from olives picked from the ground after naturally ripening, rather than being shaken prematurely from the tree, and pressed within 24 hours. The name "extra virgin" can be used only for oil that is less than 1 percent acidity and made from the first pressing, which gives the finest and fruitiest of any olive oil and is the most expensive.

virgin - less care is taken in the picking of the fruit for this olive oil. It does not have to be from the first pressing, as with extra virgin. Its acidity is less than 2 percent.

light - a misleading appellation, as it doesn't indicate low-calorie: all olive oil has the same number of calories. "Light" refers to color and fragrance.

olive paste - see OLIVADA.

olla - a tall, pot-bellied pot made of iron, copper or earthenware in which many traditional Spanish soups and stews are cooked.

olla gitana - Spanish for "gypsy stew," a stew featuring mainly vegetables and beans.

olla podrida - a Spanish stew, literally "rotten pot," made with beef, pork, chicken, chickpeas, chorizo and various seasonal vegetables, stewed in the **olla.** See also COCIDO, PUCHERO.

Olney, Richard - see profile on page 464.

oloroso - see SHERRY.

Olympia oyster - an edible, flat, small slow-growing oyster, *Ostrea conchaphila,* also known as *O. lurida,* found on the rocky North American west coast from Alaska to Panama, but particularly in protected bays and inlets of the Pacific Northwest. The only oyster native to Puget Sound, it was threatened in the 20th century by harvesting and pollution; now, a protected species in Canada, it is making a comeback. Restoration projects have also been undertaken along the California and Washington coastlines. About the size of a silver dollar, it has a smoky flavor and is often eaten **on the halfshell**.

omakase - a Japanese restaurant order that means "let the chef decide," in other words, the diner asks, allows and trusts the chef to choose the meal.

ombra - Italian for "shade," a Venetian expression meaning to have a glass of wine at a neighborhood bar, a nod to when wine was marketed by itinerant salesman, who would take their rest in the shade to keep themselves and their wines cool. Today, *ombra* is accompanied by small tapa-like snacks called *cicheti*.

omega-6 fatty acids - a type of essential fatty acid that works in conjunction with **omega-3 fatty acids** to ensure proper brain function, normal growth, healthy bones and skin, and a well-regulated metabolism. Essential fatty acids are not produced by the body, so they must be consumed in foods. Omega-6 fatty acids are ingested in the forms of linoleic acid (found in vegetable oils) and arachidonic acid (found in meats). Good sources are sunflower, safflower, cottonseed, corn and soybean oils; egg yolks; and meats, particularly organ meats. Deficiencies in North America are extremely rare, because the diet is rich in sources of omega-6 (much of it coming from the oils used in packaged foods) — so rich, in fact, that the average North American consumes 10 times the amount necessary for good health. Maintaining the proper balance between omega-6s and omega-3s is crucial to staving off diseases, as an imbalance can lead to inflammation, heart disease, arthritis and even asthma. The key is usually adding more healthy omega-3s, in the form of fish oils, etc., to the diet to balance the amount of omega-6s consumed in other common foods.

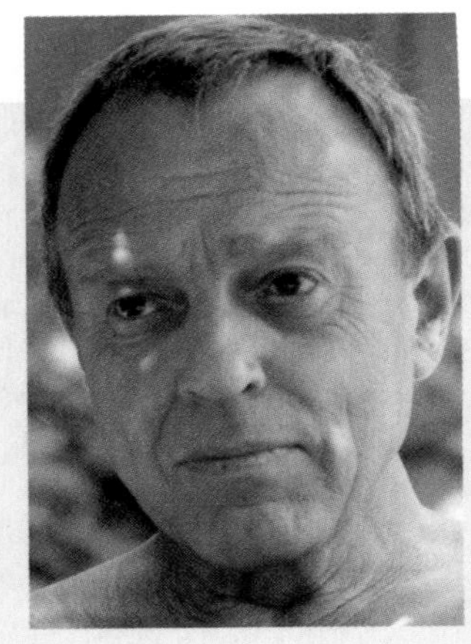

Olney, Richard (1927–1999) - food and wine writer, cookbook author and pioneer, who introduced French country cooking to Americans. Born in Marathon, Iowa, he left university with the intention of becoming a painter and, at 24, moved to Paris in 1951. There, he led a charmingly bohemian life, a member of a smart set of mostly homosexual British and American expatriates, which included the writer James Baldwin and filmmaker Kenneth Anger. His career as a culinary writer began when the magazine *Cuisine et Vins de France* invited him to become its first American contributor. His column was a great success, and his new career was launched.

Although Olney was no stranger to **haute cuisine** and his fondness for first-rate wines was legendary (he could be relied upon to arrive for dinner with an extraordinary vintage or two tucked under his arm), it was French home cooking that spoke to his soul. His first book, *The French Menu Cookbook* (1970), described as "a personal gastronomic manifesto," championed simplicity and the then unheard-of seasonal approach to cooking. He followed with *Simple French Food* (1974). Generally considered his masterpiece, it carried on the tradition of linking dinner with the garden's earthly delights. His approach to cooking was often compared to that of **Elizabeth David,** with whom he became fast friends. "I don't like recipes," he said. "They keep cooks from using their intuition, and intuition is precisely what so much of cooking is about." Yet, his recipes were precise and well crafted, incorporating a solid sense of the technique required to produce excellent results.

During his time, Olney wielded considerable influence in the food world, much of it derived from sources other than his cookbooks. His books never sold particularly well, possibly because, as **Julia Child** once suggested, he did little to promote them. He was the chief consultant responsible for all 27 volumes of the impressive Time-Life cookbook series, and his close relationship with chefs Jeremiah Tower and **Alice Waters,** which helped to shape the development of "California cuisine," influenced the development of many culinary professionals. It is said that Alice Waters keeps a copy of *Simple French Food* in the kitchen at Chez Panisse. In 1983, Olney made publishing history when he sued cookbook author Richard Nelson for copyright infringement for "stealing" 39 of his recipes. The theft was unmistakable, as it included the prose that accompanied Olney's recipes, and Nelson settled out of court. Richard Olney died in his sleep at his beloved hillside cottage in Provence in 1999.

omega-3 fatty acids - a type of essential fatty acid that works in conjunction with **omega-6 fatty acids** to ensure proper brain function, normal growth, healthy bones and skin, and a well-regulated metabolism. Because they are not produced by the body, these fatty acids must be consumed in foods. Fatty fish, such as mackerel, herring, sardines, tuna and salmon, are particularly rich sources of the two most easily absorbed omega-3 fatty acids: eicosapentaenoic acid (EPA) and docosahexaenoic acid (DHA). Soy foods, flaxseeds and walnuts are rich sources of alpha-linolenic acid (ALA), which converts to EPA and DHA in the body.

The consumption of omega-3 fatty acids is particularly important in people who have, or are at risk for, cardiovascular disease or heart attack. Omega-3s help prevent cholesterol from turning into artery-clogging plaques. They also lower blood pressure, decrease irregular heartbeat and decrease the level of triglycerides in the blood. Omega-3s are also helpful in preventing or reducing inflammation, especially in the case of arthritis.

The human diet should contain a 1:1 ratio of omega-3s to omega-6s, but, thanks to the large amounts of vegetables oil in many packaged and prepared foods, most North Americans consume 10 times as many omega-6 fatty acids as omega-3s. Maintaining the proper balance between omega-6s and omega-3s is crucial to staving off disease: an imbalance can lead to inflammation, heart disease, arthritis and even asthma. The solution is to add more healthy omega-3s, in the form of fish oils, etc., to the diet, rather than just cutting down on omega-6-rich foods.

omelet - also **omelette.** Generally, a breakfast or lunch dish made of beaten eggs, seasonings and often milk or water, cooked in butter until firm. It can be plain or filled with a wide variety of savory or sweet fillings, served flat or folded over.

omelette Norvégienne - see BAKED ALASKA.

oncom - an Indonesian fermented food, similar to **tempeh**, made from the compressed residue (the press cake) left after oil is extracted from peanuts, or from **okara** or soy, that is treated with *Neurospora sitophila* mold. Similar to tempeh, the oncom is sold in cakes (the mold gives them a characteristic orange color), which are sliced, sometimes battered, and stir-fried.

one-pot cooking - as it sounds, the cooking of a whole meal in one pot, a necessity in places short on cooking facilities, fuel or space, or when the cook has little time to fuss. Classic dishes, such as **arroz con pollo** from the Caribbean, **New England boiled dinne**r or **pot-au-feu,** make a virtue of one-pot cooking. Current electric slow cookers prove the lasting popularity of this easy style of meal making.

onigiri - also **rice ball.** A ball or patty of seasoned, cooked rice often served as a snack or as part of a **bento box** lunch in Japan, found increasingly in Japanese cafés and markets in North America. Onigiri are usually flattened rounds or triangles and are often covered with a sheet of **nori** and/or sesame seeds. Some are also filled with pickles, such as **umeboshi,** fish roe, flaked cooked salmon or even Western-style tuna salad. *Yaki onigiri* are brushed with soy sauce and briefly pan-fried to give them a crusty finish on both sides.

onion - from the Latin word *unio*, meaning a "single large pearl," which lead to the French word *oignon* and the English "onion." Onion is an edible bulb of a plant, *Allium cepa,* with a dry, yellow outer skin and crisp, layered, white flesh. Onions, along with shallots, leeks, chives and garlic, belong to the Allium family, of which there are 325 members. All have the characteristic onion smell, which is caused by volatile acids beneath the skin. Archeological and historical records show that onions have been cultivated for more than 5,000 years. They're believed to have originated in Asia, and their easy cultivation suggests that their use proliferated quickly. The onion was widely eaten in Egypt, where it was considered a sacred fruit, the symbol of eternity and the sun god, because of its sphere-like shape; the concentric rings of the sliced onion represented heaven, hell, earth and the universe. There's an inscription on the Great Pyramid that records how many onions, radishes and garlic were consumed by the laborers who constructed it. The total is 1,600 talents of silver (1 talent of silver is the equivalent of 57 pounds/26 kg). In fact, onions were even found in Tutankhamen's tomb. In Europe, onions were known and used extensively by the Greeks and Romans. In addition to the flavor they added to other foods, onions were thought to make soldiers brave. Greeks preparing to compete in the Olympics would consume pounds of onions and even drink onion juice for extra energy. By the Middle Ages, onions were a common vegetable throughout Europe and one of the few available equally to commoners and kings.

Onions were believed to have the power of absorbing poison, so they were examined carefully before cooking, as a bad onion was considered poisoned. A raw onion was said to be a quick cure for a cold and able to prevent baldness. No vegetable as well known as the onion could pass through medieval history without collecting its share of superstitions. In Elizabethan days, peeled onions were hung about the house to collect diseases that would otherwise afflict its inhabitants. To foretell droughts and blizzards, one could cut an onion on Christmas Eve to produce 12 onion cups, put salt in each, line them up in a row,

onions

ONION VARIETIES

The onion bulb begins forming when exposed to a certain amount of daylight and is classified accordingly. Short-day onions have been exposed to 12 to 13 hours of daylight, while intermediate and long-day varieties have had upwards of 14 hours.

SHORT DAY

Bermuda - a thick, flat bulb with a mild, sweet taste, available white (known as Crystal Wax) or yellow; does not store well.

Noonday - one of the sweetest onions available, grown in Noonday, Texas.

Texas Super Sweet - large, yellow, often as big as a baseball; stores better than all other short-day varieties.

Vidalia - also **Yellow Granex**. A thick, flat bulb sweet enough to eat raw, made famous by the onion-growing area of Vidalia, Georgia; does not store well.

White Granex - also **Miss Society.** With the same characteristics as a yellow onion, but stores better and has pearly white flesh.

INTERMEDIATE

Sweet red - a large, red, flattened globe with a short storage life.

LONG DAY

Cimarron - large, yellow, mildly pungent, with a medium storage life.

Spanish - white or yellow, weighing up to 3 pounds (1.5 kg), with a long storage life; a favorite for fried onion rings.

Walla Walla - sweet, yellow, the pride of Washington State, with a short storage life.

assigning each a month of the year. If, the next morning, the salt was found to be wet, that month would be wet. To prognosticate in matters of love, an Irish maiden would take four onions on Christmas Eve, placing one in each corner of her room, each named for a man of her acquaintance. The man whose onion sprouted first before Twelfth Night (January 6) would become her husband.

Christopher Columbus brought the onion to the New World on his second voyage in 1493. Ulysses S. Grant refused to march his army during the American Civil War until his onion stock was replenished. Because onions contain vitamin C, they probably helped the soldiers fight off scurvy and other diseases associated with malnutrition. They were also prized medicinally, with claims that onions could cure almost anything, from dog bites and earaches to poisonous snakebites. Onions were even prescribed for warts; those afflicted were supposed to cut an onion in half, rub it on the wart, tie the onion halves back together and bury them. When the onion decayed in the ground, the wart was guaranteed to disappear. Research shows that onions may help guard against many chronic diseases; onions contain a **flavonoid** called quercetin, which may protect against cataracts, cardiovascular disease and some types of cancer. The same sulfuric compounds that have been credited with the health benefits of onions also are responsible for bringing on tears.

There are more than 1,000 onion varieties, including Vidalia, Maui and Bermuda, to name only a few. The National Onion Association organizes the categories into "fresh summer" or "storage winter," available in white, yellow and red. Fresh summer onions, such as Vidalias and Mauis, have a shorter shelf life than storage winter onions, which are available year-round. At 87 percent of the overall onion crop, yellow onions are the most readily available and are often used in soups, casseroles and sandwiches and for grilling. White onions have more of a bite than red or yellow, so they're more commonly used in salsas and other Latin dishes. Red onions are usually used raw, as they tend to be the mildest. **Dehydrated onions** are manufactured through a drying process, which preserves the natural integrity of the onion without any loss of flavor, color or aroma. They are available kibbled, minced, chopped, granulated and powdered. Their shelf life is two years, and most of them have a large amount of **MSG** added. See also CHIVE, GREEN ONION, LEEK, PEARL ONION, SCALLION, SHALLOT.

onion bhaji - deep-fried, battered, chopped or sliced onions served as an appetizer or on the side. For this classic Indian dish, the onions are usually halved, then thinly sliced, dipped in a batter containing **besan,** eggs and water, and seasoned with cayenne pepper, coriander, cumin, garlic and/or turmeric.

onion flakes - ready-made seasoning of chopped, dried onion; when added to liquid or semi-liquid dishes (such as dips, soups and stews), they rehydrate. See also ONION.

onion powder - ready-made seasoning of finely ground, dried onion.

onion ring - a battered, deep-fried single ring of an onion, often served with pub fare, such as hamburgers or fried fish. Some onion rings are coated with a crumb mixture, while others use a smooth batter, such as the type use to make tempura.

onion salt - ready-made seasoning of onion powder and salt.

onion seasoning cube - finely ground, dried herbs and onion compressed into a cube, wrapped and sold for use in dips, sauces, soups and stews.

onions farcis - see STUFFED ONIONS.

onion soup - see FRENCH ONION SOUP.

ono - see WAHOO.

on the half shell - the serving presentation of a clam, mussel and, especially an oyster on the lower half of its shell. Oysters may be raw, grilled or steamed and served alone on their shells — usually six, arranged in a circle on an oyster plate or on crushed ice — or with caviar, lemon slices and, especially in Louisiana, hot sauce on the side. The shell is a natural scoop used to tip the whole oyster into the mouth.

on the rocks - a term denoting an alcoholic liquor poured over ice cubes (the "rocks") in a glass and served, undiluted by mixer.

oolichan grease - a diet staple of the First Nations of the Pacific Northwest, used as a cooking oil, to enrich food and traded as a commodity. The oolichan (also known as eulachon) is a small, silvery fish from the smelt family, which lives in glacier-fed rivers from northern California to the southern Bering Sea. White settlers called them "little candlelight fish" for the grease that was extracted from them and used as candle oil. The Tsimshian of the Nass River in British Columbia refer to them as "salvation" or "savior" fish, because they are the first fish to come down the river at the end of winter, when stores of food have all but run out. See also SMELT.

oolong tea - see TEA.

opah - see MOONFISH.

opal basil - see BASIL.

open crumb - see CRUMB.

open date - see EXPIRATION DATE.

opihi - see LIMPET.

oplet - see SEA ANEMONE.

orach - see GOOSEFOOT.

orange - any of a variety of citrus trees, *Citrus sinensis*, bearing fruit with juicy, orange flesh and skin, cultivated in the Indus Valley as early as 4000 BC. From their native soil in Southeast Asia, where they have been cultivated for centuries, oranges successfully took root in the Near East and North Africa in the 9th century and in southern Spain and Portugal in the 12th century. Thanks to the 16th-century Spanish and Portuguese explorers, oranges acclimated themselves to the semi-tropics of North and South America. As early as 1750, it was discovered that citrus fruits could prevent and cure scurvy. Columbus is responsible for bringing the orange to the New World.

Despite its frequent anachronistic appearance in major Renaissance paintings of the Last Supper, the orange was not consumed at the gathering. A millennium later, crusaders returning from the Holy Land reported having seen oranges there, which no doubt influenced Titian, Fra Angelico, Correggio, Botticelli and other painters, who all painted still lifes with

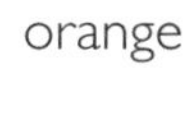
orange

ORANGE VARIETIES

Oranges are often identified by a brand, such as Jaffa (from Israel), Outspan (from South Africa) and Sunkist (from the U.S.), as well as quality, color, juice content and size. There are three main varieties of oranges: sweet, loose-skinned and bitter.

Sweet oranges are juicy and very aromatic, good for eating and juicing. They may or may not have seeds and are usually hard to peel. The three most popular sweet varieties are **navel, Valencia** and **blood oranges,** navel being the best known. The navel, named for its appearance at its base, is actually an interior smaller fruit that grows as the exterior fruit grows. Also known as **"navelina,"** it is almost always seedless and is not a modern variety; it was described and illustrated as early as 1646. The variety of navel orange we call **Washington** was already being grown in Brazil in 1820. Fifty years later, a missionary stationed there sent 12 trees, in tubs, to the Department of Agriculture greenhouses in Washington, D.C. Two of the trees were carried to Riverside, California, and became the sole source for the extensive planting in Orange County. For years, navels went by three different names: **"Bahia,"** from the part of Brazil where they originated; **"Washington,"** for their first home in the U.S.; and **"Riverside,"** for their commercial origin.

Loose-skinned oranges are so named because their skin slips off easily. The mandarin and tangerine are such varieties and can be sweet or tart.

Bitter oranges are believed to be native to Southeast Asia, but there are records showing that they've been growing in Sicily as far back as AD 1002, brought there by Arabs. For more than 500 years, they were the only orange known in Europe and were the first to reach the New World, when Spaniards introduced them to St. Augustine, Florida. These oranges are too bitter to eat raw, but are delicious cooked, as in marmalade and the classic French **bigarade** sauce. Bitter oranges are also used to make essential oils and candied peel. Their flowers are used to make **neroli oil** and **orange flower water,** as well as **Cointreau, curaçao** and **Grand Marnier liqueurs.** The two best-known bitter oranges are **Seville** and **bergamot.**

oranges. And during this time, citrus fruits were introduced to the Mediterranean from China by way of India. Where orange trees do grow, they flourish, so much so that in many places they're a symbol of fertility. In Sardinia, the wedding limousine is usually a cart pulled by oxen with oranges attached to their horns. In Crete, the bride and groom are sprinkled with orange flower water on their wedding day to make the marriage happy, prosperous and fruitful. Even in the U.S., brides often carry orange-blossom bouquets or wear wreaths of them in their hair. By the Renaissance, oranges had become a symbol of wealth and opulence. The Medici family incorporated them into their coat of arms as five golden balls.

The word "orange" has it roots in the Sanskrit *naranga* and may be linked to the Tamil word *naru*, meaning "fragrant." The initial "n" survived in *naranja*, the modern Spanish word for orange. But the "n" dropped out for the modern Italian *arancia*. Also, some etymologists hypothesize that "o" as the first letter of the modern word came about, in part, under the influence of *or*, the Old French word for "gold." See also CITRUS, CLEMENTINE, MANDARIN ORANGE.

orange beef - a Chinese dish in which the beef is flavored with dried, hard orange peel.

orange blossom honey - see HONEY.

orange curaçao - see CURAÇAO.

orange flower water - also **orange blossom water.** A liquid flavoring agent made from the blossoms of bitter oranges, such as the **Seville orange.** When the blossoms are distilled, they create **neroli oil,** which floats to the top of the mixture and is skimmed off; the remaining watery liquid is orange flower water. Orange flower water was widely used as a perfume in Europe, but became a common flavoring ingredient by the 17th century. It is still used today, both in perfumery and to flavor sweets, such as the pistachio-based Lebanese version of **baklava.**

orange lentil - see LENTIL.

orange pekoe - see TEA.

orange roughy - also **slimehead.** A cold- and deep-ocean fish named for its red upper body and blue-tinted belly, which turns orange out of the water. It is also found in the North Atlantic, but the main commercial catch is off the southern coast of New Zealand; this harvest began in the 1970s and, by 2000, it was worth $84 million NZD (about $58 million US dollars) a year. Most orange roughy is filleted, then frozen for export to consumers, who value its delicately flavored, flaky, white flesh. Uncaught, an orange roughy can expect to live about 150 years.

orca bean - see CALYPSO BEAN.

Ordinaire, Pierre - see ABSINTHE.

orecchiette - see PASTA.

oregano - the common name of several freely spreading species of the *Origanum* genus (which also embraces O. *majorana* or sweet **marjoram**) used in cooking. Native to the Mediterranean basin, many are hardy to zone 5 and have become a favorite perennial in sunny North American herb gardens since the Second World War (the story goes that soldiers brought back both the herb and an appetite for it). Oregano, particularly O. *vulgare* cultivars, has a sharp scent and mint-tinged flavor that survives drying, so it's commonly sold, dried and crumbled, alone and in ready-made Italian seasoning mixes, but oregano is also sold fresh in most supermarkets. A must-have herb in many pasta sauce and pizza recipes, oregano leaves are also used to make oil that's touted as a natural health elixir. *Lippia graveolens*, known as Mexican oregano and a familiar seasoning in Mexican and Tex-Mex cuisine, is indigenous to the American Southwest and Central America where it was used in traditional folk medicines. See also MARJORAM.

oregano

oregon grape - see BARBERRY.

oreillette - also **auricle, bugne, carnival fritters.** A pastry fried in oil, crunchy or soft, and powdered with sugar. French for "little ear," a sweet biscuit so named because it curves and folds during frying, originally prepared during Lent. A similar pastry is made in the Middle East, where it's called *hojuelos de Haman*, or "Haman's ears," and in Afghanistan, where it's called *goas-e-feel*, or "elephant's ears."

orejas ears - see PALMIER.

organic - a term indicating a specific manner in which food is grown and processed. Organic farming must maintain and replenish the fertility of the soil, without the use of toxic and persistent pesticides and fertilizers. Processing must be done with minimal use of artificial ingredients, preservatives or irradiation. Organic farming is now practiced in approximately 100 countries with more than 76.5 million acres (31 million hectares) worldwide under organic management. Australia is the world leader with 30 million acres (12.1 million hectares), followed by China with 8.6 million acres (3.2 million hectares) and Argentina is third with 7 million acres (2.8 million hectares). North America has nearly 3.7 million acres of organic farmland (1.5 million hectares).

organ meat - edible organs, such as the brain, heart, kidneys, liver and spleen. See also PLUCK.

orgeat - also **orgeat syrup.** A sweet, almond-flavored syrup that is nonalcoholic, used to flavor drinks (especially cocktails) or foods, made from almonds, sugar, and rose water or orange flower water. The word comes from the Middle French "orge," meaning barley, which was an ingredient in the original formula for orgeat.

Oriental cocktail - a classic cocktail mixed with two parts blended or **rye whiskey,** one part **Cointreau** or **triple sec**, one part sweet **vermouth** and the juice of half a lime, shaken with crushed ice, then strained into a cocktail glass and garnished with a brandied cherry.

Oriental eggplant -also **Asian eggplant.** See EGGPLANT.

Oriental radish - see DAIKON.

Orinoco banana - also **burro banana.** A short, three-sided banana with pinky flesh that is said to taste of strawberry, usually used for cooking. Hardy to zone 8, this banana is grown in gardens along the U.S. Gulf Coast or in greenhouses as an ornamental, but it is named after the region in Venezuela familiar from Gabriel Garcia Márquez's *100 Years of Solitude*. See also BANANA.

ormer - see ABALONE.

ornamental kale - see FLOWERING KALE.

Oro Blanco - a grapefuit-pomelo cross developed by the University of California. Fragrant blossoms develop into yellow fruit with a thick rind surrounding a small but sweet portion of flesh, good for eating fresh, squeezing into juice or adding to salads.

orris - the peeled, dried and powdered roots of the orris plant — whose flower is the iris, *Iris germanica,* native to the Far East — yield orris extract, which is used in ice cream, candy and baked goods. The root is often used in Russia to flavor a drink made of honey and ginger that is usually sold in the streets. In Italy, especially in Tuscany, large areas of agricultural lands are used to cultivate these irises, where they are locally known as *giaggiolo*. Barefooted women weed the plant's rows, and later whole families work together trimming and drying the roots.

ortolan - also **garden bunting.** This bird is so tiny and tender, it can be eaten bones and all. Frequently mentioned by Roman writers and in medieval accounts of feasting, they're now all but extinct and a rarity on the table. French law allows them to be netted only three weeks of the year; even though it's forbidden to serve ortolans in restaurants, they continue to be captured and fattened for private enjoyment. The little bird weighs only $1\frac{1}{4}$ ounce (36 g); it can quadruple its weight in less than a month's time.

orzo - see PASTA.

osetra caviar - see CAVIAR.

osso buco - braised shank, usually veal, with a rich tomato-and-onion sauce, originally from Milan; Italian for "bone with a hole," from the Latin *os*, meaning "bone."

ostrich - the world's largest bird (an adult male can weigh 400 pounds/181 kg), introduced on North American menus in the early 1990s. The red meat of *Struthio camelus* is similar to beef, but has considerably less fat. Tender cuts can be broiled, fried or grilled; less tender cuts can be braised or roasted. The meat cut from the powerful legs of this fast, but flightless bird is usually ground. Some cuts are dried for jerky. Farmed in Africa for more than a century, ostrich is touted by modern-day producers as being more environmentally friendly than other livestock raised for meat, as it requires less room, feed and water. The eggs, each of which is the rough equivalent of two dozen chicken eggs, are also eaten.

ostrich

Oswego tea - see BERGAMOT.

Othello - a custard-filled sponge cake with a chocolate icing.

oursin - French for "sea urchin." See also SEA URCHIN.

outlaw soup - see BAKONYI BETYÁRLEVES.

ouzo - an anise-flavored liqueur from Greece. The best ouzo is said to come from the island of Lesvos, made from a specific combination of pressed grapes, herbs, berries, aniseed, star anise, licorice, mint, wintergreen, fennel, nutmeg, coriander, cinnamon and cardamom. It's distilled in copper pot stills and placed in barrels until its distinctive taste is obtained. Ouzo and other anise-flavored liqueurs, such as **arak,** pastis, Pernod and raki, turn an opaque white when mixed with water, the result of their inherent anise oil dissolved in alcohol.

oven - see MODERATE OVEN, SLOW OVEN.

oven-braise - see BRAISE.

oven thermometer - see THERMOMETER.

over easy - a method of frying an egg on one side until the white is set, then flipping it over and cooking it for no more than 15 seconds, so the center of the unbroken yolk is still soft (it should be served immediately).

ovo-lacto vegetarian - see VEGETARIAN.

oxtail soup - a soup of ox (or beef or veal) tail with vegetables, barley, herbs and sherry, now a classic English soup, believed to have been introduced to England by French refugees fleeing during the revolution.

oyster - any of a family of various saltwater bivalve mollusks found all over the world. The Romans, true gourmets that they were, appreciated oysters. Fabius Rutilius, a Roman consul, died after eating more than 30 dozen of them. Louis XV ate them with tartar sauce. Early Americans found the shores of New York laden with oysters. Native Americans were eating oysters when the English arrived; the colonists made them an important part of their own diet. Abraham Lincoln and his wife, Mary Todd, when they lived in Springfield, Illinois, hosted oyster feasts at which oysters were eaten by the dozens. There were oyster houses in every eastern city, and oyster peddlers in the streets. In the 1840s, there were places that offered all the oysters you could eat for only six cents, although it was said that the proprietors usually slipped a bad oyster onto the plate to keep customers from eating too many. In 1877, 50,000 oysters a day were sold at New York's Fulton Fish Market, which, even then, was 60 years old. (It was finally torn down in 1969.) The Grand Central Oyster Bar & Restaurant in New York opened in 1913. It still serves oyster stew made according to its original recipe.

Oysters are most often named after the places where they are found. Bluepoint and Cape Cod oysters are from the East Coast of the U.S.; Caraquet and Malpeque are from Eastern Canada; Sydney Rocks are from Australia; and Belons, the most expensive of all oysters, are from the town of the same name in France. The only exception is the Portuguese oyster, which is not from Portugal, but from France.

The **Atlantic oyster** is also known as **Eastern oyster.** It has an elongated shell, 2 to 5 inches (5 to 12.5 cm) across, and is found along North America's Atlantic coast. It is sold under different names, depending on where it was harvested. The best-known varieties include the **Bluepoint, Cape Cod, Chesapeake** and **Malpeque.** Bluepoint is the name now used generally for any medium-size Atlantic oyster. It is believed that baymen coined the name after noticing "a blue haze" as they returned to the oyster-rich shore of Long Island. The fame of this oyster reached England, where Queen Victoria had them shipped to her. She loved them above any other varieties, and insisted that their rough shells be sanded clean before they were served in Buckingham Palace. See also OLYMPIA OYSTER.

oyster cap - see OYSTER MUSHROOM.

oyster crab - see CRAB.

oyster cracker - a tiny hollow cracker made in the shape of a shell, square, circle or octagon, traditionally served with seafood chowder in New England, developed specifically to be served with oyster stew.

oyster knife - see CLAM KNIFE.

oyster mushroom - also **oyster cap, pleurote, pleurotte, shimeji, tree mushroom.** A common name for *Pleurotus ostreatus*, an oyster-shaped fungus, which grows on tree trunks and rotting

oyster mushroom

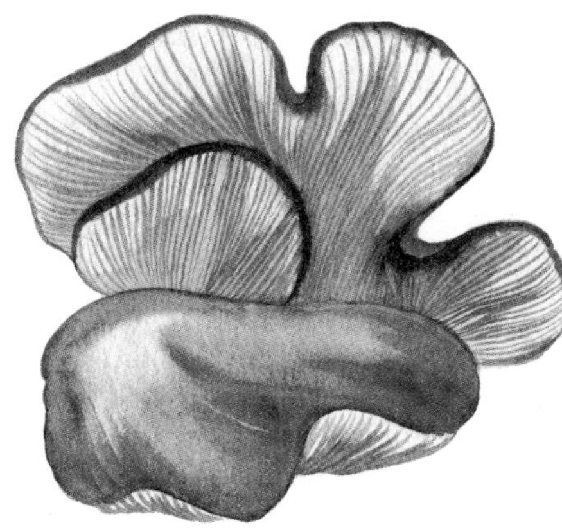

stumps in the wild, but is also commercially cultivated. It is available canned, dried or fresh; the latter can be found year-round in Asian markets. It has a slightly licorice scent and a peppery taste.

oyster plant - see SALSIFY.

oyster plate - a specially designed plate for serving oysters. Although a Dickens' character in *The Pickwick Papers* once observed that "poverty and oysters always seem to go together," the lowly bivalves rose to become all the rage in the Victorian era, and the well-to-do wanted a fancy way to serve them. Manufacturers, such as Limoges, Minton and Wedgwood, responded with plates ranging from small ones (each shaped like a broad, shallow scoop and designed for a single oyster) to platters for a dozen. In between, single-person serving plates, usually with six wells arranged in a circle, were designed for oysters with, or without, their half shells. Often highly colored and lavishly decorated with real and imaginary marine life (such as swirling mermaids, sardines and sea gods), these antique plates are still such sought-after collectibles that their collectors have formed their own international society.

oyster sauce - an Asian condiment made from oysters, brine and soy sauce.

oysters Bienville - a 1930s dish of oysters on the half shell, laid on a bed of rock salt, then covered with a **béchamel** sauce, containing bread crumbs, chopped garlic, peppers and onion, mushrooms, shrimp and white wine, and baked; named after French Canadian explorer Jean-Baptiste le Moyne, Sieur de Bienville, who established a settlement at New Orleans in 1718.

oysters Rockefeller - created in 1899 by **Jules Alcatiore,** who was 30 at the time, at the old New Orleans restaurant Antoine's, founded in 1840 by his late father. Jules apprenticed under the eye of his mother for six years; he was then sent to France, where he worked in the kitchens of Paris, Strasbourg and Marseille. He became the chef of the Pickwick Club in 1887, when he returned to his native New Orleans. The dish, which he named after the scion of the Standard Oil Co., John D. Rockefeller (because it's so rich), begins with washed raw spinach, which is put through a food chopper twice with equal amounts of parsley and green onion tops. Four or five drops of hot pepper sauce are sprinkled over this mixture, along with salt and pepper and finely ground browned bread crumbs. Butter is then rolled in and kneaded thoroughly to create the sauce, to which a little absinthe may be added. The oysters on the half shell are placed in a baking pan filled nearly to the top with rock salt and baked in a 450°F (230°C) oven for five minutes until the edges of the oysters shrink inside the shell.

ozone - a naturally occurring gas in the Earth's atmosphere that, when added to water for bottling, acts as an antimicrobial agent, leaving the water clean and pure enough to drink. Ozone kills bacteria and viruses and removes compounds that can give water an unpleasant taste, and it leaves no taste of its own, making it a less objectionable disinfectant than chlorine. Ozone is made by exciting the molecules in oxygen (O_2) so that they divide into individual atoms and recombine as ozone (O_3). It is an unstable gas, so, when exposed to air and warmth, it quickly converts back to oxygen, leaving behind no environmentally unfriendly by-products.

ozoni - also **zoni.** A traditional Japanese chicken-and-vegetable soup ladled over **mochi** cakes (grilled or plain) and often served on New Year's morning. Daikon, **dashi,** edible chrysanthemum leaves, **kamaboko, mizuna,** shrimp, spinach and **yuzu** zest are common ingredients. In eastern Japan, ozoni is usually clear, but in western Japan, the addition of miso makes it slightly opaque.

p

papaya

paan - **1.** also **paan masala, pan, quid.** An Indian preparation of **betel leaf, betel nuts,** lime paste and spices, often used as an after-dinner mouth freshener. A washed betel leaf is spread with some lime paste, then sprinkled with the other ingredients, which can sometimes also include tobacco, coconut and small pieces of candy. The leaf is then folded into a triangle and pierced with a clove to hold the package together. The paan is chewed and some of the juice and betel nut residue is spit out. The juice is a bright red color that can stain the teeth and gums (and anything else it lands on). Paan is offered at the end of a meal and at ceremonial occasions, such as weddings. It can also be found on almost every street corner in India, as well as in Indian neighborhoods in North America. **2.** a synonym for **betel leaf** itself.

Pablum - brand name for a ready-to-use, vitamin-enriched baby food, originally made with wheat germ, alfalfa, oatmeal, cornmeal, wheat meal and other ingredients, with a bland taste. Invented by three Canadian doctors, Theodore Drake, Alan Brown and Frederick Tisdall, at The Hospital for Sick Children in Toronto, Canada, it was first sold to the public in 1930. The name Pablum is taken from the Latin word *pabulum*, meaning "food."

Pacific littleneck clam - also **rock cockle.** *Protothaca staminea*, a recreational and valuable commercial catch harvested from California to Alaska. The adult clams lead sedentary lives on the sand, mud or rock in estuaries and along the shore; rarely moving, they are vulnerable to predation by birds, fish and otters, as well as fishermen and pollution. Pacific littlenecks are available canned and frozen, or fresh in their shells. See also CLAM.

Pacific littleneck clams

Pacific pompano - a relatively small, slender, oval fish, *Peprilus simillimus*, with shiny, silvery scales and mild-flavored, dark flesh. Harvested from Baja, California, north to Queen Charlotte Sound off British Columbia, Pacific pompano is related to the Atlantic **butterfish.** Fresh specimens are sold in spring and summer, whole or with the heads removed and usually about 10 inches (25 cm) long; frozen fish are also available. See also POMPANO.

Pacific sturgeon - see STURGEON.

paddy-straw mushroom - see STRAW MUSHROOM.

padek - a Laotian fermented fish sauce containing pieces of fish, such as the locally caught glass fish. Padek has a strong smell and pungent flavor, and is added to many cooked poultry, meat and vegetarian dishes; it is also used with fresh foods, such as fruits and salads. See also FISH SAUCE.

pad thai - a Thai stir-fry of rice noodles, chicken, shrimp, tofu, peanuts, eggs, bean sprouts, garlic, chiles and **nam pla.**

paella - a Spanish rice dish whose most distinctive ingredient is saffron, its name meaning "frying pan," for the wide, shallow iron pan in which it's cooked. Although there are many variations, its most common ingredients include chicken, rabbit, chorizo, mussels, clams and other seafood. Paella made in Valencia and Barcelona tends to be made predominantly with chicken and seafood.

paillard - a very thinly pounded piece of meat, usually sautéed or grilled, after a dish made by a 19th-century Parisian restaurateur of the same name.

pain - the French word for "bread."

pain au chocolat - a flaky croissant or puff pastry dough wrapped around a bar of chocolate (then sometimes glazed with an egg wash and sprinkled with sugar) and baked. Specially made bars of semisweet chocolate are sold for the filling.

pain au levain - the general term for French breads leavened with natural starters instead of yeast, with thick, leathery crusts, soft, spongy interiors and a slightly sour flavor.

pain perdu - slices of stale, leftover bread (the name is French for "lost bread"), dipped in beaten egg, then fried in clarified butter. Made

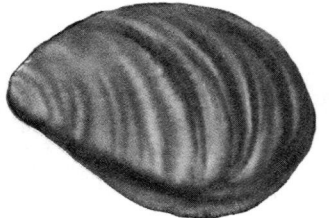

since medieval times and traditionally eaten as a dessert on feast days, such as Easter, and other special occasions, it was sometimes dipped in wine and almost always served with honey, spices and sugar, making a luxury of economy. Nowadays, pain perdu — sprinkled with confectioner's sugar, or served with fresh fruit, maple syrup or preserves — is usually served for breakfast. See also FRENCH TOAST.

pak choy - also **pak choi.** See BOK CHOY.

pakora - a small Indian fritter consisting of a ball of spiced cheese, chicken, meat, fish, fruit, seafood or vegetables, covered in a **besan** dough and deep-fried. A popular, portable street food, pakora are also served as appetizers and snacks, and floating in soups, such as **karhi.**

palacsinta - a crêpe-like Hungarian pancake, made in both savory and sweet versions. The savory dish is made by layering a stack of pancakes with a meat, seafood and/or vegetable mixture, then serving it with a cream sauce spiced with paprika. Sweet palacsinta are often rolled around fruit jam or preserves, then dusted with confectioner's sugar, or filled with a mixture of cream cheese, lemon zest and raisins, then served with a chocolate or creamy vanilla sauce.

palate - **1.** the roof of the mouth, which separates it from the nasal cavity, found in vertebrates. The fleshy back portion (called the soft palate) from such animals as beef cattle and buffalo, has traditionally been sold as **variety meat,** but is rare in butcher shops today. **2.** the sense of taste. To say, for example, that someone has a "good palate" means that person has a discerning, discriminating sense of taste. **3.** a wine term meaning the taste itself. Connoisseurs combine "palate" with other words to describe the feel, sensation and taste of a particular wine.

pale ale - see ALE.

palm cheese - fermented, pickled **hearts of palm.**

palm heart - see HEARTS OF PALM.

palm kernel oil - extracted from the kernel of the seed (or nut) inside the fruit of the palm tree, *Elaeis guineensis*, high in lauric acid and similar to coconut oil. It varies in color from white to yellow and remains solid at room temperatures, making it very useful for soaps.

palmier - also **elephant ear, palm leaf.** A flaky confection made of puff pastry, sprinkled with sugar to sweeten the dough and add a sparkly finish, sometimes dipped in or topped with melted chocolate or a sweet glaze. The palmier gets its name from its distinctive shape, which looks like elephant ears. *Palmier* means "palm" in French, thus its alternate name. Also known as **orejas ears** in Mexico.

palmita - see HEARTS OF PALM.

palm leaf - **1.** see PALMIER. **2.** a leaf cut from a palm tree, used by indigenous peoples to wrap packets of grains, meat and vegetables for cooking (the leaf itself is not eaten); or to weave sieves used in cooking and fishing. Fresh-cut young palm leaves are also used as cattle fodder, particularly in South America.

palm oil - an edible oil extracted from the fleshy layer of the fruit of the West African palm tree, *Elaeis guineensis*, reddish orange in color and very high in saturated fat; used to make soaps and candles, margarine and cooking fat. See also FATS, PALM KERNEL OIL.

palm sugar - sugar made by boiling down the sap of any of a variety of palm trees and drying the crystals in the shapes of logs, loaves or cakes. Palm sugar is unrefined and therefore quite flavorful, crumbly and moist like brown sugar. See also GUR, JAGGERY.

palm syrup - palm sap boiled until it reduces and thickens into a dark, dense, sweet syrup. Palm syrup is used in Asian and Indian cooking as a dipping sauce, sweetener and in baked goods and confections. Spices or flavorings, such as almond or vanilla, may be added to dress it up.

palm wine - see ARAK.

palmyra - see TODDY PALM.

palo cortado - see SHERRY.

pan - **1.** Spanish for "bread." **2.** a generic term used to describe various broad, usually shallow, cooking containers, almost always made of metal. They may have a lid (a saucepan), one handle (a sauté pan), or two (a paella pan), a removable rack (a roasting pan), or be ridged (a grill pan), or perforated (a pizza pan).

panaché - see SHANDY.

panada - **1.** a generic term from the Latin word *panis*, meaning "bread," given to a paste made of bread crumbs, flour or occasionally rice mixed with liquid ingredients, such as melted butter, egg yolk, milk, stock or water. A thick **béchamel** used as a base for soufflé is one example; **choux pastry** is another. **2.** a traditional English porridge-like soup of boiled bread crumbs, sometimes sweetened and flavored with wine. In the French version, *panade*, potatoes or rice may stand in for the bread.

Panama orange - see CALAMONDIN.

pan bagnat - also **pan bagna.** A kind of sandwich, a specialty of the French county of Nice, consisting of a split baguette moistened with olive oil and filled with any combination of tuna, anchovies, tomatoes, onion and hard-boiled eggs. Creative individuals may expand the ingredients to include zucchini, capers, celery, parsley, basil leaves, sliced peppers or vinegar, but whatever ingredients are used, it is critical that the bread be liberally doused in olive oil (the name means "bathed bread"). Once it is prepared, the loaf is traditionally tightly wrapped, weighted down and refrigerated to allow the juices to soak into the bread. Pan bagnat is traditionally served for lunch, as an hors d'oeuvre or at picnics.

pan-broil - to cook in an uncovered skillet with little or no fat.

pancake - also **flannel cake, flapjack, griddle cake, hotcake.** A flat batter cake that is cooked on both sides in a frying pan or on a griddle. Many countries have their own versions of pancakes, varying in degrees of thickness and fillings from the paper-thin French crêpe to the savory Japanese pancake **okonomiyaki.** See also AEBLESKIVE, BAO BING, BLINI, BLINTZ, BOUQUETTE, CRÊPE, DOSA, KATAYEF, LATKE, MANDARIN PANCAKE, OKONOMIYAKI, PANNEKOEKEN, PALACSINTA, SILVER-DOLLAR PANCAKE.

Pancake Day - see FASTNACHT.

pancake syrup - also **mock maple syrup.** A generic term usually applied to a ready-made alternative to maple syrup, which mimics its color and taste (real or faux maple flavoring is added). They are usually corn syrup based and always less expensive. Homemade versions can be made with brown sugar and caramelized white sugar, boiled with a bit of butter and vanilla. The term also encompasses brown-rice syrup, fruit syrups and light molasses.

pancetta - from the Italian *pancia*, meaning "belly," a seasoned, cured and rolled pork belly, best when it has equal parts lean meat and fat.

panch - see PUNCH.

panchan - also **panchon.** Colorful, small Korean dishes, usually salty and spicy, served as starters or side dishes. In restaurants, panchan, such as dried fish, **kimchi** and pickled vegetables and seaweed, may be served as appetizers, compliments of the house.

panch phora - also **panch phoron.** A Bengali blend of five spices, named for the Hindi words for "five" (*panch*) and "seeds" (*phora*). Seeds of cumin, fennel, **fenugreek,** mustard and **nigella** are the usual ingredients, but in some mixes **anise** seeds, **cassia** leaves or chiles may be included. When cooking, this mix is often fried in hot **ghee** or oil, to release flavor and fragrance, before the other ingredients are added.

pancit - see PANSIT.

pandan - also **daun pandan, kewra, pandanus leaves, screwpine leaves.** The lance-like leaves of the screwpine tree, used to add fragrance, a green tint and a delicate flavor — it's been compared to butterscotch — to savory and sweet Asian foods. The leaves are often scarified with the tip of a knife or the tines of a fork, or broken open by tying each in a small knot, to

pandan

release the juice, before they're added to the cooking pot. They may also be pressed to produce juice, which is added to dishes, such as custard. Whole leaves are used to wrap poultry or seafood before cooking. Frozen leaves, which lack the full flavor of fresh, are available, as is the bottled essence.

pan de aqua - a crusty breakfast bread eaten in the Caribbean and Puerto Rico, often with a cup of *café con leche*, the Spanish version of **café au lait.**

pan de muerto - Spanish for "bread of the dead." This sweet, egg-rich yeast bread — spiced with aniseed, glazed with a syrup of orange juice and zest and sugar, and sprinkled with **colored sugar** — is baked to celebrate *Dia de los Muertos* (Day of the Dead). Bone-like protuberances may be rolled from a portion of the dough and attached to the loaf, or the whole loaf may be shaped like a skull; the bread, along with other special food and drink, is often taken to the cemetery for an all-night vigil. Despite its name, the Day of the Dead is a happy celebration. On November 1st of each year, the dead come back to visit the living; the living remember the dead, remind them that they are not forgotten and reflect that the living will join them soon enough. A huge holiday throughout Mexico, the Day of the Dead is also observed by Hispanic North Americans, who now number about 41 million in the U.S. alone.

pan di Spagna - meaning "Spanish bread," an Italian sponge cake similar to the French **génoise.**

pandowdy - a classic American one-crust deep-dish pie that is almost a pudding. Sliced apples or other fruits are combined with butter, spices and brown sugar, maple syrup or molasses, then topped with a biscuit-like batter. Partway through the cooking, the crust is cracked and pushed into the filling, so it softens as it absorbs the thickened juice. These days, it is often baked; in colonial times, it was cooked in a covered pot over the fire. Pandowdy is usually served with ice cream or heavy or whipped cream. See also GRUNT.

pan drippings - liquid fat and juices released by meat, poultry and other foods as they cook. These may be used to baste a roast or turkey as it cooks, for example, as the basis for gravies and sauces, or served simply as **jus.**

pané - French for "breaded."

pane - Italian for "bread."

paneer - also **panir.** A fresh, unripened Indian cheese made by draining curdled cow's milk to make the soft cheese **chenna,** then pressing and drying it until it is the texture of firm tofu. Cubes of paneer are used in many Indian dishes, one of the most famous and ubiquitous on Indian restaurant menus being *palak paneer* (also known as *saag paneer*), a creamy melange of cubed paneer and spinach, heavily spiced and sometimes enriched with the addition of cream and caramelized onions. Paneer can also be used in sweets, such as *rasgula,* which are balls of paneer mixed with semolina, almonds, pistachios, sugar and spices, boiled in a sweet syrup.

panettone - a tall egg-rich cake with candied fruit, customarily served at Christmas and Easter. A 15th-century legend claims that the cake was made by a Milan baker, whose attractive daughter was courted by an aristocrat named Toni, who offered to work as an apprentice in the bakery. The cake became quite popular and came to be called *pane di Toni* or Toni's bread.

panforte - Italian for "strong bread," a Tuscan Christmas cake with candied fruits, cinnamon, coriander, nutmeg, cloves, pepper, walnuts, honey and orange and lemon peels. A wrapped piece of the cake is used in a Christmas game similar to shuffleboard: the cake is thrown onto a long striped table, and the one who throws it the farthest, without letting it fall from the table, gets to keep the cake.

pan-fry - to cook in an uncovered skillet with a little fat.

panhas - see SCRAPPLE.

panini - a traditional Italian sandwich of cheese, meat and vegetables. Made in a hinged panini maker or press (similar to a waffle iron, but with a "floating" lid that accommodates various thicknesses), the panini is pressed together and browned between two ridged grill plates.

panino - Italian for "roll."

panir - see PANEER.

panko - also **Japanese bread crumbs.** A coarse, dry, large bread crumb used to coat fried foods.

panna cotta - also **crema cotta.** An Italian dessert that originated in Piedmont in the early part of the 19th century and translates as "cooked cream." Panna cotta is a cloud-like confection of barely jelled cream, usually flavored with citrus and served with a caramel, chocolate or fruit coulis. It has been said that a Hungarian immigrant woman, whose version contained egg, coffee and vanilla, first made the dessert in the Langhe district of Piedmont.

pannekoeken - a Dutch pancake, similar to a crêpe, often sprinkled with confectioner's sugar and served with fresh fruit.

panocha - see PENUCHE.

pansit - also **pancit.** A Philippine dish, often made with shrimp, chopped sausage and vegetables, served over fried noodles. Cooked in a wok, with broth added partway through, pansit varies with the chef and may also contain other ingredients, such as chopped chicken, pork or squid, and can be topped with chopped green onion, hard-boiled egg or peanuts. Made with rice noodles, it's called *pansit bihon;* made with wheat-flour noodles, it's called *pansit canton.*

pansotti - see PASTA.

pan strainer - a circular or half-moon shaped metal mesh or perforated melamine or metal strainer that is held against the rim of a pan or pot to keep solid food inside, while liquids are drained off.

pansy - a member of the violet family, *Viola wittrockiana*, that is grown as an ornamental plant and also for its delicate edible flower petals. It comes in a number of colors and was originally bred from the wild violet, also known as the **Johnny-jump-up.** Larger varieties may have their petals plucked, while smaller varieties may be eaten whole. They are lovely and mild in salads. See also EDIBLE FLOWERS.

pansy

pantothenic acid - see B VITAMINS.

pantry - a room or closet generally entered from the kitchen, for provisions, silverware, china and glassware, originally used to store bread, from the Latin *panis,* meaning "bread."

panzanella - a classic Tuscan bread salad containing the basic ingredients of fresh basil, crusty bread, garlic, olive oil, red onions, red wine vinegar and tomatoes. Stale bread is usually used; it is cut in cubes and may be moistened in water or browned in oil before it's added. Other ingredients, such as capers, diced cucumbers or a sprinkling of grated Parmesan, may be added at the whim of the cook.

panzarotti - **1.** a type of crescent-shaped pizza now popular at North American pizzerias. The dough is folded over fillings, such as cheese, herbs, meat and diced vegetables in tomato sauce — pinched together to seal it around the curve, and baked. **2.** a Neapolitan dish of ravioli — filled with cheese, herbs and meat, and sometimes dipped in a beaten egg-and-water mixture — fried in oil until golden, then eaten hot. **3.** a festive and sweet Corsican yeast fritter made with a batter of milk-cooked rice mixed with brandy, eggs and lemon zest, then dusted with sugar and served piping hot.

pao duce - see PORTUGUESE SWEET BREAD.

papadam - see PAPPADAM.

papain - an enzyme derived from papaya and used as a meat tenderizer and in both conventional and folk medicine.

papaya - also **pawpaw.** This exotic fruit, *Carica papaya*, was luscious enough to be called "food of the angels" by Columbus when he discovered it in the Caribbean. Throughout history, papayas have been used to clean and soften the skin, ease indigestion and tenderize meat. They contain an enzyme called **papain,** which is extracted from the skin and used as a meat tenderizer. Pear-shaped, 5 to 6 inches long (12.5 to 15 cm), with a cavity filled with round black seeds, the papaya's flesh is sensuous and juicy, its color ranging from red and pink to orange,

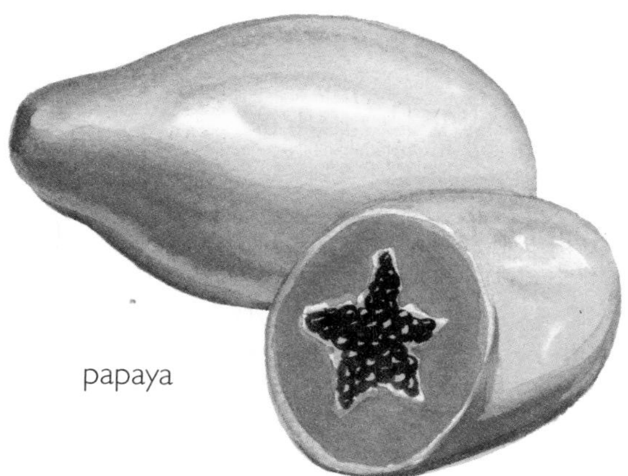
papaya

tasting a little bit like apricot and ginger. The seeds are edible and can be cooked or cured in brine like capers. Papaya can also be cooked as a vegetable when still green. It is often used to make preserves and pickles, and is available in spring and summer.

papillon - French for "butterfly," referring to the shape of a small pastry or cookie.

papillote - **1.** French for "paper wrapper," a frilly paper used to dress the end of a rib bone on chops or crown rib roasts. **2.** *en papillote* means an individual portion of poultry, fish or meat wrapped in parchment paper with some aromatics and sealed tightly and baked. The contents steam in their own savory vapor and the parchment paper puffs up; it is slit at the table.

Papin, Denis - see profile below.

pappadam - also **papadam, poppadum.** An East Indian flatbread made from chickpea or lentil flour, rolled out wafer-thin and fried or grilled. They can be plain or flavored with a variety of spices, such as black pepper or garlic. Pappadams puff up to almost twice their original size when deep-fried, but deflate as they cool.

pappardelle - see PASTA.

paprika - dried sweet pimiento, *Capsicum annum*, ground into a fragrant, mild-flavored red powder, used to add color and flavor to dishes (such as Hungarian goulash) and as a garnish, sprinkled over foods (such as **deviled eggs**). Hungary is credited with the development of paprika early in the 1600s, but it wasn't until the mid-19th century that the peppers were cored before they were dried, then ground. With the seeds removed, the powder is less hot. Hungarian paprika is dark red; the Spanish version, paler. See also CHILE PEPPERS.

paprika chicken - see PAPRIKÁS CSIRKE.

paprikás csirke - also **paprika chicken.** A classic Hungarian stew, containing chicken, onions and sweet peppers, seasoned with paprika, served with sour cream and small, egg-pasta dumplings called *galuska*.

paradise nut - also **sapucaia, sapucaya.** An indigenous nut of Brazil, *Lecythis usitata*, eaten locally fresh out of hand, and in confections and desserts. Each large, woody shell holds several nuts, which become rancid quickly, so they must be used soon after harvest. This has limited their potential as an export crop, but their nut meal and oil are commercially produced.

paraffin wax - also **baker's wax.** A tasteless, translucent, food-grade white wax with a low melting temperature, which is sold in blocks. Home cooks melt and use it to seal jars of jams and jellies, and as an ingredient in confections, such as those requiring a final dip into melted chocolate. It is also used as a coating for some fruits and vegetables to seal the skin and add shine.

para nut - see BRAZIL NUT.

Papin, Denis (1647–1712) - French scientist and inventor of the pressure cooker, Papin earned a medical degree in 1669, but he spent his life doing scientific research. In Paris, Papin worked with Dutch scientist Christiaan Huygen, a friend of philosopher and mathematician René Descartes, conducting air-pump experiments until 1675. He then went to London to work with British physicist Robert Boyle, which led to the development of the steam engine. In 1679, Papin invented the "steam digester," or pressure cooker, a lidded, airtight container that confined steam under very high pressure, raising the boiling point of water, with a safety valve to release pressure as needed, to avoid explosion.

parasol mushrooms

parasol mushroom - also **umbrella mushroom.** A summer and autumn fungus, *Macrolepiota procera*, from the Lepiota family, found standing tall on grassy hillsides, often near trees, the size of the mushroom making it easy to find. Named for the way its cap opens when mature, it has excellent flavor. The stalk should be discarded, because it's tough and fibrous. The genus name, *Lepiota procera*, derives from the Latin word *lepis*, meaning "scale," and *procerus*, meaning "tall." It should be picked young, before it starts to wrinkle.

paratha - also **paranta, parantha.** A griddle-fried, unleavened Indian bread usually made with butter or **ghee,** salt and wheat flour. Small balls of dough are rolled out, brushed with butter or ghee, folded and rolled again several times, then fried until they are crisp and golden. The layers separate somewhat as they cook, becoming flaky. Parathas are often used to make roll-ups of spicy meat and vegetable mixtures.

parboil - to partially boil foods, especially root vegetables, before roasting or adding to other quick-cooking foods, so that all foods will be ready at the same time. See also BLANCH.

parboiled rice - see RICE.

parch - to brown, dry and/or slightly toast small foods, such as beans, corn kernels, grains or peas, in dry heat.

parchment paper - a silicone-coated cooking paper used to line baking sheets and cake pans, resistant to both moisture and grease, wrapped into a package to steam-cook savory items **en papillote.**

pare - to remove the thin outer layer or peel of fruits, vegetables, fish and meat. See also PARING KNIFE.

pareve - also **parve.** A Jewish cookery term describing a neutral food that includes neither animal nor dairy products, such as fish, eggs, grains, vegetables and fruit. In a kosher kitchen, animal and dairy products must be stored, prepared and eaten separately, but pareve products, since they fall into neither camp, can be prepared and eaten with either.

parfait - a dessert served in a tall glass to expose layers of sweet ingredients, which may include any combination of fresh fruit, custard, coulis, ice cream, whipped cream, syrups or sauces.

parfait d'amour - a type of light purple liqueur, popular in the late 1800s and early 1900s, flavored with lemon or orange, and flowers, such as roses or violets. Vanilla, and sometimes cinnamon, cloves and coriander, are added.

paring knife - a knife with a very short blade, usually 2 to 4 inches (5 to 10 cm) long, used for **paring** and small cutting tasks.

paring knife

parisa - a Texas take on **steak tartare,** allegedly the legacy of Alsatian immigrants to the state, made with raw lean ground beef, grated cheese, onions and chiles. Some cooks sprinkle lime or lemon juice over the top, the idea being that the citrus juice will "cook" the meat, similar to the chemical "cooking" that takes place when citrus juice is mixed with raw shellfish in **seviche.** Parisa is served on saltines as an appetizer, usually washed down with plenty of cold beer.

Paris-Brest - a classic French dessert consisting of a circle of baked **choux pastry,** cut in half, then filled with praline-flavored cream. Topped with minced or slivered almonds, it is dusted with confectioner's sugar. The dessert, its form and its name were created to celebrate the famous bicycle race between the two cities.

Parisienne sauce - **1.** a **velouté,** thickened with cream and egg yolks, used primarily with fish and poultry (also called **allemande sauce**). **2.** a sauce made with creamy **petit Suisse** cheese, chervil, lemon juice and oil, used to dress cold asparagus.

Parisienne scoop - a bowl-shaped, sharp-edged scoop attached to a short handle, designed to core or cut balls from fruits and vegetables, or other tender items, such as scallops. The scoops come in various sizes and some are double-ended with a small and large cutting bowl on either end. It is also used to scoop up spheres of soft foods, such as butter or ice cream, balls of cream cheese or crab salad, for hors d'oeuvres or truffle mixture. See also MELON BALLER.

Parker House roll - a soft, white yeast roll named after the place where it was invented, the venerable Parker House restaurant in Boston, which is also credited as the birthplace of **Boston cream pie.** Parker House rolls are made by folding a disk of rolled-out bread dough in half, so that a crease forms on top as the roll rises. The rolls are a regular sight on holiday and Sunday dinner tables across New England.

parly - also **parley.** See SCOTTISH PARLIAMENT BISCUIT.

Parma ham - a fine-quality raw ham, or *prosciutto crudo,* hails from northern Italy's province of Parma, specifically in and around the village of Langhirano. Specially bred Parma pigs are fed chestnuts and calcium-rich whey, a by-product of local Parmesan cheese making. Parma hams are trimmed to maintain a traditional "chicken leg" shape. The ham is seasoned, salt-cured and air-dried, but not smoked. The curing process can take up to 18 months. Parma ham is served thinly sliced and eaten raw as an appetizer; the rind can be used to flavor soups. See also PARMESAN, PROSCIUTTO.

Parmentier - used in reference to dishes featuring potatoes, named to honor the pharmacist Antoine-Augustin Parmentier (1737–1813), who introduced potatoes to France.

Parmesan - a hard, heady, Italian cheese, produced since at least AD 1200, first mentioned in writings by Adamo Salimbene, a monk living in Parma at the time. Boccaccio's references to it in the *Decameron* (in 1364) show that, by the 14th century, Parmesan was well known not only in his native Florence, but also all over northern Italy. In another document, we find Bernardo Navagero, a 16th-century Venetian emissary to the Vatican, gossiping to the doge that "the Holy Father is getting fat, being very partial to Parmesan cheese, of which he eats plenty." And in 1568, Bartolomeo Scappi, a Dominican in charge of Pope Pius V's household, published a cookbook that decreed Parmesan the best cheese on earth.

Parmesan is by far the best known of the Italian hard cheeses. There are two basic types, **Parmigiano-Reggiano** and **Grana Padano,** the former considered to be superior and, to many, the only Parmesan. Its production is strictly limited to the provinces of Parma, Reggio Emilia, Modena, Mantova and Bologna. On April 1, production begins with the milk from local cows that graze in the area's rich pastureland, and it ends promptly on November 11. Parmigiano-Reggiano is made completely by hand in an artisan's tradition that is hundreds of years old. The milk is partially skimmed, with some of the whey from the previous day's cheese making added. The mixture is then cautiously heated before **rennet** is added to encourage the curdling. The remaining whey is fed to local pigs fated to become **Parma hams,** and the curds

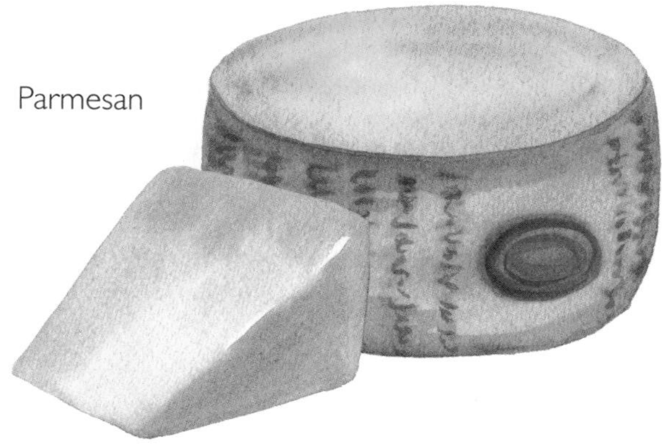
Parmesan

are put into wheel-shaped forms, where the cheese will age for at least two years. It takes about 130 gallons (490 liters) of milk to make one wheel, which weighs about 70 to 80 pounds (32 to 36 kg). Truly fine Parmesan may be aged for up to seven years. During this time, it's nurtured like fine wine, until it turns a pale golden color with a slightly grainy, crumbly consistency and a nutty, mildly salty flavor. To distinguish Parmigiano-Reggiano from other lesser-quality Parmesans, small dots spelling out its name are etched around the entire circumference of the wheel.

Parmesan knife - see CHEESE KNIVES.

parmigiana - a popular method of preparation at Italian-American restaurants, in which a cutlet, such as veal or chicken, or eggplant slices are dipped in egg, then a mixture of bread crumbs and Parmesan cheese and fried. The fried base is then topped with tomato sauce and a slice of mozzarella cheese and broiled until the cheese is melted. See also VEAL PARMIGIANA.

Parmigiano-Reggiano - see PARMESAN.

parr - a young salmon between 1 and 3 years old with vertical stripes. The parr lives in its native stream before becoming a **smolt,** which is distinguished by silvery scales, allowing it to live in salt water. It is then able to begin its migration to the sea for the first time.

parrotfish - also **uhu.** Any of several species, living in subtropical and tropical seas around the world, belonging to the family Scaridae. Named for their beak-like jaws, which hold fused teeth, their head shape and brilliant colors, parrotfish grow from 1 to 6 feet (30 to 180 cm) long. As they scrape coral reefs and rocks to obtain the algae that is their primary source of food, they take in rock and coral as well; after digestion, this crushed material becomes sand (a large parrotfish is said to produce a ton of the stuff every year). Archeological studies show that their flesh has long been a favorite food in the Caribbean, where they are added to chowders and stews, grilled and poached in coconut sauce. They remain a delicacy in Hawaii, where they have traditionally been baked, dried, fried, poached, steamed or eaten raw. The single species living in the Mediterranean is still harvested for food; other species are sought after by diners in Asia.

parsley - a biennial, *Petroselinum crispum*, that has been grown all over the world for thousands of years, the best known of all herbs. Parsley is native to the Mediterranean region of southern Europe. Before it became a part of Italy, Sardinia featured parsley on its currency. Parsley had such strong status for the Greeks that they wore it to banquets. They believed that it sprang from the blood of Archemorus, the foreshadower of Death, whose nurse carelessly placed him in a bed of parsley, where he was devoured by serpents. Regarding it as the "herb of oblivion," they decorated tombs with parsley. Homer tells us that warriors fed their chariot horses parsley and mentions it as part of Circe's pleasant lawn in *The Odyssey*. Greek poet Theocritus writes; "At Sparta's palace, 20 beauteous maids/The pride of Greece, fresh garlands crown'd their heads/With hyacinths and twining parsley dress'd, Graced/joyful Menelaus' marriage feast." They also used it for medicinal purposes and fashioned it into a crown for the winners of the Isthmian and Nemean games.

Parsley has a strange particularity: it's poisonous to most birds and lethal to birds in the parrot family. Our word for it derives from the Greek *petroselinum*, meaning "rock celery," referring to its natural habitat. Parsley is rich in vitamins A and C, calcium, iron and manganese and was used to fight scurvy among sailors on long voyages. The leaves and roots were also brewed into a tea that served as a folk remedy for menstrual, respiratory and urinary

complaints. Today, the leaves and stems of both **curly parsley** and flat-leaf parsley (**Italian parsley**) are commonly used by even the most herb timid cooks in flavored butters, egg dishes, salads, sauces, soups and stews. A sprig of curly parsley is also a ubiquitous garnish beside many main dishes (wise diners eat their parsley; the high chlorophyll content makes it a natural breath freshener). Although it is a biennial and hardy to zone 5, many gardeners treat parsley as an annual since first-season plants are considered the most tasty and tender. See also ITALIAN PARSLEY.

parsley root - also **Hamburg parsley, turnip-rooted parsley.** *Petroselinum hortense,* cultivated for its root, which is white, slender and carrot-like, used in soups and stews or as a vegetable on its own. This parsley's popularity in Europe may help account for its alternate name. Care must be taken, though, for the leaves and roots of a wild parsley look-alike, poison hemlock, are deadly poisonous.

parsnip - a biennial plant, *Pastinaca sativa,* from the Ombelliferes family, its early Roman name coming from its resemblance to a long, tapered farming implement of the time (*pastinum*), used to make deep, even holes for planting.

Beloved in France and in other parts of Europe, parsnips are closely related to carrots, celery and fennel, with much of the same characteristic sweetness. They probably originated between the Mediterranean area and the Caucasus to the northeast. Tiberius, who seems to have been the emperor of the gourmets as well as the Romans, used to have parsnips imported from the area along the Rhine River, where they grew wild, which was a tricky endeavor: water hemlock, which looks very much like parsnip, is poisonous.

By the mid-16th century, parsnips were being cultivated extensively in Germany, and they were a staple for the poor. Early British settlers introduced parsnips to North America. Even the Delaware and Powhatan Indians planted them. But they were never really appreciated in the U.S. because of their very mild flavor (or lack of it, to some) and because they grew too slowly to be profitable. Massachusetts, Illinois, Washington and northern California are the largest producers, since parsnips need cold weather to convert their starch to sugar. The parsnip grows to be about 7 to 12 inches (17.5 to 30 cm) long, and its texture resembles that of the turnip, with fruity yellowish flesh that has a hazelnut aftertaste.

parson's nose - the rectal bump on a fowl, also irreverently known as the **"pope's nose,"** thought to have been a Catholic sobriquet from the time of James II; *sot-l'y-laisse* is the French idiom, meaning "only a fool would leave it behind," referring to the bit of meat, considered a delicacy, just above it.

partridge - there are many varieties of this rasorial bird, similar to the grouse in size, but without the ruffed plumage. Hunting seasons restrict its availability; it can be roasted, stewed or cooked in a casserole. Young birds especially should be roasted and served with their own juices. When roasting, one bird should be allowed per person.

partridge

partridgeberry - see LINGONBERRY.

parve - see PAREVE.

pasilla pepper - see CHILE PEPPER.

paskha - rich molded cheese served in Russia to celebrate the end of Lent. A sweet mixture of butter, candied or dried fruit, cream, curd cheese and nuts is shaped in a pyramid-shaped mold with a perforated base (traditional carved wooden molds impress religious symbols into the mixture). The finished paskha is decorated with sprigs of **angelica** or pieces of fruit or nuts (often spelling out the initials "XB," which stand for "Christ is Risen" in the Cyrillic alphabet) and served with **kulich.**

passata - smooth or slightly textured puréed tomato pulp, used in Italian apéritifs, pasta sauces, soups and stews. The tomatoes are pushed through a **passata machine** or a fine sieve or mesh, leaving the skin and seeds behind. Some passata is cooked with other ingredients to make blends used in cooking. One such blend combines plain passata with puréed carrot, celery, onion and pancetta. It is cooked with olive oil, pork shoulder and wine; the pork is removed, then a small amount of tomato paste is slowly stirred in and the mixture is cooked until it is reduced to a brown and glossy, thick sauce.

passata machine - a hand-cranked mill for making **passata.** Tomatoes are pushed into a broad funnel on top, then drawn through a fine, stainless-steel mesh to remove the seeds and skins and produce a smooth sauce. Most come with a separate collection bowl, which fits under the mill. Some versions come with a suction base designed to grip the countertop or work surface. Passata machines can also be used with other soft fruits, such as lemons and limes, and vegetables.

Passe-Crassane - see PEAR.

passion fruit - the fruit, *Passiflora edulis*, of the passion flower plant, so named because Jesuit missionaries in South America saw symbols of the Crucifixion in the flower's exquisite, intricate bloom; the early meaning of "passion" being "suffering," as it relates to Christ's suffering on the cross. In its stems, they saw the whips; and in its showy filaments, they saw the crown of thorns. They compared its leaves to spears, its stamens to hammers, its 10 sepals to the faithful apostles present at the Crucifixion and other parts to nails, flesh wounds and a halo. Any other fruit with wrinkled, moldy skin would be considered ready for the garbage — but not so with this exotic fruit. The plant the missionaries found was a purple-skinned one indigenous to South America, also known as "purple granadilla." This round, pale fruit, about the size of an egg, is picked when the skin is smooth and reaches its peak of ripeness when its skin wrinkles. Passion fruit can be eaten fresh or used to make preserves, sauces and ice cream. It's most readily available in the summer. The seeds are edible and are traditionally sprinkled on top of the dessert **Pavlova.** See also LILIKOI.

passion fruit

pasta - well established in Italy before Marco Polo returned from China in 1295, despite the popular claim that noodles are of Asian origin. Historians tell us that the Romans and probably the ancient Greeks ate pasta, the latter giving the name *laganon* to a flat cake cut into strips, which the former called *laganum*, a dish composed of dough strips roasted on hot stones, not boiled in water. (Latin references to *pastillum* speak of bread and not pasta.) Some scholars assume that the ancient Persians ate a form of noodles they called *rishta*, while other say that the first form of boiled noodles arrived via the Arab invasions, between the 7th and 13th centuries. In the 1154 book *Kitab Rugiar*, an Arab geographer named Al-Idrisi described details of pasta making on a large scale in the town of Trabia (near Palermo), which exported pasta throughout the Mediterranean. He used the Arab word *itriyah* for the long strands of dough, which came into the Sicilian dialect as *tria*, still used today as a synonym for "spaghetti." Certainly, the environment of southern Italy was ideally suited to growing durum wheat, so the assumption that pasta was there before Marco Polo's time is quite likely.

The fame of pasta really broadened in the 14th century, when bakeries in southern Italy started to sell pasta as an alternative to bread. Then, as now, pasta was the first course of an Italian meal in the south, although in the poorest areas it constituted a complete meal. Its popularity filtered up to the north of Italy, and by the 19th century, giant factories had been set up to produce vast quantities of pasta, which became a vital part of Italian cooking. Pasta is fortified with vitamins that are light-sensitive. If you transfer pasta from its cardboard carton to a decorative glass jar, use it within one or two months. To store it longer, keep it in an airtight container in the dark; pasta will keep in this fashion for about 18 months.

PASTA SHAPES

acine di pepe - "pepper berries," tiny squares with rounded corners.

agnolotti - "priests' caps," crescent-shaped and stuffed.

alphabet - also **alfabeti.** Pasta shaped like letters and sometimes numbers, used in soup. See also PASTINA.

alphabet

anelli - "rings," also **anellini,** "small rings," and **anelloni,** "large rings."

angel hair - also **capelli d'angelo,** meaning "angel hair," fine, delicate and long.

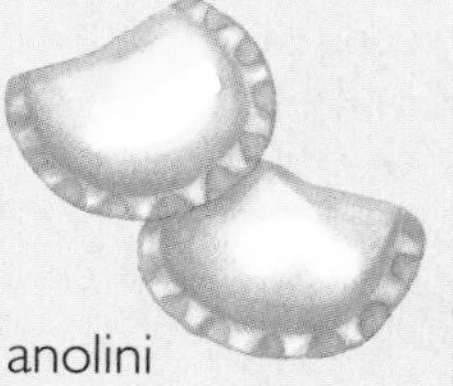

anolini

anolini - half-moon shaped, stuffed ravioli with crimped edges.

barbina - long and thin, like **capellini,** often sold coiled in nests.

bavettine - "little ribbons," narrow linguine.

bigoli - long and thick, made of whole wheat.

bucatini - long, hollow strands, thicker than spaghetti, *buco* meaning "hole," **bucatoni** being the larger version.

calamarata - "squid rinds," broad rings of pasta shaped like **calamari.** A smaller version is called **calamaretti.** Often made into the dish of the same name.

calamarata

campanelle - also **gigli.** *Campanelle* means "little bells" or "bellflowers," and *gigli* means "lilies." Both are shaped like ruffle-edged cones resembling open flowers.

canestrini

canestrini - "little baskets," small hourglass shapes, often used in soups.

cannaroni - also **zitoni.** Wide tubes.

cannelloni - "large reeds," hollow tubes, usually stuffed and baked.

capelli d'angelo - see ANGEL HAIR.

capellini - thin strands, slightly thicker than angel hair.

cappelletti - "little hats," a round, stuffed pasta.

casareccia - long, narrow, twisted tubes.

cavatappi - "corkscrew," short, thin, ribbed spirals.

cavatelli - small rounds with rolled edges that look like hotdog buns.

cellentani - hollow-ridged corkscrews, good for chunky sauces and pasta salads.

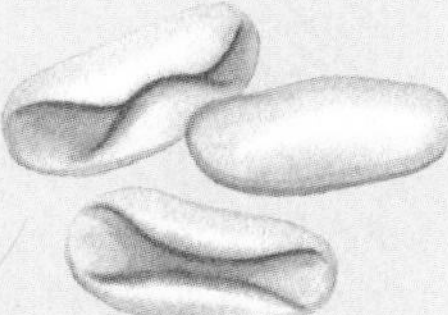

cavatelli

cencioni - "little rags," small, thin ovals, good for soaking up liquidy sauces.

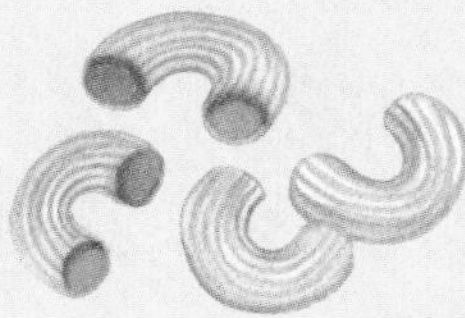

chifferi

chifferi - short, fat, curled tubes, usually ridged and similar to elbow macaroni in appearance.

chitarra - "guitar," for the wire-strung instrument they're made on, which cuts sheets of pasta into long, flat strands, from the Abruzzo region of Italy.

conchiglie - "conch shells," usually ribbed, *conchiglioni* meaning "large shells." **Conchigliette** are tiny versions of conchiglie, often used in soups.

conchiglie

corzetti - round, relatively flat, stamped with various patterns.

creste di galli - "cockscombs," curved, with a ruffled outer edge.

ditali - "thimbles," very small, **ditalini** being an even smaller version.

elbow macaroni - short, curved tubes. See also MACARONI.

elicoidali - "spiral" or "helixes," tube-shaped pasta similar to **rigatoni,** with ridges running around the tube in a spiral or helix fashion.

farfalle - "butterflies" or "bows ties," **farfallini** is the diminutive.

farfallini - see PASTINA.

farfalle

fedelini - also **fidelini.** "Little faithfuls," thin spaghetti, slightly thicker than angel hair. See also CAPELLINI.

fettuccine - also **fettucini.** "Little ribbons," thin, flat egg noodles.

fusilli

fidelini - see FEDELINI.

fusilli - "little springs," short spirals.

garganelli - a type of hand-rolled fresh pasta made with eggs, which looks like a ridged quill, similar in shape to **penne,** but with ridges that run across the width of the tube, not the length.

gemelli - "twins," two strands of spaghetti twisted together.

gigli - see CAMPANELLE.

gnocchi

gnocchi - small, ripple-edged shells or potato dumplings.

gramigna - "weed," short and grass-like.

lasagna - flat, wide noodles, often with ruffled edges.

linguine - "little tongues," narrow and long.

lumache - "snails," large shells, usually stuffed.

macaroni - tubes of various lengths, anglicized word for the Italian *maccheroni.*

maccheroni – Italian for "macaroni."

mafalda - ribbon pasta with crinkled edges and straight ends, usually about ¾ inch (2 cm) wide, and available in short pieces of about 1½ inches (4 cm) long or long ones of about 10 inches (25 cm) long.

mafalda

manicotti - "little muffs," large tubes, usually stuffed.

mostaccioli - "little mustaches," tubes cut on the diagonal, similar to **penne,** but larger.

occhi di lupo - "wolf's eyes," large tubes.

occhi di passeri - "sparrows' eyes," tiny circles.

orecchiette - "little ears," tiny, thumb-imprinted disks.

orzo - "barley," tiny grains, usually cooked in soups. See also PASTINA.

pansotti - triangular pasta shapes, stuffed until they look pot-bellied, then crimped or sealed along scalloped or straight edges, commonly filled with chopped fragrant herbs, or puréed nuts and cheese, or grated cheese and last night's pot roast, shredded.

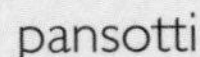

pansotti

pappardelle - broad, flat ribbon noodles.

pastina - a generic term embracing the small pasta, such as **alphabet, farfallini, orzo** and **stellette,** usually used in soups.

penne

penne - "quills" or "pens," short, diagonally cut tubes.

radiatore - "radiators," ruffle-edged spirals that look like radiators.

ravioli - square stuffed pasta.

rigatoni - large, ribbed **macaroni.**

rotini - short spirals.

seashell - see CONCHIGLIE.

rigatoni

semi de melone - Italian for "melon seeds." Flat, oval pasta shapes with pointed ends, which resemble their namesake; used primarily in soup.

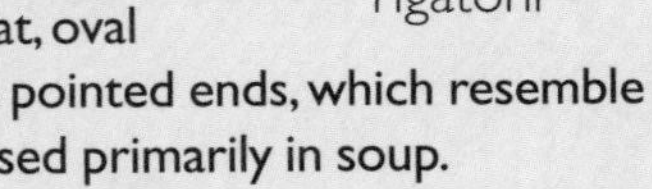

spaghetti - "little strings," long, thin, round strands, **spaghettini** is its diminutive.

stelle - also **stellette.** Star-shaped (*stella* is Italian for "star") pasta, often used in soup. See also PASTINA.

tortellini - "little twists," small, stuffed, pinched into a round shape.

tortellini

vermicelli - "little worms," thin strands of spaghetti.

ziti - "bridegrooms," thin tubes of various lengths.

zitoni - see CANNARONI.

pasta al forno - a generic Italian term for baked pasta dishes, such as the familiar lasagna or a Sicilian specialty of baked eggplant, meatballs and pasta.

pasta alla bolognese - also **pasta bolognese.** A generic Italian term for pasta served with a thick sauce of meat (usually beef) and vegetables. See also BOLOGNESE.

pasta alla Norma - a specialty of Sicily. It was named after the opera *Norma*, by Vincenzo Bellini, who was born in Catania; this dish is spaghetti served with tomato sauce, fried slices of eggplant and ricotta cheese.

pasta asciutta - a generic Italian term for pasta served plain or, more often, with a dressing or sauce, such as pesto or marinara.

pasta de guayaba - see GUAVA PASTE.

pasta e fagioli - a soup whose primary ingredients are pasta and beans (*fagioli*).

pasta filata - a cheese-making technique in which the curd is mechanically stretched, as opposed to the **grana** technique, in which the curd is stirred. Mozzarella is the best-known pasta filata cheese. The technique results in cheese that becomes stringy when melted.

pasta in brodo - a generic Italian term for "pasta in broth."

pasta nocciola - see HAZELNUT PASTE.

pasta primavera - a light dish usually made with long pasta and tender-crisp fresh vegetables, served with a simple oil-and-garlic sauce. The name comes from the Italian word for spring, "primavera."

pasta puttanesca - see PUTTANESCA SAUCE.

pastel - Spanish for "cake."

pastelito - a Cuban version of the **empanada,** which is also popular in Florida. The puff pastry may enclose a savory, spicy meat mixture or a sweet fruit filling, such as apple, **guava** or quince.

paste tomato - see TOMATO.

pasteurized milk - for thousands of years, milk carried potential diseases. In 1860, the French scientist, chemist and founder of modern bacteriology, Louis Pasteur (1822–1895), found a simple method of destroying bacteria in milk; today, the process is called "pasteurization." Pasteurizing arrests or prevents fermentation by heating milk, usually to a temperature of 145° to 162°F (63° to 72°C), so as to destroy undesirable bacteria but leave untouched other desirable organisms. Nevertheless, milk will still sour due to the presence of lactic acid bacteria, which are not destroyed by the pasteurization process. See also MILK.

pastilla - see BASTILA.

pastillage gum paste - see GUM TRAGACANTH.

pastille - French for a lozenge or candy shaped like a small disk, from the Latin *pastillas*, meaning "small loaf," also believed to be named for Giovanni Pastilla, one of Marie de' Medici's pastry cooks.

pastina - see PASTA.

pastis - **1.** an anise-flavored liqueur similar to **Pernod,** made by macerating a combination of aniseed and licorice root in alcohol. It is extremely popular in France, especially in Provence, where it is considered the regional drink of choice. **2.** any of a number of French yeast-leavened pastries.

pastitsio - also **Greek lasagna.** A traditional, Greek baked pasta dish containing cheese (often **kefalotyri**), chopped oregano, ground meat (usually lamb, but sometimes beef) spiced with cinnamon or nutmeg, macaroni and tomatoes, arranged in layers. **Béchamel** sauce is poured over the top, then the casserole may be sprinkled with bread crumbs and/or grated cheese before it's baked. Although it's called Greek lasagna, this dish is firmer and less "saucy" than its Italian cousin.

pastrami - a highly spiced lean beef, usually brisket, but may be other cuts such as plate, shoulder or round, that has been dry-cured, smoked and then cooked.

pastry - **1.** any of several doughs used for piecrusts or tarts, made of flour, fat, salt, liquid and possibly sugar, with or without eggs. **2.** a term used loosely for any sweet, baked food, such as pies, tarts, cakes, cream puffs, cookies, petits fours.

pastry blender - a traditional pastry-making tool consisting of a series of sturdy, but flexible cutting wires or fine blades (usually six) looped

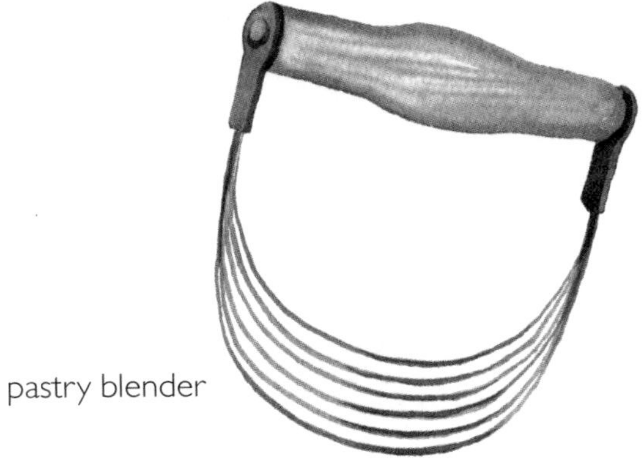
pastry blender

into a U shape, set into a metal plate on each end, which is attached to a cylindrical, horizontal handle. Repeatedly lifted and pressed through cold butter, lard or shortening set in a bowl of dry ingredients, it cuts the fat into smaller and smaller pieces. The loop of wires or blades extends far enough from the handle that warmth from the pastry maker's hands isn't transferred to the pastry mixture; for the same reason, as well as for comfort, the handle is usually made of wood (some models have a metal thumb rest at one end).

pastry brush - a small brush with a flat or round head (traditionally made with sterilized hog's bristles), joined to a wooden handle and used to brush pastry with beaten egg or milk washes, or melted fruit-jelly glazes. Many cooks find other uses for these small brushes, such as coating muffin pans with melted butter, basting a cooking bird with pan juices or brushing pizza sauce onto a round of prepared dough. A classic, but less common model used for applying light washes, such as egg white, to delicate pastry is made from several goose feathers either tied or woven together up their quill ends. Pastry brushes made with nylon and silicone "bristles" are also available. They are nonabsorbent and easy to clean, but brushes made with natural bristles or feathers, which have many microscopic projections, are considered more gentle on pastry and more efficient at picking up and transferring liquids.

pastry chef - also **pâtissier.** A specialized chef in a professional kitchen who is trained in making pastries and other baked goods, one of the positions in the kitchen brigade system created by French chef **Auguste Escoffier** in the late-19th century. See also BRIGADE SYSTEM, CHEF, ENTREMETIER, GARDE MANGER, POISSONIER, RÔTISSEUR, SAUCIER, SOUS CHEF, TOURNANT.

pastry cloth - a sturdy, cotton-canvas rectangle that is lightly rubbed, then sprinkled with flour and used as a nonstick work surface for rolling out pastry and easily transferring it to a baking or pie dish. Pastry cloths may have weights and/or a frame to fix them in place on the countertop or table. Newer versions may have a plastic coating. Usually cleaned by brushing off any loose flour or pastry, they are rolled — often around the rolling pin — for storage (folding produces creases, which mar the pastry). Although some traditional pastry chefs would never dream of washing their pastry cloths, others insist that regular washing (with thorough rinsing) is a must.

pastry cream - a firm custard sauce, which can be used to fill cakes, profiteroles, éclairs, known in French as *crème pâtissière*.

pastry crimper - spring-type, metal tongs with serrated ends, used to pinch and seal together pastry edges. In skilled hands, the same crimper can be used to produce decorative edges ranging from a simple fluted pattern to a herringbone design.

pastry cutter - usually a metal band attached end-to-end and formed into shapes, such as circles, diamonds, flowers, ovals or squares, used to cut out pastry shapes. Some cutters consist of a single band with a rolled top edge, which is comfortable to hold, and a sharp, sometimes beveled, bottom edge that cuts cleanly through delicate dough. Other classic French versions, consist of two bands: a fluted cutting band welded onto a smooth top band with a rolled top edge. Most pastry cutters are at least 1½ inches (4 cm) deep; large ones may have an arched handle on top. High-end plastic replicas are also available.

pastry flour - see FLOUR.

pastry jagger - see PASTRY WHEEL.

pastry marble - a rectangular slab of smooth marble, used as a work surface on which to roll out pastry. Usually about ¾ inches (2 cm) thick, pastry marbles are heavy enough to stay put. The nonabsorbent stone naturally stays dry (so the pastry is less likely to stick) and cool (so the pastry is more likely to keep its proper consistency).

pastry wheel - also **jagging wheel, pastry cutting wheel, pastry jagger.** A revolving metal or wooden disk attached to the end of a vertical, usually wooden, handle, used to seal together the edges of pastry. A notched-edge wheel is used around the rim of a pie, for example, to impress a decorative pattern as it seals the top and bottom crusts together. Some notched-edge pastry wheels have edges designed to cut as well as crimp; they can be also used to cut wavy-edged strips of pastry for weaving latticework top crusts. Some pastry wheels have sharp, even edges designed to cut through delicate layers of puff pastry, for example; models with finger guards are recommended.

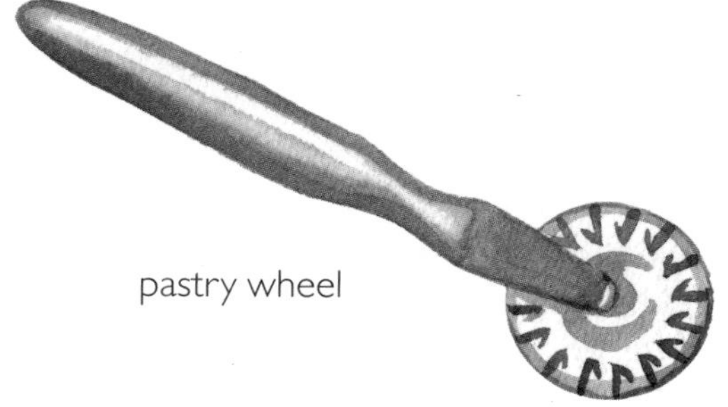
pastry wheel

pasty - see CORNISH PASTY.

pata negra - see JAMÓN IBÉRICO.

pâte - French for "paste" or "dough."

pâté - French for "pie." A baked savory mass, served hot or cold, made from ground meat, usually pork, veal or liver, mixed with small pieces of other meats, such as ham, bacon or fowl, as well as pork fat, herbs, wine, port, cognac or other spirits, and sometimes truffles. *Pâté en croûte* is a pâté covered and baked in a pastry crust; *pâté en terrine* is a pâté baked and served cold from its baking dish, which is also called a **terrine.**

pâte à choux - see CHOUX PASTRY.

pâte brisée - a rich, **short-crust pastry** with more fat in relation to flour than a regular pie crust, used for rich tarts and flans. It usually doesn't contain much sugar, infrequently contains eggs and is nowhere near as sweet at **pâte sucrée.** The name means "broken pastry," because the dough is crumbly in texture.

pâté de campagne - a classic, coarse-textured, country-style French pâté, usually made with seasoned ground chicken livers, pork and veal and black olives, sandwiched between slices of bacon (or sometimes **caul**) in a **terrine,** then cooked in a **bain-marie,** chilled and served cold. Calvados, cognac or white wine may be added to the meat mixture.

pâté de foie gras - see CLAUSE, JEAN-PIERRE; FOIE GRAS.

pâté en croûte - see PÂTÉ.

pâté en terrine - see PÂTÉ.

pâte feuilletée - French for "leaf pastry." See PUFF PASTRY.

pâte sucrée - a classic, **short-crust pastry**, containing egg yolks and sweetened with sugar, that is used for dessert tarts and pies.

patis - fish sauce from the Philippines; a fermented liquid made by mixing fish or tiny shrimp with brine and allowing the mixture to ferment for months, drawing off the liquid and then steeping it in the sun before it is bottled. It is not as highly regarded as the Vietnamese **nuoc nam,** the Thai **nam pla** or the Japanese **shottsuru.** See also FISH SAUCE.

pâtisserie - **1.** a generic French term for baked confections, such as sweet cakes, cookies and pastries. **2.** the French name for a bake shop or tea room that sells and serves patisserie. **3.** the art of making pastry.

pâtissier - French for "pastry chef."

Patna rice - see RICE.

pato real - see MUSCOVY DUCK.

patra leaf - also **colocasia leaf.** The edible leaf of the **taro** plant, used in Asian cookery. In India, for example, it is spread with a paste of seasoned **besan,** rolled up tightly, steamed, then sliced and deep-fried; they are served warm, garnished with chopped coriander, grated coconut and sesame seeds.

patty - **1.** minced fish, meat, poultry or vegetables, patted or pressed into a thin round, such as a hamburger or potato patty, for frying, grilling or roasting. **2.** a round, thin, soft sweet, such as the familiar chocolate-covered peppermint patty (after which the freckled-faced **Peanuts** cartoon character is named).

pattypan - **1.** a small, round scalloped summer squash. See also SQUASH. **2.** a pan to bake patties, not unlike a muffin tin, used for baking small, filled puff pastry.

Patum Peperium - a spiced anchovy relish used mainly as a spread and for canapés. Very close to the French **anchoïade** and called by the name of **gentleman's relish** in England, possibly because it was invented by an Englishman, John Osborn, in 1828. The secret recipe has been passed down from generation to generation by word of mouth. Today, it is made in Elsenham, England, where the original recipe is still used.

paua - see ABALONE.

paupiette - a French culinary term for a piece of finely sliced beef, fish, lamb, turkey or veal that is spread with **forcemeat,** and sometimes wrapped with bacon, then skewered or tied, and fried or braised. Occasionally, a blanched cabbage leaf substitutes for the fish, meat or poultry. One famous such dish is *sole en paupiette*. See also ROULADE.

pavé - French for "paving." **1.** a layered **génoise,** filled with buttercream (or sliced, chilled rice pudding) and frosted, that is shaped like a square paving stone. **2.** a square of savory mousse with a covering of aspic, or a sweet dessert mousse.

Pavlova - a classic dessert consisting of a fluffy, slightly crisp meringue base topped with whipped cream and slices of fresh fruit, most often kiwi fruit, passion fruit and strawberries, traditionally sprinkled with passion-fruit seeds. Created by an Australian chef — some say in honor of the 1929 visit there of Anna Pavlova — it has become the national dessert of Australia and New Zealand. Debate still rages as to whether or not the dish was actually named for the delicate Russian ballerina who danced her way through the early 1900s and was invariably described as "ethereal." But there's no denying that a billowy, white Pavlova is reminiscent of the ruffles of a tutu or the feathers of a swan (Pavlova was renowned for her role as the dying swan in Tchaikovsky's ballet, *Swan Lake*), and it is as airy and light as its namesake.

pawnhas - also **pawnhoss.** See SCRAPPLE.

pawpaw - see PAPAYA.

pea - a small, edible, round green legume, which grows in a pod on a vine, originating in Persia about 10,000 BC, spreading to Asia Minor, Palestine, Greece and then Rome. The earliest peas were very different from those we eat today. They grew wild in bogs and were as large as marbles and probably as tasty. Archaeologists believe they were always eaten toasted and peeled, like chestnuts. In 1865, Austrian botanist Gregor Johann Mendel was studying peas and pollination when he discovered that various dominant recessive characteristics depend on certain basic units, which science would later name "genes." See also BLACK-EYED PEA, CHICKPEA, SNOW PEA, SUGAR SNAP PEA.

PEA CATEGORIES

whole pea pods - entire pod is eaten young and fresh, such as the sugar snap pea and snow pea. See also MANGE-TOUT.

shelled pea - eaten shelled; also called baby pea, early pea, English pea, garden pea, June pea or sometimes called by its French name, *petit pois*.

field pea - grown specifically to be used dried; includes the black-eyed pea, chickpea, cowpea, green split pea and yellow pea.

pea bean - see NAVY BEAN.

peacemaker - a New Orleans specialty, consisting of a loaf of French bread scooped out in the center, buttered lavishly and filled with hot oysters. It was said that, in the early days of New Orleans, a Creole husband coming home in the morning hours would stop at a bakery in the French Quarter to buy one to take home to his wife, who was likely to be fuming because he'd stayed out so late.

peach - first discovered in Persia by the conquering army of Alexander the Great, who believed they originated there, hence their botanical name, *Prunus persica*. Also called Persian apples. But the luscious, juicy peach actually came from China 2,500 years ago, a far cry from the fruit we find in the market today. The first peaches were small, hard, sour and almost inedible. Still, the Chinese treasured them as a symbol of longevity and immortality. From China, peaches traveled along age-old caravan routes to the Near East and then to Greece and Rome. According to a modern currency conversion, a peach cost the equivalent of $4.50 in Rome during the

1st century BC and remained a luxury for centuries thereafter. Peaches were brought to the New World by Spanish, French and English explorers and settlers. Columbus was said to have brought the very first ones. The governor of Massachusetts Bay Colony requested that peaches be included among the first seeds sent to the colony in 1629.

Next to the apple, the peach is the most widely cultivated fruit tree in the world. Today, the U.S. produces one-quarter of the world's supply of peaches. It ranks as one of the four most popular North American fruits (the others being apple, banana and orange) and has more than 2,000 varieties, classified as **freestone,** for fruit that doesn't cling to the stone, and **clingstone,** for fruit that does. Freestones are popular for eating fresh and for canning and drying, while the clingstones, which have paler flesh, are useful for poaching, because they keep their shape and flavor. Usually, peaches are not sold by variety; they are more commonly sold by the color of their flesh — either "white" or "yellow." **Yellow peach varieties** include Flaming Fury, Crimson Lady, Candor, Derby, Sugar Time, Sweet Scarlet, Princess Gayle and Sweet September. **White peach varieties** include Spring Snow, Snow Prince, White Dragon, Ivory Princess, White Lady, Summer Sweet and Snow Giant. See also BLOOD PEACH.

peach Melba - created in 1894 by the great French chef **Auguste Escoffier** to honor Dame Nellie Melba, an Australian opera singer performing Wagner at Covent Garden and dining at the Savoy Hotel as a guest of the Duke of Orleans. Escoffier had never heard her sing, but knew she was partial to peaches and ice cream. The dish was later embellished with *sauce Cardinale*, raspberry purée with **Kirsch** and almonds.

peach palm - see HEARTS OF PALM.

pea crab - also **oyster crab.** See CRAB.

pea eggplant - see EGGPLANT.

peanut - also **groundnut.** The fruit of a perennial, *Arachis hypogaea*, which originated in South America, most likely Bolivia or Peru. The plant produces little, yellow flowers, which have the same life cycle as the morning glory. The buds open at sunrise; they're fertilized during the morning; and then wither before noon. A few days later, the floral stump will, on its own, extend, bend and penetrate the ground between 1 and 3 inches (2.5 and 7.5 cm). To harvest, the entire plant is extracted from the ground, laid to dry for a few days and then the nuts are separated from the bush. The Aztecs were already cultivating the peanut, which they called *tlacacahuatl*, in the 15th century, long before the arrival of the Spanish and the Portuguese. In the early 1500s, the Portuguese introduced peanuts to Africa and the Philippines.

The peanut's cultivation as a significant U.S. crop is rooted in African-American history. Slaves grew and ate peanuts, but their masters used them only as feed for swine. But the modest legume's profile would change drastically with the Civil War. Severe oil shortages soon led to the promotion of peanut oil for both human consumption and industrial use. Tasted and appreciated by Union soldiers, the peanut emerged from the conflict with an excellent reputation for good taste. Still, it wasn't until 1896 that the peanut was

transformed by its champion, **George Washington Carver** (1864–1943), the African-American agriculturalist who began his studies on peanuts and revolutionized farming in the South by developing more than 300 products from the peanut, making it into a $200 million industry by 1938.

Today, Asia and Africa are responsible for 90 percent of the world's production of peanuts, followed by India, China, the U.S., Nigeria and Indonesia.

peanut butter - a blend of ground shelled peanuts, vegetable oil and salt, originally devised by a St. Louis physician to nourish elderly patients and invalids. In 1903, Dr. Ambrose Straub patented a peanut-grinding machine. At the St. Louis World's Fair the next year, peanut butter was first introduced to the North American public, although Peruvians and Africans have been enjoying peanut paste for centuries. The process to keep the oil and peanut butter from separating was invented in 1923. It was vegetarian John Harvey Kellogg who really began to promote peanut butter in the early 1900s. His brother, Will, who founded the cornflake empire, then took up the torch.

peanut butter chips - as a follow-up to the ever-popular chocolate chips and to satisfy the North American appetite for all things peanut, peanut butter–flavored chips for baking were created in the latter half of the 1900s. Since both are often used in the same recipe, Hershey's introduced combination chocolate-peanut butter chips in 2002.

peanut oil - an excellent oil for frying, because of its neutral flavor and ability to take high heat. However, today's growing number of nut allergies has made the use of peanut oil dangerous, and in order to appease their clientele, many restaurants now clearly indicate on their menus if peanut oil is used on the premises.

pea pod - see POD PEA.

pear - a fruit of the genus *Pyrus*, grown by the Greeks and introduced to all the lands conquered by the Romans. By the Middle Ages, you could find pear trees in the gardens of European castles and monasteries. By the 17th century and for more than 100 years, cultivating pears was a popular hobby for wealthy gentlemen. A fierce rivalry flourished among aristocratic landowners in southern Europe. It became very fashionable to enter one's own estate-grown pear varieties in international horticultural exhibitions. Many of the varieties developed by these amateurs are still grown today. Jean Baptiste Van Mons (1765-1842), a prominent Belgian pharmacist and physicist, was perhaps the most prolific pear breeder of all time. Over a 60-year period Van Mons bred more than 40 superior varieties of pear. It is said Van Mons had at one time 80,000 seedlings growing in his garden. Van Mons loved to share his observations and plants with other fruit enthusiasts. To that end, he developed the first successful method of transporting cuttings and seedlings over vast distances, even as far as the United States. The Bosc pear, named after French horticulturist Louis Bosc, is thought by some observers to be a variety first developed by Van Mons.

The full names of some varieties, mainly those originating in Belgium, have the word *beurre* in their names to describe the soft, buttery, melting quality of the flesh. For this reason, pears are sometimes called "butter fruit." The first pear tree was planted on American soil in 1630, and pear trees are so hardy that they can bear fruit for a century or more. (For Pear Varieties see right.)

pearl onion - also **button onion.** An onion that is picked before it has reached full size, often used for pickling. It's available in white, yellow, pink, red and brown.

pearl sago - pellets of ground **sago** starch, shaped by pressing it as a paste through a sieve, then allowing the resulting "pearls" to dry. Ivory and opaque before they're cooked and translucent afterward, pearl sago is used in Asia and India for drinks, such as **bubble tea**, where it is used as a substitute for tapioca, and sweets, such as pudding.

pearl tea - see BUBBLE TEA, TEA.

peasemeal - milled, roasted yellow peas. Available in different grinds, this colorful, flavorful flour is popular in Scotland for making **bannock.**

pease porridge - a **mush** made from yellow split peas, which has been eaten in Britain for centuries, as the nursery rhyme declares, hot or cold or — in the pot — nine days old. About 400 years ago, a variation was created: the mush was wrapped in cloth (along with butter, mint,

PEAR VARIETIES

Anjou - light green with a yellow tinge when ripe, white flesh and a sweet flavor.

apple pear - see ASIAN.

Asian - also **apple pear, Chinese pear, Japanese pear, Nashi pear, nijisseiki, Oriental pear, salad pear, sand pear.** A firm, but juicy pear that ranges from golden brown to yellow green. It is noticeably more crunchy than European or North American varieties of pear. There are more than 100 varieties of pears, most of which come from Japan. **Nijisseiki,** a Japanese hybrid, is one of the most popular Asian pears around the world and is now grown in North America where it is also known as "20th Century."

Red Bartlett

Bartlett - bell-shaped with green-and-yellow speckled skin, representing 70 percent of the U.S. crop, first introduced by Enoch Bartlett in Massachusetts, brought from England, where it's called **William's Bon Chrétien.** Red Bartlett is essentially a Bartlett with bright red skin.

Bosc - long, with a distinctly tapered neck, sandy-textured brown skin and creamy flesh.

Chinese pear - see ASIAN.

Comice - rotund, with thick green skin and flesh that's sweet, juicy and buttery.

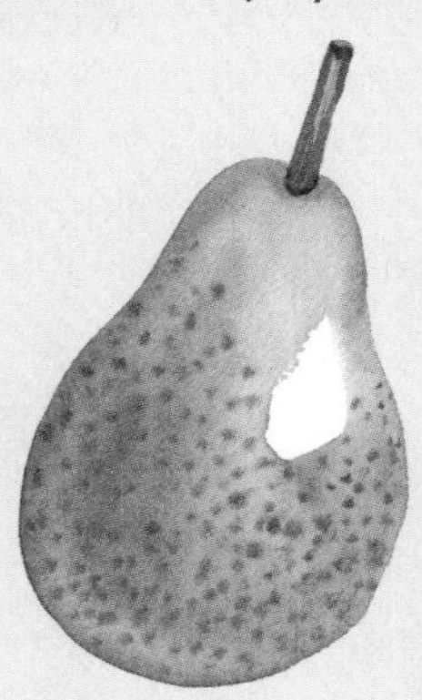

Forelle

Forelle - known as a great snacking pear, small, golden variety with a blush of red.

Japanese pear - see ASIAN.

Nashi pear - see ASIAN.

nijisseiki - see ASIAN.

Oriental pear - see ASIAN.

Passe-Crassane - a fairly new variety, a pear and quince hybrid, from California that tastes like an **Anjou** and a **Comice.**

salad pear - see ASIAN.

sand pear - see ASIAN.

Seckel - the smallest variety, with reddish skin, used more in cooking than for eating raw.

William's Bon Chrétien - see BARTLETT.

sugar, pepper and, if available, an egg), then simmered in a pot to make a more solid dish, pease pudding. Impatient cooks can now find the pudding in tins; it is still a common side dish for **Jiggs' dinner.**

pea shoots - **dau miao, dow miao, dow miu.** Tender, young spiraling stems, with newly opened leaves attached, harvested from the tips of pea plants (most often snow peas), which offer a taste reminiscent of peas, spinach and watercress all at once. Available in Asian markets, they are added to salads and, just before serving, to stir-fries.

pea soup - also **French-Canadian pea soup, habitant soup.** A hearty, traditional soup of the early farmers (called *habitants)* and settlers in Acadia and Quebec, made with ingredients such as dried yellow peas and salt pork, which kept well through the winter. Today, chopped ham often stands in for the salt pork, but the usual peas, with grated carrot, minced onion and **salted herbs,** remain. The **Newfoundland pea soup** version of the soup is similar, but contains larger chunks of carrot, along with chopped potato and turnip, and is served with doughboys (dumplings).

pecan - a nut from the hickory family. The name comes from the Algonquian word *pacane*, meaning "nut to be cracked with a rock," the fruit of an imposing tree that originated in the Mississippi Valley. The nuts were one of the staples of the Native American diet before the arrival of the Europeans. The pecan tree was a great source of fascination for Thomas Jefferson, who often wrote to his friends requesting nuts, eventually planting hundreds of pecan trees and generously sharing his yield with friends. On March 25, 1775, George Washington planted pecans at Mount Vernon from nuts sent to him by Jefferson. Three of the trees are still growing on the bank of the Potomac River. According to tradition, some of the pecan trees at the St. George Tucker House in Williamsburg, Virginia, grew from pecans that Jefferson gave to Tucker.

The U.S. has cultivated the pecan extensively, especially in Texas, New Mexico, Louisiana, Mississippi, Georgia and Florida. There are more than 300 varieties of pecan trees; one of them is adapted to cold climates and can be found growing in Canada. The first graft was made in 1846 by a Louisiana slave named Antoine, who was said to have grafted 126 trees in his lifetime. In the 1960s, Australia became a major producer, with Israel following suit in the 1970s.

The pecan tree can live hundreds, or even thousands, of years and can reach more than 16 feet (5 m) in height. Its flowers, not surprisingly, look like those of the hazelnut tree, since they belong to the same family. It takes 10 years for the tree to produce profitably, but from that time on, it can easily produce more than 400 pounds (180 kg) of nuts yearly. Pecans should be eaten within three weeks of harvesting, because their high oil content makes them go rancid quickly. See also HICKORY NUT.

pecan flour - see NUT FLOUR.

peccary - also **javelina, musk hog.** A tusked, wild mammal indigenous to the Americas, with a range that extends from the southern U.S. through Central and South America. Tough survivors in harsh environments, peccaries are classed as herbivores, but will eat anything (even prickly cactus and small animals) in a pinch. They resemble small, bristly pigs, but physical differences, such as hooves and their powerful musky smell, set them apart. Locally, "piglets" are often captured and kept as pets until they are big enough for the family cooking pot.

pecorino - from the Italian *pecora*, meaning "ewe" or "sheep," in all probability the oldest Italian cheese, dating back to ancient Rome. Then, as now, the cheeses were shaped and laid on *canestri*, rush mats strung together like hammocks, to let the cheese air-dry. Sicilian pecorino is still called *canestro* after these rush mats. All Italian cheeses made from ewe's milk are known as pecorino, but they vary a great deal in texture and flavor, from soft and mild to dry and strong.

pectin - a gelling agent, stabilizer and thickener sold as a syrup or powder, used in jellies and preserves, which pectin allows to gel because it imparts the requisite level of acidity. Pectin also occurs naturally in some fruits, at its optimal level when the fruit is just ripe; just before and just past maturity, the pectin will fail to set the juice naturally. Fruits with enough natural pectin to form a gel include crab apples, tart apples, quinces, sour blackberries, sour boysenberries, most plums, cranberries, lemons and wild grapes (Eastern Concord variety). Fruits low in pectin, requiring supplementary pectin to set, include cherries, ripe blackberries, grapefruit, grapes, melons and oranges. Fruits always requiring added pectin are peaches, pears, figs, apricots, elderberries, strawberries, raspberries, Western Concord grapes, guavas and pomegranates. Commercial pectins are made from apples or citrus fruits, and are available in both powdered and liquid forms, which are not interchangeable in recipes.

peccary

Pedro Ximénez - see SHERRY.

peel - **1.** (n.) also **rind.** The outermost layer, or skin, of a fruit or vegetable. **2.** (n.) also **baker's peel, pizza peel.** A wooden or metal tool with a large, flat, smooth paddle-shaped head and a long handle, used for slipping dough, such as for pizza or bread, into a hot oven, so that the baker doesn't have to reach into it. **3.** (v.) to remove the peel or rind of a fruit, using a paring knife or vegetable peeler. See also PARE.

peewee - see EGG SIZES.

Peking cabbage - see PO TSAI.

Peking duck - also **Beijing kao ya. 1.** an elaborate Chinese dish consisting of a duck that has had air pumped between its skin and flesh; the skin is then coated with honey and the bird is hung until the skin dries. This treatment makes the skin very crisp and golden, and the flesh very moist. Then, the duck is cooked in a specialized barrel oven, similar to a convection oven. The meat is cut into thin slices, each with a piece of skin; it is usually served rolled in very thin pancakes (called **bao bing**), Chinese onions and a special sauce. In the original recipe, long before Peking duck was called by that name, only the skin was offered to the guests, then the meat was taken back to the kitchen to be cooked with bean sprouts at an additional charge. The bones of the duck were used in duck soup, which also had an additional charge, and the dish was known as "Duck Three Ways." **2.** a breed of large, snow-white ducks of Chinese origin extensively raised in the U.S., usually referred to simply as Peking.

Peking sauce - see HOISIN SAUCE.

pekmez - a traditional, thick Turkish molasses made from grape juice that is used in cooking and as a health tonic. A variation called **dibs** has been made in Syria for centuries.

Pekoe - see TEA.

pemmican - from the Algonquian word *pime*, meaning "fat" or "grease," a staple of North American Indians, and later settlers, made of lean, dried meat that has been pounded into a paste, with melted fat added to bind and preserve it, usually carried on journeys in leather pouches. The Blackfoot used buffalo in their pemmican, cutting the meat into thin strips to dry, like jerky. Blackfoot pemmican was often mixed with crushed cherries and used in soups.

penne - see PASTA.

penne arrabbiata - see ARRABBIATA.

pennyroyal - the smallest species of mint, *Mentha pulegium*, native to Europe, Asia and North America, known by a number of odd names, among them "run by the ground," referring to how it grows, and "lurk in the ditch," for where it might be found. There are many dubious medicinal claims made for pennyroyal from relief of headaches to an antidote to hysteria. However, the best use for it is in a dog's bed where it will repel fleas.

pennyroyal

penuche - also **panocha.** A type of fudge originally from Mexico, now popular in the United States, made with coarse Mexican brown sugar called *panocha*, for which it is named. It sometimes contains nuts, such as walnuts or coconut. The American version substitutes regular brown sugar (sometimes mixed with corn syrup) as the sweetener.

peperonata - an Italian stew of red and yellow bell peppers, onions and tomatoes, possibly accented with garlic, fresh herbs and/or black olives. Served hot or cold, it can be used as a sauce for grilled or roasted meat or fish, pasta or plain potatoes. It also makes a delicious filling for omelets and is often served as a spread over grilled country bread.

peperoncini - see PEPPERONCINI.

pepián sauce - a classic, savory Mexican **mole** made with puréed seeds (such as pumpkin, sesame and squash) and nuts (such as almonds or peanuts), mixed with chopped hot chile pepper, garlic, herbs and onions, and oil. It is used as a marinade, poured on cooked foods as a sauce and served as a condiment on the side.

Homemade pepián ingredients vary with the cook; many ready-made versions of the sauce are also available.

Pépin, Jacques - see profile below.

pepitas - green pumpkin seeds used whole or hulled, raw or roasted in Mexican cooking. Pepitas may be puréed for **mole,** sprinkled on salads or soups, used in baked goods, or roasted and seasoned with cayenne pepper, garlic, salt and onion powder to eat as a savory snack.

pepparkakor - see PFEFFERNÜSSE.

pepper - see CHILE PEPPER, PEPPERCORN, SWEET PEPPER.

peppercorn

peppercorn - the most ubiquitous of spices, pepper accounts for one-quarter of the world's spice trade, starting out as small, green berries growing on vines in India, Indonesia, Malaysia, Brazil and Africa. The unripe berries can be dried or pickled as green peppercorns or dried to make black peppercorns or left on the vines to ripen and turn red, and then skinned and dried into white peppercorns. **Pink peppercorn** and **Szechwan pepper** are not really pepper, but actually berries from entirely different plants. See also CHILE PEPPER, SWEET PEPPER.

PEPPERCORN TYPES

Lampong - medium-hot, earthy with a woody undertone, the primary peppercorn grown in Indonesia, on the island of Sumatra.

Malabar - strong, full flavor with a definite pine undertone, from the Malabar Coast of southwest India.

Muntok - a white peppercorn, full-flavored but less pungent and with less of a pine undertone than black peppercorns, grown on the island of Bangka in Indonesia and named for the island's main port.

Sarawak - nutty and a bit fruitier than other peppercorns, they can have the husks removed to make white pepper or dried to make black pepper; from the region of Sarawak on the island of Borneo, in Malaysia.

Tellicherry - large in diameter, with a rich, spicy, aromatic flavor, from the city of Tellicherry, in northwest India.

Pépin, Jacques (1935–) - French chef, columnist, author and television host, Pépin began his culinary apprenticeship at the age of 13 in the town of his birth, Bourg-en-Bresse, near Lyon. Before moving to the U.S. in 1959, he was a personal chef to French dignitaries, among them Charles de Gaulle. For 10 years, he was director of research and new development for the Howard Johnson Co., a period during which he earned a master's degree in 18th-century French literature at Columbia University. He is the Dean of Special Programs at the French Culinary Institute in New York and founder of the American Institute of Wine and Food. For nearly a decade, innumerable aspiring cooks studied and referred to his two authoritative instructional books, *La Méthode* (1976) and *La Technique* (1979). He has written 21 books, columns for *The New York Times* and co-hosted two television programs with his daughter, Claudine. With Julia Child, Pépin taped 22 episodes of *Julia and Jacques Cooking at Home*, which won an Emmy Award in 2001. In 2006, Pépin received a Lifetime Achievement Award from the International Association of Culinary Professionals.

pepper Jack - a type of **Monterey Jack** cheese flavored with flecks of chopped hot peppers, usually jalapeños. Firmer, richer **Sonoma Jack** cheese is sometimes studded with hot peppers, too.

peppermint - a more pungent offspring of the spearmint, in use since biblical times. The main component of the mint's peculiarly refreshing active oil is menthol, widely used in many items on the market, including cigarettes, candy, liqueurs, toothpaste, mouthwash, cough drops, rubbing creams and room deodorizers. Menthol is a remarkable substance. At low concentrations, it raises the threshold temperature at which the cold receptors in our skin begin to discharge: it makes a warm mouth feel cool and cool drinks feel colder. In larger doses, it can be used as an anesthetic.

peppernodder - see PFEFFERNÜSSE.

pepperoncini - also **golden pepper, peperoncini, Tuscan pepper.** Slender, short sweet peppers popular in Mediterranean foods. The Italian variety ripens from green to red; the sweeter Greek version, also called "golden pepper," ripens to yellow-green. Usually dried, then pickled, pepperoncini are mild and salty, and are often served as an antipasto, in Greek salad and on top of pizza. This pepper is rated at 100 **Scoville units** or less.

pepperoni - a highly seasoned pork-and-beef sausage, commonly served on pizza.

pepper pot - also **pepperpot.** A kind of soup or stew seasoned with pepper. The best-known version is **Jamaican pepper pot soup,** usually made with the leafy green **callaloo,** pigs' tails and incendiary Scotch bonnet peppers. It is often finished with coconut milk. **Philadelphia pepper pot** is almost as well known. Legend has it that this version originated at Valley Forge, during the American Revolutionary War, when George Washington's cook used the ingredients at his disposal, tripe and black peppercorns, to make soup for his commander. Later versions of this soup substituted sea turtle or meat for the tripe and often added dumplings to the pot.

pepper steak - see STEAK AU POIVRE.

pepperweed - see MACA.

pequín - see CHILE PEPPER.

perch - the popular name of certain spiny-finned, freshwater fish of the genus *Perca,* from the Greek *perkos,* meaning "dark-colored," much appreciated by both the Greeks and Romans.

perilla - see SHISO.

periwinkle - also **bigaro, sea snail, winkle.** Any of a number of marine gastropod mollusks of the genus *Littorina,* eaten more frequently in Europe and Japan than in North America. They are available live in some fish markets and can also be found pickled in jars, usually in Asian or gourmet grocery stores. They are best cooked briefly (overcooking can make them tough), and are often served simply dressed as an appetizer or in the French manner of serving escargots, that is, tossed with garlic butter.

periwinkle

Pernod - anise-flavored liqueur produced by entrepreneur Henri-Louis Pernod in the distillery he opened in the French town of Pontarlier in 1805. He was the first to legally produce this type of anise liqueur after absinthe was outlawed. The drink is mixed with water, the usual ratio being one-third Pernod to two-thirds water. See also OUZO.

perry - a fermented cider-like beverage made from pear juice, predominantly in England.

Persian apple - actually a name for peaches. Although they are native to China, peaches were first imported to Europe by the Romans about 2,000 years ago, from Persia and given this name. See also PEACH.

Persian walnut - also **English walnut.** A walnut with a native range from eastern Europe to the Himalayas, now grown commercially in

North America in California. Unlike other walnuts, the shell of *Juglans regia* parts easily from the nut.

persillade - from the French *persil*, meaning "parsley," a sprinkling of the herb, finely chopped, or a mixture of parsley and garlic or shallots sprinkled over meat or fish.

persimmon - nicknamed "apple of the Orient," the national fruit of Japan, where it's been cultivated for about 1,000 years, although it came originally from China. The persimmon as we known it, *Diospyros kaki*, came to North America with Commodore Perry in 1852, and many varieties were grafted onto Native American rootstock. The persimmon native to North America is the *Diospyros virginiana*, the one that Native Americans called *putchamin*, *pasiminan* or *pessamin*.

In 1863, Logan Martin, a young Indiana entrepreneur, brought two buckets of wild persimmons to market in Louisville, Kentucky, and had such success that he began growing persimmons commercially. For more than 40 years, "Persimmon Martin," as he was known, shipped wild persimmons from his hometown, principally to New York.

Indians showed the settlers how to make persimmon beer and bread. A certain John Bradbury, while traveling in the Missouri territory in 1809, gave details of his encounter with an Osage chief, who offered him "a delicious gingerbread," which turned out to be a combination of yellow cornmeal and wild persimmon.

The persimmon is a member of the same family as ebony, and its hard wood was once highly prized for making the woods in golf clubs. A particularity of this brilliant orange fruit is that its skin reaches full color before the fruit is ripe, so that many people eat the persimmon too soon and find it unpleasantly astringent and bitter to eat. The fruit is ready to eat when it's so soft that it feels as if it could lose its shape if it wasn't encased in skin, smooth enough to spoon out like a pudding.

Hachiya persimmon

PERSIMMON VARIETIES

The fruit can be eaten fresh or cooked and is often candied. It's available from midsummer to midwinter.

Fuyu - a small variety with a flat bottom, looks very much like a medium-size tomato. For marketing purposes, most of the persimmons found and grown in the U.S. have Asian names.

Hachiya - a large variety, bright orange, slightly elongated tomato-shape that almost comes to a point at the bottom.

Peruvian carrot - also **Peruvian parsnip.** See ARRACACHA.

pescatarian - also **pescetarian.** An almost-vegetarian who consumes fish and seafood, but no meat. Some pescatarians eat fish and poultry, but no red meats (beef, lamb, pork); some include dairy products in their diets and others don't. The term derives from the same Latin root of the Italian *pesce* and the Spanish *pescar*, both words for "fish." See also VEGETARIAN.

pestle - a club small enough to hold upright in one fist over a mortar, and used to pound foods into a paste or powder. A larger, long-handled version, called a "purée pestle," is used to force soft foods through a sieve. See also MORTAR AND PESTLE.

pesto - an Italian sauce that gets its name from *pestare*, the technique of crushing or grinding its ingredients (basil leaves, garlic, olive oil and pine nuts) in a mortar (*mortaio*) and pestle (*pestello*). Historians believe pesto to be a descendent of the Roman **garum** sauce, part of a family of sauces mostly acidic and aromatic in character, very unlike our modern oil-based pesto and its many variations, which include combinations of mint, coriander, parsley, almond, pistachio and walnut.

Peter Heering - a rich, red fragrant Danish liqueur credited to **Peter Frederik Heering,** a Copenhagen grocer who created the first batch for his customers in the late 1700s. Made from Scandinavian Stevns cherries, it is aged in oak for three years. Sipped as an apéritif or after-dinner drink, it may also be added to cocktails, such as the **Singapore Sling,** or poured over ice cream. See also CHERRY LIQUEUR.

Petit Brie - see COULOMMIERS.

petit déjeuner - French for "breakfast."

petite marmite - in French, "small kettle," created in Paris in 1867 by chef and restaurateur Modeste Magny for a vegetable soup served from a small, tabletop earthenware pot. Magny's restaurant is where the writers George Sand and Gustave Flaubert met for the first time.

petit four - elaborately decorated miniature cake, the name being French for "little oven," referring to the small ovens used to bake them during the 18th century. These bite-size cakes first presented at the court of Louis XIV, were so tender and rich, they had to be served immediately after they were taken out of the oven.

petit-gris - see SNAIL.

petit pain - French for "roll" (or "little bread").

petits pois - a French term for tiny peas gathered when still very sweet and tender.

petit-Suisse - a Swiss cream cheese named for the young Swiss cowherd who first suggested adding a little fresh cream to the curd of the local cheese, resulting in one of the softest and fluffiest such cheeses in Europe.

petticoat tails - a Louisiana shortbread from a recipe brought to America by Scottish immigrants, often baked in molds shaped like various pieces of women's undergarments. However, their name more likely arises from 16th-century Scotland, where one of Mary Stuart's francophile courtiers called them *petits gastels*, which later became *petits gateaux*, meaning "little cakes."

Peychaud, Antoine - see COCKTAIL, SAZERAC.

Pfeffernüsse - also **pepparkakor, peppernodder. 1.** a dark, spicy, spherical cookie enjoyed at Christmas. In her book, *Around the Year with the Trapp Family*, Maria Augusta von Trapp — of the famous *The Sound of Music* family — wrote that these are Austrian cookies, but Germans (the name is German for "peppernuts") claim this cookie as their own. Most European countries have their own version, however. Almost all are sweetened with corn syrup, honey or molasses, and contain ground spices, such as anise, cinnamon, cloves, ginger, nutmeg and — no surprise, given their name — black pepper. Today's cooks may add lemon juice and zest, chopped nuts and raisins, then dust the baked cookies with confectioner's sugar or frost or glaze them. Akin to **jawbreakers,** in size, shape and crunch, Pfeffernüsse are often dunked in coffee to make them more chewable. American Mennonites make softer versions (some with all the spices, some with anise only); the dough is rolled into long ropes, then cut into short sections and laid close together, end to end, on the baking sheet to make a cookie version of **pull-aparts. 2.** a traditional crusty, spiced Russian yeast bread, sweetened with homemade **watermelon syrup.**

pH - a measure of acidity or alkalinity (the lowercase "p" stands for "potential," the uppercase "H" is the chemical symbol for hydrogen). The value is plotted on a standard scale with pH levels that change tenfold between the numbered increments and range from 0 through 14. Values moving from 0 through 6 indicate descending levels of acidity (lemon juice hovers around 2); values moving from 8 (egg white sits about here) through 14 indicate ascending levels of alkalinity. On this scale, 7 is neutral; pure water has this value, which is why some bottled water producers boast of their "pH balanced water." Food processors add acidifiers to some foods, such as pie fillings and puddings, to lower their pH. This helps prevent the growth of toxic bacteria, in particular, *Clostridium botulinum*, which causes botulism. Since the pH level affects the aroma, color, flavor and taste of a wine (and how it will age), vintners also watch the pH of their products carefully. During winemaking, a low pH inhibits bacteria, while it assists fermentation; in the finished wine, a pH of between 3 and 3.5 is desired.

phalsa - also **shukri.** A large shrub, indigenous to India and Southeast Asia, which bears clusters of sweet-tart purple-black berries, used in desserts, drinks and syrups. The fresh leaves are applied as an acne treatment and also used as animal fodder. Since the fruit should be used within 24 hours after it is picked, commercial cultivation of *Grewia subinaequalis* takes place close to cities. Recently, tests have been undertaken to determine whether phalsa would be a viable crop in the southern United States, such as Georgia.

pheasant

pheasant - a game bird, *Phasianus colchicus*, of striking plumage. From the Middle Ages to about the 18th century, it was the tradition to set aside the head and tail and to reassemble the cooked bird in its plumage to bring it to the table. There are many varieties all over the world; the type we know in North America was imported from Shanghai in the late 19th century.

phenols - also **phenolic compounds.** A group of naturally occurring acidic compounds found in a variety of foods that give them certain colors, flavors and acidity. In wines, phenols play a large role, coming from grape skins, seeds and stems, as well as from oak barrels in which some wines are aged. **Tannins,** also called polymeric phenols, are responsible for a wine's astringency and **mouth feel. Anthocyanins,** the reddish purple pigments in grape skins, are other phenolic compounds present in red wine in great quantities, determining the richness of the wine's color. The flavor compound vanillin, which is found in oak barrels and leaches into wine that is aged in them, is another example of a phenol.

phenylethylamine - a chemical in chocolate nicknamed "chocolate amphetamine" that along with the stimulants caffeine and theobromine (just two of the 300 or so chemicals in chocolate) is thought to cause an emotional high and a feeling of contentment. Perhaps it's no wonder that, on average, each person around the globe consumes about 12 pounds (6 kg) of chocolate in as many months.

Philadelphia cheese steak - also **Philly cheese steak.** See CHEESE STEAK.

Philadelphia pepper pot - see PEPPER POT.

Philadelphia-style ice cream - also **New York–style ice cream.** An American type of ice cream made without egg yolks, based solely on cream, sugar and flavorings, yielding a rich result that is not as silky and smooth as **French ice cream.**

Philippine nut - see PILI NUT.

pho - the classic Vietnamese beef noodle soup, made with **banh pho** and thin slices of (usually rare) beef in a spicy, extremely flavorful, fragrant broth. The dish is served with a plate of fresh garnishes that diners can add as they like, including cilantro, Asian basil, sliced chiles, bean sprouts and wedges of lime to squeeze over top. Pho has become an urban staple in many cities across North America, thanks to the influx of Vietnamese refugees, who immigrated to North America during the Vietnam War in the 1970s and set up restaurants serving their native specialties.

phosphorus - a mineral necessary to sustain life. Phosphorus, usually in phosphate form, is found in cereals, dairy foods, dried beans and peas, meat, nuts and seeds, and in many multivitamin pills. In Canada, the **RDI** (Recommended Daily Intake) for phosphorus is 1100 mg; in the U.S., the **RDA** (Recommended Daily Allowance) is 1000.

phulka - a paper-thin, dinner-plate size **chapati** made with whole wheat flour that is often enriched with butter, buttermilk or **ghee.** Cooked on a hot, ungreased iron griddle called a "tava," each side is fried until it's blistered and freckled with brown, then, after flipping it back onto the first side, light pressure is applied to make it puff up. Experienced cooks flip the phulka with their fingers, instead of a spatula and, if they have a gas oven, puff them up directly over the open flame. Phulka are usually eaten hot off the griddle and simply buttered with ghee. See also CHAPATI, ROTI.

phyllo - also **filo.** An exceedingly thin pastry dough, phyllo gets its name from the Greek word for "leaf," used in many Greek and Near Eastern savory dishes and desserts, often brushed with butter and layered, as in **baklava, spanakopita** and **bastila.**

phylloxera - the American vine louse, which affects grapevines, first seen in Kew, England, in 1863, currently found on every continent and island in the world, with few exceptions. Indigenous North American vines, having been partly immune to this pest, are now largely used in European and other vineyards as the stems upon which the various species of *Vitis vinifera*, the European vine, are grafted.

physalis - also **love-in-a-cage.** A generic name given most often to **cape gooseberry** (*Physalis peruviana*), but also used for **ground cherry** (*P. pubescens*) and **tomatillo** (*P. ixocarpa*). The dry, paper-like husk that encloses each fruit may have earned the plant's nickname, lovein-a-cage. While these physalis are edible, Agriculture and Agri-Food Canada warns that some of their cousins, imported from Asia and now naturalizing along roadsides in eastern Canada, can be toxic to humans and their pets.

picada - **1.** a classic savory sauce from Catalonia, in northeastern Spain, usually comprised of almonds, herbs, spices and bread crumbs pounded together in a **mortar and pestle** or puréed in a blender. Picada is traditionally added to dishes after they have finished cooking, as a thickener and flavor enhancer. Contemporary chefs experiment with picada by introducing untraditional ingredients to the blend and adding them at different stages in the cooking process. **2.** a sweet paste made of dry bread crumbs, cocoa powder, oil and possibly brandy, pounded or puréed together and used as a coating or stuffing for entrées, such as duck, fish or lamb. **3.** in Mexico, a salsa made with avocado, chile peppers, coriander, onions and tomatoes, and served with **chicharrón** (crisp pork rind). **4.** in Chile, a small, simple and inexpensive family-style restaurant. **5.** in Argentina, an array of **hors d'oeuvres** in small dishes, served, usually with **vermouth,** as a snack or small meal.

picadillo - a Spanish and Mexican dish of chopped or ground pork, veal and tomatoes, Spanish for "ground meat."

picante - Spanish for "piquant," hot or spicy. Throughout the American Southwest, the Caribbean, Mexico and South America, it's an adjective often applied to any dish cooked with hot sauce or salsa.

piccalilli - an East Indian pickled relish resembling a chutney, consisting of cauliflower, gherkins and onions blended in mustard sauce with pungent spices, used mainly with cold meats and cheeses.

piccata - an Italian dish made of thinly sliced rounds of veal (or, occasionally, of chicken, fish or other meat), dredged in flour, then sautéed in a mixture of lemon juice and seasoned butter. Served with a sauce made from the pan drippings, more lemon juice and wine, the piccata is usually garnished with chopped parsley.

pickerel - from "pike," the name applies to several small freshwater fish of the pike family. The meat is white, flaky, quite bony and somewhat dry, although sweet-tasting; it is usually poached in **court-bouillon.** See also NORTHERN PIKE.

pickling cucumbers

pickle - **1.** (v.) to preserve or **cure** a food in a salty, flavored brine or vinegar solution. **2.** (n.) a food that has been pickled in brine or vinegar, such as cucumbers, cocktail onions, peppers or hot pepper rings. See also BREAD-AND-BUTTER PICKLE, DILL PICKLE, TSUKEMONO.

pickling cucumber - any one of a number of cultivars, including several "burpless" varieties that are designed to produce straight, stubby cucumbers with crisp, firm flesh and knobby but tender skin for pickle making. Home canners who grow their own are advised to check their vines every other day, since cucumbers develop so quickly. For sweet pickles, the cucumbers should be picked at less than 2 inches (5 cm) long, for dills, between 4 and 6 inches (10 and 15 cm). See also KIRBY CUCUMBER.

pickling salt - also **canning salt, canning and pickling salt.** Pure, fine-crystal salt with no impurities or additives, such as iodine and/or anti-caking agents, which darken pickles and make brines cloudy. Pickling salt can be used in the same manner as table salt, but other sources of iodine should be included in the diet to prevent thyroid diseases caused by iodine deficiency.

pickling spice - a ready-made spice mix usually containing whole allspice berries, bird's eye chiles, black peppercorns and cloves as well as dill, fennel and mustard seeds, crushed bay leaves and cinnamon. The whole spices are added to the brine for foods, such as pickled cucumbers, eggs, green tomatoes, salmon and walnuts, or appetizers, such as **Solomon Gundy.** Wrapped whole in cheesecloth, they may be added to the pot when cooking crab, sauces, soups or stews, then removed before the food is served, or crushed and added to a roast, such as **brisket.**

picnic - a casual, friendly meal taken on a day trip, eaten outdoors, usually in summer, from the French *piquer,* meaning "to pick at food," and *nique*, meaning "something small or inconsequential." Originally, "picnic" referred to an informal meal in which everyone paid their share or brought their own dish.

picnic ham - made from the front leg of the pig, called the "picnic shoulder," which is fattier and less expensive than the hind, usually smoked, served baked, sliced and pan-fried, or boiled.

pico de gallo - also **salsa Mexicana.** A fresh salsa of coarsely chopped chile peppers (usually jalapeño or serrano), coriander, onions and tomatoes, tossed with lemon or lime juice, then served immediately or briefly chilled. Since the green peppers, red tomatoes and white onions share the colors of their flag, Mexicans like to claim — and name — this salsa as their own. Some cooks add other ingredients, such as chopped **jicama,** avocado, cucumber and radishes. "Pico de gallo" is Spanish for "rooster's beak," and some say this refers to the salsa's sharp, spicy kick, which is like a rooster's peck.

pie bird

pico de gallo seasoning mix - a ready-made mixture of lime powder, chile peppers and seasonings, with all the hot, spicy flavor of the famous salsa of the same name. The mix is a popular seasoning for fresh fruits, such as mangoes, melons, oranges and papayas, as well as corn, **jicama** and other vegetables.

picon - **1.** a bitter, orange-flavored French apéritif made with **cinchon** and gentian, and named after Gaeten Picon, who created it in the 1830s. It's usually labeled "Amer" (French for "bitter") Picon. A companion drink to beer and white wine, picon is mixed into various cocktails and is also the main ingredient of Basque picon punch, which combines brandy, grenadine, seltzer or soda water and picon, and is garnished with curls of lemon zest. **2.** a sharp, Spanish blue cheese made from cow's, ewe's or goat's milk.

pie - any of various dishes of meat, vegetables or fruit that are baked in a pastry crust, with or without a top crust. The word is said to be derived from "magpie," from medieval times in France, when live birds were baked under a crust just enough to stun them; when the pie was opened, they would fly out "to the merriment of all present."

Pies originated as main-course dishes with meat, vegetables and spices. Mince pie was made of highly spiced, chopped meat and fruits in gravy. The sweet fruit pie, served as a dessert, came much later. To North Americans, "pie" refers to something baked under or in a pastry crust. See also PÂTÉ.

pie à la mode - see À LA MODE.

pie bird - also **pie chimney, pie funnel, pie vent.** A broad-bottomed, hollow, usually ceramic, funnel traditionally shaped like a singing bird with its head thrown back and its beak open. It is set upright in the center of a pie before the filling is added and left protruding through the top crust. As the pie bakes, the bird acts as a vent for heat and steam, and prevents the juices from bubbling over. Bakers have used these apparently playful, but actually practical, vents for hundreds of years. Early ceramic and glass versions, some handmade and some embossed with the trademark of their makers, are avidly collected, especially in the United Kingdom and the U.S.

pie dish - also **pie pan, pie plate.** A rimmed, round pan usually made of heatproof ceramic, glass or metal, available in various sizes, most often 8-, 9- and 10-inch (20, 23 and 25 cm) diameters. Most have a side that slopes to the center, so an angled pie server can slip down the side and cleanly lift out each piece. The standard depth is 1½ inches (4 cm), but a deep-dish version, often used for both dessert and main-dish pies, is usually 2 inches (5 cm) deep, and may have two small, opposite handles extending from the rim. Special fruit-pie dishes have a groove around the rim that traps any bubbled-over juice and prevents spills from burning on the bottom of the oven. And some specialty versions have a wide, fluted rim that serves as a mold for shaping the edge of the crust. Some pie makers prefer the even heating of a ceramic dish; others like to see the bottom crust browning through a clear, heatproof glass model. And for picnics and potlucks, disposable foil pie dishes are available.

pie fork - a fork having broad, stubby tines (and often an extra-sturdy cutting tine on the left-hand edge), designed to slice through, slip under and lift bite-size pieces of pie neatly to the mouth. Shorter in the handle than its complementary dinner fork, a pie fork is not used for stabbing food, so has tines with duller, rounded tips.

pieds et paquets - see PIGS' FEET.

pie plant - see RHUBARB.

pierogi - see PIROZHKI.

pie weights - marble-size, usually round, ceramic or stainless-steel weights, which, distributed evenly over an empty, unbaked pie or tart shell, keep the bottom from warping or pulling away from the pan as the pastry bakes. You can also use large, dried beans or a cupful of rice, instead.

pig - a young swine, less than 125 pounds (56 kg), of either sex, before it has reached the age of sexual maturity, when it becomes a hog. A piglet is a nursing pig. A sow is a mature female pig. See also PORK.

pigeon - any of a number of different birds of the genus *Columba*, about 1 pound (500 g) each, found in many parts of the world, from Europe to North America to North Africa. Pigeons are farm-raised and hunted in the wild. They can be stuffed and roasted whole, grilled or braised, or turned into the classic dish pigeon pie, or **squab** pie, named after the immature form of the pigeon.

pigeon pea - also **gandule, no-eyed pea.** A beige bean that takes the name "pea" from its shape, size and sweetish flavor. A staple of the Caribbean, used extensively in rice dishes and soups, they're probably best known in Trinidad's pigeon pea soup and jug-jug, from Barbados, a dish derived from haggis, brought by Scottish exiles after the Monmouth Rebellion. Since this bean has no dot or "eye" (unlike, for example, the black-eyed pea), it is also called "no-eyed."

pignolo - pl. **pignoli. 1.** The Italian term for pine nut. **2.** sweet sugar cookies — popular throughout southern Italy — flavored with almond paste and pine nuts.

pigs' feet - also called **trotters** in Britain. Classified as **variety meat,** pigs' feet are actually the ankles with the feet attached. After simmering in **court-bouillon** for up to six hours, pigs' feet are served with the broth, or fried, grilled or broiled. The meat may be used in salads, soups or stews, added to sausages or served in *pieds et paquets*, a regional dish of Provence. Billie Holiday sang about them in *Gimme a Pigfoot (and a Bottle of Beer)*. A favorite bar food, pickled pigs' feet are a staple in **souse.**

pigs in a blanket - also **dogs in a blanket, pups in a blanket, saucijzenbroodjes. 1.** a quick campfire snack or hors d'oeuvre from the 1950s, made by wrapping refrigerated prepared crescent- or dinner-roll dough around a cocktail wiener, hot dog or cooked sausage; in some versions, a slice of American cheese is wrapped around the meat, first, under the dough. They may be skewered with toothpicks, which hold them together and act as handles to pick them up. **2.** a type of Dutch-American sausage roll, popular in the Midwest. Ground beef, pork, sausage or turkey (or a combination of one or more) are mixed with beaten egg, bread crumbs and spices, such as curry, nutmeg and paprika, then divided into individual portions and rolled up in squares of puff pastry or sour-cream dough and cooked.

pigweed - see EPAZOTE.

pike - see NORTHERN PIKE.

pilaf - also **pi-laff, pilau, pilaw.** From the Turkish *pilav* and the Persian *pilaw,* meaning "boiled rice," pilaf is a method of preparing rice. In Greece, it's a simple boiled rice dish, which can be mixed with pine nuts or raisins, if desired. In eastern Mediterranean countries, it's a mixture of rice, lamb or chicken, fruits (raisins, currants, apricots or prunes), nuts, vegetables and seasonings. In Iran, where it's called *polo,* it's made with rice, lima beans, lamb, dill, pepper and cinnamon. Today, the term is more often applied to the method of cooking the rice lightly in butter or oil with a chopped onion, stirred over the heat until the grains are slightly cooked, and then adding a broth or stock before boiling.

pilchard - see SARDINE.

pili nut - also **Java almond, Philippine nut.** The sweet kernel produced by about 75 different trees, growing from Africa through India and Asia to the Pacific, that belong to the *Canarium* genus. A major source of fat and protein for people in these regions, pili nut is cultivated most extensively in the Philippines; much of its harvest is exported to Hong Kong and Taiwan for use in traditional **mooncakes.** Roasted and sugared, the pili nuts are a popular snack sold by Philippine street vendors and are used in a variety of foods, such as sweet potato pudding. The kernels are also used in the production of chocolate, ice cream, marzipan and other confections. Oil is pressed from them, as well, and young shoots of the large shade trees are eaten in salads.

pili-pili - see PIRI-PIRI.

Pi Lo Chun - see TEA.

pilot's bread - see HARDTACK.

Pilsner - see BEER.

Pilsner glass - a tall trumpet-shaped glass with a narrow bottom and a flared top, used to serve **Pilsner beers** so that the maximum amount of effervescence is retained. A **Black Velvet** is excellent served in this type of glass if a Champagne **flute** is not available.

pimentón - very hot, Spanish smoked paprika. Its intense color and flavor spice up chili, egg dishes, spiced roasted nuts, paella, stews and all kinds of Southwest foods; it is added to marinades and rubs, as well. It's usually available in three grades, which may be labeled "bittersweet," "sweet" and "hot" or *dulce, agridulce* and *picante.*

pimiento - also **pimento. 1.** a heart-shaped, sweet red bell pepper, often sliced as a garnish or stuffed into pitted green olives. Most of the crop is grown for the production of paprika, but pimiento is also used as an ingredient in salads, chili, stews, or roasted on its own, or cored, stuffed and cooked. It is available bottled, canned or fresh. It is rated at 500 **Scoville units** or less. **2.** the common name of the *Pimenta dioica* tree from which allspice berries are harvested. See also CHILE PEPPER, PAPRIKA, SWEET PEPPER.

pimiento cheese - a mixture of chopped canned pimientos, grated Cheddar or shredded American cheese, mayonnaise, salt and pepper that is a popular sandwich spread and topping for grilled hot dogs and hamburgers, especially in the southern U.S. Spicy ingredients, such as cayenne pepper, mustard and Worcestershire sauce, are sometimes added.

Pimm's Cup - the quintessential cocktail of the annual Royal Ascot horse race and British summer afternoons, a Pimm's Cup is made with **Pimm's No. 1 liquor,** lemonade or lemon-lime soda, a twist of lemon and a slice of cucumber. Some aficionados claim that it's not a real Pimm's Cup unless Champagne, not lemonade, is the mixer.

Pimm's No. 1 liquor - an English gin-based liquor flavored with a secret blend of herbs, quinine and bitters, invented by a London oyster bar owner by the name of James Pimm in the 1840s, originally taken as a digestive tonic. After the Second World War, the Pimm's line expanded to include a range of flavored liquors: No. 2 was made with whiskey, No. 3 with brandy, No. 4 with rum, No. 5 with rye and No. 6 with vodka. The only variety other than the original No. 1 now in production is the vodka-based

No. 6, although it is increasingly hard to find. Tea-colored and citrusy in taste, Pimm's No. 1 is the base of the staggeringly popular English cocktail **Pimm's Cup.**

pimprenelle - see SALAD BURNET.

piña colada - a cocktail consisting of rum, cream of coconut and pineapple juice or crushed pineapple, blended with ice until thick and smooth, served in a cocktail glass with a wedge of fresh pineapple and a maraschino cherry. The name is Spanish, *piña* meaning "pineapple" and *colada* meaning "strained," because the pulp from the pineapple is strained out.

pinang - see BETEL NUT.

pinch - a common yet imprecise measure for a tiny amount of a dry ingredient, such as a spice or salt, equal to the amount one can pinch between the tip of the thumb and forefinger. See also DASH.

pineapple - a tropical fruit, *Ananas comosus*, of the Bromeliaceae family, believed to have originated in Brazil, where they were called *na-na*, meaning "fragrance" or "excellence." On November, 4, 1493, Columbus, on his second voyage to the Caribbean, landed ashore on the island of Guadeloupe where he and his crew became the first Europeans to taste the pineapple. Looking a bit like a pine cone and tasting sweet like an apple, the fruit was soon dubbed "pineapple."

pineapple

The best-known relative of the pineapple is Spanish moss, the gray-green fringe that hangs from trees in some of the southern U.S. states.

The first description we have of the pineapple dates from 1493, from Gonzalo de Oviedo y Valdes, who wrote that the *piñas* "combined the flavor of melons, strawberries, raspberries and pippin apples." Everyone who tasted the fruit, when it first appeared in Europe, raved about it, except Charles V, king of Spain, who refused to taste it for fear of being poisoned. Louis XIV was very hostile to pineapple because, when he was first offered the fruit, he greedily bit into it, with all its prickly "eyes." Louis XV, on the other hand, ordered a special hothouse for the cultivation of the fruit.

Pineapples were growing in India by 1548 and, by the end of the next century, had been planted by missionaries and navigators in parts of Africa and China. In 1790, a Spanish adventurer named Don Francisco de Paula Y Marin brought pineapples to Hawaii. English horticulturist Captain John Kidwell, living in Hawaii in 1885, developed the first practical method of farming pineapple. By 1901, with Captain Kidwell's knowledge in hand, American agriculturalist James Dole created a thriving Hawaiian pineapple business, canning and exporting the fruit to grocery store shelves all over North America. The exporting of Hawaiian pineapples was such a success the tropical island's name, for a good part of the 20th century, became almost synonymous with the fruit.

The pineapple plant can produce fruit almost indefinitely, but from a commercial standpoint, each plant is allowed to bear fruit for five to 10 years only; then, the field is replanted. It's available year-round and makes an excellent dessert fruit. It can be bought fresh or canned (in chunks, rings and diced). The pineapple has long been a symbol of hospitality; it appears often as a door-knocker design, stenciled on walls and carved on antique bedposts. In Victorian England, English growers rented pineapples to their friends to grace the center of a festive table.

pineapple guava - see FEIJOA.

pineapple upside-down cake - a white cake baked in a pan in which canned, sliced pineapple rounds have been laid in a syrup of brown sugar and butter on the bottom; the cake is turned over onto a platter to reveal the glazed fruit topping. It's usually served cold, with vanilla ice cream or whipped cream. This particular version of **upside-down cake** became popular after the 1920s, when pineapple, once an expensive luxury, became common — out of a can — in North American kitchens, and an active Hawaiian Pineapple Growers Association developed recipes to promote its product as an exotic, affordable addition to almost any dish.

pine mushroom - see MATSUTAKE.

pine nuts - also **pignoli, pigñon, snoober.** The naked seeds, *Pinus pinea,* found in the cones of many different species of pine tree. Pine nuts are mentioned in the Bible and were eaten by the Romans. In Mexico and the southern U.S., they were an enduring staple of the indigenous diet. In the Middle East, they're popular in **dolma.** Because they're rich and creamy, pine nuts were eaten during Lent, when most foods of substance, including meat and cheese, were forbidden. Like peanuts, they're eaten raw or roasted and salted, often used in soups, sauces, stews and confectionery. A pine tree started from seed will take about 75 years to reach a commercial level of pine nut production. Pine nuts are known as *pignolo* in Italian, *piñón* in Spanish and *pinion* in French.

pinga - see CACHAÇA.

pink bean - also **habicheula rosada.** This oval pink legume is grown around the globe. With proper storage, the dried beans will keep indefinitely. The older the beans, the longer the cooking time; when cooked, they triple in volume. Popular in Caribbean, Creole and Southwest cuisine, pink beans are used in refried-bean and rice dishes, salads, soups — such as Hawaiian **kau kau** — and stews, and can stand in for kidney or pinto beans. See also BEAN.

Pink Lady - a cocktail usually made with gin, **Grenadine,** lemon or lime juice, egg white and cream, shaken together with ice, then strained into a stemmed glass. See also WHITE LADY.

pink lentil - see LENTIL.

pink peppercorn - the berry from the South American native plants, *Schinus molle* and *S. terebinthifolius* (also called Christmas berry and pepper tree) and not a true peppercorn at all. After importation to the southern U.S., *S. terebinthifolius* quickly naturalized and became a threat to native plant species, especially in California and Florida. Under cultivation on Réunion Island in the Indian Ocean, in contrast, it became a lucrative crop. Packed in France and often labeled *baies roses,* these pink peppercorns were popularized in **nouvelle cuisine,** as much for their looks as for their delicate taste.

The pink berries, picked just before they are fully ripe, have hard, sweet kernels with a resinous flavor. The berries are sold at premium prices alone — dried, pickled or packed in water — or in ready-made, "rainbow" mixes that often include black and green peppercorns from *Piper nigrum* (true peppercorns), often with whole allspice added for an extra kick. Encased in clear peppermills, these attractive mélanges are a fixture at some upscale eateries. Since the flavor is overpowered by the other ingredients, however, some chefs recommend using pink peppercorns on their own. A light touch is also recommended — pink peppercorns are slightly toxic, so they should not be consumed in large quantities. And don't confuse them with the "true" red peppercorns — mature berries of *P. nigrum* — seen in southern India and often sold still on their stems. These have a mellow and sweet, but genuine peppery flavor. See also PEPPERCORN.

pink tangelo - see LAVENDER GEM.

pinole - **1.** toasted or baked, finely ground cornmeal used by indigenous people in the American Southwest and Mexico. Its name derives from the Nahuatl word *pinolli.* Early settlers in Virginia called it **rockahominy;** they prized it for its keeping qualities and easy portability. **2.** finely ground meal made from **chia seeds,** grains or **mesquite** seeds, called "beans." **3.** a drink made from pinole. The Hopi are known to have made some version of this; today's recipe usually contains baked cornmeal simmered with cinnamon, milk and sugar.

piñón - pl. **piñones.** The Spanish name for pine nut.

Pinotage - a grape variety mostly restricted to South Africa, created by crossing the Cinsault grape (from the Rhône) with the Pinot Noir.

pinto bean - a tan bean with red markings, sold dry or canned, from the Spanish, meaning "painted." See also BEAN.

pinwheel cookie - also **rolled cookie.** A round cookie with an attractive spiral design. For one version, the mixed dough is rolled flat then spread with a filling, such as **lekvar,** rolled up, jelly-roll fashion, wrapped tightly with plastic wrap and refrigerated for about four hours until firm. Then the roll is unwrapped and sliced into thin rounds, revealing the spiral of dough and filling, and baked. For another version, the mixed dough is halved. A flavoring or coloring agent, such as cocoa powder or food coloring, is mixed into one half; the other is left plain. Each dough is rolled flat, and one is layered on the other; then the double layer is rolled up, wrapped, refrigerated, sliced and baked, as above.

pinwheel sandwich - also **rolled sandwich.** This round finger sandwich with a spiral design is made from one slice of bread and a soft, fine-textured filling, such as cream cheese or deviled ham. After removing the crust, a square sandwich loaf is cut horizontally, then each long slice is buttered and spread with filling. Starting from one end (small, colorful garnishes, such as gherkins, olives or sliced radishes, are often lined up along this end first to form the center of the pinwheel); the long slice is rolled up, jelly-roll fashion, wrapped tightly with plastic wrap and refrigerated for about four hours until firm. The roll is unwrapped and cut into thin rounds, revealing the spiral of bread and filling.

pip - **1.** (n.) part of a plant capable of germination and propagation of another plant of the same type. The term is usually used for medium-size seeds, such as those from apples or watermelon. **2.** (v.) to remove the pips. See also KERNEL, SEED, PIT.

piper - see GURNARD.

pipérade - a stew of sweet peppers, tomatoes and onions mixed with egg that is a specialty of the Basque region of France. It is traditionally seasoned with *piment d'Espelette*, a medium-hot pepper grown in the region, and served with **jambon de Bayonne,** a famous salt-cured ham produced in the area.

pipikaula - Hawaiian-style homemade or ready-made jerky, its name meaning "cow" *(pipi)* and "dry" *(kaula)*. Thin slices of beef (everything from tenderloin to flank steak and, off the islands, venison, may be used) are rubbed with coarse sea salt, marinated in a mixture usually containing brown sugar, minced garlic and ginger, oil, red pepper flakes and soy sauce. Laid in the hot sun, hung inside a drying oven or smoked over a mesquite fire, the strips become chewy and somewhat dry. Pipikaula may be eaten on its own as a snack, but it's also added to salads (such as a Hawaiian seaweed salad, **poke**), stews, even sushi.

piping - to push a creamy, dense substance, such as **choux pastry,** cream cheese, frosting, softened butter or puréed meat, through the nozzle of a soft, funnel-shaped **piping bag.** Slow, even pressure and a steady hand, along with a variety of removable tips, can create an array of decorative shapes and swirls.

piping bag - a conical cloth bag, fitted with one of various screw-on nozzles. Soft mixtures, such as **choux pastry** dough, frosting, whipped cream or stuffing, are spooned into the wide, open top to partially fill the bag. The top edge is folded down, or simply gathered and grasped, forcing the mixture out of the nozzle to shape dough for cookies, such as **langue-de-chat,** create frosting **rosettes** and swirls, or pipe cheese into **manicotti.**

Pippin - see APPLE.

piquillo

pique-nique - French for "picnic."

piquia - see SOUARI NUT.

piquillo - a narrow, pointed sweet red pepper, organically grown in Lodosa, in northern Spain. Hand-picked, roasted over a wood fire, then hand-peeled and packaged, these peppers are sought after for their intense flavor. Available not-quite-ripe green or ripened red, whole or in pieces, piquillo may be stuffed with cheese, meat or seafood mixtures, added to dips and salads, fried with herbs in oil or simply eaten alone as a snack.

piri-piri - also **pili-pili.** A tiny, hot pepper, piri-piri means "pepper-pepper" in Swahili, the pan-African language. Brought to Europe by Columbus on his second voyage to the New World, the pepper was introduced by the Portuguese to their African colonies Angola and Mozambique and spread from there. Although used in many African cuisines, the pepper is best known as a Portuguese ingredient, sold marinated in oil, as a powder and as a purée. Best known in *frango grelhado con piri-piri* (grilled chicken marinated in piri-piri), the condiment is also added to meat, vegetables and fish by anyone who loves spicy condiments. Its heat is rated at 30,000 to 50,000 **Scoville units,** the equivalent of cayenne. See also CHILE PEPPER.

pirozhki - also **piroshki, pierogi.** Eastern European dumplings or turnovers, with savory or sweet fillings, in potato, yeast, short crust or puff pastry dough.

pisco - a 90-proof South American brandy made from white **muscat** grapes, first grown only in Peru, but now in Chile as well. Each country grows its own grapes, produces its own pisco and considers its brandy not only the best, but its very own national drink. The Pisco Sour, a quick-to-prepare pre-dinner cocktail made with **angostura bitters,** egg white, lemon or lime juice and simple syrup, shaken with ice, is certainly de rigueur in Peru. Another pisco cocktail called *Leche de Monja* (nun's milk) takes a little longer to make: one or two uncooked eggs in their shells are immersed in lime juice and refrigerated for two or three weeks until the shell softens, then all is puréed, after which the pisco and some sugar is stirred in (drinkers declare it delicious).

pissaladière - an onion-and-anchovy tart, originally from Nice but now found all over southern France. It's name comes from *pissala,* an anchovy paste that originally topped the tart (anchovy fillets are used today). It is made from bread dough that is similar to a pizza crust, with a crisp bottom, filled with thinly sliced onions and anchovy fillets. Traditionally, it is made in a long rectangle and cut into squares.

pistachio - the seed, *Pistacia vera,* of a small Persian tree, a relative of the cashew, cultivated for at least 3,000 years and gathered in the wild long before that. When ripe, the pistachio's shell opens at one end and is naturally tan in color, but in the 1930s, importers began dyeing the shells bright red to disguise blemishes that occurred during harvesting and to make them more attractive to consumers, a practice rarely seen today because of our modern appreciation for foods in their natural state.

pistolet - French for "pistol." A classic Belgian or French long, crusty roll.

pistou - the French equivalent of pesto, used mostly as a key ingredient and garnish for the Provençal vegetable soup *au pistou.* The word comes from the Provençal *pistar,* meaning "to crush or grind," from the Latin *pistare.*

pit - also **stone. 1.** (n.) the hard, often large, single seed of the fleshy fruits, such as cherries, dates, olives or peaches, which are called **drupes. 2.** (v.) to remove the pits. See also KERNEL, PIP, SEED.

pita - also **pocket bread.** A round Middle Eastern flatbread with a pocket, used for centuries to serve the function of plate and utensil, because the ingredients of a meal can be put inside. Developed by Arab nomads, who baked it during their caravan travel, the pita was used to take pit-roasted meats off their skewers (kebabs) by grabbing the meat with an open pita in one hand and sliding it off its spit.

pitahaya - also **pitaya.** See DRAGON FRUIT.

pith - **1.** the bitter, soft white spongy layer of a citrus peel that encloses the flesh. **2.** a term sometimes used to denote bone marrow.

pizza - a flat circle of baked yeast dough, topped with ingredients, such as anchovies, artichoke hearts, one or more cheeses, chopped herbs and vegetables, olive oil, tomato or other sauce, and sliced meats, sausage or seafood. Certain combinations denote a particular style — chopped ham and pineapple, for example, are "Hawaiian." Pizzerias sprang up all over the world after Italian immigrants brought the dish to America, although it was not until the Second World War that it became well known throughout the rest of Italy. Today, pizza is found everywhere. See also DEEP-DISH PIZZA.

pizza cutter - also **pizza wheel.** A sharp, rotating circular blade is affixed to the end of a sturdy, molded handle, so it can roll over pizza, slicing straight down through the crust with the

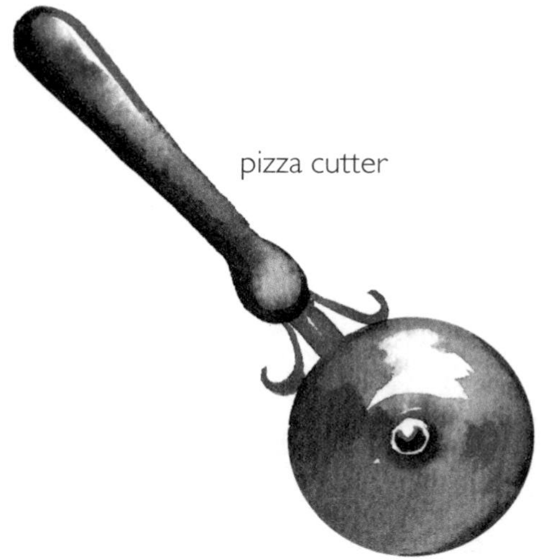
pizza cutter

minimum disruption to the toppings. A good model will have finger and thumb guards on the handle.

pizza pan - a circular, perforated metal pan for cooking pizza. The holes allow the bottom of the crust to crisp as it cooks. Different diameters, as well as deep-dish and nonstick versions, are available.

pizza peel - see PEEL.

pizza stone - see BAKING STONE.

pizza wheel - see PIZZA CUTTER.

pizzelle - a sweet, thin waffle-style biscuit made with a special iron or press, often served plain or with ice cream, or rolled and stuffed with sweetened ricotta cheese.

plaice - from Middle English *plaice,* Middle French *plais* and Late Latin *platessa,* a member of the flounder family, more flat and square than the halibut. North American plaice, or "dab," (also called "Canadian plaice"), is found in deeper waters than the European variety, which is much bigger and has different coloring.

plantain - **1.** a starchy tropical fruit resembling a banana, a staple of tropical cuisine, only eaten cooked. From the Latin *planta,* meaning "sole of the foot," because of the shape of the plant's leaves. Plantain can grow to 20 feet (6 m) in height; they were first grown in Southeast Asia, but are now grown extensively in India, Egypt, West Africa, the Pacific Islands and South America. **2.** a bitter, but edible leafy plant native to North America, considered a wilderness-survival food by many backpackers, but a weed by many gardeners. With the stringy ribs and veins removed, the young leaves can be boiled or steamed for greens.

plantation soup - a rich Southern soup made with butter, chile pepper, coconut milk, cream, oysters and **plantain,** with garlic, herbs and onions added for seasoning.

Planter's Punch - a classic, taste-of-the-tropics cocktail made with grapefruit and orange juice, light rum and sweet-and-sour mix, served over ice in an **old-fashioned glass.**

plastic wrap - also **cling film.** Clear, thin plastic film that sticks to itself, used to create an airtight covering around food. A Dow Chemical employee, **Ralph Wiley,** discovered the original substance in 1933. Transformed into fine sheets, it was called Saran (for reasons unknown) and used as a protective coating for aircraft and car seats. Dubbed Saran Wrap and marketed as a food covering beginning in 1953, it quickly took over from waxed paper. Its clinginess allowed it to completely seal and protect cooked or raw food from air, moisture and odors. Soon other manufacturers brought out their own versions of plastic wrap, some designed for special uses, such as freezing and microwaving. Concerns about its production, which uses polyvinylidene chloride — and public worry that harmful chemicals might transfer from the wrap to foods during such processes as microwaving — have resulted in changes. Cling film (as it's commonly known in the United Kingdom) is now available chlorine-free, as are plastic wraps made from polyethylene.

plaice

plate - **1.** (n) a rimmed, usually circular dish on which food is served. Used in the Western world since Roman times, plates have traditionally been made from clay, glass, metal and, in colonial America, from wood. The latter, called "trenchers" or "treen," had deep sides like today's pie plates, were sometimes shared and were often reversible to offer a clean surface for more than one course. By the late 1800s, most households had an array of crockery, including a host of plates designed to hold everything from a pat of butter to a salad to a generous portion of dinner. In North America, giveaway china could be collected at some gas stations, grocery stores and movie theatres right through the 20th century. From an average diameter of less than 9 inches (23 cm) in the 1700s, the size of the flat dinner plate peaked in the late 1900s, at the height of **nouvelle cuisine.** Throwaway paper plates were introduced in America in 1904, but some societies have used food, such as flatbread, as single-use, edible plates for centuries. **2.** see BEEF CUTS. **3.** (v) to arrange food on a plate, prior to serving.

Platina - see SACCHI, BARTOLOMEO.

pleurote - see OYSTER MUSHROOM.

Pliny - see profile below.

plonk - British slang for cheap wine.

ploughman's lunch - basic, hearty British fare consisting of thick slices of bread served with cheese and pickles, and washed down with beer. This lunch is still a popular pub meal.

plover - a wading shorebird. Harvested from the wild in Europe, plover is raised commercially in North America and considered a delicacy on both sides of the ocean. In the past, plover was one of the few birds not eviscerated before it was roasted; this was thought to improve the flavor. Cooked in their speckled shells, the small eggs are also eaten as a treat.

pluck - **1.** (n.) the organs, especially the heart, liver and lungs, of a bird or animal used as food (after losing one's guts, it would seem, one is no longer plucky). **2.** (v.) to pick and pull off fruit from a tree or feathers from a bird. In the latter case, the bird is usually chilled first so the flesh is firm and the feathers pull more easily, then plucked from back to front.

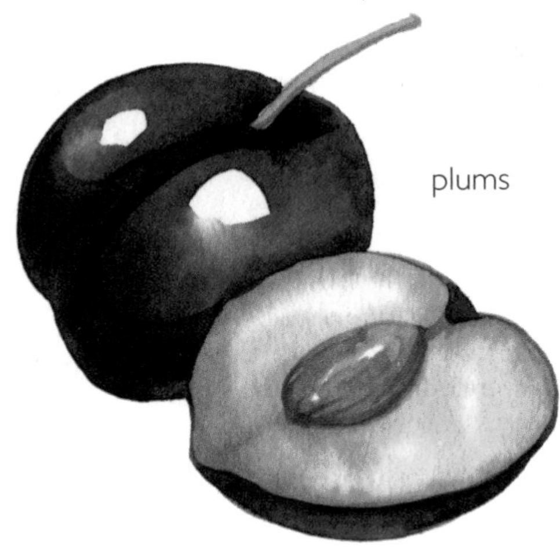

plums

plum - of the genus *Prunus domestica*, an oval or globe-shaped fruit with an oblong seed, native to most temperate climates. When dried, it becomes a prune. In most cases, plums will ferment if dried without removing the stone. Prunes, then, are varieties that can be dried without removing the pit. Plums were part of the diet of prehistoric Swiss lake dwellers (who lived in villages found in or near lakes), in whose ruins plum pits have been found. Plums were gathered and eaten by Stone Age tribes in Europe.

The plum is native to China and has been grown there since ancient times. About 300 years ago, plums were introduced to Japan. When the famous American horticulturist Luther Burbank brought them to California a century ago, they were called "Japanese plums," and the name stuck, even though it's not accurate, because they originally came from China. There are also native American plums, but none is produced commercially in any

Pliny (AD 23–79) - Roman historian and naturalist, author of *Natural History*, an encyclopedia of plants, animals, edible foods and geographical data covering the then-known world. His Latin name was Gaius Plinius Secundus, or, as we know him in English, Pliny the Elder, to distinguish him from his nephew and namesake. Pliny died in Stabiae, near Pompeii in AD 79, attempting to help the survivors of the volcanic eruption.

Plunkett, Roy J. (1910–1994) - American industrial chemist, inventor of **Teflon.** On completing his doctorate at Ohio State University in 1936, Plunkett went to work for DuPont, where he stayed until 1975. His first assignment was working with Freon, the company's trademarked refrigerant, as well as testing chemical reactions on another refrigerant, called TFE (tetrafluoroethylene). In testing a pressurized cylinder that refused to discharge, Plunkett found that the gas had solidified into a white powder. Its molecules bonded and turned into a resin with an impenetrable shield of fluorine atoms. He found a way to duplicate the chemical reaction in the lab and, in 1941, he patented the process and trademarked the name Teflon. Its first applications were for industrial and military use, but since the 1960s, it has been widely used in cookware.

quantity. California alone grows about 40 varieties commercially. When the first Pilgrims landed, Indians from New England to Florida were enjoying plums. True plums were introduced by the colonists and soon cultivated.

Perhaps the best-known plum is the Damson, named after Damascus, which were originally cultivated in the Caucasus and then spread to the Mediterranean before the time of Christ. Damsons are also known in England as "greengage," introduced in the early 18th century by Sir William Gage, the husband of Cecilia Culpeper, the daughter of the famous British herbalist **Nicholas Culpeper.** In France, they were introduced as *Reine Claude* in the 16th century. See also PRUNES.

plumcot - a cross between a plum and an apricot. See also PLUOT.

plum duff - see PLUM PUDDING.

plump - to immerse dried fruit in liquid. The fruit absorbs the moisture, increasing in size and tenderness.

plum pudding - also **plum duff.** A steamed or boiled dessert, rich with raisins, other dried fruits, spices, and scotch or brandy. Plum pudding has never contained plums, but is so named because, during the 17th century, "plum" meant raisin. It was first called "Christmas pudding" in an 1850s novel by Anthony Trollope. It was a holiday tradition to bake four symbolic charms into the pudding, each bestowing its unique blessing on whomever found it: a silver coin would bring wealth for the coming year; a tiny wishbone, good luck; a silver thimble, thrift; a small anchor, safe harbor. The custom of dousing Christmas pudding with brandy and setting it alight just before bringing it to the table is believed to be a carryover from ancient winter-solstice fire rituals.

plum tomato - see TOMATO.

plunger pot - see FRENCH PRESS.

Plunkett, Roy J. - see profile above.

pluot - a cross between a plum (two-thirds) and an apricot (one-third), a fairly new fruit developed late in the 20th century by Floyd Zaiger, a Nebraskan-born biologist, who spent more than two decades looking for the perfect fruit. The **aprium** is also a plum and apricot cross, but it has a higher percentage of apricot than plum.

Plymouth cheese - made since 1890 in Plymouth, Vermont, originally by the Plymouth Cheese Corp., which was co-founded by Calvin Coolidge's father, and now by Frog City Cheese. Plymouth is a raw-milk cheese that traditionally was hand-kneaded, as were all cheeses before the task became mechanized. The full technique involved stirring and kneading by hand, salting, pouring and pressing the curds into molds, wrapping in cheesecloth and dipping into four coats of wax for aging. Today, many of the hand-processing techniques are still used although there is some mechanized stirring and pressing now involved. Plymouth is a moist cheese, with many small holes and a slightly sour, rich taste, available from mild to sharp, with crushed red peppers, rosemary or caraway seeds.

poach - to cook food immersed in liquid just below the boiling point.

poblano chile - see ANCHO CHILE, CHILE PEPPER.

po' boy - see POOR BOY.

pocket bread - see PITA.

pod - **1.** (n.) fruit consisting of a usually crisp, long and slender, two-sided casing, containing several seeds, that becomes brittle as it matures. **2.** (v.) to remove the casing from the seeds, as for example, podding or shelling peas.

pod pea - a completely edible pea, including the pod, developed by Dr. Calvin Lamborn, a world-renowned plant breeder from Idaho; introduced in 1979. Two well-known varieties are **sugar snap peas** and **snow peas.** See also PEA.

Pogo - see CORN DOG.

poha - the **cape gooseberry,** as it's known in Hawaii.

pohole - see FIDDLEHEAD.

pohutukawa honey - see HONEY.

poi - a Hawaiian specialty made from cooked, puréed and fermented **taro** root, tasting very sour and not to everyone's liking. Poi is a Hawaiian staple and a ceremonial food imbued with meaning. When it's on the table, those sitting around it must not argue or speak in anger.

poinsettia salad - a salad of small tomatoes, each sliced partway down into eight segments joined at the base, then gently opened into a flower, with some of the "petals" slightly twisted. A spoonful of mayonnaise, decorated with tiny pieces of pimiento, creates the flower center. Featured in **Fannie Merritt Farmer**'s famous cookbook, poinsettia salad is considered a folkloric American recipe, but it still shows up on many holiday dinner tables.

point, à - see À POINT.

Point, Fernand - see profile right.

poire - French for "pear."

poire belle-Hélène - also **poire Hélène.** See BELLE HÉLÈNE.

poires Cardinal - also **Cardinal pears.** A dessert of fruit poached in vanilla syrup and **Kirsch**-raspberry sauce and sprinkled with almonds, so named because the carmine color of the sauce resembles that of a cardinal's robe.

Poire Williams - a clear French **eau de vie** made with a variety of pear known in France as William's Bon Chrétien, which North Americans call Bartlett. The first William's Bon Chrétien came to the U.S. from England and was planted in Massachusetts in 1799, in the orchards belonging to Enoch Bartlett, who commercialized the pear under his own name.

pois - French for "peas."

poisson - French for "fish."

poissonier - cook in a professional kitchen who prepares fish, one of the positions in the kitchen brigade system created by French chef **Auguste Escoffier** in the late-19th century. See also BRIGADE SYSTEM, CHEF, ENTREMETIER, GARDE MANGER, PASTRY CHEF, RÔTISSEUR, SAUCIER, SOUS CHEF, TOURNANT.

poivrade - **1.** a classic French peppery vinegar-and-wine sauce, traditionally served with beef or game, such as **venison.** Vegetables (such as carrots and shallots) and herbs are often cooked in the sauce, then strained out before the poivrade is served. **2.** a small, purple artichoke popular in France. Harvested when young and tender, it may simply be eaten fresh, with salt, or sliced and served in a vinaigrette. It can also be braised, puréed for soup, steamed or stuffed with rice.

poivre - French for "pepper."

poivre mignonette - see MIGNONETTE.

poke - **1.** pronounced *pokay*, a Hawaiian version of **sashimi.** Chunks of various kinds of inexpensive raw fish are seasoned with salt, soy, sesame oil, chiles, chopped seaweed and ground kukui nuts (a nut native to Hawaii), arranged casually on a plate. **2.** also **pigeon berry, poke salad, poke salat, pokeweed.** *Phytolacca americana*, an indigenous perennial, which grows up to 10 feet (3 m) tall in high, dry woodlands throughout the eastern and southeastern United States and parts of northern Mexico. The tuberous roots, shoots and mature leaves are poisonous, but the tender, young leaves, picked in spring before they redden, are a traditional cooked green in the American South. As a precaution, however, they must be cooked in two successive pots of boiling water (the liquid is drained off the leaves and discarded between boilings). Perhaps the last commercial canners of poke leaves (called *poke salet*) in the country, the Allen Canning Co. in Arkansas, stopped

Point, Fernand (1897–1955) - French master chef and restaurateur, often cited as the father of **nouvelle cuisine.** Point was born into a culinary family, who ran a small restaurant in Louhans. As a young boy, Point spent a lot of time in the kitchen with his mother and grandmother, who were both excellent cooks; he later cooked with his father, Auguste, who noticed his son's talent early and encouraged him to apprentice in good kitchens, which he did. Point went to Paris and cooked at Foyot's and at the Hotel Bristol. He went to Evian and worked at the Hotel Royal, cooking alongside Georges Bocuse, whose famous son, Paul, would begin his career years later as an apprentice to Point. Back in Louhans, Auguste decided to buy a restaurant. In 1922, he and Fernand found a property in Vienne, just north of Lyon, owned and run successfully for more than 20 years by a well-loved chef named Leon Guieu; Vienne is along the well-traveled route between Paris and the Côte d'Azur, which was deemed very good for business. Point christened the place La Pyramide for the town's Romanesque pyramid, and officially opened in 1923. Fernand Point was 26.

La Pyramide became a culinary hub for both gastronomes and cooks, and Point developed a reputation for attentive cooking and meticulous preparation. His philosophy of cuisine was beginning to take shape. Although **Auguste Escoffier** was still alive and his presence and influence were widely felt, Point was not interested in paying homage to the classics by recreating them. He acknowledged the master, but believed that the classics were a base on which to build an evolving cuisine. Still, his fundamental principles — local ingredients in season — never wavered. Point also distinguished himself by getting out of the kitchen. At the time, a chef never wandered into the dining room. Point regularly went out to speak to his guests, ask their opinion and often compose their dinner on the spot, in a creative collaboration that individualized his preparations. He kept the room limited to 50 seats, and the menu, which changed daily, never had more than 20 items.

Point's book *Ma Gastronomie* (My Gastronomy) is short on recipes and long on principles and ideals. Point remained true to his pronouncement, "The duty of a good cook is to transmit to the next generation everything he has learned and experienced." His greatest legacy is the long list of brilliant chefs who worked with him, learned from him and passed on his ideas. Most notable among them are **Paul Bocuse,** Alain Chapel, Francois Bise, Louis Outhier, and **Jean** and **Pierre Troisgros.** In the years before his death in 1955, Point worked closely with Paul Mercier, who succeeded Point as chef, working under the direction of Point's wife, Marie-Louise, affectionately known as Mado, whom he had married in 1930 and who remained involved in all aspects of the restaurant's business until her death in 1986.

production in 2000, citing a dwindling demand. The purple berries, which earned this plant its "pigeon berry" nickname, were a longtime source of dyestuff and are said to be safe, cooked in pies.

pokeweed - see POKE.

polenta - made of cornmeal, a traditional dish of northern Italy, which both Venice and Lombardy claim to have invented. The Greeks ate various cereal porridges called *poltos*. The Romans made a savory porridge that they called *puls*, using **farro;** the tradition continued in northern Italy, where gruels were prepared from local cereals, such as buckwheat, barley and oats. Corn was only introduced to Italy from the New World in the 17th century; soon afterward, it was being grown in all the northeastern regions of the country.

Traditionally, polenta was cooked in a *paiolo*, a special copper pot, which hung in the fireplace; it was stirred for at least an hour with a special long-handled spoon made of chestnut or acacia wood and served for breakfast, lunch or dinner (sometimes all three). In Italy, the piping-hot polenta is first poured onto a white cloth and then placed on a wooden board. Polenta was traditionally cut with a wooden spatula or a thick cotton thread. Today, many brands of packaged "instant" polenta, which cook in three to five minutes (in the microwave or on the stove), are available.

Polish sausage - see KIELBASA.

pollack - a species of marine fish belonging to the cod family.

pollo - from Italian and Spanish, meaning "chicken." Dishes include *pollo all' arrabbiata*, a classic chicken dish, from the Italian, meaning "angry chicken"; *pollo alla diavola*, a spicy grilled chicken, from the Italian, meaning "the way the devil likes it"; *pollo alla scarpariello*, meaning "chicken shoemaker's style," little bits of tender chicken meat on the bone. Its name is said to come from the way eager diners' fingers fly into their mouths while eating this dish, reminiscent of a shoemaker as he works away with a mouthful of tacks, repeatedly reaching to his lips for one more.

pollo asado - Spanish for "roast chicken." In Mexican and U.S. Southwest cooking, the chicken is often treated to a lime juice marinade that includes chile pepper among the seasonings and spices, before it's roasted in the oven or over the grill. Pollo asado is so popular that at least one ready-made seasoning mix is available.

Polonaise - also **à la Polonaise.** **1.** a French culinary term, meaning "of Poland" or "in the style of Poland," most often applied to dishes of asparagus, broccoli or cauliflower, topped with butter-fried bread crumbs, crumbled hard-boiled egg yolk (or the whole egg), and chopped parsley or other herbs. **2.** stacked slices of light, rich yeast bread saturated with **Kirsch** or rum, filled with layers of candied fruit and pastry cream, then topped with meringue and sliced almonds and browned in the oven. The finished creation is also called a *brioche polonaise*.

polony - **1.** a type of dry, highly seasoned, partially cooked pork or beef-and-pork sausage, familiar in Britain, Europe and North America. **2.** In Britain, another name for bologna.

polvorones - see MEXICAN WEDDING CAKES.

polyunsaturated fat - see FATS.

pomace - also **marc.** A crushed mass of fruit containing seeds, skin, pips and pulp, left after the liquid is pressed out. Derived from the same root as the French *pomme*, meaning "apple," this term is used to describe the residue of apples from cider making, but is also applied to the residue of grapes from wine making and that of olives from oil production. Pomace is used to make some brandies and other spirits, and is also used as livestock fodder.

pomander - from *pomme d'ambre*, meaning "amber apple." Since the Middle Ages, the ordinary pomander was a simple apple covered in spices and rolled in ambergris as a preservative. The pomander made most often is an orange studded with cloves. Up until the mid-19th century in Europe, it wasn't Christmas without a pomander. Historically, pomanders were also carried around in perforated boxes to let their scent escape, or hung from a person's belt or chain or string around one's neck, like the "bauble to contain ye pomander" that Henry VIII of England gave his daughter: a precious golden globe ornament decorated with 12 emeralds.

pomegranate

pomegranate - the crimson fruit, *Punica granatum*, of a tropical tree, with a thin, hard rind and as many as 600 tart, juice-filled seeds. Pomegranate juice is used as a flavoring in summer drinks, and in parts of the Middle East, it's included in soups. Its indelible red juices are used to dye the beautiful handmade rugs of the area and to make "true" grenadine. (Most of the "grenadine" now on the market is made with sugar water, and artificial color and flavor.)

In the West Indies, it's used widely in cooking and preserves. The word pomegranate comes from the Old French *pomme garnete*, meaning "seedy apple," although it bears no botanical relation to that fruit. According to Middle Eastern legend, there are 613 seeds in each pomegranate, one for each of the mitzvahs, or good deeds, of Hebrew tradition. King Solomon had an entire orchard of pomegranate trees, and the pillars of his temple were decorated with carvings of lilies and pomegranates. The prophet Mohammed instructed everyone to "eat pomegranate, for it purges the system of envy and hatred." In Syria and Lebanon, it's traditional for a new bride to stamp on a pomegranate at the entrance of her new home for fertility, abundance and a happy life.

pomegranate juice - a sweet-tart juice derived from pomegranates. Used to make **Grenadine,** the juice was considered medicinal in ancient times. Now, with recent studies showing that it is rich in antioxidants and may help reduce hardening of the arteries, pomegranate juice, in bottles, is becoming a familiar item on supermarket shelves.

pomegranate molasses - also **pomegranate syrup.** A bittersweet, dense, dark syrup, made by reducing pomegranate juice, commonly used in savory and sweet dishes throughout the Middle East and nearby parts of Russia. It can also be used in cordials and salad dressings.

pomegranate seeds - also **anardana.** Dried pomegranate seeds, still encased in their flesh (now dark and wrinkled) and sometimes crushed, which are used as a garnish or ingredient in many traditional Asian, Indian and Middle Eastern dishes. Harvested from varieties, often wild, that produce fruit too bitter to eat fresh, the dried seeds can be used in desserts, meat dishes, **pilafs** and salads.

pomelo - also **Bali lemon, Chinese grapefruit, pummelo, Shaddock.** A giant citrus fruit, *citrus grandus*, native to southeastern Asia and Malaysia, the largest of all citrus, similar to the grapefruit. It has a coarse thick skin with a light yellow to pink flesh. Also known as shaddock, after Captain Shaddock, an English sea captain, commander of an East Indian ship, who is said to have first brought the seed from East India to Barbados in the late 1600s. It is eaten in Asia during Chinese New Year, because it is believed that eating pomelo the last day of the year and at the beginning of the new one will bring prosperity and good fortune.

pomelo

pomme - French for "apple."

Pomme d'api - also **Lady apple.** See APPLE.

pomme de terre - French for "potato."

pommerance - dried, ground orange zest.

Pommery - see MUSTARD.

pommes à la dauphinoise - see DAUPHINOISE POTATOES.

pommes allumettes - see ALLUMETTE.

pommes Anna - see POTATOES ANNA.

pommes Dauphine - see DAUPHINE.

pommes frites - see FRENCH FRIES.

pommes soufflé - see SOUFFLÉ POTATOES.

pomodoro - Italian for "tomato."

pomology - the study of fruit and its cultivation, from the Latin *pomum*, meaning "fruit," and the Greek *logos*, meaning "discourse."

pompano - a fish from the Florida coast, the West Indies and the Gulf of Mexico, from the Spanish *pámpano*, meaning "vine tendril," referring to its thin shape. See also PACIFIC POMPANO.

pone - see CORN PONE, SWEET POTATO PONE.

Pont l'Évêque - a small, square cheese, pale yellow in color, with a whitish-orange rind, one of the world's oldest cheeses, dating back to the 13th century, when it was called d'Angelot, for the Normandy village where it was produced.

pony - **1.** a glass for measuring liquors or liqueurs, similar in form to a **jigger,** but holding only 1 ounce of spirits. **2.** the amount of liquor contained in a pony, as in "a pony of amaretto."

ponzu - a traditional sweet-sour Japanese dipping sauce for steamed dumplings. Homemade or ready-made, it usually contains boiled soy sauce, **bonito** flakes, lemon, lime or **yuzu** juice (or finely grated rind), and **mirin**

or rice wine vinegar, and may contain seaweed. North American cooks use it with grilled meat, seafood and vegetables, and, whisked with oil, as a dressing for noodle dishes.

poor boy - also **po' boy.** A New Orleans sandwich made with whatever one likes from deli meats to fried oysters; what is not negotiable among purists, however, is the bread: it must be French, crusty and with a soft center. When the city of New Orleans decided to convert streetcars into buses in 1925, 10,000 workers and sympathizers marched in a bloody strike that resulted in numerous injuries and even deaths. Brothers Bennie and Clovis Martin, restaurant owners and former streetcar workers, showed their support by offering to feed any "poor boy," or union member, who entered their restaurant. They told the strikers, "We are with you till hell freezes, and when it does, we will furnish blankets to keep you warm." What makes it "po" is its humble origin, a way to get a sustaining meal as conveniently and inexpensively as possible. See also SUBMARINE SANDWICH.

poori - also **puri.** A deep-fried, unleavened Indian bread. Different types of flour (such as **besan** or wheat) may be used. The flour is mixed with **ghee** or oil and water, or simply with water, into a stiff dough, then rolled into wafer-thin rounds. Deep-fried, the rounds puff up. After they are rolled out, a savory mixture (such as spiced, chopped vegetables) or sweet filling (such as spiced, sweetened lentils or roasted sesame seeds) may be spooned onto the center. Then, after the edges are folded over it, the filled dough is rolled again into a flat round, before deep-frying. Poori is served with dishes such as curries. In Indian grocery stores, ready-to-fry packaged poori are available. Bombay vendors sell bite-size versions, called *panipuri*, with a seasoned stuffing of minced onion and puréed chickpea and potato, and hot, sweet chutney.

poor knights - also **poor knights of Windsor.** A late 18th-, early 19th-century English version of **pain perdu,** made by dipping bread slices (often cut into strips or "soldiers") into a mixture of cream, beaten egg, sugar and nutmeg or cinnamon, then frying and serving them crisp and golden brown with butter, jam, sugar or rose water.

poor man's lobster - see MONKFISH.

pop - slang, especially in Canada, for "soda."

popcorn - a variety of Indian corn that pops open when heated, first recorded as a product of Aztec life, used primarily for decoration; similarly, the Incas cultivated popcorn to use decoratively for burials. Early popcorn makers could expand a kernel of popcorn to 15 times its original size; now, they can puff a kernel to 40 or more times its original size, with 4 cups (1 L) of popcorn containing only about an ounce (30 g) of corn.

popcorn ball - a home-cooked confection made by drizzling a heated corn-syrup mixture over cooled, freshly made popcorn, tossing it together, then (with buttered or moistened hands, so they don't stick) shaping the popcorn into softball-size spheres. Some cooks add chopped candied cherries or nuts for extra color and crunch.

popcorn rice - see WILD PECAN RICE.

popcorn shrimp -bite-size pieces of deep-fried shrimp.

pope's eye - the lymphatic gland from the middle of a leg of mutton, viewed by epicures as a delicacy. Samuel Johnson, the 18th-century lexicographer, defined "pope's eye" as "the gland surrounded by fat in the middle of the thigh; why so called I know not." In Germany, the pope's eye is called *Pfaffensbisschen*, meaning "priest's bit." In France, it also has a religious connection, but one that is more sinister, *l'oeil de Judas*, meaning "Judas's eye."

pope's nose - see PARSON'S NOSE.

popover - a rich dough of butter, eggs, milk and flour cooked in a tall, greased custard cup or **ramekin** that puffs up and out over the rim as it bakes. Under a crusty golden top, the soft interior is filled with air. Similar to **Yorkshire pudding,** a popover turned out of its cup is traditionally served with gravy and roast meat, but may be served for breakfast with butter, jam or syrup. Diced apple, blueberries, grated cheese or chopped herbs may be added to popover dough to create savory or sweet versions.

poppadum - see PAPPADAM.

poppy - from the genus *Papaver* and the Middle English *popi,* a bright flower with copious seeds. In times of famine, the leaves were used as a

substitute for spinach. The petals, which yield a potent red coloring, can be used to make inks. *Somniferum,* the poppy's botanical name, means "sleep-bringing," a reference to the milky juices from the unripe pods, which are the source of opium and its well-known derivatives, morphine and codeine. Paracelcus (1493–1541), a Swiss alchemist credited with the introduction of opium and mercury into pharmacopoeia, was the first one to extract laudanum, an opium-based painkiller, from the poppy for medical research. In 1530, he published the ingredients of certain of his concoctions, including gold leaf and other whimsical bits and pieces, but it was later revealed that he was really only making a distillation of opium.

poppy seed cake - see SEED CAKE.

poppy seed oil - extracted from poppy seeds, which are 40 to 45 percent oil, used mainly as a salad or cooking oil.

poppy seeds - used in food since before biblical times, mixed with wine and honey for the Roman table and fed to athletes competing in the first Olympic games. Poppy seeds are said to stimulate the appetite. They are opium-free, because opium is found in the pod and not the seed itself. Although it's hard to tell because of their size, poppy seeds are kidney-shaped, and it takes 900,000 seeds to make 1 pound (500 g). Holland is a major exporter.

porcini - a variety of wild Italian mushroom, closely related to the French *cèpe*. They are particularly flavorful, plump and meaty, hence their name, which means "little pigs." See also CEP.

porgy - the name for a dozen or so varieties of fish found mostly in the warmer waters of the Atlantic and the Mediterranean, also called **bream,** jolthead, pink, white or silver snapper, scup, sheephead and whitebone. They're delicious and mild-flavored, with firm, white flesh and lots of bones, making them difficult to fillet.

pork - the name given to the flesh of the hog. Our domestic pigs are descendants of the European wild boar, *Sus scrofa*, drawings of which were found in prehistoric caves near Neolithic farming communities, made about 3000 or 4000 BC. The first people to taste roast pork were probably the Chinese. Neolithic sites excavated in China show that pigs and dogs were the only domestic animals there at the time. In ancient Greece, pork was a mainstay of banquet feasts, and Romans of all classes were fond of pork, especially ham and bacon. Roman historian and naturalist **Pliny** noted that a talented cook could derive more than 50 different flavors from pork, whereas most animals offered only one.

Trichinosis, once associated with pork, and caused by eating raw or undercooked meat infected with the larvae of a species of worm called *Trichinella* (the roundworm is killed by cooking at 140°F/60°C), is now rarely an issue thanks to improved feeding techniques that do not allow raw intestines from slaughtered hogs to be fed to pork. (For Pork Cuts see page 518.) See also TEMPERATURE.

PORK DEFINITIONS

barrow - also **stag.** A castrated male hog.

boar - an uncastrated male hog.

gilt - a young female pig.

hog - a pig weighing more than 120 pounds (54 kg).

pig - a young swine of either sex before it has reached the age of sexual maturity, weighing less than 125 pounds (57 kg).

piglet - a nursing pig.

pork - the name given to the flesh of a hog.

porker - a young weaned pig, fattened for slaughter.

sow - a mature female.

stag - see BARROW.

PORK CUTS

Unless otherwise stated, roasting is the preferred cooking method.

arm roast - cut from the top part of the **shoulder** at the front leg.

belly - lower side(s) remaining after the loin and spareribs have been removed; the source of bacon.

blade roast - also **Boston butt, shoulder blade roast.** From the top of the shoulder, usually tied to cook evenly and keep its shape.

blade steak - cut from the shoulder butt, usually pan-fried.

Boston butt - see BLADE ROAST.

center-cut pork roast - see LOIN CENTER RIB ROAST.

crown rack - also **crown roast.** The entire rib section tied into a ring, the bones from the chops giving the appearance of a crown.

ham - cured and smoked meat from the hind leg, excluding the shank. A whole ham includes the upper leg and a portion of the foreleg. The remainder of the foreleg is the shank.

leg - includes the hind leg bone, lean, usually made into ham, but makes an excellent roast.

loin - from the back, between the ribs and the hip.

loin blade roast - from the shoulder end of the loin, cut into either a five- or seven-rib roast.

loin center rib roast - contains rib bones, also sometimes called **center-cut pork roast.**

loin chops - high-quality chops containing part of the tenderloin.

picnic cut - see SHOULDER.

rib chops - from the rib end of the loin, braised or pan-fried.

ribs - from the rib area along the back; usually includes portions of the backbone and rib bone. **Back ribs,** also called **baby back ribs,** are from the blade and center parts of the loin, making them meatier than spareribs, though they are smaller. **Country-style ribs** are the meatiest type, cut from the sirloin and ribs. They are sold in thick slabs or individually.

shoulder - front part, which also includes the butt (the end of the shoulder), also called a **picnic cut,** used in sausage making.

shoulder blade roast - see BLADE ROAST.

sirloin chops - cut from the end of the loin, usually pan-fried.

sirloin cutlets - tender and boneless, sometimes braised.

spareribs - taken from the lower ribs and breastbone. See also SPARERIBS.

tenderloin - the highest quality, most tender and leanest cut, safely served "pink" for gourmets who appreciate how much more succulent pork is when cooked this way.

porker - a young weaned pig, fattened for slaughter. See also PORK.

porridge - the name given to any cereal or **pulse** steeped in hot water or milk, usually made of oatmeal, an ancient food of Celtic origin. In Britain, porridge is eaten with syrup and/or sugar, whereas in Wales, Ireland and Scotland, it's eaten unsweetened.

port - a wine with grape brandy added before the fermentation is complete, more complex than other fortified wines. Port falls into two categories: wood-aged and bottle-aged. Wood- or cask-aged ports, which mature in wood casks and are then bottled, include Ruby, Vintage Character, Late-Bottled Vintage, Tawny, Colheita and White varieties. White is popular in Europe, but rarely found in the U.S. Bottle-aged ports, which spend only a brief period of time in barrels and do most of their maturing in the bottle, include Vintage (the finest), Single-Quinta and Crusted varieties. Port is made only in Portugal, in the Douro River Valley. The area was officially demarcated by the Portuguese in the 18th century.

porter - a dark, very bitter, mildly alcoholic beer first brewed in London in 1730 as a substitute for a drink called Entire, a popular mix of ale and beer. Entire was advertised as being richer and more nourishing than ale, intended for porters, carters and other heavy laborers who would find in the brew's potency the ability to accomplish tasks that no spirit drinker could perform. Its dark color was derived from roasted, unmalted barley and sometimes a dash of licorice. In the British Isles, porter was overtaken in popularity by bitter stout in the 19th century, and the last porter was brewed in Dublin in 1973. Porter is still brewed today in East Germany, North and South America, Africa, China, Denmark, Hungary, Poland and Russia.

porterhouse steak - a steak cut of beef, considered superior by many, cut from the large end of the short loin including meat from the tenderloin. The name is said to come from "porter house," a coach stop in the early 19th century where travelers would stop for something to eat, particularly steak and ale.

portobello mushroom - a very large, mature cremini mushroom, dark brown, flavorful and meaty, that can grow as large as 5 inches (12.5 cm) in diameter. See also MUSHROOM.

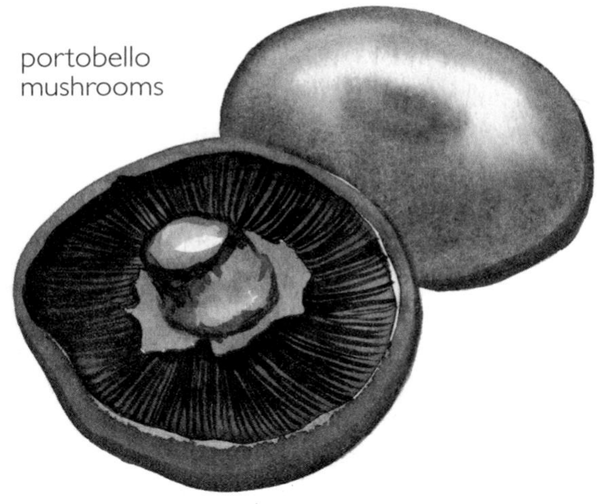

portobello mushrooms

Port Salut - also **Port du Salut.** A soft, pungent, yellowish cheese, first made by Trappist monks of the abbey in Entrammes, in northern Touraine, a province in France. During the French Revolution, the Trappists left France, but returned in 1815 and named the inlet where they landed on the Normandy coast *le Port du Salut,* meaning "the port of salvation," as well as their cheese, which they soon resumed making. They were so successful that, by 1873, Port du Salut was renowned throughout Europe. Today, Port Salut, also known as **Trappist cheese,** is made in Trappist abbeys everywhere, but is also made by many secular cheese makers who don't have any Trappist affiliations.

Portuguese bean soup - see KAU KAU.

Portuguese sweet bread - also **Hawaiian bread, pao duce.** A soft, sweet bread made with a rich dough containing butter and eggs. Some bakers flavor the dough with ginger, or lemon or pineapple juice. Traditionally, shaped into a round and cooked on a flat surface (rather than shaped into a loaf pan), it emerges from the oven topped with a golden dome. Centuries ago, Portuguese fishermen and explorers brought the recipe to their ports of call; from the late 1700s on, some sailors jumped ship to make Hawaii their home, hence the bread's alternate name.

posole - also **pozole.** See HOMINY.

posset - **1.** a medieval hot drink of spiced and sweetened curdled milk that was thought to have healing properties. Later, with the addition of cream, bread crumbs, eggs, spices (such as cinnamon, mace and nutmeg) and wine, it evolved into a pudding that was popular at weddings. The top was eaten with a spoon, and the liquid that seeped to the bottom was sipped. A special posset cup, with a spout that emerged near the base, made this easier to do. The Scots added honey, oatmeal and whiskey to their version. **2.** a contemporary, semisolid dessert made from cream cooked in a saucepan with superfine sugar; after removing it from the heat, lemon juice is stirred in and the mixture thickens, similar to a custard. Sherry or another spirit may sometimes be added, and the dish is often served with fresh or preserved fruit.

pot - **1.** (n.) a deep, round vessel with a flat bottom, used for cooking, often with a tight-fitting lid and one or two handles at the top. It is commonly used as a generic term for many different shapes and sizes of cooking pans. **2.** (v.) to preserve a food in fat, an old-fashioned method of preservation that is rarely used today, except in the case of a meat **confit.** The food is cooked in a large amount of fat, then poured into a pot, where it is covered with more fat, which hardens and seals out air and bacteria, keeping the food fresh and ready to eat.

potable - a word meaning "suitable for drinking," often used to describe water that has been judged safe for human consumption. Often used as a noun for anything drinkable, in particular an alcoholic beverage.

potage - French for "broth" or "soup."

potage de blé - French for "corn soup." A classic recipe of French Canada, this rich soup is made with butter, celery, corn, leeks or onions, milk, salt and pepper, cooked together, then puréed. Whipping cream is stirred in before serving. Brought to the U.S. by the Acadians, who settled in Louisiana in the late 1700s, perhaps, the dish is now considered a traditional Cajun recipe as well, but often chile pepper is added to spice things up.

potage printanier - French for "**spring soup**" and one of the dishes ordered by "man of the world" Prince Oblonsky, when he dines at a St. Petersburg restaurant, early in Leo Tolstoy's novel *Anna Karenina*.

potager - French for "for the pot." A term denoting a kitchen garden.

potassium - a mineral that regulates blood pressure and fluids in the body, and is considered essential for the proper functioning of the digestive system, the kidney, muscles (including the heart) and nerves. Either too much or too little can cause health problems, so taking a supplement, without a physician's recommendation, is not recommended. Eating lots of fruits, legumes and vegetables provides adequate potassium for the average person.

potato - an edible tuber, *Solanum tuberosum*, native to South America. Spanish explorers to South America were the first Europeans to come in contact with the potato in the early 1500s. They brought it back to Spain and from there it eventually spread across Europe. John Hawkins, a seafaring British adventurer, is credited with bringing the first South American potato to England in 1563. However, it was not

POTATO VARIETIES

baking potato - see RUSSET.

blue - originated in South America, readily available in the U.S., especially in the fall, with a medium starch level; they have a subtle nutty flavor; sometimes called "purple potatoes."

Idaho - see RUSSET.

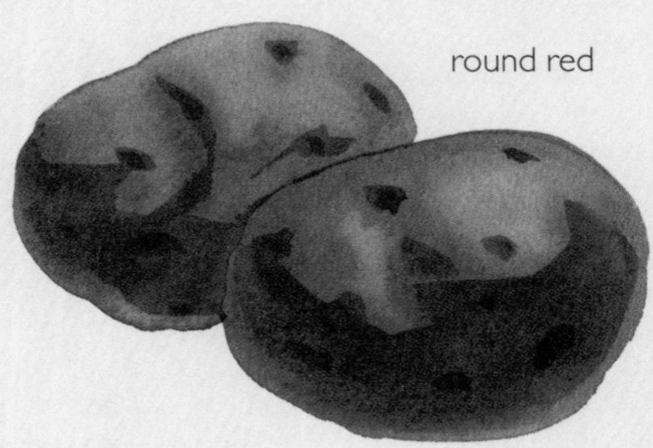

round red

round red - firm, smooth and moist, ideal for salads, roasting, boiling and steaming.

round white - best known as an all-purpose potato, smooth, light tan with a medium starch level; they keep their shape well after cooking.

russet - also known as **baking potato, Idaho.** The most popular potato in the U.S., used for baking, mashing and frying, because it has a low water and sugar content. Its flesh can vary from creamy white to light golden.

sangre - round, red potato with white flesh, excellent in soups and stews, because it maintains its shape during cooking; also good baked and in potato salad.

yellow - has a dense, creamy texture, one of the best choices for mashed potatoes, widely available in the U.S. **Yukon Gold** is a variety of yellow.

Yukon gold - gold-fleshed, with a creamy texture, a North American favorite, ideal for baking, boiling and frying.

Yukon gold

until after Sir Francis Drake returned with a batch of Chilean potatoes in 1585 that it began its rocky start to eventual widespread popularity. The queen's cook would throw them away and serve only the leaves. The wealthy reviled them as flavorless and only fit for the poor. People distrusted the fact that they reached maturity underground. In Scotland, Presbyterian ministers told parishioners that eating potatoes was blasphemous, because there was no reference to them in the Bible. Yet, by 1650, they had become a staple of the Irish diet, and their cultivation had begun to spread throughout Europe. Irish settlers brought them to the New World.

During the late 1700s in France, a military pharmacist named Antoine-Augustin **Parmentier** was the first to recognize the potato's merits, but the French would have none of it: since the potato belongs to the nightshade family, it was assumed to be poisonous. Parmentier did manage to win over Louis XVI, who let him grow potatoes at Versailles and allowed them to be pilfered by the Parisian poor. The king started wearing the potato's delicate white flower on his jacket, and Marie Antoinette took to wearing the flowers in her hair. Frederick William III of Prussia (1770–1840), sensing that the potato could boost Prussia's tired economy and feed the poor, issued what has been called "The Brandenburg Potato Paper," an edict ordering farmers to plant potatoes or risk having their ears and nose cut off, which quickly made potatoes a dietary staple.

In the late 1800s in southern Italy and Sicily, potatoes were believed to be inedible and even poisonous: if you wanted to get rid of an enemy, you wrote his name on a piece of paper, fastened it to a potato, buried it, and the enemy would soon join the potato. Europe would wait a long time before the potato gained prominence there. Ireland adopted the potato after the Royal Society of London promoted it as a relief food, primarily because it was a nutritious, rugged and abundant crop, able to provide sustenance for nearly 10 people per acre of land per year, which fueled the population explosion in the early 1800s. Unlike any other food, the potato contains most of the vitamins needed for sustenance. But by mid-century, the Irish had become so dependent upon this crop, that its failure created a famine. The 1840s saw a disastrous potato blight hit not just the British Isles, but Europe as well. The Irish famine cut the population in half, through either emigration or starvation. An effective fungicide was not found until 1883, by the French botanist Alexandre Millardet.

Potatoes can be purple, yellow, golden, pink or orange. Never eat a potato that has germinated or has a green tint to the skin, as this shows an elevated solanine content, which, in large amounts, can be lethal. Baking a potato with the skin will preserve the highest level of nutrients. Boiling a potato without the skin causes a 30 percent nutrient loss; when mashed, the loss can reach 75 percent. A potato stored for more than six months can lose about 50 percent of its vitamin C content. See also FINGERLING POTATO, MASHED POTATOES, NEW POTATO.

potato baker - a spiked rack on which whole potatoes are impaled for baking or grilling.

potato chips - invented in 1853 by a Native American named **George Crumb,** the chef at the Moon's Lake Lodge in Saratoga Springs, New York, after a guest who had ordered french fries whined that they were too thick, sending them back to the kitchen twice. Chef Crumb decided to slice the potatoes paper-thin, which crisped up beautifully when cooked. The guest was thrilled. This style of potato became a signature of the restaurant and were called **Saratoga Chips.**

potatoes Anna - also **pommes Anna.** A French dish of thinly sliced potatoes brushed with clarified butter, baked in a shallow dish and inverted, served cut into wedges. It was the 1866 invention of Adolphe Dugleré, proprietor and chef of the famed Café Anglais in Paris, as an accompaniment to a roast or poultry. It was dedicated to Anna Deslions, the "lioness of the boulevards," a famous fashionable courtesan, although some claim the dish was named for actress Anna Judic, also known as Anna Damiens.

potatoes au gratin - see SCALLOPED POTATOES.

potato flour - see POTATO STARCH.

potato fritters - see RELLENOS DE PAPA.

potato masher - a hand-powered kitchen tool for mashing drained, boiled potatoes or other

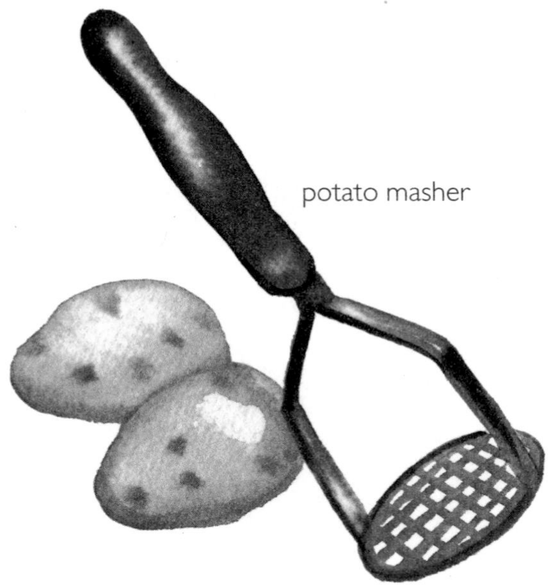
potato masher

cooked root vegetables, such as carrots and turnips. Older models have a zigzag of metal attached at right angles to a cylindrical, upright handle, which is grasped in one fist; newer models often have a perforated disk of metal or sturdy plastic at the working end, instead. Other, less common, models are designed with a horizontal handle, similar to that of a pastry blender.

potato pancake - **1.** a pancake or **latke** made with grated potato. **2.** a pancake made with potato starch, instead of wheat flour. This gluten-free version is popular with people who have celiac disease.

potato puff - a small, barrel-shaped nugget of deep-fried minced potato, similar in texture to commercial hash browns, often served to children as an accompaniment to meat or sandwiches and dipped in ketchup.

potato ricer - see RICER.

potato salad - a side dish of cooked diced potatoes, usually dressed with mayonnaise; most often with chopped onions and celery. **German potato salad** refers to cooked potatoes dressed with a hot vinaigrette made with bacon fat, usually served over vegetables. Potato salad was mentioned in 1597 by English botanist **John Gerard** in *Herball or Generall Historie of Plantes*, in which he reports that potatoes were roasted in ashes and dressed in salt, vinegar and oil, "every man according to his own taste."

potato starch - also **potato flour.** A fine, gluten-free flour produced by grinding cooked, dried potatoes, used as a thickener, interchangeable with cornstarch.

potato whiskey - whiskey made with fermented potato mash, usually illicit. See also MOONSHINE, POTEEN.

pot-au-feu - French for "pot on the fire," a peasant dish into which all kinds of odds and ends are thrown and long simmered. **Jean Anthelme Brillat-Savarin,** author of *La Physiologie du Goût* (The Physiology of Taste), defined it as "a portion of beef destined to be treated in boiling water lightly salted so as to extract the soluble parts" — in other words, ordinary boiled beef. Some attribute its origin to Henry IV, who promised that every peasant would have a chicken in the pot each Sunday, which was called *poule au pot* or chicken stew. Today, it is a hearty stew of vegetables and various meats.

pot barley - see BARLEY.

pot cheese - a fresh, salt-free cheese, similar to cottage cheese, but drained longer, giving it a drier texture. See also FARMER'S CHEESE.

pot de crème - French for "pot of cream." A rich, sweet custard, flavored with caramel, chocolate, **espresso** or, traditionally, vanilla, baked in small custard cups or **ramekins** set in a **bain-marie.** So popular has this dessert proved, that porcelain pots, resembling deep, lidded cups with matching saucers, have been specially made for it by the likes of Coalport and Limoges.

potée - also **hochepot.** A classic, rural, French slow-cooked stew, usually made and served in a ceramic pot and containing pork (this could be bacon, a ham hock, a pig's head or sausage) with cabbage, navy beans, potato and root vegetables, such as carrot and turnip. Regional variations may include duck, eel or mutton as the meat, or in addition to the pork; unlike a **pot-au-feu,** a potée does not usually contain chicken or beef. See also HOTCHPOTCH, POT-AU-FEU.

poteen - also **potheen.** Illicit Irish whiskey made with fermented grain or, more often, potatoes. Early settlers in North America set up their own stills once their land was cleared and was producing crops. See also MOONSHINE.

potherb - a leafy green, eaten on its own (fresh and raw, or boiled or steamed in a pot) or added as seasoning to such dishes as meat pies, soups or stews.

pot-lifting tongs - strong and sturdy, scissor-type tongs designed to lift heavy pots without handles from the heat, or jam jars from simmering water. The working ends of the tongs are usually curved to form an ellipse or circle that accommodates the rim of a pot or the neck of a jar. The tongs may be finished with square or triangular loops (the inside surface is usually ridged to provide a better grip), or with one curved and one straight end, which fit over the top and the lip of a pan, respectively. These tongs are made of metal, but some versions have wooden handles, so they can be grasped comfortably even when the pot is hot. See also TONGS.

pot liquor - also **pot likker, potlikker.** Not a type of alcoholic liquor at all, pot liquor is the rich cooking liquid left after vegetables or meats are simmered, considered a treat in the American South, often served as a complement to **corn pone** or **cornbread.** Pot liquor is high in vitamins and other nutrients, which leach into the water as the vegetables or meat cook. Pot liquor from the Southern staple **collard greens** is especially prized for its flavor and deep-green color.

potluck - **1.** a communal meal to which the participants each bring a dish to donate to the common "pot," which everyone will share. Since there is usually no planning of the whole menu, the diners serve themselves from what shows up, by luck, on the table. In many recipe books, some dishes are earmarked for such suppers, by virtue of being easy to prepare in large quantities, quick to reheat on the spot or convenient to transport. **2.** to accept a last-minute invitation to dine (or take potluck) on a meal for which no particular preparations have been made by the cook.

pot pie - an American invention, first mentioned in print in 1792. In 1951, Swanson made its first pot pie as a frozen entrée.

pot roast - meat, usually beef, cooked slowly and gently with liquid, vegetables and herbs, ideal for the cheaper, tougher cuts of meat, ensuring maximum tenderness and flavor.

po tsai - also **Chinese leaf, Peking cabbage.** A cabbage relative that looks similar to and is often confused with napa cabbage with tightly packed, crisp, light green leaves with wide white stems at the base. Po tsai is mild and has a delicate cabbage flavor and can be used in any dish that calls for Chinese cabbage.

pot sticker - a Chinese dumpling, made with **wonton wrappers** filled with vegetables, ground meat and seasonings, whose name warns what can happen during cooking. In Shanghai, where they're said to have originated, they're called *wor tip*, which translates as "pot stick," and in Beijing, they're called *chiao-tzu*, or "little dumpling." The legend has it that they were created by accident, when an imperial chef forgot them on his stove. Today, they're first blanched in water and then pan-fried. The classic technique is to cook them in a pot with specific amounts of water and oil together, skillfully measured so that, by the time the water evaporates, the dumpling will be cooked and the remaining oil will fry it for its final color and crispness.

potted shrimp - a spread or molded appetizer of shrimp, either minced or puréed or sautéed in butter, containing a variety of seasonings, pressed into ramekins and chilled before serving. The traditional accompaniment is toast.

Pouchong - see TEA.

poularde - French for "fowl." A term denoting a sterilized hen, fattened for food; the female equivalent of a **capon.**

Poularde Tosca - chicken stuffed with rice and served with braised fennel, created by **Auguste Escoffier** and named for the opera singer Dame Nellie Melba to celebrate her title role in the 1900 Puccini opera.

poulet - French for a "tender, young chicken."

poultry - any domestic bird bred for the table, such as chicken, turkey, duck, goose, quail, pheasant, guinea hen or squab. The chickens consumed in the modern world are descended from *Gallus gallus*, an old jungle fowl from the pheasant family (Phasianinae), bred in the Indus Valley more than 4,000 years ago. Records show that Mesopotamian farmers bred ducks and that, by 1000 BC, geese were already popular in what is now Germany. Modern domestic ducks are believed to be descendants of the wild mallard, *Anas platyrhyncha*, except for the Muscovy duck, which originated in South America.

The modern goose owes its ancestry to the graylag, *Anser feras*, a large, gray European goose, so named because it is the last of its species to leave England for its annual migration.

Today's modern turkey is not the wild turkey the Pilgrims found in 1620, but rather the descendant of a turkey domesticated by the Aztecs in Mexico and later taken to Spain by the conquistadors. From Spain, the turkey traveled to England, and about 150 years ago, the domestic turkey finally reached the U.S. In the last 80 years, poultry production in the U.S. has grown from 30 million **broilers** to more than 350 million. See also CHICKEN, DUCK, GOOSE, TEMPERATURE, TURKEY.

poultry seasoning - ready-made dried seasoning mix for chicken and turkey dishes, particularly stuffing. (It's also suitable for pork.) It contains herbs and spices, such as marjoram, nutmeg, rosemary, sage, thyme and black pepper.

poultry shears - sturdy scissors with curved, often spring-loaded blades, used to cut through the bones and flesh of poultry. The lower blade is usually serrated and may be notched near the hinge to grip small bones. The handles may resemble those of regular scissors or of secateurs (small shears used for pruning).

pound cake - a rich, golden cake named for its ingredients: a pound of butter, a pound of flour and a pound of sugar; eggs, sometimes divided into whites and yolks, then beaten separately before adding to the batter, are the leavening agent. A small amount of vanilla or lemon zest may be added to boost the flavor. In Britain, halved candied red cherries are mixed in to make a version called "cherry cake." Neither version is frosted. Pound cake can be cut up and used to make a **trifle.**

pousse café - **1.** a French term denoting an alcoholic after-coffee **chaser,** such as a liqueur. **2.** a potent cocktail in which spirits are gently poured into a tall glass, one at a time and left unstirred to create layers of color. The classic version includes ingredients such as Bénédictine, crème de cacao, crème de menthe, curaçao, cherry liqueur, grenadine and triple sec.

poussin - also **squab chicken.** A free-range baby chicken that is fed organic corn, barley and soy, and is slaughtered between 4 and 6 weeks of age.

poutine - **1.** french fries covered with gravy and cheese curds, invented in 1957 by restaurateur **Fernand Lachance** in Warwick, Quebec. It spread quickly across the country, where it's now available at fast-food chains. **2.** a small, very delicate river fish in Provence, also called *nonat*, usually fried.

poutine gravy mix - a ready-made mixture, usually containing dehydrated vegetables and seasonings, to create the gravy for the classic French-Canadian treat, **poutine.**

powdered baking ammonia - see AMMONIUM BICARBONATE.

powdered egg white - dried, pasteurized egg white, which cooks can reconstitute and substitute for fresh egg white. In recipes that call for raw egg white (no longer recommended, because of the risk it may carry salmonella) this is the perfect replacement. See also MERINGUE POWDER.

powdered garlic - see GARLIC.

powdered milk - also **dried milk, dry milk.** Air-dried pasteurized milk particles.

powdered sugar - see CONFECTIONER'S SUGAR.

pozole - also **posole.** See HOMINY.

prahoc - a Cambodian fish paste made with eviscerated fish, which are scaled, washed and pressed under banana leaves, then salted, sun-dried, pounded into a paste and left to ferment.

prairie chicken - a type of grouse, *Tympanuchus cupido pinnatus*, once found throughout the western Plains states, but today only in Texas, where it's still considered a delicacy.

prairie oyster - **1.** a cocktail of unbeaten egg yolk, Worcestershire sauce, Tabasco, malt vinegar, salt and pepper; a favorite of bartenders 100 years ago as a cure for hiccups. It is also a traditional hangover remedy. **2.** also **cowboy caviar, fries, Montana tendergroins, Rocky Mountain oysters.** A misnomer or curious euphemism for the fried **testicles** of a bull, lamb or pig, considered a delicacy in France and Italy,

A B C D E F G H I J K L M N O P Q R S T U V W X Y Z

expensive and not widely available. They can also be braised or poached. In almost all cattle-producing states, there are festivals and fairs that feature a prairie oyster cookout. In 2003, at the Montana Testicle Festival, sometimes called the Testy Festy, more than 8,000 people showed up to consume "4,500 pounds of carefully prepared, beer-marinated, secret-recipe-breaded, deep-fried bull testicles."

praline - a culinary term for roasted, chopped pecans poured into melted sugar and left to harden like brittle, used to flavor or garnish desserts, named for a 17th-century French nobleman whose chef invented it. A praline, pronounced "praw-leen," is a New Orleans candy patty made with sugar, cream and pecans.

praline paste - a homemade or ready-made sweetened paste of ground nuts, such as almonds, hazelnuts or pecans, used in cakes, confections and pastries. After storing, the oil may separate and float on the top, but can be stirred back in.

prawn - **1.** a close relative of the shrimp that generally lives in fresh water (although it tends to migrate to salt water during the spawning season), with a thinner body and long legs. **2.** small crustaceans related to and shaped like lobsters, such as the **Dublin Bay prawn,** langoustine and Danish lobster. These tiny lobsters are often called **lobsterettes** as well. **3.** a generic term applied to very large shrimp, not wholly accurate, although widely used.

prawn cracker - see SHRIMP CHIP.

preheat - setting the required temperature for a broiler, grill or oven ahead of time, so it's ready to go when the food is ready for cooking. Most baking requires a preheated oven, but some dishes, such as those cooked in a **clay baker,** are started in a cold oven.

prepared mustard - also **made mustard.** A creamy, tangy condiment that is a combination of dry ingredients (powdered mustard, seasonings and spices) and wet (beer, honey, vinegar or wine). Prepared mustards may be grainy or smooth and vary in color. See also MUSTARD.

preservative - a substance added to a food to increase its shelf life, preventing decomposition and oxidation, which can lead to spoilage and loss of color and flavor. Preservatives are also antimicrobial, preventing the growth of viruses, bacteria, molds, yeast and other fungi, which can cause spoilage or fermentation. Many common food items are preservatives, used since the dawn of time to keep food fresh for longer; among these are sugar, salt and vinegar. Others are more recent chemical additives, such as sodium benzoate, potassium sorbate and propionic acid, all of which are antimicrobials commonly added to packaged foods. Certain vitamins, such as vitamin C (often seen under the name "ascorbic acid") and vitamin E (the active form of which is known as "tocopherol"), are also added as preservatives because they are antioxidants, preventing changes in color and flavor and keeping fats in the food from going rancid. Sodium nitrite and sodium nitrate are other well-known preservatives, used to cure meat and prevent it from going bad. Both are commonly used to make bacon, ham and other preserved meats.

preserve - a generic term embracing a variety of methods, including canning, drying, freezing, pickling, salting and smoking, to keep food unspoiled and flavorful enough to eat long after it is caught, harvested or slaughtered and ensure human survival between seasons.

preserved lemons - also **salt-cured lemons.** A widely used Moroccan condiment, these lemons are pickled in a brine made from salt and freshly squeezed lemon juice, usually seasoned further with bay leaves, cloves, coriander seeds, peppercorns and/or stick cinnamon. All the ingredients are put into a canning jar and allowed to pickle at room temperature over the course of a month or two. Preserved lemons are intensely fragrant and add a pleasantly assertive salty, lemony note to many Moroccan dishes, including the signature Moroccan stew, **tagine.** They can be used either as a condiment at the table (cut into tiny pieces and eaten with stews) or as a flavoring during cooking. The leftover brine also makes an excellent addition to salad dressings or cocktails, such as **Bloody Marys.**

preserves - chunks of fruit, simmered and thickened with sugar, usually in a large **preserving kettle,** then stored in sterilized, airtight containers. **Pectin** is often added to help the mixture thicken and gel or set. Until the advent of easily available ready-made preserves, "putting up" homemade preserves for the winter was a traditional activity from midsummer through fall. Preserves may be used as a spread for sandwiches or toast, a topping for custard, ice cream or yogurt or as a filling for layer cakes, pies and tarts.

preserving sugar - see SUGAR.

pressed caviar - see CAVIAR.

pressed cookie - a special-occasion cookie, made with a smooth dough that is pushed through the tip of a cookie press, or pastry or piping bag, designed to form shapes, such as flowers, snowflakes and swirls. See also COOKIE.

pressed duck - a French dish of roasted duck, also known as *canard à la presse*. Once the duck is roasted, the breast and legs are removed and the carcass is then "pressed" tableside in an elaborate device known as a **duck press,** made specifically for this reason. Paris's La Tour d'Argent, the world's oldest and most celebrated restaurant (1582), is particularly famous for its pressed duck recipe, revived in 1890 by then-owner Frédéric Delair, who found it in an old cookbook. For more than 100 years, La Tour d'Argent has offered numbered ducks as part of its menu. If you order duck, you get a postcard with the serial number of your duck stamped on it as a souvenir (the restaurant raises its own ducks on its own farm specifically for the restaurant).

pressed tofu - see TOFU.

press pot - see FRENCH PRESS.

pressure cooking - a method of cooking by steam in a specially constructed saucepan with a tight-fitting lid at a very high temperature.

pretzel - a snack, either soft or hard, often salted and glazed, shaped into a loose knot and poached in water before baking. The name comes either from the Latin *pretium*, meaning "reward" (given to children who have been good), or the Old High German *brezitella*, derived from the medieval Latin *brachiatellum*, meaning "little arm or branch." The design supposedly came from German monks in AD 610 as a symbol of arms folded in prayer.

prick - to pierce tiny holes in food to create vents for steam in pie crusts or whole vegetables when baking them, for example, or to release fat from sausages and keep their casings from splitting when frying or grilling them.

prickly pear - see CACTUS, NOPALES.

primavera - Italian for "spring." An Italian culinary term for dishes containing colorful, fresh, or sometimes blanched, vegetables. **Pasta primavera** is a classic example.

prime rib - also **standing rib roast.** See BEEF.

princess bean - see WINGED BEAN.

prix fixe - a French phrase meaning "fixed price," usually consisting of several courses. See also À LA CARTE, TABLE D'HÔTE.

probiotic - a food-industry term describing a product, such as yogurt, to which live microorganisms, such as *Lactobacillus acidophilus*, have been added. When consumed, these encourage the growth of beneficial bacteria in the gut and enhance the health of the digestive system from top to bottom. They are also believed to help prevent infections in the urinary tract and vagina.

processed cheese - see AMERICAN CHEESE.

produce - cultivated fruits and vegetables grown for market.

profiterole - a French dessert, small cream puffs, made from **choux pastry,** savory or sweet, whose name comes from *profit*, meaning "a small gratuity or gift." The French pastry **croquembouche** is made with them.

pronghorn - see ANTELOPE.

proof - **1.** (n.) the alcohol content of distilled liquors and other spirits. Twice the alcohol percentage of the spirit (for example, 80 proof is 40 percent alcohol by volume). The word comes

pretzel

from the old method of testing the quality of liquor by mixing it into a little gunpowder and holding it over a flame. If it ignited, the spirit was said to be "proved," indicating that it contained at least 50 percent alcohol (100 proof). If it only fizzled, the spirit didn't prove and was labeled inferior. Modern distilleries use sophisticated hydrometers or other techniques to determine the proof of liquor. The alcohol content of wine is given as a percentage. White wines average 12 percent, and red wines are about 14 percent. The alcohol content of beer is between 3 and 8 percent. "Light" or lower-calorie beers have fewer calories and are closer to 3 percent alcohol content. Liqueurs, such as sherry and dessert liqueurs, contain 40 to 50 percent alcohol and tend to be higher in calories. **2.** (v.) to determine that yeast is usable for baking by combining it with warm water and a pinch of sugar, then letting it stand undisturbed in a warm place for up to 10 minutes. If the solution becomes foamy and bubbly, the yeast is alive and will cause bread to rise. If there is no activity, the yeast should be discarded and fresh yeast substituted.

prope thermometer - see THERMOMETER.

prosciutto - Italian word for cured ham, raw (*crudo*) or cooked (*cotto*). See also PARMA HAM.

prosecco - a grape variety whose resulting fresh, neutral wine is suitable for turning into sparkling wine. The fermentation of the late-ripening prosecco grapes is sometimes interrupted by frost in the winter months; as a result, the wine still has some carbon dioxide and residual sugar in the spring. The history of the success of this wine started in the 19th century, when Antonio Carpenè and three partners founded a company with the intention of producing Champagne. However, they produced instead Prosecco di Conegliano-Valdobbiadene, which became a popular and fashionable tipple. Today, approximately 20 million bottles of **spumante** are produced annually by means of secondary fermentation in pressurized tanks. If the product of this tank fermentation process is bottled after one month of storage with a bottle pressure of at least three atmospheres, it may legally be labeled spumante, or sparkling wine. If it does not reach this pressure, it must be labeled **frizzante,** or fizzy or semi-sparkling wine. Prosecco spumante commands a higher price than frizzante; however, in qualitative terms, the difference between the two isn't always detectable. Prosecco wines from the Cartizze zone, which generally have more residual sugar, are often more expensive, but seldom better than Prosecco originating from the zone of the same name.

protein - one of three essential sources of energy (along with carbohydrates and fats) required by the body; protein also assists in building and repairing bones and tissues. The general rule of thumb is that an adult should consume one gram of protein for every kilogram of body weight each day. With an amino-acid composition that classifies them as "complete proteins," dairy foods, eggs, fish, meat and poultry are the best dietary sources of protein; fruit, grains, nuts and vegetables are just down the list.

Proust, Marcel - see profile below.

Provimi veal - see VEAL.

provolone - a salty, often smoked cow's milk cheese from the south of Italy.

Prudhomme, Paul - see profile on page 528.

prune - a dried plum, popular in French cuisine as a savory ingredient, usually with game, pork and pâtés; as a sweet filling for pastry; or as a preserve. Because North Americans think of prunes primarily as a digestive aid, the U.S. Food and Drug Administration reclassified them

Proust, Marcel (1871–1922) - French writer and author of *Remembrance of Things Past* (1913–1927), which was inspired by a visceral memory from childhood that came to Proust while he was having tea and toast one day. Proust gives the book's protagonist the same experience, but with a **Madeleine,** instead: "No sooner had the warm liquid, and the crumbs with it, touched my palate, a shudder ran through my whole body, and I stopped, intent upon the extraordinary changes that were taking place."

Prudhomme, Paul (1940–) - American chef, restaurateur and entrepreneur. Louisiana native and the last born to a family of 13 children, Prudhomme was 7 years old when he first tried his hand at cooking. At his mother's side, he learned to work with fresh, seasonal ingredients out of necessity, because the family didn't have a refrigerator. In his 20s, he traveled extensively, learning various cooking styles and techniques. With his late wife, K Hinrichs Prudhomme, he opened K-Paul's Louisiana Kitchen in 1979, in New Orleans's French Quarter. It has become one of the most famous restaurants in the U.S., popularizing a style of Cajun cooking unique to the state's southwest region. Prudhomme has written seven books and developed a signature spice mix sold in more than 30 countries. He also produces his own **tasso** and **andouille,** two seasoned pork specialties of Louisiana. Prudhomme is best known for his blackened dishes in which fish and meat are coated in hot spices and charred in cast-iron pans over a very high heat.

in 2000 as "dried plums," so that the unglamorous connotation might fade and give the fruit's image and producers a boost. The marketing campaign also pointed out that prunes have the highest level of antioxidants of any fruit or vegetable.

Prunes come mostly from the Agen plum, a French variety, introduced to the U.S. by Pierre Pellier in 1856. The tree was named for a French district known for its prunes, and grafted successfully to the wild American plum. California boasts more than 80,000 acres (32,000 hectares) of prune plum orchards in the San Joaquin and Sacramento valleys, which provide 70 percent of the world's supply. See also PLUM.

prune butter - see LEKVAR.

prune jam - see LEKVAR.

prunelle - also **prunella.** A sweet, brandy-based liqueur made by soaking the stones of **sloe** plums, which give it a delicate, almond flavor. Some versions use the pulp as well; some have added vanilla. Depending on the brand, the color varies from pale green to dark amber.

psyllium - the common name for plants of the *Plantago* genus, whose seeds are used in high fiber products, particularly breakfast cereals. A powder made from the ground seeds and husks can be bought at health food stores. It is a good source of soluble fiber, which can help keep blood cholestrol low. As a thickener, it is been used in ice cream and frozen desserts. In 1998, the U.S. Food and Drug Administration authorized the Kellogg company to print on some of its products the therapeutic properties of psyllium. See also DIETARY FIBER.

puchero - Spanish for "stew." It is also a Spanish cooking term, used in Mexico, Central and South America, the Philippines and Spain, to describe a traditional "mixed" stew. Along with vegetables, it is not unusual to find chunks of chicken, beef, ham, pork and sausage in this one dish, which is often served at family reunions and other special occasions. See also COCIDO, OLLA PODRIDA.

pudding - **1.** a generic term denoting a soft, sweet, and usually cooked, dessert that includes **suet pudding;** custard cooked with eggs and milk, which may contain starchy food, such as tapioca, rice or **sago;** or a batter, bread or sponge pudding, such as a **charlotte. 2.** in Britain, a generic term for dessert itself. **3.** a baked good made from an egg-rich batter, such as **Yorkshire pudding. 4.** a savory, cooked dish, such as **haggis. 5.** a sausage containing blood, fat and meat, such as **blood pudding.**

pudding spice - see MIXED SPICE.

pudla - a golden, Indian pan bread or griddle cake, made from a **besan**-and-water batter, fried in a small amount of **ghee** or oil. A variety of ingredients, including cumin seeds, ground cayenne pepper, turmeric, lime juice, minced chiles or diced tomato, may be added.

Pueblo bread - also **Pueblo adobe bread. 1.** a baked bread made by the Pueblo Indians of the U.S. Southwest, using flour, lard, yeast and water that is cooked in a preheated adobe wood oven. **2. bannock** or fry-bread made by the

Pueblo, using a simple dough of baking powder, flour, salt and warm water, kneaded lightly, then formed into patties and fried in lard.

puerco para freir - precut pork for making **carnitas,** a traditional Mexican dish of seasonal pork butt or shoulder.

Pu-erh - see TEA.

Puerto Rican cherry - see ACEROLA.

puffball mushroom - a spherical, edible mushroom from the Lycyoperdacai family found in fields and open woodlands in late summer and early fall, and usually noticed and picked when they are from softball to soccer ball size. The young flesh should be firm and pure white right through, with a consistent, smooth texture (there should be no discoloration or sign of gills; the latter indicates that the specimen is a toxic mushroom, not a puffball). Puffballs may simply be sliced into "steaks" and fried in butter, or chopped or sliced and dehydrated for use in soups and stews.

puffed cereal - invented in the early 1900s by **Alexander P. Anderson,** an accidental result of an experiment in which grains exploded into puffy masses of starch. He then placed the masses under high-pressure steam until the vapor expanded, puffing out each small morsel. The Quaker Oats Co. was the first company to market puffed cereal, which they introduced to the public in 1904 at the St. Louis World's Fair and sold as a snack. In 1913, Puffed Rice and Puffed Wheat hit the market as breakfast cereals.

puffed rice - see MURMURA.

pufferfish - also **balloon fish, blowfish, fugu, globefish, swellfish.** When it feels threatened, the pufferfish becomes twice its size by swallowing water. Its liver, muscles, skin and ovaries contain tetrodotoxin, a powerful poison that has no antidote. Fugu, the Japanese pufferfish, is prepared by specially trained chefs, who can safely discard the poisonous parts of the fish without contaminating the rest of the fish. Still, many Japanese diners have died from eating this poisonous delicacy. Only a few people in Japan are authorized or licensed to work with the fish, and some people feel they are immune for whatever reason to the poison or are driven by pure bravado. In 1975, a Kabuki actor insisted on being served the fish's innards.

pufferfish

He died, and the chef was given an eight-year suspended sentence and put on probation for two years.

puff pastry - from a dough of the same name, used to make very light and flaky pastries, including **allumettes, croissants, Napoleons** and **palmiers.** The dough must be rolled out and folded repeatedly (up to seven times), with several layers of butter. One of the most delicate and time-consuming of doughs, when it is baked, the moisture in the butter creates steam between the layers, causing them to separate. The invention of puff pastry (the French term is **pâte feuilletée** or leaf pastry or **mille-feuille** in French, meaning "1,000 leaves") is credited to Claude Gellée, a 17th-century landscape painter and amateur cook, also known as Claude Lorrain, after the place of his birth in France. Italian authorities, on the other hand, are unanimous in naming Florence as its birthplace, noting it was expressly cited in a 1525 decree issued by the Council of Ten in Venice, which condemned puff pastry and other dishes as grandiose. Also, batches of puff pastry were served at the wedding of Marie de' Medici and Henry IV of France.

pull-aparts - a savory or sweet yeast bread made with individual balls of dough placed, side by side, in a pan. After baking, they are easily separated, by hand, into individual buns or servings. See also MONKEY BREAD.

pulled pork - a classic barbecue dish from the southern United States. Pork shoulder or butt is cooked very slowly over a long period of time, until the meat is so tender that it can be pulled off the bone. Roughly shredded and tossed in the chef's special barbecue sauce, it is served on fresh buns, often accompanied by homemade pickles and coleslaw.

pulled tea - see TEH TARIK.

pullet - see LAYING HEN.

Pullman loaf - also **Pullman bread, sandwich loaf.** A long, rectangular loaf named after George Mortimer Pullman, the 19th-century American railroad owner and industrialist who, by necessity, was also the instigator of many space-saving techniques and tools in his popular dining-car kitchens. The bread is baked in a similarly shaped lidded pan known, not surprisingly, as a "Pullman pan." Long and narrow compact kitchens are also given the "Pullman" designation.

pulque - a sacred drink of the Aztecs, made from the fermented sap of the maguey plant, also known as **agave.** Tequila and mezcal, sometimes called pulque brandies, are produced by distilling pulque. See also TEQUILA.

pulse - the dried edible seeds of certain leguminous pod-bearing plants, which include beans, lentils and peas.

pulverize - to crush into a powder. In a kitchen, a mortar and pestle or the side of a broad knife blade often do the job.

pummelo - see POMELO.

pumpernickel - a dark, coarse sourdough bread, a favorite in Eastern Europe, usually containing a higher proportion of rye flour than wheat flour, as well as molasses, which adds color and flavor.

pumpkin - fruit from the trailing vine, *Cucurbita pepo*, from the Greek *pepon*, meaning "large melon." Pumpkin is a member of the Cucurbitaceae family, which includes cucumber, squash and watermelon. Pumpkin seeds are called **pepitas. Pumpkin pie** is best made from "pie pumpkins," a variety of pumpkin that is harvested when they reach soccer-ball size so they are more dense with sweet flesh rather than seed cavity, which is more typical of the larger jack o' lantern pumpkins used for carving at Halloween. Seeds from plants related to the pumpkin date back to about 7000 BC. Native Americans had been eating pumpkins several centuries before the arrival of the Pilgrims. Around the time of the first Thanksgiving, it was traditional to serve the pumpkin with its crown and seeds removed, the cavity filled with milk, honey and spices, then baked until tender.

pumpkin

pumpkin pie - a baked, single-crust pie filled with puréed, cooked pumpkin mixed with eggs, cream or milk, vanilla and ground spices, such as allspice, cinnamon, cloves, ginger, mace and nutmeg; dried orange zest is sometimes added. Topped with swirls of whipped cream, it has been the traditional ending to North American Thanksgiving meals since the early 1900s, although English recipes for the pie date back to the late 1600s. The stewed pulp of fresh "pie pumpkins" (varieties with more dense, sweet flesh than seed cavity, which are harvested when they reach soccer-ball size) can be used, but most cooks start with canned purée, available with or without added spices.

pumpkin pie spice - a ready-made mixture usually containing ground allspice, cinnamon, cloves, ginger and nutmeg.

pumpkin seed - see PEPITAS.

pumpkin seed oil - also **pumpkin oil.** Oil made by pressing roasted pumpkin seeds to extract their liquid fat. First pressed in Styria, Austria, and still commonly available there, pumpkin seed oil has a strong flavor and can be overpowering in large quantities, so it is often used sparingly as an accent or in conjunction with other oils. It is rich in zinc, vitamin E and essential fatty acids, and is therefore a common ingredient in nutritional supplements.

punch - **1.** from the Hindi *panch*, meaning "five," for its original ingredients: tea, **arak,**

sugar, lemons and water, introduced to England by colonial army officers who had lived in India, but with the addition of Jamaican rum, which was cheap and abundant at the time; sometimes served hot. Today, in the French West Indies, a punch or *ti'punch*, an abbreviation of Creole for *petit*, is one part pure sugarcane syrup for two parts rum, topped with a wedge of fresh lime. **2.** to "punch down" risen yeast dough to push out and release any air bubbles before it is baked; depending on the recipe, the dough may need punching down more than once.

punt - also **kick-up.** The dimple or hollow in the base of a wine bottle that dates back to the days when they were hand-blown. Said to strengthen the base and provide a place to grasp when pouring the wine, this shape also allows bottles to be stacked and stored efficiently in special racks during the winemaking process.

Punt e Mes - Piedmont dialect meaning "point and a half," an extremely bitter, Italian red vermouth made with white wine and flavored with a well-guarded secret blend of herbs; part of the 19th-century custom of turning vermouth into bitters. Depending on their taste buds, lovers of vermouth will ask for a number of "points" of bitters to be added to their glass. One evening in 1870, or so the legend goes, a Turin stockbroker who had had a particularly stressful day trading, absentmindedly raised his hand to order some vermouth with bitters, using a motion he'd used countless times before on the trading floor. "Punt e mes!" he uttered mechanically. Everybody giggled at his confusing a stock bid with a drink order, but the name stuck.

pupu platter - also **pu pu platter.** A sampler platter of appetizers customarily served in Hawaiian, Polynesian and Polynesian-style Chinese restaurants in North America, from the Hawaiian word *pupu*, meaning appetizer or finger food. In Hawaii, pupu is the term for any type of appetizer, raw or cooked, cold or hot. Pupu platters on the mainland are generally the darling of the tiki bar circuit, usually Chinese-style appetizers, such as spareribs and wontons, with accents of pineapple or coconut as a nod to the pupu's Hawaiian ancestry. Pupu platters are served in a divided wooden dish with a small glowing brazier in the center for grilling or warming tidbits at the table.

pupusa - a deep-fried circular pastry filled with savory morsels: cheese and beans, **chicharrones,** vegetables or chicken are some of the most common and beloved fillings. The dough is made from **masa,** the same coarse ground corn used to make corn tortillas. Pupusas are a popular street snack in El Salvador that have made their way north to larger cities in North America along with Salvadoran immigrants.

purée - **1.** (n.) a preparation attained by mashing and sieving meats or vegetables after they've been cooked, or fresh fruit, such as raspberries and strawberries. **2.** (v.) to grind or mash fresh or cooked foods into a smooth, thick, but semi-liquid state, using a blender or food processor, or pressing it through a sieve by hand.

puri - see POORI.

purple basil - see BASIL.

purple olive - see OLIVE.

purple wax bean - see BEAN.

purslane - a herb with a rubbery and succulent stem and tear-shaped leaves, common in the warm regions of Europe and the Americas. It's name comes from the Latin *portulaca* and the Old French *pourcelaine*. Purslane, *Portulaca oleracea*, grows wild in India, where it's been eaten for thousands of years. It's widely cultivated in the Middle East and was introduced to England during the Tudor period, becoming a favorite on the Elizabethan table. It must be harvested before it blooms, and tastes slightly tangy and spicy. It can be eaten raw or cooked. The stems can be marinated in vinegar, like capers. In the Middle East, it's used in a salad called **fattoush.**

purslane

puttanesca sauce - a classic Italian sauce, originating in Naples, made with anchovies, capers, garlic, tomatoes and olives, served with pasta and seafood, as well as rice and vegetables, such as potatoes. Its name supposedly comes from *puttana,* Italian for "whore." Two popular tales suggest the name refers to either the sauce's wonderful aroma used to entice men into the bordello, or that the sauce was cheap and speedy to throw together, presumably between clients.

Puy lentil - also **French green lentil.** A dark French lentil, which varies in size; it is highly regarded and is considered the best of its type, because, like the green (or continental) lentil, it retains its shape when cooked. Originally grown in Puy, France, it is now grown in Italy and North America.

Pyrex - a heat- and shock-resistant glass, developed in 1915 by Eugene C. Sullivan and William C. Taylor for Corning.

pyridoxine - see B VITAMINS.

pysanky

pysanka - pl. **pysanky.** A Ukrainian Easter egg covered in colorful, intricate patterns, made by the women of each household in the last week of Lent, following their own special, handed-down designs. The smoothest, most perfectly shaped eggs are chosen. Using a stylus tool filled with melted beeswax, the artists draw on linear designs and outlines, usually of stylized natural forms, such as flowers or sunbursts. When the wax hardens, each egg is dipped into vegetable dye; the waxed lines and shapes resist the dye, the remainder of the shell absorbs the color. The process can be repeated with more drawings and darker and darker dyes, to add a new color each time. An unmarried women who planned to give one to her intended was warned to cap both ends of the egg with her design, to ward off baldness in her future spouse.

q
quiche

quahog - see CLAM.

quail - also **bobwhite.** A small, short-tailed, nonmigratory bird, that was historically hunted as game, but is now farmed for consumption. Its lean flesh is dark and flavorful. There are 130 species of quail, and its name is said to have come from the sound of its cry.

California Quail

Quark - soft, fresh, unripened cow's milk cheese, prepared in a fashion similar to cottage cheese, with the consistency and flavor of sour cream, usually found only in specialty stores in North America, but widely available in Germany and Austria. It's called *Quarg* in Central Europe.

quatre épices - French for "four spices," which are black pepper, nutmeg, cloves and ginger (or cinnamon), also known in France as *toute épices*, because of its spicy taste and smell. Quatre épices are used in the making of **charcuterie,** bases, broth and simmered dishes. In the Middle East and Arab countries, stews, shish kebabs and meat with dried fruit are seasoned with a local version of quatre épices. In Egypt, it's mixed with flour to flavor bread and cakes.

quatre mendiants - a French dessert of dried figs, raisins, hazelnuts and skinned almonds, whose colors recall the humble attire of the four mendicant (or "begging") orders of friars: the black friars (Dominicans, raisins); the white friars (Carmelites, skinned almonds); the gray friars (Franciscans, figs); and the hermits (Augustinians, hazelnuts).

quattro formaggio - Italian for "four cheeses," a style of dressing pizza or pasta, usually a selection of four types: fresh, dry, soft and firm, such as in ricotta, Parmesan, Gorgonzola and provolone.

quattro stagioni - Italian for "four seasons," a pizza on which each of the four quarters has a different topping, often over a base of fresh tomato sauce. The toppings vary, but classic ingredients include artichokes, clams, mushrooms, mussels, olives mixed with anchovies, and pancetta.

Queensland nut - see MACADAMIA NUT.

QUARK VARIETIES

Doppelrahmstufe - German for "double cream stage," 60 to 85 percent fat.

Frischkäse - generic term for "fresh cheese" made from skim milk, usually takes the form of a solid mass made by adding more cream to Quark. The cream is mixed in after the curd has separated from the whey, which creates its creamy texture and taste.

Labfrischkäse - aslo **Labquark.** Made with mainly rennet and little or no starter.

Rahmfrischkäse - fresh, unripened cream cheese, usually sold in small, foil-wrapped cubes. Made by adding more cream to **Speisequark**.

Schichtkäse - German for "layer cheese." Fresh, unripened curd cheese, combining layers of skimmed milk and whole milk curds.

Speisequark - means "farmer's cheese," contains more fat than **Rahmfrischkäse** and is sold plain or mixed with fruit.

Topfen - from Austria, made from whole and skim milk, sometimes mixed with butter, eggs and spices.

quenelles - a dumpling, a specialty of Lyon, where they're made of pike (*quenelles de brochet*), although they can be made of either fish or meat, very finely minced, mixed with cream, bread and spices, then formed into small ovals and poached, usually served with a cream sauce.

quesadilla - a flour tortilla filled with any combination of shredded cheese, cooked meat and/or refried beans, folded in half and toasted or fried, from the Spanish *queso*, meaning "cheese."

quesilla - see ASADERO.

queso - Spanish for "cheese."

queso anejado - also **cotija.** A white cow's milk cheese from Mexico that is quite pungent and salty. Queso anejado comes in two forms: dry and hard, like Parmesan cheese; and semidry and crumbly, like feta. It is often crumbled or grated and used as a garnish for tacos, beans and soups. The name means "aged cheese" in Spanish. See also QUESO AÑEJO.

queso añejo - also **queso enchilado.** A firm, aged Mexican cow's milk cheese, similar to **queso anejado** but with a gentler flavor. It is usually formed into blocks and rolled in chili powder, which gives it its other name, *queso enchilado*, which means "cheese seasoned with chile." *Queso añejo* means "aged cheese" or "vintage cheese" in Spanish.

queso blanco - a mild Mexican cow's milk cheese similar in texture to mozzarella, good for eating plain, broiling or frying. The name means simply "white cheese" in Spanish.

queso enchilado - see QUESO AÑEJO.

queso fresco - a soft, grainy, crumbly Mexican cheese made from cow's or goat's milk; mild and fresh tasting, excellent crumbled over enchiladas or baked dishes. The name means "fresh cheese" in Spanish.

queso fundido - Spanish for "melted cheese," a dip that can be made with one cheese (such as **chihuahua**) or with a mixture of two or three (goat's cheese, Monterey Jack, mozzarella), chopped **chorizo,** garlic, **poblano chiles** and wine. For an appetizer or party snack, it is served with soft flour tortillas or tortilla chips.

quetsch - **1.** a blue plum, grown in the Alsace region of France, famously used in jams, pies, tarts and **eau de vie. 2.** a type of clear, potent (80 proof) brandy or eau de vie, similar to **Slivoviz,** produced in Alsace. It is enjoyed straight or mixed with **Grand Marnier** and orange juice in a cocktail called the Grand Quetsch.

quetsch

quiche - a pastry shell filled with a savory custard made of eggs, cream or milk, and a variety of other ingredients, including onions, ham, mushrooms, other vegetables and seasonings. This French open tart originated in Lorraine, where it was made with lard.

quick bread - a bread made without kneading or rising, its leavening from baking powder or soda. Muffins and biscuits are examples of quick breads. See also UNLEAVENED BREAD.

quick-cooking barley - see BARLEY.

quince - a golden, round fruit, *Cydonia oblonga*, resembling a pear, consumed for more than 4,000 years throughout the Mediterranean. The Egyptians considered it a symbol of fertility and love. Quince must be cooked or baked before

quince

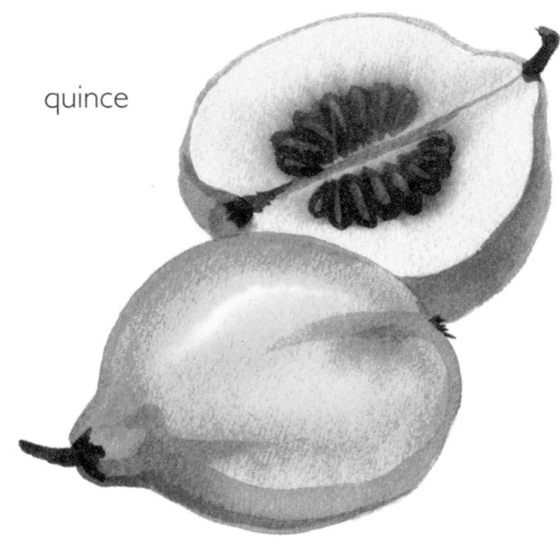

eating and makes very good preserves and jellies, because of its natural pectin. Quince jelly, called *membrillo* in Spain and *marmelo* (from which "marmalade" derives) in Portugal, is a common breakfast item in both countries and has been part of the Spanish diet for centuries. When Spanish missionaries went to Mexico in the 16th century, they were unable to have quince paste, because no quince grew there. Instead, they satisfied their craving with guava paste.

quinine - a bitter alkaloid from the bark of the cinchona tree, native to the mountains of Central and South America, used especially to flavor tonic water.

quinine water - see TONIC WATER.

quinoa - an ancient nutritious grain, a staple of the Incas, who called it *quinoa*, meaning "the mother grain." Quinoa must be rinsed before cooking, because its outer hull contains saponin, a bitter resin that would otherwise impart a disagreeable taste. Quinoa is the Spanish derivation of *kinua* or *kinoa*, from Quechua, the family of languages spoken by the indigenous people of Peru, Bolivia, Ecuador, Chile and Argentina.

quins - colorful, small candies shaped as everything from autumn leaves to dinosaurs to Christmas trees to Easter eggs, arranged or sprinkled on cakes and confections. The origin of the word is unclear, but perhaps it comes from "sequins," which are also small and colorful.

r
rambutan

rabbit - a mammal of the hare family. Domesticated rabbits are eaten for their fine-textured flesh. The mostly white meat can be prepared in any way suitable for chicken. Wild rabbits have a stronger flavor than domesticated rabbits.

raccoon - indigenous to North America, first introduced to the settlers by Native Americans, still considered exceptional table meat in the southern U.S., especially in **Cajun** cooking. Raccoons have characteristic black rings on their tail, and their nickname "bandit" describes the famous distinctive black facial mask over their cheeks, eyes and nose. The average raccoon weighs about 17 pounds (7.7 kg) and is nowadays trapped more for its hide than its meat.

rack of lamb - see LAMB.

raclette - **1.** a cow's milk cheese from Switzerland with a mild, nutty taste, similar to **Gruyère. 2.** a Swiss dish of cheese exposed to heat (usually an open fire) and scraped off as it melts, served with potatoes, bread and gherkins. The name comes from the French *racler*, meaning "to scrape."

radiatore - SEE PASTA.

radicchio

radicchio - a red-leafed chicory, *Cichorium intybus*, used in salads, originally from the Veneto region in northern Italy, with green leaves that turn red as the temperature falls. Although radicchio has been cultivated in southern France for a long time, Italy has cultivated it since the 16th century and is the world's primary producer. There are two main varieties, Verona and Treviso. Verona has burgundy red leaves with white ribs. It grows in a small loose-leafed head similar to butterhead lettuce. Treviso leaves are narrow and pointed. They are tighter and have tapered heads. The color varies from pink to dark red with white ribs.

radish - a member of the mustard family, *Raphanus sativus*, grown for its crisp, sharp-tasting root. The ancient Egyptians cultivated the radish and called it "moon." It was also known to the Mesopotamians and in various regions of the Near East more than 4,000 years ago. Introduced to China about 500 BC, radishes were cultivated and eaten, mainly pickled, in Asia for thousands of years, eventually making their way to Greece and Italy. *Raphanos*, Greek for "radish," also means "sprouts easily," referring to how quickly and easily the radish grows. They were also cultivated for medicinal purposes, specifically to treat coughs and hemorrhages. While the Athenians made replicas of beets in silver and turnips in lead, gold was reserved for radishes. *Radix*, the Latin word for radish, means "root."

Radishes reached England in the middle of the 16th century. A little more than a century later, a London publication blamed the plague on radishes, among other things. Nearly two centuries later, the great Italian composer Rossini esteemed them so highly that they became one of the subjects of his composition called "Four Hors d'Oeuvres." (The other three were butter, anchovies and pickled gherkins.) Radishes can be solid red, pink, white, purple or black; they can be round, oval or oblong and range in size from that of a cherry to a baseball. Yet, whatever form they take, they almost all taste the same. Radish seeds can be germinated and eaten like alfalfa sprouts. The greens are a delicacy when eaten young and can be prepared like spinach. See also DAIKON.

radish sprouts - see KAIWARE.

Radler - German for "cyclist," refreshment created for a group of thirsty cyclists in 1922 in the Bavarian Alps by an innkeeper who was running out of beer but had a good supply of lemonade so combined the two. See also SHANDY.

raft - see CONSOMMÉ.

ragoût - a thick, flavorful, spicy stew of meat and/or vegetables, from the verb *ragoûter*, meaning "to bring back someone's appetite." See also BURGOO.

ragù - see BOLOGNESE.

raifort sauce - also **horseradish sauce.** A generic name for sauces made with horseradish (*raifort* in French). Grated horseradish, heavy or sour cream, salt, sugar and lemon juice or vinegar are the usual ingredients, but bread crumbs, moistened with milk, may be added. Since heat diminishes the keen flavor and smell of the horseradish, raifort sauces are usually uncooked. An exception is the cooked English version called **Albert sauce,** a butter sauce made with stock and egg yolks, mustard and wine vinegar.

rainbow trout - also **silver trout, steelhead.** A freshwater fish that also adapts to salt water, *Oncorhynchus mykiss* can be found filleted or whole, fresh or frozen in supermarkets or caught in the wild (its fighting spirit makes it a good catch for sportfishermen). Common in North America, it is stocked in the Great Lakes and caught along the Pacific shore. Popular for its firm, tasty flesh, rainbow trout has been exported for aquaculture to countries around the world. See also TROUT.

raisin - **1.** a dried grape, made from **Thomson seedless** and **Muscat grapes,** from the Latin *racemes*, meaning "cluster of grapes." **2.** French for "grape."

raisiné - **1.** a brown, syrupy Swiss concentrate of apple or pear juice simmered and stirred for hours until it caramelizes. A harvest-time specialty, it may be poured over potatoes or, mixed with cream and eggs, used as a filling for tarts. **2.** a style of jam made in Burgundy, France, which has no sugar added to sweeten it; chunks of fruit are stewed in grape juice or wine. Not a preserve, this jam does not keep for long, so it's eaten with bread soon after it's made.

raisin pie - also **funeral pie.** A pie traditionally served at funerals of Old Order Mennonites and Old Amish; it can be made during any season and keeps well when prepared a day or two before the funeral, because it does not need refrigeration. Also called Rosina Pie (*rosina* is German for "raisin").

raita - an Indian salad of thick yogurt mixed with chopped vegetables (cucumber, eggplant, potatoes or spinach) or fruit (bananas or mangoes), served as a foil for spicy dishes.

rambutan - a cool, sweet fruit, *Nephelium lappaceum*, with a large stone and thick red shell covered with short hooked hairs or bristles, native to Malaysia and a close cousin of the lychee fruit, from the Malay *rambut*, meaning "hair." Sometimes called **hairy lychee.**

ramekin - also **ramequin. 1.** a small dish, usually ceramic, in which such a dish is baked and served. **2.** a couple of centuries ago, a *ramequin* was bread toasted with a mixture of offal, meat and vegetables, all blended with cream. It's a derivation of the German *ramken*, from *rahm*, meaning "fresh cream," thus it came to mean "a little dish with cream."

ramen - **1.** long, thin, spaghetti-like noodles usually served in soup with other ingredients, originally exported to Japan from China. *Ramen* is the Japanese pronunciation of the Chinese *lo mein*, meaning "boiled noodles." Made of wheat, sometimes with egg added, the off-white noodles are available dried, fresh or frozen, kinky or straight, and loose or pressed into slabs. In 1958, Momofuku Ando, the founder of Japan's Nissin Foods, pioneered the process of turning traditional ramen noodles into the now-familiar instant packaged noodles. In North America since about 1970, this instant version — packaged with a pouch of dehydrated herbs and seasonings — has become a popular quick soup for a snack or small meal. Chopped vegetables and cooked fish, meat or poultry are added to the noodles to make a more substantial meal. **2.** a dish made with ramen noodles.

ramp - see WILD LEEK.

ranch dressing - a salad dressing made with mayonnaise, buttermilk, herbs and spices, used on salads and as a dipping sauce for crudités or other appetizers. The first ranch dressing was created in the late 1950s by **Steve Henson** and served exclusively at his Hidden Valley Guest Ranch, near Santa Barbara, California. The guests loved the tangy buttermilk dressing so

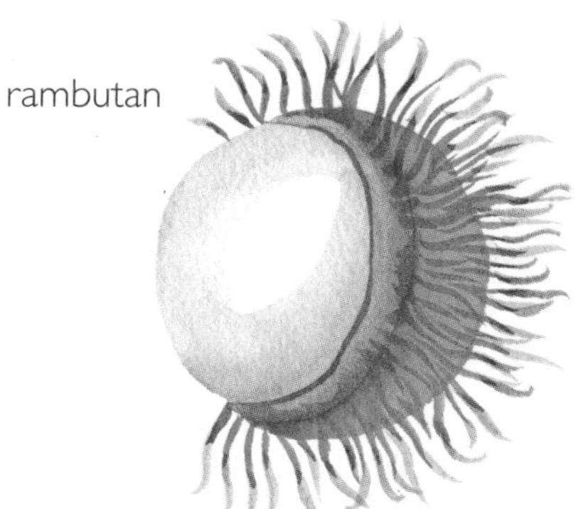
rambutan

much, they convinced him to package his secret spice blend so that they could make it at home, and the famous Hidden Valley Original Ranch salad dressing was born. Today, hundreds of versions are available, and the dressing — original or imitations — can be found on the shelves of almost any North American grocery store.

ranchero sauce - a generic term for a spicy, tomato-based homemade or ready-made salsa, used in Mexican and U.S. Southwest cooking. The basic recipe includes chopped chile and sweet peppers, garlic, lemon juice, onion and tomatoes, mixed fresh. Dressed-up versions may be cooked and contain beer, chopped celery, cumin, oregano and chili or Worcestershire **sauce.** Ranchero sauce is served with fish and meat dishes. It's also a dip for tortilla chips or a topping for hamburgers, omelets and pasta.

rape - **1.** also **broccoli rabe, rape turnip.** A bitter, leafy green of the genus *Brassica,* beloved in Italian cookery. Grown for sheep fodder in some parts of the world, it is now cultivated primarily for its seeds, from which **rapeseed oil** is produced. **2.** the plant matter left (seeds, skins and stems) after grapes are crushed for wine.

rapeseed oil - see CANOLA OIL.

rape turnip - see RAPE.

rapini - see BROCCOLI RABE.

rare - referring to meat lightly cooked, with a red center. The name comes from an Old English term *hrer,* meaning "lightly broiled or underdone."

rarebit - see WELSH RABBIT.

rascal stew - see SONOFABITCH STEW.

rascasse - see SCORPION FISH.

ras el hanout - a hot North African spice mix, its name meaning "top of the shop," used in soups, stews and **tagines,** that's considered fit for a king. An array of 20 to 50 ground spices, such as black pepper, cardamom, cinnamon, cloves, cumin, ginger, paprika and turmeric, and in Tunisia, sometimes rosebuds; or in Morocco, sometimes hashish — merge into a rich, mellow blend.

rasgulla - also **rasagolla, rosogolla.** See DAS, NABIN CHANDRA.

rasher - a single thin slice of bacon or ham.

raspberries

raspberry - a red, golden or black berry from the plant, *Rubus,* belonging to the rose family, thought to have come from Asia Minor. Roman records date the raspberry back to the 4th century AD. The Crusaders found them on their way to Jerusalem and wrote odes to their beauty and perfume. The English are responsible for the raspberry's cultivation throughout the Middle Ages, exporting it to the U.S. in the late 18th century. The black raspberry is indigenous only to eastern North America, its development taking second place to that of the more popular red variety.

ratafia - also **ratafee, ratifia. 1.** a liqueur flavored with fruit kernels, such as cherries and peaches, or bitter almonds. Depending on where ratafia is made, the fruit pits may be steeped in either apple cider, wine or grape juice, possibly with brandy or marc. The term may come from the Latin phrase *Res rata fiat,* a toast made when treaties were ratified in Europe and where cordials were often served during the ceremony. See also NOYAUX. **2.** a macaroon-like biscuit flavored with ratafia.

ratatouille - a French dish from Provence of sautéed eggplant, tomato, sweet pepper, onion, garlic, olive oil and herbs, originally from Nice, from the verb *touiller,* meaning "to mix or stir."

rau ram - see VIETNAMESE MINT.

ravigote - a white wine and vinegar sauce flavored with butter and a mixture of shallots, tarragon, chives and chervil, from the French *ravigoter,* meaning "to refresh," referring to the vinegar's tartness. The sauce was the creation of the legendary French chef **Antonin Carême.**

ravioli - an Italian dish of small squares or rounds of pasta dough stuffed with cheese, meat or vegetables. *Rabiole* is the name in the Genovese dialect, where the dish originated, meaning "bits and pieces" or "odds and ends," referring to how they were originally filled. The city of Cremona also claims to have created ravioli, which may have derived from the Latin *ravoglere*, meaning "to wrap." See also PASTA.

raw foodist - someone who eats only uncooked, unfrozen and unprocessed organic food (mainly fruits, meats, seeds and vegetables). A few raw-food proselytizers surfaced during the late 1800s, but the movement only entered the mainstream a century later. Proponents claim that cooking or freezing foods is unnatural, and damages or destroys the nutrients and essential enzymes (some will consume dairy or meat products that are cooked below 115°F/46°C). Taking their cue from healthy animals in the wild — that also dine *au naturel* — they believe their diet can help them avoid degenerative diseases. Opponents point out that most animals in the wild become "raw food" themselves before they get old enough to develop age-related problems. They also caution that it can be extremely difficult to plan a raw-food diet that adequately addresses the nutritional needs of growing children. Also, many nutrients in foods, such as those found in carrots, are better absorbed by the body when they are partially cooked.

raw milk - see MILK.

raw sugar - see SUGAR.

ray - see SKATE.

razor clam - also **jackknife clam.** A generic term for Pacific coast clams, *Siliqua patula*, found in sandy beaches from Alaska (where it has been commercially harvested since the early 1900s) to southern California, or the Atlantic coast clam, *Ensis directus*. Both are named for their resemblance to a long, folding old-fashioned straight razor. Digging clams is a favorite sport for many oceanside residents: the clams' speed in disappearing down into the sand (it takes only seconds) gives them a fighting chance to escape. The cleaned catch may be steamed in their shells at a clambake, or **butterflied** and battered, then fried in butter.

RDA - also **RDI.** Nutritional guidelines listing the recommended levels of essential nutrients, such as fat, fiber and carbohydrates, minerals and vitamins, required for health. Called RDA (Recommended Daily Allowance) in the United States and RDI (Recommended Daily Intake) in Canada, these guidelines are developed, updated and approved by the respective federal governments. Nutritional information on packaging is often listed as percentages of RDA or RDI.

RDI - see RDA.

reamer - a kitchen utensil used for juicing halved citrus fruit, with a handle at one end and a ridged head that tapers to a point on the other.

Reblochon - a rich, creamy, mild-flavored cheese from the mountainous Savoie region of France, where the cheese is ripened in caves. Its name means "second milking" because the French herdsmen who originally made it used milk from a second (illegal) milking, which was withheld (*lait de rebloche*) when the tax collectors came to check the milk yields. The farmers did not milk the cows dry, but finished the milking after the inspectors had gone.

reconstitute - to restore liquid, most often water, to concentrated or dehydrated foodstuff (such as powdered milk, dried soup mixes and dried noodle-and-vegetable dishes) before cooking or consuming it.

red bean - see KIDNEY BEAN.

red beans and rice - a dish from the U.S. South, consisting of red kidney beans cooked with onions, ham, bacon or salt pork, served with rice and ham. The dish is popular,

razor clams

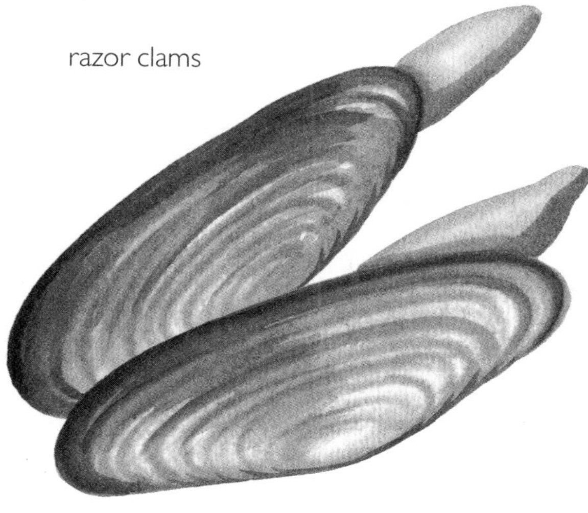

especially in Louisiana, where it's called "Monday dish," because, on laundry day, it could be left to simmer, allowing the beans to become tender and creamy, and be ready when the laundry was done.

red bell pepper - see SWEET PEPPER.

red cabbage - a smooth-leafed, purple-red cabbage that is eaten cooked or raw. The **anthocyanins** associated with its color are considered an important antioxidant, which makes a red head of cabbage an even healthier choice than a green one. See also CABBAGE.

red chief lentil - see LENTIL.

red chile sauce - a Southwestern or Tex-Mex sauce used as a topping for enchiladas, made from ground dried red ancho or pasilla chiles and seasoned with garlic, salt and often oregano and/or cumin. Green chile sauce is made from fresh or dried green chiles and seasoned in the same way.

red cooking - a Chinese technique of braising poultry, meat or vegetables in "red sauce," which lends them a characteristic color and taste. Recipes vary with the chef, but most red sauce contains dark and light soy sauce, ginger, sherry or rice wine, and star anise. Some contain **Chinese five-spice powder,** scallions and orange zest. Bottled red sauce is also available.

red curaçao - see CURAÇAO.

red currant - see CURRANT.

red curry paste - see CURRY PASTE.

red deer - see ELK.

Red Delicious apple - see APPLE.

redeye gravy - from the U.S. South, a reduction of pan drippings from fried ham, water and hot coffee, usually served with ham and biscuits.

redfish - see OCEAN PERCH.

red flannel hash - a traditional New England dish of chopped beets, potatoes, onion and bacon fried until it's brown and crispy, often served with cornmeal.

red food coloring - see ANILINE, COCHINEAL.

red grouper - see GROUPER.

red mullet - also **goatfish.** A thin-skinned, bright crimson fish common on European menus and a favorite with Mediterranean cooks. A "mullet" by common name only, red mullet actually belongs to the Mullidae family and, unlike the real mullet, has two whisker-like barbels under its chin. After gutting, medium and large-size mullet may be added to **bouillabaisse,** grilled or drizzled with olive oil and baked on a bed of herbs. Small ones can be cooked whole, but chefs are advised to remove and reserve the liver — considered a delicacy on its own or in a sauce — first.

red rice - see RICE.

red salt - also **alaea salt.** An expensive Hawaiian sea salt mixed with local volcanic red clay (alaea), which gives the granules a distinctive reddish tint and high iron content. Best used as a finishing salt on any dish where the salt will be visible or where its texture will be noticeable. See also SALT.

red snapper - see SNAPPER.

red split lentil - see LENTIL.

reduce - to boil a liquid rapidly to thicken the consistency and concentrate the flavor.

reduction - the thickened sauce that results when liquids are reduced.

red velvet cake - see VELVET CAKE.

red whortleberry - see LINGONBERRY.

red wine - a wine made from red grapes, such as **Pinot Noir** or **Cabernet Sauvignon.** Red wine turns red thanks to pigments called **anthocyanins** in the grape skins, which are allowed to remain in contact with the grape juice after pressing. The skins, as well as the stems, of the grapes also contribute **tannins** to the wine, which give it a certain amount of acidity and act as a preservative. Red wines can be cellared for much longer than white wines because of their tannin content. See also BLUSH WINE, WHITE WINE, WINE.

red yeast - a wild yeast, sold dried and used mainly for fermenting Asian vinegars.

refresh - see SHOCK.

refried beans - boiled pinto or red beans, mashed, then fried in oil with minced **chipotle** pepper and onion. Refried beans are used as an ingredient in other foods or as a side dish. The thick, pasty spread is a common ingredient in

chilaquiles, enchiladas and tacos. The English name is a mistranslation of the Spanish *frijoles refritos*, meaning "fried" (not "refried") "beans." See also TEX-MEX.

refrigerator cookie - see ICEBOX COOKIE.

refritos - see REFRIED BEANS.

Reggiano Parmigiano - see PARMESAN.

Rehoboam - see WINE BOTTLES.

Reichl, Ruth - see profile below.

reindeer - a domesticated, large-antlered (both male and female), herbivorous deer, *Rangifer tarandus*. The reindeer has been the centuries-old diet of nomadic herdsmen, such as the Sami people, in northern Europe and Eurasia, who drive them hundreds of miles over land and water to their seasonal pastures. Radioactive contamination of the vegetation they eat, particularly lichens, means that many northern reindeer now accumulate dangerous levels of radioactivity in their flesh. Farmed commercially in such places as Alaska and northern British Columbia, reindeer meat, which is available fresh, frozen and processed into sausages, has been in greater demand recently, due to the **mad cow disease** scare. The caribou of North America are considered the same species, but are wild. See also CARIBOU, DEER.

relax - a term used in pastry making to describe the dough's **rest** after forming and before rolling or cutting, which allows the flour's gluten to rest, making the pastry less likely to shrink while baking.

relish - a pickled or cooked condiment made with vegetables or fruits.

rellenos de papa - also **potato fritters.** A Latin American dish consisting of balls of mashed potato, stuffed with a spicy, seasoned mixture of ground beef or pork and chopped garlic, onion, peppers, pimiento, prunes and raisins, rolled in cornstarch and deep-fried.

rémoulade - a sharp French sauce of mayonnaise, mustard, pickles, capers, various herbs and anchovies; served cold as a sauce most often for fish, similar to **tartar sauce.**

rémuage - also **riddling.** See MÉTHODE CHAMPENOISE.

render - to heat fat from an animal or fowl at a low temperature, so that it melts into a liquid and separates from any tissue. The liquid fat is carefully strained to remove any remaining fine solids before it is cooled. The resulting pure fat must be refrigerated until it is used. See also SCHMALTZ.

renkon - see LOTUS ROOT.

rennet - an organic substance containing the enzyme **rennin,** used in cheese making, causing milk's solid particles to break from the water content and form a solid mass. Rennet is usually taken from the stomach linings of young animals, especially calves, but it can also be produced from some fungi. In the days when the dressed stomachs of young lambs were used as drinking vessels (goatskin bladders are still used as wine jugs in some countries), cheese would form naturally from milk carried in them and,

Reichl, Ruth (1948–) - American restaurant critic, author and food editor, who returned *Gourmet* magazine to prominence after taking over as editor in 1999. Despite her academic training as an art historian, Reichl began her culinary life in the early 1970s in California, where she co-founded a cooperative Berkeley restaurant. She freelanced as a food writer and critic, and published her first book, *Mmmmm: A Feastiary,* in 1972. Reichl became food editor and restaurant critic at the *Los Angeles Times* in 1984 and took over as restaurant critic at *The New York Times* in 1993. In a departure from her predecessors, who never veered from rating only formal, classical French restaurants, Reichl would rate the city's ethnic establishments and grant star status to a noodle house, for example, if deserving. Since her first book, Reichl has written three more memoirs: *Tender at the Bone: Growing Up at the Table* (1998), *Comfort Me With Apples: More Adventures at the Table* (2001) and *Garlic and Sapphires: The Secret Life of a Critic in Disguise* (2005). In 2004, she edited *The Gourmet Cookbook,* a collection of more than 1,000 recipes from the magazine's history.

when the whey was poured off, a curd would remain that was solid enough to be shaped with the hands. To this day, in certain parts of Turkey and Pakistan, cheese is cured in goatskin or sheepskin bags.

rennin - a digestive enzyme secreted by the stomach lining of mammals that is used to curdle milk when making cheese or sour cream. Most commonly derived from the stomachs of calves or goats (usually unweaned animals, since they require a high concentration of rennin in order to digest their all-milk diet), it may be sold as a liquid, powder or tablet. Rennin, derived from plant enzymes, is used to make kosher or vegetarian foods, and in the production of some classic Italian and Spanish cheeses. See also RENNET.

rest - see RELAX.

restaurant - from the French *restaurer*, meaning "to restore." The first French restaurant was born in Paris in 1765. Before then, all food prepared for sale was the product of strictly protected guilds: *rôtisseurs* provided roasted meats; *pâtissiers* made poultry items, pies and tarts; *tamisiers* made breads; and *vinaigriers* made sauces and the stews known as *restaurantes*, meaning "restoratives," referring to how one could expect this dish to restore one's energy. In 1765, an enterprising tavern owner named Boulanger decided he wanted to sell his own version of a restorative, a stew of mutton in white sauce, breaking the cardinal rule of offering foods of his own making, to order, rather than from a fixed menu at a fixed time, as inns were permitted to do at the time. The guilds promptly shut him down and brought a legal suit against him, claiming his trade violated the guilds' rights. The case went all the way to the French parliament, involving King Louis XV himself, who decided in Boulanger's favor, paving the way for all future restaurateurs. The first restaurant resembling our modern version appeared in Paris in 1782. Antoine Beauvilliers opened La Grande Taverne de Londres, with well-attired waiters serving patrons in an elegantly appointed room and a "cave" of fine wines to complement its exclusive cuisine.

resto-pub - a term used to describe a restaurant-bar that serves up better food than the usual pub fare, often with live entertainment.

retsina - an ancient Greek **aromatized wine** flavored with pine resin, described as a noble drink by connoisseurs and as a close cousin to turpentine by its detractors. Love it or hate it, this white or rosé wine is best served chilled and is considered an excellent complement to the herbaceous dishes of Greek cuisine. Retsina is said to have developed circa 700 BC, when pine resin was used to seal **amphorae** to prevent wine from going bad. The aromatized wine that emerged became an acquired taste and was deliberately infused with pine sap thereafter.

Reuben - a sandwich of corned beef, Swiss cheese and sauerkraut on rye bread, served either cold or grilled. There are two conflicting stories about the origin of the sandwich. Arthur Reuben, owner of Reuben's Delicatessen at Madison and 59th in New York City, claimed to have created the first one for Annette Seelos, an actress briefly famous for an appearance in a Charlie Chaplin movie in 1914. However, food wholesaler Reuben Kay (also Kolakofsky) claimed to have invented the sandwich in Omaha, Nebraska, in 1925 during a poker game, using whatever could be found in the kitchen. In 1956, Fern Snider, chef of the Rose Bowl Restaurant in Omaha, entered the Reuben in a national competition and won.

rhea - a large, flightless bird of the family Rheidae, Rhea americana or Rhea pennata, similar to the ostrich and emu but smaller than both, farmed in North America for its lean meat, which is lower in fat and cholesterol than chicken. Rhea meat is similar to beef in flavor and texture and can be used in all types of recipes. It is at its best when cooked slowly over low heat or quickly seared, like a steak. It can be overcooked very easily because it is extremely low in fat.

rhizome - a long, bulbous and thickened plant stem that grows under the earth (or, in aquatic plants, underwater), from which shoots grow up and roots grow down. Gingerroot and lotus root are just two examples of edible rhizomes.

Rhode Island clam chowder - see CLAM CHOWDER.

rhubarb - also **pie plant.** *Rheum rhabarbarum* (Latin for "barbarian rhubarb"), a hardy perennial native to Asia where it was cultivated for its medicinal, rhizomatous roots. Beginning about the 10th century, travelers slowly brought

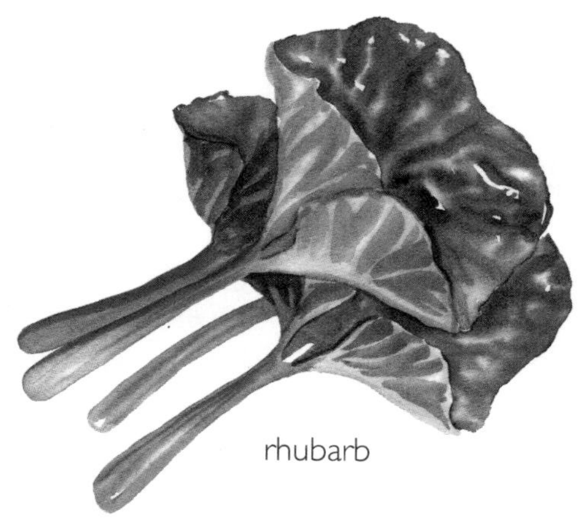
rhubarb

rootstalks to Russia, Turkey, then farther west; by the 1800s it was cultivated in kitchen gardens in North America and sold in markets along the eastern seaboard. The large glossy leaves are toxic, containing oxalic acid which causes symptoms ranging from digestive upset to respiratory failure, coma and death. The exceedingly tart, fibrous and thick red stalks of modern cultivars are the only part of the plant commonly eaten today, cut-up, sweetened and stewed (then served plain or as an accompaniment to custard, pudding or yogurt), mixed with a sweet fruit (such as strawberries) in jam, or used on its own in crisps, crumbles or tarts, or, most famously, in pies. In parts of Europe and the Middle East, rhubarb is usually used in savory dishes. A low-maintenance favorite for home gardeners who enjoy its long spring harvest, rhubarb is also grown commercially and greenhouse-grown stalks are available much of the year. Botanically a vegetable, rhubarb was classified as a fruit by a U.S. Customs Court in 1947 (the ruling was important because vegetables were charged a higher duty).

rib - **1.** see BEEF, PORK. **2.** a celery stalk.

ribbon sandwich - a striped **finger sandwich** made from three stacked slices of bread (sometimes alternating white with whole wheat) and one (or more than one) soft, fine-textured filling, such as cream cheese or deviled ham, layered in between. After removing their crusts, square sandwich loaves are cut horizontally, then the long slices are buttered, spread with filling, stacked, wrapped tightly with plastic wrap and refrigerated for about four hours until firm. The long sandwich is unwrapped and cut into narrow sandwiches across the width, revealing the "ribbons" of bread and filling.

riboflavin - see B VITAMINS.

ribollita - Italian for "boil again," a rustic Tuscan bean soup thickened with bread. It was originally a method for stretching leftover minestrone, which was boiled again the next day with the addition of bread.

rib steak - see ENTRECÔTE.

rice - from the Greek *oryza,* a grain that has been cultivated for at least 7,000 years. Alexander the Great came across rice during his travels through Mesopotamia and carried samples of rice back to the Mediterranean Basin, where it was well received by the Greeks and Romans. In the 5th century BC, Sophocles made mention of rice in his tragedies. Rice did not become popular in Italian cooking until the 16th century, when it began to be cultivated on a large scale in the Po Valley. Traditionally, rice has played a much greater part in the cooking of northern Italy than in the south. **Catherine de' Medici** brought rice with her to France, where it was cultivated in the Rhône Valley.

The cultural role of rice is best expressed idiomatically. In China, losing or quitting a job is described as "breaking the rice bowl," in reference to the effect it's likely to have on one's food supply, and getting a new job is described as "buying heavy rice." A typical modern Chinese greeting is: "Have you had your rice today?" The Japanese word for "cooked rice" is the same as the word for "meal." The importance of rice is also displayed in industry: *honda* means "main rice field," and *toyota* means "bountiful rice field." When the Thai call their family and friends to a meal, they say, "Let's eat rice." In India, it's said that grains of rice should be like two brothers: close but not stuck together.

Clues to a society's ethos lie in how its people name their chief staple. In Cantonese, rice is called *mai,* meaning "agriculture," while in Mandarin, it's called *me,* meaning "culture." In Japan, it's called *gohan,* meaning "a full meal," in Sanskrit, *vrihih,* meaning "life-giving seed." The Thai word for rice translates as "food with wings to fly." In Korea, it's translated either as "God's tears" or "God's fears." The Greeks call it *oryza sativa, oriza* meaning "of Oriental origin" and *sativa* meaning "sown."

There are three styles of rice. **Long-grain** rice is the most widely consumed, almost five times longer than its width, light and fluffy, remaining

RICE VARIETIES

There are more than 2,000 different varieties of rice. The following are among the most popular:

Arborio - an Italian-grown short-grain rice, traditionally used in making risotto, because its high starch content gives the dish its characteristic creaminess.

basmati - a long-grain fragrant variety that has been aged to reduce the moisture content and enhance its unique bouquet; imported exclusively from Punjab province in the foothills of the Himalayas. *Basmati* means "queen of fragrance."

black - an aromatic whole-grain rice, usually used in desserts, which turns its cooking water a deep shade of purple. There are several varieties of black rice: Chinese or "Forbidden Black," Thai Black Sticky Rice and Black Japonica, which was developed in the U.S.

brown - the whole unpolished grain with outer husk removed and bran layers intact.

Calrose - developed after the Second World War in California by agricultural researchers who wanted to create high-quality rice that would thrive using minimal water and mechanical harvesting.

cargo - also **paddy.** Cargo rice has been dehusked but not refined in any way.

carnaroli - a high-starch, Italian short-grain rice, often used for risotto.

Carolina - a popular and versatile hulled and polished long-grain rice; it remains firm, fluffy and separate when cooked; cultivated mainly in California, Texas, Louisiana and Arkansas. See also PATNA.

converted - see PARBOILED.

Della rice - a variety of rice developed in the U.S., a cross between long-grain and basmati rice, fragrant and fluffy like **basmati** but plumper.

glutinous rice - see STICKY.

Indica - one of the three main groups of rice (Japonica and Javinica being the other two). Varieties of Indica rice, such as basmati, are usually longer grain and grow near the equator.

instant - partially cooked and dehydrated, so that the kernels can reconstitute quickly with little water; the least nourishing of any rice.

Japonica - a medium- to short-grain rice.

jasmine - a Thai long-grain rice with a distinctive scent released during cooking; sold in both white and brown varieties.

mochi - a short-grained and glutinous rice, often pounded to make confections.

paddy - see CARGO.

parboiled - also **converted.** Rice that has been soaked and steamed under pressure and dried before milling, retaining more nutrients than conventionally milled white rice; a technique developed 2,000 years ago.

Patna - a firm long-grain rice, named for the Indian city on the Ganges where it's grown; imported during the 19th century to South Carolina by East Indian laborers from the West Indies, which is how it also became known as **Carolina**.

red - an aromatic whole-grain rice, with a brownish red outer layer, grown in many parts of the world, including Bhutan and the Carmargne area of France.

sticky - also **glutinous rice, sweet.** A long-grain rice, popular in Thai, Chinese and Japanese cuisines, it cooks to a sticky texture.

sweet - see STICKY.

Texmati - an aromatic cross between American long-grain and basmati rice, grown primarily in Texas.

vialone nano - a white rice grown in the Mantua and Veneto regions of Italy. Although its round, stubby grains (*nano* is Italian for "dwarf") have a high starch content, the rice is not sticky and absorbs flavors and liquids well; this makes it a top choice for risotto.

Wehani rice - long-grain red-brown rice, mildly sweet and nutty, unmilled and cooked like brown rice. It splits lengthwise slightly when cooked.

white - rice with the husk and bran removed, often enriched with vitamins and minerals to compensate for the nutrients lost in processing.

separate when cooked, grown mostly in the U.S., Thailand, Surinam, Indonesia, Vietnam and India. **Medium-grain** rice is two to three times longer than its width, tender and moist, often clinging together when cooked, grown mostly in China, Egypt and Italy. **Short-** or **round-grain** rice is short, plump and almost round, and when cooked, the grains are soft and cling together, releasing almost 15 percent starch into the cooking water; it is cultivated in Japan, California, Egypt, Spain, Italy and Portugal and is also known as "Japonica."

Much of Asia's cultivation of rice is still carried out by hand, following traditional techniques. The land is prepared by plowing, fertilizing and then smoothing the field flat. Seedlings are begun in beds and transplanted into a flooded field, with irrigation controlled by a system of canals and dikes. Flooding controls the growth of weeds that inhibit the seedlings' growth. The fields are drained before the harvest. Paddy rice is prolific. Often one growing season can yield two harvests.

The milling of rice entails removing the husk, leaving what we know as brown rice, the intact kernel still covered in layers of bran. Polishing is the next step: the rice travels through a wire-brush machine to remove the aleurone layer and its inherent fat content, which would otherwise leave rice with a short shelf life. Sugar is sometimes added to brighten its sheen. See also WEHANI RICE, WILD RICE.

rice ball - see ONIGIRI.

rice bean - native to Southeast Asia, the rice bean, *Phaseolus calcaratus*, is grown in limited amounts in China, India and the Philippines. It's named because of its rice-like taste.

rice bran - see BRAN.

rice flour - a flour made from white rice that has been pounded into a fine powder, used in baked goods and as a thickener. Brown rice flour is ground from whole-grain brown rice and used for baking, cooking and to make gluten-free pastas. See also FLOUR.

rice flour noodle - see RICE STICK NOODLE.

rice honey - see RICE SYRUP.

Rice Krispie square - a sticky, no-bake bar cookie made from Rice Krispie cereal stirred together with a warmed mixture of butter, melted marshmallows and vanilla, pressed into a pan to cool and set, then cut into squares. Creative cooks stir in extras, such as chocolate chips, peanuts and peanut butter, raisins and sprinkles. The cold breakfast cereal was introduced by Kellogg Co., in 1928; the cookie recipe followed shortly after in 1933 and has been a mainstay for North American moms ever since.

rice milk - a homemade or ready-made milky drink made by blending together cooked rice with warm water, a sweetener (such as sugarcane syrup) and flavorings (such as vanilla), then straining out any small, solid particles. Many brands offer an enriched version with added calcium and vitamins. The lactose-intolerant and vegetarians love it.

rice paddle - a stubby paddle-like blade, sometimes slightly curved, attached to a long handle. Made of bamboo or wood, it is used as a lifter, server and stirrer, and also to toss foods while stir-frying. In North America, some rice cookers and sushi mats are sold with their own rice paddles.

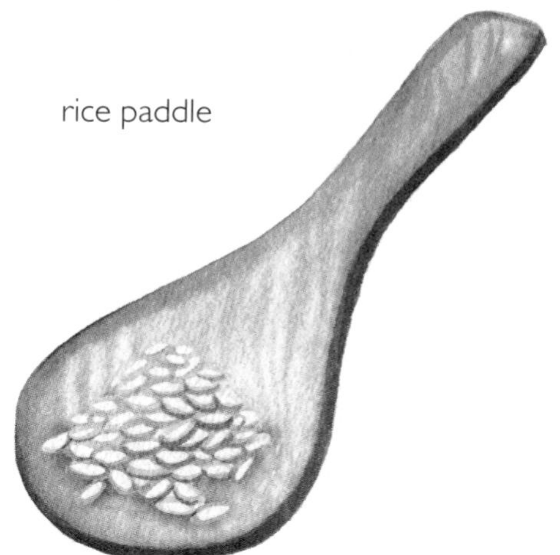
rice paddle

rice paper - an edible product sold in brittle sheets or rounds, dipped into warm water to soften, used to wrap salad rolls, fish or other foods, easily forming a seal when wet. It is usually steamed, although it can also be fried. It does not come from the rice plant, but rather the pith of the stem of an Asian tree, *Tetrapanax papyrifera*, also known appropriately as the rice paper plant.

rice pudding - a creamy dessert made with rice, milk, sugar and eggs, often flavored with spices and raisins. The first recorded mention of rice pudding is from the Romans. The centurions called it an "aqueous brew of rice and water" and ate it after a battle to clear their heads. The Gaels refined it a little by adding cream, but it was the Benedictine monks, during the Middle Ages, who made it more palatable by adding dried fruits, honey, eggs and brandy, and seasoning it with cinnamon, mace and cloves.

ricer - a culinary tool resembling a large garlic press, used to mill cooked potatoes, so named because the extruded food is reduced to soft, rice-size particles. The ricer is also an excellent tool for making chestnut purée.

rice stick noodle - also **rice flour noodle.** A type of Asian noodle made from rice flour andzwater, made in a wide variety of thicknesses and widths, some flat and wide (such as **banh pho**), some thin and round (such as rice vermicelli). These noodles are frequently used in Vietnamese, Thai, Malaysian and Chinese cuisines in stir-fries, soups, cold spring rolls and so on. They come dried and packaged in bundles and need to be soaked for about 20 minutes in hot water to make them edible. See also ASIAN NOODLES.

rice syrup - also **rice honey, yinnie syrup.** A homemade or ready-made golden, light, sweet syrup made by fermenting, then boiling whole-grain rice (usually brown). A sweetener with complex sugars, it adds a slight butterscotch flavor to baked goods and confections, salad dressings and sauces; vegans use it as a honey substitute.

rice vermicelli - vermicelli made with rice flour, rather than semolina flour. See also PASTA.

rice vinegar - also **Chinese vinegar.** The Chinese have been using rice to make vinegar for more than 3,000 years. There are basically three kinds of rice vinegar. **White rice vinegar** is colorless, similar to Western vinegars, but less acidic and milder; it is used extensively in stir-fries, sweet-and-sour dishes and in pickling. **Red rice vinegar** is darker in color, with a unique blend of sweetness and tartness; it makes an excellent dip and is a key ingredient in **shark's fin** soup. **Black rice vinegar** is dark, with a deep, smoky flavor, made with glutinous or sweet rice, although millet or sorghum are sometimes used instead. However, the best black rice vinegar is made with only rice, water and salt. Black rice vinegar is often used in braises, as a dipping sauce and a substitute for balsamic vinegar.

There are differences between rice wine and rice vinegar, which many people confuse. Enjoyed by the Chinese for more than 4,000 years, rice wine is made using a fermentation process involving yeast, which transforms the sugars from glutinous rice into alcohol. When making rice vinegar, the fermentation process goes one step further, adding bacteria to turn the alcohol into acid. It's easy enough to confuse the two, since they often sit side by side at the grocery store. The fact that rice vinegar is also called "rice wine vinegar" doesn't help matters. See also RICE WINE.

rice wine - not a wine, but a cooking condiment widely used in Asian cooking, made using a fermentation process involving yeast which transforms the sugars from glutinous rice into alcohol. Not to be confused with **sake;** although sake is a rice wine, the two are made very differently. When making rice vinegar, the fermentation process goes one step further, adding bacteria to turn the alcohol into acid. Rice vinegars are generally made from the lees (dregs) of the wine. Both, especially those from Japan, tend to be mild and sweet, and add a bit of acidity to dressings and cooking. The Chinese red and black varieties are also used as condiments, but still are characterized as mild vinegars. There are also Korean varieties, some of which are much stronger. See also RICE VINEGAR.

rice wrappers - see RICE PAPER.

riche sauce - see DIPLOMAT SAUCE.

rickey - a refreshing, tart cocktail made with liquor, lime juice and soda water. Rickeys can be made with almost any liquor, but the gin rickey is perhaps the best known. A gin rickey turns into a **Tom Collins** with the addition of sugar and a switch from lime to lemon juice.

ricotta - Italian for "recooked," referring to the process of reheating the leftover whey from cheese making (particularly provolone and mozzarella), with the addition of a little fresh milk. Ricotta is a soft-curd cheese made from either cow's or sheep's milk and has a fat content of only 20 percent. This type of cheese has been made for centuries, inspiring many imitations. A Maltese version (*rkotta*) is made from cow's milk and seawater.

ricotta salata - a pressed, white Sicilian cheese made of ewe's milk. Dense and somewhat dry, it has a sharp, salty flavor (*salata* is Italian for "salted" or "salty.") Crumbled, it may be sprinkled over fresh salads, grilled vegetables or pasta dishes.

riddling - also **rémuage.** See MÉTHODE CHAMPENOISE.

rigatoni - see PASTA.

rijsttafel - a Dutch interpretation of a traditional Indonesian feast: hot cooked rice served with an elaborate array of side dishes, such as soups, satays, **sambals,** curried meats and seafood, condiments, vegetables and fruits. The name means "rice table." The concept was imported to the Netherlands as a result of its colonization of Indonesia in the 1700s and 1800s. A traditional rijsttafel contained a huge number of dishes, upwards of 40 separate ones in some of the most opulent cases, and could take hours to consume. Today, this style of eating is still popular in the Netherlands and in Indonesia (as well as in Dutch restaurants in other countries), but the table tends to be set with fewer dishes than it was during the excesses of colonial rule.

Rikyu - see SEN RIKYU.

rillettes - a French dish made from meat (usually pork, but also duck or salmon) slowly cooked, mashed and preserved in its own fat, packed into small pots and eaten like a **pâté,** usually on small pieces of toast. See also CHARCUTERIE.

Rioja - often referred to as Spain's Bordeaux, despite the fact that the region's wines are more similar to Burgundies, because of their supple, earthy, often refined qualities. For more than a century, La Rioja has been considered Spain's pre-eminent wine region; it is especially renowned for red wines made from the Tempranillo grape. The region may have got its name in the 11th century from the tiny Rio Oja, one of the seven tributaries of the Ebro River, which flows through the region. But there are several other alternate theories. One is that the name comes from the Ruccones, a pre-Roman tribe that inhabited the region. Another is that its name comes from *roja,* Spanish for "red," possibly referring to the rose-colored soil. Yet another theory is that its name comes from the Basque *eria ogia,* meaning "land of bread," since the region is also known for cereal crops.

ris - French for "sweetbreads."

riso - Italian for "rice."

risotto - an Italian rice dish made by lightly sautéing short-grain rice, such as Arborio, Baldo, Carnaroli or Vialone Nano, with onions in butter and then gradually adding stock as the rice cooks. The mixture must be stirred almost constantly; the result has a creamy consistency, although the grains remain distinct and slightly al dente.

rissole - **1.** a turnover of puff pastry, enclosing a savory filling (such as **forcemeat**) or a sweet one (such as spiced fruit) that is fried, or given an egg wash, then baked. A dusting of sugar often tops sweet versions. **2.** a small ball-shaped mixture of minced seasoned fish, lentils, meat, nuts or vegetables (most often partly cooked potato) or cheese, or a combination, usually rolled in bread crumbs then fried in butter until browned and crisp. (Sometimes, shaped in a disk or finger.) Served as a starter or side dish, rissoles may be accompanied by sauce. The French verb, *rissoler,* means "to brown." Brave barbecue chefs risk blackening theirs on a grill.

Ritz, César - see profile below.

river pear - see ANCHOVY PEAR.

Riverside orange - see ORANGE.

Ritz, César (1850–1918) - Swiss hotelier whose name has become synonymous with style, elegance and luxury, like his hotels. Before meeting French chef **Auguste Escoffier** at Monte Carlo's Grand Hotel in 1884, Ritz had worked his way up from hotel groom and headwaiter to hotel manager. Ritz and Escoffier created a modern hotel industry that began when they were both recruited to join the newly opened Savoy in London in 1890. Their successful partnership led to the opening of the Carlton in London, the Grand Hotel in Rome, as well as a string of Ritz hotels in Paris, London, New York, Montreal and Philadelphia. Because of his reputation for elegance, luxury, quality and style, "ritz" has come to describe the same.

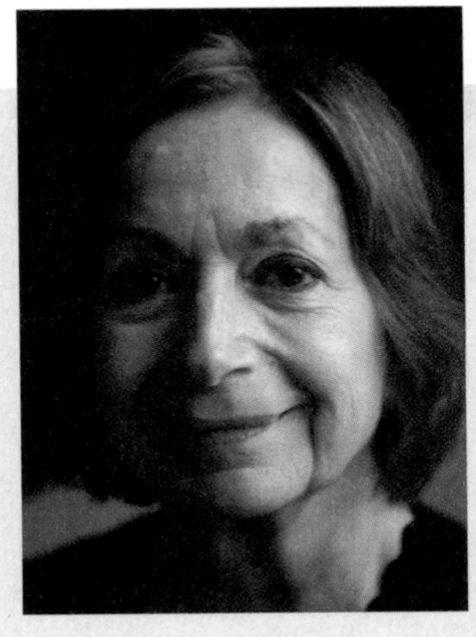

Roden, Claudia (circa 1940–) - cookbook author, culinary historian and television personality. Born in Cairo, she was educated there until she was 15 years old, a member of a close and cultured community, which she described as "a continuation of the Belle Epoque in an annex of Europe." This idyllic existence came to an end in 1956 after the Suez crisis, when Jews were banished from Egypt. Her family eventually settled in London, where Claudia studied art after completing her education in Paris. Married and feeling very much an exile, Roden began to collect recipes from friends and family members as a way of preserving one aspect of their blissful Cairo life. Many of her most vivid memories revolved around food and she later defined her work as "the fruit of nostalgic longing for... a food that was the constant joy of life in a world so different from the Western one."

Her first book, *A Book of Middle Eastern Food* (1968) immediately became a classic, introducing the Western world to a panoply of exotic delights; foods, such as pomegranates and figs; dishes, such as tabbouleh and couscous; and seasonings, such as saffron and tamarind. A diligent researcher and evocative writer, she situated recipes in a social and historical context, no mean feat since regional cookbooks were few and far between and recipes tended to belong to an oral tradition handed down from mother to daughter. The author of five other books on subjects, such as coffee, picnics and Italian food, she also hosted a BBC television series, *Mediterranean Cooking with Claudia Roden* in the 1980s.

In 1996, she published *The Book of Jewish Food,* an intensely personal collection of "ancestral memories" containing more than 800 recipes documenting the Ashkenazi and Sephardi traditions. The theme of exile runs between the lines of this work, which tells the story "of an uprooted migrating people and their vanished worlds." It is a masterpiece of cultural anthropology, for which she received the prestigious Glenfiddich Cookbook of the Year Award and the **James Beard** Foundation Cookbook of the Year. As the writer Simon Schama said, "Claudia Roden is no more a simple cookbook writer than **Marcel Proust** was a biscuit baker. She is, rather, memorialist, historian, ethnographer, anthropologist, essayist, poet, who just happens to communicate through *ta'am* — taste."

riz - French for "rice."

roast - **1.** (v.) to cook with dry, hot air on all sides, either enclosed in an oven or by rotating on a spit. **2.** (n.) a piece of meat cooked in this manner.

roasted garlic - garlic that has been roasted until soft and spreadable, used on its own as a spread or added to savory dishes, sometimes even added to sweets, such as roasted garlic ice cream. This wildly popular flavoring is made by slicing the top off a whole head of garlic so that each clove is slightly exposed. The garlic is then drizzled with olive oil, wrapped in foil to prevent it from drying out, then roasted until the cloves are soft and browned. The cloves are then squeezed out of their papery shells. Roasting garlic significantly reduces its pungency and caramelizes some of its natural sugars, making it nuttier and sweeter than raw garlic. See also GARLIC.

roasted red pepper - a red bell pepper that has been roasted or grilled over an open flame until its skin chars, then skinned and seeded. These peppers can be used in recipes or eaten on their own, and are a recently ubiquitous ingredient in North American cuisine. Roasted red peppers are often associated with Italian cuisine, where they are frequently a feature on **antipasto** platters.

roasters - see CHICKEN.

rocambole - also **giant garlic, sand leek, Spanish garlic.** A milder variety of garlic, *Allium scorodoprasum*, indigenous to northern Europe and now cultivated there. It is used in a similar way as leeks and shallots. Imported to North America, it has now naturalized along the shores of Lake Michigan and Lake Superior.

rockahominy - see PINOLE.

rock bun - also **rock cake.** A small, dense, British cake or bun containing candied peel and currants or raisins that is dropped by spoonfuls onto a baking sheet, which gives it the rough, rocky appearance for which it is named.

rock candy - see AMORPHOUS SUGAR.

rock cockle - see PACIFIC LITTLENECK CLAM.

Rock Cornish game hen - also **Cornish hen.** A cross between the White Rock and Cornish breeds of chicken, weighing up to 1½ pounds (750 g). Very popular in North America and used for baking, broiling and roasting. They were introduced in 1965 by Donald Tyson, of Tyson Foods, as a specialty item that could be taken to market sooner because they mature in 28 to 30 days, compared to chickens, which take 43.

rocket - see ARUGULA.

rock lobster - also **spiny lobster.** See LOBSTER.

rock salt - see SALT.

rock salmon - see CAPE SHARK.

rocks glass - see OLD-FASHIONED GLASS.

rock sugar - see SUGAR.

Rocky Mountain oysters - see PRAIRIE OYSTERS.

rocky road - **1.** a chunky combination bar cookie and candy made with melted chocolate (chips or squares), chopped nuts (usually almonds, peanuts or, in the American South, pecans), marshmallows and varying other ingredients, such as beaten eggs, butter, sweetened condensed milk or vanilla. The mixture is stirred together in a double-boiler, poured into a pan to cool, then cut into squares that resemble a piece of dark pavement embedded with bits of rock. **2.** a homemade or brand name ice cream flavor made with chunks of chocolate, marshmallow and nuts.

Roden, Claudia - see profile left.

Rodier, Father Clément - see CLEMENTINE.

roe - fish eggs or sperm (the former is called **"hard roe,"** the latter is called **"soft roe"** or **milt.** Some eggs, notably the sought-after, but now banned, sturgeon roe from the Caspian Sea, are salted and/or smoked, pasteurized and vacuum-packed as caviar. Spooned onto buttered **blinis** or toast (a crystal spoon is recommended, since metal is suspected of tainting the taste of the caviar), it is savored with a sip of chilled champagne or vodka. Hard and soft roe from various fish, such as carp, cod, herring, lumpfish, mackerel, salmon, trout and whitefish, may also be sold fresh or frozen for use cooked or raw in hors d'oeuvres, salads and sushi, and in famous dishes, such as the Greek **taramosalata.** Each has its own characteristic color, texture and **mouth feel;** some are smooth, some are crunchy. Of necessity, the fish are killed before or when the roe is removed, but — to save the marine equivalent of the geese that lay the golden eggs — new extraction methods are being developed to leave the fish alive and able to produce more roe. See also MILT.

Rohwedder, Otto Frederick - see profile below.

Rohwedder, Otto Frederick (1880–1960) - American inventor of a commercial machine to slice bread. Rohwedder was an Iowa jeweler and owned three stores, but by all accounts, 1912 was the year he started thinking seriously about building a bread-slicing machine. Convinced that his invention had commercial merit, he sold his stores and began working on the design. In 1917, a fire destroyed his factory and its contents, including his prototype and blueprints. During the decade it took to recoup his losses and reassemble investors, Rohwedder worked as an investment and security agent. By 1928, his first saleable bread-slicing model was complete, and he was ready to apply for his patent. Rohwedder's machine made it possible for the Continental Baking Co. to introduce sliced Wonder Bread in 1930, which originally struggled to find its market but became one of the best-known food brands of all time. Because of Rohwedder's invention, the pop-up toaster, which was invented by Charles Strite in 1926 and which had languished on store shelves for years, began to take its place among the modern kitchen's essential appliances. The original 1928 model of Rohwedder's machine is part of the Smithsonian Institution's collection in Washington.

roker - see SKATE.

roll - **1.** (n.) a single serving of yeast-bread dough rolled into a crescent or spiral, tied into a knot or cut into rounds and then baked. Rolls are a ubiquitous starter in many restaurants, served in baskets with butter pats. **2.** (v.) to roll out and flatten foodstuff, such as dough, using a rolling pin. **3.** (v.) to roll up a thin sheet or slice of foodstuff, such as a cabbage leaf, slice of cake or slab of meat, around a filling, jelly-roll fashion.

rolled barley - see BARLEY.

rolled cookie - see PINWHEEL COOKIE.

rolled oats - also **oatflakes.** Steamed, halved, hulled oat kernels (**groats**) that have been rolled to flatten them into flakes, in a process invented in 1877 by the Quaker Mill Co. of Ohio. The dry flakes are used in cakes, cookies and squares, **haggis, muesli,** porridge, trail mix and even as a filler for hamburgers and meat loaf. See also OAT.

rolled roast - a boneless cut of meat, such as pork loin, that is sold rolled and tied with twine. It can be roasted as is, or opened and spread with a savory filling, then re-rolled, cooked and sliced into pinwheels.

rolled sandwich - see PINWHEEL SANDWICH.

rolling boil - a liquid that is bubbling and energetically boiling that cannot be calmed by stirring; a very fast boil.

rolling cookie cutter - see COOKIE CUTTER.

rolling pin - also **baker's pin.** A long cylindrical kitchen utensil, with or without handles, used to roll out pie, pastry, cookie or bread dough. Rolling pins can be made from almost any material, from plastic to stainless steel to porcelain, but the most popular materials are wood and marble. A French rolling pin is simply a long cylinder of wood with no handles, which allows the cook more contact with the dough and the ability to "feel" it as it's rolled out. The typical North American rolling pin has handles on both ends, with a metal rod through the center of the barrel and ball bearings inside so that the handles spin independently of the barrel. Tapered rolling pins are similar to the long, straight French pins, but they taper at both ends, allowing the cook to turn them quickly and easily when rolling out a circle. There are also grooved rolling pins for rolling out puff pastry, embossed pins for making **Springerle,** and **hardtack** rolling pins for rolling out and **docking** flatbreads or crackers so they don't puff up while baking.

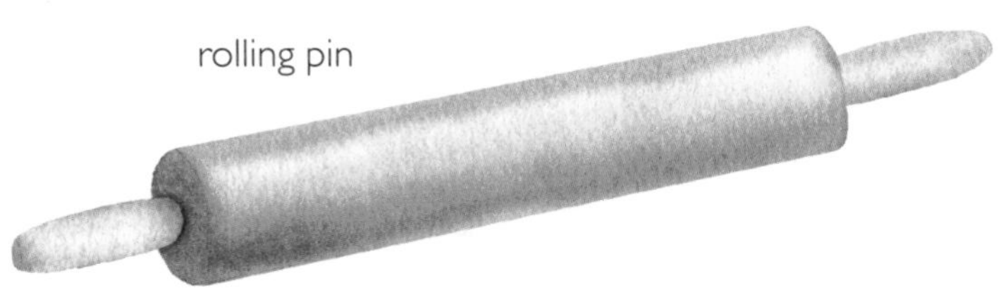
rolling pin

rollmop - see HERRING.

roll-up - a **griddle cake** or flatbread, such as **lefse** or tortilla, rolled around a savory filling including chopped or shredded cheese, cooked meat, rice and cooked or fresh vegetable mixtures. It can also have a sweet filling, such as cream cheese, cinnamon, fruit and sugar. Savory mixtures may also be rolled inside a lettuce, lotus or grape leaf, or **nori**, or a slice of cheese or sliced meat.

roly-poly pudding - a whimsical name for a pudding of suet or a biscuit-dough crust spread with jam, rolled up and baked or steamed.

romaine lettuce - see LETTUCE.

Romanesca cauliflower - also **summer cauliflower.** A *Brassica* indigenous to northern Italy, which forms a conical, lime green head composed of smaller, conical florets. The crisp, raw florets add a nutty taste to salads; the steamed vegetable on its own or in a mélange is served as a side dish.

Roman mushroom - see CREMINO.

Romano cheese - a hard, salty cheese, named after the city of Rome. The many types include the most well-known **pecorino** Romano made from sheep's milk, which is also made in the U.S. from cow's milk. The sharp-tasting **Caprino Romano** is made from goat's milk and the milder-tasting **vacchino Romano** is made from cow's milk.

romano bean - see CRANBERRY BEAN.

Roma tomato - also **plum tomato.** see TOMATO.

Rombauer, Irma S. (1877–1962) - author of *The Joy of Cooking,* one of the best-loved and bestselling cookbooks of all time. Born Irma von Starkloff in St. Louis to a prominent German-American family, she spent almost five years in *fin de siecle* Germany when her father was appointed consul to Bremen, an experience that provided her with ample opportunity to sample Europe's *grande cuisine.* After returning to America, she had a brief, but (in her words) "turbulent and intense" relationship with a Princeton graduate determined to become a writer. Believing the young man to be a ne'er do well, her family put a stop to the romance and instead of marrying Newton Booth Tarkington, who went on to become a bestselling author, she became Mrs. Edgar Rombauer, lawyer's wife and St. Louis society matron. That year, in 1899, Tarkington's first and highly successful novel, *The Gentleman from Indiana* was published.

The couple had two children, a daughter Marion in 1903 and a son Edgar Jr. in 1907. Although Edgar senior was a good provider, he likely suffered from a mood disorder. On February 3, 1930, he shot himself, leaving Rombauer a widow with two children and a legacy of $6,000. To everyone's surprise, since she had never shown the slightest interest in cooking, Rombauer decided to spend her inheritance on self-publishing a cookbook and began soliciting recipes from relatives and friends. She may not have known much about food preparation but she did know her audience — busy women like her who didn't enjoy spending time in the kitchen but wanted an assurance of good results. Utilizing her social connections, Rombauer found a printer and invested half her assets to print 3,000 copies. The first edition of *The Joy of Cooking* appeared in 1931 and the response was good from the start.

By 1932, Rombauer was revising the book and pitching it to publishers. When the Bobbs-Merrill Co. accepted it for publication, Rombauer made her first misstep. Assuming that her social skills qualified her to represent herself, she didn't engage a lawyer and was brow-beaten by Laurance Chambers, the bombastic bully who negotiated on behalf of the firm. She agreed to assign copyright to her self-published edition as well as the new one, a mistake that likely cost her family millions of dollars over the years. Her long relationship with the company was acrimonious, involving ongoing complaints about "Author's Alterations" charges and high discount sales, all of which are fully documented in Anne Mendelson's thorough and entertaining biography, *Stand Facing the Stove.* Even so, the book sold well and by the 1940s a copy of *The Joy of Cooking* could be found in a million homes.

The book went through numerous editions and over time Rombauer's health declined. By 1951, she saw the need for a succession plan and enlisted the help of her daughter. Although **Marion Rombauer** was a trained artist and her passion was gardening, not cooking, she shared her mother's talent for connecting with her audience. She introduced several innovations, including a section on healthy eating and symbols to denote recipe peculiarities, such as a snowflake for frozen ingredients. By the time Irma passed away after a long illness at the age of 84, *Time* magazine referred to the book as "a staple like salt." At that point, Marion, who had already assumed full responsibility for the book, enlisted her son, Ethan, to work with her. The only member of the family with any culinary training — at his parents' urging he had attended the Cordon Bleu Cooking school in Paris — Ethan inherited *The Joy of Cooking* when his mother passed away in 1976. He has been actively involved in the most recent editions of the book, which by 1997 had sold more than nine million copies in hardcover alone.

Rombauer, Irma S. - see profile above.

Rombauer, Marion Becker (1903–1976) - see ROMBAUER, IRMA S.

Rome apple - also **Rome Beauty.** See APPLE.

Rome Beauty - see APPLE.

Romesco - a robust sauce originating in Tarragona, a village in Catalonia, Spain, named for a specific type of dried, sweet red pepper. A brilliant shade of red, Romesco is made by pounding dried red peppers, garlic and nuts in a mortar. It is thickened with fried bread and traditionally served as an accompaniment

Root, Waverly (also **Waverley**) (1903–1982) - journalist, food writer and culinary historian, born in Providence, Rhode Island, and sent to Paris in 1927 as a correspondent for the European edition of the *Chicago Tribune*. Like other journalists of the era, Root's European explorations were subsidized by an expense account and, not uniquely, during the course of doing his job he developed a deep appreciation for food and wine, eventually retiring from news to devote himself to writing about his favorite subjects. His almost 50-year sojourn in Europe produced countless articles on culinary subjects for a variety of publications, and a number of books, including *The Food of France* (1958), *The Food of Italy* (1971) and *Food* (1980). Encyclopedic in scope, these collections of erudite essays, rather than recipes, are personal and charming explorations, which draw on a wide range of knowledge to elucidate the subjects in excellent and engaging prose. Explaining that he dropped his list of recommended restaurants from the 1977 edition of *The Food of France* because a book would not be able to keep up with the pace of change, Root felt compelled to provide his readers with alternatives, by, for instance, offering tips on judging a restaurant by its posted menu ("a sloppily presented menu is likely to indicate a sloppily run kitchen," his charming exposition on deconstructing an establishment from the doorway began). Reluctantly, he recommended the red Michelin guide, which although it has the virtue of keeping up to date, "is not infallible." "As it happens," he recounts, "the only two completely inedible meals I have ever had in France were both in restaurants to which Michelin had given a star." Root's autobiography, *The Paris Edition: The Autobiography of Waverly Root, 1927–1934* was published posthumously in 1987.

to grilled fish or seafood. Citizens of Tarragona celebrate the arrival of spring with a feast known as Calçotada, where calocats, a local green onion, are grilled over a wood fire, then dipped in Romesco sauce.

roomali roti - also **rumali roti.** A popular Indian flatbread, its name coming from *roomal*, meaning "handkerchief," because the bread is rolled as thin as a handkerchief and then folded like one. It's baked on a griddle that looks like an upturned wok.

root beer - originally, a low-alcohol, naturally fizzy drink created by Philadelphia druggist **Charles Hires,** who fermented sugar and yeast with a combination of roots, herbs and barks. Today, it's a nonalcoholic carbonated beverage colored with caramel and flavored with natural and artificial flavorings.

root beer plant - see HOJA SANTA.

root vegetable - edible corm, rhizome or tuber, such as a carrot, potato, sweet potato or **taro.** Called geophytes, these "roots" are actually swollen stems, which store energy for the plants in the form of starches. Nutritious, they are a staple of many traditional diets, not least because they are easy to keep between growing seasons, without refrigeration.

Root, Waverly - see profile above.

ropa vieja - Spanish for "old clothes," a Cuban dish of flank steak that has been poached all day with onions, green peppers and garlic, then shredded, making the meat look like rags; served with its stewing liquid and vegetables.

Roquefort - one of the three most famous blue cheeses (**Stilton** and **Gorgonzola** are the others), and one of the most beautiful of France, made solely from the milk of sheep that graze on the stony soil of land reserved specifically for them.

According to a popular, but probably apocryphal, tale, one day a shepherd boy left his sandwich of bread and cheese inside the entrance of a cave to chase after a pretty maiden. Young love being what it is, he soon forgot about the sandwich; when he found it weeks later, the bread and cheese were blue with mold. Because he was young and hungry, he ate the cheese, mold and all, and discovered that the blue part was the most delicious.

In the 9th century, the monks of St. Gall, not far from the village of Roquefort sur Soulzon, after which the cheese is named, served Emperor Charlemagne the cheese. Charlemagne apparently didn't like the cheese at first but eventually grew so fond of it he demanded to be supplied with the cheese each year.

In 1407, Charles VI issued a decree restricting the name "Roquefort" to only the cheese made in the Roquefort district of the Causses, south of Bordeaux, and by 1411, the decree began to be strictly enforced by the government. Today, to make sure that the cheese will have plenty of blue veins, bread with the *Penicillium roqueforti* culture is layered in the curd. All genuine Roquefort cheese is aged six months, cured in the limestone caverns of Mount Combalou, and bears the symbol of a sheep printed in red.

roquette - see ARUGULA.

Rorer, Sarah Tyson - see profile below.

rose - an edible flower of the genus *Rosa*, the subject of numerous legends spanning 3,000 years. In Greek mythology, the red rose came from the blood of the goddess Aphrodite, whose foot got stuck on a thorn while she was trying to help Adonis. According to a Turkish legend, the red rose was stained by the blood of Mohammed. Greek historian Herodotus said that the rosebush built up thorns only after the fall of the Garden of Eden.

The ancient cultures of both Greece and Rome cultivated roses for decoration in centerpieces at banquets and for crowning bridal couples. Similarly, Native Americans crowned their brides with rose petals and also used roses for medicinal purposes. William Penn, returning to the colonies in 1699, brought with him from England 18 rosebushes. Later, John Adams started planting roses at the White House; his plantings later became the Rose Garden.

Petals, hips and buds are still used in culinary preparations, especially in Scandinavia. Petals are used in salads and candy, while **rose water,** in particular, is used in Middle Eastern cuisines. Rose petals, with the bitter white heel removed, may be crystallized and used in salads, with fruits, for decoration or as a general flavoring. Bright red rose hips are used in jams, purées and sauces, or to make a sweet syrup high in vitamin C. See also EDIBLE FLOWERS.

rose hip - also **rose haw.** The bitter but edible fleshy fruit of a rose left at the base of each blossom after the petals fall, often made into jelly, tea, wine and syrups. The small hips develop on hybrid garden roses and are usually removed before they begin to develop, to encourage further bloom. The hips on *Rugosa*, species and wild roses, are usually left alone, and can develop into cherry-tomato size fruits. Related to pome fruits, such as apples, pears and quinces, rose hips are extremely high in vitamin C.

rose-hip jelly - a jelly made from simmered, fresh, ripe rose hips, sugar and, often, lemon juice; to bump up the pectin content and help the jelly set, some apples or crabapples are often added to the pot, as well. Since the seeds are covered in tiny hairs, which irritate the digestive tract, many recipes advise seeding the hips before cooking them. The hips have such a high concentration of vitamin C that a nonreactive pot is recommended for jelly making, to avoid discoloration of the finished product.

rose-hip tea - a fragrant, pink beverage made by pouring boiling water over dried, crushed and seeded rose hips, then covering and steeping the mixture. Some tea brewers like to place a stick of cinnamon or a whole clove into the steeping pot; others stir in few spoonfuls of honey before serving the tea. Some bakers add a little tea to their batters for flavoring. Ready-made rose-hip tea bags and loose tea mixtures are available.

Rorer, Sarah Tyson (1847–1937) - American teacher, writer, founder of the Philadelphia Cooking School and the country's first dietician. Rorer was born in Richboro, Pennsylvania, and was educated at East Aurora Academy in New York State. In 1870, she moved back to the Philadelphia area, where she met her husband, William Albert Rorer, and had two sons; the couple later separated. After taking one cooking class, she wrote, "I saw the great possibilities of right living and a well-organized school of domestic science," and began studying the chemistry of food in earnest. She began attending lectures at Woman's Medical College in Philadelphia, where she would later lecture as a national authority on dietary science, after an extensive self-directed education. Rorer ran the Philadelphia Cooking School, which she opened in 1884, for 18 years. She was also a prolific writer and editor of more than 75 books and pamphlets. She was the owner and editor of *Table Talk* magazine and a staff writer of the *Ladies Home Journal* for 14 years.

roselle - also **Florida cranberry, Jamaican sorrel, lemon bush.** A flowering shrub, *Hibiscus subdariffa,* from which the red pectin-rich flower calyces are picked and used fresh or dried to make colorful drinks, jam and jelly, and to flavor rice and vegetable dishes. Native to India and Malaysia, this subtropical and tropical plant is thought to have traveled across the Atlantic during the slave trade. Now naturalized throughout much of Central America and the West Indies, it was planted throughout southern Florida as both an ornamental and a food plant. Roselle jelly has long been a regional favorite with home canners in Florida.

rosemary - a strong-flavored herb with silvery green needle-like leaves from an evergreen shrub, *Rosmarinus officinalis,* which can grow up to 15 feet (4.5 m) in height. Because this minty herb grew wild along the seacoast, the Romans called it *ros marinus,* meaning "sea spray" or "sea dew," which later became "rosemary," no doubt influenced by the traditional association between the Virgin Mary and her floral symbol, the rose. It was believed that rosemary never grew any taller than Christ, reinforced by the fact that, after a plant attained 33 years of age, it might grow in girth, but never in height. It was said that, originally, the plant had white flowers, but that during her flight to Egypt, the Virgin Mary threw her blue cloak over a plant of rosemary while she and the baby Jesus rested in its shade; in remembrance of this honor, the flowers turned blue.

rosemary

In the Middle Ages, it was used not only for its medicinal qualities, such as a hair restorer, but also as a symbol of the declaration of courtly love, faith and remembrance. It's one of the main ingredients in the perfume Queen of Hungary Water, a distillation that is mentioned in herb and perfume books as one of the first alcohol-based perfumes. During the 12th century, the Welsh physicians of Myddvai, a small parish in South Wales, known for its medical university, depended heavily on rosemary. Their recipes are charming: "Put the flowers or leaves under your head in bed and you will not be troubled with disagreeable dreams or oppressed with anxiety of mind. Also, if you procure a spoon made of the stock or root of this shrub, in the day you drink some broth with it, you will not receive harm from poison and you will be preserved all that day against thunder and lightning as well as injuries and assaults."

Rosemary has always been associated with fidelity and memory and consequently figured prominently in both weddings and funerals. In some Central and Eastern European countries, it's customary to put a rosemary branch in the hands of the dead, a practice that started with the Romans. The connection between death and love are combined in Ophelia's remark in *Hamlet,* as she distributed the herb: "There's rosemary, that's for remembrance; pray you, love, remember." Anne of Cleves wore a wreath of rosemary at her wedding to Henry VIII. Supposedly the plant was introduced to England in the 14th century when the wife of King Edward III, Queen Philippa, received some plants from her mother, the Countess of Hainault, as a powerful shield against the plague. The original eau de cologne was made from a rosemary infusion. Rosemary contains **flavonoids** and other substances that may stimulate the immune system, improve digestion and increase circulation. In Provence, they still make a rosemary tisane using the same recipe as several centuries ago, a simple infusion of rosemary with honey and spices.

rosette - **1.** a deep-fried Scandinavian cookie, made from a plain, egg-rich dough, using a **rosette iron.** Depending on the head of the iron, the cookies may be open, fretwork hearts, flowers or snowflakes, which are dusted with icing sugar after cooking and cooling, or they may be shells, similar to **timbale,** into which savory or sweet fillings can be spooned. **2.** a piped shape of pleated concentric circles — often seen in frosting on a cake, for example, or cream cheese on an **hors d'oeuvre** cracker — that suggests the overlapping petals of a small rose. **3.** a familiar radish crudité and garnish, rendered by slicing half-moons down and around its length, then soaking the cut radish in cold water until the "petals" open. **4.** a type of French all-pork sausage, named for the color and shape of its natural **sausage casing,** which is sliced and served as an appetizer or snack.

rosette iron

rosette iron - a tool to make deep-fried **rosettes** that consists of an interchangeable, heavy metal head, such as cast aluminum, and a wooden-tipped metal handle. The head is dipped into hot oil to heat it up, then into the batter and back into the oil again to fry the cookie.

rose water - a scented liquid distilled from rose petals, widely used in Indian, Southeast Asian and Middle Eastern cookery, as well as in perfumes.

rosé wine - see BLUSH WINE.

rosogolla - see DAS, NABIN CHANDRA.

Rossini - a name given to various chicken, egg and **foie gras** dishes, as well as a salad dressing with **truffles,** a sauce and **tournedos** in honor of the great Italian musician Gioacchino Rossini (1792-1868). Although he claimed to be one of the laziest men alive, Rossini was a prolific worker — the music for his beloved *The Barber of Seville* (which debuted in 1816) was composed in 13 days and, by the time he stopped writing operas at 37, he had one to show for every year of his life. After that, aside from writing the occasional small piece for voice or piano, Rossini lived the good life in France for another 40 years and became known for his love of food and drink.

rösti - a patty of fried shredded potatoes of Swiss origin, similar to a **latke.**

rotary mixer - also **egg beater.** A lightweight, hand-held, hand-cranked upright utensil with two fixed beaters, used for mixing and beating semi-liquid or liquid food.

rote Grütze - German for "red groats." This classic, thick stew of red fruits, such as cherries, currants, raspberries and strawberries (with a few blackberries and blueberries thrown into the pot for good measure), is cooled and served as a dessert with a little milk or cream, or as a topping for **curd cheese,** custard or ice cream. During cooking, arrowroot or cornstarch is often added to thicken it. No sugar is used, however, as it's meant to be tart.

roti - **1.** in India, a common everyday Indian wheat flour bread. **2.** in the Caribbean, both the bread and the packet of food served in it, usually curried meats and vegetables. *Sada* is roti bread made with plain white flour; *dalpuri* is made with split pea flour.

rôti - French for "roast" or "roasted."

rotini - see PASTA.

rotisserie - a cooking device with a rotating spit inside an oven or next to a broiling element, on which meat or other foods are roasted, or a restaurant serving meats and fish cooked using this equipment. In the kitchen **brigade system,** the **rôtisseur** is the cook who roasts meat.

rotisserie chicken - a whole, unstuffed chicken — often marinated or seasoned with a spice rub first — grilled or roasted on a slowly revolving spit so it cooks evenly, basted with its own juices. Although many home barbecues now have the accessories required to do the job, rotisserie chicken is probably seen most often through the windowed ovens in grocery stores. Precooked and convenient, these rotisserie chickens are now a common ingredient in many easy-on-the-cook recipes.

rôtisseur - cook in a professional kitchen whoprepares roast meats and poultry, one of the positions in the kitchen brigade system created by French chef **Auguste Escoffier** in the late-19th century. See also BRIGADE SYSTEM, CHEF, ENTREMETIER, GARDE MANGER, PASTRY CHEF, POISSONIER, SAUCIER, SOUS CHEF, TOURNANT.

roughage - **1.** a somewhat old-fashioned term for the indigestible plant fibers, found in such foods as whole meal cereals and grains, that are believed to promote bowel health. **2.** a generic term referring to the food that contains these plant fibers. See also DIETARY FIBER.

rouille - French for "rust," for the color of this fiery emulsified sauce traditionally made with raw garlic, egg yolks, chiles, garlic, saffron and olive oil; sometimes mixed with fish stock, because it's the classic accompaniment to **bouillabaisse** and other fish stews.

roulade - also **bird, braciola, paupiette.** A thin slice of meat (veal, pork, lamb or even chicken) rolled around a filling of cheese, bread crumbs, mushrooms or forcemeat. It is then tied and browned, then roasted or braised in wine or stock. *Roulade* is French for "roll." *Braciola* is the Italian term for a roulade. See also JELLY ROLL.

Rouladen - the German take on **roulade.** There are many variations, such as Rinderroulade (sliced bacon fat, gherkins and onions rolled in thin slices of beef, then seasoned and slowly braised; it's often served in its own dark gravy, with **Spaetzle** and red cabbage and potatoes on the side). At least one German manufacturer produces a pre-mixed spice blend for Rouladen.

round - see BEEF.

roundfish - see FISH.

roux - a classic thickener, made of a slowly cooked mixture of fat and flour (usually using the same amount by weight of each), used in French cuisine to thicken cream and cheese sauces, soups and stews and give them a silky, smooth texture and nutty flavor. **White roux** is made by melting and clarifying butter in a heavy-bottomed saucepan, then adding the flour; it is stirred constantly to keep it smooth and heating evenly, and is cooked for five minutes. **Blond roux** is made the same way, but cooked for 10 minutes, until it's golden; **brown roux** is cooked for 15 to 20 minutes and is occasionally made with pan drippings or beef or pork fat. **Dark roux,** a variation on the classic roux, is famous in Cajun and Creole dishes. Made with bacon or duck fat, lard or peanut oil instead of the butter, it must be watched carefully and stirred constantly over high heat for almost half an hour until it's brown, but not burned (some cooks swear by a cast-iron pot). It should have the color of black coffee and a rich, smoky flavor. See also BEURRE MANIÉ.

Roux, Albert and Michel - see profile below.

Roux, Albert and Michel (1935–) (1941–) - French brothers, chefs and restaurateurs credited with inspiring the development of England as a notable culinary nation. Both Roux brothers began their traditional French apprenticeships at 14. They led separate, yet similar, lives until they reconnected later in their professional lives. Michel spent two years at the British Embassy in Paris and later became personal chef to Cécile de Rothschild. Albert went to England to work for Nancy Astor. Meeting up again in 1967, the brothers opened Le Gavroche in London. In 1972, they opened The Waterside Inn in Bray-on-Thames, just west of London, which has held its three-Michelin-star status for more than 20 years. Today, Michel Jr., Albert's son, is Le Gavroche's executive chef. Alain, Michel's son, mans the stoves at The Waterside Inn. Since 1982, the brothers have administered the Roux Scholarship, which has mentored a new generation of British cooking talent.

rowan berries

rowan berry - the small, edible fruit of various *Sorbus* species, including the North American native, *S. americana* (commonly called dogberry or mountain ash) and its European cousin, *S. aucuparia* (known as rowan). In autumn, these shrubby trees produce clusters of brilliant orange-red, berry-like, fruit with a tart, astringent taste that mellows slightly after a frost (any resemblance to a **rose hip** is not surprising; they share the same Rosaceae family). The parasorbic acid in the fruit causes digestive distress, but is neutralized by boiling it into jam (sometimes with other, sweeter fruits) or jelly (used as a condiment for game).

Traditionally collected from the wild, the fruit and flowers have a long history as medicinal ingredients in European folk remedies and flavoring in cordials and spirits. In Britain, northern Europe and Scandinavia, the tree itself was believed to have divine, magic, and restorative powers. A small bundle of twigs could protect a home from ghosts and lightening strikes; tied to a cowshed, it kept the milk from souring; tied to a bridle, it prevented fairies from kidnapping the traveller on horseback. In a graveyard, a living tree safeguarded departing souls, while dead branches were used as dowsing rods and Druid staffs. In North America, indigenous peoples (such as the Algonquin, who called mountain ash the "bear-fruit tree" ate the edible berries and brewed an antiseptic wash from the inner bark. Early settlers cooked the fruit into pies and preserves and concocted their own home remedies. Thrushes so enjoy feasting on the fruit that these trees are also called "birdcatchers."

Royal Ann cherry - also **Napoleon cherry.** One of the most important sweet-cherry cultivars grown commercially in North America. Yellow-skin blushed with red, the cherry is eaten out of hand, used in baking, candy making and canning, and is the variety commonly dyed and used to make maraschino cherries. See also CHERRY.

royal duck - see MUSCOVY DUCK.

Royal Gala apple - see APPLE.

royal icing - made of confectioner's sugar, egg whites and lemon juice, and often colored with food dyes, becoming hard when it dries, used mostly for making cake decorations.

royal jelly - a nutritious, vitamin-rich secretion from the throats of bees that is fed to bee larvae, especially queen bee larvae, in a colony, used as a supplement or added to human health drinks or foods (similar to the way ginseng is). Royal jelly is especially popular and widely available in Asia, but it is becoming a well-known human supplement in North America as well. The thick, milky liquid is touted as an immune-system strengthener, a cold and flu preventive, a wrinkle fighter and a brain-power booster, among hundreds of other claims.

royal soup - historically, in countries with monarchies, the soup reserved for the royal family. With a few variations, it was almost always a hybrid between a broth and a stew, made with an assortment of fowl and venison. The legendary French chef **Antonin Carême** said the soup included macaroni, leeks, carrot, celery, bouquet garni, slivered almonds, eight egg yolks, parsley, a whole fat *poularde* (a fat chicken suitable for roasting) and a whole ham, both poached in the vegetable broth. Later on, Napoleon requested a royal soup of his own. But the finest and most respected of royal soups emerged from the Caucasus and is still served today on special occasions, such as the birth of a baby boy, or the return of the oldest son from a long service in the military, or a long voyage or pilgrimage.

A 1,500-year-old manuscript saved by Armenian monks makes mention of a "royal" or "victory" soup: two centuries before, when an Armenian king went to war and came back victorious, it was his solemn duty to go into the forest and bring back all sorts of wild birds and venison. He would bring the game to the palace steps, where coppersmiths had placed a huge kettle. After his servants had cleaned the various meats, the king, with his own hands, would prepare the royal soup and serve it to the princes and princesses of his court, who in turn would serve the public, who would come from every part of the country to celebrate the victory.

Roy Rogers - a so-called kiddie cocktail or **mocktail** for boys. Named after the popular singing cowboy and Saturday matinee hero, this drink contains cola and **Grenadine**, garnished with a maraschino cherry and a slice of orange. A lucky boy might get a swizzle stick in his drink, as well. The girls' version is **Shirley Temple.**

rub - also **dry rub.** A combination of spices and seasonings rubbed on the outside of a piece of meat before it is grilled, barbecued or roasted to infuse it with flavor as it cooks. Rubs used for Southern barbecues often contain sugar, which caramelizes and forms a crust on the outside of the meat, sealing in juices and adding a rich dark color.

ruby port - also **ruby Porto.** A blended, fortified dessert wine produced in Portugal that owes its deep red color and fruity flavor to its youth (both would mellow with age). Ruby port, chilled or not, is enjoyed with flavorful cheeses, fruit and nuts, and may be used to poach fruit or in salad dressing or sauce. See also PORT.

rucola - see ARUGULA.

rue - a robust evergreen, *Ruta graveolens*, whose leaves were believed to have therapeutic properties. Still used in Italy for **grappa,** rue was associated with regret and melancholy. Since Dioscorides noted that weasels always eat rue before hunting for snakes, it was considered the best antidote for poison. It was also used for many centuries to induce abortion. King Mithridates VI of Pontus (120–63 BC) became king while still a child. His mother (said to have assassinated her husband, Mithridates V) ruled in her young son's stead. Afraid that his mother might kill him, Mithridates went into hiding and started ingesting small doses of rue and other poisonous herbs to immunize himself against assassination attempts.

The Romans brought rue across northern Europe to Britain, where it did not gain favor until the Middle Ages, when it was one of the herbs carried in nosegays by the rich as protection from evil and the plague. The Greeks believed that rue stolen from a neighbor's garden did better than a plant acquired honestly. Because brushes made from rue were, at one time, used to sprinkle holy water at the ceremony preceding High Mass, it was also called the "herb of repentance." Rue even played a hand in the design of playing cards, as it was used as an early model for the suit of clubs. Also, like rosemary, it was placed near the judge before prisoners were brought out, as protection from the pestilence-ridden jails and fever.

Rue was famous for preserving eyesight and was said to promote second sight. Both Leonardo da Vinci and Michelangelo were quoted as saying that the herb could enhance inner vision. Rue can make a wonderful addition to any salad, but should be used with caution because it can cause irritation like poison ivy. Rue is still used today as a natural insecticide. Its leaves are gathered early in the morning, dried in the shade, powdered and sprinkled over the infested plant.

rue

rugelach - traditional Hanukkah cookies made with rich dough containing butter and cream cheese (or sour cream). The dough is rolled flat and spread with apricot or peach preserve and a mixture of cinnamon, sugar and ground raisins and walnuts, then cut into triangles. Starting at a straight edge, each piece is rolled around the filling into a crescent. *Rugelach* means "little twists" in Yiddish. Before baking, some cooks brush on beaten egg to glaze the cookies, then sprinkle them with sugar. See also BUTTERHORN.

rugulau - see ARUGULA.

rum - a liquor distilled from sugarcane, the origin of the name is obscure, but the word has been around since the English settled in Barbados in the 1620s. One possible derivation is from the Latin for sugar *saccharum*. Another is the English word rumbullion, which means "great tumult," possibly because the first versions of the drink may have been a bit unpalatable, described in an early account as a "hot hellish and terrible liquor." For a time, rum was also called Kill-Devil. As time passed, the manufacturing technique improved and the tasty spirit we know today emerged. Rum is made from sugarcane by-products, such as molasses, by a process of fermentation and distillation. The distillate is a clear liquid. **White rum** is the distillate diluted to 40 percent alcohol. Gold and **dark rum** require aging in oak barrels from one to seven years. Most rum today is made in the Caribbean.

rumaki - an **hors d'oeuvre** of Japanese origin consisting of bacon wrapped around a slice of water chestnut and a piece of chicken liver, skewered with a toothpick and broiled until the bacon is crisp and the liver is cooked.

rumali roti - see ROOMALI ROTI.

rum baba - see BABA AU RHUM.

rum ball - a favorite spherical Christmas candy — or is it a cookie? — made with vanilla-wafer crumbs and ground walnuts, honey and rum, mixed then rolled by hand into bite-size balls, and covered in snowy confectioner's sugar. Some versions use cocoa powder, graham-cracker crumbs or macadamia nuts and add a shot of espresso to keep the ball bouncing.

rum cake - see BLACK CAKE.

rum extract - a ready-made rum-flavored substitute for the real thing, commonly used in baked goods, sauces and specialty coffees. The rule of thumb is to replace the amount of dark rum called for in a recipe with twice as much rum extract (2 tablespoons/25 mL of extract for every 1 tablespoon/15 mL of rum, for example). Replace light rum with only 20 percent of the amount called for (1 tablespoon/15 mL of extract for every 5 tablespoons/75 mL of rum). But if the recipe needs real spirits to fuel a flambé, extract won't do the job.

rumpot - also **Rumtopf. 1.** a mixture of fresh soft summer fruit immersed in sugar and rum, preserving it for midwinter celebrations. The rumpot is started as soon as the first spring fruits are harvested. In a large, airtight glass jar or glazed crock, clean hulled fruit is added, along with sugar, then rum is added until it's about "two fingers" higher than the fruit. Kept in a dark place, the rumpot is stirred occasionally and more fruit, sugar and rum are added as the season progresses. Apricots, blueberries, currants, blackberries, gooseberries, peaches, plums, raspberries and strawberries are common ingredients (apples, pears and citrus fruits are not). Small fruits are left whole; large ones are chopped. With the occasional stir and top-up of rum, the pot is traditionally saved (at least three months should elapse after the addition of the last fruit) until Christmas. The fruit is then enjoyed alone, as a topping for cake, cheesecake, custard, ice cream or pudding, or as a sweet relish for meat. Any sweet liquor that is left can be sipped from a glass. **2.** a glazed ceramic crock especially designed for making rumpot. The tall, lidded crock usually has two sturdy handles at either side of the rim, the name "Rumtopf" emblazoned across the neck, and colorful, decorative fruit designs worked into the glaze. Most hold 20 cups (5 L).

rump roast - see BEEF.

rump steak - see BEEF.

runner bean - also **case-knife bean, scarlet runner bean.** A vigorous climbing twining bean grown for its edible pods and, just as often, simply for its showy red flowers. Native to Central America, where indigenous peoples have cultivated it for its edible bean pods and roots for about 2,000 years, *Phaseolus coccineus* was brought to England as an ornamental, but quickly became a favorite (cut into short lengths and cooked) on British dinner plates. The pods range from 6 to 12 inches (15 to 30 cm) long; the mottled beans inside range from white to pink to purple. Runner beans may be eaten whole when they are small and tender; mature beans are often removed from the pod and sliced open down the center before they are added to the pot. Perennial in warm regions, runner beans are only hardy to zone 7 so are treated as an annual by North American gardeners. See also BEAN.

runza - also **bierock.** A small German- or Russian-style meat pie made with ground beef, cabbage or sauerkraut, onions and spices, encased in a yeast dough and baked. These pies came to North America with immigrants as an easy-to-eat portable convenience food, often eaten by farmers and laborers who couldn't go home for lunch. Runzas are well known in the central U.S. states of Nebraska, Iowa and Kansas.

rush nut - see CHUFA.

rusk - a slice of yeast bread baked a second time until it's crisp, dry and golden brown, similar to Italian **biscotti** and the German **Zwieback**.

russet apple - see APPLE.

russet potato - see POTATO.

Russian dressing - originally made with mayonnaise, pimientos, chives, spices, ketchup and caviar, the last ingredient likely responsible for the name, although today it's made without caviar.

Russian tea cakes - see MEXICAN WEDDING CAKES.

Rusty Nail - a classic cocktail made with 1½ ounces of **Scotch,** ½ ounce of **Drambuie** poured over lots of ice in an **old-fashioned glass,** garnished with a twist of lemon. The popularity of the drink or its moniker has spawned innumerable pubs and restaurants of the same name.

rutabaga - also **swede.** A fairly modern root vegetable, *Brassica napobrassica,* is thought to be a cross between the turnip and cabbage, introduced to England at the end of the 18th century, where they were known as swedes, because *rotabagge,* meaning "baggy root," comes from a Swedish dialect. A bit larger than its cousin, the turnip, with larger and bulkier leaves, the rutabaga has yellowish flesh and skin. The white-fleshed variety is rare and difficult to find in any market. Rutabaga can be boiled and mashed, as it's served in Scotland to accompany haggis. In the American Midwest, it's mashed and candied. In Finland, it's served in casseroles with cream and spices. Rutabagas were the base of the European diet during the Second World War, introduced by invading German troops, and became a symbol of famine. Most of the U.S. supply comes from Canada, which explains why Americans call them "Canadian turnips."

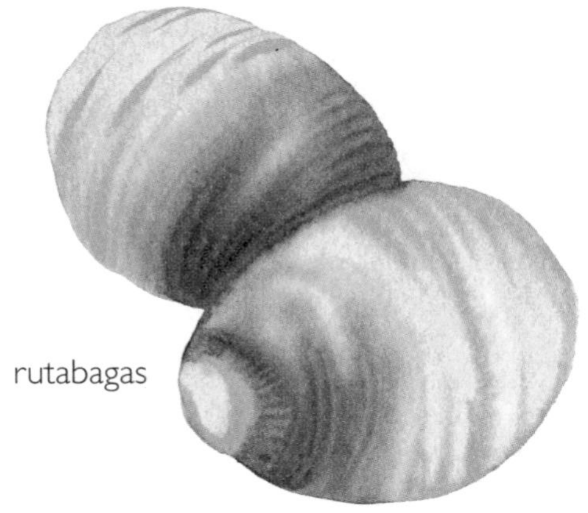
rutabagas

rye - a grain, *Secale cereale,* similar in composition to wheat, which probably originated in Southwest Asia. In Europe, rye is used mainly for making black bread and **crispbread** (mostly in Scandinavia). It contains less gluten than wheat and so does not rise as well. Rye is also used in the manufacture of liquor: whiskey in North America, gin in Holland and rye-tinged beer in Russia.

rye whiskey - see WHISKEY.

S

starfruit

saag - a Indian dish of creamed spinach (or another leafy green, such as chard), seasoned with curry powder, **garam masala,** garlic, **ghee,** ginger and/or onions. Kashmiri-style saag may be warmed up with hot chiles and **asafetida,** cumin, fennel, **fenugreek** and turmeric.

Saanen - a hard Swiss cheese made from cow's milk, similar to **Sbrinz,** aged six or seven years, more than twice the usual time. There are claims that certain Saanen cheeses have remained edible for 100 years. Historically, the wheel-shaped cheese would be put away in a cellar upon the birth of a child and be brought out for his or her engagement.

sabayon - made by steadily whisking egg yolks over a **bain-marie** until the mixture becomes frothy, smooth and nearly doubled in size. Savory sabayons begin with a strained reduction of vinegar, herbs and spices, to which the yolks are then added and whipped. Continuous, strenuous whisking prevents the eggs from scrambling from overlong contact with the hot metal of the bowl. Sabayon is the base for **hollandaise** and **béarnaise sauce,** and can also be made sweet, with a reduction of sweetened wine, Champagne or liqueur, served by itself, with fruit or gratinéed under a broiler to add color and volume. See also SABAYON GLACÉ, ZABAGLIONE.

sabayon glacé - a dessert sabayon made with a liqueur, such as **Grand Marnier,** piped or spooned into a coupe glass or goblet, and chilled or frozen, then topped with **chantilly cream** or whipped cream and fruit or grated chocolate. See also SABAYON, ZABAGLIONE.

sablé - a rich, crumbly French butter cookie, often flavored with citrus peel or dipped in chocolate. *Sablé* means "sandy" in French, which describes the melt-in-the-mouth fine, dusty texture of this cookie. See also SAND TART.

sablefish - also **Alaska cod, Alaskan black cod, black cod, butterfish.** A fish, a member of the Anoplopomatidae family found in the North Pacific, which gets its name from its black or dark green skin. Despite its other names, it does not belong to the codfish or butterfish family. The world's largest sablefish population is found in the Gulf of Alaska. The skin is pearly white, firm, oily, exceptionally flavorful and delicious, outstanding smoked or grilled. Often available smoked as smoked black cod.

Sabra liqueur - a bittersweet, rich, orange-chocolate liqueur that is native, as the name "sabra" implies, to Israel and made with homegrown oranges.

saccharin - an artificial sweetener, developed at Johns Hopkins University in the late 1800s, more than 300 times sweeter than sugar, with only one-eighth of a calorie per teaspoon (5 mL). See also ACESULFAME POTASSIUM, ARTIFICIAL SWEETENERS, ASPARTAME, SUCRALOSE.

Sacchi, Bartolomeo (Platina) - see profile below.

Sachertorte - also **Sacher torte.** A rich, layered, chocolate torte filled with apricot jam and coated in chocolate, this Austrian specialty is usually served in the Viennese style, with a generous dollop of whipped cream. Invented near the turn of the 20th century by the Sacher family, noted restaurateurs and hoteliers, the authentic version of this torte is still served today at Vienna's Hotel Sacher.

Sacchi, Bartolomeo (Platina) (1421–1481) - Italian humanist, historian and author of *De Honesta Volupate et Valetundin* (On Right Pleasure and Good Health), a food handbook published in 1480. Sacchi was born near Cremona, which is translated as *Platina* in Latin, hence the moniker by which he is best known. He went to live in Rome in 1462 and worked as a tutor and "abbreviator," writing papal briefs for Pope Pius II. He was discharged by Pius' successor Pope Paul II, and Sacchi's protestations landed him briefly in jail. But he soon returned to writing, producing histories and philosophical works. With Pope Sixtus IV, Sacchi was once again in the Vatican's favor and began writing *Lives of the Popes,* which he completed in 1474. Sacchi's food handbook was considered his most important work, notable for its originality, classical influences and the Arabist ideas prevalent in the European thinking of the day, particularly about the principles of health.

sack - from the French *sec*, meaning "dry," the English name given to dry, white 16th- and 17th-century wines from Spain and the Canary Islands, a term used by Shakespeare to denote sherries and today often used interchangeably with sherry.

sacred trinity - see TRINITY.

saddle - a single cut of meat encompassing the backbone and both loins, most often lamb, veal or venison. Tender, it is usually roasted.

safe internal temperatures for meat - see TEMPERATURE.

safflower - also **bastard saffron.** A plant, *Carthamus tinctorius*, originally cultivated in Egypt but found also in southern Europe, North Africa, parts of Asia, and India, where it is known as *koosumbha*, safflower is prized chiefly for its brightly colored flowers, which yield red and yellow dyes and a saffron substitute. The name comes from a combination of "saffron" and "flower." Today, we know of safflower as a polyunsaturated oil extracted from its seeds.

safflower

saffron - the dried, cured stigmas from the crocus, *Crocus sativus*, which looks a lot like its cousin, the garden crocus, part of the iris family (Iridacae), a purple flower with three red stigmas (female) and one yellow stamen (male), the most expensive spice in the world. Saffron is grown by division of the bulbs in autumn; if the plant is propagated from seed, it will take three years before any flowers appear.

It comes from the Arab *assfar, za'faran, zafaran or zahfaron*, meaning "yellow," for the characteristic color it imparts. Saffron first appeared in ancient Babylon and China as early as 2600 BC and is native to Asia Minor, cultivated there for thousands of years, mentioned in many classical writings, including the Bible. Saffron is the *Karcom* of the Hebrews (Song of Solomon).

In medieval England, so much was grown in Essex that the town of Saffron Walden was actually named after the aromatic. In Greek mythology, Zeus, the king of the gods, had a bed of saffron. Greek myth attributes the plant's creation to Hermes, the messenger and inventor. Hermes accidentally killed Europa's infant son Crocus; blood flowed from his head and was scattered on the ground, where the god at once changed it into the little flowers with their precious pistils. Ancient Greeks used saffron as an aphrodisiac, to perfume a bath and as a remedy for sleeplessness. Cleopatra and the pharaohs used saffron for both sacred and sensual purposes.

With coriander and cumin, saffron is part of a triumvirate of Middle Eastern spices that nomadic Arabs took first to the African region that would become Morocco and then, later, to Spain and Iran, where most of the world's saffron is now produced. It can also be found in Egypt, Kashmir and Turkey. Saffron reached England in the Middle Ages; during the Renaissance, Venice was the commercial capital of its trade. Saffron was generally used medicinally to reduce fevers and calm nerves. It was also widely used for perfumes, dyes and to flavor food and beverages, but too much of it could have a narcotic effect.

In 1649 in **Nicholas Culpeper**'s *The Complete Herbal*, it says, "The use of it ought to be moderate and reasonable, for when the dose is too large, it produces a heaviness of the head and sleepiness. Some have fallen into an immoderate convulsive laughter, which ended in death."

In culinary terms, saffron is considered savory, but has been used in breads and sweets since medieval times. The West connects saffron to its significant role in paella, risotto and bouillabaisse. In India, it's used to flavor desserts and ice creams but also in religious rituals. True Arabian coffee is said to have saffron and cardamom. The saffron crocus is harvested in late October and early November, usually between dawn and 10 a.m., because it blooms at dawn and the stigmas must be removed promptly from the blooms or they will wither and lose color and fragrance. The stigmas, three filaments one-fifth the width of a matchstick, are removed by hand, allowed to dry and cure, then taken to market. The statistics are staggering: it takes 14,000 stigmas to produce 1 ounce (28 g) of saffron; 850,000 flowers for 2 pounds (1 kg); and 400,000 stigmas for

1 pound (500 g), which explains why saffron is the world's most expensive spice.

saffron rice - a generic term for various rice-with-saffron combinations cooked in countries that circle the Mediterranean and in India. In addition to the saffron threads, which tint the rice sunny gold, the dish may contain such ingredients as almonds, cardamom, cashews, chicken or vegetable stock, cinnamon, cloves, **ghee,** molasses, onion and raisins. Saffron rice is central to **paella.** See also SAFFRON.

Saga blue - a soft, rich, blue-veined Danish cheese with a light, edible rind. This **double-crème cheese** is considered mild but flavorful; the texture is likened to that of **Brie.** It can be eaten on its own with fruit or wine, or used in savory tarts or crumbled over salads.

saganaki - a Greek appetizer or first course of epic drama, consisting of a thick slab of pan-fried **kefalograviera** or **kasseri** cheese doused with **ouzo** and **flambéed** at the table. The fire is doused with the juice from a lemon wedge, and the cheese is served with bread. Some restaurants and home cooks prefer to dispense with the drama and simply serve the fried cheese with a squeeze of lemon juice over top.

sage - a herb, *Salvia officinalis*, with gray-green furry leaves. The Aryans, distant forebears of the Persians and the Hindus, used sage, and the Egyptians used it as a powerful medicine against a lengthy list of complaints. It was very highly esteemed as a medical herb in Greece and Rome (the Romans called it "the sacred herb"), and it was used in England before the arrival of tea to make infusions for drinking and for medicinal purposes. In the Middle Ages, it was called *salvia salvatrix*, meaning "sage the savior," for its numerous applications and its health-giving properties.

Sage symbolizes wisdom and immortality. An ancient French proverb asks, "Why should a man die whilst sage grows in his garden?" An old English song proclaims, "He that would live for aye — must eat sage in May." Sage is one of the most popular herbs used in Provence, where a popular proverb states, "He who has sage in his garden needs no doctor." In the 18th century, the love of sage by the Chinese was so great that they would trade two crates of their best tea for a crate of sage. Winston Churchill liked sage tea as much as French Champagne and Cuban cigars and once wrote, "We are happier in many ways when we are old than when we were young. The young sow wild oats, the old grow sage."

Sage is a perennial but should almost always go in a pot, because it does not tolerate the cold and must be brought inside for the winter. (This is why, after being imported by the Romans, it died out in most of northern Europe and had to be re-imported in the 11th and 12th centuries.) Sage contains thujone, a natural chemical compound responsible for sage's antiseptic properties, which makes it invaluable for use as a gargle and mouthwash. Some people burn sage as an incense, but pregnant women should not burn it or eat or drink excessive amounts because sage is known to decrease milk supply; sage tea, however, is recommended when women are weaning. In the Mediterranean Basin today, many people will still not use anything but a sage stem as a toothbrush.

sage

sage cheese - also **green cheese.** English cheese flavored and marbled with green by the addition of minced sage leaves (Lancashire sage) or juice pressed from the leaves (Sage Derby cheese) during the cheese making.

sago - dried, starchy granules obtained from the pith of the tall, Asian sago palm, used as a food for invalids in cakes, soups and milk puddings and as an ingredient in some Scandinavian dishes, such as the Danish *sagosuppe*. Sago is predominantly used as a thickener, often in soups, as well as for stiffening textiles.

sagu de mandioca - also **sagu de vinho tinto.** South American dessert of **sago** simmered with semisweet red wine, sometimes spiced with ground cinnamon and cloves, and often served with cream or whipped cream. In **Brazilian red wine tapioca,** homegrown tapioca stands in for the sago.

Sahni, Julie (1945–) - Indo-American cooking teacher, writer and authority on Indian cuisine. Born in India, Sahni went to New York City in the late 1960s to study architecture at Columbia University. She worked in her field for nearly a decade before realizing that her true calling was teaching and writing about Indian food. Her first book, *Classic Indian Cooking* (1980), has gone into 29 printings and remains a definitive source for Moghul or northern Indian cuisine. She has also written *Classic Indian Vegetarian and Grain Cooking* (1985), *Moghul Microwave* (1990), *Savoring Spices and Herbs* (1996), *Julie Sahni's Introduction to Indian Cooking* (1998), *Indian Regional Classics* (2001) and *Savoring India* (2002). She opened a cooking school in Brooklyn, New York, where she lives, and conducts culinary-cultural tours of India. She has taught in her native country, at Boston University, New York University and the New School for Social Research. She has also lectured at the Smithsonian Institution, the National Geographic Society and the Asia Society.

Sahni, Julie - see profile above.

saibashi - see OHASHI.

sailor's tobacco - see MUGWORT.

St. Basil bread - see VASILOPITTA.

Saint Germain - **1.** a French culinary term, named after Comte de Saint-Germain (a mysterious figure, said to have been an alchemist, musician and spy, who moved among the powerful of Europe, including the court of King Louis XV) that is given to dishes containing fresh green peas, whole or puréed. For soup, the peas are simmered with fresh lettuce heart and onions, a little butter and sugar and a **bouquet garni.** The latter is removed, then the vegetables are pushed through a sieve and light stock is added to make soup. After reheating, butter and minced herbs are whisked in and the soup is served, garnished with croutons or whole peas. The purée, made from fresh peas simmered in a similar manner, may have egg yolk or heavy cream mixed in. It is often served as an accompaniment to meat. **2.** a French style of cooking and serving fillet of sole. Seasoned with salt and pepper, the fish is coated with melted butter and dipped in bread crumbs, then grilled and served with **béarnaise sauce** and small, fresh potatoes.

Saint-Honoré - also **gâteau Saint-Honoré.** A Parisian gâteau named for the patron saint of pastry cooks, consisting of a ring of baked puff pastry topped with a row of caramel-glazed cream puffs filled with **chantilly cream.** It's said that a Mr. Chiboust was the man who invented chantilly cream; he had a pastry shop in Rue Saint-Honoré in Paris.

St. John's bread - see CAROB.

St. Lucy's buns - see LUSSEKATTER.

St. Peter's fish - see TILAPIA.

Sakai, Hiroyuki - see profile on page 568.

sake - also **saki.** A traditional Japanese alcoholic drink made from rice, colorless, slightly hazy, non-carbonated and usually served warmed. Contrary to popular belief, sake is not a spirit (because it's not distilled), nor is it a wine (it's not macerated), but rather a special type of beer brewed from a grain base. The rice is washed, steamed and fermented with a yeast-like fungus. Primary fermentation takes 30 to 40 days, after which more rice and water are added to generate a secondary fermentation lasting eight to 10 days. The alcohol content varies between 14 and 17 percent by volume. The word *sake* comes from Osaka, where it was originally made.

salad - from the Latin *sal*, meaning "salt," perhaps referring to how cold food generally needs more seasoning than hot. The name *zelada*, or "salad," was first applied to a dish that appeared on festive tables in 15th-century Milan. It was actually a kind of salty ragoût flavored with preserves, mustard and lemon and decorated with marzipan. It was served in individual cups, a novelty at the time. The Roman contribution was the hot salad, largely green vegetables, blanched and stewed with herbs. Probably the French were the first to improve the Roman epicure **Apicius'** plan by mixing fresh salads with herbs. By the year 1500, the royal salad bowl in neighboring England counted 35 ingredients.

The word "salad" is often used interchangeably

Sakai, Hiroyuki (1942–) - Japanese chef, restaurateur, author and "Iron Chef French." Born in Kagoshima and best known for his fusion of French and Japanese cuisines, Sakai began his apprenticeship at 17, but cut it short two years later because he didn't find the instruction to his liking. After a stint cooking at the Hotel Oriental in Perth, Australia, Sakai studied with Fujio Shito, Japan's top chef cooking in the French style. In 1981, he opened La Rochelle in Tokyo, which still stands, named for a French town he had once visited and loved. Sakai first appeared on Fuji TV's *Iron Chef* program in 1994 as the French specialist, when his predecessor, Yutaka Ishinabe, retired. Sakai has published four books and opened a second La Rochelle in 2002. He is always introduced on the program wearing a signature red chef uniform, holding a pear.

with its ingredients, particularly leafy greens, but refers specifically to a cold dish of raw or cooked elements dressed with an oil-based sauce. For centuries, wild, leafy plants were collected and eaten raw, particularly in spring. During the time of Roman England, a preference for eating beet greens expanded to include lettuces, cucumbers, carrots, endive and sorrel, which were already part of the Roman diet. Six centuries later, medieval monks were planting these ingredients in their herb gardens. It wasn't until the turn of the 17th century that a number of accounts were written that shed light on the beginnings of our modern salads. The subject was engaging enough to produce *Acetaria: A Discourse of Sallets* in 1699 by Englishman John Evelyn. In 1796, the notion of a winter salad was introduced by **Amelia Simmons** in *American Cookery*, the same year that Sidney Smith published *An Herb Sallad for the Tavern Bowl*, in which the subject was given poetic treatment, such as his directions for tossing a salad: "Let onion odours lurk within the bowl and half suspected, animate the whole." Three years later, an herbal compendium listed 35 ingredients used in salads. Among the most famous salads known in the U.S and Canada are the Salmagundi (1726); Waldorf (1896); Caesar (1924); and Cobb (1937).

salad bar - a self-serve, often all-you-can-eat array of fresh fruits and vegetables, croutons, dressings and other salad fixings that is now ubiquitous in restaurants across North America. Although *Merriam-Webster's Collegiate Dictionary* dates the first usage of the term to 1937, the familiar salad bar where diners graze today — depending on the storyteller — was introduced to mid-priced restaurants in Waikiki, Hawaii, in the late 1950s or in Chicago in the 1970s. Everyone seems to agree, however, that Wendy's was the first fast-food chain with salad bars. Appealing to health-conscious patrons who wanted to load up on fresh fiber, some early salad bars held a hidden threat: **sulfites,** sprayed onto the produce to keep it crisp, colorful and moist. The sulfites caused a serious, occasionally fatal reaction among susceptible consumers, especially asthmatics. In Canada and the United States, the preservative is now banned for use on fresh produce that is sold to be served raw.

salad bowl lettuce - a type of leaf lettuce with varieties that range from pale green to red.

salad burnet - a valuable perennial culinary herb, *Sanguisorba minor* and *Poterium sanguisorba*, best used fresh in salads and savory omelets. The French, who call it *pimprenelle*, have used it since the Middle Ages for medicinal preparations and to flavor some excellent **eaux de vie.** It is also used to make herb butters and cheese and to infuse vinegar with its characteristic cucumber flavor.

salad dressing - a sauce tossed with salad greens that adds flavor and bumps up the **mouth feel**. Often containing chopped herbs and seasonings, dressings may be creamy mixtures based on mayonnaise, sour cream or yogurt or vinaigrettes mixed with clear, plain or herbed vinegars (or acidic juices, such as lemon or tomato) and oil. One rule of thumb is: the more delicate the salad ingredients, the lighter the dressing. Another is: mix a vinaigrette with one part vinegar to three parts oil. Chunky or dense ingredients, such as those in a bean or potato salad, may be mixed with the dressing an hour or more before mealtime, so they can absorb the flavor of the dressing. Leafy salad greens, on the other hand, are typically tossed with the dressing just prior to serving.

salade composé - a French cooking term denoting a carefully arranged salad, such as **salad Niçoise.** Since tossing would spoil the salad's design, any dressing is drizzled over the arrangement.

salade Niçoise - named for the Provençal town of Nice, a **composed salad** of lettuce, tomatoes, blanched green beans, anchovies, tuna, olives and hard-boiled eggs, topped with a vinaigrette.

salal - also **lemonleaf.** A low evergreen shrub that produces dark purple juicy berries from the heath (Ericaceae) family, related to blueberries and cranberries, native to North and South America, the West Indies, Japan and Australia. *Gaultheria shallon*, its botanical name, is named after Dr. Jean-François Gaultier (1708-1758), a French Canadian botanist and physician. Although its alternate name is lemonleaf, the leaves do not taste of lemon, but are used ornamentally most often for corsages and dried flower wreaths.

salamander - **1.** an eye-level gas broiler common to most professional kitchens used to brown the top of food. **2.** a colonial cooking implement with a cast-iron plate, attached to a handle and legs (giving it the look of its namesake), which was heated in an open fire until it was red-hot, then held close to the surface of food to brown, crisp or toast it. Modern salamanders look quite different: most consist of a small but thick, cast-iron disk attached to the angled end of a long metal rod that has a wooden handle at its opposite end. They are still used to crisp and brown foods, such as dishes topped with cheese or custards topped with caramel or sugar mixture.

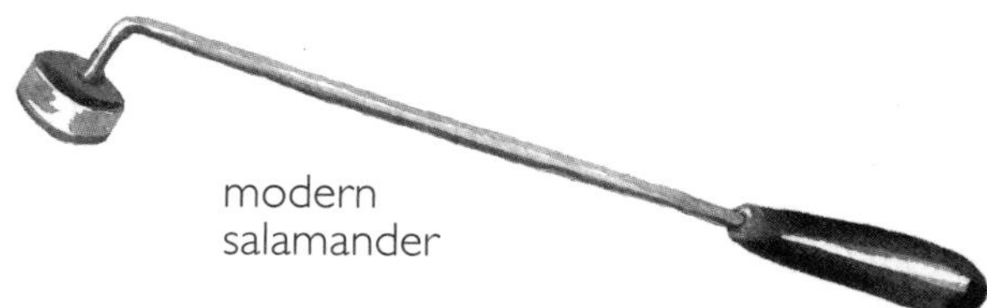

modern salamander

salametti - see SALAMI.

salami - from the Italian *salare*, meaning "to salt," for a type of cured sausage made from pork or beef, usually flavored with garlic and spices, rarely smoked. (For Salami Types see below.)

salam leaf - also **Indonesian bay leaf.** An aromatic leaf, *Eugenia polyantha*, used in the cuisine of Indonesia and Malaysia, where the plant naturally grows. The leaves may be simmered fresh and whole in dishes (such as curries) or used to line banana leaves

SALAMI TYPES

There are hundreds of different varieties of salami available, some only in their country of origin, many of which have made the trip to North America. The following are some common versions found in North American grocery stores.

cacciatorini - a type of Italian salami, a **dry sausage** produced in the Val d'Aosta region of northern Italy, made from pork and beef or just pork, seasoned with spices and wine, with a delicious garlicky flavor. Cacciatorini are short, only a few inches long, perfect for cutting into thin slices to serve on bread or crackers as an appetizer. Because they are dried for several months, cacciatorini last a long time and have dense, flavorful, meaty centers, perfect for the hunters (*cacciatori*) who often carried the sausages with them for a quick, portable lunch.

calabrese salami - pork, coarse texture, similar to **Genoa salami** but seasoned with hot peppers to make it spicy. Named after Calabria in Italy.

Genoa salami - pork, beef, veal or all pork, large diameter, air-dried, may or may not be smoked, highly seasoned with garlic and other spices so that it's quite piquant; originally from the city of Genoa in Italy.

hard salami - pork and beef, medium diameter, garlicky with a coarse texture, drier than other types of salami.

Hungarian salami - pork, large diameter, coarse-textured, well spiced with garlic and paprika, either mild or hot.

salametti - mini versions of popular types of large-diameter salami, such as **Genoa** or **calabrese.**

for wrapping pieces of fish or poultry for grilling. Outside this region, the leaves are only available dried.

salicornia - see SAMPHIRE.

Salisbury steak - a sautéed patty of ground beef, egg and bread crumbs served with gravy, named in 1888 for Dr. James H. Salisbury, a physician who advocated a daily intake of well-cooked ground meat, at least three times per day.

Sally Lunn - the name of a large tea cake very popular during Colonial times and still made in Virginia. A popular tale suggests Sally Lunn is named after a young woman from Bath, England, who, in the 18th century, created the sweet yeast bread that bears her name and supposedly sold them in the streets for more than 30 years. (A Sally Lunn teashop still exists in Bath today where they sell the popular buns.) Some now doubt whether Sally Lunn really existed and suggest other sources for the name, such as *solilem*, a French breakfast cake, thought to come from *soleil et lune*, meaning "sun and moon," because of its color and shape, symbolizing the bread's golden top and white bottom. They were sold in the streets with cries of the bun's French name, which sounded like "Sally Lunn" to English ears.

salmagundi - also **Salmagundi.** A 17th- and 18th-century composed salad (the ingredients are carefully assembled, rather than tossed together) of cold chicken, anchovies, boiled eggs, green beans, boiled onions, grapes and dressing, although there are an infinite number of suggested ingredients, which may be why the word has also come to mean "miscellany." The name has come to be used metaphorically for any curious mixture. It is spelled in almost as many ways as the dish can be prepared: salamagundy, salad Magundy, salad à Magundy, salmagundy and Solomon Grundy.

Salmanazar - see WINE BOOTLES.

salmis - also **salmi.** A rich game bird stew, sometimes including rabbit, with both minced and partially roasted birds, mushrooms and often truffles, then reheated in a wine-based sauce. The name first appeared in France at the beginning of the 14th century, although the dish may have originated even earlier.

salmon - any of a large family of fish found in the northern waters of the Atlantic and Pacific oceans, returning to freshwater rivers to spawn. Salmon was an important food source for many Native Americans. Many 18th-century domestic servants demanded contracts that stipulated that they not be served salmon more than twice a day. That gives a good indication of just how common the fish once was in our rivers and streams. Today, although wild Atlantic salmon, *Salmo salar*, is recovering from the devastation of the mid 19th century, it remains a protected species.

We have two major sources of salmon: wild Pacific and farm-raised Atlantic. There are five major species of wild Pacific salmon: **chinook** (also called king), chum (dog), **coho** (silver), pink (humpback) and **sockeye** (red or blueback). Of these, chinook, coho and sockeye are considered the best for eating fresh. Prime salmon has deep orange, almost red flesh and a full, fatty flavor. Fish farms raising Atlantic salmon, which originated in Norway, are now found throughout the world. The early efforts by the Norwegians resulted in a nice-looking fish, but it was overly lean and not very flavorful. Currently, however, farm-raised Atlantic salmon from Maine, the Maritime Provinces of Canada (especially New Brunswick), the Pacific Northwest and Chile are all consistently excellent. Salmon is extremely rich in omega-3 fatty acids. The name comes from the Latin *saltare*, meaning "to jump," reflecting its predisposition to leap from the water during mating season. See also PARR.

salmonberry - a wild North American raspberry with bright wine-red flowers

sockeye salmon

that bloom between March and May; the multicolored all-purpose berries were well known to Native Americans, who considered them an important traditional food source.

salmon candy - see SMOKED SALMON.

salmonella - a bacterium that causes food poisoning, named after American veterinarian David Salmon. Every year, approximately 40,000 cases of salmonellosis are reported in the U.S. Salmonella lives in the intestinal tracts of humans and other animals, including birds, and is usually transmitted to humans by eating foods contaminated with animal feces. Raw foods of animal origin are commonly polluted with the bacteria, but, luckily, thorough cooking kills salmonella bacteria. Salmonellosis can cause diarrhea, fever, abdominal cramps, joint pain, irritation of the eyes and painful urination. It is usually treated successfully with antibiotics.

salmon steak - a boneless slab of flesh, cut crosswise from the widest part of the cleaned fish, often broiled, grilled or poached.

salmon trout - see LAKE TROUT.

salmoriglio - a 17th-century Sicilian sauce still served today, historically served with swordfish, made of salt, lemon, oregano and garlic, the translation of which became its name: *sale*, *limone*, *origano* and *aglio*.

saloop - see SASSAFRAS.

salpicon - a mixture of finely ground or diced meat, mushrooms and other aromatics, bound together with a thick sauce and used to fill **vol-au-vents** or to top **croustades**.

salsa - a cold Mexican sauce made of tomatoes, chiles, onions, cilantro, olive oil and fresh lime juice. **Salsa verde,** also known as Veracruz, is the green version of this sauce, similar in composition, except that its main ingredient is **tomatillo**.

salsa Mexicana - see PICO DE GALLO.

salsa verde - **1.** the "green sauce" typical of northern Spanish (particularly Cantabrian and Basque) cooking, especially in the classic **hake** dish *merluza en salsa verde*, made of vibrant green minced parsley, olive oil, garlic and white wine or fish stock. Not to be confused with the Mexican salsa verde made with tomatillo. **2.** see SALSA.

salsify - also **oyster plant, vegetable oyster.** A root vegetable, *Tragopogon porrifolius*, a native of central and southern Europe for more than 2,000 years, it is grown for its long, white edible roots, which grow to be about 12 inches (30 cm) long and have a delicate oyster flavor. Its French nickname is *doigts de mort*, meaning "fingers of the dead," because of its long, tapered roots, which look like whitish fingers. Belgium is the world's largest producer of salsify. It's also called **oyster plant** or **vegetable oyster** because its flavor, when cooked, is similar to that of oysters. The English name is "John-go-to-bed-at-noon" because its purplish flowers close at midday. **Scorzonera,** also black salsify, has a black root.

salt - sodium chloride, a white, granular substance used to season and preserve food. Salt is a crystallized compound that plays a major role in regulating the body's fluid balance, making it essential to human life. It is used as a seasoning, preservative, cooking medium (for instance, salt-crusted fish) and cooling agent (for example, when making ice cream). Salty is one of the **five basic tastes,** the others being bitter, sour, sweet and **umami**. Salt comes from two basic sources: underground deposits, which are mined, and seawater, which is evaporated. This produces two kinds of salt, rock salt and sea salt. Both run the gamut in terms of texture, from coarse to finely grained.

The very first tax was a levy on salt, imposed by Chinese emperor Hsia Yu in 2200 BC. In ancient China, even coins were made of salt. Egyptian mummies were preserved using salt. Roman legionnaires were paid in salt, hence the word "salary." Other words, such as "sauce" and "salad" are also derived from it. The expression "not worth his salt" came from payment in salt for a slave. There are more than 300 mentions of salt in the Bible. Jesus called his disciples "the salt of the earth," a testimonial observed during Roman Catholic baptismal ceremonies by placing a few grains of salt on the child's tongue. The main sources of salt in ancient times were dry coastal areas near the Mediterranean. Early trade routes (these and many of the first roads were established for transporting salt) centered around Spain, Italy, Greece and Egypt. Many of the caravan trade routes were developed to transport salt, and ancient cities, such as Genoa, Pisa and Venice, became salt market centers.

The French salt tax, known as *la gabelle*, is said to have played a role in provoking the revolution in 1789. Salt was highly charged politically in India under British rule, when the government's monopoly on the sale and production of salt required that Indians buy salt from the government, at its rates, when salt could be found easily and for free. Mahatma Gandhi led his famous "long march" and general strike against this imposed salt tax.

Salt changes the density of water, raises its boiling point and lowers the freezing point

TYPES OF SALT

artisanal sea salt - see SEA SALT.

canning salt - see PICKLING SALT.

Celtic gray salt - see SEA SALT.

fleur de sel - see SEA SALT.

kosher salt - a coarse-grained refined **rock salt,** which may contain additives to prevent caking, but does not contain iodine, giving it a fresher, cleaner taste than regular table salt. A favorite of chefs, because it is readily available and inexpensive, its name evolved from its use in kosher butchering — the large absorbent crystals remain on the surface of meat drawing out the blood, a component of koshering.

pickling salt - also **canning and pickling salt, canning salt.** A fine-grained refined salt, which lacks anti-caking agents and iodine, both of which negatively affect the pickling process.

rock salt - most of the table salt consumed in North America is refined fine-grained rock salt. In the process of refining, the salt is stripped of its minerals and treated with anti-caking agents. Since the 1920s, iodine has been added to prevent goiter, a thyroid condition linked with inadequate consumption of iodine-rich fish and seafood.

There is also an extremely coarse non-food grade rock salt used to melt ice on winter roads and in the freezing compartment of some ice cream makers.

There are a small number of specialty rock salts that are unrefined. These include **Indian black salt,** which has a strong sulfuric taste and is used as a condiment in India and **Himalayan pink salt,** a mineral-rich salt, which is mined at high altitudes and transported down the Himalayan mountains by yak.

sea salt - sea salt can be either refined or unrefined. Refined sea salt is made when seawater is boiled in large vats to the point of evaporation. Unrefined sea salt is harvested from seawater that evaporates naturally, retaining its natural minerals. It does not contain additives. Most sea salt is coarse-grained, although some finely ground varieties are available. There are many kinds of sea salt, each reflecting the unique environments from which it is harvested. **Artisanal sea salt** is harvested by hand, the most famous being ***fleur de sel*** (the flower of salt), which is the sweet white layer that blossoms on the top of the salt pond. *Fleur de sel* is harvested in France and Portugal. ***Sel Gris*** or **Celtic gray salt,** is a coarse gray mineral-rich salt from the west coast of France. **Maldon Salt** is a delicate white salt harvested in Maldon on the English coast. **Halen Môn**, another delicately flavored salt is harvested in Wales. Specialty stores now carry a wide variety of sea salts from places, such as Italy, Bali and Japan.

A number of **colored sea salts** deserve mention. These include **Peruvian pink sea salt,** pink flake salt from the Murray River in Australia, and **Hawaiian red sea salt,** which gets its color from the clay of the salt ponds where it is harvested. More and more producers are also enhancing the flavor of sea salt through various methods. **Smoked sea salts,** such as Danish Smoked Salt and Hawaiian Smoked Kai Salt, are usually coarse brownish salt, smoked over different types of wood and used as condiments. Some producers are also blending sea salts with herbs and spices or other ingredients, such as truffles and citrus zest, to produce **flavored sea salts,** which are used as a condiment.

seasoned salts - usually made from refined salt, which is mixed with ingredients, such as celery seed, dried onion and garlic, or various herb mixtures.

table salt - see ROCK SALT.

to below zero. Salt is used to draw out water and bitterness from cucumber and eggplant. Although cooks have always been taught not to salt a marinade or to only salt meat just before cooking because salt has a tendency to draw moisture from food, it has become fashionable to salt food, particularly meat, early, both in a marinade and even a day before cooking, for what amounts to a short "cure." The flesh changes color, texture and flavor without excessive loss of moisture. Salt's best-known contribution has been to food preservation, which preceded refrigeration. See also SALT SUBSTITUTE.

salt box - a wooden box for storing salt, with a high back that extends above the box and has a hole through the top for a hook, and a lid that slopes down to the front from its hinge at the back. Ubiquitous in Colonial times, a salt box was hung near the stove, so that the cook had easy access for a pinch. Early New England homes that shared a similar shape in reverse (two stories at the front, sloping sharply down to one at the back) were named for this then-common kitchen item. See also SALT CROCK.

salt cod - cod that has been salted and then dried. It was Basque fishermen who first discovered that salt preserved cod and made its mild flesh tastier. Prior to that, cod was only dried and did not last as long. Salt cod is used to make the French dish **brandade.** See also COD.

salt crock - a small, traditional storage crock for salt used in Britain, Europe and North America. The semicircular container (with a flat, high back that extends above the bowl and has a hole through the top for a hook) was usually made of stoneware; a wooden lid, hinged at the back, was fastened over the container. A salt crock, like a **salt box,** was hung near the stove so the cook had easy access for a pinch. Most households had a wall model, and perhaps a small, lidded stoneware salt crock for the table (similar to a jam pot) as well. Their disappearance in North America is linked to the advent of so-called "anti-caking" salt sold in a moisture-resistant package with its own pouring spout, in the early 1900s (the first on the market, Morton Salt, boasted "When it rains, it pours.").

salt cured - see CURE.

salted herbs - also **herbes salées.** A mixture of fresh, minced onions and chopped herbs layered in a stoneware crock with salt and left for several days at room temperature; the fresh ingredients create their own brine, but sometimes water is added to help this along. A simple mixture of minced onions and chopped chives is a staple of Acadian cuisine. In the Charlevoix region of Quebec, the mixture includes celery, grated carrot, parsley and savory, as well. Salted herbs are used in fish and meat dishes, and in soups and stews.

saltfish - salted dried fish, often salt cod, eaten frequently in the Caribbean, especially in Jamaica, where the national dish is saltfish and **ackee.**

saltimbocca - an Italian dish of thinly sliced veal rolled up or folded with **prosciutto** and a sage leaf in the center, sautéed in butter and then finished with white wine. The name is a contraction of *salta in bocca,* meaning "jumps into the mouth," suggesting that a mouthful of the dish is so tasty, it cannot help but jump by itself into one's mouth.

saltpeter - potassium nitrate, a white crystalline salt used in gunpowder, fertilizers, medicine and in the preservation of various meats, such as ham, bacon, corned beef and sausage, also called "niter."

salt pork - a layer of very fatty pork cut from the sides and belly, salt- or brine-cured, used primarily as a flavoring.

salt-raised bread - also **salt-rising bread.** Wheat-based bread usually leavened with a fermented mixture of cornmeal or potato pulp, salt, sugar and warm milk or water. Salt-raised bread is an alternative to sourdough-type bread (made with a **sourdough starter**); both have traditionally been made when yeast is not readily available. A Shaker salt-raised bread recipe from the early 1900s uses a leavening mixture made in a two-step process: scalded milk is combined with cornmeal and set in a warm place until the naturally occurring bacteria in the milk causes it to ferment and bubble. It's then added to a heated mixture of more milk, baking soda, salt, shortening and sugar and, removed from the heat until it ferments to create a sponge starter.

salt substitute - a sodium-free seasoning used as an alternative to salt. Salt substitutes are either made to mimic salt or to add other flavor so that salt is not missed in a dish. Mimics are often made partially or completely of potassium chloride, which looks like salt but leaves a slightly bitter aftertaste that salt does not. They can throw off the body's salt-potassium balance, which is critical to good health, so they should be used with caution. Salt substitutes that add flavor rather than mimicking salt are usually made of a blend of herbs and seasonings that contain no sodium. While they do add flavor, they don't enhance the flavor of foods in the same way that salt does.

saltwater taffy - see TAFFY.

salty - see FIVE BASIC TASTES.

salty black beans - see FERMENTED BLACK BEANS.

sambal - a southeast Asian condiment made from chile peppers. There are various kinds of sambals, depending upon the ingredients added. For instance, **sambal oelek** is simply ground chiles, possibly with a bit of sugar and salt. **Sambal udang** also includes shrimp, and **samabl bajak** is likely to contain a multitude of ingredients, such as nuts, garlic, galangal and Kaffir lime leaves. Sambals are usually served as an accompaniment to other dishes. Occasionally, the word sambal is used to describe a spicy savory dish.

sambal belacan - see BELACAN.

sambar - **1.** a South Indian powdered spice blend made of dry-roasted ingredients that are cooled and ground. The mix is variable, but commonly starts with **asafetida,** black peppercorns, chili powder, dal, turmeric and coriander, cumin, fenugreek and mustard seeds. Sambar is used to flavor pulse and vegetable dishes. **2.** the name given to both a South Indian lentil broth and a lentil curry.

Sambuca - from the botanical name for the elder, *Sambuca nigra*, an Italian liqueur flavored with oil from the elder, white elder blossoms and licorice. The custom of serving this drink neat and with three coffee beans is said to represent the Father, the Son and the Holy Spirit; others say it's for health, wealth and happiness. Many Italians call it *con la mosca*, meaning "with the fly" and crunch the beans as they drink the liqueur.

samosa - an East Indian deep-fried triangular pastry filled with vegetables and/or meat, often served with a dipping sauce.

samovar - a Russian urn with a spigot, used to boil water for tea, sometimes very elaborately decorated with brass or copper, from the Russian *samo*, meaning "itself," and *varit*, meaning "to boil."

samp - coarsely ground, dried, hulled corn. It is used as a thickener for soups and stews, or boiled, fried or shaped into cakes, either on its own or with other ingredients mixed in. On Long Island, early settlers are said to have had a pot of samp constantly simmering on the fire; beans, salted beef or shellfish would be added, as available, to make a meal. See also HOMINY.

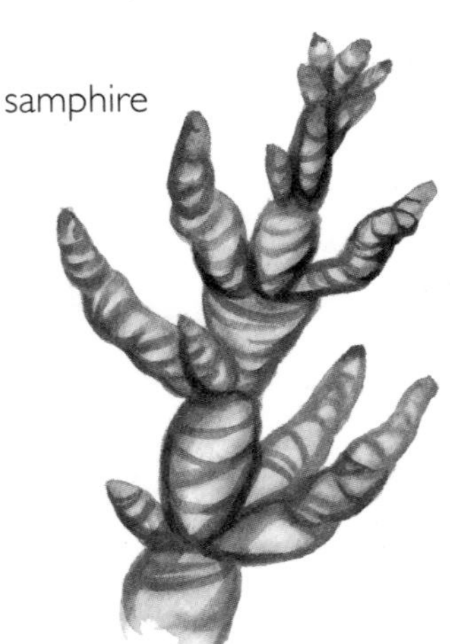

samphire

samphire - also **glasswort, salicornia.** A European herb of the parsley family that grows on coastal cliffs, with fleshy leaves; used principally in salads, but can also be cooked or pickled. Shakespeare refers to samphire growing on the white cliffs of Dover in *King Lear*.

samshu - a liquor distilled in China and the Malay Peninsula from rice or millet, from the Chinese *shao chiu*, meaning "spirit that will burn."

Samsoe - a Danish Emmental-style cheese, named for the island where it originated, with a yellow interior, small holes and a distinctive, nutty, slightly sweet flavor.

santaka chile - see BIRD'S EYE CHILE, CHILE PEPPER.

sandalwood - the dried bark of a southern Indian tree, *Santalum album*, distilled to yield an essential oil that contains the aromatic sanatol, used in ice cream, candy, baked goods and fragrances. Fragrant, finely ground sandalwood powder and chips are sold in Indian grocery stores. Prized for its scent, sandalwood is also thought to help cool the body in a hot climate.

sand dab - a generic term for various edible lean- and sweet-fleshed Pacific **flounders** found off the North American coast. Cleaned and gutted, they are often quick-fried or grilled whole, simply seasoned with a little olive oil, salt and pepper, and served with a lemon wedge.

Sanders, Colonel Harland - see profile below.

sand leek - see ROCAMBOLE.

sand shark - also **dogfish shark, ground shark.** An edible fish, *Carcharias taurus*, found from Cape Cod and south along the Atlantic seaboard. Although it's a predator, it is described as "sluggish" and spends much of its time on the seabed. The commercial fishery off Nantucket, Massachusetts, dwindled after about 1925, and today sand shark is mainly of interest to sportfishermen.

sand tart - a classic American sugar cookie washed with egg white before it's baked, then dusted with cinnamon-and-sugar "sand." The sand tart has been around for more than a century. See also SABLÉ.

sandwich - named for the 18th-century British gambler Sir John Montagu, fourth Earl of Sandwich, who refused to leave the gaming tables long enough to eat a proper meal, instead asking to receive a lunch of meat tucked inside bread.

sandwich cake - **1.** another term for a **strata.** **2.** another term for a Victoria sponge.

sandwich cookie - a generic term for a cookie made with two baked circles or slices with a layer of chocolate, buttercream, frosting, ice cream, jam or marshmallow filling in between.

sandwich loaf - see PULLMAN LOAF.

sandwich mixto - see CUBAN SANDWICH.

sangaree - a generic term encompassing various cold, sweetened alcoholic drinks, containing red wine and topped with a garnish of grated nutmeg. The mixture may combine red wine with citrus juice and soda water; beer and red wine with sweetened lemon-sugar syrup over ice; or a spirit (such as brandy, rum or whiskey) with port wine poured on top. The name, with its blood-red reference, may be derived from the word "sanguine" or a corruption of the word "sangria." See also SANGRIA.

Sangiovese - one of Italy's most well-known red grape varieties, used to make **Chianti, brunello di Montalcino** and **Vino Nobile di Montepulciano,** all important wines of the Tuscany region. The grape is thought to have originated there, but the natural genetic mutations in the grapevines mean that today there are a number of different clones that are currently identified under the Sangiovese umbrella, including Brunello, Prugnolo and Sangioveto. The variety of microclimates in Tuscany also means that the wines produced from these grapes don't have the same flavor or character from vineyard to vineyard, lending complexity and interest to the wines of the region.

Sanders, Colonel Harland (1890–1980) - American cook, entrepreneur and founder of Kentucky Fried Chicken (KFC). Born in Henryville, Indiana, Sanders began cooking at the age of 6, when his father died, leaving him to care for his two younger siblings while his mother worked. He worked at a variety of odd jobs throughout his adult life, and studied law by correspondence. In 1930, at the age of 40, Sanders was running a Kentucky gas station and began to cook for his patrons when he realized that they needed to do more than just refuel their cars. He cooked and served from his personal lodgings on-site and later moved to a properly outfitted restaurant, which he would operate for the next nine years. When he learned that a new interstate was going to bypass his restaurant, Sanders saw that his business wouldn't survive. He sold what he could, paid his creditors and set out, in his 60s, to sell fried-chicken franchises. By 1964, he had more than 600 outlets in the U.S. and Canada, which he sold that year for $2 million. In 1971, the company had 3,500 franchised and company-owned outlets worldwide and was valued at $285 million.

sangria - a chilled red wine punch with fruit and mineral water (and sometimes with a spirit), which takes its name from the Spanish *sangre*, meaning "blood," with modern versions also being made with white wine. See also SANGAREE.

sangrita - a savory Mexican drink mixed with lime, orange and tomato juice, and seasoned with Tabasco and Worcestershire sauces, minced onion, celery salt, freshly ground pepper and salt. Some barkeeps vary the ingredients, adding chili powder, grenadine or salsa. Even though it's fiery and served chilled, it's a classic chaser for tequila.

sansho - see SZECHWAN PEPPER.

Santa Claus melon - also **Christmas melon.** A football-shaped **muskmelon** with green, waxy skin, mottled with yellow, and pale green-yellow, sweet flesh that is similar to honeydew in flavor. Uncut, it keeps well. Like the jolly red-suited gentleman, this melon is usually seen in December.

Santa Claus melon

santoku - see JAPANESE KNIVES.

Santos coffee bean - see COFFEE.

sapodilla - also **naseberry.** The fruit of an evergreen, *Manilkara zapota*, originally from Central America, which secretes a white latex-like substance called chicle, used in making chewing gum, and produces delicious egg-size fruits that are reddish brown in color and taste like an apricot. The Aztecs called the fruit *tzapotl*, which the Spanish interpreted as *sapodilla*. The tree can reach more than 100 feet (30 m) in height and yields between 2,000 and 3,000 fruits per year.

sapote - a Mexican and Central American fruit, *Pouteria sapota*, whose fragrance is one of the most delicate of the tropical fruits, akin to those of pears and apricots. Its flavor is more evocative of apricots and bananas, and its texture, when ripe, is creamy and custard-like. Also called "custard apple" in the West Indies.

sapsago - also **green cheese, Schabziger.** A hard Swiss cheese intended for grating and seasoning, made from soured skim and whole milk. Sapsago is pale green due to powdered clover added to the curd.

sapucaia - also **sapucaya.** See PARADISE NUT.

Saratoga chips - see POTATO CHIPS.

Sarawak peppercorns - see PEPPERCORNS.

sardine - small, young, fatty fish that can be eaten fresh, but are more often salted and preserved in brine or oil, or tinned in various sauces. Among the fish using the name "sardine" are **pilchards** from Europe and California and some members of the herring family, such as the **brisling** or **sprat.** The name probably originated because pilchards caught off the coast of Sardinia were the first to be preserved in oil.

sarsaparilla - the roots of a Mexican tree, *Smilax aristolochiaefolia*, that yields a bitter, licorice-flavored extract used in soft drinks, ice cream, candy and baked goods.

sartù - from the French *surtout*, meaning "above all," a superlative reflecting the scarcity and high cost of rice in Bourbon Naples, when this large rice **timbale** was first made. Cooked rice is packed into a bowl or casserole with meats, cheese and sauce, then baked and turned out onto a platter. It looks like a golden brown cake but, when cut, the savory mushroom sauce, tiny meatballs and sausages that constitute the filling spill out.

sashimi - very thinly sliced raw fish, served without sushi rice.

Saskatoon berry - also **June berry, serviceberry, shadberry.** Found in the wild by Isaak Thiessen in 1904 near Waldheim, Saskatchewan, but also found all over western North America, Saskatoon berries resemble blueberries. They weren't taken to market until 1972. There are four varieties:

Thiessen, Martin, Smoky (the most common) and Northline. They're harvested in early summer, before six in the morning to keep both the berries and the pickers cool, then sorted by hand in walk-in coolers. The plant is hardy enough to withstand –40°F (–40°C) while dormant through the winter. This versatile berry is used in pies, cheesecakes, smoothies, muffins, cookies, jams and jellies. Even a type of wine is made from the fermented berries.

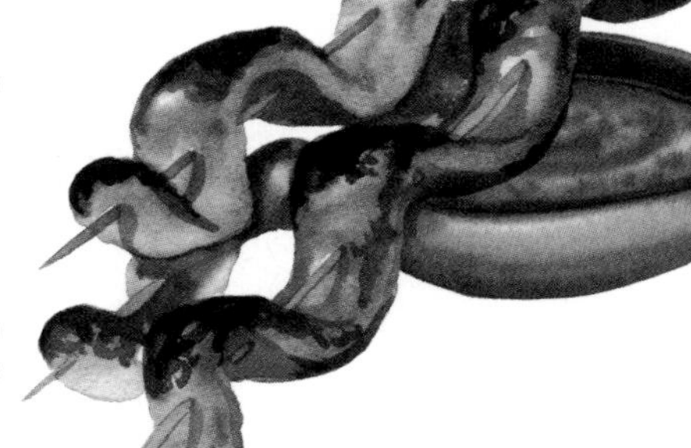
satays

sassafras - also **saloop, tea tree.** *Sassafras albidum*, an indigenous, North American tree which grows as a shrub in the northern limit of its range in Ontario and as a large tree in the American South. Early 16th-century explorers discovered that native Americans liked to chew its sweet, spicy root (hence one of its other names, cinnamon tree) and brought it back to Europe and Britain (some credit the Spanish, some the English). New World settlers simmered a concoction of maple sap and sassafras root pulp to make a spring tonic and medicinal tea (hence another name, ague-tree). And in Victorian England, saloop — a beverage of sassafras tea and hot milk — became a popular pick-me-up. The bark and roots were also brewed into a red dye. The dried, powdered leaves are used, especially in the Gulf Coast region of the U.S., as **filé,** the thickener for gumbo.

Sassafras continued to be used in drinks (giving root beer its characteristic taste), candies, folk medicines and other consumables, as well as cosmetics and toothpaste, into the 20th century, until it was discovered that the volatile oil found in its roots contained safrole. After experiments showed that safrole caused cancer in mice and rats, such use of sassafras oil and safrole was banned in 1960 in the United States. Products that contain significant amounts of safrole are still banned by both the U.S. and Canada. And despite current claims from some health-foodists (and faddists), the scientific community cautions against the use of home-brewed sassafras tonics.

satay - also **saté.** Strips of meat, fish or seafood skewered for grilling, satays come from Southeast Asia; originally an Indonesian/Malay dish, where it is served with peanut sauce.

satoimo - see TARO.

satsuma - a small, Japanese almost-seedless orange similar to the tangerine in appearance and taste, with loose, smooth skin and pale orange flesh. It's good for juicing and can be used in preserves, but is usually eaten fresh. In 1876, George R. Hall introduced them to Florida. The name is credited to the wife of the U.S. minister to Japan, General Van Valkenberg, who sent trees home in 1878 from Satsuma, the name of a former province where the fruit is believed to have originated. See also MANDARIN ORANGE.

saturated fat - see FATS.

sauce - **1.** an appetizing liquid served with a food to enhance or complement its flavor, which can vary in density and thickness. In *L'Art de la cuisine française*, published in 1833, 19th-century chef **Antonin Carême** created the methodology of classifying sauces at the beginning of French cooking's modern history. He set out four "mother sauces," out of which innumerable combinations could be made. **Espagnole,** or brown roux and brown (roasted) beef or veal stock, is used to make demi-glace, a strong reduction of Espagnole, which becomes bordelaise with red wine, and marrow sauce (*sauce à la moelle*) or Moelle with white wine and shallots. **Velouté,** blond (colorless) roux and white (unroasted) chicken stock, is used to make Suprême sauce, a reduction of velouté finished with cream. **Béchamel,** white roux and milk, becomes Mornay with grated Gruyère and Parmesan, and Cardinal sauce with fish stock, truffle essence, lobster butter and cayenne pepper. **Mayonnaise** and **hollandaise** share the category of **emulsified** sauces. Mayonnaise is the base for **aïoli** (garlic) and **rouille** (red pepper). Hollandaise is the base for béarnaise (tarragon), paloise (mint), Choron (tomato) and Foyot (demi-glace). Vinaigrette is an unofficial fifth category, well known to most home cooks, based on a three to one ratio of oil to vinegar. In 1933, the great French chef **Auguste Escoffier** published *Le Guide Culinaire,* which modernized, codified and simplified Carême's work, and added tomato to the pantheon of mother sauces. **2.** a slang term for booze.

sauce allemande - see ALLEMANDE SAUCE.

sauce Isigny - see HOLLANDAISE.

sauce piquante - French for "piquant sauce." A type of hot, sharp and spicy brown sauce, made of chopped gherkins, parsley and shallots, vinegar (the acidic ingredient that makes it piquant), wine and seasonings, served with beef and pork.

sauce verte - French for "green sauce." A sauce such as mayonnaise, or less often hollandaise, mixed with one or more minced (or blanched and puréed) herb or leafy green, such as dill, spinach, tarragon or watercress.

sauce whisk - also **French whisk.** See WHISK.

saucier - cook in a professional kitchen who prepares sauces, stocks and stews, one of the positions in the kitchen brigade system created by French chef **Auguste Escoffier** in the late-19th century. The importance of a good stock is so important that **Escoffier** said, "It is the production of perfect stocks that the sauce cook should devote himself." In his 1903 book *Le Guide culinaire* (A Guide to Modern Cookery) Escoffier wrote, "Indeed, stock is everything in cooking, at least in French cooking. Without it, nothing can be done." See also BRIGADE SYSTEM, CHEF, ENTREMETIER, GARDE MANGER, PASTRY CHEF, POISSONIER, RÔTISSEUR, SOUS CHEF, TOURNANT.

saucisse - French for "sausage."

sauerbraten - a German specialty of roast beef marinated in a sweet-and-sour marinade for several days, then browned and simmered slowly in the marinade, usually served with noodles, boiled potatoes or dumplings; *sauerbraten* means "sour roast."

sauerkraut - fermented shredded cabbage in brine, brought to Europe by Genghis Khan in the 12th century, having learned the technique from the Chinese. When he became aware of its nutritive value, Captain James Cook took 25,000 pounds (11,340 kg) of sauerkraut on his second Pacific expedition, losing only one sailor to scurvy in more than 1,000 days, thanks to sauerkraut's high vitamin C content. Because it was pickled, it lasted a year without going bad. *Sauerkraut* is German for "sour cabbage."

Saulnier, Louis - see profile below.

sausage - from the Latin *salsus,* meaning "salted." Sausage is any of a variety of ground meats (including game) or poultry stuffed into a **sausage casing.** Sausage types range from coarse-textured to fine, and mild-flavored to spicy, and may be wet (called "fresh sausage," these are made with uncooked meat) or dry (made with cooked meat). Sausages may be brined, dried or smoked, sold in links (like fresh pork sausage), in fat lengths (like bologna) or encased in plastic in bulk (to form into patties, add to stuffing or wrap another food, such as **Scotch eggs**). Many sausages contain fillers, such as grain or **rusk,** as well as seasonings, such as minced apple, garlic, herbs, mushrooms, peppers (chile and sweet varieties) and onions, cracked peppercorns and salt. Devised as a way to use all of a slaughtered animal, including the blood, fat and organs, and preserve some of the meat for long afterward, sausages are made in almost every culture; they were eaten in ancient China, Greece, Rome and Sumeria. Ironically, given their raison d'etre, sausages are also made for vegetarians now. **Vegetarian sausages** may include minced or puréed nuts, pulses, tempeh, tofu and vegetables, as well as herbs, spices and seasonings; some are made to imitate the look, feel and flavor of meat. See also ALHEIRA, ANDOUILLE, ANDOUILLETTE, BANGERS,

Saulnier, Louis (19th–20th century) - French chef and author of *Le Répertoire de la cuisine.* As a student of French chef **Auguste Escoffier,** Saulnier made his name by recording classical French cuisine as executed by his mentor. The 1914 book is still the most authoritative record of classical French cuisine, listing the dish's or sauce's names, ingredients and cooking techniques, but never quantities. Because of Saulnier's book, Escoffier is often attributed with the creation of 422 egg dishes.

BAUERWURST, BIERSCHINKEN, BIERWURST, BIRNENFORMIGE SALAMI, BLOOD SAUSAGE, BLUTWURST, BOCKWURST, BOLOGNA, BOTULISM, BOUDIN BLANC, BOUDIN NOIR, BOUDIN ROUGE, BRATWURST, BRAUNSCHWEIGER, BREGENWURST, BUTIFFARA, CAMBRIDGE SAUSAGE, CERVELAS, CERVELAT, CHARCUTERIE, CHAURICE, CHIPOLATA, CHORIZO, COPPA, COTECHINO, CRÉPINETTE, CUMBERLAND SAUSAGE, DERMA, DRISHEEN, DRY SAUSAGE, EXTRAWURST, FAGGOT, FRIZZES, GELBWURST, GOETTA, HEAD CHEESE, HOT DOG, ITALIAN SAUSAGE, KABANOS, KATENRAUCHWURST, KIELBASA, KISHKA, KNACKWURST, KNOBLAUCHWURST, LANDJAGER, LAP CHEONG, LEBERKÄSE, LIVERWURST, LOUKANIKA SAUSAGE, LUGANEGA, MERGUEZ, METTWURST, MORTADELLA, PEPPERONI, POLONY, ROSETTE, SALAMI, SAUSAGE CASING, SAVELOY, SUMMER SAUSAGE, TEEWURST, THURINGER SAUSAGE, TOSCANA, VIENNA SAUSAGE, WEISSWURST, ZUNGENWURST.

sausage casing - the flexible artificial or natural container used for sausage. Since they absorb moisture and other flavors, natural casings are preferred for sausages that will be cooked in sauces or stews. Salted, cleaned intestines and stomach linings are the traditional casings for sausages and haggis, respectively. Other natural casings include the small intestines and stomachs of pigs and sheep, and the large and small intestines of beef and oxen; in the past, bladders, esophagi, fish innards and uteruses have also been used. Although many sausages are still made with natural casings, edible artificial casings, such as those made from cellulose (a plant-based material) or collagen (an animal product) are increasingly being used. Nonedible plastic casing is used to contain sausage meat meant for use as an ingredient for patties or stuffing. See also SAUSAGE.

sausage pricker - a knife with a broad, short blade and a handle with pins extending from its tip. The blade is used to slice the links apart; the pins are used to pierce the skins so the sausages don't explode as they cook.

sausage roll - puff pastry wrapped around a whole sausage (often precooked) or hand-formed cylinder of minced sausage meat and baked. Frozen sausage rolls are a popular appetizer and party food.

sauté - from the French *sauter,* meaning "to jump," to fry foods quickly in a shallow pan, tipping the pan downward to let the food collect at the far side of the pan and then flicking the pan quickly up and back, which lifts the food into the air, stirring it while it cooks.

sauté pan - a pan similar in shape to a skillet but with a wide, completely flat bottom, usually of heavy-gauge metal, such as tin-lined copper or stainless steel, for sautéing foods over high heat. Sauté pans typically have taller sides than skillets (about 3 inches/7.5 cm high), which are perfect for containing pan sauces made after foods are initially sautéed.

Sauternes - a sweet French dessert wine made from Sémillon and **Sauvignon Blanc** grapes, rich, nectarous and well balanced, so that it is not cloyingly sweet. The grapes are left on their vines and are infected with **botrytis cinerea,** which concentrates their sweet juice and deepens their flavor. The juice is fermented for more than a year to make the final wine. Both the long fermentation process and the large number of grapes it takes to make a bottle of Sauternes means that it is an expensive wine to purchase.

Sauvignon Blanc - from the French *sauvage*, meaning "savage," a white grape varietal indigenous to France, used in making the famous Château d'Yquem. In a flash of marketing genius, California wine maker Robert Mondavi changed its name to

Sauvignon Blanc

Fumé Blanc in the 1960s, *fumé* meaning "smoked," referring to the wine's soft, smoky flavor. It quickly became very popular, with sales surpassing those of Sauvignon Blanc even to this day.

savarin - created by the **Julien brothers,** two 18th-century Parisian brothers who were famous pastry chefs, named for **Jean Anthelme Brillat-Savarin**, author of *La Physiologie du goût* (The Physiology of Taste), because the author is purported to have given the elder brother the secret liquid used to soak the cake, a sponge ring filled with fresh fruit or cream, and usually drenched in rum. This cake distinguishes itself from **baba au rhum** because it's baked in a ring mold.

saveloy - an English version of **cervelat** sausage, a dried, highly seasoned sausage traditionally made of cow or veal brains, but today made with young salted pork and **lights,** tinged red by **saltpeter,** which is legal in England. The name comes from the Latin *cerebellum,* in French *cervelle*, meaning "brain."

savoiardi - see LADYFINGER.

savory - **1.** either of two related herbs — summer savory, *Satureja hortensis,* and winter savory, *Satureja montana* — both having small, narrow, gray-green leaves. Winter savory is the stronger of the two, with a pungent flavor like that of thyme, marjoram and rosemary; summer savory has a similar, but milder flavor. Savory is among the most documented traditional herbs; Roman naturalist **Pliny** refers to 14 different species in his writings. In late medieval France, the herbs were used extensively for their medicinal value. The herb also had a reputation as an aphrodisiac because its botanical name *Satureja* was said to come from Satyrs, the half-goat, half-man amorous Greek deities, who lived in fields of savory. The Greeks used it for an infusion to soothe earaches, toothaches, relentless diarrhea or enteritis. Roman midwives swore by it as an antiseptic during childbirth. Savory reached Britain at the time of the Roman Conquest, and it appears on Charlemagne's list of herbs. According to a 17th-century French writer, "These modest little plants look as if they were intended to bloom in the cloistered gardens of the good nuns," referring to their delicate fragrance and the fragile appearance of their flowers. **2.** a word used to describe food that is piquant as opposed to sweet.

savory

savoy cabbage - more mildly flavored than its white counterpart, with a loose head of curly, wrinkled leaves in shades of green and purple.

savoy cake - a classic, airy, white sponge cake often made with seven eggs (with the yolks and whites whisked separately) and a one-to-one combination of potato flour and wheat flour. A delicate flavoring, such a lemon zest, is also added. The fine-textured cake is usually served plain, but it can be dressed up by baking it in a sugar-dusted mold. In her famous *Book of Household Management,* **Mrs. Isabella Beeton** recommends slicing any stale leftovers and slow-cooking them to make "Italian rusks," but most cooks save the slices for trifle.

sawarra nut - see SOUARI NUT.

Sazerac - called "America's first cocktail," it was invented by **Antoine Peychaud,** a New Orleans pharmacist in the 1830s. Originally, it contained absinthe and Sazerac de Forge et Fils cognac, along with **bitters** of Peychaud's own manufacture. The cocktail was named after the cognac and the city's Sazerac Coffee House, a popular watering hole of the mid-1800s, where it was served (the recipe for the cocktail included rye whiskey later on). After the coffeehouse was sold to Thomas Handy in 1870, a bar and a company that distilled, bottled and distributed spirits opened and operated under the Sazerac name. The Sazerac

Company still markets the original bitters — called Peychaud's Bitters — today.

Sbrinz - also **spalen.** A hard Swiss cow's milk cheese produced in rounds and aged from two to three years. Said to be one of the first and oldest cheeses produced in the Alps, Sbrinz is a pungent, nutty-flavored, dark yellow cheese enclosed in a tan rind. It can be sliced thin or formed into rolls for hors d'oeuvres (one classic appetizer layers it with dried beef and sliced tomato), or grated over pasta or potato dishes, soups and stews. When aged for less than two years, it's called **spalen.**

scald - **1.** to heat milk to just below the boiling point. **2.** to briefly plunge fruits and vegetables into boiling water and then into ice water to loosen the skins for peeling.

scale - to remove the scales from a fish.

scallion - a young onion with long, shallow green leaves and an undeveloped bulb, also used to describe a young shallot or leek.

scallop - **1.** a marine bivalve mollusk, *Pecten maximus*, with a distinctive fan-shaped shell, the symbol for St. James, called *Santiago* in Spain, where the world's best-known shrine to the saint is erected, and St. Jacques in France, where scallops are used in the dish **Coquilles St. Jacques.** A **bay scallop** is a tiny variety of the scallop, usually no bigger than a marble. Bay scallops are considered sweeter and more delicate than the more common, less expensive **sea scallops,** which are larger, up to 2 inches (5 cm) in diameter, with sweet flesh that is not quite as tender and delicate as that of the bay scallop. **2.** a thin round or oval boneless slice of meat or fish, known as *escalope* in French.

scalloped potatoes - layers of thinly sliced boiled potatoes in cream sauce, baked in a casserole. Many versions are made with thinly sliced onions and grated cheese layered between the potatoes. For a main dish, chopped ham may be added, as well. For **potatoes au gratin,** the dish may be topped with bread crumbs or crushed crackers tossed in melted butter before baking. See also DAUPHINOISE POTATOES.

scaloppine - a thin slice of meat, usually veal, dredged in flour and sautéed, from the French **escalope,** meaning "thin slice of meat."

scamorza - an Italian cheese related to mozzarella, yellow in color, with a firm but supple texture, originally made from buffalo milk, although cow's milk is used today.

scampi - **1.** a large **prawn. 2.** a North American dish of large shrimp sautéed with garlic, white wine and lemon juice.

scant - a recipe term written, for example, as "a scant tablespoon" or a "scant cup," meaning slightly less than the level measure.

scape - see GARLIC SCAPE.

Scappi, Bartolomeo - see profile below.

scarlet runner bean - see RUNNER BEAN.

scavece - see ESCABECHE.

Schabziger - see SAPSAGO.

schaleth - see CHARLOTTE.

schav - from the Yiddish *shtchav,* meaning "sorrel," a cold sorrel soup, made with sorrel leaves, onions, salt, lemon juice, sugar and eggs, served with sour cream, a favorite soup of Eastern European Jews.

schiuma - Italian term for the foam on top of espresso.

schmaltz - also **schmaltz.** A pale yellow rendered chicken fat used in Jewish cooking

Scappi, Bartolomeo (circa 1520–1570) - Italian papal chef and author, Scappi was the private chef to numerous Vatican cardinals and two popes, most notably Pius V, who kept Scappi's creative spirit tightly reined, because the pontiff preferred very simple preparations. He is also remembered for his banquet in honor of Charles V, while in service to Cardinal Lorenzo Campeggi. In 1570, Scappi wrote *L'Opera* (The Work), a dialogue between a master chef and his apprentice, remarkable for its vast technical knowledge, new baking methods and original dishes. The book brought Scappi recognition and fame during his lifetime, and was reprinted six times until the middle of the next century. In his 1570 book, *Cooking Secrets of Pope Pius V,* he included the first picture of a **fork.**

as a nondairy substitute for butter. It's added to mixtures, such as chopped liver, or blended with minced fruit, herb or onion, as a spread. Schmaltz is German, meaning "fat." See also RENDER.

schmaltz herring - see HERRING.

schmear - a generic term related to the English "smear" and the Yiddish word "shmeer" from the German *schmiere*, meaning to "grease." It is used to describe a creamy food, such as mayonnaise or butter, that has been spread onto a bagel, cracker or slice of bread.

Schnapps - also **Schnaps.** From the German, meaning "dram of liquor," a strong, colorless alcohol distilled from potatoes or grain, made in Germany, Scandinavia and the Netherlands and flavored in many ways, the two best known being peppermint and peach. This lip-smacking, tangy liquor derives its name from the Middle Low German *snappen*, meaning "to snap at."

Schnecken - see BUTTERHORN.

schnitzel - German for "cutlet," a thin slice of meat, usually veal, dipped in egg and breaded and then fried. See also VEAL.

schnitz un knepp - a Pennsylvania Dutch ham-and-apple stew with dumplings, literally translated from the German, meaning "apples and buttons."

Schonfeld, Reese - see profile below.

scone - a baked tea cake, either sweet or savory, usually served with butter and preserves, although originally cooked on a griddle and made with oats. They are most often triangular-shaped, but are also available in a variety of shapes, including round and diamond. Scones are named after the Scottish town of the same name, famous for being the home of the Stone of Destiny (the Stone of Scone or the Coronation Stone), where the kings of medieval Scotland and Ireland were crowned.

score - to make cuts in a food's surface before cooking: for decorative purposes, as in a baked ham; to prevent curling, as with a fillet of fish; to allow deeper infusion of flavor from a seasoning or a marinade, as is done with a leg of lamb before tying it for roasting; to ease the rending of fat, as with the fat of a duck's breast; and to tenderize, as with certain cuts of meat that benefit from severing some membranes with a series of crosscuts, as with what's known as minute steak. "Score" comes from the Old Norwegian, meaning "to cut."

scorpion fish - also **rascasse.** A white-fleshed fish found in temperate waters worldwide, including the Mediterranean. Given its bulging eyes, downturned mouth and squat body (decorated with an assortment of bumps, spikes, stripes and whiskers), perhaps only a cook or another rascasse could find it attractive. Although it's good roasted whole with herbs and wine, it is best known, cut into chunks, as an essential ingredient of **bouillabaise.**

scorzonera - also **black salsify.** see SALSIFY.

Scotch - also **Scotch whisky.** See WHISKEY.

Scotch barley - see BARLEY.

Scotch bonnet chile - see CHILE PEPPER.

Scotch broth - Scottish soup of beef, lamb or mutton simmered with barley, carrots, turnips, onions, leeks and parsley.

Scotch egg - a hard-boiled egg wrapped in sausage meat, dipped in beaten egg, breaded and then fried, usually eaten cold.

Schonfeld, Reese (mid-1930s–   ) - American media executive who launched television's Food Network in 1993, changing how the world views chefs and cooking. With an undergraduate degree from Dartmouth College, and a master's degree and law degree from Columbia University, Schonfeld set out in the 1950s to work in broadcast news. In 1975, he created the Independent Television News Association, the first satellite-delivered television news service. In 1979, he co-founded CNN, the world's first 24-hour news channel, with Ted Turner. He began developing his ideas for a food channel in 1992 and debuted the first program a year later from a one-bedroom New York City apartment. In the beginning, the network aired six hours of programming, repeated four times daily, for an audience of 6 million subscribers. Ten years later, the network was running 60 programs for an audience of more than 79 million worldwide.

Scotch pie - a single-serving, double-crust mutton pie baked in a straight-sided tin. A traditional working man's dinner, the pie is made with a rim of pastry that extends above the top crust; this contains the "extras," such as hot gravy, mashed potatoes and the like, which are spooned onto the hot pie before serving.

Scotch oats - see STEEL-CUT OATS.

Scotch woodcock - a savory British dish of toast topped with anchovy paste and scrambled cream and eggs.

Scottish fancy - a rather plain cookie (despite its name) made with eggs, salt, sugar, oats and vanilla. Occasionally, to really get fancy, some of the oats are replaced with shredded coconut.

Scottish parliament biscuit - also **parly, parley.** A crisp, brown ginger cookie sweetened with black treacle or golden syrup. Named for the 17th-century Scottish parliamentarians who were among its first and most enthusiastic consumers, the biscuits are said to have been created by an Edinburgh baker, Mrs. Flockhart, who served them to the aristocracy. They became so popular that soon street vendors were selling them to the common folk. In recognition of the opening of the new Scottish Parliament in the late 20th century, at least one Scottish cookie maker vowed to renew commercial production of the biscuits.

Scoville units - a measurement (SU) established in 1912 by chemist Wilbur Scoville as a way to measure the **capsaicin,** or heat, of a hot pepper; the higher the unit, the hotter the pepper.

scrapple - also **panhas, pawnhas, pawnhoss.** A Pennsylvania Dutch term for a way of using up a pig's scraps during butcher season. While pig intestines were used for sausage casings and pig's ears and snouts for **head cheese,** scrapple was made with pork shoulder, pork liver, cornmeal, onions, cloves and herbs, packed into loaves and cooled, then sliced and fried in shortening. Eaten at breakfast with ketchup, maple syrup or molasses, scrapple is still a regional favorite in Pennsylvania Dutch country. The German name for this dish, *panhas*, was brought to North America by immigrants from Westphalia.

screech - a liquor named for the cry it evoked from an American serviceman who, imitating his Newfoundland host, downed his first taste of it all in one go, or so the legend goes. It was originally none other than Jamaican rum received in a trade for salt fish. When the Canadian government took over the licensing and sale of liquor in the early 20th century, it began selling the rum in unlabeled bottles. Popularity of the drink quickly spread, and seizing the opportunity, the government began labeling and selling screech, Newfoundland's best-selling liquor.

Screwdriver - a classic cocktail mixed with orange juice and vodka, served over ice.

screwpine leaves - see PANDAN.

scrod - young cod or haddock.

scrunchions - cubes of salt pork, fried until crispy and golden, a Newfoundland specialty. In pubs and restaurants, they are often served with fried cod's tongues or fish.

scup - see SEA BREAM.

scuppernong - a bronze variety of the **muscadine** grape with sweet yellow-green fruits, used for eating out of hand or for making a sweet wine of the same name. The fruit was immortalized in Harper Lee's classic novel *To Kill a Mockingbird,* in which the narrator, Scout Finch, describes the rules for what to do with found money: "Finders were keepers unless title was proven. Plucking an occasional camellia, getting a squirt of hot milk from Miss Maudie Atkinson's cow on a summer day, helping ourselves to someone's scuppernongs was a part of our ethical culture, but money was different."

scurvy grass - see SEA KALE.

sea anemone - a sea-dwelling invertebrate of the order *Actiniaria* that attaches itself to rocks or coral, brightly colored and similar in appearance to a flower, eaten in France and the Mediterranean region. In Mediterranean markets, the **snakelocks** or **oplet** anemone is often available and is served fried or used in soups. The French *tomate de mer* (meaning "tomato of the sea" for its bright red tomato-like appearance) is another type regularly consumed, although it is considered less tasty and is usually only used as a part of a wide-ranging fish soup.

A B C D E F G H I J K L M N O P Q R S T U V W X Y Z

black sea bass

sea bass - the name given to as many as 500 species of firm, white-fleshed marine fish, not always related. The white sea bass is actually a member of the drum family but is so named because its firm, white flesh is very similar to that of the sea bass. Although great numbers of sea bass can be found off the California coast, many of them come from Mexico. The giant sea bass was originally classified as part of the Serranidae family, to which the grouper belongs, but was reclassified as part of the Percichthyidae, or perch, family for their physical similarities. **Black sea bass** is from the Serranidae family, found along the U.S. Atlantic coast as well as in the eastern Gulf of Mexico. See also CHILEAN SEA BASS.

sea biscuit - see HARDTACK.

sea bream - also **scup.** The name given to a large group of edible, relatively small, bony fish. This group includes *Archosargus rhomboidalis*, which is harvested along the western Atlantic from New Jersey to Rio de Janeiro, *Sparus aurata* (called "gilt-head bream" and "dorade" in England and France, respectively, and characterized by a gold spot behind the gill), found on the eastern shore of the Atlantic and in the Mediterranean, and *Sparus pagrus*, found in Mediterranean and Caribbean waters. Also found in the Indian and Pacific oceans, sea bream are aqua-farmed, as well. Since the late-20th century, at some Japanese fish farms, enthusiastic anglers can practice hooking and playing battery-powered, inedible, silicone sea bream, created by the Mitsubishi company.

sea-colewort - see SEA KALE.

sea crayfish - also **spiny lobster.** See LOBSTER.

sea cucumber - also **bêche de mer, iriko, sea slug, trepang.** A marine invertebrate with a long, cylindrical body, sea cucumber is usually sold dried, at which point it's called **trepang,** a popular ingredient in Chinese cuisine.

seafoam - see DIVINITY.

seafood - all marine animals, fish and mollusks that are eaten by humans.

Seager ham - from Suffolk, England, a ham cured in a sweet pickling solution of brine and syrup, then dried, smoked and aged.

sea kale - also **scurvy grass, sea-colewort.** Growing abundantly on Europe's western seaboard, rich in vitamin C, sea kale is a hardy perennial, which grows to about 2 feet (60 cm) in height. It has asparagus-like shoots and large, shiny, curled green leaves, which is why it's often mistaken for cabbage sea kale, *Brassica oleracea*.

seal - **1.** (n.) a migrating marine mammal found in cold Arctic waters, where it summers in herds, and up to 3,000 miles (4,800 km) south along North American coastlines. A traditional subsistence food, seals, such as the gray seal (*Halichoerus gryphus*) and the harp seal (*Phoca groenlandica*), have long been commercially caught for their meat, skins and oil, and have been an important traditional food source among the Aleuts in the Bering Sea, Icelanders, the Inuit and Newfoundlanders. The Aleuts use the dark meat (likened in flavor to beef liver) for roasts, sausages, soups and stews; the flippers are salted and stored in barrels. In Newfoundland, seal-flipper pie (a pot pie made with chopped carrots, onions and turnip, flippers and salt pork) is still a specialty. Seal meat is available in some specialty markets; the oil, rich in **omega-3 fatty acid,** is sold in some health food stores. **2.** (v.) to form or fasten an airtight barrier by wrapping cling film over a bowl of salad, for example, and adhering it around the rim to keep it fresh; pouring a layer of paraffin wax on homemade jam to prevent spoilage; or pinching together the top and bottom edges of a perogi or pie crust.

sea pie - **1.** a stovetop pie made by stewing chunks of meat in gravy seasoned with herbs, then topping it with a suet crust. This was a favorite hearty meal made by boatmen traveling the inland channels of Britain on barges that weren't equipped with ovens. **2.** also **cipaille.** A traditional dish (called *cipaille* in Quebec) often cooked over an open fire or on a stovetop, consisting of pastry dough layered with a combination of game fowl, different meats and/or poultry. The meat is cut from the bones, then the bones are simmered for stock while the pie dough is mixed. The bottom of a heavy, lidded pot or Dutch oven is lined with dough; after topping with chunks of meat, some of the stock is poured over. This process is repeated once or twice, then the filled pot is topped with a last layer of dough, the lid's put on and the pie is cooked for several hours. One late-18th-century recipe from the American seaboard calls for a combination of pigeons and pork; early settlers in Quebec used game, such as deer, moose or rabbit. Minced herbs and spices, such as cinnamon, cloves and nutmeg, flavored the dish if they were available; potatoes were an occasional addition.

sear - a method of frying over high heat that browns the surface of the meat, beginning the process of caramelization, which adds flavor. It is frequently used for meat that is to be cooked slowly for a long time. The fat must be very hot before the meat is added to the pan or the juices will run. After the meat has been browned and seared, the heat is lowered. The word comes from an earlier English term, meaning "to harden, to dry out."

sea robin - see GURNARD.

sea salt - see SALT.

sea scallop - see SCALLOP.

seashell pasta - see PASTA.

sea slug - see SEA CUCUMBER.

sea snail - see PERIWINKLE.

season - **1.** (n.) to accentuate the flavor of food with salt, spices, herbs, oil-based marinades, wine, beer and spirits, aging, curing, smoking, etc. **2.** (v.) to ready a new cast-iron pot or renovate an ill-used one for use. The inside of the pot is lightly coated with oil, then heated in a **moderate oven** for several hours to seal the porous surface and prevent foods from sticking.

seasoned salt - also **seasoning salt.** Refined salt containing several spices, including oregano and black pepper. It can be used in all savory and meat dishes. See also SALT.

seasoning mix - a ready-made mix of herbs, spices or a combination of both, such as Italian seasoning or pumpkin pie spice, prepared to suit particular cuisines or dishes.

sea urchin - also **oursin, whore's eggs.** A soft marine invertebrate enclosed inside a squat, spherical, spiny shell. The French have a special tool, a *coupe oursin*, to scoop out the inside. Only a portion — called the "coral" after its color — is edible. Often eaten raw with a drizzling of lemon juice or used in sushi, the coral may also be made into a paste and spread on toast or added to egg dishes, sauce or soup. Considered a delicacy in France and Japan, sea urchins are not a popular seafood in North America. Maine fishermen call them "**whore's eggs,**" but keep hauling them out of the Atlantic for sale to an eager Asian market.

sea urchin

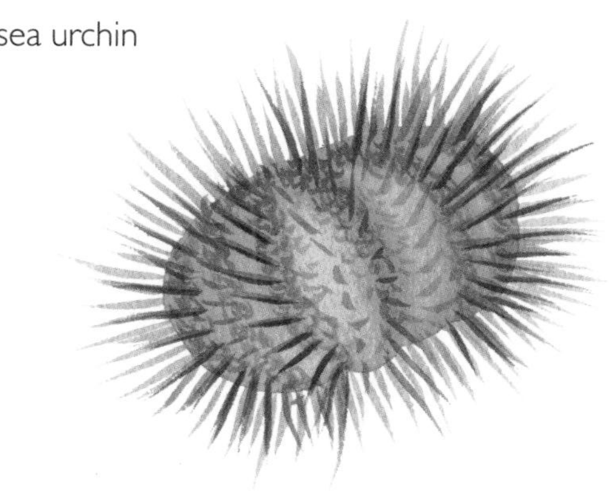

seaweed - a sea plant and an Asian dietary staple since 600 BC, kelp being the North American variety familiar to coastal fishing communities. Seaweed is consumed in Scotland; Irish moss, *Chondrus crispus*, has been used as a remedy in Ireland since the early 1800s. **Nori, kombu** and **wakame** are Japan's best-known varieties, now consumed in great quantities in the West because of the enormous popularity of Japanese food. **Laver** is a variety found off the coast of Britain, Ireland and Wales, traditionally served simply on toast with oatmeal or with grilled Welsh cured bacon. When it's mashed and boiled, it's turned into laverbread. Recently, modern chefs have taken an interest in laverbread, putting it in pasta, battered deep-fried mushrooms and seafood pizzas.

sec - a term used to describe a **still wine** that is **dry.** Confusingly, when sec is used to describe a sparkling wine, such as Champagne, it means a wine that it is fairly sweet. See also DEMI-SEC.

Seckel pear - see PEAR.

sediment - see LEES.

seed -**1.** (n.) part of a plant capable of germination and propagation of another plant of the same type, and often a nutrient-rich food source. The term is usually used for small seeds, such as sesame or poppy seeds. **2.** (v.) to remove the seeds. See also KERNEL, PIP, PIT.

seed cake - a classic butter-rich, plain, sweet cake or pound cake, with whole caraway seeds, lemon or orange zest, and sometimes a few tablespoons of whiskey mixed into the dough. Often, the finished cake is simply sprinkled with confectioner's sugar. Other small seeds, such as anise, sesame or poppy seed may be used instead to add fragrance, flavor and texture.

seitan - also **wheat meat.** A chewy meat substitute made by kneading gluten flour with water and seasonings to form a dough-like substance (or kneading regular wheat flour with water, then washing to remove the starch, leaving only the stringy gluten protein). The resulting combination is then cooked in broth. Seitan is a common food in Asia and is popular in vegetarian cooking. It soaks up flavors well and has a texture similar to that of cooked chicken, so it is a good addition to savory stews, stir-fries and other dishes. See also FU.

seize - a culinary term used to describe the sudden clumping of melting chocolate into a solid lump, usually precipitated by contact with steam or the inadvertent introduction of another liquid. A small amount of butter or oil, stirred into the seized, still-warm chocolate, can restore its softness and sheen.

sel - French for "salt."

selenium - a trace mineral important to good health but only necessary in minute amounts, usually obtained easily through food sources, such as nuts, fish, meat and enriched grain products. Brazil nuts are the most potent source of selenium, and only a handful provides more than a week's worth of the mineral. The selenium content of the soil directly relates to the selenium content of foods grown in it, so not all foods normally considered high in this nutrient are.

self-basting turkey - a turkey injected with a solution intended to make it more flavorful and tender. The components of the injected solution can vary from company to company, ranging from turkey broth to butter to emulsifiers and artificial flavors, which render during cooking, basting the bird. A self-basting turkey is meant to be extremely juicy when done.

self-rising flour - see FLOUR.

sel gris - see SALT.

sell-by date - see EXPIRATION DATE.

seltzer water - from Niederselters, a German village famous for its sparkling mineral springs since the 18th century, a term applied to any naturally sparkling spring water, which is charged with carbon dioxide gas under pressure.

semi de melone - see PASTA.

semidry - a term used to describe a **still wine** that has a very small amount of residual sugar, just slightly sweeter than **dry** wines. See also OFF-DRY.

semifreddo - an Italian dessert of custard or mousse with whipped cream or beaten egg whites folded into it, sometimes layered with cake or fruit or spooned into a crumb crust, chilled in the freezer until the custard mixture is firm but still spoonable. Its name means "half cold" in Italian to describe the half-frozen texture of the custard.

semisweet chocolate - see CHOCOLATE.

semolina - a coarsely ground durum wheat flour where the bran and germ have been sifted out, very light in color and texture, used for making pasta, gnocchi, cereals, couscous, puddings and soups. From the Italian *semolina*, a diminutive of *semola*, meaning "bran," and *similia*, meaning "very fine wheat flour." See also FLOUR.

Sencha Makato - see TEA.

sendai miso - see MISO.

Sen Rikyu - see profile right.

sereh - see LEMONGRASS.

sereh powder - a ready-made seasoning of finely ground, dried lemongrass used mainly in Asian, Indonesian, Malaysian and Thai dishes.

serrano - see CHILE PEPPER.

serrano ham - see JAMÓN SERRANO.

serrated knife - a knife with a scalloped blade usually used for cutting hard, baked goods (such

Sen Rikyu (1522–1591) - Pre-eminent master of the Japanese tea ceremony who established a standard of spiritual etiquette. The ceremonial serving and drinking of tea originated in China and took hold in Japan during the 12th century, when Buddhist monks began drinking tea to stay alert for lengthy meditations. By the middle of the 15th century, Rikyu's mentor, Murata Shuko, had established "The Way of Tea," a code governing all aspects of the ceremony, from the size and decor of the room to appropriate subjects of conversation. Rikyu is remembered for accomplishing *Wabi-cha,* which translates literally as "desolation," but refers to a broader Zen concept: only through desolation and poverty can a person find spiritual wealth by looking within. Rikyu's favorite disciple was Furuta Oriba, who became master after Rikyu's death but was forced to commit suicide when he became implicated in a political conspiracy.

as biscotti and crusty bread), soft, spongy baked goods (such as angel cake) or slicing tender fruit (such as tomatoes).

serviceberry - see SASKATOON BERRY.

servuga caviar - see CAVIER.

sesame - a tropical Asian plant, *Sesamum indicum,* cultivated for its shiny, beige, mildly flavored seed: a food, a flavoring agent and a source of oil. From the Greek *sesamon,* sesame was cultivated in Mesopotamia as early as 1600 BC. It was popular in Greek and Roman cuisine and grew extensively in Africa, its point of departure for North America as part of the slave trade. Black seeds are Japan's favorite, with a hearty, slightly bitter flavor. Brown and red seeds are rarer. The seeds get their color from their hulls, and although they taste delicate and sweet when raw, toasting deepens and enriches their flavor. Tahini is a paste of raw sesame seeds widely used in Middle Eastern cuisine; the Chinese make a paste with roasted seeds. In South Carolina, Georgia and New Orleans, "benne wafers" are sesame-seed cookies that get their name from the West African word for sesame. *Simsim* is the Arabic word for sesame seed. The expression "open sesame" was inspired by how sesame seeds suddenly pop out of their seedpods when fully mature. See also BENNE.

sesame butter - homemade or ready-made spread made with puréed, unhulled toasted sesame seeds. It is darker and denser than tahini, which is made with hulled raw seeds.

sesame oil - a fragrant, long-keeping oil with a nutty flavor that is pressed from sesame seeds and used in both savory and sweet dishes. Two types are made: Light sesame oil, produced from unroasted seeds and pale gold in color, is used in dressings, marinades, sautés and stir-fries. Dark sesame oil, often used in Asian cooking, is made from toasted seeds and amber in color. Since it burns easily, it is often added as a flavoring near the end of cooking, drizzled over food or used as a condiment. Nutritious and high in polyunsaturated fats, sesame oil is sold in many health food stores. It is also used in prepared foods, such as margarine, as well as cosmetics and pharmaceuticals.

sesame seed paste - see TAHINI.

set - a term used to describe the action in foods, such as custard, jam or jelly, which change — often as a result of heating, then chilling — from a liquid to a "set," semisolid.

seto fuumi - a Japanese seasoning compound of dried seaweed, tuna, sesame seed and monosodium glutamate.

Setúbal - fortified wines of the Setúbal peninsula, about 20 miles (32 km) south of Lisbon in Portugal, made predominantly from Muscat grapes. Setúbal is made principally from two types of Muscat grapes known in Portuguese as *Moscatel de Setúbal* (Muscat of Alexandria) and *Moscatel roxo* (purple Muscat).

seven-minute frosting - a classic, fluffy meringue frosting made by constantly beating a mixture of cream of tartar, egg whites, sugar, vanilla and water in the top of a double-boiler over rapidly boiling water until it forms **soft peaks.** The whole process takes about seven minutes, hence the name. The mixture is then transferred to a bowl where flavorings, such as caramel syrup, melted chocolate or shredded coconut, can be stirred in and beaten until it's thick enough to spread.

sevian noodles - also **chickpea noodles, sev.** Crispy, deep-fried Indian thread noodles made of **besan,** sevian noodles may be added to appetizers, main or side dishes, or eaten on their own as a snack.

seviche - also **cebiche, ceviche.** Originally a Spanish dish, adopted in Central and South America, especially Peru, Ecuador and Mexico, seviche is fish and shellfish "cooked" while marinating in lime juice, seasoned with olive oil and various herbs and spices, often served as an appetizer. Acids, such as those from citrus fruits, vinegar and sometimes wine, can cook delicate flesh like that of fish in just a few hours. Supposedly, the name comes from English-speaking people saying, "See the beach," where Peruvian fisherman ate their fish directly from the sea with just lemons and salt, the locals transforming the phrase into *seviche*.

Seville orange - see ORANGE.

shabu-shabu - a Japanese dish of very thin slices of beef and raw vegetables that each person cooks for himself or herself in a pot of hot broth sitting on a source of heat in the center of the table. Once cooked, the ingredients can be dipped into an assortment of sauces. See also SUKIYAKI.

shad - see HERRING.

shadberry - see SASKATOON BERRY.

Shaddock - see POMELO.

shad roe - the orange **roe** from a **shad,** long considered a delicacy in America. **Fannie Merritt Farmer** included five recipes for shad roe in her famous *The Boston Cooking-School Cook Book*, published in 1896. In two of the recipes, it's made into sauces for the fish; in the others, it's the star — sliced and fried or sautéed, or baked whole in a tomato sauce. Shad roe is available fresh only in the spring, but canned or frozen all year. See also ROE.

shallots

shake - see MILKSHAKE.

shallot - a member of the onion family, *Allium ascalonicum*, very subtle in flavor, the darling of French cuisine. Any haute cuisine recipe for sauce or soup will probably call for these delicately flavored members of the lily family. **Pliny** thought shallots took their name from the ancient Middle Eatern trading town of Ascalon, where they were believed to have originated. In fact, they came from Asia Minor. During the Crusades, they were brought back to Europe as a "new" food and were immediately adopted by the French. The Spanish explorer Hernando de Soto is said to have introduced shallots to the U.S. during his Louisiana explorations in the 16th century. In time, French settlers to Louisiana made the shallot an important ingredient in their cooking. The Latin name for shallots is *escalonia*.

shandy - also **panaché, Radler, shandygaff.** A half-and-half mixture of beer and — in British pubs, where the drink was born — lemonade or ginger beer served over ice. Elsewhere, ginger ale or a fizzy, lemon-lime beverage (such as 7 UP or Collins Mix) may stand in for the lemonade. The word "shandy," coined circa 1691, meant crack-brained, spirited, prophetic and wild. It was only in 1888 that "shandy" was first used to describe the drink. Enough of the brew, perhaps, led to the behavior of the same name. Called *panaché* in France and *Radler* in Germany.

Shaoxing wine - a Chinese rice wine from the province of Shaoxing. It is drunk warm, like sake, and used extensively in Chinese cooking. The best varieties may be aged for as long as a hundred years, but those commonly available in the West are likely to be "cooking quality." Available in Chinese markets rather than liquor stores, they are quite salty and not suitable for drinking. Sake, dry vermouth and dry sherry are acceptable substitutes.

sharbat - a homemade or ready-made Asian cold drink made from crushed or puréed fruits, sweet melons, spices and/or nuts, sugar and water, that is poured through a sieve into serving glasses. Some versions are flavored with flower petals or flower water. Often garnished with a mint leaf and served with crushed ice, sharbat is thought to be the precursor of sorbet.

shark - a member of a large group of primitive carnivorous fishes with skeletons made of cartilage, the smaller varieties being the most edible. Sharks can range in size from the tiny Spined Pigmy shark at 7 to 8 inches (17.5 to 20 cm) to the gargantuan Whale shark that can grow to 46 feet (14 m). See also CAPE SHARK, DOGFISH, NURSEHOUND, SAND SHARK.

shark's fin - considered a prestigious food in China, eaten for hundreds of years, believed to be beneficial to the heart, lungs, kidneys, liver and complexion. The dorsal fin is considered to be the best, although the two side, bottom and tail fins are all used in Chinese cooking, especially shark's fin soup. The Japanese are the biggest consumers of this expensive delicacy, probably because the Japanese believe it's a powerful aphrodisiac.

sharpening steel - also **butcher's steel, steel.** A long, thin, rough-textured carbon-steel rod with a handle, used to straighten the edge of a chef's knife. When the cutting edge of the knife is drawn over the steel, the steel straightens the edge, which bends invisibly as the knife is used. It is important to draw both sides of the knife edge over the steel the same number of times so that it is as even and true as possible. The proper angle at which to steel a knife is 20 to 30 degrees, which can be achieved if the knife is placed flat against the steel, then the back of the knife raised by about 1/4 inch (0.5 cm). If the knife edge has become dull, the knife needs to be sharpened on a **whetstone** before it is steeled.

Sharp, F.G. - see UGLI FRUIT.

shashlik - see SHISH KEBAB.

shawarma - the Middle Eastern version of the Greek **gyro,** a cooking method for either lamb or chicken, in which a large amount of thinly sliced, marinated meat is placed on a rotating skewer and roasted; cooks cut shavings of the meat from the mass as it cooks and serve it on pita bread with cucumbers, tomatoes and condiments. In Turkey, it's called *doner kebab*.

shea butter - also **galam, karite.** A refined vegetable fat extracted from the seeds of the *Butyrospermum paradoxum*, or karite nut tree, which is native to arid regions of west Africa. The unprocessed seeds have long been exported to Britain and Europe, where they are made into shea butter. The smooth, flavor- and fragrance-free fat is used as a baking ingredient and in the manufacture of chocolate, margarine and many cosmetics. Harvesting the seeds has traditionally been the job of rural, usually poor, women. The United Nations Development Fund for Women actively supports the efforts of these small-scale producers to export the seeds — nicknamed "women's gold" — to world markets. The women save some of the seeds to pound, raw or roasted, into homemade butters for their own baking or soap making.

shears - see KITCHEN SHEARS.

sheepberry - see NANNYBERRY.

sheep's stomach - the natural casing for traditional puddings, such as **haggis.**

sheet gelatin - see GELATIN.

shell - **1.** (n.) the rigid casing of a crustacean or mollusk, an egg, a fruit, a nut or a turtle. **2.** (n.) a usually thin crust containing the filling of a pie, tart or tortilla. **3.** (n.) a piece of shell-shaped or **conchiglie** pasta. **4.** (v.) to peel off (or crack and remove) a husk, pod or shell to get at the food inside.

shellfish - a freshwater or saltwater invertebrate with a shell or carapace, mostly edible, falling into two categories: crustaceans (including lobster, crab, crayfish and shrimp) and mollusks (including snail, clam, oyster and squid).

shepherd's pie - a casserole of cooked ground or chopped meat (traditionally lamb or mutton, but also beef) with gravy and sometimes cooked vegetables, topped with mashed potatoes and baked to golden brown; originally a way to use up leftovers.

sherbet - a frozen dessert similar to ice cream but made with fruit juice, sugar and water; it can also contain milk and eggs. The name comes from a Turkish word designating a Middle Eastern drink of sweetened fruit juice and water, from the Arabic word *sharâb*, meaning "to drink." See also SORBET.

sherrified - see MADERIZED.

sherry - a fortified wine whose name comes from Jerez de la Frontera in the south of Spain, a region planted exclusively with white grape varieties, primarily Palomino. Along with nearby coastal Sanlúcar and Puerto de Santa Maria, Jerez produces most of the world's sherry and some say the world's best. Jerez was known as *Xera* by the Greeks and *Ceret* by the Romans. By the early Middle Ages, the Arabs called the region *Sekeris*, and northern Spanish Castilians called it *Xeres* and later *Xerez*. By the late 19th century, it had become Jerez de la Frontera, the town marking a cultural divide between the north and south. From the Castilian pronunciation (*hare-ETH*), British importers called it JER-ez, then JER-ee and finally "sherry." The wine is made in a range of styles, falling into two categories: **fino** is dry, pale, straw yellow, light and fresh, with a long, crisp finish. An **oloroso** is sweet, deep amber to warm amber brown, medium- to full-bodied, with sweet wines added, often called a **cream sherry.** See also SACK.

SOME NOTABLE SHERRIES

amontillado - amber brown, rich, nutty, full-bodied.

brown - a very sweet, heavy, deep brown oloroso, almost totally out of fashion.

cream - a pale, soft oloroso.

manzanilla - a fino exclusively from Sanlúcar, distinctively fresh-tasting.

palo cortado - a rare **amontillado** with a more refined flavor

Pedro Ximénez - considered to be the ultimate brown sherry, opaque, heavy and sweet, with a highly concentrated acidity; rarely offered commercially.

shichimi togarashi - see TOGARASHI.

shiitake - also **black forest mushroom, golden oak mushroom, Japanese black mushroom.** A widely used Asian mushroom, *Lentinus edodes*, from *shii*, meaning "oak," and *take*, meaning "mushroom." Grown on the wood of dead deciduous trees; native to China and Japan, but now grown throughout the world. The spawn is planted in holes or wedges cut into the logs, and crops last for three to six years.

shi lian zu - see LOTUS SEED.

shimeji - see OYSTER MUSHROOM.

shiner - see MOONFISH.

shinshu miso - see MISO.

ship biscuit - see HARDTACK.

shirataki - noodles made from a by-product of the root of the devil's tongue plant, *Amorphophallus rivieri*, cultivated in China and Japan, from the Japanese, meaning "waterfall."

Shirley Temple - a so-called kiddie cocktail or **mocktail** for girls. Named after the curly-headed, cute and dimpled child star, this drink contains club soda, ginger ale or lemon-lime soda and **Grenadine**, garnished with a maraschino cherry and a slice of orange. A lucky girl might get a teeny paper parasol in her drink, as well. The boys' version is **Roy Rogers.**

shiro goma - see GOMA.

shirred eggs - eggs covered in milk or cream and sometimes topped with bread crumbs, baked in a small dish or cup until the whites are firm.

shish kebab - also **kabob, kebab, shashlik.** Chunks of meat, fish or vegetables pierced by a wooden stick so that they will hold together for quick grilling or broiling, from the Turkish *shish*, meaning "skewer," and *kebab*, meaning "roasted meat." Its history can be traced to Caucasus Mountain nomads, who would cook small pieces of their meat on the ends of their swords held over an open fire. The Turkish introduced kebabs to the Middle East, while Afghan traders introduced them to India following the advent of the **tandoor** oven, which required long skewers on which to cook meats. They were called *seekh kebabs* and were sometimes also shallow- or deep-fried. Numerous cultures have their own versions. See also BROCHETTE, SATAY, SOUVLAKI, YAKITORI.

shish taouk - Lebanese chicken kebabs. See SHISH KEBAB.

shiso - also known as **beefsteak plant, perilla.** An Asian annual herb, *Perilla frutescens*, with green-and-red serrated leaves and a distinctive

shiitake

flavor, similar to mint. Shiso is often used decoratively, as with sashimi, or deep-fried in tempura, but it has a wide range of uses. Shiso was part of the cuisine of ancient China, but today it's almost exclusively used in Japanese-style cuisine. Not native to North America, the plant has naturalized extensively and is now considered an invasive alien. In Texas, ranchers are warned to keep herds away from the plants, which are toxic to livestock when they are flowering.

shock - also **refresh.** To chill a blanched or boiled food in ice water to stop the cooking process.

shoestring potatoes - finely shredded or julienned potatoes deep-fried in oil until crisp, so called because the long shreds look like shoelaces.

shojin ryori - see EISAI.

shoofly pie - a famed dessert from the annals of Pennsylvania Dutch cooking, filled with molasses, brown sugar and butter, so named because, being so sweet, it would attract flies while cooling at the kitchen window. Each time the cook passed the window, he or she would yell, "Shoo, fly!"

shooter - **1.** a single serving or shot of straight whiskey or other spirit, usually served in a shot glass. **2.** a powerful mixture of spirits, usually undiluted and dubbed with an arresting name, such as "Slammer" or "Suicide," served in a shot or shooter glass (ranging from 3 to 8 ounces, the latter are larger than a standard 1½-ounce shot glass). Dessert shooters may be topped with nonalcoholic ingredients, such as chocolate sauce and whipped cream. **3.** an oyster — sauced with horseradish, Tabasco and vodka — served in a shot glass.

shorba - the word for "soup" in many Islamic countries.

shortbread - a butter-rich biscuit from 15th-century Scotland, originally made with finely ground oats, usually baked for Christmas and New Year's, with innumerable variations, although seldom straying far from flour, butter and sugar.

shortcake - a sweet, rich North American biscuit or cake, split in half and filled with fruit (especially strawberries) and topped with whipped cream.

short-crust pastry - also **short paste, short pastry.** The most common pastry, used for the base of a tart or pie, either sweet or savory. The high ratio of fat to flour (the higher the fat content, the "shorter" or more crumbly the pastry) gives the crust a crumbly rather than flaky texture. See also PÂTE BRISÉE, PÂTE SUCRÉE.

shortening - a firm, flavorless, pure-white vegetable fat made from hydrogenated oil, such as cottonseed, soybean and sunflower oil, that is often used for deep-frying, frying and as an ingredient in baked goods and frostings. One well-known brand, Crisco, was introduced in 1911 as a cheaper choice than butter and an alternative to animal fat, such as lard. In response to health concerns over the consumption of trans fats produced during the hydrogenating process, Crisco introduced a new type, called Zero Grams Trans Fat Per Serving All-Vegetable Shortening, in 2004. See also HYDROGENATION, LARD.

short ribs - see BEEF.

shot - **1.** one to 1½ ounces of alcoholic spirit measured in a shot glass of that same standard size. **2.** a small, unspecified amount of alcoholic or nonalcoholic liquid, such as a shot or dash of espresso, lemon juice or vanilla.

shot glass - also **jigger.** A small, flared glass that is supposed to hold a standard 1½ ounces of liquor, although there are more generous versions that hold 2 ounces and stingier ones that hold only 1 ounce. It is the standard measuring glass at bars for mixing cocktails.

shoti - a powder thickener made of the dried, starchy zeodary rhizome in India, which may be used as a substitute for arrowroot. See also ZEODARY.

shottsuru - fermented fish sauce made by pickling sandfish with salt and malted rice. See also FISH SAUCE.

shoyu - see SOY SAUCE.

shred - to cut food into thin strips or shreds using a knife or the holes on a grater. See also GRATE.

shrikhand - a spiced, sweetened Indian dish made of sieved curds or yogurt. Usually, it is spiced with ground cardamom, and saffron is mixed in to give it a golden color. Rosewater or mango pulp (or that of banana, grapes or orange) may also be added. Shrikhand is served chilled, sometimes garnished with slivers of pistachio nuts or sparkles of **varak.** The dish is so popular in India that home cooks can buy special machines to make it.

shrimp - any of various 10-legged crustaceans found in oceans worldwide, with shells that can be light brown, pink, red, gray, yellow, gray-green or dark green, which change color after cooking. There are hundred of species in two categories: warm-water and cold-water, the latter generally being smaller and more succulent. See also PRAWN, SCAMPI, SHELLFISH.

shrimp boil - see CRAB BOIL.

shrimp chip - also **kroepoek, krupuk, prawn cracker, shrimp cracker.** A crisp, deep-fried snack often eaten in Asia and available in Asian markets in North America as well. The chip is made from tapioca starch or rice flour and shrimp, and fried until puffy and Styrofoam-like in texture (there are also dried uncooked versions that can be fried at home for a fresh, warm chip). Store-bought shrimp chips are usually dyed a pinkish, shrimp-like hue and are, as their name implies, strongly flavored with shrimp or prawns. The Indonesian name for shrimp chip is *krupuk* which was adopted and transliterated by Dutch settlers as *kroepoek*. Shrimp chips are a popular snack in the Netherlands as well.

shrimp cocktail

shrimp cocktail - an easy, ever-popular appetizer of chilled, cooked shrimp usually hooked, side by side, over the rim of a Martini glass (for a single serving) or low bowl and served with lemon wedges and tangy dipping sauce. The tomato-based sauce contains sharp, spicy ingredients, such as chili sauce, horseradish, Tabasco and Worcestershire sauce. Ready-made sauce and frozen rings of cooked shrimp make this even easier to prepare.

shrimp cracker - see SHRIMP CHIP.

shrimp Creole - a classic shrimp stew containing chopped bell pepper, celery, garlic, onions and tomatoes, seasoned with bay leaves, cayenne pepper and thyme, served piping hot over rice. Like all traditional recipes, this dish varies with the cook. Some add an extra vegetable, such as sugar snap peas; others add a sweet ingredient, such as molasses.

shrimp paste - also **kapi, mam tom, terasi, trassi.** Ground, fermented, salted shrimp that is formed into cakes and dried, or stored as soft, thick paste, then added to curries, marinades, rice, sauces and soups. With its intense fishy, salty flavor, a little goes a long way; its powerful smell lessens with cooking. See also BELACAN.

shrimp sauce - see PATIS.

shrimp spice - see CRAB BOIL.

Shropshire blue - a sharp, creamy but firm, blue-veined cow's milk cheese that is aged for three to six months. Used to lend a pinkish tinge to the cheese, **achiote seed** also colors the orangey-brown rind. Despite its name, Shropshire blue was created in Inverness, Scotland, and is now produced in England. Delicious on a cracker or crumbled on soup, it's also considered good eating on its own, washed down with a British brown ale or fortified wine.

shrub - **1.** a combination of fruit, fruit juice, sugar and spirits, allowed to age, then puréed and mixed with a carbonated beverage. Some hikers add Gatorade to the mix. **2.** a mixture of an acidic liquid, such as lemon juice or vinegar, with fruit juice, sugar, and water or soda water, served over ice.

shuck - to remove the outer layer from something, as a shell from an oyster or the husk from an ear of corn.

Shui-Hsien - see TEA.

shukri - see PHALSA.

Siamese ginger - see GALANGAL.

Sichuan pepper - see SZECHWAN PEPPER.

Sidecar - a classic cocktail made with two parts brandy, one part lemon juice and one part triple sec, such as Cointreau, served over ice in a sugar-rimmed glass garnished with a twist of orange.

Siegert, Dr. Johann Gottlieb Benjamin - see ANGOSTURA BITTERS.

Siena cake - a long-keeping, spicy **panforte** baked at Christmas. It is named after its Italian city of origin. In the Middle Ages, Siena was a stopping point for caravans on the silk-and-spice route to the East.

sieve - also **strainer. 1.** (n.) A receptacle made of mesh or perforated material that allows liquid or small, fine particles to be strained out of mixtures. They can be any shape — from tall and conical to short and round — and are usually made of metal or plastic, often with a handle or two on the side. See also COLANDER. **2.** (v.) to remove liquids or small particles from a mixture by pouring it through a sieve or strainer.

sift - to pass dry ingredients, such as flour, cocoa powder or confectioner's sugar, through a fine-meshed kitchen utensil or sieve to remove lumps, blend ingredients and incorporate air to make ingredients lighter.

sikana - see CASSABANANA.

Silberwasser - also **Silverwasser.** A clear German liqueur that has flakes of silver foil suspended in it, usually flavored with anise and caraway seeds.

silken tofu - see TOFU.

silk melon - also **silk squash.** See ASIAN OKRA.

Silpat - brand name for a sheet of silicone-covered glass mesh, sold as a baking-pan liner. Available in various sizes, nonstick and reusable, it requires no greasing and often stands in for parchment paper.

silver beet - see CHARD.

silver-dollar pancake - a small, coin-size pancake made by dropping a spoonful of batter onto a griddle. Silver dollars became such a favorite breakfast order at diners and roadside restaurants in the mid-1900s that special griddles, impressed with several mini-pancake shapes in each, are now available. The small griddle cakes are also used as the base for bite-size appetizers and hors d'oeuvres.

silver leaf - see VARAK.

silver skin - connective tissue of fine, silvery membrane found in meats. Since it prevents the penetration of marinades and shrinks as it cooks (causing the meat to curl), the silver skin must be removed before marinating or cooking.

silver trout - see RAINBOW TROUT.

Silverwasser - see SILBERWASSER.

simmer - to cook a liquid, or a food immersed in a liquid, at just below boiling point, 185° to 190°F (85° to 88°C).

Simmons, Amelia - see profile below.

simnel cake - a traditional, dense, fruit-filled and spicy British cake made for Mothering Sunday. On this fourth Sunday in Lent, children were customarily released by their employers to visit their mothers and their "mother churches." The cake keeps so well that some, or all of it, may be saved for Easter. Different cities had their own shape and style of simnel cake, but most contained candied peel, chopped almonds, currants, **mixed spice** and sultanas. (English cookery expert Delia Smith adds a can of mincemeat to hers.) The version from Shrewsbury, home to the celebrated cathedral, is the one most well known today. It

Simmons, Amelia (18th century) - American cook and author of the first American cookbook. Apart from information surrounding the publication of her book *American Cookery* (1796), little is known about Simmons' life. From the preface of her book, we learn that she was orphaned, lacked a formal education and saw this as the reason she entered domestic service. She was considered an excellent cook, based on discerning ingredient choices and the sophisticated cooking techniques in her book. *American Cookery* distinguished itself by citing uniquely American foods, such as cornmeal and pumpkin, and Simmons was the first cookbook author to cite pearlash as a leavener, which Colonial women used before the advent of baking powder. The book was also responsible for the words "cookie" and "slaw" appearing in print for the first time.

Sinclair, Upton (1878–1968) - American writer whose novel *The Jungle* (1906) exposed the appalling working conditions and sanitation practises of the Chicago meatpacking industry. Sinclair was born in Baltimore, Maryland, and financed his studies at New York City College by writing dime novels, moving on to Columbia University in 1897. He published five novels in five years before writing *The Jungle*, which brought him critical and financial success and which led to the implementation of the Pure Food and Drug Act the same year. Sinclair was a member of the Socialist Party for many years and wrote many historical novels about social issues of the day, such as *King Coal* (1917), about the 1914 Colorado miners' strike; and *Dragon's Teeth* (1942), about Germany's Nazi downfall during the 1930s, which earned him the Pulitzer Prize for fiction in 1943.

contains a center layer and covering of homemade almond paste or marzipan, and 11 balls of marzipan — representing the true apostles — are arranged in a circle on top.

simple syrup - also **sugar syrup, sugar water.** A clear syrup commonly made by carefully boiling one part sugar to one part water until the sugar dissolves; thicker or thinner syrups can be made by using more or less sugar, respectively. Flavorings, such as lemon zest, mint leaves or the pulp of a vanilla pod, can be added, then sieved out after boiling; or fruit juice, liquid flavor extracts or spirits can be used. After cooling, the syrup can refrigerated for weeks before use. Simple syrup can brushed onto baking, such as **génoise** cakes, splashed into beverages, such as iced tea or **Margaritas,** or used to glaze or preserve fruit.

Simpson lettuce - a **leaf lettuce** with loose, crinkled, crisp leaves. Considered easy to grow and slow to bolt, it is a variety sold to home gardeners by many mainstream and heritage seed houses. See also LETTUCE.

simsim - also **sim sim.** The Arabic name for "sesame seed."

Sinclair, Upton - see profile above.

Singapore sling - a classic cocktail made with cherry liqueur, such as **Peter Heering,** gin and grenadine, shaken with ice, poured into a highball glass, then topped with soda and garnished with a maraschino cherry and an orange slice. More complex slings may have shots of angostura bitters, Bénédictine, Cointreau and lime and pineapple juice added, as well. The original was mixed at Singapore's Raffles Hotel circa 1915 — a contemporary haunt of such writers as Joseph Conrad, Noël Coward and Somerset Maugham.

singing hinny - a griddle cake imported from the United Kingdom, which is especially popular in Nova Scotia. Butter, cream of tartar, currants, flour, lard, milk, salt and sour cream are mixed into a stiff dough, which is rolled and cut into rounds. The frying hotcakes sizzle or "sing" as they cook ("hinny" and "hinnie" are local terms for "honey," and a term of endearment for small fry in the North of England and Scotland).

single fillet - see FILLET.

single Gloucester - see GLOUCESTER.

single-malt scotch - see WHISKEY.

sippet - **1.** a small sop, a piece of solid food, such as bread, for dipping into a liquid. **2.** fried or toasted bread used for garnish. See also CROUTON.

sirloin - from the French *surlonge*, meaning "on or above the loin," a cut of beef just in front of the round. See also BEEF.

sirup - see SYRUP.

sizzling rice soup - a Chinese dish in which dried, ready-made or homemade cakes of cooked rice are deep-fried, immediately placed in individual serving bowls, then topped with hot soup. When the liquid hits, the rice crackles, snaps and sizzles.

skate - also **banjo, ray, roker.** A flat, thin fish with large, wing-like pectoral fins that give it a characteristic diamond or square shape. Only

the fins are eaten. Sold fresh or frozen, the flesh is firm (not flaky) and white. It may be baked, fried, grilled or poached; traditionally, it is served with **beurre noir.**

skewer - a long, thin, pointed metal or wooden rod used to hold meat in place or to hold several small pieces of meat and/or vegetables together for cooking, as in a shish kebab or *brochette*, as they're called in French.

skillet - **1.** a long-handled kitchen pan, commonly called a frying pan. **2.** from the Middle English *skelet*, a three- or four-footed pot or kettle for cooking in the hearth.

skim - to clean a liquid by drawing a skimmer or slotted spoon across its surface to remove a layer of fat and/or scum.

skimmer - a flat perforated ladle or slotted spoon used for skimming fat and scum from the surface of liquids, especially stocks, soups and casseroles.

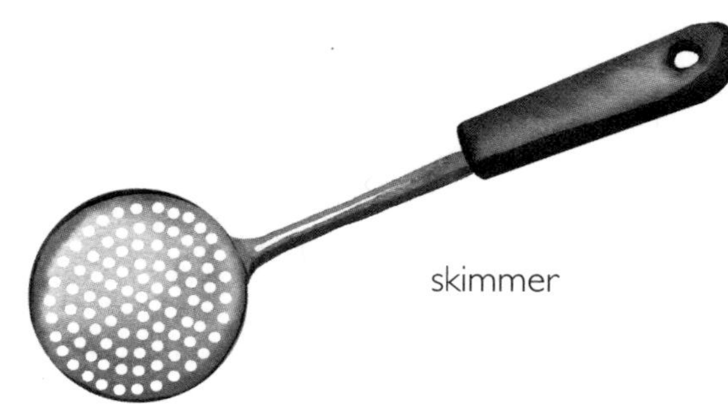

skim milk - see MILK.

skipjack tuna - see TUNA.

skirlie - a somewhat bland, Scottish side dish or stuffing, dubbed the poor man's **haggis.** Chopped onion is sautéed in beef suet or drippings; the oatmeal is added and cooked, then stock is poured into the pan and the skirlie cooks until the oatmeal absorbs the fat and liquid. Mild-mannered, skirlie allows the flavor of rich game birds to shine, and, in more modest kitchens, accompanies **tatties** and **neeps.**

skirt steak - a long, thin flap of flavorful but tough meat from the steer's diaphragm, which is attached to the inside of the rib cage.
See also BEEF.

skordalia - a Greek dip or garlic sauce made of puréed garlic, lemon, olive oil, parsley and thickened with baked potatoes, sometimes ground nuts are added, served with meats and fish, and as a dip for bread, used to accompany fried zucchini and eggplant strips or deep-fried codfish.

skyr - a cooked, curdled mixture of milk, **rennet** and buttermilk with bacterial cultures or sour cream. After standing at room temperature for several hours, it is strained to remove the whey, then whipped to a creamy consistency and served with cream, fruit and sugar. Called Iceland's national dish, protein-rich skyr has been a staple there since the first settlers arrived; with so little arable land, Icelanders raise cattle primarily for dairy products, rather than meat.

slab bacon - a large chunk of bacon that allows the cook to slice it to the desired thickness, unlike packaged pre-sliced bacon, which is all the same thickness.

slab cake - from 18th-century England, the industrial name for a factory-made cake, sold by weight.

slaw - see COLESLAW.

slice - **1.** (n.) a cut piece or serving of food, such as bread, cheese, meat or pie. **2.** (n.) a kitchen utensil resembling a triangular spatula, used for lifting foods, such as cakes and fish. **3.** (n.) a term used in some parts of western Canada for a bar cookie. For example, a New York slice means **Nanaimo bar. 4.** (v.) to cut food into broad, thin pieces.

slimehead - see ORANGE ROUGHY.

sliver - **1.** (n.) a long, very thin portion, as with pie or cheese; almonds are often slivered to accentuate their long, narrow shape. **2.** (v.) to cut food into thin, tapered strips.

Slivovitz - a plum **eau de vie,** the national drink of the former Yugoslavia, from the Slavic *sliva,* meaning "plum."

sloe - a tiny, tart, purple plum-like fruit of the blackthorn, *Prunus spinosa,* used to flavor liquors, particularly gin, and in preserves.

Sloppy Joe - **1.** a sandwich of ground beef, cooked with chopped green pepper, garlic and onion, mixed with seasoned tomato sauce and served on a bun. It is thought to have evolved from a loose-meat sandwich served in an Iowa restaurant in the 1920s. Named, perhaps, after a famous bar in the Florida of the 1930s, this drippy, but delicious American original quickly became a familiar item on restaurant menus and a favorite with budget-minded home cooks, who could make it from scratch or use a commercial sauce and seasoning mix. By the end of the century, upscale vegetarian versions of this everyman's sandwich, with ground lentils and mushrooms standing in for the beef, were being served up on pita bread. **2.** a slang term, popularized in the 1940s, denoting a coffee shop, diner or restaurant that serves cheap, quick food.

slow cooker - an appliance consisting of a metal casing containing the heat source (electrical coils) and a stoneware insert with a tight-fitting lid. Because they cook on very low heat, from about 200°F (93°C) on the Low setting to 300°F (150°C) on High, slow cookers can be safely left to cook on their own for long periods of time. Invented in the 1970s as a device for cooking beans, the appliance fell out of favor for many years but enjoyed a renaissance in the 1990s, when it was identified as a convenience tool that met the needs of busy families by enabling them to prepare long-simmering meals, while being away from the house all day. **Crock-Pot** is the registered trademark of the Rival slow cooker.

Slow Food - an international movement, founded in 1989, devoted to protecting the right to taste by emphasizing artisanal methods of food production and preparation. All facets of the food chain are represented, from growers and harvesters to artisans and chefs. The movement emphasizes organic production, if possible, as well as traditional methods of preparation, with a view toward producing more healthful and delicious food while achieving equilibrium with the environment.

slow oven - a recipe term referring to an oven temperature of about 200° to 300°F (100° to 150°C). Dating from the time when cooks used woodstoves with nonexistent or unreliable thermostats, a slow oven was one in which the cook's hand could tolerate the heat for 60 seconds. See also HOT OVEN, MODERATE OVEN.

slumgullion - a stew or hash containing any bits of leftovers, coined during the California Gold Rush. Slumgullion was the term the miners used for the mud left in the sluice after panning for gold, and also the thin watery stew made from leftovers.

slump - see GRUNT.

slurry - **1.** a mixture of flour and water, also called **whitewash,** added to simmering sauces, soups and stews as a thickener; or a mixture of cornstarch and water added to stir-fries to add gloss and thickness to the sauce. Either needs to be cooked for some minutes afterward to combine with the flavor of the dish. **2.** an alcoholic or nonalcoholic drink, akin to a **slush,** usually mixed with fruit, fruit juice or flavored syrups, then puréed with ice. **3.** one of any nutritious puréed food preparations eaten by people with dysphagia (difficulty swallowing), caused by a stroke or a neurological condition, such as multiple sclerosis.

slush - an alcoholic or nonalcoholic drink or punch, mixed first, then frozen until slushy. There are slush versions of most favorite cocktails. See also GRANITA.

smallage - see CELERY SEED.

small ale - also **small beer.** A malt-liquor beverage usually containing less than 1 percent alcohol and sometimes brewed, as a less expensive beverage, from mash already used to make full-strength ale. Given the boiling in the brewing process and the alcohol in the finished product, it was a safer drink than water in the less-sanitary past of Europe and colonial North America, so it was commonly served to children as a healthy alternative. And Benjamin Franklin, it was reported, enjoyed a glass at breakfast. See also NEAR BEER.

smelt - a small, slender, trout-like fish with silver skin and delicate, rich, oily flesh, from the Osmeridae family, related to the **grayling,** a member of the salmon family. **Candlefish,** also known as eulachon and oolichan, is a smelt found all along North America's Pacific seaboard. It got its name because, being very fatty, particularly during spawning, it was dried, skewered and burned for light by Native Americans.

Smithfield ham - see VIRGINIA HAM.

Smithfield Market - London's famed wholesale meat market, believed to have taken its name from "smooth field," the historic site of jousts, tournaments and executions, where in the 16th century, Queen Mary executed 300 Protestants, leading to her moniker "Bloody Mary."

smoked food - a method of flavoring foods by either a **hot** or **cold smoking** method. In the former, the food is cooked during smoking; in the latter, the food is salted in spiced brine, drained and smoked slowly (up to 10 hours) over hardwood chips.

EXOTIC WOOD CHIPS AND HARDWOOD

fruitwood - wood from apple, cherry, peach and other fruit trees imparts a pleasant sweetness and special aura to grilled foods. Flavors tend to be mild as opposed to smoky.

grapevine - known for centuries in Europe, which has an almost never-ending supply of it, it's the latest addition for North American chefs to use in grilling, burns very hot like mesquite, imparting a light smokiness.

hickory - responsible for the robust smoky flavor in the best barbecued ribs. It's available in chips, which should be soaked in water for 30 minutes before being distributed evenly over the fire.

mesquite - a dense hardwood from Mexico and the Southwest, cured in sealed adobe structures to produce charcoal but also made into chips, and burns very hot and long.

oak - a widely available wood that burns long and slowly to produce a perfect glow for grilling.

smoked haddock - also **Finnan haddie.** Originally from the Scottish village of Finnan in Aberdeenshire, this haddock is cured over peat smoke, usually eaten as is with a rich milk sauce or flaked in an omelet; sometimes, it's an ingredient in **kedgeree,** the classic English breakfast dish of fish and rice.

smoked salmon - perhaps the most popular of smoked foods, originally done for preservation, but since the days of refrigeration, done mostly for flavor or texture. The salmon first undergoes a curing stage, in which salt simultaneously penetrates the flesh and draws out the moisture, which hinders the growth of bacteria that will spoil the fish. **Cold-smoking** temperatures range between 70° and 90°F (21° and 32°C), producing milder, raw-textured flesh. This process, when used for the duration of a day to several weeks, will preserve the fish by drying it. **Hot-smoking** temperatures range between 120° and 180°F (49° and 82°C), producing fuller flavors and thorough cooking, ensured when the internal temperature is maintained at 145°F (63°C) for 30 minutes. The flavors of hot smoked fish are dependent on the characteristics of the wood burned, such as alder, maple or apple wood, all common types used to smoke fish.

Hot smoking can be used to produce salmon **jerky,** the sweet-salty version of which is called **Indian candy** or **salmon candy.** Another name for this type of jerky is **squaw candy,** a controversial term because the word "squaw" is considered offensive by some. *Squaw* is the word in the Massachuset language for "woman," but detractors say that the word has been used as an insult to belittle Native American women since European settlers first encountered them hundreds of years ago. The term "Indian candy" is considered only slightly less offensive, and "salmon candy" considered the best alternative. The term **Indian-smoked salmon** often refers to salted, hot-smoked salmon, but is also sometimes used as a synonym for **Indian-cure salmon,** or salmon that has been brined and cold-smoked for up to two weeks, yielding another form of chewy jerky.

Kippered salmon is the name given to salmon that has been scored or cut into chunks and soaked in a mildly salty brine, then hot-smoked. It is also the term for salmon that has been dry-salted, then painted with a flavoring mixture (usually brown sugar and rum) then hot smoked. See also LOX, SALMON, SMOKED FOOD.

smoke point - the measurement of how much heat an oil can sustain before breaking down, spoiling the quality of its flavor and smell, imparting an unpleasant flavor to foods. The higher the smoke point, the better it is for frying, because a high temperature allows foods to fry quickly without burning or absorbing excess fat.

COMMON SMOKE POINTS

350°F (180°C)	butter
360°F (185°C)	vegetable shortening
375°F (190°C)	olive oil, lard
400°F (200°C)	canola oil, semi-refined walnut oil
450°F (230°C)	vegetable, grapeseed, corn, peanut, safflower, soy and sunflower oils
520°F (270°C)	avocado oil

smolt - see PARR.

smoothie - also **smoothee.** A cold beverage made by mixing fruit with yogurt, ice cream, milk and sometimes ice, in a blender.

s'more - a campfire dessert made by sandwiching a marshmallow roasted over a fire and a thin square of chocolate between two graham wafers; from the idea that a person always wants "some more."

smorgasbord - from the Swedish *smorgas*, meaning "bread and butter" or "open-faced sandwich," and *bord*, meaning "table," referring to an assortment of hot or cold appetizers and/or a full buffet meal, although, in Sweden, this is only the first course of a meal.

smorrebrod - a Danish open-faced sandwich eaten with a knife and fork, literally translated as "smeared bread," a popular lunch often accompanied by a glass of **aquavit.**

snack - a small amount of food, especially one eaten between meals. The name describes the action, literally a "snatch" or morsel hastily taken.

snail

snail - **1.** a gastropod mollusk with a shell. When the ancient Romans brought grapevines to France, they also brought one of their favorite foods, the snail. Today, the large black Burgundy, or vineyard, snail is considered to be the premium food snail, and an entire ritual has developed around its consumption in the French wine country of the same name and wherever snails are available. The *petit-gris* snail, as its name indicates, is smaller and gray and is found in the southern part of France. **2.** see BUTTERHORN.

snail dish - see SNAIL PLATE.

snail fork - a small, usually two-pronged fork with long, fine and slightly curved tines, designed to dig a snail out of its shell.

snail plate - also **snail dish.** A rimmed, heatproof dish having six or more depressions, each of which is designed to hold a snail immersed in buttery sauce. Snail plates may have one or two handles, or none.

snail tongs - an implement designed to be held in one hand so its opposing, spoonlike ends secure the shell, slippery with sauce, while the diner wields the **snail fork** with the other hand to dig out the snail.

snakelocks - see SEA ANEMONE.

snap bean - see GREEN BEAN.

snapper - name of a fish from the Lutjanidae (or Lutianidae) family found mostly in warm water, such as in the Caribbean, but also found off the coast of England. Best known is the edible **red snapper.** Not all snappers are edible but they all have red skin with firm, white flesh. Snappers are carnivorous, with large mouths and sharp teeth.

snaps - see AQUAVIT.

snickerdoodle - a cookie from Colonial New England, where it's still a Christmas favorite, made with cinnamon and nutmeg.

snifter - a brandy or cognac glass, with a short stem and a large bowl that tapers upward. The bottom of the bowl is intended to be held in both hands, to warm the brandy while swirling to release its aroma. The glass's narrow opening captures the bouquet, which is best experienced by dipping the nose in the bowl and sniffing, hence the name.

snifter

snipe - a marsh-dwelling bird with a long, straight bill, related to the woodcock and native to Europe, subject to the same availability restrictions as most other game birds. Snipe is best roasted and can be cooked under the broiler or grill, because it's so small.

snoober - the Middle-Eastern name for "pine nut."

snow - a light dessert made of stiffly beaten egg whites, sugar and cream with added flavorings, such as lemon juice or apple purée.

snowball cookies - see MEXICAN WEDDING CAKES.

snow cake - first mentioned in **Fannie Merritt Farmer**'s *The Boston Cooking-School Cook Book,* published in 1896, a loaf cake made airy with stiffly beaten egg whites.

snow cone - a sweet, cool, crunchy treat of crushed or shaved ice drizzled with colored, flavored syrups (usually fruit-flavored), served in a paper cone. Machines to make snow cones and the syrups are sold for both commercial and home use.

snow pea - also **mange-tout.** Eaten whole, cooked or raw, snow peas are green, finger-length pods containing underripe peas, used extensively in Chinese cooking. The French call them *mange-tout,* meaning "eat it all."

soak - to steep in liquid before cooking or serving, to eliminate strong flavors and impurities or to help soften the ingredient. Anchovies are soaked in milk to make them less salty; dried pulses need to be soaked overnight in water to tenderize and reduce cooking time; and sweetbreads are soaked to remove impurities.

soba - a Japanese buckwheat noodle, Japan's most popular, served in its many *soba-ya* restaurants, often presented cold in *zaru* bowls (a bamboo sieve-like plate), garnished with **nori** and horseradish. See also YA.

sockeye salmon - see SALMON.

soda - **1.** a generic term for any soft drink. **2.** see BAKING SODA. **3.** see ICE CREAM SODA. **4.** see SODA WATER.

soda bread - a quick bread leavened with baking soda and an acid, usually buttermilk or **sour milk.**

soda cracker - an unsweetened, sometimes salted, cracker containing bicarbonate of soda and cream of tartar as the leavening agents.

soda water - also **club soda, seltzer water.** Effervescent due to carbon dioxide and a small amount of baking soda. It's also the base of some soft drinks. The sodium bicarbonate in soda water can help settle an upset stomach. See also CARBONATION, MINERAL WATER, SOLVAY PROCESS.

sodium - an essential mineral, known as salt or sodium chloride (or by its mineral name, halite), necessary for the proper functioning of cells and the digestive, muscular and nervous systems. It is estimated that the average North American consumes too much (about 4 to 5 grams daily) and, given the link between a diet high in salt with such conditions as hypertension, many people are trying to lower their salt intake. The current recommendation is to consume less than 2,400 milligrams of

snow peas

sodium per day, which is about 1 teaspoon (5 mL) of table salt. See also SALT.

soffrito - an Italian mixture used to flavor numerous dishes, including risotto and most soups, consisting of onion, parsley and (historically) lard or olive oil (although garlic, celery or carrot are also used, depending on the flavors of the final dish), sautéed until a light golden brown. See also SOFRITO.

sofkee - a traditional drink made from pounded dried corn by indigenous peoples, such as the Seminoles of the American Southeast. Cooked in a pot, it resembled thin gruel and was imbibed hot or cold. Special spoons with broad, flat, spade-shaped bowls were carved from tree branches and used to ladle out the sofkee. See also MUSH.

soft peaks - a term used to describe egg whites or whipped cream beaten until soft peaks form. You can tell they are soft peaks because when you lift the beaters they will rise and then slump slightly, losing their shape. See also STIFF PEAKS.

sofrito - a Latino condiment-style sauce with as many recipes and interpretations as there are cooks. The ingredients common to most are **achiote seeds,** which color the sauce red, salt pork, ham, onions, garlic, sweet green peppers, cilantro and parsley, some cooks add saffron; popular in Puerto Rico and Cuba, with roots in Spanish cuisine. See also SOFFRITO.

soft-ball stage - see TEMPERATURE.

soft cheese - see CHEESE.

soft-crack stage - see TEMPERATURE.

soft drink - a carbonated nonalcoholic beverage.

softneck garlic - see GARLIC.

soft roe - see MILT, ROE.

soft-serve ice cream - see ICE CREAM.

soft-shell clam - see CLAM.

soft-shell crab - see CRAB.

soft wheat – wheat with a low amount of protein in the kernel, so it does not develop gluten as well as **hard wheat,** making it better for delicate, tender baked goods, such as cakes. See also WHEAT.

soju - a generic name for a Korean spirit distilled from rice, grain or, most commonly, sweet potatoes. Different varieties are available. Some are sweet versions made with fruit; some medicinal soju are made with ginseng.

sole - from the Latin *solea,* meaning "sandal," because its shape suggests the sole of a shoe, a flatfish dating back to the Romans, who called it *soleo jovi,* meaning Jupiter's sandal. **Dover sole** is so called not because it's caught near Dover, England, but because that city was the port through which the best sole was shipped to London fish markets. English sole, also known as lemon sole, is not really sole but **flounder.** See also FISH.

sole Véronique - see VÉRONIQUE.

Solomon Gundy - a traditional salt-herring snack in Maritime Canada. After soaking in water for a day, the fillets are layered with onion slices in a jar, then a solution of **pickling spice,** sugar and vinegar is poured on top and the jar is sealed until the dish is served, often with sour cream and sometimes, in Nova Scotia, with oatcakes.

Solvay process - named for Belgian chemist Ernest Solvay, who invented soda water by discovering a process in 1861 to make sodium carbonate, bicarbonate of soda and sodium hydroxide through an interaction of common salt, ammonia and carbon dioxide. The same process is used today.

somen - a very thin, round, white wheat-flour noodle, popular in Japanese cuisine, often served in soups or cold with an assortment of julienned toppings and a soy-sesame sauce in the classic summer dish *hiyashi somen.* They are usually sold dried in bundles tied with a paper ribbon. A variation, called **tamago somen,** is made with egg yolk (buckwheat flour and green tea may be ingredients, as well). See also ASIAN NOODLES.

sommelier - a restaurant or hotel wine steward, with an extensive knowledge of wine; how it should be served, stored and purchased; and, in particular, the ability to select wines best suited to a specific food, most often to each course within a meal. Historically, the work done by the person known as the sommelier, usually as part of a royal court or aristocratic household, was characterized principally as a caretaker of food, drink, provisions, furnishings, baggage and belongings, as during a journey.

Sommier comes from the French *bêtes de somme*, or "beasts of burden." A monastery's sommelier was the monk responsible for crockery, linen, bread and wine. During the French Renaissance, a sommelier paid for the title and position of being part of a royal retinue and was responsible for stocking food and wine for journeys, keeping the provisions in a carriage called a *somme*. In an aristocratic household, the sommelier chose the wines, table settings and desserts. Simply stocking provisions, however, was not the sommelier's most important job; his most important responsibility was to ensure the condition of the perishables. He did this at great risk by taking a bite of each food and a sip of each wine before it was presented to his lord. If an enemy had poisoned the food or wine, the sommelier was the first to know.

Today, Italy has more sommeliers than any other country in the world: about 8,000, according to the Italian Trade Commission. In the U.S. and England, sommeliers aspire to attain the prestigious Master Sommelier Diploma awarded by the Court of Master Sommeliers, headquartered in London. The title has only been awarded in the U.S. since 1987. As of 2006, there were 74 Master Sommeliers in North America, 13 of them women. (There are a total of 120 Master Sommeliers worldwide.) Master Sommelier Angelo Tavernaro opened the first U.S. sommelier school in Las Vegas in January 2001.

sondesh - see DAS, NABIN CHANDRA.

sonofabitch stew - also **rascal stew.** A cowboy dish containing a range of ingredients, including a newly killed overweight calf and its heart, liver, tongue, sweetbreads, brain, marrow and pieces of tenderloin. It's been called many different names over the last century or so, often after someone for whom there is a collective disdain, such as Cleveland stew, named for the U.S. president who was thought to not have the interests of cattlemen at heart.

Sonoma Jack - a firmer, more flavorful version of **Monterey Jack** cheese, made in Sonoma County, California. A rich cow's milk cheese, Sonoma Jack is available young and semifirm, or aged and dry, similar to **Dry Jack.** It also comes flavored with a variety of ingredients, such as jalapeños, pesto, garlic, sweet onions or mushrooms.

Sontheimer, Carl - see profile below.

sop - **1.** (n.) a small piece of solid food used to dip into a liquid. **2.** (v.) to absorb or soak up; to use a piece of bread, for example, to mop up gravy or sauce so it can be consumed.

sopa - Spanish for "soup."

sopa de albóndigas - Spanish for "meatball soup." See ALBÓNDIGA.

sopa borracha - Spanish for "drunken soup." A Spanish dessert, similar to a trifle, consisting of a sponge cake soaked in a spirit, such as brandy, rum or wine (or a syrup made from one or more spirits), served with **chantilly** cream and fruit. The cake may be cut into layers and sandwiched with custard, or the center may be carved out and filled with cream and syrup. See also TRIFLE.

Sontheimer, Carl (1914–1988) - American engineer, epicure, entrepreneur and inventor of the Cuisinart food processor. Born in New York, Sontheimer spent his boyhood years in France. He earned his engineering degree at the Massachusetts Institute of Technology (MIT), where he invented a microwave direction finder used on a NASA mission to the moon. During the 1960s, he launched and profitably sold two companies, one an engineering firm and the other an electronic firm. In 1971, he set out on his retirement by revisiting France and his love of cooking. The same year, Pierre Verdon introduced the French market to Le Magi-Mix, a home version of his industrial Robot-Coupe, which was, and still is, widely used in professional kitchens. Sontheimer saw Verdon's product demonstrated at a cooking show, acquired a licensing agreement and spent two years refining what would become known as the Cuisinart. In 1987, he sold Cuisinart for $42 million.

sopaipilla - a puffy, hollow square of deep-fried pastry invented in New Mexico 200 years ago and considered the consummate Southwest treat. Sopaipillas are often served as a dessert, topped with honey or syrup and sprinkled with confectioner's sugar and/or cinnamon. They can also serve as a savory main course or snack when stuffed with refried beans and green chili sauce.

sopa seca - also **Mexican rice.** Spanish for "dry soup." **1.** a classic rice dish cooked in Mexico. Uncooked rice is browned in oil with chopped garlic, onions and tomato, then chicken broth, chopped green and red bell peppers, and herbs are added. **2.** a baked Spanish dish of grated or shredded cheese layered with thin pasta (such as angel hair or vermicelli, which is browned in oil beforehand) and a tomato sauce containing chopped chile pepper, coriander, garlic, onions and sautéed sliced chorizo. **3.** a baked casserole from northern Portugal made with leftovers. Chopped vegetables and chopped or shredded meat are layered in a deep dish with thick slices of bread, then stock is poured over it, chopped mint is scattered on top.

sorbet - a smooth frozen dessert made from fruit juice and sugar; unlike sherbet, sorbets never contain dairy products. The first recorded sorbet was a mixture of fruits crushed with snow and honey, given by Nero to his guests circa AD 60. But the Chinese should be credited with inventing a device to make sorbets and ice cream long before the birth of Christ. They poured a mixture of snow and saltpeter on the outside of a container filled with syrup, which is the same principle used in today's ice cream makers. They shared the technique with the Arabs, who began making syrups chilled with snow, called *sharbats*, from which the modern word is derived. The Arabs taught the Italians, and the Italians taught the French. In 1565, the artist-inventor Bernardo Buontalenti was commissioned by **Catherine de' Medici** to learn how to freeze a honey-based drink, which became the first sorbet for the court of France. See also ICE CREAM, SHERBET.

sorbetière - French name for an "ice cream maker."

sorbitol - a naturally occurring sweetener extracted from fruit, such as apples, berries and cherries, and sea algae and seaweed. Under various brand names it is available in crystal or liquid form as a low-calorie, nutritive sugar substitute. It is also used in confections and prepared foods for its smooth **mouth feel** and as an emulsifier, humectant (which helps keeps products moist) and thickener.

sorghum - any of several grasses of the genus *Sorghum*, related to millet. In parts of the Middle East, Africa and China, it's used to make flour, and in other parts of the world it's used for animal feed. It's also used to produce a sweet syrup that was once as common as maple syrup in the U.S.

sorrel - also **sour grass.** Any of several plants of the genus *Rumex*, in the buckwheat family, all of which are, to a greater or lesser degree, sour due to oxalic acid. Its stem resembles a thin version of rhubarb and has a similar tangy flavor. The Romans and the Egyptians used sorrel for its digestive properties. Historically, it has been very popular throughout Europe. French and British cuisine gave the plant an important presence in the kitchen. As early as the Middle Ages, herbalists noticed that sorrel was an effective herb for treating scurvy. Early English settlers in New England imported the plant to North America. The leaves may be added to green salads, cooked like spinach or used in the making of sauces or soups, such as **schav.** It's best to use only young leaves, because its flavor gets stronger with age and can easily become overwhelming.

Sorrel comes from the Old French *surele* and the Old High German *suer*, meaning "sour." It's also been known as "cuckoo bread," because the ancient Romans believed that the bird ate the leaves to clear its throat before singing, and "hallelujah," because the young leaves were best for cooking during Easter, when the sounds of "Hallelujah!" filled the church.

sotanghon - thin, translucent, bean noodles from the Philippines used in dishes, such as **pansit,** and soup.

sot-l'y-laisse - see PARSON'S NOSE.

souari nut - also **piquia, sawarra nut.** The stones from drupe fruits harvested from several *Caryocar* trees, which are native to South America. The grapefruit-size fruit have green skins and yellow flesh. Inside, the kidney-shaped fatty nuts or stones (slightly larger than Brazil nuts and four to a fruit) are covered in bumpy red shells. Once peeled, they

souari nut

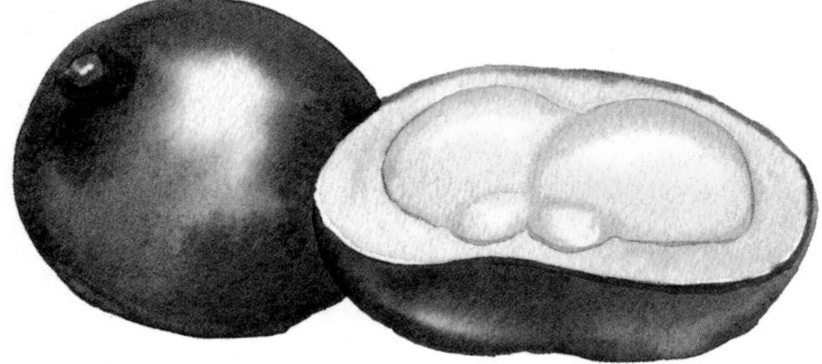

are eaten fresh or used in baked goods and liqueurs. Oil is extracted from the nuts and used in cooking. The pulp is also eaten with meat as a condiment.

Soubise - a **béchamel** sauce with the addition of puréed onions, purportedly invented by Charles de Rohan, Prince de Soubise, but more likely created by his chef, Marin, widely regarded as one of the greatest of the 18th-century chefs.

soufflé - a sweet or savory baked dish made with custard or **béchamel** sauce combined with whipped egg whites, meaning "blown," "breathed" or "whispered," suggestive of its airiness and fragility, invented by chef **Antoine Beauvillier** in 1782. In 1841, the great French chef **Antonin Carême** went into great detail about the method of making soufflés in his book *Le Pâtissier Royal*. The dish has a reputation for difficulty and proneness to accident, which it does not deserve.

soufflé potatoes - also **pommes soufflé.** The fortuitous result of a cooking mistake that became a classic of French cooking. On August 26, 1837, King Louis-Philippe and Queen Marie-Amélie were traveling the inauguration train route between Paris and Saint-Germain; on their arrival, a grand banquet of roast beef and fried potatoes was to be served. The chef began frying his potatoes according to schedule, but the train was late, so he took them out of the fryer before they were fully cooked, planning to put them back as soon as his royal guests arrived, but once drained, the potatoes shriveled. When he put the limp potatoes back into the very hot oil, a miracle happened. The sliced potatoes puffed up into golden bubbles, and when "the soufflé potatoes" were served, they were a triumph.

soul food - traditional African-American food of the South, the term coined in the 1960s, characterized by yams, black-eyed peas, collard greens, chitterlings, ham hocks and cornbread.

soup - any combination of meat, fish and vegetables cooked in a liquid, thick or thin, smooth or chunky, hot or cold. The word itself did not come into use until the Middle Ages. Some say the word "soup" comes from the sops of bread that were dipped in the broth; others claim it's the other way around. It's possible that the word was born naturally from the sound made when hot soup is drunk from the ladle or cup. Or that it came from the Old French *souper,* meaning "to sup." Supper was the meal when soup was served as the main course. The word originally meant thick soups containing bits of meat and vegetables, which the French now call *potage*. Clear soup was not perfected until much later. Soup can also be made from some types of fruit, in which case it's almost always served cold.

soup du jour - from the French for "soup of the day." In North America, it's a term that often tops a restaurant's list of daily specials.

sour - **1.** see FIVE BASIC TASTES. **2.** a type of cocktail, such as a whiskey sour, in which liquor is mixed with citrus juice, sugar and sometimes ice.

sour cream - a thick cream that has been artificially soured. Old World sour cream was nothing more than heavy, sweet cream allowed to sour in the warmth of the back of an old coal stove; it was rather thin and varied from mildly tart to quite acidic. Modern dairy technology has created a cultured product in which special bacteria are added to the cream through a series of exposure to extreme heat and pressure, achieving a thick texture and consistent taste. Sour cream can be brought to a boil without curdling. See also CRÈME FRAÎCHE.

sourdough - a bread, usually rye and some French varieties, made with a fermented starter that develops over a number of days, with or without yeast (flour and water will ferment into a leavening, and sometimes grapes are used). Alaskan and Canadian prospectors and pioneers came to be called "sourdoughs" for their reliance on it.

Starters can be kept alive a long time. Bakers take what they need for a current batch and then make another starter, to which the old one is added as the active leavening ingredient, and it continues to propagate. Some Alaskans today claim to possess sourdough starters a century old, passed down from generation to generation. Emotions run high about the precise rules for the care and feeding of a family-inherited starter. By the same token, some San Franciscans claim that the reason for the pre-eminence of San Francisco sourdough over all other sourdoughs is the peculiar bacterial microclimate of the Bay Area, which cannot be duplicated elsewhere.

sour grass - see SORREL.

sour mash - one of two methods of fermentation used to make American-type whiskeys, the other being sweet mash. Sour mash whiskey must spend less than 72 hours in the fermentation process. It's prepared by using approximately one-third of a working yeast from a previous fermentation.

sour milk - "turned" (or spoiled) milk or milk that has been intentionally soured in a controlled manner, usually with the addition of an acid, such as lemon juice, often in recipes calling for buttermilk when none is on hand, also known as fermented milk.

sour mix - see SWEET-AND-SOUR MIX.

soursop - also **guanabana**. A tropical fruit, *Annona muricata*, that is native to the West Indies and northern areas of South America, from the custard-apple family, now cultivated elsewhere as well. Related to the **cherimoya** and ilama, soursop is very juicy and used to make tropical drinks. In the French West Indies, the unripe fruit is sometimes cooked as a vegetable.

sous chef - chef that is second-in-command in a professional kitchen reporting to the executive chef and running the kitchen when the chef is absent. The sous chef oversees the preparation and presentation of the food. One of the positions in the kitchen brigade system created by French chef **Auguste Escoffier** in the late-19th century to bring order to the professional kitchen. The name comes from the French *sous*, meaning "under." See also BRIGADE SYSTEM, CHEF, ENTREMETIER, GARDE MANGER, PASTRY CHEF, POISSONIER, RÔTISSEUR, SAUCIER, TOURNANT.

souse - **1.** pieces of pork in a vinegar-spiked gelatin base to which dill pickles, sweet peppers and bay leaves are sometimes added. **2.** to preserve. See PICKLE. **3.** a drunkard.

sous vide - also **Cryovac.** French for "under vacuum." The process of putting a food inside a plastic bag, then vacuum-packing it (that is, sucking all the air out of the bag) to change the texture or flavor of the food, or to preserve it for later cooking. The food may be cooked inside the bag in boiling or simmering water, or decanted for eating as is. The pressure exerted on the food during vacuum packing actually changes the structure and composition of the proteins, fats and starches that it contains. A watery fruit, such as watermelon, is rendered drier, with a dense, crisp texture similar to that of an apple. Meat or fish cooked inside the sealed bag in a pot of boiling water retains all its juices and flavors, resulting in a flavorful and aromatic dish that has lost none of its nutrition during cooking. The hermetically sealed bags also increase the storage time for the food, preventing any contamination by bacteria or other impurities that could render it dangerous. The technique was developed in France in the 1970s as a means of providing single servings of precooked food to upscale French restaurants. The alternate name Cryovac is a trademarked name for the bags, plastic films and machines made by Sealed Air Corp., used to vacuum-pack foods for restaurant, home and commercial applications. The name comes from *cryo-*, meaning "frozen," and "vac," short for vacuum.

South African hake - see CAPE CAPENSIS.

Southern Comfort - an amber-colored, 100-proof brand-name American liqueur made with bourbon and peaches.

southern flour - see FLOUR.

southernpea - see BLACK-EYE PEA.

souvlaki - also **souvlakia.** A Greek kebab made of chunks of meat (especially lamb, but also pork or chicken) marinated in lemon juice, oil, oregano and other seasonings, grilled and served with **tzatziki** on a plate with potatoes and salad or in a bun with chopped onions and tomatoes.

sowans - a traditional Scottish porridge made from oat husks and finely ground meal steeped in water, then strained. In some parts of Scotland, it was eaten on Christmas Eve.

soybean - also **soya bean.** A legume, *Glycine max,* native to East Asia. Soybeans have been cultivated in China for more than 3,000 years, since the Chou dynasty; it is one of the oldest plants cultivated by humans. The Chinese considered soybeans one of the five grains of life, along with rice, barley, wheat and millet. The cultivation of soybeans was introduced to Europe at the beginning of the 18th century by a German botanist and in the Americas in the the late 18th-century, but mass production of soybeans only started in the U.S. in the 1930s. Today, the U.S. produces 50 percent of the world production. The discovery of margarine was due in part to research that started with the production of soybean oil. If the beans are harvested young, before they become oily and starchy, they can be eaten with or without the outer skin.

soybeans

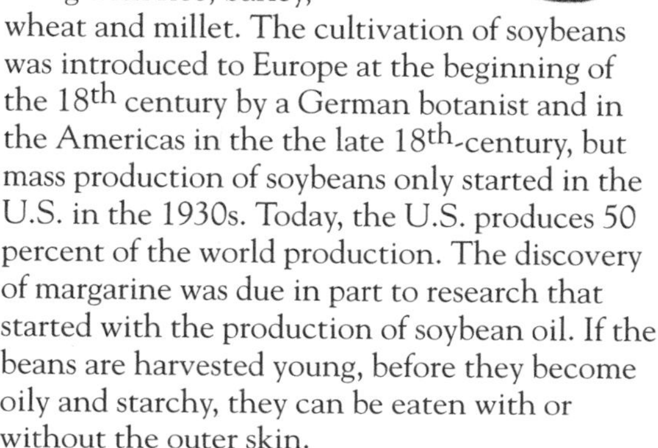

Soy flour has no gluten and consequently cannot rise, although it has two to three times more protein than wheat flour. The flour is usually used in baking or to thicken sauces, but its strong flavor requires that only small quantities be used in any given recipe. If roasted, the beans can be a coffee substitute, with a faint similarity in flavor. Soy milk, which is extracted from the beans, looks like and can be used instead of cow's milk.

Setsubun is the Japanese bean-throwing festival held every February 3rd to herald the coming of spring: each family member scatters roasted soybeans inside and outside the house while chanting to cleanse away the evil spirit of winter and invite spring in. Then, to ensure good fortune for the coming year, each person eats the same number of beans as his or her age.

soybean curd - see TOFU.

Soyer, Alexis Benoît - see profile below.

soy flour - see FLOUR.

soy mayonnaise - a version of this favorite sauce in which soy replaces the eggs normally used in the classic recipe, making this mayonnaise palatable for **vegans.**

soy milk - a protein-rich beverage made from soybeans, resembling milk but containing no lactose, saturated fat or inherent calcium, although many brands now offer fortified versions.

soy nuts - homemade or ready-made snack made with soy beans that are soaked, drained, then roasted until crunchy and golden brown. Often sold plain in health food stores, soy nuts are also available salted, spiced or covered in chocolate or a coating of praline.

soy oil - also **soya oil, soybean oil.** Extracted from crushed soybeans, which are 20 percent oil, popular, inexpensive and rich in protein, with a high smoke point.

soy paste - also **miso, natto, tempeh.** Soy pastes are made from soy, either fermented or unfermented. Japanese miso is a fermented type, made by cooking the beans, mixing them with *koji* (steamed rice treated with the fungus

Soyer, Alexis Benoît (1809–1858) - French chef, social advocate and military food reformer. Born the youngest son of a grocer in Meaux-en-Brie, Soyer began his apprenticeship in 1821 and went to London in 1830, where he spent the next seven years cooking for aristocracy. He became chef of the Reform Club, where he prepared a famous breakfast for 2,000 guests to celebrate Queen Victoria's coronation in 1838. By mid-century, as a result of many impassioned letters written to the papers about the Irish famine, the British government sent him to Dublin to open relief kitchens. Three years before his death, Soyer went to the Crimea to advise the army's kitchen, where he reformed the military field and hospital diet and worked with Florence Nightingale. He wrote several books; recently, culinary historians have discovered that one of them, *The Pantropheon: Or A History of Food and Its Preparation in Ancient Times* (1853), was actually written by someone else, save one chapter.

Aspergillus oryzae), salt and water and then inoculating with yeast. The miso is then left to ferment for several months. Natto is a similar preparation, in which the cooked beans are inoculated with *Bacillus natto*, producing a dark, sticky substance. In Indonesia, **tempeh** is a fermented bean cake made by inoculating the beans with a previous batch of tempeh; the mold used is *Rhizopus oligosporus*. Unfermented bean pastes are prepared as tofu or Chinese bean curd and as the sweet red bean paste used in confectionery.

soy sauce - also **shoya, soya sauce.** A condiment developed by the Chinese in the early 13th century, during the Sung dynasty, to add flavor to rice, oil, vinegar and tea, it quickly became a dietary staple of the poor. Soy sauce, called *shoyu* in Japan, is a thin almost black sauce used extensively in the East, largely in place of salt. It is made by fermenting soybeans with roasted wheat or barley and salt, then filtering, pasteurizing and bottling the liquid. The sauce's consistency can range from very thin to very thick. The Japanese make a **light soy sauce,** which has a thinner consistency and a saltier flavor than darker varieties. Japanese soy is preferred when a darker sauce will ruin the appearance of a dish, or when a lighter flavor is desired, especially when serving seafood. **Dark soy sauce** is popular throughout Asia. It is slightly richer than light soy sauce and tends to have a chocolate brown color, and a pungent, rather than overly salty flavor. **Mushroom soy sauce** is a dark soy sauce from China, made with straw mushrooms with a deep rich flavor. **Tamari** is a Japanese soy sauce that has a rich texture and intense flavor. See also TAMARI.

Spaetzle - also **Spätzle.** German for "little sparrow," spaetzle is a German, Austrian and Swiss side dish of tiny, irregular dumplings, made from a batter of flour and water (and sometimes eggs) forced through a special colander-style tool directly into boiling water.

spaghetti - see PASTA.

spaghetti alla Caruso - created for the great Italian operatic tenor **Enrico Caruso** in a small ninth-floor kitchen of the Knickerbocker Hotel by chef Louis P. De Gouy, with tomatoes, mushrooms and chicken livers.

spaghetti and meatballs - meatballs served together with pasta and tomato sauce. In Italy, meatballs and spaghetti would not have shared the same plate. Traditionally, they would have been served as separate courses, during a leisurely, multi-course meal. Served together to speed up the meal and to provide a meat-and-potatoes pairing of protein and starch, spaghetti and meatballs only became a couple on North American restaurant menus in the 20th century. For most contemporary North Americans, the combination has become the quintessential Italian main dish.

spaghettini - see PASTA.

spaghetti squash - see SQUASH.

spalen - see SBRINZ.

Spam - canned meat concocted by the U.S. Hormel Foods Corp. in 1937, made of finely ground pork, seasoned and cooked right in the can. The company offered a $100 prize for the best name, and it was won by Kenneth Daigneau (the actor brother of Hormel VP Ralph Daigneau) for his amalgamation of the words "spiced ham."

spanakopita - a Greek dish of phyllo pastry filled with sautéed spinach, onions, feta cheese, egg and seasonings.

Spanish garlic - see ROCAMBOLE.

spanish lime - see HONEYBERRY.

Spanish olive - see OLIVE.

Spanish onion - see ONION.

Spanish thyme - see LEMON VERBENA.

spareribs - a long, narrow cut of pork, from the lower ribs and breastbone, not in any way "extra," as the name suggests, but an English alteration of the Low German *ribbesper*, meaning "pork ribs roasted on a spit or spear." The same idea is still reflected in the modern German word for spareribs, *Rippenspeer*, which literally means "spear ribs." The English so embraced the Old German that they distorted the word to *ribspare* and use it to refer to spareribs to this day. See also PORK.

sparkling wine - any wine that is effervescent, such as Champagne. See also STILL WINE.

Spartan apple - see APPLE.

spatchcock - to cut a young chicken or small game bird down each side of the backbone or between the wings and thighs, then open it out flat to **butterfly** it. Stuffing may be added between skin and breast, then a pair of long metal skewers is often inserted, crisscross, to hold the spatchcocked bird flat while it is grilled, breast side up. Opening up the bird speeds the cooking, which keeps the meat moist.

Spätlese - a German wine label term for ripe grapes picked later in the harvest, used to make medium-weight wines. German grapes used for winemaking are classified and labeled according to their ripeness, not necessarily their sweetness, and by the weight, or body, of the wines they produce, from thin and light-bodied to syrupy and full-bodied. Spätlese wines can vary from **dry** to sweet. See also AUSLESE, BEERENAUSLESE, KABINETT, TROCKENBEERENAUSLESE.

spatula - a kitchen implement with a variety of shapes. The flat, narrow, usually flexible blade is used to spread icing. The wider, square blade, set on an angle, is used to turn foods such as hamburgers and pancakes. Spatulas are made of metal, wood or rubber, from Latin *spatha,* meaning "broad sword."

spatulas

speakeasy - also **blind pig.** An establishment that sold alcohol illegally during Prohibition in the U.S. Speakeasies were the breeding grounds of jazz, flappers and excessive drinking that marked the turbulent Roaring Twenties in dry America. These establishments required patrons to say a code word quietly through a slit in the door before it was opened, hence the name "speakeasy," in this case "easy" meaning "quietly."

spearfish - see MARLIN.

spearmint - see MINT.

speck - Italian cured bacon, aromatic, usually salted, smoked and served thinly sliced, like **prosciutto.**

speckled trout - see BROOK TROUT.

speculaas - also **spéculos, windmill cookies.** Thin, flat Dutch spice cookies baked during the Christmas season. In the past, carved wooden molds were used to impress raised designs, such as St. Nicholas, a man and woman (each has a separate cookie, but together they are called "the lovers" and are eaten to ensure fertility) and, of course, windmills. A type of ginger cookie, speculaas typically contain myriad spices, such as allspice, anise, cardamom, cinnamon, cloves, coriander, mace and nutmeg, and many recipes top that off with a pinch of black pepper. The patron saint of sailors, St. Nicholas was called "the one who sees," hence the cookie's name.

spelt - one of the oldest known grains, harvested in Europe for more than 9,000 years and in Asia long before that. It lost favor in Europe during the mid-19th century but has recently come back into fashion for its nutritive and culinary merits. Related to wheat, a grain of spelt looks much like a grain of hard winter wheat. It's extraordinarily enduring and flourishes in ruthless climates, often without the need of pesticides, fertilizers or even much warmth. Spelt is among the most nutritious grains, higher in protein, carbohydrates, iron, thiamin, riboflavin, niacin and other vitamins and minerals than whole wheat. Because it contains gluten, spelt flour can be substituted for wheat flour.

Spencer, Dr. Percy - see MICROWAVE OVEN.

spice grinder - see GRIND.

spice Parisienne - also **French spice, mélange classique.** A homemade or ready-made fragrant French blend of herbs and spices. A variable mix, it often includes dried, crumbled or powdered bay leaf, marjoram, rosemary, sage and thyme, along with ground allspice, cinnamon, cloves, mace, nutmeg and white pepper. Considered a "warm" mixture, it is used for savory dishes, including the traditional *boudin noir aux pommes* (blood sausage and apple).

spices - aromatic seasonings obtained from parts of plants other than the leaves (in which case, they're usually called herbs), dried, whole or ground. As the Romans conquered Europe, they brought back fruit trees, wine and cultivated cabbage, as well as a heavy spice habit, which may have been exacerbated by the culture's tendency toward the excessive consumption of food. One historian claims that a renewed interest and indulgence in spices followed from the 9th-century visit to Charlemagne of Haroun al-Rashid, the Caliph of Islam immortalized in *The Book of One Thousand and One Nights*. In any case, sauces of the time match or even outdo those of the Roman gourmet **Apicius** in piquancy. Up to the late 14th century, a comparison of recipes for green sauce would suggest that the English had more native herbs and spices to choose from, or at least appreciated them more than the French. See also ADVIEH, ALLSPICE, ANARDANA, ANISE, ASAFETIDA, BERBERE, CARAWAY, CARDAMOM, CAYENNE PEPPER, CELERY SEED, CHILI POWDER, CINNAMON, CLOVE, CORIANDER, CUMIN, CURRY POWDER, FENNEL, FENUGREEK, FIVE SPICES, GARAM MASALA, GINGER, GRAINS OF PARADISE, MACE, MIXED SPICE, MUSTARD SEED, NUTMEG, PAPRIKA, PEPPERCORN, QUATRE ÉPICES, RAS EL HANOUT, SAFFRON, SAMBAR, SPICE PARISIENNE, STAR ANISE, SZECHWAN PEPPER, TIRPHAL, TURMERIC, ZA'ATAR, ZEODARY.

Spickgans - smoked goose breast from Germany that has first been cured with salt, saltpeter, sugar and pepper.

spider - a long-handled cast-iron frying pan, so named because it originally had legs attached for standing it over coals in the fireplace; or a long-handled strainer whose grid has the appearance of a spider's web.

spinach - a leafy green vegetable, *Spinacia oleracea*, originally found growing wild near the Iranian desert lands of Dasht-e-Kavir, transplanted to Persian gardens, where it was cultivated mainly to satisfy the appetite of cats. In Persia, spinach was, and is still, known as *isfanakh*, meaning "a green hand." In AD 827, the Saracens introduced spinach to Sicily, the Moors introduced it to Spain, and the Arabs in the Middle East took it to Greece. It first appeared in England and France in the 14th century, probably via Spain, and it gained quick popularity because it appeared in early spring, when other vegetables were scarce and when Lenten dietary restrictions discouraged consumption of other foods. It's mentioned in the first known English cookbook, *The Forme of Cury* (1390) where it's referred to as *spinnedge* and/or *spynoches*, which echo the Spanish word for spinach, *espinaca*. But it's said that the original Arabic name was *esbanash*.

spinach

As vegetables go, spinach is a newcomer to most of the world. In fact, as late as the 16th century, the English were still calling spinach "the Spanish vegetable." The ancient Medes prescribed 12 washings for every leaf of spinach that went into a pot — 11 in water, meant to free the leaves of its dark, earthly associations, and the 12th in human tears (to season it with God's wisdom). The famous comic strip character Popeye the Sailor Man made his debut in 1929, courtesy of E.C. (Elzie Crisler) Segar. The somewhat cowardly sailor soon proved to be a fighter whose prodigious strength was derived mainly from spinach, which he swallowed by the canful. American spinach consumption increased by 33 percent in the next few years, as a favorite food for children, and Popeye ("I'm strong to the 'finich' 'cause I eats me spinach") was credited with most of the increase.

spiny dogfish - see DOGFISH.

spiny lobster - see LOBSTER.

spirit - a general term for a distilled alcoholic beverage. See also ALCOHOL, LIQUOR, NEUTRAL SPIRIT.

spit - a metal rod on which meat is skewered, then turned as it cooks over a grill or open fire, or in an oven, so that it cooks evenly and bastes itself as it roasts.

splake - a tasty, hybrid fish, produced from **brook trout** sperm and **lake trout** eggs, introduced into the Great Lakes and other smaller North American waters, and a favorite of ice fishermen. The name is a combination of "speckled trout" (a common name for brook trout) and "lake trout." Unlike many hybrid species, splake are not sterile so a self-sustaining population now exists in many lakes. One of the largest recorded catches weighed in at almost

21 pounds (9.5 kg), hooked in Lake Huron's Georgian Bay in the 1980s. See also TROUT.

spleen - also **milt.** The dark red organ that helps fight infection and keep blood healthy in vertebrates. A **variety meat** used in **forcemeat, paté** and sausages as well as in old-country favorites, such as *gefilte miltz* (Jewish stuffed spleen), *guastelle* (Sicilian spleen sandwiches) and *Milzsuppe* (German spleen soup).

Splenda - the brand name under which sucralose is used as a non-nutritive sweetener in beverages and food, and marketed for consumer use. Sold in granular form, it is available in small, premeasured packets designed for hot beverages, large bags, and in brown- and white-sugar blends for home baking. See also ARTIFICIAL SWEETENERS, SUCRALOSE.

split - see WINE BOTTLES.

split pea - see PEA.

sponge - **1.** a leavener for bread made from flour and water and allowed to ferment for several hours or days to encourage the growth of wild yeast present in the flour. Many bakers add some commercial yeast to the mixture at the beginning to start the fermentation process quickly. As the sponge ferments, it takes on the characteristic sour flavor that is so prized in sourdough breads and **pain au levain.** The yeast in the starter can be kept alive in two ways: any leftover sponge can be kept and regularly "fed" with more flour and water and used when it's convenient, or a piece of the leavened bread dough can be added to the next batch of dough and allowed to grow in that environment.
2. an old-fashioned dessert made with gelatin and fruit juices or purées. The gelatin mixture is cooled until almost set, then beaten until frothy and combined with stiffly beaten egg whites. Whipped cream is often added to the mixture to give it a richer dimension. The dessert is light, airy and quite malleable, as the gelatin can be flavored with any kind of fruit.

sponge cake - a light, airy cake leavened with stiffly beaten egg whites and made without shortening.

sponge gourd - **1.** see ASIAN OKRA.
2. see LOOFAH.

sponge pudding - a soft cake or cake-and-sauce combination made from sponge cake batter, baked or steamed in a pudding basin. Lemon sponge puddings are quite popular and yield a soft cake top and a thick lemon sauce on the bottom. **Castle puddings** are another classic example of a sponge pudding.

spoom - a foamy dessert of sorbet lightened with a mixture of egg whites and simple syrup that has been whisked to a froth. Spirits, such as sweet white wine or sherry, may also be added.

spoon - thought to be the oldest of the three vital Western eating implements, the two others of course being the **fork** and **knife**. The first spoon was probably a shell attached to a stick, which made scooping water from a stream more efficient than a cupped hand. Spoons made of wood came with the discovery of fire and cooked food. (The word "spoon" comes from *spon*, an old Anglo-Saxon word, meaning "chip of wood.")They were at first used for stirring soup or gruel, which was then drunk from a bowl; only later did humans begin using the spoon directly for eating. See also ICE CREAM SCOOP, LADLE, MARROW SPOON, MEASURING SPOON, MELON BALLER, SPORK, TASTING SPOON.

spoon bread - a pudding-like cornbread served as a side dish, so named because its soft consistency allows it to be eaten with a spoon.

spork - **1.** an eating utensil with a spoon-shaped bowl at the business end, tipped with (usually) four short, sharp points. Cheap plastic models of this fork-spoon hybrid were ubiquitous in fast-food restaurants of the late-1900s, and pricey stainless-steel and titanium versions are now sold to backpackers. Specialty sporks, designed for use with the left or right hand, are used by people with limited mobility.
2. a brand-name canned, spiced pork **lunch meat** —the Canadian cousin of **Spam** —

spork

produced by Burns in the mid-1900s. In the 1941 issue of its special catalog, called the *Eaton's Camp and Cottage Book*, the famous Canadian department store promoted Spork as "a summer camp necessity."

spotted dick - also **plum duff, spotted dog. 1.** an English **suet pudding** or **roly-poly** wrapped in a cloth, then boiled or steamed. The spots come from the raisins in the dough. The slighty off-color moniker comes from the word "dick," first meaning a firm cheese in the early 1900s, then becoming an interchangeable term for "pudding." But even stout-hearted Britons can balk at a name which smacks of a social disease. Apparently gripped by new-millennium madness, a hospital in Gloucestershire temporarily replaced the "spotted dick" on its menu with "spotted Richard" to save sensitive diners any embarassment. In 2002, the BBC was able to report that spotted dick had made a full recovery three years later and was now back on the menu. **2.** an Irish soda bread with currants or raisins added to the dough.

spotted dog - see SPOTTED DICK.

spotted dogfish - see NURSEHOUND.

sprat - also **brisling.** A small fish, closely allied to the common herring and the pilchard, often canned in oil. See also SARDINE.

Springerle - a German anise holiday cookie, stamped using a wooden roller or mold that presses or imprints a design or scenic image into the dough. The name comes from an old German dialect, meaning "little knight."

springform pan - a round, metal baking pan with a tall removable side, used to bake cheesecakes and other sticky or crumbly confections that are hard to remove from a regular cake pan. The removable side has a spring-like clip in the middle that tightens it against the lip of the pan bottom for baking, and expands to allow the side to be cleanly lifted away when the cake is done.

spring lamb - see LAMB.

spring roll - similar to an **egg roll** but smaller and more delicate. The meat or vegetable filling is wrapped in rice paper in Vietnamese and Thai versions and a dough wrapping in Chinese ones, and deep-fried or sometimes steamed.

spring soup - also **potage printanier, zuppa primaverile.** A soup, traditionally made with the first fresh, seasonal produce, such as asparagus, leeks and nettles, and sometimes chicken or **veal;** there is a version in almost every culture.

sprinkles - also **jimmies.** Tiny, cylindrical candies often chocolate with a colorful coating sprinkled on cakes, doughnuts and ice cream.

spritz - **1.** (n.) a small splash of liquid added to a drink, such as "a spritz of lime juice." **2.** (n.) a short, rich cookie dough usually made with a large amount of butter and pressed through a cookie press into festive shapes, a specialty of Scandinavia. **3.** (v.) to splash or spray with a liquid, as bread dough is spritzed with water during baking to create a thick, crackly crust.

Spritzer - a cocktail of one part white wine to two parts soda water, from the German *spritzen*, meaning "to spray."

sprouts - young shoots sprouting from seeds, which develops in as few as five days. Its culinary cultivation is an ancient Asian art. In recent years raw sprouts have emerged as a recognized source of food-borne illness involving the pathogenic bacteria salmonella and E. coli 0157. Alfalfa and clover sprouts are cited as the most risky for contacting a food-borne illness, but all raw sprouts may pose a risk. Cooking sprouts significantly reduces the chance of illness. See also ALFALFA, BEAN SPROUTS, CHIA SEEDS, KAIWARE, MUNG BEAN.

sprouting broccoli - see BROCCOLI.

spruce beer - an alcoholic or nonalcoholic beverage made from the tips of spruce branches and their tender buds and needles. Popular in Georgian England, spruce beer was shipped across the ocean by British and European sailors, who were encouraged to concoct and drink their own, once they made landfall, to ward off scurvy. The brew, which usually contains gingerroot, hops, molasses and yeast, can be enjoyed fresh or allowed to ferment. The Fortress of Louisbourg in Nova Scotia has a recipe dating from the 1700s. North American homebrewers continued to ferment spruce beer (in the East, maple syrup was often added) into the 1940s, and at least a few **microbreweries** in Alaska are still bottling it. The taste and aroma of spruce beer has been likened to that of paint thinner, but is said to mellow with time.

spuma - Italian for "foam" or "froth" and the name given to a savory or sweet **mousse** served as an appetizer or dessert, respectively.

spumante - see PROSECCO.

spumone - also **spumoni.** From the Italian *spuma*, meaning "foam" or "froth," spumone is Italian ice cream molded in strips in a variety of colors and textures, and sometimes including nuts and candied fruits.

spun sugar - **1.** the fine, glassy golden threads of hardened, boiled sugar seen on classic desserts, such as **croquembouche.** A mixture of cream of tartar, sugar and water is heated to the caramel or hard-crack stage, then a fork or whisk is dipped into it. Pulled out, the fork pulls strands of sticky sugar from each tine. These can be immediately set onto a dessert or dish as a garnish or, before they cool, laid flat on waxed paper in strips, in a grid or in shapes, such as stars. They may also be crisscrossed into or over a mold to form a three-dimensional basket or dome, or wound around a wooden spoon handle to make a nest. Brittle when fresh, spun sugar softens quickly in humid air, so it's used quite soon after it's made. **2.** a colorful confection of superfine strands of spun sugar served up at concession stands at fairs and fall festivals. See also COTTON CANDY.

spur dog - see DOGFISH.

Spy apple - see APPLE.

squab - a young pigeon specially bred for the table, 4 to 5 weeks old and weighing between 12 and 14 ounces (340 and 400 g). Popular breeds include the Homer, Mondain and King.

squab chicken - see POUSSIN.

square - a **bar cookie** cut into a square, instead of rectangle.

squash - of the genus *Cucurbita pepo*, a fruit of the gourd family, found to have been growing in Mexico and Central America 7,000 years ago, from the Native American *askootasquash*, meaning "eating green." Unlike the tomato, which has undergone a great physical transformation since its Aztec or Incan ancestor, the squash looks as it did to Columbus. A Native American staple, squash was one of the "three sisters" of vegetables grown together in a manner directed by the spirits: corn for its stalk; beans that climbed the corn; and squash to creep along the surrounding ground to keep weeds away. Squash was introduced to Europe upon the explorers' return, embraced most enthusiastically by the Italians. By the time the Pilgrims arrived on the continent, squash had spread throughout North America.

Squashes are categorized as either winter or summer, based on their longevity. **Winter squashes** take longer to ripen (as long as three months), are harvested in cool weather and can be stored for months at a time. They include acorn, butternut and hubbard varieties. **Summer squashes,** which include crookneck, pattypan and zucchini, are a warm-weather crop, bred to be harvested before their skins harden, and are grown on bush-like plants that don't creep, as winter squashes do. Summer squashes are often grouped by shape, such as scalloped, "necked" or cylindrical. (See Squash Varieties on page 612.) See also PUMPKIN.

squash blossom - the edible, nutritious flower of the pumpkin, squash and zucchini. The large yellow to orange blossoms should be picked soon after they open, early in the day they are to be used. A popular ingredient in Mexico, where they are called *flor de calabaza* ("flower of pumpkin"), squash blossoms are used there in crêpes, fruit salads, soups and quesadillas. They can also be battered and deep-fried on their own or, as the Italians do, stuffed with a soft cheese first, then fried. And, of course, they make the perfect, pretty summer garnish. See also EDIBLE FLOWERS.

squash blossoms

SQUASH VARIETIES

SUMMER SQUASHES

crookneck - usually yellow, with a long, thin, curved or straight neck.

pattypan - small, round, flattened and scalloped, green, yellow or white, with tender flesh resembling **zucchini.**

pattypan

zucchini - cylindrical, green, yellow or white, including such Italian varieties as **caserta** and **cocozelle.**

WINTER SQUASHES

acorn - also **pepper.** Dark green or yellow, sometimes striped, with fibrous flesh.

banana - long, narrow and yellow, with finely textured bright orange flesh.

bohemian - see DELICATA.

buttercup - a squat gourd with creamy orange flesh; the ambercup variety is bright orange, and the autumn cup is dark green with white stripes.

butternut - beige, with bright orange flesh, a narrow cylinder with a bulbous end containing the seeds.

carnival - gold-fleshed, beige with orange spots and pale green striped with dark green spots, often with both these markings but split horizontally, one on the top and the other on the bottom.

delicata - also **bohemian, sweet potato.** Beige or yellow, long and narrow, with green stripes.

gold nugget - also **oriental.** Round, with orange rind and flesh.

hoka - see KOBACHA.

hubbard - grown in many varieties, including green and gray, with the hardest skin of all winter squashes, allowing it to keep a long time.

Japanese pumpkin - see KOBACHA.

kobacha - also **hoka, Japanese pumpkin, kabocha.** Japanese for "squash," from the **buttercup** variety, whose flesh is dry and flaky when cooked.

oriental - see GOLD NUGGET.

pepper - see ACORN.

spaghetti - bright yellow, long and narrow, so named because its cooked flesh becomes long fibers that resemble spaghetti.

sweet dumpling - tiny, squat and round, beige with dark green stripes.

sweet potato - see DELICATA.

turban - often used ornamentally because of its distinctive, whimsical appearance, orange with green, beige and white striping, its shape split horizontally with a globular swelling whose coloration is usually different from the rest of the vegetable.

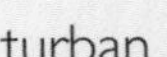
turban

squaw candy - see SMOKED SALMON.

squid - any of various mollusks with a long, slender body, elongated head, 10 sucker-bearing tentacles and firm, mild-tasting flesh. See also CALAMARI.

Sriracha - a bottled hot sauce, made from chile peppers, vinegar, salt and sugar. This popular table condiment, named after Sriracha, the city in Thailand where it originated, is used like ketchup in Southeast Asia and in western restaurants serving regional food.

Stadtländer, Michael (1957–) - Canadian chef and innovative restaurateur and the only Canadian chef to have a restaurant rated in the top 10 in the world. Born in Germany and raised on a farm, Stadtländer underwent a traditional European apprenticeship that began at 15. He served in the German Navy and took a chef's position in Stuttgart. It was at the Grand Hotel National in Lucerne, Switzerland, in 1980, where Stadtländer met Canadian chef Jamie Kennedy, who convinced him to come to Toronto to open the restaurant Scaramouche. Städtlander opened two restaurants of his own, Stadtländer in 1984 and Nekah in 1987. His career took another sharp turn in 1992, when he and his wife, Nobuyo, bought a 100-acre farm in Singhampton, Ontario, north of Toronto and opened Eigensinn Farm. They serve dinners to only 12 guests at a time, using primarily organic ingredients, often produce or meat grown and raised by the owners themselves. In 2003, London's *Restaurant* magazine named Eigensinn Farm the ninth top restaurant in the world.

stabilizer - a food additive, such as **guar gum, gum arabic, gum tragacanth** or **xanthan gum,** used to improve a food's texture or consistency, or to keep emulsions from separating.

Stadtländer, Michael - see profile above.

stainless steel cookware - made from a steel alloy containing chromium, used to make pots, pans, bowls and utensils, resistant to corrosion and rust. Stainless steel cookware does not react with the chemicals, particularly acids, in some foods, such as tomatoes and vinegar, which can discolor the food and taint the taste. See also CAST-IRON COOKWARE, EARTHENWARE, ENAMELWARE, NONREACTIVE COOKWARE, NONSTICK FINISH.

stalk - the main stem of a plant, such as asparagus, or one of several stems, such as celery or rhubarb.

standing rib roast - see BEEF.

standing rump roast - see BEEF.

stand mixer - see MIXER.

staple - a basic, primary foodstuff, such as corn, rice or wheat, around which the diet of a culture or region revolves; or an everyday foodstuff, such as bread, cheese or milk, that most cooks always keep on hand.

star anise - the seed of a small Chinese evergreen, *Illicium verum*, from the magnolia family, having the same essential oils as anise. The tree can live for more than 100 years, and it takes at least six years to bear fruit. It is one of the dominant spices in **Chinese five-spice powder**.

starfruit - also **carambola.** A waxy yellow-orange fruit, *Averrhoa carambola*, starfruit is tart and juicy and can be eaten raw or sautéed. It gets its name for its star shape when sliced crosswise. Believed to have originated in Sri Lanka, it has been well known in Southeast Asia for centuries.

Starking apple - see APPLE.

starter - **1.** used in making sourdough breads, made with water, flour and sometimes yeast and/or milk, left at room temperature for 24 to 48 hours, during which time it develops two groups of micro-organisms produced by its natural fermentation: bacteria, including lactobacilli, and natural yeasts, including saccharomyces. The bacteria generate the characteristic sour flavor, while the yeasts generate carbon dioxide to make the bread rise.

A starter will alter, depending on its milieu: a San Francisco starter used in New Zealand may not get the same results, because it's a live culture that reacts to its environment. If a starter is kept in the refrigerator, it must be brought to room temperature at least once a week; a third is removed to either bake in bread or is disposed of; and then its original ingredients are added in again. This keeps the starter healthy, alive and reproducing. At one time, starters were handed down from mother to daughter. Famous bakeries maintain their

distinctively flavored bread by keeping alive a starter that can be as many as 100 years old. See also SOURDOUGH. **2.** see APPETIZER.

Stayman Winesap apple - see APPLE.

steak - a slice of meat (usually beef) or fish cut to be cooked as an individual portion, often by broiling, barbecuing, etc., from the Old Norse *steik*, related to *steikja*, meaning "roast on a spit."

steak and kidney pie - a quintessential savory pie of the British Isles containing chunks of beef and beef kidney, and chopped onions and mushrooms, in a dark, thick sauce flavored with a bay leaf, brown ale, a pinch of mustard powder, thyme and a dash of Worcestershire sauce. Early versions used oysters in place of the mushrooms. In pubs or at home, it's often served with peas and mashed potatoes.

steak au poivre - also **pepper steak.** Beefsteak coated with pressed-on coarsely ground pepper or whole green peppercorns, then quickly broiled or fried, and served with butter or pan **jus.** The classic French version calls for rump steak. Once it's cooked, it's kept warm while brandy, white wine and veal stock are combined with the pan drippings, then reduced to a syrupy sauce to serve with the steak. Some chefs add cream to the sauce; others flambé the sauce, using cognac or whiskey.

steak-frites - the quintessential French bistro dish of grilled beefsteak served with **french fries** (known simply as *frites* in French).

steak tartare - also **beef tartare, tartare steak.** Hand-chopped beef, blended with egg yolk and various condiments, served raw. It was named for the Tartar horsemen, who ate tough meat made more palatable by shredding. In France, horsemeat was traditionally used for steak tartare, where it's known as *bifteck à l'Américaine*.

steam - to cook food (especially vegetables) by moist heat. Food is placed in the top half of a steamer or a perforated pan over boiling water.

steamed bread - bread, such as **Boston brown bread,** that is steamed, rather than baked. Most steamed breads are cooked in two-part cylindrical molds; some molds are ridged down their length to demarcate individual slices. Coffee or soup cans often stand in for these molds in home kitchens.

steamed buns - buns, such as the Chinese *mantou*, cooked in bamboo steamers; they are steamed, rather than baked.

steamer clam - a long-necked soft-shell clam found on the East Coast, a traditional New England delicacy eaten steamed with melted butter. See also CLAMS.

steam-pressure canner - see CANNER.

steel - **1.** (n.) see SHARPENING STEEL. **2.** (v.) to straighten the edge of a knife using a sharpening steel.

steel-cut oats - also **Irish oats, Scotch oats.** Crushed or sliced whole husked oat kernels. Coarse-textured and not rolled into flakes, steel-cut oats are chewy even when cooked. See also OATS, ROLLED OATS.

steel-ground flour - flour made by crushing the grains between huge hammers or rollers. The high heat that is generated by the machines damages or destroys some of their nutrients and removes the germ. Sold in grocery stores, all-purpose flours ground this way are enriched or fortified with added vitamins and nutrients. See also FLOUR, STONE-GROUND FLOUR.

steelhead - see RAINBOW TROUT.

stein

steep - to soak in or infuse a hot liquid with flavor, such as tea in water, herbs in hot oil, saffron in hot wine, etc. See also INFUSION.

stein - a tall, heavy, round mug, sometimes made from glass or metal (such as pewter) but usually made of ceramic, used for serving large quantities of beer. It is a traditional German drinking vessel, its name likely derived from the German word *Steingut*, meaning "stone goods" or "stoneware" for the material from which it was traditionally made.

stelle - also **stellette.** See PASTA.

stemware - a generic term for a drinking glass with a stem, such as a goblet or flute.

steppe cheese - a mild, soft, yellow-tinted Russian cheese, now produced in Europe as well.

stevia - also **kaa-he-he, sweet leaf.** A sweet, perennial herb, *Eupatorium rebaudianum Bertoni*, native to Paraguay, where the Guarani people, who call it *kaa-he-he*, have traditionally harvested it from the wild to sweeten hot drinks, such as **maté.** Since cultivation was begun in the early 1900s, stevia has been grown and used to make various drinks and foodstuffs in Asia and parts of Europe, as well as South America, but it has not yet received government approval as a commercial food additive in either Canada or the U.S. Health food and herbal stores do sell it as a dietary supplement, however. The leaves are used dried, fresh or in powdered form. Stevia is also available in liquid or concentrated syrup. Its boosters claim that stevia is an all-natural, calorie-free sweetener that is suitable for use by diabetics; in North America, government scientists have yet to complete testing to confirm its long-term safety when consumed in large quantities. Only a little is needed at a time, however, as it is 300 times sweeter than table sugar.

stew - **1.** (v.) to boil gently for a long time, simmering till tender, usually in a covered pot, from the Old French *estuver* and the Greek *typhos*, meaning "steam" or "vapor." **2.** (n.) a dish prepared in this way, usually containing meat and vegetables in a sauce. See also BRAISE.

Stewart, Martha- see profile on page 616.

sticky bun - also **honey bun. 1.** a small, glazed bun made with yeast dough rolled around cinnamon and raisins. A layer of honey or a mixture of melted butter, corn syrup and brown sugar is poured into the baking pan or muffin-tin cups, then the uncooked buns are placed on top. When the baked buns are turned out, the glaze sticks to their tops and sides. Some versions contain chopped citrus zest, candied fruit and/or nuts; in others, chopped or whole candied fruit and nuts are set in the bottom of the pan, in the honey, before the dough is set on top. **2.** a generic term for any bun with a sticky, sweet glaze applied during or after baking.

sticky rice - also **mochi rice.** See RICE.

stifado - also **stifatho.** A classic, fragrant Greek dish of braised chunks of beef, olive oil, red wine, tomatoes and handfuls of small, whole pearl onions. The seasonings vary with the cook, but most stifado contains a bay leaf, cinnamon, minced garlic, oregano, rosemary and thyme. Feta cheese may be crumbled over individual servings.

stiff peaks - a term used to describe egg whites or whipping cream beaten until sharp, stiff peaks form. They are stiff peaks when the beaters are pulled up and they still hold their shape. Egg whites beaten to this stage also achieve a glossy, silvery sheen. See also SOFT PEAKS.

still - a colloquial term for "distillery," often one where moonshine is produced.

still wine - any wine that is not effervescent, of any color or level of sweetness. See also SPARKLING WINE, TABLE WINE.

Stilton - a strong, English blue-veined cheese made from whole cow's milk, aged for four to six months, with a pale yellow interior, a creamy, crumbly texture and a natural brownish rind. Stilton has been made without interruption since 1730. In the early 1900s, Stilton makers formed an association to control how this cheese should be made and where: only in Derbyshire, Nottinghamshire and Leicestershire. Stilton is punctuated with tiny holes, where it has been pierced by stainless-steel needles to allow air to penetrate.

Stilton scoop - a shallow, long bowl set on a long handle. Invented during Queen Victoria's reign, it was designed to scoop cheese from inside a whole Stilton crust. It may share the shape of a small shovel, but this tool is usually executed in silver, with aristocratic ornamentation on the handle. The scoop is beautiful, but some Stilton connoisseurs prefer a knife.

Stinger - a classic cocktail mixed with three parts brandy and one part white crème de menthe, served over ice, garnished with a twist of lemon. In a variation called the "bee stinger," blackberry brandy is used. In the "vodka stinger," vodka replaces the brandy and green crème de menthe replaces the white.

stinging nettle - see NETTLE.

stinking gum - see ASAFETIDA.

stinking willie - see TANSY.

stir-fry - **1.** (v.) to cook small pieces of meat and/or vegetables quickly over very high heat, stirring constantly, with very little heat, often using a wok. **2.** (n.) a dish cooked in this manner.

stirkees - see AETTEKEES.

stirrup cup - a drinking vessel given to a person mounted on a horse upon their departure or arrival from a long journey, often shaped like the head of a hound, fox or fish, or a clenched fist.

Stewart, Martha (1941–) - cookbook author, television and magazine personality, lifestyle guru and America's first self-made female billionaire. Born Martha Kostyra in New Jersey, she was one of six children of Polish-American parents, from whom she acquired a strong sense of self-discipline as well as basic skills in domestic arts, such as gardening, decorating and cooking. Her legendary work ethic was evident from an early age. Winning a partial scholarship to New York City's tony Barnard College, Stewart capitalized on her wholesome good looks, working part time as a model to pay her university expenses. While at Barnard, she met her future husband, Andy Stewart, then a Yale law student. Their daughter, Alexis, was born in 1965. After a career as a stockbroker, Stewart began running a catering business out of her home in 1976. Within 10 years, the business was making $1 million a year. During this time, she became involved in restoring the family home, an 1805 farmhouse in Westport, Connecticut, and began to develop her profile as a national figure, writing for women's magazines.

In 1982, she published *Entertaining*, the first of her many lavishly illustrated books. It was a huge success, and *Martha Stewart's Quick Cook* followed in 1983. Although it may not have been evident at the time, the books were positioning Martha Stewart as a brand. Full-color productions, usually photographed in Stewart's exquisitely restored farmhouse, were propped using her extensive collection of antique china, glassware, table linens and cooking utensils. The books portrayed Stewart at the hub of a magical world of elegance and style, all of which owed its existence to her. The presentation for a simple fall dinner featuring frittata in *Quick Cook* is a case in point. The copy begins: "Years ago, when Andy and I visited Spain and the Balearic Islands, we discovered in Ibiza what the natives called frittatas — huge, thick omelets baked in the oven and filled with potatoes, onions, sometimes chorizo, peppers, and olives." Stewart goes on to talk about how often she and Andy eat frittatas, because they have their own hens and other ingredients that might be used. On the facing page is a sumptuous shot of the frittata ingredients, including a bowl full of eggs; through the doorway is an image of Stewart feeding the hens that provided dinner. It was the mass market's introduction to what has since been dubbed "gastro-decor-porn" and the launch of the Martha Stewart phenomenon.

By 1987, Stewart had a $5-million contract to develop products for Kmart. Soon after, she launched her own magazine, *Martha Stewart Living*, and a television show. In 1990, her marriage ended in divorce. By 1999, Martha Stewart Living Omnimedia was an IPO on the New York Stock Exchange, and her personal worth was estimated at $1 billion. But the bubble was soon to burst. In the fall of 2003, Martha Stewart was investigated for insider trading and was subsequently found guilty of lying to investigators regarding a suspicious stock trade. She served five months in jail. Her trial and personal tribulations gripped the world: was she a target as a powerful woman with a reputation for being imperious and, at times, irascible, or were the shareholders in her company the victims of her greed as the value of their stock tumbled? No matter. Within months of her release from prison, Stewart was back on her feet, with a new prime-time reality television show (not a runaway success in the ratings, but an outstanding promotional opportunity for Martha, the brand) and a bestselling book. Still the "personification of gracious living," the post-prison Stewart displayed some of the mettle that fueled her journey from Nutley, New Jersey, to the world of the super-rich and sent an unmistakable signal to those who had written her off. In the next phase of her career, the purveyor of homemaking magic had every intention of debunking the myth that in America there are no second acts.

stock - a flavorful liquid made from any combination of bones, meat, fish, vegetables and seasonings, simmered over several hours and strained. See also BROTH, SAUCE.

stockfish - fish that has been dried naturally outdoors on stones or wooden racks. Cod is most often used but pollack, haddock and other white fish are also used in stockfish production.

stockpot - a straight-sided, tall lidded pot with two generous loop-style handles on opposite sides of the rim. **Nonreactive** stainless-steel versions are recommended, as are stockpots with a thick, aluminum base that evenly distribute the heat. Some versions have a spigot near the base, which lets the stock be drained off, leaving the fat (which rises to the surface) behind. Primarily used for making soup stock, a stockpot should be roomy enough to accommodate a large marrow bone or whole chicken, but various sizes are available. Stockpots are also useful for cooking lobster and pasta, and simmering huge batches of applesauce or preserves.

Stollen - a traditional spicy German Christmas bread, which originated during the Middle Ages and is still made today, with eggs, sugar, milk, raisins, currants, citrus peel, cinnamon and nutmeg.

stone - **1.** see PIT. **2.** see PIZZA STONE.

stone crab - see CRAB.

stone-ground flour - flour made by grinding the grains between two grooved revolving millstones, often granite. Historically, water- and wind-powered grist mills ground grains into flour this way; nowadays, it's mainly small, organic producers that do so, and their mills are usually electric. The nutritional benefit is still debated, but this method grinds slowly, retains the germ and avoids the high heat, which is believed to destroy nutrients and encourage the meal from the fatty germ to become rancid. Stone-ground flour is available in health food stores. See also FLOUR, STEEL-GROUND FLOUR.

stout - a strong, dark English and Irish ale, stronger, sweeter and heavier in body than **porter,** brewed from roasted malt or barley.

stovies - see HOTCHPOTCH. A Scottish stew of sliced onions and potatoes, traditionally braised with whatever meat or seafood was available: from leftover chunks of the Sunday "joint" to bacon, corned beef, limpets or mutton. There is still debate over whether "stovies" is derived from the French, **etouffée,** or merely a variation on "stew." Either way, in Scotland and the north of England, "stovies" has become a common term for a braised dish or stew.

stracchino - a family of Italian cheeses originally made in the plains of Lombardy from the milk of cows passing through on their way south for winter grazing; from *stracca*, meaning "tired," referring to the cattle and the long distances they traveled to pastures. Cheeses in this family include **Gorgonzola** and Taleggio.

stracciatella - an Italian soup made by adding beaten eggs and cheese to a hot broth, from *straccia*, meaning "rag," referring to how the ingredients form yellow and white ribbons that resemble little scraps of cloth.

straight up - see NEAT.

strain - to remove unwanted solids from a liquid mixture by pouring it through a sieve, strainer or cheesecloth.

strainer - see SIEVE.

strata - **1.** a dish consisting of cubed or sliced bread, layered with fillings, such as fruits or vegetables, meat or seafood and, almost always, cheese. Beaten eggs, sometimes mixed with cream or milk, are poured over the assembled dish and allowed to soak in for several hours before the strata is baked. An easy entrée to prepare ahead (whether it's a down-home ham-and-cheese version or an upmarket Brie-and-crab casserole), this dish is also a delicious way to use up stale bread. **2.** see SANDWICH CAKE.

strawberries Romanoff - a simple, but sophisticated dish of hulled, fresh whole strawberries, **macerated** in orange juice and orange liqueur (such as Cointreau or Grand Marnier), then served in their liquor, topped with whipped cream. American innovations include vanilla ice cream folded into the whipped cream and a drizzle of chocolate over each serving. The dish was created in the 1800s for Czar Nicholas I (of the Russian Romanoffs).

strawberries

strawberry - of the genus *Fragaria*, valued for its therapeutic properties in ancient Rome (it's an excellent source of vitamin C) and cultivated in Europe since the Middle Ages; a low plant bearing usually reddish, conical berries covered in tiny straw-color seeds, so named either for these specks or possibly because the plant's stumps are straw-like. Strawberries are not actually berries. Botanists refer to them as a false fruit, a pseudocarp or multiple fruit. The external "seeds" that dot the outside are technically the fruit, with miniature seeds inside, while the juicy red flesh is merely a receptacle for the "fruit."

The English have been eating strawberries and cream for centuries. This was the dish that inspired an Englishman to say, "Doubtless the Almighty could make a better berry — but He never did." Wild strawberries grow on many continents and in many climates. There are records of the alpine strawberries that the French called *fraises des bois*, meaning "strawberries from the woods," being cultivated as far back as the 15th century. In 1712, a French explorer/spy, Captain Amédé Frézier, while checking Spanish fortifications on the Chilean coast, stumbled on the wild beach strawberry, *Fragaria chiloensis*, a variety as "large as walnuts," and brought it back to Europe. Early colonists in North America were amazed to see strawberries growing in abundance. In Maryland, one wrote, "Wee cannot sett down a foote but tred on strawberries." Roger Williams, the nonconformist minister who founded Rhode Island, said, "This strawberry was the wonder of all fruits growing naturally in these parts...where the Indians have planted, I have many times seen as many as would fill a good ship..." These strawberries, which the Indians crushed and mixed with meal to make bread, were named *Fragaria virginia* and were carried to Europe, where they were received enthusiastically. Later, some French growers found that Chilean strawberries bore fruit if planted next to Virginia strawberries and called the resulting crossbreed a pineapple strawberry, *Fragaria ananassa*.

In the 1830s, Charles Mason Hovey, an American horticulturist managed to successfully crossbreed several varieties of strawberries; it was the first fruit variety bred originally in the U.S. It was named after its "inventor" and quickly became popular nationally. Wilson was a new variety developed 30 years later and quickly won popularity. But strawberries stayed a locally produced, limited-season crop until after the Second World War. The big change came with the introduction of the University variety, developed by the University of California Agriculture Station in 1945. Experimentation continues to come up with hardier, more prolific strawberries that produce for a longer season and can be shipped long distances.

strawberry huller - miniature metal tongs (about thumb-length) with a sharp-edged rounded end on each arm; the disks are pinched together around the stem and leaves of a strawberry, then pulled away to remove them. A strawberry huller can also be used to remove small bones from fish when preparing it for cooking.

strawberry pear - see DRAGON FRUIT.

strawberry shortcake - see SHORTCAKE.

straw mushroom - also **paddy-straw mushroom.** Highly prized and grown on the straw left in rice paddies after harvest, straw mushrooms are fairly small, with elongated dome-like caps. In China, their country of origin, they're served as a mark of respect to guests, featured in vegetarian recipes and in steamed or fried chicken dishes.

straw mushrooms

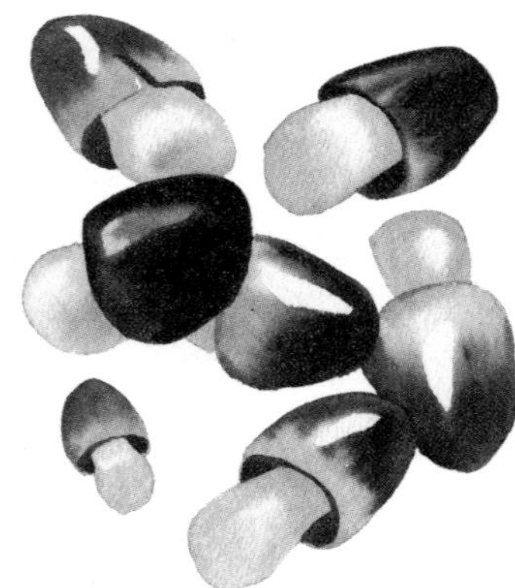

straw potatoes - potatoes cut into thin strips, about 3 inches (7.5 cm) long — slightly longer than **matchsticks** — and deep-fried.

Strega - a proprietary name for a popular Italian liqueur flavored with orange and herbs. *Strega,* meaning "witch," was named in 1860, creating a mystique for the liqueur by linking it to the legend of the witches of Benevento, its town of origin, famed for a mythical love potion that promised to unite forever any couple who drank it.

streusel - a crumbly mixture of flour, sugar, butter and sometimes spices, as a topping for baked goods, from the German, meaning "sprinkle."

string bean - see GREEN BEAN.

string-bean paté - see MOCK CHOPPED LIVER.

string cheese - stretchy ropes of mild, semisoft cheese that can be pulled apart into separate strands. Usually salty, it is available plain or seasoned and is appreciated as a tasty, portable snack by campers, backpackers and people who like to play with their food.

striped European eggplant - see EGGPLANT.

stroganoff - see BEEF STROGANOFF.

stromboli - **1.** a **calzone,** traditionally filled with mozzarella cheese and pepperoni. This hot treat originated in Philadelphia (where the Italian population burgeoned in the late 1800s), but it's named after a small, sometimes red-hot island, the cone of a still-active volcano, off the coast of Sicily. **2.** a sandwich made of crusty bread, sliced in half horizontally, then filled with a mixture of chopped garlic, onion and sweet pepper, cooked ground meat or sliced sausage, shredded cheese, Italian seasoning, mushrooms and tomato sauce, wrapped in foil and baked.

strudel - German for "whirlpool," most likely in reference to how its dough is rolled several times around its filling, creating a swirl of pastry that becomes flaky when baked. Many food historians connect strudel to **baklava** because of the similar thinness of their pastry, but baklava is built in layers, while strudel's layers are the result of rolling. Strudel pastry must be made with high-gluten flour, which gives it tremendous elasticity; it is difficult to prepare and handle. The dough is rolled to a certain thinness and then stretched by hand until it is nearly transparent, often covering an entire table. Classic Austrian strudel is filled with apples, raisins and cinnamon. Savory strudels with meat and vegetables are also common.

stud - to insert a cut piece of food, such as a slivered pistachio, or a whole item, such as a clove, partway into a semisolid or solid foodstuff, such as a cake, cookie, fruit or vegetable, or piece of meat.

stufato - Italian for "stew."

stuff - to fill a carved-out or naturally occurring cavity with fruit, meat, pasta, poultry, seafood or vegetables with a sweet or savory dressing or filling.

stuffed derma - see DERMA.

stuffed egg - a British favorite, a hard-boiled egg is cut in half and the yolk removed, then replaced after being mashed together with a mayonnaise mixture of various fillings, including ham and watercress, minced herbs, or tomato and horseradish. Easily assembled ahead, then chilled, stuffed eggs are usually served on a bed of lettuce or parsley.

stuffed onions - also **onions farcis.** A classic dish of hollowed-out onions filled with minced beef, lamb or pork, herbs, onion, and bread crumbs or rice, usually slow-roasted in a buttery sauce or stock, in shallow pan.

stuffing - see DRESSING.

sturgeon - large, long-lived fish belonging to the Acipenseridae family that occur in temperate zones in Asia, Europe and North America. *Acipenser huso* in the Black and Caspian seas, known as Beluga sturgeon, provide the world's premium caviar. Torpedo-like in shape and covered in rows of bony, protruding plates, sturgeon are often referred to as "living fossils," since fossilized remains show they have changed little since prehistoric times. Some are saltwater fish that swim into freshwater rivers to spawn; others are confined to large freshwater lakes and rivers. North American species include *A. fulvescens*, known as lake sturgeon and once common in the Hudson and Mississippi rivers, now found throughout the Great Lakes, and *A. transmontanus*, known as Pacific or **white sturgeon** and the largest freshwater fish on the continent, which is found in Pacific-coast river systems from Alaska to Mexico. The former can grow up to 7 feet long (2 m); the latter to 20 feet (6 m). Sturgeon routinely live more than 100 years (one, caught in the 1950s in Lake of the Woods in Ontario, was estimated to be 153 years old). They take about 25 years to reach their reproductive years. This slowness to reproduce, coupled with environmental degradation and over-harvesting means that many are now on endangered-species lists. See also CAVIAR.

su - high-quality Japanese rice vinegar used in preparing sushi rice, salad dressings and in marinades.

suan la tang - a very spicy Cantonese soup, meaning "sour and hot," which it is.

submarine sandwich - also **hero sandwich, sub.** A sandwich consisting of a long bun filled with cold cuts, cheese, lettuce, tomatoes, pickles, olives, peppers and mayonnaise. See also POOR BOY.

sucanat - a brown granular sweetener made by evaporating natural, unrefined sugarcane juice. Sucanat is not refined, like granulated white sugar, so it is often used by people who are interested in natural, unprocessed food. It can be substituted for an equal measure of white or brown sugar.

succotash - a dish of corn and lima beans, often also with sweet peppers, one of the first dishes given to the Pilgrims by Native Americans, originally made of corn and kidney beans and perhaps dog meat, all cooked in bear fat. The Narragansett called it *msickquatash*, meaning "boiled kernels of corn."

sucking pig - a pig of up to 6 weeks of age that is fed only mother's milk, slaughtered at between 2 and 6 weeks of age (experts claim that 3- and 4-week-old pigs yield the tastiest flesh) and roasted whole for festive occasions. "Suckling pig" is a common term for this dish, but it is a misnomer: mothers suckle their young, while the young suck. The dish is well-known and loved in Portugal, where it is called *leitão assado;* in Spain, where it is known as *cochinillo asado;* and in France, where it is known as *cochon de lait*.

sucralose - a sweetener derived from table sugar — indigestible and, therefore, non-nutritive — that is used in confections and beverages. About 600 times sweeter than sugar, it is stable at high heats, so it can be used in baked and cooked foods. See also ARTIFICIAL SWEETENERS.

sucrose - a name for common sugar, obtained from sugarcane, sugar beets and other plant sources containing glucose and fructose.

suds - a slang term for beer, earned by its frothy head of foam.

suet - the fat surrounding the kidneys and loins of beef and mutton, which yields tallow, from the Middle English *sewet*, meaning "hard animal fat." It's used to make suet pudding.

suet pudding - a savory or sweet pudding with the hard fat from around the kidneys of beef or mutton as its main ingredient. Since at least the Middle Ages, plain, so-called **white puddings** (in contrast to **black puddings**) were made of bread crumbs, flour and suet, sometimes stuffed into natural **sausage casings,** such as intestines or stomach linings, or wrapped in a pudding cloth and boiled. Often sliced, then fried in meat drippings, these were customarily served to start a meal. More complicated savory versions may have contained currants, herbs, onions and pieces of root vegetables and fowl or meat, such as bacon, beef, mutton, pigeon or rabbit. By the mid-Victorian era, savory suet puddings were available from street vendors. At the same time, sweet versions, such as plum pudding, served as dessert, were becoming popular. Today, most have less suet and may be baked, boiled or steamed, but many still contain some grated carrot as the token root vegetable. Thanks to their promotion by celebrities, such as English cookery expert Delia Smith, suet puddings are making a comeback. See also DUFF.

Suffolk ham - an expensive English ham that has been soaked in molasses for a sweet, rather than salt cure, a process that turns its skin a deep golden brown.

sufganiyot - a deep-fried jelly or jam doughnut, a traditional Israeli favorite during the Jewish celebration of Hanukkah (the name means "sponge dough"), now becoming popular in North America as well. While each doughnut is still warm, a small slit is cut into the center and jam, jelly or marmalade is pushed inside. The doughnut is then rolled in confectioner's or granulated sugar and set on a rack to cool. Aside from their good taste, sufganiyots may be appreciated for their symbolic value: their shape suggests the cycle of life, and their hidden treasure is a reminder to look within. And, like **latkes,** another Hannukah food cooked in oil, sufganiyots serve as a reminder of the miracle of the small quantity of oil that lasted eight days.

sugar - any of a group of simple carbohydrates occurring naturally, especially in fruits and honey. Most often, the word is applied to the sweet powdered substance refined from sugarcane or (less commonly) the sugar beet. Our ancestors drank the raw juice of the sugarcane. Later on, in order to make white sugar, the juice was cooked until syrupy, then hardened and dried.

Sugarcane was first cultivated in India 2,500 years ago and was called *karkara* in Sanskrit. The recorded history of cane sugar began when a member of Alexander's army mentioned it in 325 BC. It had reached China

TYPES OF SUGAR

Barbados sugar - see MUSCOVADO.

brown - white sugar with molasses.

caster - see SUPERFINE.

coarse - see CRYSTAL.

colored sugar - homemade or ready-made sugar, colored with food coloring, used to decorate baked goods and confections. In the home kitchen, it can be made by adding a few drops of liquid food coloring to sugar in a plastic bag or jar, then sealing it and shaking the sugar. Sugar cubes can also be colored (and slightly flavored, as well) by rubbing them against the clean rind of an orange or other citrus fruit.

confectioner's - also **icing, powdered sugar.** A granulated sugar crushed into a powder, with about 3 percent cornstarch added to prevent clumping.

crystal - also **coarse, decorating sugar, decorator's sugar, sugar crystals.** Granules are four times the size of those of granulated sugar.

decorating sugar - also **decorator's sugar.** See CRYSTAL.

Demerara sugar - a coarse-textured brown sugar, originally from Demerara, Guyana, similar to **muscovado** and **turbinado** sugars.

flavored sugar - homemade or ready-made sugar, flavored with fresh or dried citrus zest or flower petals or leaves, gingerroot, nuts or spices; used in cold or hot beverages and desserts. In the home kitchen, whole dried spices, such as aniseed or cloves, can be pounded together with sugar in a mortar and pestle, or pulsed together with sugar in a food processor. Alternatively, a cinnamon stick, lemon-geranium leaf or a dried, split vanilla pod can be placed with the sugar in an airtight container until the sugar absorbs the flavor.

granulated - also **white sugar.** A refined, general-purpose sugar.

icing sugar - see CONFECTIONER'S.

moist sugar - see MUSCOVADO.

muscovado - also **Barbados sugar, moist sugar.** An unrefined sugar with a strong molasses flavor, it is the product of the very first boiling of sugarcane, dark brown in color and slightly coarser and stickier than most "regular" brown sugars.

powdered sugar - see CONFECTIONER'S.

preserving sugar - fully refined, coarse-grained white sugar, which resists clumping when immersed in simmering fruit mixtures; used for making jams or preserves. The separate crystals dissolve more quickly than other sugars.

raw - the remains from sugar processing, following the extraction of molasses and sugar crystallization.

rock sugar - brittle and clear, crystallized cane sugar with a softer, mellower sweetness than granulated sugar. Despite its golden color, it has no aftertaste of caramel or molasses.

sugar crystals - see CRYSTAL.

superfine - finely ground **granulated sugar**, known as **caster** or **castor sugar** in England.

turbinado - a raw sugar that has been steamed cleaned in a centrifuge, light brown in color with a coarse grain, closer to refined sugar than raw. The surface molasses is removed in the washing process, but the sugar retains a slight molasses flavor.

white sugar - see GRANULATED.

by 100 BC. The Japanese did not have it until AD 700, although by AD 400 it was widely cultivated in the Middle East. Legend has it that during the T'ang Dynasty (AD 618–907) in the Plan-Shan mountains in China, a monk named Tsen let his donkey come down the mountain one day and eat up the cane plantation belonging to a man named Noang-chi. As compensation for the damage, the monk taught Noang-chi how to make sugar.

Sugar derives from the Arabic *sarkar,* meaning "grain," and appeared in England in the 13th century. The Roman historian and naturalist **Pliny** called it a kind of honey made from reeds. So did the crusaders, who brought it back to Europe for the first time in 1148. The sweetener would soon be priced above honey. But until the 16th century, when cane sugar from the West Indies became readily available and inexpensive, the world depended mainly on honey as its sweetener. It remained expensive until Columbus introduced canes into Hispaniola, now Haiti and the Dominican Republic, in 1493. Despite setbacks, its cultivation spread throughout the islands, and sugarcane became, and still is, a main source of sweetener. See also GUR, JAGGERY, KHANDSARI, PALM SUGAR, TEMPERATURE.

sugar apple - see SWEETSOP.

sugar banana - see BABY BANANA.

sugar beet - see BEET.

sugarcane - a tall perennial grass, *Saccharum officinarum*, from tropical climates, cultivated for the sap in its stalk, used to make sugar, syrup, spirits, such as rum, and **basi,** sugarcane wine. Sugarcane has been known for at least 2,200 years. Alexander's army saw sugarcane during its conquest of India in 326 BC, and the Arabs were responsible for much of its spread as they took it to Egypt in AD 641 during their conquests. The crusaders took it to Spain, where it's been cultivated since AD 1150. Columbus transported sugarcane from the Canary Islands to Hispaniola (now the Dominican Republic and Haiti) on his second voyage in 1493. The main U.S. producers of sugarcane are Hawaii, Texas and South Carolina.

sugar pea - see SUGAR SNAP PEA.

sugar pie - also **brown sugar pie.** An open-faced or lattice-topped pie filled with a mixture of brown sugar and cream, a traditional treat in Quebec, where it's called "tarte au sucre." The recipe sometimes calls for maple sugar instead of brown sugar, which is no surprise, since the province of Quebec is one of the largest maple syrup producers in the world. If the pie calls for maple syrup, however, it's no longer a sugar pie, but rather a maple syrup pie (*tarte au sirop d'erable*).

sugarplum - a small candy made by coating dried or candied fruits with an sugar icing mixture.

sugar snap pea - also **Chinese pea pod, pea pod, sugar pea.** A legume, a cross between the English pea and the snow pea, with a high natural sugar content, whose tall vines grow rapidly. The sugar snap pea has edible pods, even when grown to full maturity. See also PEA.

sugar substitutes - see ARTIFICIAL SWEETENERS.

sugar syrup - see SIMPLE SYRUP.

sugar syrup stages - see TEMPERATURE.

sukiyaki - a Japanese, one-pot, **nabemono**-style dish of bite-size pieces of meat (usually beef) or poultry and vegetables, cooked in a broth (such as **dashi**) containing **mirin** and soy sauce on a shallow iron pan. Noodles and tofu may be part of the meal. Before eating each cooked bit, diners dip it into beaten, raw egg. Legend says that sukiyaki — a combination of the Japanese *suki*, meaning "slice" and *yaki*, meaning "broil" — was first cooked by long-ago Buddhist field workers with an appetite for meat despite their avowed vegetarianism (but not anxious to defile their kitchens), who secretly caught and cooked game on their plow blade. Since sukiyaki is a communal dish, cooked and shared at the table, it's also called "the friendship meal."

sulfite - a compound containing the sulfite ion; a salt of sulfurous acid. Since sulfites help deter bacteria and insects, prevent discoloration and oxidization and prolong shelf life, they are a common food preservative in a wide range of foods, including baked goods, citrus juices, dried fruit, preserves, trail mix, tomato paste and wine. Sulfites are also used to produce some packaging (cellophane) and as a disinfectant during food processing. In asthmatics, people allergic to aspirin and others, sulfites can cause adverse reactions ranging from cramps and nauseau to full-blown anaphylactic shock

(Health Canada lists sulfites as "one of the nine most common food products causing severe adverse reactions"). As a consequence, regulations throughout North America require that the presence of sulfites be listed on package labels; it may be listed as Potassium bisulfite/metabisulfite, Sodium bisulfite/dithionite/metabisulfite, Sulfur dioxide, Sulfiting agents or Sulphurous acid. See also SALAD BAR.

Sullivan, Thomas - see profile below.

sultana - **1.** a small, but plump amber-green grape native to Turkey, where it has been grown since ancient times for winemaking; hundreds of thousands of tons of sun-dried sultana raisins are now produced in the Aegean region of that country. In North America, where they are grown for table grapes, juice making and, of course, for raisins, sultanas are called **Thompson seedless grapes. 2.** the raisin made from a sultana.

sumac - the dried, furry, maroon to purple fruits of *Rhus coriaria,* the so-called elm-leaved sumac indigenous to the Mediterranean and the Middle East that is used as a flavoring and spice. Powdered sumac is used in Middle Eastern dishes, such as kebabs and pilafs, and is an ingredient in the spice mixture **za'atar;** whole dried berries are soaked in liquid to make refreshing, tart and fruity-tasting beverages. In North America, Native Americans traditionally used the fruit from *R. aromatica*, also known as "lemon sumac," for culinary and medicinal purposes, and made poultices from the bark and leaves. Since some related shrubs (such as *R. vernix*, found in North American wetlands) produce toxic oils, sumac is best bought, rather than hand-harvested by amateurs.

sumac

summer cauliflower - see ROMANESCA.

summer coating - see CONFECTIONERY COATING.

summer flounder - see FLUKE.

summer pudding - a traditional English dessert made by filling a bread-lined dish with a variety of lightly cooked soft fruits. The top is covered with more bread, and the whole is pressed and left to sit overnight, then turned onto a plate and served with cream.

summer sausage - any of various dried or smoked sausages that can be kept without refrigeration.

summer savory - see SAVORY.

summer squash - see SQUASH.

sunchoke - see JERUSALEM ARTICHOKE.

sundae - a dish of ice cream served with one or more sweet sauces, fruits, nuts and/or whipped cream. Stories about the origin of the ice cream sundae are legion, hotly contested and often completely fabricated, as was a version touted by H.L. Mencken about two rival Wisconsin ice cream parlors creating the sundae. Common to nearly all stories, unsurprisingly, is that it was invented at a soda fountain, but it could have been in Wisconsin, Virginia, Illinois or New York. The sundae may have come about in response to a law forbidding the sale of sodas on Sunday, and so the soda syrup was served on ice cream instead. It may have been called a "sundae" because the versions made with chocolate syrup were too expensive to be sold every day; or because they were often enjoyed after church; or because they were special and reserved for Sunday.

sun-dried tomato - a tomato that has been dried in the sun, turning

Sullivan, Thomas (19th–20th century) - American tea importer and inventor of the tea bag. Sullivan is said to have invented the tea bag in 1908, when his customers requested samples of his tea and shipping small quantities in the usual metal canisters proved too costly. He fashioned a silk pouch containing a small quantity of tea, which his customers put directly into the pot, thinking this had been Sullivan's intention. By the 1920s, tea bags were being made commercially, eventually using gauze and later paper. Today, only 5 percent of the world's tea is made from loose leaves.

dark red, with a chewy texture, sold dried or packed in oil.

sunflower - a tall, bright yellow flower, *Helianthus annuus*, which originated in Peru and Mexico and was not introduced to Europe until the 16th century. The Spanish conquistadors found Incan sun priestesses wearing sunflower crowns and pure-gold sunflowers adorning their temples to honor the sun god. Related to the Jerusalem artichoke, the sunflower has a wide variety of uses. The stems are used to make paper; the leaves are used in salads, frying oils and cattle fodder; and the product of a second pressing of the oil is used to make soap and candles, which in turn are used for art supplies. A famous Russian flatbread is made from roasted and ground sunflower seeds, and, of course, there are the universally well-loved roasted seeds, eaten plain as a snack food.

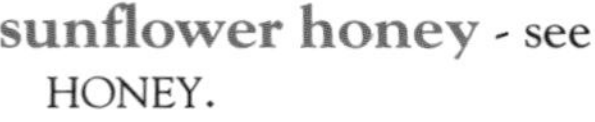

sunflower

sunflower honey - see HONEY.

sunflower oil - extracted from sunflower seeds, light in taste and color, excellent as both a cooking and salad oil. Sunflower oil has the highest vitamin E content of all vegetable oils and has a combination of monounsaturated and polyunsaturated fats, with low saturated fat levels.

sunny side up - a method of frying an egg only on the bottom so its unbroken, soft and sunny yellow yolk faces up.

sunomono - meaning "vinegared things," a Japanese salad of raw or cooked vegetables, fish or meat in vinegar.

superfine sugar - see SUGAR.

supper - from the Old French *souper,* meaning "to sup," the same origin of the word "soup," most likely because, in the Middle Ages, soup was supper's main course. Today, supper is usually the evening meal. From the 1600s to the mid-1900s, supper was often a very late evening meal for the rich.

suprême - a French term, historically, for the breast and wings of poultry and game birds removed in one piece when raw; in modern cooking, a boneless breast of chicken, sometimes with a single wing bone. Suprême is also a term used to describe a dish that is made of the finest ingredients and prepared in a special way.

suprême sauce - a **velouté** with heavy cream, for fish, poultry, vegetables and dishes that will be gratinéed.

surf and turf - a North American menu term for an entrée with both meat and seafood, such as steak and lobster.

surimi - see WHITING.

surume - seasoned dried cuttlefish or squid, often eaten as a snack with beer in Japan, also a well-known Hawaiian treat, thanks to the influence of a large number of Japanese immigrants who came to work in Hawaii in the late 1800s and early 1900s.

survival food - see FAMINE FOOD.

sushi - raw and sometimes cooked fish, thinly sliced and formed by hand onto vinegared rice. A relatively new technique, sushi derives from an Asian method of preserving fish that originated in the 8th century. In Japan, by the 17th century, the technique had evolved into seasoned fish packed with rice and stored under a stone weight and water to be fully fermented without air for as long as several months. The starch promoted fermentation, whose by-product, lactic acid, kept the fish from spoiling. During the 18th century, preserved fish was pressed onto vinegared rice by hand, but not until the early 19th century did raw fish appear hand-pressed onto rice in small, near-bite-size pieces. Some accounts credit Tokyo entrepreneur Hanaya Yohei with being the first to make and sell these "snacks" directly to his customers from his stall, considered to be the precursor of the sushi bar. Historically, the highly regarded art of sushi making required an apprenticeship of 10 years, but the world's burgeoning demand for sushi has shortened the chefs' training to three to four years. See also SASHIMI.

SUSHI TYPES

chirashi-zushi - seasoned sushi rice served in a bowl or dish, topped with morsels or slices of various vegetables and/or seafood, sometimes translated as "scattered sushi."

hand roll - see TEMAKI-ZUSHI.

maki-zushi - rolled sushi, consisting of a sheet of **nori** topped with any of a variety of fillings, rolled tightly into a cylinder and cut into bite-size rounds. Rolled sushi can also be made with a layer of rice on the outside of the roll and the seaweed on the inside, in which case it is called *uramaki*. *Hosomaki* are skinny sushi rolls, and *futomaki* are fat ones.

nigiri-zushi - hand-pressed sushi made by pressing a dollop of seasoned rice in the palm of the hand to shape it into a rectangle, then topping it with a slice of raw or cooked fish or rolled omelet. The piece is sometimes wrapped with a thin strip of **nori** to hold it together.

temaki-zushi - also **hand roll.** A large square of **nori** surrounding typical sushi fillings of fish, vegetables, etc., rolled into a tall cone and eaten with the hands.

sushi mat - also **Japanese sushi rolling mat, makisu, maki-zushi mat, sudare.** A flexible square mat made of thin strips of bamboo, used to tightly roll up maki-zushi (rolled **sushi**) inside a sheet of **nori.** The mat looks a bit like a bamboo window shade, with perpendicular threads woven through the bamboo strips and tied every couple of inches to hold them together. The sheet of nori is placed on the mat, then topped with seasoned sushi rice and fillings, then rolled up tightly, using the mat to support the roll along its length. Using a sushi mat prevents the roll from getting lumpy and creates an even product that won't fall apart when sliced.

swamp cabbage - **1.** the skinned core or pith cut from the wild cabbage palm, *Sabal palmetto*, Florida's state tree. (The tip, with a few tender unfurled leaves still attached, may be used as a garnish.) Since this is harvested from the central bud from which the fronds emerge, the tree is killed in the process. As a result, there are now state restrictions on the harvesting of this type of palm heart; in an informal way, this often occurs when land is being cleared for development. **2.** an old-time, down-home Southern dish of thinly sliced swamp cabbage cooked in meat seasoning, often over an open campfire. See also HEARTS OF PALM.

swamp morning glory - see WATER SPINACH.

swamp potato - see ARROWHEAD.

swan - an aquatic bird, *Cygnus olor,* whose young, called cygnets, were served on festive occasions in the courts of England and France up until the 17th century. (It is reputed that Richard the Lion Hearted first introduced swans to the Thames from Cyprus.) At a banquet given for the Bishop of Durham by King Richard II in 1387, 50 swans "graced the board." On Christmas Day 1512, five swans were provided for the Duke of Northumberland's table; on New Year's Day, four more; and 12 days later, another four. In London, cygnets are still eaten once a year, in a ceremonial and traditional manner, at the Vintners' Hall on the third week of July.

swatow mustard - see WRAPPED HEART MUSTARD.

sweat - to cook very gently in oil, butter or other fat to draw out the juices of a food so they soften without browning. Finely diced or sliced vegetables are often sweated in this way when making soups and casseroles. The pan must be covered during sweating and the heat kept as low as possible.

swede - see RUTABAGA.

Swedish limpa - see LIMPA BREAD.

Swedish meatballs - a mixture of ground beef, pork and veal, with onions, bread crumbs and beaten egg, formed into balls and sautéed until brown, then served in a gravy made of pan drippings and cream.

sweet - see FIVE BASIC TASTES.

sweet-and-sour mix - a classic mixture of lemon or lime juice and simple syrup (for calorie-counters, some commercial brands now contain **artificial sweeteners**). Since it's a common component of many cocktails, it's a staple behind the bar.

sweet basil - see BASIL.

sweetbreads - most often the thymus (near the throat) or the pancreas (near the stomach) of a young animal, particularly a calf, lamb or pig, served mostly in French or French-style restaurants as *ris de veau*. Thymus sweetbreads are elongated and irregular in shape; while pancreas sweetbreads are larger and rounder. See also VARIETY MEATS.

sweet breads - a generic term for sweet breads, such as **babka,** often served for breakfast or dessert or with coffee or tea. See also COFFEE CAKE.

sweet chocolate - see CHOCOLATE.

sweet cicely - see CICELY.

sweet cider - see CIDER.

sweetened condensed milk - evaporated milk with 40 to 45 percent sweetener in the form of sucrose, dextrose or corn syrup.

sweetie - also **sweet.** A British term for a candy or confection.

sweet leaf - see STEVIA.

sweet marjoram - see MARJORAM.

sweetmeat - a small candy or confection.

sweet orange - see ORANGE.

sweet pepper - also **bell pepper.** Crunchy and with a high water content, these peppers sweeten as they ripen from green to red. They have absolutely no heat whatsoever (0 **Scoville units**), and even their seeds are innocuous. Like all other peppers, sweet peppers contain high levels of vitamin C, and are the only peppers mild enough to consume with an eye toward nutrition. **Green bell peppers** contain chlorophyll as the coloring agent. When the pepper is cooked, it releases acids that react with chlorophyll and cause discoloration. **Red bell peppers** are nutritionally superior to green bell peppers. The level of carotene, an **antioxidant,** is nine times higher in a red bell pepper than in a green one. The red bell pepper also has twice as much vitamin C.

Christopher Columbus brought peppers back to Europe from the Americas. When he tasted the natives' food, which was seasoned with dried pepper powder, the flavor was reminiscent of pepper, which Marco Polo had brought back from the Orient; hence the name for this vegetable. See also CHILE PEPPER, PEPPERCORN, ROASTED RED PEPPER.

sweet potato - the orange-fleshed root of a vine, a member of the morning glory family, Ipomoea batatas, and not a potato at all. Despite a resemblance to the **yam,** the sweet potato is entirely unrelated. Some residue of the sweet potato, 10,000 to 12,000 years old, were found in Peruvian caves and are thought to be the ancestors of wild varieties. The Incas and the Mayas called the plant *cassiri* and grew many varieties, including one used by artists as a coloring agent.

The sweet potato is native to Central America, but may have spread to Polynesia before the arrival of the Europeans. The Spanish brought the sweet potato to the Philippines and the East Indies; the Portuguese took it to India, Asia and Malaysia. When Columbus and his shipmates ate their first boiled sweet potatoes, they compared the taste to that of chestnuts. Attempts to introduce them to Europe were unsuccessful, because the climate was not right for cultivation, and the sweet potato is still almost unknown there. It did not reach European tables from Spain voluntarily. In fact, Spanish gardeners fanatically kept the secret of its growth. Henry VIII, whose first wife, Catherine of Aragon, was Spanish, received the sweet potato as part of her dowry and liked the

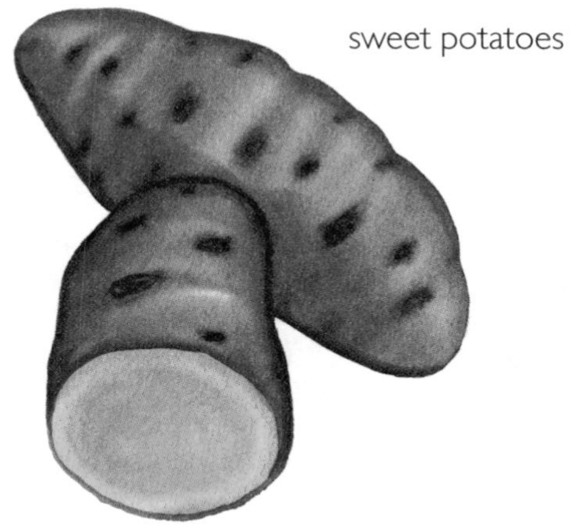
sweet potatoes

flavor so much that he insisted that Spain export them to England, which they did with some lack of enthusiasm. The king venerated them and, renowned for his appetite, was able to eat two dozen per meal. His palate was so committed to what he called "the Spanish potato" that, after his divorce from Catherine, he gave a prize of land and gold to the gardener who could grow them in Britain. The motivation worked, and by the mid-16th century, sweet potatoes bloomed all over the British Isles — but the rage was short-lived, most likely because they need a warmer climate to survive. All the plants withered in a typically wet and cool English summer and never grew there again.

In Asia, sweet potatoes are so commonplace, they're often called Japanese potatoes. Early settlers in America quickly adopted them, serving them as a staple for livestock as well as humans. It's said that sweet potatoes helped the South survive during the Civil War and the Reconstruction.

The sweet potato is remarkable for its 3 to 6 percent sugar content, which increases when it's stored at warm temperatures and during the early stages of the cooking process, because enzymes break down the starch into glucose. The sweet potato provides more calories, minerals and vitamin A, but less protein, than the white potato. The leaves are also edible.

sweet potato pie - a baked single-crust pie filled with puréed, boiled sweet potatoes mixed with eggs, cream or milk, pumpkin pie spice and vanilla. A favorite Southern pie, it may be topped with pecans in a brown-sugar glaze and served with whipped cream. He was singing about a dame, not a dessert, but songwriter James Taylor did name a tune after this dish.

sweet potato pone - a baked dish of the American South made from peeled, boiled, mashed sweet potatoes, with brown sugar, butter or margarine, eggs and vanilla. Some recipes have molasses and spices, such as cinnamon, cloves, nutmeg and **pommerance,** mixed in or brown sugar sprinkled on top before it's put in the oven. It's also popular in the Caribbean, where coconut milk or rum may be added, as well. See also CORN PONE.

Sweet red onion - see ONION.

sweet rice - also **sticky rice.** See RICE.

sweetsop - also **sugar apple.** A bumpy, conical fruit from the shrubby American tropical tree *Annona squamosa*. The skin ranges from greenish-yellow to purple; inside, the segmented flesh is soft and creamy, similar to that of a **custard apple.** It is eaten raw (without the skin) or added to desserts.

sweet tea - a favorite beverage of the American South, sweet tea is iced tea sweetened with sugar. If you ask for "iced tea" in the South, chances are you will receive sweet tea, but in other parts of the country, it will come to the table unsweetened.

sweet woodruff - see WOODRUFF.

swellfish - see PUFFERFISH.

swill - **1.** (n.) a derisive term used to describe a liquid or semisolid foodstuff, suggesting it might properly be considered pigswill. **2.** (v.) to guzzle a drink.

swine - the name given to members of the Suidae family, including pigs, boars and hogs, whose flesh is eaten under the name of "pork," from the Latin *sus*, meaning "sow."

Swiss chard - see CHARD.

Swiss cheese - a pale yellow cheese with slightly nutty flavor and large holes in its flesh, called "eyes." Swiss cheese is a North American and Australian version of a variety of cheeses originating in Switzerland, such as Emmental and Gruyère. Bacteria used in the production of Swiss cheese release carbon dioxide, which slowly form bubbles creating the eyes; in general, the larger the eyes the more intense the flavor. As well, longer aging or higher temperatures give the acting bacteria more time to produce flavor. No one can say for certain, but it is believed the first cheeses with holes began to appear during the Middle Ages.

Swiss fondue - see FONDUE.

Swiss roll - see JELLY ROLL.

Swiss steak - hardly a Swiss specialty at all, and not even an Alpine recipe. This dish of beef baked with tomatoes, onions, peppers and a range of spices may have taken its name from the English term "swissing," a word of unknown origin that refers to the practice of running cloth through a pair of rollers to tenderize it.

Butchers used a similar process for cheaper and tougher cuts of meat, running them through rollers, which created the grid pattern that inspired the name "cube steak."

Swiss water process - see DECAFFEINATION.

swivel cake stand - see TURNTABLE.

swizzle stick - a tall, slender rod used for stirring mixed drinks. In the early 1900s, hand-blown glass rods were used to stir "swizzles" (any drinks made with alcohol), but Jay Sindler is credited with inventing the 20th-century swizzle version as he drank a Martini in a Boston bar. His model, patented in 1934, had a prong on the end to spear a cherry or olive lying at the bottom of a glass. In the 1940s, with the advent of inexpensive plastic-molding technology, almost every bar, resort and restaurant served its own stick with a drink, designed as a take-away souvenir. Everything from embossed lettering and logos, palm trees and pink flamingos topped them, by the 1970s, a collection of brightly colored swizzle sticks stood in almost every home bar. Although their use has dwindled in the wine-bar culture of the last few decades, swizzle sticks are hot collectibles. One American woman has more than 50,000, including a dancing-girl stick from every province in Canada. See also MOLINILLOS.

sycamore - a fruit tree, *Ficus sycomorus*, commonly called Fig-mulberry, native to central Africa and southwest Asia, having clusters of figs on short leafless twigs. The sycamore tree is mentioned in the Bible and some Egyptian mummy caskets are made from it. The Buttonwood tree is called a sycamore in certain parts of the United States.

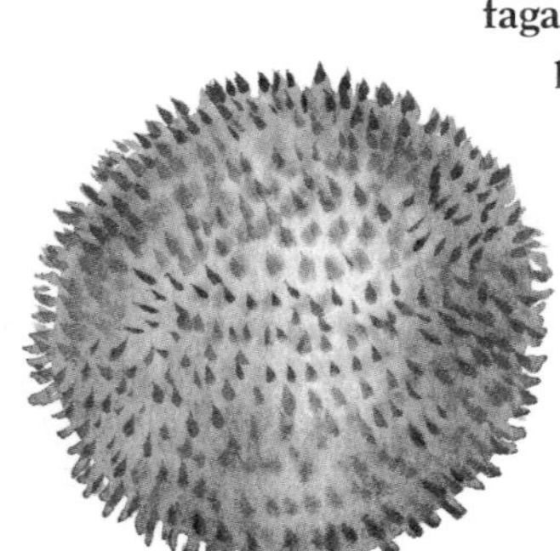

sycamore

syllabub - first mentioned in England in 1537 as a frothy mixture of cream or milk, sometimes eggs, white wine and lemon. In Colonial America, syllabub was a standard drink or dish of milk or cream with wine and other flavorings, sometimes curdled and sometimes "whipt." The simplest variety was "syllabub under the cow," made in a quick trip to the cow barn to draw fine, warm, frothy milk directly into a bowl of wine. Apple cider or other alcoholic beverages can be substituted. Determining whether it was a drink or dish depended on how much cream was used. The greater the amount of cream used, the more likely it was consumed with a spoon. Today, especially in England, syllabub is a mousse-like dessert of cream whipped with flavorings, often fruit, and a liqueur.

syneresis - a term applied to the loss of fluid from some jellies. Syneresis is more likely to occur if the acidity of the jelly is very high. Salt containing gels show increased syneresis. Currant, cranberry and some grape jellies show marked syneresis.

syrup - also **sirup.** A saturated or nearly saturated solution of sugar in water, or any sweet and somewhat viscous fluid; specifically, the final uncrystallizable fluid separated from crystallized sugar during the refining process. The word comes from the Arabic *sharâb*, meaning "drink," the same root from which we derive the word "sherbet," and the Latin *siropus*, meaning "syrup." See also CORN SYRUP, MAPLE SYRUP.

Szechwan pepper - also **Chinese pepper, fagara, flower pepper, sansho, Sichuan pepper.** The aromatic, dried berry of the prickly ash tree, *Zanthoxylum piperitum*, and not actually a peppercorn at all. As it ripens, it splits into a flower shape, hence its common name. Whole, it may be dry-roasted in a skillet to enhance the flavor before it's ground. Most often available as a powdered spice (it's one of the ingredients in **Chinese five-spice powder** and, sometimes, one of the ingredients in the Japanese seven-spice mixture shichimi **togarashi**), it is used in many Hunan and Szechwan dishes (especially in combination with anise and ginger) and in Japanese cuisine. Described as hot, minty and tongue-tingling, it's also used to season Tibetan **momos.**

t
tomatoes

Tabasco - the trademarked name for a hot sauce made from chile peppers, vinegar and salt, formulated on Avery Island off Louisiana's Gulf Coast, where New Orleans banker Edmund McIlhenny fled with his wife, Mary (née Avery), when Union troops entered the city in 1862. They settled on his in-laws' 2,500-acre island, where the Avery family operated America's first salt mine (salt was essential for preserving the meat that fed the Confederate troops). Union forces took over the island in 1863, and the McIlhennys escaped to Texas. When they returned in 1865, they found their plantation ruined and their mansion ransacked. Nothing much remained but a crop of cayenne peppers (*Capsicum frutescens*). McIlhenny crushed the peppers and mixed them with vinegar and salt, aged the mixture for a few days in wooden barrels, drained off the liquid and put the resulting piquant sauce in empty bottles. Encouraged by the response of friends, he produced 350 bottles for Southern merchants and, the next year, sold several thousand at a dollar apiece, starting a business in Cajun Tabasco sauce, which would continue its popularity as a condiment for generations.

Nothing major has changed since Tabasco was first made. Nowadays, the peppers used in the manufacture of this famous hot sauce are the *Capsicum annum* and the *Capsicum frutescens* varieties, originally from the Tabasco region of Mexico. The peppers are harvested by hand, ground to a pulp and packed into oak barrels with salt. The pulp is left to mature for more than three years before being mixed with distilled vinegar. The seeds and skins are removed by machine, and the finished product — a thin, fiery sauce — is bottled. It has a long shelf life and, like Worcestershire sauce, is used in a great number of recipes, as well as in cocktails, such as the Bloody Mary.

tabbouleh - a Middle Eastern salad, made with bulgur, mint, parsley, tomatoes, lemon juice and olive oil.

table d'hôte - French for "table of the host," now refers to a complete meal offered by a restaurant, the price determined by the entrée one chooses. See also À LA CARTE, PRIX FIXE.

table salt - see SALT.

table wine - a term used to describe a non-fortified **still wine** consumed with food. Since table wines are inexpensive enough to regularly drink with meals, they are not, by definition, of premium quality.

taco - in Mexico, a tortilla folded around a filling of meat and/or cheese, translated literally from the Spanish as "billiard cue," but also meaning "plug" and "wad." The Tex-Mex variation is a folded, crisp-fried, filled taco shell. In the U.S., "taco" first appeared in print in 1930. In 1962, Glen Bell started the national Taco Bell chain in Downey, California; Taco Bell is now owned by Yum! Brands.

taco sauce - a spicy, green or red sauce (with unripe green or ripe red tomatoes, respectively, and tomato paste as its base), containing sweet, chile and jalapeño peppers, and seasonings, that is mixed into or spooned over taco fillings. It may be homemade or purchased; bottled versions vary from mild to red hot.

taco seasoning mix - a homemade or ready-made mixture of taco seasonings, such as dried, ground chile pepper, garlic and onion.

tacqueria - see TAQUERIA.

tadka - also **tarka.** A combination of seeds and spices used in Indian cooking, which are fried in **ghee** or oil and added just before serving to enhance the flavor of a cooked dish. The term may also refer to oil cooked with whole spices until highly seasoned. This infused oil may be used in certain dishes as a cooking medium or, more often, drizzled, while still sizzling, over a finished dish.

taffy - an early 19th-century American candy made of boiled molasses, stretched and pulled to incorporate air, which lightens its color and makes it chewy. **Saltwater taffy** became associated with the boardwalk at Atlantic City, where it was sold. It became very popular later that century, sold in small pieces and wrapped in waxed paper. See also TOFFEE.

taffy apple - see CANDY APPLE.

Taggiasche - a type of small, meaty black olive grown in the Liguria region of Italy. Said to have been developed by Bénédictine monks, this gourmet variety is famous for a sweet, almond-like flavor and is used to eat and is also made into oil. See also OLIVE.

tagine - also **tajine.** Refers both to the cooking vessel and the North African stew that has been slow-cooked in it for centuries. The terra-cotta tagine has a round, medium-shallow base and a tall, tight-fitting, conical lid with a hole at its apex that allows some steam to escape, while trapping most of the steam inside to cook its contents and keep them moist. The stews are made of lamb, poultry and/or vegetables; often legumes, such as chickpeas; usually fruits, such as dates, apricots, raisins and olives; and the region's characteristic spices, including cumin, saffron, allspice and nutmeg.

tagine

tagliatelle - classic, long, flat egg noodles from Bologna, Italy, that roughly translates as "small cut-up things" or "little ribbons," from the verb *tagliare*, meaning "to cut." This specialty of the Emilia-Romagna region is said to have its origins in a nobleman's obsessive love for Lucrezia Borgia's hair. Similarly, the Italians are somewhat fanatical about their pasta, passing a law in 1972 that finally resolved a centuries-long disagreement about the correct width of tagliatelle: it must be $\frac{1}{4}$-inch (1 cm) wide.

tahini - a creamy paste made from ground sesame seeds, used extensively in the Middle East for sauces, dressings and appetizer spreads, including **baba ghanoush**, hummus and taratoor.

Tahitian walnut - see CANDLENUT.

tailgate - also **tailgate party, tailgate picnic.** A North American term referring to an outdoor gathering or celebration where food and drinks are served, buffet-style, on the opened tailgate of a pickup truck, station wagon or SUV. The term most often refers to a gathering during a sporting event, such as the Super Bowl, but can also refer to a dinner for field hands harvesting hay or lunch for a family in a public park.

Taillevent (Guillaume Tirel) - see profile below.

tajine - see TAGINE.

tako - the Japanese term for octopus, a popular topping for sushi and a common ingredient in salads and stir-fried dishes, also the base of the famous Kansai-region street food *takoyaki*, which are savory balls of pancake dough surrounding a chunk of octopus, smothered in a tangy-sweet sauce. *Takoyaki* was once considered a regional specialty but is now found in many other parts of Japan.

takuan - a Japanese pickle made of **daikon** radish, salty-sweet and pleasantly crunchy, often colored a bilious shade of yellow with turmeric. The fresh daikon is hung to dry for several days, then fermented with brown rice bran and salt for several months in wooden kegs. Slices of *takuan* are enjoyed with many different Asian dishes and are often served as part of a Japanese **bento box** lunch.

Talleyrand-Périgord, Charles Maurice de - see profile on page 632.

talmouse - a triangular puff pastry, savory or sweet, made with a cheese-flavored **choux** dough, possibly the ancestor of the cheesecake.

tamago somen - see SOMEN.

tamale - a Mexican specialty consisting of food wrapped and cooked in corn husks, banana leaves or avocado leaves, although at one time the ingredients were also wrapped in fabric and soft tree bark. Tamales first appeared about

Taillevent (Guillaume Tirel) (1310–1395) - French royal chef and author of what is considered France's first cookbook of note. While working as a young kitchen helper in French royal kitchens, Tirel was given the nickname "Taillevent," as well as a coat of arms with three stockpots bordered by roses. He became head chef to Charles V in 1373 and to Charles VI in 1381. Conflicting reports claim that each of these kings commissioned *Le Viandier,* Taillevent's 1379 book of recipes. Although the literal translation of *viande* is "meat," the word at the time referred to all solid foods, including bread, fish, poultry or vegetables. Meat itself was referred to as *chair,* meaning "flesh." The importance of Taillevent's book was his record of using bread, rather than flour to thicken sauces and soups, and a liberal use of spices, specifically cinnamon, ginger, cloves and nutmeg.

Talleyrand-Périgord, Charles Maurice de (1754–1838) - French aristocrat, statesman, diplomat, epicure and personal patron of the world's best-known chefs. A senior government official for more than 50 years, Talleyrand, as be became known, is considered a study in political survival. He missed dying by guillotine because he was in Britain and the U.S. during the Reign of Terror, but was appointed foreign minister on his return. He believed that a table set for fine dining was an ideal place for conducting political business. **Antonin Carême** was the best known of the famous chefs Talleyrand kept in his employ. Talleyrand was also a noted wit, with such *bons mots* as: "Speech was given to a man to disguise his thoughts." He was also the subject of barbs himself, the best known coming from Napoleon, who called him "a piece of dung in silk stockings."

5000 BC. They came about as a way to efficiently transport food for the warring Aztecs, Mayans and Incas, and were made in advance and cooked as needed. Tamales are labor-intensive, but can contain whatever ingredient a cook may want to use, often sweet, and can be steamed, roasted, grilled or pan-fried. Tamale has a variety of names: *bollo* in Colombia; *corunda, tamal* and *zacahul* in Mexico, depending on the region; *hallaca* in Venezuela; *humita* in Bolivia and Ecuador; *nacatamal* in Nicaragua; *pache* and *chuchito* in Guatemala; and *tamal* in Cuba, Mexico and Central and South America.

tamale pie - a dish made with **tamale** ingredients, such as beans, corn, olives, onions, tomatoes, ground beef and **nixtamal,** but layered and cooked in a baking dish or deep skillet, instead of wrapped in husks or leaves, as in a regular tamale.

tamari - a dark, thick soy sauce made from soybeans, originally made in Japan. There is a bit of confusion surrounding the name. Originally tamari referred to a soy sauce that contained little or no wheat. In the early 1960s, however, Japanese macrobiotic teacher George Ohsawa adopted the term "tamari" for his own traditional, naturally fermented style soy sauce. Soon after, Mr. Ohsawa's tamari became synonymous with "natural" soy sauce in health food stores in North America, some of which may now contain wheat.

tamarillo - an edible fruit, *Cyphomandra betacea*, from the Solanaceae family, originating in the Peruvian Andes. The tree can reach 7 to 10 feet (2 to 3 m) in height and starts producing fruit only 18 months after sprouting. The fruits are also called **"tree tomatoes"** (but the similarity ends there), and were cultivated in southern Africa under that name until 1967, when some New Zealand producers renamed them "tamarillos" for marketing purposes. They're the shape and size of large eggs, with glossy skin hiding crimson flesh, which turns gold when heated or cooked. Peeling is necessary, since the skin is bitter.

tamarillos

tamarind - also **Indian date.** An acidic fruit that grows in pods on a tropical evergreen, *Tamarindus indica*. Tamarind is best known as a souring agent in curries and a very refreshing bottled beverage sold almost everywhere in the world. One of the most delectable sherbets is made from tamarind, and it imbues cakes and pastries with an unforgettably delicious taste. The tree, which can grow to well over 80 feet (24 m) tall, is one of the world's most beautiful, with red-streaked, yellow flowers. It probably originated in East Africa, but has grown in Sri Lanka and India since prehistoric times.

tamis - also **tammy cloth.** A fine sieve, once made of cloth, now of wire mesh, used for straining stocks, sauces, custards, etc.

tammy cloth - see TAMIS.

tandoor - a tall, cylindrical clay oven, with its opening at the top, able to maintain temperatures of 500° to 900°F (260° to 480°C), fired by charcoal inside at its base. Tandoor cooking is a predominantly Indian technique, which began outdoors with nomadic tribes on the steppes of central Asia, taken to India by Moghul rulers.

The tandoor is used to bake **naan,** an Indian flatbread, by slapping the flattened dough against the sides, and to roast skewered meats or fish, usually marinated in yogurt and characteristic tandoori spices, such as cayenne, paprika, garam masala, cumin and ground coriander. The oven's temperature allows half a chicken to be cooked in five minutes, burning off the fat, crisping the skin and leaving the flesh tender and moist.

tandoori - a culinary term used to describe foods, in particular **naan** and yogurt-marinated chicken and lamb, cooked in a **tandoor.**

tandoori paste - a homemade or ready-made classic Indian mixture used as a marinade or rub that imparts a vivid red color and the flavors of cayenne, chile pepper, coriander, cumin, **garam masala,** ginger, tamarind and turmeric. See also CURRY PASTE.

tang - **1.** a distinctive, sharp scent or taste. **2.** with a capital "T," Tang is a brand-name orange-drink powder made with artificial color and flavor, but with vitamin C added; sales got a boost when U.S. astronauts on the 1965 Gemini flight took silver pouches of the "space-age" drink mix along with them.

tangelo - a yellow-orange citrus fruit, a sharp-tasting cross between a mandarin orange and the grapefruit or pomelo, tapering slightly at the stem end, good both for juicing and eating fresh.

tangelolo - see LAVENDER GEM.

tangerine - see MANDARIN ORANGE.

tangleberry - also **blue huckleberry, dangleberry, hairy dangleberry.** A sweet berry, *Gaylussacia frondosa*, which grows wild in some parts of the U.S. and can be eaten fresh or cooked.

tankard - a tall drinking vessel with a flat or short molded base, a handle and a hinged or removable cover, used for drinking beer in northern Europe since the Middle Ages.

tannia - see MALANGA.

tannin - the astringent substance found in tea leaves, the bark of trees, and the skins, seeds and stems of grapes necessary for the development of fine red wines. Tannin allows red wine to mellow with age and smooth out its character.

tansy - also **barbotine, bitter buttons, stinking willie.** An aromatic and bitter culinary herb, *Tanacetum vulgare*. In Europe during the Middle Ages, its main purpose was to preserve fresh or cooked meat (the medieval embalmer had secret recipes calling for a mixture of herbs, which included tansy). For many centuries, tansy was regarded as a superb flea and ant repellent. In Finland, it's used as a dark green dye for fine woolens. In England, it was traditionally used in puddings, breads and teas during Lent and at Easter. Today, it's more often used as a substitute for pepper, especially in salad dressings. Some say, however, that tansy's best use is as an insect repellant.

tanzenmann - a Swiss drinking vessel made of sculptured wood depicting a peasant (which forms the stem) with a basket (which forms the bowl) on his or her back. The same vessel is called *Buttenmann* in Germany.

tapa - Spanish for "lid," since it originally meant a slice of bread used to cover a glass of wine to protect it from flies, or to let the waiter know that, although you've left the table, you'll be back. Tapas, for which Spain is famous, are a variety of appetizers or snacks that often become a full meal when sufficient quantities are eaten. Common tapas include shellfish in various preparations, sausages and beans, meatballs in a sauce, wedges of *tortilla* (in Spain an omelet), steamed beans with olive oil and chiles, etc.

tangleberries

tap beer - see DRAFT BEER.

tapenade - from the Provençal *tapeno*, meaning "caper," a condiment paste from the south of France for raw vegetables, fish or meat, made with black olives, capers, anchovies and, for purists, a dash of **marc.**

tapioca - a root starch from the **yuca**, also known as the **cassava** in tropical countries, available as a flour or pearls, used as a thickening agent and to make pudding.

tapioca pudding - a creamy baked or simmered pudding made with large or small tapioca pearls (regular or "instant"), cream or milk and eggs. It may be flavored with cinnamon, nutmeg, orange zest or vanilla, or baked with sliced fruit. The bland versions are a staple **comfort food.** See also FISH EYES AND GLUE.

taqueria - also **tacqueria.** A casual eatery that serves Mexican or Tex-Mex foods.

taquito - a corn tortilla filled with a savory meat mixture, vegetables or cheese, then rolled into a cigar-shaped bundle and fried in oil, very popular in Mexico and the Southwest region of the U.S. The name means "little taco."

taramosalata - also **taramasalata.** A classic Greek dish of pink **roe** mixed with bread crumbs soaked in milk (or creamy mashed potatoes, instead), lemon juice, minced onion and olive oil. It may be used as a spread for **hors d'oeuvres** or as a dip.

taratoor - a Middle Eastern **tahini** or sesame sauce.

tarka - a mixture used in Indian cooking containing whole or ground spices (such as cardamom, cumin, mustard seed and cloves) and seasonings (such as minced garlic and dried chile pepper), cooked in **ghee** or oil, then added to a curry, soup or other hot dish a few minutes before it is served. A tarka may also be used to perk up reheated, leftover food. See also TEMPER.

taro - also **cocoyam, dalo, dasheen, eddo, elephant ear.** Grown mostly for its edible root or corm, the taro, *Colocasia esculenta*, is believed to have originated in the Pacific Islands and is now found in many tropical areas of the world. Its enormous leaves, which are shaped like elephant ears, grow to about 3 feet (90 cm) wide and 4 feet (120 cm) long. Taro has a dark brown skin, with creamy, white flesh speckled with purple. Apart from being cooked in the same way as any tuber, taro is also used to thicken gumbo. The stems and leaves should be eaten in moderation. The leaves, in particular, contain oxalic acid, a poisonous component that breaks down and becomes harmless when cooked. In Japan, taro is called *satoima* and in China *wootau*. The Hawaiians make a soup called **poi** that uses taro. See also MALANGA.

tarragon - an aromatic perennial, *Artemisia dracunculus*, with long narrow dark green leaves with an anise-like flavor. Ibn Baithar, the great 13th-century Arabian physician, claimed that tarragon sweetened the breath, was soporific and, if chewed before taking medicine, dulled any unpleasant taste. He called it *tarkhum*, Arabic for "dragon." The French named it *estragon*, meaning "little dragon." The dragon reference most likely is a reference to its roots, which are coiled in such a way that they resemble a serpent poised to strike. The Romans even used it to treat snakebites. In 1548, tarragon was introduced to England and is mentioned in herbalists **John Gerard**'s *Herball*.

tarragon

It is the only commonly used herb to come from the daisy family, the second largest family of flowering plants, and is related to wormwood. Tarragon attained its greatest culinary value and recognition in France, where it became part of the classic **fines herbes** mixture along with chervil, chives and parsley. It's also used in the French sauce **béarnaise.**

tart - **1.** (n.) a sweet or savory filling baked in a shallow pastry shell without a crust or lid on top. During the Middle Ages in France, pastries were called *tartas*. **2.** (adj.) a sour, astringent flavor, from the Old English *teart*, meaning "sharp" or "biting."

tartare steak - see STEAK TARTARE.

tartar sauce - a mayonnaise-based condiment, usually made with capers, pickles and chopped onions, traditionally served with fish.

tarte Tatin - an upside-down apple-caramel tart from 19th-century France, named after the Tatin sisters, Caroline and Stéphanie, who owned the Hotel Tatin in the heart of the Sologne, a wooded area south of the Loire at Orléans. A number of accounts provide some amusing and contradictory stories about how the tart ended up being cooked with its pastry on top, rather than vice versa. One claims that Stéphanie was distracted from her apple-caramel tart, her father's favorite, during one busy hunting season. She was in such a hurry that she'd forgotten her apples caramelizing on the stove and, not wanting to waste them because of her modest means, put the pastry on top and then served the tart warm and upside down. Another account claims she was distracted while flirting with some hunters, and yet another claims that the tart fell, which paints a sorry picture of her culinary practices. However it actually came about, it was so well received that she continued to make it this way, and word spread to the owner of Maxim's in Paris, who sent a spy to learn the technique and get its recipe. Maxim's made tarte Tatin world famous and still serves it today.

tartlet - a savory or sweet, bite-size tart often served as an **hors d'oeuvre.**

tartufo - Italian for "truffle," but also the name for a ball of chocolate ice cream, usually with a raspberry sorbet center, dusted with cocoa; so named because it's thought to resemble a black truffle.

Tasmanian leatherwood honey - see HONEY.

tasso - a Louisiana specialty of boneless pork, usually shoulder, sometimes beef, marinated, richly seasoned, usually with red pepper, **filé** powder and garlic, and heavily smoked. It's used to add powerful flavor to many Cajun recipes, including rice and beans, gumbo and jambalaya, to name only a few.

tastevin - a wine taster's tool, a small, shallow, silver cup about 3 inches (7.5 cm) in diameter, with "dimples" that facilitate the reflection of light through the wine, so that its true color and clarity can be judged.

tasting spoon - a long-handled spoon with a generous bowl, used to taste food while it's cooking, made in various lengths, in a nonabsorbent material that won't taint the taste. Porcelain is considered de rigueur for tasting spoons by French chefs, while white, which lets the color and consistency of the food easily be examined, is the preferred color. Stainless-steel versions are also available.

Tate, Sir Henry - see profile on page 636.

tatties - the colloquial Scottish name for "potatoes."

tautog - territorial fish with lean white flesh, most commonly found off the coasts of Cape Cod to Delaware, although its habitat extends from Nova Scotia to South Carolina. Its name is a Native American word and is always used in the plural, the singular being "taut."

tautog

tavern - from the Latin *taberna*, meaning "a shed," having the same root as *tabula*, meaning "board" or "table." In early England, drinking establishments were owned by vintners, who were allowed to sell only wine, and only men were allowed to enter. In 1636, a law was passed permitting owners to sell ale, beer, food and tobacco.

T-bone steak - see BEEF.

tea - originally from China, tea is said to have been "discovered" by 3rd-century BC emperor Shen Nung, an herbalist considered to be the father of medicine, who consumed hundreds of plants during his lifetime to determine their therapeutic qualities. While pruning his camellias one day, he saw a leaf from a wild bush fall into a nearby pot of boiling water, quickly turning the water brown and releasing a pleasant aroma. The origins of this wild bush are

Tate, Sir Henry (1819–1899) - English businessman, sugar refiner and art collector, who built the National Gallery of British Art in London, which was later named after him. Tate was born in Liverpool, the son of a Unitarian minister who taught poor children. Tate began an apprenticeship in the grocery trade at 13 and bought his first business by the time he was 20. He continued to acquire businesses steadily, eventually focusing solely on refining sugar. In 1876, he bought the patent for making cube sugar from its German inventor, Eugen Langen. Part of his legacy was building the National Gallery to house his vast collection. It would become known as the Tate Gallery and spawned two more galleries, in Liverpool and St. Ives. In 2000, the Tate Modern was the name given to the new home of Tate's collection, which over the century began to be recognized as a foremost modern art gallery. He was knighted in 1898, the year before he died.

described in an Indian legend about a prince called Darma. After a wild youth, the prince embraced asceticism, became a monk and went to China as a Buddhist missionary, swearing never to sleep again as self-punishment for his nights of depravity. For years, his devotion helped him keep his vow, but one day, when he was meditating on the slopes of the Himalayas, the sleep that was so long overdue finally overcame him. On waking, overwhelmed by sorrow for having broken his vow, he cut off his eyelids, buried them and set off again, tears blending with the blood on his face. Years later, passing the spot where he had made his sacrifice, he saw an unfamiliar bush. He picked the leaves and dropped them into hot water, which was his only nourishment. After the first sip, his lassitude was gone, and his spirit, swiftly motivated, reached the greatest heights of knowledge and beauty.

Tea first appeared in print in a Chinese dictionary in the middle of the 4th century. Its cultivation responded to a quickly growing demand and flourished during the next 200 years. It was first traded along the Mongolian border with the Turks, and at the turn of the 9th century, a Buddhist monk took seeds to Japan. Portuguese and Dutch traders were the first to introduce tea from China to Europe in 1560. Tea was shipped to Lisbon, and then to France, Holland and the Baltic countries. The first samples of tea made it to England sometime between 1652 and 1654 and its popularity fast replaced ale as the national drink. Sometime in the 1660s New Amsterdam's Dutch Director General Peter Stuyvesant brought tea to Dutch colonists in America. (New Amsterdam was later renamed New York by the English.) In the 1670s British colonists in Boston were introduced to tea. Oppressive taxes imposed by England made the drink impossibly expensive and led, in December 1773, to the Boston Tea Party, an act of rebellion that sparked the Revolutionary War. In Boston and at many ports of call along the East Coast, colonists dressed as Native Americans boarded trading ships and dumped their cargo of tea overboard. The excessive taxing of tea angered the English as well, and a boycott against the British East India Company's tea led to the smuggling of untaxed tea from the Netherlands.

The tea plant is hardy and can live for hundreds of years. It's cultivated to produce many young shoots and looks uncannily like a suburban hedge. Harvesting, or plucking, stretches over several months, the spring and early summer leaves yielding better tea than those from late summer and autumn. Grades of tea are largely determined by the location of the leaf on the plant and its size. The young, unopened leaf buds at the tip of the shoot rank first in quality, which decreases as the size of the leaf increases toward the lower end of the shoot. There are four principal types of tea: **green, black, white** and **oolong,** which all, surprisingly, come from the same plant. The differences lie in their treatment, processing and fermentation. See also AFTERNOON TEA, ASSAM, BERGAMOT, BUBBLE TEA, CHA, CHAI, CHAMOMILE, EARL GREY, ENGLISH BREAKFAST TEA, FAIR-TRADE, FAT RASCAL, GINSENG, HERBAL TEA, HIBISCUS TEA, HIGH TEA, ICED TEA, IRISH BREAKFAST TEA, KOBUCHA, MASALA CHAI, MATKA CHAI, MEXICAN TEA, ROSE-HIP TEA, SAGE, SASSAFRAS, SWEET TEA, TEH TARIK, TENCHAN TEA, THYME, TISANE, VERVAIN.

TEA VARIETIES

BLACK TEA

Black tea is made by allowing the leaves to wither and undergo fermentation and oxidation before being rolled and dried. The fermentation process renders about half of the tannin insoluble and turns the leaves black. Although the West calls it black tea, the Chinese call it red. China, India, Africa and Sri Lanka are the major producers of black tea.

Assam - a high-quality, all-purpose tea from northeast India, usually drunk unblended, it makes a reddish brew with a full, malty taste.

Bamboo - a strong-tasting, bitter black tea from China, so called because it's encased in dried bamboo leaves. Two rounded sections are cut off and used for an average serving.

Bo Lei - a double-fermented tea from Yunnan that improves with age. It's sometimes used to flavor confections, and it's still possible to find hundred-year-old cakes of Bo Lei in Hong Kong.

Ceylon - an unscented tea with tiny black leaves from the island of Sri Lanka, makes a bright golden infusion.

Ch'I - known as *Men* in China and *Keemun* in the West, usually used for *gongfu,* an elaborate tea ceremony often compared to the Japanese tea ceremony, with a sweet and pleasant aroma, whose leaves are processed into tiny strips.

Darjeeling - from the Indian province of Darjeeling in the foothills of the Himalayas, created in 1847 by Dr. Campbell, a British civil surgeon, who started planting the seeds, smuggled from China, as an experiment in his garden at Beechwood, Darjeeling, 7,000 feet (2100 m) above sea level. Today, connoisseurs of black tea describe it as "the Champagne of tea."

English breakfast - a favorite of tea drinkers worldwide and the tea most often enjoyed during British high tea, originally developed in Edinburgh more than 100 hundred years ago by a Scottish tea master named Drysdale. An aromatic blend of Darjeeling, Assam and Ceylon tea leaves, it soon became popular in London during the reign of Queen Victoria, who had a summer home at Balmoral Castle in Scotland. It was first marketed simply as "Breakfast Tea." Tea shops in London eventually changed the name to "English Breakfast Tea."

Irish breakfast tea - a strong, rich blend of tea, usually Assam and Ceylon, designed to be bracing in the morning. Many people only drink it in the morning due to its strength, but it's considered an all-day beverage in Ireland, usually served with an abundance of milk and sugar.

Lapsang Souchong - undergoes two distinct fermentation processes, then is smoked over burning pine chips.

Luk On - meaning "cloud mist," a very dark, strong tea with a mild flavor.

Pekoe - used to describe a whole-leaf tea. The "orange" often seen with it probably comes from the fact that the leaves used have a golden orange color when plucked, or that in China orange blossoms were sometimes added for flavor. Another suggestion is that it refers to the Dutch House of Orange. It does not have anything to do with the flavor of the tea leaves themselves.

GREEN TEA

Green tea is made by steaming, rolling and drying the leaves in such a way that they retain much of their original green color, especially the finer leaves; it is not fermented as black tea. The older leaves are often blackish gray. Green tea has little aroma and flavor when compared to black tea because of its preliminary steaming, which destroys any organisms that might give rise to volatile flavor substances. Japan, China and Taiwan are the major producers of green tea.

Bancha - a Japanese coarse, cheap grade of green tea. In the beginning of the 19th century, the term "theine," rather than "caffeine" was used to describe the stimulating agent in the tea.

Dragon Well - regarded as the crowning achievement of tea in China, customarily reserved for state dinners, going by the Chinese names of *Lung Ching* or *Loong Tsing.* A legend suggested that the tea is named for a dragon that once lived in a Hangzhou lake.

continued on page 638

Gunpowder - also called **pearl tea** by the Chinese. A grayish tea rolled up into tiny balls that resemble gunpowder pellets, hence the name, with a pungent and smoky flavor.

jasmine tea - green tea scented with jasmine flowers, often made with Chinese **Pouchong** tea but sometimes made with oolong tea as well, a popular drink in Chinese restaurants. Jasmine tea is sold in rolled whole leaf and crushed forms, loose and in tea bags.

Matcha - a Japanese green tea, whose leaves come from various varieties of tea plants blended and finely ground together, traditionally used for tea ceremonies. The best flavor, color and aroma come from leaves picked in early May and lightly steamed to avoid fermentation.

pearl tea - see GUNPOWDER.

Pi Lo Chun - meaning "green snail spring" for the tiny rolled shape of its leaves. It's said to take 80,000 leaves to make one pound (500 g) and was considered the favorite tea at the imperial court of the Ching dynasty.

Pouchong - from Fujian province, with a slightly fermented flavor.

Sencha Makato - the most popular green tea in Japan, with large leaves that provide a delicate flavor.

Shui-Hsien - also called *Soi Sin,* meaning "water spirit," from the Fujian province, with a bitter aftertaste, the favorite breakfast tea for many Chinese people. Other green teas include Young Hyson, Imperial and So Mei.

OOLONG TEA

Oolong tea is made chiefly in Taiwan and is a partially fermented tea. The fermentation period is too short to change the color of the large twisted leaf completely. It's only partially blackened.

Iron Goddess - a dark, coppery tea, usually steeped twice to make it exceptionally strong.

Pu-erh - named after the area in China where it was first harvested in Yunnan province, known in China as "medicinal tea," held in high regard. Initially, the leaves are steamed, then compressed into molds, some of which are intricately carved or embossed. The oldest known Pu-erh tea tree is more than 2,000 years old.

WHITE TEA

White tea is the least processed of all the teas, very lightly fermented, with a faint silvery color to the dried buds and a light, sweet flavor. Some varieties include Silver Needle, White Peony and Noble Beauty.

tea bag - see SULLIVAN, THOMAS.

tea ball - see TEA EGG.

tea biscuit - also **baking powder biscuit.** A small, semisweet tea cake, leavened with baking powder or soda, traditionally served with afternoon tea.

tea cake - a generic term for a usually flat, small, sweet baked good, such as a crumpet or currant scone, traditionally eaten at English teatime, often toasted.

tea egg - also **tea ball, tea infuser. 1.** a perforated metal egg-shaped sphere that is filled with loose tea, placed in a teapot, then removed when the brew achieves the desired strength. One common model has a screw-together bottom and top; the latter is fastened to a short length of chain fitted with a small hook to place over the pot rim. Another has two spoon-shaped sides that snap open and shut, fastened to a looped-wire handle.
2. a hard-boiled egg that has been tea-dyed, a Chinese specialty and street food. The shell of the hard-boiled egg is cracked in a random all-over pattern and then slowly simmered in a

tea eggs

mixture of black tea, spices and salt for about an hour. One or more flavorings such as **Chinese five-spice powder,** soy sauce and star anise may be added. When the egg is cool, the shell is picked away to reveal a crazed- or cracked-porcelain pattern on the egg.

tea infuser - see TEA EGG.

tea sandwich - see FINGER SANDWICH.

tea towel - a cloth for drying dishes. Durable, strong and able to absorb its own weight in moisture, linen makes the best tea towels. More expensive than cotton — its closest competitor in the kitchen — linen is considered much more eco-friendly to produce, as well.

tea tree - see SASSAFRAS.

Teewurst - a sausage made of finely minced pork and beef, sometimes highly spiced.

teff - at about 1⁄32 of an inch (0.8 mm) in diameter, teff, *Eragrostis tef*, is probably the smallest cereal grain on the planet. Native to Ethiopia and domesticated in that country between 4000 and 1000 BC, teff is still a staple in Ethiopian and Eritrean diets. It is usually ground into flour to make the flatbread **injera,** cooked into a nutritious porridge or used as a base for brewing alcoholic beverages.

Teflon - see PLUNKETT, ROY J.

teh tarik - also **pulled tea.** A sweet, traditional Malaysian drink of black tea with creamy evaporated milk and sweetened condensed milk. The drink is rapidly poured back and forth (hence, the "pulled") between two jugs until it's mixed and smooth.

Tellicherry peppercorns - see PEPPERCORNS.

tempeh - an Indonesian specialty made by fermenting cooked soybeans with a rhizopus, a mold. It is very similar to tofu, only firmer and with a nuttier flavor, and can be used the same way.

temper - an Indian cooking term for the technique of cooking whole or ground spices and seasonings in **ghee** or oil to intensify their flavor and fragrance; the cooked mixture is called a **tarka.** Care must be taken not to overcook or burn the spices. They should be heated just until they "bloom" and become fragrant. Some whole seeds split open; to avoid this whole spices are cooked first, with any ground spices added partway through the tempering. See also TARKA, TEMPERING.

temperature - a measurement of the heat or coldness of food, its equipment and environment, primarily to ensure proper

SAFE INTERNAL TEMPERATURES FOR MEAT

Beef, lamb and veal	
Medium-rare	145°F (63°C)
Medium	160°F (70°C)
Well-done	170°F (77°C)
Pork	
Medium	160°F (70°C)
Well-done	170°F (77°C)
Poultry	
Dark	180°F (82°C)
White	170°F (77°C)
Ground meat	
Ground poultry	165°F (74°C)
Ground beef, veal, lamb, pork	160°F (70°C)

SUGAR SYRUP STAGES, TEMPERATURES AND APPLICATIONS

The stages are named for how the syrup reacts between thumb and forefinger when dipped in ice water.

thread	230°F (110°C) for candy, fruit paste.
soft-ball	239°F (115°C) for buttercream, fondant, fudge.
hard-ball	248°F (120°C) for almond paste, Italian meringue.
soft-crack	257°F (125°C) for some caramels, soft nougat, taffy.
hard-crack	295°F (146°C) for candy, glazed fruits, pulled and spun sugar.

sanitation but also to cook in the best way possible. The **danger zone** is between 40°F (4°C) to 140°F (60°C), a range that fosters the growth of bacteria. Above the highest temperature, bacteria can't survive, and below its lowest, it can't reproduce.

tempering - **1.** a process used for melting and then cooling chocolate, usually for coating or filling molds. Tempering stabilizes cocoa butter molecules at specific temperatures and is necessary to make chocolate set properly, have a shiny gloss and creamy texture, and a crisp snap when bitten or broken. There are numerous techniques but the essentially call for the same steps. Chocolate is broken down into small pieces and melted over a **bain-marie** to 115°F (46°C). The chocolate is then cooled to various temperatures, depending on the chocolate: 86° to 89°F (30° to 32°C) for dark chocolate; 87° to 89°F (31° to 32°C) for milk chocolate; 85° to 88°F (29° to 31°C) for white chocolate. There are several methods for cooling chocolate including adding chocolate shavings or a large block of chocolate to the melted chocolate; or pouring two-thirds of the melted chocolate onto a marble slab or table and stirring with a palette knife. Poorly tempered chocolate will develop unattractive gray streaking, known as a **bloom.** **2.** to avoid shocking a cool or tepid ingredient (such as a beaten egg) to be added to a very hot ingredient (such as a pot of hot rice pudding) by stirring a little of the hot ingredient into the cool, then adding the mixture back into the hot.

temple orange - see CITRUS.

tempura - a Japanese word for something battered or deep-fried. *Koromo* is the Japanese for the flour batter used. Pieces of fish, seafood and vegetables cooked in this manner are usually accompanied with *tentsuyu,* a sauce of **mirin, dashi,** sake, soy and ginger. Modern tempura sometimes includes **panko,** white bread flakes, to provide texture and aesthetic appeal, but only deep-fried foods coated with bread crumbs are called *katsu.*

tencha tea - a green tea ground to make **Matcha,** the tea served in Japanese tea ceremonies. For several weeks before the harvest, the tea fields are shaded to protect the leaves from harsh sunlight; in the past, this was done with screens woven of reeds or straw, but cloth is used today. After harvesting and drying, the tea leaves were traditionally milled in stone grinders. To preserve the flavor and freshness, tencha is best ground shortly before use. See also TEA.

tenderloin - see BEEF.

tendon - **1.** a band of strong connective tissue that attaches bone to muscle. **2.** a Japanese dish of rice topped with **tempura**-fried shrimp, or sometimes beef, and a dashi-based sauce.

tepín - also **chiltepín.** See CHILE PEPPER.

tequila - a Mexican spirit made from the Agave plant, *Agave tequilan.* The Aztecs drank great quantities of a wine called **pulque,** made from the heart of the agave plant. The conquistadors taught them to distill their wine, and thus tequila was born.

For 400 years, the traditions and folklore of Mexico have been sprinkled with references to tequila. According to legend, pulque was discovered when lightning struck a field of agave and an aromatic nectar began to drip from the charred hearts of the plant. Revering the agave as sacred, mystical and divine, the Aztecs considered the liquid a gift from the gods and drank it at religious ceremonies.

The agave is a succulent with long, sword-shaped leaves and spiked flowers. Because its habitat is shared with the cactus, it's often mistaken for one. There are nine types and more than 100 species of agave, and, according to archaeologists, the plant has been cultivated for 9,000 years.

Often confused with mezcal, tequila is a form of mezcal in the same way that cognac is a form of brandy. Like the designation protecting cognac, true tequila is produced only from blue agave, which grows in a precisely delineated area in the Guanajuato, Jalisco, Michoacán, Nayarit and Tamaulipas states of Mexico. Tequila is double, sometimes triple, distilled. Mezcal, on the other hand, originated in the state of Oaxaca and is produced throughout Mexico from several different agave species, distilled once, although premium blends may be distilled twice. Harvested younger than those of the blue agave, which take eight to 14 years to mature, the sugar-rich agave hearts, or *piñas,* used to make mezcal are baked in pit ovens. Tequila *piñas* are baked or steamed in aboveground ovens. Tequila takes a decade to manufacture and is distilled and fermented under strict government regulations.

The *Norma Oficial Mexicana* is Mexico's tequila law, enacted in 1949, 76 years after the spirit was first exported to El Paso, Texas. "Tequila" takes its name from the town of Tequila in the state of Jalisco in central Mexico, where tequila production originated and continues to this day. The private, nonprofit Tequila Regulatory Council oversees every aspect of production, from agave cultivation to bottling to labeling. Motivated by cultural pride and to prevent foreign knockoffs, the Denomination of Origin law recognizes tequila and mezcal as distinct products of Mexico, with intellectual property rights.

Tequila Sunrise - a cocktail made with equal amounts of grenadine, orange juice and **tequila.** The latter two ingredients are poured over ice in a **highball glass** and stirred, then the grenadine is drizzled on top, creating the proverbial "rosy-fingered dawn" in an orange sky.

terasi - see SHRIMP PASTE.

teriyaki - a Japanese cooking term denoting a dish of meat, poultry or seafood, marinated in **teriyaki sauce,** then usually broiled, fried or grilled. The sugar in the sauce creates a shiny glaze.

teriyaki sauce - a Japanese sauce or marinade whose primary ingredients include soy sauce, mirin (Japanese sweet cooking wine) and ginger, from *teri*, meaning "glazed," and *yaki*, meaning "seared with heat."

terrapin - a variety of North American fresh or brackish water turtles of the Emydidae family, which includes the genus *Malaclemys*, or diamondback terrapin, distinguished by the diamond pattern on its shell. Now endangered, it is found along the Atlantic and Gulf coasts of the U.S. Terrapin is an Algonquian word, thought to mean "little turtle."

terrine - an ovenproof earthenware dish used for cooking terrines and pâtés. Terrine has come to mean the food cooked in the terrine as well as the vessel itself. Traditionally, it's oblong with a domed lid, although rectangular and round terrines are also available. They can be made of porcelain or cast iron as well as the traditional earthenware.

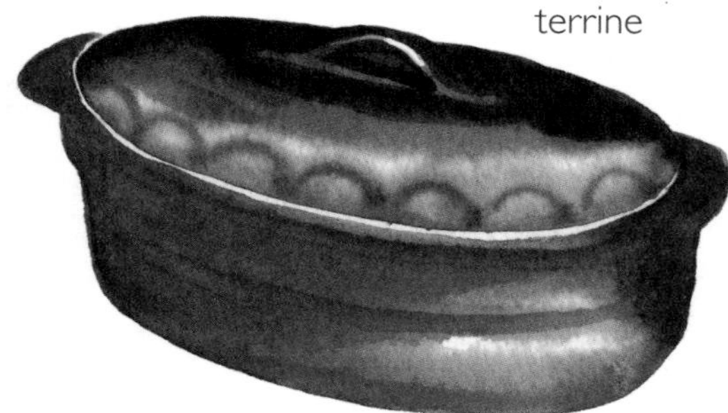
terrine

terroir - a French wine term meaning "soil," referring to the combination of a vineyard's soil type, climate, degree of slope and exposure to the sun, which imparts characteristics to the wines produced from the grapes grown there. In recent years, the term has expanded beyond wine to include all forms of agriculture as well as **artisanal** food production.

testicle - see PRAIRIE OYSTER.

Tête de Moine - a sharp cheese created by Swiss monks at a mountain abbey in the town of Bellelay, which was the cheese's original name. Renamed *Tête de Moine*, French for "monk's head," after the French Revolution, possibly because of a tax levied by the monks on local farmers, limiting their production to only one cheese per monk each year. The name could also come from how the cheese is served with its top horizontal rind removed and then cut using a *girolle*, a special tool with a spindle anchored at the center and a blade rotated by hand, which shaves thin layers of cheese, reminiscent of a monk's tonsured head.

tetilla - Spanish for "nipple," the traditional cheese of Galicia, round and pointed, like its namesake, with a yellow rind and smooth flavor.

Tetrazzini - see CHICKEN TETRAZZINI.

Texas Super Sweet - see ONION.

Texmati rice - see RICE.

Tex-Mex - a style of food combining peasant dishes and flavors from Mexico's north with Texas farm and cowboy fare, coinciding with the arrival of large numbers of Mexican immigrants after 1950. Chili con carne, which some consider to be the state dish of Texas, was unknown in Mexico and derived from the ample use of beef in Texan cooking and how well suited it was to Mexican spices. "Refried beans" is a mistranslation of the Mexican dish *frijoles refritos*, which actually means "fried beans." The combination platter of enchiladas, tacos and burritos became the unvarying standard of the Tex-Mex menu, while new dishes, such as **chimichangas** (supposedly invented in the 1950s at El Charro Café in Tucson, Arizona) and nachos (supposedly first served at a concession stand at the Texas State Fair in Dallas in 1966) were concocted to please the American palate. One Tex-Mex item that may someday rival the pizza as an extraordinarily successful ethnic dish is the fajita, introduced at Ninfa's in Houston on July 13, 1973, as *tacos al carbón*. No one knows when or where it acquired the name "fajita," which means "little belt" or "sash," referring to the skirt steak originally used in the preparation. Only in the last decade has refined, regional Mexican food established a foothold in American cities, reflecting not only the tenets of Tex-Mex cookery, but also the cuisines of Mexico City and its many regions with long-standing culinary traditions. See also CHILI CON CARNE, CHIMICHANGA, FAJITA, NACHO, REFRIED BEANS.

textured vegetable protein - also **TVP.** A processed soy food, TVP is a proprietary name owned by Archer Daniels Midland Co. and is made from defatted soy flour, a by-product of extracting oil from the soybean. The flour is then cooked under pressure, extruded and dried. TVP is sold dehydrated, either ground, to act as a substitute for ground beef, or chunked, to replace chicken. Because it's bland on its own or tastes too much like beans, TVP is often sold flavored. It's also used extensively in commercial baked goods, diet beverages and fast-food products.

Thai basil - see BASIL.

Thai bean - see ASPARAGUS BEAN.

Thai chile - see BIRD'S EYE CHILE, CHILE PEPPER.

Thai coffee - a combination of coffee and sweetened condensed milk served over ice.

Thai eggplant - see EGGPLANT.

Thai ginger - see GALANGAL.

thali - a plate on which a diner serves himself a small amount of each food, offered at a traditional Hindu meal in India. A thali can be made of any material, from precious metals to porcelain, and can even be a fresh banana leaf. An assortment of curries, chutneys, rice, pickles and breads are served at a typical Indian meal. The diner takes a small helping of each and arranges them around the edge of the thali, then combines and eats them using his right hand (the left hand is considered taboo, because it is the hand used for personal hygiene when using the toilet). In Western Indian restaurants, a thali is a set meal that includes small portions of a variety of dishes. Each dish is usually served in a small metal bowl, with all the bowls arranged attractively on a silver platter or plate with a short lip around the edge.

Theophrastus - see profile below.

thermometer - from the Greek term for "heat," a tool used extensively in cooking, mostly to measure temperatures for safety and, in the case of cooked meats, ideal doneness. Industrial freezers, refrigerators and ovens all use thermometers, the latter to ensure that the oven is actually cooking at the temperature indicated by the dial. Ovens often need to be recalibrated, and an oven thermometer will immediately alert the cook if this is the case. To keep food at its best and safest, freezers must be kept as close as possible to 0°F (–18°C), refrigerators at 40°F (4°C). See also TEMPERATURE.

thiamin - see B VITAMINS.

thickening agent - an ingredient added to thicken casseroles, custards, sauces, soups and stews. Fine, starchy powders, such as **arrowroot,** cornstarch, flour, **lotus-seed** powder or ground rice, are often added — usually after they are mixed with water into a paste or **slurry** — at the beginning of cooking. Or, to start a sauce, flour may be sautéed with butter to make a **roux,** then the **jus**, liquid or stock is slowly poured into the pan to cook and thicken. Other thickening agents, such as blood, cream and egg yolk, are added at the end to avoid the

Theophrastus (c. 372 BC–287 BC) - Greek writer, considered the "Father of Botany," he wrote two books, *On the History of Plants* and *On the Causes of Plants*. The observations in his books on the origins of plants and the medical qualities of herbs are remarkably accurate and are still used today by modern botanists. Theophrastus was Aristotle's successor to the leadership of the Peripatetic School (or Lyceum), which he helmed for 34 years. He was born in Lesbos and given the name Tyrtamus but was nicknamed Theophrastus, meaning "divine speaker" by his teacher Aristotle.

TYPES OF THERMOMETERS

candy thermometer - used to measure sugar during its various temperamental and potentially dangerous stages of cooking. If it reads up to 400°F (200°C), a candy thermometer can be used to test oil for deep-frying.

density thermometer - also **hydrometer.** Used to measure salt and sugar in pickling brines and syrups. To calibrate an **instant-read thermometer,** place it in boiling water and set to 212°F (100°C).

digital instant-read thermometer - also **digital meat thermometer.** This thermometer comes in a variety of sizes and models and is the most accurate, and therefore the safest, tool for gauging the internal temperature of cooked meat. There's no need to guess what a dial says, as the readout displays the precise temperature to the degree.

hydrometer - see DENSITY THERMOMETER.

instant-read thermometer - also **probe thermometer.** Used to read the temperature of meat to see if it has reached the desired degree of doneness. It is inserted into the meat at the end of the cooking time.

oven thermometer - reads the temperature inside a oven. It is important to have a well-calibrated oven, because the oven dial itself can sometimes be inaccurate.

probe thermometer - see INSTANT-READ THERMOMETER.

prolonged cooking or overheating that can cause them to curdle. Fresh bread crumbs, **beurre manié** or butter on its own are also used.

thimbleberry - any of several sweet-tart blackberries or raspberries native to North America, especially *Rubus occidentalis* and *R. parviflorus*, that have slightly elongated, thimble-shaped fruit, used mainly for jam and wine.

thin - to dilute mixtures, such as gravy, soup, batter or dip, by adding a liquid.

Thompson seedless grape - a grape named after William Thompson, a Scottish immigrant to the northern Sacramento Valley in California. Thompson is credited with being the first to grow grafted sultana grapes on the continent. In the 1870s, he introduced the variety for which he became famous at a local fair; it is now the bestselling grape in the United States, and one of the most commonly used to make raisins.

Thousand Island dressing - a mayonnaise-based sauce whose other main ingredients include pickles, green olives, green peppers, chili sauce, onions and hard-boiled eggs, first launched at a resort hotel on one of the Thousand Islands, in the St. Lawrence River.

thread stage - see TEMPERATURE.

three-bean salad - equal amounts of canned red kidney beans and blanched or canned green beans and yellow beans, drained and tossed with chopped onion and a simple oil-and-vinegar dressing. An easy make-ahead, this salad is ubiquitous at North American barbecues and potlucks.

three sisters - from the three fates of Greek myth to the three-sister legends told about their own trio of local mountains by Aborigines in Australia and by Native Americans on Canada's west coast, ancient stories about three sisters are a common theme. But, for many Native Americans, the term "three sisters" simply means: corn, pole beans and squash. Believed to be special gifts from the Creator, the sisters need each other to thrive, so were always planted together by Mesoamericans. And science shows that they knew a thing or three: the corn provides the perfect structure for beans twining upward to capture the sunshine, the large leaves of the spreading squash plants shade the earth, conserving moisture, and the roots of the beans add nitrogen back into the soil, enriching it for the next season's crop.

thujone - see ABSINTHE.

thumbprint - a cookie made by rolling dough into a ball for each cookie, placing it on a baking sheet, then pressing down the center with a thumb. A filling, such as cream cheese, icing, jam or peanut butter, is piped or spooned into the thumbprint before or after baking.

Thuringer sausage - any one of several spiced, pork sausages (including some **blood puddings**) named after Thuringia, a state in central Germany.

thyme - an aromatic shrub, *Thymus vulgaris*, with tiny leaves, from the same family as mint. In the south of France, where it's called *farigoule*, thyme is fed to rabbits to enhance the taste of their flesh. Thyme contains the essential oil, *thymol*. It has a long history of extra-culinary uses: its first known one was in medicine and magic. Hippocrates mentioned it, and the Romans stuffed their pillows with thyme, believing that the scent relieved melancholy and induced sleep. It was also brewed into a tea, or **tisane,** and sweetened with honey to soothe coughs. Thyme oil was used as a fumigant, an antiseptic and a remedy for colds, asthma and bronchitis, which were prevalent in ancient Rome. Since the 16th century, thyme oil has been used in mouthwashes. Thyme and its ashes were believed to guard against poisons and the bites and stings of venomous beasts and insects.

The Greeks considered thyme a symbol of vigor. They observed its stimulant properties and the beneficial effect it had on the mental powers of elderly people who regularly drank a tisane of thyme. Dionysius, the 4th-century BC tyrant of Syracuse in Sicily, perked up his palace parties by scattering thyme on the floors, because he believed it to be an aphrodisiac. His guests would crush the leaves underfoot to liberate the supposed love potion.

thyme

Thyme comes from the Greek word *thumon*, meaning to "burn as a sacrifice"; it was used as an incense to perfume the air and repel insects. There are other associations, however, for thyme with the word "courage." During the Middle Ages, a sprig of thyme was given to knights by their ladies to keep up their courage. Scarves embroidered with a bee alighting on a sprig of thyme were believed to produce the same result. Before jousting, knights were required to swear that they carried no magic herb to foil their opponents or their weapons, nor guide their own, but these embroidered likenesses gained huge popularity because, for some reason, they didn't count as betrayals of the oath.

Thyme and fairies are bound together historically in lore: fairies reveled in beds of thyme after putting their babies to sleep in the flowers, with the full assurance that passing bees would lull them to sleep. Thyme is also an important ingredient in the herb bundle **bouquet garni** and in the liqueur **Bénédictine**.

Tia Maria - a coffee-flavored liqueur that is very slightly scented with vanilla, similar but not identical in flavor to **Kahlúa.** The liqueur is made with world-famous Jamaican Blue Mountain Coffee.

tian - the French term for a shallow, rectangular or square ceramic baking dish used for making gratin-style dishes, especially Provençal recipes. It is also the name for the casseroles cooked in it. One classic recipe, potato tian, consists of potato slices layered with chopped herbs and onions, topped with cheese and drizzled with olive oil, then baked.

tidbit - any small sweet or savory bit of food, such as an hors d'oeuvre, known as "titbit" in England, from the Old English *tid*, meaning "small."

tiffin - an English word used in India and other British colonies in Asia to mean lunch, often prepared at home and delivered to the workplace on bicycle by couriers known as tiffin boys, using tiffin boxes, or shallow stacking containers held together and made easy to transport by a metal frame.

tiger lily bud - see LILY BUD.

tiger muskellunge - a short, sturdy and sterile cross of **muskellunge** and **northern pike.**

tigernut - see CHUFA.

tiger shrimp - also **tiger prawn.** A name given to *Penaeus esculentes*, *P. monodon* and *P. semisculatus*, all warm-water shrimp indigenous to the South Pacific, but now also aquafarmed. See also SHRIMP.

tikka - an Indian dish of small chunks of chicken marinated in spiced yogurt, then skewered and grilled or cooked in a **tandoor.** See also CURRY PASTE.

tilapia - also **Hawaiian sun fish, St. Peter's fish.** A relatively small fish native to Africa and the Middle East. Its abundance in Israel's freshwater Sea of Galilee earned it the name "St. Peter's fish," and it has been cultivated there for more than two centuries. These days, tilapia, from the *Oreochromis* family of fish, are extensively aquafarmed in both fresh and salt water around the world. Producers appreciate tilapia's disease resistance, speedy growth and hardiness; diners savor the firm, flaky, white flesh, which is low in fat and delicious broiled, grilled, sautéed or steamed.

ti leaf - the fibrous leaf of the Hawaiian ti shrub, from the Cordyline family, a sacred plant, similar to a small palm, which is believed to ward off evil and ensure good fortune. According to legend, before crossing a river a traveler should throw a ti leaf onto the water: if it floats, it is safe to proceed (it's said that some modern travelers still pack one in their luggage). Fresh, tender young leaves are eaten; mature leaves, which grow to about 6 inches (15 cm) wide and 29 inches (73 cm) long, are used to make roll-ups. With their central ribs pulled out, they are wrapped around portions of chicken, fish or pork, which are then cooked on hot coals (the leaf itself is discarded later). Sold dried, large ti leaves must be soaked in water to restore their pliability. See also TI ROOT.

Tilsit - a firm but springy, yellow Danish cheese shot through with small, irregular holes and covered in an orangey-brown rind. The mild flavor becomes more pungent with age. Tilsit is used in fondues, sauces and vegetable dishes, but unadorned, it's said to be best enjoyed with Danish ale. Tilsit was the name of an East Prussian town, where this cheese was first created; the town's other claim to fame was a pair of treaties known as the Treaties of Tilsit, by which Napoleon safeguarded his battlefield gains. After the Second World War, Tilsit was transferred to the U.S.S.R. and renamed Sovetsk.

timbale - French for "kettledrum," a dish baked in a mold, served turned out and upside down, maintaining the mold's shape. A timbale iron is a tool that is dipped in batter and then into hot oil to produce a pastry-like shell for either sweet or savory fillings. *Dresser en timbale*, in culinary parlance, means to heap the food on a plate or on a platter in a pyramid shape.

tin foil - see ALUMINUM FOIL.

tipple - **1.** (n.) a drink, usually alcoholic. **2.** (v.) to imbibe a large amount of intoxicating liquor by means of many small sips.

TIPS - an acronym for the gratuity given "To Insure Prompt Service." Since tips are customarily given after the fact as a reward for prompt service (such as to waiters and waitresses), "tips" is something of a misnomer.

tipsy parson - also **tipsy squire.** See TRIFLE.

tiramisù - also **tiramisu.** A rich dessert of ladyfingers drenched in espresso and Marsala or brandy, whipped mascarpone cheese and cocoa, whose name means "pick-me-up." Tiramisù is said to have originated in a restaurant called Le Beccherie, in Treviso on Italy's northern Adriatic coast, near Venice. Stories are told about Venice's courtesans, who worked in the brothel above the restaurant. According to legend, the ladies needed a "pick-me-up" to fortify themselves between amorous encounters, and tiramisù fitted the bill perfectly.

Tirel, Guillaume - see TAILLEVENT.

ti root - the edible, sweet tuberous root of the ti plant, traditionally baked and eaten throughout Polynesia, often in special communal cooking pits. See also TI LEAF.

tiropita - also **tiropitakia.** A small triangular phyllo pastry from Greece stuffed with cheese, such as feta, and baked. The name translates as "cheese pie" or "cheese pastry."

tirphal - an Indian spice used in some masala mixes, harvested from the tirphal tree, *Zanthoxylum rhetsa*, which grows in the western part of the country. After the berries are picked, they are dried in the sun and split apart; the seeds are discarded. The remaining husks, which resemble peppercorns, are bloomed to release a woody aroma and sharp flavor by dry roasting before they are used, whole, in cooking. Commonly added to legume-based dishes, tirphal is said to prevent flatulence.

tisane - a tea made with various herbs and botanicals, such as thyme, mint and chamomile, chosen for their calming or restorative effects, from the Latin *ptisana,* meaning "barley water," this being the tisane of choice during the time of Hippocrates. See also TEA.

tiswin - also **tizwin.** A fermented corn liquor, made by Apache indians, whose native name, *tulipai,* means "yellow water." Tiswin is made by soaking dried corn overnight, laying it out to sprout, drying it in the sun, grinding it into a meal, adding it to boiling water and cooking it until the liquid has evaporated by half, then refilling the pot, letting it stand, straining and leaving it to ferment. The liquid often had fruit and wheat added, as well as jimson weed (of the genus *Datura,* a toxic perennial also used in native divination, shamanism and folk medicine). Tiswin was outlawed in 1885, about the time Apaches were forced onto reservations, but the prohibition was difficult to enforce.

toad in the hole - **1.** a classic British pudding of cooked pork sausages under a puffy coverlet of crisp, golden batter. The sausages are cooked in the pan first, then, while the sausages and the fat released into the pan are still piping hot, the batter is poured over the top and the dish is put into the oven to bake. It is usually eaten hot, perhaps with gravy, mashed potatoes and onions or with butter and jam. **2.** a North American breakfast treat, consisting of a slice of bread with a hole cut in the center; lightly buttered on both sides, it is laid in a hot skillet, then an egg is broken into the center. The whole is cooked, then flipped to fry both sides, so that the egg is cooked and the bread is golden brown. Since the term "toad-in-the-hole," was already taken in Britain, this breakfast dish is called "hole-in-one." In North America, it goes by various other names: "egg in a basket," "one-eye Jack egg" and "ox-eye fried egg" (a reference to the yellow-centered oxeye daisy).

toast - **1.** (v.) the act of raising a glass within a group to honor a person and extend well wishes on special occasions. The tradition of toasting began in Greece before the 6th century BC. To assure guests that their wine was safe to drink, the host would raise his glass in a pledge of friendship and take the first sip. The Romans added a piece of toasted bread to the wine to reduce its acidity. **2.** (v.) to cook directly over or under a heat source, such as an electric broiler element or an open flame, until dry, crisp and colored anywhere from light golden to dark brown. **3.** (n.) a slice of bread that is toasted on both sides.

toaster oven - a countertop electrical appliance with a rack or pan inside for broiling foods under an electric element. It has a door that can be closed to seal in the heat, so it can also be used to bake very small items, unlike a traditional slotted toaster.

toast points - thin slices of bread with the crusts removed, then cut diagonally into quarters to make four triangles and toasted in the oven. For a humble snack, toast points may be topped with scrambled eggs; at upscale affairs, toast-point **hors d'oeuvres** may carry fancier fare, such as grilled **Brie** or scoops of caviar, lobster mousse or shrimp salad.

toban djan - see CHILE BEAN PASTE.

toddy - **1.** the sap of various tropical Asian palms and the name of the fermented beverage made from them. **2.** a hot drink made with spirits, sugar, hot water and lemon, usually in northern latitudes, probably derived from the Hindi *tari,* meaning "palm sap."

toddy palm - also **palmyra.** Indigenous tree from the Persian Gulf to Vietnam, now cultivated in such tropical places as Florida, Hawaii and Malaysia. Growing to about 100 feet (30 m) tall, *Borassus flabellifer* sprouts leathery leaves and sets smooth, brown coconut-like fruits; one tree may produce as many as 350 fruits. Immature fruits are pickled (leftovers are fed to livestock); the jelly-like kernels are canned in sweet syrup, sliced or whole, or used to make sweet cakes. Larger fruits are roasted or the juice is combined with rice to make sweet custard. The sap from the flower is called "sweet toddy" (used to make candies and **jaggery**); left to ferment naturally, then distilled, it is used to produce **arak,** palm wine or **toddy.** The starchy

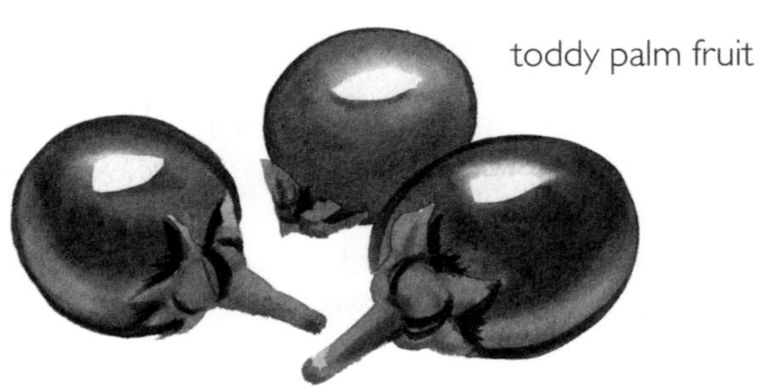
toddy palm fruit

flesh of the seedlings is eaten fresh, dried or made into **mush.** Even the roots may be roasted, skinned and eaten.

toffee - also **toffy.** An early 19th-century British confection similar to taffy but made with **treacle,** toffee is made both soft and hard, and often made with nuts. What we call **English toffee** in North America is the hard, crunchy variety, often made with a smattering of chopped nuts.

toffee apple - see CANDY APPLE.

tofu - also **bean curd, soybean curd.** A curd pressed into cakes, made from the milky liquid extracted from soybeans, its name derived from the Chinese *doufu,* meaning "curdle bean," introduced to Japan in 1212 from China, where it had been eaten for more than 2,000 years. Tofu is extremely versatile, available in firm or soft forms, eaten hot or cold, as an entrée or dessert, and even as a drink. Because it's neutral in flavor, tofu is sometimes called the "chameleon food" because it absorbs the flavors of its accompanying ingredients.

The celebrated Chinese poet Su Dong Po (1037–1101) wrote, "Tofu may be compared to milk, its skin to butter." The skin refers to the boiled soybean top layer, because when bean drink is boiled, a layer is formed on the top like skin. Modern Chinese physicians agree that the Chinese poet had a good point, because tofu is comparable to milk and its skin to butter. A Chinese book written in 1641 said, "Whenever you go to a new place and cannot get used to the foods the local people eat, you should eat tofu, which will give you time to adjust yourself to the new foods." Another Chinese herbal classic dating from 1590 said, "Tofu can eliminate toxic heat from the body and promote blood circulation." When a group of Chinese students went to study in France at the beginning of the 20th century, they brought with them a few expert tofu makers to manufacture tofu in France, which became the first European country to be introduced to it. The Chinese have a saying that tofu is everyone's favorite food, whether young or old, rich or poor, good or bad.

tofurkey - a vegan or vegetarian turkey substitute made of mashed or puréed tofu and various seasonings, often molded into the shape of a whole turkey or a boneless turkey breast for a meatless Thanksgiving main dish that can be sliced just like the real bird. Tofurkey can be stuffed with a vegetarian-friendly stuffing and served with gravy (no meat drippings in sight, of course).

togarashi - a Japanese tableside seasoning based on ground, dried red hot peppers. *Ichimi togarashi*, or simply *ichimi* (which means

TOFU TYPES

fermented tofu - a powerful smelling and tasting tofu, fermented and sun-dried, then marinated in a brine with spices and alcohol. Its assertive, cheesy flavor is an acquired taste.

firm tofu - known in Japanese as *momen-dofu,* which means "cotton tofu," or in Chinese as simply *doufu,* this is the regular tofu seen in grocery stores across North America. It is sturdy and can be cut into cubes and added to stir-fries, soups and so on, as well as grilled or fried on its own. It comes in a variety of firmnesses, from medium to extra-firm, which can be quite chewy.

freeze-dried tofu - known as *koya-dofu* in Japanese, porous and spongy in texture with more-concentrated flavor than firm or silken tofu. Freeze-drying makes this type of tofu very absorbent, so it is excellent for soaking up the liquids in which it is steeped. It comes in dry blocks and must be reconstituted in warm water.

pressed tofu - tofu pressed until the majority of its liquid is extracted to make a solid, close-textured, smooth block. Pressed tofu is usually found in Asian grocery stores; it is often marinated in soy sauce and seasoned with Chinese five-spice powder, so that it's brown on the outside with a pale, creamy interior.

silken tofu - a soft, delicate-textured tofu best used for blending in smooth sauces, soups or dips. Silken tofu is excellent in smoothies, desserts and sweet recipes, as well.

Toklas, Alice Babette (1877–1967) - confidante, cook and lover of Gertrude Stein and author of *The Alice B. Toklas Cookbook* (1954), born in San Francisco. In 1907, after moving to Paris, Toklas met Stein and became her companion for the next 39 years until Stein's death in 1946. In 1910, they moved together into what would become their famous home at 27, rue de Fleurus, where Toklas, who loved to cook, would entertain such friends as Ernest Hemingway, Pablo Picasso and Henri Matisse. After the death of Stein, Toklas wrote *The Alice B. Toklas Cookbook,* which included such chapters as Foods in French Homes, Dishes for Artists, Murder in the Kitchen and Recipes from Friends, which contained the infamous recipe for **haschich fudge.** She was not, however, the hashish queen history has made her out to be. One of the friends who contributed recipes to the chapter was the artist Brion Gysin, also a friend of Paul and Jane Bowles, and a visitor to Morocco. Haschich fudge is his contribution as was the introduction, which mentions that the recipe would be perfect for a ladies' bridge club or how in Morocco it was good for warding off the common cold. Clearly, Toklas didn't test the recipe and the odd spelling of cannabis as "canibus" in the ingredients threw her off and she innocently included the recipe in the book. In *Staying on Alone: Letters of Alice B. Toklas,* edited by Edward Burns, she wrote to a friend how shocked she was by a review in *Time* that commented on the recipe. "I was also furious until I discovered it was really in the cookbook!" Friend Thornton Wilder said no one would believe in her innocence and that she had pulled off the best publicity stunt of the year. Although the recipe did appear in the British publication of the book, it was edited out of the first American edition. Toklas also published a second cookbook *Aromas and Flavors of the Past and Present* in 1958. Toklas died in 1967 and is buried beside Stein in Le Pére Lachaise Cemetery in Paris.

"one flavor"), is only the peppers, but *shichimi togarashi*, or simply *shichimi* (which means "seven flavors"), is a mixture of seven ground spices, including Szechwan peppers, **sansho, nori,** sesame seeds, poppy seeds, dried orange peel and hemp seeds. **Nanami togarashi** is another name for *shichimi* (*nana* is an alternate way to say "seven" in Japanese).

Tokay - also **Tokaj.** Famous Hungarian white wine, enjoyed as an apéritif or dessert wine. Considered the best, Aszú Tokay is made from late-harvested grapes and is available in several levels of sweetness. All Tokay is made from locally grown grapes in the Tokaj region east of Budapest and aged in miles of centuries-old cellars carved into the rock. The Hungarian Wine Society claims Goethe, Louis XIV, Rossini, Schubert and Voltaire were among the greatest fans of this wine, which is said to serve up healthful properties as well as good taste. The story has it that Russian troops in Hungary at the end of the Second World War discovered a stash of Tokay from the 1600s, still drinkable, still delicious.

tokkuri - the Japanese name for the ceramic flask or bottle used to warm and serve sake.

Toklas, Alice Babette - see profile above.

Toll House cookie - a quintessential American cookie, created in 1939 by **Ruth Graves Wakefield** at her Toll House Inn near Whitman, Massachusetts. Substituting semisweet chocolate for baker's chocolate, of which she had run out that day, she discovered that small pieces of semisweet chocolate in a cookie dough stayed hard when baked, rather than melting, as the baker's chocolate did.

tomalley - the green-colored liver in the center of a cooked lobster, considered a delicacy by many shellfish lovers.

Tom and Jerry - a classic New Year's drink that is more of a nog than a cocktail. A "batter" (consisting of beaten egg yolk folded into an egg white beaten into stiff peaks) is put into a preheated mug, then ground allspice, cinnamon, cloves and sugar are added, followed by an ounce each of brandy and rum, and hot milk or boiling water to fill it up. After a sprinkling of ground nutmeg, the warmth of this holiday spirit is consumed. Jerry Thomas, a San Francisco bartender and author of the 1862 book, *Jerry Thomas' Bar-Tender's Guide*, is credited with the creation of the Tom and Jerry, which he publicized on a book tour throughout the U.S. and Europe.

tomatillo - also **husk tomato, jamberry.** A Mexican perennial, *Physalis ixocarpa*, originally cultivated by the Aztecs, the tomatillo looks like a green tomato wrapped in a parchment husk; it's related to the **cape gooseberry,** which is also encased in a husk. It belongs to the nightshade, or Solanaceae, family, along with the tomato, eggplant, pepper, huckleberry and potato. It's technically a berry, firmer than the tomato, about 1 inch (2.5 cm) in diameter, usually harvested when still green and tart; it turns purple or yellowish when fully ripe. The tomatillo is the most trouble-free summer crop to grow in the Northern Hemisphere; it has never suffered any of the diseases that have affected the other solanaceous vegetables, nor do insect pests bother it. It grows in every U.S. state, except Alaska. The husk must be kept on until it's ready to be eaten.

tomatillo

tomato - the fruit of a vine from the nightshade family, native to South America, originally found growing wild in the Andes. According to food historians, its Latin name, *Lycopersicon esculentum*, which means "succulent wolf peach," reflects that the tomato was thought to be as inviting as a peach but dangerous, because it was thought to be poisonous. In fact, all parts of the plant, except the fruit, are toxic. By the 16th century, when the Spanish invaded, tomatoes were widely cultivated throughout Mexico and Central and South America. Hernán Ferdinand Cortés, conqueror of the Aztecs, sent the first tomato plant, a yellow variety, to Spain, where it took some time to be accepted. People did not take instinctively to this "golden apple," which is the Latin root of *pomodoro*, Italian for "tomato." In 1596, the tomato was introduced to England, and a year later, English botanist **John Gerard** found tomato plants to be "of a ranke and stinking savour," but admired the fruit for its ornamental possibilities, which helped make the tomato a popular garden adornment. It was also known in England, as well as France, as the **"love apple,"** often given in a romantic gesture.

Spain was the first European country to use tomatoes in cooking, and Italy followed suit, but elsewhere, tomatoes were still treated with suspicion. The first red tomatoes arrived in Europe in the 18th century; a Moor carried tomato seeds from Spain to Morocco, where they became popular and grew abundantly. In his 1778 book *Il Cuoco Galant* (The Gallant Cook), Vincenzo Corrado provides a recipe for a tomato sauce, (not necessarily for dressing pasta, which came later) and also suggests a method for peeling them. Americans also resisted the tomato, but a failed act of treason came to be its salvation as a safe vegetable to eat. As the legend goes, some rivals had penetrated the White House and encouraged the cook to make President Abraham Lincoln

TOMATO VARIETIES

beefsteak - the largest, up to 6 inches (15 cm) in diameter.

cherry - small, prolific, bred to be sweet, a little larger than their namesake.

currant - mini cherry tomatoes.

grape - mini plum tomatoes.

heirloom - colorful, flavorful varieties that have been open-pollinated (within its own variety rather than bred industrially outside its variety). Available in a variety of colors, shapes and sizes.

paste - varieties with maximum flesh (no seed cavity), best suited to making paste or sun-drying.

plum - also **Roma.** Thick-fleshed and hold their shape when canned.

Roma - see PLUM.

some dishes with tomato; rather than die poisoned, as his enemies intended, the President became an enthusiastic fan, and word of the failed plot and the tomato's soundness spread. Today, tomatoes are the third largest crop cultivated for human consumption in the U.S.

tomato juice - a thin juice from cooked, seeded and skinned tomatoes, usually chilled and sipped **straight up** or used as a mix in cocktails, such as the **Bloody Mary.**

tomato paste - a concentrated paste of cooked, strained tomatoes, used to add color and flavor and thicken sauces, soups and stews. A staple in many kitchens, it is available canned or in airtight squeezable tubes, but most Mediterranean home cooks, as a matter of course, make their own. The paste is deeper in color and denser than both tomato purée or tomato sauce.

tomato purée - cooked, strained tomatoes used to add color and flavor to sauces, soups and stews. Available canned or in airtight squeezable tubes, tomato purée is thinner than tomato paste, but thicker than tomato sauce or juice.

tomato sauce - cooked, strained tomatoes, usually seasoned with garlic, herbs, onions and spices, used in many pasta dishes and stews.

Tom Collins - **1.** a classic cocktail made with gin, lemon juice, superfine sugar and club soda, all poured over lots of ice in a **highball glass,** usually served with a slice of orange skewered together with a maraschino cherry. Various theories account for the name; some believe it dates back to a sweet gin called Old Tom, while others credit this or that barman on this or that side of the Atlantic. The Russian Tom Collins (made with vodka), the Joan Collins (made with brandy) and the John Collins (made with whiskey) are just some of Tom's progeny. Homemade or commercially prepared Tom Collins mixes are also available: just add the ice and spirits. **2.** a tall, slim highball glass, often frosted, named after the drink.

tomme cheese - a generic term used for rind-covered rounds of fresh cheese produced from the skimmed milk of cows, ewes or goats (or a combination of two or more). Creamy and mild, it usually has a fat content of less than 45 percent. Made by small producers scattered throughout the French Alps, tomme cheeses, such as Tomme de Savoie, are usually named after their village or place of origin.

Tomme de Beaumont - see BEAUMONT CHEESE.

tongs - a gripping device used to hold or transfer objects, such as meat (to a plate) or spaghetti (from the water), consisting of two large arms joined together at one end with a spring-action device and with flat, circular grippers at the other, most often available in stainless steel, but also available in nylon and plastic. Some tongs consist of one band of metal that has been bent to form two bands. As well as an all-purpose tong, there are a variety of other tongs available, such as sugar tongs, asparagus tongs, barbecue tongs (with longer arms) and pot-lifting tongs. See also ESCARGOT, MEAT BALLER, PASTRY CRIMPER, POT-LIFTING TONGS, SNAIL TONGS, STRAWBERRY HULLER.

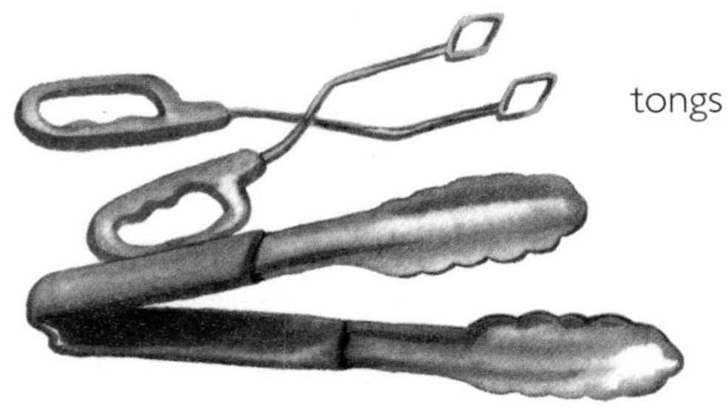
tongs

tongue - a **variety meat,** sold fresh, smoked or corned for cooking, eaten hot or cold, with or without sauce. The tongues of beef and veal are the most common, and lamb is the most tender.

tonic water - also **quinine water, tonic.** A carbonated beverage containing lemon and lime juices and **quinine** that is usually used as a mixer in cocktails. The most famous of these is gin and tonic, routinely drunk by late-19th-century British colonists in West Africa, a part of the world then called the "white man's grave." The quinine, commonly prescribed as both a preventative and a treatment for malaria, made this drink both thirst quenching and therapeutic.

tonka bean - the beautifully fragrant fruit of the tree, *Dipteryx odorata*, found principally in Guyana but also cultivated in Venezuela's Orinoco region and in Nigeria. It contains a substance called coumarin, sometimes used as a substitute for vanilla, but banned by the FDA since the 1940s as a known carcinogen. The bean is a sweet spice, not widely used, although considered well suited in recipes using coconut, walnuts or poppy seeds. Tonka beans are also used as substitutes for bitter almonds and to flavor tobacco.

tonkatsu - Japanese term for breaded fried pork. See also DONBURI, KATSU.

tonnato sauce - a traditional Italian mixture of anchovies, egg yolk, lemon juice, olive oil and tuna, usually seasoned simply with capers, black pepper and salt and puréed together into a creamy sauce. It's famous in the dish *vitello tonnato*, made of sliced cooked veal, served cold with the sauce.

toor dal - also **tur dal.** See DAL.

top loin - see BEEF.

Toronto pie - a sponge cake, sliced into two layers, filled with raspberry jam and dusted with confectioner's sugar that is a close relative of the **Victorian sandwich.** This version made its appearance in *The Home Cook Book*, a collection of recipes sent in by Canadian home cooks, published in 1887 to raise money for The Hospital for Sick Children in Toronto. Said to be the first fund-raising cookbook produced in Canada, it became the bestselling Canadian cookbook of the 19th century and was reprinted dozens of times, even in an Australian edition (it was printed again in 2002 in Canada, under its original title).

torrefaction - from the Latin *torrere*, meaning "to roast" and *facere*, "to make," the act of drying, roasting, scorching or parching by a fire or extreme heat, most often applied to coffee roasting and barrel making.

torreja - a puffy Mexican fritter served with salsa and topped with minced cilantro and green onions, or a type of French toast served with a sugar syrup infused with cinnamon and lemon peel. Other Latin American and Caribbean countries have their own particular variations on the theme, both sweet and savory.

torrone - a nougat eaten in both Italy and Spain (known there as *turrón)*, especially at Christmas, studded with almonds or hazelnuts and sometimes flavored with chocolate.

torta - **1.** the Spanish word for "cake." **2.** a popular fast food in Mexico, a grilled sandwich filled with any number of different fillings. A typical example is a layered sandwich of spicy, crumbled cooked **chorizo** sausage, sliced ham, cheese, grilled hot or sweet peppers, lettuce, tomatoes and salsa. The torta craze has recently hit larger American cities, not just in the U.S. Southwest and California, where there are large numbers of Mexican-Americans, but also cities such as New York, where the torta is considered a gourmet alternative to the usual fast-food sandwich. **3.** the Italian word for "cake," "pie" or tart."

torta dei Fieschi - a sponge cake with pastry cream and hazelnuts, a specialty of Genoa, first made in 1230 for the marriage of aristocrats Count Opizzo Fieschi and Bianca de' Bianchi. Italian bakers still make the cake on the anniversary of the wedding, and there is a love-match game played when it's served. Guests who want a slice are given a card with someone's name on it. When they've found their "mate," the two share the slice of cake together.

torta pasqualina - a centuries-old Easter specialty from Liguria, Italy, made from 33 layers of pastry, representing the 33 years that Christ lived, filled with ricotta cheese, eggs, Swiss chard, artichokes and other vegetables. Modern versions are usually made with 12 to 18 layers.

torte - German for "fancy cake." A dense cake made with lots of eggs, but little flour (bread crumbs and ground nuts are added instead), often layered with rich fillings, such as buttercream, chocolate mousse, ground nuts, jam, preserves, whipped cream and maybe a dash of brandy or liqueur. Classic examples are **Linzertorte** and **Sachertorte.**

tortellini - see PASTA.

tortilla - in Mexico, a thin, round, unleavened bread made from ground maize; in Spain, a thin, flat omelet. In southwestern Spain, a *torta* is a kind of thin pasta baked in an oven until crisp, then broken into pieces and added to soup. It's not known how many millennia the flatbread has been a staple, but it was certainly well established when the conquistadors arrived, in the late 15th century. The native Nahuatl name for tortillas was *tlaxcalli*, but the Spanish called them *tortillas*. Fresh tortillas are eaten as bread, used as a plate and spoon, or filled to make composite dishes, such as quesadillas, tacos and enchiladas.

tortoise - a generic name given to slow-moving land turtles with high, domed shells; they are almost exclusively herbivores and only occasionally consumed by humans. See also TURTLE.

tortoni - a frozen Italian dessert of rich ice cream (made from heavy cream) mixed with crumbled macaroons, finely chopped almonds and maraschino cherries, and liqueur, rum or sherry. Tortoni was an Italian immigrant who ran a popular Parisian eatery and ice cream parlor (also his namesake) throughout the 1800s, attracting a who's who of French society. Like other Neapolitans of the era, Tortoni is credited with the creation of many frosty desserts.

toscana - a large variety of Italian sausage from Tuscany, most often made with pure pork mixed with pieces of lean meat and fat.

toss - to combine ingredients by scooping under them with a utensil and lightly flicking them together until they are well mixed. Salads are usually tossed together in order to mix them with their dressings, and small chunks of meat, such as kebabs, are often tossed with a marinade to thoroughly coat them.

tostada - **1.** a Mexican tortilla, usually crisply fried and topped with meat and vegetables. **2.** a crusty bread or toasted roll eaten for breakfast in Spain, topped with marmalade or jam.

toucinho - cured pork belly, Portuguese bacon with a smoky flavor that can be sweet or hot. Used in the traditional Portuguese dish *Cozido à Portuguesa,* which is made with several smoked and fresh meats, boiled potatoes, carrots and a kale-like cabbage, known as *galician. Toucinho do Céu,* a Portuguese dessert, translates as "bacon from heaven," although it has nothing to do with bacon and is made with egg yolks and finely ground almonds.

Toulouse sausage - a small French sausage filled with coarsely chopped pork and smoked bacon, flavored with minced garlic and parsley, crushed black peppercorns and wine. Suitable for braising, frying or grilling, Toulouse sausage may also be sliced and added to salads or **cassoulets,** soups and roast fowl dishes, or broken up and formed into patties.

tourage - the French name for the technique of repeatedly rolling and folding dough to create the many fine, flaky layers (*mille-feuilles*) of puff pastry.

tournant - cook who has trained in all stations of a professional kitchen and is able to replace or fill in where needed. One of the positions in the kitchen brigade system created by French chef **Auguste Escoffier** in the late-19th century. The word comes from the French *tournant,* meaning "turning" or "revolving." See also BRIGADE SYSTEM, CHEF, ENTREMETIER, GARDE MANGER, PASTRY CHEF, POISSONIER, RÔTISSEUR, SAUCIER, SOUS CHEF.

tournedos - from the French phrase *tourner le dos,* meaning "to turn one's back," referring to one account of its origin, as explained in *Dictionnaire de l'Académie des gastronomes,* published in 1864: "In the last century, the stalls backing onto (*tournant le dos*) the central alleys of the fresh fish pavillon in the Paris Halles were assigned fish of doubtful freshness. By similarity, the name *tournedos* was given to pieces of fillet of beef that were kept for a few days in storage. A lack of discretion is said to have led to the word appearing on a restaurant menu one day; the public, not knowing its origin, adopted it." Some say the name derives from the fact that the beef fillets cook quickly and are "done before the cook has time to turn back around," but the story doesn't ring true. Perhaps a little more credible is the legendary account of Italian composer Gioacchino Rossini at the Café Anglais in Paris, at the beginning of the 19th century, and the famous dish of beef named for him (with foie gras, truffles and sauce Périgueux). A noted gourmand and friend of **Antonin Carême,** Rossini had his own table at the best restaurants in Paris and, rather than ordering what was offered by the house, he would often enter the kitchen and tell the chef what he wanted to eat. On that fateful day, Rossini, tired of the usual garnishes, told the chef which ingredients he wanted for his beef and insisted that the dish be prepared in the dining room, tableside, so that he could observe the chef. When the chef objected to Rossini's constant meddling, the maestro reportedly cried, "*Et alors, tournez le dos.*" ("So, turn your back.") Hence, the name of the preparation, "tournedos Rossini." In modern cuisine, a tournedos, usually of beef, although sometimes of fish, is a round crosscut slice from the center of the fillet.

tourte - from medieval France, a coarse, dark bread eaten by the peasant classes; in modern cuisine, a tourte is a shallow Mediterranean pie made using puff pastry, whose filling usually includes spinach or Swiss chard, as in the well-known *tourte de Haute-Provence*, but also made sweet.

tourtière - a pie dish in which to make **tourtes,** formerly earthenware. Highly praised by French chef **Antonin Carême,** tourtière comes from the Latin *tortus*, meaning, "to make round." Today, it's perhaps best known as the traditional French Canadian savory pie served on *Réveillon* (Christmas Eve, after midnight Mass), as well as throughout the holiday season, made with pork, potatoes, onions and its characteristic spices, most often including allspice, cinnamon and clove.

touton - fried rounds of bread dough. This Newfoundland specialty is often served with molasses for breakfast.

Tower, Jeremiah - see Waters, Alice.

tozzetti - Tuscan **biscotti** made with hazelnuts, instead of the usual almonds.

tragacanth - see GUM TRAGACANTH.

Traill, Catharine Parr Strickland - see profile below.

trail mix - see GORP.

trans fatty acids - see HYDROGENATION.

transparent noodles - see HARUSAME.

Trappist beer - brewed by monks of the strict-observance Cistercian order, controlled by legal regulations; it must be produced within the abbey walls, supervised by a member of the order, and its profits spent on social work. There are only six remaining abbeys where Trappist beer is still made, five in Belgium and one in the Netherlands. Trappist beer dates back to the Middle Ages, when epidemics were spread by contaminated water. Monasteries along pilgrimage routes provided food, shelter and hygienic refreshment, which came in the form of beer. There were many abbeys all over Europe: Germany alone accounted for close to 500. In Belgium, two orders brewed beer: the Bénédictines and the Cistercians.

Traill, Catharine Parr Strickland (1802–1899) - botanist, who turned her keen eye for detail and scientific nuance to domestic matters associated with emigration and settlement. The youngest of nine children of a literary family (her sister Susanna Moodie is also a well-known Canadian author of the period), as a young bride she exchanged the comforts of a genteel, but increasingly financially challenged English life for the hardships of pioneering. Two of her seventeen books deal with her experience as an immigrant and in addition to being a fascinating exploration of the heart and mind of a 19th-century woman, they are a source of extraordinary insight into the realities of homemaking in the wilderness.

The Backwoods of Canada (1836) is based on letters Catharine wrote to her mother in England, recounting her voyage, arrival and experience of settling into her new life in Canada. Resolutely cheerful, it is distinguished by her remarkable common sense and her unshakeable belief that "sound domestic economy" will save the day.

By the time she published *The Canadian Settler's Guide* (1855), Traill knew whereof she spoke, "having myself suffered from the disadvantage of acquiring all my knowledge of Canadian housekeeping by personal experience." She had seen that many women failed miserably at homesteading and provided them with an exhaustively detailed manual covering the entire range of domestic activities from home decorating and fermenting bread to raising poultry and sheep. This practical guide to settlement has often been compared to the *Book of Household Management* by **Mrs. Isabella Beeton,** although its original edition predated the English volume by almost seven years and any comparative reading of the two would highlight the dramatic differences between the audiences to whom they were addressed. No reading of Catharine's book could fail to recognize the value of homemaking as an economic activity. Traill writes precisely and elegantly on all stages of food production from sowing the seeds through harvesting, cooking, serving, storing and, where appropriate, preserving. Her section on meat includes curing and pickling as well as eating from the wild (partridges, pigeons, rabbits and squirrels, among others).

Trillin, Calvin (1935–) - American journalist, author and humorist, best known for his three books about food, despite having written nearly 20 books throughout his career. Six years after graduating from Yale in 1957, Trillin became a staff writer at *The New Yorker* and, later, a reporter for *Time* magazine and a syndicated columnist whose pieces ran in *The Nation* from 1978 to 1985. His infamous trio of books are *American Fried: Adventures of a Happy Eater* (1974); *Alice, Let's Eat: Further Adventures of a Happy Eater* (1978); and *Third Helpings* (1983). When writing about food, Trillin always mentions his family, such as poking fun at the home cooking of his childhood: "The most remarkable thing about my mother is that for 30 years, she served the family nothing but leftovers. The original meal has never been found."

Trappist cheese - see PORT SALUT.

trash fish - unmarketable types of fish that are discarded from the catch. Unsuitable for human consumption, some may be used for animal feed, for example. But as diners become more adventurous and stocks of more desirable fish decline, yesterday's discards may show up on tomorrow's dinner plate. **Nursehound,** for example, was once considered a trash fish to North Americans, but now shows up on restaurant menus. No fish is trash, of course, within its own food chain.

trassi - see BELACAN, SHRIMP PASTE.

treacle - a blend of refined syrups and molasses used to make candies, desserts and baked goods, although the English treacle tart is actually made with golden syrup. See also TOFFEE.

tree ear - see WOOD EAR.

tree mushroom - **1.** the name of a specific type of mushroom that grows on tree trunks and rotting stumps, *Pleurotus ostreatus*. See also OYSTER MUSHROOM. **2.** the generic name for many different types of mushrooms that grow on rotting tree trunks. Some are toxic, but in China and Japan, edible varieties, such as lion's mane, monkey's head and **shiitake,** have been cultivated for centuries. North Americans also produce tree mushrooms commercially, and gourmet-store growing kits — containing spawn plugs and accessories, but no logs — indicate that home cooks are cultivating them on a smaller scale, as well.

tree onion - also **Egyptian onion.** Unlike other members of its family, Allium cepa, the tree onion grows in clusters at the tops of the plant stems, but tastes and can be used like, any common variety. See also ONION.

tree spinach - see CHAYA.

tree tomato - see TAMARILLO.

tremoco - see LUPINE.

trencher - from the medieval French *trenchier,* meaning "to cut," a stale piece of flat bread used as a plate.

trepang - a Malay name for **sea slug** or **sea cucumber,** a staple among Asian cultures living near seacoasts and a delicacy in the West.

trifle - an English specialty from the Victorian age, made of layered sherry-soaked sponge or pound cake, custard and whipped cream, usually served in a glass pedestal bowl, so that the attractive layers are in full view; also known as **tipsy parson** and **tipsy squire** in Colonial times. An Italian version is called *zuppa inglese*, meaning "English soup," and the Spanish counterpart is *bizcocho borracho*, meaning "drunken cake."

Trillin, Calvin - see profile above.

Trinitario bean - see CHOCOLATE.

trinity - also **blessed trinity, holy trinity, sacred trinity.** A staple of Cajun and Creole cooking, this refers to a generous helping of chopped celery, onion and sweet green peppers, which lends a characteristic taste to such dishes as gumbos and jambalayas. The trinity is often sautéed separately, or stirred into an almost-cooked dark or brown **roux,** before it is added to the dish.

tripe - the edible stomach lining of a ruminant, a hoofed animal that digests its food in several stages, most often taken from cows but sometimes also from goats, oxen and sheep. Ruminants have three- or four-chambered stomachs: the first, called the rumen, provides plain (or smooth) tripe, also known as double tripe or *gras-double* in French; the second, called the reticulum, provides honeycomb or pocket tripe, generally tender and considered the best; the third is bible or book tripe, taken from the omasum, or third stomach; tripe from the fourth stomach or abomasum is rarely used because of its granular tissue. Although not to everyone's taste, epicureans throughout the ages have been known to appreciate tripe. It was famously loved by William the Conqueror, Rabelais and Homer. **Pepper pot** soup is a well-known recipe using tripe.

triple-crème cheese - also **triple-cream cheese.** A soft, rich cheese with 75 percent or more milk fat. **Boursin** and **mascarpone** are two examples.

triple sec - a liqueur flavored with sweet and bitter oranges that is quite sweet despite its name ("sec" usually means **dry**). Triple sec is a type of **curaçao,** of which **Cointreau** is one brand name. **Grand Marnier** is similar but is barrel-aged.

triticale - an unusually hardy hybrid grain created by American scientist **Norman Borlaug;** a crossbreed of wheat and rye, having the flavor of both. It was developed to allow people living in less fertile areas of the world to grow a nutritious, versatile grain.

tri-tip - also **bottom sirloin tri-tip.** A cut of beef from the bottom sirloin butt that must be tenderized or marinated to make it tender enough to eat. This type of steak has become very popular on the West Coast of the U.S. but is seen less frequently in the east. See also BEEF.

trocken - a German wine term equal to the English term **dry.** See also HALBTROCKEN.

Trockenbeerenauslese - a German wine label term for hand-picked grapes that have nearly dried on the vine, used to make very heavy-weight wines. German grapes used for winemaking are classified and labeled according to their ripeness, not necessarily their sweetness, and by the weight, or body, of the wines they produce, from thin and light-bodied to syrupy and full-bodied. Trockenbeerenauslese grapes are affected with **botrytis cinerea,** and the rare wine they yield is thick, sweet (very much like nectar) and extremely expensive. See also AUSLESE, BEERENAUSLESE, KABINETT, SPÄTLESE.

Troisgros, Jean and Pierre - see profile below.

trompette de la mort - see BLACK CHANTERELLE.

tropical sweet potato - see BONIATO.

trotter - the foot of a pig or calf, bought whole or split in half, used to make strong, gelatinous stock, consommé and aspic. Trotters may also be stuffed, broiled or grilled, served with a sauce, added to stews for extra richness or jellied for eating cold. See also PIGS' FEET.

trout - delicate, fine-textured fish of the Salvelinus family. They are prized by fisherman for both their beauty and flavor. See also BROOK TROUT, CHAR, LAKE TROUT.

Troisgros, Jean and Pierre (1926–1983) (1928–) - French brothers and chefs, considered to be among the founders of contemporary cuisine. They were born in Roanne, in the Loire Valley, where their parents ran the Hôtel Moderne, known locally for their mother's cooking and father's wines. The boys took naturally to cooking and apprenticed in Paris, where they met **Paul Bocuse.** They formed an indomitable team and went to work in **Fernand Point**'s kitchen. In the mid-1950s, the brothers returned to Roanne to take over the family inn. They rechristened it Frères Troisgros and earned critical praise, sustaining a three-star Michelin status for over three decades. When Jean, the elder, died in 1983, Pierre's son, Michel, took his place in the kitchen. Claude, Pierre's other son, also became a chef, living in Brazil for several years and later opening C.T. in New York City in 1994.

Troyes - see BARBEREY.

truffle - **1.** a very valuable and highly esteemed underground fungus, which until recently, couldn't be cultivated, only aged, often found with the use of pigs. (China and some other countries are now cultivating truffles on a small scale.) The black truffle, *Tuber melanosporum*, was known by both the Greeks and the Romans, who endorsed its medicinal and especially aphrodisiac attributes. Truffles were an Egyptian favorite, eaten with goose fat. But in the Middle Ages, they were thought to be manifestations of the devil. Louis XIV, however, subscribed to the earlier theory, and from his reign onward, truffles were enthusiastically consumed by all those wealthy enough to afford them.

Since the 17th century, pigs have been used to find truffles, but they developed a taste for them, so truffle pigs are now muzzled. It's also become efficient to use specially trained dogs. In Italy, these dogs can cost more than $10,000. A trained eye can spot a small hole leading under the tree, and by delicately foraging inside with a small stick, one can find a truffle. The best black truffles are said to come from the French regions of Perigord and Provence, and Piedmont, in Italy, is famous for its more subtly scented white truffle, *Tuber magnatum*. There are more than 70 varieties of truffles, and China now exports some lesser-quality truffles at a very low price. **2.** a small chocolate, often with a soft center, so named because a signature variety had an irregular round shape and was dredged in cocoa, which mimicked the appearance of the fungus.

trumpet of death - see BLACK CHANTERELLE.

truss - from the Old French *trousser*, meaning "to bundle," a method of tying up the wings and legs of poultry or a joint of meat with either butcher's cord or skewers, to secure the stuffing or maintain a neat shape for serving and carving.

tsimmes - see TZIMMES.

tsukemono - the Japanese word for pickled foods, such as **takuan** or **umeboshi,** served at Japanese meals as a complement to more delicately flavored dishes and cooked rice. Japanese pickles are heavily salted (*shio-zuke*), pickled in miso paste (*miso-zuke*) or pickled in rice bran (*nuka-zuke*), which gives them a pungent, fermented aroma.

tube steak - see HOT DOG.

tuckahoe - a Native American name meaning "edible root"; a plant whose tuber was a staple for Native Americans from New Jersey to Virginia; prolific near waterways, it's made into a flour for bread.

tuile - **1.** a thin, delicate cookie made with an almond batter, which is spread onto the baking tray, then cooks very quickly, is pliable when still warm and stiffens once it's cooled. It looks like a tile, hence its name: *tuile* is French for "tile." Tuiles are made into cups by draping a warm, limp cookie over an inverted glass or cup, or made into "cigarettes" by rolling the warm cookie around the handle of a wooden spoon. The cups are generally filled with berries and mousse, and the cigarettes are often used to garnish ice cream or sorbets, or dipped decoratively into chocolate and served as part of a selection of fancy cookies. **2.** a cheese version made by arranging circles of grated cheese (Parmesan is often used) on a parchment paper–lined baking sheet, baking them until they are melted and golden brown, then transferring them to a parchment paper–covered curved or flat surface until they cool. They are used as shells for creamy hors d'oeuvre mixtures or served alongside soup.

Tule potato - see ARROWHEAD.

tulip - also **tulipe.** A crisp, golden cookie shell, named for its shape, filled with berries or sliced fruit, Chantilly cream, **ganache,** mousse, ice cream or sorbet. A light buttery dough, made with confectioner's sugar and egg whites, is spread in circles on a baking pan. Right out of the oven, each warm cookie is draped over and gathered into a muffin or tart tin, or pressed into a fluted **brioche** mold; as it cools, it stiffens into a frilly flower shape. Any moisture in the air will be absorbed by the tulips, so they must be used soon afterward or stored in an airtight container; for the same reason, the filling is added just before the dessert is served.

tulipai - see TISWIN.

tun - see VAT.

tuna - also **tunny.** An ocean-dwelling fish from the mackerel, or Scombridae family, a very fast swimmer, which can clock 55 miles (88 km) per hour. The tuna's flesh is crimson pink, unlike that of other ocean fish, which is usually white,

TYPES OF TUNA

albacore - also **long-finned tuna.** *Thunnus alalunga,* the lightest flesh and mildest flavor, canned as "white" tuna, from the Pacific off the U.S. as well as the Mediterranean.

bigeye - *Thunnus obesus,* medium-sized, about 45 pounds (20 kg), found in the tropical and subtropical Pacific, Indian and Atlantic oceans. Like yellowfin, known in Hawai as *ahi.*

bluefin - also **horse mackerel, jack mackerel.** *Thunnus thynnus,* the preferred variety for sashimi, rich and flavorful, with dark red flesh. Bluefins are the largest tunas, weighing as much as 1,600 pounds (725 kg), found in the Atlantic, swimming as far north as Nova Scotia during spring and summer, desired both for sport and cuisine. Most of the harvest is exported to Japan and sold at a premium.

horse mackerel - see BLUEFIN.

jack mackerel - see BLUEFIN.

long-finned tuna - see ALBACORE.

skipjack - also **aku, oceanic bonito.** *Katsuwonus pelamis,* generally the strongest in flavor and with the highest fat content, a small warm-water variety, usually less than 20 pounds (9 kg), sometimes dried and sold as bonito in flakes, for use in Japanese cuisine. Also known as *aku* in Hawaii.

yellowfin - *Thunnus albacares,* second in quality only to bluefin, pale pink in color, with a stronger taste than albacore, often canned, reaching about 125 pounds (57 kg). Like bigeye, known in Hawai as *ahi.*

because the tuna's blood carries more oxygen, also allowing it to live in colder waters. Americans eat 500,000 tons (454,000 tonnes) of canned tuna each year. Canned tuna's origins reflect its proletarian status. Because of a shortage of Pacific sardines in San Pedro Bay in 1903, a southern California canner named Albert P. Halfhill decided to pack tuna instead, using flat, square sardine cans, and was surprised when sales took off. By 1913, nine plants were producing 115,000 cases a year. The canned tuna market is valued at more than $1 billion. Interest in fresh tuna has exploded with the popularization of Asian cuisine, particularly sushi.

tuna cactus - see CACTUS.

tuna casserole - a cheap and classic North American comfort food and staple of the college-students' diet, made with canned tuna, cheese, cream of mushroom soup, milk and pasta, topped with bread crumbs or crushed potato chips, and baked. The Campbell Soup Co. got tuna-casserole on kitchen tables across the continent in 1952, when it published a recipe for "Perfect Tuna Casserole" in its *Cooking with Condensed Soup* cookbook. Creative types use cream of celery soup instead of mushroom soup, or add extras, such as cashew halves, chopped green beans, onions, spinach or peppers, and toppings, such as onion rings or shrimp.

tuna steak - a boneless slab of flesh, cut crosswise from the widest part of the cleaned fish, often broiled, grilled or poached.

turban - see SQUASH.

turbinado sugar - see SUGAR.

turbot - from the Old Swedish *tornbut,* meaning "thorned flatfish," for the nodules covering the brown top of its body; native to the North Atlantic, weighing between 70 and 90 pounds (32 to 41 kg). First-century Roman poet Juvenal praised the turbot in his satires, and in the same years, the emperor Domitian convened a meeting of the Senate so that they could decide what sauce he should serve with an enormous turbot that had been given to him.

tur dal - also **toor dal.** See DAL.

turducken - a dish made famous by renowned Louisiana chef **Paul Prudhomme,** the turducken, as its fanciful name implies, is a chicken stuffed inside a duck stuffed inside a turkey. Each bird is **deboned** (except the turkey, which retains its drumsticks and wings), then laid out and covered with a layer of dressing: a cornbread dressing on the turkey, an **andouille** sausage dressing on the duck, and a shrimp dressing on the chicken. The chicken is then rolled up and placed in the middle of the duck, which is rolled up around it. This combination is then rolled up inside the turkey, which is skewered shut into its original shape. The completed turducken is then roasted for eight or more hours, depending on the weight of the birds. This enormous undertaking may actually be worth the effort, as an average turducken serves 20 or more.

tureen - a deep, usually covered, serving dish for dishes that have a liquid consistency, such as soups or stews.

turkey - a large gallinaceous bird, *Meleagris gallopavo*, with a fan-shaped tail, native to North America. In 1519, the Mayans of the Yucatán introduced Hernán Ferdinand Cortés to turkey. Turkeys appeared in England only four years later. How the turkey got its names is unclear, but there are a number of curious theories. One theory says Columbus, when he arrived in the New World believing it was connected with India, surmised the bird was part of the Indian peacock family. Thus he decided to name them *tuka*, which is the word for peacock in the language of India. Then there is the theory that says the turkey name came from the sound they make when afraid, "Turk, turk, turk." In 1538, *poule d'Inde*, "chicken of the Indies" was first served in France. The French called the hen turkey *dinde*, and the tom turkey *dindon*. The Spanish called them *pavo*. Turkey would gradually replace peacock, swan and other birds on English tables; by the end of the 16th century, peacock or swan, whose meat is tough and stringy compared to turkey, were rarely eaten again.

In 1784, when Benjamin Franklin was given a medal honoring officers of the Continental Army, he took exception to the eagle depicted on it, saying, "It looks too much like a turkey and...for my own part, I wish the bald eagle had not been chosen as the representative of our country; he is a bird of bad moral character...The turkey is a much more respectable bird, and withal a true original native of America. Eagles have been found in all countries, but the turkey was particular to ours...He is besides (though a little vain and silly, it's true, but not the worse I hope for that) a bird of courage and would not hesitate to attack a grenadier of the British guards who should present to invade his farmyard with a red coat." In some parts of the U.S., turkeys are called "bronze" or "bronze turkey."

turkey

According to the National Turkey Federation in the U.S., about 690 million pounds of turkey were gobbled up at American Thanksgiving dinners in 2004 alone. The group also claims that U.S. astronauts Buzz Aldrin and Neil Armstrong — in thanksgiving for a safe landfall, perhaps — enjoyed a foil-packed, space-food version of turkey with all the trimmings for their first meal on the moon. Increasingly, cooks who want to replace ground beef or pork with a leaner, lower-cholesterol alternative are using ground turkey in burgers, chili, meat loaf and tacos. See also TEMPERATURE.

Turkish coffee - also **Greek coffee.** While most Turks and Greeks would blanch at the equating of their favored brews, Turkish and Greek coffee (as well as coffee drunk in many Middle Eastern countries) is essentially the same. Both beverages are made of finely pulverized roasted coffee beans, boiled with water in a long-handled copper, brass or stainless-steel pot (called a **cezve** in Turkish, *ibrik* in Arabic or *briki* in Greek). For Turkish coffee, finely ground cardamom may be added to enhance the flavor. The coffee mixture is brought to a boil (without stirring) over medium heat, then, just as the foam is about to overflow, the coffee is removed from the heat and divided among **demitasse** cups. If sugar is to be added, it is added to the coffee and water at the beginning so that it is completely incorporated when the coffee is poured. There are four accepted levels of sweetness, and drinkers of a particular pot must agree at the outset how they will take their coffee: plain with no sugar, strong with little sugar, medium-sweet, or very sweet. Each cup receives some of the prized foam that forms on top of the boiled coffee. Then the cups are allowed to stand for a minute or two so that the sludgy coffee-ground mixture can settle to the bottom. A cup of Turkish or Greek coffee is never drunk completely unless the drinker wants to get an unpleasant mouthful of the bitter sediment at the bottom. See also COFFEE.

Turkish delight - a homemade or ready-made chewy and sweet jelly candy. Traditionally, a translucent green or red, and flavored with rose water, it is usually served in squares sprinkled with confectioner's sugar or coated in chocolate. Some versions contain minced nuts. Created in the late 1700s by an Anatolian candy maker named Ali Muhiddin Haci Bekir (shops bearing his name still sell candy in Turkey today), the sweet was an immediate hit with the Turkish royal court. Its popularity spread throughout Europe; Big Turk, a brand-name chocolate bar containing the jelly, is a familiar favorite in North America.

turmeric - also **curcuma.** A bright yellow rhizome from an Asian plant, *Curcuma longa*, from the Latin *terra merita*, meaning "deserving earth." The Greek physician Dioscorides mentioned it as a tonic to stimulate the appetite and as a cure for overeating and indigestion. Its powdered form was used well before the time of Christ as an economical alternative to saffron. In the Middle Ages, it was called "Indian saffron" and also used as a fabric dye, as it still is today. The ceremonial garments of monks from the Far East are dyed with turmeric. In India, a tincture based on turmeric is traditionally rubbed on the abdomen during labor and on the umbilical cord of the newborn baby as an antiseptic and for "golden" good luck. No Hindu celebration or gathering takes place without turmeric, ceremoniously and cosmetically, most notably at weddings. It's also one of the basic ingredients in Indian cooking. In the West Indies, turmeric is used to dye some margarines and dairy products. Unlike ginger, a related rhizome, which is often available fresh, turmeric is usually sold dried, as a powder, and is best stored in the dark, because it's sensitive to light.

turnip - an edible root, *Brassica rapa*, from the cabbage family, cultivated in the Middle East for more than 4,000 years, thought to be native to Russia and Scandinavia. The Romans were familiar with turnips before the time of Christ and used them for food as well as for livestock feed. The turnip was regarded as possessing a medicinal unguent for the body's outer ills. Dioscorides believed that a fresh white turnip applied to a sore foot would "renounce" the pain of the ailment immediately. The Roman epicurean **Apicius** counseled women of imminent middle age to make a thick paste of cooked turnip, cream and smashed rosebuds and to rub it thoroughly into all crevices of the face, neck and shoulders — after only two applications, these surfaces would be as smooth as a baby's thigh. Roman naturalist **Pliny** described long turnips, flat turnips and round turnips. He used the name *rapa* and *napus*; the latter term became *nepe* in Middle English and *naep* in Anglo-Saxon. When put together with the word *turn*, meaning, "make round," *naep* became "turnip." Turnips were widely consumed in the Middle Ages but fell out of grace in the 18th century, when the potato became all the rage.

turnips

A thin, whitish skin covers the flesh of the white turnip, but the root can be bright red or purple, and its slightly hairy green leaves are edible. Turnips are often mistaken for rutabagas, their distant yellow-fleshed cousin. The distinction between the two is that the turnip's leaves are directly attached to the top of the root, whereas rutabaga leaves grow around the neck. The turnip was one of the few vegetables known and available in northern Europe up to fairly modern times. It was introduced to North America by the earliest explorers and colonists. Jacques Cartier brought turnips to Canada in 1541, and they were planted in Virginia and Massachusetts in the 1600s.

turnip greens - the slightly hairy leaves of turnips, best eaten when they are crisp, tender and young, sharp-flavored but still sweet. Considered a soul food and traditionally simmered with salt pork or ham hocks, these nutritious greens can be boiled, sautéed, steamed or stir-fried, alone or combined with mustard greens. Since they wilt quickly and don't transport well, turnip greens are available fresh only in season, but are also canned and frozen.

turnip-rooted parsley - see PARSLEY ROOT.

turnover - folded-over pastry with a sweet or savory filling.

turntable - also **lazy Susan, swivel cake stand.** A rigid circle of ceramic, plastic, metal or wood that revolves on a base. Large-diameter models are customarily set in the center of the tables at Chinese restaurants, so that diners can turn to the dish they want and serve themselves. Smaller versions are used as cheese or hors d'oeuvres trays on buffet tables. Turntables held on a pedestal atop a stable, sturdy base are used by cake decorators, enabling them to work at a comfortable height to pipe frosting, for example, in one continuous motion right around a cake.

turophile - an aficionado or lover of cheese, from the Greek *turos*, meaning cheese.

turrón - see TORRONE.

turtle - **1.** a water or land reptile whose body is covered by a shell, into which it can withdraw for protection. It is most often served in a soup, cooked with sherry, for which the water turtle is best suited. Several historic recipes for the flippers reveal that they were highly prized by connoisseurs. Turtles have been eaten by Catholics during Lent since the 17th century, when the Vatican categorized them as a fish and sanctioned their consumption. The availability of the meat is now limited because of conservation concerns, but turtle meat is still available in specialty markets, especially in Florida and the Carolinas, where there is a proliferation of turtle farms. In the East, markets are filled with turtles of numerous species, mostly due to an Asian taste for the meat, a cultural history of their medicinal use and a thriving exotic pet trade, although conservationists worry that this degree of harvest may endanger world stocks. See also TERRAPIN. **2.** a brand-name candy, a Turtle, made by Nestlé, consisting of pecans and caramel covered in chocolate. **3.** a generic term, named after the candy, used to describe cakes, cookies and pies that contain caramel, chocolate and pecans.

turtle bean - see BLACK TURTLE BEAN.

Tuscan pepper - see PEPPERONCINO.

tutti frutti - Italian for "all fruits." **1.** a type of ice cream, containing finely chopped, candied, fresh and/or dried fruits. To make the classic version, candied fruit is macerated in **Kirsch** before it's added to the ice cream. **2.** a dessert consisting of two pastry layers, sandwiching finely chopped candied or cooked fruit, that is soaked in apricot syrup, frosted, then sprinkled with almond flakes or candied peel. **3.** the name of a fruity, artificial flavor used in candies and confectioneries. Both artificial and real fruit flavors have always been favorites for sweet treats. Back in 1888, the first American vending machine dispensed a brand-name Tutti-Frutti chewing gum in a New York city train station.

twist - **1.** a fine slice of citrus rind that curls naturally, often used as a garnish in cocktails, desserts or salads. **2.** a rope of savory or sweet dough twisted around itself and baked.

tybo - a Danish cow's milk cheese from Jutland. With a flavor that's mellow, mild and nutty, the creamy cheese, shot through with small holes, is surrounded by a yellow rind.

Tyhoid Mary - see MALLON, MARY.

tzatziki - a Greek sauce made with hung or drained yogurt, cucumber, garlic, dill and olive oil.

tzimmes - also **tsimmes.** A slow-simmered stew of fruits, vegetables and/or meat served as part of a celebration, particularly at the Jewish New Year, Rosh Hashanah. The sweet dish is eaten to ensure a happy and prosperous coming year, especially one version of tzimmes, honey-glazed carrots (the sliced carrots represent gold coins and are a symbol of good fortune, and the honey represents the hope of a sweet year to come). Tzimmes can also include brisket slow-cooked with brown sugar, chunks of squash, cinnamon, dried apricots and prunes, honey and orange juice. The word comes from two German words, *zum* and *essen*, meaning "eat."

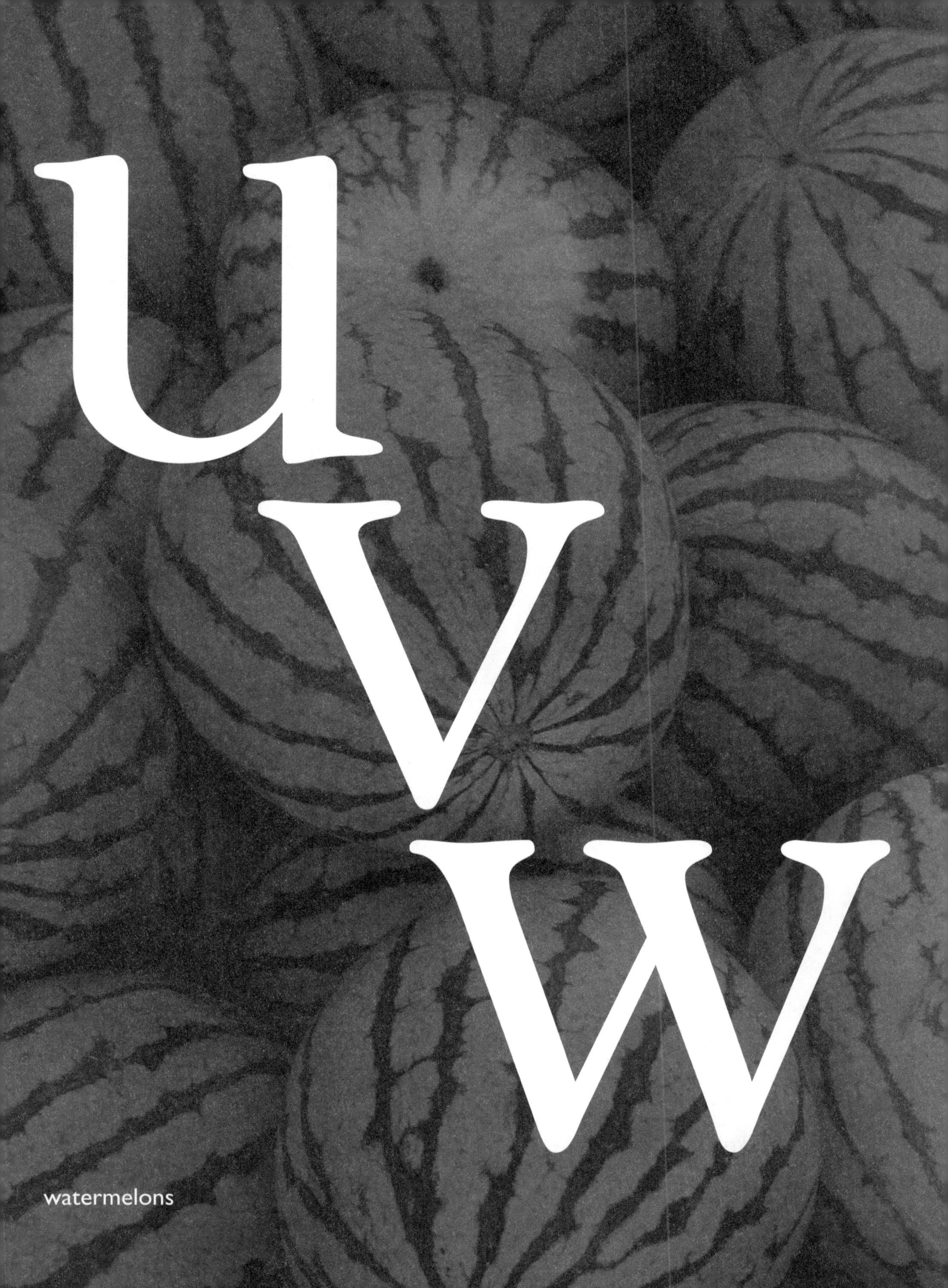
u
v
w
watermelons

udo - a Japanese woodland plant, *Aralia cordata*, that bears starbursts of white flowers followed by purple berries in the fall, but only the fresh, young stalks, traditionally harvested in the spring, are eaten. To preserve their crispness, they are added raw or after quick blanching to salads and added to hot dishes, such as soup, at the last minute. Perhaps because it grows wild, udo has also been used as a **famine food.**

udon - a long, round, white Japanese noodle, most often made with wheat and served in broth with a near-infinite variation of additions.

Ugli fruit - a fairly new addition to the citrus family, which looks like a knobby grapefruit; developed in Jamaica about 1915 or 1916 by **F.G. Sharp,** owner of Trout Hall Estates. The Ugli fruit is believed to be a cross between a grapefruit and a tangerine, although the **pomelo** may have also played a part. In an effort to increase its recognition, some vendors have taken to labeling it "Uniq" or "Unique" fruit.

Ugli fruit

uhu - see PARROTFISH.

ullage - a bottle with a faulty cork, which has allowed some of the wine to escape. An ullage bottle of Champagne, provided the loss of wine has not been excessive, may be excellent, whereas an ullage bottle of Bordeaux or Burgundy is always flat and poor. "On ullage" refers to a cask of wine that is no longer full to the **bung** (a stopper used in the hole of a wine cask), a dangerous condition for any wine, if left so for any length of time.

umami - see FIVE BASIC TASTES, MONOSODIUM GLUTAMATE.

umbrella mushroom - see PARASOL MUSHROOM.

umeboshi - pickled salted plums, a very popular type of Japanese **tsukemono** served with rice to soften its assertively sour, salty flavor. It is commonly touted as a digestive aid in Japan and is often recommended for people with a sour or upset stomach. See also BAINIKU.

unagi - the Japanese word for eel, often served grilled and basted with a salty-sweet barbecue-style sauce, used either as a sushi topping or on top of plain rice to make the dish *unadon*, or **donburi** topped with unagi.

univalve - a single-shelled, single-valved mollusk, such as a snail.

unleavened bread - bread made without leavening, such as yeast, baking soda or baking powder. **Matzo** and **lavash** are two well-known types of unleavened bread. See also BATTER BREAD, LEAVENING, QUICK BREAD, YEAST BREAD.

unmold - to invert and turn an aspic, cake, custard, ice cream, jelly or pudding out of the mold in which it was cooked or chilled and set. Dipping the mold in hot water helps loosen aspics and jellies; dipping it into cold, then tepid water helps loosen ice cream. Greasing and flouring the pans, or using nonstick or silicone bakeware, helps baked goods come out cleanly and in one piece.

unripened cheese - consumed when fresh, usually made from acidified skim milk to which milk fats are added at the curd stage. The finished product usually has a high moisture content and has been made since the 4th century BC.

unsalted butter - butter produced with no salt. Preferred by most Europeans and by North American bakers and chefs who want to eliminate or control the amount of salt in their cooking, unsalted butter is also less likely to burn in a frying pan or fight with the sweet flavors in confections. Added salt does slow down the growth of bacteria in butter, however, so whether it's frozen or refrigerated, unsalted butter doesn't keep as long as the salted variety.

unsaturated fat - see FATS.

unsweetened chocolate - see CHOCOLATE.

upo - see BOTTLE GOURD.

upside-down cake - a cake baked in a pan that has first been covered with a layer of butter and sugar, then fruit and finally the cake batter, served inverted, revealing the caramelized and glazed fruit on top.

urad dal - also **urd dal.** See DAL.

USDA plant-hardiness zone - see GROWING ZONE.

use-by date - see EXPIRATION DATE.

usuba - see JAPANESE KNIVES.

uszka - Polish for "little ears," egg-and-flour dumplings stuffed with mushrooms, served in soups.

vacchino Romano - see ROMANO.

Vacherin - a Swiss or French cow's milk cheese, with 45 to 50 percent milk fat, often served with a spoon. Several quite different cheeses share this name. The **Fribourg Vacherin** is semisoft and may be used in **raclette** or baked in dishes. The **Mont d'Or Vacherin** is made only in autumn, in both Switzerland and France.

In the early 1800s, a goat cheese called *chevrotin* (from the French *chèvre*, meaning "goat") was very popular, but a shortage of goat's milk forced the cheese makers to use cow's milk instead, using the same fabrication methods. They changed the name to *Vacherin*, from the French *vache*, meaning "cow."

vacherin - a French ice cream dessert traditionally consisting of several baked meringue rings stacked together and filled with vanilla ice cream or chantilly cream and fruit.

Valençay - a French goat cheese with an amazing story. Valençay was originally shaped like a perfect pyramid. On Napoleon's return from his disastrous campaign in Egypt, he stopped at the castle in Valençay. On seeing the cheese that reminded him of the Egyptian pyramids, he drew his sword and chopped off the top, creating the shape for which it's now known. During production, the drained curd is cast in a mold, then removed, covered with salted charcoal ashes and ripened in a well-ventilated room at 80 percent humidity. **Affinage** takes three weeks, after which a natural mold covers the surface.

Valencia orange - see ORANGE.

Valpolicella - a generic term given to wines produced in the Veneto region of northern Italy, an area of fertile valleys and foothills lying between the Alps and Lake Garda that has been inhabited by humans since prehistorical times. The wines produced here range from dry, light, young table wines (usually paired with baked eggplant, lamb or pork) to aged, full-bodied wines to rich, sweet dessert wines. All are considered fragrant and fruity, and most are served chilled, not cold.

vandyke - to cut the rind of citrus fruit and the skin of melons and tomatoes into zigzag shapes to make them look more attractive. Fish tails that are cut into "V" shapes are also described as "vandyked."

vanilla - a dark pod, *Vanilla planifolia*, the seed (not a bean, as it's often described) of a vine from the orchid family. Vanilla is native to the tropical rain forests of southeastern Mexico and Central America. Once it's picked, the pod is instantly dipped into boiling water to stop its growth and then placed in the sun to "sweat" for 10 to 20 days. Curing takes six to nine months, the process creating an enzyme reaction that changes glucovanillin to **vanillin,** the substance that gives the pods their characteristic flavor and aroma. While they cure, they must be kept warm. They eventually brown, become pliable, and develop a fine, white crystalline coating of vanillin. The most highly prized is Mexican vanilla, and second is Madagascar or Bourbon vanilla. Guyana, Guadeloupe and Martinique also produce the pods. More than 75 percent of all vanilla is grown in Madagascar and Reunion, where the pods are actually marked with the grower's brand to prevent vanilla rustlers from stealing the crops.

The name comes from the Spanish *vainilla*, meaning "little scabbard." Before the Europeans found it, vanilla had long been used by the Aztecs to flavor a drink called *xocalatl*, made with crushed cacao beans. Montezuma offered it to Hernán Ferdinand Cortés and his men when they reached what is now Mexico City. Bernardino de Sahagun, a Franciscan monk, was the first European to convey interest in vanilla in his 1560 book *Historia General de las Cosas de Nueva España* (General History of the Things of New Spain), which gave us the story *xocalatl*. The reason that real vanilla is so expensive is because it's hand-pollinated. Between 1875 and 1925, artificial vanillin was chemically synthesized from the essential oil of cloves, and

vanilla

recently, it's been made from the lignin of wood wastes. However, by U.S. law, any product labeled "vanilla extract" must derive from true vanilla.

vanilla essence - sold in grocery stores in the United Kingdom, products labeled "vanilla essence" are the equivalent of imitation vanilla extract in North America; in gourmet and specialty shops, though, vanilla essence is a stronger version of pure vanilla extract.

vanilla extract - see VANILLA.

vanilla liqueur - homemade or ready-made liqueurs flavored with vanilla. Homemade versions are usually based on brandy or vodka: together with granulated sugar, chopped split vanilla beans are immersed in the spirit and shaken; after storing in an airtight container for about two months, the mixture is strained to obtain the liqueur.

vanilla powder - finely ground, dried vanilla beans used to flavor baked goods, coffee, custards, ice cream and puddings. Not as likely to lose flavor when heated, the powder is considered superior to the more commonly available vanilla extract. When substituting, depending on the quality, the rule of thumb is to use one-quarter to one-half the amount of powder for the amount of extract called for in the recipe. Vanilla powder is sold in gourmet and specialty stores.

vanilla sugar - sugar flavored with vanilla. See also SUGAR.

Vanillekipferl - a type of biscuit meaning "vanilla crescent," very popular in Germany and Central Europe, usually made at Christmas from a rich pastry-type dough containing almonds and flavored with vanilla and lemon peel.

vanillin - see VANILLA.

varak - also **vark.** An edible precious metal in very thin sheets, of gold or silver, used to decorate desserts and other foods, used since the Middle Ages for wrapping pâtés and roast birds. Today, it is used in confectionery and cake decorations. Silver varak is a very thin film of sterling silver, most often used in Indian cooking to garnish special sweets and rice dishes.

varenyky - half-moon or square, Ukrainian savory or sweet dumplings made with unleavened dough wrapped around a filling, such as grated cheese or cottage cheese, ground meat, hard-boiled eggs, mashed potatoes, minced onion, sauerkraut or shredded cabbage (or combinations of some or all of these), or fruit. After the filling is wrapped and the edges of the varenyky are sealed, the dumplings are boiled.

varietal wine - a type of wine that is produced from a single variety of grape and identified by its grape variety (Chardonnay, Pinot Noir or Zinfandel to name a few), rather than by its region (as are the French wines, Champagne, Bordeaux or Burgundy).

variety meat - also **offal.** A euphemism for any part of an animal used for food that is not one of the skeletal muscles. Variety meats include brains, cheeks, tongue, liver, intestines, feet, pancreas, lungs, kidneys, heart, tail, testicles, stomach, thymus and spleen. See also BATH CHAPS, CHITTERLINGS, FRIES, GIBLETS, LIGHTS, MELT, ORGAN MEAT, OXTAIL SOUP, PIGS' FEET, PLUCK, SWEETBREADS, TONGUE.

vark - see VARAK.

vasilopitta - also **St. Basil bread.** A Greek bread baked for New Year's Day, which is also the feast day of St. Basil, founder of the Greek Orthodox Church. The sweet dough is commonly flavored with cinnamon, orange zest and ouzo, given an egg wash, then sprinkled with slivered almonds before it's baked. Afterward, a slit is cut into the base and a coin inserted into the cake. Sliced just after midnight on New Year's Eve or first thing the next morning, vasilopitta is traditionally cut according to ritual. Depending upon local custom, the first slice is for Jesus Christ or the Virgin Margin, the second for St. Basil or the family's patron saint, and the third is always for the house. Then each family member, from the eldest on down, gets a turn — whoever finds the coin, of course, gets the best luck for the year ahead.

vat - also **tun.** A large vessel for holding liquids during fermentation.

Vatel, François - see profile right.

Vat 69 - a blended Scotch whiskey, available in various proofs, made in Scotland since 1882. William Sanderson, its producer, joined a group of his countrymen establishing distilleries in the 19th century — James Chivas, John Dewer,

Vatel, François (1631–1671) - French royal steward, often thought of as the chef who killed himself because he didn't have enough fish to serve for dinner. Vatel wasn't, in fact, a chef, but a ploughman's son, working for the aristocracy. The only account of his demise comes from a letter written by Madame de Sévigné (Marie de Rabutin-Chantal), a writer whose work spawned an epistolary genre of French literature. Her detractors point out that the account was secondhand, while her supporters defend her reputation for accuracy. As she tells it, Vatel was at the docks, waiting for his order of fish at 4 a.m., after working for 12 days without sleep, because of the elaborate preparations required for a visit from Louix XIV. He was already upset that there had been insufficient roast for two tables the night before, because of numerous uninvited guests. When the first fish purveyor arrived with his small catch, telling Vatel that this was all he had, Vatel misunderstood him to mean that this included all available fish. Mortified that another shortage would destroy his reputation, he went to his quarters, impaled himself on his sword and killed himself — but only after three tries, as his wounds proved. Not long after, boatloads of fish began to arrive, since Vatel had placed his order far and wide.

William Teacher and John Walker, among others — who are still famous for their Scotch. Their new businesses got a boost from *Phylloxera vastatrix*. At the time, French vineyards were falling victim to this parasite, which attacked and killed the vines at the roots and reduced French exports of brandy and wine to the British Isles to a trickle. The Scotch distillers, of course, were only too happy to pour their golden spirits into any glasses going empty.

veal - in the United States, veal is meat from immature animals of the bovine species. The minimum age for slaughter is 3 weeks and the maximum about 3 months. The best meat comes from animals 4 to 8 weeks of age and may be of either sex. Veal has been a luxury ever since the Sumerians first began taming the wild cattle wandering the plains of Mesopotamia, who ate the animals young whenever they could be spared from their prime purposes for milk and as draft animals. The Romans were quick to take up the enjoyment of eating the tender meat of young animals and were already enjoying suckling pig and young lamb. To protect the dwindling breeding stock from the excesses of the Roman table, 3rd-century emperor Alexander Severus forbade the slaughter of calves. During the Middle Ages, veal made its way into **blancmange,** which literally means "to eat white." Although it's known as a sweet preparation today, it was originally savory, a veal stew made white with almond milk. A faint evolutionary line can be drawn to *blanquette de veau*, a stew of veal with cream.

The French have always loved veal. King François I was said to have demanded veal daily. Its popularity was likely due to the influence of Italian cooking. introduced by

CUTS OF VEAL

boneless leg rump roast - usually rolled and tied to keep its shape, often braised.

breast - a fairly lean cut with the lower ribs, sometimes stuffed or braised.

breast riblets - long cuts with ribs, usually braised.

cutlet - an extra-lean meat cut from the leg, usually sliced thinly and pan-fried.

leg rump roast - an irregularly shaped roast with round muscles, usually braised.

loin chop - with the tenderloin removed, braised or pan-fried.

rib chop - with part of the chine bone, usually braised or pan-fried.

rib roast - with up to 12 ribs and part of the chine bone.

shoulder blade steak - with blade bone, ribs and backbone, sometimes braised.

stewing veal - boneless chunks, usually from the shoulder or shank, best braised.

Catherine de' Medici when she married King Henry II. One particular cut of veal, the "scallop," has a curious military history. It's said to have originated in Spain and was introduced to Milan when the city was part of the Spanish Empire in the 16th century. The scallop is the emblem of Spain's patron saint, St. James, carried by the troops of Charles V. When Milan was later occupied by Austrian soldiers under Marshal Radetsky, he introduced the **scaloppine** to the Viennese imperial kitchens of Emperor Franz Josef, where it became the famed **Wiener schnitzel.**

In the U.S., veal farmers take bull calves from the herd when they are 100 to 120 pounds (45 to 55 kg) and raise them for 18 to 20 weeks until they are about 300 pounds (136 kg). They feed the calves a diet based on milk or soy-based formulas, which produces the firm, pale pink flesh for which veal is best known. **Provimi,** a shortening of "protein, vitamins and minerals," is another name for milk-fed veal.

veal cordon bleu - see CORDON BLEU.

veal Marsala - a dish of veal **scallopine,** mushrooms and **Marsala** wine. The mushrooms are sautéed in butter, then the veal is dredged in flour and pan-fried in butter. The pan is then **deglazed** with Marsala wine, which is cooked down to a thick, rich sauce and served with the veal and mushrooms.

veal Orloff - a braised loin of veal sliced thinly, horizontally, then each slice is spread with a mixture of puréed sautéed mushrooms and onions, then reassembled and tied, covered with more of the purée, **béchamel** and Parmesan cheese, and browned in the oven.

veal Oscar - sautéed veal cutlets topped with **béarnaise,** crabmeat and asparagus spears, said to be named for Sweden's King Oscar II. It is also credited to Oscar Tschirky, maitre d'hôtel of the old Waldorf Hotel on New York's Fifth Avenue, who is also credited as the source for **Waldorf salad.**

veal parmigiana - also **veal Parmesan.** A fried veal cutlet with a coating of seasoned bread crumbs and Parmesan cheese, served covered with tomato sauce.

veal scaloppine - also **veal scallopini.** Thin oval or round slices of veal cut from the leg fillet. Usually dredged in flour and sautéed, veal scaloppine are often served in tomato sauce with garlic, green pepper, mushrooms and onions, on a bed of egg noodles.

veau - French for "veal."

vegan - a person who does not eat any animal products, including meat, fish, eggs or dairy products. See also VEGETARIAN.

Vegemite - a salty sandwich spread from Australia made from leftover brewer's yeast, vegetables and spices, first made in 1922 by an Australian named Fred Walker. In 1935, the recipe and manufacturing methods were sold to Kraft Foods. The main change to the original recipe in recent years has been the reduction of salt content from 10 percent to 8 percent. Every year, 22.7 million jars of Vegemite are manufactured in Australia. See also MARMITE.

vegetable - see FRUITS AND VEGETABLES.

vegetable gelatin - see AGAR-AGAR.

vegetable marrow - see ZUCCHINI.

vegetable oil - any of various edible oils that are extracted from plants, their seeds, fruits or nuts.

vegetable oil spray - a ready-made product containing vegetable oil and usually the emulsifier lecithin, as well, which is sprayed onto pans, pots and grills before they are heated to prevent food from sticking. See also COOKING SPRAY.

vegetable oyster - see SALSIFY.

vegetable pear - see CHAYOTE.

vegetable protein - see TEXTURED VEGETABLE PROTEIN.

vegetable shortening - see SHORTENING.

vegetable soybean - see EDAMAME.

vegetable yeast extract - see NUTRITIONAL YEAST.

vegetal - a disparaging wine term used to describe a wine that has a predominant "green" smell or taste of asparagus, sweet peppers, leaves, unripe grapes or a whole vegetable garden, sometimes described as "grassiness" or "weediness." A subtle vegetal taste may be desirable, however, in some wines, such as Carbernet Sauvignon.

vegetarian - a person who does not eat meat. A **vegan** does not eat any animal products, including meat, fish, eggs and dairy products. An **ovo-lacto vegetarian** eats eggs and dairy products, but not meat. A **lacto vegetarian** eats dairy products, but not meat or eggs. A **fruitarian** eats only fruit, nuts and seeds, but not vegetables, meat or fish products (including eggs and dairy products). See also FLEXITARIAN, PESCATARIAN.

vegetarian sausage - see SAUSAGE.

veitchberry - also **king's ace berry.** From the genus *Rubus*, a cross between the raspberry and blackberry.

velouté - a sauce made from a white stock thickened with white **roux**, versatile in that it can be flavored in many ways, the base for many other sauces. Velouté is considered one of the five "mother sauces" from which almost all classic French sauces are derived. See also SAUCE.

velvet cake - a classic American cake. **White velvet cake** is made with lots of eggs, beaten and added separately so the stiffly beaten egg whites, folded into the batter last, can lend the cake an airy texture. The classic **Fannie Merritt Farmer** recipe calls for a sprinkling of blanched, shredded almonds and confectioner's sugar before the cake goes into the oven. A Southern variation is the dense, intensely chocolate, **red velvet cake** that is thought to be the forerunner of devil's food cake. Buttermilk makes it moist, and cocoa powder adds the chocolate. The color comes from a generous dose of red food coloring or puréed beets (some recipes call for baby food beets). For contrast, this cake is usually frosted with white cream cheese or, less often, buttercream icing.

Velvet Hammer - a smooth-to-swallow cocktail that packs a surprising punch, mixed with ingredients that vary with the bar. A classic recipe calls for almost-equal parts of triple sec, crème de curaçao and cream, shaken with crushed ice, strained into a Martini glass, then sprinkled with ground nutmeg. Other versions use Cointreau, vodka and Tia Maria with the cream.

velvet stem mushroom - see ENOKI.

vendaloo - see VINDALOO.

venison - see DEER.

vent - a slit or opening cut into a pie crust to allow steam to escape. Used instead of a **pie bird,** vents are often cut in decorative patterns that reveal the color and contents of the dish.

verbena - see LEMON VERBENA.

verjuice - also **verjus.** The acidic juice from tart, unripe fruits, especially apples and grapes, formerly in demand as a substitute for vinegar or lemon juice, as in medieval times, when lemons were not common. Technically not a vinegar, because it isn't fermented, verjuice is still used today in commercial mustards and in Middle Eastern cooking. Verjuice is also a natural by-product of wine making. To strengthen grape vines and allow them to produce full-flavored fruit, wine makers often thin the vines when the grapes are just beginning to ripen and press these grapes to produce verjuice, from the Latin *viridis*, meaning "green," and *jus*, meaning "juice."

vermicelli - see PASTA.

vermouth - an aromatized wine, meaning it has been fortified with alcohol, usually brandy, and steeped with botanicals, such as angelica, calamus root, cinnamon, cloves, wild thyme, coriander, orange peel, lemon peel, elderberries, quassia, chamomile, gentian, quinine and nutmeg. Vermouth is available red, known as "sweet," or white, "dry," and is sometimes served alone, especially in Europe, but most commonly mixed with liquor to create Martinis and Manhattans. **Punt e Mes** was the first commercial vermouth, introduced in 1785. A winery that would become famous for its vermouth was the house of Cinzano, which predates the production of Punt e Mes but whose output was for local consumption only. The wines are prepared chiefly in the French and Italian Alps; Italian vermouth is usually darker and sweeter than the French.

Véronique - a dish of fish or meat prepared or garnished with seedless white grapes. The original version was **sole Véronique,** sole poached in white wine, topped with **white sauce** and garnished with grapes, created by **Auguste Escoffier** in 1903 as a tribute to the comic opera *Véronique* by André Messager, which was playing in London at the time.

vervain - an herb, *Verbena officinalis*, used especially to flavor liqueurs and infusions. Shakespeare, as well as many ancient manuscripts, referred to vervain as the "herb of grace," *herbe sacrée* and *Herba Veneris* because it grows on Mount Calvary and was believed to be one of the herbs used to cleanse the wounds of Jesus. In medieval times, it was used to make an astringent tea to remedy bladder infections. Vervain was carried as a talisman by ambassadors undertaking hazardous assignments. It was also worn for protection against snakebite, as a good-luck charm, to keep away the evil eye and to improve eyesight. The Romans credited aphrodisiac qualities to the plant and wrote volumes about its use in the making of love potions and spells. The gathering of vervain was integrated into Druid rituals and has been long associated with magicians, alchemists and sorcerers.

vervain

vialone nano - see RICE.

viand - usually used in the plural, a synonym for victuals, provisions, food prepared for consumption or foods that comprise a meal, from the Middle French *viande* and medieval Latin *vivanda*, meaning "food."

Vichy carrots - carrots, cut into thin rounds then gently simmered together with salt and sugar (and sometimes bicarbonate of soda) in a small amount of Vichy water until all the moisture is absorbed. Served sprinkled with minced parsley and dotted with small pats of butter, Vichy carrots often accompany chicken or veal.

vichyssoise - a cold leek and potato soup, often garnished with chives, first served in 1917 to celebrate the opening of the roof garden at the old Ritz-Carlton Hotel on Madison Avenue at 46th Street in New York. It was created by **Louis Diat,** the Ritz's chef, who, it's said, named it after his hometown of Vichy in France, inspired by a potato soup his mother had made him when he was a child.

Victoria sponge - also **sandwich cake, Victorian sandwich.** A classic British dessert of sponge cake with jam or jelly sandwiched between cake layers magically revived thanks to the Harry Potter books. Lemon curd is sometimes substituted for the jam, and the cake may be dressed up with a simple dusting of confectioner's sugar.

Vidalia onion - see ONION.

Vienna roll - see KAISER ROLL.

Vienna sausage - a very short, canned hotdog, usually used to make **hors d'oeuvres,** such as **pigs in a blanket,** or served at cocktail parties. They are fully cooked, usually smoked, and can be eaten straight out of the can.

Viennese coffee - fresh, strong coffee sweetened as the drinker desires, served hot in a tall glass topped with a generous dollop of *Schlagobers* (whipped cream). In Viennese coffee houses, which reached their height of popularity in the 19th century and attracted a steady crowd of musicians, politicians, scientists and writers of the day, coffee is customarily served with a glass of water on the side. Some Viennese coffees are flavored with "warm" spices, such as cinnamon or cloves.

Vietnamese mint - also **laksa leaf, rau ram, Vietnamese coriander.** An herb with a hot, peppery flavor and lemony, minty scent, used in Vietnamese cooking and traditional medicine. Sold fresh in specialty food shops (it doesn't dry well), it can be added to curries, salads, sauces, soups and stir-fries.

vin - French for "wine."

vinaigre - French for "vinegar."

vinaigrette - an emulsion of oil and vinegar that often also contains herbs, spices, shallots, mustard, etc. Strangely enough, the word was originally the name for a small box of perforated gold or silver, for holding aromatic vinegar in a sponge.

vinarterta - a classic, special-occasion Icelandic white cake, flavored with almond and vanilla, baked in six to eight separate layers. When baked by "New Icelanders" — descendants of those who settled on the North American prairies — it's filled with a puréed mixture of prunes or dates (back home, apricots or rhubarb may be used, instead), sugar and a spice, such as ground cardamom or cloves, then covered in almond frosting.

vindaloo - also **vendaloo.** A very spicy curry from Goa, in southwestern India, one of the hottest curries available. It was originally made with pork, but beef, chicken and lamb are now used as well. The meat is marinated in a spicy mixture of hot peppers, tamarind, mustard seeds, cumin and other spices. The Portuguese first brought the dish to Goa making it with wine vinegar and garlic — the word is from *vinho d'alho*, meaning "wine and garlic marinade."

vindaloo curry paste - see CURRY PASTE.

vin de paille - French for "wine of straw." A classic wine traditionally made in the Jura area of France from grapes laid out to dry on mats of straw. This sweet wine is often served with a cheese or dessert course.

vinegar - from the Latin *vinum*, meaning "wine," and *acer*, meaning "sharp or sour," although it's not sour wine, contrary to popular belief. Vinegar is the result of the oxidation of ethanol in wine, cider or beer. Roman legions put wine vinegar into their drinking water to purify it, and Cleopatra once dissolved a perfect pearl in vinegar to win a wager with Mark Antony that she could host the most expensive meal in history. Both the Greeks and the Romans had special vessels for the table in which vinegar was kept for dipping bread. And in 13th-century Paris, vendors sold vinegar from barrels rolled in the street. Flavored vinegars, such as mustard and garlic, were available even then. Vinegar is also, but less commonly, made from other sources, such as champagne, coconut, honey, palm toddy, raisins and raspberries.

Wine vinegar is made by vinegar yeasts in wine, which can occur naturally, but are usually added to guarantee consistent results for

TYPES OF VINEGAR

apple cider vinegar - see CIDER VINEGAR.

balsamic vinegar - made from the cooked and concentrated **must** of white grapes in the area around Modena and Reggio Emilia in Italy, with a somewhat syrupy texture and a rich, deep mahogany color. The name "balsamic" means "balm-like," reflecting its digestive character.

cane vinegar - made from sugarcane juice, is golden and mellow, but not sweet. It is made on a small scale in Louisiana, but is perhaps most widely produced in the Philippines, where it is a staple called *sukang iloko*.

Chinese vinegar - see RICE VINEGAR.

cider vinegar - also **apple cider vinegar.** This vinegar is made from apple pulp and has a slightly sweet apple flavor.

herbal vinegars - made by completely immersing plant material, such as dried herbs or whole, small chile peppers, in warmed (not boiled) vinegar, then allowing it to stand for one or two months, sealed, until the vinegar becomes infused with their flavor. The plant material is then carefully sieved out; decorative whole, fresh stems of herbs, such as dill, for example, may be put into the bottle of finished vinegar. Delicately flavored herbs are best paired with a mild vinegar, and stronger-flavored herbs with more robust vinegars. Herbal vinegars are used in salad dressings and marinades; small amounts may be added to sauces, soups and stews.

malt vinegar - made with mashed malted barley, heated with water and fermented into a crude type of beer. The vinegar is then filtered, matured and colored with caramel. Used for pickling and in Worcestershire sauce.

rice vinegar - also **Chinese vinegar.** There are basically three kinds: white rice vinegar is colorless, similar to Western vinegars, but less acidic and milder, used extensively in stir-fries, sweet-and-sour dishes and in pickling. Red rice vinegar is darker in color, with a unique meld of sweetness and tartness, makes an excellent dip. Black rice vinegar is dark, with a deep, smoky flavor, made with glutinous or sweet rice, often used in braises, as a dipping sauce and a substitute for balsamic vinegar. **Su vinegar** is a high-quality rice vinegar used in preparing sushi rice.

wine vinegar - made by vinegar yeasts in wine, which can occur naturally but are usually added to guarantee consistent results for commercial production.

commercial production. These yeasts form what's known as a vinegar mother, a floating, cloudy raft of yeast cells, which convert the alcohol into acetic acid. A vinegar mother can also be made at home by adding a piece of bread to stale wine and leaving it at room temperature. In the previous century, vinegar mothers were passed down from mother to daughter, kept alive with the same principles that keep sourdough **starters** alive. The minimum level of vinegar's acetic acid, required by law in Britain and the U.S., is 6 percent for wine vinegars and 4 percent for all others.

Vinegar is a stimulant to the palate, making the taste buds more receptive to other flavors. Plain white vinegar is derived from malt, rye and barley and is too strong for most tastes. The most adaptable is wine vinegar, made from red or white wine. See also BALSAMIC VINEGAR, CIDER VINEGAR, DISTILLED VINEGAR, MALT VINEGAR, MOTHER OF VINEGAR, RICE VINEGAR, VERJUICE.

vine leaves - leaves, such as **grape leaves,** used to wrap fillings for **dolmades** or roll-ups. During cooking, some flavor or fragrance from the leaves is imparted to the filling.

vine-ripened - a term denoting **produce,** usually tomatoes, that is allowed to fully ripen on the vine — naturally — before it is harvested. It can be deceptive, however; the term has been used by growers who use ethylene gas to "ripen" tomatoes on the vine.

vineyard - an area planted with grapevines, usually for winemaking, and usually chosen for its **terroir.** Many European winemaking regions have vineyards that have been under cultivation for centuries.

vino cotto - also **mosto cotto.** Italian for "cooked wine." A sweet syrup made by boiling down non-fermented grape juice to one-third of its original volume. One or more spices, such as a stick of cinnamon, are occasionally added during the cooking. The syrup is used in baked goods, such as *buccellato*, desserts, dressings, marinades, and glazes for meat, poultry, seafood and vegetables — even as a dip for biscotti. In Italy, a version of vino cotto, called *mosto cotto*, is traditionally made during the grape harvest, cooking the juice and **must** to one-fifth of its original volume; after skimming, the syrup is poured into wooden casks to age. Popular as a warm drink and an ingredient in cooking, it was long believed to have healing properties. In some rural communities, the syrup was rubbed onto the limbs of newborns to help them grow strong.

Vino Nobile de Montepulciano - a red wine from the town of Montepulciano in Tuscany, made primarily from Prugnolo grapes (a clone of the well-loved **Sangiovese** grapes that are the basis of **Chianti**), with small amounts of Canaiolo, Malvasia and/or Trebbiano grapes blended in for balance. To be called Vino Nobile, the wine must be aged in wooden casks for a minimum of two years. A good Vino Nobile de Montepulciano is sharply acidic but balanced, with a spicy flavor, but less-balanced versions can be bracingly tart and astringent. The wine takes it name from the town where it is produced and was dubbed *vino nobile*, or "noble wine," in the 18th century, when it was the preferred tipple of noblemen, clergy and artists.

vino santo - a wine from Montepulciano in Tuscany, made from white Grechetto, Malaysia Toscana and Trebbiano Toscano grapes, its name is attributed to Cardinal Bessarione in 1440, who exclaimed upon tasting it, "*Ma questo è un vino santo!*" ("My, but this is a holy wine!"). In fact, for hundreds of years, it was the Catholic communion wine. Vino santo is traditionally a dessert wine, usually served with biscotti. Occhio di Pernice is the most well known and the most expensive of all the vino santo varieties.

Vins Délimités de Qualité Supérieure (VDQS) - see APPELLATION D'ORIGINE CONTRÔLÉE.

Vins de Pays - see APPELLATION D'ORIGINE CONTRÔLÉE.

vintage - the year a wine's grapes were picked or the wine was made (not bottled). A good vintage is a year that produced good wines, usually due to favorable weather conditions. A vintage wine is the product of a single year's harvest, while a non-vintage wine is a blend from two or more years. The word "vintage" is often erroneously used to mean "a very good year." In fact, it only means very good wine when applied to Champagne. The name comes from the Latin *vindemia*, meaning "vintage," and *vinum*, meaning "wine"; the French word *vendange* has the same source.

vintner - a person who sells or makes wine, from the Latin *vinum*, meaning "vine," and the Old French *vinetier*, meaning "wine merchant."

viola - see VIOLET.

violet - also **viola.** An ornamental plant, *Viola odorata*, whose leaves and flowers (when the buds just open) are culinary delights, used also medicinally. Before the rose took its place, the violet was the flower of love. It was an emblem for both Aphrodite and her son Priapus, a fertility god. The Greeks called it *Ione*, after the myth about Zeus changing his mistress Io into a white heifer, giving her violets to eat, to divert his wife Hera's suspicions. The Romans were fond of violet leaf salads and wore violet necklaces and bracelets to prevent intoxication when drinking. They made violet wine, preserves, perfume and a beauty cream of violets and goat's milk. In the Middle Ages, the violet was prized for its expectorant properties, as a mild laxative and as a poultice for fresh wounds. Napoleon, while in exile in St. Helena, promised he would return with the spring, meaning when the violets blossomed again. The favorite toast of his supporters and officers was to "Corporal Violet," in reference to his self-appointed nickname, because of his fondness for the flower.

violet

In the Victorian age, the violet stood for modesty and humility. During courtship, a man who sent violets to his beloved was saying, "I am dying of love for you but dare not say so."

There are about 500 varieties of violets. The leaves and the flowers are sweet and delicate, today used mostly in decorative confections, often candied, but also in salads. Violets are the main ingredients in the French liqueur Parfait Amour and in violet-flavored lozenges. See also EDIBLE FLOWERS.

Virginia ham - also **Smithfield ham.** The renowned product of Smithfield, Virginia, named after the famed butchers' district in London, which predates Shakespeare. The town was officially founded in 1752, but settlers in the area were exporting hams and bacon to England as early as 1639. Just over two centuries later, Queen Victoria placed an order for six hams a week from Smithfield, Virginia. In 1926, because so many imitation Smithfield hams were being sold, the Virginia General Assembly passed legislation specifying that "genuine Smithfield hams [are those] cut from the carcasses of peanut-fed hogs, raised in the peanut belt of the State of Virginia or the State of North Carolina and which are cured, treated, smoked and processed in the town of Smithfield, in the State of Virginia." Such ham, cured for a year or longer, smoked and aged, is dark reddish-brown in color and has a deep, rich, well-developed, salty flavor.

virgin olive oil - see OLIVE OIL.

virtù, Le - see LE VIRTÙ.

Visser, Margaret - see profile below.

vitamin - an organic compound necessary for proper bodily function. Vitamin deficiencies, like amino acid deficiencies, were fought by trial and error long before their chemistry was understood. Scurvy, a debilitating disease

Visser, Margaret (1940–) - Canadian academic and author of *Much Depends on Dinner: The Extraordinary History and Mythology, Allure and Obsessions, Perils and Taboos, of an Ordinary Meal* (1986).

Visser's popular book explores the rich anthropological background of a simple supper of chicken and rice. South African by birth, Visser was educated at the Sorbonne and became a professor of classics at the University of Toronto, where she taught Greek and Latin for 18 years. Her other books, also bestsellers, are *The Rituals of Dinner: The Origins, Evolution, Eccentricities and Meaning of Table Manners* (1991), *The Way We Are: Collected Essays* (2000), *The Geometry of Love: Space, Time, Mystery and Meaning in an Ordinary Church* (2000) and *Beyond Fate* (2002).

characterized by infections, tenderness, general hemorrhaging and anemia, plagued sailors on long voyages in the 16th and 17th centuries. About 1750, a Scottish physician, James Lind, discovered that oranges and lemons not only cured, but also prevented scurvy, and 50 years later the British navy ordered shipboard rations of limes (hence the nickname "limey").

We now know that these fruits are effective against scurvy because of their vitamin C content. In 1911, while studying beriberi (a disease caused by thiamine/B_1 deficiency), a Polish chemist named Casimir Funk discovered that an extract of rice hulls prevented the disease and, guessing the chemical nature of the substance, called it "vitamine," a contraction of "vital" and "amine." When it was discovered, a few years later, that the active material was not an amine, a nitrogen-containing compound, the final "e" was dropped.

vitamins B - see B VITAMINS.

vitello - Italian for "veal."

viticulture - the cultivation and science of growing grapes for wine, from the Latin *vitis*, meaning "vine," and *cultura*, meaning "culture."

vodka - a distilled liquor made from rye, wheat, potato or rice, although corn is also used today. A fermented mash from one of the grains is distilled at a high proof, which eliminates the elements that would otherwise convey flavor and aroma to the vodka. The liquid is then filtered through special charcoal, which occasionally lends a very faint trace of flavor to the finished product. Lastly, distilled water is added and the vodka is bottled.

The word vodka is actually a generic term. In both Russian and Polish, it's a diminutive of *voda*, meaning "water," following the prevalent European linguistic custom of referring to all distillates firstly as a form of water, as in *aqua vitea*, strong distilled liquor. Historical documents place vodka's first appearance in Russia in a monastery between 1438 and 1478, after the Russians learned distillation from Italy. In Russia, vodka drinking has spawned many rituals. Russian hussars drank from glasses balanced on their elbows, and today's soldiers put their awards in vodka glasses to "wash" them as a sort of blessing. At funerals, mourners salute the dead by drinking a glass of vodka straight to the bottom. Anton Chekhov, the 19th-century author, wrote "Although vodka is white, it paints your nose red and blackens your reputation." Vodka is by far the most fashionable single liquor in the U.S.

vol-au-vent - a puff-pastry shell usually filled with a savory mixture. The legendary French chef **Antonin Carême** claimed credit for its creation. On taking it out of the oven, he said that it looked so light, it could *vol au vent*, meaning "fly away in the wind."

vol-au-vent cutter - a metal box, usually four-sided, with cutting blades along its outside edge and an open duplicate of the same shape formed by cutting blades inside, bridged by a handle on top. The blades are designed to pass neatly through the puff passtry without pressing the cut edges together, which would inhibit the pastries from puffing.

Vouvray - a generic designation of white wines (ranging from still to sparkling and dry to sweet), produced near the village of Vouvray in the Loire Valley in France.

voyageur stew - a traditional French Canadian dish containing chunks of beef, bison or venison, salt bacon or pork, onions, root vegetables (such as carrots, potatoes and turnips) and herbs, simmered slowly in beef broth. Depending on the cook, ingredients, such as maple syrup, mushrooms, wild rice and wine, may also be added to the pot.

wagashi - a generic Japanese term for sweets. Most are made from beans, fruits and grains, and many are delicately flavored with green tea. See also OKASHI.

wagyu beef - see KOBE BEEF.

wafer - a crisp, thin biscuit or cookie that can be either sweet or savory.

waffle - a batter cake cooked on a two-sided iron with honeycomb imprints. The Greeks cooked flat cakes between two hot metal disks, a technique that continued throughout the Middle Ages, when they were known as *oblies*. Geoffrey Chaucer mentioned them in *The Canterbury Tales*, and many a poet sang their praises, buying his cakes piping hot on the street or at a stall. With the invention of the honeycomb waffle iron in the 14th century by the Dutch or the Germans (the debate rages on), the cake became known as *wafel* in Dutch, *waffel* in German and *wafla* in French (later called *gaufrette)*; it was made into thin cookies, rather than today's thick, fluffy breakfast food. Thomas Jefferson brought the first waffle maker to the U.S. from Holland in 1789, a pair of irons with tongs, and introduced waffles at a White House dinner. Because of his enthusiasm, "waffle parties" became very popular, and by the 1800s street vendors were selling them with butter and molasses or maple syrup. The electric waffle iron was invented toward the end of the 19th century, soon making its way into nearly every North American home, popular also on Sunday nights. In Baltimore, kidney stew served on waffles is a traditional Sunday evening meal. See also BELGIAN WAFFLE, GAUFRETTE.

wahoo - **1.** also **kingfish, ocean barracuda, ono.** A fish of the subtropical and tropical waters of the Atlantic, Caribbean, Indian and Pacific oceans. Prized by cooks for its sweet, white flesh and by Florida sportfishermen for its fight, *Acanthocybium solanderi* has been clocked at almost 47 miles per hour (75 kilometers) chasing prey. Perhaps because it is solitary and doesn't gather in large schools, wahoo is not much of a commercial catch, except in parts of the Caribbean and South America, where it is sold fresh, frozen, salted or spice cured. **2.** a small, red-berried shrub, *Euonymous atropurpurea*, that is native to eastern North America. Long used as a medicinal plant by indigenous peoples, the plant (and all its parts) can be highly toxic, so ingestion by home herbalists is not recommended.

Wait, Pearle - see COOPER, PETER.

wakame - a Japanese edible seaweed, *Undaria pinnatifida*, available dried and fresh, although rarely outside Asia. Used in soups and salads, it can also be toasted the same way as **nori** or crumbled and used as a condiment. **Mekabu,** the sporophyll or spore-bearing leaf of the wakame plant, is traditionally made into a medicinal tea.

Wakefield, Ruth Graves - see TOLL HOUSE COOKIE.

Waldorf salad - a salad of chopped apples, celery and mayonnaise introduced in 1893 by Oscar Tschirky, maîitre d'hôtel of the old Waldorf Hotel on New York's Fifth Avenue, where the Empire State Building now stands. Tschirky became a bestselling cookbook author in the 1920s. Modern versions of his salad include nuts.

Walla Walla onion - see ONION.

walleye - also **old marble eyes, yellow walleye.** *Stizostedion vitreum*, found in the Great Lakes and other smaller freshwater lakes, and considered a good game fish. Fished commercially (especially in Green Bay in Lake Michigan and Saginaw Bay in Lake Huron) during the mid-1900s, the stock eventually declined. By the 1970s, restocking programs resulted in a population rebound, particularly in Lake Erie. Available fresh or frozen in grocery stores, walleye can be cooked any number of ways, but sportfishermen often like them best dipped in a beer batter and cooked over a campfire. Because of their large, glassy eyes, which enable them to feed at night, walleye are nicknamed "old marble eyes" by sportfishermen in the North American Midwest.

walnut - the edible, furrowed, two-lobed nut encased in a hard, spherical shell produced by various *Juglans* species. The name is derived from the Old English *wealh*, meaning "foreigner," originally given to the Persian walnut, *J. regia*, to differentiate it from the island's abundant, wild hazelnuts. Now known, confusingly, as English walnut, this Persian or royal walnut is native from southeast Europe through to China. Other species include the North American *J. californica* (California

walnuts

walnut), *J. cinerea* (butternut or white walnut) and *J. nigra* (black walnut). Eaten by the Iroquois, white walnuts quickly became a common food of the early settlers. Today, walnuts are eaten fresh or roasted, on their own or used in baked goods, confections, pasta dishes, salad dressings, soups and stews. Ripe and unripe, they are pickled and preserved in sweet and savory syrups and condiments, especially in Asia. Walnuts are also ground into meal and cold-pressed into oil (usually used in uncooked dishes, since heating lessens its flavor). See also SOUARI.

walnut flour - see NUT FLOUR.

walnut liqueur - see NOCINO.

walnut oil - extracted from the meat of the walnut, which is 60 percent oil and has a high level of iodine; used in France since the middle of the 19th century, but known in the Middle East since the Middle Ages. Walnut oil is healthy, flavorful, perfect for salads, but can be used in cakes as well. It's also pricey and has a short shelf life, so it should be kept refrigerated.

wapiti - see ELK.

warqa - Moroccan for "leaf"; also an Arabic word meaning "dove" or "pigeon," which is usually the meat used for **bastila** or "pigeon pie." Warqa is a very thin pastry used to make the pie *bastila*. Warqa pastry begins as a spongy dough that is tapped or slapped against a hot convex sheet of pounded metal, a kind of pan called a *tubsil*, set over a hot charcoal brazier, in a series of overlapping concentric circles to form a large film of pastry.

wasabi - also **wasabe.** A strong, sharp Japanese condiment, similar to horseradish, from the root of a plant, *Wasabia japonica*, originally grown only in Japan. It is available as a paste or powder, which is reconstituted with water, used as a condiment, most often with sushi and sashimi; used carefully because of its spicy potency. It can sometimes, although rarely, be found fresh in specialty markets.

Washington orange - see ORANGE.

Washington pie - see MARTHA WASHINGTON PIE.

wassail - a traditional English beverage of spiced and sweetened beer or wine, which sometimes included lemon peel, eggs and slices of toast. The custom was for the master of the house to toast his guests by drinking from a bowl and saying, "*Wass heal,*" Saxon for "Be well," and passing the bowl along, each guest doing the same.

water bath - see BAIN-MARIE.

water biscuit - also **water cracker.** A plain, crisp, dry cracker usually made with shortening. The water biscuit's neutrality allows the flavors of whatever it accompanies to take prominence.

water chestnut - either of two unrelated edible aquatic bulbs, *Eleocharis dulcis* or *Trapa natans*, originally from southern China, consumed in Asia since time immemorial. The water chestnut occupies an important place in Chinese, Vietnamese and Japanese cuisine, first used medicinally in China, from which its cultivation spread to India and Madagascar. Today, China is still the major producer of water chestnuts. In North America, we know them from specialty stores, where they're sold canned, most commonly the *Eleocharis dulcis* variety. The *Trapa natans* variety is cultivated in some Asian countries and Europe. Both varieties are grown in shallow lakes, swamps and slow-running rivers. Like rice, they need large quantities of water. In Asia, they're often cultivated in rice paddies, where they're planted in spring and harvested the following fall when the rice paddies are drained.

The *Eleocharis dulcis* variety looks like the regular chestnut, rounded and from 1 to 1½ inches (2.5 to 4 cm) in diameter. The top is slightly flattened and has a little tuft where a green sprout will germinate if the chestnut is not harvested. The bulb is hidden in a rough dark brown skin under which a thin brown skin further protects the white, crispy, juicy, sweet, aromatic flesh. The *Trapa* has two varieties, *T. bicornis*, which is ornamented by two curved horns, and *T. natans* with four horns. They're sometimes called "Jesuit nuts" because they were used for centuries to make rosary beads. These varieties were once extremely popular in Europe, but they're now all but forgotten. The bulbs of these varieties cannot be consumed raw, because they all contain some toxic substances that are neutralized by the cooking process.

water-chestnut powder - also **water-chestnut flour.** A starchy powder of finely ground, dried water chestnuts, used in Asian cooking as a thickening agent for dishes such as sauces and soups, and in confections.

water cracker - see WATER BISCUIT.

watercress - a plant, *Nasturtium officinale*, with small, dark green leaves and a peppery, slightly bitter taste. Watercress will grow wild wherever there's shallow, slow-moving water, but it's native to Asia Minor and the Mediterranean. It has a lot of landlocked relatives: peppergrass (also called curly cress), upland cress, lamb's cress, cuckoo flower, lady's smoke, mayflower, pennycress and even nasturtium. Both Xenophon, the ancient Greek general, and Xerxes, the Persian king, ordered their soldiers to eat it to keep them healthy. The Greeks and the Persians found watercress in good supply, and we can find mention of it in Greek literature dating back to 100 BC.

Historically, watercress has always been tied to bread: either eating some while making bread or eating some with bread. In the early 1800s in England, watercress was a staple of the working class breakfast, eaten between two pieces of bread. If the family was too poor to buy bread, they ate it on its own, so watercress came to be known as "poor man's bread." Irish monks were said to survive for long periods of time eating only bread and watercress and referred to it as "pure food for sages." Early settlers brought watercress to the U.S., and it can be found at every point of the compass. Not long ago, you could gather it from edges of small streams while on hikes or camping trips. Now, widespread water pollution makes it safer to stick to commercially produced watercress.

water ghost - see OCTOPUS.

watermelon - a large melon of the genus *Citrullus*, with a very high water content and flesh that can be pink, red, white or yellowish orange. They are originally from Africa, but have been grown in the Middle East and the warmer parts of Russia for thousands of years. They reached southern Europe with the Moors early in the Christian era. Watermelons arrived in China about 1,000 years ago and came to the Western Hemisphere and the Pacific Islands with European colonists. In Naples, there's a saying that watermelon is "the only way to eat, drink and wash your face at the same time."

Watermelons have been common in Europe, Asia and Africa for so long that botanists were not quite sure where they had originated until the middle of the 19th century. Famed explorer Dr. David Livingstone settled the question when he discovered watermelons growing wild in the remote interior region of Africa, where they were used as canteens, stored as a source of water (watermelons are 91 percent water) for the dry seasons and taken on long journeys, when water might not be available. Today, the watermelon is grown in most tropical countries and in the warmer parts of America and Europe; it's available from summer to early autumn. It can be either round or oblong, and when ripe, the skin should be a rich, dark green or green variegated with dark gray. For vine-ripened sweetness, the stem end should be slightly sunken and calloused.

watermelon

watermelon syrup - a traditional Russian sweetener made by boiling the juice pressed from watermelon pulp, skimming and stirring it regularly, until it reduces to a thick liquid that is almost as viscous as molasses. Lacking other sweeteners, peasants produced it from homegrown melons, then used it in baking, such as **Pfeffernüsse.** A popular processed-sugar alternative for back-to-the-landers (one of their bibles, the magazine *Mother Earth News*, calls it "Nature's neatest natural nectar" and offers a recipe for home cooks that recommends boiling the juice down to one-seventh of its original volume), watermelon syrup is also available, premade, for use in fancy cocktails, gourmet coffees and smoothies.

water process decaffeination - see DECAFFEINATION.

Waters, Alice - see profile below.

water spinach - also **swamp morning glory.** A South Asian creeper, *Ipomea aquatica*, with long, pointed leaves. The leaves and tender stalks are chopped, then steamed or added to stir-fries and the fillings for egg rolls and **dim sum** (not unlike real spinach, it shrinks a great

Waters, Alice (1944–) - activist and restaurateur, credited with popularizing simple, but delicious American food. Born in Chatham, New Jersey, Waters was a politically active student during the tumultuous '60s. She graduated from the University of California at Berkeley in 1967 with a degree in French Cultural Studies and was a crusading spirit committed to improving the world. A year in France had made her aware of the connection between farmers' markets and flavorful food, and her passion for cooking inspired her to open a restaurant, so that she could cook more often for her friends, a pastime she preferred to teaching, her first career.

Chez Panisse, named for a character in a trilogy of French films made in the 1930s, opened in 1971. The restaurant was as much a reflection of Berkeley's counter-culture ideals as its commitment to producing simple and delicious food. Like the good country restaurants in France it emulated, Chez Panisse had no aspirations to producing **haute cuisine.** Staffed by a collective of talented amateurs, including the chef **Jeremiah Tower,** whose over-the-top flair helped to put the restaurant on the map, it was for many years a seat-of-the pants operation, which lost money. However, the absence of professional expertise inspired some great innovations. The single daily menu reflected how Waters cooked at home, and recipes from cookbooks by such writers as **Elizabeth David** and **Richard Olney** provided the repertoire, because the cooks weren't trained chefs.

Gradually, the restaurant became a success. Writing to a friend in 1978, **M.F.K. Fisher** said: "The food is the best I have eaten in America...in a public place I mean." Although Chez Panisse began as a spot where young Americans could put their stamp on French food, it evolved into something completely original. Its inspiration shifted from France to California, and it became known for its impeccable locally produced ingredients and commitment to sustainability. Its influence expanded far beyond the restaurant's walls. As *Gourmet* magazine editor **Ruth Reichl** said in a profile of Waters produced for public television, "When you go to your local farmers' market, you have Alice to thank. . . When you buy an organic vegetable at your supermarket, you have Alice to thank, and when you eat really simple, great food in a restaurant, Alice Waters has had a hand in that."

Ever the activist, in 1996 Alice established the Chez Panisse Foundation to support food-related public-education projects, such as The Edible Schoolyard at a Berkeley middle school, which involves students in growing and preparing the food they eat. When her daughter, Fanny, attended Yale University, Waters conceived the Yale Sustainable Food Project, which does much the same for university-age students living in a dorm. Explaining her vision to one journalist, she said, "I imagine a curriculum in the public schools that can begin in preschool and go all the way through graduate school, getting more and more complex as you go along. Conceivably, kids in high school could run their own café and get credit for it — credit for eating their own school lunch." It's a radical and delicious notion, and Alice Waters is just the person to pull it off.

deal when it's cooked). The edible trumpet-shaped flowers, which range from white through pink to purple, are also used as a garnish or an ingredient. Invited into home gardens in North America, it has become an invasive alien, threatening warm, wet areas such as the Florida Everglades. Stems up to 70 feet (21 m) long creep overland, colonize new territory and form impenetrable masses of stems. Known throughout Asia, it is called *kangkung* (Indonesia, Malaysia and the Philippines), *ong choy* (in China), *pak bung* (in Thailand) and *rau muong* (in Vietnam).

waterzooï - a classic Flemish soup-cum-stew made with freshwater eels and fish (or, less often, chicken), simmered with herbs and vegetables in **court-bouillon** (egg yolks and white wine may also be added to the broth), then topped with crisped bread crumbs, butter and **crème fraîche.**

wax bean - see BEAN.

waxed paper - also **wax paper.** Said to have been invented by Thomas Edison, waxed paper is made by coating tissue paper with paraffin wax, which is mechanically forced through the tissue's pores to penetrate and cover both sides.

wax gourd - see WINTER MELON.

wedding cake - originally known as a "great cake," a variation of the English fruitcake, spiced and with nuts, sometimes made by women before being betrothed as a way to display cooking abilities. "Great cakes" are still made in the Caribbean and some former British colonies. Until the 19th century, pieces of wedding cake were crumbled over the bride and groom, later replaced by tossed rice. The modern white wedding cake became fashionable just prior to the Civil War, when finely ground flour, baking powder and baking soda became cheaper and more available.

Today, wedding cakes are usually three-tiered affairs but recently have reached new heights with celebrities ordering elaborate creations. In 2004, the wedding cake for Mariska Hargitay, a star on the television show *Law & Order*, was 7 feet (210 cm) tall with six tiers, topped with Swarovski crystals in the bride and groom's initials.

Wehani rice - long-grained red-brown rice, aromatic, mildly sweet and nutty, related to **basmati,** unmilled and therefore cooked like brown rice. It splits lengthwise slightly when cooked. See also RICE.

Weisswurst - German for "white sausage." A pale, parboiled German sausage made of finely ground veal. Bland and smooth, this specialty of Munich benefits from its usual accompaniment — mustard — and is a tradition at Oktoberfest.

wekiwa - see LAVENDER GEM.

well - a term used in recipes to describe a depression formed in one or several mixed dry ingredients in a container or on a pastry board into which a liquid is poured before blending.

well-and-tree platter - a classic design for a large, rimmed, oval platter named after the channels in its surface, which catch and pool the juices draining from the cooked meat or poultry placed on top. Several short, tapering channels branch out from a central "trunk," which runs the length of the platter and ends in a deeper well at its base.

Wellington - see BEEF WELLINGTON.

Welsh rabbit - also **Welsh rarebit.** Cheddar cheese spiced with mustard and melted, often with ale or beer, then served on toast. This dish is said to have been the invention of a Welsh nobleman who was entertaining a large group and ran out of game, so he served cheese to the remainder of his guests and called it "Welsh rabbit."

Welsh siot - a traditional Welsh drink made from broken oatcakes steeped in buttermilk. For centuries, this nourishing drink was served to strengthen workers during the hay harvest. Special ridged rolling pins were used to crush the oatcakes.

Wensleydale - an English cow's milk cheese sometimes made as a blue-veined variety. White Wensleydale is traditionally eaten with apple pie.

Western eggplant - see EGGPLANT.

Western sandwich - also **Denver sandwich.** A sandwich containing an omelet made with diced ham, onion and often green peppers.

West Indian cherry - see ACEROLA.

West Indian pumpkin - see CALABAZA.

Westphalian ham - one of the most famous of the German hams, from pigs fed on acorns, dry-cured and smoked over beech and juniper wood. See also HAM.

wet cure - to cure a piece of meat, usually a ham, by soaking or injecting it with a brine of salt, sodium nitrite and/or sodium nitrate, sugar and seasonings. The brine quickly penetrates the flesh, shortening the curing time — an asset for most large-scale ham manufacturers. A wet-cured ham is usually lightly smoked, but it can be air-dried if desired. See also CITY HAM, COUNTRY HAM, HAM.

whale - any of a number of large ocean-dwelling mammals of the order *Cetacea*, once hunted extensively for its flesh, baleen, bone and oil, still eaten today as a delicacy in Asia and Scandinavia, and a traditional food of the Inuit of northern Canada and many other native communities around the world. Many different species of whale are commonly hunted for food, including the minke, beluga, pilot, narwhal, gray and sperm whale. Whale meat is often served raw, sliced paper-thin, as a type of **sashimi,** but it is also cooked in hundreds of different ways.

wheat

wheat - the grain of an annual grass, *Triticum*, native to the Mediterranean and southwestern Asia, used to make everything from bread to cereal to cakes and also as a thickening agent.

Wheat was one of the first grains cultivated by humans, during the Neolithic Age, about 11,000 years ago. Bread wheat was growing in the Nile Valley by 5000 BC, in China by 2500 BC and in England by 2000 BC. Mythological references to wheat usually recount the providing of food magically and in abundance. Triptolemus, whom Plato called "the minister of the gifts of Demeter" was given wheat seeds by Demeter and an order to sow them from the air, using a one-wheeled chariot that she'd made herself, drawn by a winged dragon. And Dionysus, the god of wine, had three granddaughters — Oeno (wine), Spermo (wheat) and Elais (olive oil) — whom he empowered with the ability to change water to wine, grass to wheat and berries to olives, so that no one would have to starve. They were also charged with stocking the fleet heading out to war with Troy. Agamemnon was so impressed that he wanted to abduct them, but Dionysus saved them by turning them into doves.

Wheat varieties include **hard wheat** that has a high amount of protein in the kernel, excellent for developing strong gluten strands, so therefore good for use in yeast-leavened breads. **Soft wheat** has a low amount of protein in the kernel, so it does not develop gluten as well as hard wheat, making it better for delicate, tender baked goods, such as cakes. **Durum** is a very hard wheat, with high gluten used mostly in making semolina, from the Latin *durus*, meaning "hard." The **wheat endosperm** is the interior layer of a kernel of grain, inside the outer covering of bran and surrounding the germ in the center. The endosperm is rich in starch and protein, but not high in vitamins and minerals. All-purpose flour is ground from the endosperm of wheat kernels and does not contain the germ or the bran. **Wheat gluten** is the starch element of wheat, also known as essential or vital gluten, which is extracted from the wheat during a washing and rinsing process and used mainly as an additive to dough. **Wheat bran** is the outer layer of the wheat kernel and is very high in carbohydrates, calcium and fiber. **Wheat germ** is the isolated highly nutritious core, or germ, of the grain, rich in minerals, vitamins and protein, with a pleasant nutty taste. Because it has a high oil content that causes it to go rancid quickly, it should be stored in the refrigerator. **Cracked wheat** is whole wheat grains that are crushed into coarse fragments.

The world's output of wheat is staggering: (in millions of tons) China, 112; India, 65; U.S., 62; Russian Federation, 36; France, 33; Canada, 26. See also BOULANG, BREAD, CEREAL, FLOUR, KAMUT, WHEAT BERRY, WHEAT GLUTEN.

wheat beer - a beer made from malted wheat, pale in color.

wheat berry - a husked whole kernel of wheat with its surrounding nutritious bran intact. Red (hard) wheat berries are high in gluten and relatively unprocessed, while white (soft) wheat berries have undergone greater processing and have a higher carbohydrate content and less gluten. See also FARRO.

wheat bran - see FLOUR, WHEAT.

wheat germ - see WHEAT.

wheat gluten - a protein present in wheat. Its long molecules act as a binder, making bread dough stretchy, for example, and the baked product chewy. Since it has such an effect on strength and texture, gluten is present in varying proportions in flours manufactured for different purposes. Cake and pastry flour, called "soft flour," has a low gluten content. Bread flour, called "hard flour," has more gluten. And pasta flour has the highest concentration.

wheat meat - see SEITAN.

whelk - any of a group of gastropod mollusks found in salt waters around the world. They have a spiral shell and a tough, but flavorful foot or adductor muscle.

whetstone - a fine-grained, hard stone over which cutting blades are drawn (at an angle of about 20 degrees is recommended) to hone them. For sharpening kitchen knives, a whetstone may be shaped into a long, slender cylinder and attached to a handle (often with a flange at the top that serves as a hand guard), or cut into a brick and fitted with a nonslip base for use on countertops. Versions made of Carborundum, ceramic or high-carbon stainless steel are also available.

whey - the residue of milk after most of the fats and other solids have coagulated into the curd.

whey butter - a salty, strong-flavored butter churned from any cream present in **whey** (usually made after the whey is drained off during cheese making). An **artisanal,** rather than a large-scale commercial product, whey butter may be found at some farmer's markets and specialty stores.

whey cheese - cheese made by heating **whey,** with or without added cream or milk, to concentrate it and create curds; it is then drained and pressed into molds. Italian ricotta is a familiar example. Today's whey cheeses are often vacuum-packed to ensure product safety and prolong shelf life. Traditional **artisanal** versions are usually made from ewe's or goat's cream, milk and whey, and may be drained and pressed by packing each into cheesecloth gathered tightly around the ball of cheese, then hung. Some whey cheeses, such as the Greek anthotyros, are available fresh or dry (fresh, it is mild flavored and soft; dried, it has a rich, salty flavor and is hard enough to grate).

whip - **1.** (n.) an airy, "little-nothing" dessert made with stiffly beaten egg whites or whipped cream folded into a mixture containing chocolate, fruit purée or gelatin. **2.** (n.) an alternate name for a whisk. **3.** (v.) to beat ingredients (such as cream or egg whites) to incorporate air and make them light and fluffy.

whipped butter - butter that is whipped until aerated and light and fluffy. It's sold in tubs as a spread.

whipped topping - a generic term used to describe dessert topping designed to have the taste and texture of whipped cream. Prepared frozen and refrigerated versions, as well as dry mixes, are available, many calorie-reduced.

whipping cream - see CREAM.

whisk - also **balloon whisk, whip.** An indispensable kitchen utensil, the whisk is used for aerating and whipping ingredients, such as cream, eggs and egg whites, as well as for emulsifying sauces, such as mayonnaise and **beurre blanc.** It's made of a series of looped usually stainless-steel wires (silicone-coated wires and bamboo are also used) held together by a handle. It works on the principle that as the wires move through the liquid, they create vacuum streams, which are promptly filled with air — an exercise that, when repeated steadily for a few minutes, fills heavy cream with enough air to become fluffy whipped cream. (For Types of Whisks, see page 680.)

whiskey - also **whisky.** A distilled spirit made from the mash of fermented grains, such as barley, rye and corn, Whiskey is short for *whiskybae,* which comes from *usquebaugh,* which evolved from the Irish *uisce beathadh* and the Scottish Gaelic *uisge beatha,* meaning "water of life." Like tequila and rum, whiskeys are aged in barrels to impart color and mellow the flavor.

TYPES OF WHISKS

There are a number of specialized whisks, including the following:

balloon whisk - has a bulbous working end consisting of about 10 fine, looped wires, used to quickly whip air into egg whites and whipping cream. If the kitchen only has room for one, a 12- or 14-inch (30 or 35 cm) version is recommended.

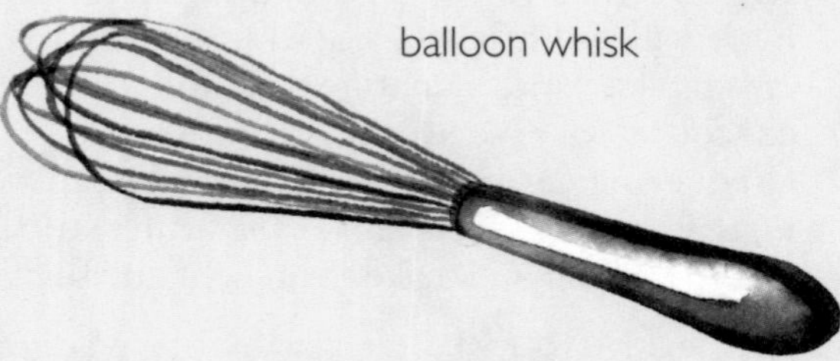
balloon whisk

bamboo whisk - also **bamboo broom.** A stubby brush made of flexible strips of bamboo, tightly wrapped together at the top end. Considered an essential in Chinese kitchens, it is used to sweep and swirl water inside a wok when cleaning it.

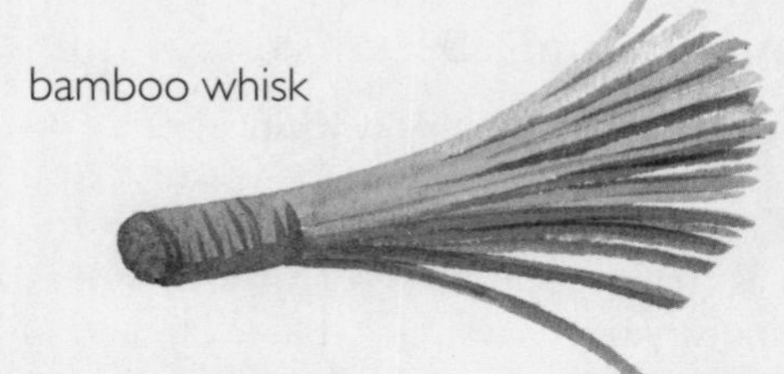
bamboo whisk

batter whisk - has a pear-shaped working end consisting of two sturdy, widely spaced, looped wires, used to mix thick batters for bar cookies or pancakes. The widely spaced wires allow the batter to slide through without clumping.

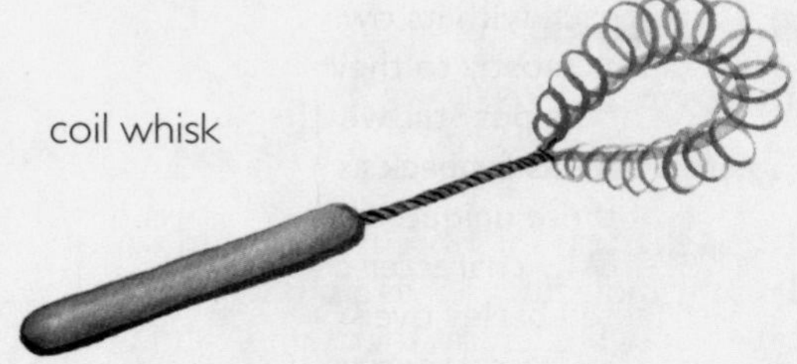
coil whisk

coil whisk - has a flat working end consisting of a stem topped by a circle of rigid wire, around which a finer wire is coiled; used to blend shallow mixtures in a bowl or pan.

flat whisk - has a working end with the top and side silhouette of a slightly upturned spoon, consisting of four looped, sturdy wires; used to blend flour with melted butter when making a roux or to deglaze pans.

French whisk - also **sauce whisk.** This whisk has an elongated oval working end consisting of about 10 sturdy, looped wires; used to blend dense or heavier sauces, such as hollandaise, or thick custards, such as pastry cream. Since they are used with hot and cold mixtures, they often have wooden handles, which don't conduct the heat.

nonstick whisk - has a working end consisting of loops of heat-resistant, silicone-coated wire or stiff nylon, designed not to scratch enameled or nonstick cookware.

sauce whisk - see FRENCH WHISK.

Whiskies made in Scotland and Canada are spelled "whisky," without the "e." (For Whiskey Varieties, see page 681.)

Whiskey Sour - a classic cocktail mixed with confectioner's sugar, lemon juice and whiskey, usually served over ice, garnished with a maraschino cherry and an orange slice.

white bean - the name used for a number of different beans, including pea beans, great Northern beans, marrow beans, navy beans, soissons, small whites, *cannelli* in Italy, *haricots blancs* in France (because they're the mature, dried white pod of the French *haricots verts*). In 1620, Pilgrims copied Native American women, who cooked these beans with deer fat and onions. They added pork fat and brown sugar and the connection between Boston and beans was created.

white cabbage - see CHINESE CABBAGE.

white chocolate - see CHOCOLATE.

white currant - see CURRANT.

WHISKEY VARIETIES

Scotch - a **single-malt Scotch,** produced in a single distillation from an individual distillery. More than 100 distillers make single-malt Scotch, each with its own characteristics, particular mostly to their region, water, peat, shape of the pot still, weather and aging casks. Some date as far back as 1494. Common to each of these unique whiskeys is malted barley. Their smoky character comes from "firing" germinated barley over coal and peat. Single malts are also categorized by their region of origin: Highland malts are the most popular, thought to have the greatest balance; Lowland malts are the lightest in flavor and color; Islay malts are the heaviest and most full-bodied.

Blended - can be a combination of single malts or grain whiskeys. As many as 25 individual whiskies can be used in a blend, and the precise proportions are unique to the individual maker. Although single malts are increasing in popularity, sales of blended Scotches still greatly exceed them.

American whiskey - bourbon does not refer to all American whiskey, as some believe, but rather specifically to the spirit that derives its name from the county in Kentucky where it was first made. Bourbon uses 51 to 79 percent corn and is aged a minimum of two years (although most bourbon distillers age their product longer for the sake of quality). Once the amount of corn used in the mash reaches 80 percent, it officially becomes **rye whiskey.** Most large bourbon distillers also produce rye. **Tennessee whiskey** is made similarly to bourbon, except that it undergoes a charcoal filtering before aging.

Canadian whisky - distilled from a mash of wheat, corn, rye and barley, corn being the dominant ingredient. It's aged in oak barrels for a minimum of three years, then blended to achieve its characteristic smoothness. Dating back to the 1800s, it became popular during Prohibition, when Canada and the U.S. passed whiskey back and forth over 3,000 miles (4,800 km) of river and lake borders.

Irish whiskey - accounts for the smallest share of the U.S. whiskey market. As in Scotland, the Irish produce both single-malt and blended whiskies, which some think are superior to those produced in Scotland. The production methods are similar to those used to make Scotch, except that rather than drying the malt over a peat fire, the Irish use closed kilns, which eliminates the smokiness of Scotch and creates a full-bodied, smooth, malty character.

white eggplant - see EGGPLANT.

whitefish - a freshwater fish known for its white flesh, usually prepared like bass and pike, and highly regarded as a smoked fish.

white goods - a term to distinguish colorless alcohols, such as vodka, gin, white rum, white tequila, etc., from **brown goods,** or whiskey, brandy, dark rum, etc.

White Granex - see ONION.

White Lady - a cocktail usually made with gin, **Cointreau,** and lemon juice, egg white and cream, shaken together with ice, then strained into a stemmed glass. See also PINK LADY.

white lightning - see MOONSHINE.

white-meat tuna - see ALBACORE.

white mushroom - see BUTTON MUSHROOM.

white pudding - see SUET PUDDING.

white rice - see RICE.

white rice vinegar - see RICE VINEGAR.

white roux - see ROUX.

white rum - also **light rum**. See RUM.

White Russian - see BLACK RUSSIAN.

white sapote - also **zapote blanco.** *Casimiroa edulus* (said to be named after 18th-century Spanish botanist Cardinal Casimiro Gomez de Ortega), which produces edible fruit. Indigenous to Central America, the trees range from 20 to 60 feet (6 to 18 m) tall. Scentless yellow flowers develop into ovoid greenish yellow–skinned fruit right through the summer. The skin isn't eaten, neither are the half-dozen

white sapote

bitter, large white seeds, but the creamy white to yellow pulp — unsuitable for canning or freezing — is eaten fresh, topped with cream and sugar, or sliced into fruit salad. Franciscan monks started seedlings in California in the 19th century, but it is grown there now only as an ornamental. It is cultivated for its fruit throughout the Caribbean, Central America, Mexico, along the Riviera and in New Zealand, however.

white sauce - see BÉCHAMEL.

white stock - stock made from beef, veal, chicken, fish or vegetables that hasn't been browned by roasting. See also BROWN STOCK.

white sturgeon - see STURGEON.

white tea - see TEA.

white toque - the tall, white hat proudly worn by the head chef since the days of the ancient Assyrians. The number of folds in the toque, which should be 100, indicated the number of ways a chef should know how to cook an egg. French chefs accompanying their aristocratic employers escaping the French Revolution introduced the tall, white toque to Britain, along with French cooking. However, in the 1800s and early 1900s, master chefs continued to wear a short black cap that caught soot that fell from the chimney, where cooks operated spits in hearth ovens. The short cap was also more convenient when carrying platters down the corridor to the dining room.

white velvet cake - see VELVET CAKE.

white walnut - see BUTTERNUT.

white wheat flour - see FLOUR.

white wine - a wine made from green grapes, can be dry, such as **Sauvignon Blanc** or **Chardonnay,** or off-dry, such as **Gewurtztraminer** or **Riesling.** The grapes are picked and transported as quickly and gently as possible, then crushed with minimal pressure so that the skins do not release their tannins into the juice and make it sour. A dry white wine is one in which there is little residual sugar left after fermentation. An off-dry white is made by stopping fermentation before it is complete by adding a bit of sulfur dioxide, which stops the action of the yeasts and leaves a higher amount of residual sugar. See also BLUSH WINE, RED WINE, WINE.

whiting - also **hake.** A slender, white-fleshed marine fish with a delicate flavor that is fished for North American markets in the northern Pacific and Atlantic oceans, but is also found extensively along the coasts of South Africa, South America and the Mediterranean. Because of its abundance, whiting is often processed into **surimi,** from the Japanese meaning "minced fish," a fish product that attempts to imitate expensive seafood, such as crab.

whole-grain barley - see BARLEY.

whole wheat flour - see FLOUR.

whore's eggs - see SEA URCHIN.

whortleberry - see HUCKLEBERRY.

wiener - also **weenie, wienie.** A common term for a frankfurter or hot dog.

Wiener schnitzel - a Viennese specialty of thinly pounded veal, breaded and fried, classically garnished with lemon, olives, anchovies, hard-boiled egg, capers and parsley.

wild celery - see ALEXANDERS, CELERY SEED.

wild leek - also **ramp.** From the onion family, the wild leek, *Allium tricocca,* has long, oval green leaves, with a small, slender bulb and a strong onion-garlic flavor. It can be found in the spring growing on the floor of moist open woods. If left to go to seed, by early summer the wild leek will have grown into a tall stalk, from 6 to 18 inches (15 to 45 cm) in height, with a spray of pale yellow flowers on top.

wild mushroom - see MUSHROOM.

wild mustard - see CHARLOCK.

wild pecan rice - also **popcorn rice.** An aromatic, hybrid, long-grain rice grown in Louisiana, named not for its parentage, but for its distinctive nutty taste (and, when cooked, its popcorn-like smell). Popular throughout the southern U.S., it's available brown or white.

wild rice - also **Indian rice.** The grain from a perennial grass, *Zizania aquatica*, wild rice is similar to white rice only in that both are cereals of the grass family and they like to grow in shallow water or mud flats. Wild rice is the only grain besides corn that is cross-pollinated. The panicles of blooms show female blossoms on the crest and male pollen-bearing flowers at the base. As they bloom in succession down the stem, it takes weeks for all to be pollinated. The first Europeans to taste wild rice in the New World were French settlers from Brittany, who disregarded the Chippewa *mahnomen*, meaning "seeds from the wild," and instead nicknamed it *folle avoine*, meaning "crazy oats."

Wild rice was known to Native Americans: the Sioux called it *msickquatash*, the Iroquois *mausamp* and the Crow *rockahominy*. In Minnesota, to harvest wild rice during its short, three-week season, residents must buy a special license. No power motors are allowed on the rice lakes, only canoes. One person "poles" the canoe through the paddies while another, seated in front, bends the stalks into the boat and knocks off the rice with a wooden stick. The high price of hand-harvested wild rice is always given as the reason for its low consumption, but when harvesting of paddy rice became mechanized in the late 1980s, California became the leading producer and its price promptly came down. Paddy-grown wild rice is usually several dollars less than lake-grown wild rice, the former being smoother and darker and usually takes longer to cook.

wild turmeric - see ZEODARY.

Wiley, Ralph - see PLASTIC WRAP.

Wilhelm IV, Duke - see BARLEY.

William's Bon Chrétien - also **Bartlett.** See PEAR.

wilted salad - also **killed lettuce.** A salad of cleaned, crisp greens, such as arugula, buttercrunch or romaine lettuce, spinach or watercress, tossed in a dressing of hot bacon grease. Chopped garlic or onions may be sautéed in the bacon grease, and such ingredients as honey, powdered mustard, soy sauce and vinegar may be stirred into it while it's heating; the hot dressing causes the greens to wilt. A topping of crunchy bacon bits is optional. Called "killed lettuce" by cooks living in the mountains along the spine of the eastern United States, this traditional salad was often assembled with wild-picked greens.

windmill cookie - see SPECULAAS.

Windsor bean - see FAVA.

wine - an alcoholic drink made from the fermented juice of grapes. The plant's Latin name, *Vitis vinifera*, translates loosely as "the vine that bears wine." The dawn of wine is placed, rather broadly, between 6000 and 4000 BC, in Mesopotamia and areas surrounding the Caspian Sea. Early Mesopotamia pottery depicts royalty partying with what looks like glasses of wine. A Persian fable gives credit for the discovery of wine to a princess who believed she had fallen out of favor with the king. Distraught and feeling hopeless, she attempted to poison herself with some spoiled grapes from a jar marked "poison." The king, who was known to keep grapes in a jar to have them conveniently at hand, had found this particular batch no longer sweet and considered them unfit to eat. Rather than dying, the princess became giddy, light-headed and eventually fell asleep, and woke up feeling that her worries of the day before had completely disappeared. The king quickly noticed the change in her, and she confessed to its source. He ordered a quantity of this beverage to be made and shared it in celebration with his court.

Wine is believed to have come from the southern Caucasus, located between Turkey, Armenia and Iran, which is more or less where Noah, well known for his love of wine, is believed to have landed his ark after the Flood. According to Genesis, one of the first things Noah did was to plant wine grapes: "And Noah began to be a husbandman, and he planted a vineyard: and he drank of the wine, and was drunken" (*Gen. 9:20–21*).

The spread of wine to Europe came via Greece during the 17th century BC. Homer documented the cultivation of wine in both *The Iliad* and *The Odyssey*. The Romans are given credit for developing viticulture in Western Europe during the 11th century BC.

Of all the pleasures and privileges of power, none was rated more highly than the possession of a vineyard. The highest favor bestowed by the Roman emperor Julian was the gift of a vineyard prepared — actually planted and pruned — by his own hands. The Romans also invented cooperage (containers used for storing and aging wines) and perhaps even the first glass bottles, and imported both grapes and wine to England, France, Spain and Germany, which quickly began developing burgeoning viticultures of their own.

The oldest known chemically confirmed traces of wine were found in a jar about 7,000 years old that was excavated by a University of Pennsylvania Museum expedition at Hajji Firuz Tepe, a Neolithic settlement in the northern Zagros Mountains of Iran. The analysis was carried out by Professor Patrick McGovern of the University of Pennsylvania Museum and colleagues. The jar dates from 5400 to 5000 BC; the tests also showed that terebinth tree resin had been added to the wine, probably to preserve it. See also AMARONE, APPELLATION D'ORIGINE CONTRÔLÉE, AROMATIZED WINE, ASSEMBLAGE, ASTI SPUMANTE, AUSLESE, BANYULS, BARBARESCO, BARDOLINO, BARLEY WINE, BAROLO, BÂTONNAGE, BEAD, BEAUJOLAIS, BEERENAUSLESE, BLANC DE BLANCS, BLANC DE NOIRS, BLUSH WINE, BORDEAUX, BOTRYTIS CINEREA, BRUNELLO DI MONTALCINO, BURGUNDY, BYRRH, CABERNET FRANC, CABERNET SAUVIGNON, CATAWBA GRAPE, CAVA, CHABLIS, CHAMPAGNE, CHARACTER, CHARDONNAY, CHARMAT METHOD, CHÂTEAUNEUF-DU-PAPE, CHENIN BLANC, CHIANTI, CLARET, COGNAC, COOKING WINE, CÔTES-DU-RHÔNE, CRU, DELAWARE GRAPE, DESSERT WINE, DOM PIERRE PÉRIGNON, DUBONNET, ELDERBERRY, ENOLOGIST, FERMENTATION, FINING, FORTIFIED WINE, GAMAY, GEWURZTRAMINER, GRAPE, GRAPPA, GRENACHE, HIPPOCRAS, ICE CIDER, ICE WINE, KABINETT, KIR, LAMBRUSCO, LATE HARVEST, LIEBFRAUMILCH, LILLET, MADEIRA, MARECHAL FOCH, MARSALA, MERITAGE, MERLOT, MÉTHODE CHAMPENOISE, MUSCATEL, MUST, NEBBIOLO, NONVINTAGE, OFF-DRY, PH, PHENOLS, POMACE, PORT, PROOF, PROSECCO, RED WINE, RETSINA, RIOJA, RUBY PORT, SANGIOVESE, SAUTERNES, SAUVIGNON BLANC, SCUPPERNONG, SEC, SEMIDRY, SETÚBAL, SHERRY, SOMMELIER, SPARKLING WINE, SPÄTLESE, STILL WINE, TABLE WINE, TANNIN, TASTEVIN, TERROIR, TOKAY, TROCKEN, VALPOLICELLA VARIETAL WINE, VERMOUTH, VIN DE PAILLE, VINEYARD, VINO NOBILE DE MONTEPULCIANO, VINO SANTO, VINTAGE, VINTNER, VITICULTURE, VOUVRAY, WHITE WINE, WINE BOTTLES, WINE-TASTING TERMS, ZINFANDEL, ZYMURGY.

wineberry - the fruit of a bramble, *Rubus phoenicolasius*, native to the mountains of China and Japan, introduced to the U.S. in 1889; a handsome ornamental climber that bears small, orange-red berries that look pretty, but taste bland.

wine bottles - the size of wine bottles has been standardized around the world, with the regular single bottle of wine containing 750 mL. There are a variety of smaller and larger bottle sizes that are commonly seen on North American store shelves, including the **split** (which holds 187 mL, or one-quarter of a standard bottle), the **half-bottle** (which holds 375 mL, or, as the name implies, half a standard bottle) and the **magnum** (which holds 1.5 L, or double a standard bottle). Other, much larger bottles are harder to find, but are also standardized and called by colorful, often biblical names. These include the enormous **Nebuchadnezzar** (which holds 15 L, or the equivalent of 20 regular bottles of wine), the **Balthazar** (which contains 12 L) and the **Salmanazar** (which contains 9 L). In between these behemoths and the smaller common bottles, there are other standardized sizes — the Jeroboam, the **Rehoboam,** the Methuselah and the Imperial — but the wine-making regions of Bordeaux and Champagne in France disagree on their measurements, so they contain different amounts depending on where the wine was made.

wine cooler - **1.** a chilled beverage mixed with a still wine, a bubbly ingredient, such as club soda or sparkling water, and, usually, a fruit juice. **2.** a tall, thick ceramic or marble cylinder, often placed on the buffet or dining table, which accommodates a chilled bottle of wine up to the neck, absorbs the coolness and keeps the bottle at the same temperature without any condensation on the glass. **3.** a tableside ice bucket, usually draped with a linen napkin, in which a chilled bottled of wine is kept cool. **4.** a prefrozen thermal blanket that wraps around a wine bottle to quickly cool the contents.

wine gum - a firm, rather rubbery, gum sweet particularly popular in the United Kingdom. Their rich, translucent colors and mellow fruit flavor are all they share with wine, however. Londoner Charles Gordon Maynard, the son of a strict teetotalling Methodist, created the first of the actually spiritless wine gums in 1909.

Winesap apple - see APPLE.

wine-tasting terms - see ACRID, AGGRESSIVE, AMARO, AMPLE, ANGULAR, AROMA, ASTRINGENCY, BACKWARD, BALANCED, BIG, BLUNT, BOTTLE STINK, BOUQUET, BUTTERY, CHEWY, CORKED, CRISP, DRY, EXPANSIVE, FINISH, FLABBY, FLAT, FLESHY, FOXY, FRUITY, FULL-BODIED, GRASSY, GREEN, HALBTROCKEN, HERBACEOUS, JAMMY, MADERIZED, MOUTH FEEL, NOSE, PALATE, VEGETAL.

wine vinegar - see VINEGAR.

winged bean - also **goa bean, Manila bean, princess bean, winged pea.** A tuberous rooted, twining plant, *Psophocarpus tetragonolobus*, all of which — including its pale blue flowers — is edible. Rich in protein, the plant is considered a good crop for subsistence farmers in tropical regions worldwide. The pods, which commonly reach a foot (30 cm) long, sport four frilly, papery "wings," for which the plant is named. Grown commercially in such places as Florida on a small scale, most winged beans are grown in North America as annual ornamentals or novelties by home gardeners, but some specialty produce markets do sell them. When mature, the beans can be eaten fresh or dried, and are similar to cranberry beans in flavor, something like a starchy green bean or a soybean. In Indonesia, versions of tofu and **tempeh** are sometimes made from winged beans, and the beans can also be made into a beverage that is similar to soymilk. Virtually all parts of the plant are edible, from the earliest seed sprouts to the leaves to the tuber at the base of the plant. Interestingly, when the beans get ripe enough, they split open with a loud pop, giving them their Latin name, *Psophocarpus*, which is derived from the Greek, meaning "noisy bean."

winged beans

winkle - see PERIWINKLE.

wintergreen - also **checkerberry.** An evergreen, *Gaultheria procumbens*, native to eastern North America, with glossy, green leaves and small, red berries. The leaves produce an oil that is used to flavor candy and chewing gum, and they can also be made into tea.

winter melon - also **wax gourd.** A large, oblong, waxy-skinned melon, *Benincasa hispida*, thought to be native to southern China. Winter melons keep well for many months. Chunks of the white flesh are commonly added to Asian soups; whole melons may be seeded, stuffed and roasted. Winter melon can be grown as an annual in North America.

winter squash - see SQUASH.

Wiper, Joseph - see KENDAL MINT CAKE.

wiri-wiri - see CHERRY PEPPER.

wishbone - the Y-shaped bone at the front of the breastbone in a bird, basically the two clavicles (collarbones) joined together at the bottom. An age-old tradition, breaking the wishbone has become a Thanksgiving ritual in North America. Two competitors each hold one side of the wishbone and pull to see who breaks off his own side plus the joint at the top. The winner makes a wish, which, according to legend, will come true if he keeps it to himself.

witloof - see ENDIVE.

wok - a round-bottom pan with curved sides, allowing even heat distribution and easy tossing of ingredients, originally used in Asian cooking.

wolfberry - see GOJI BERRY.

wonton - a Chinese dumpling consisting of one or two thin sheets of dough enclosing a small amount of chopped, seasoned meat or seafood (often barbecued pork or shrimp) and/or vegetables, or, less-commonly, a sweet dried-fruit and nut mixture, in the center. Wontons may be boiled, simmered in soup or steamed; cooked this way, they stay chewy, soft and pale. They may also be deep-fried until the **wonton wrapper** is bubbled, crisp and golden; they are then served with dipping sauce. Like other dumplings from other cultures, wontons might well have been invented to stretch the scarcest, most precious ingredients, such as meat.

wonton soup - a clear broth with chewy, soft wontons floating in it and, often, a few thinly sliced pieces of meat or seafood (usually matched with the wonton filling) and vegetables, as well. For North American take-out, there's often a garnish of chopped onions.

wonton wrapper - also **wonton skin, won ton wrapper.** A type of rolled-out noodle, similar to a sheet of fresh lasagna, used to wrap around a savory filling to make a **wonton.** Wonton wrappers come in different thicknesses. The thin ones work well to make wontons for use in soup, and the thicker ones work well to make fried wontons.

woodchuck - see GROUNDHOG.

woodcock - a bird related to the snipe but with a more robust bill and short legs, native to Europe and America, but now found worldwide. As with all game fowl, woodcock should be hung for about two weeks to allow bacteria to tenderize the flesh, without breaking the skin until plucking. One woodcock is the usual serving per person, usually roasted, braised, broiled or grilled. If roasted, it's usually not drawn or decapitated, although the gizzard is removed. The entrails are considered a great delicacy.

wood ear

wood ear - also **black fungus, cloud ear, elephant ear, Judas' ear mushroom, kikurage, tree ear.** A mushroom of the genus *Auricularia*, found growing on tree stumps in China, the wood ear is usually only available dried and has a crunchy texture and a bland flavor.

Woodhouse, John - see MARSALA.

woodruff - also **sweet woodruff.** A perennial herb, *Asperula odorata*, native to Europe, with a distinctive taste. Its leaves can be used fresh or dried, infused in Champagne, Bénédictine, punch, **tisanes** and *Mai-Bowle* ("May punch"), a woodruff-infused wine drink traditionally made for May Day in Germany.

wootau - see TARO.

worcesterberry - an American species of **gooseberry,** *Ribes divaricatum*, a small, black fruit thought to be a hybrid of a gooseberry and a black currant.

Worcestershire sauce - one of the most popular of all bottled sauces, it's aromatic and pungent with a distinctively sweet-and-sour flavor. The sauce is a very dark brown with 25 percent visible sediment; you must shake the bottle before use. Although Lea & Perrins' recipe is secret, the principal ingredients for the standard recipe are old and mature anchovies, West Indies tamarinds, vinegar, sherry, brandy, soy sauce, pork liver, salt, sugar, cayenne, black pepper, coriander, mace, shallots and caramel. The tamarinds, anchovies and pork liver are simmered in vinegar, the liquor of which is then strained and combined with the other ingredients. The sauce must then mature for at least six months to bring out the full flavor before being bottled. Worcestershire sauce has a long, almost venerable shelf life and is used in many recipes, especially soups, sauces, gravies, tomato-juice drinks and salad dressings.

wormseed - also **worm weed.** See EPAZOTE.

wormwood - a bitter, aromatic herb, *Artemisia absinthium*, historically used to treat intestinal worms. The name is a corruption of an older word having no connection with worm or wood, "ware-mood," once considered to be a "mind preserver" (from some old notion as to its virtues). The plant has been celebrated since the early 19th century for its flavoring of **absinthe.**

wrapped heart mustard - also **Chinese mustard, swatow wrapped.** A Chinese vegetable with bright green, long, shiny and wrinkled leaves, which form a sheath up the center, then flare out (almost like the petals of a flower) around its pale green tip, hence the "wrapped heart" name. Its sharp, biting taste is tamed by cooking it in stir-fries, simmering it in soups and pickling it in a sauerkraut-like mixture.

Wrigley, William - see CHEWING GUM.

Wurst - German for "sausage."

XYZ

zucchini flowers

xanthan gum - a food additive made from corn syrup, used as a thickener, stabilizer and emulsifier. See also GUM ARABIC, GUAR GUM, GUM TRAGACANTH.

xerophagy - Latin for "dry eating." A term usually used to describe a type of fast, during which only dry foods are eaten. Followers of the Greek and Russian Orthodox churches, for example, eschew dairy products, eggs, fish, oil, meat and wine at certain times in Lent.

Xuanwei ham - see YUNNAN HAM.

---

ya - a Japanese suffix meaning store or shop, for example, an *okonomiyaki-ya* specializes in **okonomiyaki** (halfway between a pancake and a pizza); a *ramen-ya* specializes in **ramen**; a *soba-ya* is where **soba** noodles are made, cooked and eaten; a *sushi-ya* specializes in **sushi**; a *teishoku-ya* is a restaurant that sells teishoku (set menus); a *tempura-ya* specializes in **tempura** dishes; a *tonkatsu-ya* serves tonkatsu (deep-fried breaded pork cutlets); an *unagi-ya* specializes in **unagi** (freshwater eel); a *sukiyaki-ya* specializes in **sukiyaki**; a *yakiniku-ya* specializes in Korean-style barbecue foods; and a *yakitori-ya* specializes in **yakitori** (grilled chicken skewers).

yakimono - a Japanese name for appetizers, usually bite-size pieces of meat that are marinated, then skewered and grilled.

yaki nasu - a classic Japanese dish (and popular North American restaurant order) of grilled, spiced eggplant with **bonito** flakes, often served with **miso** sauce.

yakinori - sheets of toasted, dried seaweed. See NORI.

yakitori - a grilled Japanese kebab, usually of chicken and vegetables, dipped in a sweet, soy-based sauce called *tare*, with which it's also basted, or simply seasoned with salt, or *shio*.

yam - a vine tuber of the genus *Dioscorea*, completely unrelated to the sweet potato, with which it's frequently confused. The yam is less sweet, grows in mostly tropical and subtropical regions, and can reach 40 pounds (18 kg) in weight. Its flesh can be white, yellow, pink or dark brown and is rich in starch, with a high mucus content that gives it a creamy consistency when cooked. Archaeological sites lead us to believe that the yam was cultivated in Africa and Asia more than 10,000 years ago. It's one of the most consumed foods in the world, a staple throughout South America and the West Indies. Its name comes from *nyam*, a West African term that made its way into Portuguese and Creole, meaning "to eat." The Latin genus name commemorates Dioscorides, the 1st-century Greek naturalist and physician. Today, progesterone extracted from wild Mexican yams is fermented to manufacture synthetic cortisone to treat arthritis. Hormones based on yam extracts are used in birth control pills. There are many varieties of yam, the principal being *D. alata*, which is indigenous to Africa and Asia. In Africa, yams are mashed, peppered and spiced to make *fufu* and used in *kalajoum*, a chicken stew with peppers and coconut.

yanagi - see JAPANESE KNIVES.

Yankee bean - see NAVY BEAN.

Yankee pot roast - an economical American meal, an inexpensive cut of beef that is browned, then cooked slowly in a slow cooker or in a Dutch oven on the stove or in the oven. A small amount of liquid, such as beef stock, tomato juice or water, is added at the beginning of cooking, to help make the meat moist and tender; root vegetables are added later to create a one-pot meal. See also POT ROAST.

yard-long bean - see ASPARAGUS BEAN.

Yarg - a mild, white English cow's milk cheese, made into wheels and wrapped in nettle leaves, with a downy, white rind. Its name is the inventors' surname (Jennifer and Allan Gray) spelled backward.

yarrow - an herb, *Achillea millefolium*, a European perennial that now grows in the U.S., considered one of the most distinctive for both its strong aroma and appearance. The plant was part of the pharmacology of the ancient Greeks and Romans and was used during the Trojan War, 3,000 years ago: Achilles packed it on his wounded comrade's arm, hence the name *Achillea*. It is recorded that 46 native American tribes used yarrow for 28 ailments that

responded to the herb. The 1st-century Greek physician Dioscorides smeared yarrow on ulcers, and 16th-century English botanist **John Gerard** recommended yarrow to relieve "swelling of those secret parts." Today, the dried leaves are commonly used as a food coloring and brewed as a tea.

yassa chicken - a Senegalese stew usually made with carrots, celery, chicken, lime juice and onion, seasoned with black pepper and chile pepper. Ingredients and seasonings vary and may include cumin, Dijon mustard, garlic and leeks. In North America, this is a popular dish for Kwanza and may be served alongside couscous, rice, stewed tomatoes or yams.

yautia - see MALANGA.

yearling - see LAMB.

yeast - many species of single-cell fungi that grow quickly in warm temperatures and react differently in different conditions, including altitude. Most yeast used in baking and fermenting is derived from *Saccharomyces* strains. In breadmaking, when it is open to the air, the growing yeast creates carbon dioxide which causes the dough to rise, producing a small amount of alcohol in the process; inside brewing vats, where little air is available, yeast converts sugar into alcohol, creating a small amount of carbon dioxide in the process. Yeast is also used in the production of various other foods and drinks, including chocolate, cheese, kefir, pasta and soy sauce. It is available powdered (in several active varieties used for baking and beer, cider and wine making, and in a non-active form — a by-product of beer making, called **"brewer's yeast"** — used as a dietary supplement), in fresh yeast cakes (used for baking), in yeast **starters** (called sponges and used for sourdough breads), as a paste (used as a nutritional spread) and, in Asian markets, formed into balls (used for making rice wine). See also ACTIVE DRY YEAST, NUTRITIONAL YEAST, VEGEMITE.

yeast bread - bread made with yeast as a leavening agent. The yeast feeds on the sugar in the dough and releases carbon dioxide gas, which is trapped by strands of **gluten** and causes the bread to rise. See also BATTER BREAD, QUICK BREAD, UNLEAVENED BREAD.

yeast extract - concentrated, sometimes flavored or vitamin-enriched, yeast used in powdered or pellet form in the food industry. It is also a generic term used to describe the savory, brown paste (familiar under the brand names Marmite or Vegemite and beloved of Britons, Europeans and vegans) that is used as a spread for crackers or toast, and added to soups, stews and vegetable dishes. See also NUTRITIONAL YEAST.

yebeg wat - a classic Ethiopian stew of marinated chunks of lamb spiced with **berbere** that is showing up on more and more restaurant menus in North America.

yellow berry - see CLOUDBERRY.

yellow curry paste - see CURRY PASTE.

Yellow Delicious apple - see APPLE.

yellow-eyed pea - curved, off-white bean, with a yellow spot or eye, used in Southern dishes, such as **hoppin' John.** See also BLACK-EYED PEA.

yellowfin tuna - see AHI, TUNA.

Yellow Granex - see ONION.

yellow passion fruit - see LILIKOI.

yellow potato - see POTATO.

yellow sapote - see MAMEY SAPOTA.

yellow walleye - see WALLEYE.

yerba maté - the dried leaves of a South American shrub from the holly family, used chiefly in Argentina, Uruguay and Paraguay to make a refreshing, energizing, tea-like beverage. The native way to drink maté is to place the leaves in a hollowed, dried calabash gourd and fill it with boiling water. A *bombilla* is the special tube, usually made of silver, with a strainer at one end, which is put into the drink, through which it's sipped, shared with friends and passed around communally.

yerba santa - see HOJA SANTA.

yinnie syrup - see RICE SYRUP.

yin-yang bean - see CALYPSO BEAN.

ylang-ylang

ylang-ylang - the flowers of a large tree, *Cananga odorata*, native to the Philippines, steam-distilled to obtain their oil, which has a strong, floral scent and a bitter, aromatic taste; used in soft drinks, ice cream, candy and baked goods.

yogurt - milk with additional milk solids added, heated to above regular pasteurization temperatures, then cooled to 108°F (42°C), to which bacterial cultures are then added and left to incubate for four to six hours. Armenian immigrants Rose and Sarkis Colombosian produced the first commercial American yogurt in 1929 and began selling throughout New England in 1940, while Daniel Carasso, whose father founded Danone (named after Daniel) in Spain in 1919, founded Dannon Milk Products in New York in 1942. Danone first put fruit in yogurt in 1947 for novelty and to balance its sourness, to which the market wasn't yet accustomed.

yogurt cheese - a soft, unripened cheese made by placing plain yogurt in a sieve lined with cheesecloth or in a paper coffee filter and allowing the **whey** to drain off for several hours. The resulting creamy, spreadable cheese can be used as an alternative to cream cheese or sour cream.

yokan - sweet, **azuki** bean jelly, a traditional Japanese treat, made from **agar-agar,** azuki-bean paste and sugar. The clear, colorful jelly is shaped into small bars or squares that may have beans suspended inside and taste of chestnut, green tea or persimmon, and elegantly wrapped.

York ham - a firm, tender, world-renowned English ham, originally from York, noted for its delicate taste; salt-cured, lightly smoked and sometimes coated with bread crumbs.

York's cheese - see CAMBRIDGE CHEESE.

Yorkshire pudding - an accompaniment commonly served with roast beef and gravy, made from a batter of eggs, milk and flour and baked in hot beef drippings. This English specialty began to appear on menus in the U.S. during the middle of the 19th century. It was originally made by pouring the batter into the dripping pan under a roast. In England, giant Yorkshire puddings are sometimes served as pub food, filled with everything from baked beans to chicken curry.

yosenabe - a Japanese **nabemono** comprising broth and seasonally available poultry, seafood and vegetables. Kept hot on a small gas cooker on the dining table, this one-pot dish is often served in winter as a communal meal, with diners around the table each taking a turn. Ready-made yosenabe broth mixes (often miso- or soy-based) are available.

youngberry - a *Rubus* hybrid of a loganberry-type cultivar, with a trailing blackberry, know as a **dewberry.** Created by its namesake, one B.M. Youngberry, a Louisiana plant breeder, early in 1905, it remains popular thanks to its juicy, sweet fruit.

yuba - also **bamboo yuba, bean stick.** The protein-filled skin that forms on soy milk when it is heated. The skin is gently removed, then dried flat or in sticks. Yuba is then rehydrated under a damp towel or by soaking in water, and used as a meat substitute or on its own in Asian cuisine, especially in China and Japan. Yuba has a delicate, nutty flavor, which blends well with most other ingredients. It is sometimes called "bamboo yuba" because it looks like a long rod of bamboo.

yuca - also **yucca.** See CASSAVA.

Yukon gold - see POTATO.

Yule log - see BÛCHE DE NOËL.

Yunnan ham - **Xuanwei ham.** Salty, smoky-tasting, traditionally cured ham produced for centuries in the Chinese province of Yunnan (most particularly in the city of Xuanwei). This ham became famous in the West by winning a gold medal at the 1915 Panama-Pacific International Exposition in San Francisco. It is found in butcher shops in China. In North America, it is available canned, if at all; some cooks use **Smithfield ham** in its place.

yuzu - a bitter, highly scented Japanese citrus fruit, used when its thick rind is still green or after it ripens to orange in the fall. The juice or rind lend sharp flavor and fragrance to a variety of dishes; finely grated or sliced, the rind is used to garnish fish or vegetable dishes. Earlier in the season, one of its white flowers may be used to decorate soup. Jars of ready-to-use juice are available, as is an "instant" powdered form.

---

za'atar - also **zaatar, zahtar, za'tar, zatar.** An Arabic word that is used in many Middle Eastern countries to refer to both the herb thyme and a spice mixture whose main ingredient is ground sumac, also containing thyme, wild marjoram and sesame seeds. *Za'atar* literally means "thyme."

zabaglione - also **zabaione.** A dessert or dessert sauce made by strenuously whipping egg yolks, sugar and usually **Marsala** over a **bain-marie** until the mixture is creamy and frothy, served warm or cold, often with berries, traditionally with fresh figs. Zabaglione is often prepared tableside, using a copper bowl. Its origin and inventor are often contested, but it's generally believed to have been created in the early 16th century, possibly by San Pasquale Bayon, a Spanish friar, gifted cook and parish priest of Turin's San Tommaso church. See also SABAYON.

Zahidi dates - see DATES.

zakuska - Russian for "hors d'oeuvre."

zalabia - a crunchy, Middle Eastern waffle that is thought to be the prototype for the waffle ice cream cone. Variously described as a cruller, doughnut, fritter and waffle, in its home region a zalabia may be made by pouring or spooning batter into boiling oil; the cooked golden fritters are then dipped in sugar syrup flavored with lemon juice and rose and orange-blossom water, then dusted with cinnamon and confectioner's sugar. At the 1904 St. Louis World's Fair, however — so the story goes — a Middle Eastern immigrant was cooking zalabias between two hot metal plates that impressed the pastries with the familiar waffle grid pattern. To help out a nearby vendor, who was selling ice cream but had nothing left to serve it in, the baker began rolling his zalabias into cones for the ice cream — and the rest is history.

zampone - also **zampone di Modena.** A hollow pig's trotter stuffed with Italian pork sausage, a specialty of Modena, Italy.

Zante grape - also **black Corinth grape, champagne grape.** A tiny, bubble-like, seedless, sweet black grape, grown mainly for drying into currants. It is cultivated primarily in California and its birthplace, Greece.

zapallo - see CALABAZA.

zapote blanco - Spanish for "white sapote." See WHITE SAPOTE.

Zara - the former name of Zadar, a town in Yugoslavia where **maraschino liqueur** originated and still is produced. Sometimes, maraschino is called *Zara*.

zarzuela - a popular Spanish stew, made with many varieties of fish and shellfish, from the Spanish *zarzuela*, a kind of lyric or comic opera in which song is intermingled with spoken dialogue.

zeodary - also **wild turmeric.** *Curcuma zeodaria*, belonging to the ginger family. In Asia and India, the dried yellow rhizomes are ground for spice that has a camphorous, warm gingery flavor. It is used in Asian curries and Indonesian seafood dishes. The tubers are also used to make a starchy thickener and the lemony leaves to flavor fish dishes.

zeppole - an Italian doughnut, chewier, fluffier and a lot greasier than the North American kind, best served hot with confectioner's (icing) sugar sprinkled over top.

zeroa - the roasted shank bone of a lamb, present on the Seder plate at the Jewish Passover meal. Not usually eaten at the meal, the bone represents the lamb sacrificed in the biblical temple. Vegetarians often replace the zeroa with a broiled beet; red, it symbolizes the blood of the lamb.

zest - **1.** (n.) the rind of citrus fruit, used for its color, aroma and inherent flavorful oil. **2.** (v.) to remove the zest, usually with a zester, which cuts the rind into strips while peeling.

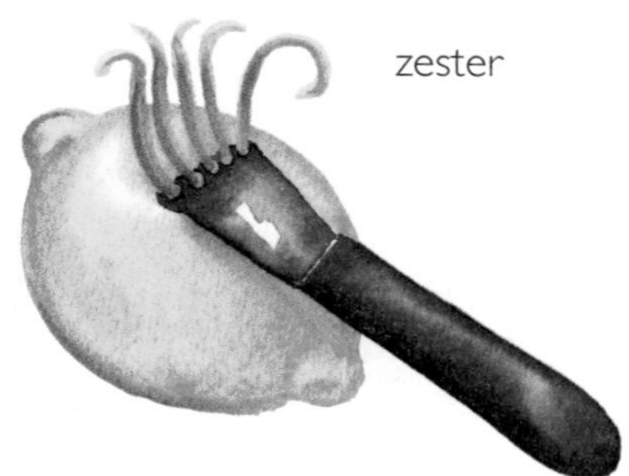

zester

zester - an angled blade edged with five small cutting holes, set into a short wooden handle, used to cut fine shreds of citrus zest. The blade is pressed against the rind and pulled across the surface. See also MICROPLANE GRATER.

zhug - a hot, spicy herb paste from Yemen, made from a purée of black peppercorns, cardamom, chile pepper, cumin, fresh coriander or parsley, garlic and salt (some cooks add caraway seeds as well). Olive oil can be added to make it into a sauce. Zhug is used as a condiment or topping (sometimes accompanied by yogurt) for egg, meat and vegetable dishes, soups and stews, and as a dipping sauce.

zinfandel - **1.** a red-black grape variety grown extensively for wine production on more than 50,000 acres of vineyards in the United States, particularly in California. In the Napa Valley, the University of California at Davis has a research station, Heritage Vineyard, where a collection of zinfandel cuttings is cultivated and conserved. The parent grape for the American zinfandel can be traced back to Europe, but mystery still surrounds its original home; some evidence points to Italy, some to Croatia. Since the juice from the grape is clear, it can be used to produce both red and white wines. The unevenly ripening grapes in each cluster, an unusual characteristic for wine grapes, is credited with giving the wines their range, from acid to fruity to deep. The popularity of both the grapes and their wines has prompted the cultivation of this variety in Argentina, Chile, Australia, New Zealand, France and Italy, as well. **2.** various wines made from the zinfandel grape, including white, blush types, rosés and reds (both fruity and full-bodied).

zingara - Italian for "gypsy," a white wine sauce made with **demi-glace,** mushrooms, truffles, ham and tongue, all finely chopped and highly spiced with cayenne pepper.

ziti - see PASTA.

zitoni - see PASTA.

Zola, Émile - see profile below.

Zombie - a fruity but powerful cocktail made with three kinds of rum (amber or gold, dark and white), pineapple juice, superfine sugar and a liqueur, such as apricot liqueur, crème de menthe or crème de noyaux. Instead of sugar, simple syrup or sweet-and-sour mix may be added. Poured over ice in a **highball glass,** a zombie is usually garnished with a green maraschino cherry, mint leaves and a pineapple slice on a skewer. See also CRÈME DE, NOYAUX.

zoni - see OZONI.

Zola, Émile (1840–1902) - French novelist, Zola used scenes involving food, eating and drinking to dramatic and literary effect in nearly all his novels. *Le Ventre de paris* (The Belly of Paris, 1873) was set in Les Halles, the large food market in central Paris, where the protagonist, after escaping from jail, finds himself famished and surrounded by all the food that will fill Parisian bellies, but only those who could afford to buy. Ironically, he becomes a food inspector. In *Germinal* (1885), Zola's social commentary about 19th-century bourgeois life in France, he described wealthy diners enjoying a rich, extravagant meal in a comfortable dining room, while outside, striking miners scour the roadside for wild greens, calling out their strike anthem, "Du pain, du pain," meaning, "Bread. We want bread."

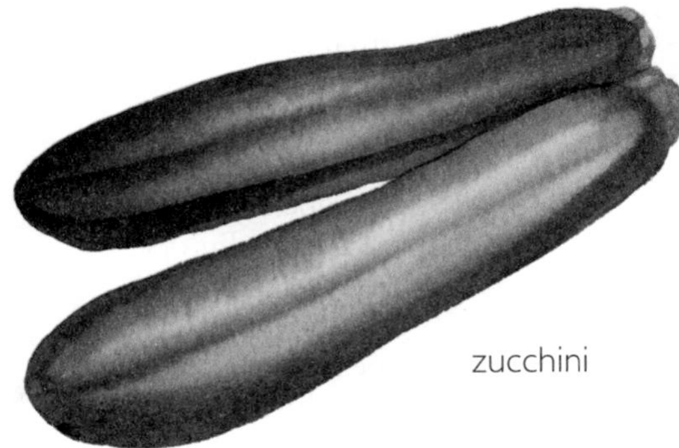
zucchini

zucchini - also **courgette, marrow squash, vegetable marrow.** A long, cylindrical vegetable, usually with the same diameter and half the length of an English cucumber. Zucchini is a summer squash that can be green or yellow, with white flesh and many tiny, soft seeds surrounded by semifirm pulp. It's grown throughout Europe and North America. Its French and British name is *courgette*, which is French for "little squash." See also SQUASH.

zucchini flowers - also **courgette flowers.** The edible flower that forms at the end of an immature zucchini, used as a food in Italian and French cuisine, usually stuffed with a savory filling and/or breaded and deep-fried. See also EDIBLE FLOWERS, SQUASH BLOSSOMS.

zucchini corer - a very long, slender, straight blade, pointed at the tip and curved around its width, used to core zucchinis for the stuffed zucchini dishes enjoyed throughout the Mediterranean and Middle East. The blade, which commonly has a double-bladed peeler slot near the base and may have teeth along all or part of its outside edges, is usually set into a short handle.

zuccotto - a domed-shaped dessert, an Italian version of a chilled **charlotte.** Triangular slices of pound cake are fitted inside a round-bottomed bowl to line it completely, then doused with one or more liqueurs (such as amaretto, Cointreau, cognac, curaçao or maraschino). Stiffly beaten whipped cream containing chocolate shards and chopped almonds and/or hazelnuts and dried fruit is then spooned on top, almost to the rim, and a thin circle of cake (sometimes chocolate for contrast) is placed on top. After chilling to set all the ingredients, the dessert is turned out onto a platter for serving. Ladyfingers, Madeira cake or sponge cake sometime stand in for the pound cake and, occasionally, strawberry preserves are spread inside the cake. Some cooks claim this that this sweet dome was created in honor of a famous cathedral in Florence; others claim it as a Tuscan dish designed to resemble a cardinal's skull cap called *zuccotto* in a local dialect.

Zungenwurst - a spicy, German sausage containing large chunks of meat, usually tongue.

zuppa - Italian for "soup."

zuppa inglese - the Italian version of trifle, which translates literally as "English soup," from the root verb *inzuppare*, meaning "to drench." Developed in 19th-century Naples, zuppa inglese is made with layers of brandy- or rum-soaked sponge cake and custard, sometimes with cream and candied fruit, covered with meringue and baked briefly for color. See also TRIFLE.

zuppa primaverile - Italian for **spring soup.**

Zwieback - German for "twice baked" or "biscuit," bread that has been baked and sliced and then baked again until it's dry and crisp, similar to biscotti and rusk.

zymology - the science of **fermentation.**

zymurgy - the name for a branch of chemistry dealing with fermentation, as in brewing, wine making and the preparation of yeast and vinegar, from the Greek *zume*, meaning "to leaven."

Library and Archives Canada Cataloguing in Publication

Rolland, Jacques, 1945–
The food encyclopedia : over 8000 ingredients, tools, techniques and people / Jacques L. Rolland and Carol Sherman with other contributors.

Includes bibliographical references.
ISBN-13: 978-0-7788-0150-4
ISBN-10: 0-7788-0150-0

1. Food — Encyclopedias. 2. Cookery — Encyclopedias.
I. Sherman, Carol II. Title.

TX349.R644 2006 641'.03 C2006-902452-9

Bibliography

Acton, Eliza. *The Best of Eliza Action* (Elizabeth Ray, editor) (Penguin Books, 1974)

Aidells, Bruce and Denis Kelly. *The Complete Meat Cookbook* (Houghton Mifflin, 2003)

Aitken, Kate. *Kate Aitken's Canadian Cookbook* (Whitecap Books, 2004)

Anderson, Kenneth N. and Lois E. Anderson. *The International Dictionary of Food & Nutrition* (Wiley, 1993)

Aron, Jean-Paul. *The Art of Eating in France* (Peter Owen, 1975)

Ayton, John. *The Glutton's Glossary: A Dictionary of Food and Drink Terms* (Routledge, 1990)

________. *An A-Z of Food & Drink* (Oxford University Press, 2002)

Babinski, Henri. *Encyclopedia of Practical Gastronomy by Ali-Bab* (McGraw Hill, 1974)

Barber, Katherine (editor). *Canadian Oxford Dictionary (Second edition)* (Oxford University Press, 2004)

Bardi, Carla. *Prosciutto* (McRea Books, 2002)

Barer-Stein, Thelma. *You Eat What You Are: People, Culture and Food Traditions* (Firefly, 1999)

Beard, James. *James Beard's American Cookery* (Little Brown, 1972)

________. *Beard on Food* (Running Press, 1974)

Beeton, Isabella (editor). *Mrs. Beeton's Book of Household Management (A First Edition Facsimile)* (Jonathan Cape, 1968)

Benoît, Madame (Jehane). *Encyclopedia of Canadian Cuisine* (Canadian Homes Magazine, 1963)

Bernasconi, Carlo and Christian Teubner. *The Complete Italian Cookbook* (Transedition, 1999)

Bibliothèque de l'Arsenal, Ursula Baurmeister and Sabine Coron. *Livres en bouche: cinq siècles d'art culinaire français, du quatorzième au dix-huitième siècle exposition* (Hermann, 2001)

Black, Rene. *The Rene Black Cookbook* (Henry Holt Company, 1955)

Bladholm, Lynda. *The Asian Grocery Store Demystified: A Food Lover's Guide to all the Best Ingredients* (Renaissance Books/St. Martin's Press, 1999)

________. *The Indian Grocery Store Demystified: A Food Lover's Guide to the Best Ingredients in the Traditional Foods of India, Pakistan and Bangladesh* (Renaissance Books/St. Martin's Press, 2000)

________. *Latin & Caribbean Grocery Stores Demystified: A Food Lover's Guide to the Best Ingredients in the Traditional Foods of Mexico, Peru, Chile, Argentina, Brazil, Venezuela, Colombia, and the Caribbean Islands including Cuba, Puerto Rico & Jamaica* (Renaissance Books/St. Martin's Press, 2001)

Bloom, Carole. *The International Dictionary of Desserts, Pastries, and Confections* (Hearst Books/William Morrow, 1995)

Boxer, Arabella and Philippa Back. *The Herb Book* (Peerage Books, 1989)

Bricklin, Mark. *Nutrition Advisor* (Rodale Press, 1994)

Brillat-Savarin, Jean Anthelme. *The Physiology of Taste* (Counterpoint, 1949)

Brookes, Phillips V. *Kitchen Utensils: Names, Origins, and Definitions Through the Ages* (Palgrave Macmillan/St. Martin's Press, 2004)

Campbell, Susan. *The Cook's Companion: The Complete Manual of Kitchen Implements and How to Use Them* (Chancellor Press, 1985)

Carême, Antonin. *L'Art de la cuisine française* (Au Dépot de Librairie, 1854)

________. *Le Cuisinier parisien* (Au Dépot de Librairie, 1858)

Chanticleer Press. *National Audubon Society Field Guide to North American Mushrooms* (Alfred A. Knopf, 1981)

Child, Julia. *The French Chef Cookbook* (Alfred A. Knopf, 1968)

________, Louisette Betholle and Simone Beck. *Mastering the Art of French Cooking, Volume One* (Alfred A. Knopf, 1961)

________, *Mastering the Art of French Cooking, Volume Two* (Alfred A. Knopf, 1974)

Claiborne, Craig. *The New York Times Cook Book* (Harper & Row, 1961)

Cooper, Artemis. *Writing at the Kitchen Table: Elizabeth David, The Authorized Biography* (Penguin books, 2000)

Courtine, Robert J. *The Hundred Glories of French Cooking* (Farrar Straus & Giroux, 1973)

Crocker, Pat. *The Healing Herbs Cookbook* (Robert Rose Inc., 1999)

David, Elizabeth. *Mediterranean Food* (Penguin Books, 1955)

________. *French Country Cooking* (Penguin Books, 1959)

________. *Italian Food* (Penguin Books, 1963)

________. *French Provincial Cooking* (Penguin books, 1964)

________. *Spices Salt and Aromatics in the English Kitchen: Volume I* (Penguin Books, 1970)

________. *English Bread and Yeast Cookery* (Penguin Books, 1977)

Davidson, Alan. *The Oxford Companion to Food* (Oxford University Press, 1999)

________ (editor) with Helen Saberi. *The Wilder Shores of Gastronomy: 20 Years of the Best Food Writing from the Journal Petits Propos Culinaires* (Ten Speed Press, 2002)

D'Avila-Latourrette, Brother Victor-Antoine. *Fresh from a Monastery Garden* (Doubleday, 1998)

Delage, H. et G. Mathiot. *Je sais cuisiner* (Albin Michel, 1945)

Della Croce, Julia. *Italy: The Vegetarian Table* (Chronicle Books, 1994)

Dias, Anthony Blue. *The Complete Book of Spirits. A Guide to their History, Production and Enjoyment* (HarperCollins, 2004)

Dorling Kindersley. *Wines of the World* (Dorling Kindersley, 2004)

Dowell, Philip and Adrian Bailey. *The Book of Ingredients* (Penguin, 2001)

Escoffier, Auguste. *The Escoffier Cook Book and Guide to the Fine Art of Cookery* (Crown Publishers, Inc., 1969)

Farmer, Fannie Merritt. *The Boston Cooking School Cook Book* (Little, Brown, 1918)

Finlayson, Judith. "A Beard in the Kitchen, But no hair in the soup." *Weekend Magazine* (January 31, 1976)

________. "Beyond Fish and Chips, Extraordinary English cooking from the kitchens of Elizabeth David and Jane Grigson. *The Canadian* (January 15, 1977)

________. *The Healthy Slow Cooker* (Robert Rose Inc., 2006)

Fitch, Noel Riley. *Appetite for Life: The Biography of Julia Child* (Doubleday, 1997)

Fitzgibbon, Theodora. *The Food of the Western World: An Encyclopedia of Food from North America and Europe* (Quadrangle, 1976)

Fortin, François (editor). *The Complete Food Guide* (Könemann, 1999)

________ and Serge D'Amico. *The Visual Food Encyclopedia: The Definitive Practical Guide to Food & Cooking* (Wiley Publishing, 1996)

Fussell, Betty. *I Hear America Cooking* (Viking, 1986)

Gibault, Georges. *Histoire des legumes* (Librairie Horticole, 1912)

Gibbons, Euell. *Stalking the Wild Asparagus* (David McKay, 1970)

Giblin, James Cross. *From Hand to Mouth: Or, How We Invented Knives, Forks, Spoons, and Chopsticks & the Table Manners to Go With Them* (Thomas Y. Crowell, 1987)

Glezer, Maggie. *A Blessing of Bread: Recipes and Rituals, Memories and Mitzvahs* (Artisan, 2004)

Gomez de Silva, Guido. *International Dictionary of Gastronomy* (Hippocrene Books, 2003)

Gottschalk, Dr. Alfred. *Histoire de l'Alimentation et de la Gastronomie depuis la Préhistoire jusqu'à nos jours* (Hippocrate, 1948)

Green, Aliza. *Field Guide to Produce: How to Identify, Select, and Prepare Virtually Every Fruit and Vegetable at the Market* (Quirk Books, 2004)

Grigson, Jane. *Charcuterie and French Pork Cookery* (Penguin Books, 1970)

________. *Good Things* (Alfred A. Knopf, 1971)

________. *English Food* (Macmillan, 1974)

Grimes, William. *Eating your Words: 2000 Words to Tease your Tastebuds* (Oxford University Press, 2004)

Grosser, Arthur E. *The Cookbook Decoder or Culinary Alchemy Explained* (78 rpm Press, 1981)

Harris, H. William and Judith S. Levey (editors). *The New Columbia Encyclopedia (Fourth Edition)* (Columbia University Press, 1975)

Hartley, Dorothy. *Food in England* (Macdonald and Jane's, 1975)

Heaton, Donald D. *A Produce Reference Guide to Fruits and Vegetables from around the World* (Haworth Press Inc., 1997)

Hemphill, Ian. *The Spice and Herb Bible* (Robert Rose Inc., 2000)

Herbst, Sharon Tyler. *The New Food Lover's Companion (Third Edition)* (Barron's Education Series, 2001)

Hibler, Janie. *The Berry Bible* (HarperCollins, 2004)

Hughes, Holly. *Best Food Writing 2002* (Marlowe & Company, 2002)

Hunt, David (editor). *Native Indian Wild Game, Fish, and Wild Foods Cookbook* (Fox Chapel, 1992)

Hutton, Wendy. *A Cook's Guide to Asian Vegetables* (Periplus, 2004)

Ingram, Christine. *Vegetables: An A-Z Reference and Cook's Kitchen Bible* (Southwater/Anness Publishing, 2000)

________. *Cooking Ingredients: The Ultimate Photographic Reference Guide for Cooks and Food Lovers* (Hermes House/Anness publishing, 2002)

________. *The World Encyclopedia of Cooking Ingredients* (Lorenz Books/Anness Publishing, 2002)

James, Kenneth. *Escoffier, The King of Chefs* (Hambledon and London, 2002)

Jenkins, Steven. *Cheese Primer* (Workman, 1996)

Joachim, David. *The Food Substitutions Bible* (Robert Rose Inc., 2005)

Jordan, Peter. *The New Guide to Mushrooms* (Ultimate Editions/Anness Publishing, 1996)

________ and Steven Wheeler. *The Practical Mushroom Encyclopedia* (Southwater/Anness Publishing, 2000)

Kennedy, Diana. *The Art of Mexican Cooking* (Bantam Books, 1989)

________. *The Essential Cuisines of Mexico* (Clarkson Potter, 2000)

________. *From My Kitchen, Techniques and Ingredients* (Clarkson Potter, 2003)

Kuh, Patric. *The Last Days of Haute Cuisine, America's Culinary Revolution* (Viking Penguin, 2001)

Kurlansky, Mark. *Cod: A Biography of the Fish that Changed the World* (Alfred A. Knopf, 1997)

________. *Choice Cuts: A Savory Selection of Food Writing from Around the World and Throughout History* (Penguin Books, 2002)

________. *Salt: A World History* (Alfred A. Knopf, 2002)

Labensky, Steven, Gaye G. Ingram and Sarah R. Labensky. *Webster's New World Dictionary of Culinary Arts (Second edition)* (Prentice Hall, 2001)

Laudan, Rachel. *The Food of Paradise: Exploring Hawaii's Culinary Heritage* (University of Hawaii Press, 1996)

Leclerc, Henri. *Les épices. Plantes condimentaires de la France et des colonies* (Masson 1929)

Lewis, Edna. *The Taste of Country Cooking* (Alfred Knopf, 1976)

________ and Scott Peacock. *The Gift of Southern Cooking* (Alfred A. Knopf, 2003)

MacNeil, Karen. *The Wine Bible* (Workman, 2000)

Mallett, Gina. *Last Chance to Eat: The Fate of Taste in a Fast Food World* (W.W. Norton & Company, 2004)

Marks, Gil. *The World of Jewish Cooking* (Simon & Schuster, 1996)

_______. *The World of Jewish Entertaining* (Simon & Schuster, 1998)

Massee, William. *Massee's Wine-Food Index* (Bramhall House, 1962)

Mayer, Paul. *Quiche and Soufflé Cookbook* (Nitty Gritty Productions, 1972)

McGee, Harold. *On Food and Cooking (Revised Edition)* (Scribner, 2004)

Mendelson, Anne. *Stand Facing the Stove: The Story of the Women Who Gave America the Joy of Cooking* (Scribner, 2003)

Mistretta, Giorgio. *The Italian Gourmet* (Gold Street Press, 1992)

Monselet, Charles. *L'Almanach gourmand* (Librarie du Petit journal, 1862-1870)

Montagné, Prosper. *Larousse Gastronomique: The World's Greatest Culinary Encyclopedia* (Clarkson Potter, 2001)

Morton, Mark. *Cupboard Love: A Dictionary of Culinary Curiosities (Second revised edition)* (Insomniac Press, 2004)

Nathan Joan. *Jewish Cooking in America (Expanded edition)* (Alfred A. Knopf, 1998)

Olney, Richard. *Simple French Food* (Wiley, 1992)

_______. *Lulu's Provencal Table* (Ten Speed Press, 2002)

Page, E.B and P.W. Kingsford. *The Master Chefs: A History of Haute Cuisine* (Edward Arnold, 1971)

Reardon, Joan. *Poet of the Appetites: The Lives and Loves of M.F.K. Fisher* (North Point Press, 2004)

Reichl, Ruth. *Endless Feasts: Sixty Years of Writing from Gourmet* (Modern Library, 2003)

Revel, Jean-Francois. *La sensibilité gastronomique de l'Antiquité à nos jours. Un festin en paroles* (J.J. Pauvert, 1979)

Riely, Elizabeth. *The Chef's Companion: A Culinary Dictionary (Third edition)* (Wiley, 2003)

Rival, Ned. *Grimod de la Reynière: Le gourmand gentilhomme.* (Le Pré aux Clercs, 1983)

Roden, Claudia. *A New Book of Middle Eastern Food* (Penguin books, 1986)

_______. *The Book of Jewish Food: An Odyssey from Samarkand to New York* (Alfred A. Knopf, 1996)

Root, Waverley. *Food: An Authoritative and Visual History and Dictionary of the Foods of the World* (Simon and Schuster, 1980)

_______. *The Food of France* (Vintage books, 1992)

Rosten, Leo. *The Joys of Yiddish* (McGraw-Hill, 1968)

Rowinski, Kate (editor). *The Quotable Cook* (The Lyons Press, 2000)

Sahni, Julie. *Classic Indian Cooking* (William Morrow and Company, 1980)

Schenone, Laura. *A Thousand Years Over a Hot Stove: A History of American Women Told Through Food, Recipes, and Remembrances* (W.W. Norton & Company, 2003)

Schneider, Elizabeth. *Uncommon Fruits & Vegetables: A Commonsense Guide. An Encyclopedic Cookbook of America's New Produce from Arugula to Yuca* (HarperCollins Canada, 1986)

_______. *The Essential Reference: Vegetables from Amaranth to Zucchini* (William Morrow, 2001)

Schott, Ben. *Schott's Original Miscellany* (Bloomsbury, 2002)

________. *Schott's Food & Drink Miscellany* (Bloomsbury, 2004)

Shannon, Ellen. *Dictionary of Culinary Terms: A Guide to the Vocabulary of the Kitchen* (Hippocrene Books, 1998)

Simon, Andre. *A Concise Encyclopedia of Gastronomy* (Overlook Press, 1981)

________ and Robin Howe. *A Dictionary of Gastronomy* (Rainbird Reference Books, 1970)

Sinclair, Charles. *A Cook's Dictionary: International Food & Cooking Terms from A to Z* (Bloomsbury, 2004)

Smith, Andrew F. (editor in chief). *The Oxford Encyclopedia of Food and Drink in America* (Oxford University Press, 2004)

Swinnerton, Jo (editor). *The Cook's Companion* (Robinson Books, 2004)

Tannahill, Reay. *Food in History* (Crown Trade Paperbacks, 1988)

Toklas, Alice Babette. *The Alice B. Toklas Cookbook* (Michael Joseph, 1954)

________. *Staying on Alone: Letters of Alice B. Toklas* (Edward Burns, editor) (Vintage Books, 1975)

Tower, Jeremiah. *California Dish: What I saw (and Cooked) at the American Culinary Revolution* (Free Press, 2003)

Trager, James. *The Food Book* (Flare Book, 1972)

Traill, Catharine Parr. *The Backwoods of Canada* (McClelland & Stewart, 1966)

________. *The Canadian Settler's Guide* (McClelland & Stewart, 1969)

Vaswani, Suneeta. *Easy Indian Cooking* (Robert Rose Inc., 2004)

Visser, Margaret. *Much Depends on Dinner* (McClelland & Stewart, 1986)

________. *The Rituals of Dinner* (HarperCollins, 1991)

Voorhees, Don. *Why do Donuts have Holes? Fascinating Facts about What We Eat and Drink* (Citadel Press, 2004)

Waldo, Myra. *Dictionary of International Food and Cooking Terms* (MacMillan Company, 1967)

Walter, Eugene. *Hints & Pinches* (Hill Street, 2001)

Werle, Loukie and Jill Cox. *Ingredients (Revised edition)* (Konemann, 1998)

Whiteman, Kate, Jeni Wright and Angela Boggiano. *Italian Ingredients Cookbook* (Lorenz Books, 1997)

________. *The World Encyclopedia of Fish and Shellfish* (Lorenz Books/Anness Publishing, 2000)

________ and Maggie Mayhew. *The World Encyclopedia of Fruit* (Lorenz Books/Anness Publishing, 2001)

Williams, Chuck (editor). *Williams-Sonoma Kitchen Companion: The A to Z Guide to Everyday Cooking Equipment & Ingredients* (Time Life, 2000)

Wolf, Bert, Emily Aronson and Florence Fabricant. *The New Cooks' Catalogue: The Definitive Guide to Cooking Equipment* (Alfred A. Knopf, 2000)

Wolf-Cohen, Elizabeth. *The Cook's Companion* (Quantum Publishing/Barron's, 2003)

Zabar, Abbie. *The Potted Herb* (Stewart, Tabori and Chang, 2000)

Photography Credits

Page 14 - Ferrán Adrià: Courtesy of El Bulli.

Page 16 - Kate Aitken: Courtesy of Canadian Broadcasting Corporation Archives.

Page 51 - Henri (Ali-Bab) Babinski: Courtesy of Photo collections ENSMP.

Page 69 - James Beard: Courtesy of James Beard Foundation.

Page 70 - Catherine Esther Beecher: Courtesy of The Schlesinger Library, Radcliffe Institute, Harvard University.

Page 75 - Mrs. Isabella Beeton: Public domain.

Page 78 - Madame Jehane Benoît: © John Reeves. The University of Saskatchewan Archives.

Page 83 - Clarence Birdseye: Courtesy of Birds Eye Foods, Inc.

Page 93 - Paul Bocuse: Courtesy of Paul Bocuse.

Page 96 - Gail Borden: Public domain.

Page 97 - Norman Ernest Borlaug: © The Nobel Foundation.

Page 139 - George Washington Carver: Frances Benjamin Johnston, photographer / Library of Congress.

Page 155 - Chef Boyardee (Hector Boiardi): Courtesy of Cleveland Public Library.

Page 162 - Julia Child: © Bettmann / CORBIS.

Page 175 - Craig Claiborne: Courtesy of The Culinary Institute of America.

Page 218 - Elizabeth David: © Topfoto / PONOPRESSE.

Page 233 - Alain Ducasse: © Mikael Vojinovic.

Page 250 - Auguste Escoffier: Courtesy of Musée Escoffier de l'Art Culinaire-France-06.

Page 256 - Fannie Merritt Farmer: Courtesy of The Schlesinger Library, Radcliffe Institute, Harvard University.

Page 264 - Mary Frances Kennedy Fisher: © Bettmann / CORBIS.

Page 320 - Marcella Hazan: Courtesy of Marcella Hazan.

Page 335 - Marjorie Husted: Courtesy of General Mills Archives.

Page 346 - Madhur Jaffrey: © Robbie Jack / CORBIS.

Page 358 - Ella Eaton Kellogg: Courtesy of Willard Library.

Page 361 - Graham Kerr: Courtesy of The Kerr Corporation.

Page 366 - Ray Kroc: Courtesy of McDonald's Restaurants of Canada Limited.

Page 368 - Peter Kump: Courtesy of The Institute of Culinary Education.

Page 381 - Edna Lewis: John T. Hill, courtesy of A.A. Knopf.

Page 385 - Mary Johnson Bailey Lincoln: Courtesy of the Division of Rare and Manuscript Collections, Cornell University Library.

Page 395: Harry MacElhone - Courtesy of Harry's New York Bar, Paris, France.

Page 411 - Nobuyuki (Nobu) Matsuhisa: © Steve Sands / New York Newswire / CORBIS.

Page 413 - Harold McGee: Courtesy of Harold McGee.

Page 436 - Anton Mosimann: Courtesy of Mosimann's.

Page 464: Richard Olney: Courtesy of the family of Richard Olney.

Page 496 - Jacques Pépin: Courtesy of Tom Hopkins / Jacques Pépin.

Page 511 - Roy J. Plunkett: Courtesy of Hagley Museum and Archives.

Page 528 - Paul Prudhomme: Courtesy of Magic Seasoning Blends, Inc.

Page 543 - Ruth Reichl: Courtesy of Bridgett Lacombe / Gourmet Magazine.

Page 550 - Claudia Roden: Courtesy of Jason Lowe - David Higham Associates UK.

Page 558 - Albert and Michel Roux: Courtesy of Redleaf Communications Ltd.

Page 567: Julie Sahni: Courtesy of Jerry Routolo Studios.

Page 568 - Hiroyuki Sakai: Courtesy of The Culinary Institute of America / 2000.

Page 575 - Colonel Harland Sanders: © Bettmann / CORBIS.

Page 594 - Upton Sinclair: Courtesy of The Schlesinger Library, Radcliffe Institute, Harvard University.

Page 601 - Carl Sontheimer: Courtesy of Cuisinart.

Page 616 - Martha Stewart: © Steve Sands / New York Newswire / CORBIS.

Page 648 - Alice Babette Toklas: Carl van Vechten, photographer / Library of Congress.

Page 654 - Calvin Trillin: Courtesy of The Institute of Culinary Education.

Page 655 - Jean and Pierre Troisgros: Courtesy of Michel and Marie-Pierre Troisgros.

Page 671 - Margaret Visser: Courtesy of Margaret Visser.

Page 676 - Alice Waters: Thomas Heinser. Courtesy of Alice Waters.

Every effort has been made to contact and obtain permission for the photographs in this book. If omissions or errors have occurred, we encourage you to contact us at foodencyclopedia@robertrose.ca.

More Great Books from Robert Rose

BESTSELLERS

ISBN 0-7788-0146-2
ISBN (13): 978-0-7788-0146-7
$29.95 Canada / $24.95 U.S.

ISBN 0-7788-0145-4
ISBN (13): 978-0-7788-0145-0
$24.95 Canada / $19.95 U.S.

ISBN 0-7788-0151-9
ISBN (13): 978-0-7788-0151-1
$27.95 Canada
ISBN 0-7788-0148-9
ISBN (13): 978-0-7788-0148-1
$22.95 U.S.

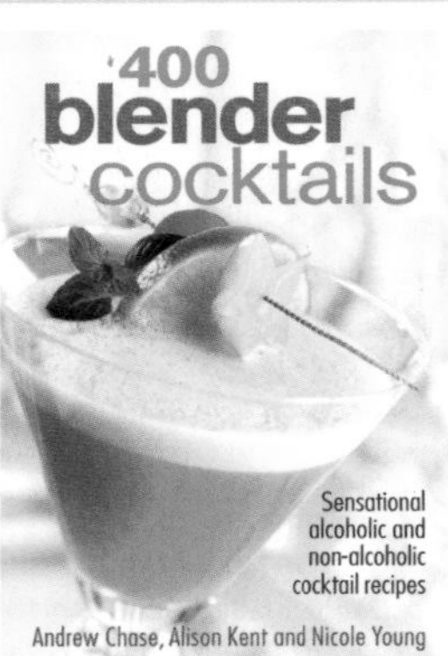

ISBN 0-7788-0142-X
ISBN (13): 978-0-7788-0142-9
$24.95 Canada / $19.95 U.S.

ISBN 0-7788-0130-6
ISBN (13): 978-0-7788-0130-6
$27.95 Canada / $21.95 U.S.

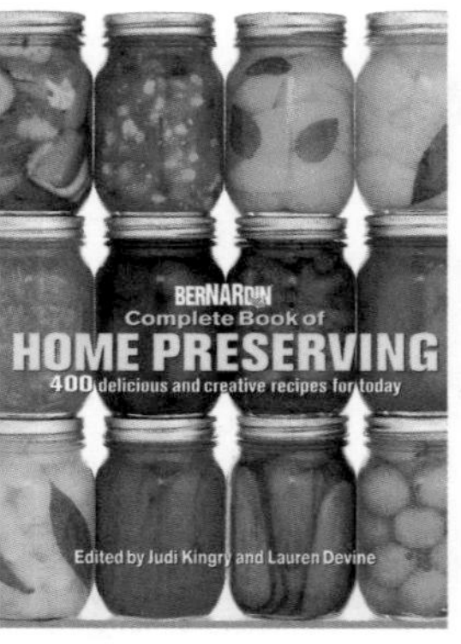

ISBN 0-7788-0137-3
ISBN (13): 978-0-7788-0137-5
$27.95 Canada

ISBN 0-7788-0131-4
ISBN (13): 978-0-7788-0131-3
$19.95 U.S.

ISBN 0-7788-0135-7
ISBN (13): 978-0-7788-0135-1
$24.95 Canada / $19.95 U.S.

BAKING BESTSELLERS

ISBN 0-7788-0144-6
ISBN (13): 978-0-7788-0144-3
$24.95 Canada / $19.95 U.S.

ISBN 0-7788-0147-0
ISBN (13): 978-0-7788-0147-4
$27.95 Canada / $22.95 U.S.

ISBN 0-7788-0125-X
ISBN (13): 978-0-7788-0125-2
$29.95 Canada / $24.95 U.S.

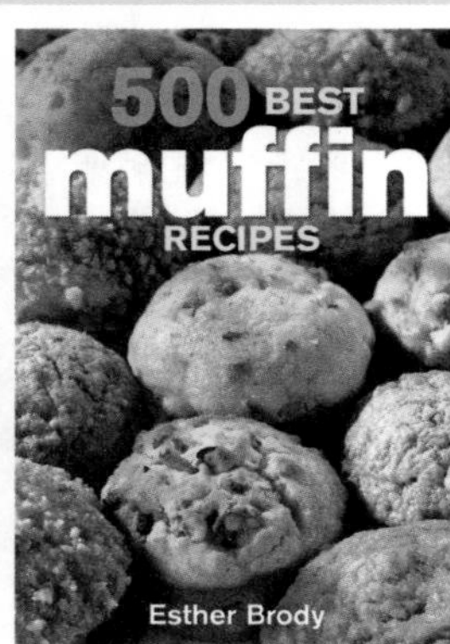

ISBN 0-7788-0071-7
ISBN (13): 978-0-7788-0071-2
$24.95 Canada / $19.95 U.S.

APPLIANCE BESTSELLERS

ISBN 0-7788-0143-8
ISBN (13): 978-0-7788-0143-6
$29.95 Canada / $24.95 U.S.

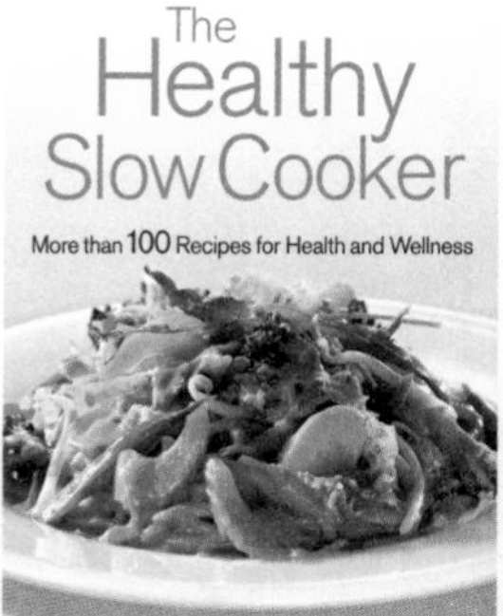

ISBN 0-7788-0133-0
ISBN (13): 978-0-7788-0133-7
$27.95 Canada / $22.95 U.S.

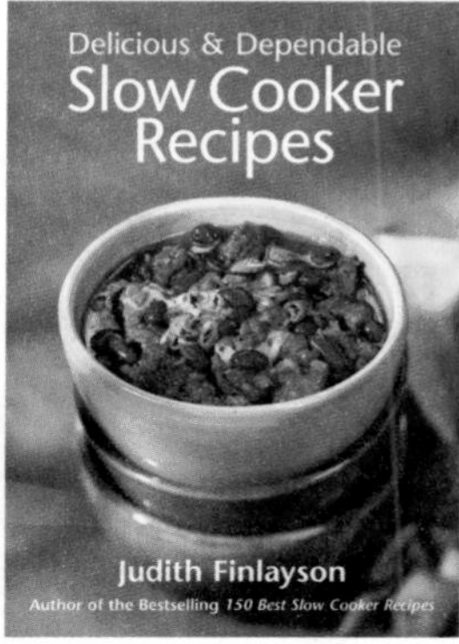

ISBN 0-7788-0052-0
ISBN (13): 978-0-7788-0052-1
$27.95 Canada
ISBN 0-7788-0053-9
ISBN (13): 978-0-7788-0053-8
$22.95 U.S.

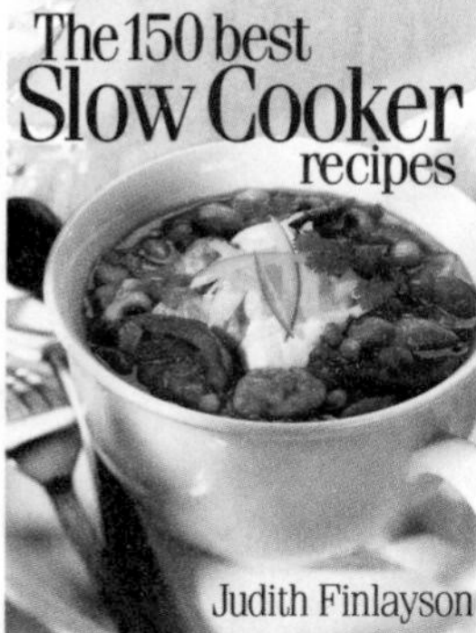

ISBN 0-7788-0041-5
ISBN (13): 978-0-7788-0041-5
$27.95 Canada
ISBN 0-7788-0038-5
ISBN (13): 978-0-7788-0038-5
$22.95 U.S.

ISBN 0-7788-0104-7
ISBN (13): 978-0-7788-0104-7
$19.95 Canada / $18.95 U.S.

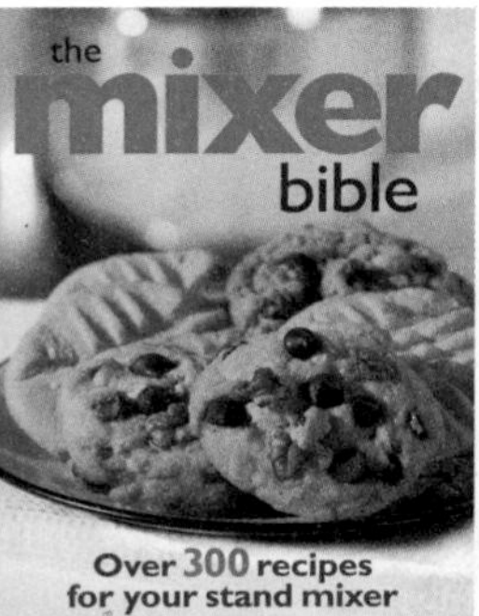

ISBN 0-7788-0124-1
ISBN (13): 978-0-7788-0124-5
$24.95 Canada / $19.95 U.S.

ISBN 0-7788-0109-8
ISBN (13): 978-0-7788-0109-2
$24.95 Canada / $19.95 U.S.

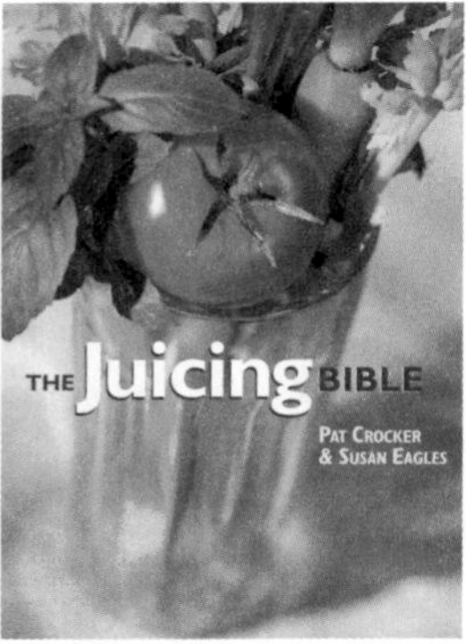

ISBN 0-7788-0019-9
ISBN (13): 978-0-7788-0019-4
$24.95 Canada / $18.95 U.S.

BABY BESTSELLERS

ISBN 0-7788-0136-5
ISBN (13): 978-0-7788-0136-8
$24.95 Canada / $19.95 U.S.

ISBN 0-7788-0149-7
ISBN (13): 978-0-7788-0149-8
$24.95 Canada / $19.95 U.S.

ISBN 0-7788-0118-7
ISBN (13): 978-0-7788-0118-4
$19.95 Canada / $18.95 U.S.

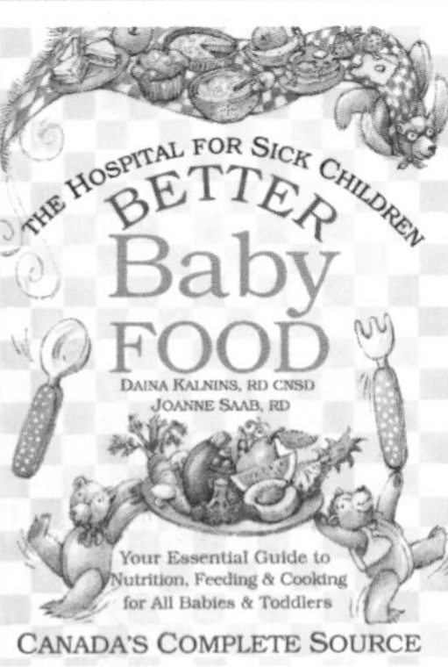

ISBN 0-7788-0030-X
ISBN (13): 978-0-7788-0030-9
$24.95 Canada
ISBN 0-7788-0027-X
ISBN (13): 978-0-7788-0027-9
$18.95 U.S.

Also Available from Robert Rose

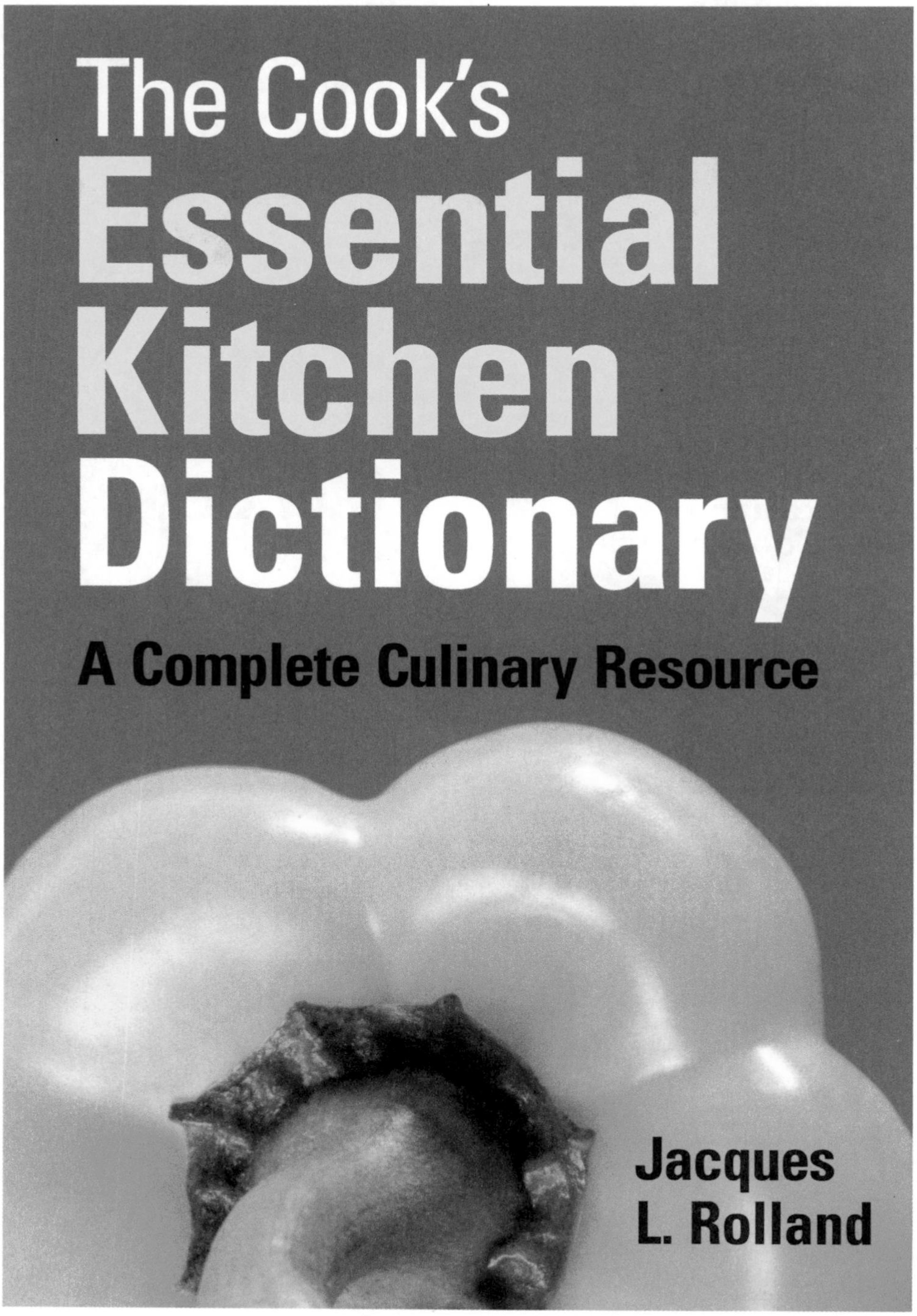

The Cook's Essential Kitchen Dictionary

A Complete Culinary Resource

Jacques L. Rolland

ISBN 0-7788-0098-9 13-digit ISBN 978-0-7788-0098-9

$19.95 CAN / $14.95 U.S.

For more great books, see previous pages